T0295722

Strategic Management for Tourism, Hospitality and Events

Strategic Management for Tourism, Hospitality and Events is the must-have text for students approaching this subject for the first time. It introduces students to fundamental strategic management principles in a tourism, hospitality and events context and brings theory to life by integrating a host of industry-based case studies and examples throughout.

This fourth edition has been fully revised and updated to reflect the major changes in strategic direction for these industries due to the most significant global crisis ever, as well as significant technology advances and issues related to sustainability.

New features and topics in this fourth edition include:

- New international tourism, hospitality and events case studies from both SMEs and large-scale businesses are integrated throughout to show applications of strategic management theory. New Technology Focus short cases are included, as well as longer combined sector case studies on topics such as COVID-19 impacts.
- A new chapter on sustainability and corporate social responsibility explores how the principles of sustainability can be incorporated into the strategy of tourism, hospitality and events organizations.
- Technology is integrated into all chapters, looking at big data, artificial intelligence, the external political environment, social media and e-marketing, absorptive capacity and innovation.
- Impacts and implications of COVID-19 are discussed, considering industry responses, financial implications and future emergent strategies.
- A contemporary view incorporates the broad range of academic literature and industry developments that have emerged in recent years and provides a particular focus on smaller organizations, recognizing their key role.
- Web support for tutors and students provides explanations and guidelines for instructors on how to use the textbook and case studies, additional exercises and video links for students.

This book is written in an accessible and engaging style and structured logically, with useful features throughout to aid students' learning and understanding. It is an essential resource for tourism, hospitality and events students.

Nigel G. Evans taught strategy and tourism management for many years in the UK at Northumbria and Teesside Universities, where he was Deputy Dean of the Business School, and at overseas institutions in Hong Kong and Malaysia. In an earlier career he worked for a London-based international tour operator. He has published widely in the tourism and management fields, and his teaching spans MBA and specialist tourism, hospitality and events programs.

Strategic Management for Tourism, Hospitality and Events

Fourth Edition

Nigel G. Evans

Routledge
Taylor & Francis Group

LONDON AND NEW YORK

Designed cover image: © Getty Images

Fourth edition published 2024
by Routledge
4 Park Square, Milton Park, Abingdon, Oxon, OX14 4RN

and by Routledge
605 Third Avenue, New York, NY 10158

Routledge is an imprint of the Taylor & Francis Group, an informa business

First edition published by Routledge 2003
Third edition published by Routledge 2019

British Library Cataloguing-in-Publication Data
A catalogue record for this book is available from the British Library

Library of Congress Cataloging-in-Publication Data
Names: Evans, Nigel, 1955- author.
Title: Strategic management for tourism, hospitality and events / Nigel G. Evans.
Description: Fourth edition. | Abingdon, Oxon ; New York, NY : Routledge, 2024. |
    Includes bibliographical references and index. |
Identifiers: LCCN 2023019082 (print) | LCCN 2023019083 (ebook) |
    ISBN 9781032331829 (hardback) | ISBN 9781032331836 (paperback) |
    ISBN 9781003318613 (ebook)
Subjects: LCSH: Tourism—Management. | Hospitality industry—Management. |
    Strategic planning.
Classification: LCC G155.A1 E927 2024 (print) | LCC G155.A1 (ebook) |
    DDC 910.68/4—dc23/eng/20230426
LC record available at https://lccn.loc.gov/2023019082
LC ebook record available at https://lccn.loc.gov/2023019083

ISBN: 978-1-032-33182-9 (hbk)
ISBN: 978-1-032-33183-6 (pbk)
ISBN: 978-1-003-31861-3 (ebk)

DOI: 10.4324/9781003318613

Typeset in Iowan Old Style
by Apex CoVantage, LLC

Printed in Great Britain by Bell & Bain Ltd, Glasgow.

Access the Instructor and Student Resources: www.routledge.com/cw/evans

To my wife Michelle and daughters Lydia, Megan and Laura, who kept me going throughout the writing of the fourth edition with love, support and tea, and our sadly missed Labrador, Leo.

Contents

List of figures   *xxiii*
List of tables   *xxvii*
List of short illustrative and technology focus cases   *xxix*
List of key concepts   *xxxv*
Preface   *xxxvii*
List of abbreviations   *xli*
Study guide   *xliii*

Part 1 Strategy and the tourism, hospitality and events contexts   1

1. Strategy and strategic objectives for tourism, hospitality and event
   organizations   13
2. Introduction to strategy for tourism, hospitality and events   44

Part 2 Analyzing the internal environment   85

3. Tourism, hospitality and event organizations – the operational context:
   sources of competitive advantage   89
4. Tourism, hospitality and event organizations – the human resources context   136
5. Tourism, hospitality and event organizations – the financial context   176
6. Tourism, hospitality and event organizations – the products and
   markets context   219

Part 3 Analyzing the external environment and SWOT   277

7. The external environment for tourism, hospitality and event
   organizations – the macro context   280
8. The external environment for tourism, hospitality and event
   organizations – the competitive context   307
9. SWOT analysis for tourism, hospitality and event organizations   351

Part 4 Strategic options   363

10. Competitive strategy for tourism, hospitality and event organizations   368
11. Strategic directions for tourism, hospitality and event organizations   399
12. Strategic methods of development for tourism, hospitality and event
    organizations   425
13. Strategic evaluation and selection for tourism, hospitality and event
    organizations   482

Part 5 Strategy in action   517

14. Strategic implementation for tourism, hospitality and event organizations   520
15. International and global strategies for tourism, hospitality and event
    organizations   570
16. Sustainability strategy for tourism, hospitality and event organizations   616
17. Strategic management for tourism, hospitality and event organizations –
    strategy in practice   626

Part 6 Case analysis for tourism, hospitality and events   637

Case study summary   642
Case/chapter correlation   644
Case 1 Competing or cooperating in the airline industry: strategic alliances or
        going it alone?   646
Case 2 Thomas Cook vs TUI: survival of the fittest   656
Case 3 Queensland Australia: tourism and events – strategic positioning
        and promotion   668
Case 4 IHG – competing on the world stage   681
Case 5 RX – strategic issues for a leading events management company   694
Case 6 Airbnb: back to the future – a 'disruptor' for global hospitality   707

Glossary   *721*
Subject index   *731*
Name index   *749*

Detailed contents

List of figures   *xxiii*
List of tables   *xxvii*
List of short illustrative and technology focus cases   *xxix*
List of key concepts   *xxxv*
Preface   *xxxvii*
List of abbreviations   *xli*
Study guide   *xliii*

Part 1 Strategy and the tourism, hospitality and events contexts   1

Introduction   2
The strategy process   2
    Strategic analysis   3
    Strategic choice   4
    Strategic implementation and management   4
    The feedback link   5
    Study progress   5
Strategy in tourism, hospitality and events (*THE*) contexts   6
    Tourism management   7
    Hospitality management   8
    Events management   8
    Tourism, hospitality and events management – an integrated approach   9
Small business focus   10
Summary   11
References   11

1 Strategy and strategic objectives for tourism, hospitality and event organizations   13
Introduction and chapter overview   13
Learning objectives   13
1.1 What is strategy?   14
    1.1.1 Definition   14
    1.1.2 Chandler's definition   15

1.2	The elements of strategy		16
1.3	The practice of strategy		17
	1.3.1	Mintzberg's 5 Ps	17
1.4	Levels of decision making		21
	1.4.1	Strategic-level decisions	21
	1.4.2	Tactical-level decisions	23
	1.4.3	Operational-level decisions	23
	1.4.4	Congruency and 'fit'	24
	1.4.5	Time and planning horizons	24
1.5	Objectives		25
	1.5.1	Types of objectives	25
	1.5.2	Hierarchy of objectives	26
	1.5.3	Mission, vision and values – overview	26
	1.5.4	Mission and mission statements	27
	1.5.5	What does a mission statement contain?	30
	1.5.6	Vision and values	32
1.6	The content of corporate objectives		33
	1.6.1	Economic objectives	34
	1.6.2	Social objectives	34
	1.6.3	Growth or market share objectives	35
	1.6.4	Competitive advantage objectives	35
1.7	How do businesses set objectives?		35
	1.7.1	The stockholder approach	35
	1.7.2	The stakeholder approach	36
	1.7.3	Stakeholders and objectives	36
1.8	Stakeholders and corporate governance		39
	1.8.1	Corporate governance and sustainability	40
Small business focus			40
Chapter summary			41
References and websites			42
2	Introduction to strategy for tourism, hospitality and events		44
Introduction and chapter overview			44
Learning objectives			44
2.1	Tourism, hospitality and events as service industry sectors		45
	2.1.1	Goods and services	45
2.2	Summary of the key characteristics and their implications for *THE* managers		45
2.3	Service product characteristics		46
	2.3.1	Intangibility	47
	2.3.2	Heterogeneity	49
	2.3.3	Inseparability	51
	2.3.4	Perishability	52
2.4	*THE* – seven specific characteristics		55
	2.4.1	Ownership	55
	2.4.2	High cost	56

	2.4.3	Seasonality	57
	2.4.4	Ease of entry/exit	60
	2.4.5	Interdependence	61
	2.4.6	Impacts of tourism	65
	2.4.7	The effect of external shocks	73
Small business focus			77
Chapter summary			79
References and websites			79

Part 2 Analyzing the internal environment   85

Internal analysis		86
Internal analysis overview		86
Study progress		86
Purposes of internal analysis		86
The components of internal analysis		87
The strategic process		87

3   Tourism, hospitality and event organizations – the operational context:
sources of competitive advantage   89

Introduction and chapter overview			89
Learning objectives			90
3.1	The sources of competitive advantage		90
3.2	Resources		92
	3.2.1	Categorization of resources	92
	3.2.2	Resource challenges for *THE* managers	93
3.3	Analyzing resources		97
	3.3.1	Analysis by category	97
	3.3.2	Analysis by specificity	99
	3.3.3	Analysis by performance	99
3.4	Competences and capabilities		99
	3.4.1	How core competences 'work'	100
	3.4.2	Distinctive capabilities	104
3.5	Core competence, distinctive capability and competitive advantage		106
	3.5.1	Sustainable competitive advantage	107
	3.5.2	The 'VRIO' framework	108
	3.5.3	Dynamic capabilities	108
	3.5.4	How dynamic capabilities are developed	110
3.6	Knowledge management as a source of competitive advantage		111
3.7	Value-adding activities		112
	3.7.1	What is value adding?	112
	3.7.2	The value-adding process	113
	3.7.3	The value chain	113
	3.7.4	Analysis of the value chain	115
	3.7.5	Core activities, non-core activities and outsourcing	119

3.8   The Profit Impact of Market Strategy   122
3.9   The service profit chain   122
3.10   Service-dominant logic   124
       3.10.1   S-D logic and co-creation of value   127
Small business focus   128
Chapter summary   130
References and websites   131

4   Tourism, hospitality and event organizations – the human resources context   136
Introduction and chapter overview   136
Learning objectives   136
4.1   The importance of human resources in *THE*   137
4.2   Employment and working conditions in *THE*   139
4.3   Management of the guest–employee encounter   143
4.4   Human resources and service quality   145
       4.4.1   Humans vs machines in *THE*   148
4.5   The human resource audit   149
       4.5.1   The contents of a human resource audit   150
       4.5.2   The outcomes of a human resource audit   151
       4.5.3   Human resources as critical success factors   152
4.6   Organizational culture   155
       4.6.1   The determinants of culture   156
       4.6.2   Why is culture important?   156
       4.6.3   The cultural web   160
4.7   Cultural typologies   164
       4.7.1   Handy's culture types   164
       4.7.2   Miles and Snow's culture types   165
       4.7.3   Hofstede's cross-cultural differences   166
Small business focus   169
Chapter summary   170
References and websites   171

5   Tourism, hospitality and event organizations – the financial context   176
Introduction and chapter overview   176
Learning objectives   176
5.1   Financial resources in *THE* contexts   177
5.2   An introduction to financial analysis   179
       5.2.1   Capital intensity   179
       5.2.2   Financial structure and profitability   181
       5.2.3   The balance sheet   181
       5.2.4   The profit and loss statement   182
5.3   Sources of corporate funding   182
       5.3.1   Share capital   183
       5.3.2   Rights issue capital   184
       5.3.3   Retained profit as a source of capital   186

		5.3.4	Loan capital	186
		5.3.5	Comparison of share capital and loan capital	187
	5.4		Sources of finance: strategic significance	188
		5.4.1	Sources of finance: company comparison	188
		5.4.2	Other sources of capital	190
	5.5		Cost of capital	191
		5.5.1	Why calculate the cost of capital?	191
		5.5.2	Costs of debt capital	193
		5.5.3	Costs of share capital	193
		5.5.4	Weighted average cost of capital	193
	5.6		Key techniques of financial analysis	194
		5.6.1	Longitudinal analysis	195
		5.6.2	Cross-sectional analysis	196
		5.6.3	Ratio analysis	199
		5.6.4	Performance ratios	199
		5.6.5	Efficiency ratios	201
		5.6.6	Liquidity ratios	201
		5.6.7	Investors' ratios	202
		5.6.8	Financial structure ratios	202
		5.6.9	Using ratios in financial analysis	203
	5.7		Limitations of financial information	203
	5.8		Foreign exchange risk management in *THE*	204
		5.8.1	Transaction exposure	207
		5.8.2	Translation exposure	208
		5.8.3	Economic exposure	208
		5.8.4	Managing foreign exchange risk	209
	5.9		Cash management	209
		5.9.1	Cash flow risk analysis	211
		5.9.2	Cash flow forecasting	212
	Small business focus			216
	Chapter summary			217
	References and websites			218
6	Tourism, hospitality and event organizations – the products and markets context			219
	Introduction and chapter overview			219
	Learning objectives			219
	6.1		Strategic marketing for competitive advantage	220
	6.2		Understanding markets	221
	6.3		Market attractiveness	221
	6.4		Defining markets	223
		6.4.1	Market – definition based on product	224
		6.4.2	Market – definition based on need satisfaction or function performed	225
		6.4.3	Market – definition based on customer identity	226
		6.4.4	Market – combined definition	226

6.5   'STP' marketing   227
6.6   Market segmentation   228
       6.6.1   Four approaches to segmentation   230
       6.6.2   Criteria for segmentation   231
       6.6.3   Sociodemographic segmentation   232
       6.6.4   Geographic segmentation   233
       6.6.5   Psychographic segmentation   233
       6.6.6   Geo-demographic segmentation   236
       6.6.7   Benefit segmentation   237
       6.6.8   Business-to-business marketing   238
6.7   Targeting   239
6.8   Product positioning   241
       6.8.1   Tourism destination positioning   244
       6.8.2   Adjusting the marketing mix   247
6.9   Products   248
       6.9.1   Product definition   248
       6.9.2   The product life cycle   250
       6.9.3   The tourism area life cycle   254
       6.9.4   Product life cycle critique   255
       6.9.5   S-curve (technology life cycle analysis)   255
6.10   New product development   258
       6.10.1   New product idea generation   259
       6.10.2   New product screening   260
       6.10.3   New product development   260
6.11   The product portfolio   262
       6.11.1   The Boston Consulting Group matrix   262
       6.11.2   Utilizing the BCG matrix   265
       6.11.3   Limitations of the BCG matrix   266
       6.11.4   Composite portfolio models   267
Small business focus   268
Chapter summary   270
References and websites   271

Part 3 Analyzing the external environment and SWOT   277

External analysis and SWOT   278
       External analysis and SWOT overview   278
       Study progress   278
       Levels of external analysis   278
       SWOT analysis   279

7   The external environment for tourism, hospitality and event
    organizations – the macro context   280
    Introduction and chapter overview   280
    Learning objectives   281

7.1		The macro environment	281
	7.1.1	Conducting macro-environmental analysis	282
	7.1.2	Limitations of macro-environmental analysis	282
7.2		'STEEP' analysis	284
	7.2.1	Using STEEP analysis	286
	7.2.2	What to analyze	286
	7.2.3	Sociodemographic factors	287
	7.2.4	Technological factors	289
	7.2.5	Economic factors	292
	7.2.6	Environmental factors	295
	7.2.7	Political, governmental, legal and regulatory factors	298
	7.2.8	The relationships between the STEEP factors	301
		Small business focus	301
		Chapter summary	302
		References and websites	303

8		The external environment for tourism, hospitality and event organizations – the competitive context	307
		Introduction and chapter overview	307
		Learning objectives	307
8.1		Industries and markets	308
8.2		Industry analysis	309
8.3		Porter's five forces model of industry analysis	310
	8.3.1	The threat of new entrants to the industry	312
	8.3.2	The threat of substitute products	316
	8.3.3	The bargaining power of buyers	317
	8.3.4	The bargaining power of suppliers	318
	8.3.5	The intensity of rivalry among competitors in the industry	320
	8.3.6	The five forces framework and profitability – a summary	325
	8.3.7	Limitations of the five forces framework	325
8.4		Clustering	328
8.5		A resource-based approach to environmental analysis	332
	8.5.1	Competitive and collaborative arenas	332
	8.5.2	Limitations of existing frameworks of analysis	332
	8.5.3	The resource-based framework	333
	8.5.4	Resource-based model – a summary	337
8.6		Strategic group analysis	338
8.7		Competitor profiling	339
8.8		Critical success factors and key performance indicators	342
		Small business focus	344
		Chapter summary	346
		References and websites	346

9   SWOT analysis for tourism, hospitality and event organizations   351
     Introduction and chapter overview   351
     Learning objectives   351
     9.1   SWOT analysis in *THE* contexts   352
     9.2   SWOT – general principles   354
     9.3   SWOT implementation   356
     Small business focus   359
     Chapter summary   361
     References   361

Part 4 Strategic options   **363**

     Strategic options for tourism, hospitality and events contexts   364
            Strategic options overview   364
            Study progress   364
            Formulating, evaluating and selecting options   364
            Levels of strategy   365

10   Competitive strategy for tourism, hospitality and event organizations   368
     Introduction and chapter overview   368
     Learning objectives   369
     10.1   How competitive advantage is achieved   369
     10.2   Strategy formulation in *THE* contexts   370
     10.3   Competitive strategy overview   372
     10.4   Michael Porter's generic strategies   373
            10.4.1   Cost leadership strategy   374
            10.4.2   Differentiation strategy   380
            10.4.3   Focus strategy   384
            10.4.4   Critical evaluation of the generic strategy framework   385
            10.4.5   The strategy clock framework   388
     10.5   Competence-based strategy   389
            10.5.1   The 'VRIO' framework   390
            10.5.2   Dynamic capabilities   390
            10.5.3   Developing dynamic capabilities   391
     10.6   Core competence, generic strategy and the value chain – a synthesis   392
            10.6.1   Where to exploit core competences and strategies   394
     Small business focus   395
     Chapter summary   396
     References and websites   397

11   Strategic directions for tourism, hospitality and event organizations   399
     Introduction and chapter overview   399
     Learning objectives   400
     11.1   Growth strategies   400
            11.1.1   Growth – Igor Ansoff's product–market framework   400
            11.1.2   Market penetration   402

		11.1.3	Market development	403
		11.1.4	Product development	406
		11.1.5	Diversification	408
	11.2	Stability strategies		414
	11.3	Retrenchment strategies		415
		11.3.1	Involuntary retrenchment	416
	11.4	COVID-19 crisis response strategies		417
	11.5	Risk and balance		419
	Small business focus			420
	Chapter summary			422
	References and websites			422

12 Strategic methods of development for tourism, hospitality and event organizations — 425

	Introduction and chapter overview			425
	Learning objectives			426
	12.1	Alternative strategic methods		426
	12.2	Organic (internal) growth		427
	12.3	Mergers and acquisitions		430
		12.3.1	The effects of mergers and acquisitions	433
		12.3.2	Synergy – the main objective of M&A	434
		12.3.3	Motivations for M&A	435
		12.3.4	Potential failure factors with M&A	436
		12.3.5	Government policy and integrations	437
	12.4	The relational approach to strategic management		439
	12.5	Joint development		440
		12.5.1	Categorizing forms of joint development	442
		12.5.2	Joint development in *THE*	443
	12.6	Strategic alliances		444
		12.6.1	Strategic alliances in *THE*	446
		12.6.2	A conceptualization of the collaborative process for international airlines	448
		12.6.3	Motivations for strategic alliance formation	449
		12.6.4	Potential difficulties with strategic alliances	450
		12.6.5	Partner selection in strategic alliances	452
	12.7	Public–private partnerships		454
	12.8	Franchising		460
	12.9	Management contracts		463
	12.10	Cooperative networks		466
		12.10.1	Hospitality consortia	467
		12.10.2	Referral networks	469
	12.11	Methods of strategic development: a comparison		469
	12.12	Methods of retrenchment		472
		12.12.1	Reasons for disposal	473
		12.12.2	Shareholders and disposals	473
	Small business focus			475

| | | Chapter summary | 476 |
| | | References and websites | 476 |

13		Strategic evaluation and selection for tourism, hospitality and event organizations	482
		Introduction and chapter overview	482
		Learning objectives	483
	13.1	Identifying strategic options	483
		13.1.1 Competitive strategy decisions	484
		13.1.2 Direction of development – product and market decisions	484
		13.1.3 Strategic method decisions	485
	13.2	Applying evaluation criteria	486
	13.3	Suitability	488
		13.3.1 Screening	489
	13.4	Feasibility	491
	13.5	Sustainability	495
	13.6	Acceptability	496
	13.7	Reaction of stakeholders	496
	13.8	Returns	497
	13.9	Financial tools for evaluating returns	498
		13.9.1 Investment appraisal – introduction	498
		13.9.2 Payback method	499
		13.9.3 Breakeven analysis	500
		13.9.4 Accounting rate of return	501
		13.9.5 Discounted cash flow methods	501
		13.9.6 Net present value	502
		13.9.7 Internal rate of return	502
		13.9.8 NPV and IRR compared	502
		13.9.9 Limitations of the financial tools	503
	13.10	Non-financial tools for evaluating returns	504
		13.10.1 Cost–benefit analysis	504
		13.10.2 Impact analysis	506
	13.11	Risk	507
		13.11.1 Scenario planning and sensitivity analysis	509
	13.12	Strategic evaluation in emergent strategies	511
		Small business focus	512
		Chapter summary	514
		References and websites	514

Part 5	Strategy in action	517
	Strategic implementation and strategy in practice for tourism, hospitality and events	518
	Study progress	518

14 Strategic implementation for tourism, hospitality and event organizations   520
    Introduction and chapter overview   520
    Learning objectives   521
    14.1 Implementation and the strategic process   521
    14.2 Aspects of strategic implementation   523
    14.3 Implementation – resources   523
           14.3.1 Matching strategy with resources   525
           14.3.2 Developing and controlling resources   528
    14.4 Implementation – configuration of culture and structure   529
           14.4.1 Cultural suitability   529
           14.4.2 Miles and Snow's typology and cultural postures   529
           14.4.3 Organizational structure   530
           14.4.4 The 'height' of structures   531
           14.4.5 The 'width' of structures   533
           14.4.6 Complexity of structure   533
           14.4.7 Methods of divisionalization   535
    14.5 Implementation – managing and leading change   538
           14.5.1 Inertia – identifying barriers to change   539
           14.5.2 Understanding change – Kurt Lewin's three-step
                   model   539
           14.5.3 Understanding the context of change   541
           14.5.4 Leading and managing change   546
           14.5.5 Leadership and management styles   548
           14.5.6 The role of the 'change agent'   549
    14.6 Implementation: *THE* contexts   551
    14.7 Implementation: communicating, coordinating and measuring   557
           14.7.1 Communicating, coordinating and measuring – a practical
                   technique for implementing strategy   557
           14.7.2 The balanced scorecard: overview   558
           14.7.3 BSC as part of the strategy process   559
           14.7.4 BSC in practice   559
           14.7.5 BSC – potential difficulties   563
    Small business focus   564
    Chapter summary   565
    References and websites   566

15 International and global strategies for tourism, hospitality and event
    organizations   570
    Introduction and chapter overview   570
    Learning objectives   571
    15.1 Internationalization and globalization   572
    15.2 Globalization of markets and industries   573
           15.2.1 Market homogenization   573
           15.2.2 Global configuration of activities and outsourcing   576
           15.2.3 Deglobalization   580

15.3   Internationalization and globalization models   580
         15.3.1   Multi-domesticity   581
15.4   Porter's global generic strategies   582
         15.4.1   Configuration and coordination of internal activities   583
15.5   The competitive advantage of nations or regions   585
         15.5.1   Porter's diamond framework   585
15.6   Yip's globalization driver framework   587
         15.6.1   Market globalization drivers   588
         15.6.2   Cost globalization drivers   592
         15.6.3   Government globalization drivers   594
         15.6.4   Competitive globalization drivers   596
         15.6.5   Using the globalization driver framework   596
15.7   Key strategic international decisions   599
15.8   Market entry decisions   599
         15.8.1   Decision criteria   599
         15.8.2   Location of value-adding activities   601
         15.8.3   Market development methods   602
         15.8.4   Internal development methods   602
         15.8.5   External development methods   603
15.9   A conceptualization of market entry   604
15.10 Globalization and market entry strategy – a focus on
        hospitality   605
Small business focus   607
Chapter summary   610
References and websites   611

16 Sustainability strategy for tourism, hospitality and event organizations   616
Introduction and chapter overview   616
Learning objectives   616
16.1   Business sustainability: meaning   617
         16.1.1   Sustainability and competitive advantage   619
16.2   Sustainability strategy: principal issues   620
Small business focus   623
Chapter summary   624
References and websites   624

17 Strategic management for tourism, hospitality and event organizations –
    strategy in practice   626
Introduction and chapter overview   626
Learning objectives   626
17.1   The growth of THE and the managerial challenges presented   627
         17.1.1   Strategic management in THE contexts   627
         17.1.2   Approaches to the study of strategic management   628
17.2   Strategy in practice   629
         17.2.1   Factors determining how strategy is presented   629

17.2.2   Styles of strategy presentation   630
17.2.3   The 8 Cs of presentation   631
17.2.4   Strategy presentation: an example   631
Chapter summary   635
References   635

Part 6 Case analysis for tourism, hospitality and events   **637**

Introduction   638
What do case studies cover?   638
Reading and studying the case   639
Doing the analysis   640
Case study summary   642
Chapter/case correlation   644
Case study 1   Competing or cooperating in the airline industry: strategic
                alliances or going it alone?   646
Case study 2   Thomas Cook vs TUI: survival of the fittest   656
Case study 3   Queensland Australia: tourism and events – strategic positioning
                and promotion   668
Case study 4   IHG – competing on the world stage   681
Case study 5   RX – strategic issues for a leading events management company   694
Case study 6   Airbnb: back to the future – a 'disruptor' for global hospitality   707

Glossary   *721*
Subject index   *731*
Name index   *749*

Figures

P1.1	A schematic of the strategic process	2
1.1	Levels of strategic decision making	21
1.2	The stakeholder map	37
2.1	Seasonality of air fares between London and New York	58
2.2	The sectors and subsectors of tourism, hospitality and events	63
2.3	Examples of the impacts of tourism on destination areas	66
P2.1	The strategic process	88
3.1	The links between resources, competences and core competences	101
3.2	The links between resources, competences and competitive advantage	103
3.3	A simplified dynamic capabilities framework	110
3.4	A simplified schematic of the value-adding process	114
3.5	The value chain	115
3.6	The value system	118
3.7	The service profit chain	124
4.1	A model of the tourist experience and moments of truth	145
4.2	The 'virtuous circle' linking human resources with business success	146
4.3	The cultural web	160
5.1	A representation of the principles of a balance sheet	181
5.2	Air New Zealand passenger revenue 2019	185
5.3	Air New Zealand passenger revenue 2021	186
5.4	Sources of finance for three *THE* companies	190
5.5	A simple longitudinal analysis: Air New Zealand annual sales revenue (2008–21)	196
5.6	A simple longitudinal analysis: Air New Zealand annual net profits (2008–21)	196
5.7	A simple longitudinal analysis: Air New Zealand fuel costs (2008–21)	197
5.8	A longitudinal analysis of Air New Zealand return on sales (2008–21)	200
6.1	Product positioning	242
6.2	The services marketing mix	247
6.3	The product life cycle and its implications	251

6.4	Strategic implications of online distribution vs brochure distribution for *THE* companies	257
6.5	A feasibility study process for a visitor attraction	261
6.6	The experience effect	263
6.7	The Boston Consulting Group matrix	264
6.8	The GE-McKinsey matrix	267
7.1	The main features of STEEP analysis	283
8.1	Porter's five forces framework	311
8.2	Concentration and market structure	321
8.3	Las Vegas hotel occupancy rates	322
8.4	The resource-based model of strategy	333
8.5	Strategic group analysis for hotels in a particular town	345
9.1	The logic of SWOT analysis	356
P4.1	The levels of strategy	365
P4.2	The three components of business-level strategy formulation	367
10.1	The generic strategy framework	373
10.2	A simplified understanding of cost leadership and differentiation strategies	374
10.3	The strategy clock	389
10.4	A simplified dynamic capabilities framework	392
11.1	The Ansoff matrix	400
11.2	Market penetration: Premier Inn UK	403
11.3	The directions and methods of diversification	408
11.4	Patterns of related diversification	410
11.5	Diagonal diversification in *THE*	412
12.1	Methods of strategic development	426
12.2	Interorganizational cooperative objectives	441
12.3	A categorization of interorganizational forms of joint development	443
12.4	Conceptualization of the collaborative strategy process for international airlines	449
12.5	The benefits of consortium membership for independent hotels	467
12.6	Methods of growth employed by selected international hotel groups (% of total rooms)	471
12.7	Buy, ally or DIY matrix	471
13.1	The strategic evaluation process	487
13.2	The breakeven point for selling seats on an aircraft	501
14.1	The linear rational (prescriptive) strategic process	524
14.2	The height of organizations	532
14.3	The centralization–decentralization continuum	533
14.4	An example of a 'hybrid' divisional structure for a vertically integrated travel company	536
14.5	An example of a matrix organizational structure for an international travel company	536
14.6	Lewin's model of change	539
14.7	The urgency for change	544
14.8	A model of types of change	545

14.9   Successfully transforming organizations   548
14.10   The McKinsey 7-S framework   551
14.11   Achieving competitive advantage in *THE* through strategic
         implementation: a conceptualization   552
14.12   Strategy as a continuum involving BSC   560
14.13   The four perspectives of BSC   561
14.14   A tourism destination organization's strategy map   562
15.1   Global–local continuum   582
15.2   Porter's global strategy framework   583
15.3   Configuration and coordination for international strategy   584
15.4   Porter's diamond analysis of the competitive advantage of nations   585
15.5   A framework describing drivers for globalization   587
15.6   A conceptual framework: drivers of entry success   605
16.1   Deriving competitive advantage from sustainability strategies   620

Tables

1.1	Comparison of strategic operational and tactical decisions	22
1.2	A hierarchy of objectives	26
1.3	A summary of stakeholder groups	37
2.1	A summary of key *THE* characteristics and their implications for managers	46
2.2	Vertically and horizontally integrated structure of TUI Group	65
3.1	Resource analysis: Marriott International	98
3.2	The VRIO framework for testing competitive resources	109
3.3	Primary activities	116
3.4	Secondary activities	117
3.5	Classification of internal and external linkages	119
3.6	Outsourcing: the airline industry	121
3.7	The transition from G-D logic to S-D logic	126
4.1	Comparison of possible intermediaries encountered in purchasing a typical package holiday or a concert ticket	144
4.2	Summary of the strategic implications of Miles and Snow's typology	166
4.3	Summary of Hofstede's cultural dimensions	168
5.1	A simplified balance sheet for AirAsia	182
5.2	A simplified profit and loss account for AirAsia	183
5.3	Summary of the major advantages and disadvantages of share and loan capital	187
5.4	Summary of the strategic significance of different sources of finance	189
5.5	A simplified cash flow forecast	213
5.6	'Interjet' – cash flow forecast	214
6.1	Penetration by hotel groups in selected countries (2013)	223
6.2	Main benefits sought in types of events and attractions	225
6.3	Consumer segments in the main constituent parts of tourism, hospitality and events	230
6.4	Sociodemographic segmentation variables	234
6.5	Selected Queensland tourist destinations – positioning summary	245
6.6	Implications of the product life cycle	251
6.7	Using the BCG matrix in strategic planning	266

7.1	Key measures of airline performance	294
7.2	The five freedoms of the air	300
8.1	Porter's five forces and profitability – a summary	326
8.2	Summary of Whitbread plc's present strategies (2022)	341
9.1	SWOT analysis applied to tourism in Macao	353
9.2	Some possible factors in a SWOT analysis	358
9.3	Obstacles to small firm business performance in tourism	360
10.1	Summary of the major frame conditions affecting THE	370
10.2	The main features of the low-cost airline model	378
10.3	Key features of generic competitive strategies	385
10.4	The VRIO framework for testing competitive resources	390
10.5	Possible relationships between generic strategies and core competences in relation to the value chain	393
10.6	Leveraging existing resources	394
10.7	The advantages and disadvantages of a niche competitive strategy	396
11.1	Typology of crisis response strategies	417
11.2	European airline COVID-19 crisis response strategies	418
12.1	The potential advantages and disadvantages of pursuing organic growth	429
12.2	A summary of the motivations for mergers and acquisitions	435
12.3	A summary of potential failure factors for mergers and acquisitions	437
12.4	Focus of interorganizational activity in THE	444
12.5	Summary of the advantages and disadvantages of franchising	463
12.6	A comparison of franchising, management contracts and managing or leasing hotels	470
13.1	Summary of the criteria used for evaluation	487
13.2	Summary of rankings for strategic options	491
13.3	A ten-point checklist on internal feasibility	493
13.4	A four-point checklist on external feasibility	494
13.5	NPV worked example of two hotel projects (Part 1)	503
13.6	NPV worked example of two hotel projects (Part 2)	504
13.7	Business risks: Live Nation	509
14.1	Resource audit	527
14.2	The advantages of centralization and decentralization	533
14.3	Considering the context of change within organizations	541
14.4	Styles of leading change	549
14.5	Strategic implementation in relation to service product characteristics	553
14.6	Strategic implementation in relation to THE management characteristics	555
14.7	The four perspectives of Discover Halifax's balanced scorecard	563
15.1	Potential sources of economies of scale and scope in international services	574
15.2	A summary of the globalization drivers	588
17.1	Factors determining the way in which organizations present their strategies	629
17.2	Differences in the presentation of an organization's strategy	630
17.3	The 8 Cs of strategy presentation	631
17.4	Suggested guidelines for the presentation of strategy	632
17.5	What a strategy document might look like – IHG	633

Short illustrative and technology focus cases

Case		Geographical focus	Page
1.1	A journey from Berlin to Paris	Europe	16
1.2	Plan, ploy and pattern strategies: a Northern European tour operator	Europe	18
1.3	Position and perspective strategies: hotels and airlines	Global	20
1.4	Levels of decision making: an Australian events management company	Australia	23
1.5	Decision-making time horizons: a hotel group	Global	25
1.6	Vision, mission and values: AirAsia	Asia	28
1.7	Vision, mission and values: VISIT FLORIDA	USA	31
1.8	Stakeholders: the Australian Council of National Trusts	Australia	38
2.1	The importance of human resources in delivering services: London 2012 Olympic 'Games Makers'	UK	49
2.2	Managing heterogeneity: Radisson Hotels	Global	51
2.3	Airline and hotel loyalty programs	Global	56
2.4	Managing variations in seasonal demand: Jet2 plc	Europe	59
2.5	Tourism in the Maldives: living with climate change	Maldives	68
2.6	Boracay, Philippines	Philippines	70
2.7	Grootbos, South Africa	South Africa	71

2.8	The effects of COVID-19	Global	74
2.9	The effects of 11 September 2001: Accor Hotel Group	Global	75
2.10	Crisis management: Ryanair and Icelandic volcanic ash	Europe	77
2.11	Association of independent tour operators	UK	78
3.1	Resource analysis: Marriott International	USA & Global	97
3.2	Core competence: Ashfield Event Experiences	Global	102
3.3	Core competences: British Airways	UK	105
3.4	Outsourcing: the airline industry	Global	121
3.5	Co-creation of value at Airbnb	Global	128
4.1	A 'pulsating' organization: the Australian Open tennis championships	Australia	138
4.2	Learning and development at Accor Hotels	Global	140
4.3	Empowerment at Ritz-Carlton	USA & Global	143
4.4	Humans vs machines	Global	148
4.5	Critical success factors: China's Home Inns	China	153
4.6	'Eventful cities': Edmonton, Canada	Canada	157
4.7	Organizational culture: Southwest Airlines	USA	158
4.8	Application of the cultural web at WestJet	Canada	162
5.1	The importance of finance: to hospitality managers	Global	177
5.2	Capital intensity: Carnival Cruises and Travel Counsellors	Global & UK	180
5.3	Refinancing: Air New Zealand	UK	185
5.4	Air New Zealand: financial management in a volatile sector	New Zealand	194
5.5	Exposure to foreign exchange risks: in a German airline and UK tour operator	Germany & UK	204
5.6	Foreign exchange exposure: Live Nation	USA	205
5.7	Transaction exposure: a UK outbound tour operator	UK	207
5.8	Translation exposure: An American-based hotel company	USA	208
5.9	Economic exposure: a European specialist tour operator	Europe	209
5.10	The importance of cash management: Live Nation	USA	210

5.11	Seasonality of cash flow: a UK outbound tour operator	UK	212
6.1	Market concentration: worldwide hotels	Global	222
6.2	Trailblazers holidays in India	India	235
6.3	Benefit segmentation: Mpumalanga, South Africa	South Africa	238
6.4	Targeting business travelers	Global	240
6.5	Product positioning: Marriott and IHG	Global	243
6.6	Destination positioning for tourism and events in Queensland, Australia	Australia	245
6.7	First-mover advantage: Dubai and Singapore as international travel hubs	UAE & Singapore	253
6.8	'Disruptive innovation' in hospitality: the rise of Airbnb	USA & Global	256
6.9	Introducing new technology: Boeing's 'Dreamliner'	USA & Global	257
7.1	'Megatrends' shaping tourism	Global	285
7.2	Sociodemographic factors: aviation	Global	288
7.3	'Smart' tourism, hospitality and events	Global	289
7.4	VR and AR enhancing heritage tourism	Global	290
7.5	Aviation: technology advances	Global	291
7.6	Economic factors: aviation	Global	294
7.7	Environmental program as a source of competitive advantage: Scandic Hotels	Europe	296
7.8	Environmental factors: aviation	Global	297
7.9	Political factors: aviation	Global	299
8.1	Brand loyalty: Hong Kong Dragon Boat Festival	Hong Kong	313
8.2	Competitive rivalry: Las Vegas hotel occupancy rates	USA	322
8.3	Forces driving competition: the European airline industry	Europe	327
8.4	Clustering: Italian meetings and conventions	Italy	330
8.5	Clustering of hotels: Premier Inn	UK	331
8.6	Market-leading products: Inkaterra, Peru	Peru	335
8.7	Strategic group analysis: Wyndham Hotel Group	USA & Global	339
8.8	Competitor profiling: Whitbread plc	UK	340
8.9	CSFs: Canadian destination marketing organizations	Canada	343

9.1	SWOT analysis applied to Macau	China	353
10.1	Achieving economies of scale through technology: Expedia Group	USA & Global	375
10.2	Experience curve effects: Merlin Entertainments Group	UK	377
10.3	Cost leadership: the airline industry	Global	378
10.4	Differentiation using collaboration and technology: the Edinburgh Festival	UK	380
10.5	Differentiation using design and innovation: W Hotels	UK & Global	383
10.6	Pursuing a 'hybrid' competitive strategy: Singapore Airlines	Singapore	386
11.1	Applying the Ansoff matrix: the arts in the UK	UK	401
11.2	Market penetration: Premier Inns	UK	402
11.3	Market penetration: Holiday Inn expansion into Eastern Europe	UK & Eastern Europe	404
11.4	Market development: GI events in Asia-Pacific	France & Asia-Pacific	405
11.5	Product development: Club Med	France & Global	407
11.6	Unrelated diversification: HNA Group	China	413
11.7	Turnaround: Holiday Inn Hotels	UK & Global	415
11.8	COVID-19 airline crisis response strategies	Global	418
12.1	Organic growth: Messe Frankfurt event management organization	Germany	428
12.2	Organic growth: Accor Hotels	France & Global	430
12.3	Mergers in the international airline industry	Global	431
12.4	Mixed methods: RX Exhibitions	UK & Global	432
12.5	Acquisitions: Marriott acquires Starwood in the world's largest hotel deal	USA & Global	434
12.6	Merger control: European tour operators	Europe	438
12.7	Joint ventures: Alibaba and Marriott e-commerce collaboration for Chinese domestic and outbound tourism growth	China & USA	445
12.8	Strategic alliances: international airlines	Global	447
12.9	Strategic alliances: Hilton strategic alliance develops into a full merger	USA & UK	451
12.10	Radisson: one name, two companies operating a strategic alliance	USA & Europe	453
12.11	PPPs: managing event venues – the Colorado Convention Center	USA	455

12.12	PPPs: Busan International Film Festival	South Korea	456
12.13	PPPs: Baltimore Inner Harbor – a model for waterfront redevelopment	USA	457
12.14	PPPs: Marketing Manchester	UK	459
12.15	International growth through franchising: fast foods and car rental	Global	460
12.16	Franchising: Holiday Inn Hotels	USA & Global	461
12.17	Management contracts: SkyWest Inc.	USA	465
12.18	Hospitality consortium: Best Western	USA & Global	468
12.19	Sale of non-core assets at TUI	Germany & Europe	474
13.1	Suitability: foreign airline access to US markets	USA	488
13.2	Screening: international growth for Kenes events management company	Switzerland & Global	489
13.3	Feasibility: access to scarce resources at London's Heathrow Airport	UK	492
13.4	Feasibility: Chinese budget hotel brands fight for market share	China	493
13.5	Sustainability: MSC Cruises switch to LNG	Global	495
13.6	Acceptability of strategic options: easyJet	UK & Europe	497
13.7	Evaluation: the Olympic bidding process for the Tokyo 2020 Olympic Games	Japan	506
13.8	Risk analysis: Live Nation	USA	508
13.9	Sensitivity analysis: Air New Zealand	New Zealand	510
14.1	Resource audit for a hotel group planning growth in East Asia	East Asia	526
14.2	Linkages between culture and structure: easyJet	UK	534
14.3	Cultural change at easyJet and Ryanair	UK & Ireland	540
14.4	Strategic drift: Calgary First Night Festival	Canada	543
14.5	Strategic change at Lufthansa: the impact of the COVID-19 pandemic	Germany	545
14.6	BSC at Discover Halifax, Nova Scotia	Canada	563
15.1	Outsourcing activities for airlines: Qantas	Australia	579
15.2	Market globalization drivers: BCD, international corporate travel management	Netherlands & Global	589
15.3	Globalization and personalization	Global	590
15.4	Internationalizing events: rugby sevens	Global	597
15.5	Market entry decisions: TUI enters and leaves Russia	Germany & Russia	600

15.6	Hospitality globalization and market entry strategy: IHG	UK & Global	606
15.7	Born global companies: Skyscanner travel search engine	China & Global	609
16.1	Sustainability strategy: Hurtigruten Group	Norway	621
16.2	Sustainability strategy: Contiki Tours	Global	622

Key concepts

Resources
Deliberate and emergent strategy
The focus of strategic decisions
Mission, vision and values
Packages and tour operators
Capacity, occupancy rate, load factors and attendance rate
Breakeven point
Barriers to entry and contestability
Understanding tourism impacts
Competitive advantage
Free resources
Competence leveraging and competence building
Markets, industries and strategic groups
Knowledge and organizational learning
Value added
Service-dominant logic
Human resource gaps
Critical success factors
Power distance
Paradigm
Capital
Share value and share volume
Rewarding providers of debt and shareholders
Working capital
Financial statements
Efficiency
Needs and wants
Market segmentation
The human life cycle metaphor for products
Price elasticity of demand (Part 1)
Competitive and macro environments
Fiscal and monetary policy

Industries and markets
Strategic business unit
Economies of scale and scope
Switching costs
Direct and indirect substitutes
Market structure
Clusters
SWOT
Price elasticity of demand (Part 2)
Combined market value
Prescriptive strategy
The time value of money
Social costs and benefits
Structure follows strategy?
Tall and short structures
Who is the boss in *THE* contexts?
Successfully transforming organizations
Multinational and transnational companies
Travel and tourism are different
Economies of scale and scope
Learning curve
Sustainability strategy: clarification of meaning

Preface

The purpose of the text is to provide a comprehensive coverage of the strategic management field but to contextualize it to the particular characteristics of the tourism, hospitality and events (*THE*) fields. The book follows a logical and structured sequence through the subject area and regular Questions and Think Points enable readers to test their knowledge. Each part of the book is clearly introduced, and the chapters follow a common template.

The fourth edition has been updated throughout and amended in several respects, particularly:

- The latest thinking relating to strategy and the *THE* fields has been included.
- References have been updated so that key points can be followed up in greater detail.
- The implications of the COVID-19 pandemic are considered at various points in the book and in several case studies.
- Case illustrations have been updated throughout the book and new cases added, including several focusing on the impacts of technology.
- The chapter focusing on strategic direction and competitive strategy has been split into two separate chapters.
- An additional chapter focusing on sustainability strategy has been added, reflecting the key importance of sustainability issues in these fields.

This international text is aimed at being the textbook of choice for three important groups of readers:

- Students studying strategy and/or marketing (probably in their final undergraduate year or at the postgraduate level) as part of their studies in *THE*
- Students and researchers who have chosen to study tourism, hospitality or events management organizations for their dissertation, projects or assignments (at the undergraduate and postgraduate levels) who want to understand the unique characteristics of the industry and to gain knowledge of the relevant literature
- Managers and practitioners working in *THE* (or seeking a career in these sectors) who want to gain an understanding of the challenges faced by managers and some of the managerial responses that can be considered.

Putting aside definitional debates, fundamentally:

- 'Strategy' is about making you think ahead regarding key issues affecting organizations.
- 'Strategic management' is about giving you concepts, frameworks, tools and techniques to help you do so.

Consequently, this book aims to make readers think ahead about the key issues facing THE organizations and provides concepts, frameworks, tools and techniques to help you do so.

The first edition of this text was published in 2003, with the second and third extended editions appearing in 2015 and 2019, respectively. The book has proved to be popular with students and academic colleagues around the world; hence the need for this fourth edition. This text builds on the previous editions, but much has changed in the intervening years, including the COVID-19 pandemic from which industry worldwide is still recovering; consequently, this edition is completely updated and its scope extended.

The text is global in its orientation and, in combining tourism, hospitality and events, recognizes the inextricably linked nature of these sectors. The text is contemporary in that the broad range of academic literature that has emerged in recent years is incorporated, as are recent industry developments. It is argued that the three sectors can and should be brought together at the *strategic* level, because at this level (unlike the operational level) there is a great deal of commonality between them.

The book contextualizes and applies relevant material from the strategic management and THE literature. The book also takes an international approach to what are inherently internationally oriented industry sectors. This approach is reflected in the following:

- The application of concepts and principles
- Links to a wide range of relevant literature enabling further study
- A particular focus on smaller organizations, recognizing that they form an important part of these sectors
- Taking an explicitly international approach for what are inherently internationally oriented sectors
- Emphasis on key points affecting this industry in particular
- Use of examples, short illustrative cases and a series of longer cases drawn from across the industry and focusing on different parts of the world

There are, of course, many existing strategic management titles, and this text attempts to replicate their comprehensive coverage. There are, however, comparatively few textbooks which apply strategy to services contexts and, in particular, to the service sectors of THE. These service sectors are intricately linked and have grown to represent one of the world's most important and fastest-growing industries.

The strategic management challenges facing managers in service contexts are often different in a number of ways from the challenges facing managers in manufacturing industries. These different challenges reflect the characteristics of services. Furthermore, THE represents a distinctive set of services that entail an understanding of their own specific characteristics. Hence, it is appropriate that a dedicated text should consider the strategic implications of managing in this important and rapidly developing industry.

Clearly, there are many examples to illustrate a text such as this, and I have chosen those that I consider to be relevant, that can provide access to meaningful information, that can link with the academic material, or for which I have personal experience. However, I recognize that other illustrations could have been chosen. I would like to encourage readers to submit further contributions and illustrations (which would be fully attributed) for inclusion on the companion website that supports this book and that contains further material. Any feedback on this edition would also be gratefully received.

I would like to thank colleagues who have commented on parts of this book. I would also like to thank the team at Routledge, particularly Harriet Cunningham, Jennifer Hicks and Jen Gardner, and my wife Michelle and daughters Lydia, Megan and Laura for all of their help and support throughout the book's production.

Nigel G. Evans
ngevans@sky.com
March 2023

Abbreviations

AITO	Association of Independent Tour Operators
AR	augmented reality
B2B	business to business
B2C	business to consumer
BSC	balanced scorecard
CEO	chief executive officer
CSF	critical success factor
CSR	corporate social responsibility
CTM	corporate travel management
EU	European Union
GDS	Global Distribution System
GHG	greenhouse gases
GRI	Global Reporting Initiative
GSP	gross state product
GSTC	Global Sustainable Tourism Council
IATA	International Air Transport Association
ICAO	International Civil Aviation Organization
IISD	International Institute for Sustainable Development
IMO	International Maritime Organization
IoT	Internet of Things
KPI	key performance indicator
LNG	liquified natural gas
NAFTA	North American Free Trade Agreement
OECD	Organization for Economic Cooperation and Development
OVE	overnight visitor expenditure
P&L	profit and loss
plc	public limited company
PPP	public–private partnership
R&D	research and development
RevPAR	revenue per available room

RTO	regional tourist organization
SBU	strategic business unit
SME	small and medium-sized enterprise
SWOT	strengths, weaknesses, opportunities and threats
TBL	triple bottom line
THE	tourism, hospitality and events
UN	United Nations
UNESCO	United Nations Educational, Scientific and Cultural Organization
UNWTO	United Nations World Tourism Agency
VR	virtual reality
VRIN	valuable, rare, inimitable and nonsubstitutable resources
VRIO	value, rarity, inimitability and organizational capability
WACC	weighted average cost of capital
WCED	World Commission on Environment and Development
WTO	World Trade Organization
WTTC	World Travel and Tourism Council

Study guide

How to use this book

Strategic management is studied in a structured way following a logical sequence.

The principles and concepts developed in studying strategic management are applied to the tourism, hospitality and events sectors.

Additionally, the book is enhanced with learning features to:

- Reinforce your learning
- Provide you with opportunities to explore topics further
- Test your knowledge as you study

The many examples and short and longer cases provide you with:

- Experience of organizational issues that you might not encounter directly
- Illustrations of the concepts of strategic management applied to relevant examples
- Opportunities to actively participate in strategic analysis, choice and implementation and presenting results persuasively
- Illustrations of the linkages in strategic decisions in one part of the organization that have impacts on other parts
- Illustrations of the holistic nature of strategic decisions that often require knowledge of other subject fields such as marketing, finance and human resource management

Each part of the five parts of the text is introduced and linked to the previous and subsequent chapters so you can clearly see the progress you have made in your learning and what lies ahead. Further supporting materials are available online at www.routledge.com/evans.

Each chapter contains:

- Introduction and chapter overview
- Learning objectives

- Small business focus
- Chapter summary
- References and websites

To bring the subject alive, aid understanding, provide examples applying theory to practice and make it memorable, throughout the book you will find sections that highlight and illustrate the material:

DEFINITION/QUOTATION

Encourages you to engage with primary sources.

KEY CONCEPT

Highlights important principles that underpin your understanding.

STRATEGY IN PRACTICE

Illustrates how as a manager you might implement elements of strategy.

SHORT CASE ILLUSTRATION

Provides you with examples of how strategy actually works in real situations taken from *THE* contexts.

TECHNOLOGY FOCUS

Provides you with examples of how technology is changing the sectors of *THE* and how it affects strategic decision making.

THINK POINTS

Provides you with review and discussion questions to enable you to test your knowledge and understanding as you progress through the book.

CASE STUDIES

The longer case studies (contained in Part 6 of the book) enable you to analyze organizational issues that it might not be possible to encounter directly and to consider them appropriately.

Part 1

Strategy and the tourism, hospitality and events contexts

Introduction

This introduction to Part 1 of the book has two purposes in that it provides readers with:

- An introduction to the approach that this book takes to the study of strategy – *The Strategy Process*
- A rationale for the approach taken by this book in applying strategic management tools, techniques and concepts in the context of the tourism, hospitality and events sectors – *Strategy in a Tourism, Hospitality and Events (THE) Context*

The strategy process

Why do we often refer to strategy as a *process*? The answer is that it is never a once-and-for-all event – it goes on and on.

There is a need to continually review *strategic objectives* because the environment within which organizations operate is continually changing. The purpose of strategy is to make an organization fit into its environment. By achieving this, the probabilities that it will survive and prosper are enhanced.

Part 1 of this book is concerned with introducing the subject matter of strategy in a specific context, namely, that of tourism, hospitality and events (*THE*).

Thus, in Part 1:

- Chapter 1 discusses concepts, definitions and the nature of objectives.
- Chapter 2 highlights the particular characteristics of tourism, hospitality and events that are relevant to understanding the way in which organizations within the industry are managed in a strategic way.

In practice, the strategic management process has three main components or stages, as shown in Figure P1.1.

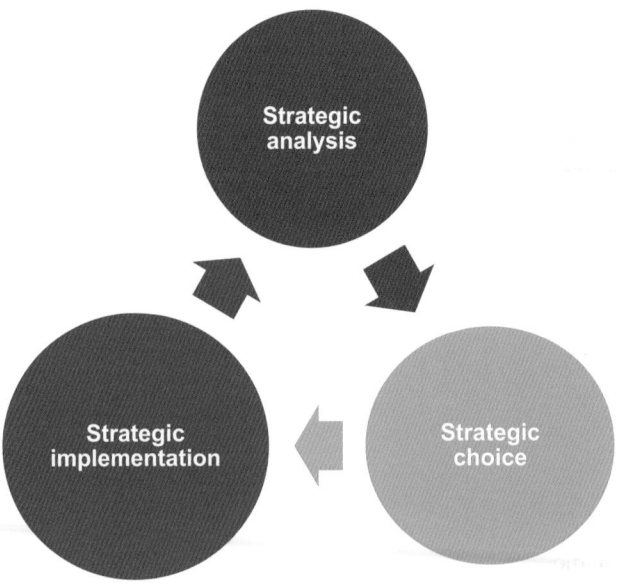

Figure P1.1 A schematic of the strategic process

Strategic analysis

The purpose of strategic analysis is to gather information and to analyze it systematically and thoroughly. None of us would be wise to make an important decision about anything in life without adequate and relevant information, nor would *THE* organizations.

There are two main stages in strategic analysis.

- Strategic analysis involves an examination of an organization's internal environment (internal analysis). This takes the form of a thorough analysis of the internal processes and structures of a business in much the same way as a doctor might carry out a thorough medical examination on a person. The purpose of internal analysis is to establish what the organization is good at (its strengths) and what it is not so good at (its weaknesses). We discuss the internal environment in Part 2 of this book.

For the purposes of strategic analysis of the internal environment, the organization is broken down into its constituent parts and the *THE* context of each is considered in turn. The operational context is covered in Chapter 3, with the human resources context, the financial context, and the products and markets contexts considered in Chapters 4, 5 and 6 respectively.

- The second stage in strategic analysis involves an examination of the organization's external environment (*external analysis*). This takes the form of a thorough analysis of two 'layers' of external environment: the *micro* or *near* environment and the *macro* or *far* environment. The external environment will be encountered in Part 3 of the book.

The macro environment contains a range of influences that have an impact not only on an organization in an industry but also on the whole industry itself. It follows that a single organization is usually unable to affect the factors in the near environment, but successful strategy usually involves learning to cope and adapt to changes. This book explains the far environment in terms of five main areas of influence – sociodemographic, political, economic, environmental and technological – which are discussed in Chapter 7.

The near environment comprises the industry in which the organization competes. The organization is usually affected by the factors in this environment, and it may be able to have some influence over it. The near environment, which is discussed in Chapter 8, is sometimes referred to as the *competitive environment*, because it is within this sphere that an organization competes, both for its resource inputs and to sell its product outputs.

From the information gathered from the external analysis, we seek to establish which influences represent *opportunities* and which are, or might develop into, *threats*.

Once we have established the organization's internal *strengths* and *weaknesses* and its external *opportunities* and *threats*, the challenge becomes the selection of an appropriate strategy. Such a strategy is required to address the weaknesses and threats while at the same time building on the identified strengths and exploiting opportunities. It is important to understand that a detailed internal and external analysis is a necessary prerequisite for producing a summary of the strengths, weaknesses, opportunities and threats – the *SWOT*. In other words, the SWOT emerges from the internal and external analyses and is a summary of the main results.

The process sometimes involves an additional stage of condensing the SWOT into a survey of the *key issues*. These are the most pressing or most important elements of the SWOT statement – those that require the most urgent action or that the strategy should be particularly designed to address. The SWOT is discussed in Chapter 9.

Strategic choice

The second stage in the strategic process involves taking the important information gathered from the strategic analysis stage and using it to make an intelligent and informed strategic *selection* or *choice* of the most appropriate courses of action for the future. These strategic choices are covered in Part 4 of the book. Specifically, strategic choices are required for *THE* organizations (or their constituent parts) in relation to three key aspects:

- How the organization will *compete*
- What *strategic direction* will the organization take
- What *methods* will be utilized by the organization

These aspects of strategic choice are discussed in Chapters 10, 11 and 12.

It is at this stage that the importance of the strategic analysis can be appreciated. If insufficient or flawed information from the analysis has been gathered, the strategy selection process will not be built on solid foundations. In other words, inappropriate strategic options could be selected.

Strategic selection therefore begins with an examination of the strategic analysis. Once we are acquainted with it, we normally generate a list of the options open to the organization, paying particular attention to how each option will address the key issues. After this, we evaluate each option using a number of criteria. Finally, the most appropriate strategic options are selected. Strategic evaluation and selection are covered in Chapter 13.

Strategic implementation and management

The third stage in the strategic process involves taking the selected strategic options and actually putting them into practice. The implementation and management of chosen strategies are discussed in Part 5 of the book.

This is a complex stage of the process because it concerns putting detailed aspects of the strategy into practice. It involves actually carrying out the strategy, and this brings into focus a number of other managerial issues. There are a number of areas we need to be aware of to effectively implement a strategy for *THE* organizations. Implementation, which is covered in Chapter 14, typically involves a consideration of the following:

- The adequacy of the organization's resource base
- The readiness of the organization's culture and structure to undertake the changes in the proposed strategy
- The leadership and management of any changes that are needed to implement the strategy
- The way in which the strategy and changes arising from its implementation will be communicated, both internally within the organization and externally

THE are sectors that are inherently international in their outlook, and the world is becoming increasingly global in terms of consumer demands. Consequently, it is important that the global and international issues of strategy be considered as part of the implementation of strategy. The ways in which organizations position themselves in respect to their geographic coverage and international presence are covered in Chapter 15.

Organizations and destinations have faced increasing pressures in recent years to be more active in their approaches to the sustainability of the natural environment. Thus, Chapter 16 considers how the issues of sustainability can be considered by *THE* organizations and incorporated into a 'sustainability strategy' as part of the organization's overall strategy.

The final chapter of the book (Chapter 17) has two purposes:

- To briefly consider different approaches it is possible to take in applying strategy in *THE* contexts
- To consider the way in which the strategy that has been developed – usually termed *the strategic plan* – should be presented

In implementing the strategic process, it is necessary to be aware not only of changes occurring to the internal and external environment but also of changes to the subject matter itself. Strategic management is a complex area of study. Though in this book we study a particular view of the subject matter, there are alternative views that could be taken, and the subject matter is continually evolving. Chapter 17 considers the present and future trends occurring in the study of strategic management to give students some understanding of the complexity and evolving themes of the subject.

The chapter also considers, in a practical sense, how the strategy should be presented in a way that is clear, coherent and convincing for internal and external stakeholders.

The feedback link

Finally, the progress of strategy is monitored continually through feedback from the implementation stage back to the analysis stage. As a strategy proceeds, it may have an effect on the organization's internal environment, and it may also have an effect on the external environment. In addition, independent influences may have brought internal or external changes about since the strategic analysis was first carried out.

To ensure that the selected strategy is still appropriate, therefore, a review of the strategic analysis is necessary. If nothing has changed, the company may decide that no amendment to the strategy is necessary. If the environment (internal or external) has changed, however, some modification to the strategy may become necessary. Environments are changing ever more quickly, and thus there is a need for organizations to maintain flexibility so that they can respond quickly and decisively to any changes.

The final part of the book, Part 6, comprises a number of long case studies taken from different parts of *THE*. The purpose of the case studies is to allow students to apply the knowledge they have gained from the other parts of the book in addressing the range of issues presented. Students should ask themselves the question, 'If I was a manager in this *THE* context with the information provided what would I have done?' There is not necessarily a 'right' answer, because there may be severable feasible ways of moving forward. The strength of an answer lies in the way in which the details are analyzed, the tools and techniques applied and the way in which strategy is formulated and implemented.

Study progress

Thus, the book is divided into five parts that follow the *strategic process* in a logical sequence and a sixth part containing a number of long cases.

The diagram below is replicated (in modified form) at the start of each part. The chapters being studied in the part are highlighted to indicate the progress you are making in studying the book's contents and to indicate where the chapters are placed within the overall strategic process, which follows a logical sequence.

Part 1		Part 2	Part 3	Part 4	Part 5
Strategy and the tourism, hospitality and events contexts		Analyzing the internal environment	Analyzing the external environment and SWOT	Strategic options	Strategy in action
Chapter 1	Chapter 2	Chapters 3, 4, 5 and 6	Chapters 7, 8 and 9	Chapters 10, 11, 12 and 13	Chapters 14, 15, 16 and 17
Strategy and strategic objectives for tourism, hospitality and events organizations	Introduction to strategy for tourism, hospitality and events				

Strategy in tourism, hospitality and events (*THE*) contexts

This text utilizes strategic management concepts and principles in a *THE* context through

- The application of concepts, tools and techniques
- Citing a wide range of relevant literature to allow students to probe particular issues further
- An emphasis on key points affecting these sectors in particular
- The use of short illustrative examples and longer case studies

Each chapter contains specific references to *THE*, but it should be stressed that this book is strategic management *for THE*, thereby implying that the theory is largely generic (through services rather than manufacturing oriented), *but* it is adapted and applied to the needs of these particular sectors.

The book explicitly recognizes that these sectors (which are closely aligned) are service based rather than manufacturing and therefore certain aspects of strategic management are particularly emphasized and the language used is modified accordingly. *For example*, the word 'operations' is used in place of 'production', and the *intangibility, heterogeneity, inseparability* and *perishability* of service-based products specifically will be emphasized.

It is recognized that there are some difficulties with this approach. *THE* sectors, although similar and linked, are distinctive to some degree. It can be argued that 'tourism' (and the travel industry that facilitates it), 'hospitality' and 'events' sectors represent separate sectors with their own literature and constructs.

In this book, however, the view is taken that:

- They are inextricably linked.
- The distinctions are outweighed by the similarities between them.
- Any difficulties can be successfully overcome.

Thus, the sectors can be studied at the *strategic* level together. It is important to stress this point. Whereas at the strategic level (high level decision making) it is sensible to study the three closely linked sectors together, it may be far less sensible to do so at the more detailed operational level.

> **For example:** *The operational detail of managing a tour operator will be very different from managing a hotel because they operate in very different ways, requiring different skills. However, at the strategic level, in terms of decisions like how resources are allocated, how*

they compete and the importance of human resources and customer service, they may have very similar sets of issues and, indeed, may in many cases be parts of the same organization.

In fact, it can be further argued that not only is it possible to cover the three sectors together at a strategic level but that it is desirable to do so. This is because the three sectors of *THE* are highly interrelated and there are many examples of cross-ownership. The demand and supply in one sector have direct effects on other parts of *THE* and, in many cases, there are shared ownership structures across the three sectors.

We now turn to a brief discussion of the individual sectors we consider in this book.

Tourism management

Tourism (and the international travel industry that has grown up to support it) is a vast and complex industry:

- That is highly fragmented in its ownership and control
- That has a wide diversity of products and destinations
- Whose development is often divided between public and private sectors

The UNWTO defines tourism as:

> Activities of persons traveling to and staying in places outside their usual environment for more than one day but not more than one consecutive year for leisure, business or other purposes. (Chadwick,1994:65)

Tourism such as pilgrimages or visiting other cities and states to trade has taken place throughout history. The origins of what is often termed *mass international tourism* are more recent and are usually traced back to Thomas Cook in 1850's Britain (Withey, 1998; Hamilton, 2006; Holloway and Humphreys, 2020) As a highly structured sector of many economies, it can primarily be viewed as a creation of more recent times. Its rise has been traced by a number of authors, including Gee et al. (1997), Fletcher et al. (2017), Page (2019) and Holloway and Humphreys (2020). Since the early 1950s the growth of tourism both domestically in developed countries and internationally has been phenomenal in its scale and remarkably resilient to periodic economic and political adversity (Evans, 2012).

The growth has been uneven spatially and has taken place against the backdrop of dramatic changes in the business environment. This dynamic environment creates both managerial opportunities and dilemmas for both private sector leaders and public sector policymakers. Given the dominance and drive of the private sector in the development of tourism and the growth in the services that support this, a business management approach to tourism studies has evolved over the past 25 years or so (Evans, 2012), which this book addresses at a strategic level.

Tourism products have a number of characteristics that are of relevance to the way in which they are managed and are thus relevant to any business-oriented study of tourism. Some of these characteristics are shared with other service products, whereas others are, if not unique, certainly of particular relevance to travel and tourism products in particular. The characteristics are thus highly distinctive and warrant specific study in this book.

The operational management issues can be viewed as being highly context specific, varying greatly according to the type, location and scope of the business and thus beyond the scope of this book. They are, however, discussed in, for example Goeldner and Brent Ritchie (2011), Holloway and Humphreys (2020), Fletcher et al. (2017) and Page (2019). The operational issues also vary greatly between tourism, hospitality and events management, so although it is possible to take a combined approach to the study of the three sectors at a strategic level, such an approach is not possible at an operational level.

Hospitality management

Although hospitality is recognized as one of the largest industries, it still remains as a composite of diverse subsectors. In a wide-ranging review of the problems of delineating hospitality, Ottenbacher et al. (2009) pointed out that there is still no consensus on the scope and exposure of this field as a whole among academics and hospitality professionals. However, in common usage the hospitality industry is often associated with the tourism industry, but most people relate it to hotels and restaurants (Barrows et al., 2012). Widening the definition of hospitality slightly, Harrison and Enz (2005:23) argued that the hospitality industry 'primarily consists of businesses that provide accommodation, food, and beverage or some combination of these activities'.

This provides a working definition of hospitality that provides an understanding of the subject matter which is followed in this book.

Notwithstanding the problems associated with the term, many hospitality and hotel management courses have grown up around the world, and in many cases tourism and/or events also appear in the title of such courses, thus giving a practical illustration of the close linkages that exist.

The definitional difficulties described serve in many ways to demonstrate the close interaction between tourism and hospitality and the fuzziness and flexibility of the boundaries between the two. Indeed, several definitions combine the hospitality and tourism fields (Ottenbacher et al., 2009) under the umbrella of 'travel and tourism' (e.g., Walker, 2016). Certainly, tourism and hospitality are closely related and are not mutually exclusive, because hospitality is at least partly concerned with providing for the needs of tourists.

Although the approach taken here is to consider strategic management, together with tourism and events management, Harrington and Ottenbacher (2011) adopted a different approach. They summarized research related to strategic management specifically in the context of hospitality, albeit recognizing the definitional difficulties involved. Indeed, more recent research recognizes the inability to clearly untangle tourism and hospitality at the strategic level by combining the two (Harrington et al., 2014; Singal, 2015; Köseoglu et al., 2019).

Events management

The conceptual problems in defining the hospitality management field are to a large extent replicated in events management. Indeed, it can be argued that the definitional problems are even more acute because, unlike hospitality:

- The subject area has been studied for a shorter period of time.
- The industry has few recognizable brand names (a measure of its fragmentation).
- The literature in the field is both more sparse and of more recent origin.

It is generally accepted (and it is the approach adopted in this book) that events management is concerned with managing in the following contexts:

- Event management companies
- Concerts and performances
- Festivals
- Exhibitions
- Meetings and conferences

The subject area is emerging, and Getz and Page (2016:595) define event studies as 'the study of all planned events, with particular reference to the nature of the event experience and meanings attached to events and event experiences'.

In a further discussion of the events field of study, Getz (2012) recognized the interactions with other related applied fields such as tourism, leisure and sports studies. Events interact in that they are used for various purposes and in the nature of the experience, but within the related fields planned events are only one phenomenon of many that are relevant. In identifying the often crucial role of events in destination development and marketing, Getz (2012) identified five core roles in that events:

- Attract tourists whose spending generates economic benefits
- Create positive images for the destination and help brand it
- Contribute to place marketing by making cities more livable and attractive to investors
- Animate cities, resorts, parks, urban spaces and venues, making them more attractive
- Act as catalysts for urban renewal, infrastructure development, voluntarism and improved marketing capability

Connell et al. (2015) also emphasized the important interrelationship between events and tourism. Events act as a bridge between the market for visitor attractions created by tourists and the use of events to fill the gaps in the off-peak season created by seasonal drops in tourism demand. A growing specific literature is emerging on events management, and new insights and research agendas are being reported, marking the maturing of the subject field (Getz and Page, 2016; Wilson et al., 2017; Draper et al., 2018; Laing, 2018; Dolasinski et al., 2021).

A number of textbooks cover the operational aspects of the subject matter and support the growth of events and events management as a field of study, including Bowdin et al. (2011), Goldblatt (2014), Raj et al. (2017) and Getz and Page (2019). In addition, there are many more practical books from the event practitioner's point of view.

However, there are currently no texts (to the author's knowledge) that consider events in a purely strategic way and that integrate events with the study of tourism and hospitality.

Tourism, hospitality and events management – an integrated approach

The previous sections illustrate the complexity of studying *THE* as industrial sectors, because there is debate as to sector boundaries and clearly there is a large degree of interrelation and overlap between them.

In each of the fields of study, many courses have emerged in recent years around the world – some of which consider the fields separately, whereas others combine the fields under a plethora of titles. In addition, a large body of both academic and commercial literature has emerged in each of these fields, and quite a large number of peer-reviewed international journals have become established. Some of these journals are dedicated to one of the fields (e.g., *Tourism Management*, *Event Management* and the *International Journal of Hospitality Management*), whereas others combine the fields (e.g., the *Journal of Hospitality and Tourism Research* and the *Journal of Convention and Event Tourism*). Though the titles might appear to make the sector boundaries clear, the content that the journals cover is not as clear because it frequently crosses over. For example, main articles in *Tourism Management* cover hospitality issues or particular events arranged for tourists.

Much of the relevant literature concentrates on detailed operational or context-specific aspects of *THE*. At this detailed operational level, it is unarguable that *THE* are (although still linked)

usually highly distinctive. The operational issues raised in managing an airline, a resort destination or a music concert, for example, are highly context specific and thus require individual
treatment.

At the strategic level, however, a more integrative approach is possible and, given the obvious com-
monalities, helpful. Thus, in this book, the view is taken that at the 'strategic' as opposed to the
'operational' level, the distinctions between tourism, hospitality and events are far less important.
Operationally they may be very different, but at the strategic level (which we are concerned with),
they are not. Each of the three sectors are *service* sectors sharing similar characteristics and, in many
cases, they overlap and interact. Consequently, tourism, hospitality and events can successfully be
included within the remit of this book.

> For example: *Tour operators engaged with organizing tourism may also own or manage
> accommodation and manage events of various kinds.*

The approach here will be to include the three sectors together because many of the companies
involved are integrated. Examples are sought from a range of different organizations of differing
sizes, spread throughout the sectors (and their subsectors), and the illustrations are taken from
around the world.

Tourism, hospitality and events share many of the same characteristics and issues for management
that are considered in various parts of this book. These shared features include the following in that
they are all sectors with:

● Products that are service based
● A scope that is international
● A heavy reliance on human resources for successful delivery
● Perishable and intangible products
● Emphasis on the importance of customer service
● Wide use of *price discrimination* and *yield management* techniques
● Rapidly changing means of distribution

Small business focus

A further relevant issue relates to scale. Though the tourism and hospitality industries can be identified broadly as a certain subset of mostly larger companies (such as airlines, hotel groups and tour
operators) providing services to customers and tourists, they also encompass a diverse, highly fragmented network of SMEs and other organizations. This is particularly relevant in these industries.
The events sector is also highly fragmented, with relatively low *barriers to entry* and represents a
wide-ranging and diverse set of organizations with few large companies or generally recognizable
brands.

Much of the strategic management literature relates primarily to larger businesses and is sometimes
viewed as being irrelevant for smaller organizations such as those in the sectors we are concerned
with. However, many of the principles embodied in the literature are applicable to smaller businesses (and also not-for-profit organizations and public sector bodies), but they often need to be
applied in a rather different way. Therefore, the approach adopted here is to focus primarily on
larger scale businesses, but each chapter also contains a specific section illustrating the relevance of
strategic management for SMEs.

SUMMARY

This part discussed the approach this book will take to the study of strategic management in a *THE* context. The part introduced the three parts of the strategic process: strategic analysis, strategic choice and strategic implementation and the importance of recognizing strategy as a continuous process requiring a feedback loop.

The part went on to introduce the individual sectors – tourism, hospitality and events – and describe the definitional debates that surround these sectors. An argument was proposed as to why these three sectors could be studied together at the strategic, but not the operational, level and that the approach adopted by the book would be to integrate the three strands of THE.

Finally, the aspect of scale was discussed in that many strategy books focus on larger scale organizations, but this book also includes discussions of particular relevance to smaller organizations.

REFERENCES

References

Barrows, C., Powers, T. and Reynolds, D. (2012) *Introduction to Management in the Hospitality Industry*, 8th ed., New York: John Wiley & Sons.

Bowdin, G., Allen, J., O'Toole, W., Harris, R. and McDonnell, I. (2011) *Events Management*, 3rd ed., Abingdon, UK: Routledge.

Chadwick, R. (1994) 'Concepts, definitions, and measures used in travel and tourism research', in J. R. Brent Ritchie and C. Goeldner (Eds), *Travel, Tourism and Hospitality Research*, 2nd ed., New York: John Wiley, 47–61.

Connell, J., Page, S. J. and D. Meyer (2015) 'Visitor attractions and events: Responding to seasonality', *Tourism Management*, 46: 283–298.

Dolasinski, M. J., Roberts, C., Reynolds, J. and Johanson, M. (2021) 'Defining the field of events', *Journal of Hospitality and Tourism Research*, 45(3): 553–572.

Draper, J., Thomas, L. Y. and Fenich, G. G. (2018) 'Event management research over the past 12 years: What are the current trends in research methods, data collection, data analysis procedures and event types?' *Journal of Convention and Event Tourism*, 19(1): 3–24.

Enz, C. A. (2009) *Hospitality Strategic Management: Concepts and Cases*, New York: John Wiley & Sons.

Evans, N. G. (2012) 'Tourism: A strategic business perspective', in T. Jamal and M. Robinson (Eds), *The Sage Handbook of Tourism Studies*, Thousand Oaks, CA: Sage, 215–234.

Fletcher, J., Fyall, A., Gilbert, D. and Wanhill, S. (2017) *Tourism Principles and Practice*, 6th ed., Harlow, UK: Pearson.

Gee, C. Y., Makens, J. C. and Choy, D. J. L. (1997) *The Travel Industry*, 3rd ed., New York: John Wiley.

Getz, D. (2012) 'Event studies: Discourses and future directions', *Event Management*, 16(2): 171–187.

Getz, D. and Page, S. J. (2016) 'Progress and prospects for event tourism research', *Tourism Management*, 52: 593–631.

Getz, D. and Page, S. (2019) *Event Studies: Theory, Research and Policy for Planned Events*, 4th ed., Abingdon, UK: Routledge.

Goeldner, C. R. and Brent Ritchie, C. R. (2011) *Tourism: Principles, Practices, Philosophies*, 12th ed., New York: John Wiley.

Goldblatt, J. (2014) *Special Events: A New Generation and the Next Frontier*, 7th ed., New York: Wiley.

Hamilton, J. (2006) *Thomas Cook: The Holiday Maker*, Stroud, UK: Sutton Publishing.

Harrington, R. J., Chathoth, P. K., Ottenbacher, M. and Altinay, L. (2014) 'Strategic management research in hospitality and tourism: Past, present and future', *International Journal of Contemporary Hospitality Management*, 26(5): 778–808.

Harrington, R. J. and Ottenbacher, M. C. (2011) 'Strategic management: An analysis of its representation and focus in recent hospitality research', *International Journal of Contemporary Hospitality Management*, 23(4): 439–462.

Harrison, J. S. and Enz, C. A. (2005) *Hospitality Strategic Management: Concepts and Cases*, New York: John Wiley & Sons.

Holloway, C. and Humphreys, C. (2020) *The Business of Tourism*, 11th ed., London, UK: Sage.

Köseoglu, M. A., Law, R., Okumus, F., Barca, M. and Dogan, I. C. (2019) 'Evolution of strategic management research lines in hospitality and tourism', *Journal of Hospitality Marketing and Management*, 28(6): 690–710.

Laing, J. (2018) 'Festival and event tourism research: Current and future perspectives', *Tourism Management Perspectives*, 25: 165–168.

Ottenbacher, M., Harrington, R. and Parsa, H. G. (2009) 'Defining the hospitality discipline: A discussion of pedagogical and research implications', *Journal of Hospitality and Tourism Research*, 33(3): 263–283.

Page, S. (2019) *Tourism Management*, 6th ed., Abingdon, UK: Routledge.

Page, S. and Connell, J. (2020) *Tourism: A Modern Synthesis*, 5th ed., Abingdon, UK: Routledge.

Raj, R., Walters, P. and Rashid, T. (2017) *Event Management: Principles and Practice*, 3rd ed., London: Sage.

Singal, M. (2015) 'How is the hospitality and tourism industry different? An empirical test of some structural characteristics', *International Journal of Hospitality Management*, 47: 116–119.

Walker, J. R. (2016) *Introduction to Hospitality Management*, 5th ed., Upper Saddle River, NJ: Pearson.

Wilson, J., Arshed, N., Shaw, E. and Pret, T. (2017) 'Expanding the domain of festival research: A review and research agenda', *International Journal of Management Reviews*, 19(2): 195–213.

Withey, L. (1998) *Grand Tours and Cook's Tours: A History of Leisure Travel, 1750 to 1915*, London: Aurum Press.

Chapter **1**

Strategy and strategic objectives for tourism, hospitality and event organizations

Introduction and chapter overview

Strategic thinking and strategic management can be viewed as the most important activities undertaken by any business or public sector organization. Strategic decisions are the key decisions that have to be taken by any organization, and from the strategic decisions that establish the framework a series of more detailed operational decisions can be made. How skillfully these activities are carried out will determine the eventual long-term success or failure of the organization.

In this chapter, the basic concepts of strategy are introduced. Definitions of the word *strategy* are discussed, and then we explore the levels of decision making in successful strategic management (at the strategic and operational levels). These are defined and the links between the levels are discussed. Finally, we discuss the nature of strategic objectives – who is responsible for setting them and what they are essentially about.

LEARNING OBJECTIVES

After studying this chapter, you should be able to:

- Define *strategy* and *strategic management*
- Explain Mintzberg's 5 Ps framework of strategy
- Appreciate the importance and organizational context of strategic decision making
- Distinguish between deliberate (prescriptive) and emergent strategy

DOI: 10.4324/9781003318613-2

- Explain what strategy often means in practice
- Distinguish between *strategic, tactical* and *operational* decisions
- Explain the meaning of mission, vision and values and describe the typical contents of these statements
- Analyze examples of mission and vision statements from relevant tourism, hospitality and events (*THE*) contexts
- Explain what is meant by *hierarchical congruence* and why is it important
- Employ the stakeholder model to explain how strategic decisions are arrived at
- Explain the most typical types of objectives that are sought through strategic management and how they might be written
- Explain the shareholder and stakeholder approaches to corporate governance
- Understand how the strategy concepts introduced in the chapter can be applied to relevant *THE* contexts

1.1 What is strategy?

Strategy is a complex study area in that it involves:

- Few (if any) *facts* that can be learned
- Many views put forward by academics, practitioners and consultants, which can sometimes appear contradictory
- A lot of jargon – where different words are used to describe essentially the same aspect *or*, conversely, the same words are used to describe aspects of strategy that are essentially different
- A vast academic and commercial body of literature
- Different schools of thought and approaches adopted by various academics and consultants involved in this field
- Dealing with a dynamic set of circumstances
- Integrating subject matter from other academic fields

In this book we attempt to find a way through this complexity by presenting the material in a logical order and by trying to present views on the subject matter that are widely accepted, taught and practiced.

This book is titled *Strategic Management* **for** *Tourism, Hospitality and Events*, and for the sake of brevity we will use *THE* throughout this book.

The implication of this title is that, though there are aspects of strategic management that need to be particularly stressed in the context of these three sectors, the conceptual material is largely generic. That is, most of the conceptual material is relevant for many industrial sectors (including *THE*) but the way in which it is applied will vary because of the particular nature of the sectors in question. As we will see in Chapter 2, there are some aspects of *THE* that are distinguishing features and that we consequently need to pay particular attention to.

1.1.1 Definition

The question, 'What is strategy?' seems to be an obvious starting point. However, the answer to the question (as implied above) is rather more complicated than it might at first appear. The growth of the subject of study has led to the use of the term strategy (and strategic management) in various ways, and numerous definitions have emerged.

Fundamentally, though, putting aside the definitional debates, we can distinguish between strategy and strategic management:

- 'Strategy' is about making you think ahead regarding key issues affecting organizations.
- 'Strategic management' is about giving you concepts, frameworks, tools and techniques to help you do so.

Many organizations operating in *THE* (as in other sectors) are hindered by short-termism, concentrating on the most pressing immediate tasks at hand rather than looking ahead and taking a longer-term view. This is perhaps understandable given the pressures of modern business but is not the most sensible way to manage.

It is extremely difficult for organizations to plan ahead (in the same way as it is difficult to forecast the weather or foresee future interest rate movements), because there are so many aspects of uncertainty and change. Concepts, frameworks, tools and techniques have been developed to facilitate the process of strategic management. The overall aim of strategic management is thus to develop a framework for thinking ahead; that is, for planning strategically.

Historically the term strategy has military roots, with commanders employing strategy in dealing with their opponents. Indeed, dictionaries often continue the military theme, defining strategy as 'the art of war'. In viewing strategy in such a way, the fundamental underlying premise of strategy becomes the notion that an adversary can defeat a rival (even a larger more powerful one) if it can outmaneuver the rival.

As it is in the military arena, so it is in business: organizations attempt to outmaneuver rivals. In so doing, strategies have to be developed that rely on various disciplines such as marketing, finance and human resource management.

Since the beginning of commercial transactions, businesses have had strategies determining their future courses of action. It is only since the 1960s, however, that the subject area has been widely considered as a topic of academic interest and hence widely taught in business schools and business-based courses.

The subject is also widely taught as part of *THE*-related courses. As we progress through the book, the *THE* literature relevant to each part of strategic management will be introduced. In some areas of the strategy (e.g., strategic alliances, which are covered in Chapter 12, and market entry strategy and globalization, which are covered in Chapter 15), the range of *THE* literature is quite extensive, whereas in many others it is far less so.

The range of literature also varies considerably in terms of its coverage of the three sectors we are considering, with the literature applying business concepts to events generally being more recent and less extensive than the literature in relation to tourism and hospitality. For an overview of recent research developments in this field, see, for example: Harrington et al. (2014), Okumus et al. (2017) and Köseoglu et al. (2019). There are also some general texts that consider strategy and planning in *THE* contexts, including Enz (2009), Olsen et al. (2013), Moutinho and Vargas-Sanchez (2018), Paterson (2016), Tribe (2016) and Okumus et al. (2019).

1.1.2 Chandler's definition

A number of writers have tried to sum up the meaning of strategy succinctly to make it easier for students to understand. One such definition, which, despite its longevity, is still widely quoted and adapted, was offered by Professor Chandler of Harvard Business School in 1962.

> ### DEFINITION/QUOTATION
>
> Strategy is the *determination of the basic long-term goals and objectives* of an enterprise and *the adoption of courses of action* and *the allocation of resources* necessary for carrying out these goals.
>
> (Chandler, 1962, emphasis added)

1.2 The elements of strategy

This definition clearly shows the three elements (or components) of strategy. The italics in the definition above emphasize long-term goals, actions to achieve the goals and allocation of resources:

- The *determination of the basic long-term goals* and objectives concerns the conceptualization of coherent and attainable strategic objectives. Without objectives, nothing else can happen. If you do not know where you want to go, how can you act in such a way as to get there?
- The *adoption of courses of action* refers to the actions taken to arrive at the objectives that have been previously set.
- The *allocation of resources* refers to the fact that there is likely to be a cost associated with the actions required to achieve the objectives. If the course of action is not supported with adequate levels of resources, the objective will not be accomplished.

The Short Case Illustration below uses the analogy of a journey to illustrate the three elements of Chandler's definition of strategy.

1.1 SHORT CASE ILLUSTRATION

A journey from Berlin to Paris

By way of analogy, we can consider a journey, say, from Berlin to Paris.

Your **objective** is clear: it is to arrive in Paris when traveling from Berlin. However, in making this journey, there are various courses of action available to you. You might travel by train, by car, by coach or by plane. You might travel on certain days or at certain times of day. You might take advantage of certain concessionary fares, and you might make a booking through an intermediary such as a travel agent, internet search site such as Expedia, or directly with the principal company (the airline or train company).

Thus, as a result of the desire to travel to Paris from Berlin, a whole range of options need to be considered and detailed decisions have to be taken as to which options to select. Hence, strategy contains three elements:

1. Your objective is clearly stated as arriving in Paris at a certain date and time.

2. To achieve this objective, certain actions are necessary and are chosen from a range of alternative options available. It might be decided that flying is the best option. Thus, a specified flight is booked through a travel agent, and a plane is boarded at the airport.

3. However, the actions could not be achieved if they could not be resourced. You need the resources of a plane with a suitably qualified pilot, an airport, money to pay for your flight and other such 'inputs'. If any one of these is missing, you will be unable to meet your objective.

When we consider organizations, we often talk about resources, which are divided up into various types. The Key Concept below considers what we mean by resources.

KEY CONCEPT

Resources

Resource inputs (sometimes called *factors of production*) are those essential inputs that are essential to the normal functioning of the organizational process. These are the inputs without which an organization simply could not continue to exist or meet its objectives. We can readily appreciate that human beings rely on certain vital inputs such as air, water, nutrition, warmth, shelter, etc., but organizations have similar needs. An organization's resource inputs fall into four key categories:

1. *Financial resources* – money for capital investment and working capital. Sources include shareholders, banks, bondholders, etc.

2. *Human resources* – appropriately skilled employees to add value in operations and to support those that add value (e.g., supporting employees in marketing, accounting, personnel, etc.). Sources include the labor markets for the appropriate skill levels required by the organization.

3. *Physical (tangible) resources* – land, buildings (offices, accommodation, warehouses, etc.), plant, equipment, stock for production, transport equipment, etc.

4. *Intellectual (intangible) resources* – inputs that cannot be seen or felt but that are essential for continuing business success; for example, 'know-how', legally defensible patents and licenses, brand names, registered designs, logos, 'secret' formulations and recipes, business contact networks, databases, etc.

1.3 The practice of strategy

The number and range of academics, consultants, authors and practitioners claiming to be involved in strategy in some way is vast. Given this diversity, it is unsurprising that, notwithstanding how we might formally define the term strategy, in practice the term has been used in numerous ways.

It was this multiplicity of uses of the term that led Professor Henry Mintzberg of McGill University in Montreal, Canada, originally writing in the late 1980s (Mintzberg, 1987), to propose his '5 Ps' of strategy.

1.3.1 Mintzberg's 5 Ps

Mintzberg suggested that nobody can claim to own the word 'strategy' and that the term can legitimately be used in several ways. A strategy can be:

- A plan
- A ploy
- A pattern of behavior
- A position in respect to others
- A perspective

Note – It is important not to see each of these 5 Ps in isolation. One of the problems of dividing ideas into frameworks, like the 5 Ps, is that they are necessarily simplified. The 5 Ps are not mutually exclusive; that is, it is possible for an organization to show evidence of more than one interpretation of strategy.

PLAN STRATEGIES

Most people use the word strategy in regard to planning. It tends to imply something that is intentionally put in place whose progress is monitored from the start to a predetermined finish. Some business strategies follow this model. 'Planners' tend to produce internal documents that detail what the company will do for a period of time in the future (say, 5 years). It might include a statement on the overall direction that the organization will take in seeking new business opportunities as well as a schedule for new product launches, acquisitions, financing (i.e., raising money), human resource changes, marketing, etc.

PLOY STRATEGIES

A ploy is generally taken to mean a short-term strategy and is concerned with the detailed tactical actions that will be taken. It tends to have very limited objectives and may be subject to change at very short notice. Mintzberg described a ploy as, 'a manoeuvre intended to outwit an opponent or competitor' (Mintzberg, 1987:14). He pointed out that some companies may use ploy strategies as threats. They may threaten to, say, decrease the price of their products simply to destabilize competitors.

PATTERN STRATEGIES

A 'pattern of behavior' strategy is one in which progress is made by adopting a consistent form of behavior. Unlike plans and ploys, patterns 'just happen' as a result of the consistent behavior.

1.2 SHORT CASE ILLUSTRATION

Plan, ploy and pattern strategies: a Northern European tour operator

A large tour operator that operates to various Mediterranean destinations offering holidays mainly to Northern Europeans might operate *plan*, *ploy* and *pattern* strategies in various parts of its business.

- *Plan* – A large tour operator, for instance, might decide that it plans to implement a strategy concerned with expanding its share of the market and that this will be achieved by setting prices at lower levels than competitors and by acquiring smaller firms.

- *Ploy* – Though the tour operator concerned has an overall strategy that includes offering lower price levels than competitors, it might also develop a short-term ploy. The company might suddenly discount its prices within six weeks of customers' departure to destabilize its competitors and to sell excess capacity.

- *Pattern* – In keeping with the consolidation that has taken place in the industry, the tour operator concerned in this illustration might have acquired a small specialist operation offering summer villa and apartment holidays to a particular Greek island to a small but loyal group of customers. This might be viewed as following a *pattern* strategy. The company is unlikely to produce elaborate plans – simply renewing contracts with property owners and transport providers annually. If offered a new villa on favorable terms, the operator would probably contract the property and feature it on its website without thinking about it. It is an opportunity that is taken because it appears too good to miss. However, the tour operator would probably not feature a hotel in Majorca because that would be outside their pattern of business behavior.

Questions

Consider other *THE* situations you are familiar with and provide an example of:

1. A *plan* strategy

2. A *ploy* strategy

3. A *pattern* strategy

Such patterns of behavior are sometimes unconscious, meaning that one does not even realize that they are actually following a consistent pattern. Nevertheless, if it proves successful, it is said that the consistent behavior has *emerged* into a success. This is in direct contrast to planning behavior.

KEY CONCEPT

Deliberate and emergent strategy

There is a key difference between two of Mintzberg's 5 Ps of strategy – *plan* and *pattern*. The difference is to do with the source of the strategy. He drew attention to the fact that some strategies are *deliberate*, whereas others are *emergent*.

Deliberate strategy (sometimes called *planned* or *prescriptive* strategy) is meant to happen. It is preconceived and premeditated and usually monitored and controlled from start to finish. It has a specific objective.

Emergent strategy has no specific objective. It does not have a preconceived route to success, but it may be just as effective as a deliberate strategy. By following a consistent pattern of behavior, an organization may arrive at the same position as if it had planned everything in detail.

The difference between these is fundamental in studying strategy. In practice, few companies have a totally deliberate or totally emergent strategy but have a combination of the two to some degree. To have a totally deliberate strategy would imply a lack of flexibility, which would be dangerous for any organization when the environment can change quickly and fundamentally. To have a totally emergent strategy could also be dangerous in that it possibly implies a lack of forward thinking.

POSITION STRATEGIES

A position strategy is appropriate when the most important issue to an organization is perceived to be how it relates to or is positioned in respect to its competitors or its markets (i.e., its customers). In other words, the organization wishes to achieve or defend a certain position.

In business, companies tend to seek such things as market share, profitability, superior research, reputation, etc. It is plainly obvious that not all companies are equal when such criteria are considered.

THINK POINTS

What are Mintzberg's 5 Ps of strategy?

- Define and distinguish between deliberate and emergent strategy.
- What are the three components of strategy as described by Chandler?

PERSPECTIVE STRATEGIES

Perspective strategies are about changing the culture (the beliefs and the 'feel', the way of looking at the world) of a certain group of people – usually the members of the organization itself. Some companies want to make their employees think in a certain way, believing this to be an important way of achieving success. They may, for example, try to get all employees to think and act courteously, professionally or helpfully.

1.3 SHORT CASE ILLUSTRATION

Position and perspective strategies: hotels and airlines

Many *THE* companies such as international airlines or hotel operators have enviable reputations for reliability and quality, whereas others are not so fortunate.

- *Position* – Competitors with a reputation to defend will use a position strategy to ensure that the reputation they enjoy is maintained and strengthened. This may include advertising and public relations activities, but it may also include a focus on other activities such as improving or adding product features or pricing incentives. Marketing messages may even extend to pointing out the deficiencies in competitors' products while pointing out the positive features of their own. International hotel groups and some airlines have also developed a number of subbrands to ensure that they are able to have apposition they can defend in every segment of the market.

- *Perspective* – This view of strategy is often of central importance to many *THE* companies because they rely on delivering services of consistent quality. In *THE*, the quality of service delivery is often judged by the quality and attitude of those members of staff who are involved with delivering services. Consequently, many *THE* companies invest heavily in developing a strong organizational culture that focuses heavily on the attitude of employees and their quality. Many large hotel groups and airlines, for example, go further and feature such a culture as a core strength. Employees (usually smiling!) are frequently featured in their advertising and other promotional activities because it is the quality of their encounter with customers that is seen as being the key factor in achieving a high degree of customer satisfaction.

Questions

Consider other *THE* situations you are familiar with and provide an example of:

1. A *position* strategy

2. A *perspective* strategy

1.4 Levels of decision making

It is useful at this stage to gain an understanding of what characterizes strategic decisions. Management decisions in an organization can be classified into three broad and sometimes overlapping categories: strategic, tactical and operational. These can be illustrated as a hierarchy (see Figure 1.1) in which higher level decisions tend to shape those at lower levels of the organization.

Strategic, tactical and operational decisions within an organization differ from each other in terms of their:

- Focus
- Level in the organization at which they are made
- Scope
- Time horizon
- Degree of certainty or uncertainty
- Complexity

The differences between the three levels of decision making are summarized in Table 1.1.

1.4.1 *Strategic-level decisions*

Strategic decisions (which are our primary focus) are concerned with:

- The acquisition of *sustainable competitive advantage* (in a commercial organization)
- Setting long-term objectives
- The formulation, evaluation, selection and monitoring of strategies to achieve these objectives

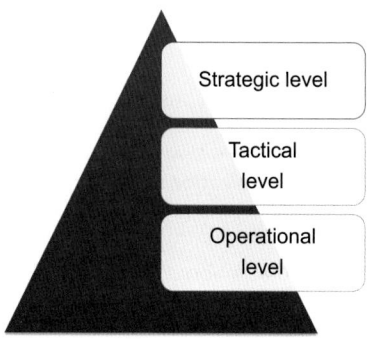

Figure 1.1 Levels of strategic decision making

Table 1.1 Comparison of strategic operational and tactical decisions

	Strategic	Tactical	Operational
Focus of decision	Achieving competitive advantage	Implementation of strategy	Day-to-day operations
Level of decision making	Senior management/ board of directors	Head of business unit or functional area	Supervisory
Scope	Corporate/entire organization	Business unit or functional area; e.g., marketing	Department
Time horizon	Medium to long term (years)	Medium term (months to years)	Short to medium term (weeks to months)
Certainty/uncertainty	High uncertainty.	Some uncertainty	High certainty
Complexity	Highly complex	Moderately complex	Comparatively simple
Examples	Decisions to launch new products, enter new markets, take over competitors, investment decisions	Decision to advertise adjust prices, alter product features, etc.	Scheduling of work rotas, reordering supplies, etc.

Strategic decisions normally have a number of characteristic features in that they:

- Are made by senior managers (usually directors)
- Affect the whole organization (or a substantial discrete part of the whole organization
- Are medium to long term in nature
- Are complex and often based on uncertain or incomplete information

Managers at the strategic level require multiconceptual skills – the ability to consider the effects of multiple internal and external influences on the business and the possible ways in which strategy can be adjusted to account for such influences.

KEY CONCEPT

The focus of strategic decisions

Strategic developments for an organization imply that strategic decisions have to be made. Strategic decisions are decisions that:

- Are of major importance to an organization's future development
- Require a substantial commitment of resources (financial and other) by an organization
- Involve choices that have to be made about the deployment of finite resources between competing strategic options
- Are complex in nature and often based on incomplete information

- Are normally made by senior managers
- Involve key changes that need to be carefully managed
- Have an impact over a medium to long term period (more than 1 year) rather than short term (less than 1 year)

1.4.2 Tactical-level decisions

Tactical decisions are concerned with how strategic-level objectives are to be met and how strategies are implemented. They are dependent on overall strategy and involve fine-tuning and adjustment. They are usually made at the head of business unit, department or functional area level, and they have an effect only in parts of the organization. They are normally medium term and semi-complex and usually involve some uncertainty but not as much as at the strategic level.

1.4.3 Operational-level decisions

Operational decisions are concerned with the shorter-term objectives of the business and with its day-to-day management. They are dependent on strategy and tactics. These decisions are made at the junior managerial or supervisory level, are based on a high degree of certainty and are not complex.

The different levels of decision making are illustrated in the case of a hypothetical Australian events management company in the following Short Case Illustration.

1.4 SHORT CASE ILLUSTRATION

Levels of decision making: an Australian events management company

Total Event Solutions (TES) is a hypothetical events management company based in Sydney, Australia. The company has successfully operated in that market for many years organizing conferences, meetings, exhibitions and other events for both large and small clients in the local region and throughout the state of New South Wales. The market is extremely competitive, and many of the larger companies TES works with have stated that they have difficulties in extending their working relationship with TES, though they are very satisfied with the service they have received. This is because the larger companies they represent have a nationwide presence and they need a partner to manage events that can also work on a nationwide basis.

TES's board of directors met and decided that to prosper in the future and compete effectively with national and international rivals in the market, TES had to expand to cover the entire Australian market. It was determined that it would do so by opening branch offices in each of the country's other state capitals. However, to expand too rapidly can be an extremely risky aspect of business and lead to so-called overtrading. In such a situation, though the underlying business may be sound, investment may mean that cash flow is negative for a period of time and thus has to be financed in some way. This occurs because financial and other resources need to be deployed before sales are achieved and revenue flows in. If there are unexpected adverse changes to the business environment or levels of expected sales are not achieved, those providing finance (generally shareholders or banks) might withdraw the finance, thereby leading to potential business failure.

Consequently, the board of directors laid down the condition that national coverage should be achieved not immediately but within 5 years through a phased opening of state offices in the key cities of Melbourne, Perth; Adelaide, Brisbane, and Hobart. The CEO and his senior team subsequently met to consider the growth plan and determined a schedule for opening the offices, which involved a phased opening over 5 years starting with Melbourne and Brisbane in the subsequent year. As in every year, sales targets were set for the Sydney office and new annual targets were set for TES's first new offices that would be opened in the coming year in Melbourne and Brisbane.

Questions

1. Distinguish between strategic-, tactical- and operational-level decisions in the TES example.

2. Explain what is meant by the term *overtrading*.

1.4.4 Congruency and 'fit'

The success of strategy rests on a very important, but rather obvious, principle. Once the strategic-level objectives have been set, the tactical and operational objectives must be set in such a way that they contribute to the achievement of the strategic objectives. In other words, the tactical and operational decisions must 'fit' the strategic objectives. This introduces the concept of *hierarchical congruence*; that is, that objectives set at various levels must be aligned with each other in such a way that each level of organizational decision making contributes to the organization's overall strategic objectives.

The decision-making framework can be visualized as a hierarchy shaped as a pyramid (as in Figure 1.1). The top, where the strategic decisions are made, is thin, whereas the bottom (operational decisions) is wider. This representation is meant to show that strategic decisions are taken infrequently, whereas tactical and operational decisions are taken more often. Strategic decisions are few and far between, tactical decisions are taken with increasing frequency and operational decisions are taken weekly, daily or even hourly. For every one strategic decision, there may be hundreds of individual operational decisions.

THINK POINTS

- Explain the meaning and significance of the term 'hierarchical congruence' for an organization.
- Why is hierarchical congruence important in successful strategy?

1.4.5 Time and planning horizons

One of the key differences between the levels of decision making in organizations is the timescale with which they are concerned. It is usually considered that the higher up the organization, the longer the timescale management is concerned with. This is certainly true in most manufacturing companies. However, in service organizations, such as *THE* organizations, the situation is often somewhat different.

Service delivery is of prime importance to service-based companies, and consequently relatively senior staff can often be involved to some degree in operational decision making. In the delivery of services it is vital that managers ensure that the service provided is:

- Delivered to specified quality standards
- Capable of being replicated
- Resilient (i.e., service standards can resist unexpected changes)

The differing time horizons for decision making are illustrated in the Short Case Illustration of a group of hotels.

1.5 SHORT CASE ILLUSTRATION

Decision-making time horizons: a hotel group

A group of hotels demonstrates the different levels of decision making and the differing time horizons that are usually involved with each level.

In a group of hotels, most of the staff will be concerned with ensuring that the daily bookings run to schedule and are delivered satisfactorily. The manager and senior hotel staff will, however, have wider concerns. They will probably have weekly, monthly and annual budgets and sales targets to hit. These requirements of their roles means that they will need to consider the hotel's position up to a year ahead. The chief executive of the whole group of hotels may have a longer time frame because they and their senior team may be considering what the potential threats and opportunities in the marketplace might be and how this particular hotel group might respond.

Questions

1. Explain why the hierarchy of decision making might be different in some service-based companies such as those in *THE*.

2. Why is service delivery likely to be so important to all managers at every level in this case?

Strategic management involves taking account of a large number of *environmental* variables (considered in Part 2 of this book). The further ahead a manager seeks to plan, the more uncertainty is introduced into the analysis.

1.5 Objectives

1.5.1 *Types of objectives*

The different levels of decision making are reflected in the way in which organizations set objectives. Objectives can be written in two forms:

- *Closed* – Stated in quantitative terms, specific in form and timescale
- *Open* – Stated in qualitative terms, general in form and timescale

Table 1.2 A hierarchy of objectives

Level of hierarchy	Focus	Type	Timescale
Mission	Strategic – Overall organization	Open	Long term
Values	Strategic – Overall organization	Open	Long term
Vision	Strategic – Overall organization	Open	Medium to long term
Corporate objectives	Strategic – Overall organization	Primary – Closed Secondary – Open and closed	Medium to long term
Business objectives	Strategic/tactical – *SBU*	Closed	Medium term
Unit/team objectives	Operational	Closed	Short term
Personal	Operational	Closed	Short term

It is important at the outset to understand two important points about the way in which objectives are used in practice in organizations:

- Objectives take different forms (open or closed) at the various levels of the organization (see Table 1.2).
- Objectives can be described in different ways; that is, organizations will use varying terminology to describe their objectives.

Objectives in an organization are often portrayed as a hierarchy in which the organization sets out:

- An overall enduring purpose by way of – its *mission*
- The way in which the organization will carry out its activities – its *values*
- A desired future position it is trying to reach – its *vision*
- How the mission and vision will be translated into specific targets – *corporate objectives, business objectives, unit or team and personal objectives*

1.5.2 Hierarchy of objectives

The hierarchy of decision making in organizations is reflected in a hierarchy of objectives as shown in Table 1.2. The mission, values, vision and corporate objectives can be cascaded down the hierarchy of the organization. In this way, the overall mission and vision for the organization are translated to give meaning for each constituent part and, in some cases, each individual employee in their business, unit or team and personal objectives.

1.5.3 Mission, vision and values – overview

An organization's mission, vision and values can be viewed as manifestations of an organization's identity – its 'personality' – which is visible to both internal groups within the organization and often external groups (stakeholders) as well.

A great deal of management literature has been devoted to the successful adoption of statements relating to missions, vision and values (see, for example, Kemp and Dwyer, 2003; Sufi and Lyons, 2003; Kantabutra and Avery, 2010; Powers, 2012; Alegre et al., 2018; Law and Breznik, 2018; Lin et al., 2018). In essence, the intention is that the statements should be clear and inspiring so that employees have a common framework of objectives they can understand and aspire to and external stakeholders have a clear view of what the organization is striving to achieve.

Here we encounter some of the confusion that is often evident in dealing with strategy, because different terminology can be encountered to describe essentially the same aspect and the position of different aspects of strategy can be altered.

> For example: *Terminology such as 'strategic intent', 'company philosophy' and 'corporate goals' can sometimes be encountered to describe the mission and vision. In some cases the mission might be subordinated to vision (rather than the other way round) – which is more usual.*

In some organizations the mission, vision and values are not labeled at all, or the values are incorporated into the mission statement. Thus, organizations create different presentational norms (the presentation of strategy is discussed further in Chapter 17) and use varying terminology or no terminology at all. However, the differing terminology should not blind us as to the purpose of such statements. The intent is clear:

> The statements are intended to create a clear framework for decision making within the organization and are disseminated through the organizational hierarchy, as shown in Table 1.2.

KEY CONCEPT

Mission, vision and values

The *mission*, *vision* and *values* of organizations can take many forms in different organizations, and different words can often be substituted for these terms. Much discussion has also taken place in the academic literature about what is entailed in each of these concepts, the usefulness of these statements and how they should be presented. One view of what each of the statements is trying to achieve is presented below. An organization's

- *Mission* – describes what the organization does

- *Vision* – sets out some desired future state; it articulates, often in bold terms, what the company would like to achieve.

- *Values* – state how managers and employees should conduct themselves, how they should do business and what kind of organization they should build to help the organization achieve its mission

Source: Adapted from Hill et al. (2020)

1.5.4 Mission and mission statements

Powers (2012) argued that management professionals generally agree that the critical first step in planning is the definition of an organizational mission. A mission statement articulates the fundamental purpose of the organization and often contains several components (Hitt et al., 2019), among them:

- Company philosophy
- Company identity or self-concept
- Principal products or services
- Customers and markets
- Geographic focus
- Obligations to shareholders
- Commitment to employees

The mission is the objective that subsumes all others beneath it; for some organizations the mission is very easy to articulate, but for large commercial businesses it tends to be more complex. Differing views for writing mission statements have emerged, and though there does not appear to be universal acceptance of any one particular format or set of attributes, Powers (2012) usefully summarized the different approaches. Williams (2008) assessed the mission statements in relation to their performance of larger American companies in the Fortune 1000 list. Similarly, in a study of Dutch mission statements, Sidhu (2003) concluded that mission statements can lead to superior performance.

Some organizations attempt to frame their mission in a formal statement, which is often to be seen adorning office walls, printed on employee identity cards and published in annual reports. Mission statements are commonly found both in the commercial sector and in the noncommercial (*not-for-profit*) sector. Because the mission statement represents a long-term perspective, it often is retained by organizations for many years, despite the many changes that may occur within the organization and in the external environment.

The Asian low-cost airline AirAsia, for example, has a long-established vision and mission statement, shown below together with its associated values statement.

1.6 SHORT CASE ILLUSTRATION

Vision, mission and values: AirAsia

Our vision

To be the largest low-cost airline in Asia and serving the 3 billion people who are currently underserved with poor connectivity and high fares.

Our mission

- To be the best company to work for whereby employees are treated as part of a big family
- Create a globally recognized ASEAN brand
- To attain the lowest cost so that everyone can fly with AirAsia
- Maintain the highest quality product, embracing technology to reduce cost and enhance service levels

Values

- Dare to Dream – Progress comes from innovation. Both require change to happen.
- People First – Care for our people, care for our guests.
- Make it Happen – Learn fast and deliver more with less.
- Be Guest-Obsessed – Understand deeply what our guests want. Then give them more than they expect.
- One AirAsia – We are one airline, with one vision and one people.
- Safety Always – Safety is everyone's responsibility; it starts with you.
- Sustainability Spirit – Acting today for a better tomorrow.

Source: www.airasia.com

A mission statement has a number of possible purposes. It can be used to clearly communicate the objectives and values of the organization to the various *stakeholder* groups, and it can be argued that it assists in achieving *strategic congruence*.

In other words, it sets a framework for the setting of other objectives, so that they are developed in a consistent manner at different levels of the organization. It may also have an effect in influencing the behavior and attitudes of employees, although this is somewhat debatable because anecdotal evidence suggests that many employees have not, in fact, read their organization's mission statement.

A mission statement can be seen as the starting point for an organization's entire planning process because it requires senior management to seriously consider where the firm is now and where it should be in the future. This point is emphasized by two leading management writers in the quotation below.

> **DEFINITION/QUOTATION**
>
> In business like in art, what distinguishes leaders from laggards, and greatness from mediocrity, is the ability to uniquely imagine what could be.
>
> (Hamel and Prahalad, 1994:25)

However, establishing an organization's mission is not easy or without controversy and, as a result, styles and content vary enormously, as leading management writer Peter Drucker points out in the quotation below.

> **DEFINITION/QUOTATION**
>
> Defining the purpose and mission of the business is difficult, painful and risky. But it alone enables a business to set objectives, to develop strategies, to concentrate its resources and to go to work. It alone enables a business to be managed for performance.
>
> (Drucker, 1974:94)

Campbell and Yeung (1998) emphasized that though the mission statement itself is clearly important, it is also important for managers to instill a 'sense of mission' in employees. The success of the mission requires the behavior of employees to match the values of the company, but such harmony is difficult to achieve and requires the mission as it is implemented to become embedded as part of the organizational culture.

One view of what effective mission statements should contain is provided below.

STRATEGY IN PRACTICE

Effective mission statements

The mission statement should be:

- **Clearly articulated** – simple to comprehend so that employees and other stakeholders can clearly understand the principles and values that will guide them in their dealings with the organization. The statement must be specific enough to have an impact upon the behavior of individuals.

- **Relevant** – appropriate to the organization in terms of its history, culture and shared values. The mission should not be too broad or too narrow. Too broad may result in lack of focus. Too narrow may mean factors that are potentially important to the organization will be overlooked.

- **Current** – an unchanged mission statement may no longer be able to act as a driving force guiding the organization into the future.

- **Positive in tone** – written in such a way that encourages commitment and energizes or inspires employees.

- **Individual** – sets the organization apart from other organizations establishing its individuality, if not its uniqueness, through an emphasis on the advantages of the organization based on an objective assessment of organizational strengths and weaknesses.

- **Enduring** – cannot be continually altered, because this would be confusing, so they are likely to remain in place for a number of years. Consequently, they must be written to allow for some flexibility.

- **Adapted** – written with various target audiences in mind, some for employees only, some for shareholders and other external groups and others for all audiences. The information and style should reflect the relevant target audience.

Source: Adapted from Stone (1996)

1.5.5 What does a mission statement contain?

The style, content and terminology of mission statements vary enormously. Some are long and detailed, whereas others are short and to the point. Some are focused on a particular audience (such as employees or customers), whereas others are written with multiple target audiences in mind. There are probably no 'rights' or 'wrongs' of how it should be presented or what it should contain; it all depends on the organization and its culture.

In assessing mission statements, the reader will find many examples of the use of language that is ambiguous in its meaning or is questionable in its use of 'hype' to inflate the image of the organization. In practice, many mission statements contain a statement on the aspects listed below.

STRATEGY IN PRACTICE

Mission statement content

In practice, mission statements usually contain one or more of the following:

- Some indication of the industry or business the organization is mainly concerned with
- An indication of the realistic market share or market position the organization should aim toward
- A brief summary of the values and beliefs of the organization in relating to key stakeholder groups such as customers and employees
- An indication of the ownership or control of the organization
- A summary of the geographical location or scope of organizational activities

In addition, specific and highly context-dependent objectives are sometimes expressed in the mission statement.

A further example of a mission statement taken from a tourism destination organization is presented in the following Short Case Illustration.

1.7 SHORT CASE ILLUSTRATION

Vision, mission and values: VISIT FLORIDA

VISIT FLORIDA, the state's official tourism marketing corporation, serves as Florida's official source for travel planning to visitors across the globe. VISIT FLORIDA is not a government agency but rather a not-for-profit corporation created as a PPP.

As the state's number one industry, Florida received 126.1 million visitors in 2018, who spent more than $67.2bn, and 1.4 million people were employed in the industry.

Purpose:

Brighten the lives of all

Vision:

Establish Florida as the No. 1 travel destination in the world

Mission:

Strengthen Florida's share of the global travel market

Goal:

Maximize the economic impact of travel and tourism to Florida

Objective:

Generate $100 billion in tourism-related spend by 2020

Values:

Make an Impact
Work Purposefully & Live Passionately
Innovate
Source: www.visitflorida.org

1.5.6 Vision and values

As with the mission, there is no firm, generally accepted definition of vision or values, and different styles with various features can be encountered.

Although strategy and leadership writers have proposed different characteristics that a vision *should* have, some commonly shared characteristics can be identified. Kantabutra and Avery (2010), for instance, identified seven characteristics that might be found in vision statements that are perceived as making a difference to organizational performance.

STRATEGY IN PRACTICE

What do 'powerful' visions look like?

- *Conciseness* – Visions should be easy to communicate and remember.

- *Clarity* – Visions directly point at a prime goal. They can be understood without extended presentation and discussion.

- *Future orientation* – Visions that are powerful do not consist of a one-time, specific goal or productivity target (e.g., sales or profit) that can be met and then discarded.

- *Stability* – Visions do not shift in response to short-term trends, technology or market changes. They must be flexible enough to weather fluctuations.

- *Challenge* – Visions that are effective are challenging because they motivate staff members to try their best to achieve desired outcomes.

- *Abstractness* – Visions that are abstract suggest a longer-term goal that also allows for individual interpretations.

- *Desirability or ability to inspire* – Powerful visions must be highly desirable and inspiring. They state a goal that directly inspires staff.

Source: Kantabutra and Avery (2010)

As individuals, we have a set of values that govern the way we behave, and so it is with organizations. Organizations will have a set of guiding principles (i.e., values), though they may not be explicitly expressed in a statement, or they be subsumed within the mission statement.

The organization's values can be viewed as the philosophical principles that the great majority of its members hold in common (Haberberg and Rieple, 2001). The values are normally enduring and often closely associated with the organizational leadership because they set the parameters within which the organization operates.

1.6 The content of corporate objectives

In strict terms, the most important of all objectives is to simply survive as a going concern. Other objectives depend on the type of organization and the nature of its environment. The objectives are not necessarily mutually exclusive in that an organization can usually pursue more than one type of objective at the same time. Two leading writers referred to them as 'the end the firm seeks and the criteria the firm uses to determine its effectiveness' (Glueck and Jauch, 1988:12).

The objectives can be written in a *closed* manner – that is, stated in quantitative terms and specific in relation to form and timescale – or in an *open* manner; that is, stated in qualitative terms and general in form and timescale.

Objectives are essential to the successful accomplishment of the managerial function in any formal organization in that they:

- Provide a sense of direction
- Provide a standard of measurement and a means of controlling performance
- Project an image of the organization's style

Corporate objectives translate the mission and vision into specific long-term targets that can usually be quantified and measured. Corporate objectives are strategic-level objectives that can be used as a starting point in setting *business* and tactical or *operational objectives*, which are more detailed objectives set lower down the organizational hierarchy. Business objectives will usually relate to important constituent parts of the overall organization – often termed *strategic business units* (SBUs), whereas operational objectives will usually relate to smaller units or teams within each SBU.

Corporate objectives normally:

- Relate to the whole organization
- Apply to the medium to long term*
- Are set by senior management
- Relate to a number of key areas of concern
- Can be pursued simultaneously

*Note – Time horizons vary considerably and will depend largely on the nature of the business, especially the lead time taken to launch new products and services. In some sectors, where heavy capital expenditure is required, development is time-consuming lead times may be long, whereas in others lead times can be much shorter. As a working rule, the long term is often considered to be 5+ years, the medium term 1 to 5 years, and the short term under 2 years.

> **For example:** *In many cases in service industries such as THE, lead times can be comparatively short, because launching a new destination or new route or planning and staging most events can be achieved relatively quickly. However, where large capital investment is required, as with hotel construction or new aircraft or cruise ship purchases, lead times are likely to be quite long.*

Care must be taken in writing corporate objectives so that they are clear and easily understood.

> ### STRATEGY IN PRACTICE
>
> #### Objective writing is a 'CRIME'
>
> A common view is that objective writing is a **CRIME** in that corporate objectives should be:
>
> - **C:** *Communicable* – capable of being easily communicated down the line to the work-force and other internal and external stakeholder groups
> - **R:** *Realistic* – capable of being achieved within the timescale
> - **I:** *Internally consistent* – consistent with the overall organizational mission, the operational objectives and the strategy for achieving the objectives set
> - **M:** *Measurable* – capable of being quantified so that they can be measured and whether the objectives have been achieved is possible to assess
> - **E:** *Explicit* – written in clear unambiguous language, precise in relation to both targets set and timescale

Corporate objectives often relate to economic and social concerns and to matters of growth and competitive advantage. The main issues addressed by corporate objectives will now be considered.

1.6.1 Economic objectives

Economic objectives are those that can be measured in financial ways. For commercial organizations, objectives will usually include measures such as *return*. Return is an accounting term to describe the proportion of either sales or investment capital that is left over as profit. In commercial organizations, the economic objective is often referred to as the *primary objective*, with other objectives being *secondary* to the achievement of the financial objective.

Return on sales, sometimes referred to as profit margin, is an indication of how well the company has controlled its costs, and *return on assets* (or *return on capital employed*) is an indication of how efficiently the company has used its investors' money. Both of these are important business objectives – to provide sufficient return to retain some profits for future investment and to provide investors with a dividend on their shareholding.

Not-for-profit organizations also have economic objectives, but they are measured in different ways. Organizations like destination marketing organizations, museums, charities and government departments tend to measure economic performance by using *cost–benefit* or *value-for-money* objectives. These organizations usually rely in large part on income over which they have little control; it may, for example, be fixed by central or local government. The objectives set will typically involve extracting the maximum benefit in terms of outputs from the income they receive.

1.6.2 Social objectives

It should not be assumed that all organizational objectives are financial in nature. Many exist, either in part or totally, to deliver social benefits. Many publicly funded organizations such as museums, art galleries, heritage attractions and so on exist to deliver services to society in general. Charities exist primarily to provide social benefit to one or more purportedly worthwhile constituencies. For organizations of this type, economic objectives may be secondary to their desire to deliver socially desirable ends.

Commercial organizations are also gradually adopting social objectives in their strategic planning as part of what they view as their *corporate social responsibilities* (CSRs). Although they are usually subordinate to their economic objectives, commercial organizations may espouse social or environmental causes that they purport to believe in. They may, for example, recognize the social value of supporting local community projects or seconding (at their own expense) some of their people to serve with charities.

1.6.3 Growth or market share objectives

At some stages in the life of an organization, objectives concerning growth and expansion become among the most important. This is especially true of businesses that must grow and maintain market position to 'keep up with' or 'keep ahead of' competitors.

Size and market position offer a number of advantages, and it is these that an organization seeks when growth is a key objective. Size gives an organization economy of scale advantages in both product and resource markets. It means that a larger organization attracts resource inputs at preferential unit costs compared to smaller concerns and its larger presence in its product markets increases its *pricing power* and its ability to subjugate competitors. We will consider the basis for this type of objective in more depth in Chapter 11.

1.6.4 Competitive advantage objectives

Finally, and importantly, many strategic objectives concern the company's position in respect to its competitors. Competitive advantage objectives concern how the company's position compares to others – especially to competitors. The objectives are limited to ensuring simply that 'we beat you' or 'we are better than you'. Superior performance is the only objective, and if a company can achieve ascendancy over its nearest competitors, the objective will have been accomplished.

1.7 How do businesses set objectives?

Earlier in this chapter, we introduced the idea that strategic objectives, because they represent the most important level of decision making, are set by an organization's senior management, usually the board of directors. In setting objectives, however, senior managers are likely to be influenced by a range of different groups that have an interest in the organization.

Who or what influences the senior management in their objective setting? Two broad schools of thought have emerged: the stockholder approach and the stakeholder approach.

1.7.1 The stockholder approach

The stockholder approach argues that businesses exist primarily for their owners (usually shareholders). Accordingly, any business behavior that renders profit performance suboptimal is not only theft from shareholders but will also, eventually, lead to a level of business performance that will harm all other groups, include employees, customers and suppliers.

Nobel Laureate Professor Milton Friedman (1970) contended that the moral obligation of business is to increase its profits. Friedman argued that the one and only obligation of company directors (who are the legal agents of shareholders' financial interests) is to act in such a way as to maximize the financial rate of return on the owners' shares. As he memorably and succinctly put it: the 'business of business is profits' (1970:195).

1.7.2 The stakeholder approach

There are many examples of different stakeholders, and the term is defined below.

DEFINITION/QUOTATION

A stakeholder can be defined as:

> Any group or individual who can affect or is affected by the achievement of an organization's objectives.
>
> (Freeman, 2010:46)

This definition draws in almost everybody that is or may be potentially involved in the life of an organization. It consequently goes without saying that not all stakeholders are equal in their influence on an organization's objectives.

The stakeholder approach, as advocated, for example, by Donaldson and Preston (1995), Campbell (1997) and Freeman (2010), argues that organizations (like individual people) are characterized by their relationships with various groups and individuals such as employees and customers. A group or individual qualifies as a stakeholder if it has a legitimate interest in the organization's activities and thus has the power to affect the firm's performance and/or has a stake in the firm's performance.

The implications of this proposition are far-reaching. In essence, *stakeholder theory* argues that shareholders are neither the sole owners of a business nor the sole beneficiaries of its activities. Though shareholders are undeniably one stakeholder group (in a commercial business), they are far from being the only group who expect to benefit from business activity and, accordingly, are just one of the groups that have a legitimate right to influence a company's strategic objectives. Some of these groups are internal to the organization and others are external.

Stakeholder groups that might be able to exert an influence over the setting of objectives are shown in Table 1.3.

1.7.3 Stakeholders and objectives

One widely used and useful model for understanding how stakeholders exert influence on an organization's objectives was proposed by Mendelow (1991). According to this model, stakeholders can be 'ranked' depending on two variables: the stakeholders' *interest* and *power*.

- Stakeholder *power* refers to the *ability* to influence the organization.
- Stakeholder *interest* refers to the *willingness* to influence the organization.

In other words, interest concerns the extent to which the stakeholder cares about what the organization does.

Table 1.3 A summary of stakeholder groups

Internal stakeholders	External stakeholders
Board of directors	Shareholders
Employees collectively	Creditors (existing and potential)
Individual employees (e.g., founding entrepreneur)	Suppliers (existing and potential)
Employees' representatives (trade unions, trade associations, etc.)	Customers (existing and potential)
Functional business areas (marketing, finance, human resources, etc.)	Trade bodies (e.g., tourism associations)
Geographical areas of the organization (e.g., Europe, Asia, etc.)	Pressure groups (e.g., environmental)
SBUs	Competitors (current and future, national and international)
	Government (legal, fiscal and regulatory impacts)
	Private individuals
	Regulatory bodies (e.g., IATA)
	The local community

It then follows that:

$$\text{Stakeholder influence} = \text{Power} \times \text{Interest}$$

The actual influence that a stakeholder is able to exert will depend on where the stakeholder is positioned with respect to the ability to influence and willingness to influence. A stakeholder with both high power and high interest will be more influential than one with low power and low interest. We can map stakeholders by showing the two variables on a grid comprising two intersecting continua as shown in Figure 1.2). Mendelow's *power–interest matrix* was developed further by Bourne and Walker (2005, 2008) as the *Stakeholder Circle,* which aims to improve the chances for success stakeholder engagement by identifying ways to develop effective relationships with key stakeholders.

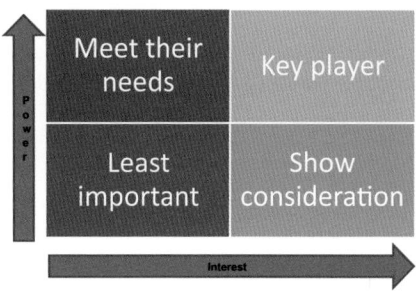

Figure 1.2 The stakeholder map

Source: Adapted from Mendelow (1991)

Once constructed, the map can be used to assess two aspects:

1. Which stakeholder is likely to exert the most influence on the organization's objectives
2. The stakeholders that are most likely to be in potential conflict over strategic objectives (where two or more stakeholders are in close proximity in the high power/high interest part of the map)

The managing director and the board of directors are examples of stakeholders with both high power and high interest. This is because they lead and manage the business and depend on it for their jobs and their positions within the organization give them power with which to implement their decisions. The local community (in most cases) will not concern itself with the setting of organizational objectives and have limited power to impose its views. Organizations will have a range of stakeholders, some of whom might have opposing views.

In applying stakeholder theory and stakeholder mapping in *THE* contexts, quite a large literature has emerged, particularly in relation to *sustainable* approaches to business. Indeed, it is now widely accepted that stakeholder consultation is necessary for sustainable tourism development to occur (Hardy and Pearson, 2018).

Roxas et al. (2020), for example, argued that tourism planning and development has increasingly revolved around sustainability concepts and issues but that addressing these concerns has become increasingly challenging. By appealing to the fundamental principles and practices of sustainability and how stakeholder involvement and participation are fused into sustainable tourism development, the authors develop a 5-point tourism stakeholder framework. The framework seeks to explain how tourism stakeholders can harness their roles to effectively govern destinations.

In applying stakeholder theory to event tourism contexts, Todd et al. (2017) provided insights into stakeholder groups recognizing that the survival and continued success of hallmark events is dependent on those groups of 'primary' stakeholders who are most involved and engaged. Getz et al. (2006). discussed multiple case studies of various types of festivals in two countries to reveal how festival managers work with stakeholders and who they are by utilizing stakeholder classification techniques.

THINK POINTS

- Explain what is meant by a mission statement.
- In what ways might a mission statement help in achieving strategic objectives?
- What is a stakeholder, and in what ways might stakeholders influence objective setting?
- Explain how the power–interest map helps to identify the most influential stakeholders.

The Australian Council of National Trusts, for example (see the following Short Case Illustration), will have a wide range of stakeholder views that need to be considered.

1.8 SHORT CASE ILLUSTRATION

Stakeholders: the Australian Council of National Trusts

The National Trust of Australia is a community-based nongovernmental organization committed to promoting and conserving Australia's indigenous, natural and historic heritage through its advocacy work and its custodianship of heritage places and objects.

The Australian National Trust movement was established in New South Wales in 1945 by Annie Wyatt, who, along with a group of other citizens, raised community consciousness of widespread destruction of the built and natural heritage in Sydney. The National Trust movement quickly spread across Australia, with the other states establishing National Trust offices throughout the 1950s and 1960s. The Northern and Australian Capital Territories were the last to establish a National Trust (in 1976). Each state's and territory's national trust is a fully autonomous entity in its own right and responsible for managing its own affairs.

The National Trust of Australia relies heavily on community support generated through membership subscriptions, sponsorship, donations and bequests, property admissions and retail sales. Of the collective total operational revenue generated by the organization, less than 10% is sourced from government.

Collectively the organization owns or manages over 300 heritage places (the majority held in perpetuity), manages a volunteer workforce of 7,000 and employs about 350 people.

Questions

1. Identify the principal stakeholder groups in this case.

2. Which stakeholder groups are likely to be the most influential, and why do you consider this to be the case?

Source: www.nationaltrust.org.au/

1.8 Stakeholders and corporate governance

Corporate governance has a key role in strategic management. 'Good' governance underpins the corporate mission, values and vision; ensures compliance with legal requirements and government regulations; and encourages transparency in management. Crucially for our purposes, because governance is concerned with who controls and manages the organization, governance has a key role in setting the strategy for an organization.

As a result of well-publicized corporate failures, frauds and unfairness in terms of how business is conducted, corporate governance has become a subject of widespread discussion around the world since the early 1990s, not least in the academic literature. For a full discussion, see, for example, Mallin (2016), Du Plessis et al. (2018) and Solomon (2020). In *THE* contexts, specific corporate governance issues have also been explored by, for example, Guillet and Mattila (2010), Bramwell (2011), Scott and Marzano (2015), Yameen et al. (2019) and Li and Singal (2021).

The importance of corporate governance arises largely from the separation of the role of management and ownership in controlling modern organizations. The interests of shareholders are sometimes viewed as conflicting with the interests of managers, because shareholders are usually primarily concerned with financial returns, whereas managers, it is argued, have to consider a wider range of views from other stakeholders such as employees, bankers and the community.

Increasingly the concept has evolved to address the rise of CSR and sustainability issues (addressed in Chapter 16) and the more active participation of both shareholders and other stakeholders in corporate decision making (Claessens and Yurtoglu, 2006). Definitions of corporate governance vary widely, and this diversity reflects reality, in that corporate governance takes different forms in different countries and is applied in various ways to different types of organizations. Indeed, it has been pointed out that no two countries handle corporate governance in precisely the same way (Jacoby, 2005). One common definition is presented below.

DEFINITION/QUOTATION

So, what exactly is corporate governance? One widely quoted definition is that:

> It comprises the laws and practices by which managers are held accountable to those who have a legitimate stake in the corporation.

Defining who has a legitimate stake is less straightforward than it sounds. Shareholders are a key constituency, and usually their interests are represented by the board of directors.

Source: Jacoby (2005)

A key theme of corporate governance is the role of the board of directors. In most organizations it is the board of directors that makes the key decisions that affect the organization, including the framing of strategy. Typically, the board comprises:

- Executive directors, who are full-time senior managers in the organization
- Nonexecutive directors, who are part-timers brought in for their expertise to provide an independent view
- In some countries (particularly in Europe), workers' representatives

The board chair can be an executive or nonexecutive, and another key figure on the board is the CEO, who normally is responsible for managing the organization on a day-to-day basis. Most corporate governance codes recommend that the roles of the chair and CEO in an organization be separated, because they have different responsibilities, and one of the responsibilities of the chair is the appointment of the CEO. However, despite this guidance, there are in practice many instances where the roles are in fact combined and carried out by the same person.

Though detailed corporate governance provisions vary around the world, a key theme of guidelines issued by governments is that boards should operate independently of the management of the company, thereby highlighting the role of the independent nonexecutive directors. In this way, as Lynch (2021:225) pointed out, there is a separation of the interests of the organization represented by the stakeholders and the control of the organization carried out by the directors.

1.8.1 Corporate governance and sustainability

Boards have come under recurring pressure in recent years (exerted by stakeholder groups) for their organizations to be more responsive to the sustainability of the natural environment and also to consider their social role in society (see, for example, Aras and Crowther, 2008; Scherer and Voegtlin, 2020). Analysis of the natural environment is considered in Chapter 7, and sustainability strategy is discussed in Chapter 16.

Small business focus

SMEs are often sadly neglected in the strategic management literature, with a concentration on large internationally diversified corporations instead. Many of the tools and techniques that have been developed are certainly primarily explained in the context of such enterprises, but in many cases they can be applied appropriately to smaller enterprises.

One of the key facets about *THE* sectors is that in most cases they are highly fragmented. Whereas vehicle or aircraft manufacture are examples of highly *concentrated* industries with production dominated by a few large corporations, this is not normally the case in *THE* sectors. Some large international diversified companies have developed in *THE* sectors (and continue to do so); nevertheless, it is true that these sectors remain highly fragmented, particularly in developing countries.

The larger companies (such as TUI, Marriott, AirAsia, Carnival Cruises) will certainly be used as examples in this book, but it is important to remember that even in highly developed economies there is often a much larger number of SMEs that have less well-known brand names.

Indeed, in one of the sectors we consider (events management), arguably no strong internationally recognized brand exists and instead there is a plethora of SMEs. In each of the component parts of *THE*, many smaller businesses and organizations exist and many family enterprises continue to thrive, because entry costs are often low and individuality and service flexibility are often valued most by customers.

Small businesses are certainly different from larger businesses in several respects. They are likely to be competing in a limited number of markets with a limited range of products, and they are often 'private' companies as opposed to 'public' companies, making access to finance more difficult. However, many of the strategic concepts, tools and techniques discussed in this book are applicable to SMEs or can be adapted for them.

> **For example:** *Unless the company is specializing in a particular market segment (and has established a specific niche), it is likely to face significant competitive pressures. Thus, those areas of strategy we will consider that deal with competitive strategy (Chapter 10) are particularly relevant in this context.*

In this chapter we introduced the notion that strategy is essentially about 'thinking ahead' in considering the most important issues an organization faces. Furthermore, the mission, vision and values and setting objectives were considered in this chapter. These aspects of strategic management, it can be argued, are valid regardless of organizational size. For SMEs, competitive pressure, the dynamic nature of the environment and the expectations of stakeholder groups (such as banks and other investors) mean that thinking ahead is of vital importance just as they are to their larger competitors.

CHAPTER SUMMARY

This chapter discussed the meanings of the terms *strategy* and *strategic management* and introduced the concepts of deliberate and emergent strategy. It went on to explain the components of strategy before discussing the levels of strategic decision making in organizations and the important concepts of strategic congruence and hierarchy of objectives. The concepts of mission, vision and values were introduced and the role of stakeholders in objective setting was discussed. The main 'types' of objectives were explained, their content was discussed and how organizations set their objectives was considered. The stakeholder vs stockholder approaches to objective setting were discussed and stakeholder mapping was introduced as a means of identifying key groups when setting relevant and realistic objectives. Finally, the issue of corporate governance was introduced, and the notion of separating responsibility for key strategic decisions was discussed.

REFERENCES AND WEBSITES

References

Alegre, I., Berbegal-Mirabent, J., Guerrero, A. and Mas-Machuca, M. (2018) 'The real mission of the mission statement: A systematic review of the literature', *Journal of Management and Organization*, 24(4): 456–473.

Aras, G. and Crowther, D. (2008) 'Governance and sustainability: An investigation into the relationship between corporate governance and corporate sustainability', *Management Decision*, 46(3): 433–448.

Bourne, L. and Walker, D. H. (2005) 'Visualising and mapping stakeholder influence', *Management Decision*, 43(5): 649–660.

Bourne, L. and Walker, D. H. (2008) 'Project relationship management and the Stakeholder Circle™', *International Journal of Managing Projects in Business*, 1(1): 125–130.

Bramwell, B. (2011) 'Governance, the state and sustainable tourism: A political economy approach', *Journal of Sustainable Tourism*, 19(4–5): 459–477.

Campbell, A. (1997) 'Stakeholders: The case in favour', *Long Range Planning*, 30(3): 446–449.

Campbell, A. and Yeung, S. (1998) 'Creating a sense of mission', in S. Segal-Horn (Ed.), *The Strategy Reader*, Oxford, UK: Blackwell, 284–295.

Chandler, A. D. (1962) *Strategy and Structure*, Boston: MIT Press.

Claessens, S. and Yurtoglu, B. (2006) 'Corporate governance and development', *The World Bank Research Observer*, 21(1): 91–122.

Donaldson, T. and Preston, L. E. (1995) 'The stakeholder theory of the corporation: Concepts, evidence, and implications', *Academy of Management Review*, 20(1): 65–91.

Drucker, P. F. (1974) *Management: Tasks, Responsibilities, Practices*, New York: Harper and Row.

Du Plessis, J. J., Hargovan, A. and Harris, J. (2018) *Principles of Contemporary Corporate Governance*, Cambridge, UK: Cambridge University Press.

Enz, C. A. (2009) *Hospitality Strategic Management: Concepts and Cases*, 2nd ed., Hoboken, NJ: John Wiley & Sons.

Freeman, R. E. (2010) *Strategic Management: A Stakeholder Approach*, Cambridge, UK: Cambridge University Press.

Friedman, M. (1970) 'A theoretical framework for monetary analysis', *Journal of Political Economy*, 78(2): 193–238.

Getz, D., Andersson, T. and Larson, M. (2006) 'Festival stakeholder roles: Concepts and case studies', *Event Management*, 10(2–3): 103–122.

Glueck, F. and Jauch, L. R. (1988) *Strategic Management and Business Policy*, 3rd ed., New York: McGraw Hill.

Guillet, B. D. and Mattila, A. S. (2010) 'A descriptive examination of corporate governance in the hospitality industry', *International Journal of Hospitality Management*, 29(4): 677–684.

Haberberg, A. and Rieple, A. (2001) *The Strategic Management of Organisations*, Harlow, UK: FT Prentice Hall.

Hamel, G. and Prahalad, C. K. (1994) *Competing for the Future*, Boston: Harvard Business School Press.

Hardy, A. and Pearson, L. J. (2018) 'Examining stakeholder group specificity: An innovative sustainable tourism approach', *Journal of Destination Marketing and Management*, 8: 247–258.

Harrington, R. J., Chathoth, P. K., Ottenbacher, M. and Altinay, L. (2014) 'Strategic management research in hospitality and tourism: Past, present and future', *International Journal of Contemporary Hospitality Management*, 26(5): 778–808.

Hill, C. W., Schilling, M. A. and Jones, G. R. (2020) *Strategic Management: An Integrated Approach Theory*, Boston: Cengage Learning.

Hitt, M. A., Ireland, R. D. and Hoskisson, R. E. (2019) *Strategic Management Cases: Competitiveness and Globalization*, 13th ed., Boston: Cengage Learning.

Jacoby, S. (2005) 'Corporate governance and society', *Challenge*, 48(4): 69–87.

Kantabutra, S. and Avery, G. C. (2010) 'The power of vision: Statements that resonate', *Journal of Business Strategy*, 31(1): 37–45.

Kemp, S. and Dwyer, L. (2003) 'Mission statements of international airlines: A content analysis', *Tourism Management*, 24(6): 635–653.

Köseoglu, M. A., Law, R., Okumus, F., Barca, M. and Dogan, I. C. (2019) 'Evolution of strategic management research lines in hospitality and tourism', *Journal of Hospitality Marketing and Management*, 28(6): 690–710.

Law, K. M. and Breznik, K. (2018) 'What do airline mission statements reveal about value and strategy?', *Journal of Air Transport Management*, 70: 36–44.

Li, Y. and Singal, M. (2021) 'Corporate governance in the hospitality and tourism industry: Theoretical foundations and future research', *Journal of Hospitality and Tourism Research*, 46(7): 1347–1383.

Lin, Y. H., Ryan, C., Wise, N. and Low, L. W. (2018) 'A content analysis of airline mission statements: Changing trends and contemporary components', *Tourism Management Perspectives*, 28: 156–165.

Lynch, R. (2021) *Strategic Management*, 9th ed., London: Sage.

Mallin, C. (2016) *Corporate Governance*, Oxford. UK: Oxford University Press.

Masterman, G. (2014) *Strategic Sports Event Management*, Abingdon, UK: Routledge.

Mendelow, A. (1991) Proceedings of 2nd International Conference on Information Systems, Cambridge, MA: Plenum Publishers.

Mintzberg, H. (1987) 'Five Ps for strategy', *California Management Review*, 30(1): 11–24.

Monks, R. A. and Minow, N. (2011) *Corporate Governance*, London: John Wiley & Sons.

Moutinho, L. and Vargas-Sanchez, A., eds. (2018) *Strategic Management in Tourism*, 3rd ed., Wallingford, UK: CABI.

Okumus, F., Altinay, L. and Chathoth, P. (2019) *Strategic Management in the International Hospitality and Tourism Industry*, 2nd ed., Abingdon, UK: Routledge.

Okumus, F., Köseoglu, M. A., Morvillo, A. and Altin, M. (2017) 'Scientific progress on strategic management in hospitality and tourism: A state-of-the-art', *Tourism Review*, 72(3): 261–273.

Olsen, M. D., West, J. and Tse, E. C. (2013) *Strategic Management in the Hospitality Industry*, 3rd ed., Harlow, UK: Pearson.

Paterson, D. (2016) *Strategic Management for Tourism and Hospitality*, Forest Hills, NY: Willford Press.

Powers, E. L. (2012) 'Organizational mission statement guidelines revisited', *International Journal of Management and Information Systems*, 16(4): 281–290.

Roxas, F. M. Y., Rivera, J. P. R. and Gutierrez, E. L. M. (2020) 'Mapping stakeholders' roles in governing sustainable tourism destinations', *Journal of Hospitality and Tourism Management*, 45: 387–398.

Sautter, E. T. and Leisen, B. (1999) 'Managing stakeholders – A tourism planning model', *Annals of Tourism Research*, 26(2): 312–328.

Scherer, A. G. and Voegtlin, C. (2020) 'Corporate governance for responsible innovation: Approaches to corporate governance and their implications for sustainable development', *Academy of Management Perspectives*, 34(2): 182–208.

Schwaninger, M. (1986) 'Strategic business management in tourism', *Tourism Management*, 7(2): 74–85.

Scott, N. and Marzano, G. (2015) 'Governance of tourism in OECD countries', *Tourism Recreation Research*, 40(2): 181–193.

Sidhu, J. (2003) 'Mission statements: Is it time to shelve them?', *European Management Journal*, 21(4): 439–446.

Solomon, J. (2020) *Corporate Governance and Accountability*, New York: John Wiley & Sons.

Soteriou, E. C. and Roberts, C. (1998) 'The strategic planning process in national tourism organizations', *Journal of Travel Research*, 37: 21–29.

Stone, R. A. (1996) 'Mission statements revisited', *SAM Advanced Management Journal*, Winter: 31–37.

Sufi, T. and Lyons, H. (2003) 'Mission statements exposed', *International Journal of Contemporary Hospitality Management*, 15(5): 255–262.

Todd, L., Leask, A. and Ensor, J. (2017) 'Understanding primary stakeholders' multiple roles in hallmark event tourism management', *Tourism Management*, 59: 494–509.

Tribe, J. (2016) *Strategy for Tourism*, 2nd ed., Oxford, UK: Goodfellow.

Williams, L. S. (2008) 'The mission statement a corporate reporting tool with a past, present, and future', *Journal of Business Communication*, 45(2): 94–119.

Yameen, M., Farhan, N. H. and Tabash, M. I. (2019) 'The impact of corporate governance practices on firm's performance: An empirical evidence from Indian tourism sector', *Journal of International Studies*, 12(1): 208–228.

Websites

www.airasia.com
www.nationaltrust.org.au/
www.visitflorida.org

2

Introduction to strategy for tourism, hospitality and events

Introduction and chapter overview

Formulating *THE* strategy represents a complex set of challenges for managers operating in these sectors because of the nature of the products being sold and because of the distinctiveness of the environment in which these sectors exist.

In particular, strategy is informed by the fact that *THE* products are 'services' rather than 'goods' (physical products), which has certain implications for managers in these sectors. Furthermore, *THE* products have certain specific features that, if not unique, are certainly highly distinctive characteristics, in comparison with other service sectors.

In this chapter we consider the nature of service products and the particular distinctive characteristics of *THE* products. An understanding of these features and the managerial implications that flow from them is necessary in that it informs and underpins the strategy formulation process.

LEARNING OBJECTIVES

After studying this chapter, you should be able to:

- Define goods and services
- Describe the key characteristics of service products and how they are relevant to *THE* organizations
- Explain the defining characteristics of *THE* products in particular
- Assess the implications of the key features of *THE* products for managers working in the sector
- Explore some of the ways in which managers respond to the key features of *THE* products

DOI: 10.4324/9781003318613-3

2.1 Tourism, hospitality and events as service industry sectors

2.1.1 *Goods and services*

In a book on strategy for tourism, hospitality and events, it is appropriate to consider the nature of the products that comprise the central themes that we will be studying. If you have studied business or economics before, you will recall that there are two basic types of product: goods and services.

- Goods are *tangible* – products you can own
- Services are *intangible* – products made on your behalf or for your benefit (i.e., you do not own service products but instead you have use of them)

> **For example:** *As a customer you do not own an aircraft seat on a flight, a hotel room or an event that you attend but instead you make use of the services offered.*

We make this distinction because it has a fundamental effect on managing in these sectors of industry. Products in *THE* have a number of key or defining characteristics that are important because they are of relevance to how managers make decisions in these sectors. Some of these characteristics they share with other service products, which are discussed in the following section. Some other characteristics can be viewed as characteristics of *THE* products in particular.

These defining characteristics are relevant to *THE* managers and are discussed later in the chapter.

Importantly, this framework, which distinguishes between:

- Goods and services
- *THE* services and other services

underpins this entire book, because it has fundamental implications for managers operating in the industry. Furthermore, this distinction provides a justification for studying strategy using a specific, contextualized text rather than one of the generic texts that are available.

The differences between goods and services (and, to a lesser extent, the particular characteristics of *THE* products) have attracted a relatively large body of academic literature. Evans (2016) summarized the literature and produced a conceptualization of the management implications arising from these differences.

The next sections of this chapter will highlight the:

- Four defining characteristics of services that have been highlighted in the literature
- Seven characteristics that are important aspects of *THE* services in particular
- Managerial implications of these characteristics

2.2 Summary of the key characteristics and their implications for *THE* managers

This chapter will consider a total of 11 defining characteristics of *THE* – 4 of these are common in many service sectors, *but* 7 are particularly important to *THE* settings.

Whichever might be the case, it is important that managers working in *THE* be aware of these characteristics (or factors) and consider the managerial implications associated with each. The strategy that organizations put in place should reflect an understanding of these characteristics and the impacts they might have on the organizations concerned.

Table 2.1 A summary of key *THE* characteristics and their implications for managers

Characteristic	Summary (examples)	Managerial implications (examples)
Intangibility	Products cannot be tested or sampled	Effective promotion and distribution are essential
Inseparability	Production and consumption take place at the same time	'Front-line' staff must deliver good service
Perishability	Products cannot be stored	Stimulate demand so all products are sold at the required time
Heterogeneity	Products are not identical	Good, well-trained staff are essential
Ownership	Customers use services rather than own them	Loyalty programs are important
High-cost product	Often a relatively expensive purchase	Customers need reassurance about reliability
Seasonality	Products often have very seasonal demand patterns	Different seasonal prices charged
Ease of entry/exit	Often relatively low barriers to entry	Product differentiation
Interdependence	The subsectors of *THE* are closely linked	Coordination or control of the supply chain
Impact on society	Tourism has a high impact on society	Produce 'sustainable' products
External shocks	Prone to external shocks, beyond manager's control	Have contingency plans in place

Table 2.1 summarizes the key characteristics of *THE* we will explore in this chapter and provides examples of their implications for managers.

2.3 Service product characteristics

Services are diverse, with substantial differences between different forms of services (Contractor et al., 2003). There are inherent difficulties involved in defining and categorizing services, because they embody business activities as diverse as tourism, transport, real estate, professional services (legal, accounting etc.), education and health care (Gummesson et al., 2010).

In classifying the diversity of services, one factor relating to the inseparability of production and consumption of *some* services is fundamental to the consideration of services of which *THE* are a part.

For many internationally traded services, decoupling of production and consumption is possible (Blomstermo et al., 2006). Production and consumption of these *separable services*, as they have been termed (Ekeledo and Sivakumar, 2004), can be decoupled so the producer and consumer do not need to be in the same place at the same time. These 'hard services' include, for example, software and architectural services, where the product can be delivered electronically or through some other tangible medium and often such products can (at least to a degree) be standardized and mass produced (Blomstermo et al., 2006).

With 'soft services' (by way of contrast), production and consumption occur simultaneously. Such services are highly intangible and require a high degree of buyer–seller interaction. *THE* products can be categorized as soft services, in that the consumption of the service and its delivery (normally) have to be simultaneous. This is closely linked to the immobility of the intangible resources (skills, knowledge, brand names, goodwill, patent rights, etc.) on which the product relies (Evans, 2016).

From the mid-1980s onwards, wide acceptance of the so-called IHIP characteristics to describe the major features distinguishing services from goods was observable (Moeller, 2009). They represent four distinctive features of services when compared with manufactured goods, following the work of Zeithaml et al. (1985). The IHIP characteristics are:

- Intangibility
- Heterogeneity
- Inseparability
- Perishability

However, the IHIP characteristics (summarized in relation to *THE* by Edgett and Parkinson, 1993; Moeller, 2009; Reisinger, 2010) have also attracted some criticism (see, for example, Lovelock and Gummesson, 2004).

The reasons for such criticisms are twofold (Moeller, 2009). Firstly, the traditional dichotomy between services and manufacturing has meant that marketing has changed. Many manufacturers emphasize the added service they provide in support of their products and, conversely, service providers are attempting to provide more tangible aspects to their products. Secondly, the development of information and communication technologies can 'water down the applicability of most of the IHIP characteristics of service' (Moeller, 2009:359). Though this may be true in some cases, such as in overcoming the inseparability of production and consumption and perishability in education through the development of interactive web-based materials, the critique's applicability to *THE* and other soft services is far less clear.

Though it is difficult to argue with the examples cited by Gummesson et al. (2010), such as the tangibility of a service provided by a surgeon in performing an operation, it can be argued that the IHIP characteristics continue to have validity in most soft service settings including *THE*.

The IHIP categorization may indeed lack validity in many 'hard' services (where there can be a separation of production and consumption), but this is not the case with regard to soft services where simultaneous production and consumption are necessary. Indeed, it will be argued that, far from being irrelevant, other characteristics should be added to the IHIP characteristics identified because of their particular significance to *THE*.

Thus, there are a number of factors that make services (such as *THE*) different from physical goods, and though they are important to *THE* organizations, they may also be important for other types of organizations in other services. We will consider each of the IHIP characteristics in turn.

2.3.1 Intangibility

Services cannot normally be seen, touched, smelled, tasted, tried on for size or stored on a shelf prior to purchase. Their *intangibility* makes them harder to buy, because they cannot be tested, but easier to distribute, because there is no physical product to distribute.

The fact that *THE* products are not normally physical objects but amalgams of 'invisible' services does create certain problems for organizations operating in these sectors. To overcome this intangibility, such organizations sometimes attempt to create some form of tangible offering that potential customers can relate to, such as a free gift, T shirts sold at a concert or free streaming, which shows product features. It also means that managers have to ensure that promotional activities are effective and that distribution of the product enables potential customers to gain access to the product so that purchases can be made. In some cases, it might also be possible to try out the product prior to acquiring it.

> For example: *A buyer working for a tour operator, event manager or travel intermediary might be able to sample the food, accommodation and facilities prior to contracting a hotel supplier. However, the exact quality of the accommodation and meals the customer will receive is still intangible. This is because the quality of the accommodation or the meals that the customer actually receives (or their perception of them) may be different from those sampled prior to contracting.*

With the growth in ownership of DVD players, personal and tablet computers and smart phones, tour operators, destinations, hospitality providers and event organizers are able to record or stream the features of their products for viewing by potential customers. This takes away some of the uncertainty the customer may have when buying these services before they are actually provided. Similarly, brochures, 'flyers' and pamphlets promoting THE products help to overcome the intangibility problem, which is why so much effort, expense and creativity are devoted to their design.

Intangibility is also one of the reasons that products in *THE* are often 'packaged' together; that is, different elements are put together and sold as a single product. Because the products cannot be tested or compared prior to purchase (because they are intangible), dealing with recognized suppliers that will package the products makes it more convenient for consumers and gives them confidence in the products they are buying. Thus, tour operators, event organizers and hoteliers will often sell transport, accommodation, events and other services together as a single package.

KEY CONCEPT

Packages and tour operators

A 'package' can be defined as a prearranged combination sold or offered for sale at an inclusive price of not less than two of the following three elements:

1. Transport

2. Accommodation

3. Other tourist services ancillary to transport or accommodation and accounting for a significant part of the package.

The growth of the package has been a major cause of the increase in the holiday market in Europe and elsewhere since the 1950s. The role of the package company (often referred to a as a 'tour operator') goes beyond that of the wholesaler, in that they not only purchase or reserve the separate components in bulk but, in combining these components into an 'inclusive tour', they also become producers in the holiday market. The traditional appeal of the tour operator's product has been to offer a complete holiday package at the lowest price to a population often lacking the linguistic knowledge or the knowledge and confidence to organize independent travel.

In recent years, tour operators have come under increasing pressure as the internet and the growth of low-cost airlines have enabled consumers to construct their own packages and low-cost airlines have taken away the cost advantages offered by charter airlines operated by the major tour operators. Notwithstanding these changes, tour operators and the packages they provide remain major features of the holiday market in many tourist-generating countries. The major international tour operators involved also wield enormous power in tourist destinations owing to the 'buying power' that they have.

2.3.2 Heterogeneity

Services, unlike mass-produced manufactured goods, are never identical. One hotel in a chain of hotels, one person's holiday or one person's experience of an event will never be identical to another. The human element and other factors in delivering services ensures that services will be *heterogeneous*; that is, varied.

THE products are human resource intensive – that is, 'people oriented' – and the human factor plays a key role. The experiences in all aspects of *THE* are closely linked to the attitude, competence and personality of those charged with delivering the particular service (see Chapter 4).

> *For example: The enjoyment gained from a foreign holiday cannot be separated from the personalities who go to make up that holiday – the personnel employed in the travel agency, the airline crew, the hotel staff, the tour operator's representative, employees at destination attractions and, of course, the other holidaymakers. All of these have a role to play in ensuring that the holiday meets or exceeds the customer's expectations.*

The importance of human resources is illustrated by the London Olympic Games in the Short Case Illustration below.

2.1 SHORT CASE ILLUSTRATION

The importance of human resources in delivering services: London 2012 Olympic 'Games Makers'

The London 2012 Olympic and Paralympic Games required a vast army of volunteers – termed the 'Games Makers', and their role in making the games such a success has been widely acclaimed. However, with such a vast army of heterogeneous volunteers, there was a significant managerial challenge to ensure that a good customer experience was achieved.

Almost a quarter of a million people applied to be Games Makers, from which the final 70,000 were selected to carry out countless crucial tasks. Significantly, nearly half of those appointed had never volunteered before. All Games Makers were offered the chance to complete a customer service qualification as part of their job.

According to Ian Hembrow, a senior consultant writing in the *Guardian* (5 September 2012), three factors really stand out about the Games Makers' achievement:

● *A specific, time-limited challenge:* Games Makers were not asked to sign up as volunteers forever but just to do their bit to help make this historic event happen and run smoothly.

- *Playing to strengths:* Games Makers were carefully screened and matched to the roles that suited them best and made the most of their skills and personalities.

- *Something in return:* The Games Makers were well briefed, properly trained and kitted out with high-quality tools for the job, from Maglite torches to Adidas clothing and footwear. Most of all, they were made to feel a vital part of something important and got the satisfaction of knowing they had done a job well.

Questions

1. Does this case illustrate whether heterogeneity is 'good' or 'bad' when delivering services in *THE* contexts?

2. What key lessons about motivating staff might be drawn from the experience of Games Makers?

Listening to and understanding the customer, anticipating customer needs and giving a high priority to customer satisfaction are key attributes to encourage in staff, particularly those in front-line positions. To many customers, the contact person *is* the organization in their eyes. The organization is only as competent, knowledgeable, courteous and reliable as the person who represents it. In most cases the person in the front line representing the company is not a member of the senior management team but a relatively junior member of staff: a waiter, receptionist, air steward, etc.

> **For example:** *The importance of front-line staff in terms of customer service is illustrated by the case of an airline and its staff. The ability of an airline pilot to successfully fly the plane you might be traveling on is of prime importance for safety, and it is assumed the pilot is suitably qualified. However, passengers rarely meet the pilot, and it is the check-in staff, air stewards, ground handling staff, etc., who are more likely to frame attitudes toward customer service.*

Human behavior, however, is highly variable, and it is difficult for an organization to ensure that its employees display good customer relation skills all of the time. Similarly, the organization has no influence over the behavior of the customer. The customer's attitudes and behavior will also contribute to the pleasure gained from hospitality received, an event attended or a holiday. This means that there is an uncontrollable element inherent in the operation of a *THE* product that can lead to the customer being dissatisfied or disappointed with the service delivery.

To take account of this problem, it is important that accurate and timely information be provided in advance to the potential customer to manage their expectations. This will reduce the risk of the customer purchasing an unsuitable *THE* product at the outset. Special attention also has to be paid to the personnel who will deal with the client on a face-to-face basis. It is necessary to make certain that they have suitable personalities and attributes for dealing with customers and that they receive appropriate and regular training and development so that they are aware of expectations and how to deal with customers.

Heterogeneity should not necessarily be viewed as a negative factor, though clearly it presents managerial challenges. In many cases with regard to *THE* products, the customer is actually attracted by heterogeneity. Tourists would become bored if every tourist destination was identical. Hotel chains strive to maintain consistent brand attributes, while at the same time trying to differentiate each hotel location through varying design features. Customers would be less likely to pay high prices for concert tickets if each performance was absolutely identical.

The attraction of heterogeneity for customers is understandable, but it does make it very difficult for potential purchasers to evaluate services and for managers to deliver products of a consistent quality, as illustrated by the Short Case Illustration of Radisson Hotels below.

2.2 SHORT CASE ILLUSTRATION

Managing heterogeneity: Radisson Hotels

Radisson Hotels were developed by the privately owned Carlson group of companies, which included the international Carlson Wagon-lit travel business based in Minneapolis, USA. The hotel businesses (outside North and South America) are now owned by a Chinese-controlled consortium led by Jin Jiang International Hotel Group.

Radisson Hotel Group is one of the world's largest and most dynamic hotel groups, with nine distinctive hotel brands with more than 1,100 hotels in destinations around the world. The portfolio of hotel brands includes Radisson Blu, Radisson, Radisson RED, Park Plaza, Park Inn by Radisson, Country Inn and Suites by Radisson and Prizeotel. Radisson has grown rapidly in recent years, despite problems elsewhere in the hotel sector, because it focused on management contracts and franchising in its hotels rather than on real estate investment; that is, another company owns the physical structure of the hotels.

Radisson owns and manages very few of these hotels, with most of them operating as franchises; that is, they are managed by franchisees operating in partnership with Radisson.

The challenge for a company such as Radisson is to ensure that the same levels of quality are provided around the world, when:

- Staff come from many cultural and linguistic backgrounds.
- Locations vary greatly in their geographical, climatic and cultural characteristics.
- Customer expectations are for a consistent brand experience irrespective of location.
- The company does not actually own the buildings in which it operates.

The strength of a brand such as Radisson relies on such standards being ensured, but in practice it is a very difficult management task, because even communicating effectively with worldwide locations in different time zones can be problematic.

Radisson relies heavily on alliances with local 'quality' hoteliers, places a great emphasis on training, has a consistent statement of vision and values, standardizes procedures where possible, carefully words all of its management and franchising agreements and has sophisticated international communications.

Source: www.radissonhotelgroup.com

2.3.3 Inseparability

The production and consumption of services including those in *THE* sectors are inseparable.

> For example: *To take advantage of a music festival event you have to be at the event at the time it is taking place. In other words, the event is being delivered (produced) at the same time as you are listening to it (consuming). Similarly, for you to make use of an air flight*

or a bus service, both you and the means of transport must make the journey at the same time; that is, the service is provided and consumed simultaneously.

The implication of this *inseparability* is important for managers in service sectors such as *THE* in that the consumers of the service have direct experience of the production of that service. They are, in effect, in the 'service factory' at the time of production. This has profound implications for the staff and managers in service industries.

When a physical product is purchased, it usually comes packaged and the customer is likely to assess the product purely upon its product features (such as taste, size, specification, reliability, durability, quality etc.). Managers have time to plan these aspects of product management to ensure that customers' satisfaction is achieved. The circumstances under which the product is produced and how it is delivered are usually of little relevance to the customer.

In the case of a service product, however, the position is often different. Customers are likely to be very concerned about the way in which the product is delivered; that is, the level of customer service.

> **For example:** *At a hotel reception desk or the welcome desk for an exhibition or convention, the customer is likely to notice if the reception staff are rude or unwelcoming. Conversely, the customer will also appreciate the production of the product if the reception staff are efficient, courteous and helpful.*

The task of satisfying customers for the provider of a service is in many ways much more difficult than it is for the manufacturer of a product. With the provision of a manufactured product there is a time delay between the production of the product and its distribution and consumption. This delay allows for mistakes to be rectified. In service industries such as *THE* sectors, the position is somewhat different.

Because production and consumption are inseparable (because they occur simultaneously), there is no chance to correct errors. Everything should be 'right the first time, all the time', and any mistake can prove very costly in terms of lost future custom. How service personnel conduct themselves in the customer's presence – what they say, what they don't say, how competent they are, how personable they are or how presentable they are – can determine whether the customer buys from the business again. If mistakes are made (as inevitably they will be), how these are followed up and dealt with is crucial in determining customer loyalty.

The implications of inseparability for managers in *THE* sectors are that it places a great emphasis on the importance of front-line staff, who need to be carefully selected, well trained and have the appropriate skills and aptitude for customer service roles.

2.3.4 Perishability

Because production and consumption are simultaneous, *THE* services are instantly perishable if they have not been sold at the time they are offered.

> **For example:** *An event that takes place and is not full to capacity, an empty train seat, an unoccupied hotel bedroom and an unsold holiday all represent lost opportunities. They are sales that have not taken place and that can never be recovered; that is, they are services offered on a certain date and they cannot be 'stored' for when demand increases. The income foregone cannot be recovered.*

If a scheduled flight leaves for its destination less than full, this is a suboptimal position for the airline, with the empty seats representing revenue that cannot be recovered at a later date. That is, the service provided (by the airline) is irrefutably *perishable*.

Unlike manufacturers of goods, service providers cannot just keep on producing services and store them for future sales. Striking the correct balance of capacity and sales (supply and demand) is extremely difficult and represents a key managerial challenge for those operating in *THE* sectors.

KEY CONCEPT

Capacity, occupancy rate, load factors and attendance rate

In *THE*, capacity refers to the number of people who can be accommodated at an event, in a hotel, on an aircraft or bus, at a resort, at a destination, etc. For example, a hotel may have a capacity of 300 and an aircraft might be able to seat 130. The important figure, however, is how much of the capacity is actually used at any time, and it is often referred to in different ways. This is normally the:

- *Occupancy rate* for accommodation
- *Load factor* for transportation
- *Attendance numbers* (or attendance rate) for events and venues
- *Carrying capacity* for destinations and resorts

    For example: *If a hotel is only full on a quarter of the nights in a year, then it is paying the 'fixed costs' (building costs, mortgage payments, taxes, etc.) on the empty rooms without any income from them. The management of capacity is particularly important when considering seasonality and also explains why prices fall in the low season – to maintain as high an occupancy rate as possible to help to cover the hotel's total costs.*

The problems of perishability can be made even more acute in *THE* by fluctuating demand for services but a relatively fixed supply. Demand can vary during the day, during the week or from season to season of the year.

> For example: *Many resort hotels are full for only a few months of the year. Capacity may therefore be insufficient to meet demand at peak times but in excess of what is required at slack times. Similarly, the demand for visits to an art exhibition may be greatest during holiday periods and when people are not generally working; that is, weekends and evenings. Consequently, during these busy periods, numbers attending may have to be restricted (because the exhibition has a given capacity level), whereas at other times there is excess capacity.*

Demand can fluctuate for all sorts of reasons, such as seasonal changes, changes due to the level of economic activity, changes due to climatic conditions, changes due to publicity or advertising and changes in trends and fashions. Changes in demand can also occur very suddenly and can have a dramatic impact on service suppliers.

> For example: *Following the terrorist attack on the Twin Towers in New York in September 2001, the airline industry worldwide faced a major and immediate downturn in demand that could not have been foreseen and that continued to be felt for a number of years. Conversely, the rapid slide in the value of the Turkish lira in the summer of 2018 led to a steep increase in demand for Turkish holidays among international tourists. More recently, the onset of the COVID-19 pandemic in early 2020 led to an immediate and dramatic fall in demand for all THE products around the world.*

Supply, however, is often much more difficult to alter (than demand), at least in the short term.

> **For example:** *A hotel has a fixed bed stock (number of beds) that it has to try and fill. A scheduled airline has an obligation to fly between advertised points regardless of the number of empty seats on the aircraft. The aircraft capacity cannot be altered. A tour operator or an event organizer enters a contractual obligation, often months in advance. In the case of a tour operator, there may be an agreement to fill a certain specified number of rooms or, in the case of an event organizer, agreements may be put in place with event locations and event participants as to the maximum permissible number of participants. All of the supply arrangements listed here can be very difficult to alter, at least in the short term.*

The management challenge, therefore, is to ensure that the organization is operating at full capacity for as much of the time as possible. To be successful, the organization will need carefully designed actions; for instance, to stimulate demand, lengthen seasons or offer appropriate pricing levels to manage and 'smooth out' occupancy levels, load factors and attendance figures.

KEY CONCEPT

Breakeven point

In *THE*, the *breakeven point* is often referred to as a crucial stage to reach in operating the particular service that the organization is involved in delivering.

The breakeven point is the point at which costs or expenses and revenue are equal; that is, there is no net loss or gain, and the activity has 'broken even'. Beyond that point, all costs have been met by revenues, so the revenues received are profits or surplus. This can often be more easily understood in relation to what is being delivered.

Thus, a coach operator with a 54-seat coach may have a breakeven point of 30 seats; a concert venue might have a capacity of 1,200 seats at which a breakeven point is reached when 1,000 tickets have been sold.

In reality, the situation is not always quite so clear, because seats on the coach or concert tickets might be sold at different price levels, but clearly it is helpful if managers have some knowledge of when the breakeven point is likely to be reached. Analyzing the breakeven point through *breakeven analysis* (see Chapter 13) is an important task for many *THE* managers.

THINK POINTS

- Explain the meaning of the terms intangibility, inseparability, perishability and heterogeneity in *THE* contexts.
- Why might heterogeneity be valued by many *THE* customers, and what challenges might this present for *THE* managers?
- Explain why perishability is affected by the difficulties of changing supply in the short to medium term in many *THE* settings.

2.4 *THE* – seven specific characteristics

The four IHIP characteristics of services (explained in the preceding section) change the emphasis of a manager's task when compared to the task of dealing with physical products. The characteristics apply to all 'soft' service products to some degree – which include banking, insurance and professional services (legal, accounting, etc.). Thus, the characteristics considered previously, though certainly applicable to *THE* sectors, are not unique to these sectors but applicable, to some extent, across all service sectors.

Seven further characteristics can be identified that are particularly applicable to the *THE* sectors (though to varying degrees within the three sectors). Consequently, these characteristics have a particular influence on decision making for managers operating in these three sectors.

The seven further factors that are relevant in *THE* contexts are:

* Ownership
* High cost
* Seasonality
* Ease of entry/exit
* Interdependence
* Impact on society
* Effect of external shocks

Though most of these characteristics are factors that are not unique to *THE* sectors, they are certainly very important to any consideration of strategic management in such contexts (Singal, 2015; Evans, 2016). This is highly significant to how organizations and destinations are managed. The seventh of these factors, however, the impact on society, is (arguably) unique to tourism, in that no other service sector can claim to have such a visible and profound impact on society.

Each of the seven characteristics (which were discussed fully by Evans, 2016) will be considered in turn.

2.4.1 Ownership

When a customer buys a manufactured product, there will usually be a document, such as a receipt, that transfers ownership from seller to buyer. When a consumer buys a service, he or she does not usually receive ownership of anything tangible.

> **For example:** *A car is hired but ownership is not transferred, a hotel room is reserved for a period of time but nothing in it is ever owned by the customer, a concert ticket provides access to the concert venue only for the time that the concert is taking place. Even a credit card actually remains the property of the issuing company.*

Service buyers are therefore buying only access to or use of something, which has important management implications. Because transfer of ownership is not involved, the tasks of building a relationship with customers, retaining their custom and building brand loyalty become more difficult.

Loyalty schemes such as the frequent flyer programs operated by many airlines and frequent guest programs operated by hotel groups are examples (as illustrated in the Short Case Illustration below) of managerial responses to the problems of building brand loyalty in *THE* organizations.

Quite a large academic literature has emerged that explores the building of relationships with customers and loyalty programs in a *THE* context. See, for example, McKercher et al. (2012), Rahimi et al. (2017) and Almeida-Santana and Moreno-Gil (2018) for a critique and literature review in a tourism

Part 1

context; Gartner and Ruzzier (2011) in relation to tourist destinations; Gallarza et al. (2012) in relation to tourism services; Kayaman and Arasli (2007), Hsu et al. (2012), Xie and Chen (2014) and Rahimi et al. (2017) in relation to hospitality; and Lu and Cai (2011) in relation to exhibition events.

2.3 SHORT CASE ILLUSTRATION

Airline and hotel loyalty programs

When American Airlines launched the first major frequent flyer program in 1981, few imagined how successful airline loyalty (frequent flyer) programs would become (DeKay et al., 2009). The reasons for the success among consumers was investigated by Dolnicar et al. (2011). American Airlines' *AAdvantage Program* (the largest) has about 70 million members. The increasingly sophisticated frequent flyer programs not only engendered loyalty but the 'big data' sets provided by the programs permitted airlines to gather vast amounts of marketing data. Indeed, as Knorr (2019) pointed out, the larger international airlines were big data pioneers (predating hospitality, for instance), which provided more precise data to create individual traveler profiles. This allowed for tailored customer offerings, including pricing and customized offers for ancillary services.

Following American's example, 2 years later, InterContinental Hotels developed the first hotel frequent guest program, *Priority Club Rewards*, which now numbers over 37 million members. Loyal customers are highly attractive to businesses because they are less price sensitive and require a lower effort to communicate with (Gomez et al., 2006).

Numerous loyalty schemes have subsequently developed. DeKay et al. (2009), in comparing hotel loyalty programs and airline frequent flyer programs, pointed out that some observers have considered the hotel programs costly, financially unprofitable and poor investments (see, for example, Skogland and Siguaw, 2004; Mattila, 2006), whereas, on the other hand, several major airlines have been kept flying by creditors mainly to retain their highly profitable frequent flyer programs.

In response, hotel loyalty programs are increasingly offering more attractive rewards that are starting to be interchangeable and less restricted (Toh et al., 2008) and with fewer rules and restrictions. The entire Marriott family of hotels, for example, which includes some 30 brands including Ritz-Carlton, Sheraton, W and Le Meridien, as well as Marriott, share the same Marriott Bonvoy loyalty program (www.marriott.com).

Questions

1. Explain the characteristic of *THE* contexts to which loyalty programs represent one response.

2. Consider what problems might arise for managers in a *THE* company because of the spread of loyalty programs throughout the industry.

2.4.2 High cost

THE products often represent a relatively high-cost purchase for the consumer. Taking a holiday, buying an airline ticket and staying at a hotel are expensive. Attending events and festivals can also be very expensive when all costs are considered. Indeed, in some cases such purchases will represent the largest single item of expenditure for a consumer in a given year, and in all *THE* sectors there is often a great deal of choice, and that potential customers are very discerning.

Consequently, making such a purchase decision does not usually occur without a great deal of thought and a comparison of alternative offerings. It is not like buying a *fast-moving consumer good*, such as a bar of chocolate or a pencil, which may be bought on impulse. There may, of course, be some exceptions in *THE* where supply is limited and impulsive purchases are made, such as highly sought-after concert or sport event tickets.

> **For example:** *With regard to some events, demand far exceeds supply. In such cases there is little chance for reflection and comparison and a speedy impulse decision is necessary. When a popular band announces they are to give a series of concerts or a popular sporting event is scheduled, often potential buyers have to react quickly to ensure success in purchasing tickets. There is thus little chance for reflection, comparison or negotiation in such cases.*

The high cost of many *THE* products has important managerial implications when formulating strategy, especially with regard to marketing aspects.

Potential customers will want reassurance about the reliability of the product, the value for money the purchase represents and the quality provided. With myriad internet search sites and apps freely available, consumers have ever more accurate pricing information at their disposal, which in most cases enables price comparisons to be easily made. This places an onus on the organization to provide product features of a consistent quality and build brand values that consumers trust. It also suggests that *relationship marketing* is important, because products are less likely to be bought on impulse. Consequently, companies have to build up a relationship with customers over a period of time to provide reassurance before the purchase decision is made.

2.4.3 Seasonality

THE products often have some of the most seasonal patterns of demand for any category of product or service. Writing in a tourism context (though it also often equally applies to hospitality and events), Bull (1995:44) argued that tourism has 'less variation than the demand for Christmas cards or air conditioners, but more than nearly all high value individual purchases'.

This seasonality of demand for the product is largely related to climate but is also related to factors such as school holidays, religious festivals and historic travel patterns. Issues relating to seasonality and the appropriate managerial responses have attracted quite a lot of attention in the *THE* literature. See, for example, Baum and Lundtorp (2001), who brought together a collection of studies that draw lessons from various parts of the world that experience the effects of seasonality; Evans (2002), who discussed the financial implications; and Rosselló and Sansó (2017), who discussed tourism demand. Ferrante et al. (2018) and Dogru et al. (2019) produced seasonality comparisons for tourist destinations. Parilla et al (2007) considered the implications for accommodation, and Saito and Romão (2018) and Lozano et al. (2021) focused on seasonality in relation to Spanish accommodation. Tum and Norton (2006) discussed the effects of seasonality on the implementation and delivery of events, and Connell et al. (2015) and Sainaghi et al. (2019) considered seasonality in the context of visitor attractions and 'mega' events, respectively.

Skiing holidays, outdoor festivals and children's summer camps (which are particularly popular in North America) are three examples of *THE* provision that, for obvious reasons, have highly seasonal demand patterns. This seasonality has important managerial implications in terms of aspects of management such as managing cash flow, product pricing, managing the quantity of products supplied and dealing with labor (and wider societal) issues relating to the need to employ, motivate and retain seasonal employees (discussed in Chapter 4).

> **For example:** *The seasonality of demand often leads to a highly seasonal pattern of cash flows (which is discussed in greater detail in Chapter 6) for organizations in these sectors. The cash flow has to be carefully managed if staff and suppliers are to be paid promptly at low points in*

the cycle. Consequently, at some times of the year, companies in these sectors may have relatively large surplus cash balances to invest, whereas at other times only small amounts of cash may be available or it may even be necessary to borrow to meet cash requirements (Evans, 2002).

There are a number of managerial implications of seasonality. One way in which management can respond is to develop or acquire counterseasonal businesses; that is, to develop businesses that operate primarily at other times of the year.

For example: *Many tour operators selling mainly to Northern European markets have attempted over the years to reduce the effects of seasonality by introducing 'winter sun' and skiing products to provide cash flows for these companies when cash flow from the sales of their summer products is low.*

Another approach in parts of *THE* is to plan particular events to attract visitors at times of the year when demand is relatively low.

For example: *In the attractions sector, managing the demand and supply due to seasonality at an individual business level poses many challenges for attraction infrastructure, in that it is fixed in time and space and has a finite capacity. To address this issue in a study of Scottish visitor attractions, Connell et al. (2015) found that 70% of businesses remained open throughout the year (albeit with reduced opening hours to attract more visitors) and that 39% of attractions that stay open host special events, with the local community being a key driver of these events to supplement tourist income.*

Figure 2.1 shows the seasonal patterns for air travel on one of the world's busiest air routes between London's Heathrow Airport and New York during 2022–23.

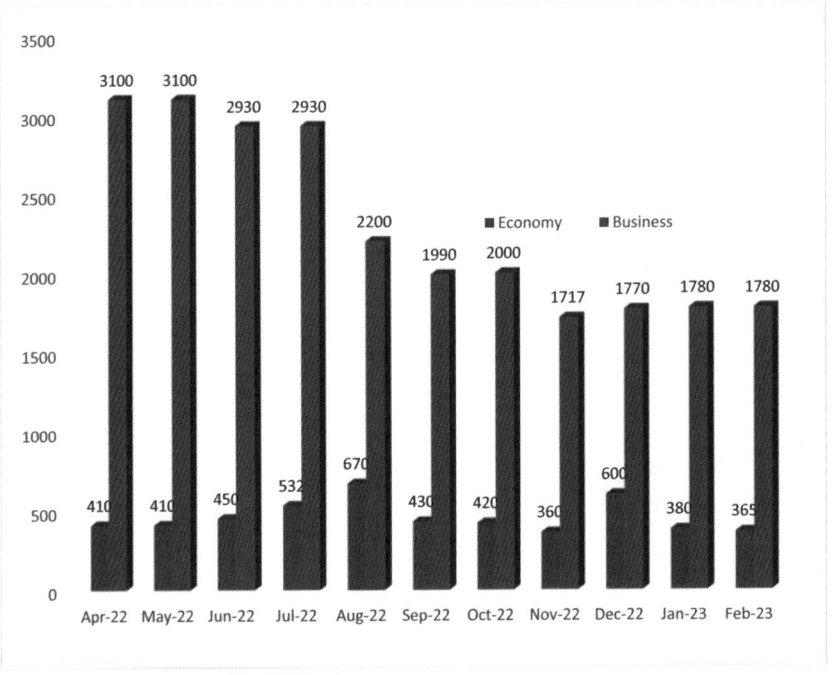

Figure 2.1 Seasonality of air fares between London and New York

Source: Adapted from www.expedia.com/ and www.opodo.com, accessed Feb. 2022

Figure 2.1 shows the seasonal fluctuation of air fares. Though numerous factors affect air fares (such as how close to the departure the booking is made), economy fares, purchased by a high proportion of leisure travelers, have a peak season in July and August (during the summer when schools are on holiday) and over the Christmas period. What is often termed the 'shoulder' seasons occur, in this case, during June, September and October, with a low season for the remaining months. Leisure travelers tend to travel during school holidays and when weather conditions are favorable, whereas business travelers (although sometimes showing some seasonal variations) often have to travel throughout the year. However, demand is slightly lower during peak summer months (in contrast to leisure travelers) and during the middle of winter when weather is poor.

2.4 SHORT CASE ILLUSTRATION

Managing variations in seasonal demand: Jet2 plc

Jet2 plc is a leading leisure travel group based in Leeds, UK, specializing in low fares provided by its airline, Jet2.com, which has a fleet of over 80 aircraft and provides package holidays from various UK regional airports. Jet2holidays is the UK's second-largest package holiday provider. The airline flies to over 65 sun, city and ski destinations across Europe and beyond, and Jet2holidays offers over 4,000 directly contracted hotels in leisure destinations in the Mediterranean, the Canary Islands and European cities.

Jet2, as with many European travel companies (depending heavily on Northern European markets), experiences a high degree of seasonality of demand. Such seasonality of demand causes some managerial problems for European-based tour operators:

- Profits are concentrated in the summer months, and losses or small profits are often incurred over the winter period. Such uneven performances experienced by many travel companies can make the financial markets uneasy and this, in turn, can lead to share price volatility.

- Large fluctuations in cash flow often occur. Typically, cash flows during the early part of the calendar year as bookings are made and paid for, but then cash is drained over the course of the summer months as the companies have to pay accommodation, airline and other expenses. Net cash levels are usually at their lowest levels during the autumn and early winter months. Many travel companies have failed owing to banks' refusal to support them through their cash-deficit months.

- 'Integrated' travel companies such as TUI and Jet2 own charter airlines. Though it is usually possible to keep the airlines flying with very high load factors over the summer season, capacity has to be carefully managed so that aircraft capacity is not underutilized during the winter. European-based companies may respond by having aircraft leased on flexible contracts; developing countercyclical business opportunities, such as skiing and winter sun holidays; or sending the aircraft to other markets, such as Canada, where there is strong winter demand.

Source: www.jet2plc.com

Questions

1. Explain the nature of the seasonality issues faced by Jet2.
2. Explain the actions managers in a company such as Jet2 might take to deal with the seasonality issues.

2.4.4 Ease of entry/exit

Barriers to entry have been a popular field of research since the seminal work of Bain (1956), and a large literature on this particular aspect of economics has developed (see, for example, Pehrsson, 2009). Barriers, which are obstacles preventing entrant firms from being established in a particular market (Porter, 1980), vary from industry to industry and from one country or trading block (such as the European Union) to another. Pehrsson (2009) categorized and summarized a number of such barriers to entry, including:

- The capital required to establish a business
- The cost incurred by customers in switching between suppliers
- Access to distribution channels

KEY CONCEPT

Barriers to entry and contestability

Barriers to entry describe the barriers preventing potential suppliers coming into the market from competing for sales. Economists talk about the relative size of the barriers and the *contestability* of markets. In recent years, *the theory of the contestable market* has become prominent, associated primarily with its proponent William J. Baumol (1982).

The theory is that what is crucial in determining prices and setting levels of supply is not whether an industry is actually a monopoly or highly competitive but whether there is a real threat of competition. A contestable market is characterized by insignificant entry and exit barriers, so there are negligible entry and exit costs (Sinclair and Stabler, 1997). The deregulation of the US airline market from the late 1970s, for example, was very much influenced by this theory in removing barriers to entry to make the airline market contestable.

In some cases, the barriers are virtually impossible to overcome – for example, where the government grants one company a monopoly to provide flights or rail services on certain routes – but in most cases barriers to entry are not insurmountable, though they vary considerably in different parts of *THE* and between different national markets.

Significant barriers to entry include:

- Government requirements for companies to hold financial bonds or licenses to operate
- Significant start-up capital requirements
- Planning restrictions
- The pricing actions and tactics of established companies

In many areas of *THE*, it is relatively easy to set up in business or, indeed, to exit from the industry; that is, entry and exit costs are relatively low (compared to some other industries). To establish an oil refinery or a vehicle manufacturing plant would require a large initial capital outlay (i.e., they are *capital-intensive* industries), but this is not the case in many parts of *THE*.

> For example: *The capital outlay to set up a tour operator, a travel agent or an event organizer is generally quite low (when compared to other industrial sectors). Many of the services included in the product are leased or are purchased as and when required.*

The greatest (up-front) cost involved is often in producing brochures, creating websites and other promotional materials and marketing the products to agents and the public. Similarly, travel agents do not generally purchase products from tour operators until the customer pays for them and so do not incur the risk of unsold stock or stock-holding costs. In recent years, the growth of internet marketing has reduced entry barriers further. Its growth has allowed many organizations in THE (and other industries) to communicate with many customers relatively cheaply rather than print and produce expensive promotional materials.

Mainly as a result of the relatively low barriers to entry, in most areas of the world *THE* is dominated by SMEs. The sectors of *THE* are generally highly fragmented, as documented by a number of authors (see, for example, Thomas et al., 1999; Pechlaner et al., 2004; McCamley and Gilmore, 2017). *THE* sectors with relatively low market entry barriers are comparatively attractive for SMEs, because various types of firms require only minor capital investments, few staff and low operating costs (Stickdorn and Zehrer, 2009).

Therefore, in many parts of *THE*, entry to the industry might be considered relatively straightforward, and this means that if one company is seen to be successful in a particular segment of the market, it is not difficult for a competitor to offer a similar product. In other parts of *THE*, however, barriers to entry may be greater.

For example: *Setting up an airline or a cruise line or building a hotel normally requires hefty capital outlays and in the case of an airline has traditionally been subject to stringent regulatory pressures. Even in these parts of THE, though, entry barriers are becoming lower as initial capital costs are avoided by such means as leasing equipment in cruising and airline operations and franchising and management contracts in hotel developments. Furthermore, the gradual removal of international regulatory barriers in the international airline industry has further lowered barriers in that sector.*

For managers, the implications of relatively low barriers to entry (or barriers which are lower that they were previously) include the need to:

- Find ways of differentiating the product, possibly on the basis of price or by adding additional features to the product that are valued by customers and that they will consequently be willing to pay for
- Establish and build a brand that is recognized and reassures customers
- Consider working cooperatively with other organizations through alliances and other arrangements

2.4.5 Interdependence

In the introduction to Part 1, the difficulties of defining and delineating the component parts of tourism, hospitality and events were considered. It was concluded that there is a great deal of overlap between the constituent parts and that at the strategic level they could usefully be considered together. Exactly where the boundaries lie is not material, but clearly there are linkages between the component parts.

Hence, the industry we are considering, *THE,* can be viewed as comprising six component sectors:

- Hospitality
- Events management
- Attractions
- Transport

- Travel organizers
- Destination organizations

Each of these sectors can be further broken down into several subsectors (as shown in Figure 2.2). Some of the subsectors, such as tour operators, are operated for profit (on a commercial basis), whereas others, such as museums and national parks, are often operated on a noncommercial basis.

The important point to note in this context, however, is that the sectors are all linked and depend upon one another; that is, there is *interdependence* between them.

> **For example:** *The hospitality sector relies on the transport sector to transport guests to and from accommodation. Similarly, the transport and hospitality sectors both rely on travel organizers and event managers to provide them with customers.*

If one subsector fails to deliver a service, it has an impact on other subsectors.

> **For example:** *The success of a music festival organized by an event management company may be judged on the arrangements for catering and accommodation provided by hospitality suppliers. Similarly, if a tour operator organizes a holiday including seats on an aircraft, the quality of the holiday will be judged partly on the quality of the airline regardless of whether the tour operator has any direct control over that airline's activities.*

THINK POINTS

- Explain the effects of seasonality on how management is carried out in *THE* organizations.
- Explain the interdependence of travel and tourism organizations.
- Provide a brief explanation of the structure of the tourism, hospitality and events sectors and explain the linkages between them.

Thus, the success of a product often depends on a *supply chain* in which there are many interdependent links. Managers need to be aware of the linkages that exist and where particular problems might occur if, for instance, demand increased suddenly. In response to the interdependence that exists, managers might try to gain greater control of the supply chain by:

- Buying suppliers, distributors or competitors
- Encouraging greater cooperation between suppliers, distributors or competitors
- Establishing rigorous quality standards for suppliers and competitors

Figure 2.2 illustrates how the various sectors in the industry 'fit' together and how the sectors interact with the transport sector at the center, implying that all sectors of *THE* rely on transport to some extent in moving customers to the place where the service is delivered. In reality, the world is not as simple as the diagram implies. Individual companies will often straddle two or more of the sectors.

One of the difficulties involved in managing such a supply chain, which is frequently owned and managed by different organizations, is that developing in an ethical and sustainable manner may be difficult to achieve. In such circumstances, it can be difficult to coordinate between the different organizations and to allocate responsibility between them to achieve sustainable and ethical

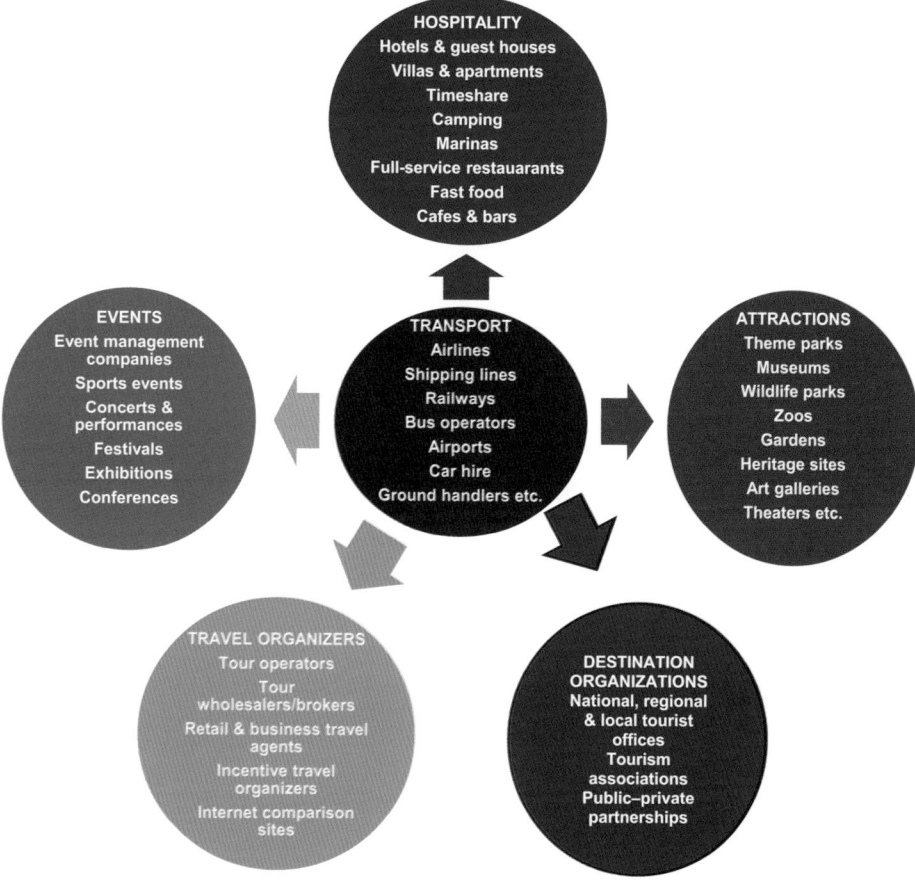

Figure 2.2 The sectors and subsectors of tourism, hospitality and events

development, as discussed by several authors (see, for example, Font et al., 2008; Sigala, 2008; Adriana, 2009; Keating, 2009). Writing in the context of heritage tourism in Northern Ireland, McCamley and Gilmore (2017) identified dissatisfaction among tourism SMEs with the supply chain. To overcome these inadequacies, SMEs engage in entrepreneurial behavior by attempting to deliver specific products and services to meet the need of tourists.

DEFINITION/QUOTATION

Tourism supply chain

A tourism supply chain is defined as:

> A network of tourism organizations engaged in different activities ranging from the supply of different components of tourism products/services such as flights and accommodation to the distribution and marketing of the final tourism product at a specific tourism destination and involves wide range of participants in both the private and public sectors.

(Zhang et al., 2009:347)

The tourism supply chain clearly illustrates the interdependence of the component parts of *THE* (and, indeed, other suppliers), because tourism supply chains involve many components – not just accommodation, transport and excursions but also bars and restaurants, handicrafts, food production, waste disposal and the infrastructure that supports tourism in destinations. This infrastructure can include the various events, festivals, exhibitions and conferences, which both create a demand for tourism in the first place and support tourists when they arrive at a destination.

> For example: *Some hotel companies organize inclusive tour packages and organize and manage events, thereby also operating in the travel organizers and events sectors. Similarly, from the 1990s, consolidation of European-based travel companies led to a small number of large pan-European travel groups being formed, operating worldwide from their European head offices under a number of different brand names (see, for example, Evans, 2001; Holloway and Humphreys, 2019). Thus, TUI AG, based in the German city of Hannover, and the Swiss-based Kuoni and Globus group of companies all became large diversified internationally diversified travel companies during the 1990s.*

These companies (to varying degrees) undertook strategies of *vertical integration* whereby a single group of companies formed to:

- Sell travel arrangements to customers through shops and online (retail distribution)
- Provide travel and accommodation arrangements (tour operations)
- Transport customers (airline and coach operations)
- Own or manage accommodation and cruising operations (in some cases)

Horizontal integration also took place whereby acquisitions, mergers and internal development occurred so that the group of companies was able to sell its products in different markets around the world.

This vertically and horizontally integrated structure (discussed in Chapter 10) can be illustrated by looking at the structure of the TUI group of companies shown in Table 2.2. TUI group, together with British-based Thomas Cook plc, came to dominate the European Tour operator sector. The position of the leading tour operators had been threatened in recent years by the growth of low-cost airline networks, internet-based providers, consumers assembling their own packages and the demand collapse associated with COVID-19.

> For example: *This is illustrated by the demise of Thomas Cook. Thomas Cook plc was a British global online/offline travel company created in June 2007 by the merger of the German company Thomas Cook AG and the UK's MyTravel Group plc, when the business was floated on the UK stock market. Thomas Cook was one of the most recognized brands in the international travel industry, with a protracted history dating back to 1841 (documented by Withey, 1998; Hamilton, 2006). Thomas Cook, however, encountered long-term financial difficulties, which eventually led to its collapse in September 2019.*

TUI Group is a German/British tourism company headquartered in Hannover, Germany that claims to be the largest tourism company in the world. The company owns and manages tour operators, hotels, airlines, cruise ships and retail stores. The company is listed on the London and Frankfurt stock exchanges.

Table 2.2 Vertically and horizontally integrated structure of TUI Group

TUI Group structure			
Holidays and experiences		Airlines and markets*	Other segments
Hotels and resorts	359 Hotels 276,000 rooms In Spain, the Caribbean, Greece, Turkey, Mexico, Egypt, Austria, Morocco and Portugal	Northern region	Tour operator and airline activity in UK, Ireland and Nordic countries Sunwing joint venture tour operator in Canada	Business activities for new markets Corporate center functions Group real estate companies
Cruises	16 cruise ships, of which 12 are part of a joint venture	Central region	Tour operator and airline activity in Germany Tour operators and in Poland, Austria and Switzerland	
TUI Musement	Delivers local services at worldwide destinations Employees in 49 countries	Western region	Tour operator and airline activity in Belgium, Netherlands and France	

*Tour operators include retail activities.

Source: TUI Group Annual Report 2021 (www.tuigroup.com)

2.4.6 Impacts of tourism

Perhaps the one area where tourism (and, importantly, the hospitality and event management sectors that support it) is unique is in its impact on society. It is probably fair to say that no other industrial service sector comes close, because tourism by definition involves the transport of people (often in large numbers) to a destination area away from home. But the impacts that tourism has are both wide-ranging and controversial.

The focus of attention is usually on the impact tourism has on host destinations. Figure 2.3 summarizes some of the impacts tourism has on host destinations. The impacts can be classified as economic, social and environmental and classified into positive and negative impacts. However, it is important to point out that the issues involved are often complex and interrelated and involve tourism together with other industrial sectors including hospitality and events.

Many destination areas have been profoundly changed by the influx of tourists. The Spanish Balearic Islands (Majorca, Ibiza, Menorca), Australia's Gold Coast, the Thai Island of Phuket, Boracay island in the Philippines and Dubai are merely examples of the way in which tourism has profoundly and visibly affected the host destinations in recent years: economically, socially and environmentally.

The impacts may rather simplistically be labeled as 'positive' or 'negative', but often whether the impacts can be viewed as positive or negative depends on whose view you take or on achieving an appropriate balance between the differing types of impact.

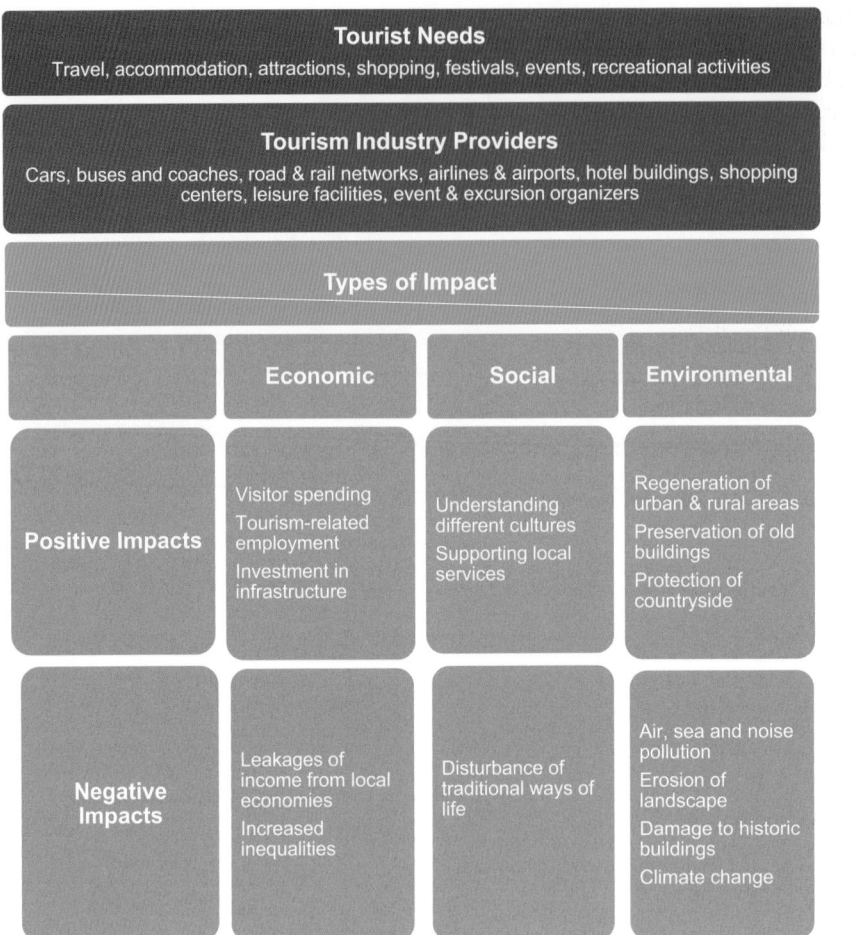

Figure 2.3 Examples of the impacts of tourism on destination areas

> For example: *If a piece of land is cleared to make way for a new hotel development next to a beach, the overall economic effect may be highly positive for the region in which it is built. However, those residents who have been displaced may not feel so positively disposed toward the development.*

Tourism can also have an impact on tourist-generating areas and on the territories affected by the travel between destinations and tourist-generating areas (Mason, 2015). The changed perceptions toward food and culture in Northern Europe and the impact of returning international students to China and India are evidence of this. Tourists (albeit long-term tourists in the case of returning students) have gained an insight into other cultures (as a result of travel) and brought back their changed perceptions, needs and wants to the tourist-generating areas.

A large tourism literature has emerged that explores the range of issues relating to the impacts resulting from development of tourism and the related, often used terms of sustainable development and responsible tourism (see, for example, Farrell and Twining-Ward, 2005; Wall and Mathieson, 2006; Buckley, 2012; Mowforth and Munt, 2015; Sharpley and Telfer, 2015; Koens et al., 2018).

Many case studies of tourism development have been published, as well as various policy responses such as the international case studies presented in Laws et al. (1998) and Mason (2015). Mbaiwa and Stronza (2010), for instance, traced the effects of tourism in the environmentally sensitive Okavango Delta of Botswana and reported that tourism development is achieving its goal of improved livelihoods for rural communities. Zhuang et al. (2019) traced the sociocultural impacts of tourism development on residents of World Heritage sites in the Guandong Province of China.

KEY CONCEPT

Understanding tourism impacts

It can be argued that tourism is different from other services in at least one important respect – its impact on society. Evans (2012:221) argued that:

> tourism is highly visible as well as invisible in its impact and is capable of making profound societal and cultural changes, not only to host destinations, but also to tourist 'exporting' areas. Though it is clear that the impacts are wide-ranging, and that some of the impacts are both easy to identify and measure while others are not, the topic is often controversial in practice and subject to much debate in the academic literature.

This controversy has been illustrated by Krippendorf (and many others subsequently).

The Swiss academic Jost Krippendorf was one of the founding fathers of the concept of 'sustainable tourism' (Müller and Lane, 2003). In his influential work *The Holiday Makers – Understanding the Impacts of Leisure and Travel* (Krippendorf, 1999), he discussed aspects of the impact that tourists have on their destination.

Krippendorf cited a leading Swiss researcher writing in the early 1960s who argued that because its focal point is people, tourism can be one of the most important means, especially in developing countries, of bringing nations closer together and of maintaining good international relations (Evans, 2012).

Krippendorf took a contrary view when he argued that this was the theory 20 years ago. Today, when traveling has become a mass phenomenon, the tale of understanding among peoples is nothing more than wishful thinking.

> I do not share this faith, nor do I know many positive experiences and examples. On the contrary, I believe that the chances for real human contact between holidaymakers and locals could hardly be less hopeful. The contact is usually only skin deep, the relationship a mere illusion. Where the main reason for traveling is to get away from things, where the tourist ignores the existence of other people, where assembly line techniques are the only way of dealing with huge numbers, where profit making rules supreme, where there are feelings of superiority and inferiority, no communication can develop.

Source: Adapted from Krippendorf (1999)

The impact of tourism is also relevant in the context of perhaps the biggest issue of our times: climate change. The tourism sector is both highly vulnerable to climate change and at the same time contributes to the emission of GHG, which cause global warming (UNWTO, 2021). Accelerating climate action – that is, efforts to measure and reduce GHG emissions in tourism – is therefore of utmost importance for the resilience of the sector. In an important study, Lenzen et al. (2018)

found that between 2009 and 2013, tourism's global carbon footprint had increased and accounted for about 8% of GHG emissions. Transport, shopping and food are significant contributors, and the authors projected that, due to its high carbon intensity and continuing growth, tourism will constitute a growing part of the world's greenhouse gas emissions.

The Glasgow Declaration on Climate Action in Tourism was officially launched at the COP26 UN Climate Change Conference held in Glasgow, Scotland, in November 2021. It proposed a coordinated plan for tourism to support the global commitment to halve emissions by 2030 and achieve net zero by 2050. The actions of the signatories are aligned with five pathways defined in the declaration: measure, decarbonize, regenerate, collaborate, finance (UNWTO, 2021).

The commitment to achieving the stated aims of the declaration has been questioned. Scott and Gössling (2022:199), for example, conceded that the declaration could prove a 'milestone' event and that it includes some positive advances. However, as the third such declaration over 20 years, the authors questioned 'whether it brings the sector closer to an action agenda commensurate with the climate emergency the sector has declared'.

In addition to the wide-ranging discussion of tourism's impact on climate change at a global scale (see, for example, Scott et al., 2012, 2019; Jones and Phillips, 2017; Dogru et al., 2019), there have been a large number of studies considering the impacts on specific destinations or *THE* sectors. See, for example, Dube et al. (2018), Hoogendoorn and Fitchett (2018) and Moyle et al. (2018) for studies focusing on Botswana, Africa and Australia, respectively. Legrand et al. (2022), in considering climate change and sustainability in relation to the hospitality sector, argued that, given their importance, an understanding of these issues is essential for all future managers in the sector.

Increasingly, these matters are also considered in the strategies of organizations in *THE* that will be considered in Chapter 16. The case of the Maldives illustrates some of the challenges tourism faces in relation to climate change.

2.5 SHORT CASE ILLUSTRATION

Tourism in the Maldives: living with climate change

The Republic of Maldives is a country with a population of about 550,000 occupying an archipelago in the Indian Ocean. The key industries are tourism and fishing. Tourism accounts for almost 28% of the gross domestic product, and over 90% of government tax revenue comes from import duties and tourism-related taxes.

The nation stands at an average height of just 1 m above sea level, making unpredictable weather patterns resulting from climate change an imminent threat to life on the 200 inhabited coral islands, a point emphasized by the country's Minister of Environment Aminath Shauna. 'Climate change is real and we are the most vulnerable country in the world. There's no higher ground for us. It's just us, our islands and the sea' (Horton, 2022). The 2004 Indian Ocean tsunami demonstrated the vulnerability of Maldives to natural disasters affecting nearly one-third of the population directly by the loss or damage to homes, livelihoods and infrastructure (www.gcca.eu/).

At the heart of the matter lies a paradox facing the islanders: a battle to survive the climate crisis while simultaneously relying on an industry that is contributing to it (Horton, 2022). Viable alternative sources of income are not readily available if the tourism industry were to collapse.

In the face of a changing climate, countries must put in place *adaptation* policies. Even assuming full global coordination on mitigation polices, global warming will not be reversed, and countries need to take steps to protect their citizens and ready their economies for a changing climate. There are numerous types of adaptation measures (e.g., educating the public, investing in climate-resilient infrastructure, better preparing for natural disasters, protecting biodiversity, sustainability measures by industry, etc.) that would result in increased resilience to climate change (Agarwal et al., 2021).

Adaptation to climate change is a priority for the government of Maldives. The National Adaptation Plan of Action identifies several foci of intervention such as critical infrastructures, tourism, fisheries, health, water resources, agriculture and coral reef biodiversity. Many of the hotels have gradually altered their practices and promote their sustainable credentials through initiatives such as marine conservation, avoiding plastic waste, recycling water, sourcing restaurant produce locally and utilizing renewable energy.

A full exploration of these topics (sustainable development and climate change) related to the impacts *of* tourism is beyond the scope of this book. However, for managers operating in *THE*, an understanding of the impacts of these sectors is important in considering how those impacts can be managed satisfactorily. The needs of the various *stakeholders* require consideration and need to be dealt with in an appropriately balanced way as part of any strategic plan (which is considered in Chapter 16).

Any discussion of the impacts of tourism usually centers on the effects of so-called mass tourism. However, in recent years, far more is being done to address the issues associated with such mass tourism through smaller-scale alternatives such as ecotourism and other forms of low-impact and responsible travel (Getz and Page, 1997). Several authors have considered whether sustainable tourism development is an achievable objective, given the impact of tourism (see, for example, Sharpley, 2020; Higgins-Desbiolles, 2021).

DEFINITION/QUOTATION

Mass tourism

Mass tourism has been defined as:

> a phenomenon of large-scale packaging of standardized leisure services at fixed prices for sale to a mass clientele.
>
> (Poon, 1993:32)

Poon (1993) identified five key forces as having been responsible for the spread of this mass, standardized and rigidly packaged tourism:

- *Consumers*: sun lust and inexperienced mass consumers
- *Technology*: jet aircraft, automobiles, computer reservations and accounting systems, credit cards
- *Production*: cheap oil, charter flights, packaged tours, hotel overbuilding, mass production
- *Management*: economies of scale, hotel and holiday branding, promotional airfares, mass marketing

- *Frame conditions*: postwar peace and prosperity, paid holidays, regulation of air transportation, incentives to attract hotel chains to establish operations

In North America and Europe, different drivers facilitated the development and spread of mass tourism. In the USA, multinational hotel chains, airlines and the growth in car usage were prevalent. In Europe, by comparison, powerful tour operators, charter flights and packaged tours to Mediterranean 'sun' destinations were the key factors in the rapid growth of mass tourism. In Southeast Asia, international tourism development has been more recent, driven at first by long-haul tourists mainly from Europe and Australasia but more recently by intraregional flows of tourists particularly from China, India and Japan.

One of the key questions facing managers in *THE* contexts today is to what extent mass tourism will continue with what some regard as its socially, culturally and environmentally harmful patterns of growth. To managers of tourism destinations, events and hospitality the question always has to be asked as to what level of visitors can be sustained without the attraction that brings visitors being irretrievably damaged; that is, what is the *carrying capacity*. The issues associated with carrying capacity and the linked issue of potential *overtourism* have been explored extensively in the literature. See, for example, Coccossis and Mexa (2017), Koens et al. (2018), Butler (2020), Tokarchuk et al. (2020) and Wall (2020).

2.6 SHORT CASE ILLUSTRATION

Boracay, Philippines

Countries in Southeast Asia are looking at ways to stem the threats of mass tourism without cutting off the cash flow of a regional tourism boom, led by China, the top source market for travelers to the region. Thailand received 35 million tourists last year, of whom nearly 10 million hailed from China. However, what is good for business can be bad for beaches. Across the region, Southeast Asia's once pristine beaches are reeling from decades of mass tourism as governments scramble to alleviate environmental degradation without curtailing a key economic driver.

Hotels and other tourist facilities have been rapidly constructed. However, all too often the commercial facilities have been poorly planned and necessary infrastructure works (such as transport links, waste disposal, provision and maintenance of public spaces) to support them have lagged behind. Development has thus reflected a desire to achieve short-term financial gain rather than a strategic approach aiming to establish a sustainable industry in the long term.

Though only 7 km long, Boracay island, situated some 300 km south of Manila, is among the Philippines' top tourism destinations. Since the early 1970s the island's white sandy beaches have led to the exponential growth of tourism numbers, with about 2 million arriving during 2017, mainly from Asian countries, including China. The island generates US$1bn from tourism and has over 500 hotels.

Drastic measures were carried out in Boracay during April 2018 when a ban on Filipino and foreign tourism was established (for 6 months) to enable facilities to treat raw sewage to be set up and illegal structures to be torn down. The abrupt decision to close Boracay forced hundreds of hotels, restaurants, tour operators and other businesses to cancel bookings and for most of the 17,000 hotel, restaurant and other tourism workers to be laid off. The move followed growing concern over the island's environmental health. Officials had warned that businesses had been releasing wastewater into the waters surrounding the island.

The threat of closure first emerged in February 2018, when Filipino President Rodrigo Duterte accused Boracay's businesses of dumping sewage directly into the island's turquoise waters. 'I will close Boracay. Boracay, it is a cesspool', he said in a speech in his home city of Davao. The rehabilitation period was used to improve the island's environment and the island subsequently reopened after about 6 months, with a limit on tourist numbers.

Source: www.itsmorefuninthephilippines.com

Questions

1. Explain how Boracay might have been developed in a more sustainable way.

2. Consider ways other than complete closure that Boracay could have adopted to deal with its issues.

It has been argued (Poon, 1993) that a 'new tourism' has emerged, the signs of which include:

- The growing demand for 'independent', nonpackaged holidays
- The growing demand for choice and flexibility
- Information technologies, such as global distribution systems (gds) and the internet, which allow customers to deal directly with companies and organizations as a means to flexibly make travel arrangements as an alternative to 'package' holidays
- Increasing environmental planning and control of tourism in host countries
- Increasing *segmentation* of travel markets to cater for differing lifestyle characteristics
- Changes in tourists' travel behavior and motivation, with more shorter breaks and activity-oriented travel
- The rapid growth of domestic, inbound and outbound tourism in many emerging markets such as China, India, Indonesia and Brazil
- A greater awareness by tourists of the potential impacts of tourism on climate change

The Short Case Illustration below illustrates some of the challenges raised by tourism and responses to these challenges at a local level.

2.7 SHORT CASE ILLUSTRATION

Grootbos, South Africa

Tourist destinations and companies are increasingly coming to realize that limits have to be placed on growth if the impacts of tourist development are not to destroy the attractions that tourists sought in the first place. In the tourism literature, the terms 'tourist carrying capacity' and 'sustainable tourism' have been used to describe the maximum desirable level of tourism development that could be sustained over a medium- to long-term period.

There are many examples from around the world of destinations, hospitality providers and event managers that are adapting their business models so that they recognize the importance of operating according to principles of sustainability. One such example is Grootbos Private Nature Reserve and Lodge in South Africa. Grootbos is a luxury camp 2 hours north of Cape Town.

Grootbos, which is operated as a charitable foundation, provides 5-star accommodation for guests, providing a crucial revenue stream. As a sustainability pioneer, Grootbos has been certified as carbon negative since 2018.

It is also an important nature reserve set in the Fynbos area. Fynbos is an area of natural heathland vegetation occurring in a small belt of the Western Cape with a Mediterranean climate that is known for its exceptional degree of biodiversity. The Grootbos nature reserve was instrumental in setting up the Walker Bay Fynbos Conservancy in 1999 and currently consists of 26 landowners who manage approximately 16,000 hectares of Fynbos.

The Grootbos private foundation also offers a number of different sustainability initiatives:

- Siyakhula Organic Farm – provides skills development in organic agriculture, sustainable animal husbandry and beekeeping to members from the local community and is run as a commercial enterprise to provide an income for Foundation projects. Beyond skills development and food production, the farm functions as research and experimentation space.

- 'Green Future' – provides annual, practical-based training programs for unemployed local people in the fields of landscaping, horticulture and ecotourism.

- 'Spaces for Sport' – offers a multipurpose facility that is considered a community development project.

The site was chosen because of its unique position in the center of three racially diverse communities. Guests are given the opportunity to plant a tree in a patch that was in a fire in February 2006. Approximately 1,000 trees have been planted to date. Each guest receives a tree planting certificate with the coordinates where the trees were planted.

Source: www.grootbos.com; www.fynbos.co.za

Questions

1. Explain the issues raised by Grootbos in relation to the impacts of tourism.

2. Explain the business model Grootbos has developed and assess its effectiveness.

The relevance of the preceding discussion on the impacts of tourism raises a number of issues for managers in *THE* sectors:

- Modern consumers are becoming ever more sensitive to the impacts of what they consume, whether it is the effect that the detergents they use might have on the environment, the amount of water used in irrigating a golf course in hot climates or the impacts that tourism has on the culture of the host community.

- An increasing number of tourism consumers are recognizing that many serious environmental deteriorations are rooted in tourism activities (Trang et al., 2019; Wang et al., 2020; Han, 2021).

Consequently, the issues of eco-friendly consumption and sustainable product development are becoming more important than ever in the contemporary *THE* sectors (Han, 2021). In successfully managing their *THE* products, managers must be sensitive to these issues in ways they often failed to be in the past.

- Though mass tourism is obviously here to stay, changes are taking place in the marketplace. Consumers are becoming more knowledgeable, experienced and sophisticated in their tastes and rather more complicated to understand. Furthermore, additional consumers are being added as emerging markets such as Brazil, Russia, India and China (the BRIC countries) develop.

- Managers have to research and attempt to understand these changes that are undoubtedly taking place. Furthermore, in the highly competitive sectors of the industry we are concerned with, they have to design their products to appeal to these changing tastes and then to promote, distribute and price the products appropriately.

- Many new forms of tourism and associated events and hospitality products have emerged to suit the needs of this vastly more discriminating travel market, including wine tourism; culinary tourism; 'dark' tourism; extreme adventures; sport, festival and event tourism; and various specialized forms of learning-based travel.

- These new forms of tourism are creating additional opportunities and challenges that managers need to research, understand, design and deliver targeted products.

2.4.7 The effect of external shocks

The sectors of *THE* are particularly prone to external shocks beyond the control of its managers.

Internal corporate shocks such as financial irregularities, by contrast, are also important to the industry, but these are not distinguishing characteristics of the industry. As events in other industries have demonstrated, they are prevalent in many industries where management has proved to be too ambitious, fraudulent or incompetent (Evans and Elphick, 2005).

THE as service sectors are unique (among service industries) in their vulnerability, because the sectors are highly exposed to risks and prone to crises as the result of external events. Unlike internal events, which can be assessed and controlled by managers, external events are beyond their control and therefore inherently provide a greater degree of risk and uncertainty.

Furthermore, the inherent characteristics of these service sectors (such as the *perishability* of the product and the *interdependence* of elements of the product) make the risks potentially very difficult to manage, because supply often cannot quickly be matched to rapid declines in demand (Evans and Elphick, 2005).

> **For example:** *A study of Indian upscale hotels (Israeli et al., 2011) found that they were not prepared to handle a crisis such as the terror attacks in Mumbai involving two luxury hotels in November 2008. The attacks reduced hotel occupancy levels to 30% for several weeks and charter tours were canceled in South India, some 2,000 km away. The result was the loss of millions of dollars of revenue for tourism, hotel and related industries.*

External shocks such as wars, pandemics, hurricanes, terrorist attacks, pollution, adverse publicity and accidents can have a dramatic and speedy effect on levels of business and disruption to planned activities and events. External shocks can quickly develop into crises and indeed can – and should – be viewed as a central concern of competent managers in the industry. The effect of COVID-19 on *THE* is difficult to underestimate and is considered in various parts of the book.

The topic has attracted quite a large *THE* literature and is considered briefly in the Short Case Illustration below.

2.8 SHORT CASE ILLUSTRATION

The effects of COVID-19

Though there are many examples of external shocks affecting *THE*, undoubtedly the COVID-19 pandemic has had the most powerful and varied impact on these sectors. COVID-19 was first detected in Wuhan in the Hubei Province of China in December 2019; subsequently, on January 30, 2020, the World Health Organization declared COVID-19 a global emergency.

Though crises are regular occurrences in tourism (Collins-Kreiner and Ram, 2020; Dolnicar and Zare, 2020; Gössling et al., 2020), the scope and scale of the impact of the COVID-19 pandemic and its impact on *THE* have been unprecedented. Ultimately, the industry around the world was forced to shut down for months, in what Aldao et al. (2021:930) termed a 'global disruptive event', leaving such devastation in its wake that strategies for recovery are in many cases unclear. The UNWTO acknowledged that tourism was one of the hardest hit industries as all parts of the industry around the world were forced to cease trading or severely curtail their activities.

The virus affected virtually all parts of the *THE* value chain. The impact of canceled events, closed accommodation, mothballed attractions and canceled flights and cruises was immediately felt in other parts of the supply chain, such as catering and laundry services. Restaurants also had to close, though in some countries a switch to takeaway/delivery sales allowed some to continue operations (Gössling et al., 2020). In a study of hospitality and restaurants, Dube et al. (2021) found that guests dropped to zero in many countries as governments across the world instituted social distancing initiatives, movement restrictions and lockdowns. COVID-19 also led to an unprecedented loss of employment and revenue, resulting in millions of jobs and billions of dollars in potential revenue lost.

Many destinations and *THE* organizations have been affected by 'natural' crises, and over the years tactics and strategies have been developed to mitigate the risks and to acquire resilience (Ritchie and Jiang, 2019). The crisis stemming from the COVID-19 pandemic, however, has presented quite different and unique challenges. Collins-Kreiner and Ram (2020) suggested that the pandemic is different in four respects:

1. The decline in travel, hospitality and tourism has been worldwide.

2. The economic collapse was more dramatic than in previous health emergencies.

3. The ongoing crisis has the potential to cause fundamental modifications in many tourism segments (Dolnicar and Zare, 2020).

4. Though the worst effects appear to be over, it is unclear (at the time of writing) how and when the crisis will end.

Questions

1. Assess the overall impact COVID-19 had on *THE*.

2. Consider how *THE* managers might prepare for a future similar external shock.

A large and varied academic literature covers 'crisis management' in *THE*. See, for example, Glaesser (2011), Mair et al. (2016), Prayag (2018), Aldao et al. (2021), Berbekova et al. (2021), Leta and Chan (2021), Le and Phi (2021), Wut et al. (2021), Ziakas et al. (2021) and Ketter (2022).

> **For example:** *Le and Phi (2021) modeled crisis management in the context of hotels in relation to COVID-19. Their model distinguishes between four phases of the crisis: 'pre-event and early symptom', 'emergency', 'crisis' and 'recovery', with appropriate managerial responses suggested for each phase.*

By their nature these events are unpredictable in relation to their geographical location, their timing and their scale and hence provide difficulties for industry managers in a number of ways:

- It is difficult to forecast such events and to foresee the full implications.
- The management steps that need to be taken can be complex at a strategic level.
- The effective implementation of management actions at an operational level is also complex and needs careful coordination of resources and communications.
- A brand that may have been assiduously developed over many years can be severely damaged or even destroyed by sudden events.
- Recovery from crises has to be planned and should stress the importance of a strategy that is flexible so that rapid unforeseen changes can be incorporated.

The terrorist attacks in New York and Washington on 11 September 2001 had an immediate effect on the industry, as illustrated by the case of Accor Hotels.

2.9 SHORT CASE ILLUSTRATION

The effects of 11 September 2001: Accor Hotel Group

Accor is a Paris-based multibrand network that, in 2001, had 3,600 hotels in 90 countries that were fully integrated in terms of sales and technology. Hotel development is based on well-known international brands (such as Sofitel, Novotel, Mercure, Ibis, Formule 1, as well as Motel 6 and Red Roof Inns in the USA) that cover the full range of hotel segments, from budget to luxury class. Accor properties are now well represented around the globe, particularly in America, Europe and Asia.

The travel industry, faced with a slowdown that was already perceptible in spring 2001, had to cope with one of the worst crises in its history after the events of 11 September 2001. The tragic events had two consequences. The first was immediate and of an unprecedented magnitude – a psychological shock. The second was the aggravation of the global economic slowdown affecting America, Europe and Asia simultaneously.

As a result of the events, some hotel investments were postponed but very few were canceled, and the group still planned 250 new hotel openings over the subsequent few years. The group was protected to some extent from the worst effects of the downturn by the diversity of its hotel portfolio both geographically and in terms of quality. However, some effects on hotel bookings were inevitable. For example, the luxury hotel industry in Paris was severely affected, whereas the economy hotel segment in Europe held up well. Thus, Sofitel's bookings dropped by 33% in October and 18% in November 2001, whereas Formule 1 and Ibis budget brands in Europe recorded an increase of 3.5% in their October bookings and 4.6% in November. In the USA, Sofitel's bookings declined by 25% to 30%, whereas Red Roof Inns and Motel 6 (budget brands) registered a limited drop of 8.2% in October and 6% in November 2001.

Source: Adapted from www.accor.com

Questions

1. Explain how Accor was affected by the 9/11 terrorist attacks.

2. Explain the managerial responses of Accor after the attacks.

Other examples include:

- The devastating Indian Ocean tsunami that occurred on 26 December 2004 was among the deadliest natural disasters in human history, with over 230,000 people killed in 14 countries bordering the Indian Ocean. In addition to the devastation in terms of the tragic loss of life, long-term effects included long-lasting impacts on tourism in Indonesia, Thailand and Sri Lanka.
- The West Africa Ebola epidemic (a rare viral disease) lasted 2½ years from late 2013, affecting almost 30,000 people, with 99% of cases in Guinea, Sierra Leone and Liberia. The majority of airlines froze flight routes, and a number of neighboring countries closed their borders with the affected countries, including adjacent countries such as Senegal and Côte D'Ivoire (WTTC, 2018). Despite no reported cases and not being directly adjacent to affected countries, tourism receipts in Gambia (a small West African country that is highly reliant on international tourism) more than halved for the 2014–15 season (Novelli et al., 2018).

Though not able to plan directly for such events, managers need to be able to:

- Identify the risks to which the organization (destination or event) may be susceptible
- Assess the possible impact of those risks
- Have contingency plans in place so that the organization is able to react quickly and effectively

---

THINK POINTS

- Why is *THE* different from other service-based sectors in relation to its impacts?
- Explain why *THE* is so susceptible to external shocks.
- Discuss why an understanding of the characteristic features of *THE* is important to managers operating in these sectors.

The contingency plans that a *THE* organization puts in place need to include detailed operating procedures for which key staff might be involved; how communications with customers, relatives and the media might be organized; and how operations can be recognized to minimize the disruption.

One approach is to spread the risks so that one crisis does not destroy the business entirely.

> For example: *A tour operator, event manager or hotel owner operating in only one country would be at risk if a war or environmental catastrophe were to occur, but by operating in several countries, the risks are spread and the overall risk is reduced.*

2.10 SHORT CASE ILLUSTRATION

Crisis management: Ryanair and Icelandic volcanic ash

In 2010, a volcano on Iceland's Eyjafjallajökull glacier caused travel chaos for Europe's airlines during April and May as vast swathes of European airspace were closed. The ash cloud moved unpredictably across much of Northern Europe, potentially threatening air safety.

The budget airline Ryanair, for example (despite protests from the airline itself that it was unnecessary), was forced to cancel 9,400 flights, which disrupted the travel plans of 1.5 million passengers. It was reported that the incident cost the Irish-based airline £42mn (€65mn).

In such unpredictable circumstances, it is important that a company:

- Communicate accurately and at an early stage with customers with regular updated information

- Provide as much operational flexibility as possible

- Be sufficiently diversified so that one serious and unpredictable incident does not lead to the organization's demise

- In the case of Ryanair, its full-year profits increased despite the severe impacts of the ash clouds.

Source: www.ryanair.com

Questions

1. Explain what the lessons of this case might be for dealing with crisis situations for *THE* companies.

2. Consider other examples of crisis situations that have occurred for *THE* organizations.

Small business focus

THE sectors can often be regarded as highly fragmented. A fragmented industry is characterized by its large numbers of small and medium-sized businesses and its lack of market leaders with a significant share of the market. The sectors do have some strong international companies, and undoubtedly both the power and the market share of these players are increasing yearly. The context varies across the sectors in that large international brands are established with regard to hotel chains, travel intermediaries, cruise lines, tour operators and airlines, whereas there are few such large internationally diversified companies currently operating in the events management sector.

However, alongside these large organizations there is a proliferation of smaller businesses, such as owner-operated guest houses and restaurants, transport operators, visitor attractions, travel agents, tour guides and resorts.

A number of the aspects discussed in this chapter are relevant to smaller businesses operating in *THE* sectors. In some cases, the characteristics that have been outlined can work against smaller businesses.

> **For example:** *In some subsectors there are high barriers to entry such as capital requirements, regulatory restrictions or well-established brand names. These barriers vary considerably between different markets, but where they exist in airlines, cruising and some hotel markets, it is difficult for smaller companies to compete.*

In other subsectors such as tour operating, acting as a travel agent or event organizer, barriers to entry are usually quite low, thereby allowing smaller companies to compete successfully.

Some of the other characteristics can at times work in favor of smaller companies in some circumstances:

- *Heterogeneity* – the desire many customers have for something that is different often means that smaller companies can provide *niche* products that are attractive to customers.

- *Inseparability* – the simultaneous consumption and production of *THE* products implies that there is a great emphasis on customer service. Though larger companies make great efforts to achieve high levels of service, it is difficult given their diversity and size to ensure that it is always delivered successfully. Smaller organizations with fewer staff and less complexity may be more agile and be able to more easily ensure that standards are maintained.

- *Ownership* – because customers have use of *THE* products rather than own them, the need to successfully build up a relationship with potential customers is implied. Many smaller companies successfully target particular types of customers or a particular market niche and build up loyalty and repeat customers through more personal communications and promotional activities.

- *Impacts of THE* – many smaller *THE* companies are able to present themselves successfully as being more sustainable in the way they operate; that is, minimizing the negative impacts of tourism that have been identified.

The Short Case Illustration below illustrates how smaller tour operators have acted collaboratively to form a trade association that stresses the particular benefits (based on the underlying characteristics we have discussed) that these SMEs are able to offer.

2.11 SHORT CASE ILLUSTRATION

Association of Independent Tour Operators

In the UK, the Association of Independent Tour Operators (AITO), founded in 1976, represents over 120 smaller tour operators that are able to successfully challenge larger tour operators through offering niche products.

The products relate to types of tourism such as adventure, battlefield, wine and gastronomy or cycling or tourism in particular parts of the world. The products offered are highly diverse, as are the companies that provide them. In some cases the particular niche segments identified are too small or new for the larger operators to have targeted them. In other cases the companies involved are competing directly with the larger operators, so they concentrate on higher and consistent levels of customer service, building up a relationship with clients and offering products that are differentiated from 'mainstream' products.

AITO stresses its sustainable tourism credentials, and potential members are scrutinized before they join to ensure that sustainable principles are adhered to. Sustainable travel guidelines for its members are based on five key objectives:

- To protect the environment – its flora, fauna and landscapes

- To respect local cultures – traditions, religions and built heritage

- To benefit local communities – both economically and socially

- To conserve natural resources – from office to destination

- To minimize pollution – through noise, waste disposal and congestion

Source: www.aito.co.uk

Questions

1. Explain which characteristics of *THE* AITO helps SMEs in competing with larger competitors.

2. Explain how belonging to AITO helps SMEs compete effectively.

CHAPTER SUMMARY

In this chapter, we introduced some of the key themes in *THE* that are relevant to strategy. These include understanding the nature of *THE* products; in this context, we looked at some of the properties of service products. These four characteristics (or properties) apply to *THE* products as they also apply to other 'soft' service sectors.

We also identified seven further factors that apply particularly to these sectors: ownership, high cost, seasonality, ease of entry/exit, interdependence, impact on society and the effects of external shocks. Understanding these characteristics and their implications for managers is key in determining the success of strategy in *THE* contexts. We will return to them, and reemphasize their importance, at several points in this book.

REFERENCES AND WEBSITES

References

Adriana, B. (2009) 'Environmental supply chain management in tourism: The case of large tour operators', *Journal of Cleaner Production*, 17(16): 1385–1392.

Agarwal, R., Balasundharam, V., Blagrave, P., Gudmundsson, R. and Mousa, R. (2021) 'Climate change in South Asia: Further need for mitigation and adaptation', IMF Working Paper 217. Washington, DC: IMF.

Aldao, C., Blasco, D., Espallargas, M. P. and Rubio, S. P. (2021) 'Modelling the crisis management and impacts of 21st century disruptive events in tourism: The case of the COVID-19 pandemic', *Tourism Review*, 76(4): 929–941.

Almeida-Santana, A. and Moreno-Gil, S. (2018) 'Understanding tourism loyalty: Horizontal vs. destination loyalty', *Tourism Management*, 65: 245–255.

Bain, J. (1956) *Barriers to New Competition*, Cambridge, MA: Harvard University Press.

Baum, T. and Lundtorp, S. (2001) *Seasonality in Tourism*, Oxford: Pergamon.

Baumol, W. J. (1982) 'Contestable markets: An uprising in the theory of industrial structure', *American Economic Review*, 72: 1–15.

Berbekova, A., Uysal, M. and Assaf, A. G. (2021) 'A thematic analysis of crisis management in tourism: A theoretical perspective', *Tourism Management*, 86: 104342.

Blomstermo, A., Sharma, D. D. and Sallis, J. (2006) 'Choice of foreign market entry mode in service firms', *International Marketing Review*, 23(2): 211–229.

Buckley, R. (2012) 'Sustainable tourism: Research and reality', *Annals of Tourism Research*, 39(2): 528–546.

Bull, A. (1995) *Economics of Travel and Tourism*, 2nd ed., Melbourne: Longman Australia.

Butler, R. W. (2020) 'Tourism carrying capacity research: A perspective article', *Tourism Review*, 75(1): 207–211.

Coccossis, H. and Mexa, A. (Eds) (2017) *The Challenge of Tourism Carrying Capacity Assessment: Theory and Practice*, Abingdon, UK: Routledge.

Collins-Kreiner, N. and Ram, Y. (2020) 'National tourism strategies during the COVID-19 pandemic', *Annals of Tourism Research*, 89: 103076.

Connell, J., Page, S. J. and Meyer, D. (2015) 'Visitor attractions and events: Responding to seasonality', *Tourism Management*, 46: 283–298.

Contractor, F. J., Kundu, K. S. and Hsu, C. C. (2003) 'A three-stage theory of international expansion: The link between multinationality and performance in the service sector', *Journal of International Business Studies*, 34(1): 5–18.

DeKay, F., Toh, R. S. and Raven, P. (2009) 'Loyalty programs: Airlines outdo hotels', *Cornell Hospitality Quarterly*, 20(3): 371–382.

Dogru, T., Marchio, E. A., Bulut, U. and Suess, C. (2019) 'Climate change: Vulnerability and resilience of tourism and the entire economy', *Tourism Management*, 72: 292–305.

Dolnicar, S., Grabler, K., Grun, B. and Kulnig, A. (2011) 'Key drivers of airline loyalty', *Tourism Management*, 32(5): 1020–1026.

Dolnicar, S. and Zare, S. (2020) 'COVID19 and Airbnb – Disrupting the disruptor', *Annals of Tourism Research*, 83: 102961.

Dube, K., Mearns, K., Mini, S. and Chapungu, L. (2018) 'Tourists' knowledge and perceptions on the impact of climate change on tourism in Okavango Delta, Botswana', *African Journal of Hospitality, Tourism and Leisure*, 7(4): 1–18.

Dube, K., Nhamo, G. and Chikodzi, D. (2021) 'COVID-19 cripples global restaurant and hospitality industry', *Current Issues in Tourism*, 24(11): 1487–1490.

Duro, J. A. and Turrión-Prats, J. (2019) 'Tourism seasonality worldwide', *Tourism Management Perspectives*, 31: 38–53.

Edgett, S., and Parkinson, S. (1993) 'Marketing for service industries – A review', *Service Industries Journal*, 13(3): 19–39.

Ekeledo, I. and Sivakumar, K. (2004) 'International market entry mode strategies of manufacturing firms and service firms: A resource-based perspective', *International Marketing Review*, 21(1): 68–101.

Evans, N. G. (2001) 'The UK air inclusive-tour industry: A reassessment of the competitive positioning of the "independent" sector', *International Journal of Tourism Research*, 3: 477–491.

Evans, N. G. (2002) 'Financial management for travel and tourism', in R. Sharpley (Ed.), *The Tourism Business: An Introduction*, Sunderland, UK: Business Education Publishers, 345–366.

Evans, N. G. (2012) 'Tourism: A strategic business perspective', in T. Jamal and M. Robinson (Eds), *The Sage Handbook of Tourism Studies*, Thousand Oaks, CA: Sage, 215–234.

Evans, N. G. (2016) 'Sustainable competitive advantage in tourism organizations: A strategic model applying service dominant logic and tourism's defining characteristics', *Tourism Management Perspectives*, 18: 14–25.

Evans, N. G. and Elphick, S. (2005) 'Models of crisis management: An evaluation of their value for strategic planning in the international travel industry', *International Journal of Tourism Research*, 7(3): 135–150.

Farrell, B. and Twining-Ward, L. (2005) 'Seven steps towards sustainability: Tourism in the context of new knowledge', *Journal of Sustainable Tourism*, 13(2): 109–122.

Ferrante, M., Magno, G. L. L. and De Cantis, S. (2018) 'Measuring tourism seasonality across European countries', *Tourism Management*, 68: 220–235.

Font, X., Tapper, R., Schwartz, K. and Kornilaki, M. (2008) 'Sustainable supply chain management in tourism', *Business Strategy and the Environment*, 17(4): 260–271.

Gallarza, M. G., Gil-Saura, S. and Holbrook, M. B. (2012) 'Customer value in tourism services: Meaning and role for a relationship marketing approach', in R. H. Tsiotsou and R. E. Goldsmith (Eds), *Strategic Marketing in Tourism Services*, Bingley, UK: Emerald, 147–162.

Gartner, W. C. and Ruzzier, M. K. (2011) 'Tourism destination brand equity dimensions renewal versus repeat market', *Journal of Travel Research*, 50(5): 471–481.

Getz, D. and Page, S. J. (1997) *The Business of Rural Tourism: International Perspectives*, Andover, UK: Cengage Learning EMEA.

Glaesser, D. (2011) *Crisis Management in the Tourism Industry*, Abingdon, UK: Routledge.

Gomez, B. G., Arranz, A. G. and Cillan, J. G. (2006) 'The role of loyalty programs in behavioural and affective loyalty', *Journal of Consumer Marketing*, 23(7): 387–396.

Gössling, S., Scott, D. and Hall, C. M. (2020) 'Pandemics, tourism and global change: A rapid assessment of COVID-19', *Journal of Sustainable Tourism*, 29(1): 1–20.

Gu, H., and Wall, G. (2006) 'The effects of SARS on China's tourism enterprises', *Tourism*, 54(3): 225–233.

Gummesson, E., Lusch, R. F. and Vargo, S. L. (2010) 'Transitioning from service management to service-dominant logic: Observations and recommendations', *International Journal of Quality and Service Sciences*, 2(1): 8–22.

Hall, C. M. (2019) 'Constructing sustainable tourism development: The 2030 agenda and the managerial ecology of sustainable tourism', *Journal of Sustainable Tourism*, 27(7): 1044–1060.

Hamilton, J. (2006) *Thomas Cook: The Holiday Maker*, Stroud, UK: Sutton.

Han, H. (2021) 'Consumer behavior and environmental sustainability in tourism and hospitality: A review of theories, concepts, and latest research', *Journal of Sustainable Tourism*, 29(7): 1021–1042.

Higgins-Desbiolles, F. (2021) 'The "war over tourism": Challenges to sustainable tourism in the tourism academy after COVID-19', *Journal of Sustainable Tourism*, 29(4): 551–569.

Holloway, C. and Humphreys, C. (2019) *The Business of Tourism*, 11th ed., London: Sage.

Hoogendoorn, G. and Fitchett, J. M. (2018) 'Tourism and climate change: A review of threats and adaptation strategies for Africa', *Current Issues in Tourism*, 21(7): 742–759.

Horton, B. A. (2022) 'The tourism paradox: Is the Maldives facing an existential crisis?', www.euronews.com/green

Hsu, C. H., Oh, H. and Assaf, A. G. (2012) 'A customer-based brand equity model for upscale hotels', *Journal of Travel Research*, 51(1): 81–93.

Israeli, A. A., Mohsin, A. and Kumar, B. (2011) 'Hospitality crisis management practices: The case of Indian luxury hotels', *International Journal of Hospitality Management*, 30(2): 367–374.

Jones, A. L. and Phillips, M. (Eds). (2017) *Global Climate Change and Coastal Tourism: Recognizing Problems, Managing Solutions and Future Expectations*, Wallingford, UK: CAB International.

Kayaman, R. and Arasli, H. (2007) 'Customer based brand equity: Evidence from the hotel industry', *Managing Service Quality*, 17(1): 92–109.

Keating, B. (2009) 'Managing ethics in the tourism supply chain: The case of Chinese travel to Australia', *International Journal of Tourism Research*, 11(4): 403–408.

Ketter, E. (2022) 'Bouncing back or bouncing forward? Tourism destinations' crisis resilience and crisis management tactics', *European Journal of Tourism Research*, 31: 3103.

Knorr, A. (2019) 'Big data, customer relationship and revenue management in the airline industry: What future role for frequent flyer programs?', *Review of Integrative Business and Economics Research*, 8(2): 38–51.

Koens, K., Postma, A. and Papp, B. (2018) 'Is overtourism overused? Understanding the impact of tourism in a city context', *Sustainability*, 10(12): 1384.

Krippendorf, J. (1999) *The Holiday Makers – Understanding the Impacts of Leisure Travel*, Abingdon, UK: Routledge.

Laws, E., Faulkner, B. and Moscardo, G. (Eds) (1998) *Embracing and Managing Change in Tourism: International Case Studies*, New York: Routledge.

Le, D. and Phi, G. (2021) 'Strategic responses of the hotel sector to COVID-19: Toward a refined pandemic crisis management framework', *International Journal of Hospitality Management*, 94: 102808.

Legrand, W., Sloan, P. and Chen, J. S. (2022) *Sustainability in the Hospitality Industry: Principles of Sustainable Operations*, 3rd ed., Abingdon, UK: Routledge.

Lenzen, M., Sun, Y. Y., Faturay, F., Ting, Y. P., Geschke, A. and Malik, A. (2018) 'The carbon footprint of global tourism', *Nature Climate Change*, 8(6): 522–528.

Leta, S. D. and Chan, I. C. C. (2021) 'Learn from the past and prepare for the future: A critical assessment of crisis management research in hospitality', *International Journal of Hospitality Management*, 95: 102915.

Lovelock, C. and Gummesson, E. (2004) 'Whither services marketing? In search of a new paradigm and fresh perspectives', *Journal of Service Research*, 7(1): 20–41.

Lozano, J., Rey-Maqueira, J. and Sastre, F. (2021) 'An integrated analysis of tourism seasonality in prices and quantities, with an application to the Spanish hotel industry', *Journal of Travel Research*, 60(7): 1581–1597.

Lu, T. Y. and Cai, L. A. (2011) 'An analysis of image and loyalty in convention and exhibition tourism in China', *Event Management*, 15(1): 37–48.

Mair, J., Ritchie, B. W. and Walters, G. (2016) 'Towards a research agenda for post-disaster and post-crisis recovery strategies for tourist destinations: A narrative review', *Current Issues in Tourism*, 19(1): 1–26.

Mason, P. (2015) *Tourism Impacts, Planning and Management*, 3rd ed., Abingdon, UK: Routledge.

Mattila, A. S. (2006) 'How affective commitment boosts guest loyalty (and promotes frequent guest programs', *Cornell Hotel and Restaurant Administration Quarterly* 47(2): 147–181.

Mbaiwa, J. E. and Stronza, A. L. (2010) 'The effects of tourism development on rural livelihoods in the Okavango Delta, Botswana', *Journal of Sustainable Tourism*, 18(5): 635–656.

McCamley, C. and Gilmore, A. (2017) 'Aggravated fragmentation: A case study of SME behaviour in two emerging heritage tourism regions', *Tourism Management*, 60: 81–91.

McKercher, M., Denisxci-Guillet, B. and Ng, E. (2012) 'Rethinking loyalty', *Annals of Tourism Research*, 39(2): 708–773.

Moeller, S. (2009) 'Characteristics of services – A new approach uncovers their value', *Journal of Services Marketing*, 24(5): 359–368.

Mowforth, M. and Munt, I. (2015) *Tourism and Sustainability: Development, Globalisation and New Tourism in the Third World*, 4th ed., Abingdon, UK: Routledge.

Moyle, C. L. J., Moyle, B. D., Chai, A., Hales, R., Banhalmi-Zakar, Z. and Bec, A. (2018) 'Have Australia's tourism strategies incorporated climate change?', *Journal of Sustainable Tourism*, 26(5): 703–721.

Müller, H. and Lane, B. (2003) 'Jost Krippendorf: Obituary', *Journal of Sustainable Tourism*, 11(1): 3.

Novelli, M., Burgess, L. G., Jones, A. and Ritchie, B. W. (2018) "No Ebola . . . Still doomed' – The Ebola-induced tourism crisis', *Annals of Tourism Research*, 70: 76–87.

Parrilla, J. C., Font, A. R. and Nadal, J. R. (2007) 'Accommodation determinants of seasonal patterns', *Annals of Tourism Research*, 34(2): 422–436.

Pechlaner, H., Raich, F., Zehrer, A. and Peters, M. (2004) 'Growth perceptions of small and medium-sized enterprises (SMEs) – The case of South Tyrol', *Tourism Review*, 59(4): 7–13.

Pehrsson, A. (2009) 'Barriers to entry and market strategy: A literature review and a proposed model', *European Business Review*, 21(1): 64–77.

Poon, A. (1993) *Tourism Technology and Competitive Strategies*, Wallingford, UK: CAB International.

Porter, M. E. (1980) *Competitive Strategy*, New York: Free Press.

Prayag, G. (2018) 'Symbiotic relationship or not? Understanding resilience and crisis management in tourism', *Tourism Management Perspectives*, 25: 133–135.

Rahimi, R., Köseoglu, M. A., Ersoy, A. B. and Okumus, F. (2017) 'Customer relationship management research in tourism and hospitality: A state-of-the-art', *Tourism Review*, 72(2): 209–220.

Reisinger, Y. B. (2010) 'Unique characteristics of tourism, hospitality, and leisure services', in J. Kandampully, C. Mok and B. Sparks (Eds), *Service Quality Management in Hospitality, Tourism and Leisure*, New York: Routledge, 15–47.

Ritchie, B. W. and Jiang, Y. (2019) 'A review of research on tourism risk, crisis and disaster management: Launching the *Annals of Tourism Research* curated collection on tourism risk, crisis and disaster management', *Annals of Tourism Research*, 79: 102812.

Rosselló, J. and Sansó, A. (2017) 'Yearly, monthly and weekly seasonality of tourism demand: A decomposition analysis', *Tourism Management*, 60: 379–389.

Sainaghi, R., Mauri, A., Ivanov, S. and D'Angella, F. (2019) 'Mega events and seasonality: The case of the Milan World Expo 2015', *International Journal of Contemporary Hospitality Management*, 3: 3.

Saito, H. and Romão, J. (2018) 'Seasonality and regional productivity in the Spanish accommodation sector', *Tourism Management*, 69: 180–188.

Scott, D. and Gössling, S. (2022) 'A review of research into tourism and climate change-Launching the annals of tourism research curated collection on tourism and climate change', *Annals of Tourism Research*, 95: 103409.

Scott, D., Gössling, S. and Hall, C. M. (2012) 'International tourism and climate change', *Wiley Interdisciplinary Reviews: Climate Change*, 3(3): 213–232.

Scott, D., Hall, C. M. and Gössling, S. (2019) 'Global tourism vulnerability to climate change', *Annals of Tourism Research*, 77: 49–61.

Sharpley, R. (2020) 'Tourism, sustainable development and the theoretical divide: 20 Years on', *Journal of Sustainable Tourism*, 28(11): 1932–1946.

Sharpley, R. and Telfer, D. J. (2015) *Tourism and Development in the Developing World*, 2nd ed., Abingdon, UK: Routledge.

Sigala, M. (2008) 'A supply chain management approach for investigating the role of tour operators on sustainable tourism: The case of TUI,' *Journal of Cleaner Production*, 16(15): 1589–1599.

Sinclair, M. T. and Stabler, M. (1997) *The Economics of Tourism*, London: Routledge.

Singal, M. (2015) 'How is the hospitality and tourism industry different? An empirical test of some structural characteristics', *International Journal of Hospitality Management*, 47: 116–119.

Skogland, I. and Siguaw, J. A. (2004) 'Are your satisfied customers loyal?', *Cornell Hotel and Restaurant Administration Quarterly* 45(3): 221–234.

Stickdorn, M. and Zehrer, A. (2009) 'Service design in tourism: Customer experience driven destination management', presented at the First Nordic Conference on Service Design and Service Innovation, Oslo, November 2009.

Thomas, R., Friel, M. and Jameson, S. (1999) 'Small business management', in R. Thomas (Ed.), *The Management of Small Tourism and Hospitality Firms*, London: Cassell, 10–25.

Toh, R. S., DeKay, F. and Raven, P. P. (2008) 'Characteristics of members of hotel frequent-guest programs: Implications for the hospitality industry', *Tourism Analysis*, 13(3): 271–280.

Tokarchuk, O., Gabriele, R. and Maurer, O. (2020) 'Estimating tourism social carrying capacity', *Annals of Tourism Research*, 86(1): 102971.

Trang, H., Lee, J. and Han, H. (2019) 'How do green attributes elicit guest pro-environmental behaviors? The case of green hotels in Vietnam', *Journal of Travel and Tourism Marketing*, 36(1): 14–28.

Tum, J. and Norton, P. (2006), *Management of Event Operations*, London: Routledge.

UNWTO. (2022) *Transforming Tourism for Climate Action*, Madrid: UNWTO, www.unwto.org

Wall, G. (2020) 'From carrying capacity to overtourism: A perspective article', *Tourism Review*, 75(1): 212–215.

Wall, G. and Mathieson, A. (2006) *Tourism: Change, Impacts, and Opportunities*, Harlow, UK: Pearson Education.

Wang, S., Wang, J., Li, J. and Yang, F. (2020) 'Do motivations contribute to local residents' engagement in pro-environmental behaviors? Resident – destination relationship and pro-environmental climate perspective', *Journal of Sustainable Tourism*, 28(6): 834–852.

Withey, L. (1998) *Grand Tours and Cook's Tours: A History of Leisure Travel, 1750 to 1915*, London: Aurum Press.

WTTC. (2018) *Impact of the Ebola Epidemic on Travel and Tourism*, London: WTTC, www.WTTC.com

Wut, T. M., Xu, J. B. and Wong, S. M. (2021) 'Crisis management research (1985–2020) in the hospitality and tourism industry: A review and research agenda', *Tourism Management*, 85: 104307.

Xie, L. and Chen, C. C. (2014) 'Hotel loyalty programs: How valuable is valuable enough?', *International Journal of Contemporary Hospitality Management*, 26(1): 107–129.

Zeithaml, V. A., Parasuraman, A. and Berry, L. L. (1985) 'Problems and strategies in services marketing', *Journal of Marketing*, 49: 33–46.

Zhang, X., Song, H. and Huang, G. Q. (2009) 'Tourism supply chain management: A new research agenda', *Tourism Management*, 30(3): 345–358.

Zhuang, X., Yao, Y. and Li, J. J. (2019) 'Sociocultural impacts of tourism on residents of World Cultural Heritage sites in China', *Sustainability*, 11(3): 840.

Ziakas, V., Antchak, V. and Getz, D. (2021) *Theoretical Perspectives of Crisis Management and Recovery for Events*, Oxford, UK: Goodfellow.

Websites

www.accor.com
www.aito.co.uk/
www.euronews.com/green
www.expedia.com/
www.fynbos.co.za
www.gcca.eu/
www.grootbos.com
www.imf.org/
www.itsmorefuninthephilippines.com
www.jet2plc.com
www.opodo.com/
www.radissonhotelgroup.com
www.ryanair.com
www.tuigroup.com/
www.unwto.org/
www.wttc.org/

Part 2

Analyzing the internal environment

Internal analysis

Internal analysis overview

The previous part of this book was concerned with considering the context of *THE* organizations that make managing in *THE* distinctive. Strategic management as a subject of study was also introduced and, specifically, objectives, mission, vision and values were considered.

In Part 2 we turn toward the internal analysis of organizations and consider in turn competences, resources and competitive advantage, followed by the human, financial and product/market aspects of internal strategic analysis. Part 2 goes on to consider the external aspects of strategic analysis.

Study progress

Part 1	Part 2				Part 3	Part 4	Part 5
Strategy and the tourism, hospitality and events contexts	Analyzing the internal environment				Analyzing the external environment and SWOT	Strategic options	Strategy in action
Chapters 1 and 2	**Chapter 3** **The operational context: sources of competitive advantage**	**Chapter 4** **The human resources context**	**Chapter 5** **The financial context**	**Chapter 6** **The products and markets context**	Chapters 7, 8 and 9	Chapters 10, 11, 12 and 13	Chapters 14, 15, 16 and 17

Purposes of internal analysis

Internal analysis is concerned with providing the management of *THE* organizations with a detailed understanding of their organizations with respect to:

- How effective current strategies are
- How effectively resources have been deployed in support of chosen strategies

In carrying out internal analysis, managers may gain insights and understanding of how *competitive advantage* might be achieved and also an appreciation of where remedial action must be taken in order to ensure survival.

This section of the book introduces and evaluates the main techniques and frameworks that can be employed to enable *THE* managers to produce a comprehensive internal analysis of their organization.

THE organizations should carry out an internal analysis for a number of reasons, including to:

- Identify resources, competences and core competences to be developed and exploited
- Evaluate how effectively value-added activities are organized
- Identify areas of weaknesses to be addressed by the formulation of future strategies and their successful implementation
- Evaluate the performance of products
- Evaluate financial performance
- Evaluate investment potential if finance is being sought from external sources
- Assess the performance and future requirements for human resources
- Provide the analytical underpinning for the 'strengths' and 'weaknesses' sections of the SWOT

The components of internal analysis

An internal analysis will usually cover some or all of the following aspects:

- Resource analysis
- Competence identification and analysis
- Internal activities analysis using *Porter's value chain* analysis
- Financial resources and financial performance
- Human resources
- Products and their position in the market

These aspects of internal analysis are covered in Chapters 3 to 6, which form Part 2 of this book. A number of tools, techniques and frameworks are introduced to help *THE* managers in carrying out the analysis and in organizing the information.

Strategy has to take a holistic view of an organization covering key aspects of activity. Sometimes modules covering strategic management in universities are referred to as 'capstone' modules, recognizing that the modules draw together detailed study of individual functional areas in a holistic manner. In studying strategy, we are concerned with studying not only the key issues of the functional areas themselves but also the interaction between them.

In some situations, it is the interaction between the functions that gives the organization a core competence or, conversely, makes the organization less competitive, rather than the way in which the functional area itself is managed.

The strategic process

Part 1 of the book introduced strategy as being a three-part process involving strategic analysis; strategic choice and strategic implementation. Figure P2.1 develops this model further and indicates the way in which internal analysis provides a firm evidence base that enables the strengths and weaknesses of the organization to be identified as part of the SWOT analysis.

Part 2

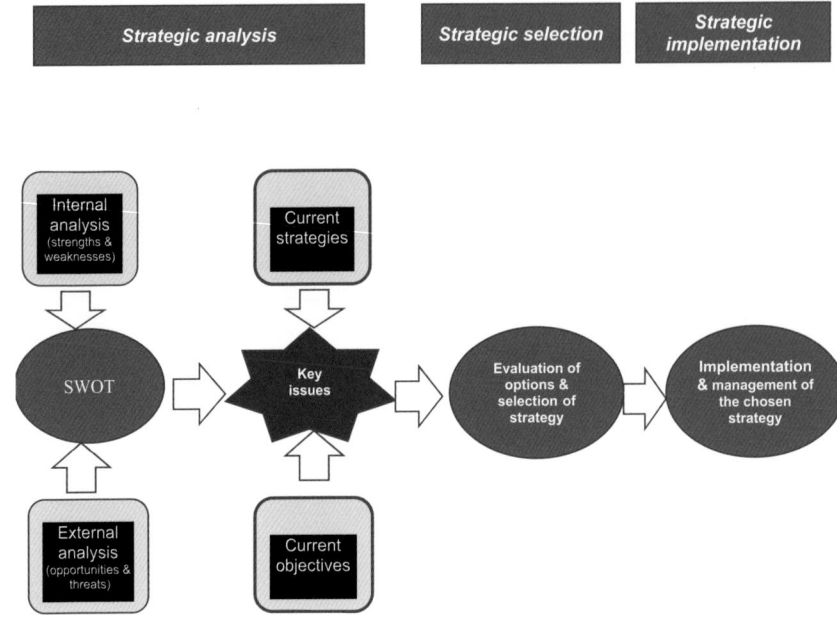

Figure P2.1 The strategic process

Chapter **3**

Tourism, hospitality and event organizations – the operational context

Sources of competitive advantage

Introduction and chapter overview

In Chapter 1 we encountered the concept of competitive advantage as one of the key objectives of business strategy. There has been considerable debate in the academic literature as to the causes of competitive advantage. Essentially, the debate asks the question, 'How do organizations achieve superior performance?'

Two positions have emerged as the most prominent: the *competitive positioning* school of thought, based primarily on the work of Michael Porter, and the *resource* or *competence* school. The analysis of competitive advantage based on these two approaches forms the basis of this chapter.

This is the first of four chapters that cover the internal analysis of *THE* organizations. This is a crucial building block in the strategy process because how can you move the organization forward successfully in the future (which is what strategic management is concerned with) unless you have a good understanding of its current position?

Subsequent chapters consider what are sometimes termed the functional areas of organizations, namely, the human resources, financial, and product and market contexts. The other key area of organizations relates to their operations.

The nature of operations is such that they are very specific to each organization. No two organizations are identical. However, they are similar in that they are trying to configure and coordinate their operational resources and processes in such a way that they add value and, in so doing, achieve an advantage over competitors – *competitive advantage*.

DOI: 10.4324/9781003318613-5

This chapter concentrates on developing an understanding of the major factors governing the level of performance of the business, namely, its resources, competences (particularly its core competences), and its so-called value-adding activities.

Much of the writing and case study examples to be found in strategy texts and academic papers relate mainly to manufacturing and the production of physical goods. Some writers have argued that different factors have to be considered in the context of services such as those considered in *THE* sectors. This has led to the development of specific conceptual models being developed such as the service profit chain and to the development of an academic framework, so-called service-dominant logic. These services-oriented topics are covered toward the end of the chapter.

LEARNING OBJECTIVES

After studying this you should be able to:

- Explain the concepts of *competences, core competences* and *resources* and the relationships between them
- Apply core competences and resources relevant to *THE* contexts
- Explain the concept of the *value chain* and the value chain framework
- Explain the relationships between core competences and core activities
- Apply the value chain framework to relevant *THE* settings
- Explain how the configuration of value-adding activities can improve business performance
- Explain the potential benefits of collaboration with suppliers, distributors and customers for *THE* organizations
- Explain why established frameworks and analytical tools may be less relevant in a service industry context
- Explain the concept of the service profit chain and how it relates to *THE* organizations
- Explain the service-dominant logic framework and co-creation of value

3.1 The sources of competitive advantage

How an organization operates is highly context specific, depending on many factors such as the size of the organization, where it is located and what sort of businesses it is operating. Managing the operations at a tourism destination will be very different from managing an annual festival or operating an airline, for instance. This chapter is concerned primarily not with the details of individual operational circumstances but with the underlying principles involved in how organizations arrange their operations. In particular, in arranging these activities, we are concerned with striving to achieve *competitive advantage*.

In all industries, including *THE*, some organizations are more successful than others. The superior performers conceivably possess something special that competitors do not have access to that allows them to outperform their rivals. Two positions have emerged as the most prominent in explaining this *competitive advantage*.

The *competitive positioning* school of thought, based primarily on the work of Professor Michael Porter of Harvard Business School (1985), stresses the importance of how the organization adds value (which is considered later in this chapter) and how the organization is positioned in respect to its competitive environment or industry (which we discuss in Chapter 8).

The alternative explanation is offered by the *resource* or *competence* school (Prahalad and Hamel, 1990; Heene and Sanchez, 1997; Barney, 2001, 2002) and is often referred to as the *resource-based view*

(RBV). The concepts we consider here (competences, core competences and competitive advantage) underpin the so-called RBV of strategy. From this perspective, it is the competences (abilities) of the business and the distinctive way in which it is able to deploy superior resources that determine the ability to outperform competitors.

Thus, in this view of strategy, the sources of *competitive advantage* lie in combining:

- The superior application of competences (skills)
- The deployment of superior resources (assets)
- Value creation for consumers

As with most controversies, it is suggested that both schools of thought have their merits. Both are partial explanations of the source of competitive advantage, and they can be viewed as complementary; that is, both types of analysis are useful in determining which organizations achieve competitive advantage.

KEY CONCEPT

Competitive advantage

Achieving competitive advantage is often seen as the overall purpose of strategy. Essentially, a business (in the commercial sector) can be said to possess competitive advantage if it is able to return higher profits than its competitors. The higher profits mean that it will be able to commit more retained profit to reinvestment in its strategy, thus maintaining its lead over its competitors in an industry. When this superiority is maintained successfully over time, *sustainable competitive advantage* is achieved. Competitive advantage can be lost when management fails to reinvest the superior profits in such a way that the advantage is not maintained.

In this text (as with other strategy texts), we tend to focus on for-profit, commercial organizations.

It is sometimes assumed that only organizations in the commercial sector have to compete – here the main driving force is the pursuit of profitability. However, this is not the case, because competition also exists among public sector and third sector (charities etc.) organizations, which are important contributors in many parts of *THE*. In these types of organizations (in which the main driver is not normally the pursuit of profit), competition takes different forms. It is demonstrated by the:

- Competition for scarce resources allocated by governments and other funding bodies
- Competition for how the service is delivered, because these bodies might have to compete with private sector organizations or PPPs
- Competition between different providers, because different organizations within the public and third sectors have to convince stakeholders that they provide value for money

Note: Strategy and *THE* texts often use the term *sustainable* (or *sustainability*) in connection with the notion of competitive advantage. However, it is also acknowledged that in *THE* texts in particular, the term is often used in different contexts to denote sustainability in relation to the physical environment. In this chapter, we use the term in relation to competitive advantage. Chapter 16 considers sustainability in relation to the natural environment.

Sustainability is achieved when the advantage resists erosion by competitive behavior (Porter, 1985), in that it cannot be copied, substituted or eroded by the actions of rivals and it is not made redundant by developments in the environment. In other words, to achieve the goal of reaching a position of sustainable competitive advantage, a business's competitive advantage must be capable of resisting duplication by other organizations (Barney, 2002).

3.2 Resources

3.2.1 Categorization of resources

In employing resources, success rests in large part on the efficiency by which the business converts its resources (inputs) into outputs. Resources fall into five broad categories:

- Human
- Financial
- Physical (e.g., buildings, equipment, stock, etc.)
- Operational (e.g., airplanes, ships, coaches, computers, etc.)
- Intangible (e.g., 'know how', patents, legal rights, brand names, registered designs, licenses, etc.)

THINK POINTS

- What are the major purposes of internal analysis?
- Define and explain the relationships between resources, competences and core competences.
- Provide an example of a core competence in a *THE* organization you are familiar with.
- Describe and distinguish between the three conceptual approaches to strategic management that have been introduced in this text.

Resources can be either *tangible* or *intangible*. They are the inputs or assets that enable an organization to carry out its activities. Tangible assets include stocks, materials, machinery, buildings, human resources, finance and so on. Intangible resources include skills, knowledge, brand names and goodwill, patent rights, operating licenses, etc. A number of writers have studied the nature and significance of intangible resources (see, for example, Fernandez et al., 2000; Galbreath, 2005; Hall 2006), and Choi and Parsa (2012) and FitzPatrick et al. (2013) considered such resources applied in relation to hotels specifically.

> For example: *Taking a resource-based view of the firm, Pearson et al. (2015) considered 36 intangible resources relating to 49 Asian airlines in relation to achieving competitive advantage. The research applied the 'VRIN framework' (discussed later in this chapter), which examines whether resources are valuable, rare, inimitable and nonsubstitutable. Resources that meet all four requirements of VRIN are considered core competences and sources of sustained advantage. The three most important resources were found to be slots, brand and product/service reputation.*

Tangible resources are obtained from outside organizations. Such resources are obtained in *resource markets* in competition with organizations from within and outside the industry. Intangible resources can often be developed within an organization but, as with tangible resources, they have a value attached to them that, although sometimes difficult to quantify (or even identify), can be bought and sold in markets. Relationships with the suppliers of resources can form an important part of the organization's core competence as, for example, with its ability to attract the most appropriately skilled human resources in the job market.

THE is different from most other industries because what economists typically refer to as *free resources* are a vital part of the product. Free resources are those resources available freely that do not require a market mechanism to allocate them.

KEY CONCEPT

Free resources

'Free' resources are those resources available in such abundance naturally, such as air, the sea, climate and culture that there is no need for an allocative mechanism (a market) to allocate them to users or consumers. However, it can be argued that free resources are also limited in supply and subject to degradation and therefore they have to be utilized carefully in 'sustainable' way.

Scarce resources, on the other hand, are the tangible and intangible resources that are limited in their supply, relative to the demand of consumers, and are therefore allocated in a market.

Bull (1995) argued that the basis for tourism lies in building on free resources (or 'renewable resources' as they are sometimes termed), with a mixture of public sector and private sector resources. Free resources together with the scarce resources are combined to form what most tourists perceive as the tourist 'product' they consume and that suppliers produce. It may be argued, as Bull (1995) pointed out, that in today's world there are few truly free resources because any human activity makes demands on the world's resources and, as a consequence, ultimately someone will have to pay a price. Indeed, the concept of *sustainable tourism* largely rests on the recognition of such a line of argument.

All resources have competing demands made on them so that if they are used for one form of activity, they cannot be used in other ways.

> For example: *a large, flat coastal area might be suitable for the development of a resort area for tourism including hotels and event venues or, alternatively, as a site for heavy industry such as steel and chemicals production. If tourism is chosen ahead of heavy industry, an opportunity to develop heavy industry on this site has been lost. The cost of this choice is known as the opportunity cost, which represents the potential economic returns that are being given up in favor of developing tourism.*

3.2.2 Resource challenges for THE managers

There are a number of challenges presented to *THE* managers in particular in the use of resources. These challenges, which will be considered in turn, relate to:

- Resource immobility
- Resource substitution

- Resource ownership and control
- Seasonality
- Low rewards
- Capacity constraints
- Time

RESOURCE IMMOBILITY

Many resources that are used cannot be moved in terms of either place or time.

> For example: *A particular beach or mountain, the Empire State Building, the culture of Spain and The Great Wall of China are geographically fixed. The alpine snows of February cannot be replicated in May, and the 'midnight sun', a tourist attraction in far northern latitudes, can be observed only during mid-summer. The Vienna Philharmonic Orchestra and the New York Marathon have their homes in those cities and represent important and prestigious parts of their cultural and sporting offerings that cannot be moved.*

RESOURCE SUBSTITUTION

It is often difficult to substitute one resource category with those of another.

> For example: *In a car factory, efficiency gains may be possible by replacing employees with machines and robots; that is, the substitution of human resources with operational resources. In the case of a luxury hotel, a concert or conference venue, an airline or a cruise ship, for instance, the quality of service is often perceived as being fundamentally linked with the quality and number of staff. Consequently, it is often difficult to replace human resources with operational resources such as computers or robots. As a result, THE sectors are usually viewed as being 'labor intensive'; that is, relying heavily on human resources in delivering products.*

RESOURCE CONFLICT AND COMPETITION

THE frequently make extensive demands on the use of certain resources, which can be in serious conflict or competition with other uses. Such resource conflict or competition may be partially resolved through pricing mechanisms by which the activity that is able to pay the most is able to use the resources. Similarly, regulatory restrictions such as the geographical zoning of areas to permit specified activities only within a particular zone may resolve some conflicts. Some degree of conflict frequently remains.

> For example: *In the UK, the competing demands of the British Army in using gunnery ranges in the Isle of Purbeck, Dorset (an area of outstanding natural beauty), and in the Northumberland National Park at Otterburn, Northumberland, are in conflict with tourist demands for unspoiled environments.*

Cultural and sporting events and tourism are often important contributors to local economies but have to compete for funding with other activities. In local settings, tourism and events often have to compete for public funding with other activities such as education, social services and health. These activities normally have far larger budgets than tourism and events, and it is difficult to argue that tourism and events should be favored in budget allocations over these crucial activities.

Recognizing this reality, government authorities throughout the world have attempted to form various types of PPPs to place promotional and organizational aspects in the private (commercial) sector. In doing so, tourism and events can form the central focus of a particular dedicated organization, rather than remain as a fringe activity in a larger body always competing for scarce resources.

RESOURCE OWNERSHIP AND CONTROL

THE managers frequently have to utilize resources that are neither owned nor controlled by the companies operating within the sectors. The lack of ownership and control of resources that is evident is a demonstration of the *interdependence* that exists between organizations operating in these sectors.

> For example: *Airlines depend on the physical resources provided by airports and the operating resources provided by air traffic control services. Although the airlines will have some influence over the way in which these resources are managed, they are rarely directly owned and managed.*

> *Projects aimed at regenerating decaying urban environments often have tourism, event venues, hotels and hospitality outlets at their heart. Such projects are often developed as PPPs. With such arrangements, the public sector (local and national government) manages and controls the overall redevelopment and provides limited funding, sometimes termed 'pump priming'. In such cases, private sector companies provide the major part of the financial resources. Examples of such PPPs include the redevelopment of Cardiff Bay in the UK, the Baltimore Waterfront in Maryland, USA, and Sydney's Darling Harbour in Australia.*

SEASONALITY

Demand for most *THE* resources, and hence the products that they contribute to, is highly seasonal (as noted in the previous chapter). This in turn is the result of factors such as climate, the distribution of holiday entitlements, the timing of events and festivals and historic travel patterns. Consequently, the price organizations pay for their resource inputs and the prices consumers pay to those organizations vary according to season.

> For example: *Many resort hotels situated in coastal areas close during the winter period and have lower rates in early spring and autumn to reflect differences in seasonal demand patterns.*

LOW REWARDS

THE sectors are often viewed as relatively low margin sectors of business. Though this is not necessarily the case, it is certainly true that the rewards from *THE* are often slow to materialize and susceptible to wide swings in cash flow and profitability.

Rewards in *THE* may be low for several reasons. The industry is often perceived as being relatively clean and pleasant, both to invest in and to work in. Consequently, employees may be prepared to work for lower wages than in other industries, and investors may be more inclined to invest in an industry that is generally viewed as interesting and 'clean'. Some destination areas are often situated in areas with few alternative land uses and employment opportunities. Thus, little competition is provided for the use of resources, thereby keeping rewards in terms of prices paid for land and development and wages paid to employees low.

For example: *The development of tourism in the Yucatán Peninsula on the Caribbean coast of Mexico has taken place over recent years in an area that is economically poorly developed and remote from major markets for goods and services. Hence, the development of hospitality and tourism in this beautiful region does not face strong competition from other industries for the use of resources and the costs of rewarding resources (in terms of land costs and wages) have been relatively low.*

CAPACITY CONSTRAINTS

The capacity of *THE* resources is frequently constrained in some way (as we noted in the previous chapter).

Thus, the *carrying capacity* for a destination is often referred to in tourism. This refers to the ability of a site, resort or region to absorb tourism use without deteriorating. The notion of carrying capacity is central to the concept of sustainability.

For example: *The rapid development of Spain's Costa del Sol from the 1950s onward demonstrates the need to constrain development. Extensive linear development along the coast to the west of Malaga led to overbuilding with poor planning controls. The relative popularity of the resort areas subsequently diminished as consumers opted for more recent and better-planned resorts elsewhere. Thus, the overuse of resources led to the carrying capacity being exceeded and deterioration in the environment that had attracted tourists in the first place.*

Similarly, the capacity of physical and operational resources in *THE* is often constrained, at least in the short to medium period.

For example: *If a hotel or a theater (physical resources) is full or an airline flight (operational resource) is fully booked, it is difficult to add capacity quickly, because the hotel, theater or aircraft accommodates a specified number of people. By contrast, if additional demand is apparent for a manufactured product, capacity can often be increased by working overtime or running production lines at a faster rate or for longer.*

Thus, in *THE*, supply is often relatively fixed (at least in the short to medium term), whereas demand can fluctuate quickly. In the longer term, capacity might be added by adding extra rooms, extending the theater or purchasing or leasing another aircraft (in the examples above).

The managerial implication of this is that managers will often (in the short to medium term) try to influence demand rather than supply. Thus, pricing levels and promotional activities will be altered to increase or reduce demand so that it matches the supply available.

For example: *It has become common for European outbound tour operators to alter prices in a very active manner in the weeks immediately prior to the date of departure, and hotels often make late alterations to their accommodation rates. This active management of prices (which can be moved upwards or downwards to inhibit or encourage demand, respectively) is a way of managing the demand so that it matches the previously fixed supply.*

TIME

Unlike the purchase of household goods or many services, *THE* consumers must also give up a scarce resource in addition to money: time. In a similar way to money, time has an *opportunity cost* attached to it; that is, other ways in which it might be spent to which a value can be attached. Though much time is spent on *THE* activities willingly, other time spent traveling to destinations or queuing at an event venue may be viewed by some consumers as a burden that, if at all possible, should be avoided or curtailed.

The managerial implication of this is that consumers may choose different products or may be willing to pay a premium for certain services. Conversely, they may take advantage of discounted prices for travel or last-minute theater tickets, for instance, in return for some extra inconvenience.

> For example: *Flights between Australia and Europe have become increasingly popular for leisure travelers in recent years as newer aircraft types have needed only one intermediate refueling stop, thereby reducing journey times. The more efficient use of time also explains why overnight long-haul flights and early morning trains are usually more expensive. The recent rapid growth in the popularity of low-cost airlines around the world is explained partly by the fact that passengers are willing to trade some degree of inconvenience for lower fares. The airlines often utilize 'secondary airports' (such as London Luton Airport in the UK or Dallas Love Field in the USA) that are further away from the main urban centers they serve or have fewer facilities and onward transit opportunities.*

3.3 Analyzing resources

When we analyze a company's resources as part of an internal analysis, several frameworks can be employed to provide a comprehensive review.

3.3.1 Analysis by category

Firstly, we might consider them by *category* – physical, operational, human, financial and intangible resources. These resources are then evaluated quantitatively (how much or how many) and qualitatively (how effectively they are being employed).

- *Physical resources* (buildings, land, materials) and *operational resources* (computers, machines, aircraft, systems, etc.) are typically audited for capacity, utilization, age, condition, contribution to output and value.
- *Financial resources* (the amount and type of finance available to the organization) are considered in terms of the balance between different types of finance and the relative cost and risks of each of these types of finance.
- *Human resources* (employees; junior, middle and senior management; board directors) are considered in terms of numbers, education, skills, training, experience, age, motivation, wage costs and productivity in relation to the needs of the organization.
- *Intangible resources* (brand, reputation, goodwill, skills, licenses and free resources) are assessed in terms of their overall value to the organization.

3.1 SHORT CASE ILLUSTRATION

Resource analysis: Marriott International

Marriott International is a leading worldwide hospitality company with its headquarters near Washington, DC, in Maryland, USA. It manages and franchises hotels under a number of recognized international brand names including Marriott, Ritz-Carlton, Sheraton, Renaissance and Courtyard. Table 3.1 summarizes Marriott's resources by category.

Table 3.1 Resource analysis: Marriott International

Resource category	Analysis of Marriott resources
Physical resources	8,000 properties with 1.4 million rooms and 30 brands in 134 counties. Properties range from luxurious (Ritz-Carlton) to budget (Courtyard and Fairfield Inn).
Operational resources	A detailed set of operating procedures for each brand that is constantly updated and refined
	Worldwide reservations system with industry-leading costs per reservation
	Common reservations system for all brands allowing for cross-selling opportunities
	Large web sales volume
	One of the largest frequent guest programs, Marriott Bonvoy, in the hospitality sector, linked to over 30 international airline programs
Financial resources	Most hotels financed by third parties, with less than 1% of properties company owned
	As a hotel manager and franchiser, significant and more stable cash flows generated than through real estate ownership
	Strong balance sheet and profitability record
Human resources	Over 125,000 employees worldwide
	Extensive staff training and advancement opportunities
	Consistently listed in *Fortune* magazine's annual list of 100 best companies to work for in USA
Intangible resources	Strong range of brand names, many of which are clear leaders within their market tiers
	Customer and owner loyalty achieved through strong rewards programs
	Distinct market positioning of each brand
	Many hotels situated at scenic locations

Source: www.marriott.com

Questions

1. Summarize the purpose of carrying out a resource analysis for a *THE* company such as Marriott.

2. What conclusions would you draw from the resource analysis of Marriott?

3.3.2 Analysis by specificity

Secondly, we can analyze resources according to their specificity. Resources can be specific or nonspecific.

> For example: *Skilled workers tend to have specialized and industry-specific knowledge and skills. Some technology, such as computer software, is for general (not industry-specific) business use, like word processing, database and spreadsheet software. Other computer software applications, like airline or hotel computer reservation systems or yield management programs, are written for highly specialized uses.*

Whereas nonspecific resources tend to be more flexible and form the basis of competences, industry-specific resources are more likely to act as the foundations of core competences.

> For example: *The specialized knowledge of procurement managers responsible for contracting accommodation in tour operators or the knowledge, expertise or training a hotel chain's front of house staff may have that can be viewed as industry leading by their companies and thereby constitute a source of core competence.*

3.3.3 Analysis by performance

Thirdly, resources can be evaluated on the basis of how they contribute to internal and external measures of performance. Internal measures include their contribution to:

- Business objectives and targets – financial, performance and output measures
- Historical comparisons – measures of performance over time (e.g., against previous years)
- Business unit or divisional comparisons – comparisons with other parts of the same organization

External measures can include:

- Comparisons with industry norms – standards of performance accepted as exemplary across the sector
- Comparisons with competitors – particularly those who are industry leaders and those who are the closest competitors and are in its *strategic grouping* (see Chapter 6)
- Comparisons with companies – in other service-based industries such as banking or insurance

By employing these techniques of analysis, an organization is able to internally and externally *benchmark* its performance as a stimulus to improving performance in the future. Performance, however, is based on more than resources, and competences must be similarly analyzed and evaluated.

3.4 Competences and capabilities

The terms *competence* and *capability*, *core competence* and *distinctive capability* are often used interchangeably in textbooks on strategy.

The notion of core competences has had a major impact on management practice and thinking, and many authors have adopted and extended the ideas. The concept of core competence is based on the work of Prahalad and Hamel (1990), Stalk et al. (1992) and Kay (1995), who advanced the idea that competitive advantage is based on distinctive capabilities. It should be noted that some authors change 'competence' to 'capability' (Stalk et al., 1992; Mooney, 2007), and Prahalad and Hamel (1990) also sometimes used the terms interchangeably in subsequent writings. Here the terms will be taken to mean broadly the same thing.

DEFINITION/QUOTATION

Competence, core competence and resources

- A *competence* is

An attribute or collection of attributes possessed by all or most of the organizations in a sector of industry

- A *core competence* is

An attribute or collection of attributes, specific to a particular organization, that enables it to produce above industry-average performance

- A *resource* is

An input employed in the activities of the business

Without competences, a business cannot enter or survive in the industry. Competences develop from resources and embody skills, technology or 'know how'.

> For example: *To operate as an outbound tour operator involved in air-inclusive 'package' tours, a company must possess a range of competences in arranging:*
>
> - *A means of distributing, marketing and selling their product*
> - *Licenses to operate the required capacity to the specified destinations*
> - *Air transportation to and from the destination*
> - *Suitable accommodation at the destination*
> - *Ground handling activities to ensure that customers are checked in for their flights and that they are transported to and from their accommodation*
> - *Every successful survivor in the industry must possess these areas of competence.*

3.4.1 How core competences 'work'

Core competences tend to be both complex and intangible, so it is necessary to explore the nature of resources and competences that underpin them before exploring the concept further. The purpose of such analysis is to allow managers to identify which resources and competences act as the foundation of existing or potential core competences. It is important to note that not all competitors in an industry will possess core competences – only those organizations that are producing above-average performance can be considered to possess core competences.

Those with only average or below-average performance possess competences and resources (without which they could not compete in the industry at all) but not core competences. For further discussion of these concepts, see Prahalad and Hamel (1990), Kay (1995), Heene and Sanchez (1997), Petts (1997), Javidan (1998) and Barney (2001). The links between competences, resources and core competences are summarized in Figure 3.1.

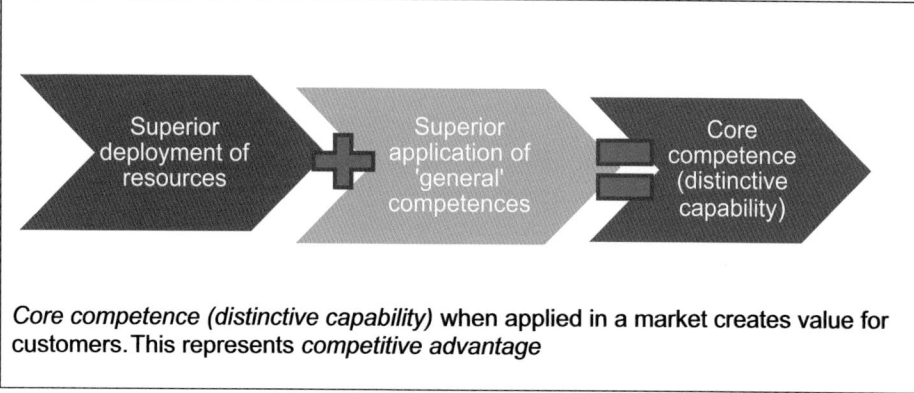

Figure 3.1 The links between resources, competences and core competences

These terms will now be considered in greater detail.

The *RBV* emphasizes that core competences arise from the way in which the organization has employed its competences and resources more effectively than its competitors. The result of a core competence (distinctive capability) is an output that customers value more highly than those of competitors, thereby achieving competitive advantage.

Prahalad and Hamel (1990) specified three tests to be applied in the identification and development of a core competence. A core competence should:

- Equip a business with the ability to enter and successfully compete in several markets
- Add greater perceived customer value to the business's products and services than that perceived in competitors' products
- Be difficult for competitors to imitate

DEFINITION/QUOTATION

Core competence

> Core competences are the collective learning of the organization, especially how to co-ordinate diverse production skills and integrate multiple streams of technologies.
> (Prahalad and Hamel, 1990:81)

Core competence arises from the unique and distinctive way in which the organization builds, develops, integrates and deploys its resources and competences.

According to Prahalad and Hamel (1990), there are many examples of core competence resulting in competitive advantage. Ashfield Event Experiences (see Short Case Illustration below), by specializing in one industry and fully understanding its requirements, has been able to build and sustain a core competence as the basis for its competitive advantage.

3.2 SHORT CASE ILLUSTRATION

Core competence: Ashfield Event Experiences

The events management sector is extremely fragmented. Low barriers to entry, few regulatory requirements and growing demand have meant that the sector has become extremely competitive, and many companies in the sector appear to offer the same range of services. Consequently, it is a competitive advantage if a company can identify its core competence and successfully promote this to build up a reputation and capability that can be sustained.

One such company is Ashfield Event Experiences (www.ashfieldeventex.com). Ashfield is a full-service global event management company that has been delivering meetings and events since the 1970s. Ashfield is a subsidiary of UK-based Inizio (www.inizio.health.com), a group of health and life sciences companies. Employees are located in offices in the UK and USA.

The company plans, researches, delivers and evaluates every element of an event, from the destination, venue, program, method of message delivery, content of presentations, team building and social activities. Many events are also held virtually, and the company has developed expertise in such delivery technology. This combination of services is not unusual for event management organizations and does not represent the application of a core competence. Unlike many events where public relations opportunities are maximized, Ashfield Event Experiences has to work in a different way.

The core competence of Ashfield lies in its specialism and how this is applied through the company's orientation. The company specializes in the health care sector, working with most of the leading pharmaceutical companies in the world, and claims to be the world's largest specialist health care event manager. This is a complex and highly regulated environment where there is often a need for specialist medical or pharmaceutical knowledge. It is also an environment where discretion and the need for both commercial and patient confidentiality are vitally important.

The experience, knowledge of the key market players, specialist health care knowledge and reassurance that there is an understanding of the sensitivity of the environment are clearly of great importance. However, as with most such companies, it is the employees who are vital in delivering the service to the required standards. Hence, the company conducts staff compliance training for all operational staff and has a medical director to ensure full knowledge of all guidelines that need to be complied with on an international basis.

Source: Adapted from www.ashfieldeventex.com

Questions

1. Explain the nature of the core competence that Ashfield exhibits in this case.

2. Consider how easy it would be for competitors to replicate the core competence of Ashfield.

Prahalad and Hamel (1990) argued that, in practice, competitive advantage is likely to be based on a very limited number of competences. These competences will allow managers to produce new and

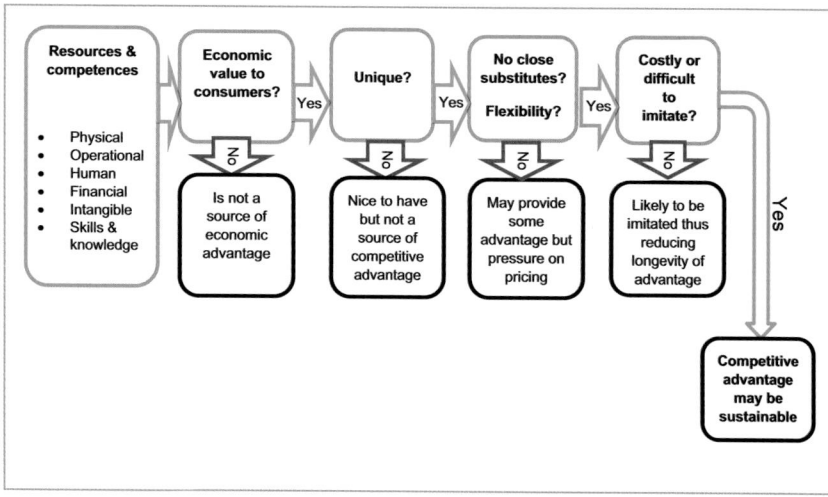

Figure 3.2 The links between resources, competences and competitive advantage

Source: Adapted from Harrison (2003)

unanticipated products and to be responsive to changing opportunities because of operational skills and the harnessing of technology.

Harrison (2003), writing in the context of hospitality, provided a model demonstrating the linkages between resources, competences and competitive advantages, as shown in Figure 3.2. The model demonstrates at a practical level some of the questions managers have to ask themselves about how resources are deployed and which competences should be sought.

Core competences can never be regarded as being permanent. The pace of change of technology and society is such that core competences must be constantly adapted and new ones cultivated. *THE* organizations normally operate in highly competitive environments and have to be responsive to changes and challenge competitors by utilizing their core competences to the full.

In a *THE* context, the core competences are sometimes the result of holding a particular market position, but they can also result from aspects of regulation or geography that are difficult for others to replicate. For a discussion of core competences in *THE* contexts, see, for example, Cetinski and Milohnic (2008), Denicolai et al. (2010), Dwyer et al. (2013), Pechlaner et al. (2014) and Marneros et al. (2021).

> For example: *Transport operators are often subject to regulatory restrictions that prevent new companies from entering the market to compete, and the beaches of Florida or the South by Southwest set of film, interactive and music festivals and conferences that have taken place every spring since 1987 in Austin, Texas, cannot be moved to different locations.*

However, in some, albeit limited, cases, core competences can be maintained over a prolonged period of time. Given the turbulent business environment in many sectors of *THE*, such adaptability is essential if competitive advantage is to be built and sustained. It is also argued that in some cases the true competitive advantage lies in the way in which core competences are combined rather than in the core competence itself. *Competence leveraging and competence building* are ways in which the identified core competences can be applied in new markets and new competences built, respectively (see, for example, Hamel and Prahalad, 1993; Y. Wang and Lo, 2003).

KEY CONCEPT

Competence leveraging and competence building

Competence leveraging

Refers to the ability of a business to exploit its core competences in new markets, thus meeting new customer needs. It can also refer to the ability of the business to modify and improve existing core competences.

Competence building

Takes place when the business builds new core competences, based on its resources and competences. It is often necessary to build new competences alongside existing ones when entering new markets because it is unlikely that existing competences will fully meet new customer needs.

3.4.2 Distinctive capabilities

Kay (1995) has taken the concept of capability (initially identified by Stalk et al., 1992) to develop a framework that explains competitive advantage in terms of what he defines as *distinctive capability*. This idea of distinctive capability has much in common with that of core competence in that it views competitive advantage as being dependent on unique attributes of a particular business and its products.

According to Kay (1995), distinctive capability results from one or more of the following sources:

- *Architecture* – The unique network of internal and external relationships of an organization that produces superior performance. These can be unique relationships with suppliers, distributors or customers that competitors do not possess. Equally, the unique relationships may be internal to the business and based on how it organizes its activities in the value chain.

  For example: *The strategic alliances that have been built up by the major international airlines in recent years are examples of using networks to strengthen the competitive position of individual airlines through shared activities and extending geographical scope. Similarly, the various marketing alliances of hotel consortia such as Best Western are examples of how independent owners of hotels can reap the marketing, branding, technology and training benefits of being part of a network of hotels.*

- *Reputation* – This stems from several sources, including superior product quality, characteristics, design, service and so on.

  For example: *Through disaster – a coach or airplane crash, a ferry sinking, a canceled concert or a hotel fire quickly erodes the reputation of the organization responsible. Though the reputation may have been built up carefully over several years, it can take only a short time for the reputation to be severely damaged.*

- *Strategic assets* – Businesses can also obtain competitive advantage from assets like natural monopoly, patents and copyrights that restrict competition.

  For example: *The dominant position of major international airlines at their 'hub' airports (such as Lufthansa at Frankfurt, United at Chicago, Emirates at Dubai, American Airlines at Dallas–Fort Worth and Delta at Atlanta) is often the result of costs expended over many years and local regulatory regimes that have allocated take-off and landing slots to these airlines over the years.*

- *Innovation* – The ability of the business to get ahead and stay ahead of competitors depends on its success in researching, designing, developing and marketing new products. Equally, it depends on the ability of the business to improve the design and organization of its value-adding activities.

  For example: *British Airways was the world's first airline to introduce flat beds for some of its business class passengers, but other airlines quickly followed its lead. However, the Short Case Illustration below suggests that the real core competences of the airline are long-standing.*

3.3 SHORT CASE ILLUSTRATION

Core competences: British Airways

In the airline sector, all airlines have the competences and resources required to operate flights between certain destinations. A company like British Airways (Kay, 1995) possesses core competences relating to its:

- Dominance of take-off and landing slots at London's Heathrow Airport
- Licenses to operate certain routes to which access is denied for other airlines
- Brand attributes that act as the basis of its reputation for high-quality service

These core competences, initially identified by the author in the early 1990s, are still valid in the contemporary market. However, it could be argued that the web of cooperative partnerships with other airlines through the 'One World' strategic alliance in allowing for greater destination choice and flexibility of arrangements provides a further area of core competence for the airline. Thus, British Airways has core competences (or distinctive capabilities in Kay's terminology) in terms of strategic assets (Heathrow slots and licenses), its reputation (brand attributes) and architecture (strategic alliance).

The possession of these core competences enables the airline to charge premium prices for its products by targeting business travelers in particular and by altering aircraft seat configurations to accommodate a greater proportion of business and first-class passengers. The airline has maintained a strong competitive position on the key transatlantic routes (partly built on its dominance at its London hub), which enjoy a strong level of premium traffic.

In this way, core competences are applied to the marketplace and thus form the basis of an organization's competitive advantage.

Questions

1. Consider what threats might emerge to challenge British Airways' core competences.
2. What steps might British Airways take to defend its core competences?

According to Kay (1995), distinctive capability (core competence) becomes a competitive advantage when it is applied in a relevant market. Each distinctive capability will have a market (or group of markets) in which the organization can achieve a competitive advantage. Competitive advantage is a relative, rather than absolute, notion and can be viewed in several ways. Organizations can enjoy a competitive advantage relative to other:

- Suppliers in the same market
- Firms in the same industry
- Competitors in the same strategic grouping

In establishing competitive advantage, therefore, it is imperative that activities be correctly matched up to the organization's capabilities. It is also important that organizations be able to fully understand the inherent differences between 'the market', 'the industry' and the 'strategic group'.

- The *market* refers to the needs of customers and potential customers.
- The *industry* an organization is in refers to a group of products linked by common technology, supply or distribution channels.
- The *strategic group* refers to those organizations that are identified as primary competitors.

KEY CONCEPT

Markets, industries and strategic groups

The Market

- Defined by demand conditions
- Based on consumer needs
- Characterized by 'the law of one price'

The Industry

- Determined by supply conditions
- Based on production or operations technology
- Defined by the markets chosen by organizations

The Strategic Group

- Defined by the strategic choices of firms
- Based on distinctive capabilities and market positioning
- Subjective in determination

Source: Adapted from Kay (1995)

3.5 Core competence, distinctive capability and competitive advantage

So, what do the concepts of *core competence* and *distinctive capability* add to our understanding of competitive advantage?

1. They provide us with insight into how an organization can build attributes which can deliver superior performance.

2. They inform the process of determining where such competences and capabilities can be exploited.

3. A core competence becomes competitive advantage when it is applied in a particular market or markets.

Chapter 10 builds on the analysis of competences and capabilities discussed here to consider how new core competences can be developed and existing ones extended as part of an organization's strategy for future development.

The process of building new core competences or extending existing ones must take into account the following considerations:

- *Customer perceptions* – Competences, capabilities and products must be perceived by customers as being better value for money that those of competitors. The organization's reputation (although difficult to measure) can be particularly important in this regard.

- *Uniqueness* – Core competences must be unique to the organization and must be difficult for competitors to emulate. Similarly, there must be no close substitutes for these competences.

- *Continuous improvement* – Core competences, products and services must be continuously upgraded to stay ahead of competitors. Product and process innovation are particularly important.

- *Collaboration* – Competitive advantage can result from the organization's unique network of relationships with suppliers, distributors, customers and even competitors. There is the potential for 'multiplier effects' resulting from separate organizations' complementary core competences being combined together.

- *Organizational knowledge* – Competences must be based on organizational knowledge and learning. Managers must improve the processes by which the organization learns, builds and manages its knowledge.

THINK POINTS

- Explain what is meant by the term 'competitive advantage'.

- Explain Porter's generic strategy framework and consider its strengths and weaknesses as an analytical framework.

- Explain what is meant by a hybrid strategy, and consider the circumstances in which it might be pursued.

3.5.1 Sustainable competitive advantage

THE organizations must strive to achieve a competitive advantage. However, if the position cannot be maintained over a period of time, it may not be worth the effort and investment necessary to achieve such a position in the first place. Sustainable competitive advantage will have been achieved:

> When an organization receives a return on investment that is greater than the norm for its competitors, and when this enhanced return persists for a period long enough to alter the relative standing of the organization among its rivals.
>
> (Finlay, 2000)

Sustainability depends on three factors:

- *Durability* – No advantage is sustainable forever, because competitors will seek to imitate it. Reputation has the potential, however, for providing long-lasting advantage, as the standing of well-known market leaders such as British Airways, TUI, Hilton and American Express testifies.

- *Transparency* – The harder it is for outsiders to understand how an organization does what it does, the harder it will be for imitators.

    For example: *Walt Disney has long been admired for how the company successfully manages and operates its theme parks and builds value from the animated characters it has created. Competitors have found it difficult to exactly replicate the successful formula.*

- *Replicability* – Once a rival understands the competences needed to copy a rival, they will need to obtain the resources necessary to replicate the rival's product. If the resources are freely available in markets, this might not pose a problem, but in some circumstances they may be limited.

    For example: *Airport take-off and landing slots, hotel rooms in popular resorts, specialist staff such as pilots, access to airline routes and access to distribution channels are all examples of resources which might be restricted for some reason.*

3.5.2 The 'VRIO' framework

The preceding sections considered some of the considerations for assessing core competences. However, perhaps what has been lacking so far is a mechanism for testing the competitive resources.

Barney (2002) provided such a mechanism in his 'VRIO' framework, which evolved from the existing VRIN framework to VRIO in the early 1990s, providing a complete framework. The change to the last letter of the acronym refers to the 'organization', which is the ability to exploit the resource or capability. Barney realized that the business must also be ready and able to utilize the resource to capitalize on its value. The sequential decision-making approach advocated by Barney questions each resource or capability in terms of its:

- *Value* – The resource or capability must have value if it is to allow the organization to choose a strategy that exploits opportunities available or responds to threats from competitors.
- *Rarity* – If the resource or capability is widely available to others, it will not provide a basis for competitive advantage and superior returns on investment.
- *Imitability* – If the resource or capability can be easily imitated or copied, competitors will do so, and so competitive advantage may be achieved temporarily but will not be sustainable.
- *Organizational capability* – An organization needs to be able to organize itself in such a way that it is capable of exploiting the resource or capability that it has identified as valuable, rare and incapable of being imitated.

A resource that meets each of these four criteria can bring about competitive advantage to the business. The VRIO framework is summarized in Table 3.2.

3.5.3 Dynamic capabilities

In recent years there has been growing recognition that though RBV, the recognition of resources with VRIN attributes (Barney, 1991) and the core competences framework (Hamel and Prahalad, 1993)

Table 3.2 The VRIO framework for testing competitive resources

Valuable?	Rare?	Costly to imitate?	Capable of being exploited by the organization?	Competitive implications	Comparative economic performance to be expected from the resource
No	–	–	No	Competitive disadvantage	Below normal
Yes	No	–	Yes/no	Competitive parity	Normal
Yes	Yes	No	Yes/no	Temporary competitive advantage	Above normal
Yes	Yes	Yes	Yes	Sustained competitive advantage	Above normal

Source: Adapted from Barney (2002)

adequately explained competitive advantage, the *sustainability* of competitive advantage required further explanation (C. L. Wang and Ahmed, 2007).

David Teece (2007:1319) argued that '*sustainable* advantage requires more than the ownership of difficult to-replicate (knowledge) assets'. The emergence of the so-called *dynamic capabilities framework* seeks to address the sustainability issue.

DEFINITION/QUOTATION

Dynamic capabilities

Dynamic capabilities can be viewed as:

> A firm's behavioral orientation constantly to integrate, reconfigure, and recreate its resources and capabilities and, most importantly, upgrade and reconstruct its core capabilities in response to the changing environment to attain and sustain competitive advantage.
> (C. L. Wang and Ahmed 2007:35)

It is important to note that the definition above emphasizes that the dynamic capabilities framework is a 'behavioral orientation' for the organization. In this way, it becomes not just a process to be carried out but a way in which the organization and its employees and leadership are orientated and behave so that the organization can respond adequately to rapidly changing environments.

The dynamic capabilities framework seeks to extend RBV to dynamic markets. The framework has achieved wide acceptance despite criticisms, and the framework has been selectively applied in *THE* contexts (Nieves and Haller, 2014; Haugland et al., 2011; Camisón Zornoza and Monfort-Mir, 2012; Evans, 2016).

Capabilities, a term widely used in the literature, refers to a firm's capacity to deploy resources, usually in combination, and encapsulates both explicit resources and tacit (or intangible) elements embedded, such as leadership and know-how (C. L. Wang and Ahmed, 2007). As such, capabilities are often firm-specific, develop over time and result from complex interactions between the firm's resources.

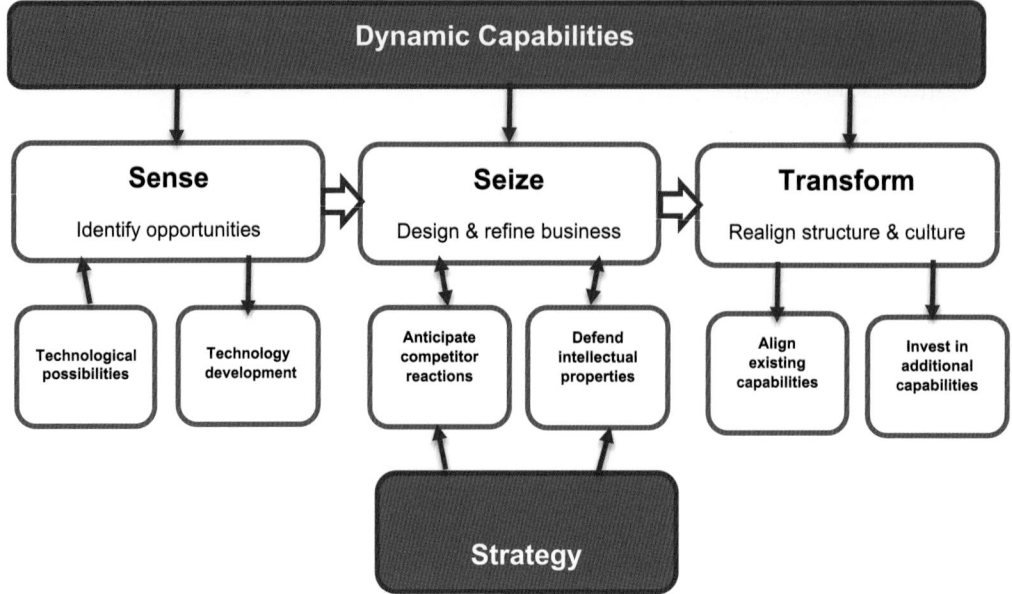

Figure 3.3 A simplified dynamic capabilities framework

Source: Adapted from Teece (2018)

The role of dynamic capabilities is to have an impact on the firm's existing resource base in such a way that it is transformed so that a firm can enhance or maintain its competitive advantage. Over a period of time, how a firm's resources are linked together internally or externally with partners, suppliers or customers can lead to a uniquely valuable combination of 'co-specialization' (Teece, 2007). The complementarity of resources is difficult for competitors to imitate and, consequently, more sustainable competitive advantage is achieved.

3.5.4 How dynamic capabilities are developed

The development of dynamic capabilities relies on three organizational activities:

- *Sensing* – describes the assessment of the opportunities and consumer needs existing outside the organization
- *Seizing* – refers to an organization's reaction to market needs to increase firm value. This involves designing innovative business models and securing access to capital and resources.
- *Transforming* – refers to renewing an organization's processes and maintaining their relevance to consumers. This requires that managers constantly streamline, improve, and alter organizational practices. Transforming is key to creating sustainable, innovative growth.

A simplified version of Teece's version of a dynamic capabilities framework is shown in Figure 3.3. In the model dynamic capabilities and strategy combine to create and refine a defensible business model, which guides the organization through *sensing*, *seizing* and *transformation*. Ideally, this leads to a level of profits adequate to allow the enterprise to sustain and enhance its capabilities and resources.

3.6 Knowledge management as a source of competitive advantage

Particularly in service organizations, knowledge has come to be regarded as the *prime* source of competitive advantage (Lynch, 2021), and a vast literature has developed on the subject and on the related concept of *the learning organization* (see, for example, Stonehouse and Pemberton, 1999; see also Korn et al. [2021], who applied the concept in the context of the Natural History Museum in Washington, DC).

In *THE* contexts, studies in hospitality (Hallin and Marnburg, 2008) and tourism (Shaw and Williams, 2009) both acknowledge the importance of knowledge management, while claiming that *THE* has been slow in recognizing its importance and adopting it in practice.

Nevertheless, Hallin and Marnburg (2008) recognized that many (somewhat anecdotal) examples exist of knowledge management practice particularly in relation to hotels and cited Accor Hotels in Germany and Hilton International as examples.

In events management settings, it can be argued that it is frequently the way in which companies use and manage the knowledge available to them that is the source of their sustainable competitive advantage. Ashfield Meetings and Events (used as an illustrative example above) derives its competitive advantage fundamentally from how it utilizes its knowledge of the health care sector and shares this knowledge through its dispersed global network employees.

> For example: *Hilton is a diversified group of hotel brands operating in over 90 countries. Delivering high-quality training and education consistently across the group is a large and complex task that Hilton has addressed through the creation of its 'university'. The Hilton Worldwide University (www.HWU.com/) is a well-established corporate university that supports all brands in the hotel group. HWU provides more than 5,000,000 hours of training each year through over 2,500 courses delivered in a wide variety of training formats, including classroom training, e-learning, webinars, e-books, live and taped programs, recommendations for on-the-job learning experiences and social learning.*
>
> *The university approach is developing a learning culture for Hilton Hotels by encouraging and offering a consistent approach to training for team members at all levels using e-learning technology in particular (Baldwin-Evans, 2006). Hilton International emphasizes knowledge sharing and on-the-job mentoring in respect to competence development among its members. In 2002 they introduced a new innovative e-learning system that is highly cost-effective and can advance generic skills in terms of communications and customer service (Hallin and Marnburg, 2007).*

KEY CONCEPT

Knowledge and organizational learning

There has been an ever-increasing interest in knowledge as a strategic asset in recent years and, more specifically, the potential for an organization to generate competitive advantage on the basis of its knowledge assets. Knowledge can be defined as 'a shared collection of principles, facts, skills, and rules' (Stonehouse and Pemberton, 1999).

Knowledge can be either explicit or implicit. The former is tangible, being clearly stated and consisting of details that can be recorded and stored. Implicit or tacit knowledge, which can be equally important, is often unstated, based on individual experience, and therefore difficult to record and store (Demarest, 1997).

Knowledge is not static but dynamic and, consequently, much has been written on the ability of organizations to successfully use information as it evolves and changes and to learn from it. The 'learning organization', as it is termed, is particularly associated with the work of Argyris (1990) and Senge (1997). Stonehouse and Pemberton (1999) maintained that in today's highly competitive environment it is not only how organizations learn from the knowledge they have but also how certain organizations 'learn about learning' that makes them likely to be the most competitively successful. Learning about learning creates an organizational context that both nurtures new knowledge and exploits existing knowledge assets (Pemberton and Stonehouse, 2000).

THINK POINTS

- Explain what is meant by *free resources* in *THE* contexts.

- Explain what is meant by *resource immobility* and *resource substitution* and explain their relevance in *THE* contexts.

- Explain the different ways in which resources might be analyzed, and explain the relationships between primary and secondary activities.

- Provide an example of a core competence in a *THE* organization you are familiar with.

- Describe and distinguish between the three conceptual approaches to strategic management that have been introduced in this text.

3.7 Value-adding activities

3.7.1 What is value adding?

Value chain analysis (Porter, 1985) seeks to provide an understanding of how much value an organization's activities add to its products and services compared to the costs of the resources used in their production. Although it has been applied widely in the manufacturing sector, several writers have applied the model successfully to a service setting. Poon (1993), for example, adapted the model to the travel and tourism industry. Fleisher and Bensoussan (2003) and Bensoussan and Fleisher (2012) offered useful insights into the application and critique of value chain analysis.

A given product can be produced by organizing activities in a number of different ways. Value chain analysis helps managers to understand how effectively and efficiently the activities of their organization are configured and coordinated. The 'acid test' is how much value is added in the process of turning inputs into the outputs, which are products in the form of goods and services. Value is measured in terms of the price that customers are willing to pay for the product.

Value added can be increased in two ways:

1. By changing customer perceptions of the product so that they are willing to pay a higher price for a product than for similar products produced by other businesses
2. By reducing production costs below those of competitors

KEY CONCEPT

Value added

In simple terms, the value added to a good or service is the difference in the financial value of the finished product compared to the financial value of the inputs. As a sheet of metal passes through the various stages in car production, value is added so that a ton of metal worth a few hundred pounds becomes a motor car worth several thousand pounds. The rate at which value is added is dependent on how well the operations process is managed. If the car manufacturer suffers a cost disadvantage by, say, holding a high level of stock or working with out-of-date machinery, the value added over the process will be lower.

Similarly, a tour operator, for instance, gathers various inputs in terms of transportation, accommodation, on-site services and ground handling arrangements and 'packages' them together and, in so doing, adds value to the customer. Efficiencies in procurement, for instance, achieved through the use of buying in bulk can be passed on to the customer.

There are clear linkages between value-adding activities, core competences, competences and resources:

- Resources form the inputs to the organization's value-adding activities.
- Competences and core competences provide the skills and knowledge required to carry out the value-adding activities.
- The more core competences can be integrated into value-adding activities, the greater the value added will be.

3.7.2 The value-adding process

Businesses can be regarded as systems that transform inputs (resources, materials, etc.) into outputs (goods and services). This is illustrated in Figure 3.4.

The activities inside the organization *add value* to the inputs. The value of the products or services is equivalent to the price that a customer is willing to pay for them. The difference between the end value (payable by the customer) and the total costs is the *margin* (the quantity that accountants would refer to as the *profit margin* – before interest, taxation and extraordinary items).

The rate at which value is added varies. If value is not being added as fast as it could be, *waste* is occurring and the organization is not operating as efficiently as it could be.

> For example: *Poor quality, low utilization, underoccupancy and an underskilled workforce are all examples of waste.*

Increased added value can be achieved through reduction in costs *or* increasing the price the customer pays for the output.

3.7.3 The value chain

Frameworks have increasingly been developed that purport to represent not merely a way of measuring the success of an organization but go further in that they offer managers a 'road map' by which they can manage (Evans, 2012:223). One of the most widely used approaches – value chain

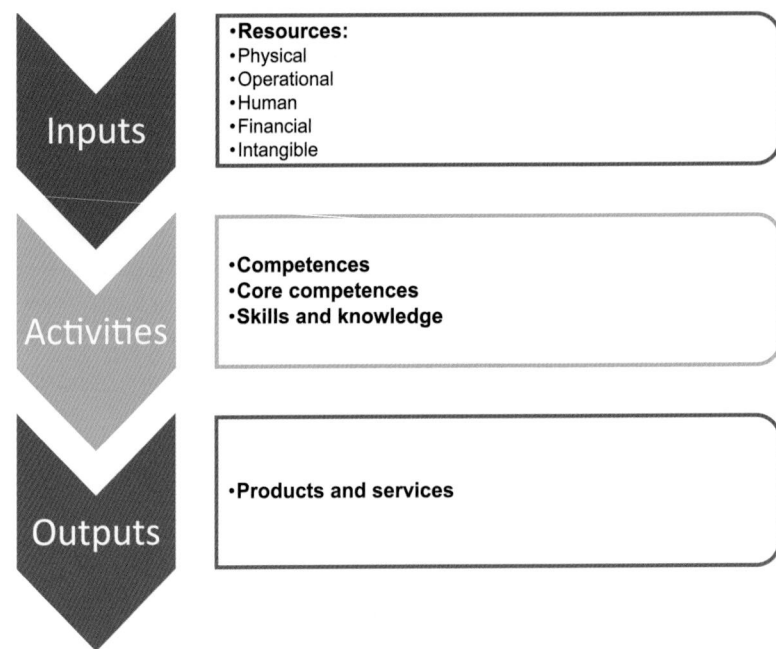

Figure 3.4 A simplified schematic of the value-adding process

analysis (Porter, 1985) – seeks to provide an understanding of how much value an organization's activities add to its products and services compared to the costs of the resources used in their production. In doing so, it seeks to help managers to understand how effectively and efficiently the activities of their organization are configured and coordinated.

The activities of the organization can be broken down into a sequence of activities known as the value chain. Fleisher and Bensoussan (2003), in their useful book that describes various analytical frameworks, methods and techniques, devoted a whole chapter to a description and critique of value chain analysis.

Although it has been applied widely in the manufacturing sector (and not so widely in a services context), several writers have discussed the model in *THE* settings, including Soteriades and Dimou (2011) and Rojas Bueno et al. (2020) in relation to the management of events; Sharma and Christie (2010) and Mitchell (2012) with regard to tourist destinations; and Ivanova and Ivanov (2015) with regard to the concept to hotels. Poon (1993) applied and adapted Porter's value chain to the tourism industry (see Figure 3.5).

The activities within the chain may be classified into *primary* activities and *support* activities:

- *Primary activities* are those that *directly add value* to the final product.
- *Support activities* do not directly add value themselves but *indirectly add value* by supporting the effective execution of primary activities.

The nature of the primary activities and the way in which they can add value vary greatly between differing types of *THE* organization according to the organizational context. By contrast, the secondary activities are common in most organizational contexts.

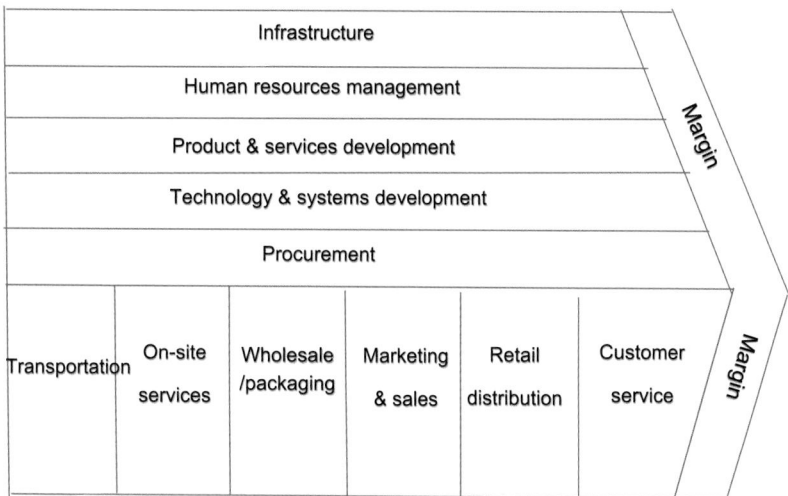

Figure 3.5 The value chain

Source: Poon (1993); adapted from Porter (1985)

Tables 3.3 and 3.4 describe the primary and secondary activities respectively relating to *THE* and how they might add value.

3.7.4 Analysis of the value chain

An organization's value chain links into the value chains of other organizations, particularly those of suppliers and distributors. Rarely does one organization alone control the whole of the value chain from product source to final customer, so how well the organization links with the value chain of other organizations is vitally important. This 'chain' of value chains is sometimes called the *value system* or *total supply chain*. Linkages with suppliers are known as *upstream* linkages, whereas those with distribution channels and customers are *downstream* linkages.

The links in the value system are shown in Figure 3.6. Questions arise from examining the value system, such as:

- Should activities be carried out within the organization or outsourced to others?
- Which organizations might be the best to partner with?
- Where do the risks lie if your organization is relying on value chains that it does not directly control?

Different types of organization will have very different value chains.

> **For example:** *The value chain of TUI group (a vertically integrated European tour operator) includes transportation of clients, arranging accommodation and retail, internet and mobile distribution. In a smaller tour operator such as the independent UK tour operator Sunvil (www.sunvil.co.uk), however, the position is somewhat different. In the case of Sunvil (which operates air holidays to Greece, Cyprus and other destinations), retail distribution and transportation are undertaken by other companies on a commercially agreed basis. Consequently, these aspects do not form a part of the company's value chain but are important elements of the value system described above. Significantly, though, internet distribution allows both the large and smaller company described above to distribute directly to customers, thereby forming part of both companies' value chains.*

Table 3.3 Primary activities

Activity	Description	Examples of how value might be added
Transportation services	Transportation to and from the destination or event and at the destination or event	• Information provision • Scheduling • Gate operations • Ticketing • Baggage handling • Passenger management • In flight/onboard services • Reservations • Route and yield management • Equipment age and specification • Timekeeping
Services on site	Services delivered to visitors at their destination or event	• Repair and maintenance of accommodation and facilities • Age and specification of accommodation and facilities • Quality of entertainment • Added services provided; e.g., valet parking, excursions • Accommodation and venue locations • Quality of company representatives
Wholesaling and packaging	Assembling or 'packaging' the product or service	• Commission and fee negotiations • Product development • Pricing • Assembling, integrating and coordinating ('packaging') aspects of the product
Retail distribution	Distributing the product to the market	• Retail locations • Choice of distribution channels • Internet search optimization • Commission levels • Cost of sales • Client database management • Customer retention levels
Marketing and sales	Making the product available to the market and persuading people to buy	• Brochure production and distribution • Advertising • Public relations • Sales force management • Managing customer loyalty programs • Point of sales materials • Developing the value of the brand

Activity	Description	Examples of how value might be added
Customer service	Installation and after-sales support	• Customer complaint management • Management and monitoring customer satisfaction • Speed of responsiveness • Client advice

Source: Adapted from Poon (1993)

Table 3.4 Secondary activities

Activity	Description	Examples of how value might be added
Procurement	Purchasing, leasing or renting of services and equipment	• Obtaining inputs at lower prices • Better contract terms • Obtaining bulk purchase discounts • Working collaboratively with suppliers
Technology and systems development	Developing and implementing technology and systems in support of primary activities	• Computer reservation systems • Internet applications • 'Real-time' sales reports • Yield management applications • Price discrimination between different customer segments
Products and services development	Developing new products, services and market opportunities	• Developing new market segments • Developing new products or enhancing existing products • Developing new destinations, new venues, new accommodation, etc. • Developing partnerships and alliances with suppliers and/or distributors
Human resource management	Recruitment, selection, training, reward and motivation	• Quality of employees and managers • Employee *empowerment* • Teamwork • Level of training • Outsourcing selected activities • Replacing human resources with technology
Infrastructure	General management, financial control and accounting, planning, legal affairs, quality control	• Speed and quality of decision making • Costs of providing infrastructure • Coherent and consistent standards • Efficient organizational structure • Communicating effectively with workforce

Source: Adapted from Poon (1993)

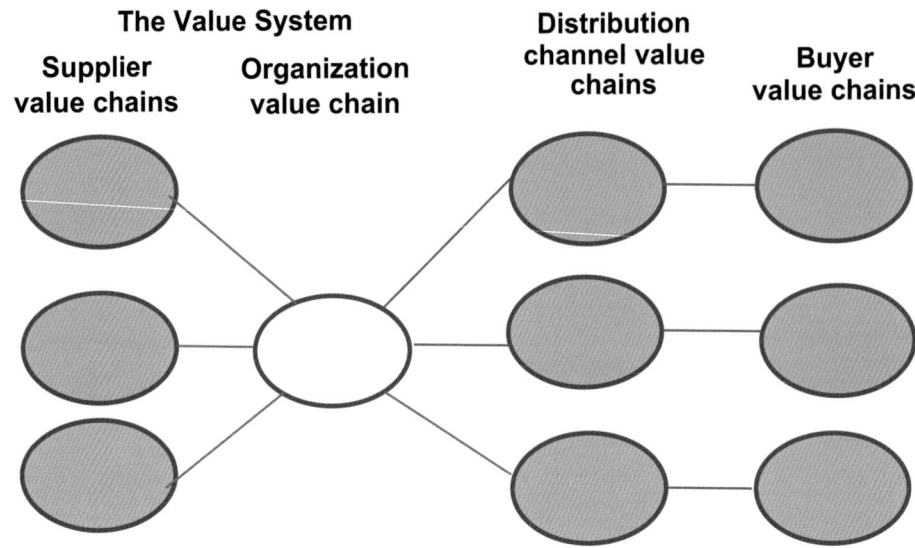

Figure 3.6 The value system

Source: Adapted from Porter (1985)

Similarly, not all of an organization's activities are of equal importance in adding value to its products. Those that are of greatest importance can be considered as *core activities* and are often closely associated with core competences.

> **For example:** *In an upscale hotel, clients are willing to pay premium prices because the level, type and consistency of customer service are of a high standard. Thus, this aspect may be of greatest importance in adding value, and the organization's core competences could be concentrated in this area. Conversely, in a budget chain of hotels (such as the Holiday Inn Express and Ibis chains operating in many countries), offering value for money, consistent standards and many convenient locations are of greatest importance in delivering value.*

A further point to stress is the importance of linkages between the component parts of the model. In some cases, a key source of value-added activity might lie in how organizations link different aspects, as opposed to the aspects on their own.

> **For example:** *For a tour operator, event manager or hotel operator, it is important that demand and supply be closely coordinated so that excess capacity that cannot be sold is avoided and so that there is enough supply to meet customer demand. This involves close linkages and coordination between the transportation, wholesaling and packaging, retail distribution and marketing and sales aspects.*

Analysis of value-adding activities helps to identify where the most value is added and where there is potential to add greater value by changing how activities are configured and by improving how they are coordinated. It is important to note that an organization's value chain is not analyzed in isolation but that it is considered in conjunction with its external linkages to suppliers, distributors and customers. Table 3.5 Provides a classification of various internal and external linkages.

A value chain analysis would be expected to include:

- A breakdown of all activities of the organization

- Identification of core activities and their relationships to core competences and current organizational strategies
- Identification of the effectiveness and efficiency of the individual activities
- Examination of *linkages* between activities for additional added value
- Identification of *blockages* that reduce the organization's competitive advantage

A useful technique in value chain analysis involves comparison with the value chains of competitors to identify the benefits and drawbacks of alternative configurations.

The aim of value chain analysis is to identify ways in which the performance of the individual activities and the linkages between them can be improved. This may involve identification of improved configurations for activities or improved coordination. It is particularly important to consider the extent to which value chain activities support the current strategy of the organization.

> **For example:** *If the current strategy is based on high quality, the activities must be configured to ensure high-quality products. On the other hand, if the organization competes largely on the basis of price, activities must be organized to minimize costs.*

3.7.5 Core activities, non-core activities and outsourcing

An increasing trend in recent years has been for organizations to concentrate on core activities associated with core competences and to *outsource* activities that are not regarded as core to other organizations for which the activities are core.

Table 3.5 Classification of internal and external linkages

Internal linkages		External linkages	
Type of activity	Example	Type of activity	Example
Primary – primary	• Interdepartmental coordination	Links with suppliers – backward linkages (upstream)	• Tour operator linking with a hotel group • Festival organizer linking with transport and accommodation providers
Primary – support	• Computer-based sales management systems	Links with distributors – forward linkages (downstream)	• Tour operator securing 'racking agreement' with a travel agency group for its brochures • Hotel group working with destination management organizations
Support – support	• Training for new technologies	Links with other companies at same stage of operations	• Airlines collaborating in some of their activities through the formation of strategic alliances

Outsourcing (which is also discussed in Chapter 14 in the context of internationalization) refers to the practice of a firm entrusting to an external entity the performance of an activity that was performed previously internally (Varadarajan, 2009) or is capable of being performed internally.

The basic premise of the concept rests on a specialist organization being able to perform a particular service more efficiently than can be achieved internally by an organization (Jennings, 1997; Quinn, 2000). This may be because a specialist organization has inherent advantages in delivering a service such as larger-scale operations leading to *economies of scale*, superior technology, superior management skills or operating in a country with lower labor costs.

Outsourcing has become a popular strategic option in parts of *THE*. It has become particularly prevalent among airline and hotel operators. See, for example, Lam and Han (2005), Bolat and Yılmaz (2009), Gonzalez et al. (2011), Espino-Rodríguez and Ramírez-Fierro (2018) and Elhoushy et al. (2020) in relation to hotels; Rieple and Helm (2008) and M. A. Abdullah and Satar (2018) in relation to aviation; and, in relation to outsourcing festivals and event management from the public to private or PPPs, see Andersson and Getz (2009) and Getz (2009).

> **For example:** *British Airways has outsourced some of its accounting and information technology functions to external suppliers, and several airlines, such as American Airlines, United Airlines and Cathay Pacific, have sold what they regarded as non-core divisions such as their repair shops and subcontract maintenance, in some cases to a joint venture. By contrast, some airlines, such as Delta and Lufthansa, are increasingly building on their existing capabilities in the maintenance function and offering this facility to other carriers (Rieple and Helm, 2008).*

Outsourcing has become common in many types of organizations in recent years, but the nature of hotel operations means that hotels are particularly suited to outsourcing activities. Indeed, outsourcing can be viewed as the norm for hotel operations. Wood (1999:2) described outsourcing as 'part of the fabric of hotel operations'. Hotel outsourcing has attracted quite a large academic literature (reviewed by Gonzalez et al., 2011). In examining the particular factors leading to hotels opting for outsourcing Lamminmaki (2011) identified the broad range of activities undertaken, the high labor content associated with many hotel activities and the volatile nature of demand for a hotel's services as significant factors. Some examples of tasks in the hospitality industry that are sometimes outsourced to other companies include laundry, pool, grounds and building maintenance, housekeeping, foodservice, information technology, reservations and financial services.

There are certain advantages to outsourcing in that staffing flexibility can be achieved, specialist expertise is brought into the organization and managers are able to focus on so-called core activities. There are, however, potential difficulties to consider in that it may be more difficult to maintain customer service standards (when staff are not directly employed by your organization) and thus the organization's culture might be jeopardized. In a study of Shanghai hotels, for example, Lam and Han (2005) found that outsourcing is not always successful. The authors pointed to China's outsourcing market as being immature in that the inadequacy of the legal framework is a hindrance to the adoption of outsourcing. Furthermore, the compatibility between the corporate cultures of the hotels and the outsourcing vendors is critical.

The advantages of outsourcing also explain why local and central government agencies around the world are often putting responsibility for tourism, including organizing festivals and events and destination management and promotion organizations, into the hands of private sector providers or into *PPPs* run at arms-length from parent bodies. This aspect of outsourcing was explored by Andersson and Getz (2009) and Getz (2009).

3.4 SHORT CASE ILLUSTRATION

Outsourcing: the airline industry

Over the last 25 years, this sector has been characterized by poor financial performance and returns that would be, according to the UK's Civil Aviation Authority (2006), 'unsustainable' in most industries. Consequently, airlines have been under enormous pressure to find ways of cutting costs and maximizing revenues to ensure survival.

One study of outsourcing in the industry focused on major international full-service, legacy (i.e., formed prior to the industry's deregulation that occurred throughout the 1980s) airlines that are broadly comparable in the customer segments they serve, as well as in their operational requirements,

The study focused on four aspects of activity (termed functions by the authors) that are commonly considered for outsourcing in the industry. The study found that, though examples of outsourcing activities in their entirety are rare (and there is differential practice between the airlines), examples of partial outsourcing were common in the sample investigated. The results are shown Table 3.6.

Table 3.6 Outsourcing: the airline industry

Airline function	Air France	British Airways	American Airlines	United Airlines	Cathay Pacific	Qantas	SAS
Plane acquisition and ownership	B	B	B	B	B	B	B
Engineering and aircraft maintenance	A	A	B	B	B	A	B
Customer sales and ticketing	B	B	B	B	B	B	B
In-flight catering	C	B	D	A	A	A	D
Corporate identity and brand management	B	B	B	B	B	B	B

Notes:

A – Undertaken wholly in-house or by wholly owned division or subsidiary
B – Partly undertaken in-house or by wholly owned subsidiary, partly outsourced
C – Wholly outsourced to partly owned subsidiary or joint venture
D – Wholly outsourced to an external supplier

Source: Adapted from Rieple and Helm (2008)

Questions

1. What do you consider the motivations for outsourcing to be in the airline industry?

2. What factors might prevent outsourcing being developed more widely in *THE* contexts?

The combination of complementary core competences (achieved through outsourcing) adds to the competitive advantage of all collaborating companies and organizations. Value chain analysis should therefore also seek to identify where outsourcing might potentially add greater value than performing the activity in-house.

THINK POINTS

- Explain the idea of the business as a value chain.
- Explain the relationships between primary and secondary activities.
- What is meant by blockages and linkages in the value chain?
- Explain with an example from *THE* what is meant by the value system.
- Provide an example of a core competence in a *THE* organization you are familiar with.
- Describe and distinguish between the three conceptual approaches to strategic management that have been introduced in this text.

3.8 The Profit Impact of Market Strategy

The Profit Impact of Market Strategy study is a major long-running study that was initiated in the 1970s by senior managers working at the American General Electric Company who wanted to know why some of their business units were more profitable than the others. The study, which has been administered by the American Strategic Planning Institute since 1975, has developed into a major database that is founded on examining thousands of companies in many industries.

One of the key findings in examining the data is that a primary determinant of profitability is market share (Buzzell, 2004), and the relationship was examined and summarized in detail by Uslay et al. (2010). The link that data appears to establish is certainly important in that several strategic management techniques that have been developed subsequently (such as the Boston Consultancy Group Matrix; see Chapter 6) apply the logic in their analyses.

However, other researchers have maintained that the relationship between profitability and market share has been exaggerated (Szymanski et al., 1993). Other researchers have also questioned the findings in relation to service companies in particular and concluded that customer loyalty is a more important determinant of profit in these companies (Reichheld and Sasser, 1990). Farris and Moore (2004) provided an overview of the project and assessed its contribution to strategy.

3.9 The service profit chain

Over the past two decades, the theory and practice of service quality and value has received considerable attention from academics and practitioners alike (Hu et al., 2009). Value has been defined according to the SERVQUAL framework developed by Zeithhaml et al. (1990:20). Value is viewed as 'the perceived service quality received relative to the service quality delivered, all of which is relative to price'.

During the 1990s, an alternative framework was introduced by a team of researchers at Harvard University: *the service profit chain* (Heskett et al., 1994; see also Heskett and Sasser, 2010). The framework assesses the sources of profitability and growth in labor-dominated service firms. Such companies are defined as those service companies where labor is both an important component of total cost and capable of differentiating the firm's service from that of its competitors.

DEFINITION/QUOTATION

The service profit chain

The service profit chain hypothesizes that:

> Profit (in a for-profit organization) or other measures of success (in for-profit organization or not-for-profit organizations) results from customer loyalty generated by customer satisfaction, which is a function of value delivered to customers. Value for customers in turn results from employee loyalty and satisfaction, which is directly related to the internal quality (or value) created for employees.
>
> (Heskett et al., 1994:165)

The service profit chain builds on the doubts raised over the veracity of the Profit Impact of Market Strategy survey in service settings in that it establishes links between profitability, customer loyalty and employees' satisfaction, loyalty and productivity. The links in the chain (Heskett et al., 1994) are as follows:

- Profit and growth are stimulated primarily by customer loyalty.
- Customer loyalty is a direct result of customer satisfaction.
- Customer satisfaction is largely influenced by the value of services provided to customers.
- Value is created by satisfied, loyal and productive employees.
- Employee satisfaction results primarily from high-quality support services and policies that enable employees to deliver results to customers.

The purpose of the service profit chain is to provide managers with a framework to help them manage such companies by enabling them to focus on (predominantly) quantifiable measures that lead to financial performance measures (Hallowell and Schlesinger, 2000) and, as such, is similar to the 'balanced scorecard' approach to strategy developed by Kaplan and Norton (2001). However, focusing as it does on the service delivery aspects of performance, the model is useful but does not represent a holistic approach to managing service-based organizations (Evans, 2012).

The service profit chain (shown in Figure 3.7) emphasizes the following three factors as key drivers of profitability and revenue growth:

- The roles of employees internal to the organization
- The way in which services are delivered
- The targeting of marketing to customers' needs

Thus, the ways in which the organization effectively utilizes its human resources and the ways in which it positions its products so that they appeal to particular target markets are two of the most important aspects of an organization's competitive strategy.

A number of authors have discussed the application of the service profit chain in a *THE* context, such as Bouranta et al. (2009) in relation to hotels and R. B. Abdullah et al. (2011) and Kim (2014) in relation to the Malaysian and Korean hospitality sectors, respectively. Prentice et al. (2017) and Solnet et al. (2018) related the concept to casinos and restaurants. O'Cass and Sok (2015) applied the concept to tourism firms, and Dodds (2007), adopting a case study approach, related how the concept has been applied to US low-cost airline Jet Blue.

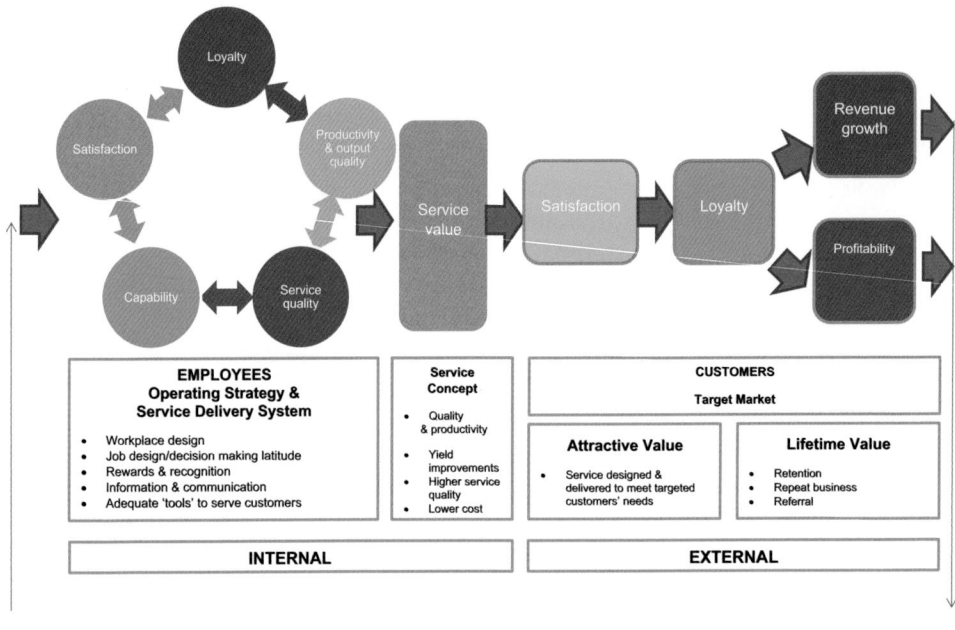

Figure 3.7 The service profit chain

Source: Adapted from Heskett et al. (1994)

3.10 Service-dominant logic

The implication of the work of Heskett et al. (1994) and the issues discussed in previous chapters is that organizations providing *THE* services are 'different' from other organizations and that lessons derived mainly from studying manufacturing companies might have to be modified in a services setting.

The provision of services, after all, represents the dominant portion of most developed economies but traditionally has received less academic attention than manufacturing. Perhaps this is partly owing to the difficulties involved in identifying, measuring and assessing the provision of the largely intangible products that services represent. The differences inherent in services apply to *THE* organizations as with others working in a services setting and, indeed (as argued in the previous chapter), there are some characteristics that, if not unique, are certainly of particular relevance to *THE* organizations.

This perceived need to study services in a different way has found a strong voice since the early years of this century through the development of a strong strand of academic thought termed *service-dominant logic* and the developing field of *services science*.

In particular, the intangibility and perishability of services have significant managerial implications and suggest that the 'soft service' provider has to be available in full from the start of the operation (Blomstermo et al. 2006; Sanchez-Peinado et al., 2007). Because the consumer and producer have to be in the same place at the same time, it can be theorized that they have a joint role in producing value. This *value co-creation* process of the organization and the consumer in tourism (Shaw et al., 2011; Harris, 2012; Cabiddu et al., 2013) provides the underlying logic for the *service-dominant logic* paradigm.

The first article on what has become known as service-dominant (S-D) logic appeared in 2004 (Vargo and Lusch, 2004) and has since been cited almost 20,000 times. Many subsequent articles (by these authors and others) have followed. In recent years, a growing literature has emerged applying the concept in *THE* settings (see, for example, Li and Petrick, 2008; Shaw et al., 2011; FitzPatrick et al., 2013; D. Wang et al., 2013; Blazquez-Resino et al., 2015; Evans, 2016; Rather et al., 2019; Font et al., 2021).

S-D logic has not been universally accepted. It has been argued and subsequently refuted (Lusch and Vargo, 2011), that S-D logic is a backward step and, specifically, it has been suggested that it 'is neither logically sound nor a perspective to displace others in marketing' (O'Shaughnessy and O'Shaughnessy, 2009:784). Others, though accepting the thrust of its logic, also noted its limitations. Campbell et al. (2013), for example, noted that S-D logic makes a useful contribution to the understanding of value, value co-creation and the consumer but also pointed to its limitations in that it does not represent a holistic theory of resources; that is, its logic is merely a way of framing the world.

At the center of Vargo and Lusch's (2008) proposition is a change in the dominant logic of marketing from exchanges of goods to service provision. Specifically, as Li and Petrick (2008) pointed out in relation to tourism, this logic focuses on:

- Intangible rather than tangible resources
- Co-creation of value rather than embedded value
- Relationships rather than transactions

THINK POINTS

- Explain the concept of the *service profit chain* and its relevance to *THE* organizations.
- Explain what is meant by *service-dominant logic*.
- Explain how *service-dominant* logic might be applied to *THE* contexts.
- Provide an example of a core competence in a *THE* organization you are familiar with.
- Describe and distinguish between the three conceptual approaches to strategic management that have been introduced in this text.

Vargo and Lusch (2004) argued that service marketing (and strategy) was built on the same goods- and manufacturing-based model as the marketing of goods and called this perspective 'goods-dominant' (G-D) logic. G-D logic suggests that the firm 'produces' value and that customers are outside the process of value creation and, as such, constitute *operand* resources; that is, resources on which an operation or act is performed to produce benefit for the producing firm. Operand resources can be contrasted with *operant* resources; that is, resources capable of causing benefit by directly acting on other resources, either operand or operant, to create benefit for consumers.

KEY CONCEPT

Service-dominant logic

S-D logic is captured in ten foundational premises (Vargo and Lusch, 2008). The central tenet of S-D logic is that service is the fundamental basis of exchange. That is, service is exchanged for service. The essential elements of S-D logic thus begin with the definition of service: the process of using one's competences (knowledge and skills) for the benefit of another party.

Perhaps the second most important tenet of S-D logic is found in its conceptualizations of value and value creation. In G-D logic, value is a property of goods and is created by the firm and distributed to 'consumers', who destroy (consume) it. In S-D logic, the firm cannot create value but can only offer value propositions and then collaboratively create value with the beneficiary. Thus, the service provided (directly or through a good) is only input into the value creation activities of the customer. Thus, value creation is always a collaborative and interactive process that takes place in the context of a unique set of multiple exchange relationships, somewhat tacitly and indirectly so, especially when service is provided through goods.

Source: Vargo (2009)

The transition from a G-D logic mindset to one embodying S-D logic is important in that it represents an underscoring of the propositions that Vargo and Lusch (2004) developed and that define S-D logic. The need for such a paradigm change also reflects the change from a manufacturing orientation to a service-dominated economic model in most developed and many developing economies. For individual organizations, including those involved in *THE*, the shift (in mindset) implies a reframing of the whole purpose of the enterprise and its collaborative role in value creation. The principal tenets of a transition from G-D logic to a S-D logic are summarized in Table 3.7.

Table 3.7 The transition from G-D logic to S-D logic

Goods-dominant logic	Service-dominant logic	Comments
Making something (goods or services)	Assisting customers in their own value creation processes	From thinking about the purpose of firm activity as making something (goods or services) to a process of assisting customers in their own value creation processes
Value as something that is produced	Value as something that is co-created	From thinking about value as something produced and sold to thinking about value as something co-created with the customer and other value creation partners
Customers as isolated entities	Customers in the context of their own networks	From thinking of customers as isolated entities to understanding them in the context of their own networks
Firm resources primarily as 'operand'	Firm resources primarily as 'operant'	From thinking of firm resources primarily as operand – tangible resources such as raw materials – to operant – usually intangible resources such as knowledge and skills
Customers as targets	Customers as resources	From thinking of customers as targets to thinking of customers as resources
Primacy of efficiency	Efficiency through effectiveness	From making efficiency primary to delivering increased efficiency through effectiveness

Source: Adapted from Vargo and Lusch (2008)

3.10.1 S-D logic and co-creation of value

Thus, importantly, S-D Logic implies a shift of emphasis from the producer producing outputs for consumption toward a process whereby value is created collaboratively as a co-creation between the parties involved.

DEFINITION/QUOTATION

Co-creation of value

Co-creation has been defined as:

> The joint creation of value by the company and the customer; allowing the customer to co-construct the service experience to suit their context.
>
> (Prahalad and Ramaswamy, 2004:8)

There are important implications that flow from this notion of co-creation of value:

- It suggests that value can only be determined following an offering of a service in that experience and perception are essential to value determination (Lusch et al., 2007). In this way, organizations cannot in themselves create value (because it is co-determined) but can only offer *value propositions*.

- If service is viewed as a process whereby it is provided for and in conjunction with another party, to obtain a reciprocal benefit, it becomes the fundamental purpose of economic exchange. That is, service is exchanged for service. In some cases goods are involved in this process (which can serve to mask the underlying service provided), but it is the competences (knowledge and skills) of the providers that are applied that represent the essential source of value created.

This represents a shift in thinking from the traditional 'firm-centric' view of value creation, in which the firm controls the value chain for its products, which it then delivers to consumers, to a 'customer-centric' view, in which the customer becomes part of the value creationg process and customers start to manage their own value chains. In this way, the economy is developing into a 'networked' economy instead of the traditional hierarchical structure. Co-creation of value has been widely adapted and applied in *THE* contexts. See, for example, Cabiddu et al. (2013), Assiouras et al. (2019), Kallmuenzer et al. (2020), Font et al. (2021), Wallace and Michopoulou (2021) and Solakis et al. (2022).

> **For example:** *Buhalis and Sinarta (2019) argued that the experiential and dynamic nature of THE leads to an increasing expectation of focusing service offerings to consumer needs using contextualized and highly personalized service and engagement online. The authors studied real-time interaction between brands and consumers, a case study of Marriott Hotels' 'MLive' real-time social marketing initiative and a number of additional case studies. The findings suggest that the integration of real-time consumer intelligence, dynamic 'big data mining' (which focuses on extracting value by identifying patterns hidden in vast data sets), artificial intelligence and contextualization can inform service offerings to empower co-creation and enhance competitiveness for THE organizations.*

It follows (from the discussion above) that transitioning from a G-D Logic mindset to one embodying S-D logic and involving co-creation of value can be regarded as an important initial step in the process of achieving competitive advantage for managers involved in leading *THE* organizations.

To work in this co-created networked economy successfully, Prahalad and Ramaswamy (2004) argued that companies need to develop a range of capabilities to successfully work with customers to deliver technology-enabled co-created platforms (Mazur and Zaborek, 2014).

The four main building blocks or groups of competences that companies should develop to effectively engage in value co-creation with customers are dialogue, access, risk assessment and transparency, which taken together form the *DART* acronym and represents a model that has been widely followed.

- *Dialogue* – represents interactivity between two equal problem solvers, eager to act together and learn
- *Access* – implies facilitating co-creation by offering the right tools for communication between customers and suppliers and also entails those marketing solutions that result in increased freedom of choice for customers
- *Risk assessment* – refers to the customers' right to be fully informed about the risks they face from accepting the value proposition
- *Transparency* – represents a retreat from the information asymmetry usually apparent between the customer and supplier and practicing the openness of information

Value co-creation is illustrated by the case of Airbnb in the following Short Case Illustration.

3.5 SHORT CASE ILLUSTRATION

Co-creation of value at Airbnb

Airbnb is an online community marketplace facilitating short-term rentals. Its phenomenal global success has enabled homeowners to benefit from their most valuable asset and for travelers to find well-located accommodation while comparing the value of competing offerings.

Airbnb and other 'peer-to-peer' short-term rental companies represent part of the broader 'sharing economy' (also sometimes called collaborative consumption; Guttentag and Smith, 2017). The sharing economy has been defined 'as consumers granting each other temporary access to underutilized physical assets ("idle capacity"), possibly for money' (Frenken and Schor, 2017:4).

In the sharing economy, consumers can be viewed as *co-creators* of value and have the potential to become entrepreneurs by dealing with their assets like solar energy, cars and, in the Airbnb context, renting out their houses and apartments (Oskam and Boswijk, 2016). This represents a shift in thinking from the traditional 'firm-centric' view of value creation, in which the firm controls the value chain for its products, which it then delivers to consumers, to a 'customer-centric' view in which the customer becomes part of the value creation process and customers start to manage their own value chains. In this way, the economy is developing into a networked economy instead of the traditional hierarchical structure.

Small business focus

Although large, powerful, diversified international organizations are emerging, in many countries *THE* is characterized by a large proportion of SMEs. In these organizations, family and private ownership are common and market entry is encouraged by relatively low barriers to entry (Getz and Carlsen, 2000). However, SME providers have to cope with competitive disadvantages, which, according to Zehrer (2009), include:

- Poor economies of *scale* and *scope*
- Minimal potential for diversification and innovation
- Inadequate information about the market
- Limited access to capital markets
- High debt-to-capital ratios

Adding to this list in a *THE* context, Abou-Shouk et al. (2012) pointed out that SMEs, particularly in developing countries, are regarded as slow adopters of technology. Notwithstanding the disadvantages identified, however, SMEs also possess certain potential advantages that can in certain circumstances be developed into core competences and provide sources of competitive advantage. Clearly, smaller organizations are likely to be able to react more quickly to market changes and offer services more flexibly than larger organizations, which have to consider wider implications and where decision making is often more centralized and consequently slower.

SMEs can also compete on more favorable terms by collaborating with each other or with suppliers and distributors, through networking and formation of marketing alliances and joint ventures; in other words, making use not only of their own value chains but utilizing the *value system*.

> **For example:** *In the UK, for example, over 120 smaller tour operators collaborate in joint marketing and distribution through the AITO to compete effectively with the large, internationally diversified tour operator companies such as TUI and Jet2.*

Independent hotel owners have also long worked collaboratively in consortia to compete effectively. A hotel consortium can be defined as 'a grouping of predominantly single, independently owned hotels that share corporate costs, such as marketing while retaining independence of ownership and operation' (Morrison and Harrison, 1998:351). Fyall and Garrod (2005) categorized five types of consortia ranging from involvement as part of a reservations system to full involvement with all marketing and purchasing aspects of the business.

Examples of hotel consortia include:

- *Best Western* – founded in 1946, based in Phoenix, Arizona, USA, it and has over 4,000 member hotels in over 80 countries, each one independently owned and managed (www.bestwestern.com).
- *HotelREZ* – established in 2004, the UK-based consortium is a global representation company providing hotel distribution and internet distribution, revenue and marketing support to over 2,500 independent hotels and small groups of hotels in over 100 countries (www.hotelrez.net).
- *Relais et Chateaux* – established in France in 1954, the consortium represents almost 600 individually owned and operated luxury hotels and restaurants in about 68 countries (www.relaischateaux.com).
- *Small Luxury Hotels of the World* – created in 1991 as the result of a merger between Prestige Hotels Europe and Small Luxury Hotels and Resorts of North America, the two groups combined to represent the collective interests of luxurious, independent hotels and resorts around the world. Based in London, the consortium has over 520 members in 80 countries (www.slh.com).
- *The Leading Hotels of the World* – founded in 1928, it is a consortium of more than 400 luxury hotels and resorts in over 90 countries. It is a German-owned company but headquartered in New York City and maintains offices in 20 cities worldwide (www.lhw.com).

- *World Hotels* – established in 1970, represents over 250 upscale independently owned hotels worldwide with reservations, marketing and revenue management support. As a subsidiary of Best Western, the group is based in Phoenix (www.worldhotels.com).
- *Your Hotel Worldwide* – established in Sweden in 1999, it represents some 90 independently owned hotels in Scandinavia and the UK (www.yourhotelsworldwide.net).

The adoption of a so-called service orientation by service businesses has become of increasing interest in recent years as a crucial factor in the enhancement of profit, growth, customer satisfaction, customer loyalty and employee satisfaction. In general terms, a service orientation is an organizational predisposition that encourages a distinctive approach to all aspects of the consumer market (Zehrer, 2009). The service orientation is extended in the service-dominant logic conceptualization originally proposed by Vargo and Lusch (2004). More specifically, Grönroos (1990) suggested six principles of services management that can be said to represent an organizational commitment to what would now be called a 'service orientation'.

These principles include the notion that decision making has to be decentralized as close as possible to the interface between organization and customer. Given their scale, SMEs should be in a more favored position to expedite decision making in a more customer-focused, responsive and flexible manner in comparison with larger competitors.

CHAPTER SUMMARY

Internal analysis centers on the identification of the organization's potential for generating competitive advantage. It is recognized that no two organizations are the same and, consequently, their operations will vary considerably. Thus, this chapter has been concerned with the underlying principles involved in how organizations arrange their operations, rather than the detail of the operations themselves.

This chapter was concerned with the way in which *THE* organizations try to configure and coordinate their operational resources and processes in such a way that they add value and, in so doing, achieve an advantage over competitors – competitive advantage. It is very important in the strategy process for organizations to have a good understanding of the resources they have available to them and how these are used to create value. Some *THE* organizations are better at doing this than others by utilizing resources efficiently, achieving core competences and applying them in markets to gain a competitive advantage.

This chapter has focused on the analysis of resources, competences, core competences, the value chain and the service profit chain. Core competences and the configuration and coordination of value-adding activities have been identified as primary sources of competitive advantage. It is important to examine the links between current strategies, core competences and core activities in the value chain because these are where the major potential for competitive advantage lies. Similarly, it is important to examine other resources, competences and activities to identify the potential for building new core competences and core activities. The analysis also helps to identify opportunities for efficiency gains by reconfiguring activities and by improving their integration to remove blockages from the system. This analysis allows a business to consider the potential of collaboration with suppliers, distributors and customers to improve performance.

The service profit chain provides a focus for analysis specifically for service-based organizations. This technique focuses particularly on the human aspects of service delivery and can be used together with value chain analysis or as an alternative. It is from all of this analysis that many of the elements of future strategy can be identified. In recent years, the academic literature has focused on a relatively new strand of thought – service-dominant logic. S-D logic attempts to distinguish between marketing and strategy in services as opposed to manufacturing and incorporates the notion of consumers being involved in the value creation process through co-creation of value.

REFERENCES AND WEBSITES

References

Abdullah, M. A. and Satar, N. M. (2018) 'The impact of outsourcing on airlines' performance: Empirical evidence from Asia and countries in the Pacific', *Airline Economics in Asia*, 7: 195–219.

Abdullah, R. B., Musa, M., Zahari, H., Rahman, R. and Khalid, K. (2011) 'The study of employee satisfaction and its effects towards loyalty in hotel industry in Klang Valley, Malaysia', *International Journal of Business and Social Science*, 2(3): 147–155.

Abou-Shouk, M., Megicks, P. and Lim, W. M. (2012) 'Perceived benefits and e-commerce adoption by SME travel agents in developing countries: Evidence from Egypt', *Journal of Hospitality and Tourism Research*, 37(4): 490–515.

Andersson, T. D. and Getz, D. (2009) 'Tourism as a mixed industry: Differences between private, public and not-for-profit festivals', *Tourism Management*, 30(6): 847–856.

Argyris, C. (1990) *Overcoming Organizational Defenses: Facilitating Organizational Learning*, Boston: Allyn & Bacon.

Assiouras, I., Skourtis, G., Giannopoulos, A., Buhalis, D. and Koniordos, M. (2019) 'Value co-creation and customer citizenship behavior', *Annals of Tourism Research*, 78: 102742.

Baldwin-Evans, K. (2006) 'Hilton highlights link between staff loyalty and e-learning: Survey investigates value and usage of online portal', *Human Resource Management International Digest*, 14(1): 36–38.

Barney, J. B. (1991) 'Firm resources and sustained competitive advantage', *Journal of Management*, 17(1): 99–120.

Barney, J. B. (2001) 'Resource-based theories of competitive advantage: A ten-year retrospective on the resource-based view', *Journal of Management*, 27(6): 643–650.

Barney, J. B. (2002) *Gaining and Sustaining Competitive Advantage*, 2nd ed., Upper Saddle River, NJ: Prentice-Hall.

Bensoussan, B. E. and Fleisher, C. S. (2012) *Analysis without Paralysis: 12 Tools to Make Better Strategic Decisions*, 2nd ed., Upper Saddle River, NJ: Pearson.

Blazquez-Resino, J. J., Molina, A. and Esteban-Talaya, A. (2015) 'Service-dominant logic in tourism: The way to loyalty', *Current Issues in Tourism*, 18(8): 706–724.

Blomstermo, A., Sharma, D. D. and Sallis, J. (2006) 'Choice of foreign market entry mode in service firms', *International Marketing Review*, 23(2): 211–229.

Bolat, T. and Yılmaz, Ö. (2009) 'The relationship between outsourcing and organizational performance: Is it myth or reality for the hotel sector?', *International Journal of Contemporary Hospitality Management*, 21(1): 7–23.

Bouranta, N., Chitiris, L. and Paravantis, J. (2009) 'The relationship between internal and external service quality', *International Journal of Contemporary Hospitality Management*, 21(3): 275–293.

Buhalis, D. and Sinarta, Y. (2019) 'Real-time co-creation and nowness service: Lessons from tourism and hospitality', *Journal of Travel and Tourism Marketing*, 36(5): 563–582.

Bull, A. (1995) *Economics of Travel and Tourism*, 2nd ed., Southbank, VIC, Australia: Longman Cheshire.

Buzzell, R. D. (2004) 'The PIMS program of strategy research: A retrospective appraisal', *Journal of Business Research*, 57(5): 478–483.

Cabiddu, F., Lui, T. W. and Piccoli, G. (2013) 'Managing value co-creation in the tourism industry', *Annals of Tourism Research*, 42: 86–107.

Camisón Zornoza, C. and Monfort Mir, V. M. (2012) 'Measuring innovation in tourism from the Schumpeterian and the dynamic-capabilities perspectives', *Tourism Management*, 33: 776–789.

Campbell, N., O'Driscoll, A. and Saren, M. (2013) 'Reconceptualizing resources a critique of service-dominant logic', *Journal of Macromarketing*, 33(4): 306–321.

Cetinski, V. and Milohnic, I. (2008) 'Company competitiveness and competitive advantages in tourism and hospitality', *Tourism and Hospitality Management*, 14(1): 37–50.

Choi, G. and Parsa, H. G. (2012) 'Role of intangible assets in foreign-market entry-mode decisions: A longitudinal study of American lodging firms', *International Journal of Hospitality and Tourism Administration*, 13(4): 281–312.

Demarest, M. (1997) 'Understanding knowledge management', *Long Range Planning*, 30(3): 374–384.

Denicolai, S., Cioccarelli, G. and Zucchella, A. (2010) 'Resource-based local development and networked core-competencies for tourism excellence', *Tourism Management*, 31(2): 260–266.

Dodds, B. (2007) 'JetBlue Airways: Service quality as a competitive advantage', *Journal of Business Case Studies*, 3(4): 33–44.

Dwyer, L. M., Cvelbar, L. K., Edwards, D. J. and Mihalič, T. A. (2013) 'Tourism firms' strategic flexibility: The case of Slovenia', *International Journal of Tourism Research*, 16(4): 377–387.

Elhoushy, S., Salem, I. E. and Agag, G. (2020) 'The impact of perceived benefits and risks on current and desired levels of outsourcing: Hotel managers' perspective', *International Journal of Hospitality Management*, 91: 102419.

Espino-Rodríguez, T. F. and Ramírez-Fierro, J. C. (2018) 'Managers' attitudes toward hotel outsourcing in a tourist destination: An approach from the benefits and risks perspective', *Tourism Management Perspectives*, 26: 143–152.

Evans, N. G. (2012) 'Tourism: A strategic business perspective', in T. Jamal and M. Robinson (Eds), *The Sage Handbook of Tourism Studies*, Thousand Oaks, CA: Sage, 215–234.

Evans, N. G. (2016) 'Sustainable competitive advantage in tourism organizations: A strategic model applying service dominant logic and tourism's defining characteristics', *Tourism Management Perspectives*, 18: 14–25.

Farris, P. W. and Moore, M. J. (Eds) (2004) *The Profit Impact of Marketing Strategy Project: Retrospect and Prospects*', Cambridge, UK: Cambridge University Press.

Fernandez, E., Montes, J. M. and Vasquez, C. J. (2000) 'Typology and strategic analysis of intangible resources: A resource based approach', *Technovation* 20(2): 81–92.

Finlay, P. N. (2000) Strategic Management: An Introduction to Business and Corporate Strategy, Harlow, UK: Pearson Education.

FitzPatrick, M., Davey, J., Muller, L. and Davey, H. (2013) 'Value-creating assets in tourism management: Applying marketing's service-dominant logic in the hotel industry', *Tourism Management*, 36: 86–98.

Fleisher, C. S. and Bensoussan, B. E. (2003) *Strategic and Competitive Analysis: Methods and Techniques for Analyzing Business Competition*, Upper Saddle River, NJ: FT Press.

Font, X., English, R., Gkritzali, A. and Tian, W. S. (2021) 'Value co-creation in sustainable tourism: A service-dominant logic approach', *Tourism Management*, 82: 104200.

Frenken, K. and Schor, J. (2017) 'Putting the sharing economy into perspective', *Environmental Innovation and Societal Transitions*, 23: 3–10.

Fyall, A. and Garrod, B. (2005) *Tourism Marketing: A Collaborative Approach*, Clevedon, UK: Channel View Publications.

Galbreath, J. (2005) 'Which resources matter the most to firm success? An exploratory study of resource-based theory', *Technovation* 25(9): 979–987.

Getz, D. (2009) 'Policy for sustainable and responsible festivals and events: Institutionalization of a new paradigm' *Journal of Policy Research in Tourism, Leisure and Events*, 1(1): 61–78.

Getz, D. and Carlsen, J. (2000) 'Characteristics and goals of family and owner-operated businesses in the rural tourism and hospitality sectors', *Tourism Management*, 21(6): 547–560.

Gonzalez, R., Llopis, J. and Gasco, J. (2011) 'What do we know about outsourcing in hotels?', *The Service Industries Journal*, 31(10): 1669–1682.

Grönroos, C. (1990) *Service Management and Marketing*, Lexington, MA: Lexington Books.

Guttentag, D. A. and Smith, S. L. (2017) 'Assessing Airbnb as a disruptive innovation relative to hotels: Substitution and comparative performance expectations', *International Journal of Hospitality Management*, 64: 1–10.

Hall, R. (2006) 'A framework linking intangible resources and capabilities to sustainable competitive advantage', *Strategic Management Journal*, 14(8): 607–618.

Hallin, C. A. and Marnburg, E. (2008) 'Knowledge management in the hospitality industry: A review of empirical research', *Tourism Management*, 29(2): 366–381.

Hallowell, R. and Schlesinger, L. A. (2000) 'The service profit chain, intellectual roots, current realities, and future prospects', in T. A. Swartz and D. Iacobucci (Eds), *Handbook of Services Marketing and Management*, Thousand Oaks, CA: Sage, 203–222.

Hamel, G. and Prahalad, C. K. (1993) 'Strategy as stretch and leverage', *Harvard Business Review*, 71(2): 75–84.

Harris, L. C. (2012) ' "Ripping off" tourists: An empirical evaluation of tourists' perceptions and service worker (mis) behavior', *Annals of Tourism Research*, 39(2): 1070–1093.

Harrison, J. S. (2003) 'Strategic analysis for the hospitality industry', *Cornell Hotel and Restaurant Administration Quarterly*, 44(2):139–152.

Haugland, S. A., Ness, H., Grønseth, B. O. and Aarstad, J. (2011) 'Development of tourism destinations: An integrated multilevel perspective', *Annals of Tourism Research*, 38(1): 268–290.

Heene, A. and Sanchez, R. (1997) *Competence-Based Strategic Management*, London: John Wiley & Sons.

Heskett, J. L., Jones, T. O., Loveman, G. W., Sasser, W. E. and Schlesinger, L. A. (1994) 'Putting the service profit chain to work', *Harvard Business Review*, March – April: 164–170.

Heskett, J. L. and Sasser, W. E. (2010) 'The service profit chain from satisfaction to ownership', in P. P. Maglio, C. A. Kieliszewski and J. C. Spohrer (Eds), *Handbook of Service Science: Research and Innovations in the Service Economy*, New York: Springer, 19–29.

Hu, H. H., Kandampully, J. and Juwaheer, T. D. (2009) 'Relationships and impacts of service quality, perceived value, customer satisfaction, and image: An empirical study', *The Service Industries Journal*, 29(2): 111–125.

Ivanova, M. and Ivanov, S. (2015) 'The nature of hotel chains: An integrative framework', *International Journal of Hospitality & Tourism Administration*, 16(2): 122–142.

Javidan, M. (1998) 'Core competence: What does it mean in practice?', *Long Range Planning*, 31(1): 60–71.

Jennings, D. (1997) 'Strategic guidelines for outsourcing decisions', *Strategic Change*, 6(2): 85–96.

Kallmuenzer, A., Peters, M. and Buhalis, D. (2020) 'The role of family firm image perception in host – guest value co-creation of hospitality firms', *Current Issues in Tourism*, 23(19): 2410–2427.

Kaplan, R. S. and Norton, D. P. (2001) *The Strategy Focused Organization*, Boston: Harvard Business School Press.

Kay, J. (1995) *Foundations of Corporate Success*, Oxford, UK: Oxford University Press.

Kim, G. J. (2014) 'Applying service profit chain model to the Korean restaurant industry', *International Journal of Hospitality Management*, 36: 1–13.

Korn, R., Chandler, K. and Marzec, C. (2021) 'Becoming a learning organization', *Curator: The Museum Journal*, 64(2): 297–311.

Lam, T. and Han, M. X. (2005) 'A study of outsourcing strategy: A case involving the hotel industry in Shanghai China', *International Journal of Hospitality Management*, 24(1): 41–56.

Lamminmaki, D. (2011) 'An examination of factors motivating hotel outsourcing', *International Journal of Hospitality Management*, 30(4): 963–973.

Li, X. R. and Petrick, J. F. (2008) 'Tourism marketing in an era of paradigm shift', *Journal of Travel Research*, 46(3): 235–244.

Lusch, R. F. and Vargo, S. L. (2011) 'Service-dominant logic: a necessary step', *European Journal of Marketing*, 45(7/8): 1298–1309.

Lusch, R. F., Vargo, S. L. and O'Brien, M. (2007) 'Competing through service: Insights from service-dominant logic', *Journal of Retailing*, 83(1): 5–18.

Lynch, R. (2021) *Strategic Management*, 9th ed., Harlow, UK: Pearson.

Marneros, S., Papageorgiou, G. and Efstathiades, A. (2021) 'Examining the core competencies for success in the hotel industry: The case of Cyprus', *Journal of Hospitality, Leisure, Sport and Tourism Education*, 28: 100303.

Mazur, J. and Zaborek, P. (2014) 'Validating DART model', *International Journal of Management and Economics*, 44(1): 106–125.

Mitchell, J. (2012) 'Value chain approaches to assessing the impact of tourism on low-income households in developing countries', *Journal of Sustainable Tourism*, 20(3): 457–475.

Mooney, A. (2007) 'Core competence, distinctive competence, and competitive advantage: What is the difference?' *Journal of Education for Business*, 83(2): 110–115.

Morrison, A. J. and Harrison, A. (1998) 'From corner shop to electronic shopping mall?', *Progress in Tourism and Hospitality Research*, 4(4): 349–356.

Nieves, J. and Haller, S. (2014) 'Building dynamic capabilities through knowledge resources', *Tourism Management*, 40: 224–232.

O'Cass, A. and Sok, P. (2015) 'An exploratory study into managing value creation in tourism service firms: Understanding value creation phases at the intersection of the tourism service firm and their customers', *Tourism Management*, 51: 186–200.

O'Shaughnessy, J. and O'Shaughnessy, N. (2009) 'The service-dominant perspective: A backward step?', *European Journal of Marketing*, 43(5/6): 784–793.

Oskam, J. and Boswijk, A. (2016) 'Airbnb: The future of networked hospitality businesses', *Journal of Tourism Futures*, 2(1): 22–42.

Pearson, J., Pitfield, D. and Ryley, T. (2015) 'Intangible resources of competitive advantage: Analysis of 49 Asian airlines across three business models', *Journal of Air Transport Management*, 47: 179–189.

Pechlaner, H., Bachinger, M., Volgger, M. and Anzengruber-Fischer, E. (2014) 'Cooperative core competencies in tourism: Combining resource-based and relational approaches in destination governance', *European Journal of Tourism Research*, 8(1):5–19.

Pemberton, J. D. and Stonehouse, G. H. (2000) 'Organizational learning and knowledge assets – An essential partnership', *The Learning Organization*, 7(4): 184–194.

Petts, N. (1997) 'Building growth on core competencies – A practical approach', *Long Range Planning*, 30(4): 551–561.

Poon, A. (1993) *Tourism, Technology and Competitive Strategy*, Wallingford, UK: CAB International.

Porter, M. E. (1985) *Competitive Advantage*, New York: Free Press.

Prahalad, C. K. and Hamel, G. (1990) 'The core competence of the corporation', *Harvard Business Review*, 68(3): 79–91.

Prahalad, C. K. and Ramaswamy, V. (2004) 'Co-creation experiences: The next practice in value creation', *Journal of Interactive Marketing*, 18(3): 5–14.

Prentice, C., Wong, I. A. and Lam, D. (2017) 'Uncovering the service profit chain in the casino industry', *International Journal of Contemporary Hospitality Management*, 29(11): 2826–2846.

Quinn, J. B. (2000) 'Outsourcing innovation: The new engine of growth', *Sloan Management Review*, 41(4), 13–29.

Rather, R. A., Hollebeek, L. D. and Islam, J. U. (2019) 'Tourism-based customer engagement: The construct, antecedents, and consequences', *The Service Industries Journal*, 39(7–8): 519–540.

Reichheld, F. E. and Sasser, W. E. (1990) 'Zero defections: Quality comes to services', *Harvard Business Review*, September – October, 105–111.

Rieple, A. and Helm, C. (2008) 'Outsourcing for competitive advantage: An examination of seven legacy airlines', *Journal of Air Transport Management*, 14(5): 280–285.

Rojas Bueno, A., Alarcón Urbistondo, P. and del Alcázar Martínez, B. (2020) 'The MICE tourism value chain: Proposal of a conceptual framework and analysis of disintermediation', *Journal of Convention and Event Tourism*, 21(3): 177–200.

Sanchez-Peinado, E., Pla-Barber, J. and Hébert, L. (2007) 'Strategic variables that influence entry mode choice in service firms', *Journal of International Marketing*, 15(1): 67–91.

Senge, P. M. (1997) 'The fifth discipline', *Measuring Business Excellence*, 1(3): 46–51.

Sharma, A. and Christie, I. T. (2010) 'Performance assessment using value-chain analysis in Mozambique', *International Journal of Contemporary Hospitality Management*, 22(3): 282–299.

Shaw, G., Bailey, A. and Williams, A. (2011) 'Aspects of service-dominant logic and its implications for tourism management: Examples from the hotel industry', *Tourism Management*, 32(2): 207–214.

Shaw, G. and Williams, A. (2009) 'Knowledge transfer and management in tourism organisations: An emerging research agenda', *Tourism Management*, 30(3): 325–335.

Solakis, K., Peña-Vinces, J. and Lopez-Bonilla, J. M. (2022) 'Value co-creation and perceived value: A customer perspective in the hospitality context', *European Research on Management and Business Economics*, 28(1): 100175.

Solnet, D., Ford, R. and McLennan, C. L. (2018) 'What matters most in the service-profit chain? An empirical test in a restaurant company', *International Journal of Contemporary Hospitality Management*, 30(1): 260–285.

Soteriades, M. D. and Dimou, I. (2011) 'Special events: A framework for efficient management', *Journal of Hospitality Marketing and Management*, 20(3/4): 329–346.

Stalk, G., Evans, P. and Shulmann, L. E. (1992) 'Competing on capabilities: The new rules of corporate strategy', *Harvard Business Review*, 63(March/April): 57–69.

Stonehouse, G. H. and Pemberton, J. D. (1999) 'Learning and knowledge management in the intelligent organisation', *Participation and Empowerment: An International Journal*, 7(5): 131–144.

Szymanski, D. M., Bharadwaj, S. G. and Varadarajan, P. R. (1993) 'An analysis of the market share – profitability relationship', *Journal of Marketing*, 57(July): 1–18.

Teece, D. J. (2007) 'Explicating dynamic capabilities: The nature and micro foundations of (sustainable) enterprise performance', *Strategic Management Journal*, 28(13): 1319–1350.

Teece, D. J. (2018) 'Business models and dynamic capabilities', *Long Range Planning*, 51(1): 40–49.

Uslay, C., Altintig, Z. A. and Winsor, R. D. (2010) 'An empirical examination of the "rule of three": Strategy implications for top management, marketers, and investors', *Journal of Marketing*, 74(2): 20–39.

Varadarajan, R. (2009) 'Outsourcing: Think more expansively', *Journal of Business Research*, 62(11): 1165–1172.

Vargo, S. L. (2009) 'Toward a transcending conceptualization of relationship: A service-dominant logic perspective', *Journal of Business and Industrial Marketing*, 24(5/6): 373–379.

Vargo, S. L. and Lusch, R. F. (2004) 'Evolving to a new dominant logic for marketing', *Journal of Marketing*, 68(1): 1–17.

Vargo, S. L. and Lusch, R. F. (2008) 'Service-dominant logic: Continuing the evolution', *Journal of the Academy of Marketing Science*, 36(1): 1–10.

Wallace, K. and Michopoulou, E. (2021) 'Stakeholder requirements and value co-creation in events', *Event Management*, 27(2): 281–299.

Wang, C. L. and Ahmed, P. K. (2007) 'Dynamic capabilities: A review and research agenda', *International Journal of Management Reviews*, 9(1): 31–51.

Wang, D., Li, X. R. and Li, Y. (2013) 'China's "smart tourism destination" initiative: A taste of the service-dominant logic', *Journal of Destination Marketing and Management*, 2(2): 59–61.

Wang, Y. and Lo, H. P. (2003) 'Customer-focused performance and the dynamic model for competence building and leveraging: A resource-based view', *Journal of Management Development*, 22(6): 483–526.

Wood, R. (1999) 'Introduction: Managerial approaches to accommodation in hospitality organizations', in C. Verginis and R. Wood (Eds), *Accommodation Management: Perspectives for the International Hotel Industry*, London: International Thomson Business Press.

Zehrer, A. (2009) 'Service experience and service design: Concepts and application in tourism SMEs', *Managing Service Quality*, 19(3): 332–349.

Zeithaml, V. A., Parasuraman, A. and Berry, L. L. (1990) *Delivering Quality Service: Balancing Customer Perceptions and Expectations*, New York: The Free Press.

Websites

www.ashfieldeventex.com
www.bestwestern.com
www.hilton.com
www.hotelrez.net
www.inizio.health.com
www.lhw.com
www.marriott.com
www.relaischateaux.com
www.slh.com
www.worldhotels.com
www.yourhotelsworldwide.net

Chapter **4**

Tourism, hospitality and event organizations – the human resources context

Introduction and chapter overview

This chapter continues the internal analysis of organizations in examining one of the functional areas that organizations are often divided into – the human context. The subsequent chapters will examine the other functional areas, namely, finance (Chapter 5) and marketing (Chapter 6).

Human resources are one of the key resource inputs to any organizational process. *THE* sectors are often said to be labor intensive (as opposed to capital intensive) in their orientation, which places an even greater reliance on the management of human resources. A thorough analysis of this resource is an important part of strategic analysis, and this chapter explains the resource audit – one of the most widely used tools for this purpose.

Closely linked to the human resource is the issue of an organization's 'personality' or 'culture'. We define culture and then go on to explain its importance to an organization. The cultural web is discussed – a model used to explain how the features of culture determine the organization's paradigm. Finally, we discuss three cultural typologies that provide frameworks for analyzing culture in organizations.

LEARNING OBJECTIVES

After studying this chapter, you should be able to:

- Define and explain the importance of human resources to *THE* organizations
- Explain the employment and working conditions in *THE* organizations

DOI: 10.4324/9781003318613-6

- Explain the importance of the guest–employee encounter to *THE* organizations
- Explain the linkages between service quality and human resources
- Explain the purpose of a human resource audit
- Describe what a human resource gap is
- Explain what a human resource audit contains and what it can be used for
- Describe human resource benchmarking
- Explain what a CSF is and how human resources can be CSFs
- Define culture; explain its determinants and why it is important
- Explain the components of the cultural web and the nature of paradigms
- Describe and apply three typologies of cultural types

4.1 The importance of human resources in *THE*

The sectors of *THE* are labor-intensive service sectors in which the human factor is often the key differentiator between different competing organizations (Evans, 2012). Employees (or groups of employees) are often critical to an organization's strategic success and thus represent what is often referred to in the literature as a *critical success factor* (CSF).

People are an important resource to most organizations, but in service-based organizations in particular, it is often the human resources (i.e., people) that represent the key factor in delivering successful performance. In contrast to most other industries, the products in *THE* are service experiences 'which are mostly intangible and highly dependent on face-to-face interactions between employees and customers' (Madera et al., 2017:48). Therefore, few people would reject the proposition that the human element in *THE* organizations is critical for service quality, customer satisfaction and loyalty, competitive advantage and organizational performance (Kusluvan et al., 2010).

Similarly, Baum (1997) considered the experience of the guest or consumer within the tourism industry to be both highly intense and intimate in a way rarely replicated in other service industries. Furthermore, their interactive experience is commonly with front-line staff, who generally are those who have the lowest status, are the least highly trained and are the poorest paid employees.

Thus, the consideration of human resource issues is vital to the successful implementation of strategy in most organizations operating in *THE* contexts. As with the other functional areas of organizations we consider in subsequent chapters (finance and marketing), we are most interested in the *key* areas of human resource management because they have an impact on the successful formulation and implementation of strategy.

However, it is important to note that in studying strategy we are less interested in the myriad detailed human resource issues that may occur in any organization but instead are interested in the broad principles relating to human resources that should guide the organization. These issues are covered in detail elsewhere. See, for example, Kusluvan et al. (2010), Mullins and Dossor (2013), Nickson (2013), Riley (2014), Van der Wagen and White (2014), Baum (2015), Hayes and Ninemeier (2016), Madera et al. (2017), Burke and Hughes (2018), Boella and Goss-Turner (2019) and Baum and Ndiuini (2020).

Given the labor intensity of most *THE* organizations and the centrality of human resources to commercial success, it is unsurprising that issues related to this field have received a considerable degree of academic attention in *THE* literature in recent years (see reviews by García-Lillo et al., 2018; Pelit and Katircioglu, 2022). In the context of tourism and hospitality, the extensive literature relating to the management of human resource issues is very much interwoven with hospitality, often being viewed as a constituent component of tourism (or vice versa). Both sectors often share similar characteristics when employing staff, and many of these characteristics are shared also by the events sector. These issues are considered in the next section.

The events sector, though sharing many characteristics with tourism and hospitality, highlights some of the issues, as follows:

- *Work is usually geared toward a particular a point in time* when the events are taking place (or the event may be repeated at regular or irregular intervals). This facet of events often gives rise to job insecurity and relatively poor working conditions, as pressure builds before and during the event and relatively high recruitment costs. However, as Bowdin et al. (2012) pointed out, if an event seeks to grow in size and attendance, each time it is repeated, a human resource strategy (as part of an overall strategy) is essential to support increased staff recruitment and to support additional and probably more sophisticated training.
- *Event teams highlight heterogeneity* (Muskat and Mair, 2020), because a variety of different values, beliefs and needs of employees and volunteers are exhibited. The heterogeneity makes motivational factors and subsequently job experiences and job satisfaction complex to manage.
- Volunteers often form an important part of the workforce and, indeed, many events such as the 2012 London Olympic Games would not be feasible without the involvement of a large-scale volunteer workforce. Recruiting, managing, motivating and controlling such a workforce present certain challenges when the normal authority engendered by the employee–employer relationship underpinned by payments and contracts does not exist (see, for example, Qi et al., 2018; Hawkins and Bonney, 2019; Holmes et al., 2021).
- *Staff numbers often have to quickly expand and then contract.* Hanlon and Jago (2004) developed the concept of the 'pulsating' organization to describe many organizations in the events sector. Many such organizations have to grow quickly as the event approaches, take on additional staff for the event itself and then quickly contract when the event finishes.

The factors outlined above give rise to specific challenges for managers in the events sector (Bowdin et al., 2012). These challenges might include:

- Obtaining paid staff of the right caliber given the short-term nature of the employment offered
- Working to short timescales to hire and select staff and to implement effective staff training
- Quickly shedding staff after the event

If volunteers are part of the workforce, specific challenges include sourcing sufficient volunteers, quality control, asserting management control, integration and cooperation with paid employees and motivation and training.

The Australian Open championships provides an illustration of some of the human resource challenges encountered in managing an annual sporting event.

4.1 SHORT CASE ILLUSTRATION

A 'pulsating' organization: the Australian Open tennis championships

The Australian Open tennis championships, together with the French and US Open and Wimbledon (UK), represents one of the four major titles on the world professional tennis circuit – the so-called grand slams. The event, held in Melbourne in January each year, provides an illustration of a 'pulsating' organization, a concept developed by Hanlon and Jago (2004) and subsequently adopted by other authors in the field (Carlsson-Wall et al., 2017; Skille et al., 2020).

Deery (2009) described the 2008 event, which employed some 4,500 staff, including 319 ball kids, 365 umpires, 195 courtesy car drivers and 45 statisticians. Most of these staff are, however, only needed during the 2-week event itself. Many of the staff work at the championships year after year, but others have to be recruited annually, with the recruiting process for the next event commencing shortly after the conclusion of the current year's event. Many volunteers as well as paid staff are employed, and rewards include access to available seats, free meals, uniforms and some free transport, as well as pay.

Questions

1. Why might the Australian Open be described as a 'pulsating' organization?

2. What would you consider the human resource challenges for managers in this case?

The general literature relating to human resources in *THE* contexts is supplemented by numerous studies considering human resource issues in particular *THE* contexts and geographical settings.

> For example: *There are many human resource challenges facing China's hotel and tourism industry. It has been argued that the key issues in this context are the lack of qualified staff at both operational and managerial levels, high staff turnover rates, the unwillingness of university graduates to enter the industry and the gap between what is taught in schools and colleges and the realities of the industry itself (Zhang and Wu, 2004). Furthermore, Liu and Wall (2005) pointed out that the provision of education and training has concentrated primarily on the preparation of hospitality personnel for large enterprises to the relative neglect of the requirements of smaller operators and the stimulation of indigenous entrepreneurship.*

4.2 Employment and working conditions in *THE*

THE represents a sizable proportion of worldwide employment, and though comparisons are difficult, it is likely that these sectors employ more than the automotive industry but slightly less than education, and employment opportunities are continuing to increase.

The WTTC (2021) estimated that when the wider impacts of the industry are taken into account, in terms of the supply chain, investment and consumer spending, travel and tourism was estimated to support over 334 million jobs – over 10% of all jobs. It had also been growing significantly, with one in four jobs created between 2014 and 2019 accounted for by travel and tourism.

However, the COVID-19 pandemic had a devastating effect, with 62 million jobs lost, leaving just 272 million employed across the sector globally in 2021 (WTTC, 2021). This decrease was felt across parts of the industry, with SMEs, which make up 80% of all global businesses in the sector, being particularly affected.

Importantly, it is not only the size of the workforce that is distinctive but also its composition. The human resources that make up the workforce in *THE* sectors are often characterized by:

- A large proportion of female employees
- A large proportion of young employees

Part 2

- A large number of part-time and seasonal workers
- High staff turnover rates
- Recruitment difficulties
- Poor levels of training
- Relatively low pay
- Mobility of labor between different employers and geographically
- Working patterns involving work at night and on weekends
- Importance of volunteer workforce particularly for large events

Each of the human resource characteristics identified can raise challenges for managers working in *THE*. The relatively high levels of staff turnover in many cases can be particularly problematic because it can lead to higher costs relating to additional recruitment activities, wasted training and development and difficulties in maintaining quality standards.

A number of studies (Dwesini, 2019; Han, 2020) have reported on the high employee turnover rates in parts of the industry and discussed strategies for retaining and motivating employees.

> For example: *Employee turnover is a challenging issue in China's hotels (as in many countries). Yao et al. (2018) reported that the average employee turnover rate of Chinese hotels in 2016 was as high as 3.34% per month, which has negative effects on the quality of services and customer satisfaction. The authors went on to suggest that too much attention has been focused on economic incentives. Though these incentives remain important, there are also significant psychological incentives affecting attitudes and staff behavior that must also be considered.*

As a result of the high staff turnover rates, many *THE* employers go to great lengths to recruit the right caliber of staff and to retain and motivate them once they have been recruited.

The case of Accor Hotels provides an illustration of the importance one major *THE* employer attaches to retention of staff through its learning and development strategy.

4.2 SHORT CASE ILLUSTRATION

Learning and development at Accor Hotels

Paris-based Accor Hotels is one of the largest international hospitality groups, bringing together some well-known international hospitality brands such as Novotel, Sofitel and Ibis.

Notwithstanding the sales-oriented language, designed to attract potential recruits and appeal to the career aspirations of its current employees, the following statements adapted from Accor clearly illustrate the importance this hotel and resorts group attaches to motivating and retaining its employees through its learning and development initiatives. Similar statements can be found on many of the websites of leading international *THE* brands, and though they are aimed at current and potential employees, the various features that are mentioned also help the companies concerned meet their objectives.

> We pride ourselves on providing our team members with access to leading training and development programs with the aim of empowering each and everyone to be actors of their own professional development and growth throughout their career at Accor.

Lifelong learning

Accor maintains that everyone working at the hotel group has opportunities for lifelong learning so that they feel valued. It is the company's aim as part of its learning and development strategy, launched in 2015, to give every one of its 'heartists' (the company's chosen terminology) the means to be independent and continually learn in order to constantly improve their skills and be able to quickly adapt to an ever-changing environment. Heartists (Heart + Artists) embody the companies culture and mindset. 'As passionate hospitality experts, we create unique and unrivalled experiences that spark emotion thanks to our team members' creativity, individual personalities, and talent journey at Accor.' The learning and development strategy is designed to be inclusive and attractive for employees but is also designed to support the global and local strategic priorities of the company.

The Accor Hotels Académie

The strategy draws in particular on the Accor Hotels Académie, the company's 'corporate university', which celebrated its 30th anniversary in 2015. The Académies' eight campuses provide training to all Accor Hotels employees. Regardless of their profession, level of training, role or tenure, the company's 'talents' receive training in excellence that Accor claims is always at the cutting edge of teaching and technological innovation. Virtual campuses to train recruits are available in countries with few or no hotel schools. The Académie also supports the company in achieving its objectives because it enables the company to support its rate of growth in different regions. The Académies delivered over 2 million hours of training in 2021.

In another major initiative, Accor Hotels set up its own internal social network in October 2015, called Yammer. Simple, intuitive and accessible via a mobile app, Yammer turns its employees into an active community that creates groups, shares news and best practices and feels connected.

Digital learning

With digital learning, Accor's employees can learn everywhere, all the time, through infographics, videos, quizzes, short e-learning modules or virtual classrooms. They can also contribute to the enrichment of the collective knowledge by connecting with other colleagues to share their expertise, learn from each other and discuss their experiences.

For example, to enhance Accor Hotels digital culture, 'Digit'all' is a mobile web-based learning solution that establishes a common base of digital knowledge for everyone in the Accor Hotels family to understand how digital is transforming the hospitality industry.

Source: Adapted from www.accor.com

Questions

1. Why does Accor give so much attention to learning and development?

2. Consider the difficulties involved in managing staff at international chains of hotels such as those managed by Accor brands.

As a counterbalance to some of the perceived negative aspects of the industry sectors (such as working 'antisocial' hours), it can be argued that it is often viewed as an attractive industry in which to work. Indeed, traveling and working in *THE* are often linked. Staff often have access to concessionary travel, and accommodation rates and opportunities are presented to attend events to meet people and to see something of the world. Furthermore many *THE* employees are situated in attractive surroundings.

For many young people (in particular) all over the world, being able to travel and undertaking tourism and hospitality work are intertwined (Duncan et al., 2013). In some cases, the attraction of the work is such that parts of the workforce can be volunteers, accepting no payment for their work (Hawkins and Bonney, 2019).

In such circumstances, the challenge for managers is to recruit and retain talented staff, take actions to motivate employees and try to ensure that an appropriate work–life balance is maintained (Deery, 2008). To be successful in these actions, employers may offer more training opportunities, career progression opportunities, travel incentives and higher levels of pay and bonuses.

Critically, though, employers need to pay attention to the design of jobs and roles through measures such as:

- *Job enlargement* – employees' jobs are made more worthwhile and interesting in that they are given a wider variety of tasks to carry out.
- *Job rotation* – employees rotate jobs so that teamwork is encouraged, knowledge and skills are gained and everyone has to take a share of less popular tasks.
- *Job enrichment* – employees are given a greater deal of discretion or *empowerment* to make decisions.
- *Job sharing* – employees' jobs are shared between two or more employees, thereby sharing burdens and responsibilities and providing cover for staff leave or sick days.

In service industries such as *THE*, managers often work in relative isolation, and many organizations or business units are relatively small. Thus, managers often work in diverse locations that are away from the central organizational support services such as sales and marketing, customer service, etc. (or organizations are too small to have such support services). It may also be the case that managers work shift patterns that mean organizational support is unavailable when called upon. However, managers can be called upon to take decisions as a result of operational difficulties or customer pressure (despite having little access to support services).

THINK POINTS

- Explain why human resources are so important to operating successful *THE* organizations.
- Identify the key differentiating characteristics of working in many *THE* organizations.
- Assess how managers in *THE* might address problems of high staff turnover rates.

Thus, empowering managers (and, indeed, all employees) to take decisions is often a vital issue for many *THE* organizations. Consequently, this issue has received quite a lot of attention in the academic literature (see, for example, Baum, 2015; Aghazamani and Hunt, 2017; Lin et al., 2017; Abou-Shouk et al., 2021; Hoang et al., 2021; Murray and Holmes, 2021).

Though they stressed the importance of empowerment, Ro and Chen (2011), for example, argued that it needs to be supported by hiring customer-oriented people, guiding them with service training, providing a valid reward system and facilitating communication of service standards to increase perceived empowerment. Cheung et al. (2012), however, writing in a Chinese hospitality context, noted the dominance of 'Western-centric' literature in the field of empowerment and questioned whether it is applicable beyond developed countries.

Managers and employers in many *THE* settings work remotely or at hours when support is unavailable. Thus, it is important for *THE* employers to understand the importance of empowering their employees so that they can take decisions and resolve issues as they occur. Such empowerment is illustrated by the following Short Case Illustration of Ritz-Carlton hotels.

4.3 SHORT CASE ILLUSTRATION

Empowerment at Ritz-Carlton

Employee empowerment can be described as enabling or authorizing employees to make decisions to solve customer issues by themselves. It is particularly advocated in services settings because of their *heterogeneity* (discussed in Chapter 2). In their contacts with customers, employees need to adapt their behaviors to the demands of each and every service encounter (Ueno, 2008) to ensure that consistent levels of service delivery are maintained. Ro and Chen (2011) emphasized the importance of careful recruitment to successful empowerment of employees in that efforts must be made to select 'empowerable' employees who can be inculcated with the skills and attitudes conducive to exercising acceptable and responsible decision making.

A few companies have embraced the concept of employee empowerment in their service delivery. The Ritz-Carlton hotel chain (a subsidiary of Marriott) is an upscale international chain with over 100 hotels in 30 countries. The company's 'gold standards' of service encapsulate the values and philosophy of the company. Among the 12 service values for staff are the statements 'I am empowered to create unique, memorable and personal experiences for our guests', and employees are encouraged to work on their own initiative with the statement 'I own and immediately resolve guest problems'.

Source: Adapted from www.ritzcarlton.com

Questions

1. What managerial difficulties is the Ritz-Carlton chain attempting to overcome through employee empowerment?

2. Consider the benefits and potential drawbacks of empowerment in this case.

4.3 Management of the guest–employee encounter

The management of the guest (or customer)–employee encounter remains one of the most difficult but ultimately most important tasks for *THE* managers (Baum, 1997; Sørensen and Jensen, 2015; Chathoth et al., 2016; Alshaibani and Bakir, 2017; Sipe and Testa, 2018). In fast-moving markets, especially in service industries that are relatively 'labor intensive', delivering the services that are the true source of sustainable competitive advantage (discussed in the previous chapter) may require:

- The ability and knowledge of people
- The ability of people to learn
- The ability of people to adapt to change

Writers on service quality have suggested that the proof of service quality is in its flawless performance (Berry and Parasuraman, 1991; Augustyn and Ho,1998), a concept similar to the notion of 'zero defects', which is often discussed in a manufacturing context. From the customer's point of view, the most immediate evidence of service quality occurs in the service encounter, or 'the moment of truth' when the customer interacts with the organization (Bitner et al., 1994).

The term 'moment of truth' is often attributed to Jan Carlzon (1987), a past president of Scandinavian Airline Systems, who used the terminology to describe every point of contact that a customer, or potential customer, has with the organization in question.

As it has been argued (Baum, 1995; Sørensen and Jensen, 2015), THE presents particular challenges in the management of moments of truth because of the *fragmentation* of the experience for many customers. For example, the purchase of a typical 'package' holiday or a concert ticket may involve contact with a wide range of intermediaries such as those indicated in Table 4.1.

The concept of the moment of truth as a manifestation of the guest/customer–employee encounter clearly has applicability throughout the three parts (traveler generator region, transit route and tourist destination region) of what Leiper (1990) called 'the tourism system'.

Baum (1997), building on Leiper's representation, produced a model of moments of truth in relation to the wide range of organizations that make up the tourism system. The model presented in Figure 4.1 recognizes that moments of truth need not carry equal weight; that is, some will be more important to customers than others, 'so that as far as the guest is concerned . . . a positive or

Table 4.1 Comparison of possible intermediaries encountered in purchasing a typical package holiday or a concert ticket

Package tour purchase: possible intermediaries	Concert ticket purchase: possible intermediaries
Retail travel agent or internet intermediary	Ticket agent, concert promoter or internet intermediary
Insurance company	Transport to and from the venue
Ground transport to and from the airport	Catering staff at the venue or providers in the locality
Airport handling agents (at outbound and inbound airports)	Sellers of merchandise associated with the concert
Immigration and customs services	Promoters of other concerts and events that may be of interest
Local ground transportation	The hotel or other overnight accommodation (if required)
Hotel or other accommodation	Artists and performers at the concert
Tour services at the destination	Emergency and first aid services at the venue
Companies selling goods and services at the destination	
Emergency services at the destination	
Service providers such as restaurants, entertainment venues, attractions, festival and event organizers	

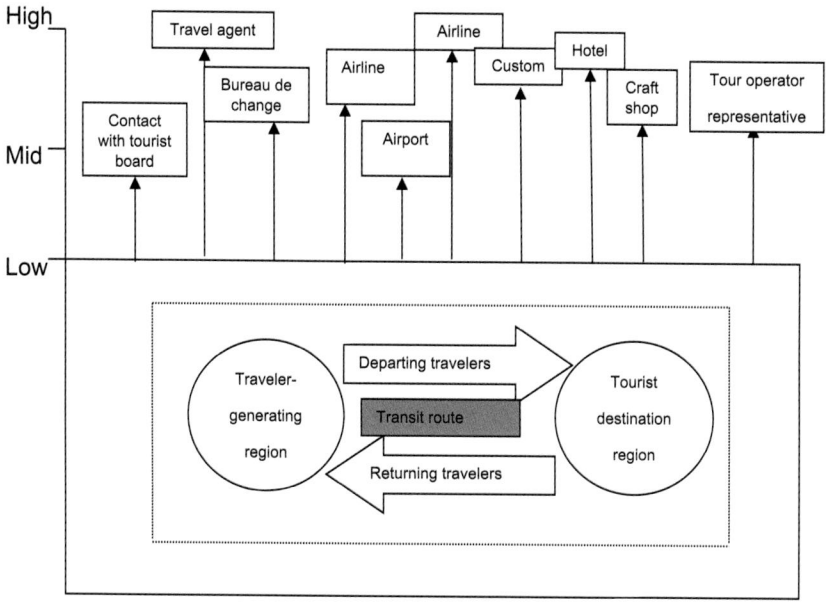

Figure 4.1 A model of the tourist experience and moments of truth

Source: Adapted from Baum (1997)

negative experience in one area may elicit a very different response to a similar experience elsewhere in the guest cycle' (Baum, 1997:93).

The model provides through its vertical axis a measure (albeit rather subjective) of the intensity and therefore the importance of the interaction to customers. In so doing, the model allows tourism managers who are responsible for the tourists' experience to attempt to predict those areas of greatest potential impact and consequently to recognize those areas where resources might be focused.

4.4 Human resources and service quality

Service quality can be viewed as an important strategy for gaining a competitive advantage in *THE* organizations, as many authors (including Baum, 1997; Crick and Spencer, 2011; Dhar, 2015; Hudson and Hudson, 2022) have outlined. The broad and expanding literature on this topic has been reviewed by Lai et al. (2018) and Park and Jeong (2019).

Service quality in *THE* is to a large degree determined by the quality and attitude of owners, managers and employees – the human resources. Quality in *THE* sectors depends on a range of human skills adopted during the service encounter. As we have seen, recognition of the centrality of human resources to the successful delivery of service quality has led to the adoption of concepts such as managing moments of truth (Carlzon, 1987) and also to what Albrecht (1992) has described as a 'spirit of service'.

In essence, human resources 'contribute to sustained competitive advantage through facilitating the development of competences that are firm specific' (Lado and Wilson, 1994:705). This link between the development of sustained competitive advantage and the quality of an organization's human resources was illustrated by Kusluvan et al. (2010):

- Services are intangible.

- Services are produced and consumed simultaneously, usually at the service provider's location.
- Customers are present or participating in the service, usually with interpersonal interaction between customers and service providers.

Owing to these features, services are made tangible in the personality, appearance, attitudes and behavior of the service provider. In this way, employees become part of the product, represent the organization and help to form the image of the organization (Kandampully, 2000; Swanson and Hsu, 2009).

In providing service quality, there are also important cross-cultural dimensions in achieving customer satisfaction that need to be considered (Weiermair, 2000; Sabiote-Ortiz et al., 2016; Su et al., 2016). It should be recognized that in many *THE* settings, delivering the service involves customers and employees who are diverse in their backgrounds, expectations, religion and cultural norms in different parts of the world. Consequently, the way in which services are delivered has to reflect and respect these differences and be adjusted accordingly. Eid and Abdelkader (2017), for example, explored the specific dimensions of service quality in a Muslim context.

Figure 4.2 illustrates how a 'virtuous circle' may be formed in service organizations such as those operating in *THE*:

1. People who are carefully selected, well trained and highly motivated are more likely to deliver services of high quality.
2. Because the quality of services offered is high, they are likely to be valued by customers, leading to customer satisfaction and loyalty.
3. This leads to the creation of a competitive advantage because a competence (delivery of high-quality services) has been successfully delivered to customers (in a market).
4. Gaining advantage over competitors leads to a high level of organizational performance and business success.

Figure 4.2 The 'virtuous circle' linking human resources with business success

5. The success of the business allows for additional resources to be deployed in rewarding existing people and recruiting additional people of a high caliber who are attracted by the success of the organization.

The most widely used model to translate theories of customer satisfaction into management practice is SERVQUAL (Soutar, 2001). The SERVQUAL model of service quality developed in the mid-1980s by Zeithaml, Parasuraman and Berry defines service quality in terms of the difference (the 'gap') between customer expectations and customer perception of service received.

Although it has been challenged on a number of grounds (see, for example, Bennington and Cumane, 1998), attempts have been made to validate the model (Rauch et al., 2015), and other models have been developed, such as those associated with Grönroos (1984) and the FESTPERF model developed by Tkaczynski and Stokes (2010) in relation to festivals and events. However, the SERVQUAL model remains important and, indeed, one leading writer (Mill, 2011:10) maintained that 'the SERVQUAL model presents *the best* mechanism to explain customer satisfaction in hospitality and tourism'.

The 'gap' in service quality occurs when the perception of service received is less than what is expected (Zeithaml et al., 1990). According to Zeithaml et al. (1990), there are five dimensions of service, which can usefully be remembered through the acronym *RATER*:

- *Responsiveness*: willingness to help customers and provide prompt service; for example, problem solving by hotel reception staff, advice offered by call centers
- *Assurance*: knowledge and courtesy of employees and their ability to convey trust and confidence; for example, level of training for flight attendants, providing itemized bills for services delivered
- *Tangibles*: appearance of physical facilities, equipment, personnel and communication materials; for example, comfort of the hotel room, facilities at the concert venue, airplane passenger features
- *Empathy*: caring, individualized attention the company provides its customers; for example, treating each customer at a restaurant individually according to their needs
- *R*eliability: ability to perform the promised service dependably and accurately; for example, train arrival times, accuracy of bills, conference running according to schedule

The gap between what customers expect and what they perceive is attributed to one or more of the following reasons (Zeithaml et al., 1990):

- Gap 1: Management does not know what guests expect.
- Gap 2: Management is not willing or able to put the systems in place to match or exceed customer expectations – service quality standards are not developed.
- Gap 3: The service–performance gap arises when employees are unable and/or unwilling to perform the service at the desired level.
- Gap 4: Promises do not match delivery.

The management task in responding to these perceived gaps is to identify effective strategic options for closing the gaps. Mill (2011) suggested that a sequential five-step approach should be adopted to address the four gaps:

1. Identify whether or not a problem exists.
2. Manage customer expectations so they are realistic with the service offering. (Gap 4)
3. Identify customer needs and expectations of quality service. (Gap 1)
4. Develop service quality standards based on customer expectations. (Gap 2)

5. Reevaluate the human resource system to hire, train and motivate employees who are willing and able to deliver quality service. (Gap 3)

THINK POINTS

- Explain the link between human resources and the quality of service delivery in *THE* contexts.
- According to Zeithaml et al., what are the five dimensions of service quality, and how might they be applied to *THE* organizations?
- Explain what is meant by 'moments of truth' and why they are crucial in *THE* contexts.

A key tool in identifying where gaps exist is the *human resource audit*, which is discussed in Section 4.5.

4.4.1 *Humans vs machines in* THE

Resource substitution (substituting one category of resources for another) is important in many industries driven primarily by technological advances. This facet is certainly an important issue in *THE* with regard to the substitution of people by operating resources in the form of various technology advances. Up to this point, this chapter has emphasized the importance of people in delivering the required standards of service in *THE*. The sectors of *THE* have been labeled as *labor intensive*, and the *heterogeneity* that using people in service delivery entails has been noted.

However, these notions are being challenged (at least to some degree) as the use of technologies such as robotics, artificial intelligence (AI), the IoT, big data, blockchain, chatbots and biometrics increasingly compete with labor resources. A number of writers have addressed these technology issues in various *THE* contexts (see Naumov, 2019; Tuomi at al., 2019; Rosete et al., 2020; Yang et al., 2020; Zeng et al., 2020; Jabeen et al., 2021; Goel et al., 2022).

> For example: *Zeng et al. (2020) documented the increased use of technology as a result of the World Health Organization declaring COVID-19 a pandemic. THE in particular was massively impacted by the lockdowns used to manage the disease, and robotics, AI and human – robot interactions gained an increased presence to help manage the spread of the disease. Though controversial in the past due to concerns over job losses and data privacy, the adoption of robotics and artificial intelligence in THE is likely to continue after the COVID-19 pandemic becomes less serious. Opportunities should be seized, the authors argued, to encourage robotic applications that enhance tourist experiences, protection of natural and cultural resources, citizen participation in tourism development decision making and the emergence of new 'high-touch' employment opportunities.*

Some of the issues relating to the adoption of technology are illustrated in the Technology Focus below:

4.4 TECHNOLOGY FOCUS

Humans vs machines

In a seemingly far-fetched context of our reality, organizations will have to decide whether the AI will allow the complete replacement of humans with robots capable of performing the necessary cognitive and emotional tasks. Or investing in balanced capacities by integrating robot–human systems . . . .

(Jabeen et al., 2022:1044)

Effectively, a robot is a machine that has been designed to automatically perform specific tasks accurately. This could include physical tasks, such as part assembly in a factory, or text or speech-related tasks. AI is perhaps the most exciting robot-related technology because it can facilitate machine learning and the performance of more complex tasks that have typically required human cognitive function. Put simply, AI is the ability for a machine to mimic this kind of cognitive ability.

Increasingly, customers are seeking self-service methods, and this makes the automation provided by robots appealing to hotels, travel agents, event venues' destination organizations and other businesses. Robots have the advantages of being able to work constantly and accurately without the need for recurring payments (unlike humans) but clearly lack the 'personal touch'.

The tourism and hospitality technology platform www.revfine.com lists a number of robotic applications in *THE*, including:

1. A robot-staffed hotel –The Henn-na Hotel in Nagasaki, Japan, is recognized as the world's first robot-staffed hotel. Robots are used on the front desk as customer information points.

2. Robot concierge – International hotel group Hilton has deployed robot technology in the form of 'Connie', an AI concierge, developed in collaboration with IBM. Connie is able to interact with visitors using speech recognition and also uses AI to learn from each interaction.

3. 'Travelmate' – Travelmate is a robotic suitcase that is able to follow its owner around autonomously, utilizing collision detection technology and 360-degree turning capabilities.

4. Chatbots for flight or hotel bookings – Online bookings revolutionized *THE* booking processes, and chatbots have started to do the same. A chatbot is a software application used to conduct an online chat conversation via text or text-to-speech, in lieu of providing direct contact with a human agent. Chatbots make use of AI to guide customers through the booking process, asking intelligent questions along the way.

4.5 The human resource audit

Decisions about the future strategy of the organization are made by people and strategies are implemented by people. The success or failure of a current strategy will depend not only on decisions made in the past but also on how those decisions are being implemented in the now by people employed by the organization. It is therefore important to ask questions about who, how and why people are doing what they are doing and what they should do in strategic implementation. In short, human resources add value, manage the business and, conversely, can make spectacular errors that can be very costly to the organization.

An understanding of the capabilities of individuals and groups in terms of attitudes, abilities and skills, as well as an understanding of how individuals relate one to another, is an important part in the preparation and development of strategy. A key 'tool' in gaining an understanding of an organization's human resources is the *human resource audit* (sometimes termed a skills audit).

The human resource audit is an investigation into the size, skills, structure and all other issues surrounding those currently employed by the organization. The audit reviews the ability of the human resources to implement a chosen strategy or a range of strategic options.

Most organizations employ accountants to maintain a constant review of financial resources, and limited companies subject themselves (by law) to a formal external financial audit each year. Human resources are another resource input and are equally important, and although they are not subject to legal verification, an organization would be foolish to pursue a strategy without a thorough review of its human resources (i.e., its people).

Once the audit has been completed, management should be able to answer the key question: Are the human resources in the organization capable of implementing the proposed strategy? If any gaps are identified, a human resource strategy (as part of the overall strategy) may be put in place to close the gap.

KEY CONCEPT

Human resource gaps

A 'gap' can occur in any area of human resource management. It rests upon a simple calculation.

> Human resource characteristic necessary for the proposed strategy – Current state of the human resource characteristic = The human resource gap.

Gaps can occur in particular skills. In *THE*, for example, skills gaps may be identified in particular areas such as knowledge and experience of computer reservation systems. It may be that the audit reveals a deficit of 30 people who can operate such systems – a negative gap. The task of the human resource department thus becomes successfully appointing, redeploying or retraining to gain the requisite number of skilled operators.

Positive gaps may also be identified; that is, surpluses of a particular type of employee. The human resource strategy thus has to put measures in place to 'dispose' of the excess labor.

Gaps may be closed by using the '5 Rs' individually or in combination. The 5 Rs are:

- **R**etirement
- **R**etraining
- **R**edeployment
- **R**edundancy
- **R**ecruitment

4.5.1 The contents of a human resource audit

The contents of a human resource audit may vary from organization to organization (see Ulrich [1998] for a discussion), depending on its size, geographic coverage and type of activity. However, a typical audit checklist might include the:

- Number of employees – the total number, by division, by location, by skill type, by grade or place in hierarchy, by age or length of service, by gender and by ethnic group
- Employee costs – usually measured by salary costs and 'add-ons' like benefits and taxes payable by the organization etc.

- Organizational structure and the position of employees within the structure
- Recruitment and selection procedures and their effectiveness
- Quality and effectiveness of training and development programs used
- Level of employee motivation and morale
- Quality of employee or industrial relations between management and employees
- Internal and external networks that employees in the organization have developed (and their effectiveness for various purposes)
- Monitoring of the effectiveness of existing human resource policies and control procedures

The information provided by the audit can provide management with important information about the state of the organization's human resources. In most types of organizations, regular audits are essential to success. However, for some organizations connected with events such as a professional football club or an orchestra, the state of the human resources is completely transparent and the audit occurs continually – although it may never be formally conducted. A football team that loses every match or an orchestra that sounds terrible will have obvious human resource skill deficits. A formal audit is hardly necessary in such circumstances.

Formal audits may be carried out by human resource specialists on a regular basis (say, annually) or whenever management needs the information for the purposes of a strategic analysis. Practitioners in this area make the point that simply following 'lists' like that outlined above is only a starting point. As points of interest are raised, such as key skill deficiencies, it is imperative that the reasons for the shortage (or surplus) be examined as an integral part of the audit.

4.5.2 The outcomes of a human resource audit

THE PROBLEM OF MEASUREMENT

The various components of a human resource audit present differing problems of quantification. We can intuitively understand that entries like employee costs, numbers, skills and shortages or surpluses can be measured in numerical terms. Industrial relations measures can usually be measured by aspects such as days lost through strikes, absentee rates, etc. Other parts of the audit present more difficulty in respect of measurement.

> For example: *How might we measure staff morale or motivation? We might be able to say that staff morale is high or low, but any 'in-betweens' might be difficult to assign a value to in the same way as for, say, employee costs. The same problems arise with the levels of staff motivation and job satisfaction. It is also probably true to say that in most organizations large disparities exist between employees in respect of these intangibles. Some employees will be highly motivated and will enjoy good morale whereas others will not. It is for these reasons that a 'checklist' approach to human resource audit is rarely possible – it usually contains some subjective assessments of some parts of the audit.*

HUMAN RESOURCE BENCHMARKING

The concept of benchmarking is one that we will encounter several times in this book. Essentially, benchmarking is a tool for comparing a feature of one organization with the same feature of another. It is particularly useful for comparison against the best in an industry for the feature in question. Followers of the best in the industry might then ask why the leader company has achieved the superior performance (see discussion of benchmarking in finance in Chapter 5 and in operations in Chapter 12). Increasingly, however, companies in the service industries are also benchmarking themselves against companies in different sectors.

For example: It may be that in the area of offering customer service, hotel companies are able to learn from practices in banking, insurance companies, airlines or car dealers.

The feature examined in a benchmarking analysis will depend upon what the organization needs to know.

For example: If a company identifies a negative gap in a key skill area that it has found difficult to close (say, of recruiting good quality graduates), a benchmark study will enable the company to find out about its competitors. If Company A is known to be able to attract the best graduates, an examination of its human resource policies will enable other companies (competitors) to benchmark their own practices against it. It may be that Company A is identified as offering the best career progression planning, the highest salaries or the best development opportunities. If this is found to be the case, competitors will want to examine their own provision in these areas to see where they can be improved.

Lead companies may also be analyzed for the ways in which they not only manage their internal human resources but also the ways in which they interact with external sources of labor.

For example: Many airlines close skills gaps by making extensive use of contract workers, 'outsource' some of their work to outside suppliers or use consultants. The ability to attract these 'mobile' workers can be just as important as attracting permanent employees.

4.5.3 *Human resources as critical success factors*

In addition to using a human resource audit to identify gaps, it can be used to establish which, if any, employees or groups of employees are critical to strategic success. These are the people that the organization's success may have been built on in the past, and it is likely that the existing structures are centered on them.

THINK POINTS

- What is the purpose of a human resource audit applied to *THE* organizations?
- What is a human resource gap, and how might the gaps be addressed by *THE* organizations?
- Explain what a human resource audit analyzes.
- Consider what the potential difficulties of a human resource audit are in relation to *THE* organizations.
- What is human resource benchmarking, and when might *THE* organizations use the technique?
- What are critical success factors?
- What are the potential difficulties with the human resource audit approach?
- What is human resource benchmarking? When might an organization use this technique?
- What is a critical success factor?

In some organizations, critical human resources may be found on the board of directors, giving strategic direction to the company as a whole. In others, they might be found in research and development, developing the new products upon which the future success will be built. Certain marketing personnel or operations managers might also be critical in some businesses.

> For example: *In some tour operators, the management of the operational aspects of tours may involve local knowledge and experience of destination areas and individual suppliers. Similarly, the organization of events such as concerts or festivals might involve the use of highly specialist staff with a range of skills such as lighting and sound engineers, stage managers, etc.*

This knowledge and experience may be held by key individuals whose sudden loss to a company could cause operational problems. Well-managed companies try to reduce this risk through measures such as documented procedures, contractual arrangements, rotating staff to widen the experience base, incentive policies for key staff and training and development procedures. These CSFs have been examined in *THE* contexts; see, for example, Getz (2004), Baker and Cameron (2008), Marais et al. (2017) and Marneros et al. (2020).

KEY CONCEPT

Critical success factors

It is usually the case that there are one or more reasons why superior performers in an industry are in the position that they are. These key reasons for success are called critical success factors (CSFs). Some companies have uniquely skilled employees, such as particularly skilled financiers, product development specialists or staff selected and trained to give exceptional levels of customer service. In these cases, the CSF is a human resource. In other businesses, the CSF might be a unique location, a brand image, an enviable reputation, a legally protected patent or license or a unique production process or technology. This is not to say that other parts of the organization are unimportant but merely that the CSF is the key cause of the success.

In terms of competitive strategy, the approach to a CSF is to defend it – in some cases at whatever cost. This usually takes the form of 'locking it in' to ensure that the advantage is maintained or that competitors are prevented from gaining the same advantage. If the CSF is in the form of a human resource, this might involve contractual arrangements providing financial incentives, long periods of notice to leave the company or the right working environment to motivate employees.

The importance of human resources as critical success factors in a business and the steps that may be taken to motivate, train and retain key staff are illustrated in the following Short Case Illustration of China's fast-growing Home Inns chain.

4.5 SHORT CASE ILLUSTRATION

Critical success factors: China's Home Inns

International hotel groups from North America and Europe announce new hotel projects in China on a nearly daily basis, and they occupy prominent sites in leading Chinese cities. However, Chinese-controlled hotel brands continue to dominate this massive, fast-developing market. The market is becoming highly competitive, particularly in the 'budget' segment (considered by Chan and Ni, 2011), though hotel groups such as Jinjiang hotels are also providing strong competition for foreign competitors in star-rated properties.

The leading chains are opening new properties at an astonishing rate, but in 2013 the largest hotel chain (according to: www.tophotelchains.com), with about 2,600 properties, is the Shanghai-based company Home Inns. Large budget chains include:

- Home Inns
- Jinjiang Inns and Jinjiang Hotels
- Green Tree Hotels
- Huazhu Hotels Group and their brands Hanting Inns and Hotels
- 7 Days Inn

Home Inns (part of the BTG group), for example, has tapped into the biggest potential market in China: domestic budget tourism. The style of the typical Home Inn is simple yet unique and certainly eye-catching. 'Its multi-story buildings have bright yellow exteriors, which are highly visible in crowded cities. Bright colors are also on display in the interiors: pink bedspreads and orange walls provide a pleasant and cosy feeling' (Zhang et al., 2013:425).

In their paper, Zhang et al. (2013) discussed the academic literature concerning CSFs and attempted to identify the relevant CSFs in the case of Home Inns (by way of contrast, Avcikurt et al. [2011] examined CSFs in a Turkish hotel context).

Although other CSFs were identified, two of the key success factors identified related to people and culture. The Chief Executive David Sun, in stressing that people are central to business success, said, 'The design, concept, and even strategies and techniques can be easily copied by others, while the core of the organization – people, cannot be duplicated in the same manner' (Zhang et al., 2013:433).

The provision of training and development opportunities for employees together with a supportive corporate culture appear to have aided retention and resulted in a comparatively low staff turnover rate of under 25%. Early in its development, Home Inns established training and development programs hosted at the Educational Institute of Home Inns in Shanghai. It is reported that new employees can be developed into unit managers within three to six years.

Culture, as the term suggests, is not something that can be directly seen or touched but is a strong invisible force for both customers and employees. Home Inns provides a written promise to create a home-like environment for customers and employees and seems to produce strong loyalty from employees. From all levels of management to the front-line workers, people in Home Inns appear to be approachable and easy to communicate with, and many employees report on the caring attitude of the company. David Sun (CEO) said, 'It is a very simple idea – if you want to keep these people, you treat them nicely by providing a nice living environment, and draw them a clear career path. We create a sense of belonging, we respect our employees, and we get along harmoniously . . . . When the staff is happy, they stay.' One example is that free meals and accommodation are often provided for staff, which is perceived as a popular benefit in cities like Shanghai, where accommodation is expensive and many employees are from other areas of the country.

Sources: Adapted from Zhang et al. (2013); Ren (2018)

QUESTIONS

1. Explain what is meant by *critical success factors* and identify what you think they are in this case.

2. What issues in relation to human resources might China's Home Inns face when expanding in China or overseas?

4.6 Organizational culture

Culture is the organizational equivalent of a human's personality. As with human personality, organizational culture can be somewhat difficult to explain and define, and consequently many different definitions exist. Edward Schein, a well-known scholar in this field (Schein, 2016) provided one definition.

DEFINITION/QUOTATION

Organizational culture

A pattern of shared basic assumptions that a group learns as it solves its problems of external adaptation and internal integration, that has worked well enough to be considered valid and, therefore, to be taught to new members as the correct way to perceive, think and feel in relation to those problems.

(Schein, 2010:18)

According to Charles Handy, a leading writer on management, culture cannot be precisely defined, because in essence it is 'something that is perceived, something felt' (Handy, 1996).

Organizational culture can vary enormously from one organization to another, as Handy (1996) pointed out. Organizations are as different and varied as the nations and societies of the world. They have differing cultures – sets of values and norms and beliefs – reflected in different structures and systems. And the cultures are affected by the events of the past and by the climate of the present, by the technology of the type of work, by their aims and by the kind of people who work in them (Handy, 1996).

Culture can thus be explained in terms of the 'feel' of an organization or its 'character' or, as it has sometimes been described, as 'the way we do things round here'. Definitions can be a bit inaccessible, but the importance of an organization's culture lies in the fact that it can be 'felt' whenever it is encountered.

From a strategic point of view, the important point is that all organizations have some sort of culture and that the culture can have a significant effect on organizational performance. Consequently, *THE* managers must attempt to understand the culture of their organization and the effect it havs (positive or negative) on organizational performance. Managers may subsequently find it necessary to take steps to implement a program that attempts to change the prevailing culture to improve performance.

The principles relating to organizational culture have remained underresearched in relation to *THE* (Bavik, 2016; but see, for example, Kyriakidou and Gore, 2005; Getz et al., 2010; Tsang, 2011; Chen et al., 2012; Pizam, 2020; Gamage and Tajeddini, 2022).

Organizations are as individual as people, and in many ways there are as many cultures as there are organizations – each one is unique. This is not to say, however, that we cannot identify common features between organizational cultures.

4.6.1 The determinants of culture

The reason why an organization has a particular type of culture is as complicated a question as asking why a human has a particular personality. It has many possible influences, the net effects of which forge culture over a period of time. Any list would be necessarily incomplete, but the most important could include the:

- Philosophy of the organization's founders, especially if it is relatively young
- Nature of the activities in the business and the character of the industry it competes in
- Nature of the interpersonal relationships and the nature of industrial or employee relationships
- Management style adopted and the types of control mechanisms; for example, the extent to which management style is *autocratic* or *democratic*
- National or regional character of the areas in which the organization's activities are located. This, in turn, can affect the *power distance*, which also influences culture.
- Structure of the organization, particularly its *height* and *width* (see Chapter 10)
- Dependence the organization has on technology and the type of technology employed

---

KEY CONCEPT

Power distance

The term is used to describe how removed subordinates feel from their superiors in a social meaning of the word 'distance'. In a high-power distance culture, inequality is accepted. in a low-power distance culture, inequalities and overt status symbols are minimized and subordinates expect to be consulted and to share decisions with approachable managers.

4.6.2 Why is culture important?

Culture is important because it can, and does, affect all aspects of an organization's activities. The metaphor of human personality may help us to understand this. Some people's personality means they are motivated, sharp, exciting to be with, etc. Others are dull, tedious, apathetic and conservative. These personality features will affect all aspects of their lives.

The same is true of an organization's 'personality'. Culture is important because of the following (not exhaustive) reasons. Culture can have an influence on:

- Employee motivation
- The attractiveness of the organization as an employer and hence the rate of staff turnover
- Employee morale and goodwill
- Productivity and efficiency
- The quality of work
- The nature of the employee and industrial relations

- The attitude of employees in the workplace
- Innovation and creativity

The point to make after such a list is simply that culture is *very* important. It is essential that management understand organization for both analyzing the organization's strategic positioning and implementation of strategy.

Many *THE* organizations have recognized the central importance of developing a strong and consistently applied organizational culture. The development of a strong culture enables the organization concerned to strive to deliver consistent standards of service but can also be used as a promotional tool not only externally for customers but also internally for employees, giving them a sense of pride and motivation. The culture is often summed up in a short advertising slogan, many of which have become synonymous with the *THE* organization in question, such as 'Now Everyone Can Fly' (AirAsia), 'We Try Harder' (Avis) and 'Incredible India' (India Ministry of Tourism).

However, building a strong sense of organizational culture is difficult in organizations such as those in *THE*, which are often dispersed and operating internationally. Developing a strong sustainable culture that can help drive an organization forward successfully often takes a long period of time.

THINK POINTS

- Providing relevant examples from *THE*, explain what is meant by organizational culture.
- Explain why organizational culture is so important to the success of organizations.
- Assess which factors determine the culture of an organization.

Most organizations operating in *THE* operate in a continuing fashion aiming to trade successfully year after year and being able to develop a successful culture on that basis. In the events sector, however, this is often not the case, because events, such as major sporting events – for example, the 2020 Tokyo Olympic Games – may be organized on only one occasion by the host city, or festivals, exhibitions and conventions may be organized on a recurring basis once a year.

Nevertheless, the successful delivery of these events may rely heavily on instilling a strong organizational culture in the workforce and volunteers enabling the festival or event to be delivered successfully. Richards (2017) emphasized that a long-term perspective is required so that events shift from short-term happenings to long-term or recurring structures. These principles are now being recognized and applied by a growing number of 'eventful' cities and regions around the world. Wynn (2016) examined the use of 'festivalization' as a means of improving quality of life, citing US examples in Austin, Texas, Nashville, Tennessee, and Newport, Rhode Island.

The case of Edmonton, Canada, below illustrates the importance of recruiting a strong volunteer workforce to deliver events and festivals successfully.

4.6 SHORT CASE ILLUSTRATION

'Eventful cities': Edmonton, Canada

Many 'eventful cities' are placing festivals and events at the heart of their development and promotional strategies, recognizing the key role that they can have in developing positive images of a location and enhancing economic activity. By way of example, Richards and Palmer (2012) cited, among others, the cases of Melbourne, Australia, which has labeled itself as 'the world's event city'; Seoul, South Korea, which has claimed to be 'one of the most eventful cities in the world'; and Reno–Tahoe territory in Nevada, USA, which has promoted itself as 'the most eventful city in America'.

Among these cities promoting themselves in this way is Edmonton in Alberta, Canada, which refers to itself as 'Canada's Festivals City', setting itself in competition with other Canadian cities Montreal and Quebec City, which define themselves in similar terms (Richards and Palmer, 2012). Edmonton, a city of about 1 million people, is somewhat isolated from other large urban centers. Edmonton hosts an array of colorful, entertaining festivals every year, including Canada's largest folk music festival, and North America's largest and longest-running International Fringe Theatre Festival. In fall 2020, Explore Edmonton, Edmonton's destination marketing organization, embarked on a process to develop the city's first Tourism Master Plan, a 10-year framework aimed at providing a common vision for growth and investment with tourism industry partners. Edmonton's status as a host city for the FIFA World Cup in 2026 will serve to focus greater international attention on the city.

Like other cities that have limited promotional budgets, Edmonton has had to rely heavily on a volunteer workforce. Since adopting this strategy of promoting itself through its festivals provision to facilitate its festivals and event programs, Edmonton has promoted a strong culture of volunteering among the population.

Sources: Richards and Palmer (2012); www.exploreedmonton.com/

Questions

1. Consider the benefits and potential difficulties that volunteers bring to events such as those in Edmonton.

2. Consider how efficiently cities such as Edmonton are able to utilize resources in providing and managing events.

The centrality of a successful organizational culture is illustrated by the cases of two airlines illustrated over the next pages: Southwest Airlines in the USA and a later follower of the airline's cultural attributes in Canada, WestJet. Southwest Airlines explicitly (and famously) places employees at the heart of what they do. To Southwest it is a simple equation: 'happy employees = happy customers' www.southwest.com/

4.7 SHORT CASE ILLUSTRATION

Organizational culture: Southwest Airlines

The culture of Southwest Airlines, which emphasizes employees as the airline's 'first customers' and passengers as the second, has been integral to Southwest Airlines' success. Dallas-based Southwest has grown significantly and profitably since its first services in 1971 and continues to do so, drawing in thousands of employees new to the airline's ways and raising questions about whether it can keep its culture intact.

In 1990, the airline had 8,600 people on its payroll, which has now risen to about 55,000. As of February 2022, the airline had over 700 aircraft all of a single type – Boeing 737 (making the airline the world's largest user of this aircraft). The airline also has flown beyond its Texas roots into other regions of the USA and today it serves about 120 destinations in eight countries.

The airline is well known for its attempts to create a 'positive' organizational culture, and many initiatives aimed at employees have been initiated. In attempts to address its organizational culture, a committee focusing on new employees was created and as turnover edges up, an internal branding campaign reminds employees of the 'freedoms' that working at Southwest brings. The airline also is in the relatively new position of having to search for applicants rather than waiting for candidates to come to it.

It takes a lot of hard work to maintain the culture, but the airline regularly finds a place toward the top on lists of best companies to work for in America. Southwest's charismatic founder and former leader, Herb Kelleher, devoted much time and energy to creating and maintaining the company's distinctive corporate culture.

Southwest now challenges the major North American 'legacy' airlines such as American, United and Delta. Originally offering flights in a triangle between Dallas, San Antonio and Houston, the idea of offering fares so cheap that people would abandon their cars for jets has proved very attractive to consumers and has been widely copied. Its low-cost operating model has been copied and adapted by numerous airlines across the world, such as easyJet and Ryanair in Europe; AirAsia, Tiger Airways and Lion Airways in Asia; and FastJet and Gol in Africa and South America, respectively. The airline's core offering is many short flights between pairs of cities, though in recent years it has been offering more long flights. Reinforcing the low fares is a culture of relaxed professionalism that includes flight attendants who might crack jokes or burst into song.

Southwest's employees appear to understand what has made the airline succeed, which provides clarity of purpose at Southwest that makes it easy to retain the culture while growing.

Throughout the company, employees are encouraged to hold 'celebrations' to mark birthdays, engagements and other milestones. Creativity also is emphasized, especially when it comes to finding relief in high-stress jobs. Customer relations workers may come to work in pajamas for a day. Profit sharing ties employees directly to company performance. Southwest built an infrastructure that ensures that when an employee does something good, many of the organization's other employees know about it. The lives of Southwest employees, along with the company's history, are highlighted on the headquarters' walls, and 'special' days are held, such as a Halloween celebration on 31 October.

To help facilitate communications, a 'culture committee' was established in 1990 aiming to do what was necessary to create, enhance and enrich the Southwest spirit, and the committee now has been replicated across the company, with local culture committees having been also been established in cities across Southwest's network. In one way or another, the committee tries to ensure that fellow workers are appreciated and that people appreciate other difficulties involved with other people's positions. A committee focusing on new employees has also been added to make sure new employees are inducted appropriately and receive proper guidance and mentoring during their early careers.

The company is also paying more attention to employee retention as turnover creeps up: an internal branding campaign established eight 'basic freedoms' of working at Southwest.

Employees, the company says, get the freedom to pursue good health, travel, learn and grow, stay connected, have financial security, work and have fun, make a positive difference and be creative and innovative.

Sources: www.southwest.com

Questions

1. Explain the main features of Southwest's corporate culture.

2. Consider the difficulties that Southwest might have in maintaining its corporate culture as it grows and develops.

4.6.3 The cultural web

Because culture is so important to successful adoption of strategy and yet is difficult to define, understand and measure, it is important to have a model that provides some understanding. One of the most commonly used ways of making sense of an organization's culture is the cultural web (Johnson, 1992). It is a schematic representation of the elements of an organization's culture in such a way that we can see how each element influences the 'paradigm' (see Figure 4.3). Each component is interrelated and has an impact on the overall cultural paradigm of the organization.

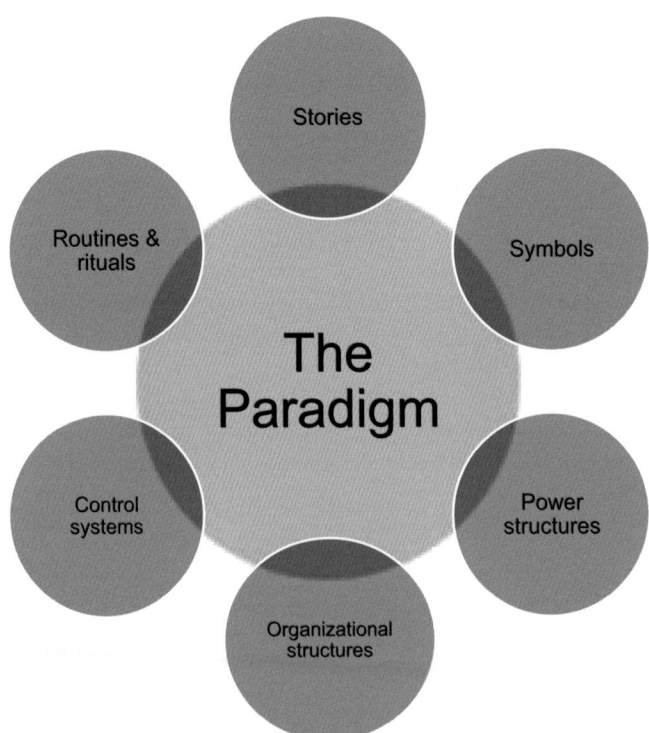

Figure 4.3 The cultural web

Source: Adapted from Johnson (1992)

Paradigm

A paradigm is a worldview – a way of looking at the world. It is expressed in the assumptions that people make and in their deep-rooted beliefs. The paradigm of an organization or a national culture is important because it determines how it will behave in a given circumstance. Given a certain moral dilemma or similar choice, we might expect the paradigms of a person living in one country or culture to lead them to arrive at different conclusions from those living in another country or culture. The aspects that cause one organizational culture to adopt one paradigm and another culture to espouse a different one are set out in the cultural web.

The main elements of the web are described below.

STORIES

Stories are those narratives that people within the organization talk to each other about and what they tell new recruits and outsiders about the organization. The stories typically recount events and people from the past and present – stories of famous victories and defeats. They tend to highlight what is considered important to the members of the organization.

ROUTINES AND RITUALS

Routines are the procedures for doing things within the organization. They are repeated on a regular basis to the extent to which they are taken as 'the way things are done'. Rituals have a longer time frame and can be either formal or informal. Formal routines and rituals are a part of the organization's practice, such as the 'long service award' or the company annual sporting event. Informal routines and rituals might include the way people behave at the annual Christmas party or the extent to which colleagues socialize (or not) after work.

SYMBOLS

Symbolic aspects concern those aspects that symbolize something to some people – a certain level of promotion, the company car they drive, the position of their office, their job title. In some companies, these symbols have no apparent importance at all. In others, they matter a great deal. How employees respond to these symbols can tell us a great deal about the culture.

STRUCTURE

The structure of an organization can mean more than just those formal relationships that are shown on an organization diagram. Informal structures can also exist through interpersonal relationships that transcend the formal structures. Some organizations have highly developed informal structures, whereas others do not.

CONTROL SYSTEMS

The ways in which activities are controlled, whether 'tight' or 'loose', is closely aligned to culture. This has a strong link to *power distance* and the nature of the activities the organization is engaged in. Control systems, by definition, concern activity in which performance is gauged against a predetermined standard, and the methods of both standard-setting and monitoring performance vary significantly according to culture.

POWER STRUCTURES

The core assumptions that contribute to the paradigm are likely to be made by the most powerful management groupings in the organization. In some companies, this power resides in the research department; in others, it will be the production people or those from another department. In some organizations, there may be arguments about what is important between one or more groupings.

Each component of the cultural web exerts its own influence on the organization's paradigm. The paradigm describes the aggregate effects of all of the cultural influences on how members of the organization look at the world.

4.8 SHORT CASE ILLUSTRATION

Application of the cultural web at WestJet

WestJet was founded in 1996 by a team of Calgary entrepreneurs as a western Canadian regional carrier with three aircraft flying to five cities. Today, the airline (Canada's second largest) offers scheduled service to over 70 destinations in Canada, the USA, Mexico and the Caribbean, with a modern fleet of over 100 Boeing 'Next-Generation' 737-series aircraft and a small number of larger Boeing 787 'dreamliner' aircraft. The airline's headquarters are in Calgary, which remains a major hub, though Toronto is the airline's largest hub.

WestJet is based on the low-cost carrier business model pioneered by Southwest Airlines and Morris Air in the USA. Its original routes were all located in western Canada, which gave the airline its name. In 2018, WestJet carried over 25 million passengers.

Stories

- Three used Boeing 737s at the start-up in 1996

- Early changes in senior management

- Taking on a well-established 'legacy' airline (Air Canada), which subsequently strengthened its dominant position with the purchase of Canadian Airlines (Canada's No. 2 airline at the time) in 2001

- Learning from other low-cost airlines and taking advantage of opportunities arising from North American airline deregulation

Symbols

- Aircraft are painted distinctively in white except for some lettering on parts of the aircraft.

- Calgary headquarters attained gold certification under the Leadership in Energy and Environmental Design (LEED) program.

- Winner of numerous awards; for example, named Canada's most trusted airline for domestic travel in 2021

Power structure

- Non-unionized, flexible workforce

- Many codeshare agreements with other airlines but not a member of any airline alliance
- 85% of employees are shareholders, giving rise to the advertising slogan 'Owners Care'.
- Head office in Canadian regional center, giving rise to strong loyalty in its home region.

Organizational structure

- Outsourcing some key business functions; for example, aircraft catering provided by local suppliers in major cities
- Strong emphasis on teamwork and WestJetters; contribution to business success 'Owners Care – sure, it's our aircraft that fly you places, but it's really our people who get you there' (www.westjet.com)
- Employee representative on the company's board of directors
- Strong leadership from experienced board of directors including a majority of nonexecutive directors

Control system

- Economies of scale through operating variants of the same aircraft type
- Extensive connectivity between the networks of WestJet and global partner airlines
- Strict adherence to budgeting, target setting and operating a 'low-cost' model
- Motivating WestJetters through share ownership scheme, competitive pay levels and other benefits

Rituals and routines

- Light-hearted attitude. Issued 'joke' press releases as part of first April Fool's Day; for example, the introduction of 'sleeper cabins' in overhead bins
- Strong ethos of community investment, environmental initiatives and sponsorship by the company and its 11,000 WestJetters (employees)
- Employees as 'owners'. 'We're looking to fill a number of positions, starting with Owner' (www.westjet.com)

Paradigm

- Value for money
- WestJetters' interests aligned with those of the company
- Growth with responsibility – to environment, communities and stakeholders

Source: Adapted from www.westjet.com

Questions

1. Consider what purpose is served by producing a cultural web for a company such as Westjet and how it might be utilized by managers.
2. Consider a *THE* organization you are familiar with and apply *the cultural web* analysis to it.

4.7 Cultural typologies

A number of writers in organizational theory have attempted to group culture types together. The thinking behind such attempts at a *typology* is that if organizations can describe their cultures by type, this would help in strategic analysis. We will briefly consider three of these attempts that might be useful in analyzing *THE* organizations in various contexts.

4.7.1 Handy's culture types

An influential writer Charles Handy (1996) suggested that organizational cultures could be divided into four broad types: power cultures, role cultures, task cultures and person cultures.

POWER CULTURES

This type of organization is dominated by either a very powerful individual or a small, dominant group. It is typified by an organization that has grown as a result of entrepreneurial flair. Strategic decisions and many operational ones are made by the center, and few decisions are devolved to other managers. Because the organization is dependent on the abilities and personality of the powerful individual, the ability of the organization to change in response to changes in the environment are sometimes limited by the center.

Power cultures are common in small entrepreneurial (owner-managed) companies and in some notable larger organizations with a charismatic leader.

ROLE CULTURES

This type of culture is found in many long-established organizations that have traditionally operated in stable environments. They tend to be very hierarchical and rely on established procedures, systems and precedent. They often respond slowly to change because it takes time for change to be recognized through the reporting mechanisms. Delays are also encountered in the slow, considered decision-making process.

Role cultures are common in traditional bureaucracies such as the civil service. The task of management in a role culture is to manage procedure. There is usually a high degree of decentralization and the organization is run by rules and established procedures.

TASK CULTURES

Task cultures are found in organizations engaged in activities of a nonrepetitive nature, often high-value, one-off tasks. Activities are normally based around flexible multidisciplinary teams with expertise in the major disciplines required to complete the project. Teams tend to be small but flexible and find change easy to identify and adjust to. Strategic planning tends to concentrate on the task at hand.

As their name suggests, task cultures can be found in organizations that are dedicated to a particular task. Consortia that work on large civil engineering projects may demonstrate task culture, as might missionary teams that work together on a medical project in the developing world.

PERSON CULTURES

Person cultures are those that exist primarily for the benefit of the members of the organization itself and, hence, they tend to be rare in commercial businesses. They can have a very different 'feel' to the other cultures because all members of the organizations work for the benefits of themselves and the other members.

They can be found in learned professional societies, in trade unions, in cooperatives, in some charities and in some religious organizations.

In reality, few organizations fit perfectly into just one classification, and they may demonstrate elements of two or more. Some diversified organizations may have divisions that fall into all categories and the cultures may change over time. Many start as power cultures and then tend toward a role culture as size increases.

In assessing the appropriateness of the four cultural types, three criteria might be used. Does the dominant culture identified:

- Fit with *prescriptive* or *emergent* forms of strategy formulation?
- Help deliver competitive advantage for the organization?
- Have the ability to cope with strategic change?

In assessing the four main cultural types, however, three important qualifications should be made:

1. Organizations change over time.
2. Several types or variations of culture often exist in the same organization as 'subcultures'.
3. Different cultures may predominate depending on the headquarters and ownership of the company.

4.7.2 Miles and Snow's culture types

Since its emergence, the typology of cultural types produced by Miles and Snow (1978) has been widely used and cited in the academic literature (see, for example, Desarbo et al., 2005; Anwar et al., 2021). Miles and Snow categorized cultures into four types, based on how they tend to react in strategic terms.

DEFENDERS

These organizations tend to seek a competitive advantage in terms of targeting niche markets through cost reduction and specialization. They tend to operate in stable, mature markets and, as the name suggests, they favor defending their current market share by service improvements or further cost savings. Defenders therefore tend to be centralized, have rigid control systems and have a hierarchical management structure that does not enjoy sudden change.

PROSPECTORS

These organizations enjoy the challenge of developing and introducing new products to the marketplace. They actively seek out new markets for their products. These favored strategies require them to constantly monitor the environment and be willing and able to respond to quickly to changes that may occur. To that end, they are decentralized and flexible.

ANALYZERS

These organizations are 'followers' and are conservative in nature. Steady growth through market penetration is the favored option because this can be achieved without radical changes to structure. Moves into new markets and products only occur after extensive evaluation and market research. They learn from the mistakes of others and tend to balance power between the center and divisions with complex control systems.

Table 4.2 Summary of the strategic implications of Miles and Snow's typology

Cultural type	Strategic implications	Environmental conditions	Organizational characteristics
Defenders	Hold on to current market position Retrench	Stable	Tight control Centralized Operational efficiency Low overheads
Prospectors	Innovate Find new market opportunities Grow Take risks	Dynamic and growing	Creative Innovative Flexible Decentralized
Analyzers	Maintain current market with moderate innovation	Moderate change	Tight control and flexibility Efficient operations Creativity
Reactors	No clear strategy React to specific conditions Drift	Any condition	No clear organizational approach Depends on current needs

REACTORS

Reactors are a bit like analyzers in that they tend to follow rather than innovate. They differ from analyzers in that they are less conservative and sometimes behave impulsively, having failed to fully consider the implications of their actions. These organizations may lack proper control systems and typically have a weak but dominant leader.

The four cultural types of Miles and Snow and their strategic implications are summarized in Table 4.2.

4.7.3 Hofstede's cross-cultural differences

Professor Geert Hofstede is an influential Dutch researcher in the field of organizational culture. His cross-cultural studies demonstrated that there are important national and regional cultural groups. The importance of these groups is that they exert a significant influence on the behavior of organizations (and societies more generally). THE is by its nature international in orientation, with organizations frequently operating across borders and working in various cultural contexts.

Consequently, it is important that managers in these sectors have an understanding of the influence of national culture and the effects the differences might have on the successful implementation of strategy (see, for example, Adekola and Sergi [2016] for a full discussion of the issues involved).

DEFINITION/QUOTATION

National culture

There is no single agreed definition of national culture, but to Hofstede (2010:6) it is:

> The collective programming of the mind which distinguishes the members of one human group from another . . . . Culture, in this sense, includes systems of values; and values are among the building blocks of culture.

Some have criticized Hofstede's work on methodological grounds, because his work was based largely on samples of employees from the company he worked for – IBM. See, for example, the critique by McSweeney (2002) and the overview by Williamson (2002). Furthermore, national cultures are subject to change over time, and important regional and ethnic variations within countries exist. In describing such cultures, it is clearly a possibility that national stereotyping will occur.

Nevertheless, his work has been widely cited, adapted by others and applied to particular circumstances. The concepts of Hofstede and others have been widely applied to cross-cultural studies in an attempt to understand why managers and employees in different parts of the world think and act in different ways.

Hickson and Pugh (2001), for example, building on the work of Hofstede and others, usefully provided an analytical journey around the world when they considered managerial and organizational differences in different parts of the world. Though arguably somewhat dated, in individual chapters they distinguished between managerial differences of 'the Anglos', the 'Latins', the 'Northern Europeans', the 'East Central Europeans', the 'Asians', the 'Arabs of the Middle East', and the 'Developing Countries'.

THINK POINTS

- Explain the concept of the cultural web and describe its components as applied in a *THE* context.

- Explain what is meant by the terms power distance and paradigm.

- Describe Handy's and Miles and Snow's cultural typologies and assess the usefulness of the concepts to *THE* organizations.

- Explain why an understanding of Hofstede's work is important to international managers operating in *THE* organizations.

Hofstede is best known for his work in developing his 'cultural dimensions theory', which encapsulates five dimensions that are considered in Table 4.3.

There are a number of strategic considerations that are raised by the outcomes of Hofstede's work that managers operating in *THE* might need to be aware of when formulating and implementing their strategic plans. These considerations might include:

- For organizations operating in one national market: *THE* employees may come from a range of countries and different cultural backgrounds, and differences in their attitudes and motivations might need to be considered when designing aspects of the strategy to be implemented,

  For example: *It is quite common for many employees at UK hotels to come from elsewhere, particularly from Eastern Europe and Mediterranean countries.*

Part 2

Table 4.3 Summary of Hofstede's cultural dimensions

Cultural dimension	Description	Findings
Power distance	• Extent to which the poorest in society are willing to accept their position or countries in which inequalities are less acceptable	• Countries such as Panama, Malaysia and Venezuela were found to accept such inequalities, whereas countries such as Ireland, Israel, Denmark and Sweden found inequalities less acceptable.
Individualism/ collectivism	• Extent to which countries are collections of individuals or are bound together as a cohesive whole	• The more individual countries included USA, UK, Australia and Netherlands, whereas South American countries tended more toward collectivism.
Masculinity vs femininity	• Extent to which countries are placed on a spectrum from masculinity to femininity	• In male-dominant cultures, there is a sharp distinction between genders, with males expected to emphasize work, power and wealth. In other cultures, there is more equality. Japan, Austria and Italy tended toward greater masculinity, whereas countries such as Sweden, Netherlands and Finland are more feminine
Uncertainty avoidance	• Extent to which members of a culture feel threatened by the unknown	• In countries where uncertainty avoidance is weak, people are willing to embrace uncertainty and ambiguous situations: precision and punctuality for meetings, for instance, were useful but not essential. These countries included Singapore, Denmark, Jamaica and Hong Kong. • On the other hand, in strong uncertainty avoidance countries, people appear to need certainty, planning and order. These cultures included those in Japan, Portugal, Greece and Belgium.
Long-termism versus short-termism	• Hofstede later added this category • It relates to the extent to which different cultures have different time horizons – long-termism versus short-termism	• Long-termism stresses the importance of taking a long view and adapting traditions to a modern context while stressing perseverance. China, Hong Kong and South Korea are examples of long termism. • Short-termism stresses the importance of quick results as well as social obligations and status. Short-termism is typified by the USA, Nigeria, the UK and Canada.

• For organizations with a range of operations in different countries: There might be a need to devise a strategy taking into account not only central headquarter issues but also local cultures styles, values and expectations.

> **For example**: *Mission statements might have to be adapted and the rate of strategic change adjusted to local circumstances.*

There might also be a need in such companies (or those with global operations) to find ways of bringing together and integrating the many cultures that exist. This might involve special integration programs to break down barriers. However, as we saw in Chapter 1, *heterogeneity* is often valued by *THE* consumers, so many companies operating in diverse international settings stress the common culture across the company but also the recognition of local cultures in their products as a way of differentiating their product offerings.

A number of authors have applied Hofstede's cross-cultural research to *THE* settings, including Reisinger and Crotts (2010), Rinuastuti et al. (2014), Li (2014), Mazanec et al. (2015) and Huang and Crotts (2019).

> For example: *Reisinger and Crotts (2010) applied Hofstede's analysis specifically to tourism. Drawing from a sample of tourists from eight countries (Australia, Greece, the UK, the USA, China, Indonesia, Malaysia and Singapore) that completed Hofstede's original survey instruments, the results showed strong support for Hofstede's national cultural measures in that only minor differences were revealed between with their study and Hofstede's work. This finding provides strong support for Hofstede's dimensions as a measure of central tendencies of visitors from different nations.*
>
> *Reisinger and Crotts (2010) also identified graphically contrasting respondents' values along the five cultural dimensions revealing that the 'between-nation' differences are relatively small when compared to the 'within-nation' variability, thus indicating that subcultures do exist within countries. The analysis also identified international regions that cluster closely together, demonstrating that national cultural differences do not end at national borders.*

Small business focus

Human resource management frequently raises particular strategic challenges for managers in smaller *THE* organizations. 'The very size of small businesses creates a special condition – which can be referred to as resource poverty – that distinguishes them from their larger counterparts and requires some very different management approaches' (Welsh and White, 1981:18). In relation to human resources, Urbano and Yordanova (2008), writing in a Spanish tourism context, argued that there are several difficulties smaller companies may face relative to larger competitors. SMEs may:

- Have less access to formal training opportunities
- Be unlikely to have human resource departments dedicated to resolving human resource issues
- Have owners and managers who are likely to combine human resources responsibility with other responsibilities
- Have more limited financial resources, limiting the adoption of costly human resource management practices
- Encounter difficulties in pursuing new approaches to people management owing to lack of information about the developments in human resources management in other companies
- Encounter problems in competing for labor with larger organizations and recruiting and training employees

Though the factors outlined above are no doubt important (and there may be others), small businesses need to design strategies to overcome the difficulties encountered and to build on other factors that might be advantageous for SMEs. For example, smaller businesses might seek to overcome their size disadvantages by:

- Working cooperatively in alliances to share resources
- Forming trade associations to share knowledge and best practices
- 'Clustering' together to achieve economies of scale in relation to aspects such as marketing and purchasing
- Using technology (such as internet applications) effectively; for example, in communicating with customers directly and providing training for employees

Notwithstanding some of the potential disadvantages smaller organizations might have relative to larger competitors, they may also have potential advantages in relation to their human resources. The task for *THE* managers in smaller organizations is then to identify these advantages and maximize their potential in the strategies they adopt. Despite extensive training and development, active policies, extensive marketing, public relations and brand building and managerial actions, larger companies frequently find it difficult to be viewed as responsive, friendly and customer focused and as having consistent service standards.

THE owners, managers and employees working in smaller organizations may be able to differentiate themselves by exhibiting superior:

- Customer knowledge
- Responsiveness to enquiries and complaints
- Development of long-lasting relationships encouraging repeat business
- Attention to detail
- Culture that is consistent across the organization and consistent with the vision and values of owners and senior managers
- Consistent and reliable standards across the organization
- Friendliness and ability to leave the customer feeling important and reassured

In addition, SMEs may be able to foster high standards of service delivery and foster a service-oriented culture by the direct day-to-day involvement of owners and managers. Rather than being remote (as in some larger organizations), managers and owners who are directly involved can seek to foster high standards.

In particular owners and managers are on hand to:

- Monitor and experience the standards directly
- Make changes quickly when required
- Impose a sense of urgency and importance when customer problems arise
- Make decisions directly and deploy necessary resources when required
- Ensure that employees are appropriately rewarded and motivated

CHAPTER SUMMARY

Both human resources and organizational culture are important parts of strategic analysis for *THE* organizations. An understanding of both of these areas is a vital part of internal analysis. The state of an organization's human resources can be assessed by using a human resource audit – a tool that has its limitations, particularly in respect of measuring intangible aspects like job satisfaction, employee morale and motivation. Nevertheless, it enables gaps (positive or negative) to be identified, the closing of which is among the issues that the strategy to be implemented must address.

Because *THE* sectors are usually highly labor intensive, it is the human resources of an organization that can frequently represent the key differentiator between organizations. In particular, the quality of the service provided in customer (or guest)/employee encounters is often critical.

The configuration of human resources in an organization is a major determinant of its culture. We can think of an organization's culture as its personality, and we can use the cultural web to analyze it. We also encountered two ways of subdividing culture types (Handy; Miles and Snow). These can also be useful tools in strategic analysis. *THE* represent highly international sectors of industry with employees of differing cultural backgrounds. It is important that cultural differences and the management implications that arise from them be recognized. This chapter considered the work of Hofstede as a way of analyzing this aspect.

REFERENCES AND WEBSITES

References

Abou-Shouk, M. A., Mannaa, M. T. and Elbaz, A. M. (2021) 'Women's empowerment and tourism development: A cross-country study', *Tourism Management Perspectives*, 37: 100782.

Adekola, A. and Sergi, B. S. (2016) *Global Business Management: A Cross-Cultural Perspective*, Abingdon, UK: Routledge.

Aghazamani, Y. and Hunt, C. A. (2017) 'Empowerment in tourism: A review of peer-reviewed literature', *Tourism Review International*, 21(4): 333–346.

Albrecht, K. (1992) *The Only Thing That Matters: Bringing the Customer to the Center of Your Business*, New York: Harper Business.

Alshaibani, E. and Bakir, A. (2017) 'A reading in cross-cultural service encounter: Exploring the relationship between cultural intelligence, employee performance and service quality', *Tourism and Hospitality Research*, 17(3): 249–263.

Anwar, J., Hasnu, S. A. F., Butt, I. and Ahmed, N. (2021) 'Miles and Snow typology: Most influential journals, articles, authors and subject areas', *Journal of Organizational Change Management*, 34(2): 385–402.

Augustyn, M. and Ho, S. K. (1998) 'Service quality and tourism', *Journal of Travel Research*, 37(1): 71–75.

Avcikurt, C., Altay, H. and Ilban, O. (2011) 'Critical success factors for small hotel businesses in Turkey, an exploratory study', *Cornell Hospitality Quarterly*, 52(2): 153–164.

Baker, M. J. and Cameron, E. (2008) 'Critical success factors in destination marketing' *Tourism and Hospitality Research*, 8(2): 79–97.

Baum, T. (1995) *Managing Human Resources in the European Hospitality and Tourism Industry – A Strategic Approach*, London: Chapman & Hall.

Baum, T. (1997) 'Making or breaking the tourist experience: The role of human resource management', in C. Ryan (Ed.), *The Tourist Experience – A New Introduction*, London: Cassell, 92–111.

Baum, T. (2015) 'Human resources in tourism: Still waiting for change? – A 2015 reprise', *Tourism Management*, 50: 204–212.

Baum, T. and Ndiuini, A. (2020) *Sustainable Human Resource Management in Tourism: African Perspectives*, Cham, Switzerland: Springer.

Bavik, A. (2016) 'Developing a new hospitality industry organizational culture scale', *International Journal of Hospitality Management*, 58: 44–55.

Bennington, L. and Cumane, J. (1998) 'Measuring service quality: A hybrid methodology', *Total Quality Management*, 6: 395–406.

Berry, L. L. and Parasuraman, A. (1991) *Marketing Services*, New York: The Free Press.

Bitner, M. J., Booms, B. H. and Mohr, L. A. (1994) 'Critical service encounters: The employee's viewpoint', *Journal of Marketing*, 58(October): 95–106.

Part 2

Boella, M. and Goss-Turner, S. (2019) *Human Resource Management in the Hospitality Industry: A Guide to Best Practice*, 10th ed., Abingdon, UK: Routledge.

Bowdin, G., Allen, J., Harris, R., McDonnell, I. and O'Toole, W. (2012) *Events Management*, London: Routledge.

Burke, R. J. and Hughes, J. C. (Eds) (2018) *Handbook of Human Resource Management in the Tourism and Hospitality Industries*, Cheltenham, UK: Edward Elgar.

Carlsson-Wall, M., Kraus, K. and Karlsson, L. (2017) 'Management control in pulsating organisations – A multiple case study of popular culture events', *Management Accounting Research*, 35: 20–34.

Carlzon, J. (1987) *Moments of Truth*, Cambridge, MA: Ballinger.

Chan, W.W. and Ni, S. (2011) 'Growth of budget hotels in China: Antecedents and future', *Asia Pacific Journal of Tourism Research*, 16(3): 249–262.

Chathoth, P. K., Ungson, G. R., Harrington, R. J. and Chan, E. S. W. (2016) 'Co-creation and higher order customer engagement in hospitality and tourism services: A critical review', *International Journal of Contemporary Hospitality Management*, 28(2): 222–245.

Chen, R. X., Cheung, C. and Law, R. (2012) 'A review of the literature on culture in hotel management research: What is the future?', *International Journal of Hospitality Management*, 31(1): 52–65.

Cheung, C., Baum, T. and Wong, A. (2012) 'Relocating empowerment as a management concept for Asia', *Journal of Business Research*, 65(1): 36–41.

Crick, A. P. and Spencer, A. (2011) 'Hospitality quality: New directions and new challenges', *International Journal of Contemporary Hospitality Management*, 23(4): 463–478.

Deery, M. (2008) 'Talent management, work – life balance and retention strategies', *International Journal of Contemporary Hospitality Management*, 20(7): 792–806.

Deery, M. (2009) 'Employee retention strategies for events management', in T. Baum, M. Deery, C. Hanlon, L. Lockstone and K. Smith (Eds), *People and Work in Events and Conventions*, Oxford, UK: CABI, 127–137.

Desarbo, W. S., Di Benedetto, C. A., Song, M. and Sinha, I. (2005) 'Revisiting the Miles and Snow strategic framework: Uncovering interrelationships between strategic types, capabilities, environmental uncertainty, and firm performance', *Strategic Management Journal*, 26(1): 47–74.

Dhar, R. L. (2015) 'Service quality and the training of employees: The mediating role of organizational commitment', *Tourism Management*, 46: 419–430.

Duncan, T., Scott, D. G. and Baum, T. (2013) 'The mobilities of hospitality work: An exploration of issues and debates', *Annals of Tourism Research*, 41: 1–19.

Dwesini, N. F. (2019) 'Causes and prevention of high employee turnover within the hospitality industry: A literature review', *African Journal of Hospitality, Tourism and Leisure*, 8(3): 1–15.

Eid, R. and Abdelkader, A. A. (2017) 'Muslim service quality dimensions in the tourism and hospitality industry: Construct development and measurement validation', *International Journal of Islamic Marketing and Branding*, 2(3): 215–231.

Evans, N. G. (2012) 'Tourism: A strategic business perspective', in T. Jamal and M. Robinson (Eds), *The Sage Handbook of Tourism Studies*, Thousand Oaks, CA: Sage, 215–234.

Gamage, T. C. and Tajeddini, K. (2022) 'A multi-layer organizational culture framework for enhancing the financial performance in tourism and hospitality family firms', *Tourism Management*, 91: 104516.

García-Lillo, F., Claver-Cortés, E., Úbeda-García, M., Marco-Lajara, B. and Zaragoza-Sáez, P. C. (2018) 'Mapping the "intellectual structure" of research on human resources in the "tourism and hospitality management scientific domain": Reviewing the field and shedding light on future directions', *International Journal of Contemporary Hospitality Management*, 30(3): 1741–1768.

Getz, D. (2004) 'Bidding on events: Identifying event selection criteria and critical success factors', *Journal of Convention and Exhibition Management*, 5(2): 1–24.

Getz, D., Andersson, T. and Carlsen, J. (2010) 'Festival management studies: Developing a framework and priorities for comparative and cross-cultural research', *International Journal of Event and Festival Management*, 1(1): 29–59.

Goel, P., Kaushik, N., Sivathanu, B., Pillai, R. and Vikas, J. (2022) 'Consumers' adoption of artificial intelligence and robotics in hospitality and tourism sector: Literature review and future research agenda', *Tourism Review*, online ahead of print.

Grönroos, C. (1984) 'A service quality model and its marketing implications', *European Journal of Marketing*, 18(4): 36–44.

Han, J. W. (2020) 'A review of antecedents of employee turnover in the hospitality industry on individual, team and organizational levels', *International Hospitality Review*, online ahead of print, https://doi.org/10.1108/IHR-09-2020-0050

Handy, C. B. (1996) *Understanding Organizations*, 4th ed., London: Penguin.

Hanlon, C. and Jago, L. (2004) 'The challenge of retaining personnel in major sport event organizations', *Event Management*, 9(1–2): 1–2.

Hawkins, C. J. and Bonney, M. S. (2019) 'Lean thinking in leisure: Continuously improving event volunteering and management', *Annals of Leisure Research*, 22(3): 362–372.

Hayes, D. K. and Ninemeier, J. D. (2016) *Human Resources Management in the Hospitality Industry*, 2nd ed., Hoboken, NJ: John Wiley & Sons.

Hickson, D. J. and Pugh, D. S. (2001) *Management Worldwide*, 2nd ed., London: Penguin.

Hoang, G., Wilson-Evered, E., Lockstone-Binney, L. and Luu, T. T. (2021) 'Empowering leadership in hospitality and tourism management: A systematic literature review', *International Journal of Contemporary Hospitality Management*, 33(12): 4182–4214.

Hofstede, G. (2010) *Culture and Organizations: Software of the Mind*, 3rd ed., New York: McGraw-Hill.

Holmes, K., Lockstone-Binney, L., Smith, K. A. and Shipway, R. (Eds). (2021) *The Routledge Handbook of Volunteering in Events, Sport and Tourism*, Abingdon, UK: Routledge.

Huang, S. S. and Crotts, J. (2019) 'Relationships between Hofstede's cultural dimensions and tourist satisfaction: A cross-country cross-sample examination', *Tourism Management*, 72: 232–241.

Hudson, S. and Hudson, L. (2022) *Customer Service in Tourism and Hospitality*, Oxford, UK: Goodfellow Publishers.

Jabeen, F., Al Zaidi, S. and Al Dhaheri, M. H. (2022) 'Automation and artificial intelligence in hospitality and tourism', *Tourism Review*, 77(4): 1043–1061.

Johnson, G. (1992) 'Managing strategic change: Strategy, culture and action' *Long Range Planning*, 25(1): 28–36.

Kandampully, J. (2000) 'The impact of demand fluctuation on the quality of service: A tourism industry example', *Managing Service Quality: An International Journal*, 10(1): 10–19.

Kusluvan, S., Kusluvan, Z., Ilhan, I. and Buyruk, L. (2010) 'The human dimension: A review of human resources management issues in the tourism and hospitality industry', *Cornell Hospitality Quarterly*, 51(2): 171–214.

Kyriakidou, O. and Gore, J. (2005) 'Learning by example: Benchmarking organizational culture in hospitality, tourism and leisure SMEs', *Benchmarking: An International Journal*, 12(3): 192–206.

Lado, A. A. and Wilson, M. C. (1994) 'Human resource systems and sustained competitive advantage: A competency-based perspective', *Academy of Management Review*, 19(4): 699–727.

Lai, I. K., Hitchcock, M., Yang, T. and Lu, T. W. (2018) 'Literature review on service quality in hospitality and tourism (1984–2014): Future directions and trends', *International Journal of Contemporary Hospitality Management*, 30(1): 114–159.

Leiper, N. (1990) 'Tourist attraction systems', *Annals of Tourism Research*, 17: 367–384.

Li, M. (2014) 'Cross-cultural tourist research: A meta-analysis', *Journal of Hospitality and Tourism Research*, 38(1): 40–77.

Lin, M., Wu, X. and Ling, Q. (2017) 'Assessing the effectiveness of empowerment on service quality: A multi-level study of Chinese tourism firms', *Tourism Management*, 61: 411–425.

Liu, A. and Wall, G. (2005) 'Human resources development in China', *Annals of Tourism Research*, 32(3): 689–710.

Madera, J. M., Dawson, M., Guchait, P. and Belarmino, A. M. (2017) 'Strategic human resources management research in hospitality and tourism: A review of current literature and suggestions for the future', *International Journal of Contemporary Hospitality Management*, 29(1): 48–67.

Marais, M., du Plessis, E. and Saayman, M. (2017) 'A review on critical success factors in tourism', *Journal of Hospitality and Tourism Management*, 31: 1–12.

Marneros, S., Papageorgiou, G. and Efstathiades, A. (2020) 'Identifying key success competencies for the hospitality industry: The perspectives of professionals', *Journal of Teaching in Travel and Tourism*, 20(4): 237–261.

Mazanec, J. A., Crotts, J. C., Gursoy, D. and Lu, L. (2015) 'Homogeneity versus heterogeneity of cultural values: An item-response theoretical approach applying Hofstede's cultural dimensions in a single nation', *Tourism Management*, 48: 299–304.

McSweeney, B. (2002) 'Hofstede's model of national cultural differences and the consequences: A triumph of faith – A failure of analysis', *Human Relations*, 55: 89–118.

Miles, R. E. and Snow, C. C. (1978) *Organizational Strategy, Structure and Process*, New York: McGraw Hill.

Mill, R. C. (2011) 'A comprehensive model of customer satisfaction in hospitality and tourism: Strategic implications for management', *International Business and Economics Research Journal*, 1(6): 7–18.

Mullins, L. J. and Dossor, P. (2013) *Hospitality Management and Organizational Behaviour*, 5th ed., Harlow, UK: Pearson.

Murray, W. C. and Holmes, M. R. (2021) 'Impacts of employee empowerment and organizational commitment on workforce sustainability', *Sustainability*, 13(6): 3163.

Muskat, B. and Mair, J. (2020) 'Managing the event workforce: Analysing the heterogeneity of job experiences', in V. V. Cuffy, F. E. Bakas and W. J. L. Coetzee (Eds), *Events Tourism: Critical Insights and Contemporary Perspectives*, Abingdon, UK: Routledge, ch. 3.

Naumov, N. (2019) 'The impact of robots, artificial intelligence, and service automation on service quality and service experience in hospitality', in S. Ivanov and C. Webster (Eds), *Robots, Artificial Intelligence, and Service Automation in Travel, Tourism and Hospitality*, Bingley, UK: Emerald, 123–133.

Nickson, D. (2013) *Human Resource Management for Hospitality, Tourism and Events*, Abingdon, UK: Routledge.

Park, J. and Jeong, E. (2019) 'Service quality in tourism: A systematic literature review and keyword network analysis', *Sustainability*, 11(13): 3665.

Pelit, E. and Katircioglu, E. (2022) 'Human resource management studies in hospitality and tourism domain: A bibliometric analysis', *International Journal of Contemporary Hospitality Management*, 34(3): 1106–1134.

Pizam, A. (2020) 'Hospitality as an organizational culture', *Journal of Hospitality and Tourism Research*, 44(3): 431–438.

Qi, H., Smith, K. A. and Yeoman, I. (2018) 'Cross-cultural event volunteering: Challenge and intelligence', *Tourism Management*, 69: 596–604.

Rauch, D. A., Collins, M. D., Nale, R. D. and Barr, P. B. (2015) 'Measuring service quality in mid-scale hotels', *International Journal of Contemporary Hospitality Management*, 27(1): 87–106.

Reisinger, Y. and Crotts, J. C. (2010) 'Applying Hofstede's national culture measures in tourism research: Illuminating issues of divergence and convergence', *Journal of Travel Research*, 49(2): 153–164.

Ren, L. (2018) 'Budget hotels in China: Recent development, changes, and challenges', in J. Zhao (Ed.), *The Hospitality and Tourism Industry in China*, Waretown, NJ: Apple Academic Press, 21–34.

Richards, G. (2017) 'Emerging models of the eventful city', *Event Management*, 21(5): 533–543.

Richards, G. and Palmer, R. (2012) *Eventful Cities*, Abingdon UK: Routledge.

Riley, M. (2014) *Human Resource Management in the Hospitality and Tourism Industry*, 2nd ed., Abingdon, UK: Routledge.

Rinuastuti, H., Hadiwidjojo, D., Rohman, F. and Khusniyah, N. (2014) 'Measuring Hofstede's five cultural dimensions at individual level and its application to researchers in tourists' behaviors', *International Business Research*, 7(12): 143–152.

Ro, H. and Chen, P. J. (2011) 'Empowerment in hospitality organizations: Customer orientation and organizational support', *International Journal of Hospitality Management*, 30(2): 422–428.

Rosete, A., Soares, B., Salvadorinho, J., Reis, J. and Amorim, M. (2020) 'Service robots in the hospitality industry: An exploratory literature review', presented at Exploring Service Science: 10th International Conference, Porto, Portugal, 5–7 February.

Ruhanen, L. and Cooper, C. (2016) 'Human resource and labor issues in Asian tourism', in C. M. Hall and S. J. Page (Eds), *The Routledge Handbook of Tourism in Asia*, Abingdon, UK: Routledge, 65–76.

Sabiote-Ortiz, C. M., Frías-Jamilena, D. M. and Castañeda-García, J. A. (2016) 'Overall perceived value of a tourism service delivered via different media: A cross-cultural perspective', *Journal of Travel Research*, 55(1): 34–51.

Schein, E. H. (2010) *Organizatonal Culture and Leadership*, 4th ed., San Francisco, CA: Josey Bass.

Sipe, L. J. and Testa, M. R. (2018) 'From satisfied to memorable: An empirical study of service and experience dimensions on guest outcomes in the hospitality industry', *Journal of Hospitality Marketing and Management*, 27(2): 178–195.

Skille, E. Å., Syversen, T. L. and Vidar Hanstad, D. (2020) 'A one-off event and the construction of organisational identity: The case of The 2016 Lillehammer Youth Olympic Games Committee', *European Journal for Sport and Society*, 17(1): 11–25.

Sørensen, F. and Jensen, J. F. (2015) 'Value creation and knowledge development in tourism experience encounters', *Tourism Management*, 46: 336–346.

Soutar, G. N. (2001) 'Service quality, customer satisfaction and value: An examination of their relationships', *Service Quality Management in Hospitality, Tourism and Leisure*, 15(4): 97–110.

Su, L., Swanson, S. R. and Chen, X. (2016) 'The effects of perceived service quality on repurchase intentions and subjective well-being of Chinese tourists: The mediating role of relationship quality' *Tourism Management*, 52: 82–95.

Swanson, S. R. and Hsu, M. K. (2009) 'Critical incidents in tourism: Failure, recovery, customer switching, and word-of-mouth behaviors', *Journal of Travel and Tourism Marketing*, 26(2): 180–194.

Tkaczynski, A. and Stokes, R. (2010) 'Festperf: A service quality measurement scale for festivals', *Event Management*, 14(1): 69–82.

Tsang, N. K. (2011) 'Dimensions of Chinese culture values in relation to service provision in hospitality and tourism industry', *International Journal of Hospitality Management*, 30(3): 670–679.

Tuomi, A., Tussyadiah, I. and Stienmetz, J. (2019) 'Leveraging LEGO® Serious Play® to embrace AI and robots in tourism', *Annals of Tourism Research*, 81: 102736.

Ueno, A. (2008) 'Is empowerment really a contributory factor to service quality?', *The Service Industries Journal*, 28(9): 1321–1335.

Ulrich, D. (1998) 'A new mandate for human resources', *Harvard Business Review*, 76: 124–135.

Urbano, D. and Yordanova, D. (2008) 'Determinants of the adoption of HRM practices in tourism SMEs in Spain: An exploratory study', *Service Business*, 2(3): 167–185.

Van der Wagen, L. and White, L. (2014) *Human Resource Management for the Event Industry*, 2nd ed., Abingdon, UK: Routledge.

Weiermair, K. (2000) 'Tourists' perceptions towards and satisfaction with service quality in the cross-cultural service encounter: Implications for hospitality and tourism management', *Managing Service Quality*, 10(6): 397–409.

Welsh, J. and White, J. (1981) 'A small business is not a little big business', *Harvard Business Review*, 59(4): 8–32.

Williamson, D. (2002) 'Forward from a critique of Hofstede's model of national culture', *Human Relations*, 55(11): 1373–1395.

WTTC. (2021) *Global Economic Impact and Trends 2021*, London: World Travel and Tourism Council, www.wttc.org

Wynn, J. R. (2016) *Music/City: American Festivals and Placemaking in Austin, Nashville, and Newport*, Chicago: University of Chicago Press.

Yang, L., Henthorne, T. L. and George, B. (2020) 'Artificial intelligence and robotics Technology in the Hospitality Industry: Current applications and future trends', in B. George and J. Paul (Eds), *Digital Transformation in Business and Society: Theory and Cases*, Cham, Switzerland: Palgrave Macmillan, 211–228.

Yao, T., Qiu, Q. and Wei, Y. (2019) 'Retaining hotel employees as internal customers: Effect of organizational commitment on attitudinal and behavioral loyalty of employees', *International Journal of Hospitality Management*, 76: 1–8.

Zeithaml, V., Parasuraman, A. and Berry, L. L. (1990) *Delivering Quality Service: Balancing Customer Perceptions and Expectations*, New York: The Free Press.

Zeng, Z., Chen, P. J. and Lew, A. A. (2020) 'From high-touch to high-tech: COVID-19 drives robotics adoption', *Tourism Geographies*, 22(3): 724–734.

Zhang, H. Q., Ren, L., Shen, H. and Xiao, Q. (2013) 'What contributes to the success of Home Inns in China?', *International Journal of Hospitality Management*, 33: 425–434.

Zhang, H. Q. and Wu, E. (2004) 'Human resources issues facing the hotel and travel industry in China', *International Journal of Contemporary Hospitality Management*, 16(7): 424–428.

Websites

www.corporate.ritzcarlton.com
www.exploreedmonton.com/
www.revfine.com,
www.southwest.com
www.tophotelchains.com
www.westjet.com

5

Tourism, hospitality and event organizations – the financial context

Introduction and chapter overview

This chapter continues the internal analysis of organizations in examining one of the functional areas that organizations are often divided into – the financial context. The previous chapters considered the operational and human resource functional areas, and Chapter 6 will examine the other functional area – marketing.

The ability to make sense of an organization's financial situation is an important part of strategic analysis. To carry out a financial analysis of an organization's situation (or of an industry), it is necessary to understand some of the fundamentals of finance and its sources.

This chapter begins with a discussion of the sources of corporate finance and then goes on to discuss the costs of the various types of capital. This information helps students to make sense of a company's financial structure before the tools of conventional financial analysis are discussed. The concept of financial benchmarking is explained and its use in analysis is discussed.

Two topics of particular relevance in *THE* contexts are outlined toward the end of the chapter: exchange rate risk and cash flow risk management.

LEARNING OBJECTIVES

After studying this chapter, readers should be able to:

● Identify the primary distinguishing aspects of financial management in parts of *THE*
● Understand what is meant by financial analysis in *THE* contexts

DOI: 10.4324/9781003318613-7

- Identify the sources of funds available to companies and the relative advantages and disadvantages of each
- Assess a company's potential for further funding based on current position, future prospects and past performance
- Understand the cost and non-cost issues involved in raising and using various forms of capital
- Understand the importance of the cost of capital
- Understand the limitations of a company report and accounts as a source of data for financial analysis
- Utilize the major techniques that can be used to analyze a company's financial position and to understand their limitations
- Analyze and understand the characteristics of foreign exchange risks in *THE* contexts
- Analyze and understand the characteristics of cash flow risks in *THE* contexts

5.1 Financial resources in *THE* contexts

Although *THE* sectors cover a wide diversity of different organizations with differing characteristics, financial management is important to all of them.

When dealing with finance much of the material is quite generic, in that the accounting conventions, ratio analysis techniques and fundamentals of raising finance are similar for *THE* organizations, as in other business fields. Nevertheless, in this chapter they will be applied to *THE* organizations to illustrate the relevant financial principles.

There are, however, also some highly significant and distinctive features of managing finance in many *THE* contexts (cash management and foreign exchange risk management), which will be discussed and illustrated toward the end of the chapter.

Financial management is concerned with the effective and efficient raising and use of funds. Like physical, operational, marketing or human resources, finance:

- Has a large number of competing uses
- Is scarce but can be obtained at a price
- Is bought and sold in markets

Financial management is concerned with managing this scarce resource to ensure that finance is:

- Available in sufficient quantities at the right time
- Obtained at the lowest possible cost
- Used in the most profitable ways

The importance of finance to hospitality managers is illustrated in the following Short Case Illustration.

5.1 SHORT CASE ILLUSTRATION

The importance of finance: to hospitality managers

Tsai et al. (2011:942) stressed the importance of good financial management for managers working in hospitality. The authors argued that 'financial management is the backbone of any business, including firms involved in hospitality (including but not limited to hotels, restaurants, and casinos)'. However, although financial management is important at all levels of hospitality organizations, the focus of financial management alters. At the property level, managers are 'charged with using owners' invested assets to enhance revenues and reduce expenses to achieve desired net profits. However, managers at the corporate level are more involved in issues related to investing excess cash and raising debt and equity capital. Dividend policy and decisions, which to some extent signal board-level views on the firm's future development opportunities, also play a significant role in hospitality finance' (Tsai et al., 2011:943).

Because the hospitality industry is relatively *capital intensive* (S. Lee, 2007; Karadeniz et al., 2009), managers at all levels are required to have adequate financial management skills and access to strategies for achieving the goal of financial management, namely, value enhancement or creation for owners.

Questions

1. Why is financial management important for hospitality managers?

2. Distinguish between the likely focus of financial management at the corporate and property levels for hospitality managers.

Most university business courses have an accounting and finance content. You may consequently be familiar with some of the content of this chapter, and this will be to your advantage. This chapter takes the material from the other modules and develops the material specifically in the context of strategic analysis. There are certain elements of finance that we need to concentrate on when carrying out a strategic analysis.

THINK POINTS

- In what respect are certain aspects of financial management characteristic of many *THE* organizations?

- Explain why an American hotel group operating hotels in Asia may be susceptible to foreign exchange risk.

- Identify the managerial implications for managers operating in high or low capital intensity parts of *THE*.

Financial management is often complex and frequently laden with specific terminology. We are primarily concerned with the impact that finance (its availability and price) will have on the adoption of successful strategies. For a more detailed examination of financial management and accounting in a *THE* context, a number of sources are available, including Evans (2002), Bowdin et al. (2011:ch. 9), Atkinson et al. (2012) and Guilding and Ji (2022). A large number of generic texts also examine financial management in detail; see, for example, Marsh (2012), Buckley (2012), Arnold and Lewis (2019) and Atrill (2019).

Finance (or the lack of it) is central to the strategic development of all organizations large and small. The most original strategies and the most complex plans for the future of a business are meaningless unless managers have considered the financial position of the organization at the outset and during the period covered by the strategy.

Thus, the ability of an organization to finance both current and future strategies is central to any analysis of the organization's position.

The success or failure of the organization is judged by its ability to meet its strategic objectives. The financial information (in the form of annual and sometimes quarterly 'corporate' financial reports) produced by organizations provides a quantifiable means of assessing success. It is important to recognize, however, that other quantifiable information, such as efficiency and productivity data, and nonquantifiable data, such as the company's image, can also be used to make such judgments. In this chapter we examine the value of information extracted from financial reports specifically as a source from which judgments can be made.

Corporate reports are, however, just one source of information about a company's financial state. Managers have a number of ways of gathering information about their own and competitors' finances, and we will discuss these later in the chapter.

5.2 An introduction to financial analysis

5.2.1 Capital intensity

Capital intensity refers to the amount of capital used in businesses relative to the other factors of production, particularly human resources. Capital-intensive industries use a large portion of capital to buy expensive equipment compared to their labor costs.

Thus, industries such as oil refining and vehicle manufacturing are often thought of as 'capital intensive'. The capital intensity of THE businesses varies enormously. Accommodation including hotels and transport, as well as airlines and cruising, is often viewed as a capital-intensive part of the industry.

Conversely, in other parts of THE, capital requirements are usually relatively low. Thus, the capital requirements in setting up a travel agent, a tour operator, an internet intermediary or an event management company, for example, are often relatively low.

The relative capital intensity of parts of the industry has three important implications for managers working in the industry.

- *Barrier to competition* – Capital intensity can often act as a barrier to new companies entering the market to compete. Often new companies or smaller companies have insufficient access to capital from the financial markets and banks, which prevents them from entering the market to compete with more established companies.
- *Long lead times* – Projects that require large amounts of capital often have very long lead times between the decision to invest and the asset becoming available. This requires careful planning and scheduling.

> For example: *if an airline decides to invest in new aircraft, it may have to raise the capital it needs to invest (from banks or financial markets), place an order with the aircraft manufacturer, have a period of aircraft testing and staff training and alter operational procedures and systems. In most cases this requires lead times of several years. Japanese Airline ANA became the 'launch' airline for the innovative Boeing 787 'Dreamliner' aircraft when it announced an order for 50 aircraft in 2004. However, the aircraft's first ANA commercial flight did not take place until 2011.*

● *Asset ownership or management* – The need for large quantities of capital can, in some parts of *THE*, be mitigated by the fact that many companies do not actually own the assets concerned (and therefore do not need to finance them) but instead manage or lease the assets.

> For example: *Compared with many other industries, the hospitality industry traditionally has a greater need for financial capital to invest in fixed assets such as land, building and equipment, and because debt is usually relatively cheaper than equity, it has been widely used as a source of capital to fund investments (Li and Singal, 2019).*
>
> *However, hotels and restaurants are often managed under management contracts or franchising arrangements, with the physical assets owned by a property company. A so-called asset-light strategy has now clearly emerged as a dominant strategy (Li and Singal, 2019). Such a strategy enables firms to give up asset ownership to focus on developing intangible assets (such as branding, loyalty schemes and additional services) that are potentially more profitable. Using a capital structure in this way allows hospitality firms to own fewer (or no) hotel or restaurant properties and invest more in technology and loyalty-based assets using franchising and management contracts (Li and Singal, 2019).*
>
> *Similarly, airlines often lease some or all their aircraft from leasing companies such as the Irish-based market leader AerCap, which owns over 2,000 aircraft.*

The contrast between Carnival Cruises and Travel Counsellors below illustrates the differences in capital intensity for two parts of *THE*.

5.2 SHORT CASE ILLUSTRATION

Capital intensity: Carnival Cruises and Travel Counsellors

Carnival Corporation & plc is a company listed in New York and London with headquarters in Miami and London. It operates some of the world's leading cruise brands, including Carnival, Holland-America, Cunard, P&O and Princess.

To grow and compete with other cruise lines, the company has to spend heavily on new cruise ships and refurbishments for its existing fleet. These investments have to be carefully planned because they have very long lead times and require substantial financial commitments over a number of years.

Carnival Corporation employs a diverse workforce of 150,000 people worldwide, and its nine cruise line brands and 87 ships account for almost 50% of the global cruise market. A total of 16 new ships are scheduled to be delivered to Carnival Corporation by 2025.

By contrast, Travel Counsellors represents a labor-intensive (as opposed to capital-intensive) part of the industry. Travel Counsellors was launched in 1994 by David Speakman and is headquartered in Manchester, UK.

The travel intermediary (which operates in the UK, Ireland, Belgium, Netherlands, UAE, South Africa and Australia) has grown substantially to become a £0.5bn business but is based on a low capital outlay business model. The company has an international network of self-employed travel counselors working from home who are paid on a commission basis based on the travel sales they achieve. Because they are self-employed, experienced and highly motivated, they are able to provide high customer service levels that are difficult to match on the internet or by traditional travel agents operating from shop premises.

Sources: Adapted from www.travelcounsellors.co.uk; www.carnival.com/

Questions

1. Explain what is meant by capital intensity.

2. Contrast the capital intensity of Carnival Corporation and Travel Counsellors and comment on the implications.

5.2.2 Financial structure and profitability

At the outset it is necessary to have an understanding of a business's financial structure. An organization's annual accounts will normally contain two key statements, which we will examine briefly:

- The balance sheet
- The profit and loss (P&L) statement

5.2.3 The balance sheet

The balance sheet is a representation of an organization's financial structure. Assets, which may be *long-term* or *current* assets, are financed (and 'matched' in the balance sheet) by capital and liabilities. Liabilities may be *current* (less than 1 year) or *long term* (over 1 year).

$$Capital + Liabilities = Assets$$

The principles underpinning a balance sheet are shown in Figure 5.1.

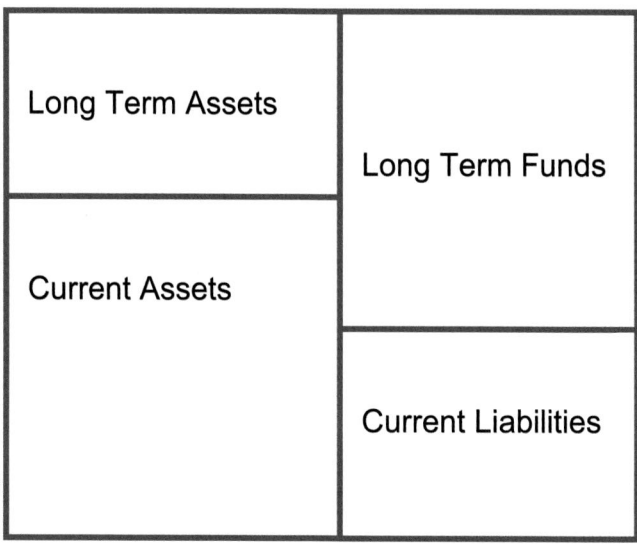

Figure 5.1 A representation of the principles of a balance sheet

Table 5.1 A simplified balance sheet for AirAsia

	Item	Value US$ (mn)	Examples
A	Fixed assets	4,872	Semipermanent assets – property, plants, vehicles, aircraft, etc.
B	Current assets	1,270	Trading assets – stock, debtors, cash
C	Current liabilities	(1,712)	Trading liabilities – creditors, overdrafts
	Net current assets or *working capital* (B + C)	(442)	
	Capital employed (A + B + C)	4,430	
D	Shareholder finance	699	Share capital, retained profits
E	Long term liabilities	3,731	Medium- and long-term loans
	Sources of finance (D + E)	4,430	

Note: Converted at rate of US$1 = 4.0 Malaysian ringgits

Source: AirAsia financial results 2019, www.airasia.com

A number of points relating to the balance sheet can be made:

- The assets of the business may be long term or current and are 'funded' by long-term funds (capital) comprising long-term loans, share capital and reserves and also by current liabilities comprising overdrafts and trade creditors.
- A proportion of the short-term assets are usually funded by long-term funding, which, unlike short-term funding (current liabilities), is difficult to take away at short notice and consequently represents a more stable form of financing. Overdrafts, for instance, can be quickly recalled by banks if they choose to do so.
- Long-term (or fixed) assets such as property, land, vehicles and aircraft are normally financed entirely by more stable financing sources; that is, long-term funding.
- The difference between current assets (comprising stock, debtors and cash) and current liabilities (comprising creditors, overdrafts and short-term loans) is called *working capital* (net current assets).

A simplified example of a balance sheet for AirAsia is shown in Table 5.1 as an example.

5.2.4 *The profit and loss statement*

The P&L statement matches the revenue earned in a period with the costs incurred in earning it. A simplified profit and loss account for AirAsia is shown in Table 5.2 as an example.

5.3 Sources of corporate funding

Financial resources, as we have already learned, are an essential input to strategic development. Capital for development can be raised from several sources, and these are summarized here.

Table 5.2 A simplified profit and loss account for AirAsia

	Item	Value US$ (mn)	Examples
A	Sales or operating revenue	3,002	Passenger and freight revenue, contract services
B	Costs or operating expenditure	(2,828)	Labor, fuel, maintenance, aircraft operations, sales and marketing, depreciation, leasing costs
C	Operating profit (A + B)	174	
D	Finance and other costs	(299)	Finance costs, foreign exchange losses and associated business losses
E	Profit before taxation (C + D)	(125)	
F	(Tax)/tax credit	57	
G	Net profit attributable to shareholders (E + F)	(68)	

Note: Converted at rate of US$1 = 4.00 Malaysian ringgits

Source: AirAsia financial results 2019, www.airasia.com

KEY CONCEPT

Capital

Accountants use the term capital to describe one particular type of 'money'. It is usually contrasted with revenue. Revenue is money that is earned through normal business transactions – through sales, rents or whatever the company 'does' through its normal activities. Capital is money that is used to invest in the business – to buy new equipment, new capacity, extra aircraft, etc. The investment of capital enables the business to expand and, through that expansion, to increase its revenue and profits in future years. Capital can be raised from shareholders, through retaining profits, through loan capital or through the disposal of assets.

5.3.1 Share capital

For *limited liability* companies, a sizeable proportion of capital is raised from shareholders (the financial owners of the company) in the form of share capital.

Historically, share capital has comprised the majority of capital for a limited company's start-up and subsequent development. In return for their investment, shareholders receive a return in accordance with the company's performance in a given year in the form of a 'dividend'. The dividend per share is an important measure by which shareholders can assess the company's success in its chosen strategy. Shares also confer to their holders a right to vote on company matters through resolutions at annual or extraordinary company meetings pro rata with the size of their holding. It follows that a shareholding in excess of 50% confers total control over a company's strategy.

Under normal circumstances, share capital is considered to be permanent – it is not paid back by the company. It is thus unlike other forms of capital (e.g., loan capital). The shareholders' return is in the form of dividends and through capital growth – an increase in the value of the shares. Shareholders who wish to divest their stock in a company must usually sell it via a stock exchange (in the case of shares in a *public* limited company) or through a private sale (in the case of a *private* company). In exceptional circumstances, some companies offer a 'buyback' of their own shares.

KEY CONCEPTS

Share value and share volume

- ***Share value*** – the price of a given company's shares at a given point in time. Like any other commodity, the forces of supply and demand determine its value. Given that in normal circumstances the supply is fixed over the short to medium term, its price is determined by how many people want to buy it. If the market has confidence in a company's prospects, its price will rise. If a company's prospects are considered poor, fewer people will want to buy its shares and the price will fall.

- ***Share volume*** – the number of shares held by a shareholder. The larger the volume, the more influential the shareholder will be in the company's affairs.

- ***Total share volume*** – the total number of shares a company has issued for sale to the stock market or to employees of the organization. Broadly speaking, larger companies have greater share volumes than smaller concerns.

5.3.2 Rights issue capital

From time to time, a company may seek to increase its capital for expansion or improve its capital structure by means of a *rights issue*. This is when a company issues new shares to the stock market, normally giving its own shareholders the first refusal *pro rata* with their current proportion of the company's share volume.

The decision to go for a rights issue may well be a strategic decision for management because it can impact ownership of the company. If existing shareholders do not exercise their right to buy, it is likely that ownership will be *diluted*; that is, shareholders will find that they own a lower percentage of share volume than they used to. A variation on a rights issue is a *placing*. A placing involves the selling of shares direct to a small number of investors, usually large financial institutions.

In the next few sections, Air New Zealand will be used to illustrate refinancing and some of the 'techniques' of financial analysis. At the time of writing, each NZ$ was worth approximately US$0.65.

Air New Zealand Limited is the flag carrier airline of New Zealand, tracing its roots back to 1940. Based in Auckland, Air New Zealand's stated purpose is to 'enrich our country by connecting New Zealanders to each other and New Zealand to the world' (www.airnewzealand.com). It operates an extensive domestic and international route network focusing particularly on the Pacific Rim. A modern fleet of about 110 aircraft is operated by the airline.

Before the COVID-19 pandemic, the airline flew more than 17 million passengers every year, with 3,400 flights per week. The airline is a member of the Star Alliance of global airline partners (which also includes Air China, Air Canada, Lufthansa, South African Airways, Singapore Airlines and United Airlines) and has an extensive domestic and international route network.

5.3 SHORT CASE ILLUSTRATION

Refinancing: Air New Zealand

Air New Zealand has an erratic recent financial history, having been largely privatized in 1989 but subsequently returned to majority government ownership in 2001 after a failed merger with struggling Australian carrier Ansett Australia.

In common with all other *THE* businesses worldwide, Air New Zealand operations were severely affected as New Zealand implemented severe lockdown restrictions in 2020 and 2021. The substantial loss of revenue, particularly for international flights (as indicated in Figures 5.2 and 5.3), resulted in the airline incurring losses. Consequently, it had to utilize its cash reserves and the government had to make loans available to the airline. Subsequently, a package of measures was announced to refinance the airline.

In March 2022, Air New Zealand launched comprehensive NZ$2.2bn recapitalization. The package was aimed at keeping the investment grading assessed by one of the international rating companies (Moody's) and to support the execution of the airline's strategic priorities.

The package of measures included an NZ$1.2bn 'rights offer', allowing eligible shareholders an opportunity to buy additional shares in Air New Zealand at a discount relative to the prevailing share price in proportion to the shares already held.

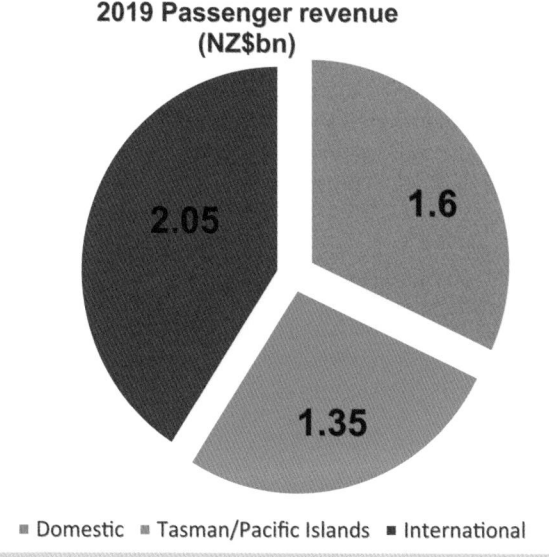

2019 Passenger revenue (NZ$bn)

2.05 — 1.6 — 1.35

■ Domestic ■ Tasman/Pacific Islands ■ International

Figure 5.2 Air New Zealand passenger revenue 2019

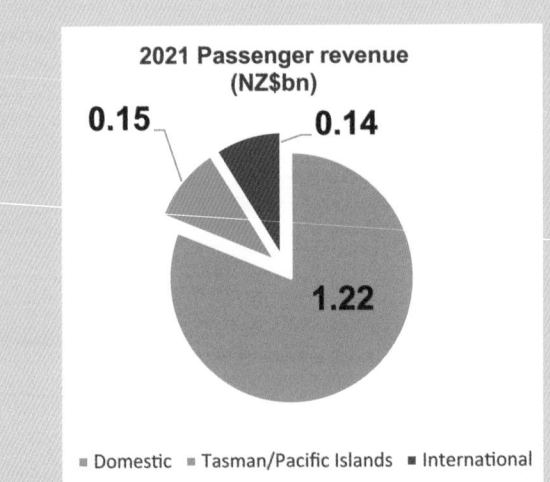

Figure 5.3 Air New Zealand passenger revenue 2021

Source: Air New Zealand annual results presentation 2021, airnewzealand.com

Questions

1. What were the financial issues Air New Zealand faced during 2020 and 2021?

2. Explain the measures the company took to address the financial issues.

5.3.3 Retained profit as a source of capital

Shareholders provide other funds for development by agreeing *not* to receive all of the company's profits in a given year. *Retained profit*, that element of operating profit not paid to shareholders in the form of a dividend, is arguably the most common method of funding strategic developments, particularly if the company is quite old in terms of years of operation. By using this form of funding, organizations save on the costs involved in using alternatives such as fees to investment banks, lawyers and accountants. It also means that management does not have to reveal or justify their strategies to others and risk their plans becoming known to competitors.

5.3.4 Loan capital

An important consideration in the use of retained profits to fund corporate development is clearly the ability of the company to actually make a profit that can be, at least in part, distributed to shareholders as dividends. Though a company may make a profit from its normal activities after taxation, some profits may be required to meet the cost of other forms of *debt finance* or loans.

Debt finance is usually shown in the balance sheet under two headings:

- *Creditors* – amounts falling due within 1 year
- *Creditors* – amounts falling due after more than 1 year

The form of borrowing with the most impact on strategic development is that falling due after more than 1 year – long-term debt.

Debt finance is normally for a set period of time and at a fixed rate of interest. The interest must be paid every year, regardless of the level of profit (often referred to as *servicing the debt*). The interest rate for this source is normally lower than the cost of share capital (when the dividend payable on the shares is taken into account).

5.3.5 Comparison of share capital and loan capital

Each of the types of capital described above has its pros and cons. Share capital has the advantage that the amount paid on the capital is dependent on company results. A company can decide not to pay a dividend if profits are poor in any given year. Loan capital, by contrast, must normally be serviced regardless of results, in much the same way that a mortgage on a house must be repaid regardless of other commitments.

Share capital is normally permanent. As long as the company exists, it has an obligation to its shareholders, who would be expected to be rewarded by dividends when profits are made. Loan capital has the advantage that it is time limited. Servicing the capital is restricted to the term of the loan (like a mortgage on a house), and when it is finally repaid in full, the business has no further obligation to the lender.

The fact that the repayment of debt finance takes precedence over dividends on shares means that shareholders bear an increased risk. If the company performs poorly, their return on investment will be small or nonexistent in a given year. Against this possibility, they usually expect to receive higher returns compared to providers of loan capital in the years when profits are good.

KEY CONCEPT

Rewarding providers of debt and shareholders

- Interest on debt capital must be paid regardless of the level of profit.
- Interest on debt capital takes priority over dividends to shareholders.
- Thus, shareholders take a greater risk and expect to be rewarded accordingly.

The major advantages and disadvantages of share and loan capital are summarized in Table 5.3.

Table 5.3 Summary of the major advantages and disadvantages of share and loan capital

	Advantages	Disadvantages
Share capital	• No fixed charges or legal obligation to pay a dividend	• Extension of voting rights
	• No maturity dates	• High issue costs
	• Issue of equity increases credit worthiness	• May increase average cost of capital
	• Marketable; i.e., can be traded	• Dividends not tax deductible
Loan capital	• Known cost and often lower cost	• Increase in risk, which may cause value of equity to fall
	• No *dilution* of equity	
	• Interest payable is tax deductible	• Need for repayment
		• Limit to amount of available funding

5.4 Sources of finance: strategic significance

Company ownership varies greatly in different countries:

- In some countries such as the UK, Australia, New Zealand, USA and Canada, there is a strong tradition of share ownership by private individuals and public share quotations on the stock exchange.
- Other countries, such as Germany, France, Italy and Spain, exhibit different patterns, with more companies owned, at least in part, by banks, private trusts, families and government institutions (Lynch, 2015).

Regardless of these differences, however, the main sources of finance can be analyzed and their strategic significance assessed.

> ### THINK POINTS
>
> - Why is money important to a business?
> - Define and distinguish between revenue and capital.
> - Define and distinguish between share capital and loan capital.

As stated in Chapter 1, strategic developments for an organization imply that they:

- Are of major importance to a company's future development
- Require a substantial commitment of resources (financial and other) by an organization
- Involve choices that have to be made about the deployment of finite resources between competing strategic options
- Have an impact over the medium to long term (more than 1 year) rather than over the short term (less than 1 year).

Because of the scope and timescale of strategic developments, some forms of finance are more suited to funding them than others. Table 5.4 considers the main categories of finance and considers their significance in finding strategic developments.

5.4.1 Sources of finance: company comparison

In Figure 5.4 the sources of finance for three well-known *THE* companies are summarized. It is, however, often difficult to obtain such detailed information for companies whose shares are not traded on major stock markets because they are not legally required to make such information widely available. Because there are many such businesses in *THE* that are 'owner-managed' or family owned and do not have a stock market quotation, obtaining details of their funding position can be somewhat difficult.

The events management sector, for example, is highly fragmented, with few large players with stock market quotations. There are also many event management operations that operate as subsidiaries of larger corporations. Many of the larger quoted hotel groups such as Marriott and Hilton, for example, have event management capabilities that rely on the parent company's balance sheet for funding and so cannot be analyzed independently in terms of their sources of finance.

Table 5.4 Summary of the strategic significance of different sources of finance

Sources of finance	Strategic significance
Reserves and retained profits	• Represent an accumulation over time. If not utilized, shareholders may demand that they be distributed to them as owners.
	• Provide cheap and noncontroversial financial sources
	• Typically the largest sources of finance for many companies
	• Often finances the majority of strategic developments
Shareholders	• They are useful to be able to access when major new strategic initiatives are envisaged
	• Relying on shareholders for further funding changes ownership, so risky in terms of retaining control
Provisions for tax and pensions	• Funds are committed for other purposes, so not really useful for strategic developments.
Debt: long term	• Can be cheap and quick to set up and retains the existing shareholder structure thereby retaining control.
	• High levels of debt (relative to equity) can be dangerous when interest rates are rising or when the economy is weak.
	• The requirement to pay interest to 'service' the debt can be a major burden on companies when earnings are weak.
Debt: short term	• Short term means repayable inside 1 year and so is only a temporary solution for major strategic initiatives.
	• Funding could be quickly withdrawn by provider, leaving the organization with a funding difficulty.

Source: Adapted from Lynch (2015)

The companies chosen for comparison (Carnival Corporation, Qantas and Accor) operate in different parts of *THE* and in differing markets and have done so with differing levels of financial success in recent years. Hence, it is unsurprising that their balance sheets demonstrate different patterns of funding. Note: the figures also exclude the most severe effects of COVID-19 because they are for 2020 for Carnival and 2019 for Qantas and Accor.

• *Carnival Corporation & plc* is a global cruise company with stock market listings in both New York and London and a turnover of about $10bn per annum. The company is one of the largest vacation companies in the world, operating a portfolio of leading cruise brands that includes Carnival Cruise Lines, Holland America Line, Princess Cruises and Seabourn in North America; P&O Cruises and Cunard in the United Kingdom; AIDA Cruises in Germany; Costa Cruises in Southern Europe; Iberocruceros in Spain; and P&O Cruises in Australia. These brands attract about 10 million customers annually (www.carnival.com).

• *Qantas* is Australia's largest airline and is also one of the world's oldest airlines, with an extensive domestic and international network serving Europe and North America as well as the Asian market through its low-cost Jetstar subsidiary. Due to COVID-19, high fuel prices, intense competition and industrial disputes, Qantas has reported several annual losses, resulting in periods of substantial restructuring and management changes The airline operates a fleet of almost 300 aircraft, and in May 2022, it ordered 12 A350–1000 planes from Airbus to be utilized on the world's longest nonstop flights from Sydney to London and New York in late 2025 (www.qantas.com.au).

- *Accor*, which is based in France, is one of the world's leading hotel operators, with a particularly strong presence in Europe. It has some 780,000 rooms in more than 5,300 hotels in about 110 countries. Its extensive brand portfolio – encompassing Rafles, Fairmont, Swissôtel, Sofitel, Pullman, Novotel, Mercure, Adagio, Ibis and HotelF1 – provides a comprehensive range of options across the luxury to economy spectrum (www.accor.com).

Some conclusions can be made through an examination of the sources of finance in Figure 5.4:

- Carnival – has a moderate level of reserves and retained profit, relatively low levels of short-term debt and high levels of long-term debt
- Qantas – has low levels of reserves and retained profit (a reflection of poor levels of profitability in recent years) and high levels of both short- and long-term debt
- Accor – has high levels of reserves and retained profit and moderate levels of long- and short-term debt

In practice, business profits can vary significantly over time. In some years, it is preferable to use loan capital, especially when interest rates are low and profits are high. In other years, when profits are lower and interest rates are higher, share capital works out cheaper. The fact that the benefits are so finely divided means that most companies opt to use an element of both.

5.4.2 Other sources of capital

Though the foregoing are the most common mechanisms of raising capital for development, others are available under some circumstances. One such method is to dispose of existing fixed assets.

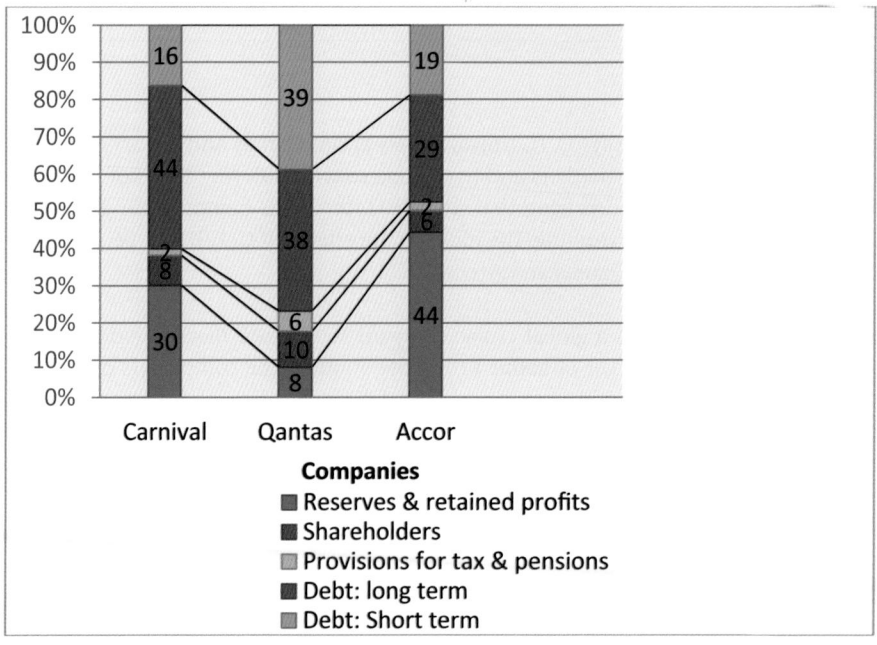

Figure 5.4 Sources of finance for three *THE* companies

Source: Annual reports (2019)

This can range from selling of an aircraft, a hotel building or a performance venue to selling a subsidiary to a third party.

Marginal improvements in a company's capital situation can be achieved by improving the management of *working capital*; that is, over the course of a financial year, small savings can accumulate to significant proportions, increasing both profitability and capital for reinvestment. This can be achieved by:

- Extending the time taken for the organization to pay creditors
- Getting debtors to pay the organization sooner
- Spreading payments by the organization, through leasing rather than purchasing assets

---

KEY CONCEPT

Working capital

Working capital is the amount of money that a company has tied up in the normal operation of its business. Working capital comprises money tied up in:

- Stocks
- Debtors (money owed to the business)
- Creditors (money the company owes)
- Cash or current bank deposits

A company's objective is usually to minimize this figure or to manage the working capital in such a way that minimizes financing costs or maximizes earnings on cash balances. This is an important source of earnings for many companies in *THE* given the seasonality with which revenue is often received.

Working capital is needed to pay for goods, services and expenses before money can be recovered from creditors. The ability of a business to pay its cash commitments as they fall due shows that it has sufficient liquidity.

Inefficient management of working capital can lead to overinvestment in working capital – overcapitalization. Conversely, undercapitalization, also known as overtrading, often occurs when a company tries to do too much, too soon with too little long-term capital. In this situation, a company can be trading profitably but runs out of cash to make payments; that is, it becomes insolvent. Warning signs of overtrading include:

- A rapid increase in sales
- A rapid increase in current assets
- Deterioration in liquidity ratios (such as the acid test ratio, which measures the proportion of current assets less stocks to current liabilities)

5.5 Cost of capital

5.5.1 Why calculate the cost of capital?

Availability of capital (where to get it from) is one issue when examining a company's capital funding, but another equally important consideration is its cost.

We learned above that providers of loans or share capital (equity) both require a return on their investments. Managers therefore need to know what return (profit) they need to make to meet the minimum requirements of capital providers. Failure to achieve this minimum will make the raising of future funds all the more difficult.

THINK POINTS

- Explain the advantages of employing share capital for development.
- Explain the advantages of employing loan capital for development.
- Explain what is meant by a 'rights issue'.
- Explain the importance of 'working capital' to successful business operation.

The *cost of capital* can be seen as the minimum return required on the company's assets, which in turn may influence the objectives of the company.

At its simplest, the cost of capital can be viewed as the annual amount payable (as a percentage) against the principal amount of money. The return payable on loans varies between lenders and over time as interest rates rise or fall.

> For example: *The cost of loans on a credit card is much higher than a mortgage loan (where the security against the loan is mainly responsible for the difference).*

The cost of capital is usually an important figure to calculate because if it works out to be too high, the development that it is intended to fund may not be viable. Given that both debt and share capital attract servicing costs, the profit returns must exceed these servicing costs to the extent that the proposal is economically attractive.

If the projected returns on a strategic development (such as a new hotel, theater or cruise liner) are not much more than the projected servicing costs, then management will have to make a judgment as to whether the investment is actually 'worth the risk'.

The whole situation is rendered more complex if debt capital is obtained at a variable rate of interest. Interest rates can vary substantially throughout an economic cycle and depend upon things such as government inflation targets, the currency exchange value and the rate of economic growth.

There are no strict rules as to the ideal capital structure – the balance between debt and equity finance – but investors will form judgments as to what they expect. The optimal structure will vary from company to company, from industry sector to industry sector and from year to year. Some companies will calculate their WACC and include factors that are difficult to quantify, such as the degree of risk faced by the industry, trends in interest rates and even the cost and availability of funds to competitors.

Generally, however, two guidelines might be that it is risky to:

- Rely heavily on short-term funding sources, because these can be quickly withdrawn. For that reason, Figure 5.1 shows current assets being partly funded by long-term funding sources.
- Have a high level of debt relative to equity ('the gearing ratio') because it risks increased costs if interest rates rise and interest payments to providers of debt have to be paid regardless of levels of profitability.

5.5.2 Costs of debt capital

The costs of debt capital are relatively easy to calculate because they tend to correspond closely to the prevailing rate of interest.

5.5.3 Costs of share capital

Calculating the cost of share capital is slightly more complex because it contains more variables. Accounting academics spend a great deal of time discussing what should and should not be included in this calculation and how each component should be weighted. Reasons for this complexity include:

- The indefinite nature of the funding
- The *opportunity cost* of undistributed profits
- Shareholders' expectations

These factors mean that some models try to include components for inflation, industry averages and attitudes toward risk.

At its simplest, the cost of share capital can be calculated as follows:

Cost of share capital (equity) as a percentage = (Current net dividend per share/Current market price of share) × 100 + Average percentage annual growth rate

---

Cost of share capital – example

If the market price for shares is 400 cents per share, the annual dividend is 20 cents and the growth in profits average 10% per annum, this gives:

Cost of share capital = (20/400) × 100 + 10% = **15%**

5.5.4 Weighted average cost of capital

The WACC can be used to determine the overall cost of funding to a company. The calculation of this information is relatively simple:

WACC = (Proportion of loan finance × Cost of loan finance) + (Proportion of shareholders' funds × Cost of shareholders' funds).

WACC – Example

Assuming that a company has $30mn of loan capital and $70mn equity funding. The cost of each type has been calculated as 5% and 15%, respectively. The calculation would be as follows:

Type of capital	Proportion	Cost (after tax)	Weighted cost
Loan finance	0.3	5%	1.5%
Shareholders' funds	0.7	15%	10.5%
Total	1.0	12.0%	

Part 2

5.6 Key techniques of financial analysis

We would usually employ an analysis of a company's financial situation as part of an internal strategic analysis, in the same way as we consider other functional areas of an organization in relation to its operations, human resources and marketing. It is necessary to understand a company's finances to make an assessment of its 'health' or its readiness to undertake a phase of strategic development.

It is also necessary to have an understanding of the interaction between finance and the other functional areas.

> For example: *The strategic marketing plan that is developed may suggest that a major expansion into a foreign market requiring the takeover of a local supplier should take place and that heavy promotional activity should support the move. Such a strategic option, however, cannot be successful unless adequate financing is available at a price that allows profits to be made.*

Three key techniques of financial analysis are:

- *Longitudinal* analysis (sometimes called trend or time series analysis)
- *Cross-sectional* analysis (or comparison analysis)
- *Ratio* analysis

A comprehensive analysis of a company's financial situation would normally involve an element of all three of these analyses. One thing to bear in mind when looking at accounting statements is that they contain numbers in isolation. An accounting number on its own is just that – a number. To make any sense of it, we must compare it with other accounting numbers.

5.4 SHORT CASE ILLUSTRATION

Air New Zealand: financial management in a volatile sector

The airline industry is notoriously volatile in terms of its revenues, costs and profits.

Some years ago, difficult trading conditions were encountered during a downturn in the world economy. The impacts can be illustrated from the following extract from the 2012 Air New Zealand shareholder review:

Air New Zealand operates in a volatile industry. On-going challenges in the global economy have continued to suppress demand, escalate oil prices and destabilize financial markets, yet tough operating conditions do not justify poor financial results. We simply must adapt our business, improve our productivity and enhance our financial performance.

The airline's shareholder review went on to point out that the Air New Zealand had undergone substantial changes and that these changes had enabled it to be well positioned to operate profitably into the future in the face of uncertain demand and high fuel costs. The challenge was how to commercialize this positioning and deliver levels of profitability in line with expectations.

In more recent years, Air New Zealand's financial position also improved as the world economy strengthened (in common with most other world airlines), with an improving earnings and revenue. And then: COVID-19 struck. During March and April 2020, the New Zealand government established tight lockdown measures that remained in place until early 2022. Airline demand reduced to almost zero at times, and sometimes the airline's network was reduced to 5% of capacity. As the 2020 shareholder review stated, 'Never in the 80-year history of our airline have we had to reduce network capacity to this extent'.

Faced with such a dramatic and prolonged drop in demand, drastic measures had to be taken. These included dropping most scheduled services, making over 4,000 employees redundant, securing a loan from the government, canceling dividend payments and reviewing all costs. In 2022 the airline issued a rights issue to secure additional funding from shareholders as part of its financial restructuring.

Covid-19 had a profound impact on the size of the airline, its balance sheet and its profits, but *downsizing* and financial restructuring enabled it to survive.

Source: Air New Zealand annual shareholder reviews and Air New Zealand annual reports, www.airnewzealand.com

Questions

1. Explain the financial challenges that Air New Zealand faced in 2020.

2. What measures did Air New Zealand take to improve financial performance?

5.6.1 Longitudinal analysis

The simplest means of assessing any aspect of a company's finances is to compare the data for two or more years and see what has increased and what has decreased over that time period and by how much. It goes without saying that the longer back in time we look, the better idea we will get as to its current position in its historical context. Many company corporate reports provide a 5- or 10-year record, and this can help us in constructing a longitudinal analysis.

The easiest way to perform this form of analysis is to conduct an initial scan of the figures to identify any major changes between the years. This involves simply looking along each line in turn and highlighting any larger than normal increases or decreases; for example, a scan of fuel expenses shown in Figure 5.7 clearly indicates that fuel costs (a large component of total costs) were highly volatile over the period.

Anomalies like these may need further investigation to find answers to the reasons for such volatility. Further investigation of the balance sheet or P&L account, together with any notes to the accounts, may provide some clues. It may be important to discover how such an increase was financed, why there was a need to carry high levels of stock and the impact on suppliers and customers.

The initial scan may need to be followed by a more detailed analysis that calculates the year-on-year increase/decrease in percentage terms. It is sometimes helpful to plot trends on a graph against time (such as in Figures 5.5, 5.6 and 5.7). This can help to highlight changes at particular points in time and to identify correlations between the various indicators.

The identification of trends, in terms of, say, turnover, costs or some items on a balance sheet (such as debtors), can therefore be valuable in our financial analysis.

Such trends should, however, be seen in their context. An organization operating in a static or slow growth market may judge a 1% year-on-year increase in turnover as a great success, whereas a company in a buoyant market would judge a 1% increase as a failure.

Part 2

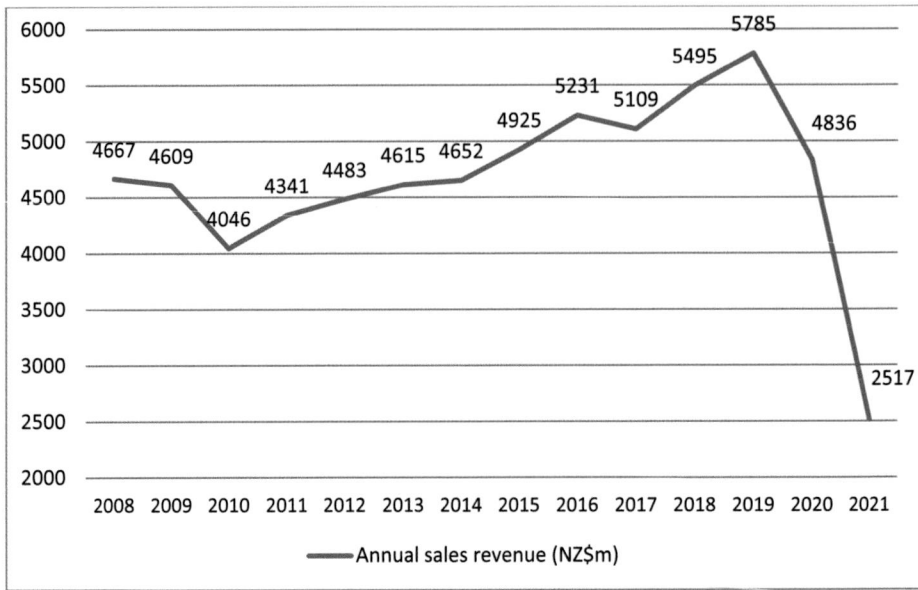

Figure 5.5 A simple longitudinal analysis: Air New Zealand annual sales revenue (2008–21)

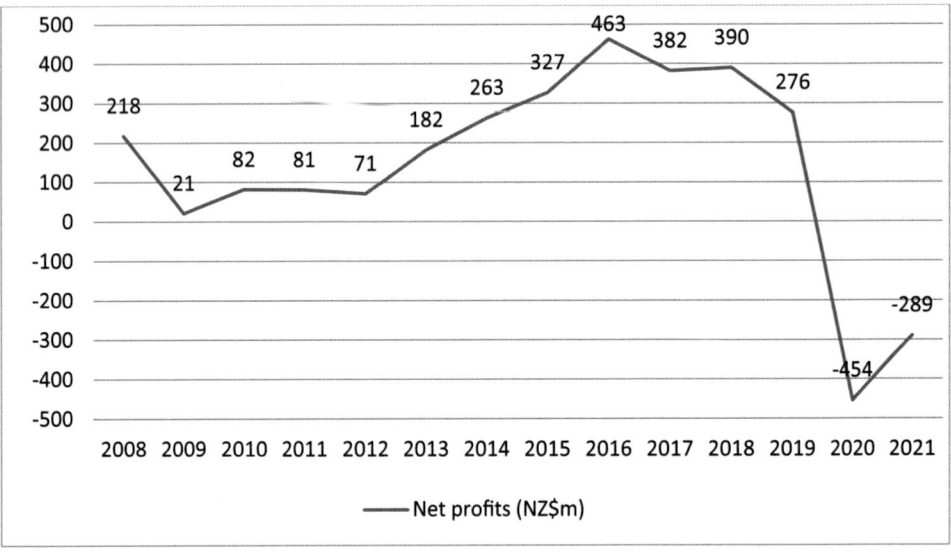

Figure 5.6 A simple longitudinal analysis: Air New Zealand annual net profits (2008–21)

5.6.2 Cross-sectional analysis

Though longitudinal analysis helps us to assess performance within the context of historical trends, it tells us nothing of the company's performance against that of competitors or of similar companies in other industries.

> For example: *If we were to identify strong sales growth of 10% a year in a longitudinal analysis of Company A's financial statements, we might be tempted to think that the*

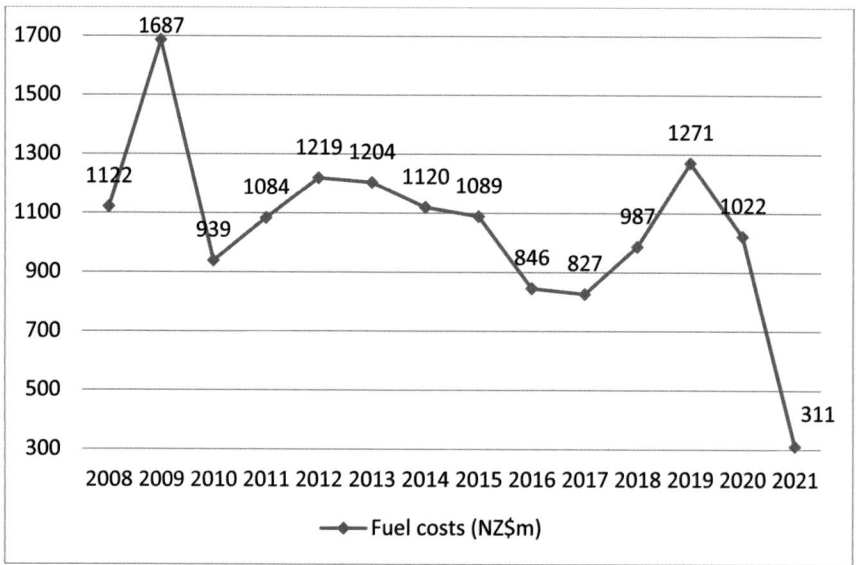

Figure 5.7 A simple longitudinal analysis: Air New Zealand fuel costs (2008–21)

company was performing well. If we were then to compare this company with one of its competitors only to find that the industry average rate of growth was 15%, we would wish to modify our initial assessment of Company A's performance.

Intercompany comparison or financial *benchmarking* is a variation on cross-sectional analysis. It usually involves an analysis of 'like' companies, usually in the same industry, but it can sometimes be an interindustry analysis.

To make the benchmarking analysis meaningful, the company selection should usually be guided by similarity by:

- Company size (i.e., comparable in terms of turnover, market value or market share)
- Industry (i.e., produce similar products)
- Market (i.e., share a similar customer base)

In practice, sample selection for a benchmarking study always involves some compromise because no two companies are in all respects directly comparable. Many companies, for example, operate in more than one industry, and this may render problematic any comparisons with another company that operates in only one industry.

Accountants and financial analysts have undertaken the practice of intercompany (cross-sectional) analysis using financial data for many years. Benchmarking, however, can be used to compare financial and, importantly, non-financial information between two or more companies. See, for example, Wöber (2002) and Schmidgall and DeFranco (2016) for discussions of benchmarking in *THE* contexts.

Benchmarking is now used to compare the effectiveness of various processes, products and procedures against others. The objective is to identify where superior performance is found in whatever variable is being used for comparison. Once the company with the highest performance is identified, the exercise becomes to explore the reasons behind the superior performance.

The benchmarking process therefore involves decisions on:

- What are we going to benchmark? (financial or non-financial data)
- Who are we going to benchmark against? (sample selection)
- How will we get the information?
- How will we analyze the information?
- How will we use the information?

The value of benchmarking is in identifying not only which company has the superior performance in a sector but also why this is the case.

> **For example:** *If our analysis throws up the fact that Company X enjoys a return on sales significantly higher than the other companies in the sector, this company would occupy the profitability benchmark in the sector. The other companies may then wish to examine the practices within Company X that give rise to this level of performance.*

For non-financial indicators, our analysis may highlight the fact that Company Y is able to attract the best-qualified people within a key category of human resources, such as the best sales and marketing professionals or computer programmers. In this case, Company Y demonstrates the benchmark in successful recruitment. Other companies who are unable to attract the best people would wish to examine Company Y to see why it is so successful in this regard.

THINK POINTS

- Distinguish between longitudinal and cross-sectional analyses.
- What are the main categories of accounting ratios?
- Explain what is meant by benchmarking.

KEY CONCEPT

Financial statements

One of the conditions usually placed on limited companies is the requirement to file an audited annual report and accounts. The details vary from country to country but usually include elements such as:

- A chairman's and a chief executive's statement
- An auditor's report
- A P&L statement
- A balance sheet
- A cash flow statement

The accounting rules by which they are to be constructed are prescribed in financial reporting standards (which vary in different countries, often making comparisons difficult) to ensure that all companies mean the same thing when they make an entry in one of the statements. When they are completed (following the company's financial year end), they become publicly available.

It is for the purposes of comparisons of this nature that cross-sectional analyses are important. As well as comparing accounting numbers like turnover, it is often helpful to compare two or more companies' ratios (see next section) such as return on sales or one of the working capital ratios.

5.6.3 Ratio analysis

The third important technique in the analysis of company performance is *ratio analysis*. A ratio is a comparison (by quotient) of two items from the same set of accounts. Given that there are a lot of numbers in a set of accounts, it will not come as a surprise to learn that a large number of ratios can be calculated – some of which are more useful than others.

Ratio analysis is an area of some academic debate and, accordingly, how ratios are expressed may vary between accounting and strategy textbooks. What is important, therefore, is to employ a consistent approach to ratio analysis, especially in *longitudinal* and *cross-sectional* analyses (discussed in the previous sections). It is also important to note that in the current context, we are considering the use of financial ratios to assess organizational *financial* performance. Importantly, there are also a series of key *operational* ratios that are often highly important to *THE* organizations in managing performance, such as load factors, occupancy rates and staff turnover (which were considered in Chapters 3 and 4).

For a discussion and examples of ratio analysis, see, for example, Fleisher and Bensoussan (2003:ch. 22) and Walsh (2011).

Care must be taken in using and interoperating ratios because the detailed specification of the ratios and the way in which accounts are presented are not always consistent. Furthermore, the results presented by the ratios vary considerably across different industries and sectors.

> For example: *Kim and Ayoun (2005) used ratio analysis to examine salient financial trends within four major sectors of THE (lodging, restaurants, airlines and the amusement sectors). Cross-sectional analysis results indicated that at least for the test period, 8 out of 13 financial ratios were statistically different across the four sectors studied.*

For most purposes, we can divide ratios into five broad categories:

1. Performance ratios
2. Efficiency ratios
3. Liquidity ratios
4. Investors' ratios
5. Financial structure ratios

5.6.4 Performance ratios

Performance ratios test how well a company has turned its inputs into profits. This usually involves comparing *return* or profit before interest and tax (PBIT) against either turnover or against its capital. This is because the rates of tax and interest payable vary. Using profit after interest and tax would distort the performance figure.

Return on capital employed (ROCE) is perhaps the most important and widely used measure of performance. It indicates the return being made compared to the funds invested. At its simplest, it is this figure that tests the gains of investing in a business as opposed to simply placing capital in a bank.

Where an organization can break down its figures by divisions or subsidiaries, individual performance can be measured and decisions relating to continued ownership (of the divisions) made.

Return on equity or *return on ordinary shareholders' funds* gives an indication of how effectively the share capital has been turned into profit (i.e., it does not take account of loan capital). This ratio should be used carefully because the capital structure of the company can affect the ratio.

Performance ratios – Examples

Each expressed as a percentage by multiplying the ratio by 100.

Return on capital employed = Profit before interest and tax (PBIT – from P&L account)/Total capital employed (i.e., one side of the balance sheet) × 100:

AIR NZ, 2019 = (381/7,621) × 100 = **5.0%**

Return on shareholders' funds = PBIT/shareholders' funds (from balance sheet) × 100:

AIR NZ, 2019 = (381/11,992) × 100 = **19.1%**

Net return on sales = PBIT/total sales (also called turnover or revenue) × 100:

AIR NZ, 2019 = (381/5,485) × 100 = **6.6%**

Return on sales, or *profit margin*, either net or gross, is a popular guide to the profitability of a company. These ratios assess the profit made per unit of currency sold. Return on sales tends to vary from industry to industry and between companies within an industry. Airlines and tour operators, for example, typically make net returns of less than 10%, whereas companies in the pharmaceuticals sector often make more than 20%. Figure 5.8 shows a graphical representation of return on sales for Air New Zealand.

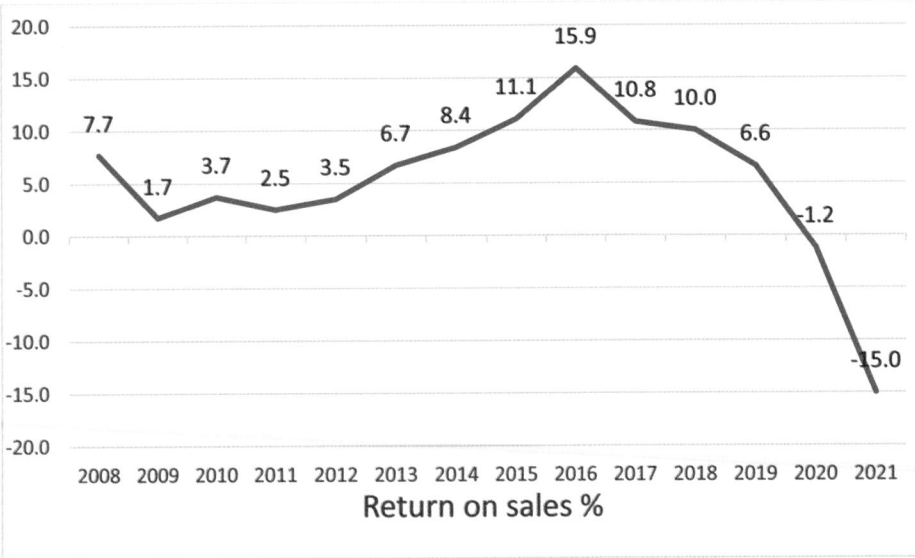

Figure 5.8 A longitudinal analysis of Air New Zealand return on sales (2008–21)

5.6.5 Efficiency ratios

These ratios show how efficiently a company has used its assets to generate sales. We can use any one of a number of a company's inputs to test against sales or profits. Common efficiency ratios include *sales per employee* and *profit per employee*, both of which test the efficiency with which a company uses its labor inputs.

KEY CONCEPT

Efficiency

The term efficiency is used in many ways – not just in accounting.

We may speak of an efficient engine on a cruise liner or an efficient ventilation system in a concert hall, for instance. At its simplest, efficiency is a comparison of a system's output to its inputs – with a view to testing how well the inputs have been turned into an output. It follows that a more efficient system will produce more output for a given input than a less efficient one. It can be expressed mathematically as a quotient.

Efficiency = (work output/work input) × 100 (to arrive at a percentage)

Efficiency ratios – examples

Sales per employee = Total sales (from P&L)/Number of employees (usually found in the notes to the accounts):

AIR NZ, 2019 = NZ$5,785mn/11,793 = NZ$490,000

Profit per employee = PBIT/Number of employees:

AIR NZ, 2019 = NZ$3,810mn/11,793 = NZ$32,307

5.6.6 Liquidity ratios

These ratios test the company's ability to meet its short-term debts – an important aspect to establish if we have reason to believe the company is in trouble. Essentially, they ask the question, 'Has the company enough funds to meet what it owes?'

The *current ratio* is the best-known liquidity ratio. It is a measure of a company's total liabilities in comparison to its total assets and is thus calculated entirely from balance sheet figures. It is used to assess the company's ability to meet its liabilities as they become due by the use of its assets such as stock, debtors (receivables) and cash.

Many textbooks suggest a ratio of 2:1 should be a target for the current ratio. These are simple guides and should not be taken as the norm for all industries.

Liquidity ratios – examples

Current ratio = Current assets/Current liabilities:

AIR NZ, 2019 = NZ$1,804/2,666 = 0.68

5.6.7 Investors' ratios

This family of ratios test for aspects of a company's performance that are important to a company's investors – usually its shareholders or potential shareholders.

Earnings per share (EPS) are calculated by dividing profit after interest and tax (called earnings) by the number of shares. It shows how much profit is attributable to each share.

The *price earnings ratio* (P/E) gives an indication of the stock market's confidence in a company's shares. It is the current market price of the company's ordinary shares divided by its EPS at the last year end. It follows therefore that the P/E varies with the share price. Broadly speaking, it is a way of showing how highly investors value the earnings a company produces. A high P/E ratio (where the price is high compared to the last declared EPS) usually indicates growth potential, whereas a low P/E suggests static profits. The P/E ratio for quoted companies is regularly published in the financial press.

Investors' ratios: Examples:

EPS = Profit after interest and tax/share volume:

AIR NZ (2019) = NZ$276mn/1,123mn = **NZ$0.25**

P/E = Price of share (as of 'today' or in accounts)/EPS at most recent year end:

AIR NZ (2019) = NZ$2.71/0.25 = **6.84**

5.6.8 Financial structure ratios

We encountered financial structure above when we discussed the relative merits of loan and share capital earlier in the chapter. The way in which a company 'mixes' these forms of capital is referred to as its financial (or capital) structure.

The relationship of debt capital to shareholder capital is referred to as the company's gearing ratio. Gearing is an indication of how the company has arranged its capital structure.

The *gearing ratio* looks at the relationship between all of the borrowings of the company (including short term borrowings) and all of the capital employed by the company. This provides a view of the extent to which borrowing forms part of the total capital base of the company and hence the risk associated with rising interest rates.

Financial structure ratios – example

Gearing = Net debt (typically all borrowings less bank and other deposits)/Net debt + Shareholders' funds × 100:

AIR NZ = 2,597/2,597 + 1,992 × 100 = **56.5%**

The gearing ratio is usually expressed as a percentage by simply multiplying the quotient by 100. In theory, the higher the level of gearing, the higher the risks to a business, because the payment of interest and repayment of debts are not optional in the same way as dividends. Traditionally a rate of over 50% is considered relatively high.

It should be noted that (as with most ratios) there are several variants of the gearing ratio that use different measures of borrowing. It is important to be consistent in the ratio that is used when comparing the gearing of two or more companies or comparing the gearing of a single company over a period of time.

5.6.9 Using ratios in financial analysis

Compared to simply looking at accounting numbers, ratios provide a way of making some sense of published accounts. However, if a ratio is placed within its longitudinal or cross-sectional context, its usefulness is maximized.

> **For example:** *If the return on sales ratio is calculated, we would usually want to know how Company A's figure this year compares not only with last year's (i.e., is it more or less?) but also with Company A's competitors. This enables us to assess how Company A is performing over time and to make a judgment on its competitive position in its industry. This is because profitability is an important indicator of competitive success.*

5.7 Limitations of financial information

For most purposes in strategic analysis, we can accept the proposition that the data we collect from a company's annual accounts are accurate and provide a truthful statement on its financial position. From time to time, however, we may need to qualify our analysis because of one or more reasons.

- *Accuracy* – Though the financial statements are audited for accuracy, other parts of the annual report are not. If our financial analysis consists of an examination of the entire document and not just the accounting sections, we would need to be aware of this. Some commentators have suggested that such disclosures may be something of a public relations and marketing exercise.

- *Historic information* – It should be remembered that the financial information in a corporate report is historical, often published up to three months after the period they represent. Though historical information can be used to judge past performance, it may have limited use in predicting future performance. The balance sheet shows the financial position at 'a moment in time' (at the year end). It does not (unlike the P&L) summarize a full year's trading, and matters can sometimes change quickly after the year end.

In an attempt to avoid this potential problem, quoted companies in many parts of the world are required to produce interim reports, normally half-yearly or quarterly and unaudited, that show their profit and turnover for that period. Companies are also required to provide information that may have a significant impact on its prospects such as changes to the board or anything that gives rise to a 'profits warning'.

- *Presentation of accounts* – Those who prepare a company's financial statements (the financial accountants) sometimes have cause to 'hide' bad news to avoid alarming the company's investors. It is possible to employ legal financial restructuring to make some figures appear better than they are. Also, although there are accounting conventions that most organizations follow, they vary in detail in different countries.

For example: *A year-on-year increase in the value of fixed assets may appear at first glance to be healthy, but it might be that the company has accumulated a high amount of debt to finance this increase. It is for this reason that we sometimes need to examine all parts of a company's financial statements to spot any countervailing bad news that has been obscured by the company in its reporting.*

5.8 Foreign exchange risk management in *THE*

Two further financial topics are particularly pertinent to *THE* settings given the characteristics of the sectors being considered. These topics involve the recognition of risks relating to foreign exchange and managing cash flow risks, through cash management. For a more detailed discussion of these topics, see, for example, Evans (2002), Arnold and Lewis (2019:ch. 22), Jankensgard et al. (2020) and Madura (2020:part 3).

Many businesses in *THE* operate internationally (across national boundaries), producing costs and revenues in various currencies. Because the rate of exchange between one currency and another varies, this produces a risk (commonly called 'exposure') that needs to be managed.

Such risks are, of course, not unique to *THE* businesses. Given the underlying nature of the business, however, the size of the exposure to movements in foreign exchange rates is often large relative to the size of the organization, far larger than for most companies engaged in other areas of the economy. The very purpose of companies such as those involved in tour operating, international air transportation or hotel groups operating internationally implies that they are operating across national boundaries and, consequently, they are exposed to foreign exchange risks.

The profitability of any company that trades internationally is affected by changes in foreign exchange rate, as stated by Lockwood (1989) in relation to *THE*:

DEFINITION/QUOTATION

Foreign exchange risks for *THE* organizations

As a large part of the travel and tourist industry is concerned with persuading and assisting people to cross national boundaries and thus to buy goods and services priced in a foreign currency, the identification and management of exchange rate exposures is vital to the profitable operation of a travel and tourist business.

(Lockwood, 1989:175)

The cases of a German airline and a British tour operator illustrate the sort of foreign exchange risks that *THE* companies are often exposed to.

5.5 SHORT CASE ILLUSTRATION

Exposure to foreign exchange risks: in a German airline and UK tour operator

Many companies in *THE* operate internationally, which produces costs and revenues denominated in foreign currencies. Because the rate of exchange between most currencies varies because the rate is set by the vast international foreign exchange markets, a risk is created. The risk is basically that planned revenues are lower and costs are higher than expected when converted into the company's home currency.

For example, a German airline may:

- Sell its tickets in many currencies
- Buy its fuel and aircraft in US dollars
- Pay most of its staff and report its profits in its home currency – euros

Similarly, a British-based outbound tour operator may:

- Receive most of its income in pound sterling
- Buy or lease aircraft and pay for fuel in US dollars
- Pay most of its staff in its home currency – pound sterling
- Pay its accommodation and other suppliers in the various currencies of the destination countries concerned

In the cases above, if the value of the US dollar and other currencies in which costs occur were to rise against the euro and pound sterling, costs would be higher, putting a strain on the profitability of the operations of the two companies.

Questions

1. Explain the nature of the foreign exchange exposure for the German airline.

2. Explain the nature of the foreign exchange exposure for the British-based outbound tour operator.

The lack of stability caused by the continual changes in exchange rates between currencies creates uncertainty. Specifically, uncertainty is created as to what:

- Foreign income will be worth when it is received
- Payments will cost when they have to be made
- The value of foreign assets and liabilities might be in the future

5.6 SHORT CASE ILLUSTRATION

Foreign exchange exposure: Live Nation

The overall foreign exchange position of a company may be complicated, and the measures taken to reduce the risks associated with foreign exchange rate movements can be illustrated by the position of a leading event management company, Live Nation.

Live Nation is the largest producer of live music concerts in the world, organizing over 30,000 events and over 100 festivals with over 86 million attendees each year. These figures are sharply lower than the pre COVID-19 pandemic figures, when 98 million people attended over 40,000 events. Live Nation, based in Los Angeles, operates in five main industries within the live entertainment business, including live music events, venue operations, ticketing services, sponsorship and advertising sales and artist management and services, with revenues of about $5.8bn.

Live Nation has operations in countries throughout the world, and the financial results of its foreign operations are measured in their local currencies. As a result, the financial results are affected by factors such as changes in foreign currency exchange rates.

The primary foreign exchange exposure includes the euro, British pound and Canadian dollar. The company primarily uses forward currency contracts in addition to options to reduce its exposure to foreign currency risk associated with short-term artist fee commitments. Live Nation also enters into forward currency contracts to minimize the risks and/or costs associated with changes in foreign currency rates on forecasted operating income and short-term intercompany loans.

At the end of 2018, the company had forward currency contracts and options outstanding with a notional amount of $100.0mn.

Source: www.livenationentertainment.com

It is important to the profitability of many companies operating in *THE* that this exposure to foreign exchange rate movements be recognized and managed appropriately. Though it is prudent to manage these risks, it is common in reality for them to be ignored, especially by smaller companies.

In all cases, risk attributed to foreign exchange rate movements arises out of uncertainty about the future exchange rate between two currencies (Evans, 2002). This risk would be minimized if it were possible to predict future rate movements. Unfortunately, it is not possible to do so with any degree of accuracy, and for a company to try to do so can be financially dangerous.

If foreign exchange rates cannot be predicted, another option might be to pass on to the customer the effects of any adverse movements in exchange rates, and hence the company would incur no impact. In most cases, however, the highly competitive nature of most *THE* businesses prevents higher costs being passed on to the customer in this way.

We can identify three different types of foreign exchange risk or *exposure* an organization may be faced with:

- Transaction exposure
- Translation exposure
- Economic exposure

These terms are defined and discussed below.

DEFINITION/QUOTATION

Foreign exchange – transaction, translation and economic risk

- *Transaction risk* is the risk that transactions already entered into or for which the firm is likely to have a commitment in a foreign currency will have a variable value in the home currency because of exchange rate movements.

- *Translation risk* arises because financial data denominated in one currency are then expressed in another currency. Between two accounting dates the figures can be affected by exchange rate movements.

- *Economic risk* arises where a company's economic value may be affected by foreign exchange rate movements causing a loss in competitive strength.

Source: Arnold and Lewis (2019)

5.8.1 Transaction exposure

Transaction exposure relates to the foreign exchange exposure where contracts have already been entered into. When a company has contracted to receive or pay an amount of money in a foreign currency at some time in the future, a risk is incurred.

The specific risk is that adverse exchange rate movements between now and the time of the eventual cash receipt/payment will increase the amount to be paid out or decrease the amount to be received. The Short Case Illustration below illustrates the risks for a UK outbound tour operator.

5.7 SHORT CASE ILLUSTRATION

Transaction exposure: a UK outbound tour operator

A UK-based outbound tour operator selling holidays to America would receive its income in the local currency; that is, pounds sterling. Most of its payments to suppliers such as hoteliers, transportation companies, ground handling staff and other suppliers would be likely to be in US dollars. To make the payments at some stage, the company would have to convert the sterling the company receives in revenue into US dollars. This would entail a risk that the US dollar might rise in value (appreciate) against sterling, thereby making the payments more expensive in sterling terms:

Assume, for instance:

- The company had costed its hotel beds in its American hotels programmed at a rate of $1.40 to the pound (i.e., £1 buys US$1.40)

- The total cost to purchase the required bed spaces was US$1,400,000.

In the case outlined above, the planned cost in sterling to the company would be US$1,400,000/1.40 = £1,000,000.

Now if the rate subsequently fell to US$1.30, the cost would increase to US$1,400,000/1.30 = £1,076,923, an additional cost of almost £77,000 to the company.

Questions

1. What would the impact to the company be if the exchange rate changed to US$1.65 to the pound rather than US$1.30 in the example?

2. Consider what steps managers in this company might take to deal with the issue in this example.

Part 2

5.8.2 Translation exposure

Translation exposure arises on the consolidation of assets, liabilities and profits denominated in foreign currency in the process of preparing consolidated accounts. Values rise and fall in the accounts when revalued every year at the current prevailing exchange rate. However, unlike transaction exposure, the real gain or loss is only realized when the asset is sold or the liability becomes payable.

The concept (also known as *accounting exposure*) is illustrated by an American hotel company in the following Short Case Illustration.

5.8 SHORT CASE ILLUSTRATION

Translation exposure: an American-based hotel company

If an American hotel company that produces its annual results in its home currency (US$) purchases a hotel in Australia, it acquires an asset (the hotel) that is priced in the local currency; that is, Australian dollars (AU$).

Each year when the balance sheet of the business is prepared, the value of the hotel would be translated into the company's 'home' currency, in this case US$, at the prevailing rate on the balance sheet date. The risk is that the hotel might therefore be worth less in US$ terms as shown in the balance sheet of the company than the cost of the asset when it was bought. This would be the case if the AU$ were to rise against the US$.

Assume, for instance:

- The company purchased the hotel when the US$/AU$ rate was 1.10; that is, US$1 buys AU$1.07
- Assume that the hotel cost AU$10mn

In the case outlined above, the planned cost in US$ to the company would be AU$10,000,000/1.10 = US$9,090,909. This is the value of the property that will be recorded at the time of purchase.

Now if subsequently the rate of the AU$ strengthened and the exchange rate changed to AU$1.15, the value of the property (recorded in the annual report in US$) would fall to AU$10,000,000/1.15 = US$8,695,652, a recorded drop in value of over US$395,000 that would be recorded in the annual accounts.

Questions

1. What would the impact be if the hotel company took out a loan of AU$10mn to pay for the hotel?

2. Explain why a country's historically volatile currency might deter investment in physical assets such as hotels in that country.

5.8.3 Economic exposure

Economic exposure (sometimes referred to as 'political exposure') arises from the effect of adverse exchange rate movements on future cash flows, where no contractual arrangement to receive or pay money has yet been made.

This kind of exposure is longer term in nature and often difficult to quantify exactly and forecast accurately and is illustrated by the case of a specialist tour operator below.

5.9 SHORT CASE ILLUSTRATION

Economic exposure: a European specialist tour operator

Suppose a specialist European tour operator operates most of its tour operating program to one country, say, Egypt. The company will have an economic exposure to that country and its currency.

In some cases, the political and economic circumstances are very uncertain, and if, for example, the government should be replaced in a violent way (as occurred in recent years in Egypt), customers will be reluctant to book holidays to that country, thereby severely limiting the revenues of the specialist tour operator.

Questions

1. What steps might the company as described here take to protect itself against economic risks?

2. What other examples of economic risk affecting *THE* organizations you are familiar with could you cite?

5.8.4 Managing foreign exchange risk

Thus, movements in foreign exchange rates lead to a number of different problems or 'exposures' for *THE* companies. These exposures can be dealt with in a number of ways. The most obvious way of dealing with such exposures is to avoid the exposures altogether, either by trading in domestic markets only or by passing the exposure over to suppliers or customers.

These alternatives are seldom possible in the competitive international sectors of *THE*, so other management methods such as the use of *forward foreign exchange contracts* or *foreign exchange options* have to be employed to reduce the risks. For a discussion of these methods, see, for example, Arnold and Lewis (2019:ch. 22) and Madura (2020:part 3)

THINK POINTS

- What are the main limitations of financial information you need to be aware of?
- What are the three categories of foreign exchange risk? Provide an illustration of each of these risks from *THE*.
- Explain the possible impact of seasonality on cash flows in *THE*.

5.9 Cash management

All companies have a need to hold cash or have the ability to borrow cash. Cash is used to pay creditors (suppliers). Cash management is concerned with investing of cash surpluses and financing of cash shortages.

During the course of trading, companies often generate cash surpluses for which there is no current requirement and that can therefore be invested for a period of time. Sometimes companies that have such surpluses are referred to as 'cash-rich', and many in *THE* are in this category, at least for part of each year, because of the *seasonality* of many businesses in these sectors (discussed in Chapter1).

THE organizations make profits predominantly from their operations, such as selling holidays, accommodation, transportation or events. However, many organizations in *THE* also derive substantial revenues from investing the cash they receive from their customers at certain times of the year. Many parts of the industry are highly seasonal, with large cash accumulations in some periods (and an exodus of cash during other times of the year).

Such a situation is illustrated by the major events and entertainment group Live Nation below.

5.10 SHORT CASE ILLUSTRATION

The importance of cash management: Live Nation

Live Nation, probably the largest entertainment company in the world, organizes and promotes concerts and festivals around the world, owns or leases concert and festival venues and sells tickets for events through its Ticketmaster operations.

The *seasonality* of the underlying businesses creates volatile cash flows that need to be planned for and managed.

> Our results may vary significantly from quarter to quarter . . . . Typically, we experience our lowest financial performance in the first and fourth quarters of the calendar year as our outdoor venues are primarily used, and our festivals primarily occur during May through to October. In addition, the timing of tours of top grossing acts can impact cash flow. The seasonality of our businesses could create cash flow management risks if we do not adequately anticipate and plan for periods of decreased activity, which could negatively impact our ability to execute our strategy, which in turn could harm our results of operations.
>
> (Live Nation, 2021:26)

Examples of seasonal effects include the concerts segment, which reports the majority of revenue in the second and third quarters. Cash inflows and outflows depend on the timing of event-related payments, but the majority of the inflows generally occur prior to the event.

It should be noted that during 2020 and 2021, due to the unprecedented closure of concert venues from March 2021 due to the COVID-19 pandemic, the company did not experience the normal seasonal cash flow trends. However, the seasonality effects would be expected to return as entertainment venues around the world reopened during 2022.

Source: Adapted from Live Nation Entertainment annual report:2021, www.livenationentertainment.com

Questions

1. Consider what the implications of the seasonality of cash flow might be for a company such as Live Nation.

2. Can you cite other examples of companies involved in *THE* with such seasonal cash flows, and what are the implications for managers in these companies?

5.9.1 Cash flow risk analysis

As discussed in Chapter 1, *THE* has one of the most highly seasonal patterns of demand for any group of products or services.

> **For example:** *In temperate climates, there is a strong tendency to travel, hold events and utilize hospitality services when the weather is more likely to be benign and daylight hours are longer; that is, spring and summer.*

Seasonality of demand for such products leads to a highly seasonal pattern of cash inflows and outflows.

Consequently, at certain times of the year, companies in these sectors may have large cash balances to invest, and at other times of the year many companies need to borrow money to maintain payments to suppliers (creditors). The industry is also *cyclical* in nature, in that cash flows are very responsive to changes in the general level of economic activity.

In terms of cash management, tour operators, event managers, travel agents and airlines, for instance, are typically quite low margin businesses. They often derive important parts of their income not from operating profits (through the selling of their services) but from interest income derived from investing cash surpluses they may be holding at certain times of the year. This source of income, though, has been rather less important in the relatively low interest rate environment that has existed around the world in recent years.

Cash builds up and declines in a seasonal way: during certain times of the year, particularly in the spring, large surplus cash balances are free to be invested until the cash is needed to pay bills during the summer season and for the remainder of the year. The size and timing of the cash balances and the interest earned from the invested balances will vary from year to year, because the profile of bookings and level of interest rates also vary from year to year.

The period of greatest risk for many *THE* companies, however, usually comes in the autumn and winter, and historically this is when many such businesses have failed. Cash balances have been run down as seasonal payments were made during the preceding summer season, and the bulk of bookings for the subsequent season have yet to be made, for which cash is yet to be received. Companies often have to rely on bank support to help them through this period.

In a case where a bank (or other party) fails to lend the necessary support, *insolvency* is the inevitable result. Insolvency has often befallen companies in these sectors when anticipated revenue from expected bookings failed to materialize. Thus, many businesses fail not because they fail to be profitable but because they run out of cash; that is, they become *insolvent* and are unable to pay their bills as they become due.

When a company reaches an insolvent position, it normally leads to the company's failure and liquidation. A company can sometimes survive for many years without making profits or making very low levels of profit, but if they run out of cash, it is difficult for them to survive, because employees and creditors must be paid.

Many *THE* companies routinely rely on banks to provide short-term finance for part of the year, but when these negative cash balances are larger or more prolonged than usual and banks feel unable to provide finance, problems occur.

Analyzing cash flow is an important strategic task that can provide a lot of information on how the company is trading at the time and indicate likely future problems.

The Short Case Illustration below indicates the sort of seasonal cash flow issues associated with many *THE* companies, in this case a UK-based tour operator. The characteristics of the tour operating business outlined have certain implications for cash flow analysis and cash management.

5.11 SHORT CASE ILLUSTRATION

Seasonality of cash flow: a UK outbound tour operator

Detailed patterns of seasonality will differ between sectors, companies and countries, but most organizations in *THE* are prone to the effects of seasonality of cash flow to some degree.

As an example, a typical UK outbound tour operator selling 'package holidays' largely to Southern Europe is greatly affected by the seasonality of the product, and this directly affects its cash flow and, in turn, its management.

Such an operator may have a number of operating characteristics:

- The bulk of holidays sold would be 'summer sun', with the season lasting from April to September and with peak months of July and August during school holidays.

- Summer sun holidays are typically booked in three distinct periods:

  - The early booking period starting in August or September is when a significant number of people book. This applies especially to families and those who are tied to taking holidays between certain dates

  - The post-Christmas period from January to March is usually the largest booking period.

  - The late booking period, from April onwards, has become increasingly significant in recent years and may be a time of intense competition as operators try to sell remaining capacity and vary prices to do so.

- Many tour operators have attempted to widen their range of activities, and reduce the effects of seasonality by, for instance, introducing 'winter sun' and skiing programs. The winter sun season normally lasts from October to April, and the skiing season normally lasts from December to April with peaks in February and at Easter. In most cases the combined size of these programs is far smaller than the summer program in terms of receipts. Bookings for the winter sun and skiing programs are taken throughout the summer and autumn, but the winter ski program in particular is subject to a great deal of late booking in late autumn and early winter as customers wait to see what snow conditions are likely for the season.

- The tour operator will have a number of seasonal costs such as airline fuel, staff working at resorts, and accommodation charges. However, the tour operator will also have a high level of costs that have to be met throughout the year, such as the costs of head office staff, aircraft maintenance and computer facilities.

Questions

1. Explain what issues the seasonality of cash flow might cause for managers in this case.

2. Explain the steps such a company might take to reduce the impact of this seasonality of cash flow.

5.9.2 *Cash flow forecasting*

One of the most straightforward financial tools is a cash flow forecast – sometimes called a funds flow forecast.

A business may have substantial assets such as cruise ships, aircraft and buildings, but creditors such as suppliers, staff and the government cannot be paid using these because they need to be paid in cash. Assets such as buildings and transport equipment can, of course, be sold for cash, but this cannot happen easily or quickly because they are *illiquid*, not liquid, assets.

Essentially, cash flow forecasting involves a forecast of the:

- Expected revenues to be received
- Costs that will be incurred
- Net cash inflows or outflows (derived from the difference between revenues and costs)

The purpose of the forecast is that it allows for potential problems and solutions to be identified. If the same procedure is carried out for each option, the most favorable can be identified or suggestions can be made to improve the forecast cash position.

Many businesses fail not because they fail to be profitable but because they run out of cash; that is, they become *insolvent* and are unable to pay their bills as they become due.

Table 5.5 demonstrates the principles of constructing a cash flow forecast. The forecast will be broken down into monthly 'chunks' and a statement will be constructed for each month in which cash outflows and inflows are shown, together with opening and closing bank balances. The closing bank balance in one month is carried over and becomes the opening balance in the following month.

Applying the principles shown in Table 5.5, Table 5.6 shows a specific (fictional) tour operator (Interjet) that exhibits the characteristics shown in the Short Case Illustration above. The table demonstrates how analysis of a detailed cash flow forecast can be used to identify underlying financial issues.

As with many *THE* businesses, the Interjet cash flow forecast shows large seasonal fluctuations that managers have to be aware of to take active steps to ensure that the difficulties are not insurmountable and are managed appropriately.

The Interjet example (Table 5.6) shows forward projections of cash flow and is intended to highlight a number of problems that can be identified and that require managerial actions to be planned such as those identified above. Clearly, with no actions being taken, the company in the example will experience future problems and will exceed its overdraft limit from Month 6 to Month 11. Without renegotiation of these facilities, the company faces a potential position of insolvency because it will have no funds available to pay its bills as they become due.

It is not possible to categorically predict whether the collective actions the company might take would be successful in the case of Interjet, because this is a simplified example. Some important

Table 5.5 A simplified cash flow forecast

	Month 1	Month 2	Month 3
Revenue	500	400	400
Expenditure	−400	−1,000	−500
Net	100	−600	−100
Balance brought forward	200	300	−300
Balance carried forward	300	−300	−400

Table 5.6 'Interjet' – cash flow forecast

	1 Apr	2 May	3 Jun	4 Jul	5 Aug	6 Sep	7 Oct	8 Nov	9 Dec	10 Jan	11 Feb	12 Mar	TOT.
INFLOWS													
Receipts from debtors	230	250	120	50	60	75	80	90	110	150	220	320	1,755
Dividend on investment							45						45
TOTAL INFLOWS	230	250	120	50	60	75	125	90	110	150	220	320	1,800
OUTFLOWS													
Payments to creditors		80		80		88		88		88		92	516
Wages & other expenses	102	77	58	103	79	59	105	80	62	108	83	63	979
Payments for fixed assets				70	10	15					5		100
Dividend payable		80											80
Corporation Tax									120				120
TOTAL OUTFLOWS	102	157	138	253	89	162	105	168	182	196	88	155	1,795
NET IN/OUT	128	93	−18	−203	−29	−87	20	−78	−72	−46	132	165	5
Bk Balance													
Opening	30	158	251	233	30	1	−86	−66	−144	−216	−262	−130	
Closing	158	251	233	30	1	−86	−66	−144	−216	−262	-130	35	

Notes:

a. As a tour operator most funds are received by customers as a deposit & subsequent payment of balance. On average this results in 3 months credit being granted to customers.
b. On average 6 weeks credit is taken from customers.
c. Capital expenditure budget:
   - New computer facilities — Month 4 — £40,000
   - Routine replacement of motor vehicles — Month 4 — £30,000
   - Computer software & programming costs — Month 5 — £10,000
   - Progress payment on building extensions — Month 7 — £15,000
   - Office furniture & equipment — Month 11 — £5,000
d. Negotiated overdraft facilities currently stand at £60,000

information is not given, such as the attitude of the bank toward the company with regard to its planned overdraft limit. However, careful consideration of the case can provide some suggested actions that could help.

> *For example: Some aspects of the company's capital budget may be considered 'business critical' (vital to the company's ongoing success), but other aspects may be far less vital and could be postponed or canceled altogether. Similarly, the amount of credit given by the company to its customers (debtors) compared to the amount of credit the company receives from its creditors might be considered. Other actions might also be considered by the company to alleviate its difficulties such as renegotiating its borrowing limits and postponing or spreading some capital expenditure.*

Interjet is a small outbound tour operator with ambitious plans. The company plans to increase its sales turnover by around 25% each year. However, like many tour operators, travel agents and other tourism businesses, the company experiences annual seasonal cash flow difficulties.

THINK POINTS

- Review the information on Interjet (Table 5.6).
- Identify foreseeable difficulties in the future cash flow position presented.
- Advise the board of Interjet on possible actions it might take to improve its forecast cash flow for the year and avoid any foreseeable difficulties.

In analyzing the cash flow forecast, it may be necessary to:

- Produce 'sensitivity analyses'; for instance, what if, sales were 10% lower/higher than expected or jet fuel prices rose by 50%?
- Produce a graph showing monthly or weekly balances may help indicate trends

Cash flow forecasts may reveal real potential problems. Failure to address them could potentially result in insolvency as creditors refuse to provide additional credit to maintain the company as a going concern. Analysis of the cash flow forecast should prompt certain questions such as:

- How easily predictable are the cash flows?
- How seasonal or cyclical are the cash flows?
- Can the company keep within its borrowing limits?
- Is the company generating enough cash to ensure its survival?
- Does the company require further credit facilities?
- How long does it take customers to pay the company?
- How quickly does the company pay suppliers and others?
- To what extent are payments *business critical*; that is, critical to the company's ongoing trading.

It is imperative that managers have a good insight into future cash flow patterns, and if problems are foreseen, they should have a set of planned actions to address them. Managers need to be able to convince banks and other creditors that their investments are safe and that credit should not be withdrawn.

Thus, there are a number of actions a company may wish to consider to alleviate perceived cash flow problems that the forecast shows for particular options, including:

- Postponing capital expenditure
- Accelerating cash inflows
- Postponing or reducing cash outflows
- Selling non-core assets
- Negotiating new lines of credit or extending existing lines
- Leasing rather than buying equipment.
- Tightly controlling costs such as salaries
- Prioritizing *business critical* expenditure over other expenditure
- Phasing payments so that they are paid when seasonal cash inflows are at their highest

---

THINK POINTS

- Explain what is meant by the term insolvency and how it can occur despite a company being profitable.

- Provide an example of a *THE* company you are familiar with that has failed owing to its insolvency and explain the underlying reasons why this might have occurred.

- Advise the board of Interjet (Table 5.6) on the forecast cash flow difficulties it is facing and when they are likely to occur.

- Advise the board of Interjet of the actions that managers might take to alleviate its difficulties.

Small business focus

Raising finance for smaller businesses in *THE* (as in other industries) is often problematic because:

- The asset backing (collateral for loans) is often lacking
- They lack managerial expertise
- Some financing sources are unlikely to be available, such as access to stock markets
- Providers of finance will demand higher returns because the risks and the setup cost are greater
- The company is less likely to have a long trading history to provide reassurance
- With smaller resources or a more limited niche market, they may be less aware of the risks or have less ability to manage them or may be particularly dependent on one market segment rather than a balanced portfolio
- With larger companies, banks and other providers of finance are likely to try harder to save failing large companies because of the large losses they might incur and negative publicity that might be generated.

Set against these difficulties for smaller companies in relation to raising finance there may be some advantages, in that owner-managers are often very close to the business and can react quickly to adapt to market changes. Banks and other lenders prefer to lend to businesses the owners have their own money invested in (as is likely to be the case in smaller businesses), because it might imply that the owner will work harder. In addition, if the business fails, the equity is lost first, meaning that a cushion is provided for the bank and other lenders. Furthermore, the owners of smaller businesses are often prepared to accept lower returns on their own investment to attract other investors and ensure long-term success.

Although in the modern world loan applications are often evaluated by computers according to centrally agreed-upon lending criteria, building up a good relationship with banks and other investors often remains important. In the financing of smaller companies, the credentials of the owners and key managers are often crucial in securing adequate financing, because if they leave the enterprise the impact is likely to be high.

It is important to realize that any time a small business seeks outside sources of finance its case almost certainly has to be presented in a formal way as part of a business plan or business case. This is because any investors will want to know what the investment is trying to achieve – is the amount of the investment sufficient to achieve the stated aims, and, crucially, how will the finance provider be rewarded and get their investment back?

In making a judgment on whether or not to invest, investors (particularly in smaller companies) may need to be satisfied that the '5 C's of credit' (W. Lee, 2019) have been addressed:

- *Character* – The general character of the owner and or key managers and specifically the probability that a person will attempt to pay off the debt and how serious their intention is
- *Capacity* – A judgment on the borrower's ability to pay. Many small businesses attempt to grow too quickly and run out of the liquidity to service their loans, which is often referred to as *overtrading*.
- *Capital* – The general financial condition of the borrower as reflected in its financial statements
- *Collateral* – The assets offered as security
- *Conditions* – General economic conditions and the specific circumstances of the borrower's industry or geographic area. In periods of economic downturn, even well-established businesses can fail and banks are reluctant to lend.

CHAPTER SUMMARY

An analysis of a company's financial position is an indispensable part of any strategic review. Decision makers need to know whether the company has the level of funding required to finance their strategies; if not, financial resources will have to be raised.

It is usually important to know where a company has obtained its capital and the cost of this capital. Both share capital and loan capital have their advantages and disadvantages for use in strategic development. It is important to note whether current levels of profitability are sufficient to service the costs of capital. In *THE* settings, it is also important to understand the relative capital intensity of the particular part of the industry being considered because it has important strategic consequences for managers.

There are a number of techniques that can be used to make sense of a company's financial statements. *Longitudinal* analysis examines trends over time; *cross-sectional* analysis compares a company's finances against its competitors; and *ratio* analysis enables us to make sense of accounts by dividing one accounting number by another. *Benchmarking* enables us to compare one company's performance on a number of fronts with similar companies.

Additionally, foreign exchange risk and cash flow risk are important facets of strategic financial risk for many *THE* companies, and this chapter has provided an overview for analyzing such risks.

Part 2

REFERENCES AND WEBSITES

References

Air New Zealand. (2021) Shareholder review, www.airnewzealand.com

Arnold, G. and Lewis, D. (2019) *Corporate Financial Management*, 6th ed., Harlow, UK: Pearson.

Atkinson, H., Jones, T., Lorenz, A. and Harris, P. (2012) *Strategic Managerial Accounting: Hospitality, Tourism and Events Applications*, 6th ed., Oxford, UK: Goodfellow.

Atrill, P. (2019) *Financial Management for Decision Makers*, 9th ed., Harlow, UK: Pearson.

Bowdin, G., Allen, J., Harris, R., McDonnell, I., and O'Toole, W. (2011) *Events Management*, 3rd ed., Abingdon, UK: Routledge.

Buckley, A. (2012) *International Finance: A Practical Perspective*, Harlow, UK: Pearson.

Bull, A. (1995) *The Economics of Travel and Tourism*, 2nd ed., Melbourne, VIC, Australia: Longman Australia.

Evans, N. G. (2002) 'Financial management for travel and tourism', in R. Sharpley (Ed.), *Travel and Tourism*, Sunderland, UK: Business Education Publishers, 345–366.

Fleisher, C. S. and Bensoussan, B. E. (2003) *Strategic and Competitive Analysis: Methods and Techniques for Analyzing Business Competition*, Upper Saddle River, NJ: Prentice Hall.

Guilding, C. and Ji, K. M. (2022) *Accounting Essentials for Hospitality Managers*, 4th ed., Abingdon, UK: Routledge.

Jankensgard, H., Alviniussen, A. and Oxelheim, L. (2020) *Corporate Foreign Exchange Risk Management*, Hoboken, NJ: John Wiley & Sons.

Karadeniz, E., Kandir, S. Y., Balcilar, M. and Onal, Y. B. (2009) 'Determinants of capital structure: Evidence from Turkish lodging companies', *International Journal of Contemporary Hospitality Management*, 21(5): 594–609.

Kim, W. G. and Ayoun, B. (2005) 'Ratio analysis for the hospitality industry: A cross sector comparison of financial trends in the lodging, restaurant, airline, and amusement sectors', *The Journal of Hospitality Financial Management*, 13(1): 59–78.

Lee, S. (2007) 'An examination of financial leverage trends on the lodging industry', *Journal of Hospitality Financial Management*, 15(1): 35–45.

Lee, W. (2019) 'Character-based lending for micro business development: Empirical insights into conceptualizing character', *Journal of Small Business and Entrepreneurship*, 34(6): 645–660.

Li, Y. and Singal, M. (2019) 'Capital structure in the hospitality industry: The role of the asset-light and fee-oriented strategy', *Tourism Management*, 70: 124–133.

Live Nation. (2021) *Live Nation Entertainment Annual Report and Accounts 2021*, www.livenationentertainment.com/

Lockwood, R. D. (1989) 'Foreign exchange management', in *Tourism Marketing and Management Handbook*, S. F. Witt and L. Moutinho (Eds), London: Prentice Hall, 175–178.

Lynch, R. (2015) *Strategic Management*, 7th ed., Harlow, UK: Pearson.

Madura, J. (2020) *International Financial Management*, 14th ed., Boston: Cengage.

Marsh, C. (2012) *Financial Management for Non-financial Managers*, London: Kogan Page.

Schmidgall, R. S. and DeFranco, A. (2016) 'How to best use financial ratios in benchmarking and decision making in clubs: Review of the decade 2003–2012', *International Journal of Hospitality and Tourism Administration*, 17(2): 179–197.

Tsai, H., Pan, S. and Lee, J. (2011) 'Recent research in hospitality financial management', *International Journal of Contemporary Hospitality Management*, 23(7): 941–971.

Walsh, C. (2011) *Key Management Ratios*, 4th ed., Harlow, UK: Pearson.

Wöber, K. W. (2002) *Benchmarking in Tourism and Hospitality Industries: The Selection of Benchmarking Partners*, Wallingford, UK: CABI.

Websites

www.accor.com

www.airasia.com

www.airnewzealand.com

www.carnival.com

www.livenationentertainment.com

www.qantas.com.au

www.travelcounsellors.co.uk/

Chapter **6**

Tourism, hospitality and event organizations – the products and markets context

Introduction and chapter overview

So far in this part of the book in relation to *THE* organizations we have analyzed the operational aspects, human aspects and financial aspects of organizations in Chapters 3, 4 and 5, respectively. This chapter examines the final part of the 'functional' aspects of the organization – products and markets. The way in which an organization relates to its markets is one of the most important aspects of competitive strategy. The idea of a market as a place where buyers and sellers come together can apply to both inputs and outputs. Product markets are those in which an organization competes for sales, whereas resource markets are those in which an organization competes for its resource inputs.

In this chapter, we discuss the key elements of this system – the nature of markets and the nature and importance of products in *THE* contexts. The way in which an organization configures itself in respect to these elements is crucial to the success of business strategy.

LEARNING OBJECTIVES

After studying this chapter, in relation to *THE*, readers should be able to:

- Explain the term *market* and describe the ways in which markets can be defined
- Understand the importance of markets and provide relevant examples from *THE*
- Explain the ways in which markets can be segmented and be able to apply the principles to *THE* contexts

DOI: 10.4324/9781003318613-8

- Understand the concepts of targeting and positioning in relation to *THE* contexts
- Explain the term product and describe Kotler's five levels of product benefit and be able to illustrate the concepts with relevant *THE* examples
- Understand the stages in and uses of the product life cycle and its derivative application in tourism – the tourist area life cycle
- Explain the concept of a product portfolio and understand the underlying cash flow implications
- Understand the composition and limitations of selected strategic models such as plc, the BCG matrix and the GE-McKinsey matrix

6.1 Strategic marketing for competitive advantage

The way in which an organization's products relate to its markets is one of the most important aspects of competitive strategy, the aim of which is to gain a competitive advantage over competitors. An organization may have great technical and operational capabilities, but these capabilities only become a source of competitive advantage when such 'distinctive capabilities' are applied in the marketplace (Kay, 1995:127). Hence, it is of critical strategic importance that managers are able to define and understand the markets in which they are operating. The next section considers various ways in which markets can be defined.

Modern management writers view marketing less as one of the main constituent departments of an organization and more as a holistic, competitive orientation for a business (Evans, 2012). Thus, marketing takes on a strategic role for an organization and, indeed, the 'strategic' dimension to marketing reflects its growing impingement on traditional 'strategic management' territory (Fyall and Garrod, 2005). Thus, the strategic management literature and the marketing academic literature are closely linked, often covering similar concepts, tools and techniques.

The intention in this chapter is *not* to cover marketing in a *THE* context in great detail (because this is done elsewhere as indicated below) but instead to concentrate on those strategic aspects of marketing that are necessary to analyze as part of a holistic understanding of organizations' strategic positioning.

Marketing as applied to specific *THE* contexts has generated a large academic literature in recent years, including a number of textbooks. Increasingly, tourism and hospitality are being considered jointly, with separate texts available for events management, or the approach of this text has been adopted, in which, given their commonality, tourism, hospitality and events are covered in a single text. See, for example, Preston (2012), Bojanic and Reid (2017), Bowie et al. (2016), Hudson and Hudson (2017), Reic (2017), Rogers and Davidson (2017), Kolb (2017, 2018), Morrison (2018), Fyall et al. (2019), Kotler et al. (2021) and George (2021).

Markets are rarely completely homogenous. Within markets there are groups of customers with requirements that are similar, and it is this similarity of needs and wants that distinguishes one market *segment* from another.

The most widely quoted author on marketing, Philip Kotler, used these differences when he proposed that the heart of modern strategic marketing can be described as 'STP marketing' namely, segmenting, targeting, and positioning (Kotler and Armstrong, 2020). In STP (or 'target marketing'), the seller distinguishes the major segments (identifiable parts) of the market, targets one or more of these segments and positions products and marketing programs so that they will appeal to the needs and wants of these chosen target segments. Kotler has also applied his approach specifically to tourism and hospitality (Kotler et al., 2021) and to destinations (Kotler et al., 1993).

Kotler's approach, which has been widely followed and adapted by other authors (see, for example, West et al., 2015; Ezeh, 2017), will be followed in this chapter because it takes a strategic view of marketing within organizations, it is easy to understand and apply and, importantly, it is widely utilized in teaching and in practice.

6.2 Understanding markets

It is important before going on to consider how organizations approach their markets to consider exactly what we mean by the term 'markets'. Economists refer to a market as a system comprising two 'sides'. The demand side comprises buyers or consumers of a product or service. The supply side produces or operates products and services.

In strategy, we often use the term slightly differently. By 'market' we usually mean a group of actual or potential customers with similar needs or wants (the demand side). We usually refer to the supply side as an industry.

The definition and boundaries of an organization's markets represent a key starting point for the formulation of strategy and provide a basis for measuring competitive performance. The analysis and definition of markets will also provide key information concerning the threats and opportunities facing an organization.

An understanding of markets is important for several reasons, because managers are able to:

- Gain an indication of the demand (and potential demand) for an organization's products and services
- Assess the potential for market growth and gaining market share over competitors
- Recognize and evaluate the number, type and capabilities of competitors
- Position products and services in the market so that they are able to develop and sustain their competitive advantage.

6.3 Market attractiveness

Managers often consider the attractiveness of a market; that is, they consider whether products offered in a particular market will deliver returns on investment that are attractive to the organization and its investors. A number of factors contribute to market attractiveness, including market size, market growth and supplier concentration.

- *Market size*. In general terms the larger the size of a market, the more attractive it will be, in that it will offer wider opportunities for a larger number of organizations. Such a market, however, will also attract powerful suppliers who will attempt to dominate it by gaining a high market share.

  For example: *The market for mass holidays to Spain from Northern Europe is large and, consequently, it is supplied by a large number of tour operators, whereas the market for activity holidays for European teenagers is far smaller and is consequently supplied by fewer companies.*

- *Market growth rate*. A growing market is normally more attractive than a static or declining market, because growing markets allow opportunities for businesses to expand in line with the growth of the market. In static or declining markets, growth for individual organizations can only be achieved by taking market share away from competitors, which can be expensive and may lead to lower margins.

  For example: *The market for fast travel between China's major cities has been growing quickly in recent years and, consequently, state (or part state-owned) airlines, low-cost airlines, rail and road services have all considerably added to their capacity. Conversely, overall hotel capacity in many English seaside resorts has been falling.*

- *Supplier concentration.* Concentration refers to the extent to which a market is dominated by its largest suppliers and is usually measured by the percentage market share of the top four or five suppliers. The Short Case Illustration below outlines the relative lack of concentration in the case of international hotels.

Large organizations, which dominate the market, will tend to have advantages over smaller organizations in terms of costs; available promotional budgets and power over customers and suppliers as to setting prices and minimizing costs. However, large organizations may find it difficult to increase their market share beyond a certain point owing to regulatory restrictions, and smaller organizations may compensate for their disadvantages.

In contrast, smaller organizations may be more flexible in their approach, know their customers' preferences more thoroughly, have access to a market niche (which is too small to attract larger organizations) and be less bureaucratic than larger competitors. In such circumstances it may be medium-sized organizations that find their competitive position is difficult to defend, because they possess neither the advantages of scale nor the benefits that small organizations may be able to exploit.

6.1 SHORT CASE ILLUSTRATION

Market concentration: worldwide hotels

The hotel industry around the world has traditionally been highly fragmented. In many countries, provision has been dominated by small operators often run by families with a single hotel.

As such, the industry remains fragmented. Branded hotel penetration has steadily increased as a long-term trend and is expected to continue to grow as consumers look to trusted brands to meet their evolving expectations.

However, this pattern is changing, with large international groups becoming more active in many countries. One of the largest global branded hotel groups IHG (which includes brands such as Intercontinental, Holiday Inn and Crowne Plaza in its portfolio of brands) estimated that about 54% of worldwide hotels are part of branded groups. Five of the leading branded hotel companies (IHG, Marriott, Hilton, Wyndham and Accor Hotels) account for approximately a quarter of the market. (www.IHG.com).

Consequently, the market is becoming more concentrated in some countries, though the position varies considerably in different national markets. IHG (2022) reported that cost remains a significant barrier to building a scale position in the industry, whether that is due to the investment required to build and maintain hotels, establish a strong loyalty program or market brands in a competitive marketplace (IHG, 2022).

A 2013 report (Clifton, 2013) analyzed the extent to which the global hotel industry had been penetrated by the leading hotel groups in terms of the proportion of total room stock that was affiliated to the hotel groups. The proportion of total hotel room stock that was affiliated to one of the 2,100 groups of hotels was measured in percentage terms and the countries were categorized.

The data (for selected markets for which data were available), presented in Table 6.1, indicate a marked difference in concentration between some national markets and others. According to this study, countries such as the USA, UAE and New Zealand have particularly high levels of concentration, whereas others such as Italy, Austria and Pakistan show evidence of a fragmented structure and low levels of concentration.

Table 6.1 Penetration by hotel groups in selected countries (2013)

>74%	50%–74%	25%–49%	10%–24%	<10%
UAE	South Africa	Finland	Croatia	Austria
Djibouti	Singapore	Spain	Portugal	Pakistan
New Zealand	Dominican Republic	France	Germany	Italy
Cuba	India	Australia	Mexico	Argentina
Monaco	Norway	Netherlands	Morocco	Paraguay
Burundi	Canada	Denmark	Saudi Arabia	Ukraine
USA	UK	Sweden	Turkey	Peru
	China	Ireland	Switzerland	
		Swaziland	Japan	
		Egypt	Russia	

Source: Clifton (2013)

Questions

1. Why is worldwide hospitality relatively less concentrated than many other industry sectors?

2. Consider what factors might make worldwide hotels more concentrated.

6.4 Defining markets

We can also define the boundaries of markets in different ways. If different companies define a market in different ways, it is not surprising that the sum of their claimed market share may add to more or less than 100%. The problem is particularly difficult in many service industries because the boundaries between them often overlap and are sometimes difficult to define, whereas the market for many manufactured products, such as cars, is obvious and relatively easy to define.

> **For example:** *The 'overseas holiday' market, may mean different things to different companies. One company might include all holidays taken abroad, whereas another company might only include such holidays taken by air or sold as part of a 'package'.*

The problem is perhaps even more difficult in a sector such as 'events' because its boundaries are difficult to define and recognize. The sector (as discussed in the Introduction to Part 1 of this book) has few recognizable brand names, a measure of its fragmentation, and there is some discussion as to the boundaries of the subject. It is, however, generally accepted (Getz, 2022) that events management is concerned with managing in the contexts of:

- Event management companies
- Sports events

- Concerts and performances
- Festivals
- Exhibitions
- Meetings and conferences

It is clearly important, therefore, that market share measures be stated explicitly with the market boundaries clearly defined.

Market share is a measure of an organization's performance with regard to its ability to win and retain customers relative to other organizations. It can be measured either by *volume* or by *value*.

- *Volume measures* concern the organization's share of units sold to the market.

   For example: *The number of air-inclusive holidays sold by a tour operator in relation to the total number of air-inclusive holidays sold over a period, the number of bed spaces sold by a hotelier relative to all bed sales or the number of event tickets sold by an event manager relative to sales made by all event managers.*

- *Value measures* concern the sales turnover of one company in proportion to the total value of the market.

   For example: *The sales turnover of one air-inclusive tour operator relative to the turnover for all air-inclusive tour operators, the value of bed sales by one hotelier relative to the value of all bed sales or the value of event tickets made by one manager relative to the value of all ticket sales.*

There are three ways in which markets are commonly defined, based on:

- *Product*
- *Need satisfaction* (or *function performed*)
- *Customer identity*

We will briefly examine each of these in turn.

6.4.1 Market – definition based on product

If someone working for an organization is asked what market they are in, a common reply will be to describe the products that sold. Thus, we would have examples like holidays or conferences and exhibitions. If the product definition is wide, this type of definition is close to describing an industry. Because government economic statistics are often produced on this basis, markets defined in this way often have the advantage of ease of measurement.

A drawback of this approach is that it sometimes fails to consider that a product may provide a range of different benefits, and different products, often derived from completely different sources, might meet the same need.

The strategic implication of this is that it could lead to a failure to recognize threats that may come from a different industry altogether, as the two examples below illustrate.

   For example: *Rapid advances in technology enable competing organizations to rapidly reach a large scale of operations and to disrupt more traditional suppliers. The growth of Airbnb, Uber and Expedia is an example of where technology companies have grown to disrupt markets and provide a threat to more traditional providers in accommodation, taxi services and travel distribution, respectively.*

For example: *Holidays, watching sport and attending arts festivals appear to be entirely different products with different markets, but they each may compete for customers' discretionary income and time (the income and time left over when essentials have been dealt with). They can also both be considered as part of the wider 'leisure' market.*

An advantage of a product-based definition of markets can be that economies of scale of operations may be gained by the sharing of particular processes. Taken to extremes, this can lead to a view of a market as the market for the products that a company happens to produce even where they appear to have little in common.

For example: *Saga Holidays is a UK-based tour operator selling holidays exclusively for the over-55 age group directly to the public. Using its database of clients, it is also able to sell other products such as financial services and insurance to the same target market.*

6.4.2 Market – definition based on need satisfaction or function performed

Consumers purchase a good or service to gain *utility*. The concept of utility (a word often used by economists) infers that whenever a consumer makes a purchase, they make a cost–benefit calculation, in that they make a judgment that the benefit they will get from the product is worth more than the price paid.

This understanding enables the organization to understand its markets according to customers' perceptions. In this view, organizations are concerned with matching the product offered with the benefits sought by the customers. The matching of the two is, however, a challenging process.

To illustrate this approach to defining markets, Table 6.2 considers the benefits being sought by visitors to various types of events and attractions

Table 6.2 Main benefits sought in types of events and attractions

Type of event/attraction	Main benefits sought
Theme park	Excitement, variety of on-site attractions, atmosphere
Beach	Suntan, sea bathing, company of others *or* solitude, water-based activities
Cathedral	History, aesthetic pleasure derived from architecture, sense of peace or spirituality
Museum or gallery	Learning something new, nostalgia, purchasing replicas or souvenirs
Theatre	Entertainment, atmosphere, status – to be able to say you were there
Leisure center	Exercise, physical challenges, competing against others
Mountains	Solitude, beauty, activities, walking
Concert, event or festival	Entertainment, support, atmosphere, status – to be able to say you were there

Source: Adapted from Swarbrooke and Page (2012)

Though a definition based on satisfying needs can lead to a more open-minded approach to the formulation of strategy, its weakness can be that very broad definitions can lead to a view of markets that do not allow a practical approach to decision making.

> For example: *A restaurant chain might define itself as being in the 'leisure' market, but it is probably wise for restaurant companies to also consider threats and opportunities that might arise from competing sources such as television, bars, computer games, holidays, etc. Opportunities only arise from leisure activities that the company's competences would allow it to enter (see Chapter 2), and threats would come from activities that would be likely to provide adequate substitute for customers' business.*

KEY CONCEPT

Needs and wants

Whenever a customer makes a purchase decision, he or she expects to gain a benefit from the product purchased. This benefit of satisfaction is usually expressed as a need or a want. The difference between the two is in the perception of the consumer – one customer's want is another's need.

The practical use of the distinction is in the price responsiveness of the product. Generally speaking, customers who need – or who believe they need – a product will be less price sensitive than those who merely want it. Hence, the greater the felt need, the more *price inelastic* the demand (see Key Concept on page 379).

6.4.3 Market – definition based on customer identity

Groups of customers have requirements in common and differ from other groups of customers. In this way, the *identity* of customers can be used to define markets.

> For example: *Consider the 'business travel market' as a quite distinct market. The market might be for products as diverse as airline flights, hotel rooms, meeting and exhibition spaces, event management services, car hire, etc. But the market could clearly be seen as the market for types of travel, hospitality and ancillary services needed by those traveling for business purposes.*

In terms of strategy formulation, the advantage of this approach is that it allows accurate targeting of the customer, so that efficient use can be made of advertising, direct mail shots, personal selling, search engine optimization, social media, etc. Its main disadvantage is that though marketing economies may be made, a number of different suppliers in the supply chain might need to be used to service the various requirements, so that the control of the quality of these suppliers becomes an issue of concern.

6.4.4 Market – combined definition

In practice, most businesses serve several markets with a range of products. They will define their markets with a combination of the ways listed here, and to the extent that one or another approach is uppermost, the advantages and disadvantages that we have already encountered will apply.

A key task for management at a strategic level is to produce combinations that gain synergistic benefits and that enable the best opportunities to be chosen and exploited. In cases where change in aspects of the technology of supply or the characteristics of markets take place so that synergies previously achievable are no longer available, a case exists for restructuring an organization to divest itself of some activities and/or to acquire new ones.

In terms of working out competitive success in markets, a key concept is that of the *served market* – that part of a market that the company is trading in. It is on that basis that the measure of market share is most meaningful.

THINK POINTS

- Explain how the term *market can* be defined and analyzed.

- Explain why a detailed definition and understanding of the market is so important for *THE* managers.

- Explain the meanings of market *attractiveness* and supplier concentration, and illustrate your answer by providing examples from *THE*.

6.5 'STP' marketing

Market segmentation has been considered one of the most fundamental aspects of marketing since Wendell Smith (1956) published his influential article in the *Journal of Marketing*. Organizations cannot realistically engage and communicate with the entire population, so the overall population, or potential market, has to be broken down into manageable chunks. Organizations can effectively engage with or, to use the terminology that is commonly used, 'reach' these chunks or 'segments'.

Thus, market segmentation is concerned with the process of dividing a market into distinct groups of buyers with similar requirements.

To Kotler (Kotler and Armstrong, 2020), the essence of modern strategic marketing can be described as *STP* marketing, namely:

- Segmenting
- Targeting
- Positioning

In STP or target marketing (which, for example, Tsiotsou and Goldsmith [2012], Weinstein and Morritt [2012], Alexander et al. [2015] and Mody et al. [2019] discuss in relation to *THE* contexts), the seller:

- Distinguishes *segments* (identifiable parts) of the market
- *Targets* one or more of these segments
- *Positions* products and marketing programs so that they will appeal to the needs and wants of these chosen target segments

In this way, organizations are able to define unique customer groups, select those they wish to serve and then integrate the *marketing mix* to establish a unified image of the product relative to the competition (Jonk et al., 2008).

Organizations widely adopt such an approach. Target marketing (as it is frequently termed) helps sellers to:

● Identify marketing opportunities better
● Develop the right product features to attract each target market
● Have the ability to adjust their prices, distribution channels and promotional activities to 'reach' the target market efficiently

The approach can be seen as focusing marketing efforts on those customers that the organization has the greatest chance of satisfying. Underpinning this strategic process are two important information requirements. The organization needs to gain an understanding of:

● The process by which potential purchasers arrive at a decision to purchase a particular product; that is, *buyer behavior*
● The structure of the market and competitive product offerings that influence buyer behavior and require attention to be given to the importance of detailed *marketing research*

6.6 Market segmentation

Markets are rarely completely homogenous. Within markets there are groups of customers with requirements that are similar, and it is this similarity of needs and wants that distinguishes one market segment from another. These 'submarkets' are known as *market segments*. By considering the extent to which the segments should be treated differently from others and which ones will be chosen to *serve*, organizations can develop *target markets* and gain a focus for their commercial activity.

DEFINITION/QUOTATION

Tourism segmentation

In justifying market segmentation as a tool for tourism, Dolnicar (2008:45) stated that:

> Tourists are heterogeneous. Market segmentation is the strategic tool to account for heterogeneity among tourists by grouping them into market segments which include members similar to each other and dissimilar to members of other segments. Both tourism researchers and tourism industry use market segmentation widely to study opportunities for competitive advantage in the marketplace.

This process of segmentation represents a powerful competitive tool. It is true that a business will prosper by giving the customer what the customer wants. Because not all customers are likely to want the same thing, identifying subgroups and attending to their requirements more precisely is a way of gaining competitive advantage.

KEY CONCEPT

Market segmentation

> A market segment is a homogeneous group of customers with similar needs, wants, values and buying behavior.

> (Hollensen, 2019:296)

As such, each market segment can be viewed as the sector of the overall market in which competition takes place. The marketer is concerned with identifying subsets of people with similar needs and characteristics that lead them to respond in similar ways to product offerings.

Hollensen (2019) identified three reasons for the increasing importance of market segmentation in developing marketing strategies:

- Population growth has slowed and more product markets are maturing, which in turn leads to more intense competition as companies seek growth through gains in market share.

- There is an important trend toward 'microsegmentation' (one-to-one marketing). In manufacturing, flexible production techniques allow cars, for instance, to be made to order to the customer's specifications. In THE, technology has allowed customers to be offered individualized tour itineraries and potential events to be offered based on past purchasing histories.

- Expanding disposable incomes, higher educational attainment and greater awareness of the world have produced customers with more varied and sophisticated needs, tastes and lifestyles.

Despite the advantages of segmenting a market, there may also be potential difficulties, as identified by Gibson (2001). The difficulties may include:

- Segmentation normally describes *current market segments* – the future position of segments may be different.

- Segmentation assumes *homogeneity within each identified segment* – this may not be the case.

- Segmentation implies competition-free segments – other competitors may identify the same segments.

- Segmentation may *identify the wrong segment* – other segments not identified may hold more opportunities.

It could be argued that it is better to be hated by half of potential customers and loved by the other half than to be quite liked by them all. The latter is a recipe for being everyone's second choice and underlines the dangers of placing too much reliance on averages in market research.

By identifying a specific market segment and concentrating marketing efforts at the segment, many organizations can build a degree of *monopolistic power* (a mini-monopoly) in the segment and thereby achieve higher profit margins than would otherwise be achievable. Many organizations that have identified a highly specific segment can succeed and gain reasonable profits by configuring their internal activities to precisely meet the needs and wants of the customer group.

For the most part, we can assume that segments exist naturally in most markets, and it is up to organizations as to how to exploit the differences that exist in the submarkets. We do, however, have to recognize that companies activities can also shape the segments to some extent. We could expect, for example, that men and women buy differently. If, in those markets, suppliers offer and promote different products to men and women, this tendency will be reinforced.

Before considering the ways in which market segments might be identified and specific segments targeted, it is useful to consider the type of subgroups that exist within the different sectors of *THE*, as shown in Table 6.3. Destination organizations are excluded because most are seen as having relevance for all of the segments identified.

6.6.1 Four approaches to segmentation

Four broad approaches are recognized in respect to the ways in which an organization can approach marketing to market segments (or submarkets)

UNDIFFERENTIATED MARKETING

This means that the organization denies that its total markets are segmented at all and relates to the market assuming that demand is homogeneous in nature. The economies of a standardized approach to marketing outweigh any advantages of segmenting the market. Undifferentiated marketing is appropriate when the market the organization serves is genuinely homogeneous in nature.

Table 6.3 Consumer segments in the main constituent parts of tourism, hospitality and events

Tourism, hospitality and events	Principal consumer segments
Hotels	• Corporate/business clients
	• Visitors on group package tours
	• Independent vacationers
	• Visitors taking weekend/midweek package breaks
	• Conference delegates
Tour operators	• Young people, singles and couples, 18- to 30-year-olds
	• Families with children
	• Retired/senior citizens/empty nesters
	• Activity/sports participants
	• Culture seekers
Transport operators	• First-class passengers
	• Club-class passengers
	• Standard-class passengers
	• Charter groups
	• Advance purchasers
	• Purchasers close to departure – 'last-minute'
Destination attractions, cultural, sporting and business events Restaurants	• Local residents in the area
	• Day visitors from outside the local area – leisure and business
	• Domestic tourists – leisure and business
	• Foreign tourists – leisure and business
	• School parties

Source: Author's categorization

DIFFERENTIATED MARKETING

Companies that adopt *differentiated* marketing recognize separate segments of the total market and treat each segment separately. Different segments need not always be different in every respect – it could be that some standard products can be promoted differently to different segments because of certain similarities or common characteristics. In other cases, the product will be substantially or completely different and marketing to each segment will necessitate a distinctive approach to each one.

CONCENTRATED MARKETING

An extreme form of differentiated marketing is *concentrated* marketing, where an organization's effort is focused on a single market segment. In return for giving up substantial parts of the market, an effort is made to specialize in just one niche, referred to as *niche marketing*.

This approach offers the advantage that the organization can gain a detailed and in-depth knowledge of its segment, which, in turn, can enable an ever-improving match between the product and the customer requirement. The disadvantage relates to the extent to which the company may become dependent on the one segment it serves. Any negative change in the demand pattern of the segment will leave the supplier vulnerable because of the narrowness of its market portfolio. Market portfolio considerations are covered later in the chapter, when the product life cycle and various models are discussed.

CUSTOMIZED MARKETING

Customized marketing occurs in cases where a market is viewed as being so diverse that an organization has to focus its marketing efforts on the needs of each individual customer. Such an approach enables the organization to modify its product or the way in which it is delivered, promoted or priced to satisfy individual requirements. Such an approach may be costly, because any potential economies of scale are lost. However, advances in technology, such as utilizing social media to enable dynamically interactive personalized social experiences (Buhalis and Sinarta, 2019) and analyzing big data sets (Ardito et al., 2019), can make such approaches easier to implement than previously was the case, leading to so-called mass customization (see, for example, Neuhofer et al., 2015).

It should be noted that companies operating with a large product range in many markets will typically use a multifocus strategy – that is, a combination of the above.

6.6.2 Criteria for segmentation

Market segmentation occurs because organizations can no longer regard markets as being uniform, where all consumers wish to purchase the same product. Thus, each organization has to divide the market into clearly defined segments, where each segment represents a discrete body of consumers, each of whom will have clearly defined needs that warrant a separate marketing strategy.

However, the method by which the marketer or strategist divides the market into segments is extremely important.

> For example: *One method might be to divide the population into groups according to eye color. We might end up with people with blue eyes, people with brown eyes and people with mixed eye colors. This would be a perfectly valid method of classifying people into groups whose members were similar to each other and dissimilar from members of other groups. But what use would it be to the marketing of a tourist destination or a cultural event? The answer, of course, is very little, because consumer needs and wants are unlikely to vary according to eye color.*

In *THE* sectors there are perhaps two major problems to consider when segmenting the market:

1. The product itself is, in many cases, highly inflexible. In other words, supply is usually fixed, at least in the short to medium term. The basic attractions of the product are to a great extent given.

> **For example:** *It is difficult to move a preplanned festival at short notice to a different date, the attractions of a tourist destination (sun, sea, mountains, etc.) cannot be altered and cruise ship or hotel capacity cannot be changed quickly.*

2. In many cases, resources are extremely limited.

> **For example:** *Destinations, attractions and national or regional tourism authorities often have very small promotional budgets, whereas the promoters of a festival or event will have a fixed promotional budget they are expected to adhere to.*

The most important aspect of market segmentation is the choice of *bases* (criteria) used to divide customers into groups. The criteria selected must be relevant to the customers' needs and/or their behavior in the market concerned.

There is no single way of segmenting a market. Each organization has to choose *bases*, or variables, that it thinks are appropriate in respect of its consumers. It must never be forgotten that there is not only a great variety of *THE* products – countries, regions, cities, agencies, airlines, tour operators, festivals and events, etc. – but that the cost of promoting and distributing these products is extremely high. This forces each provider to critically consider all expenditure and to clearly define groups of customers that are most likely to purchase the products.

In the literature and in practice, a distinction is often made between two groups of variables:

- Sociodemographic variables
- Geographic variables
- Psychographic variables  Consumer characteristics
- Geo-demographic variables
- Benefit variables } Consumer responses

Kotler and Armstrong (2020) pointed out that there is a basic distinction between geographic, demographic and psychographic variables on the one hand and behavioral variables on the other. Behavioral variables represent the responses that consumers exhibit to various marketing stimuli, whereas the other categories of variables represent characteristics of the consumers themselves.

We will look briefly at each of these means of segmentation. Segmentation has received considerable attention in the *THE* literature. For a detailed examination of the more common bases to segment markets in *THE* contexts, see, for example, Tkaczynski et al. (2009), Tkaczynski and Rundle-Thiele (2011, 2020), Morritt and Weinstein (2012), E. Kim et al. (2018), Mody et al. (2019), Dolnicar (2020), and McKercher et al. (2022).

An important point to remember is that the various bases should generally be regarded not as alternative choices for segmentation but as overlapping and complementary ways of subdividing the total market. In most cases the actual segments chosen by organizations represent a combination of bases, sometimes referred to as *matrix segmentation*.

6.6.3 Sociodemographic segmentation

This form of segmentation addresses the question of 'who buys?'

Perhaps the most common means of segmenting the market, particularly where the major *THE* organizations are concerned, is by using demographic data.

> **For example:** *Some tour operators specialize in providing packages for specific demographic groups. Contiki Tours (www.contiki.com, part of The Travel Corporation group of companies,* www.thetravelcorporation.com*) specializes in activity-based coach tours in Europe, Australia and New Zealand, Asia, Latin America and North America, aimed at the 18-to-35 age group of tourists worldwide. The company stress the activity-based nature of their holidays. Saga Holidays, on the other hand, specializes in tours and holidays for people aged over 50 predominantly located in the UK* (www.travel.saga.co.uk/).

There are a number of demographic variables (characteristics) that may be of relevance to different markets, as summarized in Table 6.4. These variables usually refer to the age, gender, income, socio-economic (income) group and stage in the family life cycle of the consumer.

6.6.4 Geographic segmentation

This form of segmentation addresses the question of 'where do they buy?'

An organization may segment its market according to the geographic location of its consumers. Similarly, it is useful to be able to make distinctions between affluent and poor areas and between various types of urban and rural areas.

> **For example:** *A visitor attraction or an event organizer will need to know where their customers are coming from to plan their strategy for attracting repeat custom and for targeting new geographical areas.*

6.6.5 Psychographic segmentation

In psychographic segmentation, consumers are divided into different groups on the basis of social class, lifestyle and/or personality; see, for example, Litvin (2006) and Park and Jang (2014).

The majority of people do not regard holidays, hospitality or attendance at events as status symbols. Rather, they are merely seeking to spend their time in the most effective ways, at the best possible price. When choosing a holiday destination, for example, some tourists might be motivated by the chance to learn about the local culture, but others might be seeking destinations that are less demanding and remind them of home.

In a frequently cited work, Plog (2001) identified a continuum of tourist types, ranging from self-inhibited psychocentric tourists to extrovert allocentric tourists (Chang et al., 2011; Ho and McKercher, 2015; Piuchan, 2018). Thus, Plog (2001) divided tourist consumers into five different psychographic traits: *allocentrics, near allocentrics, midcentrics, near psychocentrics* and *psychocentrics*. At the two extremes, allocentrics seek cultural and environmental differences from their norm, belong to higher income groups, are adventurous and require little in the way of tourism infrastructure. Psychocentrics seek familiar surroundings, belong to lower income groups, are unadventurous and require a high level of tourism infrastructure. A psychocentric New Yorker might favor Coney Island (a New York beach resort), whereas an allocentric New Yorker might favor an African Safari.

Attitudes and motivations, together with beliefs and perceptions, form the 'psychographic' profile of a consumer. Once the provider of *THE* products understands this profile, they can infer a person's buying behavior and devise the appropriate tourist products to cater for these segments of the market.

People's product interests are influenced by their lifestyle, including their day-to-day habits, work patterns, leisure interests, attitudes and values. Lifestyle segments are based on distinctive ways of living and social values portrayed by certain types of people.

Table 6.4 Sociodemographic segmentation variables

Sociodemographic variables	Comments
Age	Segmenting customers according to age bands is very common, because children's needs, for example, are clearly different to those of retired people.
Gender	Gender is a relevant segmentation criterion for many markets. Some THE products are, however, largely designed for either males or females, whereas others appeal to both sexes. Spa days, for example, which have become increasingly popular at leading hotels, are primarily aimed at female customers.
Income	The personal disposable income of the consumer can be used as a segmentation variable. Some products are targeted at consumers with high disposable incomes, such as cruises and first-class travel, whereas other products are aimed primarily at consumers with lower disposable incomes, such as camping holidays.
Level of education	Sometimes the level of educational attainment is used as a segmentation variable. This criterion has obvious value with products requiring a certain level of intellectual application, such as books, but has also been found to influence other products as well. For example, people with lower levels of education often opt for the 'safety' of well-known destinations and established events, whereas those with higher levels of education are more likely to have the confidence to try more diverse locations and events.
Family life cycle	The stage that consumers have reached in their family development can be an important variable. Two married couples with identical jobs and income levels, one with four children and the other childless will exhibit significant differences in their spending patterns. Family life cycle segments might include: • Young single people • Young couples with no children • Families with young children • Families with older children • Middle-aged couples with no children or whose children now live away from home • Retired couples • Retired single people

This approach (see, for example, Gonzalez and Bello, 2002; Scott and Parfitt, 2005; Füller and Matzler, 2008; Valentine and Powers, 2013) is sometimes felt to offer a more complete picture of the consumer than other approaches. Lifestyle market segmentation divides the market according to the consumer's way of life. This has resulted in the marketing world labelling segments with acronyms and descriptions such as:

• Yuppies – young, upwardly mobile professionals
• Dincs – double-income, no children
• Wooppies – well-off older people

- Glammies – the greying, leisured, affluent, middle-aged sector of the market
- Generation X – those born between 1965 and 1980
- Generation Y (Millennials) – those born between 1981 and 1996
- Generation Z – those born between 1997 and 2012

STRATEGY IN PRACTICE

VALS (values, attitudes and lifestyles)

Many companies now utilize proprietary methodologies and software such as VALS (Values, Attitudes and Lifestyles) for psychographic market segmentation. VALS was developed in 1978 by social scientist Arnold Mitchell and his colleagues at SRI International and is offered as a product of SRI's consulting services division. VALS draws heavily on the work of Harvard sociologist David Riesman and psychologist Abraham Maslow.

The main dimensions of the VALS framework are primary motivation (the horizontal dimension) and resources (the vertical dimension). The vertical dimension segments people based on the degree to which they are innovative and have resources such as income, education, self-confidence, intelligence, leadership skills and energy. The horizontal dimension represents primary motivations and includes three distinct types:

- Consumers driven by knowledge and principles are motivated primarily by ideals. These consumers include groups called Thinkers and Believers.

- Consumers driven by demonstrating success to their peers are motivated primarily by achievement. These consumers include groups referred to as Achievers and Strivers.

- Consumers driven by a desire for social or physical activity, variety and risk taking are motivated primarily by self-expression. These consumers include the groups known as Experiencers and Makers.

At the top of the rectangle are the Innovators, who have such high resources that they could have any of the three primary motivations. At the bottom of the rectangle are the Survivors, who live complacently and within their means without a strong primary motivation of the types listed above.

Source: Adapted from www.strategicbusinessinsights.com

A *THE* company that has taken a lifestyle approach can develop products that will appeal specifically to people with a particular way of life. One such company, Trailblazers, is discussed in the Short Case Illustration below.

6.2 SHORT CASE ILLUSTRATION

Trailblazers holidays in India

With more than half of its 1.4 billion population under the age of 25, it is sometimes referred to as India's 'demographic dividend'. The country is expecting economic growth to be spurred on by a surge of new workers. The vast increase in the number of young people is in itself driving new business opportunities. Among these opportunities are American-style summer camps serving busy middle-class parents in India's burgeoning in cities such as Mumbai and Delhi. With limited green spaces, traffic congestion, searing heat and pollution, many families are choosing to send their children to the hills during the long school holidays. The camps offer everything from music tuition to backpacking and rafting. Many such camps are based close to the old colonial-era hill stations such as Shimla and Darjeeling in the Himalayan foothills, which have served as retreats for those seeking escape from oppressive summer heat for generations (Walsh, 2013). To serve these needs, many new companies have been born.

One such company is Trailblazers Adventure Travel Pvt. Ltd. based in Mumbai. The company, established in 1994, is guided by a mission that states: 'We aspire to transform people by providing enriching experiences that unveil the secrets and wonders of the outdoors, ensuring safety in all actions, following ethical business and sustainable environmental practices' (www.trailblazersindia.com/).

To this end, under the marketing slogan 'India's Leading Outdoor School', over the past 25 years the company has designed and organized outdoor programs for some of India's leading academic institutions and corporate clients. It has grown to become one of the largest operators of residential adventure holidays for school groups and children in India.

The camps operated by the company at various locations around India and in other Asian locations are custom designed to help children learn from nature, offering an outdoor experience. At the same time, emphasis is placed on helping to develop leadership qualities, beliefs and independence of thought, all packaged in a fun way with the help of professionally trained outdoor trainers. Since its inception, Trailblazers has worked with over 600 schools and over 150,000 campers across the country.

The company has grown by developing products that deliver learning programs delivered in camps across domains of adventure, culture, nature and curriculum for students across all age groups, combining learning with outdoor activities. For example, the economics camps have been developed in recent years with the aim of bringing to life this academic discipline. This is done through outdoor adventure activities and teaching, site visits to both urban economic centers and rural agricultural communities, invited guest speakers and fun activities.

Questions

1. Explain the approach to product development taken by Trailblazers.

2. Why might Trailblazers products be attractive to the Indian market?

6.6.6 Geo-demographic segmentation

Geo-demographic segmentation seeks to combine geographic and demographic principles of segmentation and, as Konu et al. (2011) pointed out, has become more popular with the advent of geographical information systems (see, for example, Middleton et al., 2009).

Geo-demographic segmentation is based on two simple principles:

● People who live in the same neighborhood are more likely to have similar characteristics than are two people chosen at random.

- Individual neighborhoods can be categorized in terms of the characteristics of the population they contain. Any two neighborhoods can be placed in the same category – that is, they contain similar types of people, even though they are widely separated.

Geo-demographic segmentation is normally based on proprietary software systems offered by commercial suppliers such as Claritas Prizm and Tapestry in the USA, PSYTE HD in Canada, ACORN and MOSAIC systems in the UK, geoSmart in Australia and the world's largest system, CAMEO, which covers about 40 countries. Other systems have been developed elsewhere in the world.

> For example: *ACORN (A Classification of Residential Neighborhoods) was developed in the UK in the late 1970s and classifies households according to the neighborhood in which they are found. The underlying philosophy is that certain types of neighborhoods not only will display similar housing but also will have residents with similar demographic and social characteristics who will share common lifestyles and will tend to display similar purchasing behavior.*

> *The developers of a new visitor attraction in a particular area of the UK aimed at families with young children in the local vicinity could use an ACORN map of the town. This would inform the managers of the attraction of the types of residential areas in the vicinity and hence those most likely to include the target customers.*

6.6.7 Benefit segmentation

Benefit segmentation involves segmenting the market based on the perceived value or advantages that consumers believe they will receive from a particular product.

According to a much-cited article, the rationale behind this approach is that benefits sought by consumers are the fundamental reasons for the existence of true market segments, and they determine consumers' behavior much more accurately than do other descriptive variables such as demographic and geographic characteristics (Haley, 1968).

In the case of benefit segmentation (unlike the use of other variables), we are concerned with consumer responses – that is, consumer behavior – rather than consumer characteristics, and the technique has been widely applied in *THE* contexts (see, for example, Frochot and Morrison, 2000; Jang et al., 2002; Frochot, 2005; Li et al., 2009; Mackellar, 2009; W. G. Kim et al., 2011; Almeida et al., 2014; Kinnunen et al., 2019).

THE consumers are often attracted not by the product features but by the benefits they perceive they are likely to derive from their purchase. Consumers may be encouraged to buy a product if they recognize that they will benefit from it.

> For example: *Customers who purchase an inclusive tour to the Australian Outback, are not buying their package holiday simply for the flight on the airplane, the accommodation provided and the excursions that are arranged for them (which we could describe as the features of the holiday). Rather, the tourists are buying the complete package to enjoy the benefits of going away on a particular type of holiday. The holiday provides a chance to experience a different lifestyle, the opportunity to sample different forms of culture, a break from normal everyday routine and the possibility of encountering wildlife not encountered in the home environment.*

To take advantage of this knowledge, tour operators would have to identify the specific benefits that consumers in a particular market segment look for when going on holiday. When identified, the tour operator can devise holiday packages providing the specific benefits that are attractive to different market segments.

6.3 SHORT CASE ILLUSTRATION

Benefit segmentation: Mpumalanga, South Africa

Mpumalanga province lies to the east of Johannesburg in South Africa. The province contains the Drakensberg escarpment, which separates a western half consisting mainly of high-altitude grassland at over 2,000 m in places (the Highveld) and an eastern half situated at low altitude (the subtropical). The southern half of Kruger National Park, one of Africa's largest game reserves, is situated in the latter region. Tourism is a key driver in the economy of the area, so segmenting the overall tourism market in a useful way that attracts additional spending is of fundamental importance.

To understand what benefits tourists seek so that promoters can engage with distinct tourism market segments, Nduna and van Zyl (2017) undertook a benefit segmentation study of visitors to Kruger National Park. Their questionnaire aimed to identify the key benefits tourists sought so that the significant market segments could be categorized. The study identified two segments of tourists in Mpumalanga, which the authors categorized as 'nature–escapist' and 'cultured–naturist'.

The nature–escapist segment (79% of the sample) greatly appreciated spending time in a natural environment, stayed 3 nights on average and relied on blogs, TripAdvisor, social media, video clips, travel magazines and travel brochures as information sources for planning their visits and comprised mainly domestic tourists. The cultured–naturist segment valued experiences specific to Mpumalanga such as learning about new cultures; visiting local arts and crafts stalls and learning about the specific nature and wildlife of the area. The segment referred to travel magazines and brochures when planning their trips, researched their visits carefully, spent more money than nature escapists and predominantly comprised foreign visitors.

The authors argued that developing a benefit segmentation framework provides a useful tool for marketing planning.

Source: Adapted from Nduna and van Zyl (2017)

Questions

1. Explain the benefits sought by tourists visiting Mpumalanga.

2. Explain what alternative types of segmentation might be useful.

6.6.8 Business-to-business marketing

In this chapter, up to this point, we have primarily been concerned with businesses marketing to consumers (B2C) marketing and segmentation. However, in many cases in *THE*, as in other industries, organizations are concerned with marketing not directly to consumers but to other businesses – so-called B2B marketing.

The concept of B2B segmentation has demanded increasing academic attention in recent years (see, for example, Crittenden et al., 2002; Powers and Sterling, 2008; Hall, 2017; Brotspies and Weinstein, 2019; Hollensen, 2019; Cartwright et al., 2021).

B2B consumers differ in their needs, resources and buying habits. According to the widely cited model of Bonoma and Shapiro (1983), the B2B marketer typically segments organizations broadly classified into two major categories:

- *Macro segmentation* – centers on the characteristics of the buying organization and situation, thus dividing the market by such organizational characteristics as size and geographical location
- *Micro segmentation* – requires a higher degree of market knowledge and focuses on the characteristics of decisions making units within the macro segment, including buying decision criteria, perceived importance of the purchase and attitudes toward vendors

The information required for the type of B2B segmentation outlined above is often difficult or costly to acquire. Consequently, in practice, many companies find it difficult to adequately segment their B2B marketing.

The notion of *reverse segmentation*, or *supplier segmentation* as it is often referred to, has become common in recent years (Day et al., 2010; Lajimi and Majidi, 2021). Reverse segmentation highlights a process that parallels segmentation, a process by which customers select suppliers that meet particular specified criteria such as quality, financial stability, ethical stances, delivery reputation and collaborative development opportunities (Hollensen, 2019).

The implication is that a supplier that is able to exhibit appropriate reverse segmentation criteria to a customer can become significantly more attractive to buyers, not least because they demonstrate a greater degree of understanding of customer needs. Actively seeking a particular supplier segmentation variable could in itself become a significant segmentation variable, especially for those organizations seeking to benefit from long-term supplier–customer relationships such as in the car components industry or in corporate sponsorship markets (Mitchell and Wilson, 1998).

> **For example:** *Hoteliers at a particular destination resort might target consistent and reliable deliverable quality standards to build up a long-term sustainable supplier – customer relationship with incoming our operators. Similarly, a conference venue might target well-trained staff delivering high levels of customer service and culinary excellence to attract repeat custom from corporate clients.*

6.7 Targeting

When the possible range of segments has been identified and the characteristics of each of the segments has been analyzed, the *THE* organization then has to decide which market segments to target (see, for example, Jang et al., 2002; Lee et al., 2006; Camilleri, 2018; Çınar et al., 2020).

When deciding which segments to target, a number of considerations should be borne in mind in relation to the segments. Each segment should reflect the following important characteristics:

- *Market size and market growth* – Each segment should be large enough, or demonstrating growth potential, to justify further investment of time and money by the company. As part of this evaluation, an organization might consider the number and type of competitors in each segment.

  > **For example:** *It would probably be possible to construct and promote hotels solely for people in wheelchairs, but would this be a substantial enough segment of the population to ensure success?*

- *Accessibility* – Each segment should be 'reachable', in the sense that it should be possible to give the consumers in that segment appropriate information about the organization's products.

For example: *A coach or bus operator finds that most customers are single and aged between 18 and 35, but unless they live in certain geographical areas, they may be difficult to reach cost-effectively.*

● *Measurability* – Each segment should be measurable, so that the likely demand for *THE* products in that segment can be identified. Research is very expensive, and certain variables are very difficult to measure.

For example: *In deciding on their holiday, many people do so in the expectation of receiving certain benefits such as peace and relaxation or a lively night life, but it is difficult to measure such 'motivations', especially when people are sometimes unwilling to answer personal questions honestly. Some young people's true motivations for travel may be a desire to meet the opposite sex or to consume alcohol, but they may be reluctant to publicly acknowledge such motivations.*

● *Actionability* – Each segment should be actionable, in that cost-effective programs can be formulated for servicing the segments.

For example: *A small airline identifies seven market segments, but its staff and financial resources are too small to develop separate cost-effective marketing programs for each segment identified.*

6.4 SHORT CASE ILLUSTRATION

Targeting business travelers

In *THE*, business travelers are usually highly sought after because they are normally able and willing to pay higher prices than leisure customers. However, targeting a segment of 'business travelers' is overly simplistic because they do not represent a homogeneous group that can easily be targeted, meaning that marketing resources could be wasted if an attempt to do so were made.

Hence, Camilleri (2018) identified six different types of business travelers:

● *Hard Money Travelers* (or the independent business travelers) – these include business individuals traveling at their own expense

● *Soft Money Travelers* (or corporate business travelers) – these include business individuals traveling on an expense account

● *Medium Money Travelers* (or the conference or incentive business travelers) – these include business individuals traveling within a group

● *Interim Travelers* – these include business travelers who are combining personal travel with a business trip

● *Frequent Short Travelers* – these include business travelers who consistently fly a short-haul route

● *Periodic Travelers* – these include salespersons who make a round of stops on a steady itinerary

Each of the above target segments will have slightly different needs and wants and have differing attitudes toward prices to be charged. Some of the groups are more likely to be willing to pay higher prices in return for added product features such as frequent services and ticketing flexibility.

Strategists and marketers must seek to identify the most appropriate target segments and seek to analyze and understand the requirements of each of these target segments so that products can be developed and *positioned* successfully.

Questions

1. Explain why targeting a segment of 'business travelers' might not be successful.

2. What are the main factors *THE* businesses should consider when deciding which segments to target?

However, some of the long-held assumptions that limit the smallest segments that can be economically reached are likely to change. Flexible technology and augmented reality (Ghandour et al., 2021) are enabling products to be tailored to individual requirements more cheaply, thereby increasing choices available to consumers (Buhalis and Foerste, 2015). In advertising, we are used to the concept of broadcasting. In the future, we shall have to become used to the concept of *narrowcasting*, as a revolution in media takes place. If a company advertises on television and its product is only of interest to city dwellers, it is often also paying to reach rural viewers. Cable, satellite and mobile technology allows organizations to direct adverts much more accurately at prospective customers.

The same process is taking place with regard to direct marketing (mail shots) and mobile and web-based marketing, where data on buying habits and geo-demographic data allow accurately targeted marketing communications (see, for example, Skinner et al., 2018; Ramos et al., 2019). The result of this process is that great rewards are available to organizations that can come up with sophisticated targeting strategies, as opposed to straightforward 'old-style' mass marketing.

6.8 Product positioning

All organizations need to differentiate themselves and their products from competing organizations and products. Product positioning is the way in which a product or brand is perceived in relation to preferences of segments of the market and in relation to competitive products.

The perceptual image that a consumer holds about an organization or product is important because a positive and favorable image can lead to the consumer purchasing products from the organization in question, whereas a negative image inevitably results in consumers looking elsewhere for their product purchases. Thus, *THE* strategists (and marketers) must seek to match the attributes of their product and buyers' perceptions of those attributes with the needs and priorities of customers in that segment. A number of authors have considered positioning in a *THE* context (see, for example, Dev et al., 1995; S. S. Kim et al., 2005; Sahin and Baloglu, 2011; Morgan et al., 2012; Robertson and Wardrop, 2012; Rodríguez-Molina et al., 2019).

By way of example, assume that market research has been carried out that has identified that the two key attributes used by customers to rate specific airlines are:

- Price
- Quality

This enables the market position of all the main competing products in that segment to be analyzed by asking customers to rate each airline according to the two attributes of quality and price.

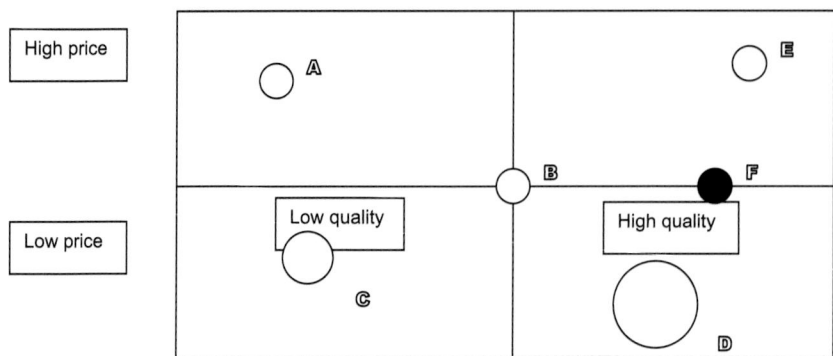

Figure 6.1 Product positioning

The customer may be asked to rate each on a ten-point scale. The results can then be plotted (see example shown in Figure 6.1) on a scatter diagram where the position of each response can be accurately marked.

The five competitors A, B, C, D and E differ in sales volume, as reflected by the sizes of the circles. The competitors' positions on the map are as follows:

- Competitor A occupies the high-quality/high-price position, sometimes termed a 'premium' position.
- Competitor B is perceived by the market as offering an average-quality product at an average price.
- Competitor C sells a low-quality product at a low price, sometimes termed a 'budget' position.
- Competitor D sells a high-quality product at a low price, sometimes termed a 'value-for-money' position.
- Competitor E sells a low-quality product at a high price, sometimes termed a 'cowboy' position.

The best position for a particular product can thus be determined. If the research carried out is successful, it will reveal an 'ideal' position not occupied by any existing product. If so, the objective of locating a group of customers with an unsatisfied need will have been achieved. It might also be the case that in crowded markets there are no positions identified that are not occupied by existing products. Such a finding, though disappointing, gives an important signal as to the viability of launching a new product.

In Figure 6.1, a newcomer to the market might give consideration to locating at position F, where a high-quality product is provided at an average price. However, in reality in today's very competitive markets, the product positioning map will probably not reveal such an obvious opportunity. The ideal product may be close to or identical to an existing product or several existing products. If so, two basic positioning choices are possible:

- Introduce a *me-too* product, replicating the attributes of existing products occupying a similar position
- Move into a gap on the product-positioning map, introducing a product bearing little similarity to any of the existing leading products

If an organization finds a group of customers with a particular requirement for a combination not currently offered, it will literally have discovered a *gap* in the market (see the 'gap' on the bottom right of the chart). More likely, it will have to make the best of subtle differences in position, because all major combinations may be filled.

However, in the B2B market, company image considerations rather than the brand image (which we have considered here) are more likely to be important in positioning. As Kalafatis et al. (2000) noted, the brand image-led positioning strategies that are prevalent in consumer goods marketing do not transfer well to business marketing.

6.5 SHORT CASE ILLUSTRATION

Product positioning: Marriott and IHG

Hotel brands are continually evolving and developing, with new niche markets being served. The larger international hotel groups (such as IHG and Marriott) all have several subbrands so that they can target different segments successfully.

As Richard Solomons, former chief executive of UK-based IHG plc, which ran brands such as Holiday Inn and Crowne Plaza, stated, 'Customers are so much more discerning today, they are much clearer about what they want' (Goodman, 2013). To illustrate the point, Solomons drew an analogy with cars: 'When I grew up, it was a saloon, sports car or convertible. Now you've got SUVs and there are big SUVs and small SUVs and so on. Most consumer categories are becoming more segmented' (Goodman, 2013). Indeed, his own group, which already encompassed brands such as Holiday Inn, Crowne Plaza, Intercontinental and, more recently, Indigo, launched a new brand in 2012. Hualuxe is a brand aimed firmly at the Chinese market and catering for Chinese tastes, as opposed to imposing Western tastes on the Chinese market.

Marriott hotel group based in Washington, D.C., currently has 30 brands (including Ritz-Carlton, Renaissance and luxury boutique brand Edition), but it is constantly searching for new niches to serve. The development of the Courtyard brand in the 1980s and 1990s and the current development of Moxy provide illustrations.

From its launch with three test hotels in 1983, Courtyard has expanded rapidly in several countries, and several hotel chains have attempted to duplicate the format. Research had identified a niche in the mid-level market that was not being filled by any hotel concept at that time.

Marriott management identified three criteria that had to be met in the design of the Courtyard concept:

- Ensure that the new concept offered consumers good value for money

- Minimize *cannibalization* (taking business away) from their other hotel offerings in the group

- Establish a market position that offered a substantial competitive advantage

Marriott developed a product positioning statement for the hotel concept that stated that the Courtyard product was to serve business travelers who wanted moderately priced hotels of consistent high quality and pleasure travelers who wanted an affordable room that was a safe base of operations. A basic conceptual framework for the product was then developed. The product would have the following features (Crawford-Welch, 1994), in that it would:

- Be tightly focused for the transient mid-priced market segment

Part 2

- Be relatively small (150 rooms or fewer) to project a residential image
- Serve a limited menu and offer less than competitors in the way of public space and amenities
- Be a standardized product managed in clusters (i.e., five to eight hotels in one area)
- Have the Marriott name attached for recognition and a 'halo' effect

Moxy Hotels is Marriott's new entrant in the economy segment, developed in partnership with the property division of Ikea Group using modular construction techniques. Moxy, launched in 2014, is growing quickly in urban locations in Europe, North America and Asia. The 3-star brand is designed specifically to target Generation Y and Millennial travelers with features such as freshly brewed coffee, large flat-screen TVs, an always open bar and 'grab and go' bikes.

As the Moxy website says, 'Marriott International's newest player in the affordable 3-star-tier segment for Millennial global nomads. It's got the power of Marriott behind it. The potency of style, innovation and tech-savviness surrounding it. And a whole lot of wattage to light up its vibrant future' (www.moxyhotels.com).

Approximately 2 of 5 million rooms in Europe are in economy hotels, but the goal is to attract the emerging next-generation travelers who do not want to sacrifice comfort and design for an affordable price.

Technology and product design combined with Marriott's hospitality experience are aimed at attracting younger customers: Generation Y and Millennials. Moxy's 17 m^2 (183 ft^2) rooms feature high-tech amenities, such as built-in universal serial bus ports and large flat-screen TVs with airplay connectivity. Each room also features a floor-to-ceiling signature art wall that is hand selected to reflect the local city or surroundings. Public spaces, meanwhile, double as design-led hangouts with food and alcohol (Mayock, 2013).

Sources: www.ihg.com, www.marriott.com, www.moxy-hotels.marriott.com

Questions

1. Consider what advantages and possible disadvantages that belonging to a powerful branded chain brings to Moxy.

2. Consider the reasons why Marriott is developing its Moxy brand.

6.8.1 Tourism destination positioning

The principles of positioning and repositioning can also be applied to destinations and events, and a large literature has developed around the subject area. See, for example, Gallarza et al. (2002), Usakli and Baloglu (2011), Pike and Mason (2011), Pike (2012), Hallmann et al. (2015), King et al. (2015), Souiden et al. (2017), Stylos et al. (2016), Shankar (2018) and Fyall (2019).

However, destinations differ from organizations in that the assumptions of strong leadership and clear goal-driven decisions to which all participants adhere may be lacking. This is because destinations may be viewed as conglomerates of attractions, operators and agencies, which each have individual objectives (Scott et al., 2000). Consequently, successful destinations need to coordinate all of the parties involved so that a strong and consistent positioning is achieved.

6.6 SHORT CASE ILLUSTRATION

Destination positioning for tourism and events in Queensland, Australia

Tourism is one of Queensland's key sectors, generating AU$25.0bn per year in over-night visitor expenditure. Tourism also directly and indirectly accounts for almost 10% of Queensland jobs and is the state's second largest export earner (behind coal). Tourism and Events Queensland (TEQ) is the Queensland government's lead marketing, experi-ence development and major events agency, representing the state's tourism and events industries.

TEQ's Strategic Plan 2022–2026 represents a new vision for Queensland as a tourism desti-nation. Its vision lies in 'inspiring the world to experience the best address on Earth' (TEQ, 2022:1). Its relaunched brand is centered on the notion of 'travel for good', which 'embod-ies a promise to travelers to leave restored and renewed. Connecting travelers with a place of diverse and rich epic wonder. A place that will change them, and eventually, the world' (TEQ, 2022:1). Ambitious growth targets have been set based on the Queensland Experi-ence Framework, which focuses on those 'Hero Experiences' (such as the Great Barrier Reef) that are the heart and soul of the Queensland story.

As the TEQ organization's name suggests, tourism and events are marketed jointly – a rec-ognition of the interconnections between the two. Thus, alongside the marketing strategy, an events strategy puts the growth of events at the heart of the organization's vision up to 2025. The events strategy markets an enhanced Queensland calendar of events using the 'It's Live! In Queensland' branding platform.

Though the new branding represents an umbrella brand to promote the whole of Queensland, the state has a unique position in Australia of having a number of strong des-tination brands, each having distinctive attributes, target markets and a sufficiently devel-oped tourist industry to warrant a portfolio approach to their management as destinations. The approach reflects the diversity and scale of Queensland (and its tourism industry) and translates into different destination images, target markets and positional and promotional programs for each destination. These are summarized in Table 6.5.

Table 6.5 Selected Queensland tourist destinations – positioning summary

Destinations	Brand positioning	Brand themes
Tropical North Queensland	Feel the natural exhilaration of an Australian Tropical Adventure.	• Great Barrier Reef • The world's oldest tropical rainforest • Tropical lifestyle and culture • Adventures • Aboriginal and Torres Strait Islander people
Townsville North Queensland	Feel the pride of discovering the essence of North Queensland in one vibrant, progressive community.	• Great Barrier Reef Centre of Excellence • Special places in nature • Eventful life in the Tropics • History and heritage

Part 2

Destinations	Brand positioning	Brand themes
Whitsunday Islands	Feel the wonder of Australia's island paradise.	• Diverse island paradise • Iconic landscapes in the heart of the Great Barrier Reef • Sailing, flying, snorkeling and diving • Airlie Beach and Mainland
Sunshine Coast	Feel the rejuvenating warmth of our beach culture.	• Innovative food • Wonders of nature • Immersive encounters • Exhilarating events • Beachside culture
Brisbane	Feel the vitality of city life with a subtropical twist.	• Vibrant • Relaxed • Urban outdoor lifestyle events • Culture • Nature at your doorstep bursting with color and life
Gold Coast	Welcoming, vibrant, diverse, fun and entertaining	• Surf • Taste • Escape • Play • Culture
Southern Queensland Country	Slow down, breathe deep and enjoy a taste of life in the country.	• Natural beauty • History and heritage • Four seasons • Authentic country life
Outback Queensland	Number one choice for an authentic Australian Outback experience and adventure for families.	• Outback adventures • Outback events • Palaeo-tourism • Heritage and locals

Source: Adapted from www.teq.queensland.com

Questions

1. Explain the potential differences in positioning a destination rather than a *THE* product belonging to a single company.

2. Explain why Queensland might need a number of subbrands, and explain their relationship to the umbrella brand.

6.8.2 Adjusting the marketing mix

Once an organization has decided how it wants to position itself relative to its competitors, it adjusts its *marketing mix* to achieve such a differentiation. The marketing mix comprises those variables that an organization can control that stimulate consumer demand. Traditionally marketers have viewed the marketing mix as being concerned with the *4 Ps* of:

- Product
- Promotion
- Price
- Place (distribution)

However, it is common (Goi, 2009; Kwok et al., 2020) for those managing in service industries to also include three further aspects, sometimes labeled the *services marketing mix*, as shown in Figure 6.2. In this way, the importance of these three further aspects of marketing in service settings is recognized.

These further *3 Ps* are:

- Personnel
- Physical environment
- Processes

A full consideration of the services marketing mix is beyond the scope of this text, because it is concerned with more detailed implementation issues often dealt with by marketers. For a more detailed discussion of marketing mix issues in *THE* contexts, see, for example, McKercher (1995), Allen et al. (2005), Middleton et al. (2009), Kotler et al. (2022), Hudson and Hudson (2017) and Kwok et al. (2020).

Here, however, we will consider the *product*, because achieving a balance between products at different stages of development can be viewed as a central strategic issue affecting resource allocation, cash flow and risk.

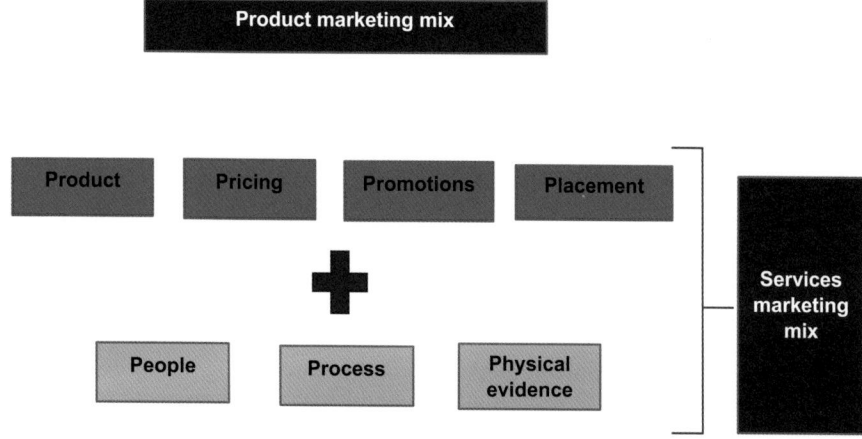

Figure 6.2 The services marketing mix

6.9 Products

6.9.1 Product definition

Having considered markets, we turn our attention to products.

Much of the strategic management literature is concerned with products and markets, and the terminology *product-market* strategy is often used.

DEFINITION/QUOTATION

Product

According to Kotler et al., a product is

> Anything that can be offered to a market for attention, acquisition or consumption that might satisfy a want or a need. It includes physical objects, services, persons, places, organizations and ideas.

(Kotler et al., 2022:30)

Importantly, of course, it is the sale of the product that provides sales revenue for the company. If a consumer buys a package holiday from one tour operator and is satisfied with that holiday or has had a good experience of an event or at a particular venue, he or she may decide to book again with the same company in the future. Therefore, the company must pay careful attention to all facets of the product to make sure that it lives up to consumers' expectations and leads to brand and/or company loyalty.

When thinking about *THE* products, it must be recognized that the 'product' does not just include the actual holiday or travel that is purchased or the visit to the tourist attraction, festival or event. The product is, in fact, all of those elements that make up the experience enjoyed by the customer. Of importance in product-market strategy is how the product features might be enhanced in a way that is valued by customers and that consequently they are willing to pay for. To do this, it can be useful to consider the product's features and benefits at a number of levels. Different suggested approaches can give a different number of levels, but Kotler et al. (2022) recommended that marketers (and strategists) recognize the product as being made up of five levels:

1. *The core product* – the main benefit the customer gains when purchasing the product.

   For example: *When a European holidaymaker goes on a holiday to Majorca, the core product may be one representing rest and relaxation, whereas the core product for a holidaymaker going to Vietnam might be somewhat different. In this instance, the core product might be to explore a newly developed international tourist destination.*

2. *The generic product* – a basic version of the product. It refers to the features of the holiday that are purchased.

   For example: *A visit to a festival might include travel arrangements to and from the festival, accommodation at the festival and 'add-ons' such as excursions to local attractions and vouchers to use at local restaurants. All of the standard features that comprise the trip to the festival, including the brochure or promotional material, are part of this generic product.*

3. *The expected product* – represents a set of attributes and conditions that buyers normally expect and agree to when purchasing a product

> For example: *Customers might normally expect certain features at self-catering apartments that might form a part of the package arrangements they book at their holiday destination, such as clean rooms, bed linen, towels, plumbing fixtures, hanging space for clothes, a quiet location and privacy.*

4. *The augmented product* – goes beyond the customer's expectations to provide something extra and desirable.

> For example: *The levels of service provided by staff in a travel or concert booking agency, those in a call center who arrange the booking or the way in which particular companies deal with customer complaints provide examples of the augmented product level. The way in which these and other services are delivered can 'add value' to the product sold and can often distinguish one company's product offering from others.*

Importantly, Kotler (2020) viewed this augmented level as being the level at which most competition takes place in the increasingly competitive market now faced by companies. To be successful in business, companies have to continually review their products (and, crucial in *THE* contexts, the way in which they are delivered) to ensure that they are superior to competitors.

However, each augmentation costs the organization resources in terms of time or money and, consequently, questions must be asked as to whether customers will pay enough to cover the extra costs involved. Augmented benefits soon become expected benefits.

> For example: *En suite rooms have moved from being the exception to the norm in most international standard hotels in the last 40 years and, more recently, internet connectivity has increasingly become the norm.*

Similarly, what is contained in the expected product in one market may be in the augmented product in another.

> For example: *Air conditioning might be a bonus in a temperate climate but a necessity in tropical or desert climates. Short-haul airline passengers may tolerate cramped seating conditions in return for lower prices, whereas this is less likely to be the case with long-haul passengers.*

This means that competitors have to continually search for still further features and benefits to add to their products. Sometimes, after a period of rivalry where competitors try to compete by adding more and more features and cost, a market segment emerges for a basic, stripped-down, low-cost version that supplies just the expected benefits.

> For example: *The emergence of the low-cost airline sector (e.g., AirAsia, Southwest Airlines, easyJet, Wizzair and Ryanair) and budget hotel brands in Europe such as Formula 1, Etap and Premier Inn in recent years can be seen in this way.*

5. *The potential product* – includes all of the augmentations and transformations that the product might ultimately undergo in the future. Whereas the augmented product describes product features included in today's product, the potential product represents the possible evolution of the product. Successful companies will therefore manage and evaluate their products very carefully. They will appreciate that some additional benefits must be provided to attract customers in competitive markets. Farsighted companies will therefore put much effort into research and development because the potential product is the product that is likely to be successful in tomorrow's markets.

6.9.2 *The product life cycle*

The product life cycle (PLC) concept is based on an analogy with living things, in that they all have a finite life. All products would be expected to have a finite life, whether long or short. The life cycle can operate at an individual product level or a product type or at a product class level, where arguably a market life cycle would be a more appropriate title.

At the individual product level, the PLC is a useful tool in product planning, so that a balance of products is kept in various stages of the life cycle.

KEY CONCEPT

The human life cycle metaphor for products

The concept of life cycle does not just apply to humans (or animals); it also applies to products, tourist destinations, festivals and events. Human beings undergo a life cycle that has a huge bearing not just on our biological changes but also on behavior; products often move through a similar cycle.

We undergo introduction when we are conceived and grow inside our mothers. After birth, we begin to grow – a process that continues until, after puberty, we reach our full height and weight. Our maturity phase is the longest. For most people, it will last from our mid-teens until the time when our faculties begin to fail us – perhaps in our 60s or 70s. When we reach old age, we begin to decline. Our eyesight may begin to deteriorate, we slow down and we may lose some of our intellectual sharpness. Finally, when decline has run its course, life is no longer viable and we die.

At the product class level, we can use the PLC concept to analyze and predict competitive conditions and identify key issues for management. It is conventionally broken into a number of stages as shown in Table 6.6. We shall explore the key issues posed by the different stages.

Each stage of the PLC has different implications for aspects of the organization and the way in which it manages its products. Specifically, managers need to be aware of the changing impact of costs, competitors, objectives and cash flow as products move through the life cycle. Figure 6.3 shows the life cycle and summarizes the main implications of these aspects.

THE INTRODUCTION STAGE

The introduction stage follows the product's initial development. It is consequently new to the market and will be bought by *innovators,* a term used to describe a small proportion of the eventual market. The innovators may not be easy to identify in advance, and there are likely to be high launch and marketing costs. Because operational (or production) volumes are likely to be low, because the product is still at a 'pilot' stage, the operational cost per unit will be high.

The *price elasticity of demand* will strongly influence whether the product is introduced at a high 'skimming' price, or a low 'penetration' price.

- *Price skimming* is appropriate when the product is known to have price inelastic demand such as with new exclusive resort developments or a first-class cabin provided by an airline serving a new destination.

Table 6.6 Implications of the product life cycle

	Introduction	Growth	Maturity	Decline
Costs	Highest costs per customer	High costs per customer	Low costs per customer	Low costs per customer
Competitors	None or few	Few	Maximum number of competitors	Declining number of competitors
Product objectives	High product awareness and trial – need to explain nature of innovation	Maximum market share before too many competitors arrive	Maximize profit while defending market share and motivate customers to switch brand	Reduce expenditure and milk the brand Cost control is vital
Cash flow	Likely to be negative as launch costs are not covered by sales	As sales grow, negative cash flow turns into a positive cash flow	Maximum positive cash flow as product has become established which allows surplus cash to be invested in other products	Strong cost controls enable a positive though diminishing cash surplus to be achieved

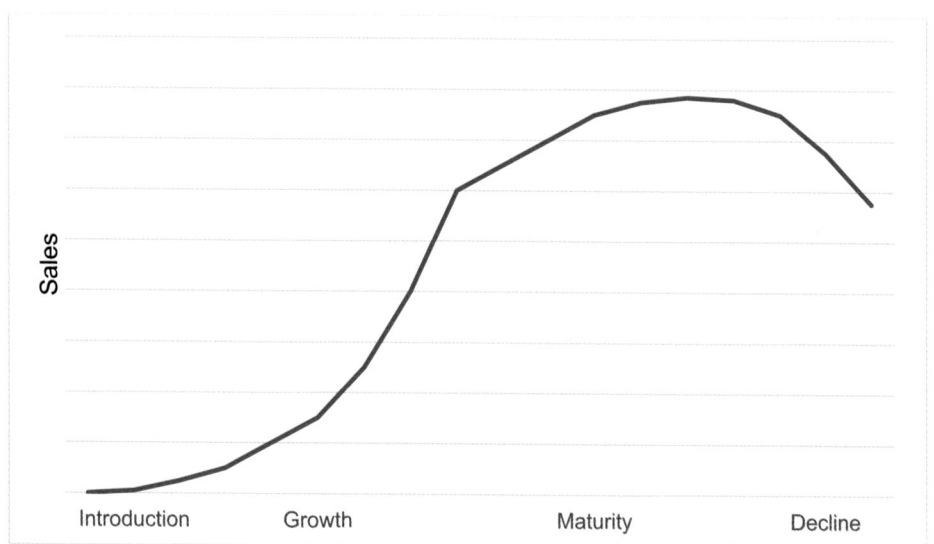

Figure 6.3 The product life cycle and its implications

- *Penetration* is appropriate for products with price elastic demand and when gaining market share is more important than making a fast recovery of development costs. A low-cost airline launching a new route or a budget hotel operator launching in a new city provide examples of such products.

KEY CONCEPT

Price elasticity of demand (Part 1)

Demand represents the quantity of a product buyers are willing and able to buy at a particular price over a specified period of time.

To an economist, demand is not quite the same as 'wants'. Everyone might want to travel on a luxury round-the-world cruise, but not everyone has the ability to pay for it. Other things being equal, we would expect the quantity of services to be demanded to be inversely related to its price. In other words, if the price is increased, lower quantities would be demanded and vice versa.

The important concept of *price elasticity of demand* measures the responsiveness of demand to a change in price – some services are very responsive, whereas others may be less so. In making pricing decisions, it is very important to understand just how responsive demand is to price changes if revenue is to be maximized.

The main factors affecting price elasticity of demand in relation to *THE* products are likely to be:

- *The availability of substitutes* – The greater the degree of competition (and hence the availability of substitutes), the more elastic (responsive) demand is likely to be. *For example*, there are many festivals throughout Europe, particularly in the summer months, and competition between them is strong, whereas the number of airlines operating on particular routes is often very limited.

- *The time period* – Over a prolonged period, consumers' demands are likely to be more elastic. *For example*, if the price of holidays from Northern Europe to Spain increases relative to those to Greece, in the short term, demand may not change very much (because arrangements and bookings have been made), but over a longer period, consumers are likely to switch demand to Greece. In other words, the price elasticity of demand for Greece is likely to increase over time.

- *Proportion of income* – The higher the proportion of a consumer's income a particular product takes up, the higher the price elasticity of demand is likely to be. *For example*, in purchasing a trivial item like a pencil, a consumer is likely to be less concerned about the price than with an expensive purchase such as an airline flight or attendance at a concert.

- *Luxury vs necessity* – Those seeking luxury are generally willing and able to pay for it and, consequently, the price elasticity of demand is likely to be lower for luxury products.

- *Business vs pleasure* – Business travelers are likely to be less price sensitive than leisure travelers because they value time and reliability and, consequently, price elasticity of demand is likely to be lower.

Source: Adapted from Evans (2002)

Pioneer companies (those that are first to the market with a particular product) are often forced, or sometimes willingly seek, to sell the product idea to an existing established product brand. The early promotion of a product idea by pioneer companies may also enable the idea to become more widely accepted as a product innovation for the market more generally and help competitors who enter the market later with *me-too* versions of the product idea.

Entering the market at an early stage is usually risky. Not only will the company be likely to incur a negative cash flow for a period but many products also fail at this stage. Against this risk is the prospect of increasing market share in the new product area faster than the 'me-toos' and, consequently, achieving so-called first-mover advantage.

First-mover advantage occurs when the first product becomes the established provider and establishes a *barrier to entry* for subsequent entries to the market.

6.7 SHORT CASE ILLUSTRATION

First-mover advantage: Dubai and Singapore as international travel hubs

A first-mover advantage can be simply defined as a firm's ability to be better off than its competitors as a result of being first to market in a new product category (Suarez and Lanzolla, 2005). It is useful to distinguish between durable first-mover advantages that improve a firm's market share or profitability over a long period and those that are short-lived. Although no advantage lasts forever, firms that succeed in building durable first-mover advantages tend to dominate their product categories for many years, from a market's infancy until well into its maturity.

Coca-Cola in soft drinks and Hoover in vacuum cleaners unmistakably demonstrate both the value and longevity of early success (Suarez and Lanzolla, 2005). Those products that follow on behind trying to catch up and copy those with first-mover advantage are often described as *me-too* products.

The growth of air transport networks and deregulation have allowed small places with relatively small populations like Singapore and Dubai to become major international tourism destinations and transportation hubs. Both Singapore and Dubai have managed to divert a significant number of passengers who stop in either of those cities on long-haul routes between Europe, Asia, the Southwest Pacific, and Africa (Lohmann et al., 2009). Dubai has been found to be one of the world's most efficient airports (Junior et al., 2021).

In both cases, integrated and complex networks have been developed, and both have enjoyed success both as hubs and through their respective airlines: Emirates and Singapore Airlines. Hubs were transformed into destinations by the complementary interaction of attractions, transport and accommodation sectors. Both used shopping 'paradises' to persuade visitors to stay.

Singapore and Dubai have both enjoyed first-mover advantages in terms of the model they have adopted, but other countries have similar geographical features that may gradually erode this. Regional rivals Kuala Lumpur (Malaysia) and Bangkok (Thailand) enjoy similar locational advantages and are now endeavoring to challenge Singapore as the premier hub of the region (Bowen, 2000). Abu Dhabi (UAE) and Doha (Qatar) and their respective airlines, Etihad and Qatar Airways, are growing and provide competition to Emirates and Dubai (Lohmann et al., 2009).

Questions

1. Explain what is meant by *first-mover advantage* and a *me*-too strategy, citing examples of both you are familiar with from *THE*.

2. Consider what advantages Singapore and Dubai might have been able to exploit in developing *first-mover* advantage.

The growth stage

During the growth stage, sales for the market as a whole increase and new competitors typically enter to challenge the pioneer for some of the market share. The competitors may develop new market segments in an attempt to avoid direct competition with the established pioneering market leader.

The market becomes profitable, cash flow becomes positive and the funds generated can be used to offset the development and launch costs. This is an important time to win market share, because it is easier to win a disproportionate share of new customers than to get customers to switch brands later on. As new market segments emerge, key decisions will need to be made as to whether to follow them or stay with the original.

The maturity stage

Maturity is reached when a high proportion of people who will eventually purchase a product have already purchased it once. It is likely to be the longest stage, but depending on the market, this could range from days or weeks to many decades or even centuries. It is important at this stage either to have achieved a high market share or to dominate a special niche in the market. It can be expensive and risky to achieve large market share changes at this time, so some companies prefer to concentrate their competitive efforts on retaining existing customers and competing very hard for the small number of new customers. In this phase, it is likely that large positive cash flows are being generated that can be reinvested in new products or in products at an earlier stage of their evolution.

To maintain and protect their position in a mature market, companies have to be vigilant in detecting changes taking place. In response to changes, organizations have to be ready to modify or improve products and how customers perceive them and to undertake product repositioning.

The decline stage

It is part of PLC theory that all markets will eventually decline, and therefore companies have to be ready to move to new markets where decline is felt to be inevitable or to be ready with strategies to extend the life cycle if this is feasible. Appropriate extension strategies could include developing new uses for the product, finding new users and repositioning the product to gain a presence in the parts of the market that will remain after the rest of the market has gone. Even where markets have reached an advanced stage of decline, there may remain particular segments that can be profitable for organizations able to anticipate their existence and dominate them.

Companies that succeed in declining markets usually adopt a 'milking' strategy wherein investment is kept to a minimum and take up any market share that may be left by competitors that have left the market because of the decline. There is a certain recognition that death will come eventually and thus any revenues that can be made in the interim are something of a bonus.

6.9.3 The tourism area life cycle

The idea of the PLC has been applied in a tourism destination context through the tourism area life cycle (TALC). The TALC model has become one of the most cited and frequently used models in the tourism literature, having been applied in various parts of the world and in various contexts (see, for example, Whitfield, 2009: conference management; Garay and Cànoves [2011]: Catalonia, Spain; Kozak and Martin [2012]: managing for profit; Liu et al. [2016]: China; Strom and Kerstein [2015] and Garcia-Ayllon [2016]: Spain).

Borrowing from the classic business literature on life cycles of products, and with strong links to other spatial economic models, Butler (2009) argued that destinations can be viewed as products and that their pattern of development closely mirrors the classic life cycle curve. According to TALC (see, for example, Butler, 1980, 2009; Ma and Hassink, 2013; Dodds, 2020), destinations go through a similar evolution to that of products but visitor numbers are substituted for product sales. Destinations move from evolution (similar to introduction in the PLC), through involvement, development and consolidation (similar to growth in the PLC) before reaching stagnation (similar to maturity in the PLC). Like the PLC, decline will inevitably follow unless actions are taken which result in rejuvenation of the destination.

The shape of the curve, the length of each stage and the length of the cycle itself are variable.

> **For example:** *Cooper et al. (1998) pointed to 'instant' resorts such as Cancun in Mexico or time share developments that move almost immediately to growth. In contrast, well-established resorts such as Scarborough on England's east coast have taken 3 centuries to move from exploration to rejuvenation.*

6.9.4 Product life cycle critique

The PLC (and its application to *THE* contexts in the form of the TALC) appears to be both widely understood and widely used (Greenley and Bayus, 1993). Fleisher and Bensoussan (2003) provided a useful overview of the concept and its application. Nevertheless, some important criticisms of the concept have been made, and it is important in using concepts of this type that they are not used uncritically and are combined with other corroborating evidence.

The first criticism that has been leveled is that though it is easy to go back into history and demonstrate all of the features of the concept, it is hard to forecast the future and, in particular, it is hard to forecast turning points. Not to try to do so at all, however, would be to avoid confronting hard strategic issues.

Another criticism is that life cycles may sometimes not be inevitable as dictated by the market but created by the ineptitude of management. If management assumes that decline will come, they will take the decision to reduce investment and advertising in anticipation of the decline. Not surprisingly, decline does come but sooner than it otherwise would have done had the investment not been withdrawn.

Moutinho (2000) detailed several criticisms of the concept in a tourism context. For the TALC, decline relates to visitor numbers exceeding capacity levels at the destination, but Moutinho (2000) pointed out that capacity is a notoriously difficult concept to operationalize because it is possible to envisage different forms of capacity threshold. Physical, environmental and psychological capacity may vary, and it may be possible to 'manage' capacity.

6.9.5 S-curve (technology life cycle analysis)

In arguing for a different approach that incorporates the role of technology changes, Brown (1991:189) stated that 'marketing literature abounds with "S" curves to depict processes which start slowly, then gradually gather pace until they move into fast growth, which continues until saturation is approached, when growth slows down and finally plateaus', the most notable of which is the PLC. A major difficulty in implementation in reality is that the PLC rarely assumes a smooth, predictable curve. There are often discontinuities in the curve. Product markets rarely develop as a single homogeneous unit; rather, they develop as a series of segments (Brown, 1991) because of the impacts derived from the introduction of new technology.

Business history contains many examples of the enormous impact the introduction of new technology and innovation can have, such as the rapid displacement of mechanical cash registers by electronic cash registers during the 1970s. Several examples can be cited in relation to the *THE* sectors, and Hjalager (2015) tried to classify 100 of these innovations.

> For example: *The introduction of jet aircraft from the 1950s and the introduction of the Boeing 747 ('jumbo' jet) in the 1970s had transformational impacts on the airline industry. Similarly, the development of the internet from the 1990s has had enormous repercussions for all industries but perhaps none more so than for travel and event intermediaries such as travel agents and booking agencies. The widespread diffusion of the internet allows customers to deal directly with travel companies and event organizers rather than going through an intermediary, allowing so-called disintermediation to take place. The internet has also allowed customers to gain far greater ability to quickly compare prices.*

6.8 SHORT CASE ILLUSTRATION

'Disruptive innovation' in hospitality: the rise of Airbnb

Airbnb is a private company, with its headquarters in San Francisco, California, that operates an online accommodation marketplace that is accessible via its websites and mobile apps. Members can use the service to arrange or offer accommodation primarily in the form of 'homestays'. The company does not own any of the real estate listings but acts as a broker receiving commission from every booking. The company, which markets itself as 'The Worldwide Alternative to Hotels' (www.airbnb.com), has grown enormously since its founding in 2008 to present a serious challenge to traditional accommodation providers.

This innovative approach to tourism accommodation developed by Airbnb (and other similar companies) can best be viewed through the lens of *disruptive innovation* theory (Guttentag, 2015). The concept was popularized by Clayton Christensen in several works (see, for example, Christensen, 2006). The theory, according to Guttentag (2015), outlines a process through which a 'disruptive' product transforms a market. A disruptive product will generally offer a distinct set of benefits, typically focused around being cheaper, more convenient or simpler. Consequently, the disruptive product appeals to the low end of the market or creates a completely new market and, using mobile and internet communications technology, is capable of growing very quickly. However, as growth continues, the disruptive products can enter the mainstream market and be copied by 'me-too' products, so maintaining momentum through growth can be challenging.

Examples of disruptive products in the recent history of *THE* products include low-cost airlines challenging established airlines, Uber (and other ride-handling apps) challenging traditional taxi firms and internet intermediaries such as Expedia and Booking.com challenging traditional travel agents.

Questions

1. Explain what is meant by disruptive innovation with regards to *THE* products.

2. Consider other examples of disruptive innovation in *THE* and assess what factors have helped them grow and the factors that may challenge growth in the future.

S-curve analysis integrates technological change into strategic planning. It accomplishes this by plotting the effort expended into a product or process technology and the resulting return, the rationale being that every technology has a natural limit to the benefits it can generate. At some point,

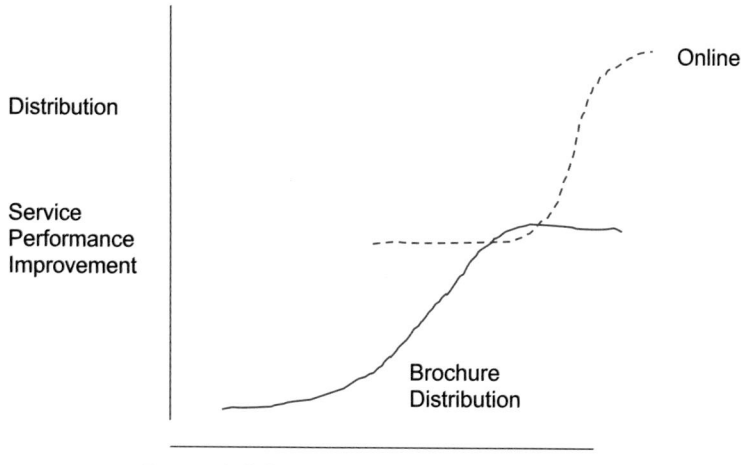

Figure 6.4 Strategic implications of online distribution vs brochure distribution for *THE* companies

increasing research and development expenditure will result in a decreasing rate of productivity growth (Fleisher and Bensoussan, 2003).

Figure 6.4 illustrates the possible effects of distribution of *THE* products through traditional brochures and through online distribution. The figure indicates that online distribution has established itself as a more effective means of distribution, though brochure distribution remains important.

The existence of more effective or efficient technologies frequently results in the existence of multiple S-curves, as shown in Figure 6.4. Rivals operating on S-curves above and to the left of the firm's current S-curve will be competitively superior in that they may have lower costs, higher quality or increased differentiation. Because this superior performance can be achieved, the challenge for managers becomes not *whether* to make a move but *when*. Switching technologies can be expensive and often involves new skills and processes.

Achieving this transition to a new technology is very difficult for most firms, and timing is of utmost importance. Making the transition too early, before the marketplace is ready to embrace the new technology, is a costly mistake. Leaving the transition too late risks falling behind competitors and may make it very difficult to catch up on the ground that has been lost.

6.9 TECHNOLOGY FOCUS

Introducing new technology: Boeing's 'Dreamliner'

Replacing older, less fuel-efficient long-haul aircraft such as the Boeing 747 with more modern fuel-efficient aircraft such as the Boeing 787 (Dreamliner) may move an airline forward technologically, and it provides a public relations opportunity for the airline and manufacturer. The Dreamliner incorporated many innovative features and was the first airliner with an airframe constructed primarily of composite materials. However, it is also expensive and requires extensive training and development work. Furthermore, it is not without risks in terms of proving a new aircraft type.

The technical difficulties (mainly with batteries) encountered by the Dreamliner after its launch illustrate the point. Two Japanese carriers, All Nippon Airlines and Japan Air Lines, were early purchasers (in 2012) of the Dreamliners and began flying the fuel-efficient aircraft to cities such as Boston and San Jose, California, that would not be profitable with larger planes.

However, in early 2013, a 4-month global suspension of 787 services was ordered by regulatory authorities after lithium-ion batteries overheated on two different planes, with one of them catching fire while the aircraft was parked. Such episodes severely dented public confidence and led to severe operating difficulties for all of the early adopting airlines, which included Ethiopian Airlines, Qatar Airways, Air India and United Airlines.

Despite initial problems (outlined by Moll and Harrigan [2018] and Schmuck [2021]), the aircraft has proved to be successful, with over 1,300 orders for the innovative fuel-efficient airliner. Boeing's technical lead has now been challenged by the latest aircraft, the A350XWB, built by Airbus, which represents a direct competitor to the Dreamliner. The European challenger to US-based Boeing delivered the aircraft, built largely from composite materials, to its first customer (Qatar Airways) at a ceremony in Toulouse, France, in 2014.

Questions

1. Explain the potential advantages and disadvantages of first-mover advantage in this case.

2. Consider other successful or unsuccessful introductions of technology in *THE* and provide a relevant example.

6.10 New product development

Changes in society, markets and economies have led to a shortening of life cycles, and this has intensified the need for most organizations to innovate in terms of the products that they offer. New products can provide the mechanism whereby further growth can take place. Increasing competition, often itself coming from new or modified products, means that innovation is frequently not an option but a necessity for many companies operating in all sectors.

However, totally new products are in reality quite rare, though they may be labeled as 'new' for marketing purposes. Many products promoted as 'new' have evolved from existing product offerings or are merely 'new' to a particular market segment, such as a particular geographical territory.

Thus, 'newness' can vary from restyling or minor modification such as the introduction of restyled promotional brochures, revamped festival schedules or new aircraft liveries to producing products that are *new to the world* and that lead to new markets being created, such as the creation of a new genre of music and the events that stem from it.

> For example: *Though blessed with beautiful scenery, superb beaches and a tropical climate, the Caribbean country of Haiti has in recent years attracted only the most intrepid of international tourists. Lack of infrastructure, political turmoil and earthquakes have all had their impacts. However, this is beginning to change and a new international market is being created as international tour operators such as Canada's Transat begin to feature the destination, which is a value-for-money destination. A further boost to the country's international tourism aspirations was provided in 2014 when the US Department of Defense announced the removal of the country from its list of 'danger zones'.*

The higher the degree of newness, the more likely it is that major gains in sales and profits will be made; at the same time, however, the risks of incurring high costs and market failure are also increased. A single new product failure, if big enough, could lead to the financial failure of an organization. It is generally accepted that a very large proportion of new products fail, although precise quantification is impossible because many new products may be kept on the market despite not meeting their original objectives.

Organizations are faced with a dilemma in the management of new product development: it is essential for further success but is also fraught with risks. The successful management of this dilemma requires a large number of new product ideas, most of which will never reach the market because they have been screened out by an appropriate screening process.

6.10.1 New product idea generation

Ideas for new products can come from many sources. The greater the range of sources used, the more likely it is that a wide range and large number of new ideas will be produced (Sowrey, 1990).

IDEAS FROM CUSTOMERS

For most organizations, the most important source of new ideas will be their customers. Terwiesch and Ulrich (2009), for example, noted that across industries, about a quarter of innovation opportunities tend to come from interactions with customers and new customer requirements.

Obtaining ideas from customers is a good way to ensure that ideas lead to products that are a result of 'market pull'. This means that there will be a market for the products that result because they are specifically requested by the customers. Surveys and focus groups can help to produce ideas. The more straightforward approaches may provide ideas for improvements, but more subtle approaches may reveal new needs.

Von Hippel (1978) showed that a very successful approach for new ideas in industrial markets was to work with lead customers (respected, technically advanced buyers) to overcome their particular problems and then sell the resulting new products to other customers. Sometimes the products may require modification at some cost. The modified products that ensue then have unique value for these customers, who are then willing to pay for the enhanced product features provided. Thus, the product enjoys the benefits of *price inelasticity of demand*.

Poetz and Schreier (2012) considered the notion of outsourcing idea generation to the users of potential products (*crowdsourcing*). The authors compared the ideas generated by a firm's professionals with those generated by users. They found that users' ideas were more frequently among the very best in terms of novelty and customer benefit.

OTHER SOURCES OF IDEAS

It is impossible to construct a comprehensive list of sources of new product ideas, but the following have proved useful in the past:

- Intermediaries such as advertising agencies, legal firms and property agents (who sometimes have their 'finger on the pulse' of market requirements)
- Consultants (who may carry out market research on a company's behalf)
- Universities and other academic institutions
- Competitors (where an organization copies a competitive product)
- Suppliers (who may have devised a way of using technology)

- Employees, sometimes through 'employee idea' schemes
- Distributors and agents for the product

6.10.2 New product screening

Once ideas for new products have been generated, a company must then sift through them to develop only those with genuine potential – a process known as *screening*. The screening process attempts to avoid two potential types of errors:

- GO errors, where products are developed that ultimately fail or do not meet objectives
- DROP errors, where ideas are abandoned that would ultimately have succeeded

GO errors are recognizable, at least by the organization that makes them, but most DROP errors are unrecognized because the project has been scrapped (unless, of course, a competitor makes a success of an idea that has been abandoned).

In practice, the screening process is normally a multistage process, with at least some kind of review at several points in the process. Because risks may be high and organizational politics may play a part, it is usually recommended that in at least one of the stages a formal process is undertaken in which the idea is evaluated against predetermined objective criteria.

6.10.3 New product development

The stages in development will vary according to the nature of the product and the work required to develop a new version, but it is important to include stages of the screening process before activities that involve the commitment of large amounts of finance and human and marketing resources, and it would not make sense to spend large amounts in developing a new product without producing evidence that there would be some demand for it. Stages in the process are typically as follows:

- Initial appraisal
- Detailed business analysis and investment appraisal
- Technical development
- Market testing
- Launch

A traditional view of the development process is that one stage should precede another. With increasing competition, reducing time to market has become very important in many industries. To reduce the time to market, some of the activities may occur simultaneously, sometimes known as *parallel processing*. This puts a premium on good communications between functions such as operations, finance and marketing.

To avoid the delays and complications that might be involved in handing a project from one function in the organization to another, multidisciplinary teams known as *venture teams* may be created, and in some circumstances the team may be given the new product to manage when it is on the market. If such a team is created, it is likely that more senior management will make the GO or DROP decisions to avoid the risk of bias of an enthusiastic but optimistic team taking over.

In some areas of *THE*, such as the development of new hotels, resort development, buying cruise liners or new aircraft and the creation of visitor attractions, new product development requires

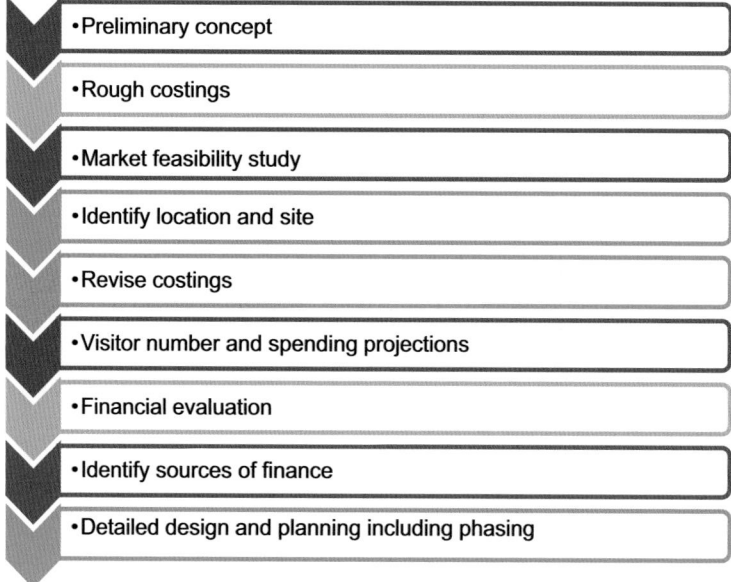

- •Preliminary concept
- •Rough costings
- •Market feasibility study
- •Identify location and site
- •Revise costings
- •Visitor number and spending projections
- •Financial evaluation
- •Identify sources of finance
- •Detailed design and planning including phasing

Figure 6.5 A feasibility study process for a visitor attraction

Source: Adapted from Swarbrooke and Page (2012)

significant capital investment. Consequently, it is common to carry out a feasibility study prior to decide whether to proceed to testing the viability of the proposed project.

> **For example:** *Swarbrooke and Page (2012) identified a nine-stage feasibility study process when assessing the viability of a visitor attraction. The stages are summarized in Figure 6.5.*

Key points of the study include:

- Assessing the *penetration factor*; that is, predictions of the proportion of people in each market segment who may visit the attraction
- Analysis of where the visitors will come from, when they will come and how much they are likely to spend
- Analysis of capital costs, estimated likely income and estimation of the breakeven level of visitors

---

THINK POINTS

- Explain why segmenting the market is so important for *THE* managers and outline the main ways in which it can be carried out.
- Explain and illustrate Kotler's five levels of product benefit using relevant *THE* examples.
- Explain what criteria might be used in selecting potential target segments.
- Explain the major differences between B2B and B2C marketing using relevant *THE* examples to illustrate your answer.

6.11 The product portfolio

All companies need to decide on an optimum number of different products to offer consumers:

> **For example:** *Should a tour operator offer only inclusive air tours to Greece, or should packages also be developed for Cyprus and Turkey? Should the travel agent specialize in high-value cruise and long-haul specialized products or products that will have more of a mass market appeal?*

The organization must not only consider the present situation, however, because consumer tastes change, tourist destinations go out of favor as new resorts are developed and competing events and festivals are continually being developed. The organization must therefore also consider the future situation, specifically:

- Which new products could be launched onto the market
- When should they be launched?

The answers to these questions will depend on factors such as:

- The resources available to the business
- The market segments to be targeted
- The needs of the consumers

Controlling the company's range of products, the so-called product portfolio, and phasing in new products as established products decline is an important function of a strategic manager (as distinct from the marketing manager), who has also to take decisions concerning the features that will be included in each product. Such strategic decisions have led to the development of a number of concepts and models, some of which are discussed in the following sections and were summarized by, for example, Brownlie (1985), Morrison and Wensley (1991), Fleisher and Bensoussan (2003) and Madsen (2017).

Since its inception as an academic field, planning for the portfolio of products to be offered (so-called product portfolio theory) has been a central theme in strategic management. The theme has attracted much attention from academics, consultants and practitioners.

The notion of a portfolio exists in many areas of life, not just for products. Underpinning the concept is the need for a business to spread its opportunity and risk. A broad portfolio signifies that a business has a presence in a wide range of product and market sectors. Conversely, a narrow portfolio implies that the organization only operates in few or even a sole product or market sector.

A broad portfolio offers the advantage of robustness in that a downturn in one market will not threaten the whole company. Against this advantage is the problem of managing business interests that may be very different in nature – the company may be said to lack strategic focus. Organizations operating with a very narrow portfolio (i.e., just one segment) can often concentrate wholeheartedly on its segment, but it can become vulnerable if there is a downturn of demand in the one sector it serves.

6.11.1 *The Boston Consulting Group matrix*

Originally developed in the early 1970s for a leading management consulting company, the Boston Consulting Group (BCG) matrix offers a way of examining and making sense of a company's portfolio of product and market interests (see Fleisher and Bensoussan, 2003). As with other models and matrices used in strategic analysis (of which there are many), the BCG matrix is a simplifying tool, and though it is long-standing, it is still widely used, cited and applied.

The model works on two parameters:

- *Relative market share* – as an indicator of the strength of the competitive position
- *Growth* – as an indicator of the potential and attractiveness of the market

A key point of the matrix is that market share and market growth provide approximations of the company's ability to generate cash. Generating cash, which is normally referred to as *cash flow*, is important because it represents the most important determinant of a company's ability to develop its product portfolio. Cash generated by successful products can be utilized in developing new products.

Also implicit in the use of the matrix are the benefits to be gained from the so-called experience effect (Henderson, 2012). It is well recognized that companies (as with people) carry out their activities more efficiently with greater experience. Lessons are learned and adjustments to processes and systems are made. The experience effect is linked to market share through a virtuous cycle (Hooley et al., 2020), as shown in Figure 6.6.

The virtuous cycle demonstrates the impact of the experience effect in that:

- A company with high market share gains more experience than its competitors.
- The experience results in lower costs.
- The lower costs mean that, at a given price, the company with the highest market share has the highest profits.

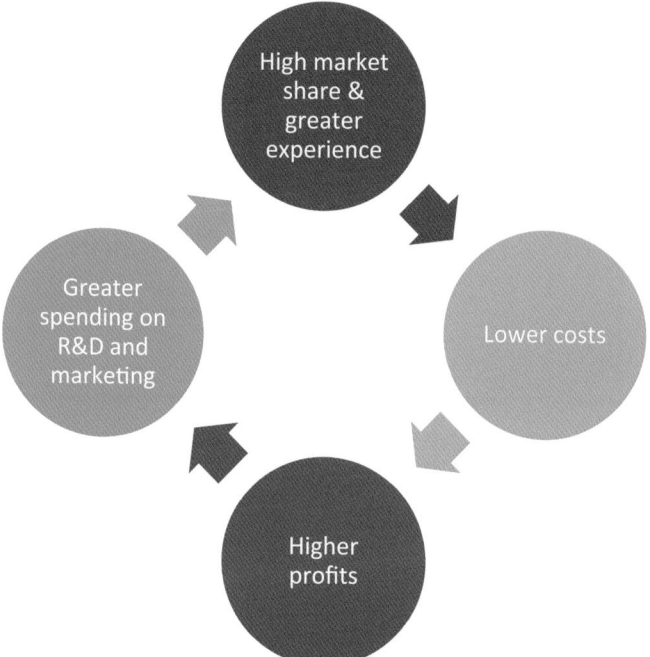

Figure 6.6 The experience effect

- The company with the highest profits or contributions from sales has more to spend on research and development or marketing, which allows it to maintain its high market share.

  For example: Applying this cycle to a tour operator in its dealings with hoteliers:

  A high market share enables the tour operator to have greater experience of dealing with hoteliers than its competitors.

  The experience represented by the large market share allows the tour operator to reassure the hoteliers that large volumes will be sold so that high occupancy rates can be achieved.

  As a consequence of the high volumes, lower room rates will be paid by the tour operator (than by its competitors) to the hotelier.

  The lower costs enable the tour operator with the highest market share to achieve the highest profits.

  The tour operator with the highest profits has more to spend on research and development or on marketing, which allows it to maintain its high market share.

A large empirical study, the Profit Impact of Market Strategy (PIMS), provides further justification for the BCG approach. Perhaps the most important finding from the PIMS study is that there is a strong correlation between a high market share and the level of profitability (Buzzell, 2004). Thus, a high market share is not an end in itself but something that is desirable because it leads (on average) to higher returns being achieved.

The BCG matrix is used to analyze the product range with a view to aiding decisions on how the products should be treated in an internal strategic analysis. Figure 6.7 shows the essential features of the BCG matrix.

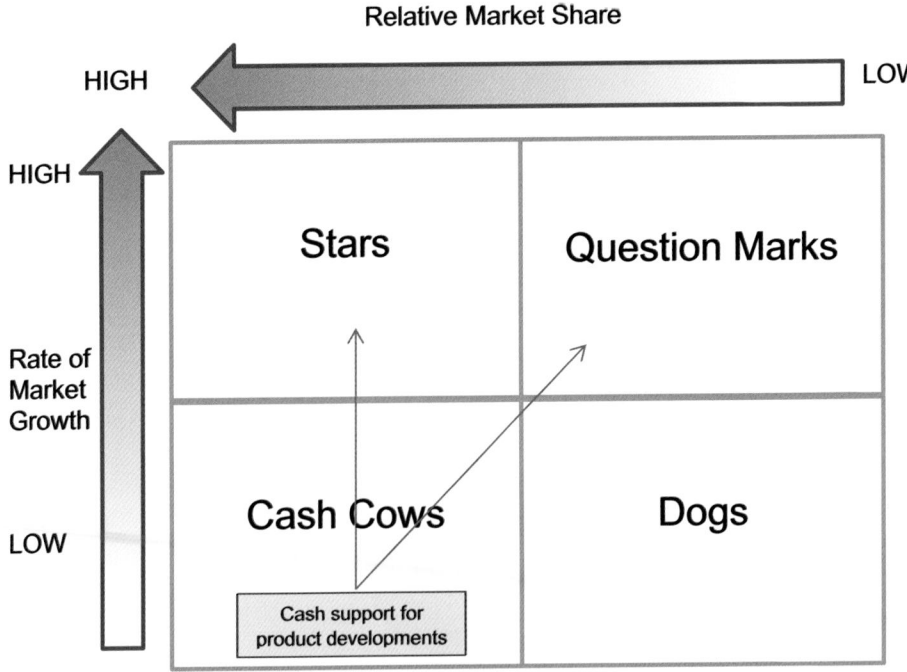

Figure 6.7 The Boston Consulting Group matrix

6.11.2 Utilizing the BCG matrix

Depending on their performance in respect of the two parameters (relative market share and growth), products are placed in one of four categories, normally (and somewhat creatively) labeled as:

- Cash cows
- Dogs
- Stars
- Question marks

We will consider each of these categories in turn.

CASH COWS

A product with a high market share in a low growth market is termed a *cash cow*. Such a product is normally both profitable and a generator of cash. Profits from this product can be used to support other products that are in their development phase. Standard strategy would be to manage conservatively but to defend strongly against competitors. Such a product is called a cash cow because profits from the product can be *milked* on an ongoing basis.

These are products associated with high positive cash flows. Consequently, these products can be used to support *stars* and selected *question marks* (as indicated by the arrows in Figure 6.7).

DOGS

A product that has a low market share in a low growth market is termed a *dog*. It is typically not very profitable or possibly loss-making. To cultivate the product to increase its market share would incur cost and risk, not least because the market it is in has a low rate of growth. Accordingly, once a dog has been identified as part of a portfolio, it is often discontinued or disposed of.

More creatively, opportunities might be found to differentiate the dog and obtain a strong position for it in a niche market. A small-share product can be used to price aggressively against a very large competitor because it is expensive for the large competitor to follow suit.

Dogs are products associated with modest positive or negative cash flow.

STARS

A product with a high market share of a rapidly growing market, and therefore with rapidly growing sales, is termed a *star*. These products may be the sales manager's dream but they could be the accountant's nightmare, because they are likely to absorb large amounts of cash even if they are highly profitable. It is often necessary to spend heavily on advertising and product improvements so that when the market slows, these products become cash cows. If market share is lost, the product will eventually become a *dog* when the market stops growing.

These are products associated with modest positive or negative cash flow.

QUESTION MARKS

A product with a low market share of a rapidly growing market is termed a *question mark*. Question marks are aptly named because they create a dilemma: they may or may not go on to become successful products as stars and cash cows. Alternatively, though they already have a foothold in a

Table 6.7 Using the BCG matrix in strategic planning

Business category	Market share thrust	Business profitability	Investment required	Net cash flow
Stars	Hold/increase	High	High	Around zero or slightly negative
Cash cows	Hold	High	Low	Highly positive
Question marks A	Increase	None or negative	Very high	Highly negative
Question marks B	Harvest/divest	Low or negative	Divest	Positive
Dogs	Harvest/divest	Low or negative	Divest	Positive

Source: Adapted from Hax and Majluf (1983)

growing market, if market share cannot be improved, they will become dogs. Resources need to be devoted to winning market share, which requires intrepidness for a product that may not yet have high sales, or the product may be sold to an organization in a better position to exploit the market. These products will be high users of cash when trying to establish them in a growth market.

These are products associated with large negative cash flow.

In summary portfolio management is concerned with balancing products and hence cash flow, so that one category of products supports the development of other categories and risks can thereby be diminished. Specifically, companies should be looking to develop question mark products into stars and stars into cash cows (moving products in an anti-clockwise direction around the matrix). Dogs should be assessed carefully and disposed of unless a viable future position can be envisaged.

Table 6.7 summarizes the strategic implications of using the BCG matrix.

Using the terminology that is usually applied to the matrix, portfolio management is concerned with:

- *Milking* surplus cash generated by cash cows
- Using the cash generated in *maintaining* stars and *investing* in selected question marks
- *Withdrawal* from dogs (if profitable niche positions cannot be established) or *harvesting* them if profitable niches can be established

6.11.3 Limitations of the BCG matrix

Accurate measurement and careful definition of the market are essential to avoid misdiagnosis when using the matrix. Critics (perhaps unfairly) point out that there are many relevant aspects relating to products that are not taken into account, but BCG never claimed that the process was a panacea and covered all aspects of strategy (Morrison and Wensley, 1991).

Above all, the matrix helps to identify which products to push or drop and when. It helps in the recognition of windows of opportunity and provides strong evidence against simple rules of thumb for allocating resources to products. However, the information needed to apply the matrix might be difficult and time-consuming to obtain and update, and some *THE* managers might feel that the effort is not worthwhile.

6.11.4 *Composite portfolio models*

The limitations of the BCG matrix have given rise to a number of other models that are beyond the scope of this text. A leading example is the General Electric-McKinsey (GE-McKinsey) matrix (see Fleisher and Bensoussan, 2003). The BCG matrix is intended for products but may be used for *SBUs* (which we encountered in Chapter 1) that are fairly homogenous, whereas the GE-McKinsey matrix is mainly applied to SBUs such as the subsidiaries of a holding company.

The model rates *market attractiveness* as high, medium or low and *competitive strength* as strong, medium or weak. SBUs are placed in the appropriate category, and although there is no automatic strategic prescription, the position is used to help devise an appropriate strategy.

Market attractiveness criteria will be set by the user and could include factors such as market growth, profitability, strength of competition, entry/exit barriers, legal regulation, etc. Competitive strength could include factors such as technological capability, brand, image, distribution channel links, operational capability and financial strength. The flexibility to include as many variables as required is useful but could lead to a lack of objectivity. Most users of the model recommend that the variables be given a weighting to establish their relative importance, which will in turn reduce the potential for bias. In practice, managers are aware that the tool is likely to be used as a basis for resource allocation and, consequently, they may attempt to influence the analysis in the favor of their own product or SBU.

The analysis gives rise to a 3 × 3 matrix as shown in Figure 6.8.

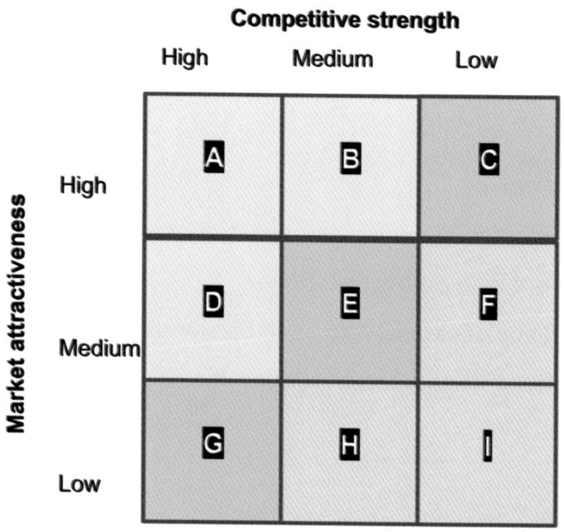

Classification			Strategic thrust
		High overall attractiveness (A, B &D)	Invest/grow
G)		Medium overall attractiveness (C, E &	Selectively improve/defend
		Low overall attractiveness (F, H and I)	Harvest/divest

Figure 6.8 The GE-McKinsey matrix

Source: Adapted from Fleisher and Bensoussan (2003: Ch.5)

Each of the cell positions has associated strategic implications:

- Cell A – The company would invest strongly in these products or SBUs because it offers an attractive strategic position where distinctive capabilities providing competitive strength can be harnessed in an attractive market.
- Cell B – The company could be aggressive and attempt to build strength to challenge competitors, or it could build selectively.
- Cell C – There is a real dilemma in that there is the difficulty of competing well against stronger competitors. The most plausible options would be to divest because the opportunity might be attractive to others or to specialize around selected niches where some strength could be built.
- Cell D – Indicates limited investment but only aimed at maintenance of competitive ability
- Cells E and F – Indicates risk minimization and prudently selecting choices for investment and expansion rather than investing in all possibilities
- Cells G and H – Indicates management of a mature or declining market to maximize earnings through highly limited investment
- Cell I – Could require divestment or minimizing investment to maintain the product or SBU as a going concern

Extreme care is required in the judgments that place products or SBUs into any one category, and the model does not directly take account of synergies between different products or SBUs. However, importantly, the model does represent a means of relating competences (of the organization) to the external environment. Consequently, the model can be viewed as taking SWOT analysis, covered in Chapter 9, a stage further.

THINK POINTS

- Distinguish between price skimming and penetration strategies.
- Explain what is meant by a product portfolio.
- Explain the importance of cash flow to an understanding of the BCG matrix.
- Explain the major benefits and potential difficulties of using the BCG and GE-McKinsey matrices.

Small business focus

Many of the marketing and product aspects considered in this chapter can be applied to small THE businesses similar to how they can be applied to larger businesses. In many cases, though, the concepts were developed primarily for large-scale businesses often with a number of products or SBUs, and many of the textbook examples used also relate to such organizations. Studies have shown that marketing in an SME context frequently works in different ways. Marketing SMEs is often characterized by:

- A focus on sales and promotion
- A lack of formal marketing plans
- The importance of the owner/entrepreneur in making marketing decisions

- The importance of personal contacts with customers and potential customers
- The role of innovation and flexibility in continually adapting products to meet customer requirements

The marketing function (if it exists) in many SMEs relates primarily to sales and promotions only, a perception that has grown from the ability of SMEs to obtain sales without planning their marketing activities (Carson, 1990; Stokes, 2000). There is frequently a lack of formal structure and conventional marketing concepts, which can be misinterpreted as not recognizing the importance of marketing (O'Dwyer et al., 2009).

However, as O'Dwyer et al. (2009) pointed out, much of the literature on SME marketing identifies the presence of a form of marketing that is unique to small firms (Carson, 1993; Stokes, 2000), because the role of entrepreneurs and innovation is of central importance and thus SMEs frequently adapt general marketing concepts, practices and theories to suit their own purposes (Carson, 1993), while maintaining a process focus and concentrating on incremental innovations (Miles and Darroch, 2006).

Central to SME marketing is the continual development of the experiential knowledge of the entrepreneurs gained by doing business (Grant et al., 2001). Thus, to a certain extent, the marketing characteristics of an SME are often derived from the experiential knowledge of the owner/manager and the firm's characteristics, such as a distinctive managerial style, independence, ownership, having limited resources and the scale and scope of operations (Carson and McCartan-Quinn, 1995).

These characteristics combine to form an inherently innate method of doing business for SME owner/managers, which enables them to focus on achieving competitive advantage through added value marketing initiatives. Traditionally, some marketing approaches have concentrated on the marketing mix: the traditional marketing paradigm of the 4 Ps (product, price, place and promotion) or the 7 Ps adopted by service marketing (product, price, place, promotion, people, process and physical evidence). However, Stokes (2000) argued that the entrepreneurs who are central to SME decision making stress the importance of promotion and word of mouth. Such entrepreneurs often identify one of the unique selling points of their business as the nature of their personal contact with customers and stress that their focus is on the *four Is* of information, identification, innovation and interaction (Stokes, 2000).

Palmer (2014) produced an overview of the potential marketing advantages that small businesses might experience that enable them to exploit being small and to achieve competitive advantages. To Palmer (2014), the competitive advantages may lie in three areas:

- Small businesses often exhibit greater adaptability than larger companies. Larger companies tend to be burdened by slower decision-making processes and become more risk averse as they grow.
- In many *THE* service environments, there are comparatively small economies of scale available, which allows larger organizations to become more efficient and dominate the market. Despite the inexorable rise of technology and the growth of international brands, this may explain why there are still many independent travel intermediaries, event management companies, tour operators and accommodation providers.
- Small businesses, often driven by an entrepreneurial owner/manager, tend to be good innovators. The internet opened up many opportunities for entrepreneurs to establish new business formats. The travel agency presents an example, because it was largely smaller businesses that were the first to innovate with web-based sales facilities, whereas the larger chains were slower to adapt and set up their own internet facilities (Palmer, 2014). This was partly perhaps because setting up web-based activities presented a potential threat to other parts of their businesses such as the capital that had been invested in setting up physical travel agency branches.

Many larger businesses are primarily concerned with developing their brand and its values. In smaller businesses, the emphasis may switch to developing a personal reputation, expressed through consistency and providing particular levels of service. The growth of boutique hotels (with under 50 rooms and having individualized design and service) illustrates this point. The growth of such hotels may be viewed as appealing to segments of buyers seeking the experience of surprise, as opposed to more monotonous standardized, branded chains (Palmer, 2014).

Smaller businesses have to seek ways of maximizing their limited budgets. A leading small business text (Scarborough and Cornwall, 2018), for example, advocated the use of so-called bootstrap marketing strategy (sometimes termed *guerrilla* marketing). Such marketing strategies are characterized as being unconventional, being low cost and utilizing creative techniques to maximize the 'bang from marketing bucks'. Though bootstrap marketing is certainly not limited to the internet, it has undoubtedly provided SMEs with a wide range of opportunities to reach their potential customers and to compete effectively with larger competitors.

> For example: *Emails can be a very blunt instrument, but a company can send out hundreds or thousands of emails at low cost and wait for the responses. However, hiring a tracking company (or purchasing relevant software) to follow up on who opened the emails, what links were clicked on and more allows SMEs to more closely target their marketing efforts. Similarly, Facebook, Twitter and Instagram (and other social media sites) provide many additional bootstrap marketing opportunities. For instance, Facebook allows companies to target social network groups that match the company's identified target demographics. Additionally, Facebook allows marketing messages to be spread when someone opts to become your 'friend'.*

In many cases in *THE*, smaller businesses can successfully compete by forming alliances, partnerships and consortia (of various types), which allow marketing resources to be pooled so that they are *leveraged* and used more effectively.

> For example: *Independent hotels are often able to compete and prosper by not using their own brand but by linking it to the brand of marketing consortia (such as Best Western, Small Luxury Hotels of the World and Consort Hotels). Accommodation providers and other SMEs may also be able to leverage additional marketing benefits in particular geographical areas by effectively utilizing networking and clustering opportunities to group together for collective advantage (Novelli et al., 2006).*

CHAPTER SUMMARY

The chapter dealt with issues concerned with defining and analyzing markets for *THE* managers. It explained how splitting markets up into segments could be used as a competitive tool and investigated different ways in which market segments might be chosen. The concept of the augmented product was considered as a tool to examine how features and benefits might be produced to provide a competitive edge.

The product life cycle showed how a number of strategic issues might be anticipated at different stages, and the management of the product portfolio dealt with the management of a whole product range or different SBUs. Aspects of product innovation were viewed by examining the processes of new idea generation and new product screening.

Finally, the chapter considered the concept of a portfolio of products at different stages of development. Two models, namely, the BCG and GE-McKinsey matrices, were outlined. These provide means by which the portfolio of products might be analyzed and provide a potential basis for the allocation of resources.

REFERENCES AND WEBSITES

References

Alexander, A., Kim, S. B. and Kim, D. Y. (2015) 'Segmenting volunteers by motivation in the 2012 London Olympic Games', *Tourism Management*, 47: 1–10.

Allen, J., O'Toole, W., Harris, R. and McDonnell, I. (2005) *Festival and Special Event Management*, Milton, QLD: John Wiley & Sons Australia.

Almeida, A. M. M., Correia, A. and Pimpão, A. (2014) 'Segmentation by benefits sought: The case of rural tourism in Madeira', *Current Issues in Tourism*, 17(9): 813–831.

Ardito, L., Cerchione, R., Del Vecchio, P. and Raguseo, E. (2019) 'Big data in smart tourism: Challenges, issues and opportunities', *Current Issues in Tourism*, 22(15): 1805–1809.

Bojanic, D. C. and Reid, R. D. (2017) *Hospitality Marketing Management*, 6th ed., Hoboken, NJ: John Wiley & Sons.

Bonoma, T. V. and Shapiro, B. P. (1983) *Segmenting the Industrial Market*, Lexington, MA: Lexington Books.

Bowen, J. (2000) 'Airline hubs in Southeast Asia: National economic development and nodal accessibility', *Journal of Transport Geography*, 8: 25–41.

Bowie, D., Buttle, F., Brookes, M. and Mariussen, A. (2016) *Hospitality Marketing*, 3rd ed., Abingdon, UK: Routledge.

Brotspies, H. and Weinstein, A. (2019) 'Rethinking business segmentation: A conceptual model and strategic insights', *Journal of Strategic Marketing*, 27(2): 164–176.

Brown, R. (1991) 'The S-curves of innovation', *Journal of Marketing Management*, 7(2): 189–202.

Brownlie, D. (1985) 'Strategic marketing concepts and models', *Journal of Marketing Management*, 1(1–2): 157–194.

Buhalis, D. and Foerste, M. (2015) 'SoCoMo marketing for travel and tourism: Empowering co-creation of value', *Journal of Destination Marketing and Management*, 4(3): 151–161.

Buhalis, D. and Sinarta, Y. (2019) 'Real-time co-creation and nowness service: Lessons from tourism and hospitality', *Journal of Travel and Tourism Marketing*, 36(5): 563–582.

Butler, R. W. (1980) 'The concept of the tourist area life cycle of evolution and implications for management', *The Canadian Geographer*, 24: 5–12.

Butler, R. W. (2009) 'Tourism in the future: Cycles, waves or wheels?', *Futures*, 41(6): 346–352.

Buzzell, R. D. (2004) 'The PIMS program of strategy research: A retrospective appraisal', *Journal of Business Research*, 57(5): 478–483.

Camilleri, M. A. (2018) *Travel Marketing, Tourism Economics and the Airline Product*, Berlin: Springer.

Carson, D. (1990) 'Some exploratory models for assessing small firms' marketing performance (a qualitative approach)', *European Journal of Marketing*, 234(11): 8–51.

Carson, D. (1993) 'A philosophy for marketing education in small firms', *Journal of Marketing Management*, 9: 189–204.

Carson, D. and McCartan-Quinn, D. (1995) 'Non-practice of theoretically based marketing in small business – Issues arising and their implications', *Journal of Marketing Theory and Practice*, 3(4): 24–31.

Cartwright, S., Liu, H. and Raddats, C. (2021) 'Strategic use of social media within business-to-business (B2B) marketing: A systematic literature review', *Industrial Marketing Management*, 97: 35–58.

Chang, R. C., Kivela, J. and Mak, A. H. (2011) 'Attributes that influence the evaluation of travel dining experience: When East meets West', *Tourism Management*, 32(2): 307–316.

Christensen, C. M. (2006) 'The ongoing process of building a theory of disruption', *Journal of Product Innovation Management*, 23(1): 39–55.

Çınar, K., Yetimoğlu, S. and Uğurlu, K. (2020) 'The role of market segmentation and target marketing strategies to increase occupancy rates and sales opportunities of hotel enterprises', in A. Kavoura, E. Kefallonitis and P. Theodoridis (Eds), *Strategic Innovative Marketing and Tourism*, Springer Proceedings in Business and Economics, Cham, Switzerland: Springer, 521–528.

Clifton, W. (2013) *The Global Hotel Industry: Big, Beautiful and Branded? Part Two*, London: Global Hotel Research Limited.

Cooper, C., Fletcher, J., Gilbert, D., Shepherd, R. and Wanhill, S. (1998) *Tourism Principles and Practice*, 2nd ed., Harlow, UK: Longman.

Crawford-Welch, S. (1994) 'The development of Courtyard by Marriott', in R. Teare, J. A. Mazanec, S. Crawford-Welch and S. Calver (Eds), *Marketing in Hospitality and Tourism: A Consumer Focus*, London: Cassell.

Crittenden, V. L., Crittenden, W. F. and Muzyka, D. F. (2002) 'Segmenting the business-to-business marketplace by product attributes and the decision process', *Journal of Strategic Marketing*, 10(1): 3–20.

Day, M., Magnan, G. M. and Moeller, M. (2010) 'Evaluating the bases of supplier segmentation: A review and taxonomy', *Industrial Marketing Management*, 39(4): 625–639.

Dev, C. S., Morgan, M. S. and Shoemaker, S. (1995) 'A positioning analysis of hotel brands: Based on travel-manager perceptions', *Cornell Hotel and Restaurant Administration Quarterly*, 36(6): 48–55.

Dodds, R. (2020) 'The tourist experience life cycle: A perspective article', *Tourism Review*, 75(1): 216–220.

Dolnicar, S. (2008) 'Market segmentation in tourism', in A. G. Woodside and D. Martin (Eds), *Tourism Management: Analysis, Behavior and Strategy*, Wallingford, UK: CAB International, 129–150.

Dolnicar, S. (2020) 'Market segmentation analysis in tourism: A perspective paper', *Tourism Review*, 75(1): 45–48.

Evans, N. G. (2002) 'Travel and tourism economics', in R. Sharpley (Ed.), *The Tourism Business: An Introduction*, Sunderland, UK: Business Education Publishers, 367–396.

Evans, N. G. (2012) Tourism: A strategic business perspective, in T. Jamal and M. Robinson (Eds), *The Sage Handbook of Tourism Studies*, Thousand Oaks, CA: Sage, 215–234.

Ezeh, P. C. (2017) 'A critical review of market segmentation, target marketing and positioning in hospitality marketing,' in D. Gursoy (Ed.), *The Routledge Handbook of Hospitality Marketing*, Abingdon, UK: Routledge, 31–40.

Fleisher, C. S. and Bensoussan, B. E. (2003) *Strategic and Competitive Analysis. Methods and Techniques for Analyzing Business Competition*, Hoboken, NJ: Prentice Hall.

Font, X. and McCabe, S. (Eds). (2019) *Marketing for Sustainable Tourism*, Abingdon, UK: Routledge.

Frochot, I. (2005) 'A benefit segmentation of tourists in rural areas: A Scottish perspective', *Tourism Management*, 26(3): 335–346.

Frochot, I. and Morrison, A. M. (2000) 'Benefit segmentation: A review of its applications to travel and tourism research', *Journal of Travel and Tourism Marketing*, 9(4): 21–45.

Füller, J. and Matzler, K. (2008) 'Customer delight and market segmentation: An application of the three-factor theory of customer satisfaction on life style groups', *Tourism Management*, 29(1): 116–126.

Fyall, A. (2019) 'Tourism destination re-positioning and strategies', in E. Fayos-Solà and C. Cooper (Eds), *The Future of Tourism*, Cham, Switzerland: Springer, 271–284.

Fyall, A. and Garrod, B. (2005) *Tourism Marketing: A Collaborative Approach*, Bristol, UK: Channel View Publications.

Fyall, A., Legohérel, P., Frochot, I. and Wang, Y. (2019) *Marketing for Tourism and Hospitality: Collaboration, Technology and Experiences*, Abingdon, UK: Routledge.

Gallarza, M. G., Saura, I. G. and García, H. C. (2002) 'Destination image: Towards a conceptual framework', *Annals of Tourism Research*, 29(1), 56–78.

Garay, L. and Cànoves, G. (2011) 'Life cycles, stages and tourism history: The Catalonia (Spain) experience', *Annals of Tourism Research*, 38(2): 651–671.

Garcia-Ayllon, S. (2016) 'Geographic information system (GIS) analysis of impacts in the tourism area life cycle (TALC) of a Mediterranean resort', *International Journal of Tourism Research*, 18(2): 186–196.

George, R. (2021) *Marketing Tourism and Hospitality*, Cham, Switzerland: Palgrave Macmillan.

Getz, D. (2022) 'Event management', in D. Buhalis (Ed.), *Encyclopedia of Tourism Management and Marketing*, Cheltenham, UK: Edward Elgar, 144–147.

Ghandour, A., Kintonova, A., Demidchik, N. and Sverdlikova, E. (2021) 'Solving tourism management challenges by means of mobile augmented reality applications', *International Journal of Web-Based Learning and Teaching Technologies*, 16(6): 1–16.

Gibson, L. D. (2001) 'Is something rotten in segmentation?', *Marketing Research*, 13(1): 20–25.

Goi, C. L. (2009) 'A review of marketing mix: 4Ps or more', *International Journal of Marketing Studies*, 1(1): 2–15.

Gonzalez, A. M. and Bello, L. (2002) 'The construct "lifestyle" in market segmentation: The behavior of tourist consumers', *European Journal of Marketing*, 36(1/2): 51–85.

Goodman, M. (2013) 'Hotels' Mr Smooth learnt all the tricks from his dad, interview with IHG hotels chief executive', *The Sunday Times*, 7 April.

Grant, K., Gilmore, A., Carson, D., Laney, R. and Pickett, B. (2001) 'Experiential research methodology: An integrated academic – practitioner "team" approach', *Qualitative Market Research: An International Journal*, 4(2): 66–75.

Greenley, G. E. and Bayus, B. L. (1993) 'Marketing planning decision making in UK and US companies: An empirical comparative study', *Journal of Marketing Management*, 9: 155–172.

Guttentag, D. (2015) 'Airbnb: Disruptive innovation and the rise of an informal tourism accommodation sector', *Current Issues in Tourism*, 18(12): 1192–1217.

Haley, R. I. (1968) 'Benefit segmentation: A decision-oriented research tool', *Journal of Marketing*, 32(3): 30–35.

Hall, S. (2017) '*Innovative B2B Marketing: New Models, Processes and Theory*, London: Kogan Page.

Hallmann, K., Zehrer, A. and Müller, S. (2015) 'Perceived destination image: An image model for a winter sports destination and its effect on intention to revisit', *Journal of Travel Research*, 54(1): 94–106.

Hax, A. C. and Majluf, N. S. (1983) 'The use of the growth-share matrix in strategic planning', *Interfaces*, 13(1): 46–60.

Henderson, B. (2012) 'The experience curve reviewed', in R. Lesser, M. S. Deimler, D. Rhodes, and J. Sinha (Eds), *Own the Future: 50 Ways to Win from the Boston Consulting Group*, Hoboken, NJ: John Wiley & Sons, 211–214.

Hjalager, A. M. (2015) '100 Innovations that transformed tourism', *Journal of Travel Research*, 54(1): 3–21.

Ho, G. K. and McKercher, B. (2015) 'A review of life cycle models by Plog and Butler from a marketing perspective', in M. Kozak and N. Kozak (Eds), *Destination Marketing an International Perspective*, Abingdon, UK: Routledge, 145–154.

Hollensen, S. (2019) *Marketing Management: A Relationship Approach*, 4th ed., Harlow, UK: Pearson Education.

Hooley, G. J., Nicoulaud, B., Rudd, J. M. and Lee, M. (2020) *Marketing Strategy and Competitive Positioning*, 7th ed., Harlow, UK: Pearson.

Hudson, S. and Hudson, L. (2017) *Marketing for Tourism Hospitality and Events: A Global Digital Approach*, London: Sage.

Intercontinental Hotel Group. (2022) *Intercontinental Hotel Group (IHG), Annual Report 2022*, www.ihg.com/

Jang, S. C., Morrison, A. M. and O'Leary, J. T. (2002) 'Benefit segmentation of Japanese pleasure travelers to the USA and Canada: Selecting target markets based on the profitability and risk of individual market segments', *Tourism Management*, 23(4): 367–378.

Jonk, G., Handschuh, M. and Niewiem, S. (2008) 'The battle of the value chains: New specialized versus old hybrids', *Strategy and Leadership*, 36(2): 24–29.

Junior, A. C. P., Hollaender, P. S., Mazzanati, G. V. and Bortoletto, W. W. (2021) 'Efficiency drivers of international airports: A worldwide benchmarking study', *Journal of Air Transport Management*, 90: 101960.

Kalafatis, S. P., Tsogas, M. H. and Blankson, C. (2000) 'Positioning strategies in business markets', *Journal of Business and Industrial Marketing*, 15(6): 416–437.

Kay, J. (1995) *Foundations of Corporate Success*, Oxford: Oxford University Press.

Kim, E., Fredline, L. and Cuskelly, G. (2018) 'Heterogeneity of sport event volunteer motivations: A segmentation approach', *Tourism Management*, 68: 375–386.

Kim, S. S., Chun, H. and Petrick, J. F. (2005) 'Positioning analysis of overseas golf tour destinations by Korean golf tourists', *Tourism Management*, 26(6): 905–917.

Kim, W. G., Park, Y., Gazzoli, G. and Sheng, E. (2011) 'Benefit segmentation of international travellers to Macau, China', *Journal of Quality Assurance in Hospitality and Tourism*, 12(1): 28–57.

King, C., Chen, N. and Fun, D. C. (2015) 'Exploring destination image decay: A study of sport tourists' destination image change after event participation', *Journal of Hospitality and Tourism Research*, 39(1): 3–31.

Kinnunen, M., Luonila, M. and Honkanen, A. (2019) 'Segmentation of music festival attendees', *Scandinavian Journal of Hospitality and Tourism*, 19(3): 278–299.

Kolb, B. (2017) *Tourism, Marketing for Cities and Towns*, Abingdon, UK: Routledge.

Kolb, B. (2018) *Marketing Research for the Tourism, Hospitality and Events Industries*, Abingdon, UK: Routledge.

Konu, H., Laukkanen, T. and Komppula, R. (2011) 'Using ski destination choice criteria to segment Finnish ski resort customers', *Tourism Management*, 32(5): 1096–1105.

Kotler, P. and Armstrong, G. (2020) *Principles of Marketing*, 18th Global ed., Harlow, UK: Pearson.

Kotler, P., Bowen, J. T. and Balaglu, S. (2021) *Marketing for Hospitality and Tourism*, 8th ed., Harlow, UK: Pearson.

Kotler, P., Haider, D. H. and Rein, I. (1993) *Marketing Places*, New York: Free Press.

Kotler, P., Keller, K. L. and Chernev, A. (2022) *Marketing Management*, Global 16th ed., Harlow, UK: Pearson.

Kozak, M. and Martin, D. (2012) 'Tourism life cycle and sustainability analysis: Profit-focused strategies for mature destinations', *Tourism Management*, 33(1): 188–194.

Kwok, L., Tang, Y. and Yu, B. (2020) 'The 7 Ps marketing mix of home-sharing services: Mining travelers' online reviews on Airbnb', *International Journal of Hospitality Management*, 90: 102616.

Lajimi, H. F. and Majidi, S. (2021) 'Supplier segmentation: A systematic literature review', *Journal of Supply Chain Management Science*, 2(3–4): 138–158.

Lee, G., Morrison, A. M. and O'Leary, J. T. (2006) 'The economic value portfolio matrix: A target market selection tool for destination marketing organizations', *Tourism Management*, 27(4): 576–588.

Li, M., Huang, Z. and Cai, L. A. (2009) 'Benefit segmentation of visitors to a rural community-based festival', *Journal of Travel and Tourism Marketing*, 26(5–6): 585–598.

Litvin, S. W. (2006) 'Revisiting Plog's model of allocentricity and psychocentricity one more time', *Cornell Hotel and Restaurant Administration Quarterly*, 47(3): 245–253.

Liu, W., Vogt, C. A., Lupi, F., He, G., Ouyang, Z. and Liu, J. (2016) 'Evolution of tourism in a flagship protected area of China', *Journal of Sustainable Tourism*, 24(2): 203–226.

Lohmann, G., Albers, S., Koch, B. and Pavlovich, K. (2009) 'From hub to tourist destination – An explorative study of Singapore and Dubai's aviation-based transformation', *Journal of Air Transport Management*, 15(5): 205–211.

Ma, M. and Hassink, R. (2013) 'An evolutionary perspective on tourism area development', *Annals of Tourism Research*, 41: 89–109.

Mackellar, J. (2009) 'Dabblers, fans and fanatics: Exploring behavioral segmentation at a special-interest event', *Journal of Vacation Marketing*, 15(1): 5–24.

Madsen, D. Ø. (2017) 'Not dead yet: The rise, fall and persistence of the BCG matrix', *Problems and Perspectives in Management*, 15(1): 19–34.

Mayock, P. (2013) Marriott CEO shares Moxy update, www.hotelnewsnow.com

McKercher, B. (1995) 'The destination-market mix: A tourism market portfolio analysis model', *Journal of Travel and Tourism Marketing*, 4(2): 23–40.

McKercher, B., Tolkach, D., Eka Mahadewi, N. M. and Byomantara, D. G. N. (2022) 'Choosing the optimal segmentation technique to understand tourist behaviour', *Journal of Vacation Marketing*, 29(1): 71–83.

Middleton, V. T., Fyall, A., Morgan, M., Morgan, M. and Ranchhod, A. (2009) *Marketing in Travel and Tourism*, 4th ed., Abingdon, UK: Routledge.

Miles, M. P. and Darroch, J. (2006) 'Large firms, entrepreneurial marketing processes, and the cycle of competitive advantage', *European Journal of Marketing*, 40(5/6): 485–501.

Mitchell, V. W. and Wilson, D. F. (1998) 'Balancing theory and practice: A reappraisal of business-to-business segmentation', *Industrial Marketing Management*, 27(5): 429–445.

Mody, M., Suess, C. and Lehto, X. (2019) 'Using segmentation to compete in the age of the sharing economy: Testing a core–periphery framework', *International Journal of Hospitality Management*, 78: 199–213.

Moll, J. and Harrigan, F. (2018) 'We went too far, and we learnt from it: Management control in the development of the Boeing Dreamliner', in M. Carlsson-Wall, H. Håkansson, K. Kraus, J. Lind and T. Strömsten (Eds.), *Accounting, Innovation and Inter-Organizational Relationships*, Abingdon, UK: Routledge, 104–129.

Morgan, N., Pritchard, A. and Pride, R. (2012) *Destination Branding*, Abingdon, UK: Routledge.

Morrison, A. (2018) *Marketing and Managing Tourism Destinations*, 2nd ed., Abingdon, UK: Routledge.

Morrison, A. and Wensley, R. (1991) 'Boxing up or boxed in?: A short history of the Boston Consultancy Group share/growth matrix', *Journal of Marketing Management*, 7(2):105–129.

Morritt, R. and Weinstein, A. (2012) *Segmentation Strategies for Hospitality Managers: Target Marketing for Competitive Advantage*, Abingdon, UK: Routledge.

Moutinho, L. (2000) 'Strategic planning', in L. Moutinho (Ed.), *Strategic Management in Tourism*, Wallingford, UK: CABI, 259–282.

Nduna, L. T. and van Zyl, C. (2017) 'A benefit segmentation analysis of tourists visiting Mpumalanga', *African Journal of Hospitality, Tourism, and Leisure*, 6(3): 1–22.

Neuhofer, B., Buhalis, D. and Ladkin, A. (2015) 'Smart technologies for personalized experiences: A case study in the hospitality domain', *Electronic Markets*, 25(3): 243–254.

Novelli, M., Schmitz, B. and Spencer, T. (2006) 'Networks, clusters and innovation in tourism: A UK experience', *Tourism Management*, 27(6): 1141–1152.

O'Dwyer, M., Gilmore, A. and Carson, D. (2009) 'Innovative marketing in SMEs', *European Journal of Marketing*, 43(1/2): 46–61.

Palmer, A. (2014) *Principles of Services Marketing*, 2nd ed., Maidenhead, UK: McGraw-Hill.

Park, J. Y. and Jang, S. (2014) 'Psychographics: Static or dynamic?', *International Journal of Tourism Research*, 16(4): 351–354.

Pike, S. (2012) 'Destination positioning opportunities using personal values: Elicited through the repertory test with laddering analysis', *Tourism Management*, 33(1): 100–107.

Pike, S. and Mason, R. (2011) 'Destination competitiveness through the lens of brand positioning: The case of Australia's Sunshine Coast', *Current Issues in Tourism*, 14(2): 1.

Piuchan, M. (2018) 'Plog's and Butler's models: A critical review of psychographic tourist typology and the tourist area life cycle', *Turizam*, 22(3): 95–106.

Plog, S. (2001) 'Why destination areas rise and fall in popularity: An update of a Cornell Quarterly classic', *Cornell Hotel and Restaurant Administration Quarterly*, 42(3):13–24.

Poetz, M. K. and Schreier, M. (2012) 'The value of crowdsourcing: Can users really compete with professionals in generating new product ideas?', *Journal of Product Innovation Management*, 29(2): 245–256.

Powers, T. L. and Sterling, J. U. (2008) 'Segmenting business-to-business markets: A micro-macro linking methodology', *Journal of Business and Industrial Marketing*, 23(3): 170–177.

Preston, C. A. (2012) *Event Marketing: How to Successfully Promote Events, Festivals, Conventions, and Expositions*, Hoboken, NJ: John Wiley & Sons.

Ramos, C. M., Almeida, C. R. D. and Fernandes, P. O. (Eds). (2019) *Handbook of Research on Social Media Applications for the Tourism and Hospitality Sector*, Hershey, PA: IGI Global.

Reic, I. (2017) *Events Marketing Management: A Consumer Perspective*, Abingdon, UK: Routledge.

Robertson, M. and Wardrop, K. M. (2012) 'Events and the destination dynamic: Edinburgh festivals, entrepreneurship and strategic marketing', in I. Yeoman, M. Robertson, J. Ali-Knight, S. Drummond and U. McMahon-Beattie (Eds), *Festival and Events Management*, Abingdon, UK: Routledge: 115–121.

Rodríguez-Molina, M. A., Frías-Jamilena, D. M., Del Barrio-García, S. and Castañeda-García, J. A. (2019) 'Destination brand equity-formation: Positioning by tourism type and message consistency', *Journal of Destination Marketing and Management*, 12: 114–124.

Rogers, T. and Davidson, R. (Eds). (2017) *Marketing Destinations and Venues for Conferences, Conventions and Business Events*, Abingdon, UK: Routledge.

Sahin, S. and Baloglu, S. (2011) 'Brand personality and destination image of Istanbul', *Anatolia – International Journal of Tourism and Hospitality Research*, 22(1): 69–88.

Scarborough, N. M. and Cornwall, J. R. (2018) *Essentials of Entrepreneurship and Small Business Management*, 9th Global ed., Harlow, UK: Pearson.

Schmuck, R. (2021) 'Global supply chain quality integration strategies and the case of the Boeing 787 Dreamliner development', *Procedia Manufacturing*, 54: 88–94.

Scott, N. and Parfitt, N. (2005) 'Lifestyle segmentation in tourism and leisure: Imposing order or finding it?', *Journal of Quality Assurance in Hospitality and Tourism*, 5(2–4): 121–139.

Scott, N., Parfitt, N. and Laws, L. (2000) 'Destination management: Co-operative marketing, a case study of the Port Douglas brand', in B. Faulkner, G. Moscardo and E. Laws, (Eds.), *Tourism in the 21st Century: Lessons from Experience*, London: Continuum.

Shankar, R. S. (2018) 'Destination personality and destination image: A literature review', *Journal of Brand Management*, 15(4): 47–60.

Skinner, H., Sarpong, D. and White, G. R. (2018) 'Meeting the needs of the Millennials and Generation Z: Gamification in tourism through geocaching', *Journal of Tourism Futures*, 4(1): 93–104.

Smith, W. R. (1956) 'Product differentiation and market segmentation as alternative marketing strategies', *The Journal of Marketing*, 21(1), 3–8.

Souiden, N., Ladhari, R. and Chiadmi, N. E. (2017) 'Destination personality and destination image', *Journal of Hospitality and Tourism Management*, 32: 54–70.

Part 2

Sowrey, T. (1990) 'Idea generation: Identifying the most useful techniques', *European Journal of Marketing*, 42(5): 20–29.

Stokes, D. (2000) 'Putting entrepreneurship into marketing: The processes of entrepreneurial marketing', *Journal of Research in Marketing and Entrepreneurship*, 2(1): 1–16.

Strom, E. and Kerstein, R. (2015) 'Mountains and muses: Tourism development in Asheville, North Carolina', *Annals of Tourism Research*, 52: 134–147.

Stylos, N., Vassiliadis, C. A., Bellou, V. and Andronikidis, A. (2016) 'Destination images, holistic images and personal normative beliefs: Predictors of intention to revisit a destination', *Tourism Management*, 53: 40–60.

Suarez, F. and Lanzolla, G. (2005) 'The half-truth of first-mover advantage', *Harvard Business Review*, 83(4), 121.

Swarbrooke, J. and Page, S. J. (2012) *Development and Management of Visitor Attractions*, 2nd ed., Abingdon, UK: Routledge.

Terwiesch, C. and Ulrich, K. T. (2009) *Innovation Tournaments: Creating and Selecting Exceptional Opportunities*, Cambridge, MA: Harvard Business School Press.

Tkaczynski, A. and Rundle-Thiele, S. R. (2011) 'Event segmentation: A review and research agenda', *Tourism Management*, 32(2): 426–434.

Tkaczynski, A. and Rundle-Thiele, S. R. (2020) 'Event market segmentation: A review update and research agenda', *Event Management*, 24(2–3): 277–295.

Tkaczynski, A., Rundle-Thiele, S. R. and Beaumont, N. (2009) 'Segmentation: A tourism stakeholder view', *Tourism Management*, 30(2): 169–175.

Tourism and Events Queensland. (2017) *TEQ Events Strategy 2025*, www.teq.queensland.com

Tourism and Events Queensland. (2018) *TEQ Marketing Strategy 2025*, www.teq.queensland.com

Tourism and Events Queensland. (2022) *TEQ Strategic Plan 2022–2026*, www.teq.queensland.com

Tsiotsou, R. H. and Goldsmith, R. E. (2012) 'Target marketing and its application to tourism', in R. H. Tsiotsou and R. E. Goldsmith (Eds), *Strategic Marketing in Tourism Services*, Bingley, UK: Emerald, 3–16.

Usakli, A. and Baloglu, S. (2011) 'Brand personality of tourist destinations: An application of self-congruity theory', *Tourism Management*, 32(1): 114–127.

Valentine, D. B. and Powers, T. L. (2013) 'Generation Y values and lifestyle segments', *Journal of Consumer Marketing*, 30(7): 597–606.

von Hippel, E. (1978) 'Successful industrial products from customer ideas', *Journal of Marketing*, 42(1): 39–49.

Walsh, D. (2013) 'Rite of passage to India: Children's activity camp hits expansion trail', *The Times*, 18 February, 11.

Weinstein, A. and Morritt, R. (2012) *Segmentation Strategies for Hospitality Managers: Target Marketing for Competitive Advantage*, Abingdon, UK: Routledge.

West, D. C., Ford, J. and Ibrahim, E. (2015) *Strategic Marketing: Creating Competitive Advantage*, 3rd ed., New York: Oxford University Press.

Whitfield, J. (2009) 'The cyclical representation of the UK conference sector's life cycle: The use of refurbishments as rejuvenation triggers', *Tourism Analysis*, 14(5): 559–572.

Websites

www.contiki.com/
www.ihg.com
www.marriott.com
www.moxy-hotels.marriott.com
www.strategicbusinessinsights.com
www.TEQ.Queensland.com
www.thetravelcorporation.com
www.trailblazersindia.com/
www.travel.saga.co.uk

Part **3**

Analyzing the external environment and SWOT

External analysis and SWOT

External analysis and SWOT overview

The analysis of the internal environment (which provides the analytical underpinning for the 'strengths' and 'weaknesses' of the SWOT) was considered in Part 2 of this book.

Part 3 of the book turns to the analysis of the *external environment* facing *THE* organizations. The analysis in the subsequent chapters provides a rigorous underpinning for the 'opportunities' and 'threats' components of the SWOT. In some ways this form of analysis can be viewed as being more complicated than internal analysis because by definition it includes everything that is happening outside *THE* organizations' control. Because such analysis potentially covers a vast array of factors, the problems lie in deciding the relevant factors to include and in categorizing them in a useful and meaningful way.

Thus, Chapters 7 and 8 are concerned with developing concepts and frameworks that help organize material appropriately and help in understanding what is occurring outside the organization concerned. Chapter 9 brings together the outcomes of the internal analysis (covered in Chapters 3, 4, 5 and 6) and the external analysis (Chapters 7 and 8) in the form of a SWOT.

Study progress

Part 1	Part 2	Part 3	Part 4	Part 5
Strategy and the tourism, hospitality and events contexts	Analyzing the internal environment	Analyzing the external environment and SWOT	Strategic options	Strategy in action
Chapters 1 and 2	Chapters 3, 4, 5 and 6	**Chapter 7** **The macro context** / **Chapter 8** **The competitive context** / **Chapter 9** **SWOT analysis**	Chapters 10, 11, 12 and 13	Chapters 14, 15, 16 and 17

Levels of external analysis

We can view external analysis on two levels:

- Firstly, the *macro environment* (sometimes called the *far, broad* or *general environment*) contains a number of factors that affect not only an organization itself but also all others in the industry. Most strategy textbooks use the STEP (or PEST) approach. In this book, in recognition of the key influence of environmental influences (in terms of the built and natural environments) in *THE* contexts, the STEP framework is widened to STEEP.

  STEEP – The sociodemographic, technological, economic, environmental and political factors are certainly beyond an individual organization's control, although in some cases an organization may be able to exert some influence over some of the factors. Consequently, strategic management rests on an organization's ability to cope with any changes in the macro environment through the successful formulation and implementation of appropriate strategies. The macro environment is considered in Chapter 7.

- Secondly the *competitive* (or sometimes termed micro, *near* or *industry*) environment is the sphere in which the organization interacts most often – usually on a day-to-day basis. Any changes in the competitive environment can affect a *THE* organization very quickly and sometimes dramatically. In most organizations, the competitive environment comprises influences from its industry and markets. In Chapter 8, two models are discussed for making sense of these important strategic influences – Porter's five force model and the resource or core competence–based model.

SWOT analysis

Chapter 9 provides the culmination of the analytical phase by bringing together and summarizing the results of the internal and external analyses in the form of a SWOT. The SWOT provides a position statement of where the organization is at the present time. Having understood the present position of the *THE* organization, the SWOT provides a firm platform for going on to consider the future in terms of the strategic options to be pursued.

Part 4 will go on to consider the formulation, evaluation and selection of strategic options, which are derived in a logical and robust way from the analysis carried out.

7

The external environment for tourism, hospitality and event organizations – the macro context

Introduction and chapter overview

THE entities – whether hotels, tour operators, travel agencies, event managers, etc. – function as open systems in that they interact with, respond to and are affected by their external environment (Jogaratnam and Law, 2006; Adema and Roehl, 2010). Thus, having an understanding of the external environment is of critical importance to most managers. Gaining such understanding is sometimes termed *environmental scanning* or *horizon scanning*, but here we will refer to it as macro-environmental analysis (see, for example, Bensoussan and Fleisher, 2013).

The most widely used technique for analyzing the macro environment is to divide the macro environment into its constituent parts, and here we use the terminology of *STEEP* analysis. STEEP analysis divides the factors in the macro environment into five categories:

- *Sociodemographic*
- *Technological*
- *Economic*
- *Environmental*
- *Political*

It is worth noting that in some texts the acronym STEP is used, with environmental factors omitted. In many other texts the STEP acronym is turned around and presented as PEST or sometimes

DOI: 10.4324/9781003318613-10

PESTEL. However, the framework for analysis is essentially the same. It is this popular framework that is explained and explored in this chapter.

After studying this chapter, students should be able to:

- Explain what is meant by the macro environment
- Explain Ginter and Duncan's mechanisms of carrying out macro-environmental analysis
- Describe the components of each of the five STEEP factors and be able to apply them to relevant *THE* contexts
- Explain how the STEEP factors are interlinked and interrelated in *THE* contexts

7.1 The macro environment

The macro environment refers to the broad environment outside an organization's industry and markets.

The macro environment is sometimes referred to as the *far* or *remote* environment because it tends to exert forces from outside the organization's sphere of influence and the forces are usually beyond the organization's control. The forces identified in the macro environment can, however, have significant impact on the industry environment in which the organization operates.

Changes in the macro environment can be of immense importance to an organization in that (amongst other important aspects) they can:

- Bring about the birth or death of an entire industry
- Make markets expand or contract
- Determine the level of competitiveness within an industry

It is therefore essential that *THE* managers be alert to actual and potential changes in the macro environment and that they seek to anticipate the potential impacts on their industry and markets.

Ginter and Duncan (1990) identified the potential benefits of macro-environmental analysis as:

- Increasing managerial awareness of environmental changes
- Increasing understanding of the context in which industries and markets function
- Increasing understanding of multinational settings
- Improving resource allocation decisions
- Facilitating risk management
- Focusing attention on the primary factors on strategic change
- Acting as an early warning system, providing time to anticipate opportunities and threats and devise appropriate responses

In many ways, analysis of the macro environment is more difficult than internal analysis because it involves *everything* that occurs outside the organization.

The problems when dealing with such a vast amount of information are:

- Assessing what should be included
- Assessing what should be left out
- Determining how the information should be organized in a rational and meaningful way

There are no simple rules governing the contents and presentation of macro-environmental analysis, as Richard Lynch makes clear in the quotation below.

DEFINITION/QUOTATION

Macro-environmental analysis

> There are no simple rules governing an analysis of the organization. Each analysis [of the macro environment] needs to be guided by what is relevant for that particular organization.
>
> (Lynch, 2018:79)

Thus, though analytical frameworks can be suggested for sorting and organizing pertinent information, the key issues are likely to be highly specific to each organization's circumstances.

7.1.1 Conducting macro-environmental analysis

For Ginter and Duncan (1990), macro-environmental analysis involves:

- *Scanning* macro environments for warning signs and possible environmental changes that will affect the organization
- *Monitoring* environments for specific trends and patterns
- *Forecasting* future directions of environmental changes
- *Assessing* current and future trends in terms of the effects such changes would have on the organization

The main features of STEEP analysis incorporating Ginter and Duncan's framework are summarized in Figure 7.1.

7.1.2 Limitations of macro-environmental analysis

We should be careful to note that macro-environmental analysis has its limitations and pitfalls.

At its root, the macro environment can be extremely complex, and at any one time there may be conflicting and contradictory changes taking place. The pace of change in many macro-environmental situations is increasing and becoming more turbulent and unpredictable, as discussed by, for example, Chakravarthy (1997), Mason (2007), Vecchiato (2015), Benítez-Aurioles (2019), Senbeto and Hon (2020) and Schoemaker and Day (2021). Not surprisingly, in recent times, a large number of authors (including a number focusing on *THE*) have pointed to the high degree of turbulence and uncertainty caused by the worldwide Covid-19 pandemic (see, for example, Giousmpasoglou et al., 2021; Herédia-Colaço and Rodrigues, 2021; Scheiwiller and Zizka, 2021).

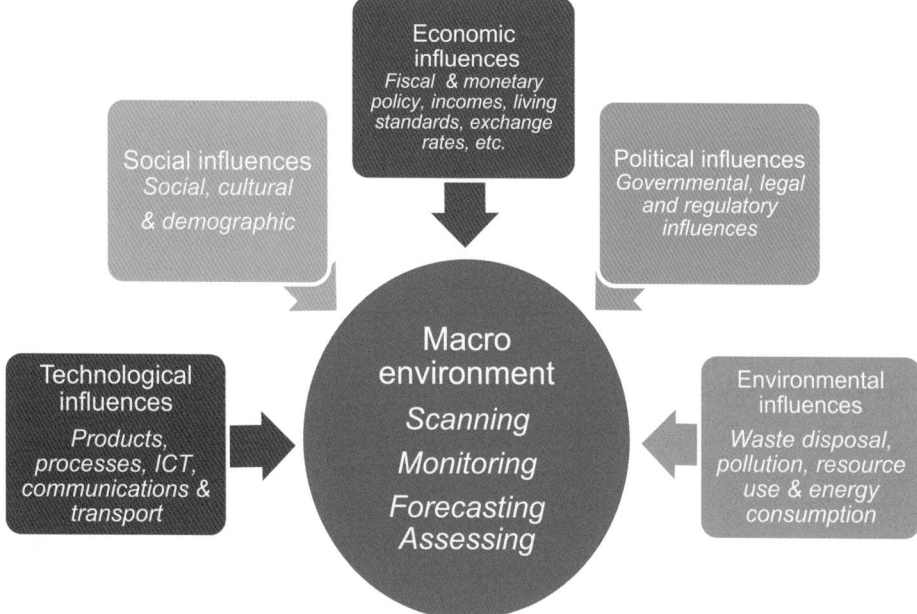

Figure 7.1 The main features of STEEP analysis

This degree of uncertainty has, to some extent, cast some doubt over the value of carrying out a macro-environmental analysis at all. By the time an organization has come to terms with one major change in the macro environment, another change often occurs that requires even more attention and action.

Accordingly, those managers that are concerned with strategic analysis must:

- Be aware of the limitations and inaccuracies of macro-environmental analysis
- Carry out the analysis or update it continuously (because it changes so frequently)
- Constantly seek to improve sources of information and techniques for its analysis
- Use the information as one source of organizational learning
- Use the information to inform future strategy

Notwithstanding these points, macro-environmental analysis is a valuable mechanism for increasing the strategic awareness of managers.

KEY CONCEPT

Competitive and macro environments

The most commonly used frameworks for analyzing the external business environment distinguish between two levels or strata of environmental influence.

- *The competitive (micro or near) environment* (considered in Chapter 8) is that which immediately surrounds a business, the parts the business interacts with frequently and

> over which it may have some influence. For most purposes, we can identify competi-
> tors, suppliers and customers as comprising the main constituents of this layer of the
> environment.
>
> • *The macro (far or general) environment* comprises those factors that can affect the whole
> industry in which a business operates. The macro environment comprises influence aris-
> ing from political, economic, sociodemographic and technological factors. The nature of
> these factors normally means that individual businesses are unable to influence them –
> strategies must usually be formulated to cope with changes in the macro environment.

7.2 'STEEP' analysis

The complexity of the macro environment makes it necessary to divide the forces at work into the
five broad categories we have already encountered (see Figure 7.1). It is important to remember that
the five categories are interrelated and constantly interact with each other.

In the process of STEEP analysis (sometimes called STEP, PEST or PESTEL analysis), it is therefore
important to explore and understand the relationships between the forces at work. It is equally
important to identify the relative importance of the factors at work for the organization, its industry
and its markets. Finally, because of the uncertainty of the effects of macro-environmental change
on the competitive environment, it is essential that a range of possible outcomes of the changes be
identified and considered.

In carrying out a STEEP analysis, it should be pointed out that some of the factors may be generic
in that they affect all industrial sectors, whereas others are specific to *THE* or a particular sector.
It should also be noted that the factors are somewhat subjective (i.e., open to opinion) and are
dynamic in that they are likely to change over time. Rate et al. (2018b) provided a review of some
of the major environmental factors in *THE* using an extended framework, which they termed SCEP-
TICAL analysis. The acronym stands for Social, Cultural, Economic, Physical, Technical, International, Communications and Infrastructure, Administrative and Institutional and Legal and Political
factors.

Some texts use the STEP or PEST acronym, thereby omitting explicit recognition of the environmental factors but considering these as part of the other factors. The approach adopted here, however,
is to explicitly recognize the central importance of environmental factors in *THE* contexts by considering them under a separate heading. It is clearly the case that there can be few industries where
the interdependence between the physical environment and economic activity is so clearly visible.

A sizeable literature has developed in *THE* that considers the macro environment. See, for example,
Costa (1995), Okumus (2004), Tum et al. (2011), Adema and Roehl (2010) and Clarke and Chen
(2012).

A further academic literature attempts to identify future trends, sometimes referred to as 'megatrends', that will shape future development of the sectors of *THE*. See, for example, Buckley et al.
(2015), Tolkach et al. (2016), Rate et al. (2018a) and Doorly (2020). A number of international
organizations, such as OECD (2018) and WTTC (2019), have also added their views on future
trends affecting *THE* to this output.

It is important to emphasize two points, however. Firstly, the analysis should be contextualized to
the particular organization being considered and should therefore be selective in the points that
are considered to be relevant. Secondly, though some of the material in the literature is highly

convincing, the future cannot be forecast with certainty, so caution and judgment should be applied in using the future trends identified, and the analysis should concentrate on what is known with certainty; that is, the present and the past.

7.1 SHORT CASE ILLUSTRATION

'Megatrends' shaping tourism

A number of academic papers and reports from international agencies have claimed to identify the megatrends that will shape the fututre of tourism and, by extension, hospitality and events. Because the future is unpredictable and dynamic, any such claims have to be treated with some caution, but studies from reputable organizations, based on a rigorous review of current and past activity, have a better chance of coming to fruition.

One such study was published by the Paris-based OECD (2018). The intergovernmental organization, which represents 38 of the world's economies, identified four megatrends that they argue will shape the future of tourism.

The four megatrends are:

- Evolving visitor demand – Changing demographics will transform the way people travel. For example, an expanding middle class creates new tourism markets, and an aging population in many developed countries will alter patterns of demand.

- Sustainable tourism growth – Developing tourism in a way that is sustainable for the 'natural' environment and the local population is key to addressing the potentially damaging impacts associated with excessive tourism

- Enabling technologies – Evolving technologies continue to reshape the way in which people work, travel and do business. The digital economy, automation, artificial intelligence, blockchain and VR/AR have the ability to make travel more affordable, efficient and accessible to many people.

- Travel mobility – The ability for people to be able to travel safely and freely across borders will be a key factor in the success and growth of the tourism sector. Transport developments will continue to be a key enabler of international tourism (as they have been in the past) in bringing consumers to commercial services and providers to global markets.

Megatrends, the report argued, capture globally relevant social, economic, political, environmental and technological changes over the long term. Such trends often unfold slowly, but they have potential for high impact and can drive the global economy and society in specific directions. It is argued that although the exact outcomes of these trends are typically uncertain, it is important that governments and organizations involved with delivering tourism services assess their implications and put policies and plans in place accordingly.

Source: Adapted from OECD (2018)

Questions

1. Explain why an understanding of sociodemographic influences might be important for a manager of an airline or a cruise line.

2. What sort of demographic factors might lead to greater air or cruise travel in the future?

- Explain the meaning of the term 'macro environment'.
- Explain how the business competitive environment and macro environment relate to each other.
- Explain the stages in a macro-environmental analysis.

7.2.1 Using STEEP analysis

Before looking at the individual elements of STEEP analysis, it is useful to consider how we might use the framework. What sort of information do we need to consider with each of the framework's elements, and how might the information be used?

The analysis is generally considered as falling into four stages.

- *Scanning and monitoring* the macro environment for actual or potential changes in social, technological, economic and political factors
- *Assessing the relevance and importance* of the changes for the market, industry and business
- *Analyzing each of the relevant changes* in detail and the potential relationships between them
- *Assessing the potential impact* of the changes on the market, industry and business

In carrying out the analysis, there are a few important points to note in that the analysis should:

- Concentrate on key strategic points; that is, those that are likely to have widespread and significant impact
- Not be an endless list of factors but should prioritize the most important ones
- Consider the timescale being considered, because the impact of factors far into the future is difficult to assess

7.2.2 What to analyze

When managers carry out a STEEP analysis as part of a strategic analysis (and the same is true of students examining a case study), they would normally examine how each factor might impact:

- *The internal parts of an organization* – The effects of STEEP factors on the organization's core competences, strategies, resources, value system and functional areas (operations, marketing, human resources and finance)
- *An organization's markets* – The effects of STEEP factors on product markets (e.g., market size, structure, segments, customer needs and wants, etc.) and the resource markets for human resources, financial resources, etc.
- *The industry in which the organization competes* – The effects of STEEP factors on the five competitive forces (buyer power, supplier power, threat of entry, threat of substitutes, competitive rivalry) identified by Michael Porter (see Chapter 8)

In the following sections, the component parts of STEEP are considered systematically. The array of potential factors in any particular organization at any time is vast. The factors are heavily dependent on the individual context of the organization (its location, sector, size, etc.). The approach adopted here is to discuss some of the generic factors and provide illustrations of some specific factors by using the airline sector throughout for purposes of illustration (for consistency), together with some further examples and further reading from other sectors.

As indicated earlier in the chapter, carrying out a macro-environmental analysis is not easy (but that is not to say that it should not be undertaken), because it is:

- Context specific – Each organization's circumstances will be different.
- Time specific – Factors identified are dynamic.
- Based on judgment – Managers may view factors identified in different ways.
- Future focused – We need to consider how the identified factors are likely to change, but we cannot predict the future with certainty.

7.2.3 Sociodemographic factors

Analysis of the social environment is concerned with understanding the potential impacts of society and social changes on a business, its industry and its markets. For most analyses, analysis of the social environment will require consideration of:

- *Social culture* (values, attitudes and beliefs) – the impact on demand for products and services, attitudes to work, savings and investment, ecology, ethics, etc.
- *Demography* – the impact of the size and structure of the population on the workforce and patterns of demand
- *Social structure* – the impact of attitudes toward work and products and services

SOCIAL CULTURE

The culture of a country in which a business operates (considered in Chapter 4) can be of particular importance. The culture of a country consists of the values, attitudes and beliefs of its people, which will affect the way they behave (or, put simply, a country's 'personality'). There are important cultural differences between all countries. Culture can affect consumer tastes and preferences, as well as attitudes toward work, education and training, corruption and ethics, credit, the social role of a business in society and many other things.

DEMOGRAPHY

Demographic trends are similarly important. Demography is the social science concerned with the charting of the size and structure of a population of people. The size of the population will obviously be a determinant of the size of the workforce and the potential size of markets. Just as important is the structure of the population. The age structure will determine the size of particular segments and also the size of the working population. The size and structure of the population will change, and these changes will have impact on industries and markets.

> **For example:** *Peluso and Pichierri (2021) considered socioeconomic variables of age, gender, education, income, health status and number of children to investigate their influence on individuals' sense of control and ability to avoid the uncertainty derived from the COVID-19 health crisis in relation to their vacation intention. The research, based on an Italian sample, showed that older respondents and those in poorer health felt less in control and able to avoid the uncertainty related to the pandemic. This, in turn, decreased their intention to take a vacation when the pandemic ends.*

SOCIAL STRUCTURE

Social structure is strongly linked to demography and refers to the ways in which the social groups in a population are organized. There are a number of ways of defining social structure, such as by sociodemographic groupings, location, population density in different areas, etc. The social structure will affect people's lifestyles and expectations and so will strongly influence their attitudes toward work and their demand for particular products and services.

Among the most important general changes in recent years in the social environment have been in people's attitudes toward the natural environment. Increasing awareness of the problems caused by pollution and the exhaustion of nonrenewable resources have caused travel and tourism organizations to rethink (in many cases) how they produce their products and the composition of the products themselves. Similarly, changes in social structure (upward mobility), lifestyle (increased leisure) and demography (aging populations in developed countries) have significantly altered many market and industry structures.

7.2 SHORT CASE ILLUSTRATION

Sociodemographic factors: aviation

A number of demographic factors point toward a greater use of air travel. These factors include:

- An increasing proportion of the population being relatively healthy and prosperous
- Increasing numbers of retired people
- A decline in average family size
- Greater international mobility of labor
- Increasing number of days of paid holiday
- Larger numbers of two-income families

All of these factors point to higher usage of air services. Leisure travel (which accounts for about 80% of trips) has grown more rapidly than business travel.

Other factors that might be considered are lifestyle trends and attitudes towards air travel and associated airport development. An increasingly mobile society where people take safe, reliable and affordable air transportation for granted is challenged by a critical society that assesses the contribution of air travel to air and noise pollution (Holloway and Humphries, 2012). This dichotomy in which the competing needs and interests of airline stakeholder groups need to be considered represents a challenge to airlines, regulators and governments.

One study (Oyewole, 2001) of the airline industry found that gender, occupation, education and marital status have an important influence on satisfaction with airline services. Another study (Jiang and Zhang, 2016), which considered service quality, customer satisfaction and loyalty in China's airline market, also found that some demographic variables such as gender, income and education had a significant impact on customer loyalty among some groups. The authors suggested that different marketing strategies should be used in targeting different segments to improve customer loyalty.

Questions

1. Explain why an understanding of sociodemographic influences might be important for airline managers.

2. What sort of demographic factors might lead to greater air travel in the future?

7.2.4 Technological factors

Analysis of the technological environment involves developing an understanding of the effects of changes in technology on all areas of a business and its activities, including:

- Products and services
- Operational processes
- Information and communications
- Transport and distribution
- Society, politics and economics

Developments in information and communications technology (ICT), like the development of personal computers, laptops and tablets, networks, satellites, cable and digital communications, the internet and mobile phone applications, together with rapid advances in software, have all contributed to revolutionizing how business is conducted in many industries.

Activities are now better coordinated, and research and development are speeded up, thus making businesses more flexible and responsive. Many activities previously carried out by middle layers of managers, which often involved collating and analyzing data from operational activities and reporting to senior managers, can now be more effectively carried out using ICT solutions.

It is beyond the scope of this book to present a full summary of all of the technological changes and their implications, which have been considered elsewhere (see, for example, Buhalis et al., 2019; Law et al., 2020).

Furthermore, the particular aspects of technology to be considered are often highly specific to a particular context. A vast contemporary literature has emerged that focuses on changes brought about by technological advances and changes that are likely to affect *THE* organizations in the future. Three examples of technology from diverse *THE* contexts are presented to illustrate the profound changes that have occurred due to the introduction of various types of technology.

7.3 TECHNOLOGY FOCUS

'Smart' tourism, hospitality and events

Effective management of *THE* operations has been greatly facilitated in recent years by digital technology in its various forms (Filimonau and Naumova, 2020; Stankov and Gretzel, 2020). Consequently, the concepts of *smart tourism* (Gretzel et al., 2015) and its extension to *smart hospitality* (Buhalis and Leung, 2018) and *smart events* (Bustard et al., 2019) have emerged. The concepts serve to underline the ever-increasing role of digital technology in building sustainable business models (Filimonau and Naumova, 2020).

Smart tourism refers to the burgeoning phenomenon in which tourism destinations, practitioners and tourists depend accumulatively on emerging ICTs that enable colossal data transformation into value proposition (Gretzel et al., 2015). The concepts of smart tourism and smart hospitality have received considerable attention in recent years (see, for example, Shafiee et al., 2019; Lee et al., 2020; Mehraliyev et al., 2020; Law et al., 2022) and can be viewed as broad terms encompassing many *THE* technology-enhanced initiatives. Indeed, the concept has to be treated with some caution because 'in practice, "smart" has become a very fuzzy concept often used to drive specific political agendas and to sell technological solutions. This is especially true in the case of smart tourism' (Gretzel et al., 2015:179).

The EU, for example, has adopted smart tourism principles and applied them to a broad variety of tourism destinations (www.smarttourismdestinations.eu/). The project focuses on how EU cities can adopt data-driven approaches to become or improve as smart tourism destinations.

Questions

1. Explain the meaning of 'smart tourism'.

2. Provide an example of how digital technology has changed an aspect of *THE* in recent years.

Emerging technologies are increasingly affecting the design and delivery of *THE* products and the experience of consumers in these sectors. The pace of change has been rapid, and further innovations are expected.

The development of these innovations (summarized by Buhalis, 2020) includes:

- The IoT (Car et al., 2019)
- Big Data Analytics (Mariani, 2020)
- Artificial intelligence (AI; Ruel and Njoku, 2021)
- Blockchain (Önder and Gunter, 2022)
- Robotics (Koo et al., 2021)
- Location-based services (Uphaus et al., 2019)
- Virtual and AR systems (Loureiro et al., 2020)

7.4 TECHNOLOGY FOCUS

VR and AR enhancing heritage tourism

Digital technologies are distorting the distinction between the real and the virtual world. This provides opportunities to increase the level of immersion within tourism experiences (Jung et al., 2016). Importantly, VR and AR are able to enhance visitor experiences at the destination itself, prior to visiting and subsequently when recollecting tourism experiences.

AR is a technology with the capacity to overlay the existing environment into a digital context, with applications including text, video, images and 3D objects. VR creates virtual three-dimensional environments that can be interacted with in a seemingly real or physical way (Jung et al., 2016).

AR and VR has been successfully applied within various parts of *THE*, enabling an increased level of visitor engagement. Bec et al (2019) considered AR and VR application in a heritage tourism context in which they recognized the ability of AR and VR to enhance the tourist experience. However, the technology can also make a contribution to addressing issues associated with heritage, including the preservation of artifacts and understanding the contested nature of heritage.

To address issues surrounding the virtual presentation of heritage and the management of digital heritage tourism experiences, the authors proposed a four-stage conceptual model to guide applications of AR and VR for tourism experience and heritage preservation (Bec et al., 2019)

Questions

1. Explain the differences between AR and VR.

2. Provide examples of how AR and VR have been applied to an aspect of *THE*.

Similarly, changes in transport technology (such as high-speed trains, sophisticated cruise ships and newer, more fuel-efficient aircraft types) have revolutionized business and changed societies and cultures. It is possible to transport tourists and businesspeople as well as materials, components and products with far greater speed and at much lower cost as a result of developments in road, rail, sea and air transport. These improvements in transport have also increased the total amount of personal and business travel that people undertake, leading to profound societal changes both in tourist 'exporting' and 'importing' regions.

Thus, it is important for organizations to monitor changes in the technologies that can affect their operations or markets. In most industries, organizations must be flexible and ready to innovate and adopt new technologies as they come along. The way in which (and the extent to which) organizations do or do not employ the latest technology can be an important determinant of its competitive advantage.

7.5 TECHNOLOGY FOCUS

Aviation: technology advances

Despite the aviation industry's heavy regulatory standards, technological advances in how parts are transported, planes are built and aircraft are maintained have been particularly rapid (Berecz, 2017). The aviation industry has never shied away from technology. Advances in aircraft development, including the ecological inclusion of better fuel efficiency, recyclability concerns and more, mean that all involved, from manufacturers to suppliers, must become early adopters of useful technology to flourish (Berecz, 2017). Undoubtedly, emerging technologies such as electric-powered aircraft and blockchain technology will have profound impacts on airlines – but perhaps their major impact on most major airlines is some way off.

Computer reservation systems such as Sabre developed by American Airlines are powerful travel marketing technology tools. The systems, developed largely in the 1960s and 1970s (with airlines in the forefront), have attained global reach, and hence they are now often referred to as GDSs. GDSs have emerged over several decades as a central feature of electronic commerce in travel providing virtual real-time connectivity between thousands of suppliers of travel inventory (airlines, hotels, car rental, tour operators, cruise lines, etc.) and hundreds of thousands of retail sellers of travel products (Sismanidou et al., 2009; Goecke, 2020).

GDSs progressively consolidated their position to only five major systems, namely, Sabre, Amadeus, Galileo, Apollo and Worldspan (the latter three now acquired by Travelport Inc. but operated separately from Travelport's Atlanta and UK data centers). Allied to the use of GDSs are the revenue management systems that have been developed. These systems, which utilize the GDS accumulated databases, allow for the yield realized to be optimized by varying prices and altering the mix between classes of tickets that are issued.

The emergence of the internet in the mid-1990s forced airlines to reshape their distribution strategy to boost their competitiveness (Buhalis, 2004). The emergence of internet search engines (such as Expedia, Travelocity and Booking.com), together with the sophisticated databases, allows for diversified distribution and communication channels to be utilized, thus creating new opportunities for airline marketing.

The aviation industry embraced the IoT, which allows electronic devices to communicate with one another without the need of a host computer. Today, maintenance, repair and overhaul professionals can communicate with plane sensors using tablets. This allows them to scan aircraft systems easily, identifying components in need of replacement or repair (Berecz, 2017).

In relation to the aircraft themselves, technological innovations continue to drive costs down and influence route structures.

> For example: The long-haul wide-body aircraft Airbus A350 has been developed by the European company Airbus. The aircraft is designed to carry 270 to 475 passengers up to 15,000 km. In this segment, the A350 is competing with the American Boeing 787 (Dreamliner). Such aircraft allow the airlines to consider introducing routes that were previously considered unviable or too long.

> In March 2022, Air New Zealand announced that it would launch the first non-stop service between Auckland and New York's JFK Airport beginning in September 2022. The 14,200-km flight, one of the world's longest, will be operated by the airline's Boeing 787–9 Dreamliner, which will be equipped with 275 seats, plus 13 Skycouches – rows of three seats that convert into a couch after takeoff.

Questions

1. Explain the meaning of the IoT and provide an example of how it might be applied in a THE setting.

2. Assess the multitude of ways in which airlines are embracing new technology.

7.2.5 Economic factors

Analysis of the economic environment will center on changes in the macro economy and their effects on business and consumers. It is important to remember that because governments intervene (to varying extents) in the operation of all countries' economies, many factors classed as political in this chapter will have important economic implications.

Broadly speaking, the regulation of a national economy is brought about by two key policy instruments – *fiscal policy* and *monetary policy*. These policy instruments, alongside factors from international markets, determine the economic climate in the country in which a business competes. From these, a number of other vital economic indicators 'flow' that affect an organization – for either good or ill.

KEY CONCEPT

Fiscal and monetary policy

Fiscal policy:

The regulation of the national economy through the management of government revenues and expenditures. Each fiscal year, a government raises so much in revenue (such as through taxation) and it spends another amount through its various departments (such as on health, education, defense, etc.). The government is able to influence the economic climate in a country by varying either or both of these sides of the fiscal equation.

Monetary policy:

The regulation of the national economy by varying the supply and price of money. Money supply concerns the volume of money (in its various forms) in the economy, and the 'price' of money is the base rate that determines the interest rate that banks and other lenders charge for borrowings.

In the UK, for example, the Chancellor of the Exchequer (a government minister) is in charge of fiscal policy, whereas monetary policy is overseen by the Monetary Policy Committee of the Bank of England.

When the effects of fiscal and monetary pressures work themselves out in the economy, they can affect any or all of the following economic factors:

- Economic growth rates (the year-to-year growth in the total size of a national economy, usually measured by gross domestic product, GDP)
- Levels of income in the economy
- Levels of productivity (i.e., output per worker in the economy)
- Wage levels and the rate of increase in wages
- Levels of inflation (i.e., the year-to-year rise in prices)
- Levels of unemployment
- Balance of payments (a measure of the international competitiveness of one country's economy against its international competitor countries)
- Exchange rates (the exchange value of one currency against another)

Economic growth, exchange rates, levels of income, inflation and unemployment will all affect people's ability to pay for products and services and hence affect levels and patterns of demand. Similarly, levels of productivity, wage levels, levels of inflation and exchange rates will affect costs of production and competitiveness. All of these indicators must be monitored in comparison to those faced by competitors abroad to provide indications of changes in international competitiveness.

7.6 SHORT CASE ILLUSTRATION

Economic factors: aviation

Aviation is a dynamic industry that continuously adapts to various market forces. Key economic market forces that impact the airline industry are fuel prices, economic growth and stage of economic development. During the COVID-19 pandemic between 2020 and 2022, the industry was severely disrupted, with many flights being canceled.

Air travel demand has closely mirrored the cyclical pattern shown by GDP figures in that it responds to cyclical upswings and downswings. However, air travel growth has far exceeded GDP growth over most periods.

Air travel has always been a strongly cyclical business. Periods of 7% to 9% annual growth of global consolidated passenger traffic alternate with years of slower rising, or declining, demand (Franke and John, 2011). The industry has reliably returned to its long-term growth rate of approximately 5% per year, and the IATA (2017) expects such long-term trends to continue (albeit spread unevenly across the regions of the globe) in their 20-year forecast through to 2036.

Many factors will influence air travel markets in the long run, from shifting dynamics in energy markets to structural economic reforms. However, ultimately, they can be viewed as affecting air travel markets through one of the three following channels (IATA, 2017): living standards, population and demographics and price of air travel.

The airline industry also has a high level of fixed costs and, consequently, average load factors and revenue measures per passenger are crucial in maintaining profitability. Load factors are measured systematically and are studied carefully by airline managers. The major measures are shown in Table 7.1.

Table 7.1 Key measures of airline performance

Measure	Description
RPK – Revenue passenger kilometers	Measure of passenger traffic = Number of paying passengers × Kilometers flown
ASK – Available seat kilometers	Measure of passenger capacity = Number of seats × Kilometers flown
FTK – Freight tonne kilometers	Measure of freight traffic = Freight tonnes carried × Kilometers flown
LF – Load factor	Measure of capacity utilization = RPK/ASK

Furthermore, fuel and aircraft prices are major expenditure items subject to fluctuations, and the international orientation of the industry means that movements in foreign exchange rates can have major effects on industry profitability. The post-2008 global recession and the COVID-19 pandemic had severe impacts on airline finances, but most airlines learned lessons from the events of 2001/2003, (following 9/11) and reacted very quickly by grounding considerable capacity and reducing their workforces.

Questions

1. Why is airline travel so cyclical?

2. Explain the ways in which airlines assess their performance.

7.2.6 Environmental factors

Environmental factors here refers to the influence of concerns for the physical environment (both the natural environment and the built environment) on *THE* organizations. In recent years, increasing concerns about ecology and 'green' issues have been an important social trend and has changed attitudes toward the effects of products and operational processes on the environment. Issues such as global climate change, ozone depletion, deforestation, extinction of species, soil erosion, desertification, acid rain, toxic wastes and water and noise pollution have become important concerns with regard to the natural environment (Peattie and Moutinho, 2000).

To such concerns regarding the natural environment might be added others concerning the built environment such as traffic and airport congestion, deteriorating buildings and historic sites, poor urban planning and visually intrusive buildings. The problems and issues identified have certain unifying characteristics in that they:

* All have international dimensions
* Are not exclusively related to tourism, hospitality and events but nevertheless have important implications for managers in *THE* sectors, among others

Whereas 30 years ago most consumers showed little concern for the long-term effects of products and processes on the natural environment, today people are increasingly aware of the need to protect it. Following various developments such as the publication of the Brundtland Report in 1987 (WCED, 1987) and the Earth Summit in Rio de Janeiro in 1992 (Grubb et al., 2019), there has been increasing commitment to the principles of sustainable development in many industries, including tourism. The term 'sustainable development' was used by the 'Brundtland Commission', which coined what has become the most often-quoted definition of sustainable development.

DEFINITION/QUOTATION

Sustainable development

> Development that meets the needs of the present generation without compromising the ability of future generations to meet their own needs.
>
> (WCED, 1987:16)

This has led to pressure on governments to introduce legislation and other measures to control pollution and limit emissions. The combined desire of consumers for products that are themselves environmentally friendly and that have been produced by 'green' methods has resulted in the realization by business organizations that there are profits to be made by being 'environmentally friendly', or at least appearing to be so.

For example: *International car rental firm Avis, founded in 1946 by Warren Avis, astutely anticipated postwar trends in postwar travel. Starting with three cars in Detroit, Avis is today a global brand, with over 5,200 rental locations in more than 165 countries. Avis (Europe, Middle East and Africa) was the first car rental company to launch a corporate social responsibility policy (in 1997) and claims to have been a 'carbon-neutral' operation since 2000. It has achieved this through initiatives such as fleets with electric- and natural gas–powered cars; offices with smart, energy-saving technology; and rigorous procedures to ensure that fuel spills and leaks are prevented. Though such measures are clearly beneficial in their own right, they also constitute an important part of the company's business strategy, in that the company is able to use its carbon neutrality as part of its competitive offer (www.avisbudgetgroup.com).*

7.7 SHORT CASE ILLUSTRATION

Environmental program as a source of competitive advantage: Scandic Hotels

Scandic Hotels, with its headquarters in Stockholm, Sweden, is the leading hotel brand in Scandinavia. Its environmental program, which is central to the brand's promotional activity, provides a source of competitive advantage for Scandic in a region where consumers are traditionally highly environmentally conscious. The hotel group's pioneering environmental programs have also been discussed in the academic literature (see, for example, Bohdanowicz et al., 2005; Chou, 2014; Phi and Waldesten, 2021).

The group, which employs over 10,000 people, has about 280 mid-market hotels mainly in the Scandinavian countries, with others located around Europe. The brand, which positions itself as offering 'value for money', places great emphasis on continual competence development of employees at all levels of the organization and on its environmental program.

Scandic's environmental program was launched in 1994 following consultation with staff, and the hotel group has won numerous awards. It was a Scandic idea to 'hang up your towel if you want to use it again' – an idea that is now the standard in the hotel industry around the world. Today, sustainability is a part of Scandic's values – an integral element of all of its operations – and the company produces a sustainability report as part of its annual reporting cycle. Employees have the opportunity to take part in training in environmental issues, and there is an environmental manager at each hotel.

The environmental program involves the continuing education of all employees and includes initiatives such as reporting their energy, water and chemical use as well as unsorted waste (since 1996). Since then, its operations have continued to show improved results. Recycled waste, for example, increased from 69% to 97% between 2015 and 2019.

Source: Adapted from www.scandichotelsgroup.com

Questions

1. Explain the ways in which Scandic Hotels make their environmental program a central part of their competitive offering.

2. What risks might there be for the company in taking such a prominent environmental stance?

The issue of the sustainability of tourist destinations, hotels, events and attractions has been widely addressed in *THE* academic literature in recent years by authors such as Getz (2009), Buckley (2012), Seguí-Amortegui et al. (2019) and Camisón (2020). A number of authors have also traced the environmental impacts of particular sectors of *THE*.

> **For example**: *Getz (2009) discussed the need for public sector involvement in successful and sustainable planning for festivals and events, and Hsieh (2012) analyzed the environmental management policies and practices of 50 hotel companies as disclosed on their corporate websites.*
>
> *Mair and Smith (2021), in introducing a special journal edition on event sustainability, argued that researchers should examine how events might contribute to overall sustainable development, rather than merely exploring how individual events could be made more sustainable.*
>
> *Graham (2018) traced environmental policies and practices at a number of airports including Oslo, Manchester, London Heathrow, and Amsterdam.*
>
> *Jones et al. (2019) outlined the main sustainability challenges facing the cruising sector and consider current industry practices. They found a marked variation in the extent to which the leading cruise companies publicly report on their sustainability strategies and achievements and argued that the cruise companies' commitment to sustainability is comparatively weak.*

7.8 SHORT CASE ILLUSTRATION

Environmental factors: aviation

Managers operating in the aviation sector need to be concerned with the environmental impacts of the industry when making strategic plans. The industry is often the focus of environmental debate, and plans for airport developments and associated infrastructure and additional airline capacity have often proved contentious. Public concerns have often thwarted potential developments for many years. The industry has responded in various ways, including technological advances to limit aircraft emissions, siting airports away from population centers and efficiencies in aircraft operating and routing procedures.

Environmental concerns in the airline sector include:

- The effects of noise
- Air pollution caused by aircraft emissions
- Impacts of developing airport and ground transportation infrastructure

Public tolerance of aircraft noise has been diminishing despite the reduction in noise levels due to the development of less noisy aircraft types (Graham, 2018). The problems associated with aircraft noise have led to ever more stringent and sophisticated noise abatement measures being introduced at most major airports. Some of the gases emitted by aircraft in flight, primarily carbon dioxide and water vapor, are GHGs that contribute to global warming and climate change. However, it is thought that aviation's contribution to global human-made carbon dioxide emissions amounts to only around 2% of the total (Brandon et al., 2018). The environmental impacts caused by the airline sector and initiatives to deal with these impacts are well documented in the academic literature; see, for example, Lynes and Andrachuk (2008) and Peeters and Bongaerts (2015).

The aviation industry recognizes the need to address the global challenge of climate change, and at the IATA Annual Meeting in Boston, USA, in October 2021, a resolution was passed by IATA member airlines committing them to achieving net-zero carbon emissions from their operations by 2050. This pledge brings air transport in line with the objectives of the Paris agreement to limit global warming to 1.5°C. This will be achieved by a combination of sustainable aviation fuel (65%), new technology (13%), infrastructure and operational efficiencies (3%) and offsets and carbon capture (19%; www.iata.org).

The increasing infrastructure (airports and ground transportation) to support airlines has often proved controversial. Thus, the agreement to proceed with a fifth terminal for London's Heathrow Airport was secured only after 10 years of public consultations, whereas Manchester Airport proceeded with building a second runway in the face of strong lobbying by environmental pressure groups.

Questions

1. Explain why airline managers need to take environmental concerns into account.

2. Consider which stakeholder groups are likely to be influential when making decisions about airport infrastructure projects.

7.2.7 Political, governmental, legal and regulatory factors

The political environment is defined as that part of the macro environment that is under the direct control or influence of the government. Governments have direct control or influence over:

- *Legislation and regulation* – this covers laws that influence employment, consumer protection, health and safety at work, contract and trading, trade unions, monopolies and mergers, taxes, etc.
- *Economic policy* – particularly over fiscal and monetary policy. Governments usually set policy over the levels of taxation and expenditure in the country and control monetary policy concerned with interest rates and the money supply.
- *Government-owned businesses* – nationalized industries. Some governments retain control over key strategic industries (such as airlines), and the way in which these are controlled can have 'knock-on' effects on other parts of the economy.
- *Government international policy* – government intervention to influence exchange rates, international trade, etc.

The objectives that a government may have regarding regulation of business will depend in large part on the political leaning of the governing party. Most governments have, however, sought to construct policy over a number of key areas of business activity:

- Control of inflation (to improve international competitiveness)
- Promotion of economic growth and investment
- Control of unemployment
- Stabilization of exchange rates
- Control of balance of payments
- Control of monopoly power, by both businesses and trade unions

- Provision of public goods like health, education, defense
- Control of pollution and environmental protection
- Redistribution of incomes (to varying degrees)
- Consumer protection
- Regulation of working conditions
- Regulation of trade

To varying degrees, all businesses will be affected by political factors. Accordingly, it is important for managers to monitor government policy to detect changes early to respond effectively.

Another important aspect of the political environment is *political risk* and its potential effects on business. Political risk is particularly important in international business. Whereas Western Europe and North America are comparatively politically stable, other parts of the world like Eastern Europe, South America, sub-Saharan Africa and parts of the Middle East, Central Asia and North Africa have undergone periods of instability. It is therefore necessary to closely monitor the political situation in these areas when trading with them, because the political risks are large. Even in more stable areas, political uncertainty can be higher during election years or when other political crises arise.

For example: *The referendum held in the UK during June 2016 resulted in a vote to leave the European Union – the so-called Brexit process. This political process, which involved the UK leaving the EU in March 2018, led to profound economic consequences for all businesses operating in the UK (including those in THE).*

7.9 SHORT CASE ILLUSTRATION

Political factors: aviation

Governments have always taken a strong interest in the airline sector (far more than any other sector of *THE*), which has traditionally resulted in a high degree of regulation and state ownership. Both of these factors have seen major changes in recent years, and these changes are continuing. Three major reasons can be put forward for this strong government involvement:

- Safety – controlling airline and airport safety
- Security – ensuring that countries have adequate air resources in times of war or disaster
- Prestige – government airline ownership of 'national flag carriers', often viewed as a symbol of national prestige

International cooperation in regulatory matters has long been a feature of the airline sector. The ICAO is a UN specialized agency based in Montreal, Canada, and was established in 1944 to manage the administration and governance of the Convention on International Civil Aviation (Chicago Convention). ICAO works with the Convention's 192 Member States and industry groups to reach consensus on international civil aviation standards and recommended practices and policies.

The IATA is a trade association of the world's airlines. Consisting of 290 airlines, representing 117 countries, the IATA's member airlines account for carrying approximately 82% of total available seat miles. IATA, headquartered in Montreal, Canada, with executive offices in Geneva, Switzerland, supports aviation and helps formulate industry policy and standards.

The political environment of the airline sector has been characterized by an extended network of national and international rules and regulations, many of which date back to the Chicago Convention of 1944 and the Bermuda Agreement of 1946. Based on the acknowledgment of the sovereignty of nations over their airspace and of the equal right for every nation to participate in air travel, the so-called five freedoms of the air were established as shown in Table 7.2.

Table 7.2 The five freedoms of the air

Freedom	Description
• First freedom	The right to fly over another country without landing
• Second freedom	The right to make a landing for technical reasons (e.g., refueling) in another country without picking up/setting down revenue traffic
• Third freedom	The right to carry revenue traffic from your own country (A) to the country of your treaty partner (B)
• Fourth freedom	The right to carry traffic from country B back to your own country (A)
• Fifth freedom	The right of an airline from country A to carry revenue traffic between country B and other countries such as C or D on services starting or ending in its home country. (This freedom cannot be used unless country C or D also agrees.)

The five freedoms were followed by a complex web of bilateral intergovernmental agreements that allowed national governments involved to maintain control over national interests related to air travel. A more liberal approach is reflected in the so-called open skies agreements granting carriers of the states involved unlimited access to the routes between airports in these states. The concept of open skies reflects a development of major importance for the airline industry: liberalization unfolding around the globe (Doganis, 2010).

In the USA (which has the world's largest airline industry), the strict regulations governing the domestic air travel market were swept away by the Airline Deregulation Act of 1978. The act abolished regulations specifying which routes the carriers were allowed to fly and controls on air fares. After deregulation, many new carriers entered the market (and many subsequently folded). Some of the newer carriers such as Southwest, JetBlue and Frontier are now substantial entities in their own right, operating low-cost operating models. Most of the largest so-called legacy carriers, such as United, American and Delta, survived but, undoubtedly, competition in the US domestic market has increased.

Subsequently, other parts of the world have followed with similar policies of deregulation. Another major trend among European and other governments is the privatization (in whole or in part) of former state-owned carriers such as British Airways, Air France and Lufthansa.

Sources: www.icao.int; www.iata.org

Questions

1. Explain why the political environment for the airline sector is different from that of any other industry.

2. Consider the effect that deregulation in various parts of the world has had on the airline sector.

7.2.8 *The relationships between the STEEP factors*

A temptation when carrying out a STEEP analysis is to think of each influence as separate when, in fact, they are often interlinked. The effects of environmental factors on organizations provide an example.

> For example: *The environmental concerns themselves (such as the use of water resources for golf course development or the building of a visually intrusive hotel in a scenic area) are issues to be dealt with within the 'environmental' category of the STEEP analysis. However, such concerns might also involve social, political and technological factors in the analysis. Thus, in the simple example of the golf course or visually intrusive hotel development above, environmental concerns raised by the developments might lead to social factors (increased awareness) that impact political factors (legislation and regulation), and the two forces together might produce technological change (products and processes that are less damaging to the environment).*

Accordingly, a macro-environmental analysis should recognize the ways in which the five STEEP factors might be linked to each other in addition to the individual factors by themselves.

THINK POINTS

- Discuss the argument that suggests that turbulence and uncertainty render analysis of the macro environment less useful.
- Explain the importance of sustainability to macro-environmental analysis in *THE* contexts.
- Explain why it is important to recognize the linkages between the STEEP elements.

Small business focus

Understanding the external environment is important for all organizations, but from a managerial perspective, the primary differentiating factor between the internal and external environment (considered in Chapters 3–6) is *control*. Whereas managers have some degree of control over the internal environment, this is rarely the case with regard to the external environment. However, in some cases, large organizations may have some influence over the external environment, or they can protect themselves against the dangers posed.

Larger organizations may, for example, be able to:

- Switch investment from one country to another
- Influence government policy

- Use financial instruments to 'hedge' against interest rate and oil price movements
- Diversify their product portfolios so a hostile external environment for one set of products (or in a particular market) may be offset by a benign environment in another

However, SMEs are far more limited in that they rarely are able to have any meaningful degree of influence over the external environment, cannot easily switch investment and have far more limited access to the financial and commodity markets (or do so at far greater cost), leaving them more exposed. Furthermore, SMEs usually have a more limited product range, meaning that weak performance in one area cannot be offset by strong performance in another.

In their study of tourism sector small business performance, Morrison and Teixeira (2004) highlighted the weak power position within the tourism sector of individual SME units. One major change in the external environment, such as an increase in interest rates, an economic recession or a catastrophic event at an event or destination, could have a profound effect on any business, but for SMEs operating in THE sectors, such changes can result in business failure (and often have).

There may also be a tendency for SME owners and managers to ignore the external environment in a belief that because they cannot alter it there is little point in attempting to understand it. This is a mistake, because though SMEs cannot alter the macro environment, because they are smaller and more agile, they can quickly alter their business models to cope with changing circumstances in ways that are not possible for larger less agile businesses. Thus, it is key to survival and business success for SMEs to scan their external environment and understand possible scenarios where uncertainty is involved, as discussed by Oreja-Rodríguez and Yanes-Estévez (2007) in their study of Spanish hotels.

It is necessary to think through the implications of each possible scenario and how the business might position itself to respond. However, by their nature, SMEs have more limited human, material and financial resources. Furthermore, SMEs often focus on allocation of resources to achieve their maximum short-term advantage, which frequently leaves them to respond to external factors as they occur rather than taking a proactive approach (McAdam, 2000). Some evidence suggests that the majority of small firms do not utilize the traditional tools and techniques of strategic planning (Meers and Robertson, 2007). To achieve success in turbulent markets, a number of writers in THE have pointed to the need for organizations to form networks or clusters to jointly achieve the advantages of size enjoyed by larger competitors (see, for example, Novelli et al., 2006; Zhang and Morrison, 2007; Gardiner and Scott, 2014; Lee et al., 2020).

Tools and models aim to clarify complex issues, and Banham (2010) introduced her 'degrees of turbulence' model to assist owner/managers of SMEs in understanding the externalities that impact their business operations. This represents an attempt to simplify and systemize external environmental scanning for smaller businesses using a numerical scoring system to gauge the relative turbulence of the environment.

CHAPTER SUMMARY

Analysis of the macro environment is primarily concerned with providing insight into the future facing an organization. The complexity and turbulence of the environment make prediction of the future problematic.

Analysis, however, informs managers in their strategic decision making. The complexity of the external environment is simplified by breaking it down into the smaller social, technological, economic, environmental and political/legal components. These environments can then be analyzed for their potential effects on the business and its competitive environment. The process of macro-environmental analysis must:

- Be continuous to cope with the pace of change
- Be selective (so that only factors of strategic significance are analyzed)
- Avoid endless lists of factors
- Recognize potential interactions between the differing aspects of the STEEP analysis

REFERENCES AND WEBSITES

References

Adema, K. L. and Roehl, W. S. (2010) 'Environmental scanning the future of event design', *International Journal of Hospitality Management*, 29(2): 199–207.

Banham, H. C. (2010) 'External environmental analysis for small and medium enterprises (SMEs)', *Journal of Business and Economics Research*, 8(10): 19–26.

Bec, A., Moyle, B., Timms, K., Schaffer, V., Skavronskaya, L. and Little, C. (2019) 'Management of immersive heritage tourism experiences: A conceptual model', *Tourism Management*, 72: 117–120.

Benítez-Aurioles, B. (2019) 'Barcelona's peer-to-peer tourist accommodation market in turbulent times: Terrorism and political uncertainty', *International Journal of Contemporary Hospitality Management*, 31(12): 4419–4437.

Bensoussan, B. E. and Fleisher, C. S. (2013) *Analysis without Paralysis: 12 Tools to Make Better Strategic Decisions*, Upper Saddle River, NJ: Pearson.

Berecz, R. (2017) '7 Technological advances changing the landscape of the aviation industry', www.aviationtoday.com

Bohdanowicz, P., Simanic, B. and I. Martinac (2005) 'Environmental training and measures at Scandic Hotels, Sweden', *Tourism Review International*, 9(1): 7–19.

Brandon, G., Zhang, K. and Rutherford, D. (2019) *Emissions from Commercial Aviation, 2018*, Washington, DC: International Council on Clean Transportation.

Buckley, R. (2012) 'Sustainable tourism: Research and reality', *Annals of Tourism Research*, 39(2): 528–546.

Buckley, R., Gretzel, U., Scott, D., Weaver, D. and Becken, S. (2015) 'Tourism megatrends', *Tourism Recreation Research*, 40(1): 59–70.

Buhalis, D. (2004) 'eAirlines: Strategic and tactical use of ICTs in the airline industry', *Information and Management*, 41: 805–825.

Buhalis, D. (2020) 'Technology in tourism – From information communication technologies to etourism and smart tourism towards ambient intelligence tourism: A perspective article', *Tourism Review*, 75(1): 267–272.

Buhalis, D., Harwood, T., Bogicevic, V., Viglia, G., Beldona, S. and Hofacker, C. (2019) 'Technological disruptions in services: Lessons from tourism and hospitality', *Journal of Service Management*, 30(4): 484–506.

Buhalis, D. and Leung, R. (2018) 'Smart hospitality – Interconnectivity and interoperability towards an ecosystem', *International Journal of Hospitality Management*, 71: 41–50.

Bustard, J. R. T., Bolan, P., Devine, A. and Hutchinson, K. (2019) 'The emerging smart event experience: An interpretative phenomenological analysis', *Tourism Review* 74(1): 116–128.

Camisón, C. (2020) 'Competitiveness and sustainability in tourist firms and destinations', *Sustainability*, 12(6): 2388.

Car, T., Stifanich, L. P. and Šimunić, M. (2019) 'Internet of Things (IoT) in tourism and hospitality: Opportunities and challenges', *Tourism in South East Europe*, 5: 163–175.

Chakravarthy, B. (1997) 'A new strategy framework for coping with turbulence', *Sloan Management Review*, 38(2): 69–82.

Chou, C. J. (2014) 'Hotels' environmental policies and employee personal environmental beliefs: Interactions and outcomes', *Tourism Management*, 40: 436–446.

Clarke, A. and Chen, W. (2012) *International Hospitality Management*, London: Routledge.

Costa, J. (1995) 'An empirically-based review of the concept of environmental scanning', *International Journal of Contemporary Hospitality Management*, 7(7): 4–9.

Doganis, R. (2010) *Flying Off Course: The Economics of International Airlines*, 4th ed., Abingdon, UK: Routledge.

Doorly, V. B. (2020) *Megatrends Defining the Future of Tourism: A Journey within the Journey in 12 Universal Truths*, Cham, Switzerland: Springer Nature.

Filimonau, V. and Naumova, E. (2020) 'The blockchain technology and the scope of its application in hospitality operations', *International Journal of Hospitality Management*, 87: 102383.

Franke, M. and John, F. (2011) 'What comes next after recession? – Airline industry scenarios and potential end games', *Journal of Air Transport Management*, 17(1):19–26.

Gardiner, S. and Scott, N. (2014) 'Successful tourism clusters: Passion in paradise', *Annals of Tourism Research*, 46: 171–173.

Getz, D. (2009) 'Policy for sustainable and responsible festivals and events: Institutionalization of a new paradigm', *Journal of Policy Research in Tourism, Leisure and Events*, 1(1): 61–78.

Ginter, P. M. and Duncan, J. (1990) 'Macroenvironmental analysis for strategic management', *Long Range Planning*, 23(6): 91–100.

Giousmpasoglou, C., Marinakou, E. and Zopiatis, A. (2021) 'Hospitality managers in turbulent times: The COVID-19 crisis', *International Journal of Contemporary Hospitality Management*, 33(4): 1297–1318.

Goecke, R. (2020) 'The evolution of online booking systems', in Z. Xiang, M. Fuchs, U. Gretzel and W. Höpken (Eds), *Handbook of e-Tourism*, Cham, Switzerland: Springer: 1–25.

Graham, A. (2018) *Managing Airports: An International Perspective*, 4th ed., Abingdon, UK: Routledge.

Gretzel, U., Sigala, M., Xiang, Z. and Koo, C. (2015) 'Smart tourism: Foundations and developments,' *Electronic Markets*, 25(3): 179–188.

Grubb, M., Koch, M., Thomson, K., Sullivan, F. and Munson, A. (2019) *The 'Earth Summit' Agreements: A Guide and Assessment: An Analysis of the Rio'92 UN Conference on Environment and Development* (Vol. 9), Abingdon, UK: Routledge.

Herédia-Colaço, V. and Rodrigues, H. (2021) 'Hosting in turbulent times: Hoteliers' perceptions and strategies to recover from the COVID-19 pandemic', *International Journal of Hospitality Management*, 94: 102835.

Holloway, J. C. and Humphries, C. (2012) *The Business of Tourism*, 9th ed., Harlow, UK: Pearson.

Hsieh, Y. C. J. (2012) 'Hotel companies' environmental policies and practices: A content analysis of their web pages', *International Journal of Contemporary Hospitality Management*, 24(1): 97–121.

IATA. (2017) *20 Year Passenger Forecast*, Geneva: IATA.

Jiang, H. and Zhang, Y. (2016) 'An investigation of service quality, customer satisfaction and loyalty in China's airline market', *Journal of Air Transport Management*, 57: 80–88.

Jogaratnam, G. and Law, R. (2006) 'Environmental scanning and information source utilization: Exploring the behavior of Hong Kong hotel and tourism executives', *Journal of Hospitality and Tourism Research*, 30(2): 170–190.

Jones, P., Comfort, D. and Hillier, D. (2019) 'Sustainability and the world's leading ocean cruising companies', *Journal of Public Affairs*, 19(1): 1609.

Jung, T., tom Dieck, M. C., Lee, H. and Chung, N. (2016) 'Effects of virtual reality and augmented reality on visitor experiences in museums', in A. Inversini and R. Schegg (Eds), *Information and Communication Technologies in Tourism*, Cham, Switzerland: Springer, 621–635.

Koo, C., Xiang, Z., Gretzel, U. and Sigala, M. (2021) 'Artificial intelligence (AI) and robotics in travel, hospitality and leisure', *Electronic Markets*, 31(3): 473–476.

Law, R., Leung, D. and Chan, I. C. C. (2020) 'Progression and development of information and communication technology research in hospitality and tourism: A state-of-the-art review', *International Journal of Contemporary Hospitality Management*, 32(2): 511–534.

Law, R., Ye, H. and Chan, I. C. C. (2022) 'A critical review of smart hospitality and tourism research', *International Journal of Contemporary Hospitality Management*, 34(2): 623–641.

Lee, Y. J. A., Jang, S. and Kim, J. (2020) 'Tourism clusters and peer-to-peer accommodation; *Annals of Tourism Research*, 83: 102960.

Loureiro, S. M. C., Guerreiro, J. and Ali, F. (2020) '20 Years of research on virtual reality and augmented reality in tourism context: A text-mining approach, *Tourism Management*, 77: 104028.

Lynch, R. (2018) *Corporate Strategy*, 8th ed., Harlow, UK: Pearson.

Lynes, J. K. and Andrachuk, M. (2008) 'Motivations for corporate social and environmental responsibility: A case study of Scandinavian airlines', *Journal of International Management*, 14(4): 377–390.

Mair, J. and Smith, A. (2021) 'Events and sustainability: Why making events more sustainable is not enough', *Journal of Sustainable Tourism*, 29(11–12): 1739–1755.

Mariani, M. (2020) 'Big data and analytics in tourism and hospitality: A perspective article', *Tourism Review*, 75(1): 299–303.

Mason, R. B. (2007) 'The external environment's effect on management and strategy: A complexity theory approach', *Management Decision*, 45(1): 10–28.

McAdam, R. (2000) 'The implementation of reengineering in SMEs: A grounded study', *International Small Business Journal*, 17(3): 305–323.

Meers, K. A. and Robertson, C. (2007) 'Strategic planning practices in profitable small firms in the United States', *The Business Review*, 7(1): 302–307.

Mehraliyev, F., Chan, I. C. C., Choi, Y., Koseoglu, M. A. and Law, R. (2020) 'A state-of-the-art review of smart tourism research', *Journal of Travel and Tourism Marketing*, 37(1): 78–91.

Morrison, A. and Teixeira, R. (2004) 'Small business performance: A tourism sector focus', *Journal of Small Business and Enterprise Development*, 11(2): 166–173.

Novelli, M., Schmitz, B. and Spencer, T. (2006) 'Networks, clusters and innovation in tourism: A UK experience', *Tourism Management*, 27(6): 1141–1152.

OECD. (2018) 'Analysing megatrends to better shape the future of tourism', OECD Tourism Papers No. 2018/02, Paris: OECD Publishing. https://doi.org/10.1787/d465eb68-en

Okumus, F. (2004) 'Potential challenges of employing a formal environmental scanning approach in hospitality organizations', *International Journal of Hospitality Management*, 23(2): 123–143.

Önder, I. and Gunter, U. (2022) 'Blockchain: Is it the future for the tourism and hospitality industry?', *Tourism Economics*, 28(2): 291–299.

Oreja-Rodríguez, J. R. and Yanes-Estévez, V. (2007) 'Perceived environmental uncertainty in tourism: A new approach using the Rasch model', *Tourism Management*, 28(6): 1450–1463

Oyewole, P. (2001) 'Consumer's socio-demographic characteristics and satisfaction with services in the airline industry', *Services Marketing Quarterly*, 23(2): 61–80.

Peattie, K. and Moutinho, L. (2000) 'The marketing environment for travel and tourism', in L. Moutinho (Ed.), *Strategic Management in Tourism*, Wallingford, UK: CAB International, 17–37.

Peeters, P. and Bongaerts, R. (2015) 'The role of aviation in sustainable development of tourism', in C. M. Hall, S. Gossling and D. Scott (Eds), *The Routledge Handbook of Tourism and Sustainability*, Abingdon, UK: Routledge, 420–429.

Peluso, A. M. and Pichierri, M. (2021) 'Effects of socio-demographics, sense of control, and uncertainty avoidability on post-COVID-19 vacation intention', *Current Issues in Tourism*, 24(19): 2755–2767.

Phi, G. T. and Waldesten, T. (2021) 'Educating sustainability through hackathons in the hospitality industry: A case study of Scandic Hotels', *Scandinavian Journal of Hospitality and Tourism*, 21(2): 212–228.

Rate, S., Moutinho, L. and Ballantyne, R. (2018a) 'Futurecast applied to tourism', in L. Moutinho and S. Vargas-Sanchez (Eds), *Strategic Management in Tourism*, 3rd ed., Wallingford, UK: CABI, 20–32.

Rate, S., Moutinho, L. and Ballantyne, R. (2018b) 'The new business environment and trends in tourism', in L. Moutinho and S. Vargas-Sanchez (Eds), *Strategic Management in Tourism*, 3rd ed., Wallingford, UK: CABI, 1–15.

Ruel, H. and Njoku, E. (2021) 'AI redefining the hospitality industry', *Journal of Tourism Futures*, 7(1): 53–66.

Scheiwiller, S. and Zizka, L. (2021) 'Strategic responses by European airlines to the COVID-19 pandemic: A soft landing or a turbulent ride?', *Journal of Air Transport Management*, 95: 102103.

Schoemaker, P. J. and Day, G. (2021) 'Preparing organizations for greater turbulence', *California Management Review*, 63(4): 66–88.

Seguí-Amortegui, L., Clemente-Almendros, J. A., Medina, R. and Grueso Gala, M. (2019) 'Sustainability and competitiveness in the tourism industry and tourist destinations: A bibliometric study', *Sustainability*, 11(22): 6351.

Senbeto, D. L. and Hon, A. H. (2020) 'Market turbulence and service innovation in hospitality: Examining the underlying mechanisms of employee and organizational resilience', *The Service Industries Journal*, 40(15–16): 1119–1139.

Shafiee, S., Ghatari, A. R., Hasanzadeh, A. and Jahanyan, S. (2019) 'Developing a model for sustainable smart tourism destinations: A systematic review', *Tourism Management Perspectives*, 31: 287–300.

Sismanidou, A., Palacios, M. and Tafur, J. (2009) 'Progress in airline distribution systems: The threat of new entrants to incumbent players', *Journal of Industrial Engineering and Management*, 2(1): 251–272.

Stankov, U. and Gretzel, U. (2020) 'Tourism 4.0 technologies and tourist experiences: A human-centered design perspective', *Information Technology and Tourism*, 22: 477–488.

Tolkach, D., Chon, K. K. and Xiao, H. (2016) 'Asia Pacific tourism trends: Is the future ours to see?', *Asia Pacific Journal of Tourism Research*, 21(10): 1071–1084.

Tum, J., Norton, P. and Wright, J. N. (2011) *Management of Event Operations*, 2nd ed., Abingdon, UK: Routledge.

Uphaus, P. O., Ehlers, A. and Rau, H. (2019) 'Location-based services in tourism: An empirical analysis of factors influencing usage behaviour', *European Journal of Tourism Research*, 23: 6–27.

Vecchiato, R. (2015) 'Strategic planning and organizational flexibility in turbulent environments', *Foresight*, 17(3): 257–273.

WCED. (1987) *Our Common Future*, Oxford, UK: Oxford University Press.

WTTC. (2018) *The Megatrends That Are Affecting Travel & Tourism Today*, London: WTTC. www.wttc.org.

Zhang, H. Q. and Morrison, A. (2007) 'How can the small to medium sized travel agents stay competitive in China's travel service sector?', *International Journal of Contemporary Hospitality Management*, 19(4): 275–285.

Websites

www.aviationtoday.com.avisbudgetgroup.com
www.avisbudgetgroup.com
www.iata.org
www.icao.int
www.scandichotelsgroup.com
www.smarttourismdestinations.eu/
www.wttc.org

Chapter **8**

The external environment for tourism, hospitality and event organizations – the competitive context

Introduction and chapter overview

In the introduction to Part 3, we encountered the idea that an organization's external environment comprises two strata: the macro environment and the competitive environment. We considered the macro environment in Chapter 7 (using the STEEP framework); in this chapter we turn to an analysis of the competitive environment.

The micro environment comprises those influences that the organization experiences frequently. For most businesses, this concerns the industries in which they operate. Businesses may compete with each other or, in some circumstances, collaboration may be more appropriate. We discuss two models for industry analysis in this chapter. We then go on to discuss the scope of collaborative behavior, before considering how competitors in an industry fall into strategic groups.

LEARNING OBJECTIVES

After studying this chapter, students should be able to:

• Distinguish between micro- and macrolevel external analysis
• Explain the importance of industry and market analysis with regard to *THE* sectors
• Describe the construction and application to *THE* of Porter's five forces framework
• Explain the limitations of Porter's five forces framework
• Define and distinguish between competitive and collaborative behavior in industries

DOI: 10.4324/9781003318613-11

- Assess and explain the limitations of the resource-based model of industry analysis
- Define strategic groups and be able to apply the concept in industry analysis for *THE* sectors
- Explain the meaning of critical success factors and distinguish them from key performance indicators

8.1 Industries and markets

Some strategic management texts wrongly use the terms *industry* and *market* interchangeably. Kay (1995) pointed out that confusing the two concepts can result in a flawed analysis of the competitive environment and, hence, flawed strategy. Modern organizations, such as *vertically integrated* travel companies, may operate in more than one industry (or industrial sector) and in more than one market.

> For example: *TUI plc, a 'vertically integrated' European travel group, operates in the airline, travel intermediary (tour operator and travel distribution), accommodation and cruising sectors of the travel industry and has major markets in Scandinavia, Continental Europe, the UK and North America. Each industry (or industrial sector) and market has its own distinctive structure and characteristics that need to be understood because they have particular implications for the formulation of strategy.*

KEY CONCEPT

Industries and markets

- *Industries* produce goods and services – the *supply side* of the economic system.
- *Markets* consume goods and services that have been produced by industries – the *demand side* of the economic system.

Industries are centered on the supply of a product or service, whereas markets are concerned with demand. It is therefore important to understand and analyze both industries and markets to assist in the process of strategy selection.

It is sometimes difficult to define a particular industry precisely. Porter (1980) defined an industry as a group of businesses whose products are close substitutes, but this definition can be inadequate because some organizations and industries produce a range of products for different markets. The importance of identifying the industry setting successfully and understanding its implications has been examined by, for example, Rumelt (1991) and McGahan and Porter (1997). It has also been pointed out (see, for example, Sampler, 1998; W. C. Kim, 2005; Porter and Heppelmann, 2014; Szalavetz, 2022) that traditional concepts of industry boundaries have become blurred as technology creates new industries and new competitors emerge to challenge existing businesses, sometimes from surprising sources.

STRATEGY IN PRACTICE

Ways of understanding markets, industries and strategic groups

Kay (1995) considered the differences between markets, industries and strategic groups. A core competence (or *distinctive capability*, to use his terminology) becomes a competitive advantage only when it is applied in a market, an industry or a strategic group.

Competitive advantage is a relative term in that an organization can enjoy a competitive advantage by reference to other suppliers to the same market, other organizations in the same industry or other competitors in the same strategic group. Demand factors determine the market, whereas supply factors determine the industry.

By way of example, Kay (1995) cited Eurotunnel and P & O Ferries. Both serve the same market and represent alternative options customers might choose to cross the English Channel between France and the UK.

However, they are in very different industries in that one is a shipping company, whereas the other is the manager of a large infrastructure project. The strategic group is viewed as the competitive battleground and is determined by classifying companies with similar strategies. Thus, Lufthansa and British Airways are part of the same strategic group, whereas Southwest Airlines, a low-cost airline operating only domestic services in the USA, would be in a different strategic group.

It is important for organizations to identify the relevant market, industry and strategic group and to understand how and why they are not the same.

Source: Adapted from Kay (1995)

Thus, whereas an industry is centered upon producers of a product or service, a market is centered on customers and their requirements (needs and wants). A particular market consists of a group of customers with a specific set of requirements that may be satisfied by one or more products. Analysis of a market will therefore involve gaining understanding of customers, their requirements, the products that satisfy those requirements, the organizations producing the products and the means by which customers obtain those products (distribution channels).

As well as selling their products in markets, businesses obtain their resources (labor, materials, equipment, land, etc.) in markets – referred to as *resource markets*. Additionally, most businesses are interested in markets for substitute products, and they will also be keen to investigate new markets for their products.

8.2 Industry analysis

Analysis of its industry and markets allows an organization to:

- Identify other industries where it may be able to deploy its core competences
- Understand the nature of its customers and their needs
- Identify new markets where its core competences may be exploited (see Chapter 3 for a discussion of core competences)
- Identify threats from existing and potential competitors in its own and other industries
- Understand markets from which it obtains its resources

Analysis of the competitive environment (industry and market) is important to the development of an organization's future strategy, as is analysis of the macro environment (covered in Chapter 7) and internal analysis (which was the subject of Part 2 of this book). The industry and market context will play an important role in shaping an organization's competences and core competences.

The core competences of a business must continually be reviewed in relation to:

- Changing customer needs
- Competitors' competences
- Other market opportunities

Industry analysis aims to establish the nature of the competition in the industry and the competitive position of the business. Industry dynamics, in turn, are affected by changes in the macro environment (see Chapter 7).

> For example: *Aging populations in many developed countries have significantly affected the demand for tourism products with the growth in cruising, escorted coach tours and long-stay holidays being but three industry responses to the trend.*

THINK POINTS

- Using examples from *THE*, define and distinguish between an *industry* and a *market*.
- What is the purpose of industry analysis?
- Explain using examples from *THE* what is meant by the term *strategic group* and distinguish how it is different from an industry.

There is a danger that industry analysis can be seen as a 'one-off' activity, but like all components of the strategic process, it should be undertaken on an ongoing basis. The industry analysis framework developed by Porter (1980) is the most widely used and is explained in the following section.

8.3 Porter's five forces model of industry analysis

Models that become widely accepted and utilized are generally simple and easy to recall. Such is the case with Porter's widely used 'five forces' model of industry analysis. The concept has been widely applied and critiqued in the *THE* academic literature (see, for example, Benson and Henderson, 2011; Tavitiyaman et al., 2011; Ivanova and Ivanov, 2015; Roper and Hodari, 2015; Emery et al., 2016; Moreno-Izquierdo et al., 2016; Nannelli et al., 2019).

Porter (1985) developed a framework for analyzing the nature and extent of competition within an industry. He argued that there are five competitive forces that determine the degree of competition within an industry. Understanding the nature and strength of each of the five forces within an industry assists managers in developing the competitive strategy of their organization. The five forces, which are shown in Figure 8.1, are as follows:

- Threat of new entrants to the industry
- Threat of substitute products
- Power of buyers or customers
- Power of suppliers (to businesses in the industry)
- Rivalry among businesses in the industry

By determining the relative 'power' of each of these forces, an organization can identify how to position itself to take advantage of opportunities and overcome or circumvent threats. The

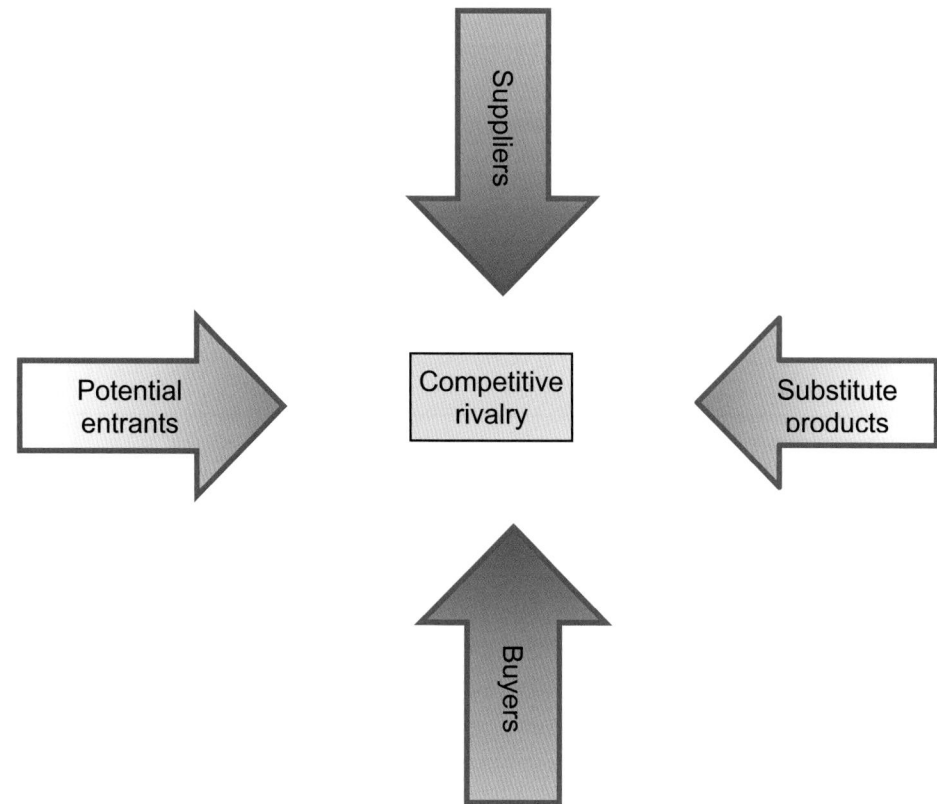

Figure 8.1 Porter's five forces framework

Source: Adapted from Porter (1985)

strategy of an organization may then be designed to exploit the competitive forces at work within an industry.

Before considering the detailed aspects of the five forces framework, a number of points should be noted:

- Although originally developed with commercial businesses in mind, the framework can provide valuable insights for most organizations, destinations or attractions.
- It is important to identify which of the five forces are the key forces at work in an industry. In many cases, one or more of the five forces prove to be 'key forces' and the strategic analysis must focus on these.
- The dynamic nature of the competitive environment means that the relative strength of the forces in a particular industry will change over time. It is therefore important for the analysis to be repeated on a regular basis to detect such changes, before competitors do so, and allow an early adjustment of strategy.
- The framework should be based at the level of the SBU rather than at the level of the entire organization (except where the organization is simple and consists of one SBU only). This is because individual organizations may be diverse in their markets and operations.

● The five forces are not independent of each other, with pressures from one competitive force having the potential to trigger changes in the other forces.

> For example: *Potential new entrants to a market, finding their route blocked, may find new routes to the market by bypassing traditional distribution channels using agents or intermediaries and sell directly to consumers. Most airlines following the low-cost model (such as easyJet, Norwegian, IndiGo, Jetstar, AirAsia, Frontier or Southwest) do not commonly use distribution through intermediaries such as travel agents and do not feature prominently on GDSs. Instead, tickets are normally sold directly to consumers (largely through the internet), thereby cutting out the intermediaries and the commission that would ordinarily have been paid to them. Thus, the bargaining power of one set of buyers (the travel agents) was reduced by the introduction of new market entrants, whereas the bargaining power of another set (consumers) was increased as a result of increased competition provided by the new entrant.*

KEY CONCEPT

Strategic business unit

In strategy, the term *strategic business unit* is widely used, usually using the acronym *SBU*. An SBU supplies goods or services for distinct market segments (Whittington et al., 2020). The term SBU is rarely used by organizations internally (because it represents management jargon); rather, the terms 'department', 'functions', 'subsidiaries' and 'profit centers' are more widely applied to distinctive parts of organizations.

An SBU allows organizations to be broken down into distinct parts that can be analyzed accordingly and appropriate strategies designed. This is useful because an individual organization may be offering many products to different segments of customers in various markets in which they may face a different set of competitors. Subdividing organizations into its constituent SBUs allows this complexity to be understood and for meaningful analysis to be carried out. Management decisions can then be made in relation to each SBU based on the analysis. In some cases, with smaller organizations, they cannot meaningfully be broken down, because they have a limited product range. In such cases the entire organization is a single SBU.

> For example: *A vertically integrated travel company such as TUI (which we cited as an example previously) operates in various sectors. In each of these the company faces different sets of competitors, suppliers and substitutes and also encounters varying regulatory processes. Thus, the competitive forces are different in each of its chosen competitive arenas.*

Each of the five forces will be discussed in turn in the context of various forms of travel and tourism organization.

8.3.1 The threat of new entrants to the industry

The threat of entry to an industry by new competitors depends on the 'height' of a number of entry barriers. *Barriers to entry* can take a number of forms.

THE CAPITAL COSTS OF ENTRY

The size of the investment required by a business wishing to enter the industry will be an important determinant of the extent of the threat of new entrants. The higher the investment required, the lesser the threat from new entrants is likely to be. The lower the required investment, the greater the threat. In some areas of *THE*, such as building a hotel or a visitor attraction, starting a cruise line or launching an airline, the capital costs are clearly quite high.

However, in some situations it might be possible to avoid or defer some capital costs by separating ownership from the management of the assets or by leasing or franchising.

> **For example:** *Separating ownership and management is common in the hotel sector, where a property company may own the physical assets but a hotel operator manages the hotel. Leasing aircraft and ships is common in the airline and cruising sectors and allows high upfront costs to be spread out over a period of time.*

In other areas of *THE* such as starting a tour operator, a travel agency, an internet intermediary or an event management company, the capital costs might be relatively low because they do not normally require the purchase of expensive assets.

BRAND LOYALTY AND CUSTOMER SWITCHING COSTS

If the companies in an industry produce differentiated products and services and customers are loyal to particular brands, potential new entrants will encounter resistance in trying to enter the industry. Brand loyalty will also be an important factor in increasing the costs for customers of switching to the products of new competitors.

> **For example:** *In some instances, tourism destination products are able to fully differentiate their products. There is only one Louvre art gallery in Paris where the* Mona Lisa *can be viewed, and the emperor penguin can only be viewed (except in captivity) in extreme southern latitudes. Similarly, there is only one Glastonbury rock festival held in Somerset, UK, in the early summer each year.*
>
> *In other instances, though competitors exist, customers may have a preference for one brand over another. In the hotel, tour operating, airline and cruising sectors, companies spend heavily on establishing their individual brands, and many consumers are relatively loyal to particular brands. Loyalty is encouraged through an array of well-developed loyalty schemes.*

8.1 SHORT CASE ILLUSTRATION

Brand loyalty: Hong Kong Dragon Boat Festival

Dragon boats have a long and colorful history stretching back in China to the third century BC. The boats are best known for energetic and fiercely competitive dragon boat races, where teams of up to 80 paddlers race the long narrow boats accompanied by the beat of a drum down to the finish line.

It all started in Hong Kong in 1976 when Hong Kong fishermen participated in an international dragon boat race (there was one foreign team – from Japan) off the northeastern coast of Hong Kong island. From such humble beginnings the event sparked an explosion of worldwide interest in dragon boat racing and transformed an ancient Chinese folk ritual into a modern international sport.

The races have now become established as an annual international event. Although scaled back in recent years because of the COVID-19 pandemic restrictions, in June 2018 over

5,000 athletes representing more than 200 teams from all over the world competed in the Hong Kong International Dragon Boat Races, with Hong Kong's iconic skyline as the backdrop.

By definition, the 'Hong Kong' dragon boat races cannot be staged elsewhere. A tradition is formed over many years and a brand backed by business sponsorship becomes established, with loyalty among the sport's participants and supporters. However, the Hong Kong dragon boat races have formed a recognized identity and brand so that Hong Kong branded dragon boat racing now takes place annually in other cities around the world, including London and New York.

Source: www.discoverhongkong.com/

Questions

1. Explain how the building of a brand has established a barrier to entry in this case.

2. Provide another example from your knowledge of *THE* of a brand becoming so well established as to create a barrier to entry.

Thus, customers cannot switch to new entrants if they want to experience these attractions or events.

However, in many cases, *THE* consumers are driven by price and exhibit little brand loyalty. Thus, consumers may switch from existing tour operators, travel agents, hotel groups, events and attractions and airlines to new entrants on the basis of a more competitive offering.

In some cases, however, switching costs are imposed through customer loyalty schemes such as the frequent flyer and guest loyalty programs operated by airlines, hotels, attractions and other *THE* suppliers. These programs (such as American Airlines' AAdvantage, Air France–KLM's Flying Blue, Hilton's HHonors and Accor Group's Le Club Accorhotels) represent powerful incentives for *THE* consumers to remain loyal to particular brands.

ECONOMIES OF SCALE OR SCOPE AVAILABLE TO EXISTING COMPETITORS

If existing competitors are already obtaining substantial economies of scale, it will give them an advantage over new competitors, who will not be able to match their lower unit costs of production.

> For example: *A new entrant offering 'package' holidays to Spain from the major European markets (Germany, the UK and Scandinavia) would face strong competition from large entrenched operators such as TUI, Kuoni and Jet2. These operators often have long-standing arrangements with accommodation suppliers in Spain and other Mediterranean destinations. Given their ability to contract bed spaces in bulk, they are able to negotiate highly favorable terms that may not be available to a smaller new entrant.*

KEY CONCEPT

Economies of scale and scope

Economies of scale and economies of scope are widely used terms in the academic literature. They are conceptually similar (and often the term economies of scale is used loosely to denote both concepts), but they are different in detail.

Economies of scale primarily refers to reductions in the average cost (cost per unit) associated with increasing the scale of operations for a single product type.

Economies of scope refers to lowering the average cost for a firm in producing two or more products.

> For example: *An airline operating to single destination may be able to achieve economies of scale by operating a larger airplane as business increases because it will probably have lower operating costs per passenger. Similarly, if further routes are added to the airline network, economies of scope may occur because the costs of maintenance, sales and marketing, check-in staff, etc., may be shared by several products (the airline routes in this case), thus bringing average costs per passenger down.*

ACCESS TO INPUT AND DISTRIBUTION CHANNELS

New competitors may find it difficult to gain access to distribution channels, which will make it difficult to provide their products to customers or obtain the inputs required.

> For example: *In the case of the tour operator cited previously, such is the shortage of some categories of accommodation in some destinations that existing operators have sometimes contracted all available capacity, thereby excluding new entrants from access to the necessary inputs. Furthermore, the existing large tour operators have established distribution channels (such as travel agents, call centers and the internet) in their major markets that they have developed over the years to provide the most cost-efficient means of distribution. A new entrant would require heavy investment to secure such access.*

THE RESISTANCE OFFERED BY EXISTING BUSINESSES

If existing competitors choose to resist strongly, it will make it difficult for new organizations to enter the industry.

> For example: *If existing businesses are obtaining economies of scale, it will be possible for them to undercut the prices of new entrants because of their cost advantage. In some cases, existing competitors may make price cuts or increase marketing expenditure to deter new entrants. It has been claimed that such predatory pricing behavior has been undertaken by the established 'full-service' airlines to deter new low-cost carriers (see, for example, Fageda et al., 2011).*

If barriers to entry make it difficult for new competitors to enter the industry, this will limit the amount of competition within it. As a result, competitors within the industry will seek to strengthen the barriers to entry by cultivating brand loyalty, increasing the costs of entry and 'tying up' input and distribution channels as far as is possible.

Conversely, potential new entrants will lobby for the removal or reduction of such barriers to allow them to enter the industry and compete for business. In other words, they will try to make the industry *contestable*.

GOVERNMENT REGULATION

In some situations, new competitors are prevented from entering the market by government or intergovernmental regulation of *THE* sectors.

> **For example:** *Provision of accommodation and services for tourists by organizations is strictly regulated within the internationally renowned national parks of the USA such as Yellowstone and Yosemite. This is in marked contrast to the largely unregulated position outside the parks.*

The institutional environment plays a very important role (in regulating competition), particularly in so-called transition countries such as China. Government intervention is a typical characteristic of the institutional environment in these transition countries (C. Wang and Xu, 2011). In such circumstances, the government intervenes not only in the formulation of investment policy but also in its implementation and even in firms' operations, particularly those of state-owned enterprises.

8.3.2 The threat of substitute products

A substitute can be regarded as something that meets the same needs as the product of the industry.

> **For example:** *An individual wishing to cross the English Channel between England and France can choose to travel by air, by cross-channel ferry or by the train service using the channel tunnel. These products all provide the benefit to the customer of crossing to France, despite the fact the ferry rail and air services are provided by different industries.*

The extent of the threat from a particular substitute will depend upon two factors:

- *The extent to which the price and performance of the substitute can match the industry's product*

Close substitutes whose performance is comparable to the industry's product and whose price is similar will be a serious threat to an industry. The more indirect the substitute, the less likely the price and performance will be comparable. Because most *THE* products (in leisure markets) are of relatively high cost and the expenditure is usually seen as a luxury rather than a necessity, the products will compete for disposable income with other high-cost items such as cars and 'white goods' (refrigerators and washing machines).

- *The willingness of buyers to switch to the substitute*

Buyers will be more willing to change suppliers if switching costs are low or if competitor products are lower priced or have improved performance. This is also closely tied in with the extent to which customers are loyal to a particular brand. The more loyal customers are to one supplier's products (for whatever reason), the more the threat from substitutes will be reduced.

KEY CONCEPT

Switching costs

One of the key strategic maneuvers in maintaining customer loyalty is increasing the cost – to the customer – of changing to a new supplier. If switching costs are high, customers will have an economic disincentive to switch and hence will tend to stay with the existing supplier. For direct substitutes, switching costs may be increased by customer loyalty schemes or promotional offers to existing customers.

For indirect substitutes, there are likely to be higher actual or perceived switching costs, because the benefits derived from a holiday or attendance at a festival are very different from those derived from buying say a new washing machine, yet they both compete for a share of consumers' disposable income.

Competitors in an industry will attempt to reduce the threat from substitute products by improving the performance of their products, by reducing costs and prices and by differentiation.

KEY CONCEPT

Direct and indirect substitutes

There are very few products for which there is no substitute. A substitute can be defined as a product that offers substantially equivalent benefits to another. This criterion – that of receiving equivalent benefits – can be met in two ways: directly and indirectly.

Direct substitutes are those that are the same in substance. Direct substitutes may simply be competitive brands or competing destinations. Emirates Airlines, Singapore Airlines, Malaysia Airlines and Thai Airways are direct competitors for air services between Southeast Asia and Europe.

Indirect substitutes are those that are different in substance but which can, in certain circumstances, provide the same benefit. Thus, international air travel and teleconferencing are different in substance, but can provide similar benefits in certain circumstances. If a meeting is required to discuss new product ideas the two indirect substitutes should be considered. If, however the purpose of the business trip is to meet potential suppliers or view new hotel or event facilities it is unlikely that teleconferencing would provide an adequate substitute.

8.3.3 The bargaining power of buyers

The extent to which the buyers (customers) of a product exert power over a supplying organization depends upon a number of factors. Broadly speaking, the more power that buyers exert, the lower will be the transaction price. This has obvious implications for the profitability of the supplier. The factors that affect the relative power of buyers include:

THE NUMBER OF CUSTOMERS AND THE VOLUME OF THEIR PURCHASES

The fewer the buyers and the greater the volume of their purchases the greater will be their bargaining power. A large number of buyers each acting largely independently of each other and buying only small quantities of a product will be comparatively weak.

For example: *The major cruise lines operating in the Caribbean (of which there are relatively few) have power over the many competing small Caribbean island destinations when deciding on their cruise schedules and negotiating port charges. On the other hand, individual travelers will have limited bargaining power when dealing with large cruise lines because there are many such customers but relatively few cruise lines.*

THE NUMBER OF BUSINESSES SUPPLYING THE PRODUCT AND THEIR SIZE

If the suppliers of a product are large in comparison to the buyers, buying power will tend to be reduced. The number of suppliers also has an effect – fewer suppliers will tend to reduce the bargaining power of buyers because choice and the ability to 'shop around' are reduced.

> For example: *Individual airlines wanting to serve London – and wanting to serve the lucrative business market in particular – are faced with a difficult situation. The three largest London airports (Heathrow, Gatwick and Stansted) are separately owned. Heathrow is by far the largest, has the greatest number of business clients and has the most connectivity with other destinations. The Heathrow to New York route in particular is one of the most lucrative in the world for business clients. This gives the London Heathrow airport operator a strong position when negotiating landing rights and their cost with airlines.*

SWITCHING COSTS AND THE AVAILABILITY OF SUBSTITUTES

If the costs of switching to substitute products are low (because the substitutes are close in terms of functionality and price), customers will be accordingly more powerful.

> For example: *Customers would not normally be financially penalized for moving their business from one Spanish resort to another or for moving a concert from one venue to another (unless contractually bound).*

It should be borne in mind that buyers are not necessarily those at the end of the supply chain. At each stage of a supply chain, the bargaining power of buyers will have a strong influence on the prices charged and the industry structure.

> For example: *In the supply chain for hotel rooms at a particular destination, the buyers include individual business and leisure customers, tour operators, travel intermediaries (such as travel agencies and internet comparison sites), airlines and other transportation groups and event promoters. The amount of power that each buyer exerts can differ substantially. Those buyers who can buy in bulk and provide the accommodation provider with guaranteed occupancy levels will be able to exert far greater pressure on the hotels in question than individual customers.*

In summary, the relative power of buyers is likely to be most powerful when:

- There are few of them and they purchase large quantities
- There are a large number of suppliers
- The size of the buyers is large relative to the size of the suppliers
- Switching costs for buyers from one product supplier to another are low
- Substitute products are available
- Switching costs between suppliers is low

When the opposite conditions apply, buyers will be weak.

8.3.4 The bargaining power of suppliers

Organizations must obtain the resources they need to carry out their activities from resource suppliers. These resources fall into the four categories we have previously encountered: human, financial, physical and intangible.

Resources are obtained in resource markets where prices are determined by the interaction between the organizations supplying a resource (suppliers) and the organizations from each of the industries using the particular resource in question. It is important to note that many resources are used by more than one industry. As a result, the bargaining power of suppliers will not be determined solely by their relationship with one industry but rather by their relationships with all of the industries that they serve.

The major factors determining the strength of suppliers are as follows.

THE UNIQUENESS AND SCARCITY OF THE RESOURCE THAT SUPPLIERS PROVIDE

If the resources provided to the industry are essential and have no close substitutes, suppliers are likely to command significant power over the industry. If the resource can be easily substituted by other resources, its suppliers will have little power.

> For example: *People with rare or exceptional skills can command higher salaries than lesser-skilled people. The musician or sports team represents the talent appearing at a concert or festival or major sporting event, for instance. The power of the personal or team brand is such that they provide the principal unique selling point for the event. Consequently, the artist or members of the sports team command high salaries because the event depends directly on their participation for its success.*

> *Similarly, the limited number of aerospace suppliers gives them considerable power. The worldwide suppliers of large jet aircraft are limited to two (Boeing in the USA and Airbus, a collaboration between France Germany, and Spain with participation by the UK), and the large-scale suppliers of jet engines are limited to four (General Electric and Pratt and Whitney in the USA, Rolls Royce in the UK and SNECMA in France).*

HOW MANY OTHER INDUSTRIES HAVE A REQUIREMENT FOR THE RESOURCE?

If suppliers provide a particular resource to several industries, they are less likely to be dependent on one single industry. Thus, the more industries to which they supply a resource, the greater their bargaining power will be.

> For example: *In some of the most developed accommodation markets such as London, Dubai and New York, hotels often find it difficult to recruit an adequate supply of staff because they have to compete for labor with many other industries. Consequently, staff members are frequently supplied from foreign countries with lower wage rates and/or higher unemployment levels. Similarly, in these locations, development land is scarce and hotels have to compete with other uses (offices, retail and residential) for suitable sites.*

SWITCHING COSTS BETWEEN SUPPLIERS

In some cases, switching between suppliers may be difficult and costly. Close working relationships may have been built up over a protracted period so that any new supplier would not have the necessary knowledge or experience required, or systems and services may have been tailored to the requirements of a particular supplier.

> For example: *An airline that operated an all-Boeing fleet of aircraft would find it difficult to switch quickly to supply from Airbus because pilots were trained for Boeing aircraft, capacity was calculated using Boeing seat configurations, engineers were trained to maintain Boeing aircraft and spares were bought for the Boeing aircraft.*

Conversely, the costs for an event management company in moving a concert in a particular city from one venue to another may be very low.

THE NUMBER AND SIZE OF THE RESOURCE SUPPLIERS

If the number of organizations supplying a resource is small and the number of buyers is large, the greater the power of the suppliers over the organizations will be in any industry. If the suppliers are small and there are a large number of them, they will be comparatively weak, particularly if they are small in comparison to the organizations buying the resource from them.

> For example: *Most of the suppliers of food and services to an international hotel group such as Sheraton are weak because they are small in comparison to the hotelier. Hotel groups will have a number of suppliers at its various locations and are able to switch suppliers, if necessary, to gain lower input costs or higher quality.*

In summary, suppliers to an industry are likely to be most powerful when:

- The resource they supply is scarce
- There are few substitutes for it
- Switching costs are high
- They supply the resource to several industries
- The suppliers themselves are large
- The organizations in the industry buying the resource are small

When the opposite conditions apply, suppliers will be weak.

8.3.5 The intensity of rivalry among competitors in the industry

Businesses within an industry will compete with each other in a number of ways. Broadly speaking, competition can take place on either a price or non-price basis.

- Price competition involves businesses trying to undercut each other's prices, which will, in turn, be dependent on their ability to reduce costs of production (operations).
- Non-price competition will take the form of branding, advertising, promotion, additional services to customers and product innovation.

KEY CONCEPT

Market structure

The markets for which an industry's businesses supply their products differ considerably in their structures. There are four basic types of market structure:

- Perfect competition
- Monopolistic competition
- Oligopoly
- Monopoly

Each of these types, which are shown in Figure 8.2, have their own set of characteristics and assumptions, which will in turn affect decision making within firms and the profits they can make. Economists refer to the degree of *monopolistic power* that companies possess – because the greater the power, the greater the degree of control companies will have over their pricing. Broadly speaking, this power increases from perfect competition (where there is none) – that is, many competitors – to monopoly (where there is a great deal); that is, no competitors.

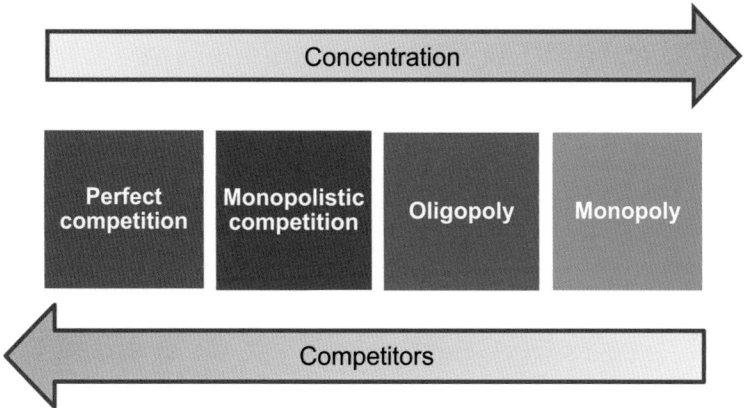

Figure 8.2 Concentration and market structure

- *Perfect competition* – a large number of small firms compete against each other. A single firm does not have any significant market power. As a result, the industry as a whole produces the optimal level of output, because none of the firms have the ability to influence market prices.

- *Monopolistic competition* – a large number of small firms compete against each other. However, unlike in perfect competition, the firms sell similar but slightly differentiated products. This gives them a certain degree of market power that allows them to charge higher prices within a certain range.

- *Oligopoly* – is dominated by only a small number of firms. This results in a state of limited competition. The firms can either compete against each other or collaborate. By doing so, they can use their collective market power to drive up prices and earn more profit.

- *Monopoly* – a single firm controls the entire market. In this scenario, the firm has the highest level of market power, because consumers do not have any alternatives. As a result, monopolists often reduce output to increase prices and earn more profit.

In some sectors of *THE*, competitive rivalry is fierce, whereas in others, it is less intense or even nonexistent because *oligopolies* or *monopolies* are formed.

> For example: *The competition among upscale hotels in Las Vegas, USA (see Short Case Illustration below) has been intense in recent years. A building boom during the 1990s and early years of the 2000s was followed by an economic slowdown after 2008 that affected occupancy rates and led to heavy discounting of room rates.*

> *This can be contrasted with rail services in many countries such as France, Italy, Germany, Malaysia and China where state-controlled enterprises hold monopoly (or near monopoly) positions.*

8.2 SHORT CASE ILLUSTRATION

Competitive rivalry: Las Vegas hotel occupancy rates

Las Vegas, Nevada, is unlike any other city in America. From its humble origins as a small desert town with a few hotels and saloons that served the workers who built the nearby Hoover Dam, the town has mushroomed, constantly adding hotels and attractions. Older hotels like the Dunes and the Sands were demolished to make room for the new properties. People travel to Las Vegas for business, with convention business having increased markedly in recent years, and for leisure driven by gaming and high-quality entertainment.

The Las Vegas Convention and Visitors Authority gathers a variety of data that are used to measure the health and growth of the economic engine that drives the Las Vegas economy. Figure 8.3 shows annual occupancy rates for Las Vegas. In 2021, some 32.2 million people visited the town, well down from the pre-COVID-19 figure of 42.5 million. The Las Vegas hotel market is intensely competitive and continually seeking ways to attract additional visitors through price incentives, refurbishment of existing facilities and new building, providing entertainment and adding attractions.

Nevertheless, overall occupancy rates fell from their 2007 peak as the economic recession following the 2008 banking crisis took its toll. Hotel occupancy levels have recovered somewhat since 2013 but are still lower than those achieved in the early years of the new millennium.

In most years, occupancy rates of over 80% are still high by most standards, but occupancy rates vary enormously between high weekend demand and lower occupancy rates during the week. Variable occupancy rates in turn lead to highly elastic pricing structures. Prices usually rise in Las Vegas on weekends and fall during the intervening period, in marked contrast to most city-based accommodation markets, which exhibit higher rates during the week to cater to business demand.

The COVID-19 pandemic severely affected occupancy rates (as with all accommodation markets) in 2020, with rates falling to 37.4%. Some recovery was evident in 2021, with rates increasing to 60.5%.

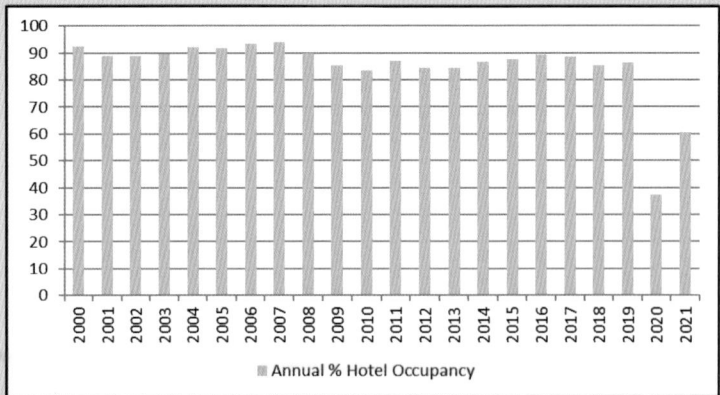

Figure 8.3 Las Vegas hotel occupancy rates

Source: Adapted from www.lvcva.com

Questions

1. Explain the pattern of demand for hotel accommodation in Las Vegas and contrast it with most other city markets.

2. Contrast the competitive rivalry in Las Vegas with a state-controlled railway company.

In highly competitive markets companies engage in regular and extensive monitoring of key competitors by such means as:

- Examining price changes and matching any significant move immediately
- Examining any rival product change in great detail and regularly attempting new initiatives in one's own organization
- Watching investment in new competing operations
- Attempting to poach key employees

In Figure 8.1 it can be seen that the other four forces point inwards toward this fifth force.

This representation is intentional, to remind us that the strength of this force is to a large extent dependent on the contributions of the other four forces that 'feed' it. The overall market structure in which industries sell their products is also important. However, there are also some additional conditions within the industry itself that may lead specifically to a higher degree of competitive rivalry. These specific factors include the following:

THE RELATIVE SIZE OF COMPETITORS

When competitors in a sector are of roughly equal size, there is a possibility that rivalry is increased as the competing companies try to gain a higher degree of market dominance, but profits fall as a result of this increased rivalry.

Conversely, in situations where there is a dominant organization, there may be less rivalry (and consequently higher levels of profitability) because the larger organization has a degree of *monopolistic power* and is often able to stop or curtail moves by smaller competitors.

> For example: *In relation to Macao, Sheng (2011) argued that there has been local underinvestment and a large influx of foreign labor, and in such circumstances large transnational enterprises may make their profits at the expense of local businesses. Therefore, Sheng (2011) maintained that it is the government's responsibility (China in the case of Macao) to regulate foreign investment in a way that is conducive to sustainable development.*

THE NATURE OF COSTS IN INDUSTRY SECTORS

If sectors of an industry have high fixed costs and thus are capital intensive, rivalry among competitors may become more intense as price-cutting becomes a way of filling capacity.

> For example: *In the cruise sector and among airlines, hotel brands and tour operators and event managers, discounting during the period close to departure, when the accommodation is required or the event is scheduled to take place is commonplace because of the inherent perishability of the product and the high level of fixed costs.*

THE MATURITY OF THE MARKETS SERVED

If the market is mature (and thus only growing slowly), competition is likely to be more intense than that in a market that is still growing vigorously. This is because in a mature market the only way for an organization to achieve higher sales is by taking market share from competitors and, consequently, rivalry is increased. In markets that are still growing vigorously, however, new opportunities are opening up for organizations and thus sales can be increased without taking market share from competitors.

THE DEGREE OF BRAND LOYALTY AMONG CUSTOMERS

If customers are brand loyal, there is likely to be less competition, and what competition there is will be on a non-price basis. If there is little brand loyalty, competition will be more intense.

> For example: *Cruise passengers have traditionally been very loyal to a particular cruise line and even to their preferred ship, whereas Northern European tourists taking packaged Mediterranean holidays are willing to switch brands freely, lured by a high level of price competition. Such brand loyalty is closely linked to a further factor – that of differentiation.*

THE DEGREE OF DIFFERENTIATION

Where products can be easily differentiated, rivalry is likely to be less intense, whereas where differentiation is difficult, rivalry is likely to be more intense.

> For example: *Continuing the example from above, it is relatively easy to differentiate a cruising product through the type, size, quality and crew of a ship. By contrast, with regard to a package holiday to the Mediterranean, tour operators may use similar types of aircraft, accommodation, ground handling agents and distribution channels and offer the same destination choice. Consequently, the opportunities to differentiate their product offerings are more limited.*

GOVERNMENT REGULATION

The degree of government regulation will have an influence on the extent of competitive rivalry in a sector. The international airline industry has traditionally been heavily regulated, with governments taking direct roles in setting intergovernmental agreements to exert control.

> For example: *International air travel between many countries has been regulated through a complex web of bilateral treaties negotiated between the governments at either end of the air routes. Although much deregulation has taken place, many restrictions still remain.*
>
> *Similarly, in the UK, the government, acting through the Civil Aviation Authority's Air Travel Organisers' Licence system, seeks to control the capacity of air inclusive tour operators. In both these cases, rivalry might be more intense if government regulation ceased to exist.*
>
> *By contrast, government controls over the international hotel sector are rare, other than through normal planning restrictions and investment incentives.*

THE HEIGHT OF EXIT BARRIERS

The height of exit barriers (the ease with which organizations can leave the sector) will have an impact on competitive rivalry. Where high capital costs have been incurred, as with the purchase of aircraft, cruise liners or the construction of hotels or visitor attractions, it may be difficult to exit from these sectors, because these assets cannot easily be put to other uses and may be difficult to sell, particularly in times of economic downturn. Consequently, overcapacity may persist in such sectors for a period of time, leading to increased rivalry between competitors. Conversely, because new capacity is difficult to add quickly, undercapacity may be an issue at certain times, leading to a decrease in rivalry between competitors.

> For example: *Issues in relation to overcapacity in some Asian hotel markets such as Hong Kong and Shanghai were discussed by Tsai and Gu (2012) and Zheng and Gu (2011), respectively, and S. K. Lee and Jang (2012) assessed potential overcapacity issues in US lodging provision.*

A high degree of rivalry will usually reduce the potential profitability of an industry and may lead to innovations that serve to stimulate consumer demand for the *THE* products being offered. In recent years, many sectors of *THE* have become more competitive as the result of the influence of several factors, including:

* Technology advances
* Government deregulation
* Government privatization
* Economic slowdown in many economies
* Removal of restrictions on foreign travel
* Removal of limits on supply

> For example: *The competition among European tour operators to secure hotel rooms and self-catering accommodation rooms at prime Spanish resorts, the competition between European cities as short break destinations, the growth of Dubai as a tourist destination, the increasingly crowded schedule of European summer music festivals and the increased competition in the air travel market between Europe and North America are all examples of increasingly competitive sectors of THE.*

THINK POINTS

* Explain how Porter's five forces framework works as a tool of industry analysis.
* What are the limitations of the five forces framework?
* Using examples from *THE*, explain what *entry barriers* are and the link between their 'height' and the likely profitability of an industry.

8.3.6 The five forces framework and profitability – a summary

As has been discussed, a relationship can be established between an organization's position in respect to the five forces and its potential profitability. Table 8.1 summarizes how the five forces can help to determine company and industry profitability.

8.3.7 Limitations of the five forces framework

Porter's five forces framework represents a good starting point for the understanding of competitive forces and has obvious value as a tool for managers seeking a better understanding of such forces. However, the framework is subject to several important limitations. The major limitations of the framework are as follows.

Table 8.1 Porter's five forces and profitability – a summary

Force	Profitability likely to be HIGHER if there is/are:	Profitability likely to be LOWER if there is/are
• Bargaining power of suppliers	Weak suppliers	Strong suppliers
• Bargaining power of buyers	Weak buyers	Strong buyers
• Threat of new entrants	High entry barriers	Low entry barriers
• Threats from substitute products	Few possible substitutes	Many possible substitutes
• Competitive rivalry	Little rivalry	Intense rivalry

IT IMPLIES THAT SUPPLIERS, BUYERS AND COMPETITORS ARE THREATS

The framework is built on the premise that suppliers, buyers and competitors represent threats that need to be tackled. However, some organizations have built successful strategies on the basis of building close working relationships with suppliers, buyers and competitors.

Collaborative (or cooperative) strategy has become an important part of the overall *THE* competitive landscape and takes a number of forms involving aspects such as *strategic* and *marketing alliances, partnering, networking* and *clustering*. In all of these activities (see Chapter 11), separate organizations (or parts of them) work together in various ways for mutual benefit, and in many cases public and private sectors work together in PPPs.

This facet of strategy for *THE* organizations has generated a broad literature, having been discussed by a number of authors, including Evans (2001), Casanueva et al. (2014), Zou and Chen (2017) and Peng and Lu (2022) in relation to airlines; Chathoth and Olsen (2003), Pansiri (2008), Ramayah et al. (2011) and Dewally and Gordon (2022) in relation to tourism and hospitality; Andersson and Getz (2009) and Zapata and Hall (2012) in relation to PPPs; Long (2000), Aas et al. (2005) and Stokes (2006) in relation to events and attractions; and Y. Wang and Fesenmaier (2007), Y. Wang et al. (2012), Garrod and Fyall (2017) and Cehan et al. (2021) in relation to destinations.

IT CLAIMS TO ASSESS INDUSTRY PROFITABILITY

Porter (1980) argued that the framework makes it possible to assess the potential profitability of a particular industry. Though there is some evidence to support this claim, there is also strong evidence to suggest that company-specific factors are more important to the profitability of individual businesses rather than industry factors (Rumelt, 1991; Karniouchina et al., 2013).

IT IMPLIES THAT THE FIVE FORCES APPLY EQUALLY TO ALL COMPETITORS IN AN INDUSTRY

In reality, the strength of the forces may differ from business to business. The framework implies that if, for example, supplier power is strong, this will apply to all the businesses in the industry. In fact, supplier power may differ from business to business in the industry. Larger businesses will face less of a threat from suppliers than will smaller ones. Similarly, businesses with strong brand names will be less susceptible to buyer power and substitutes than those with weaker brands.

Notwithstanding the criticisms, Porter's five forces analysis has been highly influential and is widely applied. As with other simplifying models, it has to be applied carefully and critically and should be used as one form of evidence to be used in conjunction with others. Dobbs (2014) provided a set of industry templates for applying the model successfully. In a widely cited article, Grundy (2006) critiqued the model and recognized its influential position in the strategy field. In the article, he argued that despite its inherent difficulties, the model is valuable and that there are a number of important opportunities for using Porter's model in an even more practical way.

The Short Case Illustration below applies Porter's five forces analysis to the European airline industry.

8.3 SHORT CASE ILLUSTRATION

Forces driving competition: the European airline industry

New entrants

- Relatively high entry barriers
- High capital costs for start-ups
- Well-established brands
- Some examples of tacit government support for national 'flag carriers'
- Shortages of airport take-off and landing slots at some major airports
- Corporate jets, low-cost carriers and regional airlines challenging larger, more established airlines

Buyers

- Decreasing customer loyalty
- Airline frequent flyer programs
- Greater choice on some routes
- Complicated and confusing fare structures
- Competition from charter carriers on some routes
- Consolidation among travel intermediaries
- Increasing consumer use of price comparison sites

Substitutes

- Development of high-speed trains across Europe
- Extensive motorway network for car usage
- Telecommunication technologies such as teleconferencing

Suppliers

- Oligopoly of aircraft and aircraft engine suppliers
- Oligopoly of aircraft leasing companies
- Local monopolies of infrastructure providers (airports and surface transport)
- National monopolies and undercapacity of air traffic control providers and air space

Rivalry among competitors

- Varies on different routes but increasing generally
- Increasing price competition and continuing quality and service competition
- Extensive use of GDS systems and internet and mobile distribution
- Sophisticated yield management systems enabling *price discrimination* to take place
- Collaboration through strategic alliances and code sharing
- Charter, regional and low-cost entrants and high-speed rail providing increased competition
- Established carriers dropping service features to compete with new entrants

Discussion

Air transport is only one example of the various sectors in which industry leaders are facing increased competition from low-cost companies. The nature of competition has changed in recent years as market liberalization has enabled low-cost airlines (LCAs) to enter the market. New operational practices, lower service levels, internet and mobile distribution and the operation of a single aircraft type keep costs at low levels in a manner pioneered by Southwest Airlines in the USA. The LCA model started in Europe in 1995. Irish airline Ryanair's Michael O'Leary visited Southwest in 1991 and adapted its model a few years later (Creaton, 2005). Subsequently, easyJet was launched as an LCA in 1995, and many others have followed.

The newer entrants to the European airline industry have induced new demand for air travel among the population, and new city pairings previously thought not to be viable have emerged. An environment of deregulation and privatization has resulted in a more open market, but congestion at several major airports, air traffic control limitations and strong entrenched airlines, sometimes benefiting from tacit government support, have limited competition on some routes. The turbulent environment has placed a high degree of pressure on airlines to adapt to survive. As a sign of adaptation, the formation of strategic alliances has become a defining characteristic of the global air transport sector.

Questions

1. Outline the factors leading to the rise of low-cost airlines.
2. How has the intensity of competitive rivalry changed in recent years in the European airline industry?
3. Comment on why it might be useful to apply Porter's five forces model in situations like the European airline industry.

8.4 Clustering

An important aspect of Porter's work relates to the importance of *clusters*. Clusters are geographic concentrations of interconnected companies and institutions in a particular field. They encompass an array of linked industries and other entities that are important to competition. The best-known international examples that are often cited include the cluster of technology companies south of San Francisco in California's Silicon Valley and Tennessee's music industry cluster centred on Nashville (see Porter et al., 2012), but many other examples exist around the world.

KEY CONCEPT

Clusters

The application of the cluster theory to *THE* sectors has long been of interest (Capone, 2015).

> Porter (1998:78) defined clusters as geographical concentrations of interconnected companies, specialized suppliers, service providers, firms in related industries and associated institutions in particular industries that compete, but also co-operate.

The clustering in a territory as a determinant of firms' competitiveness was extended some time ago to the tourism, hospitality and cultural and creative industries, which led to the coining of terms such as *tourist cluster*, *cultural cluster*, *district cluster* and *creative cluster* (Capone, 2015).

By way of an example, Porter discussed the idea of a tourist cluster in analyzing the California wine and tourist cluster. He drew attention to the host of linkages among cluster members that result in a whole greater than the sum of its parts. In a typical tourism cluster, for example, the quality of a visitor's experience depends not only on the appeal of the primary attraction but also on the quality and efficiency of complementary businesses such as hotels, restaurants, shopping outlets and transportation facilities. Because members of the cluster are mutually dependent, good performance by one can boost the success of the others (Porter, 1998).

Clusters are not only composed of interrelated firms but benefit from the presence of local institutions and governance organizations. The cluster concept focuses on the linkages and interdependencies among actors in the value chain of products, services and innovations (Capone, 2015).

Thus, clustering often involves all elements of *THE* (accommodation, tourist facilities, events, transport, etc.) working in an interrelated way supported by government and public and private bodies to improve competitiveness for all participants.

Clustering also takes place in various sectors of *THE*, and the phenomenon and its implications have been investigated in the academic literature. However, whereas manufacturing industries have been widely studied from the clustering perspective, service clusters and specifically touristic clusters have received less attention (Peiró-Signes, 2015). See, for example, Hawkins (2004), Jackson and Murphy (2006) and Novelli et al. (2006).

> For example: *Y. J. A. Lee et al. (2020) examined the importance of tourism clusters in relation to Airbnb listings in Florida. The results indicated that overall tourism clusters (especially in relation to accommodation and food services) lead to superior Airbnb performance.*

In *THE sectors*, clustering clearly takes place in terms of supplying the needs of visitors at destinations; indeed, a 'resort' can be viewed as a form of cluster development.

> For example: *Peiró-Signes et al. (2015) identified US tourist clusters using a concentration measure, the 'location quotient', and checked whether hotels located in tourist clusters obtain higher economic results than hotels outside the identified clusters. The authors found that a hotel's economic performance is indeed enhanced when in a*

cluster but that it is more pronounced within luxury and upscale hotel categories and within chain-managed hotels.

Another aspect of clustering among *THE*-oriented companies and ancillary services is that such organizations tend to cluster around transport hubs, particularly airports.

> For example: *London's Gatwick airport and nearby towns such as Crawley and Dorking host a growing cluster of travel-related firms. These companies include airlines and ancillary services but also tour operators such as British Airways Holidays, Virgin Holidays, Kuoni and Italian specialist tour operator Citalia. Companies such as these benefit from access to a hub airport, ease of access to London as an international business and professional center, access to airline partners and access to an experienced pool of labor.*

The Short Case Illustration below demonstrates the importance of clustering in the context of the Italian meetings and conventions sector.

8.4 SHORT CASE ILLUSTRATION

Clustering: Italian meetings and conventions

The meetings, incentive travel, conventions, and exhibitions (MICE) industry is one of the fastest growing segments of the tourism industry today, in both global and country-specific contexts (S. S. Kim et al., 2003). Though it is difficult to define precisely, it is clear that it is growing steadily in many countries. S. S. Kim and Chon (2009), for instance, reported the increased importance of MICE to the South Korean economy.

Bernini (2009) investigated the clustering of the convention industry in Italy. In 2004, it was estimated that Italian convention turnover was worth approximately US$28bn to the Italian economy or about 26% of the total turnover produced by the tourism and hospitality industry.

The study identified a number of clusters of convention activity. Preeminent among these are the two 'capital' clusters of Rome and Milan and a further cluster of eight 'leading convention towns': Venice, Turin, Rimini, Genoa, Bologna, Naples, Palermo and Florence. Given Italy's cultural and artistic heritage, a further cluster of minor arts cities such as Verona and Siena were also identified as being important.

Rome and Milan are the two largest Italian cities and represent the national and business capitals, respectively, and hence have many ancillary services for convention delegates such as hotel accommodation, restaurants and international airports. Both cities have about 220 convention-oriented firms, which represents about 43% of the national total. Bernini (2009:884) stated that 'these clusters are the result of the co-location of complementary firms, not involved in the same activity, which benefit from the network membership and alliance dynamics'.

Source: Adapted from Bernini (2009)

Questions

1. If you were managing a company managing conventions in Rome or Milan, what specific benefits might you hope to gain through clustering, and are there likely to be any drawbacks?

2. What other examples can you cite of clustering in *THE* sectors, and do you think clustering of such activities is likely to be more or less important in the future?

Thus, where such clusters can be identified, a mutually supportive set of enterprises exists that compete and collaborate in such a way that may give rise to competitive advantage being established.

Though clustering is usually applied in the literature to multi-organization contexts, the clustering of activities can also benefit individual organizations due to the economies of scale and scope that can be achieved.

> *For example: The advantages of clustering have long been recognized by leading hotel groups. Many such groups concentrate their development efforts on particular geographical territories to focus management expertise and to obtain economies of scale and scope. Many hotel groups, for instance, have regional or area managers whose responsibilities cover the overall activities of several hotels within a group. Clustering in this way is rather different from the clustering involving numerous companies clustering for mutual benefit; in cases of this type, clustering is done largely to achieve operating efficiencies or so-called economies of scale and scope.*

The Short Case Illustration below illustrates the importance of clustering to the UK's largest group of hotels.

8.5 SHORT CASE ILLUSTRATION

Clustering of hotels: Premier Inn

Whitbread plc uses the advantages of clusters in developing its Premier Inn brand, which has grown quickly to become Britain's largest hotel chain. In an investor presentation, the company demonstrated the advantages of clustering. At that time, there were 656 Premier Inn hotels arranged in 110 clusters. In Manchester, for example, there were 14 Premier Inn hotels that were arranged in three clusters: Manchester Trafford, Manchester City and Manchester North.

By clustering in this way, opportunities are provided for:

- Managerial expertise to be shared between hotels
- Associated costs to be shared between several sites rather than just one
- Staff to follow clear career progression standardization can be facilitated between sites
- The pooling of consumables procurement and administration
- Processes (e.g., staff training and hiring) to be streamlined within the cluster

Source: Adapted from www.whitbread.co.uk

Questions

1. Explain how the clustering involved in the Premier Inns case is different to conventions in Italy in the previous Short Case Illustration.

2. What factor might inhibit working in clusters for a group of hotels, and could clustering work on a basis other than geography?

THINK POINTS

- Using examples from *THE*, explain what is meant by *clustering* and assess its usefulness for *THE* organizations.

- Define and distinguish between competition and collaboration.

8.5 A resource-based approach to environmental analysis

8.5.1 Competitive and collaborative arenas

It is not always the case that businesses in an industry compete with each other – they might, from time to time, have reasons to collaborate with each other. Accordingly, in some 'arenas', businesses compete, whereas in others they may work together.

At the root of this understanding is the fact that organizations and industries are open systems – they interact with many environments. The arenas in which the organization operates are described below:

- *The industry* – the industry within which the organization currently deploys its resources and competences in producing products
- *Resource markets* – the markets from which the organization, its competitors and other industries obtain their resources
- *Product markets* – markets where the organization sells its products. These can be subdivided into:
  - markets for the organization's products
  - markets for substitute products
  - new markets to which the organization may be considering entry
- *Other industries* – where businesses possess similar competences to those of the organization. Such industries are important for two reasons:
  - the business may be considering entry to them
  - organizations in these industries are potential competitors who may enter the business's industry and markets

Each of these arenas must be analyzed because they directly affect an organization's competitive positioning and hence its chances of outperforming competitors.

The competitive and collaborative arena framework builds on Porter's five forces framework but explicitly recognizes that the competitive environment is divided into four separate but interrelated arenas.

8.5.2 Limitations of existing frameworks of analysis

This chapter has concentrated on explaining the traditional strategic management frameworks employed in the analysis of the competitive environment.

The resource-based approach to strategic management, which is particularly associated with the work of Jay Barney in the early 1990s (Barney, 1991) and more recently assessed by Barney et al. (2011), emphasizes the importance of *core competences* in achieving competitive advantage. In doing so, it employs a different approach to analysis of the competitive environment because several limitations (Bensoussan and Fleisher, 2013) were identified with the existing frameworks in that they:

- Do not sufficiently integrate external and internal analysis
- Presuppose that businesses are naturally competitive and not collaborative in their behavior
- Tend to emphasize product and service markets rather than those where organizations obtain their resources
- Do not adequately recognize the fact that organizations themselves may alter their own competitive environments by their competence leveraging and building activities (see the Key Concept in Chapter 3)

- Do not adequately recognize the fact that organizations currently outside a company's industry and market may pose a significant competitive threat if they possess similar core competences and distinctive capabilities
- Do not recognize that the leveraging of existing competences and the building of new ones may enable businesses to compete outside their current competitive arenas

8.5.3 The resource-based framework

A resource-based framework for analysis of the business and its competitive environment is shown in Figure 8.4. Analysis is divided into five interrelated areas:

- The organization
- Its industry
- Product markets (existing markets, markets for substitutes, potential new markets)
- Resource markets
- Other industries

The significance of each area is considered below.

THE ORGANIZATION

'The organization' concerns the configuration of the internal value chain, its competences, resources and core competences and was discussed in Part 1 of this book (particularly in Chapter 2).

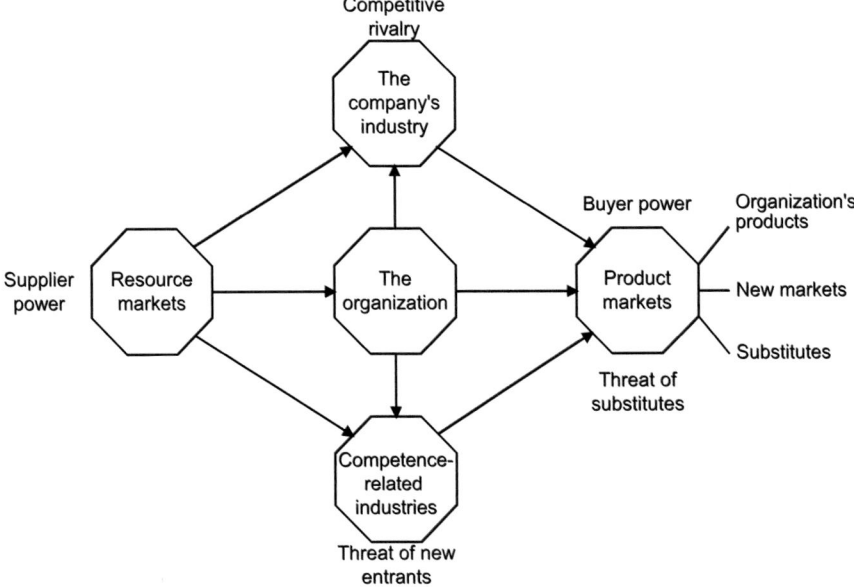

Figure 8.4 The resource-based model of strategy

Source: Adapted from Campbell et al. (2002:145)
Note: Competence-related industries are those where businesses possess similar competencies to those of competitors

The organization's industry

The organization's industry consists of the business and a group of companies producing similar products, employing similar capabilities and technology.

Analysis of the industry therefore examines the following over time (for each player in the industry):

- Skills and competences of the competitors
- Configuration of value-adding activities
- Technologies employed
- Number and relative size of competitors in the industry
- Performance of competitors (particularly in financial terms)
- Ease of entry to and exit from the industry
- Strategic groupings (see later in the chapter for a discussion of this concept)

This analysis will assist the organization in gaining greater understanding of its core competences, its major competitors and their core competences, and competitive and collaborative opportunities and threats.

Product markets

Product markets are those where businesses deploy their competences and sell their products and services. A business may operate in one or more product markets. In addition, a business will be interested in understanding markets to which it is considering entry on the basis of its core competences as well as markets for substitute products. Each of these markets will have its own characteristics, and each market can be analyzed in terms of:

- Customer needs and motivations
- Unmet customer needs
- Market segments and their profitability
- The number of competitors to the market and their relative market shares
- The number of customers and their relative purchasing power
- Access to distribution channels
- Potential for collaboration with customers
- Ease of entry
- Potential for competence leveraging
- Need for new competence building

In commercial (for-profit) settings, unless an organization's products and services are sold at a profit, the business will ultimately fail. Market-driven businesses that set out to meet existing customer needs and that anticipate their currently unmet needs and actually seek to shape the needs of their customers are likely to be the most successful.

Thus, when companies have products that have leading positions in their identified markets, they are likely to be most successful. An example of a market leading product that competes partly on the basis of its sustainable practices is provided by the Peruvian company Inkaterra, which is illustrated below.

8.6 SHORT CASE ILLUSTRATION

Market-leading products: Inkaterra, Peru

Inkaterra has pioneered and promoted sustainable tourism in Peru and at the same time operated a profitable business model. The successful coexistence of profitable commercial activities funding scientific research brought it to international prominence in 2012 with the award of the prestigious WTTC 'Tourism for Tomorrow World Conservation Award'. In the same year, Inkaterra also became the first world hotel to be recognized with the International Certificate in Sustainable Tourism by the CU Green Choice Sustainable Tourism Standard.

Founded in 1975, Inkaterra is a for-profit tourism company that actively supports scientific research and biodiversity conservation and hosts over 200,000 tourists each year. The company, which employs over 500 staff mainly drawn from local towns and villages, operates five hotels in the area of Machu Picchu (which was declared a UNESCO World heritage site in 1983) and the Madre de Dios area of the Amazon rainforest in southern Peru. The Inca settlement of Machu Picchu dates from the 15th century and is a highly sensitive site because of environmental degradation, which has been monitored by the World Monuments Fund.

Since its inception, an outstanding guest experience along with a commitment to conservation and local community benefit has been driving forces in the company's growth and development. Sustainable tourism principles and practices are used to facilitate the increased understanding among travelers of the biodiversity and cultural heritage of the Andes and the Amazon of Peru.

With the establishment of the Inkaterra Association, focused solely on biodiversity research, a model partnership was formed between a for-profit tourism company and a nonprofit research organization. Funding for scientific study of rare fauna and flora as well as education of national and international tourists about Peru's diverse tropical ecosystems and wildlife has been provided. Projects include sequestering over 3 million tons of carbon dioxide within the rainforest in the Inkaterra Ecological Reserve (monitored with the University of Leeds, UK, since 1989); a rescue center for endangered 'spectacled bears', the only South American native bear species; and the restoration of many acres of rare native cloud forest. Inkaterra hotels also practice environmentally friendly operations, including state-of-the-art irrigation systems utilizing rain and grey water and closed-pit composting and recycling, which, together with other measures, provide a dedicated 100% carbon-neutral hotel stay for guests.

Sources: Adapted from www.inkaterra.com; www.wttc.org; www.wmf.org; www.whc.unesco.org; Richter and Tveteras (2012); Sloan et al. (2013).

Questions

1. Consider why Inkaterra might be considered to be a market leading product.

2. Consider the sustainability of Inkaterra's business model.

MARKET SUBGROUPS

An important part of understanding the market is identifying subgroups within the market that share common needs. Such shared characteristics will mean that specific customer groups have different needs and act and behave differently to other customer groups (or *segments*). Fundamentally, segmentation means subdividing the total market into customer subgroupings, each with their own distinctive attributes and needs.

Customer groups are commonly segmented according to demographic variables (or 'people dividers') like age, sex, occupation, socioeconomic group, race, lifestyle, buying habits and geography (i.e., where they live). When customers are other businesses, they can be grouped by the nature of the business, organization type and size.

Each segment is then analyzed for its size and potential profitability, customer needs and potential demand, based on ability and willingness to buy. Segmentation analysis assists in the formulation of strategy by identifying particular segments and consumer characteristics that can be targeted.

The concept of market segmentation is discussed in greater depth in Chapter 6.

CUSTOMER MOTIVATIONS

Once market segments have been identified, they must be analyzed to reveal the factors that influence customers to buy (or not to buy) products. It is particularly important to understand factors affecting customer motivations like:

- Sensitivity to price
- Sensitivity to quality
- The extent of brand loyalty

Differences in customer motivations between market segments can be illustrated by reference to the market for air travel. The market can be segmented into business and leisure travel. Customers in each group have very different characteristics and needs.

> **For example:** *Business travelers are not particularly price sensitive but are sensitive to standards of service, scheduling and availability of connections. Leisure travelers, on the other hand, are generally much more price conscious and are less sensitive to scheduling and connections.*

Market research has an important role to play in building understanding of customer needs so that they can be targeted by appropriate product or service features.

Potential new markets are those where the product or service bought by customers is based on similar competences to those of the organization or where customer needs are similar to those of customers in the business's market. If conditions are favorable, the organization may consider using its current competences to enter new markets. Of course, it may also have to build new competences to be able to meet new customer needs.

RESOURCE MARKETS

Resource markets are those markets where organizations obtain finance, human resources, materials, equipment, services, etc. It is evident that businesses will normally operate in several such markets, each with its own characteristics, depending on the company-specific resources that are required. Resource markets can be analyzed in terms of:

- Number of actual and potential resource suppliers
- Size of suppliers
- Supplier capabilities and competences

- Potential for collaboration with resource suppliers
- Access by competitors to suppliers
- Nature of the resource and the availability of substitutes

By analyzing each of its resource markets, the managers of a business can identify the extent of competition they face from suppliers of resources, the competition they face from other competitors using the same resources and the potential for collaboration with suppliers (if appropriate).

COMPETENCE-RELATED INDUSTRIES

Other industries comprising businesses possessing similar competences and that often produce products or services that are substitutes for those of the business in question must also be analyzed. This analysis is necessary for three reasons, in that the organization may:

- Face a threat from other competitors possessing similar competences that may seek to enter its industry and markets
- Be able to enter industries where competences are similar to those it already possesses
- Be able to enter the markets currently served by competitors in the competence-related industry

Competence-related industries can be analyzed for:

- Key competences of the businesses in the industry
- The number and size of the businesses in the industry
- The threat from competitors in such industries that may leverage their competences to enter the markets of the business
- Opportunities for the business to leverage its existing competences and build new ones to enter competence-related industries and their markets
- Substitutability of the products of the industry for those of the business – how close the substitute product is to satisfying the same consumer demands as the business's product or service.

8.5.4 Resource-based model – a summary

The competence/resource-based model is more complex than the five forces framework but offers a more comprehensive analytical framework in that it enables an organization to:

- Establish the extent of competition within its own industry and market
- Assess the threat of competition from competitors in industries where competences similar to their own are employed
- Identify other markets that it may be able to enter by leveraging its existing competences and by adding new ones

Once adapted, the framework enables managers to understand:

- The nature of competition within the industry and markets (both product and resource) in which they operate
- The threat from competitors in other industries
- Potential opportunities in new industries and markets

> **THINK POINTS**
>
> - What is a resource market?
> - Explain how the resource-based model aids the understanding of industry analysis.
> - Compare and contrast Porter's five forces model with the resource-based view of industry analysis and assess the usefulness of both.

8.6 Strategic group analysis

A business can rarely confine its analysis to the level of the industry and markets in which it operates. It must also pay particular attention to its closest competitors, which are known as its *strategic group* (Porter, 1980). Strategic groups cannot be precisely defined, but they consist of organizations:

- Possessing (or potentially possessing) similar competences
- Serving customer needs in the same market segment
- Producing products or services of similar quality

Such analysis (see, for example, Söllner and Rese, 2001; Fleisher and Bensoussan, 2003; Gursoy et al., 2005; Short et al., 2007; Varelas and Georgopoulos, 2017) allows the managers of a business to compare its performance to that of its closest competitors in terms of profitability, market share, products, brands, customer loyalty, prices and so on. In this way, managers are able to *benchmark* the performance of their organization against their closest rivals. It is important that the closest rivals br identified carefully.

> **For example:** *Although the 'five-star' Ritz Hotel in Paris's Place Vendôme and a small guesthouse in rural France both provide the same service (providing accommodation and dining for guests), and hence are technically competitors, they operate in quite different strategic groups.*
>
> *They are unlikely to appeal to the same customers (or will appeal to the same customers but at different times), and their products, distribution channels, identities and prices are quite different. The Ritz strategic group (the grouping of hotel operators that compete with each other directly) will include other luxury hotels in Paris and key world capitals, whereas the rural French guesthouse strategic group will include other guesthouses in rural France.*

Strategic group analysis (sometimes called *competitive group analysis*) is an interesting way of analyzing the competitive structure in an industry and assessing the positioning of key competitors. By plotting how the major organizations in an industry (or a subsector within it) compete along two competitive dimensions, managers start to understand the relative position of their company and its products or services relative to major competitors.

There are three steps involved in the analysis and graphical representation of strategic groups:

- Identify the important competitive dimensions in an industry, taking into account the information you have available. Competitive dimensions are the specific factors the firms are using to compete within the industry. The competitive dimensions might include factors such as quality (perceived or actual), price, geographical scope or typical customer types.
- Construct two-dimensional plots of the competitive dimensions.

- Analyze the firm's position relative to competitors.

> For example: *In a study of Taiwan hotels, Tsang and Chen (2013) collected empirical data from 56 international tourist hotels. Five strategic groups were identified in terms of efficiency, and the hotels within the groups were ranked by attractiveness scores to reveal their competitiveness. The hotels were also assessed by progress scores to reveal how to advance to a higher level. By integrating both of these scores, a clear benchmarking path was designed for each hotel to guide inefficient hotels and identify suitable role models for excellence.*

8.7 SHORT CASE ILLUSTRATION

Strategic group analysis: Wyndham Hotel Group

Many companies produce informative, revealing and analytical presentations for investors that are usually available online. Though such presentations need to be viewed critically (because they are designed to attract investors and present the organization in the most favorable light), they nevertheless give valuable insights into the:

- Organization's financial position
- Strategic thinking of its management
- Position of the organization relative to competitors

Wyndham Hotel Group, headquartered in New Jersey, USA, is one of the world's largest and most diverse hotel companies, with over 9,000 hotels worldwide.

The company is one of the world's leading hotel groups, with leading brands in lodging franchising; 99% of its hotels are franchised as opposed to owned or managed, and it is the world's largest hotel franchisor. Hotel Brands include Wyndham, Travelodge, Days Inn, Howard Johnson and Ramada.

The company's presentation to investors portrays the company as benefiting from its diversified income streams, which delivers high levels of cash flow that it contends enables it to deliver superior growth. The asset-light franchise model provides a resilient and reliable source of fees at lower risk than other models of operation. The strategic group analysis, adapted from its presentation below, shows the company in relation to four other lodging groups: Marriott, Choice, Hilton and IHG, which comprise the strategic group constituting Wyndham's primary competitors.

Sources: Wyndham Worldwide Investor Presentation, www.wyndhamhotels.com

Questions

1. Consider why the asset-light franchise method of development is favored by Wyndham.

2. Consider potential disadvantages of this method of development.

8.7 Competitor profiling

The strategic group analysis potentially enables an organization to identify its key competitors in a way that is easily communicated to both internal and external stakeholder groups. A useful further step is to profile these key competitors to gain a more detailed insight as to:

- How and where the competitors might pose a *threat*
- Under what circumstances collaboration might be sought and thereby *opportunities* realized

This sort of analysis is very useful in providing a detailed analysis of each competitor, but caution needs to be exercised in interpreting the information gathered.

Industries and competitors are dynamic as opposed to static, and the competitors an organization faces have an interest in providing forward information that is not too useful to their rivals. Thus, the information gathered often represents mainly historical information that is in the public domain (as in the Whitbread Short Case Illustration below). Information based on future proposed changes to strategy for competitor organizations is usually much harder to obtain because it is likely be highly *commercially sensitive*.

Such an analysis might be carried out using the following headings:

- Overview
- Objectives
- Resources
- Past record of performance
- Current products and services
- Present strategies

The Short Case Illustration below applies the competitor profiling to the UK-based hospitality company Whitbread plc.

8.8 SHORT CASE ILLUSTRATION

Competitor profiling: Whitbread plc

A hotel operator seeking to expand in the UK hotel market would need to profile existing key competitors.

One of these would certainly be Whitbread plc, which has developed the leading brand of 'lodge' hotels that offer modern value-for-money accommodation with few added extras but with consistent and reliable standards. The company is traded on the London stock market and is a constituent member of the FTSE 100 index of the UK's largest companies.

Overview: The UK Company Whitbread plc was a major brewer founded in the middle of the 19th century. The end of the 20th century and the start of the 21st marked a watershed in the company's history, as Whitbread sold its breweries and then exited its pubs and bars business. After several decades of diversification, Whitbread can be viewed as one of the UK's largest hospitality companies, employing about 35,000 people with the leading lodge hotel brand and a number of food and beverage brands. Until January 2019, Whitbread owned Costa, a coffee bar chain operating in many countries and the market leader in the UK. This business was sold to Coca-Cola, with part of the £3bn sale proceeds earmarked for expansion of the Premier Inn brand.

Objectives: The priorities, on behalf of shareholders, are to grow the business and to achieve annual improvements in the return on their capital. The business is focused on growth sectors of the UK leisure market – lodging and eating out.

- To grow and innovate in the core UK market
  - Focus on a unique operating model

- Deliver best-in-class operational performance
- Further enhance and invest in the model
- To focus on strengths to grow internationally
  - Replicate UK success in Germany
- To enhance capability to support long-term growth
  - Deliver £150mn of efficiency savings over 5 years
  - Enhance digital, distribution, procurement and property capabilities

Resources: In 2022, the company had a turnover of about £1.8bn, with profits before tax of approximately £60mn. Approximately 40,000 people are employed by the company. 2020 and 2021 were challenging years because of the COVID-19 pandemic, and the company will not return to pre-COVID levels of profitability until 2023.

Past record of performance: The repositioning of the company some years ago to move away from brewing to focus on three core areas (hotels, restaurants and coffee shops) in which it possesses strong brands has shown consistent results.

Current products and services: In the hotel sector, the company has hitherto concentrated its efforts on its Premier Inn brand, which, with over 840 hotels and 80,000 rooms, is the UK's leading hotel operator. The Premier Inn brand has grown significantly in recent years and gained market share throughout the pandemic. Distressed property values caused by the economic downturn and COVID-19 and a focus on driving down building costs have provided opportunities to expand quickly in a cost-effective manner. The company has a strong and clear stance on sustainability issues.

Present strategies: See Table 8.2 for a summary of Whitbread plc's present strategies.

Table 8.2 Summary of Whitbread plc's present strategies (2022)

	Premier Inn UK	Premier Inn Germany
Market position	• UK's leading hotel chain with a long-term structural growth opportunity • Continued to gain market share during pandemic • Returned to prepandemic occupancy levels	Replicating the success of Premier Inn in Germany
Competitive and structural advantages	• Largest UK network by comfortable gap • Leading digital and direct distribution model • Strong freehold property underpinning	Significantly fragmented market with independent market share approximately 75% Flexible freehold/leasehold/acquisition model

	Premier Inn UK	Premier Inn Germany
Building strategic momentum	• Significant UK capacity additions with high occupancy	Strong customer feedback following 2-year Frankfurt trial
	• Good return on capital and fast maturity	Leveraging UK digital distribution capability
	• Best-in-class digital distribution	
Strong return on capital	• Strong capacity increase in last 5 years	Initial market entry model delivers return on capital above capital cost
	• Return on capital consistently above 13%	Further expansion has strong premium to cost of capital
Long-term structural opportunity	• Pipeline to 90,000 rooms secured	German market is 35% larger than the UK market
	• 'Line-of-sight' to over 100,000 rooms	Potential to replicate the scale and success of the UK business
	• Innovation to extend further	

Source: Categorization and analysis by author based on Whitbread plc company information available at www.whitbread.co.uk

Questions

1. Consider what you would regard as Whitbread's strengths and weaknesses if you were a manager at a competing hotelier.

2. Consider why a competitor might not want to rely too heavily in its decision making on the competitor profiling tool of analysis alone.

8.8 Critical success factors and key performance indicators

In any industry and its associated markets, there will be certain factors that are of fundamental importance to the success of the businesses operating within that competitive environment. These are known as critical success factors (see the Key Concept in Chapter 4). Competitive analysis allows managers to identify CSFs. A business must ensure that its competences and core competences directly address these CSFs.

CSFs differ between individual industries and markets. In the pharmaceutical industry, CSFs will be in the areas of research and development and production. For *THE* organizations, however, CSFs are likely to lie in areas such as the reputation of the brand, service excellence, product range, product features, distribution and innovation.

The concept of 'success factors' is attributed to Ronald Daniel of the international management consultancy firm of McKinsey and Company (Daniel, 1961). The concept was developed further into *critical success factors* by Rockart (1979).

CSFs can be viewed as those elements that are vital for a strategy to be successful. Thus, a critical success factor drives the strategy forward and makes the strategy successful; hence the use of the word 'critical'.

CSFs have been applied broadly in various *THE* contexts, with a large academic literature having emerged that applies the concept to all sectors of *THE*. See, for example, Lade and Jackson (2004) and Andersson and Getz (2009) on festivals and events; Padilla-Meléndez and Garrido-Moreno (2014) and S. Wang and Hung (2015) on hospitality; and Getz and Brown (2006), Haven-Tang et al. (2007), Baker and Cameron (2008), Hughes and Carlsen (2010), Jones et al. (2015), Marais et al. (2017) and Chingarande and Saayman (2018) on tourism and tourist destinations.

The Short Case Illustration below uses the work of Getz (2004) to illustrate the specific CSFs found to be important in relation to Canadian destination marketing organizations.

8.9 SHORT CASE ILLUSTRATION

CSFs: Canadian destination marketing organizations

Getz (2004) undertook research to gain a better understanding of the nature and competitive importance of bidding for events by destination marketing organizations in Canada, with emphasis on identifying CSFs for winning bids. Data were collected on the goals and nature of the event bidding process from convention and visitor bureaus in Canada.

The study found that Canadian bureaus were very active in bidding on a diverse range of events, especially meetings, conventions, political events and sports events. Most bureaus encouraged and assisted other local organizations to make bids and themselves concentrated on major events with city-wide economic impacts.

In this context, the most important CSFs for winning bids were found to be:

* Strong partners
* Excellent presentations
* Treating each bid as a unique process

Many respondents in the study also felt their destination needed bigger and better facilities and more marketing/bidding resources.

Source: Adapted from Getz (2004)

Questions

1. Why might Getz's research be useful for Canadian destination marketing bureaus to consider in formulating their strategies for future development?

2. Consider the CSFs for another aspect of *THE* you are familiar with.

Sometimes confusion exists about the distinction between CSFs and another popular term in strategy, namely, *key performance indicators* (KPIs).

THINK POINTS

* Using relevant examples from *THE*, explain the concepts of *strategic group analysis* and *competitor profiling*.
* Explain what is meant by KPIs and CSFs and comment on their usefulness in managing *THE* organizations.

- Using relevant examples from *THE*, explain what the limitations of *competitor profiling* might be.
- Explain the links between industry analysis and CSFs.

Whereas CSFs are concerned with those factors or elements without which the strategy would not be successful, KPIs represent a measurement tool. They are measures that quantify management objectives and enable the measurement of strategic performance.

> **For example:** *Whereas the KPI is a measure of progress toward a goal or objective, CSFs allow the strategy to be successful by, for instance, attracting new customers through putting measures in place to attract those customers:*

- *KPI = Sales rise 10% each year over a 5-year period*
- *CSF = Installation of a new customer relationship management system and enhanced booking functionality on the website (and indirectly influencing acquiring new customers through customer satisfaction).*

Small business focus

In the previous chapter, it was pointed out that large organizations may in some cases have some influence over the external environment or they can protect themselves against the dangers posed. This statement has validity for the macro level of external analysis but also for the competitive level, as discussed in this chapter.

Unlike large firms, which have some chance of shaping or influencing their competitive environment (at least to some degree), smaller organizations generally have little choice but to accept the competitive environment in which they operate. The smaller company has to focus on minimizing the harmful consequences (as best they can) and adapting to the circumstances.

To react to the competitive environment, it is necessary for the smaller business first to understand it. Consequently, analysis of some sort is of great importance to smaller businesses, just as it is to larger businesses, so that they are able to react quickly and effectively to competitive threats.

It is necessary for small business owners to explore the basis on which they are competing by fully understanding their CSFs.

> **For example:** *In a study by Avcikurt et al. (2011) of the perceptions of small hotel managers/ owners in the Aegean region of Turkey, the main CSFs were efficient use of the internet, service quality, financial performance and marketing. However, it was also found that there were some different perceptions of CSFs, depending on educational background and work experience.*

It is also vital for small businesses to understand who they are really competing against. This is not always as obvious as it may sound. Understanding who the *real* competitors are and the type of competitive threat they pose will require a focus on the particular arena in which competition takes place and may need the adaptation of relevant tools and techniques.

There are generally two possibilities with regard to identifying key competitors (Lasher, 1999). The most important competitors may be those companies that are identified as the:

- Leaders in the segments targeted
- Companies that are in some sense close

Close competitors might be competitors that are close either geographically or in a different sense.

> For example: *Close competitors might be competing for the same suppliers, pool of employees, distribution channels or destination accommodation or offering similar product features.*

Thus, when dealing with smaller companies, the scope of the analysis carried out needs to be considered carefully. Establishing the relevant scope of analysis may help identify who the key competitors might be. Furthermore, the tools and techniques of competitive analysis outlined in this chapter may need to be modified for the circumstances.

> For example: *In its analysis of competitors, a large international restaurant chain or hotel company might take a global view of competition and compare itself in the main to other international branded chains.*
>
> *However, a single family-owned restaurant or hotel may be more concerned with the local town in which it operates. Hence, the boundaries of the analysis are largely established as the boundaries of the town itself (though there needs to be some recognition that consumers are mobile and can switch to a different town). Therefore, the relevant competitors may include the international branded chains but may also include other smaller restaurant or hotel businesses operating in their vicinity.*

The family business (of which there are many in *THE*) may not have the competitive advantages of the branded chain elsewhere, but in their particular town they might be able to compete very effectively. This effective competition provided by the independent business might be on the basis of characteristics such as location, pricing or reputation for good service.

A *strategic group analysis* and *competitor profiling* could help in this situation, in that they may aid the hotelier or restaurateur in identifying the key competitors in the industry. The scope of the analysis, however, would not be on the industry regionally, nationally or even internationally but would be based on the town in which the hotel or restaurant is situated.

> For example (continuing the example above): *A strategic group analysis could be carried out on the basis of the two attributes of price and location for a single family-owned hotel business in the town, as shown in Figure 8.5. In Figure 8.5, four strategic groups are identified:*
>
> *A. Midscale branded chain hotels with moderate prices in poor to moderate locations*

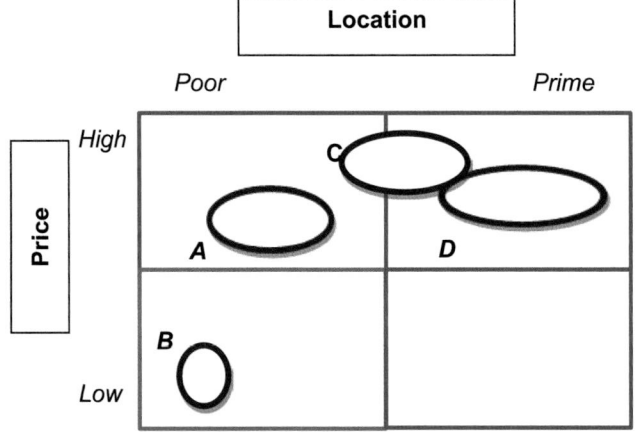

Figure 8.5 Strategic group analysis for hotels in a particular town

B. Budget branded chain hotels with low prices in poor locations

C. Upscale branded hotels with high prices in moderate locations

D. Independent hotels with moderate to high prices in prime locations

It is assumed that the independent family-run hotel in question is in Group D and is (like others in the group) well established, and this has enabled it to have a prime location, unlike the newer branded arrivals in town. The location enables the independent hotels or restaurants to charge higher prices than would otherwise be the case, enabling the independent hotel in question within this group to compete effectively in this particular town.

Following on from the strategic group analysis, a competitor profiling exercise could be carried out by the independent family-run hotel to gain a deeper understanding of the competitive positioning of each identified competitor.

In this way, some of the tools of analysis covered in this chapter are adapted to the relevant circumstances and scope of a smaller company. In different circumstances, this type of analysis might be adapted and applied to:

- A small event management company specializing in particular types of events, such as leadership development courses or firework displays
- A tour operator specializing in a particular market niche, such as selling holidays to a specific set of Greek islands that the company knows well

This chapter has also covered different ways in which smaller companies can group together in various ways to protect themselves against larger competitors. One such way is through *clustering* together with similar companies so that a city or area becomes known for certain specialisms. Smaller companies can also gain protection through collaboration and networking (touched upon in this chapter), which will be covered in greater detail in Chapter 11.

CHAPTER SUMMARY

Analysis of the competitive environment is intended to increase managers' understanding of the industry and markets in which their organization operates. The process begins with a clear identification of those industries and markets and their key characteristics. The process then allows managers to develop a detailed picture of the industry in which they operate, the markets for their products, the markets where they obtain their resources, their strategic grouping, markets that they may wish to enter in the future and industries with related competences.

This analysis will enable managers to identify:

- Critical success factors in their industry and markets
- Needs and opportunities for competence building and leveraging
- The potential for collaboration with suppliers, distributors, customers and competitors

REFERENCES AND WEBSITES

References

Aas, C., Ladkin, A. and Fletcher, J. (2005) 'Stakeholder collaboration and heritage management', *Annals of Tourism Research*, 32(1): 28–48.

Andersson, T. D. and Getz, D. (2009) 'Tourism as a mixed industry: Differences between private, public and not-for-profit festivals', *Tourism Management*, 30: 847–856.

Avcikurt, C., Altay, H. and Ilban, M. O. (2011) 'Critical success factors for small hotel businesses in Turkey: An exploratory study', *Cornell Hospitality Quarterly*, 52(2): 153–164.

Baker, M. J. and Cameron, E. (2008) 'Critical success factors in destination marketing', *Tourism and Hospitality Research*, 8(2): 79–97.

Barney, J. B. (1991) 'Firm resources and sustained competitive advantage', *Journal of Management*, 17(1): 99–120.

Barney, J. B., Ketchen, D. J. and Wright, M. (2011) 'The future of resource-based theory: Revitalization or decline?', *Journal of Management*, 37(5): 1299–1315.

Benson, A. M. and Henderson, S. (2011) 'A strategic analysis of volunteer tourism organizations', *The Service Industries Journal*, 31(3): 405–424.

Bensoussan, B. E. and Fleisher, C. S. (2013) *Analysis without Paralysis: 12 Tools to Make Better Strategic Decisions*, Upper Saddle River, NJ: Pearson Education.

Bernini, C. (2009) 'Convention industry and destination clusters: Evidence from Italy', *Tourism Management*, 30(6): 878–889.

Capone, F. (2015) *Tourist Clusters, Destinations and Competitiveness: Theoretical Issues and Empirical Evidences*, Abingdon, UK: Routledge.

Casanueva, C., Gallego, Á., Castro, I. and Sancho, M. (2014) 'Airline alliances: Mobilizing network resources', *Tourism Management*, 44: 88–98.

Cehan, A., Eva, M. and Iațu, C. (2021) 'A multilayer network approach to tourism collaboration', *Journal of Hospitality and Tourism Management*, 46: 316–326.

Chathoth, P. K. and Olsen, M. D. (2003) 'Strategic alliances: A hospitality industry perspective', *International Journal of Hospitality Management*, 22(4): 419–434.

Chingarande, A. and Saayman, A. (2018) 'Critical success factors for tourism-led growth', *International Journal of Tourism Research*, 20(6): 800–818.

Creaton, S. (2005) *Ryanair: How a Small Irish Airline Conquered Europe*, London: Aurum.

Daniel, D. R. (1961) 'Management information crisis', *Harvard Business Review*, 39(5): 111–120.

Dewally, M. and Gordon, R. (2022) 'Financial impact of partnerships on hospitality firms', *Annals of Tourism Research*, 95: 103435.

Dobbs, M. E. (2014) 'Guidelines for applying Porter's five forces framework: A set of industry analysis templates', *Competitiveness Review*, 24(1): 32–45.

Emery, P., Westerbeek, H., Schwarz, E. C., Liu, D. and Turner, P. (2016) *Managing Sport Facilities and Major Events*, Abingdon, UK: Routledge.

Evans, N. G. (2001) 'Collaborative strategy: An analysis of the changing world of international airline alliances', *Tourism Management*, 22: 229–243.

Fageda, X., Jiménez, J. L. and Perdiguero, J. (2011) 'Price rivalry in airline markets: A study of a successful strategy of a network carrier against a low-cost carrier', *Journal of Transport Geography*, 19(4): 658–669.

Fleisher, C. S. and Bensoussan, B. E. (2003) *Strategic and Competitive Analysis. Methods and Techniques for Analyzing Business Competition*, Hoboken, NJ: Prentice Hall.

Garrod, B. and Fyall, A. (2017) 'Collaborative destination marketing at the local level: Benefits bundling and the changing role of the local tourism association', *Current Issues in Tourism*, 20(7): 668–690.

Getz, D. (2004) 'Bidding on events: Identifying event selection criteria and critical success factors', *Journal of Convention and Exhibition Management*, 5(2): 1–24.

Getz, D. and Brown, G. (2006) 'Critical success factors for wine tourism regions: A demand analysis', *Tourism Management*, 27(1): 146–158.

Grundy, T. (2006) 'Rethinking and reinventing Michael Porter's five forces model', *Strategic Change*, 15(5): 213–229.

Gursoy, D., Chen, M. H. and Kim, H. J. (2005) 'The U.S. airlines relative positioning based on attributes of service quality', *Tourism Management*, 26(1): 57–67.

Haven-Tang, C., Jones, E. and Webb, C. (2007) 'Critical success factors for business tourism destinations: Exploiting Cardiff's national capital city status and shaping its business tourism offer', *Journal of Travel and Tourism Marketing*, 22(3–4): 109–120.

Hawkins, D. E. (2004) 'Sustainable tourism competitiveness clusters: Application to World Heritage Sites network development in Indonesia', *Asia Pacific Journal of Tourism Research*, 9(3): 293–307.

Hughes, M. and Carlsen, J. (2010) 'The business of cultural heritage tourism: critical success factors', *Journal of Heritage Tourism*, 5(1): 17–32.

Ivanova, M. and Ivanov, S. (2015) 'The nature of hotel chains: An integrative framework', *International Journal of Hospitality and Tourism Administration*, 16(2): 122–142.

Jackson, J. (2006) 'Developing regional tourism in China: The potential for activating business clusters in a socialist market economy', *Tourism Management*, 27(4): 695–706.

Jackson, J. and Murphy, P. (2006) 'Clusters in regional tourism: An Australian case', *Annals of Tourism Research*, 33(4): 1018–1035.

Jones, M. F., Singh, N. and Hsiung, Y. (2015) 'Determining the critical success factors of the wine tourism region of Napa from a supply perspective', *International Journal of Tourism Research*, 17(3): 261–271.

Karniouchina, E. V., Carson, S. J., Short, J. C. and Ketchen, D. J., Jr. (2013) 'Extending the firm vs. industry debate: Does industry life cycle stage matter?', *Strategic Management Journal*, 34(8): 1010–1018.

Kay, J. (1995) *Foundations of Corporate Success*, Oxford: Oxford University Press.

Kim, S. S. and Chon, K. (2009) 'An economic impact analysis of the Korean exhibition industry', *International Journal of Tourism Research*, 11(3): 311–318.

Kim, S. S., Chon, K. and Chung, K. Y. (2003) 'Convention industry in South Korea: An economic impact analysis', *Tourism Management*, 24(5): 533–541.

Kim, W. C. (2005) 'Blue ocean strategy: From theory to practice', *California Management Review*, 47(3): 105–121.

Lade, C. and Jackson, J. (2004) 'Key success factors in regional festivals: Some Australian experiences', *Event Management*, 9(1–2): 1–2.

Lasher, W. R. (1999) *Strategic Thinking for Smaller Businesses and Divisions*, Oxford, UK: Blackwell.

Lee, S. K. and Jang, S. S. (2012) 'Re-examining the overcapacity of the U.S. lodging industry', *International Journal of Hospitality Management*, 31(4): 1050–1058.

Lee, Y. J. A., Jang, S. and Kim, J. (2020) 'Tourism clusters and peer-to-peer accommodation', *Annals of Tourism Research*, 83: 102960.

Long, P. (2000) 'After the event: Perspectives on organizational partnerships in the management of a themed festival year', *Event Management*, 6(1): 45–59.

Marais, M., du Plessis, E. and Saayman, M. (2017) 'A review on critical success factors in tourism', *Journal of Hospitality and Tourism Management*, 31: 1–12.

McGahan, A. M. and Porter, M. E. (1997) 'How much does industry matter, really?', *Strategic Management Journal*, 18: 15–30.

Moreno-Izquierdo, L., Ramón-Rodríguez, A. B. and Perles-Ribes, J. F. (2016) 'Pricing strategies of the European low-cost carriers explained using Porter's five forces model', *Tourism Economics*, 22(2): 293–310.

Nannelli, M., Buhalis, D., Franch, M. and Lucia, M. D. (2019) 'The impact of the new short-term rental players', *e-Review of Tourism Research*, 17(3). https://ertr-ojs-tamu.tdl.org/ertr/index.php/ertr/article/view/529

Novelli, M., Schmitz, B. and Spencer, T. (2006) 'Networks, clusters and innovation in tourism: A UK experience', *Tourism Management*, 27(6): 1141–1152.

Padilla-Meléndez, A. and Garrido-Moreno, A. (2014) 'Customer relationship management in hotels: Examining critical success factors', *Current Issues in Tourism*, 17(5): 387–396.

Pansiri, J. (2008) 'The effects of characteristics of partners on strategic alliance performance in the SME dominated travel sector', *Tourism Management*, 29(1): 101–115.

Peiró-Signes, A., Segarra-Oña, M. D. V., Miret-Pastor, L. and Verma, R. (2015) 'The effect of tourism clusters on US hotel performance', *Cornell Hospitality Quarterly*, 56(2): 155–167.

Peng, I. C. and Lu, H. A. (2022) 'Competition effects among global airline alliances for selected Asian airports', *Journal of Air Transport Management*, 101: 102193.

Porter, M. E. (1980) *Competitive Strategy: Techniques for Analyzing Industries and Competitors*, New York: Free Press.

Porter, M. E. (1985) *Competitive Advantage*, New York: Free Press.

Porter, M. E. (1998) 'Clusters and the new economics of competition', *Harvard Business Review*, 76(6): 77–90.

Porter, M. E., Bernard, M., Chaturvedi, R. S., Hill, A., Maddox, C. and Schrimpf, M. (2012) 'Tennessee music cluster: Microeconomics of competitiveness', Harvard Business School Presentation, May 2012.

Porter, M. E. and Heppelmann, J. E. (2014) 'How smart, connected products are transforming competition', *Harvard Business Review*, 92(11): 64–88.

Ramayah, T., Lee, J. W. C. and In, J. B. C. (2011) 'Network collaboration and performance in the tourism sector', *Service Business*, 5(4): 411–428.

Richter, U. and Tveteras, S. (2012) 'The case of Inkaterra: Pioneering ecotourism in Peru', in P. Sloan, C. Simons-Kaufmann and W. Legrand (Eds), *Sustainable Hospitality and Tourism as Motors for Development*, Abingdon, UK: Routledge, 62–74.

Rockart, J. F. (1979) 'Chief executives define their own data needs', *Harvard Business Review*, 57(2): 81–93.

Roper, A. and Hodari, D. (2015) 'Strategy tools: Contextual factors impacting use and usefulness', *Tourism Management*, 51: 1–12.

Rumelt, R. P. (1991) 'How much does industry matter?', *Strategic Management Journal*, 12(3): 167–185.

Sampler, J. L. (1998) 'Redefining industry structure for the information age', *Strategic Management Journal*, 19(4): 343–355.

Sheng, L. (2011) 'Foreign investors versus local businesses: An urban economics model for tourist cities', *International Journal of Tourism Research*, 13(1): 32–40.

Short, J. C., Ketchen, D. J., Palmer, T. B. and Hult, G. T. M. (2007) 'Firm, strategic group, and industry influences on performance', *Strategic Management Journal*, 28(2): 147–167.

Sloan, P., Legrand, W. and Simons-Kaufmann, C. (2013) 'Social entrepreneurship and cultural tourism in developing economies', in M. Smith and G. Richards (Eds), *Routledge Handbook of Cultural Tourism*, Abingdon, UK: Routledge, ch. 30.

Söllner, A. and Rese, M. (2001) 'Market segmentation and the structure of competition: Applicability of the strategic group concept for an improved market segmentation on industrial markets', *Journal of Business Research*, 51(1): 25–36.

Stokes, R. (2006) 'Network-based strategy making for events tourism', *European Journal of Marketing*, 40(5/6): 682–695.

Szalavetz, A. (2022) 'The digitalisation of manufacturing and blurring industry boundaries', *CIRP Journal of Manufacturing Science and Technology*, 37: 332–343.

Tavitiyaman, P., Qu, H. and. Zhang, H. Q. (2011) 'The impact of industry force factors on resource competitive strategies and hotel performance', *International Journal of Hospitality Management*, 30(3): 648–657.

Tsai, H. and Gu, Z. (2012) 'Optimizing room capacity and profitability for Hong Kong hotels', *Journal of Travel and Tourism Marketing*, 29(1): 57–68.

Tsang, S. S. and Chen, Y. F. (2013) 'Facilitating benchmarking with strategic grouping and data envelopment analysis: The case of international tourist hotels in Taiwan', *Asia Pacific Journal of Tourism Research*, 18(5): 518–533.

Varelas, S. and Georgopoulos, N. (2017) Competition as a critical factor of the strategic planning of hotel businesses', *Strategic Management Quarterly*, 5(1–2): 16–21.

Wang, C. and Xu, H. (2011) 'Government intervention in investment by Chinese listed companies that have diversified into tourism', *Tourism Management*, 32(6): 1371–1380.

Wang, S. and Hung, K. (2015) 'Customer perceptions of critical success factors for guest houses', *International Journal of Hospitality Management*, 48: 92–101.

Wang, Y. and Fesenmaier, D. R. (2007) 'Collaborative destination marketing: A case study of Elkhart County, Indiana', *Tourism Management*, 28(3): 863–875.

Wang, Y., Hutchinson, J., Okumus, F. and Naipaul, S. (2012) 'Collaborative marketing in a regional destination: Evidence from Central Florida', *International Journal of Tourism Research*, 15(3): 285–297.

Whittington, R., Regnér, P., Angwin, D., Johnson, G. and Scholes, K. (2020) *Exploring Strategy*, 12th ed., Harlow, UK: Pearson.

Zapata, M. J. and Hall, C. M. (2012) 'Public–private collaboration in the tourism sector: Balancing legitimacy and effectiveness in local tourism partnerships: The Spanish case', *Journal of Policy Research in Tourism, Leisure and Events*, 4(1): 61–83.

Zheng, T. and Gu, Z. (2011) 'Overcapacity in Shanghai's high-end hotel sector: Analysis based on an inventory mode', *Journal of Convention and Event Tourism*, 12(4): 253–270.

Zou, L. and Chen, X. (2017) 'The effect of code-sharing alliances on airline profitability', *Journal of Air Transport Management*, 58: 50–57.

Part 3

Websites

www.discoverhongkong.com
www.inkaterra.com
www.lvcva.com
www.whc.unesco.org
www.whitbread.co.uk
www.wmf.org
www.wttc.org
www.wyndhamhotels.com

Chapter **9**

SWOT analysis for tourism, hospitality and event organizations

Introduction and chapter overview

The previous chapters in Part 2 have covered the internal analysis of organizations (Chapters 3–6) and the external environment that organizations face (Chapters 7 and 8).

It is important to bring all of the analytical work together in one place to provide a summary and a firm foundation for the next stage – formulating strategy. This work provides an opportunity to summarize the previous analysis in the form of a SWOT.

SWOT analysis is an acronym for *S*trengths, *W*eaknesses, *O*pportunities and *T*hreats. The analysis has become a major analytical tool and is firmly established in the literature. Although it is the most widely used technique for summarizing the results of the various types of analysis described in the previous chapters, it nevertheless can be implemented in various ways. Consequently, different approaches are suggested in the many texts that cover this analytical technique, but here a simple, structured and logical approach is suggested.

The chapter covers the ways in which SWOT has been applied to *THE* contexts, before considering the general principles of SWOT analysis. Finally, the chapter considers how the technique should be implemented.

LEARNING OBJECTIVES

After studying this chapter, you should be able to:

● Recognise the way in which SWOT has been applied in various *THE* contexts

DOI: 10.4324/9781003318613-12

- Explain what is meant by SWOT analysis
- Understand the coherent and logical sequence that exists between the SWOT presentation and detailed internal and external analyses
- Describe how a SWOT should be constructed
- Consider the way in which relevant points can be presented in a SWOT
- Apply the SWOT analysis principles appropriately in *THE* settings
- Understand the relationship between the SWOT analysis and strategic formulation

9.1 SWOT analysis in *THE* contexts

SWOT analysis has been widely applied in *THE* contexts. It has been applied not only to organizations operating in the sectors of *THE* but also to destinations and individual events.

> For example: *Karadakis et al. (2010) produced a SWOT in which the mega sporting event of the Athens Olympics was analyzed, and Bardolet and Sheldon (2008) produced a SWOT comparing tourism in the Balearic Islands with Hawaii and found that there are many common factors. It has also been applied at the micro level (such as an individual hotel or a particular event) and at the macro level (covering, say, an entire country or region or a group of hotels). Mondal and Haque (2017), for instance, utilized SWOT analysis in assessing strategies to develop sustainable tourism in Bangladesh.*
>
> *In applying SWOT analysis to festival managers, Carlsen and Andersson (2011) investigated how a strategic approach can be adopted in the public, private and not-for-profit sectors. The findings indicated significant differences between the three ownership types. Private and nonprofit festivals are more strategic in responding to financial opportunities, threats and weaknesses, and public festivals are more dependent on a single stakeholder and revenue source. Other significant differences exist in terms of stakeholder management and sponsorship strategies.*

In applying SWOT analysis, it is argued below that strengths and weaknesses are normally factors that are *internal* to the organization, destination, etc., and can therefore be controlled by managers, whereas opportunities and threats are factors that are *external* to the organization and consequently are beyond mangers' control.

However, in applying SWOT in *THE* settings, it is very important to recognize that *THE* organizations, destinations, festivals and events rely very heavily on the resources that are available. *THE* often relies very heavily on resources that are natural or that cannot be easily replicated or moved elsewhere. Although such resources are clearly not controlled by individual managers, they represent key factors that are given and cannot be altered. Thus, they are underlying strengths (or possibly weaknesses). As such, they can be viewed as internal to the analysis rather than external because they are integral to success or failure.

> For example: *In Chapter 2, resource immobility was discussed. The Mediterranean climate of southern Spain cannot be replicated in Northern Europe, and the grandeur of the Grand Canyon cannot be moved. Similarly, the success of the annual Salzburg Festival of classical music (which was first held in the Austrian city in 1877) to some degree depends on the fact that the famous composer Wolfgang Amadeus Mozart was born there. Conversely, the unpredictable summer climate of Northern Europe might be viewed as a weakness in trying to attract international summer visitors.*

Thus, many SWOTs applied in *THE* settings will cite climatic, geographical or social factors as strengths or weaknesses. These are resources that are relied on and consequently (although external to the organization) are integral to success, so it is argued that it is legitimate to consider them as strengths or weaknesses, rather than opportunities or threats.

> For example: *In their comparison of the Balearic and Hawaiian archipelagos, Bardolet and Sheldon (2008) cited 'the attractive climate' as a strength common to both destinations. It is clear that the climate is a key part of the attraction in both cases and that this is an underlying resource on which the destinations rely. However, it is also the case that managers in the two cases do not control the climate, but they do rely on the nature of the climatic resources as an underlying strength that supports THE and the associated businesses involved in the two archipelagos.*

The Short Case Illustration below demonstrates the use of the SWOT technique in relation to the destination of Macau.

9.1 SHORT CASE ILLUSTRATION

SWOT analysis applied to Macau

Macau, which lies on the western side of the Pearl River Delta, is one of the two special administrative regions of the People's Republic of China, the other being Hong Kong. The territory's economy is heavily dependent on gambling and tourism but also includes manufacturing.

The sustainability of tourism development has become a leading issue in Macao in recent years. Though the industry has grown dramatically over the last decade, this issue has been gaining importance in line with the growing contribution the industry makes to the territory's economy as a whole. With a population of about 650,000 and a land area of only 30.5 km², visitor arrivals have grown enormously, and the increasing significance of the tourism industry has given rise to discussions regarding social and economic consequences.

Macao is a city blending Eastern and Western cultures with a mixture of Euro-Asian architecture that attracts large numbers of international tourists. Tourism employs approximately a third of the territory's workforce and generates about 40% of the territory's gross domestic product.

Macao is renowned for its gaming activity (which is the world's largest), but the tourism industry also comprises hotel and catering businesses, recreational activities and MICE industry. MICE (meetings, incentives, conventions and exhibitions) is a commonly used term that broadly covers the arrangement of symposiums, seminars, exhibitions, expositions, trade fairs, incentive events and cultural and sporting events.

As part of an extensive analysis, the *Macao Tourism Industry Development Master Plan* (Macao, 2017) produced a SWOT as shown in Table 9.1.

Table 9.1 SWOT analysis applied to tourism in Macao

Strengths	Weaknesses
• Unique location in Pearl River Delta	Limited land and natural resources
• Unique blend of Chinese and Western culture with 500 years of cultural exchange	Limited labor force

Strengths	Weaknesses
• High reputation as gaming destination, with integrated resorts	Limited carrying capacity and tourism-supporting infrastructure
• Historic Centre of Macao – a UNESCO World Heritage site	Uneven product development, money flows overreliant on casino and gaming sector, lack of tourism product diversification
• Famous festivals and events destination, such as Macao Grand Prix (celebrating over half a century)	Limited MICE function spaces
	Relatively low capacity of airport, limited public ground transportation options

Opportunities	Threats
• Develop new reclamation areas and other potential tourism products and projects	Tourism competition from nearby regions such as Hong Kong, Zhuhai, Guangzhou and Shenzhen
• A powerful attraction to large potential Asian tourism markets	Gaming industry competition from Singapore, Malaysia, Philippines, Korea and Cambodia
• Future advantage from the development of the Guangdong–Hong Kong–Macao Greater Bay Area urban cluster	Further controls on border crossing and money flows from China
• Unique cultural background, great potential to develop cultural and heritage attractions related to arts, maritime, history, etc.	Future labor force may be insufficient to support tourism industry
• Leverage gaming incomes to support development of other potential tourism products and projects	Residents discontent with problems brought about by unmanaged tourism growth

Source: Adapted from Macao (2017); Pao (2004)

Questions

1. Explain the underlying logic behind presenting a *SWOT* in this case.

2. From a managerial perspective, what is the fundamental difference between *strengths* and *weaknesses*, on the one hand, and *opportunities* and *threats*, on the other?

9.2 SWOT – general principles

The strengths and weaknesses are based on the internal analysis of an organization (covered in Chapters 3–6), and the opportunities and threats are based on the analysis of the environment that is external to the organization (covered in Chapters 7 and 8).

The key distinguishing characteristic between the strengths and weaknesses, on the one hand, and the opportunities and threats, on the other, is the degree of *control* that managers may have.

An important point to note is that in many *THE* contexts (as noted in the previous section), the normal principles may be varied slightly. Underlying resources on which the organization, destination, festival, event, etc., rely (but that are clearly beyond the control of managers) may be considered as strengths or weaknesses. This is because they are given factors that remain in place largely unaltered.

Managers can exert control with the internal strengths and weaknesses, whereas in certain circumstances, though managers may have some influence with regard to opportunities and threats, they will not be able to control such factors.

> **For example:** *A strong balance sheet (a strength) is a result of managerial decisions; if the organization is seen as being overstaffed (a weakness), managers can address the issue through reducing staff numbers. However, changing government policies, product changes by competitors or a war breaking out (all of which might produce opportunities or threats to an individual organization, depending on the circumstances) are beyond the control of managers in an individual organization.*

KEY CONCEPT

SWOT

SWOT is the key technique for presenting the results of strategic analysis. It provides a platform on which to formulate the strategy for the future. The strengths and weaknesses should normally be based on the internal analysis of the organization, whereas the opportunities and threats should be based on an analysis of the organization's external environment.

An important differentiator between the *internal* and *external* environments is *control*. Whereas managers can control the internal environment through the decisions they make, they cannot control the external environment.

Although it is very common in practice to begin the process of formulating strategy by asking participants in a rather informal way to draw up a SWOT for their organization, such a process represents a limited use of the technique. It is, however, useful for getting the participants to become quickly and fully engaged in the process of strategy formulation (Finlay, 2000). It can also help identify the wide range of factors that might warrant more detailed investigation.

Importantly, though, the final SWOT presented should be based on a thorough, wide-ranging, detailed audit and assessment of an organization and its environment (Haberberg and Rieple, 2008). In this way, points presented are evidence based and consequently can be fully justified. Thus, the SWOT should be seen primarily as representing the end point of the analytical stage (rather than the starting point) in which findings can be presented in a clear, concise manner but that nevertheless are grounded in a robust framework of analysis.

It is useful to summarize what the SWOT is and is not:

- SWOT represents a *position statement* stating where the organization is now in relation to its environment.
- SWOT should clearly follow from a robust analysis of the internal and external environments.
- Strengths and weaknesses are normally based on the internal analysis of the organization's environment over which managers have control.

- Opportunities and threats are normally based on the external analysis of the environment facing the organization over which managers (normally) have no control.
- Strengths and opportunities represent factors that help the organization achieve its objectives.
- Weaknesses and threats are factors that may prevent the organization from achieving its objectives.
- SWOT is not the strategy in itself and should not involve making statements about what should be done in the future.
- SWOT provides a firm platform for planning for the future of the organization; that is, *formulating* the strategy, which is the next stage in the strategic process.

9.3 SWOT implementation

The SWOT is often presented as a table. Figure 9.1 shows a SWOT and its underlying logic. The task of managers with regard to each element can be summarized as follows:

- **Strengths** – Build or protect strengths so that they continue to be strengths.
- **Weaknesses** – Address weaknesses so that they become strengths in the future or are eliminated.
- **Opportunities** – Position the organization so that it is able to selectively take advantage of the opportunities available.
- **Threats** – Position the organization so that the threats are understood and the organization is protected from their impacts.

The SWOT should have a *strategic* focus in that it concentrates on those factors that:

- Have a major impact on past performance
- Have a major impact on future performance
- Distinguish the organization from its competitors

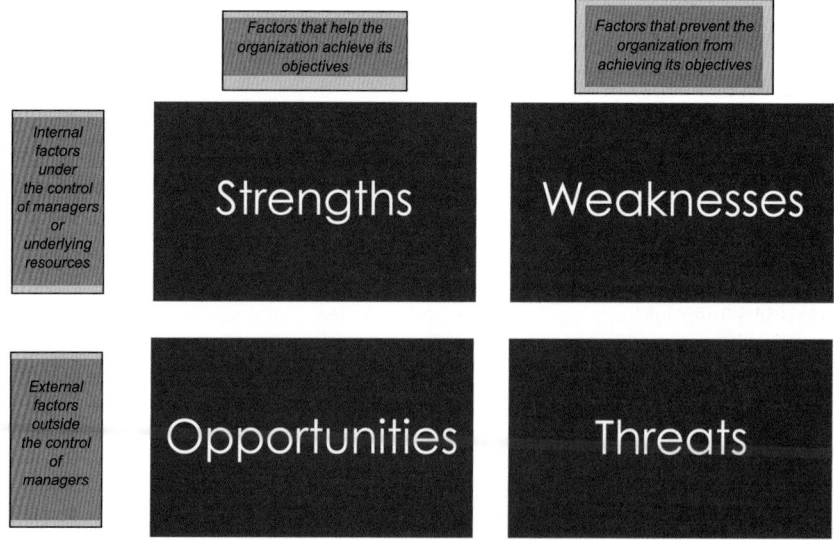

Figure 9.1 The logic of SWOT analysis

In presenting the SWOT table, a number of rules should be followed:

- *Avoid detail:* Too much detail should be avoided in presenting the SWOT, so that the key points can be clearly seen. Keep each point short and to the point so that an overview can quickly be gained. The detailed justifications for the points presented in the table should be presented separately.
- *Have a strategic focus*: The SWOT is a tool of strategic management and therefore the points presented in the SWOT must be strategic in nature rather than operational or tactical.
- *Points are often relative rather than absolute:* Many of the points presented in the SWOT may be relative rather than absolute and consequently a matter of some judgment. Thus, it is difficult to say at exactly at what level a high level of financial *gearing* becomes a weakness or a share of a particular market, load factors, occupancy levels or ticket sales become strengths.
- *Hard facts and softer factors are both important*: The SWOT should not concentrate solely on 'hard' facts (such as financial measures or market growth statistics) that can be measured or proven. Softer factors such as organizational culture or the leadership skills exhibited by managers may be more difficult to measure but are nevertheless important for organizational performance.
- *Strategic points should be prioritized and combined*: The most important points should be shown first, and points that are not key or strategic in nature should be excluded. In some cases, it may be necessary to combine points to make one large overarching point. For instance, if a SWOT is partly based on a financial analysis that indicates a strong financial position, the SWOT should not have individual points on high level of profitability, low gearing, adequate liquidity, etc., because this would confuse the presentation. The point presented in the SWOT should be that the organization has a strong financial position. The justification for making such a point would be provided by the assessments relating to profitability, gearing liquidity and so on.
- *Clear presentation:* The presentation should be specific, avoiding blandness but being realistic in its assessment.

Two common errors in producing a SWOT are outlined below.

DEFINITION/QUOTATION

Common errors with SWOT analysis

In his analysis of the problems of presenting a valid SWOT, Richard Lynch (2021:286–287) recognized two common errors:

> Probably the biggest mistake that is commonly made in *SWOT* analyses is to assume the analysis is bound to be 'correct' because it contains every conceivable issue and is truly comprehensive. This is not the case, it . . . merely demonstrates a paucity of real thought and a lack of strategic judgement about what is really important for that organization.

> Another common error is to provide a long list of points, but little logic, argument and evidence. A short list with each point well-argued is more likely to be convincing.

To keep the SWOT focused, it is suggested that a maximum of six points be presented under each of the SWOT headings. However, it might be the case that in some circumstances the overriding importance of certain points means that far fewer than six points are presented.

If, however, a greater number of points are presented, whether all of the points mentioned are truly strategic or whether some of the points represent different aspects of the same issue and therefore could be combined must be questioned.

THINK POINTS

- Explain the underlying logic that supports SWOT analysis.
- Describe the major rules that should be followed when presenting a SWOT.
- Describe some of the common errors that are made when presenting a SWOT.
- Compare and contrast examples of how SWOT has been applied in relevant *THE* contexts.

DEFINITION/QUOTATION

SWOT analysis compared to elephants

John Argenti (2018), one of the early writers on strategy, in summarizing the principles of a SWOT (originally writing in the late 1960s), famously compared the points in a SWOT to elephants. You are looking for 'strategic elephants' in that, as with elephants, the points of a SWOT are:

- A rare species
- Large but sometimes difficult to spot
- Difficult to turn around

In Table 9.2, a number of issues are presented for possible inclusion in a SWOT presentation. It should be noted that this list is indicative because the issues will vary enormously depending upon the individual circumstances.

Table 9.2 Some possible factors in a SWOT analysis

Internal	
Strengths	**Weaknesses**
• Market dominance	Market share weakness
• Core strengths	Few core strengths and low on key skills
• Economies of scale and scope	Equipment with higher costs than competition
• Low-cost position	Weak finances and poor cash flow
• Leadership and management skills	Management skills and leadership lacking
• Financial and cash resources	Poor organizational structure
• Operational ability and age of equipment	Low quality and reputation

Internal	
Strengths	**Weaknesses**
• Innovation processes and results	Products not differentiated
• Organizational structure	Dependent on few products
• Reputation	Products in mature or declining PLC stages
• Differentiated products	Low market share
• Good balance of products	
• Product or service quality	
External	
Opportunities	**Threats**
• New markets and segments	New market entrants
• New products	Increased competition
• Diversification opportunities	Pressure from customers and/or suppliers
• Market growth	Substitutes
• Competitor weaknesses	Low market growth
• Strategic space	Economic cycle downturn
• Demographic and social change	Technological threat
• Change in political and economic environment	Change in political or economic environment
• New takeover or partnership opportunities	Demographic change
• Economic upturn	New international barriers to trade
• International growth	Environmental impacts of activities
	New destinations or events

Source: Adapted from Lynch (2021)

Small business focus

Small businesses in *THE* sectors have significant hurdles to overcome in successfully competing with larger businesses, but they may also have some advantages. The SWOT must represent a realistic appraisal for SMEs that honestly represents the true position relative to the larger organizations, destinations, events, etc., that are engaged in the competitive arena.

As Palmer (2014) pointed out, small businesses are often associated with a bundle of positive attributes such as friendliness, flexibility, originality and individuality. Conversely, big businesses may be associated with negative connotations such as being impersonal, inflexible, standardized and lacking a 'human dimension'.

However, there are a number of potential factors that may inhibit small business performance that need to recognized and their impact appraised. Morrison and Teixeira (2004), for example, listed a number of such potential obstacles, which are shown in Table 9.3.

Table **9.3** Obstacles to small firm business performance in tourism

Obstacle focus	Obstacle description
Internal: owner manager	• Lack of ambition, vision
	• Lack of inclination to increase production or operations
	• Constrained resources to address gaps in managerial competences
	• Perceptions that enterprise development would negatively impact product/service quality
	• Anti-business 'hobbyist' approach to running the business
	• Protecting quality of lifestyle
Internal: business	• Multi-skilling in every category of staff necessary
	• Limited resources and capacity available to narrow skill gaps
	• Physical constraints curtail expansion
External	• Weak power position within the industry sector and markets as an individual unit
	• High dependency on externalities (external costs or benefits beyond the control of the organization)

Source: Adapted from Morrison and Teixeira (2004)

In constructing a SWOT for a smaller *THE* organization, event or destination, it might be useful to compile a simple checklist that is more focused on individual characteristics of the owner/manager than is likely in larger businesses. However, as with all SWOTs, the SWOT should be based on robust analysis of all of the relevant factors taking into account both qualitative and quantitative data as appropriate.

The following checklist might be useful in such circumstances. The questions should be asked of the organization but also of the leader/manager, because in many smaller businesses they have a pivotal role.

- *Strengths* – concerned with the attributes of the owner/manager and the business that could help the business achieve its objectives:
  - What do you do well?
  - What are your unique skills and competences?
  - What expert or specialized knowledge do you possess?
  - What experience do you have?
  - What do you do better than your competitors?
  - What are your most profitable areas of business?

- *Weaknesses* – concerned with the lack of attributes of the owner/manager and the business that may hinder the business in achieving its objectives.
  - In what areas do you need to improve?
  - What resources do you lack?
  - What parts of your business are not very profitable?
  - Where do you need further education, training and/or experience?
  - What costs you time and/or money?

- *Opportunities* – concerned with the external opportunities that may help you achieve your objectives.
  - In what ways could you do more for your existing customers or clients?
  - How can you use technology to enhance your business?
  - Are there new target audiences you have the potential to reach?
  - Are there related products and services that provide an opportunity for your business?

- *Threats* – concerned with the external threats that may hinder you in achieving your objectives.
  - What is the balance of power between your organization and suppliers and customers?
  - What are the strengths of your biggest competitors?
  - What are your competitors doing that you are not?
  - What is happening in the economy?
  - What is happening in the industry and markets you are involved with?

CHAPTER SUMMARY

SWOT is a tool that is widely used and understood by students and managers. It should represent a solid foundation for moving on to strategic formulation, but care has to be taken in implementing the SWOT to ensure that it is not bland and is fully supported by the evidence that is available. However, the SWOT analysis should not be viewed as the start of the analysis. Instead, to arrive at a proper SWOT appraisal, other analyses need to be carried out first.

This is the approach taken in this chapter, with the SWOT representing the culmination of the internal and external analyses described in Chapters 3 to 8. A rigorous analysis of the current situation provides a solid and defensible platform from which to move toward the formulation of a strategy that focuses on the future position.

SWOT analysis has been widely applied in *THE* settings, with examples cited in the references. These examples span all parts of *THE* and range from 'micro' SWOT analyses of individual hotels or one-off events through the application to individual organizations and the adaptation of the technique to areas, regions and, in some instances, entire countries.

REFERENCES

References

Argenti, J. (2018) *Corporate Planning: A Practical Guide*, Abingdon, UK: Routledge.

Bardolet, E. and Sheldon, P. J. (2008) 'Tourism in archipelagos: Hawaii and the Balearics,' *Annals of Tourism Research*, 35(4): 900–923.

Carlsen, J. and Andersson, T. D. (2011) 'Strategic SWOT analysis of public, private and not-for-profit festival organisations', *International Journal of Event and Festival Management*, 2(1): 83–97.

Finlay, P. (2000) *Strategic Management: An Introduction to Business and Corporate Strategy*, Harlow, UK: Pearson Education.

Karadakis, K., Kaplanidou, K. and Karlis, G. (2010) 'Event leveraging of mega sport events: A SWOT analysis approach,' *International Journal of Event and Festival Management*, 1(3): 170–185.

Lynch, R. (2021) *Strategic Management*, 9th ed., Harlow, UK: Pearson Education.

Macao. (2017) *Macao Tourism Industry Development Master Plan*, Macao: Directorate of Tourism Services, macaotourism.gov.mo

Mondal, M. and Haque, S. (2017) 'SWOT analysis and strategies to develop sustainable tourism in Bangladesh', *UTMS Journal of Economics*, 8(2): 159–167.

Morrison, A. and Teixeira, R. (2004) 'Small business performance: A tourism sector focus', *Journal of Small Business and Enterprise Development*, 11(2): 166–173.

Palmer, A. (2014) *Principles of Services Marketing*, 7th ed., Maidenhead, UK: McGraw-Hill.

Pao, J. W. (2004) *Recent Developments and Prospects of Macao's Tourism Industry*, Macau: Monetary Authority of Macao.

Part 3

Part 4

Strategic options

Strategic options for tourism, hospitality and events contexts

Strategic options overview

The previous three parts of this book have been concerned with an introduction to the subject matter and establishing the *THE* context, followed by chapters that studied strategic analysis both internally and externally. This culminated in the bringing together of available information (from the analyses) in the form of a SWOT.

The analysis culminating in the SWOT establishes the current position based on a rigorous examination of the information and data available. This is a necessary prerequisite for moving on to consider the strategic options available to *THE* organizations, for future development and making choices between these options.

In Part 4 we turn toward the future by identifying the strategic options *THE* organizations have available to them and making choices between them to develop their strategies for future development. In Part 4 we are concerned with making the decisions about an organization's future and the way in which it needs to respond to the many pressures and influences identified in the analysis studied in the previous chapters.

Study progress

Part 1	Part 2	Part 3	Part 4				Part 5
Strategy and the tourism, hospitality and events contexts	Analyzing the internal environment	Analyzing the external environment and SWOT	Strategic options				Strategy in action
Chapters 1 and 2	Chapters 3, 4, 5 and 6	Chapters 7, 8 and 9	Chapter 10 Competitive strategy for *THE* organizations	Chapter 11 Strategic direction for *THE* organizations	Chapter 12 Strategic methods of development for *THE* organizations	Chapter 13 Strategic evaluation and selection for *THE* organizations	Chapters 14, 15, 16 and 17

Formulating, evaluating and selecting options

Specifically, Part 4 is concerned with making choices between the strategic options that are identified and can be considered in three stages:

1. *Formulating* options for future development (Chapters 10, 11 and 12)
2. *Evaluating* between available options (Chapter 13)
3. *Choosing* which options are likely to lead to strategic success (Chapter 13)

Many *THE* organizations are complex in terms of the scope and scale of their operations and in the way they are managed. The nature of the industry is such that many such organizations may:

- Be operating internationally
- Comprise many different departments or divisions
- Have operations that are geographically scattered
- Have a large, centralized head office or a small head office with dispersed authority

Levels of strategy

As a result of this complexity, it is common to distinguish between various levels of strategic selection, although textbooks often vary in their definition and scope of these levels. Three levels of organizational strategy are discernible:

- Corporate level
- Business level
- Operational level

The main focus of this text is on the business and operational levels.

However, it should be noted at the outset that the boundaries between the levels are often unclear, particularly in smaller organizations where frequently the levels will effectively merge.

Figure P4.1 shows the three levels of strategy as a hierarchy.

Corporate-level strategy is concerned with the overall purpose and scope of an organization.

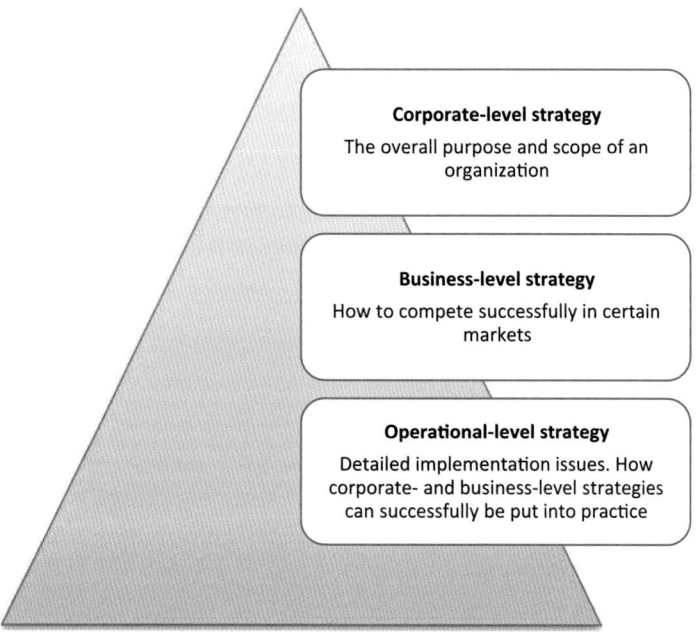

Figure P4.1 The levels of strategy

This level of strategy might include the broad determination of which business areas or geographical areas the organization might want to be involved with. Clearly, this area of strategy development is thus closely involved with the organization's mission and its manifestation in the form of a mission statement. This level of strategy is usually determined by the most senior levels of the organization; that is, the board of directors and the CEO.

For example: *Changing the focus of a business from concentrating on one sector such as manufacturing to a different sector such as hospitality may be such an issue.*

At this level of strategy, organizations are also concerned with so-called *corporate governance* issues that were considered in Chapter 2. Corporate governance is concerned with establishing and monitoring the rules, practices and processes by which a firm is controlled.

For example: *Determining the size and composition of the board of directors may be such an issue.*

Though transformational changes (such as those outlined above) occur from time to time, they tend to be far less common than the business-level decisions that organizations continually need to make. The focus of this part of the text is thus primarily at the business level of strategy.

Business-level strategy is concerned with how to compete successfully in certain markets.

The focus at this level is not normally on the entire organization (as in corporate-level strategy), except in the case of smaller organizations. Instead, this level of strategy usually focuses on breaking the entire organization down into its constituent parts; that is, its *strategic business units* (SBUs). This level of strategy will also be the concern of the board of directors and the CEO, but it will also usually involve other managers who are responsible for the individual SBUs. The concerns at this level of strategy include:

● How can *advantage* over competitors be achieved?
● Which *products or services* should be developed and in which markets should they be sold?
● What *methods* can be used to achieve competitive advantage and to develop products and services?

These three concerns of business-level strategy are addressed by *strategic formulation* of strategies by considering the

● Basis on which competition takes place – *Competitive Strategy*
● Direction which development should take place – *Strategic Direction*
● Methods by which development should be achieved – *Strategic Methods*

These three aspects of strategic formulation will be covered in subsequent chapters. Competitive strategy is considered in Chapter 10, strategic direction in Chapter 11 and strategic methods in Chapter 12.

Figure P4.2 shows the elements that need to be considered in strategic formulation and how they all form part of the business strategy.

Once strategic options for the future have been formulated (identified), it is necessary for them to be evaluated, and the most appropriate strategies should be selected. The evaluation and selection of strategies are considered in Chapter 13.

Operational-level strategy is concerned with the more detailed implementation issues relating to how the proposed corporate- and business-level strategies can successfully be put into practice.

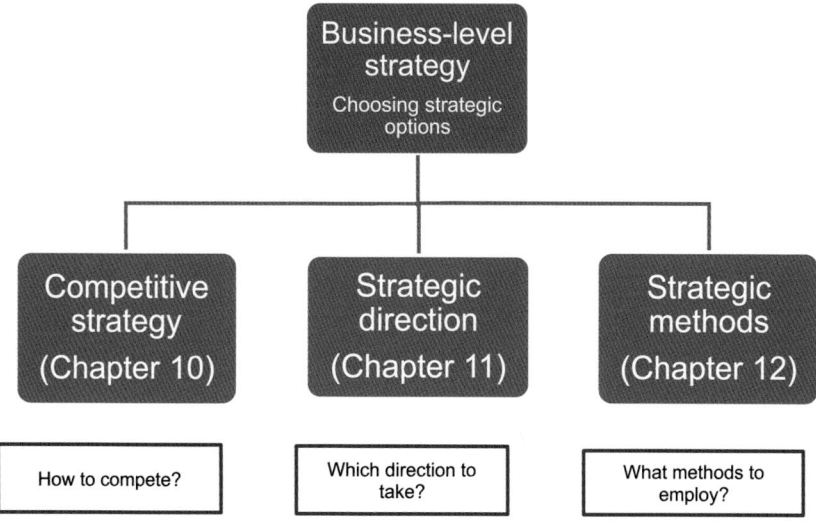

Figure P4.2 The three components of business-level strategy formulation

The concern here is how the changes arising from the adoption of corporate- and business-level strategies can be managed effectively and on the detailed decisions that have to be made in each area of the organization to implement the higher order decisions. This level of strategy will usually involve most managers and many other employees in organizations.

These issues are considered in Part 5 of this text.

Chapter **10**

Competitive strategy for tourism, hospitality and event organizations

Introduction and chapter overview

Fundamentally, strategic management is concerned with achieving sustainable competitive advantage. Thus, any organization must formulate *strategic options* for future development, evaluate them and choose those that the organization considers most likely to be successful.

Making strategic choices is concerned with:

- *Formulating* strategic options (Chapters 10, 11 and 12)
- *Evaluating* the available options (Chapter 13)
- *Choosing* the options most likely to lead to strategic success (Chapter 13)

Formulating *business strategy* is concerned with three primary issues:

- What is the basis on which competition will take place? – *competitive strategy* (Chapter 10)
- Which direction for development will be taken will be taken? – *strategic direction* (Chapter 11)
- How will the development be achieved; that is, which methods will be adopted? – *strategic methods* (Chapter 12)

Competitive strategy is considered in this chapter. Two important points are relevant before we proceed to considering the formulation of strategy.

DOI: 10.4324/9781003318613-14

- The focus of strategy at this level (often referred to as 'business' strategy) is not normally on the entire organization, except if the organization is small in size. In business strategy, the concern is usually with breaking the entire organization down into its constituent parts; that is, its SBUs.

- Although the focus here is on the business level –that is, the level of the SBU – at some stage the organization as a whole must bring the strategies of the individual SBUs together. Because resources are finite, the organization is unlikely to have the resources available to develop each SBU at the same rate, and some will offer higher returns than others. Thus, choices have to be made at the *corporate* level between the competing demands of the individual SBUs.

After studying this chapter, you should be able to:

- Understand various *THE* contexts in which competitive strategy has to be considered
- Explain the concept of competitive advantage
- Describe and evaluate Porter's generic strategy framework
- Describe and evaluate the strategy clock and Poon's tourism competitive strategy concepts
- Explain the concept of hybrid strategy
- Explain the role of core competences and distinctive capabilities in building competitive advantage
- Explain the role of the value chain in linking core competences and generic strategies
- Understand how the concepts and models discussed can be applied to *THE* contexts
- Provide illustrative examples from *THE* organizations of competitive strategy

10.1 How competitive advantage is achieved

The study of strategic management offers several explanations of how competitive advantage can be achieved and sustained. This topic was introduced in Chapter 3. This chapter focuses on two of the major explanations of competitive advantage:

- Competitive positioning
- Core competences

The *competitive positioning* approach is based largely on Porter's generic strategy framework (Porter, 1980, 1985). The *core competence* or *resource-based* view explains competitive advantage in terms of the development and exploitation of an organization's core competences. A third approach, the *relational approach*, recognizes that many resources critical to an organization's success can come from outside the organization. Consequently, the importance of interfirm working (in the form of alliances, joint ventures, franchising arrangements, etc.) is stressed. (This approach is considered in Chapter 12 as part of strategic methods.) Kim and Oh (2004) provided a useful summary and critique of the three approaches in a *THE* context.

These three approaches can be viewed as being complementary and mutually enriching rather than mutually exclusive.

10.2 Strategy formulation in *THE* contexts

As stated previously, business strategy is concerned with formulating strategies in three key issues:

- How can advantage over competitors be achieved? (competitive strategy)
- Which products or services should be developed, and in which markets should they be sold? (strategic direction)
- What methods of development should be adopted? (strategic methods)

These issues are of fundamental importance in any industry, not just in the sectors of *THE*. However, the strategic options that are formulated to address these issues and the strategy developed to take the organization forward will vary according to the circumstances of the particular industry concerned. In other words, in formulating strategy, managers must consider the wider external environmental factors affecting organizations operating in the industry or parts of it. Some texts refer to these factors as the *frame conditions.*

- *Frame conditions* are those conditions operating in the organization's commercial environment that frame (or influence) strategic decision making for a particular organization.

The frame conditions represent the major changes or trends occurring in an industry or parts of it that managers must be aware of and take into account when formulating strategy. The frame conditions may affect all organizations or only those operating in a particular sector, subsector or geographical location.

Table 10.1 summarizes some of the major frame conditions affecting *THE*. It should be stressed that this is not an exhaustive list but instead is indicative of the sort of issues that might be considered. It could well be that in certain contexts these are not the major frame conditions that need to be considered and others may be more important. It could also be that some of the issues represented in Table 10.1 manifest themselves in a different way or are relevant for different sectors in different ways than those indicated in the table.

The key point is that in formulating valid strategic options that are capable of achieving competitive advantage, managers operating in *THE* must seek to identify and understand the major changes that have occurred and continue to affect their sector of the industry.

The chapters focusing on analysis (Chapters 3–9) considered some of the issues, but Table 10.1 summarizes and groups them together for the first time in this book. Though the issues presented are not necessarily unique to *THE*, they have certainly been important in many parts of *THE* worldwide in recent years.

The sectors and subsectors are consistent with the conceptualization of *THE* considered in Chapter 2 and shown diagrammatically as Figure 2.2.

Table 10.1 Summary of the major frame conditions affecting *THE*

Frame Condition	Comments
Collaboration	Collaborating between various companies in *THE* has expanded through various types of strategic alliances, joint ventures, franchising etc., with companies attempting to gain advantages of economies of scale and scope.

Frame Condition	Comments
Cost cutting	The commercial environment has been getting ever more competitive as the economic weakness in the world economy of event years has combined with lower barriers to entry, pressure on public financing, privatization and deregulation. Companies have responded by focusing on its cost base by measures such as 'downsizing' (making the business smaller) and 'outsourcing' (buying in inputs rather than providing them internally).
Cruising	The growth of cruising in parts of the world in recent years has exceeded the growth of tourism generally.
Deregulation and Privatization	Markets have been deregulated and public companies have been privatized in parts of as governments have been under financial pressure not to provide financial support for *THE* activities.
Emerging outbound tourist markets	Many countries such as China, India, Japan, Mexico, Indonesia and Malaysia are developing large outbound tourism markets.
Emerging tourism destinations	Many countries such as China, India, Vietnam, Peru, Tanzania and the Philippines have shown rapid growth in international tourism arrivals. Existing and new built and natural attractions have been marketed.
Eventful cities	Many cities (and regions) around the world have focused on events such as festivals and conferences as a key part of their economic development and tourism strategies.
Growth of all inclusive	All-inclusive resorts and hotels have grown in popularity as consumers have sought pricing certainty, quality assurance and controlled environments.
Industry structural changes	There has been a great deal of structural change and industry consolidation in parts of *THE*. *Many* organizations have become part of vertically and/or horizontally integrated structures while others have diagonally integrated using common technology platforms.
International event management	Events and the companies which organize and manage them has been a highly fragmented business field, and dominated by domestic providers. Recent years have seen the emergence of some large diversified companies with international capabilities which add to what is already a highly competitive sector with low barriers to entry.
Internationalization	Many companies have grown, merged and formed alliances to move from domestic orientation and to increase their international presence.
Low cost competitors	Companies have emerged which focus their competitive stance on cutting out additional product features and concentrating on cutting costs wherever possible.
Public–private partnerships	In many countries public funding for *THE* has been curtailed and public authorities have wanted to involve private sector expertise and attract private capital investment.
Technology: disintermediation	Technology has had affected many parts of *THE* in many ways but perhaps the most important changes have been the growth of the Global Distribution Systems (GDS) and the internet. The internet has allowed disintermediation to take place on a large scale i.e. consumers can buy tourism, hospitality and event products directly from suppliers from their computers and mobile devices with no need for an intermediary.

(continued)

Table 10.1 Continued

Frame Condition	Comments
Technology: resource substitution & resource re-location	Many parts of *THE* are highly labor intensive which tends to be an expensive resource. It is also difficult to ensure consistent quality standards are met. Computer and communications technology have been utilized to replace labor with technology or to re-locate labor resources to where they are provided at lower cost. For example, call centers have been replaced by interactive websites for booking and price comparison, self-checking in is now common at airports and electronic information points are available at tourist sites. At the same time call centers and other functions have been relocated in many cases from 'Western' countries to countries such as India and the Philippines (known as 'offshoring') or sometimes to low labor cost localities in the same country (known as 'near-shoring').
Technology: transportation	Transport technology is continually developing, with new aircraft types being developed, cruise ships becoming larger and more sophisticated, more high-speed railways being built and increasing infrastructure such as rood and airport capacity in many parts of the world.
Value accommodation	The fastest growing part of the hotel market in many markets has focused on branded, value-based chains of budget hotels.

10.3 Competitive strategy overview

Competitive strategy is concerned with the bases on which an SBU might achieve competitive advantage in its chosen market or markets. For *THE* organizations in the private sector, competitive advantage is clear:

- Organizations need to compete with the competitors in their particular sector to gain customers and to achieve profitability for the benefit of the business owners.

Many *THE* organizations are in the public sector or are publicly funded. Thus, achieving competitive advantage is important because these organizations, as well as attractions, events and festivals, need to be able to demonstrate that they are competitive because they often have to compete with other:

- Publicly funded activities for funding and thus need to be able to demonstrate the effectiveness of the funding they receive
- Locations offering similar attractions, festivals and events
- Ways in which the services could be delivered

THINK POINTS

- Explain the meaning of *frame conditions*.
- Explain why it is necessary for *THE* managers to have a good understanding of the most relevant frame conditions.
- Provide an example of a *frame condition* relevant to a sector of *THE* you are familiar with that is not included in Table 10.1 but that you think is of importance to future development.

10.4 Michael Porter's generic strategies

Perhaps the oldest and best-known explanation of competitive advantage was given by Michael Porter in his *generic strategy* framework, which was first developed during the 1980s. Although this framework has been increasingly called into question in recent years, it still provides useful insights into competitive behavior. The framework and its limitations are considered in this section. Perhaps its main use is that it provides a framework that has an intrinsic logic, which forces managers to think about the underlying basis upon which they are attempting to compete.

According to Porter (1985), competitive advantage arises from selection of the generic strategy that best fits the organization's competitive environment and then organizing value-adding activities to support the chosen strategy. There are three main alternatives:

- *Cost leadership* – being the lowest cost producer of a product so that above-average profits are earned even though the price charged is not above average
- *Differentiation* – creating a customer perception that a product is superior to those of competitors so that a premium price can be charged
- *Focus* – utilizing either a differentiation or cost leadership strategy in a narrow profile of market segments (possibly just one segment)

Organizations that fail to make a strategic decision to opt for one of these strategic stances are in danger of being *stuck in the middle* (to use the Porter's terminology). In other words, the organization tries to both be the cost leader and the differentiator and achieves neither and, in the process, confuses consumers.

Porter argued that an organization must make two key decisions on its strategy:

- Should the strategy be one of differentiation or cost leadership?
- Should the scope of the strategy be broad or narrow?

The possible orientations that result are shown diagrammatically in Figure 10.1.

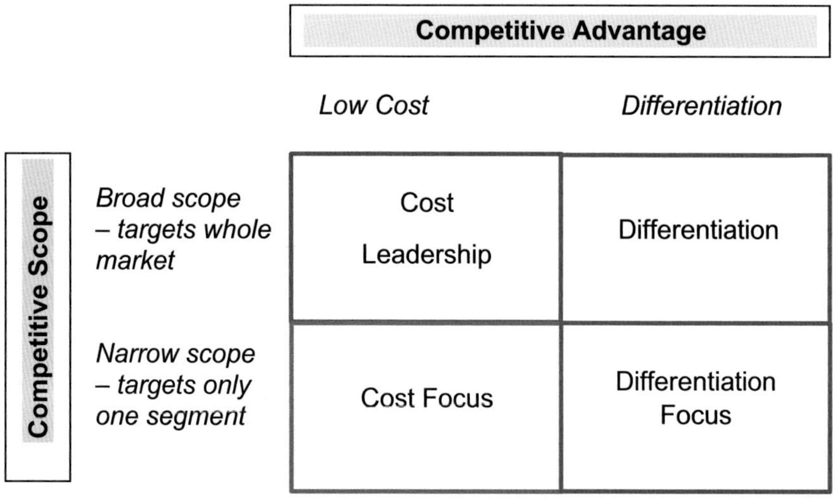

	Competitive Advantage	
	Low Cost	*Differentiation*
Broad scope – targets whole market	Cost Leadership	Differentiation
Narrow scope – targets only one segment	Cost Focus	Differentiation Focus

(Competitive Scope)

Figure 10.1 The generic strategy framework

In other words, an organization must decide whether to try to gain competitive advantage by:

- Differentiating its products and services and selling them at a premium price *or*
- Producing its products and services at a lower cost than its competitors

Higher profits can be made by adopting either approach. An organization must also decide whether to:

- Target the whole market with its chosen strategy *or*
- Target a specific segment or niche of the market.

Figure 10.2 shows a diagrammatic representation of differentiation and cost leadership. With the cost leadership strategy, an organization charges the same price as in cases where no pricing strategy is employed but derives higher profits by cutting costs. In the case of differentiation, an organization is able to charge a premium price (because it offers features consumers are willing to pay for), while maintaining costs at their initial level, thereby achieving higher levels of profitability.

10.4.1 Cost leadership strategy

A cost leadership strategy is based on a business organizing and managing its value-adding activities such that they are the lowest cost producer of a product or service within an industry. There are several potential benefits of a cost leadership strategy for a business, in that it:

- Can earn higher profits by charging a price equal to or below that of competitors because its costs are lower

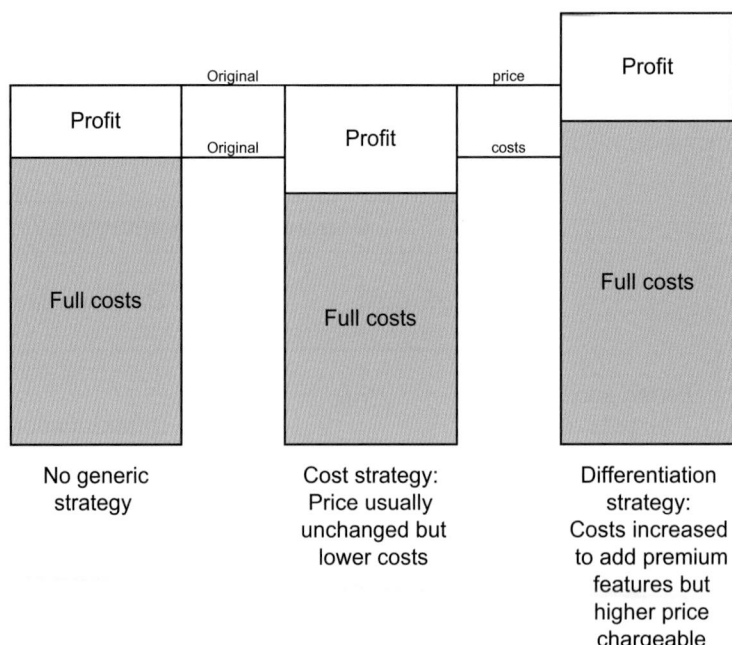

Figure 10.2 A simplified understanding of cost leadership and differentiation strategies

Note: price = full costs plus profits

- Provides the possibility of increasing both sales and market share by reducing price below that charged by competitors (assuming that the product's demand is price elastic in nature)
- Allows the possibility to enter a new market by charging a lower price than competitors
- Can be particularly valuable in a market where consumers are price sensitive
- Creates an additional *barrier to entry* for organizations wishing to enter the industry

Value chain analysis is central to identifying where cost savings can be made at various stages in the value chain and its internal and external linkages (see Chapter 3).

A successful cost leadership strategy is likely to rest on a number of organizational features. Attainment of a position of cost leadership depends on the arrangement of value chain activities. Examples of how costs savings might be achieved include the following:

- Reducing costs by copying rather than originating product design features.

  For example: *A tour operator, hotel company or event promoter might copy the design and functions of an existing website developed by competitors so that development costs are minimized.*

- Using less expensive resource inputs.

  For example: *Many 'low-cost' airlines and event organizers, among others in THE, have substituted technology for expensive labor. Telephone sales agents have been replaced by internet sales, which are much cheaper sales and are facilitated by the simplicity of the underlying product.*

- Producing products with 'no frills', thus reducing labor costs and increasing labor productivity.

  For example: *Low-cost airlines have generally eliminated free meals and free seat reservations from their products, thereby reducing costs, or require additional payments for these services.*

- Achieving economies of scale by high-volume sales perhaps based on advertising and promotion or allowing high fixed costs of investment in modern technology to be spread over a high volume of output.

  For example: *The growth of the internet and mobile technology has transformed the intermediation process between consumers and companies providing THE products and services during the last 20 years or so. Several large global players have emerged. These include Ticketmaster, a subsidiary of Live Nation Inc. for events and Travelocity, Orbitz and Trivago (all of which are subsidiaries of Expedia); US-based Booking Holdings, which runs the Booking.com website (among others); and China's Shanghai-based Trip.com Group for tourism and hospitality products.*

The Technology Focus on Expedia Inc. illustrates the rise of these intermediaries.

10.1 TECHNOLOGY FOCUS

Achieving economies of scale through technology: Expedia Group

In 1996, a small division within Microsoft launched online travel booking site Expedia.com, which gave consumers a revolutionary new way to research and book travel. Three years later, Expedia was sold, becoming a publicly traded company.

InterActive Corporation acquired a controlling interest in Expedia in 2002, and Expedia subsequently grew quickly as synergies with the parent company's other travel holdings were realized and the technology platforms were developed. The company also acquired other leading travel brands, including online travel sites Hotels.com and Hotwire and traveler reviews and opinions site TripAdvisor.

In 2005, InterActive Corporation sold its travel businesses under the name Expedia, Inc. and, since then, Expedia has evolved into what is today the world's largest online travel company, parent company to a global portfolio of leading consumer brands. In 2011 Expedia, Inc. sold TripAdvisor Media Group and retained its successful travel transaction brands. Expedia brands include Expedia.com, Hotels.com, Trivago.com, Travelocity.com, homeaway.com and Orbitz.com.

Expedia's corporate headquarters are located in Seattle, Washington, USA, with offices throughout the Americas, Europe and Asia-Pacific regions. Expedia, Inc. employs over 12,000 employees worldwide across its network of brands. Expedia's revenue dwindled from $12bn in 2019 to $5.2bn in 2020 due to the COVID-19 pandemic.

The brands that comprise Expedia Group operate websites, with localized content, for more than 200 travel booking sites in more than 75 countries and 150 mobile sites in about 70 countries. Investment in technology, shared resources among a number of brands and acquisitions have enabled Expedia to obtain economies of scale and achieve market leadership in travel web and mobile technology.

Source: Adapted from www.expediainc.com/

Questions

1. Explain the reasons why Expedia has been able to grow into a market leading position.

2. Consider the main competitive threats faced by an intermediary such as Expedia.

- Using high-volume purchasing to obtain discounts for bulk buying of resource inputs such as accommodation or transportation requirements.

  For example: *TUI has grown to a preeminent position in European tour operations, allowing the company to demand lower prices for resource inputs (such as hotels and other accommodation) than might be available to smaller competitors.*

- Locating activities in areas where costs are low or government help, such as grant support, is available.

  For example: *UK airline British Airways has located call centers at peripheral locations in the UK such as Newcastle and Glasgow where abundant, fairly cheap labor is available and where government aid in the form of tax savings is available for incoming investors. Other THE companies use outsourcing to site call centers in countries such as India and the Philippines where labor costs are lower.*

- Obtaining *experience effect* economies (see Chapter 3).

  For example: *The operator of an established theme park may be able to operate the park with lower costs than a new entrant because they might have more experience of important operational aspects such as staff scheduling and training, minimizing power costs, purchasing new rides, waste disposal, pricing and marketing incentives, buildings and ground maintenance and employing specialist staff. The Short Case Illustration of Merlin Entertainments Group below illustrates the point.*

10.2 SHORT CASE ILLUSTRATION

Experience curve effects: Merlin Entertainments Group

Merlin Entertainments is a UK-based entertainment group that operates about 140 attractions in 24 countries with well-known international brands such as Madame Tussauds, Legoland and Sealife centers as well as theme parks such as Alton Towers in the UK and Gardaland in Italy. In 2019, it was acquired by a consortium that includes Kirkbi A/S (the investment arm of the Christiansen family, which controls the Danish-based Lego Group).

Merlin delivers two types of visitor experiences: midway attractions are predominantly indoor attractions located in city centers, resorts or shopping malls, providing visits of shorter duration; theme parks are outdoor attractions offering accommodation, rides, shows and interactive experiences around a central theme. They are managed in two operating groups – Legoland Parks and Resort Theme Parks. One feature of the company is its ability to deliver development needs completely in-house. This capacity provides the experience and ability to deliver projects on time, on budget and to the required specification.

Since it was formed in 1999, Merlin's strategy has been to create a high-growth, high-return family entertainment company, a business based on strong brands and a global portfolio naturally balanced against the impact of external factors.

Working with the world's largest toy brand – Lego (a Danish company) – the company is able to roll out parks internationally using the intellectual property rights for the brand that Merlin possesses. One of these developments was Legoland Japan, Merlin's eighth Legoland park, which opened in April 2017 with more than 40 rides, shows and attractions. Extensions to the park in 2018 added a Sea Life Centre and a hotel.

Source: Adapted from www.merlinentertainments.biz/

Questions

1. Explain how *experience curve* effects might work to the benefit of Merlin.

2. Consider other examples from *THE* where *experience curve* effects may aid an organization in competing successfully.

- Standardizing products or resource inputs.

  For example: *Holiday Inn is able to franchise its concept internationally to franchisees because it has operating procedures, brand attributes, training practices, financial controls and technical support that are fairly standardized throughout the world. Similarly, Southwest Airlines is able to achieve economies in maintenance, purchasing and crew training because it operates only one aircraft type (albeit in various versions), the Boeing 737. It is the world's largest user of this aircraft type, with about 740 in service.*

Perhaps no industrial sector exemplifies the adherence to the principles of cost leadership more than the airline sector, as outlined in the Short Case Illustration below.

10.3 SHORT CASE ILLUSTRATION

Cost leadership: the airline industry

The growth of so-called low-cost airlines, which commenced with the birth of Southwest Airlines in 1971 and was facilitated by US Airline deregulation from the 1970s onwards, has been one of the major developments in global *THE*. Highly regulated airline markets were progressively deregulated in many countries following the US initiative, and this spawned many new low-cost start-ups around the world. Many of the start-ups quickly failed due to competition from existing carriers, poor financing or failure to adhere to the low-cost principles, but many have prospered and grown into substantial carriers.

Over 20 years ago, Doganis (2001) estimated that the cost advantage of low-cost carriers was on the order of 40% to 50%. Though some of the cost advantages have probably been eroded subsequently as 'full-service' airlines (such as British Airways, Singapore Airlines and United) have adopted some of the cost saving measures pioneered by low-cost airlines, low-cost airlines still strive for cost leadership by cutting out product features that are not valued and by making operations highly efficient.

Alamdari and Fagan (2005) summarized the primary features of the original low-cost model pioneered by Southwest Airlines, as shown in Table 10.2.

Table 10.2 The main features of the low-cost airline model

	Attribute	Characteristics
Product	Fare	Low, simple and unrestricted
	Frequency	High
	Network	Point-to-point
	Connections	No
	Distribution	Call centers, internet, ticketless
	Class	Single class
	Seat comfort	High-density seating
	Food	No free meals or drinks
	Seat assignment	No
	Baggage	Low weight allowances and carry-on encouraged
Operations	Aircraft fleet	Single type
	Aircraft use	High capital productivity >12 hours
	Airports	Secondary and uncongested
	Airport turnaround	20–30 minutes
	Sector length	Short (400 miles)
	Staff	High labor productivity, competitive salaries

As Alamdari and Fagan (2005:378) pointed out, some of the airlines have based their business models fairly rigidly on Southwest's fundamental low-cost principles. However, increasingly, other low-cost airlines have emerged 'that adhere to Southwest's fundamental principle of undercutting the incumbent or the alternative carrier on price while attempting to differentiate their services from those of their competitors'.

Though there are many variations of the low-cost model and, indeed, Southwest Airlines has itself deviated at least in part from some of its original principles, some of the features of the low-cost model are rarely altered, particularly the focus on point-to-point services, short sector lengths, limited number of aircraft types, high aircraft usage rates and short airport turnaround times. Though low-cost airlines have succeeded in attracting customers based on their value for money propositions, they have sometimes found difficulties in retaining customers and building a loyal customer base (Rajaguru, 2016).

Questions

1. Explain the main features of the cost leadership model exemplified in this case.

2. Explain the factors that led to the rise of low-cost airlines and consider the competitive threats such airlines might face in their future development.

A cost leadership strategy, coupled with low price, is best employed in a market or segment where demand is *price elastic* (see Key Concept below).

Under such circumstances, sales and market share are likely to increase significantly, thus increasing economies of scale and reducing unit costs further, generating above-average profits.

KEY CONCEPT

Price elasticity of demand (Part 2)

We encountered price elasticity of demand in Chapter 6. Here we further emphasize its importance in underpinning strategic pricing decisions. Economists use the term price elasticity to describe the extent to which the volume of demand for a product is dependent on its price. The coefficient of elasticity is expressed in a simple equation:

$$E_p = \text{Percentage change in quantity/percentage change in pr-ice}$$

The value of E_p (price elasticity) tells us the price responsiveness of the product's demand. If, for any given price change, E_p is more than −1, the change in price has brought about a higher proportionate change in volume sold. This relationship between price change and quantity is referred to as price elastic demand.

Demand is said to be price inelastic if the quantity change is proportionately smaller than the change in price (resulting in an E_p of less than −1). The larger the value of E_p, the more price elastic the demand and, conversely, the nearer E_p is to 0, the more price inelastic the demand.

The price elasticity of demand (the value of E_p) is dependent on the nature of the market's perception of a product. Products tend to be relatively price elastic if the market sees a product as unnecessary but desirable, as in the case of many leisure-oriented *THE* products and services or, say, chocolate. Products will tend to have relatively price inelastic demand if the customer perceives a *need* for a product rather than a *want*. The demand for many business-oriented *THE* products or services or most pharmaceutical products often exhibits relative price inelasticity of demand.

10.4.2 Differentiation strategy

A differentiation strategy is based on persuading customers that a product is superior in some way to that offered by competitors. Differentiation can be based on premium product features or simply on creating consumer perceptions that a product is superior. The major benefits to a business of a successful differentiation strategy are that:

- Its products will command a premium price
- Demand for its product will be less price elastic than demand for competitors' products
- Above-average profits can be earned
- It creates an additional barrier to entry to new businesses wishing to enter the industry

> For example: *Becerra et al. (2013) studied the impacts of differentiation in the context of the Spanish hotel industry. Their study found that differentiation had an impact on pricing decisions, in that it protects hotels from the pressure to reduce prices as competition increases.*

A business seeking to differentiate itself will organize its value chain activities to help create differentiated products and to create a perception among customers that these offerings are worth a higher price. Differentiation can be achieved in several ways:

- Creating products that are superior to those of competitors by virtue of design, technology, performance, etc.

> For example: *Over the last few years the demand for cruises has been growing quickly around the world, and the types of customers have been changing; that is, more families and younger customers are being attracted in addition to the traditional clientele of older age groups.*
>
> *Consequently, the major cruise lines have responded by adding tonnage but also by attempting to differentiate their ships in various ways. The Royal Caribbean cruise line (www.royalcaribbean.com), for instance, has targeted the family market with its four 'Oasis' class ships, which are the largest passenger ships afloat. The ships' features include a five-deck-high boardwalk, outdoor areas running down the middle of the ships that feature lush tropical gardens, a sloped-entry beach pool with surf simulators, a zip wire and a youth zone featuring a science lab and computer gaming.*

10.4 TECHNOLOGY FOCUS

Differentiation using collaboration and technology: the Edinburgh Festival

Edinburgh, the capital of Scotland, is a thriving city of over half a million people. Each year its festivals attract performers and audiences from around the world and enable Edinburgh to market itself as 'the world's favorite festival city'.

Although often referred to as 'The Edinburgh Festival', the festival has developed into a vast and complex series of 11 major festivals (held predominantly over the summer months), flowing through hundreds of venues and offering thousands of events. The festivals include the original Edinburgh International Festival (a festival of the arts and music), the Edinburgh International Film Festival, the Edinburgh Jazz and Blues Festival and the Edinburgh Festival Fringe (the world's largest arts festival featuring comedy and theater performances). Although largely organized separately, taken together the festivals constitute a vital part of Edinburgh's economy and international image.

Edinburgh's festival season was initiated with the birth of the International Festival in the postwar Britain of 1947 'to provide a platform for the flowering of the human spirit'. The festivals developed at a time before the internet, when programs were all on paper and days were planned weeks in advance, and there were far fewer such events competing for attention and custom.

Today's festival experience is very different, with a vast array of events and activities and the need to compete, requiring collaboration and technology as key points of differentiation. Rather than compete between themselves, the individual festivals recognized the power of working collaboratively for mutual advantage.

The publication of a report in 2006 served as a 'wake up' call to Edinburgh's festivals. The Thundering Hooves report (metaphorically named after the sound of the competition catching up with Edinburgh) concluded that although in the short term Edinburgh's status was secure, when viewed against the sustained development of some actively competitive cities, its enviable preeminent position was less secure.

The directors of Edinburgh's leading festivals came together in 2007 to formally establish 'Festivals Edinburgh' with a mission to support Edinburgh's festivals in sustaining and developing their position through development and delivery of collaborative projects and initiatives that support growth, product development, leadership and audiences. Since then, strategic plans have been produced covering all of the major activities, and close collaboration has been achieved particularly in relation to strategic planning, marketing, program development and infrastructure.

In the marketing field, for instance, the festivals have jointly embraced technology and developed a joint website and mobile apps. The Edinburgh Festivals website covers all of the major festivals and provides direct links to a number of free GPS-enabled apps that include useful features such as allowing customers to:

- Locate events close to the present location

- Keep track of events and plan future attendance

- Receive alerts regarding events nearby or starting soon

- Access user-generated reviews

- Read the 'Festival Buzz', which tracks shows being discussed online

- Read 'iFringe', which collects a diverse number of independent professional reviewers such as 'FringeGuru' and 'Edinburgh Spotlight' in one place for quick reference

- Contact others with 'FestAfriend', which links up with others interested in the same shows

Source: Adapted from www.edinburghfestivalcity.com

> **Questions**
>
> 1. Explain the main ways in which The Edinburgh Festivals *differentiates* itself from competitors through the use of technology.
>
> 2. In what other ways might similar festivals choose to *differentiate* themselves from competitors?

- Offering a superior level of service.

  For example: *An upscale hotel chain such as Hong Kong–based Mandarin Oriental (www.mandarinoriental.com), which operates hotels largely in Southeast Asia and major American and European cities, attempts to differentiate itself by offering a very high level of service. This is achieved, in part, by having a very high ratio of staff to guests.*

- Having access to superior distribution channels.

  For example: *A chain of retail travel agents that has been established for some time may have been able to develop a network of branches in prime retail locations (especially important in the retail sector). Although internet distribution has been increasingly important, retail travel agents remain important in many countries, offering advice, competitive pricing, convenient locations, financially protected products and the ability to put different elements of a 'package' together. Accumulating suitable sites at competitive rates would take some time and considerable expense for a newcomer to the sector.*

  For example: *Trailfinders plc (www.trailfinders.com) has operated since 1970 and currently operates from 34 retail premises in key strategic locations in the UK and Ireland. The company has built up a reputation for dealing with long-haul independent travelers and has won numerous awards. The company tends to employ agents who have themselves traveled extensively, believing that the advice they are able to offer is superior to the service customers are likely to receive from internet-based providers and other retail chains.*

- Creating a strong brand name through design, innovation, advertising, loyalty programs and public relations.

  For example: *The development by American Airlines of the world's largest frequent flyer program (AAdvantage) creates loyalty for its brand among passengers. The promotional scheme, launched in 1981, has over 70 million members. Though many of its features have been copied by other airlines, the size of its membership together with the route flexibility offered by the airline's extensive network and those of its partners (which include British Airways, Iberia and Cathay Pacific Airlines) provides competitive strength. Nevertheless, competitive pressures have led the airline to liberalize rules over the years to develop partnerships with a vast array of hotels, car rental companies and other suppliers to offer promotions. However, a major change to the program occurred in 2016, when AAdvantage began crediting miles based on the amount of the airfare, not the distance traveled. This change was accompanied by increases in miles needed for an award.*

- Leveraging distinctive or superior product promotion.

  For example: *Tourism is an important sector for the economy of the Phillipines, with the industry accounting for about 11% of the country's GDP. The 'It's More Fun in the Philippines' campaign developed for the Philippines Department of Tourism (www.itsmorefuninthephilippines.com) has won numerous advertising industry awards. The campaign,* *initiated in 2012, used social media to enlist the help of the Filipino public in creating the campaign, thus enabling the limited marketing budget to be multiplied enormously. The campaign went viral within hours of its official launch, with Filipinos using the 'It's More Fun' theme to express their own feelings on the web in numerous imaginative ways, which helped drive visitors to the country. The value of international tourism doubled from US$3.2bn in 2013 to US$6.5bn in 2017 (www.tourism.gov.ph).*

A differentiation strategy is likely to necessitate and emphasis on innovation, design, research and development; awareness of particular customer needs; and marketing. To say that differentiation is in the eyes of the customer is no exaggeration. It could be argued that it is often brand name, brand values or a logo that distinguishes one product from another, rather than real product superiority. The Short Case Illustration of W Hotels below demonstrates how a hotel company has used design and branding to create a differentiated product.

A differentiation strategy is employed to reduce *price elasticity of demand* for the product so that its price can be increased above that of competitors without reducing sales volume, thus generating above-average profits.

10.5 SHORT CASE ILLUSTRATION

Differentiation using design and innovation: W Hotels

Although they vary greatly, the term 'boutique hotel' has usually been used to describe smaller full-service hotels with luxury facilities in interesting settings. The individual hotels are distinctive and often reflect the nature of the neighborhoods in which they are located.

Boutique hotels began appearing in the 1980s in major cities like London, New York and San Francisco. The term is often attributed to New York hoteliers Ian Schrager and Steve Rubell, who opened their New York hotel, Morgans, in 1984. The growth of such hotels can be viewed as a reaction to the standardization of many hotels that form part of a chain and a recognition that younger customers are more design conscious.

Many international hotel chains have reacted to this trend by launching boutique brands of their own, though they tend to be larger than the original boutique hotels, and as they are rolled out to different locations, standardization is apparent. Intercontinental Hotel Group operates about 150 hotels using its Indigo boutique brand, and Marriott launched its Moxy boutique hotel brand, aimed at younger travelers and in urban settings, in 2013.

W Hotels is Marriott's luxury boutique hotel brand and is generally targeted at a younger clientele than its other brands, which include Marriott, Westin, Sheraton and Le Meridien. It was launched in 1998 with the W New York, and the brand has since expanded with over 65 hotels and resorts around the world.

Though the hotels vary in size and types of locations, they have a common theme of mini-malist stylish decor and informal names for categories of rooms and public areas. For example, the hotel lobbies are known as the 'living room'. W Hotels attempt to include the letter *W* wherever possible – the swimming pool is known as 'Wet', the concierge is known as 'Whatever Whenever', and so on.

Source: Adapted from: www.marriott.com and www.ihg.com

Questions

1. Explain the main elements of W Hotels' *differentiation* strategy.

2. Consider the factors that could threaten the continued development of the chain in using such a *differentiation* strategy.

10.4.3 Focus strategy

A focus strategy is aimed at a segment of the market for a product rather than the whole market. In the case of SMEs, because they are small in scale, they almost certainly have to use a focus competitive strategy to compete.

With a focus strategy, a particular group of customers is identified on the basis of age, income, lifestyle, sex, geography and other distinguishing demographic characteristics or on the benefits sought from travel and tourism products. Within the segment, a business employs either a cost leadership or a differentiation strategy.

The major benefits of a focus strategy are that it:

● Requires a lower investment in resources compared to a strategy aimed at an entire market
● Allows specialization and greater knowledge of the segment being served
● Makes entry into a new market less costly and simpler

A focus strategy will require:

● Identification of a suitable target customer group that forms a distinct market segment
● Identification of the specific needs of that group
● Establishing that the segment is sufficiently large to sustain the business
● Establishing the extent of competition within the segment
● Production of products to meet the specific needs of that group
● Deciding whether to operate a differentiation or cost leadership strategy within the market segment

Focus strategies can be developed in *THE* in a range of different circumstances by:

● Focusing on a particular group of buyers

> For example: *Contiki Tours (www.contiki.com), now a subsidiary of London-based The Travel Corporation, markets their coach-based holidays to customers in many parts of the world. The company, which was founded in the 1960s by a New Zealander as a safe and secure means for Australians and New Zealanders to see Europe, now offers tours (which combine activities and sightseeing) in North America, Australia and New Zealand and Europe. All tours are targeted at a single demographic subgroup, namely, the 18 to 35 age group.*

● Specializing on particular geographic destinations

> For example: *Sunvil Holidays (www.sunvil.co.uk), a specialist UK-based tour operator, was founded by an entrepreneur with a Greek Cypriot background. Although it has now*

diversified into other areas, the company is able to compete with larger rivals in the market for holidays to Cyprus by utilizing in-depth knowledge of the destination, a network of contacts and a loyal customer base.

• Catering for the benefits sought by a particular group of buyers or a particular product

Many organizations use a focus strategy to enter a market before broadening their activities into other related segments. Table 10.3 provides a summary of the key features of generic competitive strategies.

10.4.4 Critical evaluation of the generic strategy framework

It could be argued that none of Porter's categories should be regarded as alternatives and that in reality to categorize competitive strategy in this way is simplistic and possibly misleading. However, it does force managers, in a clear and simple way, to seriously consider the basis on which they are competing and to adjust their competitive strategy if necessary.

Porter's generic strategy framework has been the target of some criticism and discussion of its limitations (in a *THE* context, see, for example, Hendry, 1990; Parnell, 2006; Gurau, 2007; Poon, 1993).

At least six limitations of Porter's model have been identified.

Table 10.3 Key features of generic competitive strategies

Features	Differentiation	Cost leadership	Focus
Aim	• Ability to charge a premium price	To be the lowest cost supplier	Either to charge a premium price or to be the lowest cost supplier in particular segments of the market
How	• Superior product/service • Advertising and promotion • Branding • Distribution channels • Different locations • Customer care • Technology • Licenses/regulation	High-volume sales Economies of scale New technology High productivity Low-cost inputs Low distribution costs Low location costs	As for differentiation or cost leadership applied to particular segments
Strategy entails	• Changed perception • Higher price than rivals • Quality • Innovation	Price equal to or below that of rivals Acceptable quality Advertising to sell high volume	Segments and consumer needs Choose differentiation or cost leadership strategy for a segment or niche
When to use	• Price insensitive market • Established position in the market	Price sensitive market Market entry	For firms not large enough to target the whole market Firms possessing specialist skills

- A business can apparently employ a successful 'hybrid' strategy without being 'stuck in the middle'.

Porter argued that a business must choose between a differentiation and cost leadership strategy. To be 'stuck in the middle' between the two, he argued, will result in suboptimal performance. There is evidence to suggest, however, that some companies with lower than industry-average costs can nevertheless sell their products on the basis of differentiation. That is, they employ a combined or 'hybrid' strategy. The effects of innovations or economies of scale may allow a successful hybrid strategy to be employed.

> For example: *An airline flying a new fuel-efficient aircraft type may achieve the benefits of cost leadership and differentiation simultaneously. The new aircraft type differentiates the airline in the eyes of potential customers, and the fuel efficiency allows lower costs to be achieved.*

The Short Case Illustration of Singapore Airlines illustrates this situation.

10.6 SHORT CASE ILLUSTRATION

Pursuing a 'hybrid' competitive strategy: Singapore Airlines

Some authors have argued that it is possible to achieve cost leadership and differentiation at the same time (without being 'stuck in the middle') in a so-called hybrid or dual strategy. Heracleous and Wirtz (2010), for example, argued that Singapore Airlines (SIA) might be a successful example of such a strategy.

SIA has combined the supposedly incompatible strategies of differentiation – which it pursues through service excellence and continuous innovation – and cost leadership. The airline is well known for its quality, having won numerous awards including the World's Best Airline award from *Condé Nast Traveler* and Skytrax's Airline of the Year. What is less well known is its cost leadership strategy.

Using International Air Transport Association data, Heracleous and Wirtz's analysis of the years 2001 to 2009 showed that SIA's costs per available seat kilometer were just 4.58 cents. This compared with costs for full-service European airlines of 8 to 16 cents, for US airlines of 7 to 8 cents, and for its Asian competitors of 5 to 7 cents.

One reason for this cost leadership performance lies in the age of its fleet. SIA has invested heavily in its aircraft. For instance, in 2022, its passenger aircraft were 67 months old, on average (Singapore Airlines, 2022), less than half the average age of the fleets of some competitors. United Airlines, for example, has an average aircraft age of about 16.5 years (www.airfleets.net). This in turn triggers a vicious cycle:

- Because mechanical failures are rare, fewer take-offs are delayed, more arrivals are on time and fewer flights are canceled.

- New planes are also more fuel efficient and need less repair and maintenance.

- Consequently, the planes are able to spend more time flying.

- Finally, customers, of course, tend to like newer planes, thereby boosting sales.

In a later article, the same authors (Heracleous and Wirtz, 2014) presented a critique of Porter's generic strategy and concluded that in this case a paradox exists. SIA has achieved competitive advantage through effectively implementing an unconventional dual strategy: differentiation through service excellence and innovation together with simultaneous cost leadership in its strategic group of similar airlines. The authors argued that this ability to master the paradox and balance apparently contradictory competences and positions is becoming increasingly necessary (in all industries) because of the simultaneous quality and cost pressures in most industries and the advancement of technology that challenge existing business models.

Source: Adapted from Heracleous and Wirtz (2010, 2014)

Questions

1. Explain why Singapore Airlines might be considered to be pursuing a *hybrid competitive strategy* in this case.

2. Consider other examples of a *hybrid* strategy from your knowledge of *THE* organizations and consider whether such a position is sustainable.

A successful hybrid strategy will be based on a conscious decision by senior managers to combine differentiation with price and cost control, and under such circumstances a business can be successful. When a business slips into the situation unconsciously, it can still be regarded as being 'stuck in the middle' but is less likely to be successful.

- Cost leadership does not, in and of itself, sell products.

Buying decisions are made on the basis of desirable product features or price, not on the basis of the unit cost itself, which may not be known by consumers.

- Differentiation strategies can be used to increase sales volumes rather than to charge a premium price.

Porter's work does not consider the possibility that a business employing a differentiation strategy might choose not to charge a premium price but rather to increase sales and market share by foregoing the premium price for an introductory period. This criticism, however, does not fundamentally undermine Porter's thinking.

- Price can sometimes be used to differentiate.

Porter did not consider the possibility that price may be used to differentiate a product. Mintzberg et al. (1995) argued that price, along with image, support, quality and design, can be used as the basis of differentiation.

- A 'generic' strategy cannot give competitive advantage.

It is evident that to outperform competitors, a business must do things better and differently. The word 'generic' could be construed to imply that Porter is arguing that there are general recipes by which competitive advantage can be achieved. This, however, is not the case. Porter's framework is merely a framework by which competitive strategies can be grouped to assist in understanding and analysis.

- The resource/competence-based strategy has arguably superseded the generic strategy framework.

The resource-based approach argues that it is the core competences of the individual business that give it competitive advantage and not generic strategies. In fact, the two approaches do not preclude each other. The relationship between the two approaches is discussed in a later section of this chapter.

Despite the limitations outlined above, Porter's generic strategy framework continues to be widely used by practitioners and academics, perhaps for the following reasons:

- It has an underlying logic that can be easily understood.
- It has been widely disseminated and applied in textbooks and academic papers.
- It forces managers to seriously consider the underlying basis on which they are trying to compete.

Despite the criticisms, Porter's work can, in modified form, constitute the basis of a useful framework for categorizing and understanding sources of competitive advantage. One such approach is the 'strategy clock' framework developed by Faulkner and Bowman (1995) and reported by Whittington et al. (2020).

THINK POINTS

- Explain what is meant by the term 'competitive advantage'.
- Explain Porter's generic strategy framework and consider its strengths and weaknesses as an analytical framework.
- Explain what is meant by a hybrid strategy, and consider the circumstances in which it might it be pursued.

10.4.5 The strategy clock framework

The strategy clock framework develops and adds to Porter's original model and, consequently, some aspects are open to similar criticisms.

However, it is a more sophisticated approach that recognizes and deals with some of the criticisms of Porter's framework and, in particular, recognizes that in certain circumstances a 'hybrid' strategy can be successful. This model also differs from Porter's in that it focuses on prices to customers as opposed to costs to organizations. Whittington et al. (2020) argued that it represents a more dynamic view of competitive strategy than Porter's generic strategy. This framework suggests that it is possible to have a number of successful strategic positions (rather than just two) and that it is possible for strategies to change over time in moving around the clock.

The model is shown in Figure 10.3 and is followed by a brief explanation of the categories used. Note that strategies 6, 7 and 8 are strategies destined for ultimate failure in 'normal' competitive markets, because they combine high prices with relatively low benefits.

In concluding this section, the extent of differentiation, price and cost control will depend upon the nature of the market in which the business is operating. In markets where consumers show a preference for quality the emphasis is less on price and costs, whereas in markets where demand is

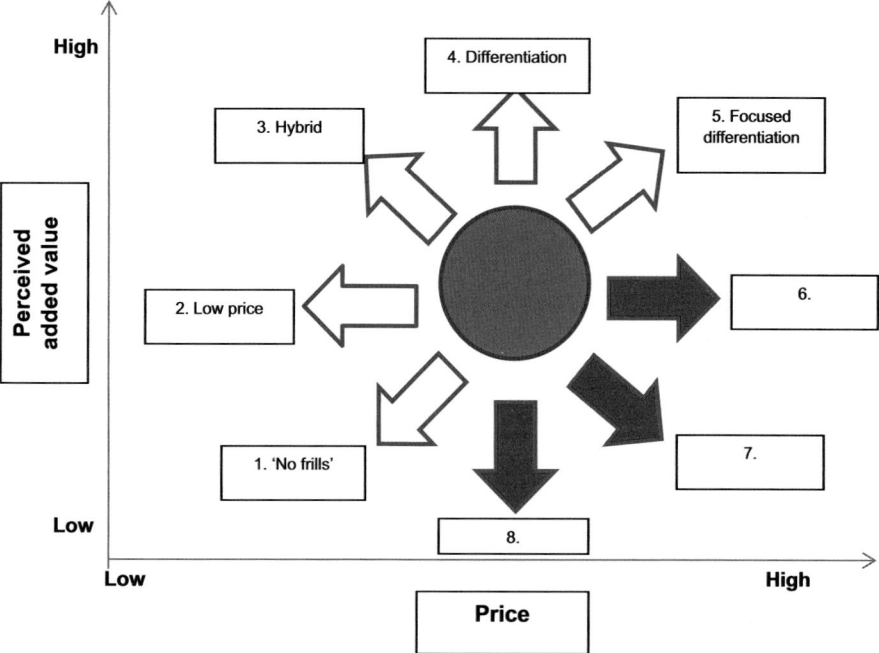

Figure 10.3 The strategy clock

price sensitive the emphasis will be on keeping both price and costs as low as possible. Of course, organizations may also seek to shape customer attitudes by advertising and promotion to modify market conditions.

10.5 Competence-based strategy

The generic strategy model is not the only one that seeks to provide an explanation of the sources of competitive advantage. The *competence-* or *resource-based view* emphasizes that competitive edge stems from attributes of an organization known as *competences* or *capabilities* that distinguish it from its competitors, thus allowing it to outperform them (see Chapter 3).

Chapter 3 explained the ways in which internal analysis makes it possible to better understand core competences by a process of deconstructing them into the component resources and competences that act as their foundation.

This chapter builds on this analysis to explore the ways in which existing competences can be extended and new ones cultivated. It goes on to examine how and where these core competences can be exploited to acquire and prolong competitive advantage.

The concept of *core competence* is based on the work of Prahalad and Hamel (1990), Stalk et al. (1992) and Kay (1995), who advanced the idea that competitive advantage is based on *distinctive capabilities*.

Prahalad and Hamel (1990) argued that competitive advantage is likely in practice to be based on a very limited number of competences. These competences will allow managers to produce new and unanticipated products and to be responsive to changing opportunities because of operational skills and the harnessing of technology.

The turbulent business environment in many sectors of *THE* requires adaptability if competitive advantage is to be built and sustained. The sustainability of competitive advantage was also considered in Chapter 3. In some cases the true competitive advantage lies in the way in which core competences are combined rather than in the core competence itself.

10.5.1 The 'VRIO' framework

Chapter 3 and the preceding sections reviewed some of the considerations for assessing core competences and their sustainability. However, what is also needed is a mechanism for testing the competitive resources.

In the early 1990s, Jay Barney provided such a mechanism in his 'VRIO' framework, which is explained in a later co-authored work (Barney and Hesterly, 2010). The sequential decision-making approach advocated by Barney questions each resource or capability in terms of its:

● *Value* – The resource or capability must have value if it is to allow the organization to choose a strategy that exploits opportunities available or responds to threats from competitors.
● *Rarity* – If the resource or capability is widely available to others, it will not provide a basis for competitive advantage and superior returns on investment.
● *Imitability* – If the resource or capability can be easily imitated or copied, competitors will do so and so competitive advantage may be achieved temporarily but will not be sustainable.
● *Organizational capability* – An organization needs to be able to organize itself in such a way that it is capable of exploiting the resource or capability that it has identified as valuable, rare and incapable of being imitated.

The VRIO framework is summarized in Table 10.4.

10.5.2 Dynamic capabilities

In more recent years, there has been growing recognition that though the resource-based view, the recognition of resources with VRIN attributes (Barney, 1991) and the core competences framework (Hamel and Prahalad, 1994) adequately explained competitive advantage, the *sustainability* of competitive advantage required further explanation (Wang and Ahmed, 2007).

Table 10.4 The VRIO framework for testing competitive resources

Valuable?	Rare?	Costly to imitate?	Capable of being exploited by the organization?	Competitive implications	Comparative economic performance to be expected from the resource
No	–	–	No	Competitive disadvantage	Below normal
Yes	No	–	Yes/no	Competitive parity	Normal
Yes	Yes	No	Yes/no	Temporary competitive advantage	Above normal
Yes	Yes	Yes	Yes	Sustained competitive advantage	Above normal

Source: Adapted from Barney et al. (2002)

David Teece (2007:1319) argued that '*sustainable* advantage requires more than the ownership of difficult to-replicate knowledge assets'. The emergence of the so-called dynamic capabilities framework seeks to address the sustainability issue.

DEFINITION/QUOTATION

Dynamic capabilities

Dynamic capabilities can be viewed as:

> A firm's behavioral orientation constantly to integrate, reconfigure, and recreate its resources and capabilities and, most importantly, upgrade and reconstruct its core capabilities in response to the changing environment to attain and sustain competitive advantage.
>
> (Wang and Ahmed, 2007:35).

It is important to note that the definition above emphasizes that the dynamic capabilities framework is a 'behavioral orientation' for the organization. In this way, it becomes not just a process to be carried out but a way in which the organization and its employees and leadership are orientated and behave so that the organization can respond adequately to rapidly changing environments.

The dynamic capabilities framework seeks to extend the resource-based view of strategy to dynamic markets. The framework has achieved wide acceptance despite criticisms, and the framework has been selectively applied in *THE* contexts. See, for example, Camisón Zornoza and Monfort-Mir (2012), Nieves and Haller (2014), Nieves et al. (2016), Evans (2016), Marco-Lajara et al. (2021) and Pereira-Moliner et al. (2021).

Capabilities, a term widely used in the literature, refers to a firm's capacity to deploy resources, usually in combination, and encapsulates both explicit resources and tacit (or intangible) elements such as leadership and know-how (Wang and Ahmed, 2007). As such, capabilities are often firm specific, develop over time and result from complex interactions between the firm's resources.

By way of distinction, the dynamic capabilities framework builds on capabilities and emphasizes the dynamism of markets and the transformational effect on resources.

The role of dynamic capabilities is to have an impact on the firm's existing resource base in such a way that it is transformed so that a firm can enhance or maintain its competitive advantage. Over a period of time, the way in which a firm's resources are linked internally or externally with partners, suppliers or customers can lead to a uniquely valuable combination of 'co-specialization' (Teece, 2007). The complementarity of resources is difficult for competitors to imitate and consequently more sustainable competitive advantage is achieved.

10.5.3 Developing dynamic capabilities

The development of dynamic capabilities relies on three organizational activities:

- *Sensing* describes the assessment of the opportunities and consumer needs existing outside the organization.

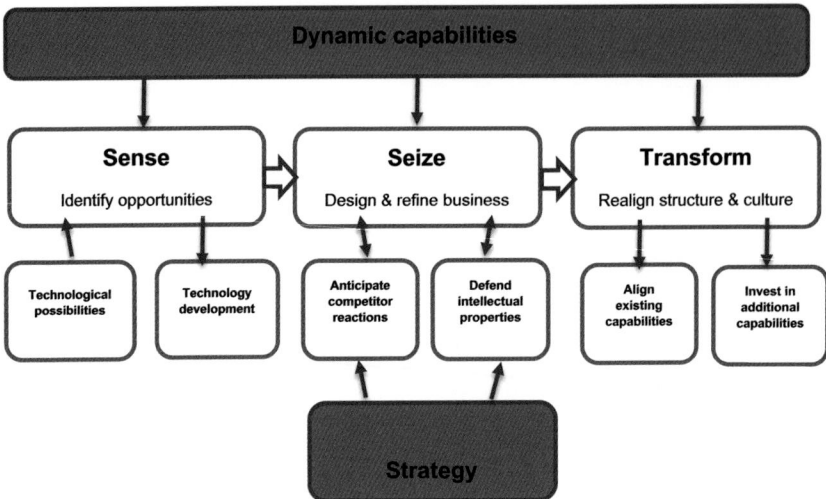

Figure 10.4 A simplified dynamic capabilities framework

Source: Adapted from Teece (2018)

- *Seizing* refers to an organization's reaction to market needs to increase firm value. This involves designing innovative business models and securing access to capital and resources.
- *Transforming* refers to renewing an organization's processes and maintaining their relevance to consumers. This requires that managers constantly streamline, improve and alter organizational practices. Transforming is key to creating sustainable, innovative growth.

A simplified version of Teece's version of a dynamic capabilities framework is shown in Figure 10.4 (Teece, 2018). In the model, dynamic capabilities and strategy combine to create and refine a *defensible* business model that guides the organization through sensing, seizing and transformation. Ideally, this leads to a level of profits adequate to allow the enterprise to sustain and enhance its capabilities and resources.

10.6 Core competence, generic strategy and the value chain – a synthesis

It has been argued (see, for example, Heene and Sanchez, 1997) that the resource-based or competence-based approach is largely incompatible with the competitive positioning or generic strategy approach advocated by Porter (1980, 1985).

Mintzberg et al. (1995), however, made the case that the two approaches are in many respects complementary rather than mutually contradictory. Perhaps the best way of illustrating the linkages between the approaches is through the value chain of the organization.

Because competitive advantage is based on the unique approach of the individual organization to its environment, it is not possible to identify a one-for-all prescription that will guarantee superior performance in all situations. Both competitive positioning and the resource-based approach, however, provide frameworks that allow broad sources of competitive advantage to be categorized for the purposes of analysis and development of future strategy.

A differentiation strategy, for example, will be likely to be dependent on core competences in areas of the value chain like design, marketing and service. Similarly, a cost- or price-based strategy may well require core competences in value chain activities like operations, procurement and perhaps marketing. It is much less likely that a cost leader will have core competences based on design and service.

Possible relationships between core competences, generic strategies and the value chain are shown in Table 10.5.

Table 10.5 Possible relationships between generic strategies and core competences in relation to the value chain

Value chain activity	Areas of competence associated with differentiation strategies	Areas of competence associated with cost/price-based strategies
Primary activities		
Inbound logistics	Control of quality of inputs	Strict control of the cost of inputs, tendency to buy larger volumes of standard inputs
Operations	Control of quality of output, raising standards	Lowering operational costs and achieving high-volume operations
Marketing and sales	Sales (and customer relations) on the basis of quality technology, performance, reputation, outlets, etc.	Achieving high-volume sales through advertising and promotion
Outbound logistics	Ensuring efficient distribution	Maintaining low distribution costs
Service	Adding to product value by high-quality and differentiated service	Minimal service to keep costs low
Support activities		
The business's infrastructure	Emphasis on quality	Emphasis on efficiency and cost reduction
Human resource development	Training to create a culture and skills that emphasize quality, customer service, product development	Training to reduce costs
Technology development	Developing new products, improving product quality, improving product performance, improving customer service	Reducing production costs and increasing efficiency
Procurement	Obtaining high-quality resources and materials	Obtaining low-cost resources and materials

---

THINK POINTS

- Outline the criticisms that have been made of Porter's generic strategy.
- Explain the factors that might make the *sustainability* of competitive advantage more likely, citing examples from *THE* you are familiar with.
- Explain the VRIO concept and how it works.
- Explain the main features of the dynamic capabilities framework.

10.6.1 Where to exploit core competences and strategies

As core competences and business strategies are developed, it is necessary to decide where they can be exploited. Core competences and strategies can be targeted toward existing customers in existing markets or new customers in existing markets. Alternatively, it may be possible to target new customers in new markets. These markets may be related to markets currently served by the organization or may be unrelated markets. The organization may also consider employing its competences in a new industry.

These decisions on where to deploy core competences are concerned with determining the *strategic direction* of the organization (which is considered in the following chapter). Once this decision has been made, decisions must be made on the *strategic methods* to be employed in following the chosen strategic direction (which is considered in Chapter 12).

The process of exploiting existing core competences in new markets is known as *competence leveraging* (Hamel and Prahalad, 1992). The notion here is that operating strategically is about not just how resources are allocated (between competing demands) but how effectively they are utilized. Some organizations are able to achieve better results than others by utilizing similar resources more effectively. In other words, competitively successful organizations are able to find less resource-intensive ways of achieving their goals and objectives; that is, 'they get more bang for the buck (dollar)'.

> **For example:** *Lynch (2021) cited the case of Walt Disney. For many years after the founder's death, the company continued to make good films and developed the California Disneyland theme park and later the Disney World theme parks focused on the Disney characters. It was only in the 1980s that the company leveraged its resources in fully exploiting its core competence (the cartoon characters it had created) by moving heavily into merchandizing, hotels, cruises and publishing.*

Generally, existing resources can be leveraged in five ways, as shown in Table 10.6.

To enter new markets, it is often necessary for the organization to build new core competences, alongside the existing core competences that are being leveraged, to satisfy new customer needs. The identification of customer needs to be served by core competences is based on analysis of the organization's competitive environment using the resource-based framework developed in Chapter 3.

Table 10.6 Leveraging existing resources

Ways of leveraging resources	Comments
Concentration	Concentrating resources on the key objectives of the organization and targeting those that will add the most value
Conservation	Avoiding waste or duplication or recycling resources, with the aim of exploiting the entire resource available to the organization
Accumulation	Exploiting all of the accumulated skills and knowledge available to an organization and combining them effectively. May involve buying in the necessary experience, skills and knowledge when necessary
Complementarity	Blending together resources and capabilities from different parts of the organization; for example, ensuring that the operational and sales and marketing activities of the organization work effectively together
Recovery	Ensuring that resources generate cash as quickly as possible, thus achieving benefits sooner rather than later

Sources: Adapted from Lynch (2021), based on Hamel and Prahalad (1992)

Chapter 11 considers alternative strategic directions an organization can pursue. Methods that can be employed in following these strategic directions are considered in Chapter 12.

Small business focus

This chapter has considered one of the three key issues in strategic formulation relating to *competitive strategy*. The chapter has also considered the frame conditions that underpin decision making in *THE*. Both provide important implications for smaller businesses.

The business strategy academic literature is heavily weighted toward larger, diversified companies, which are often multinational companies. Such companies will have multiple SBUs. These companies, by definition, have some degree of diversity, and this gives them some degree of protection against risk because if one SBU is not trading well, another might be, so one can support the other. This focus in the literature on larger companies is natural because more information on them is publicly available. In addition, as Mathur and Kenyon (2011:5) pointed out:

> Vexing management problems do not arise to anything like the same extent in smaller businesses. However, the competitive issues of strategy are just as critical for even the one-person business.

Smaller companies (SMEs) do not have the same level of protection against business uncertainties, because they are not likely to have SBUs; instead, the whole company is likely to be focused on a single product or a limited range. This has implications for the competitive strategy that smaller *THE* businesses might choose to take.

With regard to competitive strategy and Porter's generic strategy alternatives in particular, it is likely that most SMEs in *THE* will have to compete on the basis of a *focus* competitive strategy. The focus might be based on cost leadership, or more likely on differentiation, because cost leadership is normally difficult for SMEs to achieve, because their scale precludes them from reaping the benefits of economies of scale or scope.

In the often highly fragmented sectors in which *THE* companies operate, a focus (or *niche*) strategy provides a position that can be defended. This is because a particular niche has been developed where expertise, customer service or location that are not easily accessible to larger companies can be exploited.

> **For example:** *A long-established family-owned hotel or restaurant might have the best location at a particular destination, the event manager can offer a highly personalized service based on local knowledge and the tour operator specializing in particular types of activity-based holidays is able to sell on the basis of employing highly specialized staff with appropriate experience.*

The potential advantages and disadvantages of adopting such a niche competitive strategy for smaller *THE* companies are summarized in Table 10.7.

The early part of this chapter discussed frame conditions for *THE*, which were summarized in Table 10.1. All companies need to think carefully about the frame conditions affecting their own companies, and the relevant details will vary in each individual set of circumstances according to the location of the company, the markets it is involved with, the nature of its products and the scale and scope of its operations.

This last factor is relevant here. The view taken of frame conditions will be different for smaller companies as opposed to their larger counterparts. We could go through the list produced in Figure 10.1 and possibly add some additional frame conditions particularly pertinent to SMEs. However, here we take one example – that of 'internationalization'.

Table 10.7 The advantages and disadvantages of a niche competitive strategy

Niche strategy: potential advantages	Niche strategy: potential disadvantages
• Supplier becomes a specialist in serving the needs of customers in a particular niche	Notable success in the niche could lead to its growth and the niche becomes an attractive segment for new entrants
• Expertise and knowledge may make it very difficult for others to compete	Niche has to be large enough to warrant attention but not so large that other entrants will be attracted
• Newcomers discouraged from entering niche because of incumbent's expertise	Larger competitors can bring additional resources that smaller firms cannot hope to match
• If the niche is small, there is little incentive for larger companies to enter	The niche loses its attraction to customers for some reason or becomes unavailable
• Niche buyers may have relatively little power because there are few suppliers	Niche buyers gain power as other niches elsewhere or with a better offer become available

Source: Partly adapted from Lasher (1999)

> **For example:** *Though many SMEs in THE operate internationally (because of the nature of their products and markets), few will be involved with internationalization, which involves a wider commitment to international activities (see Chapter 16). However, that is not to say that the topic is not important to SMEs. This is because even if they are not at the stage of development where international activities are being developed, larger companies they have to compete with will be. Thus, for instance, an event management company could suddenly find that the particular domestic market niche the company has developed is being challenged by a foreign-based competitor coming in to challenge it for market share.*

CHAPTER SUMMARY

In formulating strategy for future development, three key issues are considered: competitive strategy, strategic directions and strategic methods. The first of these was considered in this chapter (the other two are considered in subsequent chapters).

In considering the formulation of strategy, managers in *THE* need not only consider the three key issues outlined above but also the relevant context in which they are operating. Thus, there are a number of *frame conditions* that represent the major changes and trends apparent in *THE* sectors.

The essence of competitive advantage is the ability to outperform competitors. Though it is difficult to identify the source or sources of an organization's competitive advantage precisely, it is possible to place potential sources of competitive advantage into broad categories that assist in the analysis of a business and in the formulation of its strategies for future development.

Porter's generic strategy framework, modified and enlarged by the strategy clock, which includes the concept of hybrid strategies, is useful in appraising the roles of differentiation, price and cost in achieving competitive advantage. The core competence, distinctive capability and dynamic capabilities frameworks offer a means of evaluating the part played by a business's resources, competences, relationships, reputation, innovation and assets in delivering competitive edge. The way in which the business configures and manages its value-adding activities forms the link between core competences and generic strategies. Core competences and generic strategies can be exploited in existing and new markets.

e

REFERENCES AND WEBSITES

References

Alamdari, F. and Fagan, S. (2005) 'Impact of the adherence to the original low-cost model on the profitability of low-cost airlines', *Transport Reviews*, 25(3): 377–392.

Barney, J. B. (1991) 'Firm resources and sustained competitive advantage', *Journal of Management*, 17(1): 99–120.

Barney, J. B. (2001) 'Resource-based theories of competitive advantage: A ten-year retrospective on the resource-based view', *Journal of Management*, 27(6): 643–650.

Barney, J. B. and Hesterly, W. S. (2010) 'VRIO framework', in *Strategic Management and Competitive Advantage*, Hoboken, NJ: Pearson, 68–86.

Becerra, M., Santaló, J. and Silva, R. (2013) 'Being better vs. being different: Differentiation, competition, and pricing strategies in the Spanish hotel industry', *Tourism Management*, 34: 71–79.

Camisón Zornoza, C. and Monfort-Mir, V. M. (2012) 'Measuring innovation in tourism from the Schumpeterian and the dynamic-capabilities perspectives', *Tourism Management*, 33: 776–789.

Doganis, R. (2001) *The Airline Business in the 21st Century*, Abingdon, UK: Routledge.

Evans, N. G. (2016) 'Sustainable competitive advantage in tourism organizations: A strategic model applying service dominant logic and tourism's defining characteristics', *Tourism Management Perspectives*, 18: 14–25.

Faulkner, D. and Bowman, C. (1995) *The Essence of Competitive Strategy*, London: Prentice Hall.

Gurau, C. (2007) 'Porter's generic strategies: A re-interpretation from a relationship marketing perspective', *The Marketing Review*, 7(4): 369–383.

Hamel, G. and Prahalad, C. K. (1989) 'Strategic intent', *Harvard Business Review*, 67(3): 63–76.

Hamel, G. and Prahalad, C. K. (1992) 'Strategy as stretch and leverage', *Harvard Business Review*, 71(2): 75–84.

Hamel, G. and Prahalad, C. K. (1994) *Competing for the Future*, Boston: Harvard Business School Press.

Heene, A. and Sanchez, R. (Eds). (1997) *Competence-Based Strategic Management*, New York: John Wiley.

Hendry, J. (1990) 'The problem with Porter's generic strategies . . .', *European Management Journal*, 8(4): 443–450.

Heracleous, L. and Wirtz, J. (2010) 'Singapore Airlines' balancing act', *Harvard Business Review*, 88(7/8): 145–149.

Heracleous, L. and Wirtz, J. (2014) 'Singapore Airlines: Achieving sustainable advantage through mastering paradox', *The Journal of Applied Behavioral Science*, 50(2): 150–170.

Kay, J. (1995) *Foundations of Corporate Success*, Oxford, UK: Oxford University Press.

Kim, B. Y. and Oh, H. (2004) 'How do hotel firms obtain a competitive advantage?' *International Journal of Contemporary Hospitality Management*, 16(1): 65–71.

Lasher, W. R. (1999) *Strategic Thinking for Smaller Businesses and Divisions*, Oxford, UK: Blackwell.

Lynch, R. (2021) *Strategic Management*, 9th ed., Harlow, UK: Pearson.

Marco-Lajara, B., Ruiz-Fernández, L., Seva-Larrosa, P. and Sánchez-García, E. (2021) 'Hotel strategies in times of COVID-19: A dynamic capabilities approach', *Anatolia*, 33(4): 525–536.

Mathur, S. S. and Kenyon, A. (2011) *Creating Value: Successful Business Strategies*, 2nd ed., Abingdon, UK: Routledge.

Mintzberg, H., Quinn, J. B. and Ghoshal, S. (1995) *The Strategy Process: Concepts, Contexts and Cases*, European ed., Englewood Cliffs, NJ: Prentice Hall.

Nieves, J. and Haller, S. (2014) 'Building dynamic capabilities through knowledge resources', *Tourism Management*, 40: 224–232.

Nieves, J., Quintana, A. and Osorio, J. (2016) 'Organizational knowledge, dynamic capabilities and innovation in the hotel industry', *Tourism and Hospitality Research*, 16(2): 158–171.

Parnell, J. A. (2006) 'Generic strategies after two decades: A reconceptualization of competitive strategy', *Management Decision*, 44(8): 1139–1154.

Pereira-Moliner, J., Molina-Azorín, J. F., Tarí, J. J., López-Gamero, M. D. and Pertursa-Ortega, E. M. (2021) 'How do dynamic capabilities explain hotel performance?', *International Journal of Hospitality Management*, 98: 103023.

Poon, A. (1993) *Tourism Technology and Competitive Strategies*, Wallingford, UK: CAB International.

Porter, M. E. (1980) *Competitive Strategy: Techniques for Analyzing Industries and Competitors*, New York: Free Press.

Porter, M. E. (1985) *Competitive Advantage*, New York: Free Press.

Prahalad, C. K. and Hamel, G. (1990) 'The core competence of the corporation', *Harvard Business Review*, May – June: 1–15.

Rajaguru, R. (2016) 'Role of value for money and service quality on behavioural intention: A study of full service and low cost airlines', *Journal of Air Transport Management*, 53: 114–122.

Singapore Airlines. (2022) 'Singapore Airlines Annual Report 2022, www.singaporeair.com

Stalk, G., Evans, P. and Shulmann, L. E. (1992) 'Competing on capabilities: The new rules of corporate strategy', *Harvard Business Review*, March/April: 57–69.

Teece, D. J. (2007) 'Explicating dynamic capabilities: The nature and micro foundations of (sustainable) enterprise performance', *Strategic Management Journal*, 28(13): 1319–1350.

Teece, D. J. (2018) 'Business models and dynamic capabilities', *Long Range Planning*, 51(1): 40–49.

Wang, C. L. and Ahmed, P. K. (2007) 'Dynamic capabilities: A review and research agenda', *International Journal of Management Reviews*, 9(1): 31–51.

Whittington, R., Regnér, P., Angwin, D., Johnson, G. and Scholes, K. (2020) *Exploring Strategy*, 12th ed., Harlow, UK: Pearson.

Websites

www.airfleets.net

www.contiki.com

www.edinburghfestivalcity.com

www.expediainc.com

www.ihg.com

www.itsmorefuninthephilippines.com

www.mandarinoriental.com)

www.marriott.com

www.merlinentertainments.biz/

www.royalcaribbean.com

www.singaporeair.com

www.sunvil.co.uk

www.tourism.gov.ph

www.trailfinders.com

www.whitbread.co.uk

11

Strategic directions for tourism, hospitality and event organizations

Introduction and chapter overview

Just as every product or business unit must determine an appropriate competitive strategy (considered in the previous chapter) to achieve an enhanced competitive position relative to rivals, so every organization must decide upon its attitude toward growth or alternative *directions* of strategic development. That is, should the direction taken be to expand, cut back or continue operations unchanged?

As with the other key business-level decisions (relating to the competitive stance and strategic methods), decisions related to strategic direction are usually taken at the SBU or product level, because conditions in one part of the organization may be different from those in another part.

At the overall organizational (or 'corporate') level, however, managers must also be mindful of the overall *balance* between the directions taken by individual business units, because available resources will be finite. Necessary resources may not be available to invest in all aspects of the organization simultaneously, so resources may be taken from one area to invest in another area to allow it to develop and grow.

These principles of selective investment and growth are consistent with the thinking embodied in the *product life cycle* and *portfolio models* (such as the Boston Consultancy Group matrix) that were explained in Chapter 6.

In general terms, three orientations are possible with regard to directional strategy:

- *Growth* strategies – expand the activities of the SBU
- *Stability* strategies – maintain the activities of the SBU
- *Retrenchment* strategies – reduce the activities of the SBU

DOI: 10.4324/9781003318613-15

LEARNING OBJECTIVES

After studying this chapter, you should be able to:

- Understand various *THE* contexts in which strategic directions have to be considered
- Identify the strategic directions available to organizations
- Understand and apply the Ansoff product–market model to relevant *THE* contexts
- Explain the risks associated with particular decisions on strategic direction
- Understand that organizations may need to ensure balance in their portfolio of SBUs because resources are finite
- Provide illustrative examples from *THE* organizations of strategic directions

11.1 Growth strategies

Having chosen the general orientation (such as growth), the management of an organization can then choose more specific strategies. According to Igor Ansoff (1987), growth can be broken down into four distinct categories.

11.1.1 Growth – Igor Ansoff's product–market framework

The most commonly used model for assessing the possible strategic *growth* directions an organization can follow (which is also commonly cited in the marketing literature) is the *Ansoff matrix*, shown in Figure 11.1. This matrix, which has two variables (products and markets), shows potential areas where core competences and generic strategies can be deployed. There are four broad alternatives:

- *Market penetration* – increasing market share in existing markets utilizing existing products
- *Market development* – entering new markets and segments using existing products
- *Product development* – developing new products to serve existing markets
- *Diversification* – developing new products to serve new markets

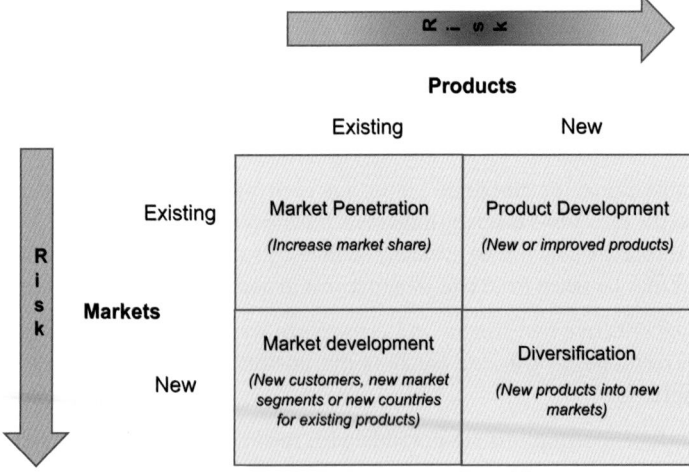

Figure 11.1 The Ansoff matrix

Source: Adapted from Ansoff (1987)

It should be emphasized that the matrix is related to the level of risk that managers are prepared to accept. Entering new markets or producing new products present areas of risk because many new products fail and managers will not have precise knowledge of market conditions when they enter new markets.

Thus, the lowest risk option is market penetration, because this option represents known markets and known products. Diversification, on the other hand, represents the highest risk category, because the organization will be entering new markets with new products.

11.1 SHORT CASE ILLUSTRATION

Applying the Ansoff matrix: the arts in the UK

Though classical music is a somewhat imprecise term, the word 'classical', when used to describe a musical style, is used by 'Western' popular culture to distinguish this kind of music from jazz, rock or other contemporary styles. Classical music audiences were broadly static in the UK between the mid-1980s and 2003, with classical music attendances during the period being in the range of 11% to 13% of the population in any given year.

Increasing participation in the arts (of which classical music is a part) has been a stated objective of UK governments, and classical music has to compete for public funding alongside other art forms. Hence, there is perceived need to develop audiences. Audience development is a planned process that involves building a relationship between an individual and the arts. It is an activity that is undertaken specifically to meet the needs of existing and potential audiences.

Barlow and Shibli (2007) argued that the Ansoff matrix provides a logical framework for evaluating strategies designed to impact customers (audience) and products (programs) in the arts. The matrix provides a clear conceptualization of products and markets that is easily understood and provides a firm basis for managerial decision making.

Applying the Ansoff matrix to audience development has the following implications:

- Market penetration – increasing the frequency of attendance and attracting lapsed attenders
- Product development – offering new programs to existing audiences
- Market development – attracting new people for the first time to the existing program
- Diversification – introducing a new program for a new audience

In applying the matrix to classical music, the authors pointed out that different positions within the matrix require different strategies. For example, in the case of market development, free or low-cost 'taster' sessions and the provision of information and reassurance may be appropriate strategies. Alternatively, pursuing a market penetration strategy may require different strategies such as providing incentives for existing concert-goers to attend more often through reduced prices for regular attendance.

Source: Adapted from Barlow and Shibli (2007)

Questions

1. Explain the concept of the Ansoff matrix and how it relates to this case.

2. Explain what the underlying purpose of applying models (such as the Ansoff matrix) to cases like this is when considering future strategy.

11.1.2 Market penetration

The main aim of a market penetration strategy is to increase market share using existing products within existing markets. This may involve taking steps to enhance existing core competences or building new ones. Such competence development may be intended to improve service or quality to enhance the reputation of the organization and differentiate it from its competitors. Equally, competence development may be centered on improving efficiency to reduce costs below those of competitors.

Mature or declining markets are more difficult to penetrate than those that are still in the growth phase, which provide more opportunities. In the case of a declining market, the organization may also consider the possibility of retrenchment or withdrawal to redeploy resources to more lucrative markets.

Market penetration is likely to be appropriate when:

● The existing market has growth potential

● Other competitors are leaving the market

● The organization can take advantage of its acquired experience and knowledge in the market

● The organization is unable (for some reason, such as lack of resources or regulatory restrictions) to enter new markets

When a business's current market shows signs of saturation, it may wish to consider alternative directions for development.

11.2 SHORT CASE ILLUSTRATION

Market penetration: Premier Inns

The concept of 'value' or 'budget' hotels has taken root in the UK (and other developed economies) over the last 25 years. In the UK, the growth of the largest brands in the budget sector – Premier Inns and Travelodge – has been rapid. The hotels, often located at convenient roadside locations, airports and city centers, offer good quality standardized rooms and are capable of accommodating a family at a reasonable price. The growth of these hotels has placed pressure on older properties and on 'bed and breakfast' establishments.

The market leader in the UK is Premier Inn, owned by the UK hospitality group Whitbread plc, which also developed the Costa Coffee brand, until its £3.9bn sale to the Coca-Cola Corporation in 2019. Unlike Costa Coffee (which Whitbread expanded rapidly into international markets), to date the company has mainly chosen to consolidate its lead position in the UK through *market penetration* with its Premier Inn brand. The company has tested international markets, notably India, the UAE and Ireland, and is now committing sizeable resources to the German market, which is 25% larger than the UK market but currently lacks a similar chain.

The brand has grown quickly, targeting its leadership position in its competitive set as shown in Figure 11.2.

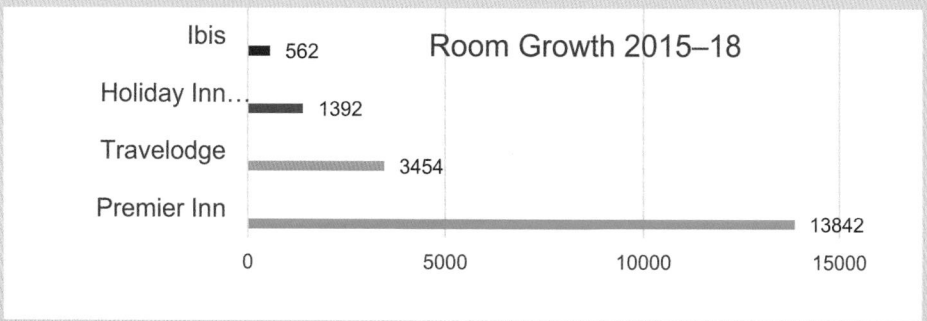

Figure 11.2 Market penetration: Premier Inn UK

Notwithstanding its current leadership position, Premier Inn continues to view opportunities for further penetration of the market in the UK and has set ambitious growth targets for the brand.

Source: Adapted from www.whitbread.co.uk/

Questions

1. Explain the rationale of expanding through market penetration for Whitbread plc's Premier Inn brand.

2. Consider why Whitbread is choosing only to invest cautiously in foreign markets for its Premier Inn brand at present.

11.1.3 Market development

Market development is based on entry to new markets, employing essentially unchanged products (although they may be modified in detail).

The new markets may be new geographical areas or new segments of existing markets. In either case, this strategic option attempts to attract new customers for the existing range of products or services. The key to success in market development is the transferability of the product as it is repositioned in new markets.

> For example: *McDonald's fast food restaurants have advanced inexorably from country to country, masterminded from its Chicago headquarters. It has done so with only relatively minor amendments to the overall product concept to take into account national cultural differences and purchasing habits. In France, for instance, alcohol is served in its restaurants, in contrast with most other countries.*

Entering new markets is likely to be based on leveraging existing competences but may also require the development of new competences (see the Key Concept in Chapter 3 for a definition of leveraging). Entering new segments of existing markets may require the development of new competences that serve the particular need of customers in these segments.

Internationalization and globalization are commonly used examples of market development. It is likely that an organization will need to build new competences when entering international markets to deal with linguistic, cultural, logistical and other potential problems.

11.3 SHORT CASE ILLUSTRATION

Market penetration: Holiday Inn expansion into Eastern Europe

Many large internationally diverse *THE* companies boast that they operate 'around the world' or have a 'global' presence. Closer inspection often reveals that there are gaps in their coverage. In reality, most companies in *THE* (as in other industries) expand into new countries in a structured and planned way, taking care to ensure that they understand the market before committing resources.

Thus, in September 2018, IHG, one of the world's largest hotel companies, announced that it was developing its first hotel project in Latvia with a Holiday Inn hotel in the center of the Latvian capital Riga. The hotel takes advantage of the surging demand in recent years for both leisure and business accommodation in Eastern Europe. Holiday Inn Riga is a key stage in IHG's Eastern European and Baltic expansion strategy, fueled by growing domestic travel; tourism from visa-free countries including China, South Korea and India; as well as a sustainable level of demand from IHG's customers in Western Europe, who are attracted by new travel experiences and low costs.

By developing additional capacity, IHG derives benefits from economies of scale and scope and builds momentum for its portfolio of brands. The development of the hotel in the historic city of Riga is the fourth announcement of an Eastern European hotel development during 2018, a region in which the company already had 25 established properties across its brand portfolio, which also includes Crowne Plaza and Intercontinental hotels.

Source: www.ihg.com

Questions

1. Explain why companies such as IHG may take a cautious approach in developing in new countries.

2. Explain the economies of scale and scope that IHG may be able to realize in Eastern Europe as a result of developing multiple properties in the region.

Market development is likely to be appropriate when:

- The existing market has no growth potential
- Regulatory or other restrictions prevent an increase in an organization's market share in its current market
- Other geographic markets or market segments offer good growth potential
- Existing products are easily transferable

The major risk associated with market development is that it centers on entry to markets of which the organization's managers may have only limited experience and, consequently, costly mistakes may be made.

11.4 SHORT CASE ILLUSTRATION

Market development: GL events in Asia-Pacific

The growth of the events industry is always fueled by the trends that shape a region's economy. Nowhere is this more evident than in the Asia-Pacific region. It has developed a vast and dynamic meetings and events industry fueled by factors such as rapid economic growth, China developing into a global economic superpower, development of high-tech infrastructure, a highly educated workforce and a vibrant business start-up environment.

People travel thousands of kilometers to attend annual events such as RISE in Hong Kong (possibly Asia's largest technology conference) and Singapore's FinTech Festival, which focuses on technology in the finance sector. Attendees expect these events to be impressive, reflecting the location and the latest event innovations.

The event management industry is diverse, fragmented and highly competitive. It is a field in which local knowledge is vital in delivering successful events because numerous suppliers and venues are usually involved and marketing requires a detailed knowledge of local media channels and target segments. For established companies in this industry, expanding into new territories can be highly risky because up-front investment is necessary before returns are likely to be forthcoming and competition from local rivals is often intense.

GL Events is a French company based in Lyon and quoted on the Paris stock exchange that offers specialized expertise for every area of the event industry in a number of countries. The group operates in the three major segments of the event industry market:

- Organizing – for trade fairs, conventions and events
- Venues management – managing 50 venues around the world
- Service provision – for sport events, exhibitions, conferences and corporate events

GL Events has been steadily increasing its global reach in recent years with a particular emphasis on Asia. It opened its Hong Kong subsidiary in 2000 before reaching out to Mainland China with the opening of its GL China office in Shanghai in 2006. A further office was added in Macau in 2008. Each of these offices combines the international experience of a major diversified events management organization with the regional expertise of a local office staffed by local employees. With local offices in place, the pace of GL Events' development in this region has accelerated. In 2018, for example, the company participated in the organization of the Asian Games in Indonesia.

Source: www.gl-events.com

Questions

1. Explain the *market development* that GL Events has undertaken in recent years.

2. Explain the core competence that GL Events is able to leverage across multiple markets.

11.1.4 Product development

Product development centers on the development of new products for existing markets.

As with the previous two growth directions, the intention is to attract new customers, retain existing ones and increase market share. Providing new products will be based on exploiting existing competences but may also require that new competences be built (such as in product research and development).

Product development offers the advantage of dealing with customer needs of which it has some experience because they are within its existing market. In a world of shortening product life cycles, product development has become an essential form of strategic development for many organizations. Product development is likely to be appropriate when:

- An organization already holds a high share of the market and could strengthen its position by the launch of new products
- The existing market has good potential for growth, with opportunities for good economic returns for new product launches
- Customer preferences are changing and they are receptive to new product ideas or new destinations
- Competitors have already launched their own new products

Although 'new' products are considered in product development, it is possible to consider new products in several different ways. There are very few products that are totally new. Holidays to the moon might be such an example. Many so-called new products are actually variations on existing products or products that are new to a particular organization. Thus, new products might be:

- Completely new to a particular organization as, for example, when a tour operator launches an airline or an events management company that organizes music festivals adds exhibitions and meetings to its product portfolio
- Developments of additional lines of existing products as, for example, when tour operators launch new destinations or a hotel group 'extends' its well-established brand from roadside locations to city
- Creation of differing quality versions of the same product as, for example, when British Airways added an additional airline class in 2000 for those paying 'full economy' (as opposed to discounted fares) when it launched its 'premium economy' class – an innovation, which has subsequently been copied by many airlines

Introducing new products is, however, highly risky, because many new products fail. There are a number of factors that could reduce the risks of failure. New products should:

- Have a market focus
- Build on existing core competences
- Involve cross-disciplinary teams in their development
- Involve good internal communications so that all within the organization are kept informed

11.5 SHORT CASE ILLUSTRATION

Product development: Club Med

In 1950, with Europe at peace, Frenchman Gilbert Trigano and Gérard Blitz, a Belgian, bought some American army surplus tents and camp beds, set them up in a pinewood on the Spanish island of Majorca and called the enterprise Club Mediterranean. The idea was a success from the start. Holiday camps were not new. In Britain, Billy Butlin's camps had provided cheap refuges from rainy summers.

It was Trigano who developed the Club Med product into a profitable business. During his four decades with Club Med, bungalows and hotels were added with the soft comforts of home. Staff were hired to do the chores and Club Med establishments spread throughout the world. Club Med became a messenger of France's perceived high standards in food, wine, language and fashion.

In the 1990s, the Club's fortunes declined as competitors copied its concepts and holidaymakers demanded more sophisticated offerings. Philippe Bourguignon, former CEO of EuroDisney, came in as CEO with a diversification strategy that involved launching gyms, bars, nightclubs and a budget version of the village – but it was not successful.

During the early part of the new century, driven by the changing expectations of its customers and another CEO Henri Giscard Estaing, the company returned to developing its core product: holiday villages. Peripheral activities were sold, and new investors were found. The villages moved upscale to the four- and five-star brackets and were aimed firmly at families seeking activities in beautiful locations. It invested heavily in renovating its villages, closed nonperforming villages and expanded into China. This move was hastened in February 2015, when the Chinese company Fosun International finalized a takeover deal for Club Med's parent company at a valuation of just over US$1bn.

The brand has regained its success by discarding non-core activities, investing heavily in product development and specifically targeting the family market, which accounts for approximately 70% of its clientele. Most villages are designed for families, with villages providing daytime supervised facilities for children.

The 70 villages situated worldwide are now divided into three different types:

- Family resorts: villages with children's clubs and activities for teenagers, offering relaxation and leisure activities and welcoming families, couples and friends

- Resorts for everyone: villages with no club facilities for children and teenagers but welcoming couples, families and friends

- Resorts for adults only: adults-only villages (from 18 years) offering entertainment, relaxation, sports and leisure activities to friends, singles or couples

Source: Adapted from www.clubmed-corporate.com/

Questions

1. Explain the *product development* that Club Med has undertaken and the reasons why it had to adopt this option.

2. Explain the reasons why a company such as Club Med would discard its 'non-core' activities.

11.1.5 Diversification

Diversification involves growth achieved through new products sold in new markets. Because it involves both markets and products that are new to the organization and of which managers have no experience, this is viewed as the option entailing the most risk. Despite the risk, there will be situations where this represents the most sensible option.

Diversification can be achieved by developing in a number of directions (which will be discussed in subsequent sections) and by utilizing a number of different methods (which will be discussed in the following chapter).

Figure 11.3 summarizes the directions and methods of diversification available to managers.

The underlying reason usually advanced by managers for diversification is 'synergy'. Synergistic benefits are created when value is created through diversification. In essence, synergy is concerned with the whole being worth more than its constituent parts, which has sometimes been expressed in strategy texts as the '2 + 2 = 5 effect'.

DEFINITION/QUOTATION

Synergy

Synergy refers to the benefits gained where activities or assets complement each other so that their combined effect is greater than the sum of the parts.

(Whittington et al., 2020:245)

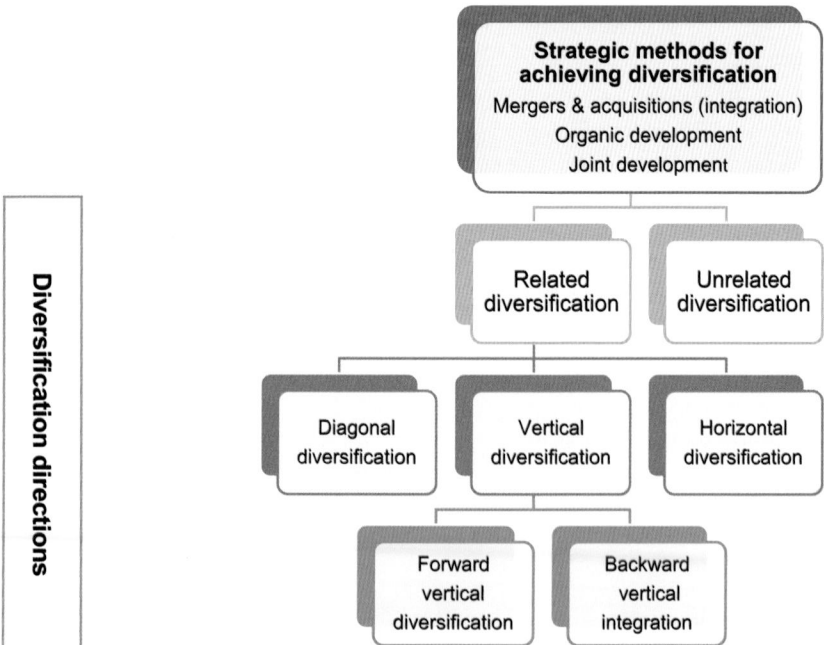

Figure 11.3 The directions and methods of diversification

In other words, the value created from controlling (or owning) various parts of the value chain is greater than when they were controlled separately because the individual elements support each other. As Lynch (2021) pointed out, though the concept is relatively easy to understand, it is rather more difficult to analyze and measure precisely. The topic has also received a great deal of attention in the strategic management academic literature. The breadth of the research was reviewed by Purkay-astha et al. (2012) and Dhir and Dhir (2015) and applied in a tourism context by Weidenfeld (2018).

More specifically, diversification is likely to be an appropriate strategic option when the organization concerned:

- Has current products and markets that no longer provide an acceptable financial return
- Has underutilized resources and competences
- Wishes to broaden its portfolio of business interests across more than one product/market segment
- Wishes to make greater use of any existing distribution systems in place, thus diluting fixed costs and increasing returns
- Wants to derive the benefits of economies of scope (see Key Concept in Chapter 8)
- Wants to spread risks
- Has a need to even out the cyclical effects in a given sector

Related diversification occurs when the products and/or markets share some degree of commonality with existing ones. This 'closeness' can reduce the inherent risks (because managers are dealing with both new markets and new products) associated with diversification. In practice, related diversification usually means growth into similar industry sectors or *forward* or *backward* in an organization's existing supply chain.

Related diversification (sometimes termed *concentric* diversification) can follow four main patterns, as shown in Figure 11.4.

Vertical backward diversification occurs when an organization seeking to operate in markets from which it currently obtains its resources (i.e., extending the value chain in an *upstream* direction).

> **For example:** *An event management company gaining a controlling stake in an event venue such as a concert theater and a tour operator developing a hotel chain or an airline are examples of vertical backward diversification.*

Upstream diversification (as it is sometimes termed) provides greater control over supplies of resources. The benefits of vertical backward diversification are that:

- Supplies are guaranteed
- The costs of supplies are internalized; that is, brought within the organization's control
- Supplies may be denied to competitors or made more expensive to acquire
- The portfolio of activities is broadened, giving protection against risk
- Potential problem areas with regard to supplies are identified and dealt with quickly

Vertical forward diversification occurs when an organization seeks to operate in markets currently served by its customers or distributors (i.e., extending the value chain in a *downstream* direction).

> **For example:** *An event management company or a tour operator developing a distribution network such as a chain of agents or call centers is an example of vertical forward diversification in that companies are taking control of aspects of their distribution and customer services.*

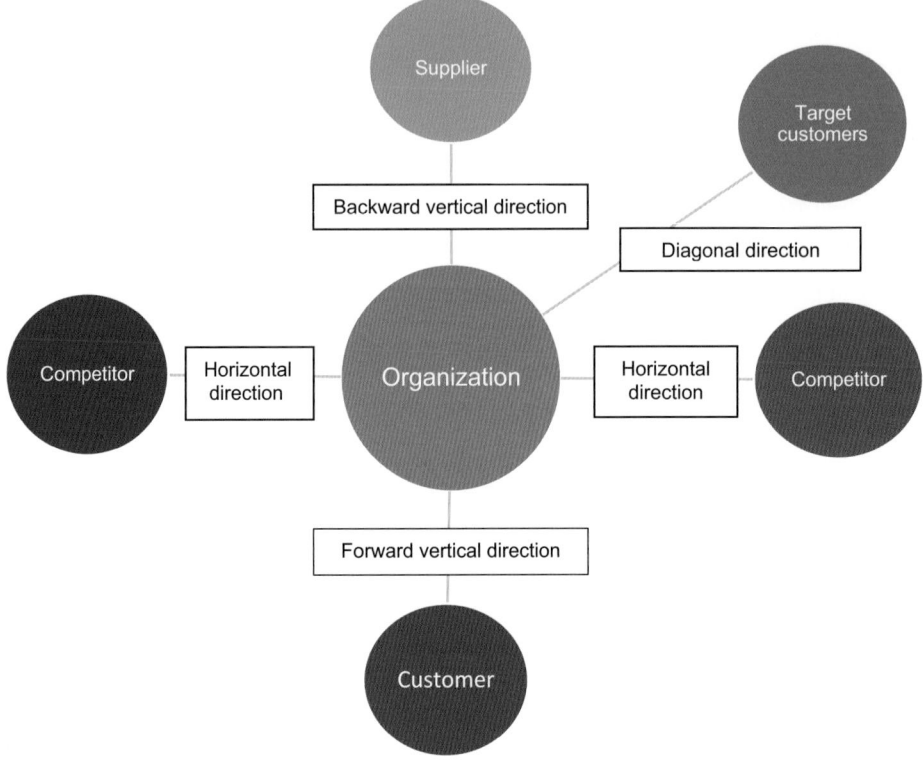

Figure 11.4 Patterns of related diversification

This form of diversification gives an organization closer contact with customers and can give significant marketing advantages in that it provides market intelligence that might not be forthcoming when dealing through an intermediary such as an independently owned chain of agents.

> **THINK POINTS**
>
> - Distinguish between market development and product development, citing examples you are familiar with from *THE*.
> - Explain what is meant by *forward* and *backward* vertical diversification.
> - Explain the four quadrants of the Ansoff matrix in relation to the risks incurred.

The benefits of vertical forward diversification are that:

- Guaranteed outlets are provided for products to be distributed
- The costs of distribution are internalized and can therefore be controlled
- Distribution outlets are denied to competitors

- Information is gathered regarding consumer purchasing behavior both for the organization's own products and for competing products
- The portfolio of activities is broadened, giving protection against risk

Note: Vertical diversification should not be confused with *vertical integration*, which concerns mergers or takeovers (acquisitions) to integrate existing organizations. That is a further decision regarding the *method* of diversification to be employed (see Chapter 12 on strategic methods).

> **For example:** *Rather than purchase an existing agency chain, the event management company or tour operator (featured in the previous two examples) might choose to develop such a chain for themselves from scratch or to work cooperatively with another company through an alliance or other arrangement.*

Horizontal diversification involves an organization entering complementary or competing markets.

> **For example:** *A tour operator working with or taking over another tour operating organization, an airline or hotel strategic alliance when two or more airlines or hotels work in a complementary manner to achieve common objectives and two event management companies in different countries working together to achieve wider geographical coverage for mutual benefit are examples of horizontal diversification.*

Note: In a similar fashion to vertical diversification, horizontal diversification should not be confused with *horizontal integration*, which is the merger with or takeover (acquisition) of a competitor. Diversification may be achieved by integrating a competitor that has been acquired, but it might also be achieved through joint developments (such as alliances) or by developing internally (see Chapter 12 on strategic methods).

The benefits of horizontal diversification are that:

- Market share is increased
- Greater purchasing power leads to more favorable rates being negotiated with suppliers and distributors
- Economies of scale are derived from the enlarged organization
- Opportunities to increase market share are denied to competitors
- Competitors may become collaborators

Related diversification has the benefit of leveraging existing competences as well as requiring the building of some new competences. In other words, it draws on existing organizational knowledge as well as requiring the building of some new skills and knowledge.

DIAGONAL DIVERSIFICATION

Service-based companies experience particular problems during growth owing to the nature of the product. In particular, the intangibility of the product and the inseparability of production and consumption lead to difficulties in targeting new segments (see Carman and Langeard, 1980). However, service-based companies such as those in *THE* may also have particular advantages that allow their core competences to be leveraged in related areas but in a different way from the horizontal and vertical axes considered so far in this chapter.

Poon (1993) referred to a fourth pattern of related diversification – that of *diagonal diversification*, also referred to as *concentric diversification* in some texts (see, for example, Kim et al., 2017). This form of diversification (common in service industries) utilizes a common platform of information utilizing technology to target a group of customers with a closely related set of products.

> For example: *Banks use their customer databases to target their customers with offers of insurance, mortgages, financial planning services and possibly travel products.*
>
> *In a similar way, Saga, a UK company that developed travel products for the over 55 group, also targets its customers with a range of financial services. Another example is American Express, the American financial services and travel group that is also involved in travel related and financial services. Many of its sales in leisure travel are to its American Express card holders.*

Diagonal diversification offers potential benefits in that it:

- Allows organizations to get close to their customers and lower costs for each product by sharing overhead across several product categories
- Allows organizations to benefit from *economies of scope* and systems savings
- Is cheaper for one organization to produce a combination of services rather than for many organizations to produce each separately

Diagonal diversification is illustrated in Figure 11.5.

UNRELATED DIVERSIFICATION

Unrelated diversification (sometimes termed *conglomerate* diversification) occurs when growth takes place in product and market areas that are completely new and with which the organization has no previous experience. The lack of experience in these products and markets serves to increase the potential risks.

Unrelated diversification carries greater risk than related diversification because it involves producing new products in unfamiliar product areas for markets with which the organization is also unfamiliar. Businesses tend to take this option when they see serious restrictions on growth potential in their existing markets, and in related markets, or when they see significant opportunities for growth in new markets. In addition, there are potential financial and risk-bearing economies of scale, opportunities to build on existing competences and the possibility of synergy.

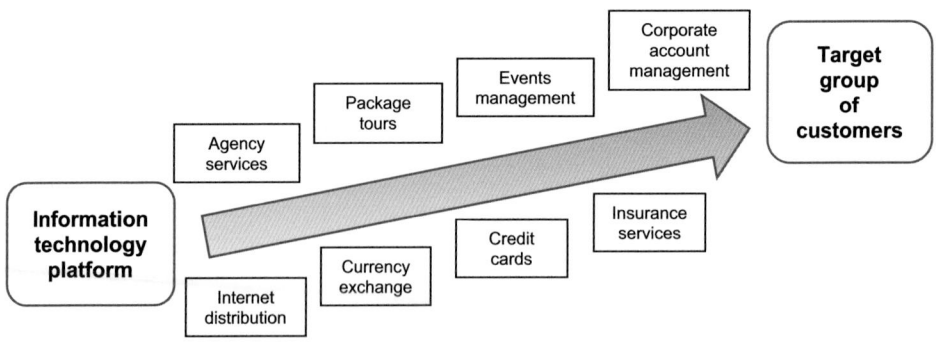

Figure 11.5 Diagonal diversification in *THE*

Source: Adapted from Poon (1993)

Unrelated diversification is far less common than related diversification in publicly quoted companies. The synergies between unrelated businesses are more difficult to achieve, although shared technology is one way in which they might be achieved. In the past, stock markets have found such conglomerates difficult to value, resulting in the so-called conglomerate discount.

Conglomerates can trade at a discount to the overall individual value of their businesses. The conglomerate discount arises because such companies are difficult to understand and they straddle several business sectors, so that they are difficult to compare with other companies.

However, unrelated diversification is still common among private companies (which do not require stock market quotations) and is still very popular in certain countries. Such conglomerate groups of companies are common in many Asian countries such as China, India, Malaysia, Thailand and Indonesia, a point that goes unrecognized in many Western-oriented texts. The Short Case Illustration below provides an example of one such conglomerate.

11.6 SHORT CASE ILLUSTRATION

Unrelated diversification: HNA Group

HNA Group Co., Ltd. was a Chinese conglomerate founded in 2000 and headquartered in Haikou, Hainan, China. It was involved in numerous industries including aviation, real estate, financial services, tourism and logistics, along with other diverse assets.

Two Chinese entrepreneurs created Hainan Airlines, a regional Chinese airline, in 1993. Following a restructuring of the airline, HNA Group was founded. Since that time, the group has carried out diversification on a massive scale, entering multiple industries such as tourism, property, logistics and financial services, as well as massively increasing the size of its core airline (Hainan) and investing in other airlines.

It also significantly expanded its involvement with both national and international companies to create a sprawling group covering numerous countries and commercial sectors. These include large stakes in several airlines in China, Africa and South America; international hotel group NH Hotels; airport services group Swissport; an office tower and a hotel in New York City; and investments in the German Bank Deutsche and Hilton Hotels.

This rapid diversification into new products and new markets, some of which were unrelated to its existing businesses, was fueled by excessively high levels of debt. It had a sprawling web of activities but there appeared to be no overall strategy guiding the growth. Instead, investments seemed to be made as opportunities arose in whichever sector that happened to be. Concerns over the sustainability of the levels of debt led to the intervention of the Chinese government in July 2017 and the halting of new loans. Overall debt in 2017 was said to have reached $94bn.

The company was *overtrading*, a situation in which companies expand their operations too quickly and risk failure due to the lack of access to adequate financial resources. Subsequently, to ease the burden, the company disposed of assets worth several billion dollars, severely curtailing the company's activities and reducing its revenues, which once stood at US$55bn. The liquidity shortage also resulted in the non-delivery of six Airbus A330 aircraft due to be delivered to the group.

On 29 January 2021, HNA Group declared bankruptcy after debt restructuring efforts failed, and several legal cases are outstanding against the company and some of its directors.

Sources: Various newspaper articles

Questions

1. Consider the reasons why conglomerates such as HNA remain successful business forms in many countries.

2. Consider the reasons for HNA's failure.

3. Although many of the businesses contained within HNA appear to be unrelated, there may be advantages in being part of a large, diverse group. Explain what these advantages might be.

11.2 Stability strategies

An organization's SBUs may choose stability (sometimes termed *persevering* in the literature) over growth by continuing current activities without any significant change in direction. Stability strategies are not the same as 'doing nothing', because to remain stable, actions have to be taken to defend the current market position from competitors. There may be several reasons for opting for such a strategic direction:

- The current environment is hostile or unpredictable, making investment required for growth unattractive
- A balance has to be maintained in the organization, so finite resources have to be deployed in other SBUs that provide greater opportunities
- A position of maturity has been reached where further growth is difficult and emphasis is placed on defending the current position

Many small business owners opt for this strategy as they are happy with their position, having found a niche that they understand and that they are able to defend.

Stability strategies can be very useful in the short to medium term but can be dangerous in the longer term as competitors start to make inroads into market share.

Wheelen et al. (2018) identified three variants of stability:

- *Pause/proceed with caution* – an opportunity to rest and reflect before continuing a growth or retrenchment strategy. It represents a deliberate attempt to make only incremental improvements until the environment changes. Such a strategy may be the result of excessive growth in the past that has led to pressures on the organization or from the need to stabilize after a period of decline.
- *No change* – a decision to do nothing new, choosing to continue current operations for the foreseeable future. Returns are adequate in the current position, so why put these returns at risk by going after growth?
- *Profit* – a decision to do nothing new in a worsening environmental position but instead to act as though the organization's problems are only temporary. The profit strategy attempts to support profits when an organization's sales are declining by reducing investment and reducing unnecessary expenditure; that is, squeezing out costs to increase margins.

11.3 Retrenchment strategies

An organization's SBU may pursue a retrenchment strategy when it is in a weak competitive position and the environment remains hostile for the alternative stability or growth strategies.

> For example: *In the period following the 11 September 2001 terrorist attacks in America, travel companies around the world chose to reduce their scale of operations in response to the severe drop in demand. AerLingus, the Irish airline, which relies on the transatlantic trade (which was particularly badly hit) for about 70% of its revenues, scaled back large parts of its operations in the wake of the attacks and looked for potential partners and sought additional sources of finance. In the poor trading conditions, which continued for several years following the attacks, two national 'flag carrier' airlines – Swissair and the Belgian airline Sabena – both went bankrupt.*

Wheelen et al. (2018) identified four variants of retrenchment:

- *Turnaround* – emphasizes the improvement in operational efficiency when an organization has problems that, though serious, are not critical (see, for example, Solnet et al. [2010] for a discussion of turnaround in relation to hotels and tourism). Analogous to a weight reduction diet, Pearce and Robbins (1994) viewed such a strategy as a two-stage process involving contraction followed by consolidation. Contraction is the initial effort to 'stop the bleeding', with general cutbacks in size and costs followed by consolidation that implements a program to stabilize the now leaner organization.

- *Captive company* – involves giving up independence in return for security, whereby management offers the company to one of its largest customers to ensure survival. The customer guarantees the survival of the company by offering a long-term contract.

- *Sell out/divestment* (see also Chapter 12) – if an organization or SBU is in a weak competitive position, it may choose to retrench through selling the entire organization or divesting those SBUs that are in a weak position to provide finance for those that are stronger.

- *Bankruptcy/liquidation* – occurs when the organization finds itself in a very poor competitive position with few prospects. Bankruptcy (sometimes called administration) involves giving up the management of the company to the courts in return for some settlement of the corporation's obligations. The court-appointed managers attempt to keep the organization as a 'going concern'. By contrast, liquidation is the termination of the organization when it is too weak to be sold to others as a going concern and any assets are sold to pay as much as possible to the organization's creditors.

The Short Case Illustration below provides an example of a turnaround at the Holiday Inn Hotel group.

11.7 SHORT CASE ILLUSTRATION

Turnaround: Holiday Inn Hotels

The international hotel brand Holiday Inn (part of the IHG Group) has expanded rapidly around the world in the last few decades largely through franchising, but the growth path has not always been smooth.

American entrepreneur Kemmons Wilson opened the first Holiday Inn hotel in 1952 in Memphis, Tennessee, after he returned from a family holiday discouraged over the lack of family and value-oriented lodging. Children stayed free, and the hotel offered a swimming pool, air conditioning and restaurant on the property. Telephones, ice and free parking were standard as well. Although commonplace today, these services were revolutionary at the time and set a standard for the hotel industry.

What Holiday Inn then proceeded to do, which had not been done before, was to standardize the style of the motels and hotels and franchised the concept to other business owners. Holiday Inns spread quickly first in the USA and subsequently to other parts of the world. However, any brand has to be kept fresh and relevant, and it became increasingly clear by the early years of this century that the 'legacy' brand had become tired, with many older properties. Though Holiday Inn brand recognition remained high, other hotel chains had overtaken Holiday Inn and sales were under pressure.

Consequently, in 2007, the company launched an ambitious $1bn rebranding initiative for its 60-year-old brand, the largest ever undertaken by a hotel chain. By 2011, Holiday Inn had removed nearly 1,200 underperforming Holiday Inn and Holiday Inn Express hotels and added 1,500 new ones, and a new logo and brand attributes were developed and rolled out across the network.

Source: Adapted from www.IHG.com and various newspapers

Questions

1. Explain why Holiday Inn had to launch its turnaround strategy.

2. Identify and explain the main elements of Holiday Inn's turnaround strategy.

11.3.1 Involuntary retrenchment

In some cases, retrenchment strategies are not chosen by organizations voluntarily but are forced upon them as the only viable option in response to external environmental pressures. The 'threat of external shocks' was discussed in Chapter 2, and it was stated that (though not, of course, unique to *THE*) these sectors are particularly prone to the threats posed by external shocks. These impacts are beyond the control of managers, though they must react to them quickly and decisively to manage the impact they have on their organizations. Such was the case with the COVID-19 pandemic, which had a dramatic and relatively fast impact on all *THE* organizations and destinations around the world.

Many organizations and destinations are affected by incidents such as cyclones, earthquakes and terrorist attacks and have developed risk mitigation and resilience strategies over the years (Ritchie and Jiang, 2019).

Though the worldwide impact of COVID-19 was clearly devastating for many parts of *THE* worldwide, estimating its total effects is clearly highly problematic, though Škare et al. (2021) attempted to do so. Furthermore, the authors argued that from the start of the COVID-19 crisis in China, the impact of the pandemic on the travel tourism industry was significantly underestimated. The COVID-19-induced shock can be viewed as being different from other crises facing *THE* in three critical respects (Dolnicar and Zare, 2020) in that the:

- Economic shock and consequent travel decline were global

- Economic shock was more dramatic, with reductions to economic growth twice as great as those caused by regular economic shocks
- Shock had the potential to trigger structural changes in certain sectors of the industry

These three criteria, it can be argued, differentiate economic shocks from the 'super-shock' caused by COVID-19 (Dolnicar and Zare, 2020). Consequently, most organizations and destinations were forced into rapidly adopting retrenchment strategies to *downsize* their activities during the pandemic to ensure survival.

11.4 COVID-19 crisis response strategies

The way in which *THE* organizations responded to the COVID-19 pandemic has been widely reported in the academic literature. See, for example, Wenzel et al. (2020) for an overview of strategic responses to the pandemic; on MICE, see Disimulacion (2020); on airlines, see Albers and Rundshagen (2020); on tourism, see Gössling et al. (2020) and Kuščer et al. (2022); and on hospitality, see Dolnicar and Zare (2020) and Le and Phi (2021). Several journals also published specific collections of COVID-19-related articles. For example, the *International Journal of Hospitality* (Rivera and Pizam, 2022) published a collection of some 84 articles on 'The Impact of the COVID-19 Pandemic on the World's Hospitality Industry'.

In dealing with the severe and relatively sudden pressures of the COVID-19 pandemic, almost all *THE* organizations and destinations adopted strategies that involved *retrenchment, stability (perseverance)* or a combination of these. Wenzel et al. (2020) usefully produced a typology of crisis response strategies that can be applied to how organizations responded to COVID-19. The typology is shown in Table 11.1.

Though all aspects of *THE* were hit hard by COVID-19, particularly during 2020 and 2021, some sectors were impacted more than others. Airlines, cruises and events were among those affected most, whereas holiday rentals and online travel agencies were relatively less affected (Borko et al., 2020). Detailed reactions to the crisis varied, but retrenchment and stability (perseverance) were universally implemented.

Table 11.1 Typology of crisis response strategies

Strategic crisis response	Comment
- *Retrenchment* – substantial cost/overhead and/or asset reductions	Tends to be effective as instruments of short-term survival of the organization through the crisis
- *Persevering* – measures to preserve the status quo of the organization and its activities	Examples include debt refinancing and more effective utilisation of resources
- *Innovating* – strategic renewal of the organization during the crisis	May be an important move in long-lasting crises that leads to re-establishment of the business at or above previous levels
- *Exit* – discontinuation of an organization's activities; can include a forced release of an unviable business or a considered strategic response to crisis	Includes freeing up committed resources for future business opportunities; not necessarily viewed as a business failure

Sources: Adapted from Wenzel et al. (2020); Albers and Rundshagen (2020)

11.8 SHORT CASE ILLUSTRATION

COVID-19 airline crisis response strategies

Albers and Rundshagen (2020) analyzed the reactions of European airlines to the COVID-19 crisis in the spring and early summer of 2020.

During the crisis peak (March and April 2020), all European airlines grounded almost their entire fleets and largely halted operations as wide-ranging travel restrictions were imposed, leading to the collapse of passenger travel. Responses to the crisis had both short- and long-term dimensions; that is, beyond the short-term retrenchment, airlines took other actions incorporating a longer-term perspective (Albers and Rundshagen, 2020).

Albers and Rundhsagen (2020) applied the crisis response typology developed by Wenzel et al. (2020) as summarized in Table 11.2.

Table 11.2 European airline COVID-19 crisis response strategies

Strategic crisis response	Comment
• *Retrenchment*	
Short-term orientation	All European airlines grounded their fleets almost completely owing to the imposed travel restrictions. Most airlines announced job cuts and/or reduced work patterns in accordance with national schemes to maintain employment.
Long-term orientation	Many airlines reduced their fleets, canceled new aircraft orders and retired larger aircraft. For example, Lufthansa retired its fleet of large Airbus A380 aircraft.
• *Persevering*	Most European airlines sought government aid through grants, loans at preferred conditions/state guarantees or subsidies.
• *Innovating*	
Crisis specific	Many airlines reconfigured some of their fleet for freight operations.
Longer term	Some new ventures and cooperation agreements were announced during this period; for example, low-cost carrier Wizz Air announced its intention to enter a number of new markets and grow ancillary services.
• *Exit*	
Failure	A number of European airlines failed and ceased operations during this period, including UK-based Flybe and Air Italy.
Withdrawals	Some airlines withdrew from some operations during this period. For example, Lufthansa's low-cost subsidiary (Germanwings) ceased trading in April 2020.

Source: Adapted from Albers and Rundshagen (2020)

11.5 Risk and balance

There are risks associated with all forms of strategic development. In relation to the strategic directions of development, the risks are:

- Smallest when development is largely based on existing core competences and when it takes place in existing markets
- Greatest when development requires entry to unrelated markets and/or products

Whether or not the risks are worth taking will depend on the current position of the organization and the state of its markets and products. Entry to new markets, whether related or unrelated, will depend on the business's assessment of the opportunities in new markets compared to opportunities in its existing markets.

> **For example:** *Decisions as to when to grow may be influenced by a country's economic performance, including cycles of strong and poorer rates of growth, or according to the political climate. Consequently, investment of finite resources in a particular foreign subsidiary may be restricted when the economy of that country is performing poorly or when there is political instability, because the opportunities do not present attractive financial returns. When the economy recovers or political stability returns, the company concerned may resume a growth strategy for that SBU by investing in that particular foreign subsidiary. Following the UK's Brexit decision to leave the European Union in a referendum held in June 2016, many investment decisions in THE (as in other industries) were delayed pending greater clarity as to what the economic impacts of Brexit might be.*

The focus of this chapter has been on the *business* level; that is, the level of the SBU. At some stage, the organization as a whole must bring the strategies of the individual SBUs together. Because resources are finite the organization is unlikely to have the resources available to develop each SBU at the same rate, and some will offer higher returns than others. Thus, choices have to be made at the *corporate* level between the competing demands of the individual SBUs.

Thus, a *THE* organization may also need to consider the issue of 'balance' in relation to the decisions it makes regarding strategic direction. Although it might want to target growth in all of its SBUs, it may not have sufficient resources and it may not be sensible to simultaneously target growth in all parts of the business.

It follows that a *THE* organization may go for growth in parts of its business where opportunities appear to be greatest and returns appear to be higher. At the same time, the business may target stability or retrenchment in other parts of the business where there are fewer opportunities and returns are lower.

In this way, a business with a number of SBUs considers the balance of products and markets, investing finite resources in those that offer the greatest returns. However, because the internal environment of organizations and the external environment faced by *THE* organizations are dynamic rather than static, the directions taken by each SBU may change over time.

> **For example:** *A vertically integrated travel company (which operates an airline, tour operations and travel intermediaries such as travel agents and websites) might want to expand its airline activities while at the same time reducing the size of its tour operations because of the market conditions pertaining to these two parts of the business. In this case, there might be overcapacity in tour operating but undercapacity in airline operations.*
>
> *An events management company might want to expand in one area of its business dealing with clients from a growing business sector, while at the same time shrinking other parts of the business that are doing less well.*
>
> *An international hotel company may see excellent opportunities to expand in certain countries because of an expanding economy but at the same time needs to contract in others because of a poor regulatory environment making the business less viable.*

THINK POINTS

- Explain why organizations do not always want to grow, and outline the alternatives.
- Explain why there are relatively few conglomerates operating as public companies quoted on the world's stock markets.
- Outline the advantages of organizations having a balanced portfolio of products in relation to the levels of risk incurred.

Small business focus

This chapter has considered one of the three key issues in strategic formulation relating to *strategic direction*.

In relation to strategic direction, the smaller scale of operations of SMEs can be both an advantage and a disadvantage. On the one hand, smaller enterprises can quickly adjust their direction in response to changes in the micro or macro environment.

Their size means that they are likely to be:

- More responsive to customer demands
- More flexible and adaptive because they do not have multiple SBUs and multiple markets to consider
- Quicker and more decisive at decision making aided by their *flatter* structures, often with a single leader (see Chapter 14)

However, SMEs in *THE* (as in other industries) are also extremely vulnerable to external environmental shocks over which they have no influence. Whereas larger organizations might have some protection (against adverse external factors) through the diversity of their operations and the size of their reserves, SMEs tend to have no such protection. Consequently, decisions on when and how to grow or, alternatively, to go for stability or retrenchment have to be taken very carefully. A poor decision could prove extremely costly because it could destroy the entire enterprise, as opposed to just a part of it in a larger, diversified company.

This factor appears to weigh very heavily in the minds of many owner managers. There is some evidence from *THE* contexts (see, for example, A. M. Williams and Shaw, 2004; Goulding et al., 2005; Bosworth and Farrell, 2011) that many entrepreneurs in reality do not try to maximize profitability, an assumption usually made in economics, but instead are satisfied at lower levels. Because profits can be seen as the reward for taking risks, this implies a risk-averse strategy being adopted by many owner managers of smaller firms. Bosworth and Farrell (2011), for instance, reported income *satisficing* behavior among tourism and hospitality businesses in rural Northumberland, UK.

The notion of *satisficing* is a behavior linked to the behavioral theory of the firm associated with the work of Cyert and March (1963). In this view of the firm (which often applies to smaller companies), once a critical level of profit is achieved, priority is attached to the attainment of other goals because the owners are satisfied with the levels of profit that have been achieved.

Notwithstanding the satisficing behavior of some SMEs, many small businesses have to take a highly entrepreneurial approach to survive and grow, which has been termed an *entrepreneurial orientation* (R. I. Williams et al., 2020). Such an approach represents behaviors associated with the extent to which firms employ an entrepreneurial ethos (Lumpkin and Dess, 1996).

Lumpkin and Dess (1996) proposed five entrepreneurial dimensions of entrepreneurial orientation, which were summarized by R. I. Williams et al. (2019). These are:

- *Autonomy* – the freedom individuals in a firm have to think creatively, make decisions and champion ideas
- *Innovativeness* – a firm's willingness to engage new ideas, embrace creativity and experimentation and seek new products, services or processes
- *Risk taking* – a firm's willingness to accept uncertainty and make resource commitments in the context of risk
- *Proactiveness* – demonstrate a forward-looking, *first-mover* approach
- *Competitive aggressiveness* – how a firm approaches its competitors

Larger companies often find it difficult to respond quickly and decisively to environmental changes, but SMEs, being smaller and often having an owner and/or founder still in place, are frequently more agile and entrepreneurial. Many owner managers exhibit such an ethos that they try to instill in their businesses as part of the organizational culture, and a number of studies (see, for example, Baker and Sinkula, 2009; Kajalo and Lindblom, 2015) have reported a positive correlation between entrepreneurial orientation and small firm performance. A number of specific *THE* studies have also explored this correlation, including Kamal et al. (2016), Fadda (2018), Peters and Kallmuenzer (2018) and Tajeddini et al. (2020).

The COVID-19 outbreak has been challenging for all *THE* organizations around the world. Though larger organizations often have the financial resources to withstand periods of low demand, they nevertheless have had to adopt strategies of retrenchment and stability to survive. Many smaller *THE* organizations ceased trading during the pandemic or downsized their activities considerably to survive.

> **For example:** *Do et al. (2022) surveyed 32 SME tour operators in Vietnam to explore their strategic responses to the crisis. Most respondents were aware of the need for restructuring and were expecting financial support from the government. The findings*

revealed that tour operators focused more on short- and medium-term strategies (i.e., retrenchment, persevering and exiting) rather than long-term planning (i.e., innovating) in response to COVID-19.

CHAPTER SUMMARY

The strategic direction of an organization determines the nature of product and market development, and the Ansoff matrix provides a simple and widely used way of conceptualizing the direction of growth. There may also be times when an organization judges that it is not the right time to grow and stability or retrenchment are considered as alternative directions of development. Retrenchment may at times be an involuntary means of development forced on organizations by internal and/or external environmental pressures. The chapter explored such circumstances in relation to COVID-19.

Finally, the issues of risk and balance were considered with regard to choosing directions of development. An organization has to consider the risks associated with each direction and the balance between SBUs because resources are finite and some SBUs may offer more attractive opportunities for returns on investment than others.

In Chapter 12, the third key issue of strategic formulation is considered, namely, the strategic methods that will be employed.

REFERENCES AND WEBSITES

References

Albers, S. and Rundshagen, V. (2020) 'European airlines' strategic responses to the COVID-19 pandemic (January – May, 2020)', *Journal of Air Transport Management*, 87: 101863.

Ansoff, I. (1987) *Corporate Strategy*, London: Penguin.

Baker, W. E. and Sinkula, J. M. (2009) 'The complementary effects of market orientation and entrepreneurial orientation on profitability in small businesses', *Journal of Small Business Management*, 47(4): 443–464.

Barlow, M. and Shibli, S. (2007) 'Audience development in the arts: A case study of chamber music', *Managing Leisure*, 12(2–3): 102–119.

Borko, S., Geerts, W. and Wang, H. (2020) *The Travel Industry Turned Upside Down: Insights, Analysis and Actions for Travel Executives*, New York: Skift Research and McKinsey.

Bosworth, G. and Farrell, H. (2011) 'Tourism entrepreneurs in Northumberland', *Annals of Tourism Research*, 38(4): 1474–1494.

Camisón Zornoza, C. and Monfort-Mir, V. M. (2012) 'Measuring innovation in tourism from the Schumpeterian and the dynamic-capabilities perspectives', *Tourism Management*, 33: 776–789.

Carman, J. M. and Langeard, E. (1980) 'Growth strategies for service firms', *Strategic Management Journal*, 1(1): 7–22.

Cyert, R. M. and March, J. G. (1963) *A Behavioral Theory of the Firm*, Englewood Cliffs, NJ: Prentice Hall.

Dhir, S. and Dhir, S. (2015) 'Diversification: Literature review and issues', *Strategic Change*, 24(6): 569–588.

Disimulacion, M. A. T. (2020) 'MICE tourism during COVID-19 and future directions for the new normal', *Asia Pacific International Events Management Journal*, 1(2): 11–17.

Do, B., Nguyen, N., D'Souza, C., Bui, H. D. and Nguyen, T. N. H. (2022) 'Strategic responses to COVID-19: The case of tour operators in Vietnam', *Tourism and Hospitality Research*, 22(1), 5–17.

Dolnicar, S. and Zare, S. (2020) 'COVID19 and Airbnb – Disrupting the disruptor', *Annals of Tourism Research*, 83: 102961.

Fadda, N. (2018) 'The effects of entrepreneurial orientation dimensions on performance in the tourism sector', *New England Journal of Entrepreneurship*, 21(1): 22–44.

Gössling, S., Scott, D. and Hall, C. M. (2020) 'Pandemics, tourism and global change: A rapid assessment of COVID-19', *Journal of Sustainable Tourism*, 29(1): 1–20.

Goulding, P. J., Baum, T. G. and Morrison, A. J. (2005) 'Seasonal trading and lifestyle motivation: Experiences of small tourism businesses in Scotland', *Journal of Quality Assurance in Hospitality and Tourism*, 5(2–4): 209–238.

Kajalo, S. and Lindblom, A. (2015) Market orientation, entrepreneurial orientation and business performance among small retailers', *International Journal of Retail and Distribution Management*, 43(7): 580–596.

Kamal, S. B. M., Zawawi, D. and Abdullah, D. (2016) 'Entrepreneurial orientation for small and medium travel agencies in Malaysia', *Procedia Economics and Finance*, 37: 115–120.

Kim, H., Hong, S., Kwon, O. and Lee, C. (2017) 'Concentric diversification based on technological capabilities: Link analysis of products and technologies', *Technological Forecasting and Social Change*, 118: 246–257.

Kuščer, K., Eichelberger, S. and Peters, M. (2022) 'Tourism organizations' responses to the COVID-19 pandemic: An investigation of the lockdown period', *Current Issues in Tourism*, 25(2): 247–260.

Lasher, W. R. (1999) *Strategic Thinking for Smaller Businesses and Divisions*, Oxford, UK: Blackwell.

Le, D. and Phi, G. (2021) 'Strategic responses of the hotel sector to COVID-19: Toward a refined pandemic crisis management framework', *International Journal of Hospitality Management*, 94: 102808.

Lumpkin, G. T. and Dess, G. G. (1996) 'Clarifying the entrepreneurial orientation construct and linking it to performance', *Academy of management Review*, 21(1): 135–172.

Lynch, R. (2021) *Strategic Management*, 9th ed., Harlow UK: Pearson.

Nieves, J. and Haller, S. (2014) 'Building dynamic capabilities through knowledge resources', *Tourism Management*, 40: 224–232.

Nieves, J., Quintana, A. and Osorio, J. (2016) 'Organizational knowledge, dynamic capabilities and innovation in the hotel industry', *Tourism and Hospitality Research*, 16(2): 158–171.

Pearce, J. A., II and Robbins, D. K. (1994) 'Retrenchment remains the foundation of business turnaround', *Strategic Management Journal*, June: 313–323.

Pereira-Moliner, J., Molina-Azorín, J. F., Tarí, J. J., López-Gamero, M. D. and Pertursa-Ortega, E. M. (2021) 'How do dynamic capabilities explain hotel performance?' *International Journal of Hospitality Management*, 98: 103023.

Peters, M. and Kallmuenzer, A. (2018) 'Entrepreneurial orientation in family firms: The case of the hospitality industry', *Current Issues in Tourism*, 21(1): 21–40.

Poon, A. (1993) *Tourism Technology and Competitive Strategies*, Wallingford, UK: CAB International.

Purkayastha, S., Manolova, T. S. and Edelman, L. F. (2012) 'Diversification and performance in developed and emerging market contexts: A review of the literature', *International Journal of Management Reviews*, 14(1): 18–38.

Ritchie, B. W. and Jiang, Y. (2019) 'A review of research on tourism risk, crisis and disaster management: Launching the *Annals of Tourism Research* curated collection on tourism risk, crisis and disaster management', *Annals of Tourism Research*, 79: 102812.

Rivera, M. and Pizam, A. (Eds). (2022) 'The impact of the COVID-19 pandemic on the world's hospitality industry', *International Journal of Hospitality Management*, Special Edition.

Škare, M., Soriano, D. R. and Porada-Rochoń, M. (2021) 'Impact of COVID-19 on the travel and tourism industry', *Technological Forecasting and Social Change*, 163: 120469.

Solnet, D. J., Paulsen, N. and Cooper, C. (2010) 'Decline and turnaround: A literature review and proposed research agenda for the hotel sector', *Current Issues in Tourism*, 13(2): 139–159.

Tajeddini, K., Martin, E. and Ali, A. (2020) 'Enhancing hospitality business performance: The role of entrepreneurial orientation and networking ties in a dynamic environment', *International Journal of Hospitality Management*, 90: 102605.

Weidenfeld, A. (2018) 'Tourism diversification and its implications for smart specialisation', *Sustainability*, 10(2): 319.

Wenzel, M., Stanske, S. and Lieberman, M. B. (2020) 'Strategic responses to crisis', *Strategic Management Journal*, 41: 7–18.

Wheelen, T. L., Hunger, J. D., Hoffman, A. N. and Bamford, C. E. (2018) *Strategic Management and Business Policy: Globalization. Innovation and Sustainability*, 15th ed., Harlow, UK: Pearson Education Limited.

Whittington, R., Regnér, P., Angwin, D., Johnson, G. and Scholes, K. (2020) *Exploring Strategy*, 12th ed., Harlow, UK: Pearson.

Williams, A. M. and Shaw, G. (2004) 'From lifestyle consumption to lifestyle production: Changing patterns of tourism entrepreneurship', in R. Thomas (Ed.), *Small Firms in Tourism: International Perspectives*, Abingdon, UK: Routledge, 109–124.

Williams, R. I., Jr., Smith, A., Aaron, J. R., Manley, S. C. and McDowell, W. C. (2020) 'Small business strategic management practices and performance: A configurational approach', *Economic Research-Ekonomska Istraživanja*, 33(1): 2378–2396.

Websites

www.clubmed-corporate.com
www.gl-events.com
www.ihg.com
www.whitbread.co.uk/

Chapter **12**

Strategic methods of development for tourism, hospitality and event organizations

Introduction and chapter overview

The previous chapters considered two aspects of strategic choice, namely, *competitive strategy* and *strategic direction*. This chapter considers the third aspect: How the development will be achieved; that is, which methods will be adopted (*strategic methods*).

In Chapter 10 we considered two approaches to competitive advantage that have been developed in the academic literature: the *competitive positioning* approach and the *core competence* or *resource-based* approach.

This chapter briefly discusses a third approach – the *relational approach* – which recognizes that many resources critical to an organization's success can come from outside the organization. Consequently, this approach stresses the importance of interfirm working in the form of business structures such as alliances, joint ventures, franchising arrangements and management contracts, all of which have become common in *THE* contexts.

The decision as to which method of strategic development to adopt is critical to the success of strategy.

The chapter considers internal (or organic) growth and then discusses the various mechanisms of external development: mergers and acquisitions and various forms of joint development involving differing types of collaborative arrangements. Finally, the chapter looks at 'downsizing' strategies such as demergers.

DOI: 10.4324/9781003318613-16

Part 4

After studying this chapter, you should be able to:

- Define and distinguish between internal and external methods of business development and to provide relevant *THE* examples
- Describe and provide illustrations of the various types of mergers and acquisitions
- Explain the motivations behind mergers and acquisitions and the reasons why they succeed or fail
- Describe what is meant by the various forms of joint development such as strategic alliances and assess with relevant *THE* examples why organizations enter into them
- Compare and contrast the circumstances in which the various methods might be used in the constituent parts of *THE*
- Explain what is meant by a 'disposal' and describe why at times *THE* organizations might pursue this pathway

12.1 Alternative strategic methods

In determining the methods by which strategic development will take place, the management of *THE* organizations must decide between three basic options. These are to:

- Develop internally (or organically as it's often called) utilizing existing available resources
- Merge with or acquire other companies or allow the company to be acquired by another company
- Develop through joint development with other organizations by making some form of collaborative arrangement

The three strategic methods are shown diagrammatically in Figure 12.1.

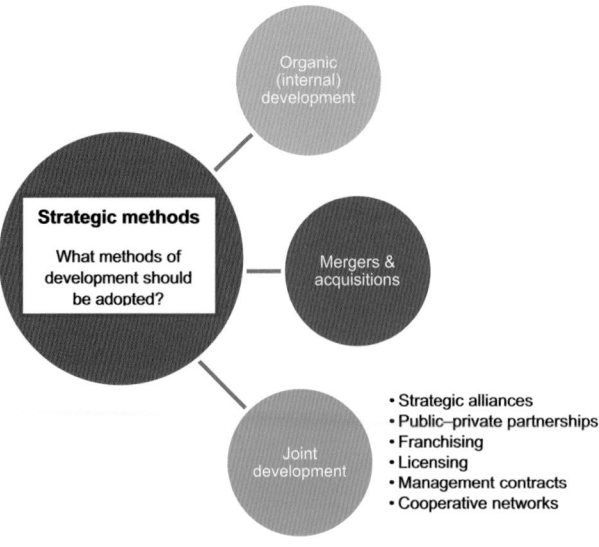

Figure 12.1 Methods of strategic development

Many organizations use each of the alternative strategic options in different circumstances. The same company may, for instance, choose to grow organically in one market, acquire another company in a second market and form a collaborative venture in a third market in recognition of the differing market characteristics that exist.

The different methods have associated advantages and risks, and the choice between them may vary at different points of the economic cycle.

Organizations operating in *THE* have to make a choice between the full range of strategic methods available. Franchising, management contracts, strategic alliances and PPPs are particularly characteristic of the sectors of *THE*, though the methods are not evenly represented in all sectors as shown later in Table 12.6. These characteristic forms of joint development are discussed fully later in the chapter.

THINK POINTS

- Using examples from *THE*, define and distinguish between internal and external business growth.

- Describe and distinguish between the three conceptual approaches to strategic management that are introduced in this text.

12.2 Organic (internal) growth

Organic growth is the most straightforward and commonest mechanism of business growth. Most companies use internal growth as their main method of growth at some time, so its popularity is obvious. The essential feature of organic growth is the reinvestment of previous years' profits in the existing business, together with finance provided by shareholders and banks. By increasing capacity (by, say, offering a larger number of holidays for sale, increasing the number of hotel rooms or managing a larger number of events), the organization takes on more employees to cope with the extra demand. In so doing, turnover increases and so does the capital (balance sheet) value of the business.

Organic growth is common during the early stages of corporate development as companies build markets and develop new products. It is also a common method of growth where access to capital markets might be restricted as with public sector organizations. Large companies may also use this method alongside external growth to consolidate market position.

> For example: *The introduction of an additional cruise ship by a cruise line and the building of an additional hotel by a hotel group are examples of organic growth. The retained profits from earlier years, possibly enhanced by additional funding provided by banks or shareholders, are channeled into the development, and the organization benefits from the increased market share and increased turnover. MSC Cruises is a division of a privately owned Swiss shipping company with headquarters in Geneva and is the third largest cruise operator in the world (after Carnival Corporation & plc and Royal Caribbean Cruises). When four LNG-fueled ships each weighing in excess of 200,000 tons enter service between 2022 and 2027, the cruise line will significantly increase its passenger capacity.*

The Short Case Illustration of Messe Frankfurt below illustrates an organization that has grown quickly by utilizing organic growth to achieve a considerable scale of operations.

12.1 SHORT CASE ILLUSTRATION

Organic growth: Messe Frankfurt event management organization

Germany, as a manufacturing and trading nation, has a long tradition of organizing international trade fairs and exhibitions, the origins of which date back several hundred years in some cases. Consequently, Hanover, Hamburg, Düsseldorf, Munich, Berlin and Frankfurt all have extensive modern exhibition spaces, which rank among the world's largest. Berlin, for example, hosts ITB Berlin, which rivals London's World Travel Market, as the world's largest event focusing on the travel and hospitality industries and their suppliers.

For example, in 1585, a small group of Frankfurt merchants requested that the town council establish regular trade fairs. Frankfurt has considerable advantages as a trading center, situated as it is at the heart of European trading routes. Modern-day trade fairs were reestablished after World War II and grew steadily in the postwar years as Frankfurt established itself as Germany's preeminent financial center (as the home of the German and European central banks and Germany's leading commercial banks) and also, crucially, as Germany's leading hub airport – a position it retains to this day.

In the postwar period, the Messe Frankfurt organization was established to organize and manage trade fairs. The Messe (Market) Frankfurt organization is a public sector body that is 60% owned by the City of Frankfurt and 40% by the state government of Hesse. The growth is partly attributable to the application of the Messe Frankfurt business model.

The increasing diversity of the products on offer quickly created a trend toward greater specialization of trade fairs. This was reflected in the 'Frankfurt principle'. Individual product groups that had previously been represented in the comprehensive multisector trade fairs for the consumer goods industry were further developed to create independent industry events. Thus, Frankfurt created market-leading trade fairs in industry sectors such as automotive, textiles, books, music, lighting and paper.

From a fairly small base in postwar Germany Messe Frankfurt has grown to become one of the world's leading exhibition end events management organizations, a position it has achieved largely through organic growth. In 2017, 140 trade fairs, conferences and exhibitions were organized at 50 venues around the world, attracting in excess of 5 million attendees. Owing to the global coronavirus pandemic and the ensuing travel restrictions and quarantine regulations, physical events around the world were canceled or restricted locally from 2019. Post-COVID-19, the company has been regaining its lost momentum and regaining its pattern of consistent growth.

The company has been able to leverage its expertise through international events, and although its center will remain in Frankfurt, crucially, about a third of the events were organized in foreign locations, which the company delivered through a network of 22 global subsidiaries. The international expansion of Messe Frankfurt, particularly in emerging markets, is an important part of the company's strategy for future development.

Source: Adapted from www.messefrankfurt.com/

Questions

1. What are the advantages and possible limits of the Frankfurt Messe business model?

2. What sort of competitive threats might Frankfurt Messe face?

The potential advantages and disadvantages of organic growth over other methods of development are summarized in Table 12.1.

Many large companies have used this method extensively in reaching their present size, but few have used the method exclusively.

> **For example:** *The Marriott International hotel corporation developed its Courtyard hotels concept organically during the 1990s, from the drawing board through to its current international market penetration in major business cities (Crawford-Welch, 1994). More recently, Marriott International developed its Moxy brand, which debuted in September 2014 with the opening of the Moxy Milan. A 'boutique hotel' concept for younger travelers, the brand is expanding fast mainly in city center locations, combining stylish design and informal service at an affordable price point (www.moxy-hotels. marriott.com).*

This method tends to be chosen in circumstances where:

- Suitable partners for joint development are unavailable
- Merger or acquisition is prevented on the grounds of cost, unavailability of suitable targets or regulatory disapproval
- Access to capital to pursue alternative methods is limited
- Directors want to maintain control
- The necessary resources and competences are available internally

The case of Accor in the following Short Case Illustration shows how this large hospitality company has primarily used organic growth, coupled with targeted acquisitions to drive growth.

Table 12.1 The potential advantages and disadvantages of pursuing organic growth

Potential advantages	Potential disadvantages
• Usually, a lower risk option in that the increase in capacity remains fully under the control of the existing management, thereby avoiding the risks of dealing with other organizations.	Usually a slower mechanism compared to external growth methods where the 'bolting on' of a new company or cooperation with other organizations is a faster route to growth than gradual growth by internal means.
• Core competences can usually be exploited and existing expertise, experience and knowledge can be capitalized upon.	Relying on the competences and resources of a single organization may lead to shortages and might mean that important opportunities are not exploited.
• Potential problems associated with the integration of differing organizational cultures are avoided.	
• Disruption to cash flows is likely to be less than with other methods. Also, other methods often require large up-front payments, whereas organic development allows investment to be spread over time.	

12.2 SHORT CASE ILLUSTRATION

Organic growth: Accor Hotels

The French group Accor, with its headquarters in Paris, is one of the world's largest hoteliers. The brands it operates under various contractual arrangements include Sofitel, Raffles, Fairmont, Swissôtel, Mercure, Pullman, Novotel and Ibis.

In recent years, Accor increased its presence around the world, though COVID-19 interrupted this expansion somewhat. Accor operates in about 110 countries around the world with about 5,300 sites and a total number of about 780,000 rooms worldwide.

The group has followed mixed methods of strategic development in that it primarily grew through organic growth supplemented by targeted acquisitions and partnerships with travel intermediaries. The group added some 10,000 rooms through two targeted acquisitions in high growth markets in which its brands were already well known: in Australia, New Zealand and Indonesia it purchased the Mantra Hotel group, and in Brazil it purchased over 20 properties from the BHG group of hotels.

However, the majority of Accor's growth has come from organic growth of its brands targeted at emerging hospitality markets, and this trend is set to continue.

To take full advantage of the dynamic growth in emerging markets, which is being led by a fast-rising middle class in search of travel and leisure opportunities, room openings have been particularly concentrated in Asia-Pacific and Latin America.

Source: Adapted from Accor.com

Questions

1. Why do you think Accor has chosen mainly to grow organically?

2. What are the potential advantages and disadvantages to Accor of this form of growth?

12.3 Mergers and acquisitions

It is difficult to open the business press without encountering details of a proposed or progressing merger or acquisition. The term *merger*, however, is sometimes replaced in such text with *takeover* or *acquisition*. The same news story may use all three terms as though the words mean the same thing. It is also common in the media and elsewhere for the terminology 'M&As' to be used as a shortened umbrella term covering all such activity.

For the purposes of a strategy text such as this, it is important to clarify the main terms generally used in connection with this process.

- *Merger:* the shareholders of the organizations come together, normally willingly, to share the resources of the enlarged (merged) organization, with shareholders from both sides of the merger becoming shareholders in the new organization.

The international airline industry, for example, has undergone a period of rapid consolidation over the last 20 years involving a number of mergers (particularly in North America). This merger activity is briefly described in the Short Case Illustration below.

12.3 SHORT CASE ILLUSTRATION

Mergers in the international airline industry

The US Airline Deregulation Act of 1978 introduced airlines operating in the USA to a new world of competitive threats and opportunities. The key change, whereby price-regulating power was removed from the Civil Aeronautics Board, enabled airlines to increase the variety of fares offered and increase the frequency by which fares were changed (Evans, 2001b). The changes the act brought forward led to the entry into the market of low-cost carriers such as Southwest Airlines and Frontier and eventually led to industry consolidation in the USA. Later deregulation in Europe has also led to some consolidation in Europe and elsewhere.

Established 'legacy' carriers in the USA had extensive networks operating 'hub-based' networks and generally had high cost bases and experienced low and variable levels of profitability. The high costs and periodic economic downturns in the sector frequently led to the major airlines incurring heavy losses, and several, such as American and US Airways, were at times close to bankruptcy. One response to these pressures has been the consolidation of the US air market that dates back to 2005 with the merger of US Airways and America West, followed by Delta merging with Northwest in 2010 (keeping the Delta name) and United merging with Continental in 2012 (keeping the United name). Discussions took place between American Airlines and US Airways about a possible merger, which was finally agreed in 2013, with the American Airlines name being retained.

Thus, 'the large eight airlines of 10 years ago are on course to become the big four, with reduced competition meaning that the remaining players have greater pricing power – the ability to raise fares after years of slashing ticket prices during market share grabs' (Parker, 2013a). The eight long-established large carriers, the so-called legacy airlines, have now consolidated into three carriers as outlined above: American Airlines (based in Dallas–Fort Worth), United Airlines (based in Chicago) and Delta (based in Atlanta). All of these airlines have come under pressure from newer low-cost rivals such as Southwest Airlines, JetBlue Airways and Frontier Airlines. Elsewhere in the world, consolidation has been less extensive, though important mergers have taken place in Europe, Latin America and Asia. For example:

- Air France merged with KLM Royal Dutch Airlines in 2004 to form Air France KLM.

- The International Airlines Group was formed in 2011 by a merger of British Airways and Spanish carrier Iberia.

- Lufthansa acquired Swiss in 2005 and Austrian Airlines in 2009.

- Latam Airlines is the result of the merger in 2012 between LAN Airlines of Chile and TAM Airlines of Brazil.

Though the level of market concentration means that much of the consolidation has probably already taken place in Europe, Parker (2013a) argued that there is a case for more mergers because there are still too many carriers.

Sources: Adapted from Evans (2001b); Parker (2013a); various newspaper articles

Questions

1. What factors favored consolidation in the international airline industry?

2. Why do many airlines historically have low and variable profit levels?

- **Acquisition:** a 'marriage' of unequal partners, with one organization buying and subsuming the other party. In such a transaction the shareholders of the target organization cease to be owners of the enlarged organization unless payment to the shareholders is made partly in shares in the acquiring company. The shares in the smaller company are bought by the larger.

RX Exhibitions, discussed in the following Short Case Illustration, provides an example of an acquisition together with other methods of development.

12.4 SHORT CASE ILLUSTRATION

Mixed methods: RX Exhibitions

Reed Exhibitions rebranded to RX in 2021 to reflect the increasingly digital and data-driven nature of the offer to customers. It is a division of the UK owned publishing and communications business Relx plc based in southwest London. The business grew rapidly prior to the pandemic, but retrenchment was forced upon the division during 2020 and with a slight recovery in 2021. Strong revenue growth, driven by a significant increase in face-to-face activity across most geographies, resumed in 2022. Revenues of about £1.1bn in 2019 fell to £360mn and £530mn in 2020 and 2021, respectively, but more recently, strong growth has resumed.

Although comparisons are difficult and industry boundaries are not easily determined in what is a highly fragmented industry, RX is a leading events management business and the market leader in exhibitions, with about 10% of world markets. Key products include London's World Travel Market, which has also spread to subsidiary locations. Other international exhibition organizers include Informa, Clarion and some of the larger German *Messen*, including Messe Frankfurt, Messe Düsseldorf and Messe Munich. Competition also comes from industry trade associations and convention center and exhibition hall owners.

Today, RX, like most large businesses, has a mix of strategic methods, as evidenced by the 2021 Relx Annual Report, which states that:

> Organic growth will be achieved by continuing to generate greater customer value by combining the best of face-to-face events with data and digital tools. RX will continue to seek organic growth through launches that are tightly focused on industries and geographies that are recovering most strongly from the pandemic.

> RX continues actively to shape its portfolio through a combination of new launches, strategic partnerships and selective acquisitions in faster growing sectors and geographies, and during the pandemic has withdrawn from markets and industries that have been particularly impacted and with lower long-term growth prospects.

The company states that these methods provide a strong platform for the recovery and longer-term success of RX.

Sources: Adapted from Relx Annual Report 2021, www.relx.com/

Questions

1. Explain the methods that Reed Exhibitions has used to grow.

2. Why might the methods used have changed at different periods in its development?

- **Takeover**: technically the same as an acquisition, but the term is often taken to mean that the approach of the larger acquiring company is unwelcome from the point of view of the smaller target company. The term *hostile takeover* describes an offer for the shares of a target public limited company that the target's directors reject. If the shareholders then accept the offer (despite the recommendation of the directors), the hostile takeover goes ahead.

> **For example:** *In early 2022, Denver-based Frontier attempted to acquire Florida-based Spirit Airlines, another US-based ultra-low-cost carrier, in a US$2.8bn cash-and-stock deal. The deal would have created the fifth-largest airline in the USA. The offer was rejected by the Spirit shareholders. Subsequently, JetBlue made a competing offer to acquire Spirit for US$3.6bn in cash that was accepted by a majority of Spirit shareholders.*

12.3.1 The effects of mergers and acquisitions

Whichever route (merger, takeover or acquisition) is taken, the result is a larger and usually a more financially powerful company. There are cases, however, where the purchasing company pays too much to acquire another company or where the high financing costs cannot be serviced satisfactorily. In these cases, the purchasing company is left financially weakened and may be subject to takeover by another company. The word *integration* is the collective term used to describe these growth mechanisms.

One of the consequences of M&A activity is that many of the well-known names of the past have disappeared, and some of today's best-known companies are relatively young in their current form.

> **For example:** *In the North American airline industry, well-known names with long histories such as Northwest, Continental, US Airways and America West have ceased to exist in the last 20 years or so as consolidation has taken place. By way of contrast, online global travel retailer Expedia traces its roots as a Microsoft subsidiary only to 1996, before it was sold by the company in 1999. Both companies retain their headquarters in Seattle.*

KEY CONCEPT

Combined market value

All public limited companies have a market value. Market value equals the number of shares on the stock market (the *share volume*) multiplied by the share price. It is taken to be a good indicator of the value of a company because it accounts for the company's asset value plus the 'goodwill' that the market attaches to the share. It follows that the combined market value of a merger or acquisition is the value of the two companies added together. It is an indication of what the company will be valued at after the integration goes ahead.

A common misunderstanding surrounding the integration process is that two organizations always come together in their entirety. In practice, much integration is the result of one organization joining with a divested *part* of another. That is, one company has made a strategic decision to withdraw from an industry or market and in an attempt to maximize the value of the resources it no longer wants (i.e., an unwanted part of the previous company structure), it sells them to another company.

The reasons why companies *demerge* and sell subsidiaries in non-core elements are addressed later in this chapter.

> ### THINK POINTS
>
> - Define and distinguish between internal and external business growth.
> - Using examples from *THE*, define and distinguish between a merger and an acquisition.
> - Summarize the reasons why a business might seek to pursue external rather than internal growth.

12.3.2 Synergy – the main objective of M&A

The overriding purpose served by integration is that of *synergy* (which was introduced in Chapter 10). Integration can be said to be synergistic when the *whole is greater than the sum of the parts*, often expressed, as noted in Chapter 10, as '2 + 2 = 5'. If the integration is to achieve synergy, the 'new' company must perform more efficiently than either of the two parties would have if they remained separate. Interestingly, in describing the strategic alliance between Rezidor and Carlson Hotel groups (described later in the chapter), the companies utilized similarly poor arithmetic in describing the benefits of their alliance as the '1 + 1 = 3' effect.

12.5 SHORT CASE ILLUSTRATION

Acquisitions: Marriott acquires Starwood in the world's largest hotel deal

In November 2015, Marriott International Inc. announced its plan to acquire Starwood Worldwide Inc. (with brands such as Sheraton, le Meridien, Westin and Four Points).

The acquisition was successfully completed in spring 2017, but the process from initial announcement to finalization was far from easy, because regulatory approvals by antitrust authorities from major countries that Marriott and Starwood were operating in, such as Canada, China, the European Union and Saudi Arabia, were needed (Dogru et al., 2018). The $13bn deal created the world's largest hotel group, with over 8,200 properties with approximately 1.5 million rooms in over 30 countries. The acquisition surpassed other large deals such as Accor's $3bn acquisition of the Fairmont, Raffles and Swissôtel brands, completed in 2015.

The acquisition was expected to create a synergy through increases in sales and profit margins and decreases in costs brought about by the larger scale of operations. As Marriott's CEO Arne Sorensen (who led the merger) stated in an interview:

> It's really about loyalty and how we can take the SPG (Starwood) and Marriott Rewards program, each of which were very strong on their own and build something that is even stronger and gives our company a higher share of wallet. Behind loyalty would be the sales force. How do we get the sales force calling on more customers with the same resources so that we can drive sales? The other piece, of course, is around margins. I think that owners in both of the legacy Starwood and legacy Marriot [sic] portfolios will benefit from the increased scale and consolidation of resources. That is, having one email program, one reservations platform, and, ultimately, one loyalty program. These are all places that we can save on spending and implement lower-cost programs.
>
> (Hughes, 2017)

Subsequently, a major IT security breach was identified in November 2018 that made headlines around the world. Marriott announced that there had been unauthorized access to a database that contained guest information relating to reservations at Starwood properties. The data breach provided an example of some of the potential difficulties that can be encountered during the assimilation phase of mergers and acquisitions.

Source: www.marriott.com

Questions

1. What are the main advantages cited for the acquisition of Starwood by Marriott?

2. What are the risks that may occur in an acquisition such as this?

Synergy is measured in terms of increased added value. Kay (1995:145) made the point that 'value is added, and only added [in an integration], if distinctive capabilities or strategic assets are exploited more effectively. A merger adds no value if all that is acquired is a distinctive capability which is already fully exploited, as the price paid will reflect the competitive advantage held.'

Accordingly, integrations that do not enable the 'new' organization to produce higher profits or consolidate a stronger market position are usually deemed to have been relatively unsuccessful. Why failures sometimes occur is discussed in a subsequent section.

12.3.3 Motivations for M&A

Though synergy is often cited as the overriding purpose for external growth achieved through integration, there are a number of more detailed potential reasons for pursuing such a strategic method. Table 12.2 presents a summary of these motivations.

Table 12.2 A summary of the motivations for mergers and acquisitions

M&A motivation	Comments
• Increase market share	Increase pricing power in an industry
• As means of entering a new market	Possibly to offset the effects of decline in current markets or to broaden the portfolio of markets in which sales are generated
• Reduce competition	Purchase a competitor or a potential competitor
• Gain control of valuable assets	Purchase a company's controlling assets such as brand names, pieces of intellectual property like patents, access rights (e.g., development land for new hotels) or takeoff and landing slots at crowded airports
• Gain preferential access	Purchase 'downstream' assets to gain preferential access to distribution channels or 'upstream' assets by purchasing a supplier to gain preferential access to inputs.
• Broaden product range	Purchase another business to exploit more market opportunities and to spread risk
• Develop new products	Acquire a business as a faster way of developing new products than carrying out research and development internally

(continued)

Table 12.2 Continued

M&A motivation	Comments
• Gain access to new technologies	New operational or information technologies may reduce costs, increase quality or increase product differentiation
• Gain economies of scale	Combine two companies to benefit from economies in areas such as purchasing, human resources and marketing
• Make productive use of underused resources	Resources might be redeployed and used more effectively. For example, finance sitting in bank accounts might be invested or productivity improved by staff working more effectively.
• Asset strip	The practice of breaking up an acquired company and recovering more than the price paid by selling the parts separately
• Enhance corporate reputation	Appropriate if the existing company name has been associated with an alleged misdemeanor

The precise nature of the integration selected will depend on the specific objectives being pursued. If, for example, market share is the objective, then it is likely that a company will seek a suitable horizontal integration. On the other hand, a vertical integration would be more appropriate if supply or distribution concerns are uppermost among a company's threats.

External growth achieved through integration is usually expensive and therefore has significant financial resource implications, not to mention sizeable expenses for lawyers and investment bankers, who are inevitably brought in to advise on the process. Accordingly, it is entered into for specific strategic purposes that cannot be served through the normal progression of organic development.

There are also often significant challenges facing managers in integrating the merged businesses. These managerial challenges for moving the merged company forward successfully might include:

- Designing an effective organizational structure
- Deciding where operations and head offices should be located
- Successfully integrating policies, processes and procedures
- Creating or modifying organizational cultures so that the two parts work together harmoniously
- Ensuring that marketing and branding of the two parts are aligned
- Planning the cash flow so that merger costs can be successfully serviced

12.3.4 Potential failure factors with M&A

The fact that mergers and acquisitions are undoubtedly popular as methods of business growth may lead us to conclude that they are always successful. In practice, this is not always true. A number of studies in *THE* contexts (particularly focusing on hospitality) have analyzed the performance of companies after integrations, and the findings (summarized by Dogru et al., 2018) are not conclusive.

The studies found that many corporate 'marriages' failed to work and sometimes ended in 'divorce' or a combined company that failed to add value for the company's owners (its shareholders). Of those that did survive, Tuch and O'Sullivan (2007), in a review of empirical research on the impact of acquisitions on firm performance, found that in the short run, acquisitions have at best an insignificant impact on shareholder wealth, whereas in the long run performance analysis reveals overwhelmingly negative returns. These findings have been broadly supported by other studies (see, for example, Hsu and Jang, 2007).

On the contrary, other studies have found that hospitality mergers create positive returns, especially for the acquiring company (see, for example, Canina et al., 2010; J. Yang et al., 2010; Chatfield et al., 2012; Dogru, 2017).

A number of 'failure factors' that suggest reasons why integrations might not work are summarized in Table 12.3.

History has shown that mergers and acquisitions work best when the initiating company follows a number of intuitively fairly obvious rules. They are designed to offset the failure factors that have been identified. Accordingly, the importance of detailed information gathering before the integration and careful analysis of the information cannot be overemphasized.

Thus, the identification of possible efficiency gains is a core issue in the analysis of mergers, and much of the evidence points to a poor record. However, there are situations in which existing suppliers are clearly not operating effectively, where there are too many smaller suppliers that lack the economies of scale and scope. Mergers in such situations can clearly produce productivity gains.

> For example: *In the early 2000s, the Chinese government pursued a strategy of merging small firms in key industries to create large enterprise groups. Two studies of Chinese airlines provide evidence of efficiency gains through mergers in this particular context. Chow and Tsui (2017) and Yan et al. (2019) studied the effect of horizontal mergers on the efficiency of the Chinese airline sector, which is dominated by state-owned or state-controlled airlines. Overall, the analysis suggested that the mergers increased the productivity of Chinese airlines. Chow and Tsui (2017) emphasized the impact of organizational learning from the airlines' prior operating experience in improving operating costs.*

12.3.5 Government policy and integrations

Government policies on mergers and acquisitions may contribute to some integration failures or successes. Many countries worldwide have adopted policies and legal underpinning providing for

Table 12.3 A summary of potential failure factors for mergers and acquisitions

Potential failure factors for mergers and acquisitions
• Lack of research into the circumstances of the target company. Failure in this aspect (often termed 'due diligence' by accountants) can result in some nasty surprises after the integration.
• Cultural incompatibility between the two parties
• Lack of communication within and between the two parties
• Difficulties in integrating the structures of the two organizations
• Loss of key personnel in the target company after the integration
• Paying too much for the acquired company and hence overexposing the acquiring company to financial risk
• Assuming that growth in a target company's market will continue indefinitely. Markets can fall as well as rise, and future trends may not follow past patterns.

merger control. National or sometimes supranational competition agencies such as the EU or the US Federal Trade Commission are often empowered to consider the competitive implications of allowing larger mergers to proceed.

Such measures are adopted to prevent anticompetitive consequences of overconcentration of power as a result of mergers and acquisitions. The relevant authorities are usually concerned with whether the concentration will impede successful competition.

The EU provides an example of the way in which individual governments (or governments acting collectively in this case) attempt to regulate and control mergers and acquisitions. European competition regulations are provided for in the Treaty of Rome, 1957 (the primary legislation of the EU). Article 86 refers specifically to mergers and acquisitions.

Article 86 is designed to prohibit the abuse of a dominant market position (i.e., a high market share). It does not prohibit monopoly as such but seeks to ensure that large businesses do not use their power against consumer and competitor interests. This indirectly acts against large companies seeking to acquire a high market share by integration.

The administrative part of the EU, the European Commission, has the responsibility for implementing Article 86. If the annual turnover of the combined businesses exceeds specified thresholds in terms of global and European sales, notification of the proposed merger must be provided to the European Commission, which must examine it. Below these thresholds, the national competition authorities in the EU Member States may also review the merger. Mergers are approved if they are found not to impede successful competition. If it is found that the merger will impede competition, it is either rejected or approved with conditions.

THINK POINTS

- Explain the reasons why mergers and acquisitions sometimes go wrong.
- Explain the measures an organization should take to increase the probability of success of a merger or acquisition.
- Providing examples, explain why public authorities try to regulate mergers and acquisitions.

The Short Case Illustration relating to consolidation of European-based tour operators below illustrates examples of mergers that were approved by the EU, albeit in one of the cases cited subject to conditions being met.

12.6 SHORT CASE ILLUSTRATION

Merger control: European tour operators

The European-based outbound tour operator sector underwent a period of consolidation during the first decade of this century. The highly fragmented sector experienced a large number of both horizontal and vertical mergers and acquisitions, and two major pan-European groups emerged. Both groups emerged in the middle of 2007 and both mergers were approved (albeit with conditions in the case of TUI).

Thomas Cook Group plc was a British global travel company listed on the London Stock Exchange. It was formed on 19 June 2007 by the merger of the German Thomas Cook AG (itself the successor to the long established British group Thomas Cook & Son) and MyTravel Group plc.

TUI Travel plc was an international leisure travel group listed on the London Stock Exchange. It was formed in September 2007 by the merger of British-based tour operator First Choice Holidays plc and the tourism division of German-based TUI AG, which owned 56.4% of the company. Subsequently, the German group TUI AG merged with TUI Travel plc to form the TUI Group with its headquarters in Hannover, Germany. The TUI Group promotes itself with the assertion that it is 'the world's number one tourism business'.

When approving both mergers in 2007, the European Commission did so on the condition that TUI sold its Irish subsidiary Budget Travel.

The EU is normally wary of approving deals that reduce the number of big market operators to just two (Buck and Blitz, 2007). However, in its findings on the Thomas Cook merger with MyTravel plc, the Commission acknowledged that the travel market had changed substantially since it reviewed and blocked the planned merger of MyTravel (then known as Airtours) and First Choice in 1999. The Thomas Cook Group subsequently failed in September 2019, though the brand name has been retained as an online-only business (www.thomascook.com).

Sources: Adapted from www.tuigroup.com; Buck and Blitz (2007)

Questions

1. Why might regulators have been concerned about the competitive impact of the mergers?

2. What competitive changes in the marketplace may have led to the mergers being approved?

12.4 The relational approach to strategic management

As Rumelt (1991) testified in a much-cited article, strategy is fundamentally concerned with explaining differential firm performance.

In searching for sources of differential performance or competitive advantage, two prominent views (which were considered in Chapter 10) have emerged:

- The competitive positioning approach
- The core competence or resource-based approach

These two perspectives focus on those resources that are housed within the firm and have certainly contributed to how firms achieve competitive advantage. In an influential article, Dyer and Singh (1998) introduced a third view.

THE RELATIONAL APPROACH

The relational approach (which Dyer et al. [2018] revisited in a more recent article) recognizes that a firm's critical resources may extend beyond firm boundaries. The main aspects of this approach were summarized well by De Wit and Meyer (2014), and the approaches were contrasted and applied in a hospitality context by Kim and Oh (2004) and in a tourism context by Pechlaner et al. (2014).

The central thesis expounded by Dyer and Singh (1998) is that a pair or network of firms can develop relationships that result in sustained competitive advantage. It can be argued that the approach is particularly pertinent in *THE* contexts because many interorganizational relationships exist in these sectors.

In studying strategy, though competition between single firms is still the main focus of attention, various ways of joint development provide opportunities to create and sustain competitive advantage. Because firms may exist as parts of larger networks of relationships with buyers, suppliers and competitors, competitive advantage can be achieved either through an exchange relationship or through the joint contribution of the specific partners (Dyer and Singh, 1998).

Organizations do not operate in isolation, as is perhaps implied by the two approaches considered previously, but instead interact with other organizations to achieve common goals. When two or more organizations move beyond a mere transactional relationship and work jointly toward a common goal, they form an alliance, partnership or network (De Wit and Meyer, 2014), the details of which we will consider in subsequent sections.

The ways in which organizations work together vary enormously in terms of their complexity, long-term sustainability and level of commitment. However, at the heart of the involvement is the understanding that working together in a cooperative manner can lead to objectives being achieved that could not be achieved by a single organization working alone. Specifically, working cooperatively may lead to objectives being attained in relation to resources, activities and products, as indicated by De Wit and Meyer (2014; see Figure 12.2).

The three approaches were put into context and contrasted in a *THE* setting by Kim and Oh (2004). As Kim and Oh pointed out, the three approaches are not mutually exclusive but instead emphasize different important aspects of strategy in achieving competitive advantage and adopting an integrated approach. They argued that to achieve long-term profitability and growth, firms should:

- Adapt themselves to the rapidly changing environment (Porter's competitive positioning)
- Continually develop new resources such as market-based resources (resource-based approach)
- Build strong relationships with customers, suppliers and other companies selling in the same markets (the relational approach)

Thus, an integrated approach to strategy is called for that draws on the three strands of thought. The challenge then for managers is not to choose one approach over another (because they are not like opposing armies in a battle) but rather to seek the advantages of the different perspectives and blend them together in an effective synthesis.

We will now turn our attention to the main ways in which organizations can work with other organizations; that is, externally, in *joint development*, to create greater value.

12.5 Joint development

Joint development is two or more organizations working together to share resources and activities to pursue common strategic objectives. This method of development has been increasingly popular in recent years and is very common among *THE* organizations seeking help and support from other organizations. Companies within the airline, hospitality and travel organizer sectors of the industry in particular, as well as ancillary services such as car rentals, are increasingly favoring joint

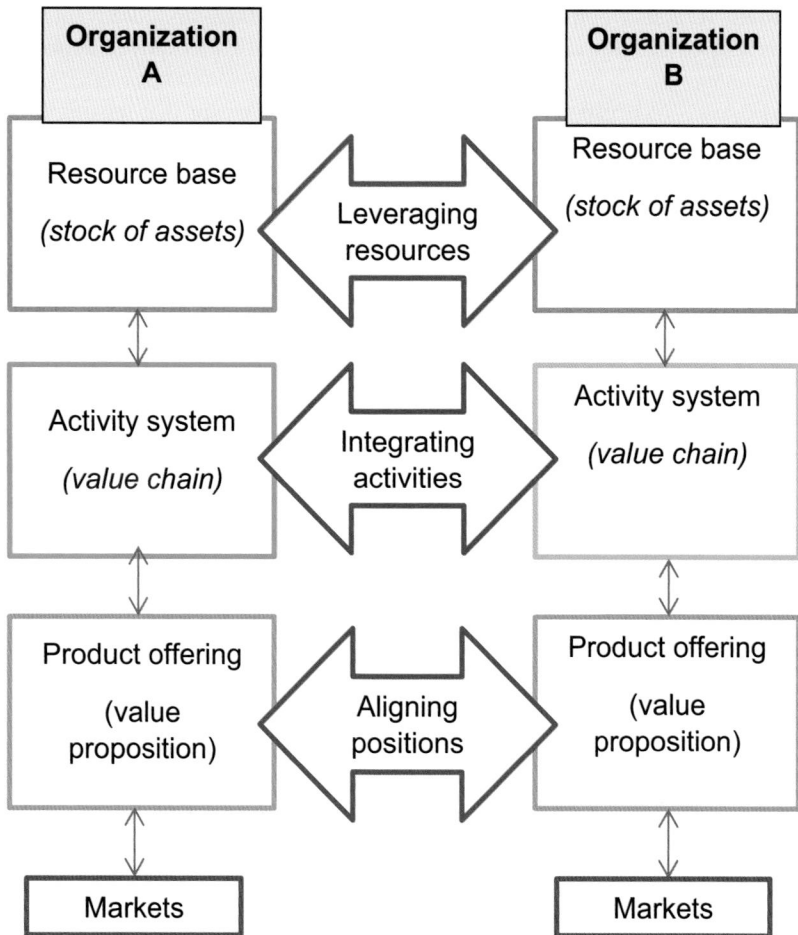

Figure 12.2 Interorganizational cooperative objectives

Source: Adapted from De Wit and Meyer (2014)

development achieved through so-called collaborative strategy as their chosen means of growth. Public sector bodies involved in events, tourism and hospitality and wider aspects of public policy are also favoring joint development by working with the private sector in so-called PPPs. It is clear that collaborative arrangements of various types have become an increasingly important strategic method of development in *THE* (see, for example, Gursoy et al., 2015), although statistical data are often lacking.

Indeed, Dev et al. (1996) asserted that throughout the 1980s and 1990s joint development in *THE* increased until the position was reached in the early 1990s at which most of the world's major airline, hotel and car rental firms were linked by a web of cross-shareholdings, joint ventures and joint sales and service arrangements. New arrangements have continued to develop in the new millennium, and existing arrangements have matured and gained increasing customer recognition.

Joint development is sometimes viewed as a 'hybrid' method of strategic development because it does not imply full integration (like mergers and acquisitions) or the 'go-it-alone' approach implied by organic development. Instead, it represents a middle way involving cooperation with partners.

Though this method of development has its own specific advantages and disadvantages, it is also a method that is favored in some cases because of the drawbacks of alternative methods:

- *Organic development* – Increasingly complex environments have meant that organizations often cannot develop adequately through using their own resources and competences alone. In such circumstances, organic development is often slow and companies are not able to achieve the required scale of operations (or cannot achieve the scale quickly enough) to compete effectively with international competitors.
- *Mergers and acquisitions* – This method might also be viewed as having serious drawbacks or may be prevented in some cases by regulatory restrictions, lack of appropriate targets or insufficient financing. This method is expensive, entails some loss of control and has often led to a loss of value for the combined company rather than value creation (Tuch and O'Sullivan, 2007).

Joint development involves companies working cooperatively as opposed to competing with each other, and *collaborative strategy* (or *cooperative strategy* as it is often termed) has become an important focus of strategic management (both in practice and conceptually) in recent years. Thus, collaborative strategies involve organizations working with rivals or other related companies to the mutual benefit of both (or all) organizations (Lynch, 2021).

In rapidly globalizing world markets, collaborative strategy is often viewed as the engine driving companies that are deficient in certain competences, resources or assets, to link together with other companies in a similar predicament to jointly derive the competitive advantages they lack on their own.

Recent years have seen the rapid rise of collaborative strategy as a favored strategic option. This point was highlighted by Faulkner (1995), who argued that collaborative (cooperative) strategy had become the counterpart of competitive strategy as a key strategic management tool.

DEFINITION/QUOTATION

Collaborative strategy

In comparing commercial organizations with the foreign policies of national governments, the famous Japanese management guru Kenichi Ohmae (1989) observed that companies are learning what nations have always known; that is, that 'in a complex, uncertain world filled with dangerous opponents, it is best not to go it alone'.

12.5.1 Categorizing forms of joint development

There are various ways in which joint development takes place, involving differing levels of cooperation between the parties involved.

Faulkner (1995) categorized collaborative relationships in relation to their degree of integration, ranging from markets to hierarchies.

- In a *hierarchy*, a central authority governs internal relationships and has the formal power to coordinate strategy and solve interdepartmental disputes (De Wit and Meyer, 2014).
- In a *market*, relationships between firms are nonhierarchical, because they interact with one another without any explicit or dispute settlement mechanism (De Wit and Meyer, 2014).

Between the two extremes, a range of interorganizational forms exist with ascending levels of integration. Strategic alliances and joint ventures represent the most integrated form of interorganizational collaboration. Any further integration represents a single corporate form subject to fully integrated decision making. At the other end of the spectrum of interorganizational collaboration are cooperative networks. Figure 12.3 illustrates Faulkner's (1995) categorization of interorganizational forms.

Many interorganizational forms can be developed between the extremes of hierarchies and markets. Todeva and Knoke (2005), for example, identified 13 basic forms of interorganizational relations appearing in the theoretical and research literatures.

12.5.2 Joint development in THE

Here we will focus on those aspects of joint development of most relevance to *THE*, namely:

- Strategic alliances and joint ventures
- PPPs
- Franchising
- Management contracts
- Cooperative networks

There are many examples of the interorganizational forms listed in the sectors that constitute *THE*. However, the examples are not evenly spread throughout the *THE* sectors.

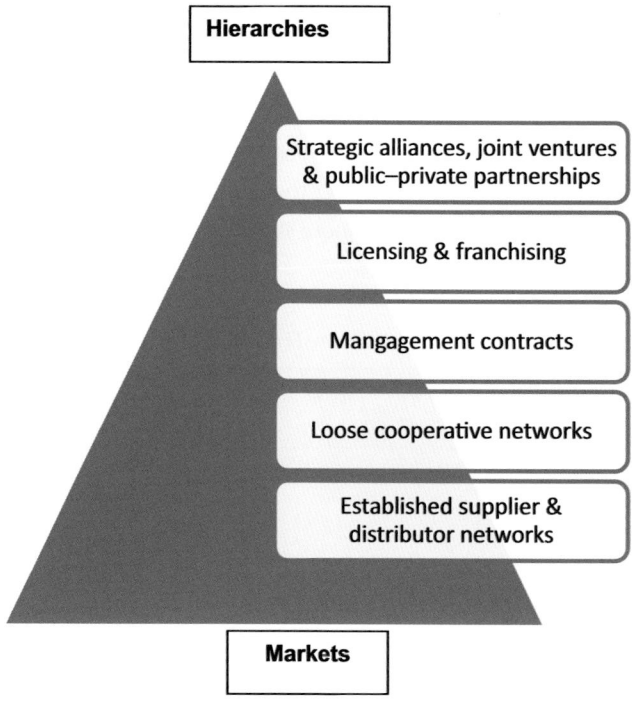

Figure 12.3 A categorization of interorganizational forms of joint development
Source: Adapted from Faulkner (1995)

As Table 12.4 indicates, the focus of interorganizational forms differs in the six constituent sectors of *THE* we identified in Chapter 2 (Figure 2.2). Thus, for example, strategic alliances are particularly prevalent with regard to transport, hospitality and travel organizers, whereas PPPs are a particular feature of attractions, destination organizations and events.

12.6 Strategic alliances

A large academic literature has emerged discussing strategic alliances since Harvard academic Rosabeth Moss Kanter's influential contributions were published in the 1990s (Kanter, 1990, 1994). The various aspects of strategic alliances such as their categorization, reasons for formation, partner selection and success and failure factors were summarized by Ireland et al. (2002), Kale et al. (2002), Tjemkes et al. (2017) and Mamédio et al. (2019) and, in *THE* contexts, by Evans (2001a, 2001b). Even though their failure rate is high, the number of alliances being formed is growing because they have the potential to create value (Ireland et al., 2002).

Though many analysts regard strategic alliances as recent phenomena, interorganizational linkages have existed since the origins of the firm as a production unit (Todeva and Knoke, 2005). The literature is far from clear as to just what constitutes a 'strategic alliance', and many definitions have emerged (see Glaister and Buckley, 1996; French, 1997).

Most writers would agree that the term strategic alliances applies largely (though not exclusively) to 'horizontal' interorganizational relationships between companies engaged in similar types of activity at the same level. Thus, in categorizing strategic alliances, most writers would exclude buyer–seller relationships, subcontracting, franchising, management contracts and licensing, where to some degree the parties involved may have opposing goals and the relationships are 'vertical' between organizations along the channel of distribution.

In a widely cited understanding of strategic alliances, Yoshino and Rangan (1995) provided three criteria for a strategic alliance:

- At least two partner firms that remain legally independent after the alliance is formed
- Sharing of benefits and managerial control over the performance of assigned tasks
- Making continuing contributions in one or more strategic areas, such as technology or products

Table 12.4 Focus of interorganizational activity in *THE*

	Transport	Hospitality	Attractions	Destination organizations	Travel organizers	Events
Strategic alliances	✓	✓			✓	
PPPs		✓	✓	✓		✓
Franchising		✓			✓	
Management contracts	✓	✓	✓			
Cooperative networks		✓	✓	✓	✓	✓

Source: Author's categorization

These three criteria imply that strategic alliances create interdependence between autonomous economic units, bringing new benefits to the partners in the form of intangible assets and obligating them to make continuing contributions to their partnership (Todeva and Knoke, 2005).

Different alliance forms represent different approaches that partner firms adopt to control their dependence on the alliance and on other partners. Bennett (1997), writing in an airline context, for example, distinguished between 'tactical' alliances, which are loose forms of collaboration that exist to gain marketing benefits, and 'strategic' alliances, which are characterized as being longer and wider in their scope and level of commitment. Thus, the many codesharing agreements that proliferate among the world's airlines can be viewed as tactical rather than strategic, because they are limited in their scope.

The distinction between *joint ventures* and *strategic alliances* is one of emphasis rather than fundamental distinguishing characteristics. A joint venture normally implies joint ownership of assets by the parties involved, the formation of separate independent operating companies for the management of the shared activities and collaboration on a relatively narrow range of activities. In practice, the distinction between the two terms is often blurred. Global distribution systems are an example of a joint venture, as discussed in the Technology Focus below.

12.7 TECHNOLOGY FOCUS

Joint ventures: Alibaba and Marriott e-commerce collaboration for Chinese domestic and outbound tourism growth

A joint venture (JV) is a commercial agreement that takes place between two or more companies (which sometimes but not always involves a joint company being established) for mutual benefit. For a JV to work there must be a shared understanding of the objectives for the JV and there must be a benefit envisaged for both companies in agreeing to this form of collaboration.

In 2018, Alibaba group, China's e-commerce platform reached a JV agreement with the American-based Marriott International hotel group. The joint working combines the e-commerce giant's in-depth knowledge of China's consumers with the worldwide hospitality presence of the Marriott group's hotel brands to upgrade the travel experience for hundreds of millions of Chinese tourists.

The JV is designed to deliver personalized trip planning services, high-quality travel experiences for Chinese outbound and domestic tourists and exclusive benefits for each company's membership clubs. Marriott will also accept Alipay, the online payments platform owned by Alibaba, and the JV will manage Marriott's 'storefront' on Fliggy, Alibaba's travel service platform, as well as the hotel chain's Chinese-language digital channels including Marriott.com and its mobile app. In addition, the JV will provide content, programs and promotions customized for Chinese travelers, enhancing offerings on those sites.

Through the partnership, Marriott is able to leverage insights gleaned from Alibaba's 500 million monthly mobile active users to better market to and engage with China's growing consumer base. As incomes in China rise, many people are looking for both higher-quality and, often, foreign goods, as well as more sophisticated travel experiences, which provides opportunities for well established players in the industry. According to Fliggy, half of China's outbound travelers are young, between the ages of 23 and 34, and the general trend among all Chinese tourists is to seek out new experiences, rather than going abroad purely to shop.

At the heart of the deal is the JV's push to fully integrate the travel experience for Chinese tourists as e-commerce and offline shopping continue to merge. To that end, consumers are now able to plan, book, pay for and manage a trip, as well as shop, eat and sightsee at their destinations, all by using the digital platforms of Alibaba and Marriott.

The two companies also look to expand the range of those experiences for Marriott and Alibaba loyalty club members. Marriott offers access to private concerts, family-focused experiences and courtside seats at sporting and other events through its rewards programs, and Alibaba members get access to personalized hospitality programs and Marriott's global concierge service. Eventually, a deeper harmonization of loyalty programs is planned. The initiative would include benefits such as status tier matching and the ability to exchange and redeem points between the two programs for travel planning and retail purchasing.

About a year and a half after the JV was established, travel website Skift reported that the collaboration was enabling the hotel giant to make inroads with a relatively new customer base – leisure travelers – a majority of whom are female and younger than 40.

Furthermore, it was reported that its 'storefront' on Fliggy (Alibaba's travel division where it sells its global hotel inventory) is a direct booking channel with costs that are lower than those available through online travel agency distribution (Schaal, 2019).

Sources: www.marriott.com; www.skift.com; www.alibaba.com

Questions

1. Outline the principal reasons for Marriott and Alibaba forming a joint venture.
2. Consider the factors that might lead to the joint venture being discontinued in the future.

12.6.1 *Strategic alliances in* THE

The formation of strategic alliances has been evident in many industries, including pharmaceuticals, vehicle manufacture and chemicals. This process has been replicated in *THE*, where they have come to form a central feature of the developing industrial structure, particularly in relation to hospitality companies and transport companies.

Many writers, including Bennett (1997), Evans (2001a, 2001b), Chathoth and Olsen (2003), Oum et al. (2000, 2004), Min and Joo (2016) and Cobeña et al. (2019), have pointed to the high level of activity in the field of *THE* alliance formation, particularly in relation to airline and hospitality companies. However, the alliances differ in:

- Their motives
- Their scope
- Their structures
- Their objectives
- The ways in which they are managed

The motivations for forming strategic alliances in *THE* are numerous and complex. It is clear, however, that in recent economic history, *THE* has been characterized by the emergence of many alliances, some of which have subsequently failed, and new realignments of companies have been forged. Long-standing 'natural' alliances between travel companies and accommodation providers that saw the ownership of hotels by railway, shipping and airline company interests as a means of extending their reach into new markets have been replaced by other arrangements as intercompany and intermodal competition has increased (Garnham, 1996).

Many examples of alliances exist in the airline and hotel sectors, although many fall short of being 'strategic' in the true sense but rather are more 'tactical' in their orientation, focusing primarily on marketing and information technology collaboration rather than wider collaboration.

In distinguishing between three levels of alliance on the basis of short-term, medium-term or long-term (strategic) relationships, Dev and Klein (1993) argued that in such a hierarchy of relationships, partners often progress from the simple short-term relationships through to complex strategic relationships but that only at the strategic level do alliances offer companies the ability to respond to the pressures of global competition and illiquidity. They argued that potential benefits from such strategic ways of working together accrue from:

- Enhanced market coverage both geographically and by segment
- Greater economies of scale in advertising, sales, distribution and purchasing
- Complementary strengths in operations and marketing

THINK POINTS

- Explain what is meant by a 'strategic alliance' and how it differs from a merger.
- Using relevant examples, explain why *THE* organizations seek to form strategic alliances.
- Explain the difference between a strategic alliance and a joint venture.

The Short Case Illustration below illustrates how airlines are attempting to gain the advantages of operating through strategic alliances.

12.8 SHORT CASE ILLUSTRATION

Strategic alliances: international airlines

The airline industry has long been characterized by agreements between pairs of airlines on particular routes. These 'bilateral' agreements are particular to the routes in question, change quite regularly and are limited to particular aspects of the airlines' operations.

Strategic alliances go much further than these bilateral codesharing agreements in that the agreements are 'strategic' in nature, involving as they do agreements that:

- Involve several airlines
- Are wide-ranging in their scope including various aspects of activities
- Are long-lasting in their impact on the airlines involved

Many of the world's international airlines now belong to one of the three major strategic alliance groupings: Star Alliance, oneworld and SkyTeam. These three alliances operate on a worldwide basis, but other important alliances operating on a more regional basis include the Vanilla Alliance operating in Africa and the Indian Ocean and the Value Alliance operating in Southeast Asia, Japan and South Korea.

In each case, the constituent airlines are trying to derive the advantages of working collaboratively as part of the strategic alliance. These advantages might include cost reductions or enhanced revenue from sharing:

- Sharing sales offices
- Sharing maintenance and operational facilities
- Sharing airport lounges
- Coordinating schedules, thereby increasing load factors and avoiding flight duplication
- Joint aircraft purchasing
- Sharing marketing expenses

The benefits for the traveler might include:

- The ability to gain access to a wider network
- Easier transfers between airlines
- Shared loyalty program incentives

Sources: www.staralliance.com; www.skyteam.com; www.oneworld.com; www.iata.org

Questions

1. What are the differences between strategic alliances and codeshare arrangements?

2. What factors have led to airlines forming strategic alliances?

12.6.2 A conceptualization of the collaborative process for international airlines

Figure 12.4 provides a conceptual model of the strategic management processes involved in the formation of strategic alliances using the airline sector as an example (though it could be adapted for other *THE* sectors).

It has been argued (Evans 2001b), and consistent with the structure of this text, that a four-stage process takes place:

- A strategic analysis of the internal organizational and external environmental 'drivers' that act as the underlying motivating reasons for alliance formation is carried out.
- Alternative strategic options are postulated and evaluated and the option of strategic alliance formation (either with or without equity) participation is chosen.
- Implementation issues are considered, including the choice of appropriate partners and issues relating to the structure and scope of the alliance.

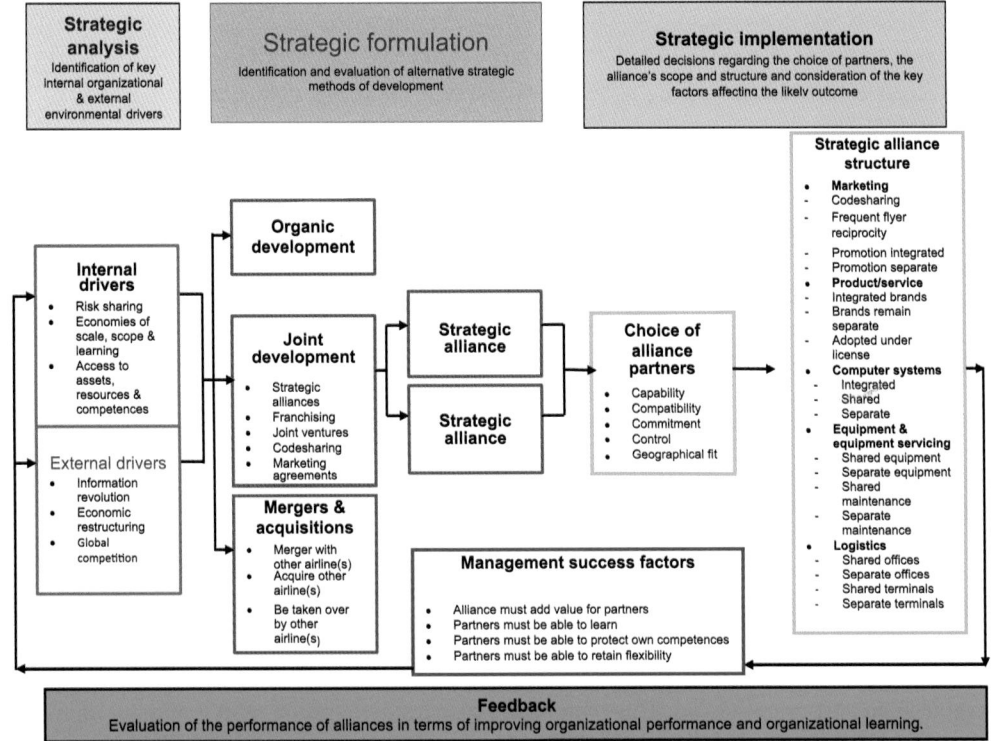

Figure 12.4 Conceptualization of the collaborative strategy process for international airlines

Source: Adapted from Evans (2001ᵃ)

- The strategic alliance is evaluated against selected criteria purporting to measure the success of the alliance. The evaluation of the alliance is fed back into the analytical phase so that any changes based on experience can be incorporated.

12.6.3 Motivations for strategic alliance formation

A number of studies have sought to identify the underlying motivations for the formation of strategic alliances (see Glaister and Buckley, 1996; Bennett, 1997; Das and Teng, 2000), and it is generally accepted that some types of external drivers need to be present.

Child and Faulkner (1998) suggested that there are six key external driving forces and four key internal needs acting as motivational forces in the formation of alliances:

External driving forces for alliance formation include:

- Turbulence in world markets and high economic uncertainty
- The existence of economies of scale and/or scope as competitive cost-reducing agents
- The globalization or regionalization of a growing number of industries
- The globalization of technology
- Fast technological change leading to ever-increasing investment requirements
- Shortening product life cycles

Internal needs for alliance formation are to:

- Achieve economies of scale and learning with one's partner
- Get access to the benefits of the other firm's assets, such as technology, market access, capital, operational capacity, products or personnel
- Reduce risk by sharing it, notably in terms of capital requirements but also in respect of research and development expenditure
- Help 'shape' the market; that is, increased scale provides more power to set prices and influence how the market operates.

The nature of the internal needs and external drivers will, of course, vary between industries and industry sectors, and the emphasis may alter in different markets and may shift over time.

12.6.4 Potential difficulties with strategic alliances

Despite their surge in popularity, international strategic alliances are often viewed as inherently unstable organizational forms. It has been noted by Porter and Fuller (1986), for instance, that alliances involve significant costs in terms of coordination, reconciling goals with an independent entity and creating competitors. These associated costs frequently serve to make alliances transitional rather than stable organizational forms and therefore rarely can they be viewed as a sustainable means of creating competitive advantage.

The failure rate associated with alliance arrangements is high, often resulting in significant costs to one or both parties concerned. This high failure rate has been reported in a number of studies. For instance, in their study of cross-border alliances, Bleeke and Ernst (1991) found that some two-thirds had run into serious managerial or financial trouble within the first two years, resulting in a high rate of failure.

In a *THE* context, strategic alliances, it can be argued, are often a second-best option, often necessary only as a result of regulatory and legal restrictions, which frequently make mergers and acquisitions problematic.

In the airline sector, where strategic alliances are commonplace, the strategic importance that many governments attribute to airlines means that there are legal restrictions on foreign ownership.

> For example: *The USA places a limit of 25% on foreign ownership of its airlines; for Japanese airlines, the limit is 33%; and the EU limits non-EU ownership of the airlines of its Member States to 49.9% (www.centreforaviation.com).*

Thus, in both cases (which are replicated in many other countries), a controlling stake in airlines is denied to foreign investors. Thus, in the airline sector, where full ownership of companies by foreign-based nationals is often prohibited and that is often characterized by a high degree of consumer loyalty to 'national champions', alliance formation has in many cases been viewed as the only viable market entry mechanism, at least in the short to medium term.

Such organizational structures can hardly be viewed as models of business efficiency and long-term sustainability and therefore must be questionable. Thus, alliances, it can be argued, are rarely stable sustainable entities, because they commonly represent the only viable market entry mechanism when regulatory and other barriers to entry effectively block other market entry modes (such as full acquisition). Additionally, many of the alliances that are formed appear in a constant state of flux, altering their shapes, sizes and partners in response to changes in the competitive environment, with partners being added or dropped and partners falling out among themselves.

One further point to note is that alliances can fail *not* because of the partners' failure to agree on substantive points but, on the contrary, because the alliance leads to the delivery of a high degree of collaboration and agreement between the partners. In cases where the results of successful collaboration are apparent, partners may be forced to merge their activities, providing that regulatory and legal restrictions do not stand in the way. The case of Hilton Hotels (see Short Case Illustration below) illustrates this facet of strategic alliances.

12.9 SHORT CASE ILLUSTRATION

Strategic alliances: Hilton strategic alliance develops into a full merger

Hilton is one of the most recognized brands in international hospitality, but the brand has not always been unified. Two arms of Hilton, Hilton Hotels Corporation in the USA and Hilton Hotels International based in the UK, were separated under different ownership in 1964 some 45 years after Conrad Hilton opened the first hotel to bear his surname in Chicago. Thus, there were two separate, fully independent companies operating hotels under the Hilton name, the American branch operating largely in North America and the British branch mainly operating Hilton hotels elsewhere in the world. From the time of the split, the relationship between the two chains bearing the Hilton name was frequently acrimonious.

The situation, which was confusing to consumers and failed to fully capitalize on a strong brand, was clearly not an optimal way of operating. In 1996, both chains appointed chairmen committed to capitalizing fully on the strength of the Hilton brand, which resulted in a 1997 agreement to form a wide-ranging strategic alliance between the two chains, covering a joint reservations system (boosted by $100mn spending on new technology), the extension of HHC's loyalty rewards to Hilton International, the adoption of joint brand identities including a new logo and joint marketing campaigns.

Though the strategic alliance improved the operational efficiency of the brand and worked well, the logical extension of the cooperation was full integration. This was achieved in 2005 when Hilton Hotels Corporation acquired the British chain Hilton International for £3.3bn. Subsequently, the company was sold to private equity group Blackstone in 2007 for $26 bn, just as the economy was moving into recession. The company returned to the stock market in 2013 as Hilton Worldwide Holdings Inc. and is now (like its rival Marriott) headquartered in suburban Washington, D.C., having moved its headquarters from California in 2009.

Source: www.hiltonworldwide.com/

Questions

1. What are the factors that led to the two parts of Hilton merging?

2. What difficulties might have been encountered after the two parts merged?

Collaboration, though often financially beneficial, nevertheless may imply that the partners are operating suboptimally, because the need for communication and management duplication imposes higher cost levels. The airline alliances have elaborate committee structures so that their member airlines' views are represented. Such structures are often viewed as overly bureaucratic, expensive and leading to slow decision making.

Though there is some inherent instability in the airline alliances mentioned, it should be noted that the alliances themselves have been operating for over 20 years (Star Alliance, oneworld and Skyteam were formed in 1997, 1999 and 2000, respectively), albeit aided by the regulatory restrictions described. It should also be noted that though the three major alliance groupings mentioned (together with several other smaller groupings) are important in the airline sector, there are also many other airlines that have yet to join any of the alliances or that have chosen not to do so.

In particular, the low-cost carriers that have proliferated around the world have developed independent models that do not involve alliance membership. Some other well-known airlines (particularly the fast-growing Middle East airlines) have deliberately chosen not to join strategic alliances, choosing to remain independent as a deliberate part of their strategic development.

> **For example:** *UK-based Virgin and the fast-growing United Arab Emirates airlines of Emirates and Etihad based in Dubai and Abu Dhabi, respectively, have chosen not to join the alliance groupings. In November 2013, the* Financial Times *quoted Emirates President Tim Clark as saying that 'it was within our DNA to chart our own destiny'. Instead, among other actions, the airline has negotiated a wide-ranging codesharing agreement with Australia's Qantas. Etihad Airlines, in rejecting alliance membership, has pursued a different strategy in that it has purchased minority stakes in a number of airlines, including now-defunct Air Berlin, Germany's second-largest carrier at the time of the purchase (Parker, 2013b), and a 49% stake in the troubled Italian airline Alitalia in 2014.*

12.6.5 *Partner selection in strategic alliances*

Despite the evident instability demonstrated by many alliances, there may be ways in which companies can form and manage alliances to ensure a longer life expectancy and a higher degree of stability. Although there are no doubt many complex reasons for alliance failures, many writers, such as Kanter (1994) and Medcof (1997), agree that poor initial selection of alliance partners is a key variable.

Medcof (1997), for instance, postulated that the first imperative in partner selection is to ensure that the proposed partner represents a good *strategic fit*; that is, the weaknesses of one partner are complemented by the strengths of the other partner and vice versa.

Four criteria were proposed (Brouthers et al. 1995) for when partners are deemed to be a good strategic fit and to determine whether a proposed partnership is likely to be workable at an operational level. These criteria, referred to conveniently as the '4 Cs', are *complementary skills*, *cooperative cultures*, *compatible goals* and commensurate *levels of risk*.

- *Complementary skills* – questions whether the prospective partners have the ability to successfully carry out their respective roles in the alliance.

Managers should form alliances only with firms that fulfill a specific need and that can contribute to the overall strength of the alliance. Without the addition of new skills, expertise or market access, there is little incentive for the respective companies to work together.

- *Cooperative cultures* – concerns the ability of the partners to work together effectively.

The criterion therefore relates to the respective corporate cultures of the partner organizations and to the working relationships between staff and management at the partners. Managers must look for opportunities to learn from partners and be sensitive to different cultural norms in different settings.

For example: *In the case of the strategic alliance that was agreed between Carlson and Redizor (see Short Case Illustration below), both companies shared strong Scandinavian roots and had successfully worked closely together before a formal strategic alliance was agreed in 2012.*

- *Compatible goals* – concerns the willingness of partners to commit resources, effort and know-how to an alliance.

In a worst-case scenario, a partner might expend only the minimum effort required to keep the alliance alive, while opportunistically leaving others to bear the brunt of the responsibilities and at the same time receiving know-how and market intelligence from alliance partners. Strategic objectives should be fulfilled through the alliance that could not have been fulfilled without the alliance being in place. In some cases, one partner may be dominant, thereby suppressing the aspirations of others. In other cases, a dominant partner may ensure the effectiveness of the alliance owing to that partner's superior expertise or market position. The key question with regard to partners is whether the system of control that the alliance puts in place allows all partners to achieve their strategic objectives.

- *Commensurate levels of risk* – concerns the appropriate balance between partners in the alliance and between risks contained within the alliance and those sheltered from it.

A strategic alliance in which one member company is taking a disproportionate share of the financial and/or operational risks is unlikely to be sustainable. In many cases, alliances are formed to reduce risks but while reducing some risks they may produce others; for example, the alliance may reduce exposure to political uncertainties but increase the risks of giving away corporate competences or financial pressures brought about by the financial weaknesses of a partner.

THINK POINTS

- What might an organization do to ensure that its strategic alliance is successful?
- Explain the difference between a strategic alliance and a tactical alliance.
- Explain why partner selection is so important in strategic alliances and what factors should considered.

Two important examples of strategic alliances relating to hotels – Hilton and the Radisson Hotel Group – below illustrate some of the points made in the preceding sections.

12.10 SHORT CASE ILLUSTRATION

Radisson: one name, two companies operating a strategic alliance

The Radisson Hotel Group is one of the largest hotel groups in the world. The group's brands include Radisson Collection, Radisson Blu, Radisson, Radisson RED, Park Plaza, Park Inn by Radisson and Country Inn and Suites by Radisson. To the casual observer it might appear to be a single entity operating in a unified manner, but in fact the hotels are managed by two companies (albeit with similar names) operating as partners in a strategic alliance.

The history and operation of the strategic alliance are slightly complex, and its sustainability in its current form is questionable. As in the case of Hilton (see previous illustration), the two arms of the alliance are partly under separate ownership and aligning activities ever more closely using the established Radisson brands. However, the management of the two parts of the group is separated, costly coordination of activities is necessary and future ownership of the group is uncertain.

The Carlson group of travel companies is a large, privately held travel group based in Minneapolis, Minnesota, with an 80-year history in the travel business. It owns significant travel assets including Carlson Wagonlit Travel, a global leader in business travel management. The group also owned the Radisson brands, which it developed itself within North America. Outside North America, however, development largely took place through a strategic alliance with the Rezidor Hotel Group and its forerunner Scandinavian Airways.

A new era for Radisson began in December 2016 when the China-based HNA Tourism Group bought Carlson Hotels and acquired its controlling stake in Rezidor. In August 2018, Radisson Hotel Group was sold to Aplite Holdings AB, a consortium led by a Chinese state-owned hospitality company Jin Jiang International. Radisson Hotels Americas operating in North and South America and the Caribbean are owned separately and became a subsidiary of US company Choice Hotels in 2022.

The two Radisson partners continue to be governed by boards of directors that are independent of each other and have authority to govern their individual businesses.

Sources: www.carlson.com; www.radissonhotels.com; www.radissonhotelsamericas.com

Questions

1. What are the advantages of the two branches of Radisson operating in a strategic alliance?

2. What factors might lead the strategic alliance to be unsustainable?

12.7 Public–private partnerships

Another form of joint development common in *THE* is PPPs, which are a response to the nature of the industry. Though Long (1997:236) wrote in a tourism context, his observation that 'the fragmented nature of the tourism industry comprised, in most areas, of large numbers of small to medium-scale enterprises, together with a wide range of interest groups from public sector agencies to community groups in destinations, is increasingly recognized' is equally valid for hospitality and events.

As a response to the fragmentation and range of public sector, private sector and community stakeholder groups, various types of arrangements to bring the interests together through collaborative arrangements in the form of PPPs are widespread in many countries (see, for example, Weiermair et al., 2008; Zapata and Hall, 2012; Pinz et al., 2018; Xiong et al., 2019).

These PPPs take many forms and often are related to achieving a set of wide-ranging objectives, which include tourism, hospitality and events organizations but may also include many other types of organizations. Often the PPPs are involved in a broader process of urban development or urban renewal that may have important tourism, hospitality and events components but also involve other elements such as housing, offices, retail developments and transport infrastructure.

In general terms, however, such partnerships normally involve the:

- *Public sector* providing the policy and planning framework and infrastructure provision together with some financial incentives
- *Private sector* being involved in providing some or all of the financial resources and managerial competences

One way in which PPPs are facilitated lies in the provision of event venues and facilities to attract visitors, which in turn attract other investment in the form of hotels, restaurants and other activities. The Colorado Convention Center provides an example of such a partnership.

12.11 SHORT CASE ILLUSTRATION

PPPs: managing event venues – the Colorado Convention Center

The USA has a number of large property management companies with sizeable international operations that specialize in event venues. However, unlike its major competitors such as Live Nation and Nederlander organization, which generally own or lease their properties, ASM Global manages many publicly owned facilities. Los Angeles–based ASM Global (a subsidiary of entertainment company AEG) claims to be the world's largest venue management company, with operations involving some 300 stadiums, convention and exhibition centers and performing arts venues concentrated in North America but with further operations in Europe and Asia. One example of a PPP involving ASM Global's private sector expertise working with a publicly owned venue is located in Denver, Colorado.

Built in 1990, the Colorado Convention Center and nearby Denver Performing Arts Complex are top economic engines driving Colorado's economy. The center is a multipurpose series of spaces located in downtown Denver, Colorado, including the 5,000-seat Bellco Theatre. It is the 12th largest convention center in the United States. The convention center hosts over 400 events annually and is owned by the City and County of Denver but has been operated under contract by ASM Global (and its predecessors) since 1994 in a PPP. The partnership is similar to numerous examples operating around the world in that public authorities provide infrastructure and own venues but bring in specialist private sector competences to manage the facilities.

Sources: www.smg.com/; www.denver.org; www.asmglobal.com/

Questions

1. What competences and resources are provided by the public and private sectors in this case?

2. What motivates public authorities to form PPPs such as the one in Denver?

PPPs have become common in *THE* in several diverse ways, such as:

- The development or regeneration of many cities
- Providing and managing music, exhibition and conference venues
- Organizing festivals and events for the benefit of both residents and tourists
- Financing and managing costly infrastructure such as railways, airports, toll highways and hotels

Public sector involvement in tourism and the visitor economy including hospitality and events is commonplace and brought about by a variety of factors (Heeley, 2001). These include the need to:

- Regulate private sector activities
- Provide nonremunerative infrastructure and superstructure
- Remove obstacles to more effective private sector performance
- Redress market failures
- Provide industry leadership and promotion

Increasingly, though, it has been recognized in many countries that in terms of government spending (at national, regional and local levels), spending on tourism, hospitality and events rates well down on the order of priorities. Such spending is often relatively insignificant both in scale and in terms of need when compared with spending on, say, health, defense, social welfare and education. Hence the need to attract private capital.

THE is, however, recognized by governments as a significant and growing contributor to revenues both directly and indirectly. Visitors directly contribute to the economy but also contribute through secondary spending by *THE* organizations that spreads to other industries and by providing positive images of destinations, thereby indirectly contributing to attracting other commercial activities.

Thus, the underlying rationale for PPPs is that the government at various levels wants to maintain an interest in *THE* (for the reasons stated above) but in many cases would like to limit its financial contribution and involve private sector finance and competences. In many cases, public sector contributions to infrastructure (such as airport and road building) are often used as 'pump-priming' to *lever* larger private sector financial contributions.

The Busan International Film Festival is an example of public and private sectors working together to create a major international event.

12.12 SHORT CASE ILLUSTRATION

PPPs: Busan International Film Festival

Busan is the largest port city and second largest city in Korea, and it is undergoing rapid deindustrialization and population aging. However, the city is also undergoing changes captured under the place branding of 'Dynamic Busan'. The focus is on constructing a hub for international sea, air and land transportation and redeveloping itself as a 'soft power' city with improved living environments, cultural and education experiences and welfare services (Seo et al., 2015).

An important and long-standing contributor to this change of emphasis is the Busan International Film Festival (BIFF). The festival was inaugurated in 1996. It has subsequently expanded to become one of Asia's largest film festivals, alongside festivals such as those held in Shanghai, Tokyo, the Hong Kong International Film Festival and the International Film Festival of India held annually in Goa. BIFF has grown steadily and attracted in excess of 200,000 visitors (prior to the COVID-19 pandemic) to the event, held in October each year. BIFF's focus is on introducing new films and first-time directors, especially those from Asian countries. The festival is also notable in that it nurtures and attracts a large youthful audience.

As with many other large public events around the world, one of the driving forces behind the success of the festival is the active PPP that supports it. BIFF relies on 'the strength and determination of institutional and governmental support and funding' (Teo, 2009:118).

Financed by Busan's municipal authorities, the Korean Ministry of Culture, Sports and Tourism, as well as the Korean Film Council, BIFF has benefited from a political stability that allows the festival to avoid entering into complex budgetary arrangements with sporadic funders and sponsors. Since 2011, BIFF has benefited from having an official exclusive venue (The Busan Cinema Center), which was largely publicly funded and is now publicly owned by the Busan local metropolitan government.

Yet, although the active involvement of local and state government ensures constancy and solidity, BIFF benefits from the financial endorsement and support of many private companies, local banks and universities.

This PPP has proved extremely effective in terms of providing stability for the festival and the necessary financial resources to a provincial Korean festival to achieve and maintain international competitiveness.

Sources: www.busan.go.kr/; www.biff.kr; Teo (2009); Seo et al. (2015)

Questions

1. Why might a PPP be effective in these circumstances?

2. What other methods might be appropriate for developing such an event?

A feature of the past 50 years has been the creation of 'hybrid' public and private sector mechanisms that have been premised on the public sector letting go of some or all of its traditional intervention and leadership accountabilities (Heeley, 2001).

In a later article, Heeley (2011) cited the cases of a number of European cities, including Oslo, Lausanne, Dublin, Barcelona, Vienna and Prague, that have established PPPs to facilitate the development of the visitor economy that *THE* activities facilitate. In the USA, many examples of real estate developments being facilitated by PPPs focused on the provision of visitor attractions, convention facilities, restaurants, hotels and event venues are evident.

One such example is the case of Baltimore Inner Harbor (see below), which has developed for over 40 years through various PPP arrangements (the details of which have changed over the years).

12.13 SHORT CASE ILLUSTRATION

PPPs: Baltimore Inner Harbor – a model for waterfront redevelopment

One case of PPP in action with tourism, hospitality and events very much at its heart that is often quoted is the case of Baltimore Inner Harbor (see, for example, Kostopoulou, 2013). A PPP has developed the Baltimore Inner Harbor waterfront over the last 45 years. Baltimore is the blueprint many other cities have studied and adapted to specific circumstances.

Toronto and Boston also started their waterfront redevelopment projects at about the same time (in the late 1970s), and subsequently many other US cities such as San Francisco, Seattle and Cleveland as well as several European port cities such as Barcelona, Spain; Genoa, Italy; and Cardiff and Liverpool, UK have followed this lead (Jauhiainen, 1995). The lessons from such redevelopment have also been applied in a Chinese setting by Xu and Yan (2000).

In the case of Baltimore Inner Harbor, a historic but rundown waterfront has been transformed through a partnership now coordinated by the Baltimore Waterfront Partnership (www.baltimorewaterfront.com). The development is multifaceted and includes tourist attractions such as the National Aquarium, Maryland Science Center and the nearby Baltimore Convention Center and Hyatt Regency Baltimore Hotel. These leisure- and business-focused attractions have acted as 'magnets' to attract further investment, and many other hotels, housing schemes and restaurants have been developed in the area.

After 50 years of development, it has been argued that further investment is needed to improve and extend facilities, and an Inner Harbor 2.0 plan is being implemented. To provide a new dynamic vision for the Inner Harbor, this master plan looks to build upon the successes of the original 1970s plan, while providing bold new ideas. The overall intent is to provide a visionary but realistic plan that can be implemented as funds are available. This includes smaller items like recommendations for consistent street furniture and lighting to larger capital projects such as the redevelopment of Rash Field (a local park).

Sources: Jauhiainen (1995); Xu and Yan (2000); Kostopoulou (2013); www.waterfrontpartnership.org

Questions

1. What direct and indirect benefits does Baltimore hope to achieve from its PPP?

2. Why does the public sector not carry out such development on its own?

In the UK, these joint development initiatives were pioneered by Plymouth in 1978 with the formation of the Plymouth Marketing Bureau. Many British cities such as Birmingham, Liverpool, Glasgow, Sheffield, Cardiff and Manchester followed in the 1990s. In these cases, and in subsequent British examples, normal visitor and convention bureau activities – that is, tourism – were supplemented by the related fields of city imaging and festivals management (Heeley, 2001). Subsequently, the partnerships were often given wider powers to provide an integrated approach to *THE* as well as inward investment and economic development activities.

THINK POINTS

- Explain the objectives that public and private sectors hope to gain from PPPs.
- What types of development in *THE* are involved with PPPs?
- Why might PPPs prove unsuccessful in some circumstances?

Manchester's reemergence in recent years as 'Marketing Manchester' (see Short Case Illustration below) illustrates this integrated approach to *THE*, inward investment and economic development.

12.14 SHORT CASE ILLUSTRATION

PPPs: Marketing Manchester

Manchester is an industrial city in the northwest of England at the center of a conurbation (Greater Manchester) of over 2.5 million people. It is famed for its manufacturing base and grew to its prominent position during the industrial revolution with an emphasis on cotton and clothes manufacture. However, it would not be thought of as a 'traditional' visitor destination, unlike its nearby historic counterpart Chester.

The city's contemporary profile is boosted by its two Premier League football teams (Manchester United and City) and through attracting many international students to its universities. Recast for the 21st century as the original modern city, Greater Manchester has experienced a contemporary resurgence marked culturally by the acclaimed reopening of the Whitworth art gallery, arts center HOME and the world-leading Manchester International Festival; by a property and investment boom that has outstripped the rest of the country; and by major changes to its governance and infrastructure.

However, during the economic downturn, the city was hard hit and has turned to attracting increasing numbers of business and leisure visitors as a way of increasing economic activity. It has done this by relying on its central position, selling events often staged at large publicly funded venues and through the activities of a PPP – Marketing Manchester.

Marketing Manchester is the agency charged with promoting Greater Manchester on the national and international stage to visitors, investors, conference organizers and students. It is the region's destination marketing organization and the tourist board for Greater Manchester.

The agency is funded through a combination of commercial revenue (including funding from Manchester Airport, Britain's third largest, for international campaigns) and public funds from the local authorities throughout Greater Manchester. It is overseen by a board comprising representatives from public sector bodies and private sector companies. Marketing Manchester works closely in partnership with the Greater Manchester Combined Authority (the strategic public local authority for Greater Manchester), Britain's national tourism organization (VisitBritain), other destination management organizations and other key stakeholders, as well as over 500 private sector partners.

Marketing Manchester's strategy dovetails with the overall Greater Manchester Strategy and the Greater Manchester Internationalization Strategy, which has a vision for Manchester to be a Top 20 global city by 2035. Its strategy for 2017–20, 'A place to visit, invest, do business, and study', has a number of strategic priorities:

- Promote Greater Manchester to priority markets and sectors
- Facilitate placemaking, collaboration and partnerships
- Become an exemplar destination marketing organization

Ambitious growth targets were set aside due to the impacts of the pandemic, and a one-year recovery plan was put in place for 2002–21. The aim in 2021–22 was to rebuild the visitor economy, bolster work in key sectors, support investment and improve confidence in visiting and staying in Greater Manchester following the effects of the pandemic.

Sources: Adapted from www.marketingmanchester.com/; Edwards and Taylor (2012); Van Den Berg (2017)

Questions

1. What are the management and governance issues that might arise in such a PPP?

2. Could the same approach be easily transferred to other cities?

12.8 Franchising

Franchising is a method involving two parties: the *franchisor and* the *franchisee*.

In return for gaining access to the brand attributes, image, marketing and other support from the franchisor such as systems and training, the franchisee usually takes a substantial portion of the financial risk (providing the capital investment) and pays fees to the franchisor. Because it involves another party providing the financial resources, it has often proved to be a fast method of expanding for many hotel, restaurant and car hire companies, among others.

Franchising is one of the most popular methods of growth in parts of *THE*. Leading industry and ancillary service brands such as Avis and Hertz (car rental companies); Marriott, Holiday Inn, Choice and Radisson (hotels); and McDonald's, Burger King and KFC (fast food outlets) have expanded primarily by pursuing the franchise method. The rise of franchising in various *THE* contexts has been explored by various writers, including Denton and Dennis (2000), Pine et al. (2000), Altinay et al. (2013), Hua et al. (2017) and Jang and Park (2019).

The Short Case Illustration below involving fast food and car rental firms illustrates the speed at which companies can grow when they have established a strong brand by adopting this method.

12.15 SHORT CASE ILLUSTRATION

International growth through franchising: fast foods and car rental

It is not a well-known name, but it is likely that Yum! Brands Inc. is familiar to most of this book's readers through its products. Yum is a fast food provider based in Louisville, Kentucky, that owns the worldwide rights to well-known brands including KFC, Pizza Hut and Taco Bell. The company formed in 1997 as the result of a sale of PepsiCo's fast food division and is a Fortune 500 company quoted on the New York Stock Exchange with revenues in excess of $6bn. The vast majority of restaurants, in over 130 countries, utilize a franchise model of operation.

Since the spin-off from PepsiCo in 1997, the company has expanded internationally. Further opportunities for international expansion are envisaged by the company (based on its three core brands), because there are about 2.5 restaurants per million people in the top 10 emerging markets, compared to 57 restaurants per million in the USA.

Enterprise Holdings is one of America's largest privately held companies. The company, with annual revenues in excess of $30bn, is based in St. Louis, Missouri, and traces its origins to the late 1950s. Enterprise Holdings controls three of the world's leading vehicle rental franchises: Enterprise, Alamo and National.

In both cases, a substantial scale and internationally diversified scope of operations have been built relatively quickly. It is unlikely that such scale and scope could have been achieved as quickly if the companies concerned had to rely on their own financial resources. The scale of capital investment required would have been massive, and the inherent risks involved would likely have deterred potential investors.

Instead, the risks and capital investment were largely dispersed among the many franchisees spread around the world. The franchises investing their own capital were incentivized to grow the businesses and were able to apply local market knowledge while being able to rely on the support offered by strong internationally recognized brands.

Sources: Adapted from www.yum.com; www.enterpriseholdings.com

Questions

1. Why have American companies been particularly successful in using this form of growth?

2. Why has franchising been so prevalent in certain parts of *THE*, including fast food, car rental and hotels, but not in others?

In capital-intensive parts of *THE* requiring a large up-front financial outlay to establish facilities or in smaller start-up businesses, franchising provides an opportunity for organizations to lower the risks and the level of investment to expand. Thus, this method of growth is particularly prevalent among hotel organizations, travel intermediaries, restaurants and ancillary services such as car hire companies, but examples are also to be found among airlines and festival end event management companies. Many small *THE* businesses have been established by becoming franchisees of larger businesses with strong brands. Some of the franchisees have themselves grown into substantial businesses by expanding through the franchise route.

In the past, a number of airlines including British Airways, Lufthansa and Air France have made franchising an important element of the strategic methods they have employed. The method has, however, become less important among airlines as acquisitions, industry consolidation, strategic alliances and codesharing agreements have often taken their place.

There are still some examples in the airline sector, such as Sun Air (www.uk.sun-air.dk), operating as a British Airways franchise, and Air Nostrum (www.airnostrum.es), operating as an Iberia franchise. These two airlines operate regional services from bases in Denmark and Spain, respectively.

Nowhere in the commercial field has franchising been more evident than among the leading international hotel groups. Progressively, most of the largest chains, to some degree, have followed this strategic method, which was pioneered by Holiday Inn during the 1950s (see the Short Case Illustration below). The big international hotel groups operate so-called asset-light business models, having sold most of their real estate assets to concentrate on brand growth through managing and franchising their hotels.

12.16 SHORT CASE ILLUSTRATION

Franchising: Holiday Inn Hotels

In 1952, an American entrepreneur, Kemmons Wilson, opened the first Holiday Inn hotel in Memphis, Tennessee, after he returned from a family holiday discouraged by the lack of family- and value-oriented lodging. Children stayed free, and the hotel offered a swimming pool, air conditioning and restaurant on the property. Telephones, ice and free parking were standard as well. Although commonplace today, these services were revolutionary at the time and set a standard for the hotel industry.

The company became a pioneer of franchising and rapidly expanded the Holiday Inn system primarily through utilizing this method of strategic growth. The brand was almost literally rolled out across the USA, following the US interstate highway system's growth across the country. On the heels of this domestic success, the brand soon found investor interest in Europe and Asia, becoming the largest single hotel brand in the world. By the late 1980s, the Holiday Inn brand could be found in many parts of the world. Go and Pine (1995:11) suggested that the franchise strategy pursued by Holiday Inn 'is among the greatest success stories in US Business'.

In operating franchises, Holiday Inn sought to apply strict operating standards and supplied franchisees with almost everything, apart from the land upon which the hotel would be built, to ensure that there were 'no surprises' (Nickson, 1997). In 1990, IHG plc, which has its corporate headquarters in London (then known as Bass plc), acquired Holiday Inn and moved the hotel headquarters from Memphis to Atlanta in the summer of 1991. Atlanta offered the corporate infrastructure, worldwide transportation access and international presence that were necessary for the company to succeed as a global business. Holiday Inn, together with its complementary brands, which include Holiday Inn Express, Crowne Plaza and Intercontinental Hotels, has grown (predominantly through franchising) into a vast international hotel grouping.

As an 'asset-light' business, IHG is a manager and franchisor of hotel brands. This means it can focus on growing fee revenues and fee margins, with limited requirements for capital, an approach that has helped the group to successfully grow its business and deliver high returns.

In 2019, IHG had about 845,000 guest rooms and about 5,650 hotels across nearly 100 countries.

Sources: Adapted from www.ihgplc.com/; Go and Pine (1995); Nickson (1997)

Questions

1. What might the potential difficulties for a franchisor such as Holiday Inn be?

2. What might the potential difficulties for a Holiday Inn franchisee be?

The franchise method can vary in its detailed implementation. It may involve fairly simple arrangements whereby one franchisee develops one unit or a single territory from the franchisor. Many Avis and McDonald's franchisees, for example, operate one or a limited number of franchise locations.

A more complex arrangement may exist when a large company purchases a *master franchise* from the franchisor, which gives the company exclusive rights to the franchise name for a region or country.

> For example: *In March 2016, Best Western Hotels and Resorts, which at that time has 22 hotels in India, signed a master franchise agreement with the Indian company Sorrel Hospitality group to expand its portfolio in India, Bangladesh and Sri Lanka. Sorrel Hospitality, based in Delhi, is responsible for Best Western's future positioning,*

growth and development across India, Bangladesh and Sri Lanka. Best Western provides its hoteliers with global operational, sales and marketing support and online and mobile booking capabilities.

Although hospitality franchise agreements resemble strategic alliances, in that two parties work collaboratively, they are dissimilar in terms of the attainment of allying partners' objectives and development of interfirm relationships through resource sharing, as explained below.

In a *THE* franchise agreement, although the two firms involved typically share assets, the risk exposure is not equally shared. The franchisor is exposed to lower risks than the franchisee, who meets the infrastructural requirements of the agreement. The franchisor meets the product, technology, marketing and training aspects of the agreement for a fixed and/or variable fee. Although the variable component of the fee changes with the level of sales, the reduced risk exposure is balanced by the fee's fixed component.

On the other hand, the franchisee's return depends purely on the cash flow generated by the franchise operation. The franchisor usually has the upper hand in the agreement. Consequently, these types of contracts do not create parity in the agreement between the franchisor and franchisee.

The reasons for the popularity of franchising among both franchisors and franchisees and possible disadvantages are summarized in Table 12.5.

12.9 Management contracts

Management contracts are a popular joint development method of international growth, particularly in the hospitality and airline sectors, and also in relation to attractions and venues.

A management contract is an arrangement under which operational control of an enterprise is vested by contract in a separate enterprise that performs the necessary managerial functions in return for a fee (see, for example, DeRoos, 2010; Ivanova and Ivanov, 2015).

The distinction between management contracts and franchising lies in the fact that management contracts involve not just selling a method of carrying out activities and the support of an established

Table 12.5 Summary of the advantages and disadvantages of franchising

	Advantages	Disadvantages
Franchisor	• Low capital costs • Ability to use brand strength to expand quickly • Use of franchisee's local market knowledge and entrepreneurial abilities	Returns may be capped Some loss of control of the brand Having to consider the interests of the franchisees as a stakeholder group Need to scrutinize the structure, organization and financial viability and capabilities of the franchisee
Franchisee	• Lower risk than going it alone • Support from a major company • Exclusive rights to a brand in a particular territory	Fees and part of profits paid to the franchise holder Risk that franchise quality deteriorates or the franchisor withdraws it

Source: Adapted from Evans (2001b)

brand (as with franchising or licensing) but also actually carrying out these activities. A management contract can involve a wide range of functions, such as:

- Operation of a facility
- Reservation, ticketing and operating systems
- Management of human resources
- Accounting and financial control
- Sales and marketing services
- Training

In the case of accommodation where management contracts are very common, utilizing this method, the ownership of the physical asset (the hotel or other accommodation) is separated from its management. The management contract is thus an agreement between a hotel owner (or other form of accommodation) and a hotel operating company, by which the owner employs the operator as an agent to assume full responsibility for the management of the property.

As an agent, the operator usually pays, in the name of the owners, all property and operating expenses from the cash flow generated through operations, retains its management fees and remits surpluses, if any, to the property owner. The property owner, on the other hand, usually provides the hotel land, building furniture, furnishings, equipment and working capital, while also assuming full legal and financial responsibility for the hotel (Olsen et al., 1991).

DEFINITION/QUOTATION

Management contracts

Conceived as a relatively simple arrangement that allowed international expansion by hotel chain operators without the risk of real estate ownership, the management contract has become an intricate and nearly essential element of the contemporary hotel industry.

While trends in management contracts have shifted with the relative bargaining power of owners and operators, the key to a successful contract is aligning the interests of all parties. Owners seek some reasonable guarantee of cash flow, while operators need assurance that they will be able to benefit from their continued operation of a property.

DeRoos (2010)

Many well-known upscale international hotel chains (such as Sheraton, Sofitel, le Meridien, Marriott, Hilton International, Hyatt, Radisson, Nikko and Shangri-La) have successfully utilized this method of expansion. Large international foodservice companies such as Compass, Sodexo and Aramark (based in the UK, France and USA, respectively) have also used this method. These companies (and many others), through being awarded management contracts, have expanded their diverse catering operations internationally to include transport facilities, sport and entertainment venues and corporate premises.

For the operating company, the management contract:

● Allows rapid expansion to take place
● Allows easy market penetration
● Involves little or no capital investment

The operating company is therefore not prone to speculative risks associated with falling property prices (and also does not benefit from rises in property values). In some cases, the operating company will, however, invest some of its own capital in the project alongside the property developer. The operating company also has an agreed rate of return built into its contractual terms.

The principal disadvantage of the management contract for the operating company is the insecurity associated with this method. From time to time management contracts come up for renewal. It is usual for the workings of the relationship to be reviewed and its success judged at this time. In practice, a change in the operating company is quite common, so that when the management contract is renewed the company operating a hotel under a management contract might change from, say, le Meridien (a Marriott brand) to, say, Hyatt.

There are also a number of the world's airlines that operate feeder or so-called regional services for other carriers. In the world's largest aviation market, the USA, this arrangement is particularly common, with a number of airlines competing to operate feeder services into the main hubs of the large international carriers. These airlines generally operate on fixed-price management contracts. Many of these airlines operate most of the functions of a full airline but fly in the colors of the so-called legacy airlines (such as American, Delta and United Airlines) and coordinate their schedules accordingly.

THINK POINTS

● Providing examples from *THE*, explain the differences between growth achieved through franchising and management contracts.

● Outline the benefits and potential difficulties of franchising for both the franchisor and the franchisee.

● Why has franchising been so successful as a growth method for *THE* and ancillary services?

● Why might PPPs prove unsuccessful in some circumstances?

This system of management contracts among airlines is illustrated by the Short Case Illustration of SkyWest Inc. below.

12.17 SHORT CASE ILLUSTRATION

Management contracts: SkyWest Inc.

Though it is a major transport company in its own right with well over 500 aircraft, Skywest Inc. is not well known to consumers. Like other 'regional' airlines such as Air Wisconsin, Republic Airways and Mesa Air operating similar models in the USA, it generally operates through management contracts with other airlines.

These airlines generally connect smaller population centers with the hubs of the major airlines. The routes generally cover shorter distances, using smaller airplanes (often Embraer or Bombadier) than the major US airline brands. For example, United may contract one of these airlines to fly between Bozeman, Montana, the principal airport for Yellowstone National Park, and its hub at Chicago's O'Hare International Airport.

Utah-based SkyWest Airlines provides air passenger services with approximately 2,000 daily departures to destinations in the United States, Canada, Mexico and the Caribbean, carrying over 36 million passengers in 2021. Most flights are operated for the 'regional' brands of major US carriers Delta Connection, United Express and American Eagle, and it uses the systems and brand identities of these airlines in operating its services.

The services are managed through two types of long-term management contracts involving codeshare agreements: 'fixed-fee' or, 'revenue sharing'. Among other features of the fixed-fee management contracts, Skywest's partners generally reimburse the company for specified direct operating expenses (including fuel) and pay a fee for operating the aircraft. Such an arrangement provides benefits for both Skywest and its partners. Skywest has a relatively stable revenue stream, access to a strong brand and an incentive to reduce costs to increase operating margins. For the partner airline for which it operates, an extensive and complex regional network is provided at a competitive agreed cost.

Under a revenue sharing management contract, the regional airline and the major airline negotiate a contract whereby the regional airline receives an agreed proportion of the revenues. All direct costs associated with the regional flight are borne by the regional airline. In such an arrangement, the regional airline bears some of the risk in that there are opportunities to increase profits as ticket prices and passenger loading increase or fuel costs decrease. Conversely, lower profits may be achieved when ticket prices and passenger loading decrease or when fuel prices increase.

Sources: Adapted from www.inc.skywest.com/; Lohmann and Koo (2013); Whyte and Lohmann (2020).

Questions

1. What are the advantages for major airlines of subcontracting services to SkyWest through management contracts?

2. What are the risks and benefits for SkyWest?

12.10 Cooperative networks

Various types of cooperative networks or consortia have been developed in *THE* (see, for example, Van der Zee and Vanneste, 2015). These networks and consortia are most evident in *THE* in two ways:

- The hospitality sector (where the method is most frequently evident) is characterized by a high degree of fragmentation, with a large number of individual or family-owned enterprises. These independently operated businesses face increasing competitive pressures from hotel chains operating branded products that enjoy marketing economies and sophisticated systems.

- *Referral networks* that have been formed whereby many of the world's major airline, hotel, car rental firms, event venues, tour intermediaries and ancillary suppliers are linked by a web of arrangements. These arrangements involve consumers being cross-referred from one supplier to other 'preferred' suppliers in the supply chain. In such circumstances, there is an inference that consumers will find that the preferred suppliers are leaders in their offerings or that they are able to offer preferential financial terms.

12.10.1 Hospitality consortia

In response to the threats of competing in arenas increasingly dominated by large companies, individually operated hotel and accommodation businesses have increasingly joined together in networks or consortia. By doing so, they are attempting to achieve the marketing, branding and systems advantages of larger rivals while maintaining their independence. In return for a fee, the individual hotel receives a range of benefits. In categorizing hotel consortia, Fyall and Garrod (2005) pointed out that the consortia vary in terms of the degree of commitment, control and cooperation involved and in the organizational formality. They also vary in terms of the financial commitments that are undertaken by their members.

The strengths and weaknesses of independent hotels and the benefits they hope to derive from joining a consortium are summarized in Figure 12.5.

Many consortia have been established in specific parts of the world, and some, such as Best Western, Relais, Châteaux and Small Luxury Hotels of the World have gained widespread international coverage. Consortia have also been formed that involve smaller chains of hotels (rather than individual properties), allowing the chains to maintain their brand attributes and to compete effectively with larger internationally diversified brands.

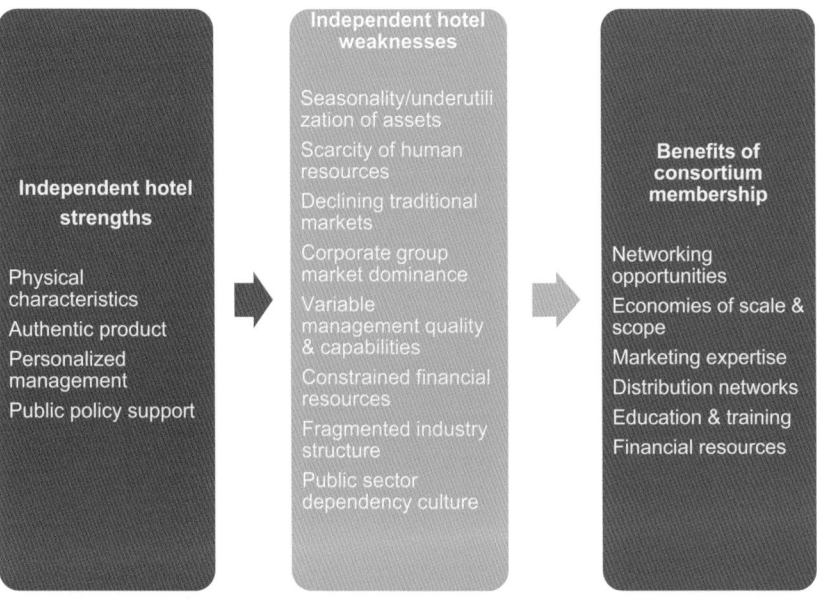

Figure 12.5 The benefits of consortium membership for independent hotels

Source: Adapted from Morrison (1994)

> For example – *Dubai-based Global Hotel Alliance brings together mainly mid- to upscale brands from around the world. Unlike Best Western, it represents smaller chains of hotels that maintain their individual branding. The alliance runs a joint loyalty scheme for customers using the hotel brands it represents. The consortium represents brands such as Park Royal, Pan Pacific and Marco Polo, which have properties across Asia-Pacific; Kempinski Hotels, a luxury brand with properties across Europe, Asia and Africa; and Leela, which is represented at key locations across India (www.gha.com).*

Best Western provides a well-known example of a hospitality consortium that has grown to a world-wide presence.

12.18 SHORT CASE ILLUSTRATION

Hospitality consortium: Best Western

Best Western traces its origins back to 1946 when it began as an informal referral system among member hotels in California. It has subsequently grown from its Phoenix, Arizona, base to a presence in over 100 countries representing over 4,700 properties, making it one of the world's largest branded chains.

The business model operated by Best Western is that it operates as a nonprofit membership association, with each member voting on aspects of the association in a way similar to a marketing cooperative. Best Western provides marketing support, reservations systems and a unified brand identity in return for fees. The hotels are allowed to keep their independent identity, though they are required to use Best Western signage and systems and to identify themselves as Best Western hotels. In the USA in particular, there are many smaller chains of Best Western hotels that are owned by the same management, though this is less common elsewhere.

Best Western offers members the potential advantage of retaining their independence while at the same time providing the benefits of a full-service, international lodging affiliation offering a global reservations system, marketing, advertising, purchasing, training and quality standards.

One way in which Best Western can be observed to have added value and supported its members is in its response to the COVID-19 pandemic.

Chan et al. (2021) reported that as a pioneer in cleaning standards, Best Western started using a variation of ultraviolet technology in 2012 to decrease microbial levels in guest-rooms. Since the outbreak of COVID-19, they have also published protocols online to showcase their enhanced standards through their 'We Care Clean' program.

Sources: Adapted from www.bestwestern.com/; Chan et al. (2021)

Questions

1. What advantages does Best Western membership provide for an individual hotel?

2. What difficulties might Best Western have in competing effectively with branded chains?

12.10.2 Referral networks

These arrangements involve consumers being cross-referred from one supplier to other 'preferred' suppliers in the supply chain, usually in a vertical or diagonal supplier relationship. These networks have proliferated in *THE* to such an extent that most hotel and airlines have suppliers that are favored partners to which they are referred, though such arrangements are less common in other parts of *THE*.

In such circumstances there is an inference that consumers will find that the preferred suppliers are leaders in their offerings or that they are able to offer preferential financial terms. The arrangements frequently involve loyalty schemes. It is common for there to be reciprocity between airline and hotel frequent flyer and loyalty schemes whereby points earned on one scheme can be credited as points in the other.

There have been changes since the advent of the internet. It was common for airlines to refer to a limited number of hotel partners with which they had a contractual or occasionally equity relationship. This is less common now as airlines usually utilize internet intermediaries such as Expedia or TripAdvisor on their sites to provide a greater range of choices.

> For example: *Pan Pacific Hotels Group (www.panpacific.com) is a global hospitality company that owns and/or manages more than 50 hotels, resorts and serviced suites across three brands: Pan Pacific, Park Royal Collection and Park Royal, encompassing more than 30 cities across Asia-Pacific, North America and Europe. Headquartered in Singapore, it is a member of Singapore-listed UOL Group Limited. With its primary focus on Asia-Pacific, it is unsurprising that it emphasizes reciprocal preferred supplier arrangements with a number of leading Asian airlines, including All Nippon Airways, Cathay Pacific, Japan Airways, Malaysian Airlines, Philippine Airlines and Singapore Airlines.*

12.11 Methods of strategic development: a comparison

Clearly, each of the strategic development methods outlined in the preceding sections – organic growth, mergers and acquisitions and joint development – have certain inherent advantages and disadvantages associated with them.

Internal development, for instance, may be relatively slow, and choosing an alliance partner that does not have complementary competences can be problematic. Mergers and takeovers can be expensive, and evidence shows that in many cases this method fails to add value for the enlarged group.

Companies operating in *THE* have to make a choice between the various methods available to them. The decision as to which method to adopt will be influenced by both internal and external factors including the competitive, economic and regulatory environment faced by the company and the availability of finance and other resources. The methods chosen may also depend on the relative strength of the organization, timing and the balance of its portfolio of activities. The choices are complex and will change over time.

Taking the accommodation sector as an example, and hotels in particular, development can be carried out by franchising, management contracts and owning or leasing property achieved by organic growth or mergers and acquisitions.

Table 12.6 gives a comparison between development through franchising, management contracts and owning or leasing hotels as summarized by the leading international group IHG. Some portfolios of owned and leased properties may have been built up organically, whereas others may have been acquired through mergers and acquisitions. In either case, the hotel group has to provide capital, which makes expansion costly and sometimes (in the case of organic development) relatively slow.

Table 12.6 A comparison of franchising, management contracts and managing or leasing hotels

Aspect	Franchised	Managed	Owned and leased
Brand ownership	IHG	IHG	IHG
Marketing and distribution	IHG	IHG	IHG
Staff	Third party	IHG usually provides a general manager as a minimum	IHG
Hotel ownership	Third party	Third party	IHG
IHG capital	None	Low/none	High
IHG income	Fee % of rooms revenue	Fee % of total revenue plus % of profit	All revenues and profits

Source: www.IHG.com

In practice, the decisions made by major international hotel groups can vary quite considerably. Notwithstanding these differences, there has been a significant shift toward the speed of development possible with so-called asset-light business models. These models of development favor franchising and management contracts as opposed to ownership and leasing.

DEFINITION/QUOTATION

The 'asset-light' hotel

> You book a room on the website of a famous international hotel chain. As you arrive to check in, its reassuring brand name is above the door. Its logo is everywhere: on the staff uniforms, the stationery, the carpets. But the hotel is owned by someone else – often an individual or an investment fund – who has taken out a franchise on the brand. The owner may also be delegating the running of the hotel, either to the company that owns the brand or to another management firm altogether. The bricks and mortar may be leased from a property firm. In some cases, yet another company may be supplying most of the staff, and an outside caterer may run the restaurants. Welcome to the virtual hotel.
> ('Why hotel chains don't own many hotels', 2009)

Figure 12.6 demonstrates how selected international hotel groups have developed using different methods. Whereas, for example, Wyndham Worldwide and IHG have grown largely through franchising, the other hotel groups have more of a balance between franchised and managed properties. In all of the hotel groups sampled, the proportion of owned or leased properties is quite low, because all of these groups (and many others) pursue 'asset-light' strategies (which were investigated by Sohn et al. 2013; Blal and Bianchi, 2019; Li and Singal, 2019; Märklin and Bianchi, 2022).

Johnson et al. (2017), drawing on the work of Dyer et al. (2004) and Yin and Shanley (2008), summarized four key variables that can aid managers in choosing between acquisitions, alliances and organic development.

The 'buy, ally or DIY [do-it-yourself]' matrix produced by Johnson et al. (2017) is shown in Figure 12.7.

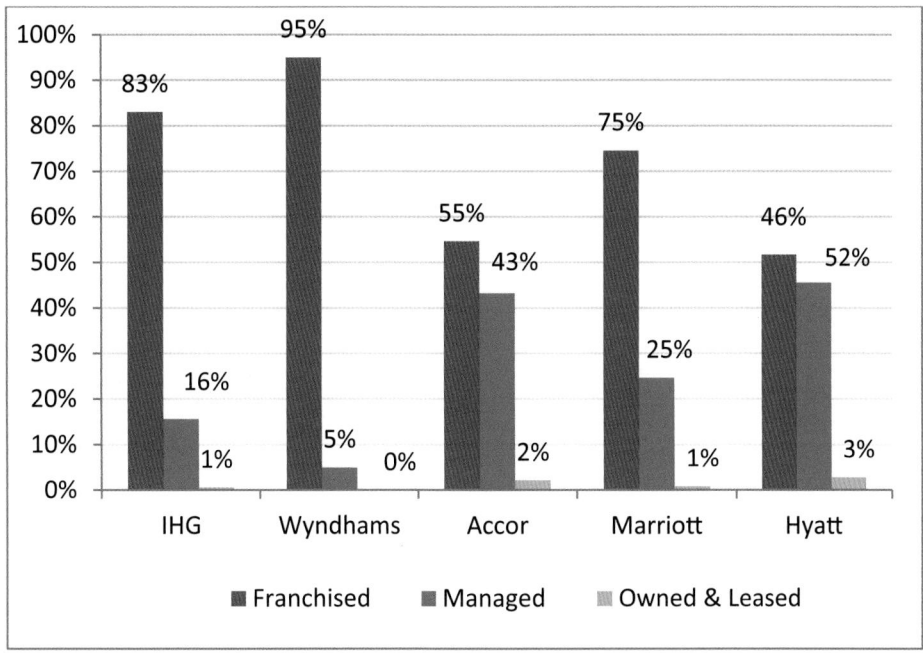

Figure 12.6 Methods of growth employed by selected international hotel groups (% of total rooms)

Source: Adapted from company websites (accessed Nov. 2022)

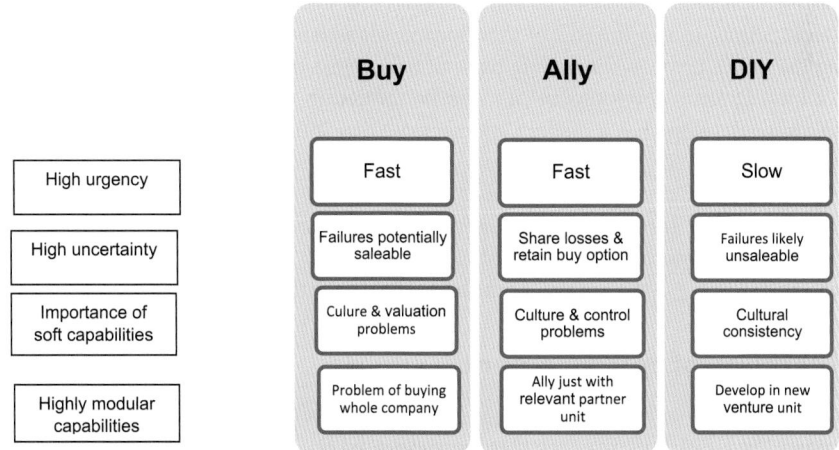

Figure 12.7 Buy, ally or DIY matrix

Source: Adapted from Johnson et al. (2017:359), based on work of Dyer et al. (2004) and Yin and Shanley (2008)

The buy, ally or DIY matrix uses four variables:

- *Urgency* – In developing a business, mergers and acquisitions can be a relatively quick method of growth. Organic growth, on the other hand, is slower, because it involves everything having to be provided from the organization's own resources and capabilities.

> **For example:** *It is unlikely that TUI would have been able to develop its tour operating business from a mainly German base to a pan-European giant without two strategic moves. The purchase in 2000 of Thomson (Britain's largest tour operator at the time) and the subsequent merger with another large quoted UK tour operator, First Choice Holidays in 2007, transformed the group.*

- *Uncertainty* – If there is a high degree of uncertainty, alliances offer flexibility in that, if success-ful, there is potential to move on to a full merger, whereas failures are shared between partners, thereby limiting losses. Acquisitions offer the chance of a resale even if the venture is not success-ful, because the assets have attracted a bid in the past, thereby demonstrating potential. A failed organic development might have to be written off because the unit concerned has never been subject to a market valuation.
- *Capabilities* – So-called soft capabilities such as people and skills are much harder to value and replicate than hard capabilities such as equipment and machinery.

Most *THE* acquisitions involve a large component of soft capabilities because they are human resource –intensive activities often with a strong reliance on brand values. Soft capabilities are also more dif-ficult to control. Consequently, organizations need to be cautious with acquisitions or when entering into joint ventures because of these potential difficulties. On the other hand, organic development in this respect can be less risky. By developing organically, an organization can ensure that these soft capabilities are developed in a culturally consistent manner using acquired knowledge and experience.

- *Modular capabilities* – The extent to which the capabilities that are being sought by an organization are 'modular' will have an impact on the favored method. If the capabilities are distributed in particular divisions or SBUs of the proposed partners, an alliance or joint venture is likely to be favorable. Such an arrangement would mean that one venture could link just with the relevant parts of the partner, leaving each partner to run the rest of their businesses independently. An acquisition could involve acquiring the whole company, including parts of no interest that have to be subsequently sold, pos-sibly at a loss. Organic development can also be favored in these circumstances because the new business can be developed as a distinct and separate division, which avoids the involvement of the entire organization.

The choice between the three alternative methods is at times restricted by regulations, available finance and available opportunities. Nevertheless, the matrix shown is a valuable tool in focusing managers on the possible options that might be available for their organizations.

12.12 Methods of retrenchment

We should not assume that business strategies are always designed to cause business growth. There are times when organizations may wish to become smaller; that is, to retrench. As with growth strategy, retrenchment (size reduction) can be achieved through various methods. Retrenchment can be achieved by:

- Organic reduction (by winding down operations in specific product areas)
- Divestment or demerger – the opposite of acquisitions and mergers
- Disengagement with partners involved in joint development

Demergers and divestments (which together are referred to as *disposals*) involve taking a part of a company and selling it off as a 'self-contained' unit with its own management, structure and employees in place. The unit may then be sold on to a single buyer (for whom it will be an acquisition) or it may be floated on the stock market as a public limited company.

Disposals occur when parent organizations wish to offload a part of its structure that is no longer in line with its core activity. They can take the form of divestments, demergers, equity carve-outs or management buyouts.

12.12.1 Reasons for disposal

There are a number of reasons why a company may elect to dispose of a part of its structure. The most prominent reasons may include:

- Underperformance (e.g., poor profitability), possibility due to poor synergy
- A change in the strategic focus of the organization, meaning some parts are no longer required
- Poor medium- to long-term prospects
- It is an unwanted subsidiary of an acquired company
- The need to raise capital to reinvest in core areas or to increase liquidity in the selling company
- The belief that it would be more productive if it were owned by another company
- Being used as a tactic to deflect a hostile takeover bid
- Being part of a process of 'asset stripping' – the process of breaking a company up into its parts and selling them off for a sum greater than that paid for the whole

---

THINK POINTS

- Explain how organizations might choose between allying, buying or DIY.
- Explain what is meant by retrenchment.
- In what circumstances might organizations consider disposals?

12.12.2 Shareholders and disposals

The most common method of corporate disposal is a 'private' transaction between two companies, which is intended to be of benefit to both parties. The seller gains the funds from the transaction and is able to focus on its core areas. The buyer gains the product and market presence of the disposal, which, in turn, will be (we assume) to its strategic advantage.

Disposals are designed to create synergy to the shareholders in the same way as integrations. We should not lose sight of the fact that business organizations are owned by shareholders, and it is the role of company directors (as the shareholders' agents) to act in such a way that shareholder wealth is maximized. If this can be achieved by breaking a part of the company off, this option will be pursued.

All organizations are constrained by resources, which are finite, and choices have to be made (as discussed in the following chapter) as to where they are best deployed in the organization. In identifying resources, it is common for organizations to discern between core and non-core assets and decide to sell the non-core assets in a program of disposals.

Assets may be deemed non-core for a variety of reasons. The assets may be peripheral to the main purposes of the business, unable to contribute to the organization's core competences, too risky, too small to warrant investment and management attention or thought not to be capable of achieving rates of return equivalent to other parts of the organization. It may also be the case that when cash flow problems arise, assets have to be sold to fund the rest of the organization so that it can continue trading.

The TUI group has made a number of disposals in recent years as part of its strategy of concentrating its resources on its core businesses and brands, as illustrated below.

12.19 SHORT CASE ILLUSTRATION

Sale of non-core assets at TUI

TUI Group labels itself as 'one of the world's leading tourism groups'. As a 'vertically integrated' tourism company, it covers the entire tourism value chain in that the company includes tour operating brands, travel agencies, airlines with over 150 aircraft, more than 400 hotels, 16 cruise liners and incoming tourist agencies in all major world markets. The TUI Group, based in Hannover, Germany, is an international tourism group that serves over 20 million customers a year. The company has dual stock market listings in Frankfurt and in London.

Like all businesses, choices have to be made about how the resources can be utilized most effectively to maximize shareholder returns. The global travel restrictions imposed during the COVID-19 pandemic had a strong negative effect on the TUI Group's earnings and liquidity – evidenced from the end of March 2020 and throughout the financial year 2021. The company's financial position became stretched and emergency funding was secured from the German government; additional capital funding was secured through two rights issues of shares.

Another response was to reconsider aspects of its strategy with regard to asset ownership, following the lead of the large international hospitality chains. TUI announced that it had completed the sale of its 49% stake in the Riu family hotel properties in a deal valued at €670mn. The proceeds of the sale of the portfolio of 21 properties will enable the company to reduce its levels of debt while continuing to utilize the hotels for its itineraries.

Chief executive Fritz Joussen said, 'The transaction enables us to further implement our 'asset-right' strategy with a clear focus on managing brand, operations, customer experience and distribution – decoupling growth in hotels from investments and hotel management and the holiday experience from property ownership' (Taylor, 2021).

The deal represents the latest in a series by the group as TUI divests cruise ships and property assets to focus on its operations and brands.

Sources: www.tuigroup.com; Taylor (2021)

Questions

1. Why is TUI engaged in a program of disposals?

2. Why do you think TUI decided to sell these particular assets?

Small business focus

This chapter indicated that there is a great deal of consolidation occurring in all parts of *THE*. As the world's large *THE* groups consolidate, they are deriving the benefits from economies of scale and scope and concentrating resources so that they can acquire the latest technology and expertise. In doing so, strong internationally recognized brands are being developed for more sophisticated and demanding customers. This growth of the large brands has been achieved by a mix of methods that vary in different parts of *THE*.

However, consolidation should not be overemphasized. Although the big brands are expanding their market shares, the sectors that constitute *THE* for the most part remain highly fragmented. Accommodation, events management, travel intermediaries, attractions and venues, festivals and exhibition organizers still have many smaller companies operating as a result of relatively low barriers to entry and the emphasis on personal service.

One of the world's largest branded hotel companies, IHG (www.Ihgplc.com) estimates that the total hotel market is about 17.2 million rooms, of which branded hotels account for only slightly over half of all rooms (54%). Its world market share is about 4.5%, for example. The large branded accommodation chains are undoubtedly increasing their share, though. IHG benchmarks itself against four large competitors. The five leading branded hotel companies (IHG, Marriott, Hilton, Wyndham and AccorHotels) account for approximately 24% of total open branded rooms.

Unlike large firms, which have some chance of shaping and controlling the environment in which they operate, SMEs have limited resources and consequently have little option but to take whatever the environment throws at them (Haberberg and Rieple, 2008). In such circumstances, the methods for strategic development SMEs adopt may be limited, and they may need to gain protection from predatory larger competitors. Thus, in many circumstances, mergers and acquisitions may not be possible because they are expensive, access to finance is often difficult for SMEs and they often end in failure.

In many cases, the only options available are likely to be organic development and some sort of joint development. Many SMEs succeed through organic growth in *THE* because they have found a particular niche that they can exploit or because they can provide competitive service delivery that is appropriately personalized. Indeed, though it is usually assumed that most businesses want to pursue growth and profitability objectives, this may not necessarily be the case with regard to some SMEs operating in *THE* sectors. Several researchers (see, for example, Getz and Petersen, 2005; Williams and Shaw, 2003; Wang et al., 2019) have identified the prominence of lifestyle motives among *THE* business owners that may preclude them from pursuing growth and profitability at the expense if their lifestyle objectives.

Some of the difficulties encountered by SMEs are, in part, overcome through aspects of collaboration, which has been viewed through the importance of networks and clusters (Morrison et al., 2004; Baggio et al., 2010; Mwesiumo and Halpern, 2017; Ness et al., 2018). Joint development has become particularly prevalent as a means of expansion for SMEs, and this chapter looked at several means by which SMEs can develop, such as by franchising and by joining marketing consortia.

Franchising has been particularly important as a growth method for hotel groups. Though Alon et al. (2012) found that hotels are significantly different from retail and business services franchises' internationalization. Franchising-related costs are highest in terms of the required capital investment for hotels, but they have proved to be increasingly important for growth in this sector. Total investment required by most hotel groups runs into many millions of dollars per hotel. By contrast, most other service franchising industries require less than $1mn in start-up costs.

The high capital requirement raises considerable risks for smaller companies, but most academic studies have considered the advantages of this method from the franchisor perspective. Only a few studies (such as Xiao et al., 2008; Brookes and Altinay, 2011; Yeung et al., 2016; Jang and Park, 2019) have studied this aspect of strategic management from an SME perspective; that is, from the viewpoint of the franchisee. In a European hotel context, Brookes and Altinay (2011) found that in selecting partners, franchisees valued factors such as the ability to retain control of assets, a perception of mutual value and risk, the similarity of organizational values and culture and the perception of a fair deal. In a study of potential Chinese hotel franchisees, Xiao et al. (2008) found that hotel chains that have strong brand awareness and supportive centralized reservation systems and offer relatively high returns on investment at relatively low franchise fees are likely to be most attractive.

Finally, SMEs in *THE* may seek the advantages of joint development by forming alliances with larger organizations. Such alliances are termed asymmetric when they involve cooperation between two companies with marked differences in terms of resource portfolio and market position (Barabel et al., 2014). In such alliances there is a risk of exploitation by the larger, more powerful partner (H. Yang et al., 2014), though there can also be an important role in terms of knowledge transfer, which can benefit the smaller, less powerful partner.

In such alliances (Pansiri, 2008; Pansiri and Courvisanos, 2010), the selection of partners is vital to ensure that there are compatible objectives. In exploring the chances of alliance success, Medcof (1997) cited four criteria that increase the chances of success (explored earlier in the chapter).

CHAPTER SUMMARY

This chapter considered the various *methods* of strategic development that are available to *THE* managers and considered a third approach to strategic management, namely, the relational approach.

Organic growth is the most common method of strategic development, because most organizations use it on an ongoing basis. It is therefore difficult to quantify the degree of internal development taking place at any time. The action that creates one organization from two is known as integration. Though there are many logical reasons why organizations select this method of development, research evidence has suggested that its success rate is not particularly high. Integrations are unsuccessful for many reasons but mainly due to a lack of research into the target company and its environment.

Various types of joint development such as strategic alliances and franchises have been considered. These are collaborative relationships between organizations that fall short of full mergers, which are particularly important in many *THE* contexts. The various forms of alliance can range from informal to highly formalized agreements, and their success often depends on the commitment of both parties to achieving the objectives of the alliance.

There are times when *THE* organizations need to opt not for growth but have to be more defensive in opting for retrenchment. There are various ways in which this can be carried out, but a disposal of assets is the most common.

REFERENCES AND WEBSITES

References

Alon, I., Ni, L. and Wang, Y. (2012) 'Examining the determinants of hotel chain expansion through international franchising', *International Journal of Hospitality Management*, 31(2): 379–386.

Altinay, L., Brookes, M. and Aktas, G. (2013) 'Selecting franchise partners: Tourism franchisee approaches, processes and criteria', *Tourism Management*, 37: 176–185.

Baggio, R., Scott, N. and Cooper, C. (2010) 'Network science: A review focused on tourism', *Annals of Tourism Research*, 37(3): 802–827.

Barabel, M., Meier, O. and Soparnot, R. (2014) 'Asymmetric alliances between SMEs and large firms in the area of innovation: Strategic determinants and cultural effects', *Gestion 2000*, 31(6): 87–106.

Bennett, M. M. (1997) 'Strategic alliances in the world airline industry', *Progress in Tourism and Hospitality Research* 3: 213–223.

Blal, I. and Bianchi, G. (2019) 'The asset light model: A blind spot in hospitality research', *International Journal of Hospitality Management*, 76: 39–42.

Bleeke, J. and Ernst, D. (1991) 'The way to win in cross-border alliances', *Harvard Business Review*, November/December: 127–135.

Brookes, M. and Altinay, L. (2011) 'Franchise partner selection: Perspectives of franchisors and franchisees', *Journal of Services Marketing*, 25(5): 336–348.

Brouthers, K. D., Brouthers, L. E. and Wilkinson, T. J. (1995) 'Strategic alliances: Choose your partners', *Long Range Planning*, 28(3):18–25.

Buck, T. and Blitz, R. (2007) 'MyTravel merger approved', *Financial Times*, 5 May.

Canina, L., Kim, J. Y. and Ma, Q. (2010) 'What we know about M&A success: A research agenda for the lodging industry', *Cornell Hospitality Quarterly*, 51(1): 81–101.

Chan, J., Gao, Y. L. and McGinley, S. (2021) 'Updates in service standards in hotels: How COVID-19 changed operations', *International Journal of Contemporary Hospitality Management*, 33(5): 1668–1687.

Chatfield, H. K., Chatfiled, R. and Dalbor, M. (2012) 'Returns to hospitality acquisitions by method of payment', *Journal of Hospitality Financial Management*, 20(1): 1–16.

Chathoth, P. K. and Olsen, M. D. (2003) 'Strategic alliances: A hospitality industry perspective', *International Journal of Hospitality Management*, 22(4): 419–434.

Child, J. and Faulkner, D. (1998) *Strategies of Cooperation: Managing Alliances, Networks, and Joint Ventures*, Oxford, UK: Oxford University Press.

Chow, C. K. W. and Tsui, W. H. K. (2017) 'Organizational learning, operating costs and airline consolidation policy in the Chinese airline industry', *Journal of Air Transport Management*, 63: 108–118.

Cobeña, M., Gallego, Á. and Casanueva, C. (2019) 'Diversity in airline alliance portfolio configuration', *Journal of Air Transport Management*, 75: 16–26.

Crawford-Welch, S. (1994) 'The development of Courtyard by Marriott', in R. Teare, J. A. Mazanec, S. Crawford-Welch and S. Calver (Eds), *Marketing in Hospitality and Tourism: A Consumer Focus*, London: Cassell.

Das, T. K. and Teng, B. S. (2000) 'A resource-based theory of strategic alliances', *Journal of Management*, 26(1): 31–61.

Denton, N. and Dennis, N. (2000) 'Airline franchising in Europe: Benefits and disbenefits to airlines and consumers', *Journal of Air Transport Management*, 6(4): 179–190.

DeRoos, J. A. (2010) 'Hotel management contracts – Past and present', *Cornell Hospitality Quarterly*, 51(1): 68–80.

Dev, C. S. and Klein, S. (1993) 'Strategic alliances in the hotel industry', *The Cornell H.R.A. Quarterly*, February: 43–45.

Dev, C. S. Klein, S. and Fisher, R. A. (1996) 'A market-based approach for partner selection in marketing alliances', *Journal of Travel Research*, Summer: 11–17.

De Wit, B. and Meyer, R. (2014) *Strategy Synthesis: Resolving Strategy Paradoxes to Create Competitive Advantage: Text and Readings*, 4th ed., Andover, UK: Cengage.

Dogru, T. (2017) 'Under- vs over-investment: Hotel firms' value around acquisitions', *International Journal of Contemporary Hospitality Management*, 29(8): 2050–2069.

Dogru, T., Erdogan, A. and Kizildag, M. (2018) 'Marriott Starwood merger: What did we learn From a financial standpoint?', *Journal of Hospitality and Tourism Insights*, 1(2): 121–136.

Dyer, J. H. and Singh, H. (1998) 'The relational view: Cooperative strategy and sources of interorganizational competitive advantage', *Academy of Management Review*, 23(4): 660–679.

Dyer, J. H., Kale, P. and Singh, H. (2004) 'When to ally and when to acquire', *Harvard Business Review*, July – August: 109–115.

Dyer, J. H., Singh, H. and Hesterly, W. S. (2018) 'The relational view revisited: A dynamic perspective on value creation and value capture', *Strategic Management Journal*, 39(12): 3140–3162.

Edwards, S., and Taylor, L. (2012) 'The exportation of event expertise: Taking best practice to international markets in the MICE sector', in N. Ferdinand and P. J. Kitchin (Eds), *Events Management: An International Approach*, Thousand Oaks, CA: Sage, 303–314.

Evans, N. G. (2001a) 'Alliances in the international travel industry: Sustainable strategic options?', *International Journal of Hospitality and Tourism Administration*, 2(1): 1–26.

Evans, N. G. (2001b) 'Collaborative strategy: An analysis of the changing world of international airline alliances', *Tourism Management*, 22: 229–243.

Faulkner, D. (1995) *Strategic Alliances: Cooperating to Compete*, New York: McGraw Hill.

French, T. (1997) 'Global trends in airline alliances', *Tourism Analyst*, 4: 81–101.

Fyall, A. and Garrod, B. (2005) *Tourism Marketing: A Collaborative Approach*, Clevedon, UK: Channel View Publications.

Garnham, B. (1996) 'Alliances and liaisons in tourism: Concepts and implications', *Tourism Economics*, 2(1): 61–77.

Getz, D. and Petersen, T. (2005) 'Growth and profit-oriented entrepreneurship among family business owners in the tourism and hospitality industry, *International Journal of Hospitality Management*, 24(2): 219–242.

Glaister, K. W. and Buckley, P. J. (1996) 'Strategic motives for international alliance formation', *Journal of Management Studies*, 33(3): 301–332.

Go, F. M. and Pine, R. (1995) *Globalization Strategy in the Hotel Industry*, London: Routledge.

Gursoy, D., Saayman, M. and Sotiriadis, M. (Eds). (2015) *Collaboration in Tourism Businesses and Destinations: A Handbook*, Bingley, UK: Emerald.

Haberberg, A. and Rieple, A. (2008) *Strategic Management: Theory and Application*, 2nd ed., Oxford, UK: Oxford University Press.

Heeley, J. (2001) 'Public–private sector partnerships in tourism', in A. Lockwood and S. Medlik (Eds), *Tourism and Hospitality in the 21st Century*, Oxford, UK: Butterworth-Heinemann.

Heeley, J. (2011) 'Public–private partnership and best practice in urban destination marketing', *Tourism and Hospitality Research*, 11(3): 224–229.

Hsu, L. T. and Jang, S. (2007) 'The postmerger financial performance of hotel companies', *Journal of Hospitality and Tourism Research*, 31(4): 471–485.

Hua, N., O'Neill, J. W., Nusair, K., Singh, D. and DeFranco, A. (2017) 'Does paying higher franchise fees command higher RevPAR?', *International Journal of Contemporary Hospitality Management*, 29(11): 2941–2961.

Hughes, K. (2017) 'Marriott's big deal: Interview with Arne Sorensen', *Lodging Magazine*, March 13, www.lodgingmagazine.com

Ireland, R. D., Hitt, M. A. and Vaidyanath, D. (2002) 'Alliance management as a source of competitive advantage', *Journal of Management*, 28(3): 413–446.

Ivanova, M. and Ivanov, S. (2015) 'Affiliation to hotel chains: Hotels' perspective', *Tourism Management Perspectives*, 16: 148–162.

Jang, S. S. and Park, K. (2019) 'A sustainable franchisor – franchisee relationship model: Toward the franchise win – win theory', *International Journal of Hospitality Management*, 76: 13–24.

Jauhiainen, J. S. (1995) 'Waterfront redevelopment and urban policy: The case of Barcelona, Cardiff and Genoa', *European Planning Studies*, 3(1): 3–23.

Johnson, G., Whittington, R., Scholes, K., Angwin, D. and Regner, P. (2017). *Exploring Strategy: Text and Cases*, 11th ed., Harlow, UK: Pearson.

Kale, P., Dyer, J. H. and Singh, H. (2002) 'Alliance capability, stock market response, and long-term alliance success: The role of the alliance function', *Strategic Management Journal*, 23(8): 747–767.

Kanter, R. M. (1990) *When Giants Learn to Dance*, New York: Simon and Schuster.

Kanter, R. M. (1994) 'Collaborative advantage: The art of alliances', *Harvard Business Review* July/August: 96–108.

Kay, J. (1995) *Foundations of Corporate Success: How Business Strategies Add Value*, Oxford, UK: Oxford University Press.

Kim, B. Y. and Oh, H. (2004) 'How do hotel firms obtain a competitive advantage?', *International Journal of Contemporary Hospitality Management*, 16(1): 65–71.

Kostopoulou, S. (2013) 'On the revitalized waterfront: Creative milieu for creative tourism', *Sustainability*, 5(11): 4578–4593.

Li, Y. and Singal, M. (2019) 'Capital structure in the hospitality industry: The role of the asset-light and fee-oriented strategy', *Tourism Management*, 70: 124–133.

Lohmann, G. and Koo, T. T. (2013) 'The airline business model spectrum', *Journal of Air Transport Management*, 31: 7–9.

Long, P. E. (1997) 'Researching tourism partnership organizations: From practice to theory to methodology', in P. E. Murphy (Ed.), *Quality Management in Urban Tourism*, London: John Wiley & Sons, 235–251.

Lynch, R. (2021) *Strategic Management*, 9th ed., Harlow, UK: Pearson.

Mamédio, D., Rocha, C., Szczepanik, D. and Kato, H. (2019) 'Strategic alliances and dynamic capabilities: A systematic review', *Journal of Strategy and Management*, 12(1): 83–102.

Märklin, P. and Bianchi, G. (2022) 'A differentiated approach to the asset-light model in the hotel industry', *Cornell Hospitality Quarterly*, 63(3): 313–319.

Marriott. (2017) *Marriott Fact Book 2017*, www.Marriott.com

Medcof, J. W. (1997) 'Why too many alliances end in divorce', *Long Range Planning*, 30(5): 718–732.

Min, H. and Joo, S. J. (2016) 'A comparative performance analysis of airline strategic alliances using data envelopment analysis', *Journal of Air Transport Management*, 52: 99–110.

Morrison, A. J. (1994) 'Marketing strategic alliances: The small hotel firm', *International Journal of Contemporary Hospitality Management*, 6(3): 25–30.

Morrison, A. J., Lynch, P. and Johns, N. (2004) 'International tourism networks', *International Journal of Contemporary Hospitality Management*, 16: 187–202.

Mwesiumo, D. and Halpern, N. (2017) 'A review of empirical research on interorganizational relations in tourism' *Current Issues in Tourism*, 22(4): 1–28.

Ness, H., Fuglsang, L. and Eide, D. (2018) 'Editorial: Networks, dynamics, and innovation in the tourism industry', *Scandinavian Journal of Hospitality and Tourism*, 18(3): 225–233.

Nickson, D. (1997) 'Research: "Colorful stories" or historical insight? – A review of the auto/biographies of Charles Forte, Conrad Hilton, J. W. Marriott and Kemmons Wilson', *Journal of Hospitality and Tourism Research*, 21(1): 179–192.

Ohmae, K. (1989) 'The global logic of strategic alliances', *Harvard Business Review*, March/April: 143–154.

Oum, T. H., Park, J. H., Kim, K. and Yu, C. (2004) 'The effect of horizontal alliances on firm productivity and profitability: Evidence from the global airline industry', *Journal of Business Research*, 57(8): 844–853.

Oum, T. H., Park, J. H. and Zhang, A. (2000) *Globalization and Strategic Alliances: The Case of the Airline Industry*, Bingley, UK: Emerald.

Pansiri, J. (2008) 'The effects of characteristics of partners on strategic alliance performance in the SME dominated travel sector', *Tourism Management*, 29(1): 101–115.

Pansiri, J. and Courvisanos, J. (2010) 'Attitude to risk in technology-based strategic alliances for tourism', *International Journal of Hospitality and Tourism Administration*, 11(3): 275–302.

Parker, A. (2013a) 'Consolidation: Concentration of carriers puts collapse on Europe agenda', *Financial Times*, 16 June.

Parker, A. (2013b) 'Gulf carriers destabilise alliances', *Financial Times*, 14 November.

Pechlaner, H., Bachinger, M., Volgger, M. and Anzengruber-Fischer, E. (2014) 'Cooperative core competencies in tourism: Combining resource-based and relational approaches in destination governance', *European Journal of Tourism Research*, 8(1): 5–19.

Pine, R., Qiu Zhang, H. and Qi, P. (2000) 'The challenges and opportunities of franchising in China's hotel industry', *International Journal of Contemporary Hospitality Management*, 12(5): 300–307.

Pinz, A., Roudyani, N. and Thaler, J. (2018) 'Public–private partnerships as instruments to achieve sustainability-related objectives: The state of the art and a research agenda', *Public Management Review*, 20(1): 1–22.

Porter, M. E. and Fuller, M. B. (1986) 'Coalitions and global strategy', in M. E. Porter (Ed.), *Competition in Global Industries*, Boston: Harvard Business School Press.

Rumelt, R. P. (1991) 'How much does industry matter?', *Strategic Management Journal*, 12(3): 167–185.

Schaal, D. (2019) *Marriott's Alibaba Joint Venture in China Is Part of Its Direct-Booking Strategy*, www.Skift.com

Seo, J. K., Cho, M. and Skelton, T. (2015) 'Dynamic Busan: Envisioning a global hub city in Korea', *Cities*, 46: 26–34.

Sohn, J., Tang, C. H. H. and Jang, S. S. (2013) 'Does the asset-light and fee-oriented strategy create value?', *International Journal of Hospitality Management*, 32: 270–277.

Taylor, I. (2021) 'TUI completes sale of €670m stake in Riu Hotel properties', *Travel Weekly*, 30 July, www.travelweekly.co.uk

Teo, S. (2009) 'Asian film festivals and their diminishing glitter domes: An appraisal of PIFF, SIFF and HKIFF', in R. Porton (Ed.), *Dekalog 3: On film Festivals*, London: Wallflower, 109–121.

Tjemkes, B., Vos, P. and Burgers, K. (2017) *Strategic Alliance Management*, Abingdon, UK: Routledge.

Todeva, E. and Knoke, D. (2005) 'Strategic alliances and models of collaboration', *Management Decision*, 43(1): 123–148.

Tuch, C. and O'Sullivan, N. (2007) 'The impact of acquisitions on firm performance: A review of the evidence', *International Journal of Management Reviews*, 9(2): 141–170.

Van Den Berg, L. (2017) *European Cities in the Knowledge Economy: The Cases of Amsterdam, Dortmund, Eindhoven, Helsinki, Manchester, Munster, Munich, Rotterdam and Zaragoza*, Abingdon, UK: Routledge.

Van der Zee, E. and Vanneste, D. (2015) 'Tourism networks unravelled: A review of the literature on networks in tourism management studies', *Tourism Management Perspectives*, 15: 46–56.

Wang, S., Hung, K. and Huang, W. J. (2019) 'Motivations for entrepreneurship in the tourism and hospitality sector: A social cognitive theory perspective', *International Journal of Hospitality Management*, 78: 78–88.

Weiermair, K., Peters, M. and Frehse, J. (2008) 'Success factors for public private partnership: Cases in alpine tourism development', *Journal of Services Research*, 3(2): 7–21.

'Why hotel chains don't own many hotels'. (2009) *The Economist*, 19 February, www.economist.com

Whyte, R. and Lohmann, G. (2020) 'Airline business models', in L. Budd and S. Ison (Eds), *Air Transport Management*, 2nd ed., Abingdon, UK: Routledge, 129–144.

Williams, A. M. and Shaw, G. (2003) 'From lifestyle consumption to lifestyle production: Changing patterns of tourism entrepreneurship', in R. Morgan (Ed.), *Small Firms in Tourism*, Oxford, UK: Elsevier, 109–124.

Xiao, Q., O'Neill, J. W. and Wang, H. (2008) 'International hotel development: A study of potential franchisees in China', *International Journal of Hospitality Management*, 27(3): 325–336.

Xiong, W., Chen, B., Wang, H. and Zhu, D. (2019) 'Governing public–private partnerships: A systematic review of case study literature" *Australian Journal of Public Administration*, 78(1): 95–112.

Xu, Y. J. and Yan, X. P (2000) 'Waterfront tourist development: The North American experience and its application to China', *Economic Geography*, 20(1): 99–103.

Yan, J., Fu, X., Oum, T. H. and Wang, K. (2019) 'Airline horizontal mergers and productivity: Empirical evidence from a quasi-natural experiment in China', *International Journal of Industrial Organization*, 62: 358–376.

Yang, H., Zheng, Y. and Zhao, X. (2014) 'Exploration or exploitation? Small firms' alliance strategies with large firms', *Strategic Management Journal*, 35(1): 146–157.

Yang, J., Kim, W. G. and Qu, H. (2010) 'Post-merger stock performance of acquiring hospitality firms', *Tourism Economics*, 16(1): 185–195.

Yeung, R. M., Brookes, M. and Altinay, L. (2016) 'The hospitality franchise purchase decision making process', *International Journal of Contemporary Hospitality Management*, 28(5): 1009–1025.

Yin, X. and Shanley, M. (2008) 'Industry determinants of the "merger versus alliance" decision', *Academy of Management Review*, 33(2): 473–491.

Yoshino, M. M. Y. and Rangan, U. S. (1995) *Strategic Alliances: An Entrepreneurial Approach to Globalization*, Boston: Harvard Business Press.

Zapata, M. J. and Hall, C. M. (2012) 'Public–private collaboration in the tourism sector: Balancing legitimacy and effectiveness in local tourism partnerships. The Spanish case', *Journal of Policy Research in Tourism, Leisure and Events*, 4(1): 61–83.

Websites

www.accor.com/
www.alibaba.com
www.airnostrum.es
www.asmglobal.com

www.bestwestern.com
www.biff.kr
www.busan.go.kr
www.carlson.com/
www.centreforaviation.com
www.denver.org
www.economist.com
www.enterpriseholdings.com/
www.gha.com/
www.hiltonworldwide.com/
www.iata.org
www.ihgplc.com
www.lodgingmagazine.com
www.marketingmanchester.com
www.marriott.com/
www.messefrankfurt.com
www.moxy-hotels.marriott.com
www.oneworld.com
www.panpacific.com
www.radissonhotelgroup.com
www.radissonhotelsamericas.com/
www.relx.com/
www.skift.com
www.skyteam.com
www.skywest.com
www.smg.com
www.southwest.com/
www.staralliance.com/
www.thomascook.com
www.tuitravelplc.com/
www.united.com/
www.waterfrontpartnership.org
www.wyndhamworldwide.com/
www.yum.com/

13

Strategic evaluation and selection for tourism, hospitality and event organizations

Introduction and chapter overview

Important decisions are never easy. To ensure that we make the right choice in any given situation, we must first be in possession of all relevant information. This is the purpose of the strategic analysis stage – to ensure that the management of a *THE* organization is fully aware of the internal strengths and weaknesses and the external opportunities and threats.

The next stage in making an important decision is being aware of *all* of the options available and making a choice between them following a process of evaluation. In the previous three chapters, various options related to the key strategic issues facing *THE* organizations were considered:

- *Competitive strategy* – How can advantage over competitors be achieved?
- *Strategic directions* – Which products or services should be developed, and in which markets should they be sold?
- *Strategic methods* – What methods of development should be adopted?

The most obvious choice is not necessarily the 'right' one. Indeed, the whole concept of 'right' and 'wrong' may itself be difficult. There may be some options (following an evaluative process) that may be obviously wrong. They just do not make any sense when they are evaluated and the organization's current situation is considered.

However, there may be several options that are considered equally 'right', or the evaluation leads to conflicting signals. In such circumstances, managers have to make a judgment based on the

DOI: 10.4324/9781003318613-17

information they have available. Because we are talking about options for *future* strategic development, it is only after a period of time elapses that the judgment can be assessed and a definitive view can be established as to whether the correct (or 'right') option was in fact chosen.

Following the generation of options, the next stage is evaluating each option using consistently applied criteria. The purpose of evaluation is to ensure that all options are assessed with equal thoroughness. Finally, strategic choice involves actually making a decision based on evaluation of the options. In other words, a choice is made between the various competing options.

This chapter considers each of these stages in turn in relation to the key strategic decisions on strategic development.

LEARNING OBJECTIVES

After studying this chapter, you should be able to:

- Describe the nature of strategic options in relation to *THE* organizations
- Explain the key areas that strategic development decisions concern
- Describe the three criteria that are applied to strategic options
- Understand the financial and non-financial tools and techniques that can be used to evaluate strategic options
- Understand examples of the ways in which *THE* organizations have utilized evaluation in choosing their strategies
- Explain the issues involved in choosing between strategic options relating to *THE* organizations
- Understand the differences between a prescriptive and emergent approach to strategy
- Explain the limitations of an 'emergent' approach to strategy when it relates to strategic evaluation and selection

13.1 Identifying strategic options

At the start of this chapter, we must remind ourselves of what makes a decision *strategic* in nature as opposed to one that is *operational*. We encountered these terms in Chapter 1 in the context of the nature of strategic objectives and in the introduction to Part 4.

Strategic decisions are taken at the highest level of an organization. They concern decisions on how the whole organization, broken down into its constituent SBUs, will be positioned in respect to its product and resource markets, its competitors and its macro influences. Accordingly, the options at the strategic level are those that offer solutions to the 'big questions' facing *THE* organizations.

Operational-level decisions are those that are concerned with how the internal parts of the organization should be configured and managed so that they can achieve the strategic objectives.

The big questions that are considered in strategic selection usually concern three major areas, all of which are discussed in detail elsewhere in this text.

- Decisions on *competitive strategy* (see Chapter 10)
- Decisions on products and markets relating to the *strategic direction* of development (see Chapter 11)
- Decisions on *strategic methods* of development (see Chapter 12)

In most cases, an organization will need to make continual decisions on all of these matters. We should not lose sight of the fact that the strategic process is just that – a process. Strategic choice is no more of a 'once-and-for-all' activity than either strategic analysis or strategic implementation. For organizations that exist in rapidly changing environments, decisions on strategic options will be required on a continual basis; hence the importance of ensuring that we have a good grasp of the issues that are discussed in this chapter.

13.1.1 Competitive strategy decisions

Decisions over the organization's competitive or generic strategy (as discussed in Chapter 10) are important, not only because they define the organization's competitive position but also because they will determine how the internal value chain activities are configured (see Chapters 3 and 10).

If the company elects to pursue a differentiation strategy, for example, the implications of this will be felt in all parts of the organization. The culture and structure will need to be configured in such a way that they support the generic strategy and the product features and quality will also reflect it. Similarly, how the organization sources and configures its resource base will need to support the strategy.

The same issues will be considered if a cost-driven strategy is chosen, although the way in which the internal activities are configured will be somewhat different.

13.1.2 Direction of development – product and market decisions

The questions over *which products* and *which markets* are extremely important because they can determine not only the levels of profitability but also the survival of the organization itself. It is likely that strategy will involve a change in the SBU or company's size. You will recall that in Chapter 10 three strategic options were considered:

- Growth
- Stability
- Retrenchment

If stability is the chosen option, this does not mean that nothing should be done, because to do so would invite competitors to increase their own market shares. In such circumstances, market share may be fiercely defended through measures such as pricing, promotional offers or increased levels of efficiency. Furthermore, even if the market share remains stable when the market as a whole is growing, the size of the overall business will increase; that is, to use the analogy of a cake, your own organization's slice of the cake may remain constant but the overall size of the cake is growing.

If retrenchment is the chosen option, decisions have to be made concerning which product or market areas should be reduced, sold off or withdrawn.

In cases where growth is the chosen strategic option the organization will pursue (see Chapter 10), decisions have to be taken about the direction of growth. These strategic choices arise from Igor Ansoff's (1987) framework. Ansoff's generic growth strategies concern whether growth will involve new or existing markets and products (see Chapter 6).

A number of further product and market decisions are normally required.

MARKET CATEGORIES

Firstly, decisions must be made about the categories of markets the business will be involved with. The organization will have to reach decisions on geographic coverage, international exposure and the benefits and risks that relate to such options (see Chapter 15).

PRODUCT FEATURES

Secondly, decisions must be made on the features the product will possess. The mix of product benefits a product will possess will strongly affect not only costs but also the position the product will assume in the market. We encountered Kotler's (1997) five 'levels' of product features (or 'benefits') in Chapter 6, and the inclusion or exclusion of any of these will have a strong bearing on any proposed strategy.

PRODUCT AND MARKET PORTFOLIOS

Thirdly, product and market decisions must include a consideration of portfolio (see Chapter 6). The extent to which the products and markets are focused or spread can be very important. A broad portfolio (presence in many product market sectors) offers the ability to withstand a downturn in one sector and to exploit opportunities that arise in any of the areas in which the business operates. Conversely, a narrow portfolio enables the organization's management to be more focused and to develop expertise in its narrower field of operation.

LIFE CYCLE CONSIDERATIONS

The final consideration to be made for products and markets concerns their life cycle positions. It is perhaps intuitive to say that products or markets that are approaching late maturity or are in decline should be of particular concern, but there is also a need to produce new products or develop new markets on an ongoing basis. Products in late maturity or in decline can produce medium to high levels of positive cash flow. New products in the introductory or early growth phases, on the other hand, often produce negative cash flows. Thus, mature and declining products can release financial resources that can be invested in new products, which can then in time move up the product life cycle toward maturity (see Chapter 6).

13.1.3 Strategic method decisions

The third area for which strategic business-level decisions are required relates to the methods or mechanisms that are to be used. A basic choice exists between:

- Internal (organic) development
- Mergers and acquisitions
- Joint development such as alliances and franchises

The choice has important implications for the:

- *Resources* that are required
- Degree of *control* over future strategic decisions
- *Speed* with which a change in the position of the SBU could be achieved
- Need to *reconfigure* the internal value chain of the organization

For example: *A tour operator has decided that its future growth method should be that of organic growth achieved through adding destinations to the existing range that it serves. In making the decision, the company's managers would be cognizant of the fact that this method usually produces slower growth than alternatives (because resources are provided by one organization only). Either alternative (some form of joint development or a merger or acquisition) would involve a step change in size and produce speedier growth.*

However, the organization's managers would also be aware that internal growth retains full control within the existing organization, with no control being ceded to other organizations. That is, the existing managers would continue to control the company, including subsequent decisions about strategy.

13.2 Applying evaluation criteria

When considering which course of action to pursue, a number of options may occur to an organization's top management. To ensure that each option is fairly and equally assessed, a number of criteria are applied.

> ### KEY CONCEPT
>
> **Prescriptive strategy**
>
> This text is primarily concerned with *prescriptive strategy*, which takes the view that a rational, evidence-based analysis of the environment will reveal options that will deliver the strategy. The options revealed in this way then have to be evaluated and choices made to select the options most likely to produce a successful outcome. Because the choices are based on logic and evidence, proponents of prescriptive strategy would argue that they are more likely to be successful than alternatives.
>
> *Emergent strategy*, on the other hand, reflects the fact that sometimes strategy is not derived from a formal planned approach (as implied above) but instead emerges from many sources, in many different ways.
>
> In reality, in most real-world situations, strategy is probably derived from both sources, as Mintzberg and Waters (1985) argued; that is, that 'realized' strategy is the product of both deliberate planning (prescriptive strategy) and also emerges in an unplanned way (emergent strategy).

For each option, three criteria are applied. To 'pass', the option must usually receive an affirmative answer to each criterion. Various acronyms have been introduced to describe the criteria, such as RACES (as described by Haberberg and Rieple, 2008), SCARE and CARES, which usually stand for resources, acceptable, consistent, effective and sustainability, which are considered in the order required by the acronym.

Here, another widely used scheme is used (see, for example, Whittington et al., 2020) – the 'SFA' framework – but here we add a fourth criterion: 'sustainability'. Thus, the evaluation framework becomes:

- **S**uitability
- **F**easibility
- **S**ustainability
- **A**cceptability

Thus, each strategic option should be considered in relation to the four criteria by considering whether the strategic option is suitable, feasible, acceptable and sustainable and enables *competitive advantage* to be achieved, as summarized in Table 13.1.

The process of evaluation is an integral part of the overall strategy process, as indicated in Figure 13.1. Note that a screening stage is introduced after suitability. Because evaluation can be costly and time-consuming, this allows options that are clearly unrealistic – that is, that are not likely to be feasible or acceptable – to be dropped for further evaluation.

Table 13.1 Summary of the criteria used for evaluation

Criteria	Key issues
Suitability	Does the proposed strategy: • Exploit *opportunities* in the environment and avoid or address the *threats*? • Capitalize on an organization's *strengths* and avoid or address the *weaknesses*? • Address the expectations of stakeholder groups?
Feasibility	Is the proposed strategy possible: • In relation to the organization's internal culture, capabilities and resources? • In relation to the organization's external stakeholders?
Sustainability	Does the proposed strategy deliver a sustainable solution: • That is more sustainable than previous strategies? • That promotes economic and social practices that benefit the organization, its employees and society? • That engages in practices that do not compromise environmental resources for future generations?
Acceptability	Does the proposed strategy deliver performance: • Outcomes that are acceptable to the organization's stakeholders? • That is superior to the current situation? • That is better than that of the organization's competitors?

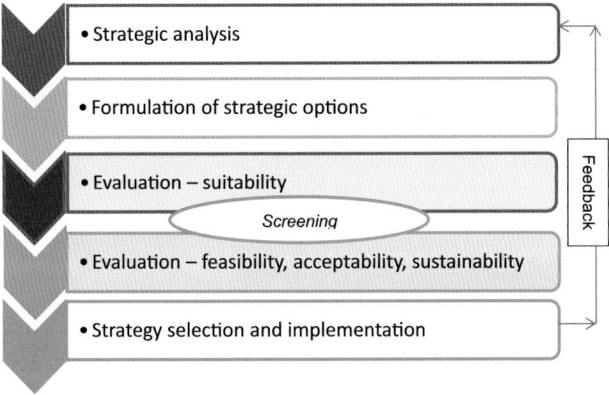

Figure 13.1 The strategic evaluation process

13.3 Suitability

- *Suitability* is concerned with assessing whether the strategy will enable the organization to achieve its strategic objectives.

A strategic option is suitable if it will enable the organization to actually achieve its strategic objectives. If it will fall short of achieving these objectives in any way, there is no point in pursuing it and the option should be discarded.

> **For example:** *If an events management organization has set one of its strategic objectives as 'to spread its market portfolio by gaining a presence in selected foreign markets', the option of increasing the company's investment in its domestic market would clearly be unsuitable.*

The suitability of options must be assessed not only in relation to the objectives that have been set but also in relation to the SWOT. The SWOT itself is, of course, the culmination of a number of analytical tools and techniques such as STEEP, five forces, value chain and the cultural web.

THINK POINTS

- Explain where strategic evaluation and selection fit into the strategic process.
- Describe the four criteria that can be used to evaluate strategic options.
- In relation to the direction of development, outline the main product–market decisions that are required.

Options might be regarded as suitable when they:

- Exploit *opportunities* in the environment and avoid or address the *threats*
- Capitalize on an organization's *strengths* and avoid or address the *weaknesses*
- Address the expectations of stakeholder groups

It is also important to recognize cases where strategic options may be unsuitable:

- Suitability may be seen in relative terms, and the various options are thus ranked according to their suitability.
- There is a need for internal consistency in the choice of options, in that the choice of competitive strategy (such as cost leadership or differentiation), the development direction (such as market development or diversification) and the development method (internal, acquisition or joint development) need to work together as a 'package'.

13.1 SHORT CASE ILLUSTRATION

Suitability: foreign airline access to US markets

The airline market in the USA is the world's largest, accounting for about 35% of world demand, though China is forecast to overtake the USA during the 2020s (www.Iata.org).

However, despite airline deregulation that took place in the 1970s and 1980s, restrictions on foreign ownership of airlines still apply. Like many governments, the USA has historically restricted foreign ownership to protect its domestic companies in the belief that it is strategically important for the country to have strong domestic industry. Foreign airlines are restricted to ownership of 25% of any US-based airline, thus preventing foreign carriers from entering the market.

For example, British Airways, a subsidiary of IAG Group, has long been reported to have sought a merger partner in the USA, and talks have been held at various times with American Airlines and US Airways (now itself part of American Airlines). However, a non-American airline seeking to grow in the USA through market penetration is restricted in its choice of strategic method.

The foreign ownership restrictions prevent the purchase of an American airline or the development of airlines by foreign-based companies. Thus, if British Airways or any other airline wanted to achieve its stated strategic objective of US airline market penetration, it would have little option but to do so through joint development opportunities, such as through alliance relationships, to develop its position in this vitally important market. This has actually occurred as cooperation with American Airlines through the oneworld Alliance. Similarly, Delta and United Airlines are members of the SkyTeam and Star alliances, respectively.

Thus, in this example, if an option of US acquisitions was proposed, it would not be 'suitable' because it would not be capable of achieving the strategic objective.

Questions

1. Explain the issue of suitability highlighted by this case.

2. What are the advantages and possible disadvantages to the country of placing restrictions on foreign ownership imposed in this example?

13.3.1 Screening

Having applied the suitability criterion, a further stage might be interjected in some cases – that of *screening*.

If certain options are clearly unsuitable, it makes little sense to expend the time, effort and expense involved in applying further criteria. Consequently, at the screening stage, a decision is made as to whether it is worth continuing with the further stages of evaluation or whether certain options should be disregarded at this stage of evaluation owing to their unsuitability.

The case of the Kenes Group, an event management company that organizes scientific conferences worldwide, illustrates why screening might be necessary.

13.2 SHORT CASE ILLUSTRATION

Screening: international growth for Kenes events management company

The management of events is a very diverse field and is highly fragmented, with many small businesses in operation. Like an advertising agency, a football team or a small travel agency, events management companies often rely very heavily on the competences of a small group of highly skilled people as their main source of competitive advantage. Consequently, such organizations have to plan their growth carefully so that they do not overburden their key resource.

The Kenes Group focuses on providing international congress organization services from its headquarters in Geneva, Switzerland, and regional and national offices in key business locations around the world. Founded in 1965, Kenes is an industry leader in organizing medical and scientific conferences and is a member of the international trade bodies ICCA (the International Congress and Convention Association) and IAPCO (the International Association of Professional Congress Organizers). The company has members in both the PCMA (Professional Convention Management Association) and ASAE (American Society of Association Executives).

Kenes Group has over 100 long-term and returning clients worldwide and has managed almost 4,000 global conferences in 100+ countries. Many of the conferences take place on an annual basis (though in different cities each year) around the world. An example is the Annual Meeting of the European Society of Pediatric and Neonatal Intensive Care (ESPNIC), whose latest meeting took place in Vienna, Austria, in May 2023 (www.clocate.com).

Although large in its chosen specialist field, there are many competitors, and the company has to consider the *suitability* of international expansion carefully before proceeding. The company has expanded its international offices. However, the company is clear that they only establish regional and national offices, if it makes sense for its clients and Kenes' quality, mission and values will be upheld by the regional and local partners that it knows and trusts.

Clearly, a company such as the Kenes Group is pursuing a strategic objective that involves spreading its market portfolio by gaining a presence in selected foreign markets. Its current executive offices, though geographically widely spread, provide global coverage through regional offices but without a presence in some key countries (such as Brazil, Russia, Canada, the UK, South Africa, Australia and Indonesia).

In such a case, management needs to consider its financial and human resources carefully and the relative attractiveness of market opportunities before expanding into new countries, and thus a *screening* process might take place to determine which countries provide the best opportunities. In keeping with this approach, a new office was opened in Lisbon, Portugal, in 2019, marking 18 office locations on four continents.

Sources: www.kenes-group.com; www.clocate.com

Questions

1. Explain why a screening process might be beneficial this case when assessing international expansion.

2. What factors might it be useful for Kenes to take into account when considering opening new international offices?

For example: *The events management company Kenes Group had set one of its strategic objectives as 'to spread its market portfolio by gaining a presence in selected foreign markets'. When the management considered its financial and human resources, as a relatively small company, it is likely that it only had sufficient resources to expand into one new country at a time. Initially it had considered six countries as possible contenders for the first expansion. A simple screening process (such as that shown in Table 13.2) might help such a company decide which country offers the best opportunities.*

In this example, the six countries are ranked from 1 to 6 (with 1 being the most attractive) on four measures. The measures chosen might vary according to circumstances, but taking these measures into account, three countries (B, C and E) appear 'suitable' and worthy of further evaluation. Country B, for example, appears to be an attractive market of a good size. The company is well placed to exploit the market in terms of its competences, but unfortunately the regulatory and general business environment only appear to be moderately favorable (compared to options C and E).

Thus, in this case, a screening process by which six alternatives are ranked allows three options to be 'screened out', allowing three (options B, C and E) to go forward for further evaluation.

The example given above is of a simple screening process based on ranking alternative options. Though conceptually simple, importantly, it relies heavily on the strength of the underlying analysis. The ranking of the options should be based on a solid analysis of the available evidence; otherwise, the screening and the ranking on which it depends will have no validity. Assessing the market attractiveness, for instance, requires a sound understanding of the dynamics of the particular market in question. This will perhaps be based on Porter's five forces framework, which was covered in Chapter 9, and other relevant analytical tools and techniques.

13.4 Feasibility

● *Feasibility* is concerned with assessing whether the strategy is capable of working in practice.

A strategic option might be considered suitable but not possible. In other words, the option is not feasible. When evaluating options using this criterion, it is likely that the options will be feasible to varying degrees. Some will be completely unfeasible, others have some potential, whereas others still are definitely feasible.

The extent to which an option is feasible will accordingly depend in practice on two areas:

1. The culture, skills and resources, which are *internally controlled* by the organization. An organization might not have the culture, skills or resources necessary to carry out the options. A deficit

Table 13.2 Summary of rankings for strategic options

Criteria	Country A	Country B	Country C	Country D	Country E	Country F
Market size	4	2	1	6	3	5
Market attractiveness	3	1	2	5	4	6
Company competences	6	2	3	4	1	5
Regulation and business environment	4	3	2	5	1	6
Total	17	10	8	20	9	22

in any of the key resource areas (physical, financial, human and intangible) will present a problem at this stage of evaluation. If an option requires capital that is unavailable, human skills that are difficult to buy in, land or equipment that is equally difficult to obtain or a scarce intellectual resource, then it is likely to fail the feasibility criteria.

13.3 SHORT CASE ILLUSTRATION

Feasibility: access to scarce resources at London's Heathrow Airport

Takeoff and landing slots are rights allocated to an airline by an airport or government agency granting the slot owner the right to schedule a landing or departure at a particular time. Usually they are referred to as a 'pair of slots' to denote the right to both take off and land.

London's Heathrow Airport, one of the world's leading international airports, has been working at or close to capacity for a number of years. The pairs of slots are a scarce resource, as they are at many busy airports around the world. The rights of airlines to operate the slots generally lie with those airlines that have operated at the airport for a protracted length of time, operating under so-called grandfather rights. Although most airlines did not originally pay for the slots but inherited them through historically operating from the airport, they protect them and rarely sell them.

Because these inherited rights are rarely relinquished by airlines, the allocated slots have gained a commercial value and can be traded between airlines. For example, in March 2020, Air New Zealand sold a mid-morning arrival slot at the airport for US$27mn because it planned to cease using the slot for its flight from Los Angeles.

Many airlines would like to establish a presence at Heathrow, a key international transit hub, some in preference to using London's second largest airport, Gatwick. However, the airlines are prevented from doing so by the lack of slots coming onto the market or their cost when they do so. It is comparatively rare for slots to be marketed because airlines that possess the valuable resource (such as British Airways, which has a dominant 54% of Heathrow slots) tend to retain them and defend their position.

Consequently, though establishing a presence at Heathrow might be a *suitable* aspect of a growth strategy for an airline, it might not be *feasible* due to the deficit in a key resource area; that is, the failure to gain access to the physical resource of Heathrow.

Source: 'How landing and take-off slots are allocated at congested airports' (2017)

Questions

1. Explain the difference between 'suitability' and 'feasibility' illustrated by this case.

2. What options might be feasible for an airline seeking to expand operations focused on London?

The checklist shown in Table 13.3 indicates some of the key internal feasibility issues to consider.

Table 13.3 A ten-point checklist on internal feasibility

Internal issue	Key questions
• Capital investment required	Do we have the funds?
• Projection of cumulative profits	Is it sufficiently profitable
• Working capital requirements	Do we have enough working capital?
• Tax liabilities and dividend payments	What are the implications, especially on timing?
• Number of employees	Are there sufficient or too many employees?
	In the case of redundancy, what are the costs associated with this?
• New technical skills required, new operational equipment required:	Do we have the skills?
	Do we need to recruit or hire temporarily some specialists?
• New products and how are they to be developed	Are we confident that we have a portfolio of fully tested new products?
	Are they breakthrough products or merely catch-up on our competition?
• Amount and timing of marketing investment and expertise required	Do we have the funds?
	When will they be required?
	Do we have the specialist expertise, such as advertising and promotions agency teams to deliver our strategic options?
• The possibility of acquisition, merger or joint venture with other organizations and the implications	Have we fully explored other strategic options that would bring their own benefits and problems?
• Communication of ideas to all those involved: how will this be done?	Will we gain the commitment of the managers and employees affected?
	Who are required to implement the required changes?

Source: Adapted from Lynch (2021:359)

2. The second area that needs to be considered with regards to feasibility relates to the consideration of competitive reactions and other considerations, which are *external* to the organization. Specifically, the acceptance of customers and suppliers, competitive reactions and necessary approvals from government or regulatory bodies need to be considered.

13.4 SHORT CASE ILLUSTRATION

Feasibility: Chinese budget hotel brands fight for market share

After learning and absorbing international practices, China's domestic hotel firms developed rapidly after 1990. Not only are these domestic firms growing in size, but many have strategically positioned themselves in different market segments. Chinese domestic branded budget chains developed prominently with a race to roll out their brands across the country to gain so-called first-mover advantage and secure a large market share. Doing so rested partly on their ability to raise capital from overseas equity markets.

One such example (Gu et al., 2012) is that of Home Inn, a budget hotel chain formed in 2002. The US$109mn the company raised from its initial public offering (IPO) from the NAS-DAQ exchange in New York in 2006 was invested in its aggressive expansion. The finance enabled the company to compete effectively with Jin Jiang Inn, China's leading budget hotel chain.

However, another Chinese budget hotel chain, 7 Days Inn, followed the development model by using what is sometimes referred to as a *me-too* strategy in strategy texts. In 2009 it raised US$111mn through the New York Stock Exchange. The company is currently ranked as one of the top five budget chain hotels in China. Its quick ascent to the top rank of budget hotel operators following its founding in 2005 was attributed to its ability to raise capital from an overseas equity market.

Thus, Home Inn used a particular funding method to expand rapidly. In pursuing this growth, however, the hotel chain would have had to consider whether it would be *feasible* for other operators to pursue a similar strategy. As it turned out, it was feasible for another chain to adopt a 'me-too' strategy and gain finance in a similar way to fund its expansion plans.

Subsequently, the Home Inn chain was acquired by a state-controlled tourism group, Beijing Tourism Group (BTG) in 2015.

Source: Adapted from Gu et al. (2012)

Questions

1. Explain why an organization such as Home Inn should consider the reactions of competitors in considering *feasibility*.

2. Explain what is meant by *first-mover advantage* and a *me-too* strategy in relation to this illustrative case.

The checklist shown in Table 13.4 indicates some of the key external feasibility issues to consider.

Table 13.4 A four-point checklist on external feasibility

External issue	Key questions
Customers	How will our customers respond to the strategies we are proposing?
Competitors	How will our competitors react?
	Do we have the necessary resources to respond?
Suppliers	Do we have the necessary support from our suppliers?
Government	Do we need government or regulatory approval?
	How likely is this?

Source: Adapted from Lynch (2021:360)

13.5 Sustainability

Global imperatives such as climate change, resource scarcity and demographic changes are increasingly forcing organizations and destinations toward more *sustainable* resources, processes and products (Höse et al., 2022). Sustainability strategy is discussed in Chapter 16.

The consequent shifts in the attitudes of consumers exacerbate the trend by leading *THE* organizations (and others) to reassess the way in which they carry out their activities; hence the need to incorporate sustainability as a criterion in evaluating strategic options (Bansal and DesJardine, 2014; Asmelash and Kumar, 2019; Cardeal et al., 2020).

Despite the preponderance of academic material, the meaning of sustainability (and its place in strategy) is often unclear. Some people restrict sustainability to 'green' environmental issues, and others use it synonymously with *corporate social responsibility* (Bansal and DesJardine, 2014). Sustainability has been commonly defined as development that 'meets the needs of the present without compromising the ability of future generations to meet their own needs' (WCED, 1987).

In this way, sustainability is about ensuring that future generations are able to experience the same opportunities as the current generation, or *intergenerational equity*, as it is often termed. The same logic, it is argued, applies to business sustainability, because most managers want their business to be at least as profitable as in the past and, ideally, for profits to grow. In other words, firms want to respond to their short-term financial needs without compromising their ability to meet future needs (Bansal and DesJardine, 2014).

Sustainability requires trade-offs, with firms choosing between investing less for smaller profits sooner and investing more for greater profits later (Laverty, 1996). This aspect of a trade-off distinguishes sustainability from CSR, though undeniably they are often used interchangeably in the literature. CSR is normally viewed as a set of organizational activities that are good for society *and* the firm (McWilliams and Siegel, 2001) and does not necessarily involve a short-term vs long term trade-off.

13.5 SHORT CASE ILLUSTRATION

Sustainability: MSC Cruises switch to LNG

MSC Cruises (www.msccruises.com/) is a privately held company based in Geneva, Switzerland, that has grown rapidly to become one of the world's largest cruise lines. After a number of years of enforced retrenchment due to the COVID-19 pandemic restrictions, it has now reembarked on its growth trajectory.

The company has ordered three 205,000 ton 'world-class' ships, which will be among the world's largest cruise liners when they are delivered between 2024 and 2027. The ships will be powered by LNG. The vessels will be able to sail with decreases in sulfur emissions and particulate matter of 99%, NOx emissions of 85% and CO_2 emissions of 20% compared with traditional fuel oil-powered ships. However, though the cost of the fuel is lower, construction costs are typically 15% to 20% higher than those for traditionally powered ships (Ma, 2022).

Triple bottom line (TBL) is a sustainability-related construct that was coined by Elkington (1997), and the terms TBL and sustainability are often used interchangeably in the literature (Alhaddi, 2015). The term has also been referred to as a practical framework of sustainability (Rogers and Hudson, 2011) that allows organizations to put a consistent and balanced focus on the economic, social and environmental value provided. The concept has also been widely applied to *THE* contexts; see, for example, Hede (2007), Stoddard et al. (2012) and Boley and Uysal (2013).

The exact measures to be built into *TBL* sustainability, however, are themselves complex and highly dependent on the contextual circumstances. The indicators to be used were discussed by Asmelash and Kumar (2019). Each organization, destination or event needs to determine its own indicators to give a fair and balanced picture.

In broad terms, the focus of TBL is on the:

- *Economic line* – economic value provided by the organization to the surrounding economic system in a way that it prospers and promotes its ability to support future generations
- *Social line* – beneficial and fair business practices for the human resources of the organization and for the community
- *Environmental line* – engaging in practices that do not compromise the environmental resources for future generations. It pertains to the efficient use of energy recourses, reducing greenhouse gas emissions, minimizing emissions, etc. (Goel, 2010).

13.6 Acceptability

Acceptability is concerned with assessing the expected performance outcomes of a strategy to determine whether they are likely to be acceptable to stakeholders.

In considering expected performance, it is useful to make an assessment following Whittington et al. (2020) on what can be termed the '3 Rs of acceptability':

- *Reactions* of stakeholders
- *Returns*
- *Risks*

In assessing the strategy for acceptability, it is sensible to consider all of the 3Rs. Consequently, the acceptability of a chosen strategy is often determined by using a range of analytical financial and non-financial tools such as those described later in the chapter. A strategic option is acceptable if those who must agree to the strategy accept the option. This raises an obvious question – who are those who agree that the option is acceptable?

13.7 Reaction of stakeholders

We encountered the concept of stakeholders in Chapter 1, and we shall return to it again in Chapter 16. The extent to which stakeholders can exert influence on an organization's strategic decision making rests on the two variables power and interest (see Chapter 1).

Stakeholders that have the highest combination of both the ability to influence (power) and the willingness to influence (interest) will have the most *effective* influence. Where two or more stakeholder groups have comparable influence, the possibility of conflict over acceptability will be heightened (see the easyJet Short Case Illustration). In most cases, the board of directors will be the most influential stakeholder. It is also important to consider the commitment from managers and employees. If important members of the organization are not committed to the strategy, it is unlikely to be successfully implemented.

13.6 SHORT CASE ILLUSTRATION

Acceptability of strategic options: easyJet

easyJet plc is a British airline based at London Luton Airport. The airline was launched in 1995 as part of the easyGroup conglomerate by Cypriot businessman Sir Haji-Ioannou (often referred to by his first name, 'Stelios') with two 'wet leased' aircraft and was floated on the London Stock Exchange in November 2000.

Subsequently, easyJet has grown rapidly as consumers took to the variant of the low-cost model pioneered by Southwest Airlines in the USA, which the airline operates. It has grown through acquisitions and by developing new operating bases across Europe. It now has operating bases across Europe, the largest of which is at London's Gatwick airport. easyJet is the second-largest low-cost carrier in Europe, behind Ryanair.

Although he stepped down from the easyJet board, Haji-Ioannou and his family remain large shareholders, with about a third of all shares. He has repeatedly clashed with easyJet's board over its strategy. His criticisms have been over several issues. His resignation from the board in 2010 was prompted by the airline's strategy, which called for the expansion of its fleet with an order to buy over 130 new Airbus aircraft. He argued that such rapid expansion of the fleet (from its 2013 level of about 200 aircraft) was unsustainable and that, instead, more money should go to shareholders in dividends. The easyJet board, however, argued that growth and fleet renewal were essential to maintain easyJet's strong European market position.

The fleet renewal and enlargement were approved by the board and new aircraft deliveries took place. Subsequently, Stelios has clashed with the board over other issues including executive pay and dividend policy. In 2016 he again made his feelings plain when he opposed the rumored takeover of a failing British rival, Monarch Airlines. 'My personal view as a shareholder', he said, 'is that easyJet should not do any acquisitions. They usually destroy shareholder value' (Young, 2016).

The issues raised by Stelios seem to have been resolved as his shareholding fell to about 15% from September 2021 as he failed to take up his allocation of shares from a 'rights offer', raising additional capital for the company.

Source: www.corporate.easyjet.com

Questions

1. Explain the issue of acceptability highlighted by this case.

2. Which of the stakeholders involved in this case is likely to be able to adopt their favored strategy, and why?

13.8 Returns

We learned in Chapter 1 that one of the key objectives in strategy is to create competitive advantage. This criterion asks a simple question of any strategic option – what is the point of pursuing an option if it is not going to result in superior performance (compared to competitors) or higher than average profitability? In other words, a strategic option would fail this test if it were likely to only result in the business being 'ordinary' or average in relation to the industry or sector norm.

This is particularly important when considering product options. For example, if a new product option is forecast to receive an uncertain reception from the market, we might well ask what the point of the launch is at all. It would be unlikely to result in competitive advantage for the business.

How do we know if competitive advantage is likely to be achieved in the future as a result of implementing the chosen strategy? We cannot be certain, because we are dealing with forecasts of the future rather than measurements of the past, but the answer lies in the *returns* that are likely to be received.

In the commercial sector, this normally relates primarily to the *financial* returns that are likely to be received as a result of implementing the strategy. For noncommercial activities the returns may be assessed in a rather different way. In these circumstances, we are more likely to be concerned with the benefits that are received relative to the costs that are incurred to achieve these benefits (so-called cost–benefit analysis).

13.9 Financial tools for evaluating returns

In the evaluation and selection stage, a number of 'tools' are available to managers that may assist in deciding upon the most appropriate option. Not all of them will be appropriate in every circumstance, and some are more widely used than others. They are used to explore the implications of the options so that the decisions that are made are based on the best possible information.

Accountants or financial analysts are usually very involved in strategic evaluation and selection because of their expertise in understanding the financial implications of the possible courses of action. Some of the tools involved can be quite complicated, so a detailed discussion of their workings is beyond the scope of this book. However, it is extremely important that decision makers (who may or may not be financial specialists) have an understanding of the financial principles involved to make sound judgments; hence the need to cover the issues and principles here.

The reader is referred to more specialized texts which cover this material in greater depth. For example, Horner (2020) is a good starting point for non-financial specialists, Arnold and Lewis (2019) give more detailed general coverage and Scholes et al. (1998) consider financial decisions specifically in a strategic management context. Specialist *THE* texts that cover this material and place it in a relevant contextual framework include Adams (2020) and DeFranco and Lattin (2006).

In Chapter 5 we considered cash flow forecasting, which is an important stage of financial analysis. Here we consider methods of investment appraisal, which usually forms part of the financial decision-making process when making a choice between differing strategic options.

13.9.1 Investment appraisal – introduction

An investment, at its simplest, is some money put up for a project in the expectation that it will enable more money to be made in the future. The additional money over and above the original investment is termed the *return on investment*. There is often a strong time element to investment appraisal techniques because the returns on the investment may remain for several years or even decades. Therefore, a factor is often built into the calculation to account for the *time value of money* (see Key Concept below).

> **KEY CONCEPT**
>
> **The time value of money**
>
> Generally, a sum of money received now is preferable to the same sum of money received at some point in the future.
>
> This time preference is so because of the time value of money and not because of inflation or risks – though both are important. In most developed and developing economies, inflation has caused the value of money to diminish over time. Even if there were no inflation and there was an absolute certainty that the amount of money would be returned, the time preference for money would still hold.
>
> The explanation lies in the concept of *opportunity cost*. If a sum is received immediately, rather than some time in the future, it can be invested in some way and yield a rate of return. Thus, the difference between present and future receipt is the opportunity cost of the investment opportunity foregone.
>
> Because future inflows of cash are less desirable than present inflows, they must be discounted at a rate of interest so that the current and future inflows of cash are equalized.

There are thus two key questions surrounding investment appraisal:

- *How much* will the organization make against each investment option?
- *When* will the organization receive its return on investment?

Key measures of *acceptability* are the *returns* that are likely to accrue from specific options and the *risks* of potential losses. Returns are based on forecasts. What risks arise if the forecast returns turn out to be inaccurate?

A common method of assessing the financial acceptability of strategic options is through the application of *investment appraisal* techniques. Various methods of investment appraisal can be used. We will briefly consider the principles involved with the five most common methods below. These are:

- Payback method
- Breakeven analysis
- Accounting rate of return
- Net present value (NPV)
- Internal rate of return (IRR) discounted cash flow (DCF) methods

13.9.2 Payback method

The first and most obvious thing that managers want to know about any investment is the *payback period*. This is the time taken to repay the investment – the shorter the better. If, for example, an investment of $1,000,000 is expected to increase profits by $100,000 a month, the payback period will be 10 months.

In practice, payback periods are rarely this short, and it is this fact that makes investment appraisal calculations a bit more complicated. When the effects of inflation are taken into account, the returns on an investment can be eroded over time. Consequently, accountants include a factor to account for the effects of inflation, usually on a 'best-guess' basis. The payback method can be justified on the grounds that it represents a simple, quick screening process.

However, it can be criticized in that it ignores the so-called time value of money and also ignores inflows after the payback period.

13.9.3 Breakeven analysis

Breakeven analysis is concerned with finding the point at which the total revenue from a project is equal to the total costs incurred.

The analysis (see, for example, Glautier et al., 2010:ch. 19) is directed toward finding the *tipping point* (breakeven point) beyond which revenue exceeds the total costs; that is, the variable and fixed costs combined. As such, it rests on a number of assumptions, including:

- Costs can be easily attributed between fixed and variable elements
- Fixed costs are constant
- Fixed costs can be allocated to particular products
- It is possible to predict the volume of sales at various prices

Nevertheless, breakeven analysis is widely understood and can easily be communicated in organizations so that employees know the sales levels that must be achieved to attain profitability of operations. It is extremely important in many aspects of *THE* for companies to know their breakeven points.

Thus, breakeven analysis is a useful and widely used tool but needs to be treated with some caution because it rests on a number of assumptions and is in itself variable. Managers should, of course, be concerned not just with the breakeven point that is calculated but in affecting it in such a way that the breakeven point is brought down. In other words, the measure of capacity (such as the load factor, occupancy rate, etc.) that we use at which breakeven is reached is lowered. To do this, managers have to look closely at their costs to ensure that they are minimized.

> **For example:** *An airline or a coach operator would measure their load factors meticulously because they are 'proxy' measures of their profitability. A certain load factor is reached beyond which profitability is achieved, and revenues over and above this tipping point add directly to the margins being achieved. Similarly, a hotel operator, restaurant or venue operator will measure room occupancy rates, covers served and tickets sold for similar reasons. Most companies will have a view on the level at which the breakeven is achieved and pass this on to employees, particularly those involved in achieving sales.*

Figure 13.2 shows a graphical representation of the breakeven point for selling seats on an aircraft (though the same principles would apply to a bus, a theater, hotel rooms, etc.).

The following points about costs and revenues should be noted:

- Some costs are fixed regardless of sales. In this case, it might apply, for instance, to staff costs for the aircraft and landing and takeoff fees and would be variable; that is, it would vary in accordance with the number of seats sold.
- Total costs = fixed costs + variable costs.

- Total revenues increase as the number of seats sold goes up.
- There comes a point at which the lines intersect, at which the revenues received equal the total costs. This is the *breakeven point*.

The difference between the revenues and total costs represents profit, and this increases quickly beyond the breakeven point. In this case, the breakeven point is at about 200 seats sold of a 350-seat aircraft, representing a load factor of about 57%.

13.9.4 Accounting rate of return

The accounting rate of return (ARR), as its title implies, is an accounting measure. It is calculated in three steps:

- Take average annual inflows over project life
- Deduct depreciation on the initial outlay
- Divide the result by the average investment over the period

The ARR can be justified (like the payback method) on the grounds that it represents a simple, quick screening process, but it can also be criticized in that it ignores the so-called time value of money.

13.9.5 Discounted cash flow methods

The two main DCF methods (NPV and IRR) are considered superior (but more complicated) than payback and ARR because such methods consider the timing of cash flows – *the time value of money*.

The time value of money is based on the notion that organizations or individuals need to be compensated for foregoing the use of money for a period of time if, for example, it has been invested in a project.

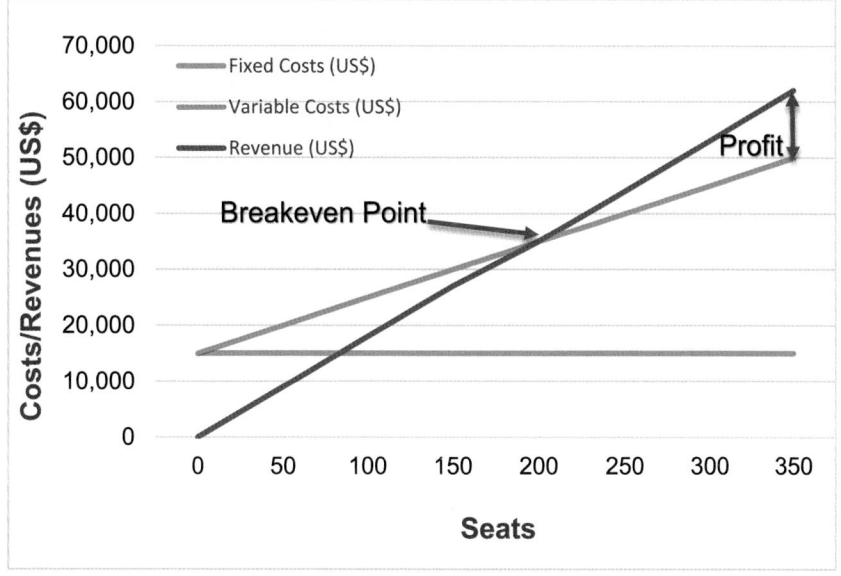

Figure 13.2 The breakeven point for selling seats on an aircraft

Such methods are based on the concept of compound interest in reverse. For example, if interest rates are 10% and a certain investment promises to pay $100,000 in one year's time, the amount we would need to invest now is:

$$\frac{\$100,000 \times 100}{110} = \$90,900$$

That is, $90,900 now is equivalent to $100,000 received in one year. It is the *present value* of $100,000.

13.9.6 Net present value

NPV is the value obtained by *discounting* the forecast cash inflows and outflows of a project at a chosen *acceptable* rate of return and taking the net total. An acceptable rate of return is the return that stakeholders would think is acceptable relative to other comparable investments.

Note: The present value of the inflows and outflows can be found by applying a discount factor from published tables.

> For example: *The discount factor applied after one year at the rate of 10% is 0.9091, after two years it is 0.8264, and so on. That is, each US dollar is worth 0.9091 after one year and 0.8264 after two years and so on. Thus, NPV involves the following steps:*
>
> 1. *Find the present value of the project's cash inflows (using discount rate tables).*
> 2. *Find the present value of the project's cash outflows (using discount rate tables).*
> 3. *If 1 minus 2 (above) is positive, the investment is worthwhile. If it is negative, the project or option should be rejected.*

13.9.7 Internal rate of return

The goal with this method is to find the interest rate at which inflow exactly equal outflows; that is, where NPV $=$ 0. Where IRR is higher than the rate deemed to be an acceptable level of return, the option should be considered financially viable.

> For example: *If 10% is viewed as an acceptable rate of return and the IRR is calculated to be 15%, the project would be deemed to be viable.*

The steps to find IRR are as follows:

1. Select an acceptable interest rate as a rate of return.
2. Discount the present and future cash inflows and outflows at this rate.
3. If the result of this step is *not* zero, return to step 1 and select a different interest rate.
4. Continue until the result is zero; that is, the interest rate at which NPV $=$ zero has been found. This is the IRR of the project.
5. If the IRR exceeds the target rate of return that has been set, the investment should go ahead.

13.9.8 NPV and IRR compared

Because it is expressed as a percentage, whereas NPV is an amount, IRR is easier to understand, but NPV is normally considered superior because:

- NPV is easier to calculate.
- IRR ignores the relative size of the investments being considered.

- IRR rates are nonadditive; that is, the rates from two or more projects cannot be added together.
- In some circumstances there may be more than one IRR.

13.9.9 Limitations of the financial tools

The limitations of the financial tools rest on the problem of the unpredictability of the future. We learned in Chapters 7 and 8 that the macro and micro environments can change, sometimes rapidly and with great magnitude. Accordingly, the actual returns that an organization makes on an investment may not always be what were expected.

In making investment decisions, there is a need to consider the effects of inflation; that is, the increase in price of goods and services over a period of time.

A distinction can be made between anticipated and unanticipated inflation. Anticipated inflation can be taken into account by investment appraisal models, whereas unanticipated inflation is one of a number of sources of uncertainty. The investment analysis is only a tool in helping to make decisions and ultimately a judgment has to be made because uncertainty will always exist when forecasting the future.

Thus, when the analysis is complete, investors may require a so-called risk premium (an additional return over and above the investment return) to compensate them for the degree of uncertainty, including inflation, that they judge to be involved. In forecasting the level of inflation for NPV calculations, the presence of inflation would erode the purchasing power (what the cash sums would buy) but would not alter the relative attractiveness of competing projects. In major economies such as those in Western Europe, North America, Japan and Australia, the level of inflation has historically been relatively stable at between 2% and 10%, with an occasional 'shock' such as in the mid-1970s when in the UK, for example, it reached 24%.

In other parts of the world, however, problems with the supply of goods and the value of currency can lead to much higher inflation levels, which have occasionally (in countries such as Venezuela and Zimbabwe) exceeded 1000% a year. A presumption of low and stable inflation will therefore tend to encourage investment rather than high and unpredictable inflation, which will discourage investment or require a large risk premium to be paid to investors as compensation for the increased levels of perceived risk.

Tables 13.5 and 13.6 show a simplified fictitious example that compares two hotel projects.

Consider the case of a (fictitious) hotel company considering an investment in a new Japanese hotel to open in 2019, before the Tokyo Olympic Games in 2020 (shown in Tables 13.5 and 13.6).

Table 13.5 NPV worked example of two hotel projects (Part 1)

Cash outflow and inflow	Period	Hotel Project A – Tokyo US$mn	Hotel Project B – Osaka US$000s
Outlay period	0	(15,000)	(15,000)
Inflow period	1	7,000	2,000
	2	5,000	3,000
	3	4,000	7,000
	4	4,000	10,000

Table 13.6 NPV worked example of two hotel projects (Part 2)

Cash outflow and inflow	Period	Project A	Project B	Present value @ 10%	Project A	Project B
Outlay period	0	−(15,000)	−(15,000)		−(15,000)	−(15,000)
Inflow period	1	7,000	2,000	0.9063	6,344	1,813
	2	5,000	3,000	0.8203	4,102	2,461
	3	4,000	7,000	0.7441	2,976	5,209
	4	4,000	10,000	0.6756	2,702	6,756
	Total				**1,124**	**1,238**

The hotelier has the option of either building the hotel in Tokyo, which would enable the company to gain good levels of occupancy at high room rates shortly after opening, or opening in another Japanese city such as Osaka, which may give more even returns over a longer period.

In this case, it is necessary to determine which project is preferable assuming:

- The company only has available funding for one of the projects
- A discount rate of 10%
- NPV provides the most effective means of investment appraisal because it considers the time value of money

In Table 13.6 above, the cash flows are discounted by a factor contained in published present value tables (included in many financial textbooks and widely available online). In this case:

- Both projects achieve a positive NPV, so both are worthwhile.
- Project B is preferable because it provides a higher NPV, though it has a slightly longer payback period.

13.10 Non-financial tools for evaluating returns

Financial evaluation of strategic options is very important, but for most organizations, other tools can also provide useful information. These may require financial information as an input, so they should be seen not as 'instead of' financial analyses but 'as well as'. They enrich the information enabling management to select the best strategic option.

13.10.1 Cost–benefit analysis

Cost–benefit analysis applies to almost every area of life, not just strategic evaluation and selection. The cost–benefit concept suggests that a money value can be put on all costs and benefits of a strategy, including tangible and intangible returns to people and organizations proposing the project. Each option will have a cost associated with it and will be expected to return certain benefits. If both of these can be quantified in financial terms, the cost–benefit calculation will be relatively straightforward. The problem is that this is rarely the case.

The major benefit of such analysis is that it forces managers to be explicit about the various factors that influence strategic choice, so that even if people disagree about the valuations included in the analysis, the material is brought out into the open and the merits of the various arguments can be compared.

The costs of pursuing one particular option will have a number of elements. Any financial investment costs will be easily quantifiable. Against this, the cost of not pursuing the next best option needs to be taken into account – the *opportunity cost*. There may also be a number of social and environmental costs, which are much harder to attach a value to.

The same problems apply to the benefits. In addition to financial benefits, an organization may take into account social benefits and others such as improved reputation or improved service. Intangible benefits are very difficult to attach a value to in a cost–benefit analysis because they can take a long time to work through in increased financial performance.

Though it is difficult to quantify non-financial benefits, it is usually possible after some calculations have been made, as well as research and negotiations between the interested parties. The technique is commonly used to assess the acceptability of strategic options, particularly in the public sector (see, for example, Scholes and Johnson, 2001) and in cases where development involves PPPs.

The technique has also been quite widely used in *THE* settings, particularly in relation to major infrastructural projects such as for transport development and also in relation to the staging of festivals and events. See, for example, Dwyer (2012) for a description of the method applied to tourism and hospitality and Mules and Dwyer (2005) and Dwyer et al. (2016), who applied the concept to sporting events.

The problems with this evaluative technique, however, are that:

- Some of the 'measures' that are used are in fact subjective judgments and consequently open to challenge.
- There is no agreed methodology and, in reality, the term covers a range of approaches.
- In many cases there are issues regarding just where the analysis should stop.

> For example: *In considering a major new airport development for a city, it would seem appropriate that the increased costs of noise and emissions and congestion should be costed. However, aircraft emissions are thought to be partly responsible for the global warming phenomena. Consequently, should the costs associated with global warming arising from increased air transport movements also be factored into the calculations, or is this aspect too remote from the project under consideration?*

KEY CONCEPT

Social costs and benefits

All organizations have an impact on the societies that are in their locality or that are affected by their products or activities. As we argued in Chapter 2, *THE* often has a profound social impact: in the home location, at destinations and in transit between the two. Although the term *social* is a bit nebulous, it is generally taken to mean the effect of the condition being evaluated on employment, social well-being, health, chemical emissions, pollution, aesthetic appearance, charitable societies, etc.

A strategic option will have an element of social cost and social benefit. We would describe a social cost as a deterioration in any of the above – an increase in unemployment, higher levels of emissions, pollution, declining salaries, etc. Conversely, a social benefit will result in improvements – increasing employment, cleaner industry, better working conditions, etc.

13.10.2 Impact analysis

When a strategic option may be reasonably expected to have far-reaching consequences in either social or financial terms, an impact study may be appropriate. Essentially, this involves asking the question, 'If this option goes ahead, what will its impact be on . . . ?'

The aspects that might be impacted will depend on the particular circumstances of the option and have been widely discussed in THE contexts. Authors such as Archer (1996), Mules (2000) and Andersson and Lundberg (2013) pointed out that impact analysis of festivals and events has been a central theme in event studies for decades. In their paper, Andersson and Lundberg (2013) studied a three-day music event in Sweden and proposed a model for measuring impacts from a sustainability perspective, and they developed a common monetary metric that could be applied in different settings.

As with cost–benefit analysis, impact analysis really describes a range of approaches because the type of analysis, the sort of questions that are asked and the measures that are important are highly context specific. In other words, the underlying principles may be the same, but the detail will vary in the cases of, say, a hotel development, an infrastructure project or festivals and events.

> For example: *With regard to a proposed development of a new theme park, the impact study might typically take into account the development's implications for:*

- *Local employment*
- *Primary and secondary levels of spending to be generated and leakages from the local economy*
- *The effect of the development on other businesses*
- *The capacity of the local infrastructure such as road and rail services but also utilities such as water and sewerage, waste disposal, gas and electricity*
- *The environmental impact on the local flora and fauna and the effects of noise pollution*
- *The aesthetic impact of the development on the local community*

In many cases, an impact study will be an intrinsic part of the cost–benefit calculation, and it suffers from the same limitations – that of evaluating the true value of each aspect that may be impacted.

13.7 SHORT CASE ILLUSTRATION

Evaluation: the Olympic bidding process for the Tokyo 2020 Olympic Games

The Olympic Games is the world's largest sporting event, and cities have to bid against each other in a highly publicized bidding process. The bids have to go through a careful evaluation process before the successful city is chosen. Though the terminology is not used, the evaluation involves a series of stages, which in essence involve suitability, screening, feasibility and acceptability.

- *Suitability* – Each competing country has a National Olympic Committee (NOC). The NOC coordinates any possible bid from the country it represents and assesses the suitability of the bid. At this stage the bid may be withdrawn because it is not deemed to be suitable and therefore unlikely to succeed, but if it passes this hurdle, the NOC formally passes the bid on to the International Olympic Committee (IOC) for further scrutiny. Cities such as Prague, Czech Republic; Saint Petersburg, Russia; and Toronto, Canada, considered making bids for the 2020 Olympic Games, but they did not do so. Rome, Italy, was to submit a bid to the IOC, but the Italian government subsequently withdrew its support and the bid was withdrawn.

- *Screening* – Following submission of their bids, the 'applicant cities' are required to answer a questionnaire covering themes of importance to a successful Games organization. This allows the IOC to analyze the capabilities and the strengths and weaknesses of the potential host cities and assess the risks involved. Following a detailed study and ensuing reports, the IOC Executive Board selects the cities that are qualified to proceed to the next phase. At this screening stage, some cities are screened out and cannot proceed. In the bidding process for the 2020 Olympic Games, Baku, Azerbaijan; and Doha, Qatar, were rejected at this stage and did not proceed.

- *Feasibility* – At the candidature stage, the accepted 'candidate cities' submit a second questionnaire in the form of an extended, more detailed, candidature questionnaire, which includes detailed financial and operational details and impact assessments. The reports are carefully studied by the IOC Evaluation Commission. The members of the Commission make 4-day inspection visits to each of the candidate cities, where they check details of the bid. The results of its inspections are passed to IOC members up to one month before the electing IOC session. Three cities were considered for selection to host the 2020 games at this stage: Istanbul, Turkey; Madrid, Spain; and Tokyo, Japan.

- *Acceptability* – The acceptability of the bids is the responsibility of members of the IOC, who each have one vote. Voting continues in rounds, eliminating cites until a city with an overall majority is chosen. Thus, in its meeting on 7 September 2013 held in the neutral city of Buenos Aires, Argentina, Tokyo was chosen to host the 2020 Summer Olympic Games.

A similar process was employed in awarding the 2024 Summer Olympic Games to Paris.

Source: Adapted from: www.olympic.org

Questions

1. Explain why the Olympic Games goes through this structured evaluation process.

2. What other stakeholders other than the IOC members may have a view on the 'acceptability' of the Olympic bids?

13.11 Risk

The third 'R' of acceptability relates to risk and uncertainty.

Most decisions about strategy are made under conditions of some uncertainty, because who can predict the future with any degree of certainty when the environment is complex and rapidly changing. There is clearly thus a risk that the outcome will be different from what was planned.

Thus, we need to have a framework for considering what would happen to the organization if the assumptions that underpin the strategy turn out to be wrong and what risks might this entail. All organizations encounter risks, some of which are fairly generic in nature, such as financial risks associated with interest rates, and others that are quite specific to each individual business situation.

It is important that managers:

- Identify the major risks that the organization encounters
- Attempt to understand the nature of the risks identified and how they are likely to change
- Plan their strategy in such a way that enables them to manage and deal with the risks

No business can eliminate risk, and because the level of returns is usually correlated with risk, it may be sensible to take on some risks that could be avoided. By doing so, managers have the opportunity to maximize returns, but it is important that a balanced assessment be made in which the relative risks and returns are considered. It is also necessary that the risks be 'owned' by particular identified managers and directors so that they are tracked, the changing implications are monitored and steps are taken to manage the risks appropriately. These steps may include:

- Just recognizing that the risk exists in the knowledge that good returns are being received
- Having a portfolio approach so that a risk in one part of the business is balanced by non-risky aspects elsewhere
- Taking active measures to control risks, such as through *hedging*, working collaboratively with partners or passing the risk to suppliers or customers

The types of risks a large *THE* business may encounter are shown in the Short Cast Illustration of Live Nation.

13.8 SHORT CASE ILLUSTRATION

Risk analysis: Live Nation

Live Nation Entertainment, Inc., based in Beverly Hills, California, claims to be the largest live entertainment company in the world and operates five main areas associated with live entertainment events: promoting music events, operating venues, ticketing services (such as Ticketmaster), sponsorship and advertising sales and artist management and services.

All businesses encounter risks, and it is important that managers identify the risks and understand the implications if adverse circumstances arise.

As part of its annual reporting, the company analyzes the business and financial risks it encounters in detail. Some of the business risks identified by the company are summarized in Table 13.7.

Table 13.7 Business risks: Live Nation

Live Nation identified business risks
• The impact of tightening labor markets
• The increased risk of litigation in the current and future environment
• A reduction in the profitability of operations
• Potential decreased willingness of artists to tour or impracticability of touring
• Potential changes to consumer preferences for consumption of live music or sporting events
• Loss of ticketing clients due to the economic impacts of the pandemic
• The inability to pursue expansion opportunities or acquisitions due to capital constraints
• The future availability or increased cost of insurance coverage
• A potential shift away from live events by sponsors and advertisers
• Incurring additional expenses related to compliance, precautions and management of the company during and after this period

Source: Adapted from Live Nation (2021)

Questions

1. Explain why a company like Live Nation needs to identify the risks it is subject to.

2. In what general ways might managers respond to the risks identified in a case such as Live Nation?

13.11.1 *Scenario planning and sensitivity analysis*

The uncertainties of the future, as we have seen, make any prediction inexact. Though an organization can never be certain of any sequence of future events, scenario planning (or 'what if?' analysis, as it is sometimes called) and its variant, sensitivity analysis, can give an idea of how the outcome would be affected by a number of possible disruptions. For a general discussion of this technique, see, for example, Fleisher and Bensoussan (2003); for a context-specific discussion, see, for example, Yeoman and McMahon-Beattie (2005) for their application of the technique to Scottish tourism and hospitality and Breukel and Go (2009), who applied the technique to the Dutch hospitality sector.

The development of computerized applications and spreadsheet applications has made this activity easier to undertake. A financial model on a spreadsheet that makes a number of assumptions such as revenue projections, cost forecasts, inflation rate, etc., can be modified to instantly show the effect of, say, a 10% increase in costs or a higher-than-expected rate of inflation. This is designed to show how sensitive the cash flow is to its assumptions – hence the name.

> For example: *An airline might produce a projection of future earnings on the basis that the average price it would have to pay for its jet fuel requirements (a major constituent of*

airline costs) is US$170 per barrel (a barrel is 42 US gallons or roughly 159 liters). The airline obviously is unable to control the price of this key input and indeed has no accurate means of forecasting it. Consequently, when forecasting its future earnings, the airline might regard it as a prudent step to produce alternative scenarios that ask the 'what if' question. The scenarios might suppose that:

A major war breaks out or the Organization of Petroleum Exporting Countries (OPEC) restricts supplies, thereby increasing jet fuel prices by 20%

Surplus supplies of jet fuel become available as a result of lower demand for air services, leading to jet fuel prices falling by 20%

Having produced the scenarios and calculated the impact of the events on the cost of jet fuel, the airline would factor the costs into its overall calculations. As a result, the airline might be able to produce a central or base earnings forecast based on the US$170 per barrel price but would also have knowledge of the effect an increase or decrease in fuel costs would have on overall profitability.

In other words, the *sensitivity* of earnings to fuel price changes would have been assessed. In some cases, the analysis might go a stage further by applying weightings to the scenarios. Thus, the airline might be fairly confident about its central assumption and assign a 50% weighting; that is, its assessment of the situation is that there is a 50% chance of the central assumption of US$170 being realized. Similarly, the company might assess the situation and feel that if the central case is not borne out, a rise is more likely than a fall and consequently 30% and 20% weightings are assigned to the rising and falling fuel price scenarios, respectively.

13.9 SHORT CASE ILLUSTRATION

Sensitivity analysis: Air New Zealand

Companies frequently assess the sensitivity of their earnings to major changes in their annual report and accounts and other company documents. This serves to warn investors and other stakeholders of the potential volatility of earnings. It also informs the stakeholders that managers are aware of the risks and of the steps they might be taking (such as *hedging*) to deal with the risks identified.

To return to an example used in Chapter 5 of Air New Zealand, in its annual reports it identified a number of risks and analyzed the sensitivity of earnings to price changes. The Air New Zealand Annual Report (Air New Zealand, 2022) stated that 'the sensitivity analyses are hypothetical and should not be considered predictive of future performance'.

The report identified key sensitivities relating to foreign currency, liquidity, equity investment prices, interest rates and jet fuel prices. In relation to jet fuel prices, for example, to alleviate this risk, management hedges a large part of its exposure to fuel price movements through the use of financial instruments.

Source: Air New Zealand (2022)

Questions

1. Explain why Air New Zealand is concerned about jet fuel prices.

2. Explain what is meant by sensitivity analysis and consider in what circumstances it might be useful to THE organizations.

Qualitative variables can also be analyzed. If an option has a high dependency on the availability of a key resource or the oversight of a key manager, a 'what if?' study will show the effect that the loss or reduction in the key input would have.

13.12 Strategic evaluation in emergent strategies

In Chapter 1 we encountered the idea that business strategies can be either prescriptive (or deliberate). That is, some strategies are planned in advance, often following a rational sequence of events – prescriptive strategies. Others are not planned in this way and are said to be emergent – they result from an organization's management following a consistent pattern of behavior.

A planned prescriptive approach can imply excessive formality, inflexibility and an overreliance on analysis. Indeed, in a well-known article on strategy, Lenz and Lyles (1985/1989) argued that too much analysis can stifle innovation and lead to paralysis (a lack of action). However, in a prescriptive approach, managers and other stakeholders can at least be assured that strategic options have been formulated, evaluated and chosen based on an evidence base.

This distinction is important when it comes to strategic evaluation. Companies that employ the deliberate model are likely to use the criteria and the tools above, whereas those that prefer the emergent model are less likely to do so explicitly. This is not to say, however, that the analytical process cannot form a part of an intelligent manager's intuitive thinking.

It is here that one of the potential limitations of emergent strategy becomes apparent. If an organization follows a deliberate process with its systematic and sequential events, it can be more certain that all possible options have been identified and evaluated before the most appropriate one is selected. When using an intuitive emergent approach that relies on patterns of behavior, one cannot be certain that the best option is taken at all times.

The contrary argument for emergent strategy is that in today's rapidly changing environments, organizations must be flexible, be adaptive and move quickly when required. A deliberate approach can mitigate against these actions because it infers a more orderly planned approach that is time-consuming and may stifle innovation and creativity. With a great deal of uncertainty, product innovation leading to rapid market changes and an ever more competitive environment, emergent approaches have become popular in the academic literature.

Henry Mintzberg's research findings, first developed during the 1980s (Mintzberg and Waters, 1985), have often emphasized the importance of emergent strategy, which arises informally at any level in an organization, as an alternative or a complement to deliberate strategy. His much-cited work the *The Rise and Fall of Strategic Planning* (Mintzberg, 2000), presents a critique of planned (prescriptive) approaches and emphasizes the need for a more emergent form of strategy.

Other writers such as Eden and Ackermann (2013) took the emergent theme a stage further when they emphasized the 'making' of strategy as a highly inclusive and action-oriented activity. The academic debates and the main features of emergent strategy and its implications for decision making have been well articulated by Lynch (2021).

In reality, most organizations probably adopt a hybrid approach that lies somewhere between the two extremes to try to obtain the advantages of a planned approach without losing the possible advantages of innovation and flexibility that might be evident in a more emergent approach. Stakeholders such as shareholders and banks tend to force many organizations down a prescriptive (deliberate) route of strategic formulation. This is because in making investment decisions, they want to see evidence that the organization has considered its strategy carefully and considered alternatives based on analysis of the evidence.

However, there has undoubtedly been recognition that strategic formulation cannot be static. In contemporary fast-moving markets, which value creativity and innovation and where barriers to entry have been removed or lowered, organizations have to maintain flexibility to compete effectively. Recognizing the advantages of more emergent approaches to strategic formulation also has particular relevance for SMEs because, for reasons we will consider below, they can gain competitive advantage over larger competitors in fast-moving markets through innovation.

The preceding discussion emphasizes the fact that strategy is not a once-only activity – the organization determines its strategy and then implements it. Instead, whichever end of the prescriptive–emergent continuum an organization chooses as the basis for strategy formulation, it must be viewed as a 'process'. The process requires continual monitoring of the implementation of the strategy, feedback provided to managers and adjustments made when necessary. The implementation issues relating to strategy will be covered in the next part of this book.

THINK POINTS

- Explain why a screening stage is often inserted between suitability and feasibility in strategic evaluation.
- Explain what is meant by the '3 Rs of acceptability'.
- Assess the limitations that emergent strategies may have at the strategic evaluation stage.

Small business focus

There is some evidence that though most organizations view strategy and strategic planning as highly important, many organizations do not use the tools and techniques of evaluation outlined in this chapter (despite the advantages in delivering rigor). This is particularly true of SMEs. Stonehouse and Pemberton (2002:855), building on the work of Glaister and Falshaw (1999), for example, stated that 'only a limited set of tools are deployed by small, medium or large organizations, though there is evidence that larger organizations are more likely to take a more structured approach and utilize the tools'. The authors also identified a short-term outlook in relation to the business planning of the companies they surveyed.

Notwithstanding the lack of formal use of the strategic tools and techniques, many SMEs have to produce regular business plans to satisfy the banks and shareholders who finance them. This forces them to take a planned prescriptive approach to strategy – albeit sometimes rather short to medium term in its outlook. But there is also a need for SMEs to continually innovate to stay ahead of competitors (which are often larger), and the theme of innovation is something that is particularly stressed in the literature relating to emergent approaches to strategy.

There is a body of research that argues that SMEs in fast-moving markets enjoy particular advantages over more established competitors largely due to their ability to innovate and adapt quickly, operating in a more emergent manner. Although this literature mainly relates to technology companies (see, for example, Christensen et al., 1998; Weinstein and Winston, 2016), it can be argued that the markets in many parts of *THE* also represent such fast-moving markets and thus place a high dependence on innovation.

Thus, innovation is a key driver in many SMEs in *THE* and a driver that can provide a strong position relative to larger competitors. See, for example, Prentice and Andersen (2003), Hjalager (2010), Sundbo et al. (2007), Gomezelj (2016), Sandybayev (2016) and Marasco et al. (2018).

In discussing innovation in tourism, Sundbo et al. (2007) concluded that among tourism firms, hotels, restaurants and transport have been seen to be the most innovative, and Prentice and Andersen (2003) pointed out that it is Edinburgh's reputation for innovation in relation to the arts that underpins its success as a multi-festival city. There are a number of examples of quite rapid market changes that have often transformed the competitive landscape in *THE*, such as the:

- Growth of low-cost airlines
- Rapidly segmenting markets for cruising
- Growth of individually styled boutique hotels
- Proliferation of new and more specialized festivals
- The 'discovery' of new travel destinations

The rapid market changes are encouraged by lower barriers to entry and the desire of *THE* consumers for products that provide consumers with experiences that are 'new', 'exciting', 'challenging' and 'different'. Such products are often also driven by style, fashion branding and status.

THE organizations providing such products are often relatively new and innovative SMEs benefiting from *first-mover* (or *early mover*) advantage. Equally, by its very nature, the openness of most parts of *THE* makes it easy for enterprises to observe what others are doing, with the result that SMEs may be able to get a 'free ride' on the investments, ideas and successes of others (Hjalager, 2002). In adopting a so-called me-too strategy, SMEs are able to adapt, extend and provide niche versions of products provided by larger companies. In some cases, innovative SBUs of larger companies, operating relatively independent of the parent company, have been innovative or have been quick to follow the innovations of SMEs (as with the boutique brands of the larger chains).

When industries are subject to rapid change as in most aspects of *THE*, there are two issues (Lynch, 2021) that established leading organizations must face. As a consequence, opportunities are presented to SMEs and new competitors.

The two issues identified are the:

- *Sunk cost effect* – Organizations that have already committed substantial resources may be reluctant to change. These resources represent those sunk into technologies or products, and though the sunk costs have already been spent, they will influence strategic thinking and may inhibit change on the part of larger companies.
- *Replacement effect* – Existing large companies have less incentive to innovate than SMEs and new entrants. This is because the existing companies already enjoy market dominance and therefore innovation would not enhance their position but just replace one technology or product innovation with another. SMEs, on the other hand, have incentive to innovate because they can gain market share and later market dominance by doing so.

> **For example:** *The operator of a hotel chain may have invested heavily in spreading the brand attribute of the hotel brand around its network. Customers grow accustomed to these attributes, and a certain expectation and brand loyalty develop. However, over time, the hotels may become 'tired' or old-fashioned and be overtaken by newer more fashionable brands. Without refreshment and innovation, the older brand gets left behind as others benefit from being more innovative.*

CHAPTER SUMMARY

The process of choosing strategic options is concerned by evaluating and selecting the best options. Options are considered in relation to the three key aspects of strategy:

- Competitive strategy
- Strategic directions
- Strategic methods

Each option is considered in turn using four overarching criteria:

- Suitability
- Feasibility
- Sustainability
- Acceptability

The acceptability phase is concerned with assessing options in relation to the '3 Rs':

- *Reactions* of stakeholders
- *Returns*
- *Risks*

A number of financial and non-financial tools and techniques can be used to evaluate the 'acceptability' of each option before the most favorable one is chosen. Finally, this chapter considered the risks inherent in an emergent strategy approach when it comes to strategic evaluation and considered the potential advantages SMEs might have in fast-moving markets that might exist in parts of *THE*.

Having chosen strategic options, organizations are faced with the issues involved in implementing the chosen strategy. This is the subject of the next part of the book.

REFERENCES AND WEBSITES

References

Adams, D. (2020) *Management Accounting for the Hospitality, Tourism and Leisure Industries: A Strategic Approach*, 3rd ed., Oxford, UK: Goodfellow.

Air New Zealand. (2022) *Annual Report*, www.airnewzealand.com

Alhaddi, H. (2015) 'Triple bottom line and sustainability: A literature review', *Business and Management Studies*, 1(2): 6–10.

Andersson, T. D. and Lundberg, E. (2013) 'Commensurability and sustainability: Triple impact assessments of a tourism event', *Tourism Management*, 37: 99–109.

Ansoff, I. (1987) *Corporate Strategy*, London: Penguin.

Archer, B. H. (1996) 'Economic impact analysis', *Annals of Tourism Research*, 23(4): 704–707.

Arnold, G. and Lewis, D. (2019) *Corporate Financial Management*, 6th ed., Harlow, UK: Pearson.

Asmelash, A. G. and Kumar, S. (2019) 'Assessing progress of tourism sustainability: Developing and validating sustainability indicators', *Tourism Management*, 71: 67–83.

Bansal, P. and DesJardine, M. R. (2014) 'Business sustainability: It is about time', *Strategic Organization*, 12(1): 70–78.

Boley, B. B. and Uysal, M. (2013) 'Competitive synergy through practicing triple bottom line sustainability: Evidence from three hospitality case studies', *Tourism and Hospitality Research*, 13(4): 226–238.

Breukel, A. and Go, F. M. (2009) 'Knowledge-based network participation in destination and event marketing: A hospitality scenario analysis perspective', *Tourism Management*, 30(2): 184–193.

Cardeal, G., Höse, K., Ribeiro, I. and Götze, U. (2020) 'Sustainable business models – Canvas for sustainability, evaluation method, and their application to additive manufacturing in aircraft maintenance', *Sustainability*, 12: 9130.

Christensen, C. M., Suárez, F. F. and Utterback, J. M. (1998) 'Strategies for survival in fast-changing industries', *Management Science*, 44(12): 207–220.

DeFranco, A. L. and Lattin, T. W. (2006) *Hospitality Financial Management*, Hoboken, NJ: John Wiley.

Dwyer, L. (2012) 'Cost–benefit analysis', in L. Dwyer, A. Gill and N. Seetaram (Eds), *Handbook of Research Methods in Tourism: Quantitative and Qualitative Approaches*, Worcester, UK: Edward Elgar.

Dwyer, L., Jago, L. and Forsyth, P. (2016) 'Economic evaluation of special events: Reconciling economic impact and cost–benefit analysis', *Scandinavian Journal of Hospitality and Tourism*, 16(2): 115–129.

Eden, C. and Ackermann, F. (2013) *Making Strategy: The Journey of Strategic Management*, London: Sage.

Elkington, J. (1997) *Cannibals With Forks – Triple Bottom Line of 21st Century Business*, Stoney Creek, CT: New Society Publishers.

Fleisher, C. S. and Bensoussan, B. E. (2003) *Strategic and Competitive Analysis: Methods and Techniques for Analyzing Business Competition*, Upper Saddle River, NJ: Prentice Hall.

Glaister, K. W. and Falshaw, J. R. (1999) 'Strategic planning: Still going strong?', *Long Range Planning*, 32(1): 107–116.

Glautier, M. W. E., Underdown, B. and Morris, D. (2010) *Accounting Theory and Practice*, 8th ed., Harlow, UK: Perason.

Goel, P. (2010) 'Triple bottom line reporting: An analytical approach for corporate sustainability', *Journal of Finance, Accounting, and Management*, 1(1): 27–42.

Gomezelj, D. O. (2016) 'A systematic review of research on innovation in hospitality and tourism', *International Journal of Contemporary Hospitality Management*, 28(3): 516–558.

Gu, H., Ryan, C. and Yu, L. (2012) 'The changing structure of the Chinese hotel industry: 1980–2012', *Tourism Management Perspectives*, 4: 56–63.

Haberberg, A. and Rieple, A. (2008) *Strategic Management: Theory and Application*, Oxford, UK: Oxford University Press.

Hagen, D. (2021) 'Sustainable event management: New perspectives for the meeting industry through innovation and digitalisation?', in L. Filho, E. V. Krasnov and D. V. Gaeva (Eds), *Innovations and Traditions for Sustainable Development*, Cham, Switzerland: Springer, 259–275.

Hede, A. M. (2007) 'Managing special events in the new era of the triple bottom line', *Event Management*, 11(1–2): 13–22.

Hjalager, A. M. (2002) 'Repairing innovation defectiveness in tourism', *Tourism Management*, 23(5): 465–474.

Hjalager, A. M. (2010) 'A review of innovation research in tourism', *Tourism Management*, 31(1): 1–12.

Horner, D. (2020) *Accounting for Non-Accountants*, 12th ed., London: Kogan Page.

Höse, K., Süß, A. and Götze, U. (2022) 'Sustainability-related strategic evaluation of business models', *Sustainability*, 14: 7285.

'How landing and take-off slots are allocated at congested airports'. (2017) *The Economist*, 4 December.

Kotler, P. (1997) *Marketing Management Analysis, Planning, Implementation, and Control*, 9th ed., Englewood Cliffs, NJ: Prentice Hall.

Laverty, K. J. (1996) 'Economic "short-termism": The debate, the unresolved issues, and the implications for management practice and research', *Academy of Management Review*, 21(3): 825–860.

Lenz, R. T. and Lyles, M. A. (1985) 'Paralysis by analysis: Is your planning system becoming too rational?', *Long Range Planning*, 18(4): 64–72. Reprinted in Asch, D. and Bowman, C. (Eds). (1989) *Readings in Strategic Management*, London: Macmillan.

Live Nation. (2021) *Annual Report*. www.livenationentertainment.com

Lynch, R. (2012) *Corporate Strategy*, 6th ed., Harlow, UK: Pearson.

Lynch, R. (2021) *Corporate Strategy*, 9th ed., Harlow, UK: Pearson.

Ma, H. (2022) 'LNG cruise ship: Top pros and cons', www.cruisehive.com

Marasco, A., De Martino, M., Magnotti, F. and Morvillo, A. (2018) 'Collaborative innovation in tourism and hospitality: A systematic review of the literature', *International Journal of Contemporary Hospitality Management*, 30(6): 2364–2395.

McCarthy, D. (2020) 'MSC Cruises adds two world class vessels, new ship class to expansion plans', www.travelmarketreport.com

McWilliams, A. and Siegel, D. (2001) 'Corporate social responsibility: A theory of the firm perspective', *Academy of Management Review*, 26(1): 117–27.

Mintzberg, H. (2000) *The Rise and Fall of Strategic Planning*, Harlow, UK: Pearson Education.

Mintzberg, H. and Waters, J. A. (1985) 'Of strategies, deliberate and emergent', *Strategic Management Journal*, 6(3): 257–272.

Mules, T. (2000) 'Globalization and the economic impacts of tourism', in B. Faulkner, G. Moscardo and E. Laws (Eds), *Tourism in the 21st Century: Lessons from Experience*, London: Continuum, 312–327.

Mules, T. and Dwyer, L. (2005) 'Public sector support for sport tourism events: The role of cost–benefit analysis', *Sport in Society*, 8(2): 338–355.

Porter, M. E. (1985) *Competitive Advantage*, New York: Free Press.

Prentice, R. and Andersen, V. (2003) 'Festival as creative destination', *Annals of Tourism Research*, 30(1): 7–30.

Rogers, K. and Hudson, B. (2011) 'The triple bottom line: The synergies of transformative perceptions and practices of sustainability', *OD Practitioner*, 4(43): 3–9.

Sandybayev, A. (2016) 'Strategic innovation in tourism. A conceptual and review approach', *International Journal of Research in Tourism and Hospitality*, 2(4): 5–10.

Scholes, K. and Johnson, G. (Eds). (2001) *Exploring Public Sector Strategy*, London: FT.

Scholes, K., Johnson, G. and Ambrosini, V. (1998) *Exploring Techniques of Analysis and Evaluation in Strategic Management*, Harlow, UK: Pearson.

Stoddard, J. E., Pollard, C. E. and Evans, M. R. (2012) 'The triple bottom line: A framework for sustainable tourism development', *International Journal of Hospitality and Tourism Administration*, 13(3): 233–258.

Stonehouse, G. and Pemberton, J. (2002) 'Strategic planning in SMEs – Some empirical findings', *Management Decision*, 40(9): 853–861.

Sundbo, J., Orfila-Sintes, F. and Sørensen, F. (2007) 'The innovative behaviour of tourism firms – Comparative studies of Denmark and Spain', *Research Policy*, 36(1): 88–106.

WCED. (1987) *Our Common Future*, New York: Oxford University Press.

Weinstein, A. and Winston, W. (2016) *Defining Your Market: Winning Strategies for High-Tech, Industrial, and Service Firms*, Abingdon, UK: Routledge.

Whittington, R., Regnér, P., Angwin, D., Johnson, G. and Scholes, K. (2020) *Exploring Strategy*, 12th ed., Harlow, UK: Pearson.

Yeoman, I. and McMahon-Beattie, U. (2005) 'Developing a scenario planning process using a blank piece of paper', *Tourism and Hospitality Research*, 5(3): 273–285.

Young, S. (2016) 'EasyJet founder says would oppose acquisitions after Monarch reports', Reuters, 19 April, www.Reuters.com

Websites

www.airnewzealand.co.nz
www.centreforaviation.com
www.clocate.com
www.corporate.easyjet.com
www.cruisehive.com
www.iata.org
www.kenes-group.com/
www.livenationentertainment.com
www.msccruises.com
www.olympic.org
www.reuters.com
www.travelmarketreport.com

Part 5

Strategy in action

Part 5

Strategic implementation and strategy in practice for tourism, hospitality and events

The previous part of this book was concerned with considering the options available to *THE* organizations for future development, evaluating the options and choosing between these options.

In Part 5 we turn toward putting the chosen strategic options into practice. Once a *THE* organization has selected the most appropriate strategic options, the organization must consider a number of key issues related to actually putting the proposed elements of the strategy into practice.

As ever, the danger can lie in this more detailed level of strategic management. However well thought-out the strategy may be, if sufficient thought is not given to the ways in which it should be *implemented* and appropriate actions that follow, it is unlikely that the strategy will prove to be successful.

Study progress

Part 1	Part 2	Part 3	Part 4	Part 5			
Strategy and the tourism, hospitality and events contexts	Analyzing the internal environment	Analyzing the external environment and SWOT	Strategic options	Strategy in action			
Chapters 1 and 2	Chapters 3, 4, 5 and 6	Chapters 7, 8 and 9	Chapters 10, 11, 12 and 13	**Chapter 14**	**Chapter 15**	**Chapter 16**	**Chapter 17**
				Strategic Implementation for tourism, hospitality and event organizations	**International and global strategies for tourism, hospitality and event organization**	**Sustainability strategy for tourism, hospitality and event organizations**	**Strategic management for tourism, hospitality and event organizations – strategy in practice**

In this stage of the strategic process, the word *implementation* is often used, which perhaps implies that it is a 'one-off' process with the strategy being implemented and then left alone. This is not the case. Strategic management should be viewed as an ongoing process because lessons learned (both successes and failures) from this stage of actioning the strategy can provide useful feedback into the analysis phase.

The external and internal environments of *THE* organizations are constantly changing so that organizations need to continually re-evaluate their environments. Changes in these may require modifications to the chosen strategies and, consequently, revisions to the ways in which they are implemented. Firms must be flexible and responsive but, at the same time, they have to remain focused on the overall aim of the strategies and not be constantly 'blown off course'. This is a delicate balancing act that is difficult to achieve in practice.

In this part of the book, a number of the most important issues connected with putting the strategy into action are considered.

- *Resources* – Implementation requires a reconfiguration of the *THE* organization's resource base. Does the organization have the inputs it needs in terms of finance, people, physical inputs and intellectual assets to carry out the strategy, and how should these resources be configured? If not, how will the resources be obtained (Chapter 14)?

- *Structure and culture* –A *THE* organization will need to bring its structure and culture into such a position that they facilitate a successful outcome. It may be that the structure and culture are not initially supportive for the strategic changes the organization is trying to implement. In such a situation the organization will need to instigate the requisite changes (Chapter 14).

- *Leadership and change* – Implementation of strategy invariably involves change. This will affect employees' roles and responsibilities and may mean redundancies or additional appointments, and external stakeholders such as shareholders will also be implicated. Change can be a difficult managerial challenge requiring strong leaders. Though some may welcome proposed changes, others may resist, thus risking the efficient implementation of the strategy. Different approaches may be adopted by leaders and managers according to the circumstances (Chapter 14).

- *Communication and coordination* – To be successful, all parts of the organization need to be aware of the overall strategy and its implications. It is likely that in most organizations the corporate objectives will be cascaded through the organization so that objectives and operational plans are set for all functional areas and SBUs (Chapter 14).

- *Internationalization* – *THE* represents inherently international sectors of industry, with consumers crossing international borders and usually relatively low barriers, preventing international growth for companies. In such circumstances, it is important to consider the approach of organizations to internationalization. International strategy is considered in Chapter 15.

- *Sustainability* – Chapter 13 includes a discussion of the issues related to sustainability. The issues are complex, and many views are expressed in the vast THE literature related to the topic. It is vital that THE organizations and destinations consider these issues, but if they are to have any relevance, a considered and appropriate strategy must be implemented. Sustainability strategy is considered in Chapter 16.

At the end of a book on strategic management for tourism, hospitality and events, it is apposite to stand back and consider a summary of the subject matter that the book has considered and to briefly consider the changing nature of the subject. Thus, the book concludes in Chapter 17 with a brief overview of the challenges that managers in THE contexts face and the strategic management approaches that managers might consider.

Finally, having studied the subject matter and its complexities and designed a strategy, we are left with the problems of how the strategy should be presented in such a way that it:

- Is clear
- Is convincing
- Can easily be communicated to internal and external stakeholders

Consequently, the practical issues of how the strategy can be presented are dealt with in the final chapter (Chapter 17).

Chapter **14**

Strategic implementation for tourism, hospitality and event organizations

Introduction and chapter overview

Strategic implementation is concerned with the issues considered necessary for the successful execution of strategy. In other words, this is 'strategy in action'.

In a prescriptive strategic process, strategic implementation would be carried out only after an organization has gathered sufficient information on its internal and external environments (the purpose of strategic analysis). After it has undertaken the process of choosing strategic options through the formulation of strategic options, evaluation of these options is followed by choosing the most appropriate options (see Chapter 13). Implementing strategy always requires making changes, sometimes relatively minor but often quite radical in nature. Hence, the implementation of strategy is closely associated with 'managing change'.

This chapter will discuss the difficulties of the strategic implementation phase, as identified in the literature, before going on to consider key areas that managers of strategic change need to consider. Throughout this text, we have emphasized that managing strategically in *THE* is somewhat different to other industrial sectors because of its defining characteristics. This applies to implementation as much as to the other aspects of strategy. Consequently, this chapter specifies the issues raised by these characteristics and suggests various actions managers might take in response. Finally, a tool to coordinate, manage and measure strategic implementation (the 'balanced scorecard', or BSC) is considered.

DOI: 10.4324/9781003318613-19

To successfully carry out a strategy, an organization must consider several key areas. The organization must consider how the strategy will:

- Be resourced
- Impact the culture, structure and internal systems of the organization
- Necessitate change and the leadership and management implications of making the changes
- Be communicated to staff and translated for all parts of the organization

This chapter discusses each of these matters in turn. Throughout this text it has been emphasized that strategy (whether in its prescriptive or emergent forms) should *not* be viewed as a one-off exercise but instead as a continual process. As part of this process, it has also been emphasized that feedback is required on how successful the strategy is so that it can be modified if necessary.

This raises the question: how do you know whether the strategy is successful or not? The strategic implementation phase of strategy is often closely linked with measuring organizational success. Thus, organizations have ways of understanding to what degree the strategic measures they are implementing are successful or not.

Various tools and techniques have been developed to help managers to:

- Implement strategy in a consistent manner across their organizations
- Measure organizational success
- Provide feedback and tracking to inform any amendments to the strategy that may be required

The best known of these tools is the BSC (which will be considered toward the end of the chapter), as a way of integrating and coordinating the strategic implementation process.

LEARNING OBJECTIVES

After studying this chapter, you should be able to:

- Describe where implementation fits into the strategic process
- Understand how the characteristics of *THE* might have an impact on the implementation process
- Explain the role of resource planning in strategic implementation
- Explain how and why corporate culture plays an important part in implementation
- Understand the link between structure and strategy
- Evaluate the essentials of change management
- Assess the management and leadership styles necessary to implement changes
- Understand how resource, cultural, structural and change management issues might be managed in *THE* contexts
- Explain the use of the BSC as a tool to be used in strategic implementation
- Provide examples of implementation issues being addressed in *THE* contexts

14.1 Implementation and the strategic process

Implementation is the process of putting chosen strategic options into action.

DEFINITION/QUOTATION

Strategic implementation

> Implementation is the system-wide action taken by firm members aimed at accomplishing formulated strategies.
>
> (Hahn and Powers, 2010)

Implementation is important to firm performance because strategies do not add value unless they are properly implemented, but it is often the aspect of strategy that tends to receive the least attention. Chebat (1999) suggested that implementation receives scant attention in the literature for two reasons. First, it is mechanistic and mundane when compared to strategy formulation and choice and, second, it is difficult to evaluate the process and generalize findings because they are usually context specific.

Most people intuitively understand that a lot of information is required before any big decision can be made.

> **For example:** *Consumers would not normally spend on most THE products – say, a holiday, hotel booking or attendance at a festival (all relatively expensive purchases) – without investigating the attractions of the destination, hotel or event and finding out something about the company providing the service before purchasing. Buying a low-value item – say, a pencil – would not warrant such analysis, because it represents a small proportion of the buyer's income.*

In the same way, an organization would be risking a great deal if it were to pursue a strategic option without first carrying out a detailed analysis of its internal and external environments.

Put simply, successful strategy choice and implementation rely on the presupposition that the organization has carried out a meaningful strategic analysis and is consequently aware of its internal strengths and weaknesses and external opportunities and threats.

It is not surprising perhaps, because it is geared more toward 'action' and less conceptual in nature, that the implementation phase of strategy has received relatively less academic attention than the analysis and formulation phases (Chebat, 1999; Kaplan and Norton, 2001; Evans, 2005; Hahn and Powers, 2010; Greer et al., 2017). Other authors have made important contributions by pointing to the difficulties inherent in the implementation phase (Epstein and Manzoni, 1998) or by calling for a reassessment of the difficulties inherent in the process (Lorange, 1998; Greer et al., 2017).

However, the fact that successful implementation is key to successful strategy has long been recognized. Several authors (see, for example, Ghoshal and Bartlett, 1987; D. Miller, 2001) pointed to the lack of successful strategic implementation as an issue affecting many businesses. S. Miller et al. (2004:202) referred to the 'implementation gap', arguing that 'organizations are slower to change and more difficult and expensive to develop than strategies are to prepare'.

Given its importance in the successful delivery of outcomes, the strategic implementation phase has attracted more attention in recent years; see, for example, Okumus (2003), Evans (2005), Hahn and Powers (2010) and Hitt et al. (2017).

14.2 Aspects of strategic implementation

To successfully put into practice (implement) a strategy, an organization will need to consider four aspects:

1. ***Resources*** – *How should the strategy be resourced?* This relates to the way in which the organization will obtain the requisite finance, human and physical resources (such as equipment and buildings) and intellectual or 'intangible' resources. All parts of the organization need to be aligned so that all parts are working toward a common vision, aim and objectives. In doing so, detailed decisions about obtaining and utilizing resources have to be made to ensure that resources are used effectively and waste and duplication are avoided.

2. ***Configuration*** – *How should the culture and structure of the organization be configured to 'fit' the proposed strategy?* Because all parts of the organization need to contribute to successful implementation, it is necessary for the structure of the organization and the organizational culture to be fit for purpose so that there are no impediments to success. This is not always the case, and in many cases the structure has to be amended and the culture changed so that there is a so-called strategic fit.

3. ***Change*** – *How should the changes arising from the strategy should be managed and led?* Implementing strategy invariably involves changes to aspects of the organization and how it positions itself. To successfully implement change, managers need to consider what type of change is envisaged and how it might be managed and led.

   Thus, strategic implementation is involved with making detailed decisions regarding three key aspects of strategy relating to resources, configuration and change.

   When these decisions have been made, it is vital (because all parts of the organization need to be aligned for successful implementation) that a fourth issue be considered. This relates to the dissemination and coordination of the strategy.

4. ***Dissemination and coordination*** – *How should the strategy be communicated and put into action?* Some research suggests that many strategies are well conceived but poorly executed. In his book, which focuses on communicating strategy, Jones (2008) reported that less than 10% of employees actually understand their firm's strategy.

   This aspect of strategy involves:

- Communicating the strategy effectively
- Coordinating the implementation of the strategy
- Measuring the success of the strategy so that modifications can be made if necessary

Thus, there is a major managerial task in terms of effectively organizing the strategic implementation task. In this chapter, we will consider one widely adopted means of managing this process: the BSC.

Figure 14.1 indicates how the implementation of strategy relates to the other major components of strategy: strategic analysis and strategic choice (formulation, evaluation and selection).

14.3 Implementation – resources

The successful management of a strategy is likely to depend on the management of many resource areas. In the same way that people and animals need the inputs of air, food, warmth, etc., also organizations need inputs to function normally. Economics textbooks refer to these inputs as the *factors of production.*

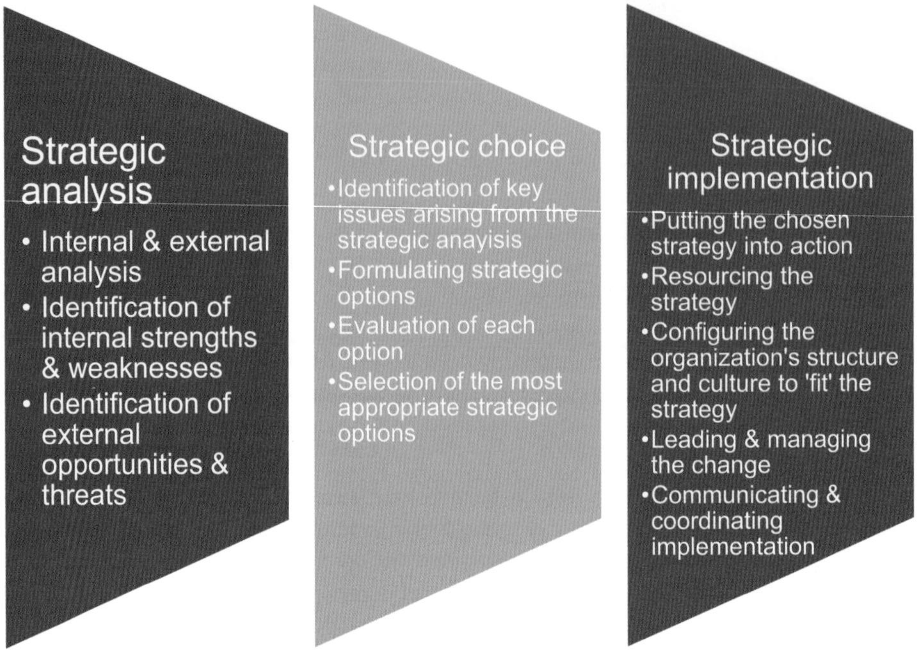

Figure 14.1 The linear rational (prescriptive) strategic process

They fall into four broad categories:

1. *Physical and operational resources* (land, buildings, plants, equipment, etc.)
2. *Financial resources* (share and loan capital required for development and expansion)
3. *Human resources* (the requisite number of appropriately skilled employees)
4. *Intellectual* or *intangible resources* (nonphysical inputs that may be necessary in some industries such as databases, legal permissions, brand or design registration, contacts, etc.; see R. Hall, 1992; Pearson et al., 2015)

In most instances, *THE* organizations must obtain resource inputs in competitive markets. Even in instances where *THE* organizations are in public control, they have to compete for resources with other publicly funded activities such as education and health or with other ways in which the services might be provided; for example, outsourcing. This means that they must also compete with other organizations for the best people, the cheapest finance, the best locations for development, etc.

> For example: *A retail travel agent setting up a new branch will want to ensure that they occupy a site that has a large number of people passing the shop window (or 'footfall', as retailers often refer to it). Other retailers may also want to gain access to such a site, so the travel agent may have to compete for this scarce resource, thus bidding up the price. At some point the price (in the form of rent) may become too great in relation to the expected revenues, so decisions have to made regarding how much can be afforded.*

Thus, all of these inputs have a cost attached to them, so careful planning for resource requirement is usually a key calculation in strategic implementation.

14.3.1 *Matching strategy with resources*

Once a strategic option has been chosen, management attention turns to assessing the resource implications of the strategy. The extent to which the resource base needs to be adjusted will, of course, depend on the degree of change the proposed strategy entails.

Broadly speaking, resource planning falls into three categories:

- Some strategies, particularly those that are not particularly ambitious, require *few changes* in the resource base. They may require, for example, a slight increase in financing to fund modest expansion or the recruitment or retraining of some human resources to meet a skill shortage in one or two areas. Conversely, of course, strategy may require the disposal of some assets or a slight reduction in the human resource base.

- Some strategies require an *increase* in the resource base to facilitate a more substantial program of growth. This usually entails two things: an internal reallocation of resources and purchasing fresh resource inputs from external suppliers. Internal reallocation entails reducing resource deployment in one area of the organization and moving it to where it is needed, say, by redeploying human resources or by selling some non-core activities to reinvest the money in the area of growth. New resources (from outside the organization) are obtained through the usual channels – from the job market, the real estate market, financial markets and so on.

- Thirdly, some strategies involve a *reduction* in the resource base to successfully manage decline. If after a resource audit an organization finds that it has too many resources (say, too many employees, too many aircraft, too many hotel properties in the wrong locations, etc.), measures will be put in place to carry out some reduction. Excess capital or physical resources can often be successfully reinvested in business areas that are in more buoyant markets, and excess human resources usually require layoffs.

To successfully implement the chosen strategic options, the resources available need to be carefully assessed through a process such as a *resource audit* (though this might have been carried out as part of the strategic analysis stage). The implementation stage allows for the information to be 'tested' in detail with regards to the chosen option specifically rather than all available options.

An audit process can be used to make assessments of any or all of the resource inputs. In Chapter 4 we discussed in some depth the human resource audit, but the same procedures can be employed to audit financial, physical or intellectual resources.

The nature of an audit of any kind (including resource audits) is for the purpose of checking or testing. Resources are audited (or purposefully checked) for:

- *Sufficiency* – is there enough for the purpose?
- *Adequacy* – is the condition, location, state or quality of the resources adequate for the purpose?
- *Availability* – are the required resources available at the time, desired price and quantities required?

> For example: *An audit of a hotel group's chain of hotels (an example of physical resources) might take the form of assessing whether the number of rooms is sufficient for current needs and any planned expansion. This might be followed by an evaluation of its adequacy – the location of the hotels relative to customers and those of competitors, the state of repair and decoration of the hotels and the ability of the hotels to support the prevailing business (leisure, business, conferences, etc.). Finally, if more resources are required or if development of the land or buildings is needed, availability is examined, of either additional property or land for development.*

THINK POINTS

- Explain where implementation fits into the strategic process.

- Explain the major features of a resource audit.

- What key considerations might managers in *THE* contexts need to consider in the implementation phase of strategy?

The Short Case Illustration below shows the approach outlined above extended to all resource categories for a hotel chain and suggests the use of a 'traffic light' approach that highlights those aspects requiring particular managerial attention.

14.1 SHORT CASE ILLUSTRATION

Resource audit for a hotel group planning growth in East Asia

As part of its strategy, a (hypothetical) hotel group may decide that it wants to expand into the fast-growth market of East Asia. A resource audit will help establish the extent to which resources are likely to be in place to support the strategy.

An audit of the hotel group's chain of hotels in East Asia (an example of physical resources) might take the form of:

- Assessing whether the number of rooms is *sufficient* for current needs and any planned expansion

- Evaluating its *adequacy* – the location of the hotels relative to customers and those of competitors; the state of repair and decoration of the hotels and the ability of the hotels to support the prevailing business (leisure, business, conferences, etc.)

- Examining *availability*, either of additional property or of permissions for development, if more resources are required or if development of the land or buildings is needed

Table 14.1 shows a full resource audit, where all of the resource categories are assessed according to the sufficiency, adequacy, and availability criteria. The table uses a traffic light coding system in which:

- Green meets the criteria

- Amber partly meets the criteria

- Red does not meet the criteria at present

The traffic light coding allows significant resourcing issues to be highlighted to allow easy communication to both internal and external stakeholders. Thus, in this case, the sufficiency of physical resources, adequacy of human resources and availability of financial resources appear to be key resourcing issues to be addressed.

Table 14.1 Resource audit

Resource category	Resource sufficiency	Resource adequacy	Resource availability
Physical resources	Additional hotels need to be built, acquired or managed in the specified region to meet the strategic objective that has been set	Hotels already in the group are adequate and performing well but require some updating in parts	Resources are being built by property developers throughout the region so that resources are available
Financial resources	A large amount of finance is supporting the rapid growth in these markets	Adequate finance is available from a range of sources including banks equity markets and government agencies at internationally competitive rates	Though hotels are being developed by property developers, there is strong competition among international hotel groups to manage, own or lease these properties. Great care must be taken to select strong assets in good locations and not to overpay for them
Human resources	There are many people who are seeking hotel careers	Though there are some skilled employees being trained by colleges and hotel groups, there is a major training requirement to provide employees with adequate skill levels and cultural awareness of the company	Employees are available at reasonable cost but there are some minor timing issues involved in bringing them into the group
Intangible resources	The hotel group has strong brand recognition and established support systems	There is some need to adapt the brand and systems for local conditions	The brand and systems should be available when the other resources have been acquired or developed

Questions

1. Explain why a resource audit is useful to the organization in this case illustration.

2. Why might a 'traffic light' approach to presentation be useful in considering an organization's resources?

14.3.2 Developing and controlling resources

To meet the resource requirements of a proposed strategy, resources are developed and then controlled to ensure that they meet the needs of the strategy.

FINANCIAL PLANNING

Financial planning takes the form of financing the proposed strategy (see Chapter 5 for a more detailed discussion of these issues). *Capital budgeting* concerns projecting the capital needs of a strategy. This is usually a relatively straightforward operation because costs can normally be forecast with some accuracy. Once the capital requirements are known, a plan is put in place to finance any shortfall. Whereas some strategies can be financed from retained profits (depending on how much retained profit the company has), others are financed from external sources such as share (rights) issues, debt capital or the issuing of corporate bonds or debentures. The pros and cons of these approaches to financing are discussed in Chapter 5.

HUMAN RESOURCE PLANNING

Human resource planning (see Chapter 4) involves projecting the human capital required for the successful implementation of the proposed strategy. It would typically take the form of forecasts of both the *number* of people required and the types of *skills and abilities* that will be in demand. If a shortfall in either of these is identified, the 'gap' will be filled by one or more of the following.

- Training, retraining or staff development – to close the skills gap by developing existing employees
- Appointing new employees – entering the labor market and competing with other employers for the requisite number of appropriately skilled employees

PHYSICAL RESOURCE PLANNING

Physical resource planning is slightly more complex than financial and human resource planning, because so many inputs fall into this category. We include in this category land, buildings, location, plants and equipment.

Some physical resources are more easily obtained than others. Most equipment is relatively easily obtained unless the requirement is very specialized. However, careful planning may be necessary because some equipment requires long lead times for construction.

> For example: *A cruise line or an airline seeking to update its fleet with new ships or aircraft would need to plan a number of years in advance to secure delivery on a particular date.*

Obtaining a particular location, land and buildings can be problematic. Businesses that have requirements for key locations and buildings of particular specifications expose themselves to the possibility of having to settle for second best if they are unable to effectively compete in these particular resource markets.

Some sectors of THE exemplify this competition for physical resources. The location of a retail travel outlet, a hotel, a visitor attraction or a festival will often be a key determinant in the success of the business. Successfully competing for prime locations will consequently be of paramount importance, especially when these locations are in short supply.

> For example: *Over the last 200 years, Hong Kong has developed into a world-class business location, but land is a precious commodity because it has a comparatively small land area. This Special Administrative Region of China has developed predominantly on Hong Kong island,*

where the central business district is located, and across the harbor in Kowloon on the Chinese mainland. On the island, especially in the central business district, the lack of suitable sites and the costs of development have forced most hotels to seek other locations. Banks and other financial institutions have been willing to pay very high prices for prime sites and, consequently, many of the new hotel developments have taken place in Kowloon, where development sites are more plentiful and where land costs (though still relatively high) are lower by comparison. Similarly, when Hong Kong Disneyland Resort (Disney's fifth resort and its second in Asia) opened in 2005, it did so on the outlying island of Lantau, where Hong Kong's international airport, Chek Lap Kok, was also developed. By doing so, the resort was able to obtain large amounts of land at moderate prices as well as gain the advantages of rapid access to the city and adjacent international airport.

INTELLECTUAL RESOURCE PLANNING

Intellectual resources – inputs that cannot be seen and touched – can be the most important resource inputs of all (see Chapter 1). Some proposed strategies require legal or regulatory permission, a database (say, of key customers in a certain market segment) or experience of dealing with certain markets.

14.4 Implementation – configuration of culture and structure

14.4.1 *Cultural suitability*

The concept of organizational culture was discussed in Chapter 4. Strategic implementation usually involves making an assessment of the suitability of a culture to undertake the strategy. In the context of implementation, culture is usually analyzed for its suitability. If we consider human personalities, we can readily appreciate that not all personalities are equally suitable for all jobs or tasks.

Some people, for example, are ready to embrace a new challenge and take to change with vigor and excitement. They enjoy bungee jumping and parachute jumps. Other people would prefer things not to change. They are conservative in nature and would be likely to turn down the opportunity to engage in risky sports. These two personality types highlight the suitability contrasts that can exist.

In Chapter 4 we encountered three typologies of corporate culture. Handy (2007) identified four types of culture – power, role, task and person – and Hofstede's cultural dimensions theory (1980) focused on international differences in relation to culture. Miles and Snow (1978) also identified four culture types by their reaction tendency, and this is probably the more useful typology in this context.

14.4.2 *Miles and Snow's typology and cultural postures*

Miles and Snow's (1978) typology (discussed in Chapter 4) divides culture types according to how they approach strategy. These distinctions are important because they tell us how each culture type will react to different strategic options.

Miles and Snow identified four categories of organizational culture:

- *Defender* cultures are suitable for organizations that exist in relatively well-defined market areas and where improving the position in existing markets is the most appropriate strategic option (e.g., market penetration). In this culture, it would be uncomfortable to develop new markets or diversification.
- *Prospector* cultures, in contrast to defenders, are continually seeking out new product and market opportunities. Accordingly, they often create change and uncertainty.

- *Analyzer* cultures exhibit features of both defenders and prospectors. They are a type of culture that is able to accommodate both stability (which defenders like) and instability (which prospectors have learned to adjust to).

- *Reactor* cultures can sometimes lack strategic focus and are consequently sometimes accused of being 'blown around' by changes in their environments. This type of culture is not innovative and tends to emulate the successes of competitors.

It is evident that the ability of cultures to undertake different strategic courses of action varies. It is likely, for example, that defender cultures and those like them would be less able to undertake a program of radical change than, say, those that exhibit prospector characteristics.

Cultural differences between *what is* and *what is required* for a strategy are one of the most important aspects of strategic implementation. Incongruities between the two present a challenge to management in respect of either changing the culture or compromising on strategic objectives such that cultural change is required to a lesser extent. We will return to the nature of change – including cultural change – later in this chapter.

14.4.3 Organizational structure

Organizational structure refers to the 'shape' of the organization.

There is no such thing as 'the perfect structure' for an organization, because compromises have to be made in their design and often are the result of ad hoc growth where parts are added over time rather than planned from the outset. For a more detailed discussion of various structural types and their relative advantages and disadvantages, see, for example, Lynch (2021:ch. 12).

However, what we are interested in is not the study of organizational structure in itself (interesting though this may be) but how it relates to the successful implementation of strategy.

In this context, it is necessary to consider whether the proposed structure will help the organization achieve the objectives that have been set as part of its strategy. In this regard, key issues include the following:

- How easy is it to change the structure when circumstances change?

- How efficient is the structure in ensuring that key information and decisions are disseminated appropriately?

- To what degree does the formal organization chart represent the way in which decision making really takes place?

KEY CONCEPT

Structure follows strategy?

In the strategic management literature, a major debate, summarized by Galan and Sanchez-Bueno (2009), has taken place over many years regarding the relationship between the strategy and structure of organizations.

Based on studies of American companies, US economic historian Alfred Chandler (1962) argued that the structure is subordinate to and therefore should follow the formulation of strategy. To D. J. Hall and Saias (1980), however, the strategic opportunities available to an organization are partly the result of its existing organizational structure so that in some cases the strategy follows on from the structure.

In a widely quoted article, Henry Mintzberg (1990:183) concluded that neither structure nor strategy takes precedence and that *both* should be considered as part of an integrated system:

> . . . structure follows strategy as the left foot follows the right in walking. In effect, strategy and structure both support the organization. None takes precedence; each always precedes the other, and follows it, except when they move together, as the organization jumps to a new position. Strategy formation is an integrated system, not an arbitrary sequence.

The main issues in designing an organizational structure are:

- Division of labor – who does what?
- Source of authority – who has the right to tell others what to do?
- Relationships – how does the structure fit together?

In attempting to resolve the key design issues, organizational structures tend to be described in terms of their:

- Height
- Width
- Complexity

In designing the structure of an organization, these three issues are taken into account in a fourth design issue concerned with devising a method of division.

14.4.4 The 'height' of structures

Height refers to the number of layers that exist within the structure. It is perhaps intuitively obvious that larger organizations are higher than smaller ones. The guide to how high an organizational structure depends on the complexity of the tasks that a proposed strategy entails.

> For example: *Contrast a small events management company with a diversified international travel group. The small company involved in organizing and managing events is competing in one location with an easily identified number of competitors and a single set of product types. Customers probably value the direct communication with the decision makers in the company, which is due to the lack of layers within the company.*
>
> *This scenario is much less complex than a multinational, vertically and horizontally integrated travel company that competes in many national markets, in several product types and with a high dependence on innovation. In such circumstances, there are likely to be a greater number of layers to the organization to facilitate its complex processes. Customers are likely to purchase the products on the basis of their attributes and are unconcerned about the internal structure of the organization they are dealing with.*

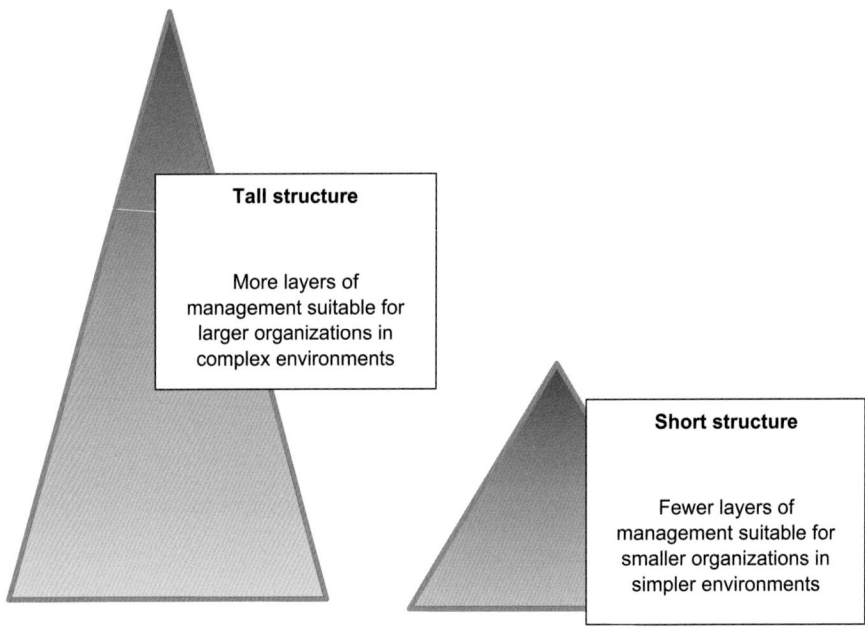

Figure 14.2 The height of organizations

Essentially, height facilitates the engagement of specialist managers in the middle of an organization who can oversee and direct the many activities that some larger organizations are involved in. Not all organizations have this requirement, and it would be more appropriate for such organizations to have a flatter structure (see Figure 14.2).

The trend in recent years has been for organizations to become flatter, because technology can provide information directly from the point of sale to the highest levels. Similarly, technology permits communications from the highest level of the company to be quickly and widely disseminated among all staff at every level. This process is often known as *delayering* and facilitates quicker decision making and faster communications between managers and operational employees who have to implement the decisions.

KEY CONCEPT

Tall and short structures

Tall structures, involving more layers of specialist managers, enable the organization to coordinate a wider range of activities across different product and market sectors. It is more difficult for senior management to control and is obviously more expensive in terms of management overhead.

Shorter structures involve few management layers and are suitable for smaller organizations that are engaged in few products or market structures. They are cheaper to operate and facilitate a greater degree of senior management control.

14.4.5 The 'width' of structures

The 'width' of organizational structures refers to the extent to which the organization is centralized or decentralized.

A decentralized organizational structure is one in which the center elects to devolve some degree of decision-making power to other parts of the organization. A centralized organization is one in which little or no power is devolved from the center. In practice, a continuum exists between the two extremes along which the varying extents of decentralization can be visualized (see Figure 14.3).

As with the height of structures, there is a trade-off between the costs and benefits of width. The advantages of centralization are mainly concerned with the ability of the center to maintain tighter direct control over the activities of the organization. This is usually more appropriate when the organization is smaller and engages in few product or market segments. Some degree of decentralization is advantageous when the organization operates in a number of markets and local specialized knowledge is an important determinant of overall success.

The principal advantages of centralization and decentralization are summarized in Table 14.2.

14.4.6 Complexity of structure

The complexity of structure is usually taken to mean the extent to which the organization observes a formal hierarchy in its reporting relationships. Strict hierarchy is not always an appropriate form of organization, especially when it cannot be automatically assumed that seniority guarantees superior management skill.

In some contexts, formal hierarchy is entirely appropriate in implementing strategy. In others, however, allowing employees to act with some degree of independence can enable the organization

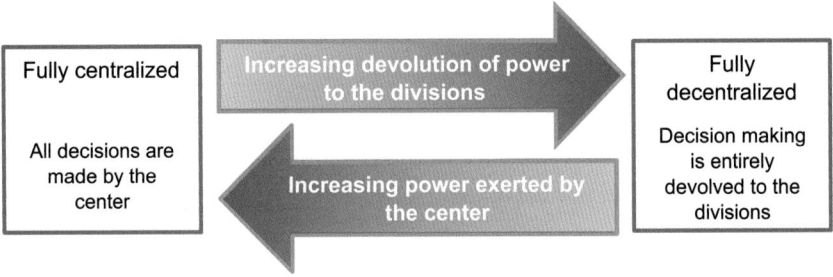

Figure 14.3 The centralization–decentralization continuum

Table 14.2 The advantages of centralization and decentralization

Advantages of centralization	Advantages of decentralization
• Managers at the center maintain tight control	Can engage in a wider range of activities
• Avoids problems of complex structures	Enables increased specialization
• Communications are quicker and cheaper	Can reduce time taken to make key decisions
• Delegation risks are avoided	Can develop and improve the skills of managers

to be more efficient. The use of matrix structures (discussed later in the chapter), for example, can result in the organization being able to carry out many more tasks than a formal hierarchical structure. Many companies go some way in this regard by seconding employees into special task forces or cross-functional teams that are not part of the hierarchical structure and that act semi-independently in pursuit of its brief.

The matrix structure is quite common in larger companies where there is likely to be greater complexity. By way of contrast, some organizations operate with little or even no formal structure. Many smaller companies operate in such a way in the belief that structures are not necessary and can impede creativity, innovation and teamwork.

> For example: *The events management sector is highly fragmented, with a large number of very small localized companies operating and low barriers to entry (and exit). Some may have just a sole proprietor or members of a single family carrying out all tasks or have a few full-time employees, with a larger number of part-time workers brought in to staff the event. In such circumstances, it is unlikely that there will be a formal structure, and informality allows all attention to be focused on achieving the task at hand.*

In this chapter, we have discussed culture and structure separately, because they are in themselves complex organizational issues with a great deal of academic literature devoted to each.

However, they can also be viewed as being intrinsically linked because the organizational structure that is adopted will have important implications for the culture the organization wants to encourage, and, likewise, if a particular culture is present that the organization wants to facilitate, this implies that a certain structural form will be favored by the organization.

The close links between structure and culture are illustrated by the Short Case Illustration of easyJet below.

14.2 SHORT CASE ILLUSTRATION

Linkages between culture and structure: easyJet

Many *THE* companies explicitly feature their organizational culture in promotional materials to:

- Attract new employees with appropriate skills and attitude
- Motivate and inform existing employees
- Promote a positive image of the organization to external stakeholders

The low-cost airline easyJet is one such company that promotes its company culture strongly. It also illustrates the strong linkages between culture and structure. The company stresses its informality, dress code and office layout, but as the quotation below demonstrates, a key part of the organizational culture at easyJet relates to the structure it adopts.

The following is a direct extract from the company's website:

> We don't believe in hierarchy or unnecessary layers of management. We do believe in giving our team a human touch that people can benefit from right across the organization. It encourages a 'one team' approach. And a strong sense of pulling in the same direction. It helps us all to keep on upping our game, whether that's coming up with better ideas or solving more and more complex problems.

Source: www.easyjet.com

Questions

1. Explain the main features of the easyJet culture and consider why these features might have been adopted.

2. Consider what difficulties easyJet might encounter in relation to culture and structure as it continues to grow.

14.4.7 *Methods of divisionalization*

The fourth and final way of understanding how structure fits into strategic implementation is by considering how the parts of the organization are to be divided.

As with all other matters to be considered in structure, the method of division is entirely dependent on the context of the company and its strategic position. It is a case of establishing the most appropriate divisional structure to meet the objectives of the proposed strategy.

Divisions are based on grouping people with a shared specialism. By acting together within their specialism, synergies can be obtained both with and between divisions. In divisionalizing an organization, the three previous factors (height, width and complexity) are underlying determinants that are taken into account.

There are five common methods of divisionalization. A company or group of companies can be divisionalized by:

- *Functional* specialism – typically, operations, human resource management (HRM), marketing, finance, etc.
- *Geographic* concentration – where divisions are regionally located and have specialized knowledge of local market conditions
- *Product* specialism – where divisions, usually within multiproduct companies, have detailed knowledge of their particular product area
- *Customer* focus – where the company orientates itself by divisions dedicated to serving particular customer types; for example, retail customers, industrial customers, etc.
- *Holding company* – where a company owns various individual businesses and the holding company acts as an investment company overseeing its investments in individual businesses, which can be wholly or partly owned but where the individual companies run largely autonomously

In many cases, a 'hybrid' approach to divisionalization might be appropriate.

> **For example:** *A (hypothetical) vertically integrated travel company that provides tour operations, has an airline and operates in online and physical travel retailing with sales in the UK, Western Europe and North America might have a hybrid divisional structure. Such a structure might have geographical, product and functional elements as shown in Figure 14.4. Each geographical region might have three product areas, each with their own functional divisions.*

A final common way of structuring an organization is the so-called matrix structure. Such a structure combines two forms of organization such as functional and geographic, as shown in Figure 14.5. In such an organization, there are dual lines of authority for employees – one vertical and the other horizontal.

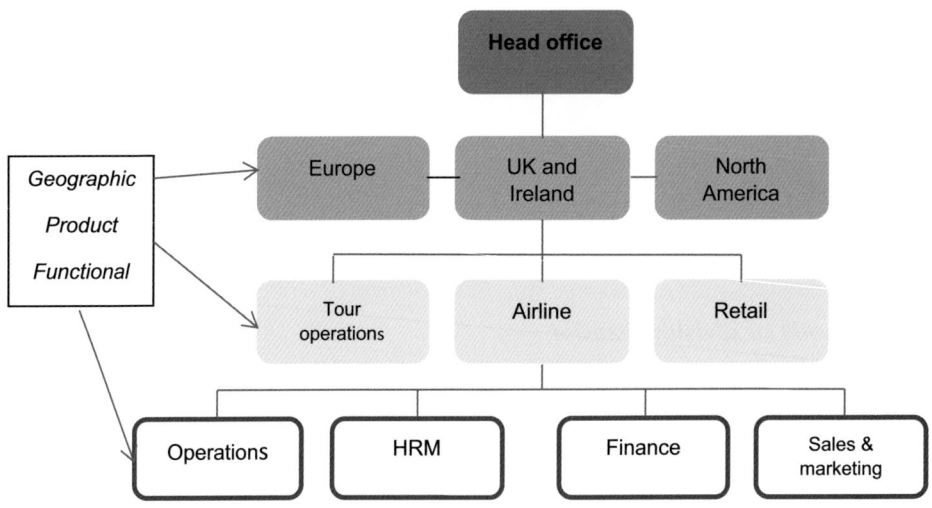

Figure 14.4 An example of a 'hybrid' divisional structure for a vertically integrated travel company

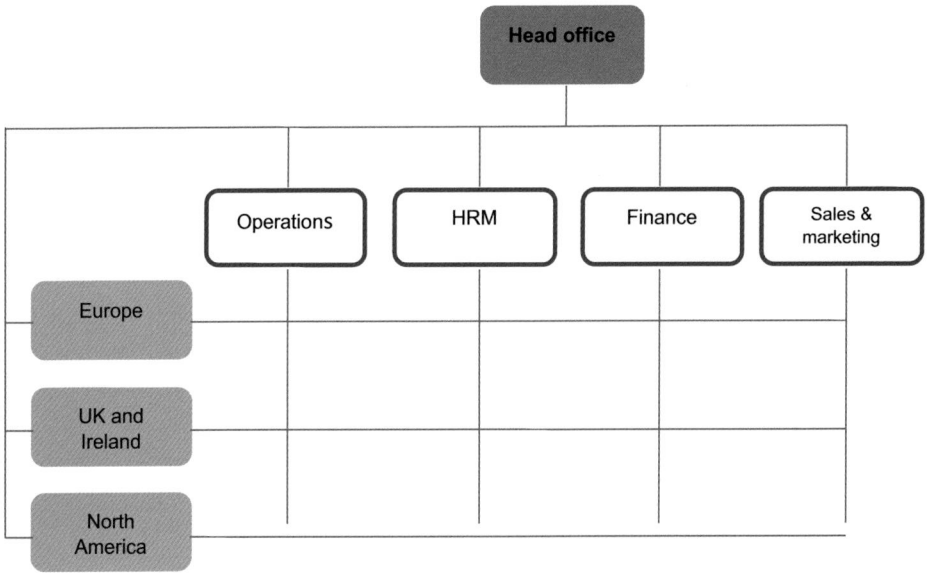

Figure 14.5 An example of a matrix organizational structure for an international travel company

For example: *In relation to HRM (as an example), the organization may have an HRM manager in each of its regions (Europe, UK and Ireland and North America). The managers will report (horizontally) to the director for these geographical regions, who will be responsible for all activities in the region, but they will also be responsible (vertically) to the HRM director, who will be responsible for all HRM activities across the company. Thus, the geographical director coordinates a team responsible for all activities in the region, whereas the functional directors will coordinate all activities related to their specialisms across the company.*

The advantages of such a structure are that it is likely to focus attention on key tasks and is adaptable. It also encourages teamwork. However, it is complex and can produce tensions between the different lines of reporting (vertical and horizontal). Many larger *THE* organizations, such as international hotel chains, travel companies and airlines, have versions of a matrix structure.

An organization is given definition and 'shape' by the formal structure it adopts, because this orders the various tasks and relationships so that they are directed toward fulfillment of the organization's objectives.

THINK POINTS

- Explain the advantages of centralization and decentralization in *THE* contexts.
- In *THE* contexts, why might a strict hierarchy not always be the most suitable structural arrangement?
- What are the five major methods of divisionalization?
- Explain the usefulness of Miles and Snow's typology to culture and implementation.

However, it is important to recognize that whatever structure is adopted, in all organizations there co-exists a pattern of informal relationships, communication and authority, which is often termed the 'informal organization'. Each part of the organization, social group, working team or group of specialists may have its own subculture, customs, norms, authority structure and goals.

The informal organization may operate for or against the interests of the formal organization. Many organizations recognize and sometimes encourage the informal organization as a way of increasing productivity and teamwork. The informal organization can usefully:

- Improve communication by means of 'the grapevine'
- Coordinate the activities of individuals and groups
- Establish unwritten but practical ways of doing things
- Provide ideas and enhancements

Conversely, the informal organization may absorb energy and time on unproductive activities.

In some *THE* contexts, this informal organization extends to a consideration of who is in charge; that is, who is the boss? Though the organizational structure as shown in the organization chart may make it clear, the reality as indicated in the Key Concept that follows might be somewhat different, and organizational leaders must strive to communicate effectively with key groups of staff.

KEY CONCEPT

Who is the boss in *THE* contexts?

The structures discussed in this section of the book appear to make it clear who 'the boss' is. It is normally the CEO based at the organization's head office, who is responsible to the board of directors.

However, there are some circumstances in *THE* where this might not be so evident. The role of specialists is important in many businesses, but in many aspects of *THE*, specialists are crucial to the successful ongoing operation of the business, and there are important managerial implications that arise from this.

Take, for example, the pilot of an aircraft, the captain of a cruise ship, the stage manager at a concert or theatrical performance or the head chef in the kitchen of a major hotel. In all of these examples, the people involved may not figure prominently in the organization chart depicting the structure of a particular organization, because there may be many pilots, captains, stage managers, chefs, etc. However, all have highly specialized skills that are crucial in service delivery. The pilot and the ship's captain, for example, are legally responsible for the safety of their aircraft or ship and thus these roles are not responsible for boosting company profitability.

Consequently, when the CEO walks onto a plane or a ship, into the concert venue or the hotel kitchen, he or she could legitimately be told (by the pilot, captain, chef, manager, etc.), in recognition of their specialist skills and responsibilities: 'Outside you are "the boss" – but here I am in charge.'

The implication of this apparent inversion of authority is that many organizations will have some key members of staff who are crucial in implementing the strategy successfully. The staff may have specialist knowledge or particular responsibilities (that determine their priorities), and implementing the strategy may not be their utmost priority. They might support the strategy but could also attempt to block it or ignore it.

Hence, it is important for senior managers to identify these individuals or groups and communicate with them appropriately to gather support for the changes that are required. This, of course, is not always easy and is not always successful. It is an aspect of *management of change* (discussed in the next section).

14.5 Implementation – managing and leading change

At its simplest, strategy is all about change. In this chapter, we have discussed the importance of an organization's resource base, its culture and its structure. To bring about strategic repositioning (e.g., in respect to products and markets), all of these may need to be changed.

Change can take different forms in different circumstances. For example, it can be viewed in four dimensions as follows:

- Continuous or discontinuous
- Incremental or transformational
- Proactive or reactive
- Broad or narrow in its scope

Different organizations exhibit differing attitudes toward change. We can draw a parallel here with different types of people. Some people are very conservative and configure their lives to minimize change. Such people will generally fear change and will resist it. Other people get bored easily and are always looking for new challenges, new jobs and so on. Organizations reflect this spectrum of attitudes. It is here that we encounter the concept of *inertia*.

14.5.1 Inertia – identifying barriers to change

Inertia refers to the force that needs to be exerted on a body to make it move. The size and shape of the body will have a large bearing on its ability to move – compare, for example, the inertia of a football to that of a train.

In the same way, different organizations present managers with issues relating to change due to varying degrees of inertia. Some are easy to change and others are much more reluctant. The willingness to change may depend on the culture of the organization, its size, its existing structure, its product and/or market positioning and even its age (i.e., how long it has existed in its present form).

For most purposes, we can say that resistance to change on the part of employees can be due to different attitudes. A number of studies in *THE* have reported resistance to change; see, for example, Okumus and Hemmington (1998), Pechlaner and Sauerwein (2002) and Kim et al. (2022). In a study of hotel managers in China, Singapore, Malaysia and Hong Kong, Jogaratnam and Tse (2004) found that few hospitality managers are used to the need to constantly innovate and influence change and that many managers are afraid to change.

Those affected by the change who resist it may do so because they:

- *Lack understanding of the details* – The reasons for the change may not have been explained to them. This particular barrier can normally be overcome relatively easily by management closing the information gap.
- *Lack trust* – They do not place their trust in the management.
- *Are afraid* –They may fear that the proposed changes will adversely affect their place in the structure, particularly in respect to their personal position or their social relationships.
- *Are uncertain about the future* – Attitudes toward uncertainty vary significantly among people, with some being much more averse than others.

14.5.2 Understanding change – Kurt Lewin's three-step model

Lewin (1947) suggested that organizational change could be understood in terms of three consecutive processes: unfreezing, moving and then refreezing (Lynch, 2021), as shown in Figure 14.6.

Unfreezing (mobilization for change)

Unfreezing involves introducing measures that will enable employees to abandon their current practices or cultural norms in preparation for the change. In many organizations, little has changed for many years, and unfreezing is necessary as a 'shaking up' phase. The impetus for unfreezing can come from either inside or outside the organization. Changing market conditions, for example, sometimes give employees warning that change will be imminent. Internally, a management shake-up, a profit warning or talk of restructuring may bring about similar expectations.

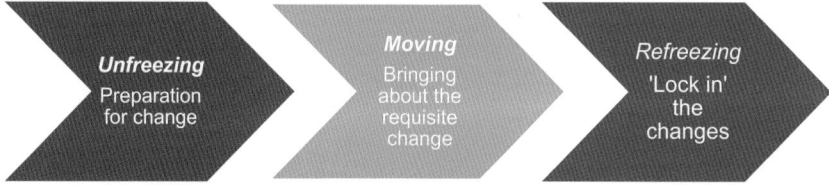

Figure 14.6 Lewin's model of change

Source: Adapted from Lewin (1947)

MOVING (MOVEMENT TO A NEW LEVEL)

Moving to the new level involves bringing about the requisite change itself. The time period given over to this phase varies widely. Structural change can usually be brought about relatively quickly. Changes in internal systems sometimes take longer (such as the introduction of new quality or information systems), and changing culture can take years.

REFREEZING (SUSTAINING CHANGE)

Refreezing is necessary to 'lock in' the changes and to prevent the organization from going back to its old ways. We would usually expect cultural changes to require more 'cementing in' than some other changes, and some resolve might be required on the part of senior management to avoid slippage.

14.3 SHORT CASE ILLUSTRATION

Cultural change at easyJet and Ryanair

Ryanair and easyJet are two airlines that have spearheaded the low-cost airline revolution in Europe since the 1990s, and both have grown rapidly to become established as substantial airlines.

The 'low-cost' model, as its name implies, is built on cutting out unnecessary costs. Consequently (though variations have emerged), low-cost airline operations usually imply cutting out additional product features, high aircraft utilization rates, point-to-point (as opposed to 'hub-and-spoke') routing, using a limited number of aircraft types, sales mainly derived online and fast airport turnaround. The airlines were also often cited for providing poor levels of customer service. In some cases, the poor levels of service became symbolic of the fact that the airline was doing everything possible to cut prices for passengers. The trade-off for low fares was a low level of service.

In a 2002 interview (Chesshyre, 2002), long-serving CEO and talisman for low-cost airlines Michael O'Leary said:

> Our customer service is about the most well-defined in the world. We guarantee to give you the lowest airfare. You get a safe flight. You get a normally on-time flight. That's the package. We don't and won't give you anything more on top of that.

But times have changed, and competitive pressures on European short-haul routes have been intensifying. The so-called full-service airlines have responded in short-haul markets in many cases by cutting costs, removing product features or developing their own low-cost subsidiaries (such as International Airline Group's Vueling and Iberia Express).

The low-cost airlines have had to adjust their own business models with regard to their culture and service standards to respond to their rejuvenated full-service competitors. The *Financial Times* reported that 'customer service has become easyJet's own weapon, wielded against rivals in the highly competitive airline market' (Wild, 2013) as the company pushed ahead with a program to transform the company's culture. 'While Ryanair was paring its core service to the bone, rival easyJet made some counterintuitive moves for a low-cost airline – offering flexible tickets and allocated seating, to woo business travelers' (Topham, 2013).

The cultural change at easyJet was facilitated through a major training program. Staff are instructed on their ABC's – attitude, behavior and communication – and are shown how unwitting actions make an impression on customers. Further initiatives to raise standards include an updated uniform; a customer charter, which includes promises from staff; and many staff around the company acting as 'customer champions' to inform and inspire colleagues. Incentives for staff in buying in to the revised organizational culture are mainly in the form of pride in the company, winning your name on an aircraft, or becoming an ambassador for UNICEF.

Sources: Adapted from Chesshyre (2002); Wild (2013); Topham (2013); www.ryanair.com/; www.easyjet.com/

Questions

1. Explain why change is necessary at easyJet and Ryanair.

2. Outline the sort of difficulties easyJet and Ryanair might encounter in trying to change their organizational cultures.

14.5.3 Understanding the context of change

Being able to manage change effectively is key to organizational survival and is probably the Achilles' heel of even very successful companies (Holbeche, 2011). To successfully lead and manage change, it is first necessary to understand change conceptually. Here we present a summary, but the subject was covered in detail by Holbeche (2011) and Balogun et al. (2016).

Before embarking on a program of change, organizational leaders need to be aware of the context of change within the organization. Table 14.3 presents some key contextual factors that a *THE* organization might need to consider before embarking on a program of change as part of its implementation of strategy.

Table 14.3 Considering the context of change within organizations

Change – contextual factor	Primary issue
• Time	How quickly is change required?
• Scope	To what degree is change needed?
• Preservation	What needs to preserved when other aspects are changed?
• Diversity	Will all parts of the organization be treated the same, or will there be room for diversity of approach?
• Experience and capability	Does the organization have experience of change and the ability to carry it through the process?
• Capacity	Are the resources required for change available?
• Readiness	How willing and able to change are the people in the organization's constituent groups?
• Power	Do the organization's leaders have the necessary power to lead the required changes?

Organizations continually need to change and need to do so at a pace that is equal to or faster than the external environment in which they operate. If they fail to do so, so-called *strategic drift* occurs.

DEFINITION/QUOTATION

Strategic drift

Strategic drift:

> Is the tendency for strategies to develop incrementally on the basis of historical and cultural influences, but fail to keep pace with a changing environment.
>
> (Whittington et al., 2020:174)

This occurs when an organization (even one that has enjoyed considerable success) responds too slowly to changes in the external environment and continues with the strategy that once served it very well. A well-known example that is often cited (though outside our focus) is that of Kodak, which in the context of film and photography failed to adapt its strategy to the rapid digitalization of the industry.

Dwyer et al. (2016) argued that tourism organization managers and destinations faced with pressures for change typically 'try to minimize the extent to which they are faced with ambiguity and uncertainty by looking for that which is familiar'. In managing for the future, difficulties occur because action is required beyond the scope of their core assumptions and routines. In essence, the organization does not understand the cause and effect of what is occurring in the external environment, resulting in strategic drift.

In the context of identified megatrends, a major challenge for *THE* organizations is identifying when their organization is at risk of or in a state of strategic drift (Dwyer and Edwards, 2009). Dwyer and Edwards (2009) recognized that there is no magic formula for avoiding strategic drift, but *THE* managers should recognize the importance of:

- Sustainable yield as an objective of the tourism organization
- Customers' needs as a driver of new product and new service development
- Proactive adoption of new technology
- A culture encouraging innovation
- Risk management, so they are prepared for any incident and can respond swiftly, confidently and appropriately
- Collaborating with other organizations to achieve efficiencies and an integrated 'value chain'
- Education and training to create an innovative and adaptive workforce

Comparatively little attention has been paid to the individual or collective viability and long-term sustainability of festivals and events in an increasingly competitive environment. Getz and Andersson (2008) emphasized important considerations for festival managers to thrive and keep abreast of the changing environment (thereby avoiding strategic drift). Data derived from 14 Swedish live music festivals confirmed the importance of attaining 'institutional status', occupying a unique 'niche' in the community, retaining committed stakeholders and practicing constant innovation.

For example: *When organizing festivals and events, there is an inherent risk of failing to adapt strategy quickly enough to changing environmental circumstances (i.e., strategic drift). There is also the risk of failure due to 'resource dependency' (on state or other sources), as well as more pragmatic reasons, including bad weather and managerial incompetence (Carlsen et al., 2010).*

The Short Case Illustration of the Calgary First Night Festival's demise illustrates the problems of strategic drift in the competitive world of festivals.

14.4 SHORT CASE ILLUSTRATION

Strategic drift: Calgary First Night Festival

Recent years have seen a huge increase in the number and range of festivals in countries around the world as localities, regions and countries compete for consumer spending. Successful festivals such as those in Edinburgh, Scotland, and Salzburg and Bregenz, Austria, can be highly lucrative for their local economies both directly and indirectly through the enhanced image of the city that they engender.

However, the environment is highly competitive. The environment is competitive in two respects: there are now many more festivals competing for public custom, and the festivals have to compete for finite public and commercial financial resources. Many festivals are highly specialized and depend on public subsidy, volunteers and sponsorship for survival. Failure to keep pace with the changes in relation to these factors is an example of *strategic drift*.

Getz (2002) cited the example of the termination of the First Night Festival in the Canadian city of Calgary, and, in a Swedish context, Nordvall and Heldt (2017) explored the failure of a family arts festival held on New Year's Eve from 1985 to 1995 that attracted up to 40,000 people. Failure was attributed not to lack of interest but to other environmental factors:

- Price restrictions were imposed, which prevented the organizers from increasing their revenue
- An initial city grant was discontinued and put additional pressure on the event
- The festival was not eligible for ongoing funding from the Calgary Regional Arts Foundation, which otherwise supports local festivals
- The volunteer festival directors were 'burned out' because of the constant fight for financial viability

Thus, failure to respond to the rapidly changing financial circumstances and an unsustainable leadership model implied that a *strategic drift* had taken place; that is, the festival's rate of change failed to keep pace with the changing external environment.

Source: Adapted from Getz (2002)

Questions

1. Explain what is meant by the term 'strategic drift' and how it is illustrated in this case.

2. What might the organizers of the festival have done to prevent failure in this case?

Two key aspects of change that managers need to determine relate to the urgency for the changes to be implemented and the nature of the change that needs to take place.

The pace at which change happens can usually be divided into one of two categories – step (often termed *transformational*) and incremental change. Incremental change, or incrementalism, has become associated with the management learning process and is associated in particular with the work of Quinn (1980); see also the assessment by Johnson (1988).

Figure 14.7 illustrates the two principal categories of change. As the terminology suggests, *step change* represents a major change implemented over a short period of time, whereas *incrementalism* involves many small steps and learning along the way so adjustments can be made as necessary.

Quinn and Voyer (1998) suggested that there are two factors that determine which is the most appropriate:

- *How urgent the need for change is* – A market crisis will typically bring about an urgent need for rapid change, whereas preparing for the introduction of a new legal regulation in 5 years' time will allow change to occur more slowly and perhaps more painlessly.
- *How much inertia is evident* within the organization's culture – The time to 'unfreeze' will depend on the level of inertia.

Step change offers the advantage of 'getting it over with'. It enables the organization to respond quickly to changes in its environment and hence to conform to new conditions without lagging behind. Disadvantages include the 'pain' factor – it may require some coercion or force on the part of management, which in turn may damage employee–management relationships.

Incremental changes offer the advantage of a step-by-step approach to change. For an organization with high inertia, it enables management to gain acceptance before and during the change process and, consequently, it tends to be more inclusive. The process is divided into a number of distinct phases, and there may be periods of 'rest' between the phases. It would be an inappropriate technique to use in situations of rapid environmental change.

Balogun et al. (2016) usefully categorized types of change in four categories in their model of types of change, as shown in Figure 14.8, defined in two dimensions:.

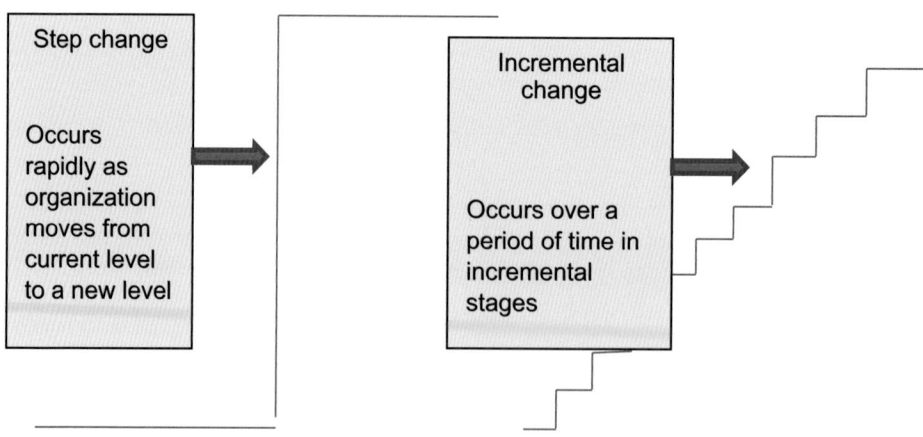

Figure 14.7 The urgency for change

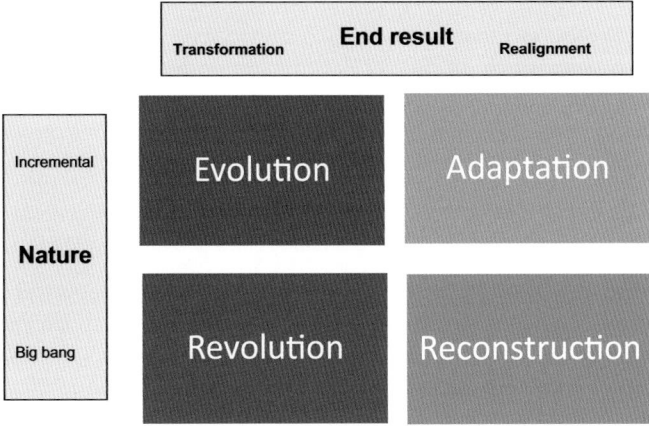

Figure 14.8 A model of types of change

Source: Adapted from Balogun and Hailey (2016)

- *End result of change* – that is, the extent of the desired change
- *Nature of the change* – that is, the speed at which the changes will be implemented

The four categories of change are as follows:

- *Adaptation* – aimed at realigning rather than transforming the organization, implemented slowly through staged initiatives
- *Reconstruction* – aimed at realigning rather than transforming the organization but occurring more dramatically and faster
- *Evolution* – a transformational change implemented gradually through different stages and inter-related initiatives
- *Revolution* – a fundamental transformational change occurring by simultaneous initiatives on many fronts, often in a relatively short space of time. It is more likely (than evolution) to be forced on staff and reactive to rapidly changing market conditions.

The Short Case Illustration of the German airline Lufthansa illustrates a strategic change process being implemented in the turbulent environment faced by airlines in recent years.

14.5 SHORT CASE ILLUSTRATION

Strategic change at Lufthansa: the impact of the COVID-19 pandemic

The German airline Lufthansa, with its main operating base at Frankfurt International Air-port, is the principal airline in a group of airlines that also includes Swiss and Austrian air-lines. International airlines have had to become adept at managing change in response to rapid and fundamental environmental changes and highly volatile records of profitability.

Bruch et al. (2005) reported that Lufthansa had shifted its shape successfully several times over the previous years since its spectacular turnaround from the brink of bankruptcy in 1991 (detailed by Bruch and Sattelberger 2000). 'The company became a master of managing strategic change despite the turbulent aviation market conditions prevalent from 1991 to 2004 by launching a series of major initiatives' (Bruch et al., 2005:98).

In 2020 and 2021, the coronavirus pandemic had an unprecedented impact on the aviation industry and led to speedy and fundamental changes to previously planned strategies.

The Lufthansa Group actively used the crisis to accelerate the group's transformation and create a good starting position to be successful in the future competitive environment. The group responded quickly and comprehensively to set up the 'ReNew' restructuring program as a reaction to the crisis-related market collapse and the changed financial situation. Liquidity outflow was successfully reduced or stopped, fixed costs were reduced in the short term by over 30% and capital expenditures were reduced by around two-thirds compared with the original planning.

In addition, voluntary and compulsory job reductions took place across the group and aircraft were temporarily parked. As a result, it was reported that by 2024, annual costs should be around 3.5bn euro lower than before the crisis.

Sources: Lufthansa (2021); Bruch and Sattelberger (2000); Bruch et al. (2005)

Questions

1. Explain what problems Lufthansa might encounter in implementing its program of change and how these difficulties might be overcome.

2. Explain the main features of Lufthansa's change program as a result of the pandemic and why it is so important for the airline group.

14.5.4 Leading and managing change

Strong management and leadership of change are vital if the planned changes are to be successful.

There are no generally accepted definitions of the terms 'management' and 'leadership'. In both cases, many definitions have emerged in the academic and commercial literature, and the meaning of both terms is subject to much debate. Hence, the terms, their meaning and their application are subject to various interpretations.

Although in common usage, the terms are often used interchangeably, and care must be taken in distinguishing between the two concepts. Kotter (2001), for example, argued that leadership and management are two distinctive and complementary systems, each having its own function and its own characteristic activities, but both are necessary for complex organizations and vital to the successful implementation of strategic changes. *Management* is about planning, controlling and putting appropriate structures and systems in place, whereas *leadership* has more to do with anticipating change, coping with change and adopting a visionary stance.

Zaleznik (2004) also perceived a difference between management and leadership. Managers are seen as fairly passive, people-centered operators intent on 'keeping the show on the road', whereas leaders seem to be more solitary, proactive, intuitive and emphatic and are attracted to situations of high risk where the rewards for success are great.

In practice, the difference between leadership and management is that:

- **Leadership** is setting a new direction or vision for a group or for oneself that others follow; that is, a leader is the spearhead for that new direction.
- **Management** controls or directs people/resources in a group according to principles or values that have already been established.

Management usually consists of people who are experienced in their field and who usually possess a good technical knowledge. Their authority derives from the position they hold.

But what is leadership? There are almost as many definitions as there are commentators. Many associate leadership with one person leading. However, four aspects stand out in the discussions:

- To lead involves *influencing others* and may derive from the position they hold or from other characteristics such as their personal qualities.
- Where there are leaders, there are *followers*.
- Leaders seem to come to the fore when there is a *crisis or special problem*. In other words, they often become visible when an innovative response is needed.
- Leaders are people who have a clear idea of what they want to achieve and why. This is often described in terms of a *vision*.

Thus, leaders are people who are able to think and act creatively in non-routine situations and who set out to influence the actions, beliefs and feelings of others. In this sense, being a leader is personal. It flows from an individual's qualities and actions. However, it is also often linked to the individual's role, such as a manager or expert.

Hence, there can be a lot of confusion. Not all managers are leaders, and not all leaders are managers. Leaders stand out by being different. They question assumptions, are suspicious of tradition and have a preference for innovation.

The study of leadership is not new. Interest in what makes effective leaders has a long history, with many examples in the literature taken from the military field. Management, by contrast, is usually viewed as a more recent phenomenon linked to the development of modern industrial practices.

DEFINITION/QUOTATION

Leadership

> The study of leadership rivals in age the emergence of civilization, which shaped its leaders as much as it was shaped by them. From its infancy, the study of history has been the study of leaders – what they did and why they did it.
>
> (Bass and Bass, 2009:4)

Kotter (2001) produced eight practical guidelines for leaders and managers seeking to transform their organizations; see the following Key Concept.

KEY CONCEPT

Successfully transforming organizations

In stressing the need for strong, effective leadership and management in organizations implementing programs of change, Kotter argued that there are eight steps to successfully transforming organizations, as shown in Figure 14.9.

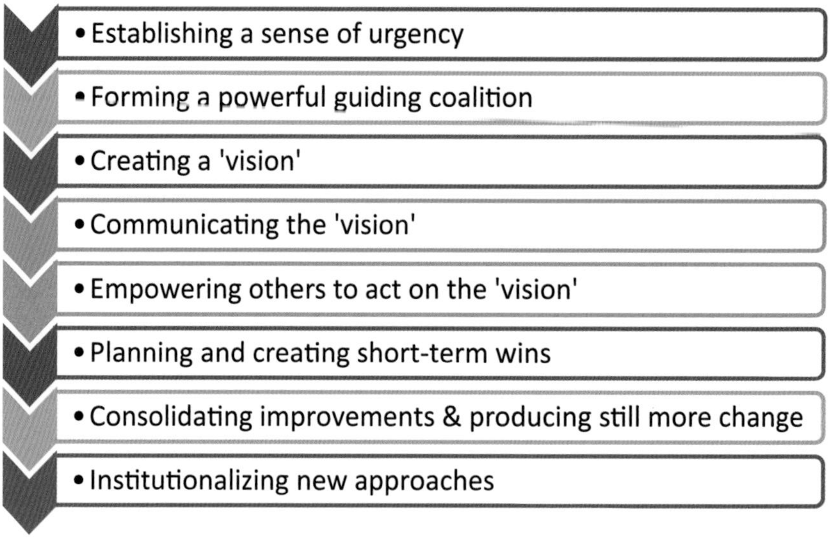

- Establishing a sense of urgency
- Forming a powerful guiding coalition
- Creating a 'vision'
- Communicating the 'vision'
- Empowering others to act on the 'vision'
- Planning and creating short-term wins
- Consolidating improvements & producing still more change
- Institutionalizing new approaches

Figure 14.9 Successfully transforming organizations

Source: Adapted from Kotter (1995)

The process of actually leading and managing strategic change leads to the consideration of a number of managerial approaches and their appropriateness in various contexts.

14.5.5 Leadership and management styles

Managers and leaders have different styles (approaches) that they adopt in implementing change in their organizations. It is true that there is no 'best' style of leading and managing strategic change (Whittington et al., 2020); instead, it is perhaps better to think of leaders needing to adjust the style they adopt according to the circumstances they encounter. This approach has become known as *situational leadership* following the work of Paul Hersey and Ken Blanchard during the 1970s (Hersey et al., 1979), which was summarized and critiqued by Graeff (1997).

THINK POINTS

- What is inertia, and how is it applied to organizational change?
- Explain Lewin's three-step model of change.
- Define and distinguish between step change and incremental change.

Building on this adaptation of leadership style according to the circumstances, Balogun et al. (2016) argued that there are five styles that can be adopted, each with associated advantages and disadvantages. The styles represent a continuum, from *coercion*, where change is forced on people, to *education and delegation*, where change is delegated. Consequently, each style may be more appropriate in some circumstances than others.

The five styles and their associated advantages and disadvantages identified by Balogun et al. (2016) are summarized in Table 14.4.

14.5.6 The role of the 'change agent'

Many writers have stressed the importance of the leadership role in successfully implementing change; see, for example, Howell and Higgins (1990) and Palmer et al. (2021). The individual or

Table 14.4 Styles of leading change

Style	Description	Advantages	Disadvantages
Education and delegation	Use small group briefings to explain things to employees. Aim is to gain support for the change by generating understanding and commitment	• Spreads support for change • Ensures a wide base of understanding	Takes a long time If radical change is required, fact-based argument may not be enough to convince others of need to change Easy to voice support but then walk away and do nothing
Collaboration	Widespread involvement of employees on decisions about what and how to change	• Spreads not only support but 'ownership' of change by increasing involvement	Time-consuming Little control (by senior management) over decisions made May lead to change outside original vision
Participation	Involvement of employees in 'how' to deliver the desired changes. May also include limited collaboration over aspects of the 'how' to change as opposed to 'what' to change	• Spreads ownership and support for change but with a more controlled framework • Easier to shape decisions	Can be perceived as manipulation
Direction	Change leaders make the majority of decisions about what to change and how. Use of authority to direct change	• Less time-consuming • Provides a clear change direction and focus	Potentially less support and commitment and therefore proposed changes may be resisted
Coercion	Use of power to impose change	• Allows for prompt action	Unlikely to achieve employee buy-in except in a crisis

'change agent' instigating change may be the key manager (usually the CEO or managing director) within the organization or the organization may bring in an external consultant for the duration of the process.

How the process of change is implemented and by whom is an interesting issue in itself. In the so-called *top-down* vs *bottom-up* discussion that has taken place in the academic literature over recent years (see, for instance, Burnes, 2017). The role of top management is clearly important, whichever style they adopt and whether they lead the change themselves or bring in external consultants to do so.

However, Beer et al. (1990) found that change programs that were directed by top management were quite likely to fail. The change programs that were more likely to be successful were those that were started at the bottom of the organization and driven by individuals or task groups who 'championed' specific aspects of change.

Beer et al. (1990) argued that top management's role in the change process is to support, but not interfere with, change; to create the climate for change to take place, specifying the general direction of change; and to communicate the successes and failures of the change process so that the lessons can be learned. Specifically, the authors recommended that the role of top management in a program of change should be to:

- *Mobilize commitment* to change through joint diagnosis and team efforts
- *Develop a shared vision* for change emanating from the task teams
- *Foster consensus* for the new vision by giving support and encouragement
- *Replace managers* who cannot work under the new system
- *Spread revitalization* to all departments without pushing from the top
- *Institutionalize change* through systems and procedures
- *Monitor and adjust strategies* in response to problems

The change agent approach in which an external person or team is brought in to implement change has been termed the 'champion of change' model. Though a disadvantage is that an external person does not know the context of the change or the personalities involved as well as an insider, there are a number of advantages, in that the change agent:

- Provides a focus for the change and personifies the process. A 'walking symbol' of change can act as a stimulus to change and can ensure that complacency is avoided.
- Will be engaged, in many cases, because he or she is an expert in the field. The person may have overseen the same change process in many other organizations and so is well acquainted with the usual problems.
- Frees up senior management's time because responsibility for the change process is delegated. Management thus gains the normal advantages of delegation.

Many management consultants vie for opportunities to advise organizations on implementing their strategies and have developed proprietary frameworks and systems to do so. One such external approach to implementing strategy is the 7-S model developed by the well-known international consultancy firm McKinsey. *In Search of Excellence*, the best-selling book by McKinsey partners Tom Peters and Robert Waterman (2015), introduced the mass business audience to the firm's 7-S model.

Whatever type of change is envisaged, the model can be used to understand how the organizational elements are interrelated and to ensure that the wider impact of changes made in one area in terms of its impacts elsewhere is taken into consideration.

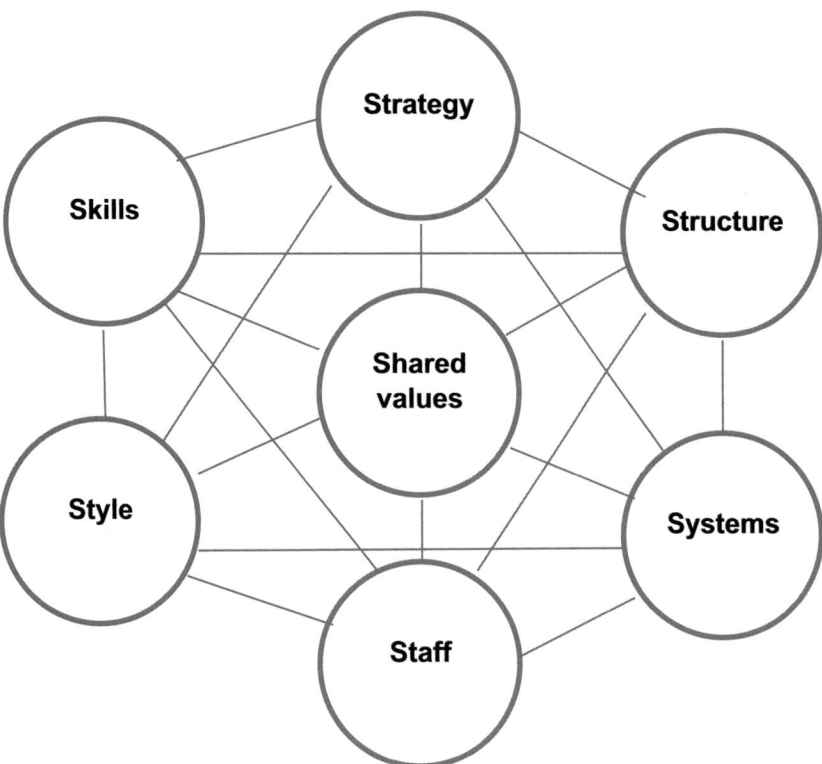

Figure 14.10 The McKinsey 7-S framework

The model, shown in Figure 14.10, is based on the notion that the seven elements (structure, strategy, systems, skills, style, staff and shared values) need to be aligned and mutually reinforcing so that the organization can perform well. In *THE* contexts, Palatková (2011), for example, applied the model to destination marketing strategy in the Czech Republic, and Gkoumas (2022) applied the model in establishing restaurant viability in Taiwan following the COVID-19 pandemic.

14.6 Implementation: *THE* contexts

In this section, we attempt to put together key aspects of this book in relation to the ways in which we have to think about strategy in *THE* contexts differently than other industrial contexts. The reason for this lies in the service contexts we are dealing with and, specifically, the defining characteristics of the sectors that make up *THE*.

The underlying premise of this book is that strategic management in *THE* contexts is in some way different in that there are certain characteristics of these sectors that managers need to consider in designing and delivering their strategies.

We discussed these characteristics in Chapter 2. Four of the characteristics, it was argued, were common in most service industry contexts and a further seven, though not necessarily unique to *THE* management, were nevertheless particularly prominent in these contexts.

The 11 characteristics and examples of the managerial implications that arose because of these characteristics were summarized in Table 2.1. Importantly, the characteristics have particular relevance for the way in which strategy is implemented in *THE* organizations. Specifically, managers in these sectors need to consider the characteristics in relation to how:

- Resources are allocated and deployed
- The organization is configured in terms of its culture and structure
- The process of change is managed and led

Thus, the ways in which these issues are addressed are affected by the particular context within which *THE* organizations operate; that is, the 11 defining characteristics. In implementing strategy, managers have to address these aspects in such a way that core competences are applied (discussed in Chapter 3) When the core competences are applied effectively in the market, competitive advantage is achieved.

This process, from defining characteristics through strategic implementation to core competences, applied in the market is shown conceptually in Figure 14.11 (and was discussed by Evans, 2015).

Figure 14.11 presents a conceptualization of how strategic implementation can be applied in *THE* contexts. Tables 14.5 and 14.6 build on the conceptualization by summarizing some of the specific services (Table 14.5) and *THE* characteristics (Table 14.6) facing managers. The tables build on the summary presented in Table 2.1 in Chapter 2.

The tables also consider the actions managers might take to respond in relation to the three aspects of resources, configuration of structure and culture and managing change (which were covered earlier in this chapter).

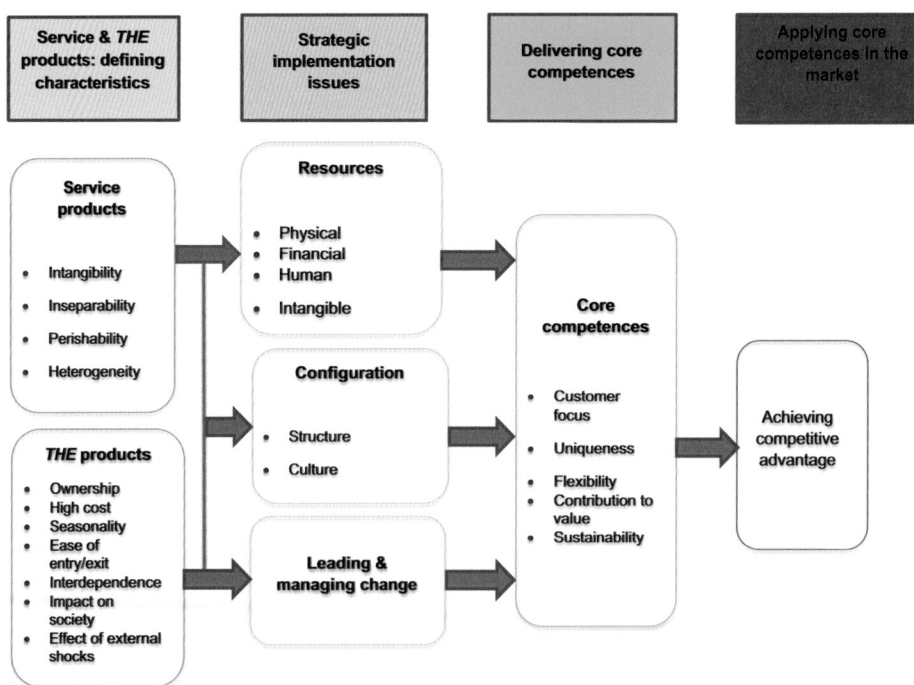

Figure 14.11 Achieving competitive advantage in *THE* through strategic implementation: a conceptualization

Table 14.5 Strategic implementation in relation to service product characteristics

Characteristic	Implementation actions: *Resources*	Implementation actions: *Configuration*	Implementation actions: *Change*
Intangibility Products cannot be tested or sampled	• Physical and virtual marketing materials must be of a high standard • Effective distribution of the products is essential • Tangible additions to the product often important	*Structure* – Front-line sales force must be well trained and able to sell the product attributes competently *Culture* – Delivering excellent service is of utmost importance to all employees	Building brand loyalty is difficult and time consuming, and brand switching is common. Therefore, managers must devote resources to positioning and building brands and recognize and manage risks to the brand
Inseparability Production and consumption take place at the same time	• There is often no opportunity to store resources, so they must be available in the right quantities and location when required	*Structure* – Front-line staff must be trained and empowered to satisfy customer demands *Culture* – 'Get it right first time' or rectify mistakes when they happen quickly and satisfactorily *Culture* – Empower staff within specified boundaries so that lapses can be overcome	Ensure that high customer service levels are maintained Front-line staff should be carefully selected, well trained and have the appropriate skills and aptitude for customer service roles
Perishability Products cannot be stored	• Supply is often fixed in the short to medium term, so pricing and other promotional methods are used to effect demand	*Structure* – Flexibility is necessary so that appropriate responses to rapid environmental changes can be implemented *Structure* – Flatter structures favor rapid decision making and information flows *Culture* – Avoiding waste and cutting costs are key drivers	Performance monitoring systems are necessary to avoid wasting resources and plan resource deployment Sudden changes in demand and supply must be carefully monitored and resources redeployed accordingly

(continued)

Table 14.5 Continued

Characteristic	Implementation actions: *Resources*	Implementation actions: *Configuration*	Implementation actions: *Change*
Heterogeneity Products are not identical	• Staff are vital in delivering excellent services, so it is essential to recruit and retain good staff, train them well, ensure that rewards are well targeted and take measures to ensure staff are well motivated • It is important to stress differentiation between the organization's own products and those of competitors	*Structure* – Ensure that structure enables information from front-line staff to quickly reach company decision makers *Culture* – Staff are a key part of the product, and service quality is of utmost importance *Culture* – Staff are empowered to make decisions	Listening to and understating the customer: anticipating customer needs and giving a high priority to customer satisfaction are important Heterogeneity should be managed in such a way that the differences are valued by the customer and that high-quality standards are maintained
Ownership Customers use services rather than own them	• Building loyalty is difficult, but promotional activities, excellent staff and loyalty schemes should be aligned toward building loyalty	*Structure* – Front-line and back office staff must act as if customers are own-ers of the product *Culture* – Strong and explicit organiza-tional values are important in building staff and customer loyalty *Culture* – Despite lack of ownership, quality of 'after-sales' service is vital for repeat bookings	Ensure that loyalty schemes are well targetec and offer value for money for customers and the organization Develop a relationship with customers through public relations, promotion and organizational image so that customers feel like they 'own the product'

Table 14.6 Strategic implementation in relation to *THE* management characteristics

Characteristic	Implementation actions: *Resources*	Implementation actions: *Configuration*	Implementation actions: *Change*
High-cost product Often a relatively expensive purchase	• Provide opportunities to sample, test or compare the product • Ensure that resources are deployed on product features valued by the customer and for which they are willing to pay	*Structure* – All levels of the organization are required to take responsibility for excellent service delivery and product enhancement *Culture* – Continuous improvement and innovation are encouraged so that products and service levels keep ahead of competitors	Continually evaluate product offering so that it is correctly positioned in the market Ensure that pricing and product information is updated and accurate Build trust with customers through relationship building
Seasonality Products often have very seasonal demand patterns	• Ensure flexible resourcing so that there is availability when required but resources can be discarded when not required • Make extensive use of part-time and volunteer workers • Carefully manage seasonal cash flows and foreign currency receipts and payments	*Structure* – Flexibility and clarity are needed to accommodate seasonal workers and ensure that they are well managed *Culture* – Inclusivity is needed so that part-time volunteers and staff do not feel excluded and are aware of organizational norms and requirements	Manage change in demand and supply balance carefully so that resources are available when required and waste is avoided in their deployment Price effectively to match seasonal variations so that revenues are maximized Take action to extend the season or minimize its impacts
Ease of entry/exit Often relatively low barriers to entry	• Resources often need to be deployed flexibly to respond quickly to competitive threats • Focus on the cost base because otherwise lower cost competitors will enter the market • New competitors can quickly emerge, so it is important to establish position in the market through differentiation and/or price • Many opportunities are available for innovative SMEs if they have the necessary resources available • Raise the height of barriers for new entrants if possible, by gaining access to resources that are denied to others, such as a resort, hotel or concert venue	*Structure* – Avoid being overly bureaucratic so that it is possible to responding quickly to new vigorous competitors *Culture* – Develop an 'open' culture where employee ideas and innovations are encouraged and incentivized appropriately *Culture* – If there is relative ease of entry and exit, develop a culture in which whether correct markets are being targeted and correct products are being offered can be constantly assessed	Products and innovations can often be easily replicated, so seek niches, specialisms, product features, brand or pacing points that can be defended Innovative SMEs can effectively compete if they utilize technology, design, service quality or a particular niche effectively

(continued)

Table 14.6 Continued

Characteristic	Implementation actions: Resources	Implementation actions: Configuration	Implementation actions: Change
Interdependence The subsectors of *THE* are closely linked	• Seek opportunities to share resources with collaborating organizations, suppliers and customers	*Structure* – Ensure a 'strategic-fit' between structures of collaborating organizations *Culture* – Work with organizations with compatible vision and values	Ensure goal alignment among partners and suppliers Communicate and share information effectively with partners, suppliers and customers Coordinate strategic planning effectively
Impact on society *THE* has a high impact on society	• Use natural resources in an environmentally responsible way • SMEs can compete effectively with larger companies by deploying resources in a way that emphasizes their 'green' credentials	*Structure* – A decentralized structure might allow for local managers to be more sensitive to local impacts and make necessary adjustments *Culture* – It may be necessary to devise a strategy that takes into account not only central headquarter issues but also local cultures styles, values and expectations	*THE* is unique among service industries in its impact. Managers in *THE* must be sensitive to this issue and emphasize the corporate responsibility of their organization Managers must be aware of changing consumers who recognize the impacts of their consumption and attempt to work with responsible suppliers New forms of tourism are creating additional opportunities and challenges that managers need to research and understand to design and deliver targeted products
External shocks Prone to external shocks beyond manager's control	• Risks vs rewards are carefully assessed and resources deployed accordingly • Spread risks through a portfolio of products and markets • Protect assets where possible; for example, through insurance, spreading their location and 'asset-light' operations	*Structure* – Flexibility is important so responses can be speedy and effective *Structure* – All employees must know how their specific role fits in and how they should respond *Culture* – Safety and security of customers is not an objective but an absolute value and cannot be compromised	Risks are identified and contingency plans are in place Managers must have an understanding of their role in unexpected circumstances Scenario planning helps in preparing contingency plans Financial risks such as foreign exchange, interest rates and fuel prices should be assessed and managed

14.7 Implementation: communicating, coordinating and measuring

This chapter has so far considered the three key aspects of strategic implementation:

- *Resources* – How should the strategy be resourced?
- *Configuration* – How should the culture and strategy of the organization be configured to 'fit' the proposed strategy?
- *Change* – How should the changes arising from the strategy be managed and led?

All of these aspects represent important dimensions of strategy implementation but do not provide a detailed coherent framework within which managers can act. Two important issues arise:

- How should the strategy be spread (or 'cascaded', as it is often termed) throughout the organization?
- How should the implementation (in a practical sense) be coordinated, managed and monitored?

Successful implementation of strategy involves all parts of an organization being successfully aligned to meet the strategic objectives that have been set as part of the strategic process. Thus, the strategy must be communicated and disseminated as part of this process. A detailed strategy may be developed for each part of the organization, such as the marketing, financial operations and human resources functional areas and the SBUs of the organization.

Thus, we now turn to the fourth issue:

14.7.1 Communicating, coordinating and measuring – a practical technique for implementing strategy

Measuring organizational success and implementing effective strategies for future success represent continuous challenges for managers, researchers and consultants (Evans, 2005). Against this background there is a continual striving to find a workable means of strategic implementation. Managers in a wide variety of industries are rethinking their performance measurement systems and means of strategic implementation.

One such means of implementation that is widely used is the BSC, which is covered in detail below.

Arguably, nowhere is the need for a consistent and coherent approach to strategic implementation more apposite than in the sectors of *THE*. A rapid switch from local and domestic competition to 'global' markets has taken place. In such markets, large international companies strive to develop and implement strategies to ensure strategic success. At the same time, innovative companies have emerged, encouraged by low barriers to entry and easing of regulatory restrictions. Increasing attention is being given to performance measurement and strategic implementation in many instances throughout *THE*.

It is against the background of the need for a comprehensive implementation technique that other approaches have been developed. The service profit chain (Heskett et al., 1997) assesses the sources of profitability and growth in labor-dominated service firms and was discussed in Chapter 3. The service profit chain's purpose is to provide managers with a framework to help them manage by enabling them to focus on (predominantly) quantifiable measures that lead to financial performance measures.

In this respect, the model is similar to the BSC approach to strategy developed by Kaplan and Norton (1996, 2001), which is discussed below. However, focusing as it does on the service delivery aspects of performance, the model is useful but does not represent a holistic approach to managing service-based organizations (Evans, 2005).

14.7.2 *The balanced scorecard: overview*

Of all of the frameworks for performance measurement and strategic implementation, the BSC technique has gained wide acceptance, particularly in the USA. Though not without its critics (see, for example, Nørreklit, 2000; Franco and Bourne, 2004), the success of the BSC is evident not only because of its intrinsic value to businesses but also because the concept has been aggressively marketed.

BSC was developed by Robert Kaplan (a Harvard professor) and consultant David Norton in the early 1990s and resulted from their experiences in implementing strategic initiatives at several US corporations.

Kaplan and Norton (1996, 2001) identified two significant deficiencies in the implementation of strategic plans:

- *A measurement gap* – Though most companies measure performance, most of the measurements used are historical, looking backwards rather than focusing on future success.
- *A strategy gap* – Many companies identified general plans, but in many cases they did not translate effectively into managerial actions. The authors claimed that many strategic initiatives had little real impact on the organization because they were not cascaded to managers and employers to use in their daily work.

BSC presents a technique for translating an organization's mission (embodied in its strategy) into more tangible measurable goals, actions and performance measures. The technique involves a range of measures (not only financial measures) because it has been argued that financial measures alone are inadequate in evaluating a company's competitive position (Stalk et al.,1992). This is particularly true of the service sector, with its focus on human resources, intangible assets and difficulties with regard to delivery of consistent product standards (Evans, 2005).

The BSC technique was documented in a number of papers in the 1990s and in greater detail in two books (see, for example, Kaplan and Norton, 1996, 2001). The later works shifted the emphasis from a system of performance measurement toward a system for managing and implementing strategy, which is our focus here.

Many other authors have helped to disseminate the technique's features, and a number of studies have documented the technique in relation to *THE* sectors and to hotels and accommodation in particular; see, for example, Doran et al. (2002), Evans (2005), Phillips and Louvieris (2005), Sainaghi (2010), Sainaghi et al. (2013, 2019), Wu and Liao (2014), Elbanna et al. (2015) and Fatima and Elbanna (2020). For case studies utilizing the technique, see Huckestein and Duboff (1999), Denton and White (2000), Vila et al. (2010) and Elbanna et al. (2022).

Crucially, the BSC approach can also be applied at different levels of an organization. Typically, the total organizational business scorecard will be mapped and specified and then be replicated in modified form for each part of the organization; that is, it can be applied with a common structure but specific and modified objectives, measures and targets to the:

- Total organization
- SBUs
- Individual operational teams
- Individual members of staff

In this way, each part of the organization contributes to the achievement of a common set of objectives and targets, which can easily be seen by internal and external stakeholders. Consequently, BSC represents a methodology for implementation that:

- Has a high degree of visibility and can easily be understood
- Can be easily and consistently be communicated to staff and other stakeholders
- Offers a high level of consistency in its approach
- Can be 'cascaded' to all parts of the organization
- Produces tangible and measurable outcomes so that the success of strategic implementation can be assessed

14.7.3 BSC as part of the strategy process

The process involves:

- Identifying key components of operations
- Setting goals for them
- Finding ways to measure progress toward their achievement

Traditional financial measures, viewed as lagging indicators of performance, are balanced with non-financial measures, which are lead indicators and serve to drive future performance. The measures are not to be viewed merely as a collection of various metrics (Kaplan and Norton, 2001) but instead are selected to show cause and effect in the implementation of the company's mission and organizational strategy.

An important preliminary step prior to choosing the scorecard goals and measures is to 'map' the strategy in detail, a process that Kaplan and Norton (2001) described in some detail.

A first stage in mapping the strategy is understanding where it fits into the overall management processes of an organization. To Kaplan and Norton (2001), strategy does not stand alone but is one step in a logical continuum that moves an organization from a high-level mission statement to the work performed by individual 'front-line' and 'back office' employees.

Implied in this continuum is a causal link that starts with individual employees and that, through collective actions, builds up to the achievement of the organizational mission. In this way, strategy becomes embedded in the organization in that strategy becomes 'everyone's everyday job' (Kaplan and Norton, 2001:9); thus, as the title of their book makes plain, the organization becomes 'strategy focused'. BSC is an integral part of the continuum because it enables implementation and monitoring of the strategy that has been formulated.

Figure 14.12 provides a representation of strategy incorporating the BSC approach (that is consistent with the approach taken elsewhere in this book). Strategy is viewed as a continuum that starts with the high-level mission and ends with personal objectives for individual employees.

14.7.4 BSC in practice

A typical scorecard normally includes four components:

- A financial perspective

Figure 14.12 Strategy as a continuum involving BSC

- An internal business perspective
- A customer perspective
- An innovation and learning perspective

The components, as shown in Figure 14.13, should not be viewed in isolation but as an integrated model in which there are 'cause-and-effect' relationships. Kaplan and Norton (2001) argued that the BSC has a 'top-down' logic, starting with the *financial outcomes*; moving on to the *customer outcomes*, which include 'the value proposition' (which defines how the organization differentiates itself for customers); and then moving on to *business processes* and *the learning and growth infrastructure*, which are the drivers of change.

For each component, the organization has to identify a number of:

- Objectives (or goals)
- Measures for gauging the degree of goal attainment
- Targets that identify progress toward achieving the goals
- Initiatives (or priorities) within the period

The cause-and-effect linkages of a strategy map are demonstrated in a tourism context in Figure 14.14. In this case, the strategy map for the tourism destination organization shows the linkages that enable staff to be aligned with the strategy, which eventually through the cause-and-effect linkages allow the organization to achieve its objectives.

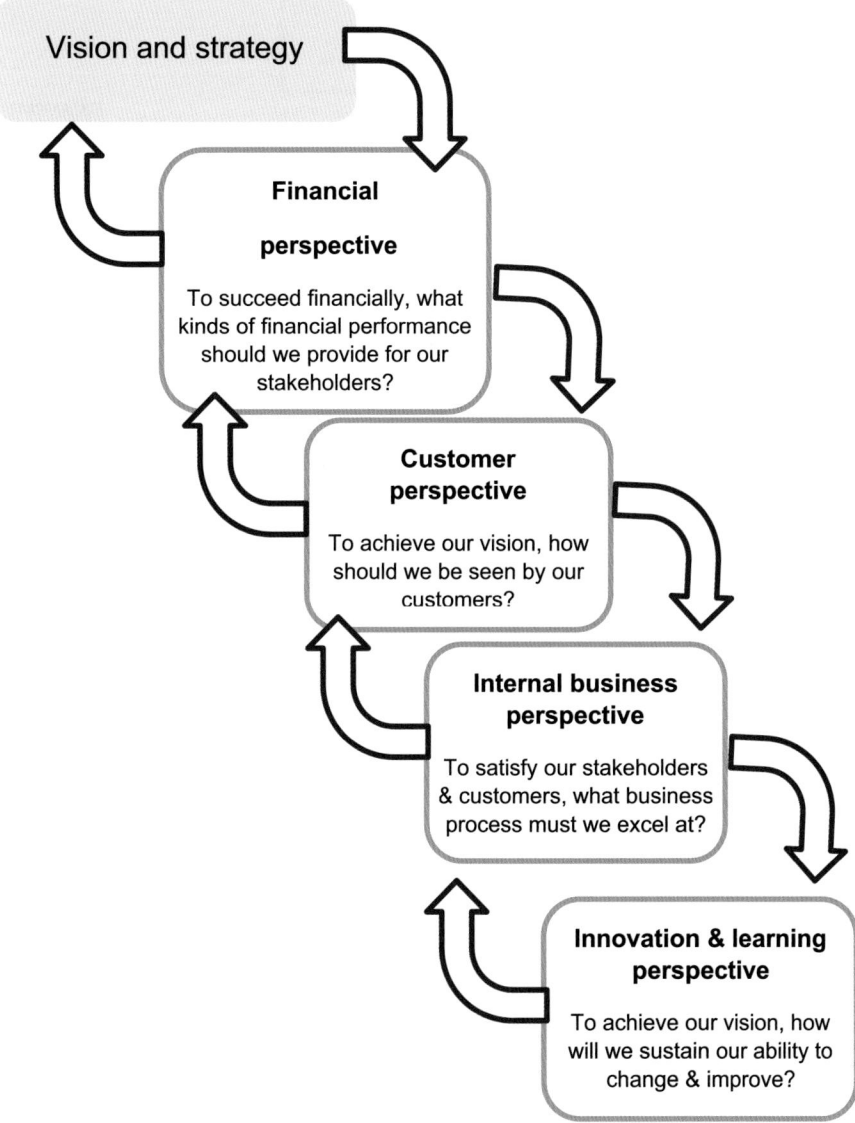

Figure 14.13 The four perspectives of BSC

Source: Adapted from Kaplan and Norton (2001: 77)

The purpose of the strategy map is to show the cause-and-effect relationships of the organization's strategic objectives in a visual manner. It demonstrates how the destination organization creates value for the tourism industry. It should also align with the performance measurement framework found in the organization's BSC.

Many organizations around the world (particularly in North America) have adopted the BSC as a tool to use in communicating and coordinating strategy. Organizations often adapt the model to suit their own set of circumstances, but the logic and usefulness of the concept remain intact.

One such organization is Discover Halifax in Canada, discussed in the Short Case Illustration below.

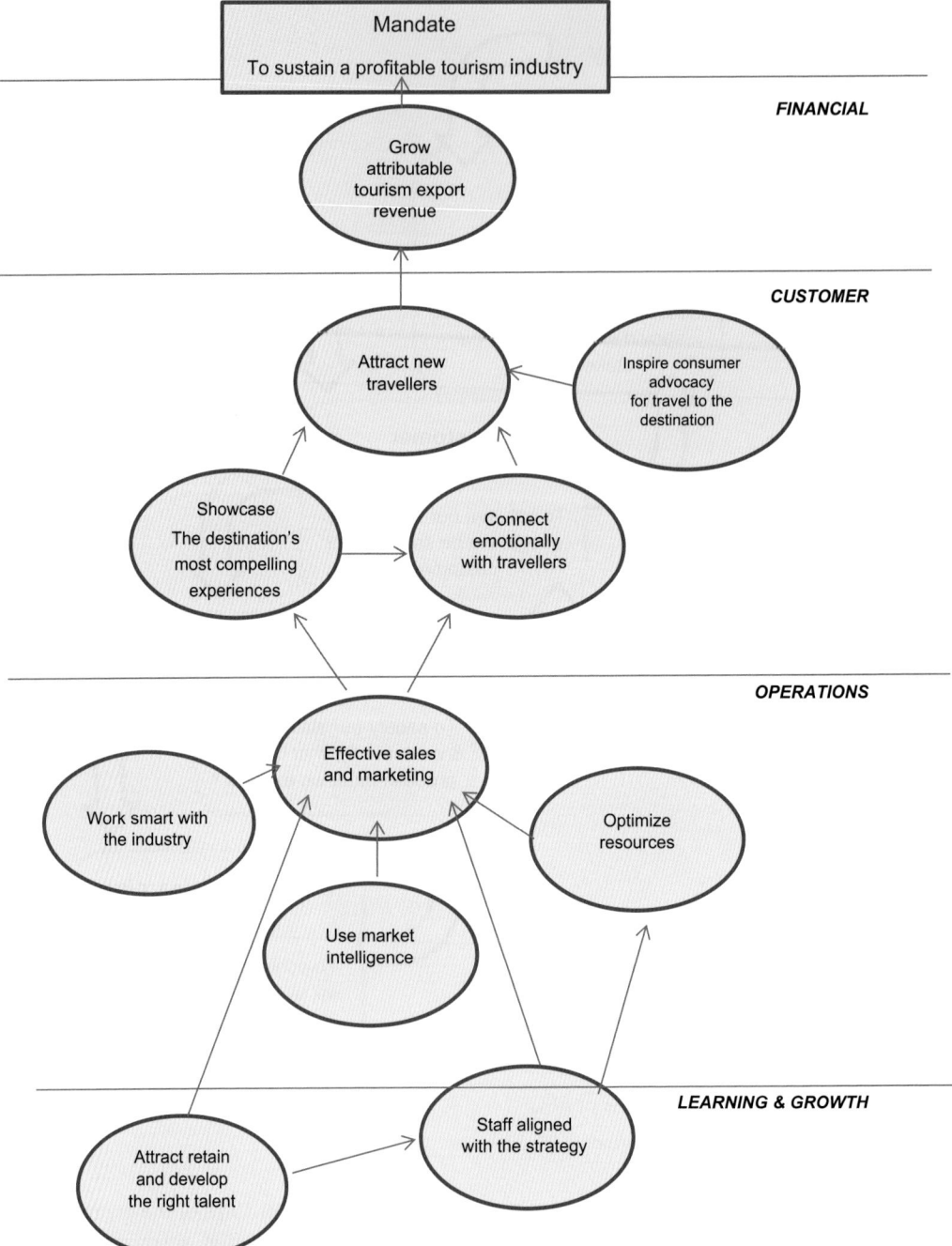

Figure 14.14 A tourism destination organization's strategy map

Source: Adapted from Canadian Tourism Commission (2012)

14.6 SHORT CASE ILLUSTRATION

BSC at Discover Halifax, Nova Scotia

Halifax is the capital and largest city of the Canadian province of Nova Scotia and the largest urban area in the Atlantic provinces of Canada. It has a population of about 500,000.

The city's tourism industry is highly developed and is a key economic driver for the city, showcasing Nova Scotia's culture, history, scenery and coastline. The city hosts many festivals and events and has seven museums and galleries. The waterfront in Downtown Halifax is the site of the Halifax Harbourwalk, a popular 3-km boardwalk.

Prior to COVID-19 (2020–21), the Halifax region enjoyed seven straight years of tourism growth, representing 5.3 million overnight visits, with visitors spending more than $1bn on tourism accommodation, attractions and services.

Discover Halifax is a nonprofit, membership-based marketing and sales organization in partnership with the Halifax regional government, the Hotel Association of Nova Scotia and participating industry members. Since its inception in 2002, Discover Halifax's goal has been to promote Halifax as a destination of choice for leisure and business travelers.

Discover Halifax has used a BSC approach for a number of years to meet its mandate of promoting the Halifax region, with the goal of being recognized as Canada's favorite city.

The BSC outlines four important categories to measure performance. For each of the stated objectives (shown in Table 14.7), detailed KPIs are set annually.

Table 14.7 The four perspectives of Discover Halifax's balanced scorecard

Customers	People	Innovation	Financial
• Grow leisure visitation	Support training and sales	Align strategy with partners	Leverage funding
• Grow group visitation	Manage and reward	Invest in technology	Improve return on investment
• Grow visitor spend with members	Support training and sales	Improve processes	Grow investment

Source: www.discoverhalifaxdmocom/

Questions

1. Explain what benefits Discover Halifax might gain by using the BSC.
2. Explain how the BSC shown here is related to the strategy map shown in Figure 14.14.

14.7.5 BSC – potential difficulties

At each stage of the development of BSC as a tool for implementation, it is necessary to be aware of potential difficulties that need to be overcome (Evans, 2005).

Evans (2005) identified three key potential difficulties:

- *Mistaking data for useable information* – A balance needs to be achieved between having enough detail to be actionable and having only enough to be meaningful and easily interpreted by managers
- *Failing to establish causal linkages between scorecard components* – Kaplan and Norton (2001) argued that each BSC measure becomes embedded in a chain of cause-and-effect logic that connects the desired strategic outcomes with the drivers that will lead to the successful achievement of these outcomes. Thus, in this way, the mapping of the BSC tells the story of the strategy in a way that is meaningful to stakeholders.
- *Failing to get the support of employees for the management system* – It is important that an understanding of strategy cascades down through an organization so that all employees are aware of strategic intent and the impact of operational activities on its delivery. Such an understanding is more easily conveyed using a tool such as BSC, which clearly establishes causal links.

THINK POINTS

- Explain how the BSC framework can be used in strategic implementation.
- What are the four perspectives in a typical BSC?
- Explain why strategic mapping is important to the BSC process.

Small business focus

The fragmentation of many parts of *THE* and the consequent importance of SMEs have been outlined throughout this book. It is largely accepted that SMEs are different in many respects to larger companies, not least when it comes to issues of strategic implementation. In particular, in SMEs:

- Formal planning systems may be less common and consequently SMEs may be more likely to tend toward more emergent approaches to strategy
- The role of the leader or entrepreneur may be more prominent
- The resources to formulate and implement strategy of their larger counterparts may be lacking

In summarizing previous research, Garengo and Biazzo (2102) confirmed these differences, in that SMEs often:

- Are operationally focused and lack formalized strategies
- Suffer from entrepreneurial behavior where performance measures are considered constraints to change
- Have limited resources and managerial capacities fueled by mainly implicit and context-specific knowledge

The reality for many small firms is that short-term survival is more important than strategic planning, say, five years hence, and never was this more evident than during the global COVID-19 pandemic. There also appears to be an inverse relationship between the age of a business and its likelihood of failure. This is perhaps because older firms have already demonstrated a successful capacity to adapt and develop and have built competences and capabilities that allow this process to continue (Haberberg and Rieple, 2008).

Thus, for many SMEs in *THE* there may be a number of difficulties when strategic implementation issues are considered. A specific but limited literature has emerged that considers these issues in *THE* contexts (see, for example, Kyriakidou and Gore, 2005; Hwang and Lockwood, 2006). In studying smaller tourism businesses in New Zealand, Ateljevic and Doorne (2004) pointed to the difficulties smaller businesses have with regard to specialist labor resources. Not only are employees expected to be specialists (e.g., chef, receptionist and guide) but they also require detailed understanding of the business and the dynamics of the industry sector.

Some of the key difficulties may relate to the availability of finance or appropriately skilled personnel, access to training programs and regulatory environments favoring larger enterprises. A further difficulty may relate to entrepreneurs being involved in *THE* for the lifestyle it offers, rather than being motivated by growth and development of the enterprise.

Notwithstanding the difficulties outlined, the implementation phase of strategy is often easier and more successful in SMEs than in larger companies. This is often because the larger the company, the greater the distance between the chief executive and front-line staff (Lasher, 1999), leading to lack of control and communication, or because of the direct involvement of the owner, who sets the standards and style of the operation (Hwang and Lockwood, 2006).

Other factors that might make implementation of strategy more successful in SMEs include:

- *Complexity* – Less complex structures make it easier to direct communications and receive feedback.
- *Centralization* – SMEs are less likely to be decentralized due to their smaller scale, so management control is easier and usually quicker.
- *Cultural consistency* – Larger organizations often have subcultures and informal cultures operating in parts of the organization, making it difficult to make changes in a consistent manner.
- *Leadership* – SMEs are often strongly associated with entrepreneurs or a small number of leaders, so it is clear where authority lies and decisions can be made quickly and decisively.

CHAPTER SUMMARY

The implementation of a selected strategy rests on the successful management of a number of issues.

An organization must firstly ensure that sufficient resources are available and in place to implement the strategy and, once acquired, resources need to be configured to support the key value-adding activities.

The culture and structure need to be assessed for their suitability to undertake the strategy and must be changed as necessary. The chapter also considered the issues surrounding the management of change – usually an important part of managing the implementation of strategy.

In this chapter, we also considered the particular context of *THE*, presenting the 11 characteristics of the industry (introduced in Chapter 2) and the possible managerial actions relevant to the implementation stage of strategy.

Finally, a BSC framework was suggested for coordinating, communicating and measuring the changes arising from implementation of strategy in a practical sense.

REFERENCES AND WEBSITES

References

Ateljevic, J. and Doorne, S. (2004) 'Diseconomies of scale: A study of development constraints in small tourism firms in central New Zealand', *Tourism and Hospitality Research*, 5(1): 5–24.

Balogun, J., Hailey, V. H. and Gustafsson, S. (2016) *Exploring Strategic Change*, 4th ed., Harlow, UK: Pearson.

Bass, B. M. and Bass, R. (2009) *The Bass Handbook of Leadership: Theory, Research, and Managerial Applications*, 4th ed., New York: Simon and Schuster.

Beer, M., Eisenstat, R. and Spector, B. (1990) 'Why change programs don't produce charge', *Harvard Business Review*, Nov.–Dec., 158–166.

Bruch, H., Gerber, P. and Maier, V. (2005) 'Strategic change decisions: Doing the right change right', *Journal of Change Management*, 5(1): 97–107.

Bruch, H. and Sattelberger, T. (2000) 'The turnaround at Lufthansa: Learning from the change process', *Journal of Change Management*, 1(4): 344–363.

Burnes, B. (2017) *Managing Change*, 7th ed., Harlow, UK: Pearson.

Canadian Tourism Commission. (2012) *Helping Tourism Businesses Prosper: Canadian Tourism Commission Corporate Plan 2013–2017*, www.destinationcanada.com

Carlsen, J., Andersson, T. D., Ali-Knight, J., Jaeger, K. and Taylor, R. (2010) 'Festival management innovation and failure', *International Journal of Event and Festival Management*, 1(2): 120–131.

Chandler, A. D. (1962) *Strategy and Structure: Chapters in the History of the American Industrial Enterprise*, Cambridge, MA: MIT Press.

Chebat, J. (1999) 'Special issue on strategy implementation and assessment research: Research on implementation deserves as much attention as strategy formulation', *Journal of Business Research*, 45: 108–109.

Chesshyre, T. (2002) Interview with Michael O'Leary, *The Times Travel Section*, 5 January.

Denton, G. A. and White, B. (2000) 'Implementing a balanced scorecard approach to managing hotel operations: The case of White Lodging Services', *Cornell Hotel and Restaurant Administration Quarterly*, 41: 16–26.

Doran, M. S., Haddad, K. and Chow, C. W. (2002) 'Maximising the success of balanced scorecard implementation in the hospitality industry', *International Journal of Hospitality and Tourism Administration*, 3(3): 33–58.

Dwyer, L. and Edwards, D. (2009) 'Tourism product and service innovation to avoid "strategic drift"', *International Journal of Tourism Research*, 11(4): 321–335.

Dwyer, L., Mistilis, N., Edwards, D. and Roman, C. (2016) *Gambling with Our Tourism Future: The Role of Research in Destination and Enterprise Strategies to Avoid Strategic Drift*, Travel and Tourism Research Association: Advancing Tourism Research Globally, www.scholarworks.umass.edu/ttra/2007/Illustrated_Papers/25/

Elbanna, S., Eid, R. and Kamel, H. (2015) 'Measuring hotel performance using the balanced scorecard: A theoretical construct development and its empirical validation', *International Journal of Hospitality Management*, 51: 105–114.

Elbanna, S., Kamel, H., Fatima, T. and Eid, R. (2022) 'An investigation of the causality in the balanced scorecard: The case of the Gulf Cooperation Council hospitality industry', *Tourism Management Perspectives*, 41: 100934. https://doi.org/10.1016/j.tmp.2021.100934

Epstein, M. and Manzoni, J. F. (1998) 'Implementing corporate strategy: From tableaux de bord to balanced scorecards', *European Management Journal*, 16(2): 190–203.

Evans, N. G. (2005) 'Assessing the balanced scorecard as a management tool for hotels', *International Journal of Contemporary Hospitality Management*, 17(5): 376–390.

Evans, N. G. (2016) 'Sustainable competitive advantage in tourism organizations: A strategic model applying service dominant logic and tourism's defining characteristics', *Tourism Management Perspectives*, 18: 14–25.

Fatima, T. and Elbanna, S. (2020) 'Balanced scorecard in the hospitality and tourism industry: Past, present and future', *International Journal of Hospitality Management*, 91: 102656. https://doi.org/10.1016/j.ijhm.2020.102656

Franco, M. and Bourne, M. (2004) 'Are strategic performance measurement systems really effective: A closer look at the evidence', in *Proceedings of the EurOMA Conference*, vol. 2, Paris: INSEAD, 163–174.

Galan, J. I. and Sanchez-Bueno, M. J. (2009) 'The continuing validity of the strategy – structure nexus: New findings, 1993–2003', *Strategic Management Journal*, 30(11): 1234–1243.

Garengo, P. and Biazzo, S. (2012) 'Unveiling strategy in SMEs through balanced scorecard implementation: A circular methodology', *Total Quality Management and Business Excellence*, 23(1): 79–102.

Getz, D. (2002) 'Why festivals fail', *Event Management*, 7(4): 209–219.

Getz, D. and Andersson, T. D. (2008) 'Sustainable festivals: On becoming an institution', *Event Management*, 12(1): 1–17.

Ghoshal, S. and Bartlett, C. (1987) 'Management across borders: New strategic requirements', *Sloan Management Review*, 43: 1–17.

Gkoumas, A. (2022) 'Developing an indicative model for preserving restaurant viability during the COVID-19 crisis', *Tourism and Hospitality Research*, 22(1): 18–31. https://doi.org/10.1177/1467358421998057

Graeff, C. L. (1997) 'Evolution of situational leadership theory: A critical review', *The Leadership Quarterly*, 8(2): 153–170.

Greer, C. R., Lusch, R. F. and Hitt, H. A. (2017) 'A service perspective for human capital resources: A critical base for strategy implementation', *Academy of Management Perspectives*, 31(2): 137–158.

Haberberg, A. and Rieple, A. (2008) *Strategic Management: Theory and Application*, Oxford, UK: Oxford University Press.

Hahn, W. and Powers, T. L. (2010) 'Strategic plan quality, implementation capability, and firm performance', *Academy of Strategic Management Journal*, 9(1): 63–81.

Hall, D. J. and Saias, M. A. (1980) 'Strategy follows structure!', *Strategic Management Journal*, 1(2): 149–163.

Hall, R. (1992) 'The strategic analysis of intangible resources', *Strategic Management Journal*, 13(2): 135–144.

Handy, C. (2007) *Understanding Organizations*, London: Penguin.

Hersey, P., Blanchard, K. H. and Natemeyer, E. (1979) 'Situational leadership, perception, and the impact of power', *Group and Organization Studies*, 4(4): 418–428.

Heskett, J. L., Sasser, W. E. and Schlesinger, L. A. (1997) *The Service Profit Chain*, New York: Simon and Schuster.

Hitt, M. A., Jackson, S. E., Carmona, S., Bierman, L., Shalley, C. E. and Wright, M. (2017) *The Oxford Handbook of Strategy Implementation*, Oxford, UK: Oxford University Press.

Hofstede, G. (1980) *Culture and Organizations: Software of the Mind*, London: McGraw-Hill.

Holbeche, L. (2011) *Understanding Change: Theory, Implementation and Success*, Abingdon, UK: Routledge.

Howell, J. M. and Higgins, C. A. (1990) 'Champions of change: Identifying, understanding, and supporting champions of technological innovations', *Organizational Dynamics*, 19(1): 40–55.

Huckestein, D. and Duboff, R. (1999) 'Hilton Hotels: A comprehensive approach to delivering value for all stakeholders', *Cornell Hotel and Restaurant Administration Quarterly*, 40: 28–38.

Hwang, L. J. J. and Lockwood, A. (2006) 'Understanding the challenges of implementing best practices in hospitality and tourism SMEs', *Benchmarking: An International Journal*, 13(3): 337–354.

Jogaratnam, G. and Tse, E. C. Y. (2004) 'The entrepreneurial approach to hotel operation evidence from the Asia-Pacific hotel industry', *Cornell Hotel and Restaurant Administration Quarterly*, 45(3): 248–259.

Johnson, G. (1988) 'Rethinking incrementalism', *Strategic Management Journal*, 9(1): 75–91.

Jones, P. (2008) *Communicating Strategy*, Farnham, UK: Gower Publishing.

Kaplan, R. S. and Norton, D. P. (1996) 'Using the balanced scorecard as a strategic management system', *Harvard Business Review*, 74: 75–85.

Kaplan, R. S. and Norton, D. P. (2001) *The Strategy-Focused Organisation*, Boston: Harvard Business School Press.

Kim, J. S., Hardin, A. and Lee, S. (2022) 'Factors influencing resistance to hospitality information system change', *Journal of Hospitality and Tourism Insights* [e-pub ahead of print]. https://doi.org/10.1108/JHTI-04-2022-0129

Kotter, J. P. (2001) 'What do leaders really do?', *Harvard Business Review*, 79(11): 85–98.

Kyriakidou, O. and Gore, J. J. (2005) 'Learning by example: Benchmarking organizational culture in hospitality, tourism and leisure SMEs', *Benchmarking: An International Journal*, 12(3):192–206.

Lasher, W. R. (1999) *Strategic Thinking for Smaller Businesses and Divisions*, Oxford, UK: Blackwell.

Lewin, K. (1947) 'Feedback problems of social diagnosis and action of frontiers in group dynamics', *Human Relations*, 1: 147–153.

Lorange, P. (1998) 'Strategy implementation: The new realities', *Long Range Planning*, 31(1): 18–29.

Lufthansa. (2021) *Lufthansa Annual Report 2021*, www.lufthansa.com

Lynch, R. (2021) *Strategic Management*, 9th ed., Harlow, UK: Pearson.

Miller, D. (2001) 'Successful change leaders: What makes them? What do they do that is different?', *Journal of Change Management*, 2(4): 359–368.

Miller, S., Wilson, D. and Hickson, D. (2004) 'Beyond planning: Strategies for successfully implementing strategic decisions', *Long Range Planning*, 37(3): 201–218.

Miles, R. E. and Snow, C. C. (1978) *Organizational Strategy, Structure and Process*, New York: McGraw Hill.

Mintzberg, H. (1990) 'The design school: Reconsidering the basic premises of strategic management', *Strategic Management Journal*, 11(3): 171–195.

Nordvall, A. and Heldt, T. (2017) 'Understanding hallmark event failure: A case study of a Swedish music festival', *International Journal of Event and Festival Management*, 8(2): 172–185.

Nørreklit, H. (2000) 'The balance on the balanced scorecard: A critical analysis of some of its assumptions', *Management Accounting Research*, 11(1): 65–88.

Okumus, F. (2003) 'A framework to implement strategies in organizations', *Management Decision*, 41(9): 871–882.

Okumus, F. and Hemmington, N. (1998) 'Barriers and resistance to change in hotel firms: An investigation at unit level', *International Journal of Contemporary Hospitality Management*, 10(7): 283–288.

Palatková, M. (2011) 'The 7-S-McKinsey model: An implementation tool of a destination marketing strategy in the Czech Republic', *Global Management Journal*, 3(1/2): 44–54.

Palmer, I., Dunford, R. and Buchanan, D. A. (2021) *Managing Organizational Change: A Multi Perspectives Approach*, 4th ed., New York: McGraw-Hill.

Pearson, J., Pitfield, D. and Ryley, T. (2015) 'Intangible resources of competitive advantage: Analysis of 49 Asian airlines across three business models', *Journal of Air Transport Management*, 47: 179–189.

Pechlaner, H. and Sauerwein, E. (2002) 'Strategy implementation in the Alpine tourism industry', *International Journal of Contemporary Hospitality Management*, 14(4): 157–168.

Peters, T. J. and Waterman, R. H. (2015) *In Search of Excellence: Lessons from America's Best-Run Companies*, London: Profile Books.

Phillips, P. and Louvieris, P. (2005) 'Performance measurement systems in tourism, hospitality, and leisure small medium-sized enterprises: A balanced scorecard perspective', *Journal of Travel Research*, 44(2): 201–211.

Quinn, J. B. (1980) 'Managing strategic change', *Sloan Management Review*, Summer: 3–20.

Quinn, J. B. and Voyer, J. (1998) 'Logical incrementalism: Managing strategy formation', in H. Mintzberg, J. B. Quinn and S. Ghoshal (Eds), *The Strategy Process*, Englewood Cliffs, NJ: Prentice Hall, 103–110.

Sainaghi, R. (2010) 'Hotel performance: State of the art', *International Journal of Contemporary Hospitality Management*, 22(7): 920–952.

Sainaghi, R., Phillips, P. and Corti, V. (2013) 'Measuring hotel performance: Using a balanced scorecard perspectives' approach', *International Journal of Hospitality Management*, 34: 150–159.

Sainaghi, R., Phillips, P. and d'Angella, F. (2019) 'The balanced scorecard of a new destination product: Implications for lodging and skiing firms', *International Journal of Hospitality Management*, 76: 216–230.

Stalk, G., Evans, P. and Sgulman, L. E. (1992) 'Competing on capabilities: The new rules of corporate strategy', *Harvard Business Review* 70: 57–69.

Topham, G. (2013) 'Ryanair: More Christmas cheer, less of the bah, humbug from Michael O'Leary', *The Observer*, 1 December.

Vila, M., Costa, G. and Rovira, X. (2010) 'The creation and use of scorecards in tourism planning: A Spanish example', *Tourism Management*, 31(2): 232–239.

Whittington, R., Regnér, P., Angwin, D., Johnson, G. and Scholes, K. (2020) *Exploring Strategy*, 12th ed., Harlow, UK: Pearson.

Wild, J. (2013) 'easyJet blazes trail on customer service', *Financial Times*, 23 December.

Wu, W. Y. and Liao, Y. K. (2014) 'A balanced scorecard envelopment approach to assess airlines' performance', *Industrial Management and Data Systems*, 114(1): 123–143.

Zaleznik, A. (2004) 'Managers and leaders: Are they different?', *Harvard Business Review*, 82(1): 74–81.

Websites

www.destinationcanada.com
www.discoverhalifaxdmo.com/
www.easyjet.com
www.lufthansa.com
www.ryanair.com
www.scholarworks.umass

Chapter

15

International and global strategies for tourism, hospitality and event organizations

Introduction and chapter overview

One of the most important considerations in the implementation of strategy is the extent to which the organization's activities are spread across geographical regions.

Some organizations are entirely domestically based, others operate in many countries and still others operate in almost all regions of the world. This chapter is concerned with a discussion of the key issues surrounding the *why* and *how* questions:

● Why do organizations expand in this way?
● How do they go about it?

The *why* questions are covered in a discussion of the factors that drive increased internationalization. The *how* questions are answered in a discussion of the *market entry* options.

This chapter considers the decisions many organizations in *THE* need to make at some time during their development related to internationalization and globalization.

In considering the international and global dimensions of strategic development, this chapter inevitably draws heavily on previous chapters. In particular, it utilizes material from Chapters 10, 11 and 12 (which considered strategic direction, competitive strategy and strategic methods, respectively), though these chapters did not specifically consider the strategic development of organizations in international or global contexts. Nevertheless, many such decisions (especially in inherently international sectors such as those of *THE*) involve international decision making. In this chapter, we

DOI: 10.4324/9781003318613-20

focus specifically on the international and global dimensions when it comes to implementing strategic decisions.

The terms *internationalization* and *globalization* are widely used both in everyday language and also in the academic literature related to business and *THE*. The terms are also often used interchangeably.

Here, the differences between the two terms as presented by the relevant academic literature are examined. Two frameworks, developed by Yip and Porter, are presented to aid our understanding of the processes involved, and these models can be usefully applied in *THE* contexts.

In considering international and global strategy, many organizations consider whether to undertake operations themselves or outsource activities to another company. Though such decisions do not always involve an international dimension, in *THE* decision making there is often an international dimension. Thus, the topic of outsourcing is considered in this chapter, and there is quite a large literature in *THE* (particularly related to hotels and airlines) that specifically relates to this topic.

The chapter also considers what is often described as *market entry strategy*. This specifically concerns considerations such as:

- What are the drivers (factors) underlying market entry?
- How should organizations seek to enter particular international markets?
- Which methods (modes) should be used to enter these markets?

The chapter presents a conceptualization (model) of market entry strategy that provides a useful way of understanding the various factors involved in considering market entry strategy and the linkages between them.

Though internationalization, globalization and market entry strategy are presented separately, they are aspects of the same set of issues. Thus, the chapter concludes by considering the aspects holistically and using the hospitality sector as an exemplar of this approach.

Because this topic area involves added complexity and risk for organizations, it may be assumed that it is not relevant to SMEs. However, it is suggested this is not the case in many smaller *THE* companies because they are inherently international in their orientation.

LEARNING OBJECTIVES

After studying this chapter, you should be able to:

- Define and distinguish between internationalization and globalization
- Explain the factors that drive globalization
- Describe and demonstrate the application of Yip's framework for analyzing the extent of globalization in an industry and market
- Explain the adaptation of Porter's generic strategy to global and international settings
- Apply internationalization and globalization concepts and frameworks to *THE* contexts
- Explain the major global strategy alternatives
- Describe the international market entry strategies
- Apply market entry strategy and conceptualization to *THE* contexts
- Explain how some *THE* SMEs have been able to internationalize rapidly

15.1 Internationalization and globalization

Business has long been international, as merchants traveled the known world to sell products manufactured in their home country and returned with products from other countries. Initially, international business simply took the form of exporting and importing.

The term *international* describes any business that carries out some of its activities across national boundaries, so clearly a large number of *THE* businesses are included in this categorization. Even smaller businesses are also often increasingly international in their outlook, taking advantage of lower entry barriers with respect to technology and deregulation and forming alliances and networks across borders. Public sector organizations are increasingly having to compete internationally and make choices about outsourcing, international collaboration and tendering against foreign competitors for domestic contracts (Whittington et al., 2020).

Globalization, on the other hand, is more than simply internationalization and has given rise to a vast literature in relation to business but also in relation to wider societal issues. Indeed, globalization can be viewed as one of today's most controversial issues and, importantly (for our purposes), *THE* is at the same time both a central part of the process that results in globalization and a part of the result.

As Hjalager (2007:438) put it, 'Travel and tourism are among the many causes and results of globalization processes.'

DEFINITION/QUOTATION

Globalization

Globalization can be defined as the increasing integration of economies, societies, and civilizations. It includes, and goes beyond, the more simple internationalization defined as relations among and within nations. Globalization is a restructuring process that works across units and affects all aspects of human life: from capital flows, through political collaboration, to the flow of ideas. It also includes environmental pollution, criminal behavior, disease and, ultimately, terror.

Hjalager (2007:437–438)

There is a growing interest in researching the internationalization process of service firms (see, for example, Blomstermo et al., 2006; Pla-Barber and Ghauri, 2012; Jensen and Petersen, 2014). A growing number of studies have focused on *THE*, and hotels in particular (Chen and Dimou, 2005; Agndal and Elbe, 2007; Altinay, 2007; Hjalager, 2007; Litteljohn et al., 2007; Williams and Shaw, 2011; Etemad and Motaghi, 2018; H. Song et al., 2018; S. Song and Lee, 2020).

> **For example:** *Hjalager (2007) traced the stages that tourism goes through in the process of globalization and pointed to the distinguishing characteristics of tourism that distinguish it from other sectors. Chen and Dimou (2005) investigated the main factors that influence the corporate development decision of international hotels with particular reference to franchising vs management contracts.*

A large multinational company is not necessarily a 'global business'. For a business to become global in its operations, we would usually expect a number of important characteristics to be in place. Global organizations usually exhibit the characteristics outlined below:

- *Convergence of customer needs* – They take advantage of the increasing trend toward a convergence of customer needs and wants across international borders in many commercial segments, such as fast foods, soft drinks and beverages, accommodation and travel intermediaries.
- *Globalized industries* – They compete in industries that are globalized. In some sectors, successful competition necessitates a presence in almost every part of the world to effectively compete in its global market.
- *Location of value-added activities* – They can, and do, locate their value-adding activities in those places in the world where the greatest competitive advantages can be gained. This might mean, for example, shifting (outsourcing) certain operations to a low-cost region.
- *Integration and coordination of activities* – They are able to integrate and coordinate their international activities between countries. The mentality of 'a home base, with foreign subsidiary interests' that has been so prevalent among traditional multinational companies is eroded in the culture of global businesses. They have learned to effectively manage and control the various parts of the business across national borders despite local cultural differences.

The development of an organization's global strategy, therefore, will be concerned with:

- Global competences
- Global sales and marketing
- Global configuration and coordination of its value-adding activities (see the discussion of value adding in Chapter 3)

KEY CONCEPT

Multinational and transnational companies

The terms 'multinational' and 'transnational' are both commonly found in the business and *THE* literatures. The two terms are often used interchangeably, but here (following Stonehouse et al., 2007) it is argued that the difference between the two is one of emphasis on the degree of centralized control.

Both multinational and transnational companies share features such as being large and having direct investments in one or more foreign countries. The foreign investments may be part shareholdings but are more usually wholly owned subsidiaries.

The difference is in the degree to which the foreign investments are coordinated. We tend to think of a *transnational* company as one that has a high degree of coordination in its international interests. It will usually have a strategic center that manages the global operation such that all parts act in accordance with a centrally managed strategic purpose.

The term *multinational* company is usually taken to mean an international company whose foreign interests are not coordinated (to a large degree) from a strategic center.

15.2 Globalization of markets and industries

15.2.1 Market homogenization

It was Levitt (1983) who first argued that changes in technology, societies, economies and politics are producing a 'global village'. By this he meant that consumer needs in many previously separate national markets were becoming increasingly similar throughout the world. It should be recognized that globalization is not without its critics. Douglas and Wind (1987), for example, critically examined the key assumptions underlying globalization and the underlying philosophy that a strategy of global products and brands is the key to success in international markets.

Segal-Horn (2004) argued that the globalization of services (including *THE*) is distinctive when compared to manufacturing. Market homogenization means that segments should be defined internationally. However, whereas in manufacturing this usually means that identical products are produced in services (where standardization is more difficult), it does not usually mean providing the same product in all countries but rather offering 'local adaptations around a standardized core' (Segal-Horn, 2004:424).

> **For example:** *In THE there are numerous examples of companies responding to market homogenization through what Segal-Horn (2004) described as local adaptations around a single core. Fast food restaurants such as Burger King and McDonald's, hotel chains such as Holiday Inn and car hire companies such as Hertz and Avis exhibit such responses.*

In assessing the viability of international strategies for services, emphasis is often placed on economies of scale and economies of scope (which were explained, for example, by Ghoshal, 1987). Indeed, Segal-Horn (2004) asserted that many industries including travel and fast food now meet the criteria of a 'global industry' (as defined by Kobrin, 1991). A global industry is thus defined in terms of the significance of the competitive advantage of international operations arising mainly from the structural characteristics of scale economies and through technological intensity.

A categorization of some of the sources of competitive advantage derived from economies of scale and scope by service companies active internationally is shown in Table15.1.

Table 15.1 Potential sources of economies of scale and scope in international services

Economies of scale	Economies of scope
• Geographic networks	IT and shared information networks
• Physical equipment	Shared learning and doing
• Purchasing/supply	Product or process innovation
• Marketing	Shared R&D
• Logistics and distribution	Shared channels for multiple offerings
• Technology	Reproduction formula for service system
• Production resources	Range of services and service development
• Management	Complementary services
• Organization	Branding
• Operational support	International franchising
• Knowledge	Training
	Goodwill and corporate identity
	Culture
	Internal exploitation of economics

Economies of scale	Economies of scope
	Reduced transaction costs
	Know-how effects
	Privileged access to parent services

Sources: Segal-Horn (2004); Ghoshal (1987)

However, Segal-Horn (2004) also stressed the 'fuzzy' industry barriers as an important and distinctive aspect of international growth for many service providers, and this facet certainly applies in *THE* contexts. Thus, much of the growth has been across rather than within industry boundaries; for example, retail/financial services, retail/leisure, leisure/travel and travel/hospitality. Consequently, she argued that service industries should most appropriately be viewed not as discrete entities but instead as fuzzy sets of activities. This can be viewed as a similar notion to the diagonal integration discussed in Chapter 12, in that economies are gained by crossing the industry boundary.

> **For example:** *The American Express group is diversified both geographically and in relation to its range of services and illustrates service growth within a fuzzy industry set of leisure/travel/financial services (Segal-Horn, 2004).*

In summary, Segal-Horn (2004) emphasized the importance of economies of scope (as well as scale) to the international growth of many service firms, a view that is asserted in the quotation below.

DEFINITION/QUOTATION

Growth through wider scope

To generalize, 'Growth' for service firms may not involve a deepening of asset structure as in manufacturing companies, but a horizontal accretion of assets across different markets and different industries (i.e., scope).

Segal-Horn (2004:425)

Similarly, a discourse in areas of *THE* (particularly relating to tourism, visitor attractions and festivals and events) has taken place that discusses issues of authenticity and sustainability in relation to the increasingly globalized pattern of economic development.

> **For example:** *See McCartney and Osti (2007) and Quinn (2005) in relation to festivals and events and Teo (2002) for a discussion of the sustainability of tourism in the face of the pressures of globalization. McCartney used the International Dragon Boat festival held in Hong Kong to illustrate the issues that arise. Paradoxically in relation to cultural events, the increasing popularity (to global audiences) can also take away from the authentic experience, becoming more 'staged' as performances for visitors (McCartney, 2007).*

However, it is now generally recognized that in some way most markets and industries are becoming more global in nature. Though there is certainly still room for interpretation of what this actually means in practice, we will examine some of the major implications of this trend for *THE* organizations.

Developments in technology and removal of regulatory barriers to make markets 'contestable' have increasingly enabled services to be spread throughout many countries. Furthermore, transport developments have not only made it easier to move products and materials between countries but also resulted in a huge increase in world travel. Such travel educates people on the products and services available in other countries and, on their return home, they often wish to have access to products and services from overseas. This trend has been reinforced by changes in information technology, particularly those related to the internet, mobile communications, cinema and television, which have been important in some aspects of cultural convergence.

The development of the WTO has resulted in huge reductions in the barriers to trade between countries since World War II. Rising income levels throughout many parts of the world have also given economic impetus to the development of global markets.

It is not only markets that are becoming more global – industries are also becoming more global. The value chains of businesses in many industries span the globe.

> For example: *In the case of a diversified international tour operator, inputs in the form of tourist destinations may be sourced from many parts of the world, with the supply from one country varying from year to year based on the costs of the destination relative to other competing destinations. The resulting changing expenditure patterns of tourists will have profound direct and indirect effects on the local economies of the specific tourist destinations. Spending patterns will not only affect direct suppliers (such as restaurants, hotels, coach operators, airports, entertainment and event venues, tourist attractions and car hire firms); indirect suppliers will also be affected. These might include garage services, food suppliers, laundry services, banking and retailing.*

THINK POINTS

- Using appropriate *THE* contexts to illustrate your answer, what do you understand the term 'globalization' to mean?
- Distinguish between globalization and internationalization.
- Explain the meaning of 'market homogenization', providing examples from relevant *THE* contexts.

15.2.2 Global configuration of activities and outsourcing

Organizations concentrate certain activities in locations where they hope to obtain cost, quality or other advantages. Other activities, like distribution, are also often dispersed around the world. How a business configures its activities across national borders can be an important source of competitive advantage. The spread of an organization's value-adding activities around the world also means that there are important advantages to be gained from effective integration and coordination of activities.

In concentrating certain activities in certain locations around the world, organizations have a key question to address: should we carry out the activities ourselves, or should the activities be outsourced to specialist suppliers?

The main reasons for outsourcing include cost savings, a focus on core competence and flexibility in management (Hsu and Liou, 2013). Although cost savings are clearly a key driver in making a decision to outsource, in their influential book, Hamel and Prahalad (1994) argued that companies that measure their competitiveness solely on the basis of price are actually contributing to the erosion of their core competences. They asserted that care must be taken to protect and nurture core competences and, consequently, products and services, which are regarded as core competences, should be produced internally.

DEFINITION/QUOTATION

Outsourcing

'Outsourcing' is the contractual relationship between a client and a provider – the supplier of some service – by means of which the latter assumes the commitment to deliver that service to the former. Outsourcing is characterized by the fact that the service might be delivered internally within the client firm, but the latter achieves some benefit from outsourcing it.

Gonzalez et al. (2011:1670)

Outsourcing has become one of the key restructuring tools for companies seeking to boost their growth and business performance (Mol, 2007), and it has been widely applied to sectors of *THE*, particularly in relation to international hotel groups and airlines. Outsourcing has also been widely discussed in the academic literature in relation to these sectors. See, for example, Lamminmaki (2005), Espino-Rodríguez and Padrón-Robaina (2005) and Promsivapallop et al. (2015) in relation to hotels; Rieple and Helm (2008) and Hsu and Liou (2013) in relation to airlines; and Borodako et al. (2015) in relation to meetings and events.

KEY CONCEPT

Travel and tourism are different

Tourism, it can be argued, is different from other services in at least one important respect. Tourism is highly visible as well as invisible in its impact and is capable of making profound societal and cultural changes, not only to host destinations but also to tourist 'exporting' areas (Evans, 2012:221). However, we can distinguish between 'tourism' as a human phenomenon and the travel industry that facilitates the phenomenon.

The terms 'travel' and 'tourism' are both commonly used. In many circumstances, they are interchangeable, or one or the other is used to denote both travel *and* tourism. Indeed, this book itself uses the term 'tourism' as a 'shorthand' expression, when really it relates to both travel and tourism.

The distinction between them may seem fine, but it has an important implication when it comes to outsourcing. There are, of course, many definitions of tourism, but one commonly used definition is:

the temporary movement to destinations outside the normal home and workplace, the activities undertaken during the stay, and the facilities created to cater for the needs of tourists.

(Mathieson and Wall, 1982:1)

Thus, tourism can be viewed as a phenomenon that is essentially an activity engaged in by human beings. It includes the act of travel from one place to another, a particular set of motives for engaging in that travel and engagement in activity at the destination (Tribe, 1997).

At the same time, 'travel' can be viewed as a vast industry, the growth of which has mirrored the dynamic growth of tourism as a human phenomenon. Viewed in this way, tourism as an activity is destination specific – it cannot move. Sydney Harbor Bridge, The Great Wall of China and the Grand Canyon are rooted in a certain place and have to be visited at their location by tourists; that is, they cannot be outsourced.

Thus, there is a widespread assumption that tourism is an exception, an industry where global mechanisms and consequences do not come fully into play. Consequently, it can be argued that tourism (as a phenomenon) cannot be 'outsourced' (Hjalager, 2007). This is due to the centrality of the 'sense of place' to tourism, and a large academic literature has examined this facet (see, for example, Tsai [2012], who studied the notion of place in relation to international tourists in Singapore). Tourists visit a particular place for the range of benefits offered, and the benefits cannot be moved or outsourced.

However, by contrast, 'travel' or, more precisely, the travel industry upon which tourism depends is not constrained by place in the same way. Its activities can and are often outsourced, an option that managers must consider.

The same arguments about the sense of place and the immovability (or lack of outsourcing opportunities) can be extended to hospitality and events – though arguably to a slightly lesser degree.

For example, it is conceivable that the Wimbledon Tennis Championships, Salzburg Music Festival, Hong Kong's famous Peninsula Hotel or the Paris International Air Show could be moved to another location. In doing so, the essential characteristics of each (which depend in large part on their location) would be lost. The brand would be weakened, and it would probably make little commercial sense to do so. Thus, in these cases, certain aspects of the business (such as sales and marketing, 'back office' administrative functions and accounting) might be outsourced, but moving the entire product offering would be very difficult.

Though outsourcing does not necessarily involve outsourcing to a different country, in many cases or with certain functions (e.g., call centers) it does, or domestic providers may have to bid against foreign-based providers. Outsourcing has given rise to its own specific terminology in terms of 'offshoring' and 'nearshoring'.

- *Offshoring* is generally taken to mean providing services in locations anywhere in the world where they can be delivered competitively through the use of technology (see, for example, Fuster et al., 2018).
- *Nearshoring* is generally taken to mean that services are located either domestically or in a foreign country that is easily accessible. Nearshoring has become a recent trend as the pricing power of offshoring destinations like China, India and the Philippines has decreased relatively due to climbing wages and fast economic growth.

The generally recognized disadvantages of outsourcing (Hsu and Liou, 2013) include:

- Information security
- Loss of management control
- Staff morale problems
- Labor union issues

Other unanticipated problems may also occur that may serve to erode the supposed advantages attributed to outsourcing. Howells (1999) argued that many companies have found that outsourcing activities have introduced unexpected complexities, added costs and friction in the value chain and can require more senior management attention and deeper management skills than initially anticipated.

15.1 SHORT CASE ILLUSTRATION

Outsourcing activities for airlines: Qantas

International airlines have experienced highly volatile trading conditions in recent years as high fuel prices, intense completion, economic recession and unexpected crises (such as 9/11 and the COVID-19 pandemic) have affected their levels of profitability.

Assessing the relative costs or strategic benefits of outsourcing in the airline industry is therefore likely to be challenging (Rieple and Helm, 2008). The factors involved are complex, full information about costs is hard to gather and the circumstances being considered are dynamic rather than static. Nevertheless, many airlines have considered outsourcing some of their activities (Al-Kaabi et al., 2007; Hsu and Liou, 2013; Gil et al., 2022), particularly in relation to maintenance, repair and overhaul but also in relation to sales and marketing and computing and technology support

Specialist companies such as Minneapolis, USA-based Navitaire (a wholly owned subsidiary of the major GDS system Amadeus) have emerged to aid airlines and other companies in facilitating the outsourcing of some of their functions. Navitaire claims to have helped over 50 airlines (particularly low-cost carriers and start-up airlines) by assuming responsibility for many key processes, including reservations, internet and direct distribution, flight operations and operations recovery, loyalty schemes and revenue accounting.

For example: Qantas Airlines of Australia has a long history of outsourcing activities, including heavy maintenance of its aircraft. Outsourcing has sometimes proved to be controversial. In 2021, it announced it was outsourcing airport ground operations at 10 Australian airports with the loss of 2,500 jobs. It subsequently lost a legal challenge, which halted the move.

Sources: www.navitaire.com/; www.qantas.com.au; www.asianaviation.com

Questions

1. Explain the potential advantages of outsourcing to an airline such as Qantas.

2. What difficulties might Qantas need to overcome in implementing outsourcing?

15.2.3 Deglobalization

The process of globalization has become contentious and attracted criticism for a variety of reasons but mostly because the income of large and/or vocal segments of the population has been threatened by the dislocation and competition of trade and investment and by the inability or unwillingness of states to compensate for these losses (Hillebrand, 2010).

Globalization comprises many elements, including cross-border flows of trade, investments, data, ideas and technology, and, of course, people, including tourists. Indeed, among the most significant outcomes of globalization has been the popularization of international travel and the accompanying global expansion of the tourism industry (Niewiadomski, 2020). However, globalization (as measured by trade flows) appears to have peaked in 2008, with a slow decline following the banking crisis of that year (Irwin, 2020).

Consequently, in recent years, a new term has become established in the economic and business literature, namely, *deglobalization* (Postelnicu et al., 2015), though literature specific to *THE* is, to date, sparce. Deglobalization, in general terms, describes the process of decreasing economic interdependence between countries and is conceptually set in contrast to the process of globalization.

The COVID-19 pandemic (between 2020 and 2022) and the war in Ukraine have added momentum to this preexisting retreat from global economic integration.

Tourism and the travel industry were hit hard by the COVID-19 pandemic. In a short space of time, international travel came to a near-complete standstill (during 2020), grounding tourists and cutting off the revenue streams the sector offers to communities, businesses and workers around the world. An estimated 50 million tourism jobs were lost during 2020. However, the industry has proved to be resilient, and international tourist arrivals (though still lower than prepandemic levels) increased by 172% between January and July 2022 compared with the previous year (UNWTO, 2022).

Policymakers and business leaders now openly question whether global supply chains are sensible and resilient and whether economic interdependence should be reduced. This extends to tourism, where it remains to be seen whether international *THE* regains its long-term growth trajectory. Niewiadomski (2020) maintained that deglobalization brought about by COVID-19 is a temporary rather that permanent phenomenon. Importantly, the hiatus represents an opportunity to eradicate the 'dark side' of tourism's growth, such as environmental degradation, economic exploitation and overcrowding.

The UNWTO, in leading policy responses to the COVID-19 downturn, accepted that it represented a pivotal opportunity for tourism (UNWTO, 2022). However, Niewiadomski (2020) reported that the path of redevelopment and transformation will not be easy and is yet to be determined.

The implication for managers of the discussion on deglobalization is that if globalization is no longer considered inevitable, managers need to carefully consider where scarce resources are invested. Would investment in domestic markets or international markets that are close be more likely to yield superior returns than attempting to compete on a global basis?

15.3 Internationalization and globalization models

There are several models that seek to explain the basis of international and global strategy. This chapter explains the frameworks developed by Porter (1986b, 1990) and Yip (1992).

- *Porter* focused on adapting the generic strategy framework to global conditions and the role of configuration and coordination of value-adding activities in securing global competitive advantage.
- *Yip* developed the concept of 'total global strategy' based on his globalization driver framework.

Although these are the models considered in this chapter, interested readers should consider the work of Hamel and Prahalad (1985), Bartlett and Ghoshal (2002) and Stonehouse et al. (2007).

Mirroring the general business literature, there is also a large developing literature on globalization and its impacts on the development of *THE* sectors, including an edited 'handbook' (Timothy, 2019).

> For example: *Wahab and Cooper (2005) considered various aspects of tourism in relation to global issues, and Hjalager (2007) reviewed the literature on the topic and examined the stages tourism goes through in the process of globalization. There is great deal of literature that focuses on the hotel and airline sectors in particular. Go and Pine (1995) and Whitla et al. (2007) included conceptual and practical insights into the globalization issues facing hotels. Hanlon (2007) and Ramón-Rodríguez (2011) outlined the unique set of factors facing aviation in relation to international and global issues. The literature relating to internationalization and globalization of festivals and events is more sparse, though Matheson et al. (2006) considered globalization in relation to Singapore festivals.*
>
> *Dwyer (2015), in addressing several of the important effects of globalization (in a THE context), identified economic development, employment opportunities, the spread of technical knowledge, the development of new markets and products, new consumer values and environmental and sociocultural changes. The paper advocated for proactive responses to the challenges of globalization if organizations are to maintain their competitive position.*

15.3.1 Multi-domesticity

Porter (1990) argued that industries can be either global or *multi-domestic*. Multi-domestic industries are those where competition in each nation is essentially independent. He provided the example of consumer banking, where a bank's domestic reputation and resources in one nation tend to have little effect on its success in other countries. The international banking industry is, Porter argued, essentially a collection of domestic industries.

Global industries are those in which competition is global. The consumer electronics industry is a good example, where companies like Sony, Apple, Siemens, LG and Samsung compete in almost all countries worldwide. The implication would appear to be that businesses should adopt a global strategy in global industries and a multilocal strategy in multi-domestic markets. Yet the situation is not so simple as this. Even markets like consumer banking are becoming more global. The trend is for most industries to become more global, but even within industries major differences may occur.

One way of viewing globalization is as a continuum from globalization through international to local or multi-domestic (as shown in Figure 15.1).

In *THE*, the large global distribution systems (such as Galileo, Amadeus and Sabre) have a global reach, whereas toward the other end of the continuum, most retail travel agents and rail and bus operators might be viewed as being at the multi-domestic end in their orientation. Large airlines often like to portray themselves as 'global' carriers, but close inspection of their route networks reveals that no carrier serves all parts of the world, and even in those countries that are served, usually only the largest city is served.

Similarly, the large international hotel chains have expanded to include many countries but rarely penetrate local markets beyond the principal cities. By way of contrast, major soft drink brands such as Coca-Cola are widely available throughout the world and are widely dispersed within individual countries.

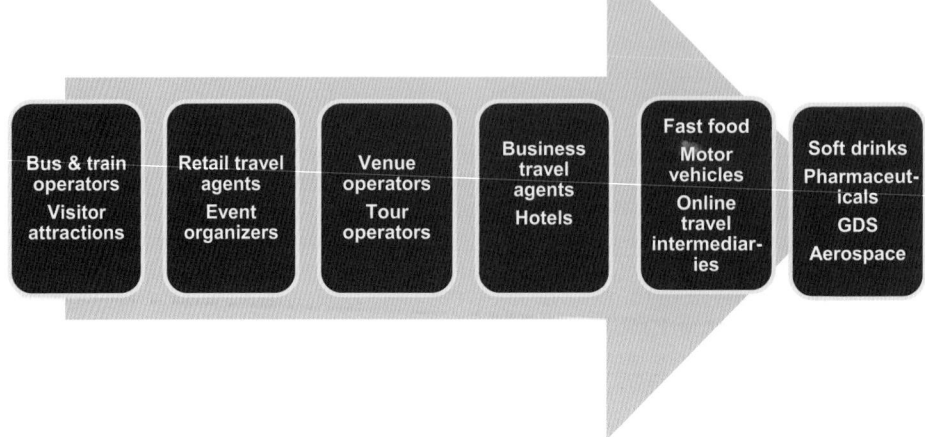

Figure 15.1 Global–local continuum

15.4 Porter's global generic strategies

Porter (1980) argued (see Chapter 8) that competitive advantage rests on an organization selecting and adopting one of three generic strategies to modify the five competitive forces in its favor to earn higher profits than the industry average. The three generic strategies are:

- Differentiation
- Cost leadership
- Focus

Porter (1986b) extended the generic strategy framework to global business. The model suggests that a business operating in international markets has five strategy alternatives (as shown in Figure 15.2). The five strategic postures are defined according to their position in respect to two intersecting continua:

- The extent to which the industry is globalized or country-centered (horizontal axis)
- The breadth of the segments (different customer groups) served by the competitors in an industry

The five strategic positions are described below.

- *Global cost leadership* – The organization seeks to be the lowest-cost producer of a product globally. Globalization provides the opportunity for high-volume sales and greater economies of scale and scope than domestic competitors.
- *Global differentiation* – The organization seeks to differentiate products and services globally, often on the basis of a global brand name.
- *Global segmentation* – This is the global variant of a focus strategy when a single market segment is targeted on a worldwide basis employing either cost leadership or differentiation.

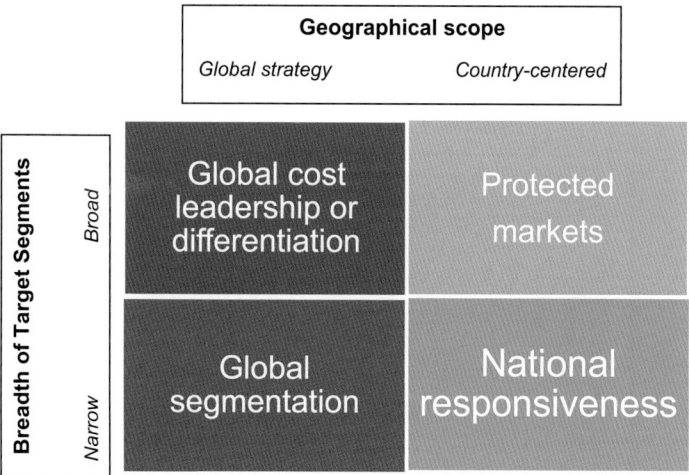

Figure 15.2 Porter's global strategy framework

Source: Porter (1986b)

- *Protected markets* – A organization identifies national markets where its particular organization is favored or protected by the host government.

- *National responsiveness* – The organization adapts its strategy to meet the distinctive needs of local markets (i.e., not a global strategy; suitable for purely domestic organizations).

The model suffers from similar flaws to those discussed in Chapter 8 relating to the generic strategy framework. As in the case of the conventional understanding of generic strategy, it is possible for a business to pursue a hybrid international strategy.

> For example: *Some of the 'low-cost' airlines such as easyJet, AirAsia, IndiGo, Lion Air and JetBlue clearly are concerned with strict adherence to cost control, as 'low-cost' suggests. At the same time, however, they are increasingly seeking to differentiate themselves from each other and from the established carriers by having very young aircraft fleets and by adding features such as priority boarding and preallocated seating to their business models.*

15.4.1 Configuration and coordination of internal activities

One of Porter's most important contributions to understanding global strategy is his work on the global value chain (1986a, 1990). Porter made the case that global competitive advantage depends on *configuring* and *coordinating* the activities of a business in a unique way on a worldwide basis. To put it another way, competitive advantage results from the global scope of an organization's activities and the effectiveness with which it coordinates them. Porter (1986a, 1990) argued that global competitive advantage depends on two sets of decisions:

- *Configuration of value-adding activities* – Managers must decide in which nations they will carry out each of the activities in the value chain of their business. Configuration can be broad (involving many countries) or narrow (few countries or one only).

- *Coordination of value-adding activities* – Managers must decide the most effective way of coordinating value-adding activities that are carried out in different parts of the world.

Part 5

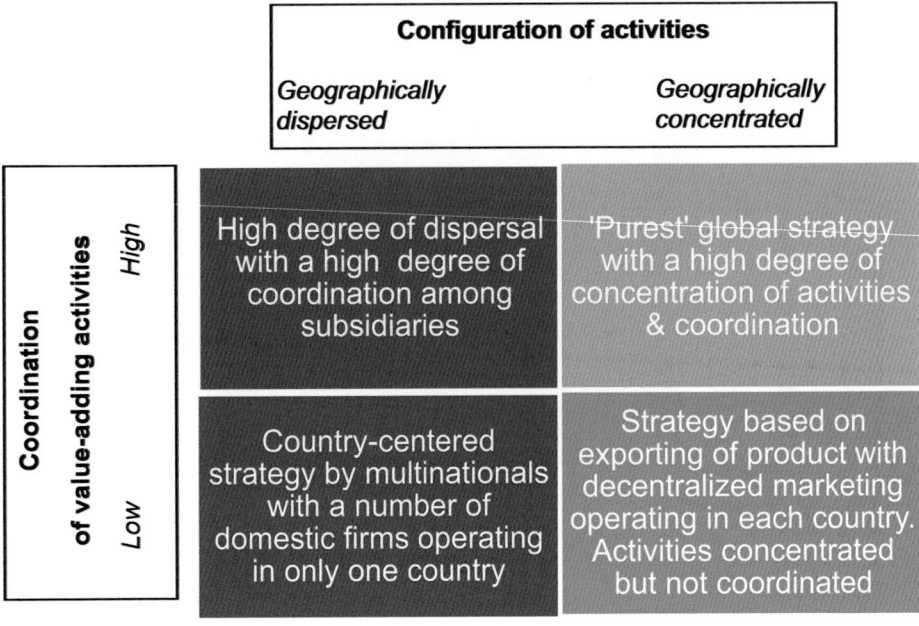

Figure 15.3 Configuration and coordination for international strategy

Sources: Porter (1986a, 1990)

Configuration and coordination present four broad alternatives, as illustrated in Figure 15.3.

In the case of configuration, an organization can choose to disperse its activities to a range of locations around the world, or it may choose to concentrate key activities in locations that present certain advantages. Many businesses concentrate their operations in countries where costs are low but skill levels are high.

> **For example:** *Many THE (and other) organizations have chosen to base call center operations and administrative 'back office' functions in countries such as India and the Philippines because they can gain access to high-quality English-speaking employees at relatively low cost.*

An organization can decide to coordinate its worldwide activities or to manage them locally in each part of the world. The latter approach misses the opportunity for global management economies of scale and scope. For Porter (1986a:12), the 'purest global strategy' is when an organization concentrates key activities in locations giving competitive advantages and coordinates activities on a global basis. In the long term, according to Porter, organizations should move toward purest global strategy to the degree practicable.

It is also the case that the degree of globalization of an industry or market may not be uniform. In other words, some aspects of an industry or market may be indicative of globalization, whereas others may be indicative of localization.

The degree of globalization of an industry can be assessed using Yip's globalization driver framework (1992). This widely used framework is generally a more useful framework than Porter's because it makes it possible to evaluate both the overall degree of globalization of an industry and which features of the industry are more or less global in nature.

15.5 The competitive advantage of nations or regions

Porter's five forces analysis (see Chapter 8) was developed during the 1980s and has proved to be highly influential in providing a framework for the analysis of a wide variety of organizations, including those in the public and not-for-profit sectors.

In a later work, Porter (1990) developed his ideas relating to competition in trying to explain why some nations, as well as some regions within countries, are more competitive than others. For a full discussion of the contribution of this framework to strategic thinking, see, for example, Snowdon and Stonehouse (2006), Stonehouse et al. (2007), Sölvell (2015) and Whittington et al. (2020).

15.5.1 Porter's diamond framework

Porter developed his 'diamond' analysis to assess the competitive advantage of nations or regions. The diamond represents a framework consisting of four factors that individually and through the linkages between them can be used to assess the degree to which a country or region enjoys a relative competitive advantage. The four factors are as follows:

- *Factor conditions* – physical resources, human resources, capital resources, infrastructure and knowledge resources
- *Market structures* – organization and strategies
- *Demand conditions*
- *Related and supporting industries*

In addition, Porter identified two further factors: *government* (which can influence any of the four factors) and *chance events* (which can shift competitive advantage in unpredictable ways). Porter's diamond is shown in Figure 15.4.

In Porter's analysis, each of these factors should be analyzed and the relative strengths or weaknesses evaluated.

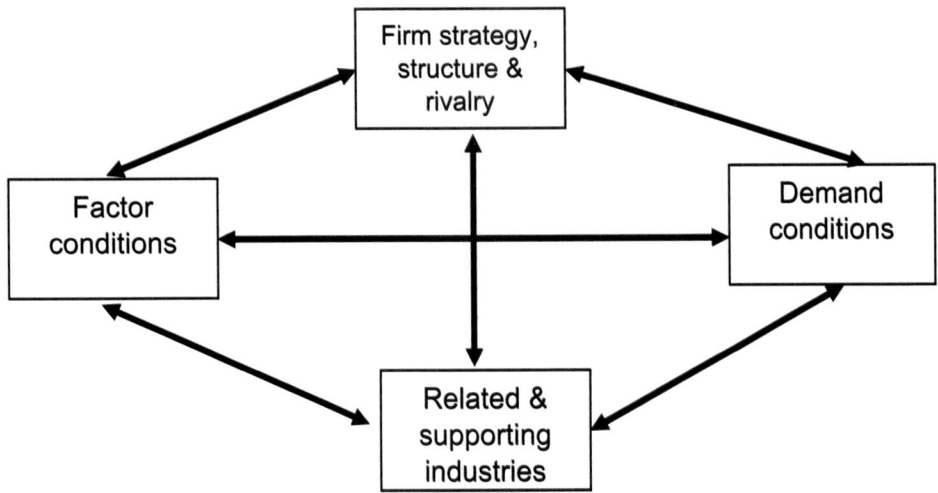

Figure 15.4 Porter's diamond analysis of the competitive advantage of nations

Source: Adapted from Porter (1990)

The diamond analysis of Michael Porter has been widely applied in *THE* settings, particularly to destinations (see, for example, Enright and Newton, 2004; Hawkins, 2004; Wahab and Cooper, 2005; Jackson and Murphy, 2006; Hong, 2009; Ribes et al., 2011; Porter et al., 2012).

> **For example:** *In their paper, Wahab and Cooper (2005) discussed Porter's diamond in a tourism context and applied the analysis to Egypt. International tourism and hospitality greatly contribute to wealth creation, as it did to Spain from the 1960s and 1970s, to Greece since the early 1970s and to Turkey since the mid-1980s (Wahab and Cooper, 2005). The authors concluded that though Egypt clearly has great potential as a tourist destination, some of the potential had (at the time of writing) still to be realized and that, consequently, the country had not yet reached a position of competitive advantage.*

The Strategy in Practice below outlines some of the steps a tourist destination area might take in practice to achieve a competitive advantage over rivals.

STRATEGY IN PRACTICE

Improving the competitiveness of a tourist destination

A list of guidelines for improving the competitiveness of a tourist destination was produced by Smeral (1998), building on the work of Porter (1990), and also later reported by Wahab and Cooper (2005). The guidelines include factor conditions (which are background considerations), of which those of specific importance to the tourism sector are (1) market structures, organization and strategies; (2) demand conditions; and (3) government.

1. Market structures, organization and strategies

- Image building within the context of global competition
- Aggressive and innovative marketing to foster growth and expansion of tourism's value-add through special interest motivations
- Information coordination and intensification of knowledge pertaining to a destination's strengths and weaknesses within a competitive environment at the international, national and regional levels

2. Demand conditions

- Expanding the destination's share of quality tourism movement from primary, secondary and opportunity markets offering them quality facilities and services
- Reducing demand seasonality through strategies aiming at guaranteeing a steady flow of tourist traffic from various markets
- Enhancing tourist receipts by concentrating mostly on higher spending tourist arrivals
- Encouraging repeat visitors through offering diversified attractions separately or in combined forms
- Holistically oriented local, regional and national policy

3. Government

- Encouragement of systematic and continuous research into tourism market trends, demand changes and innovations in leisure and tourism activities

- ● Serious and systematic control of and guidance to the travel and tourism industries to keep total quality at its most appropriate to face global competition

- ● Improving academic and professional education and intensifying quality training in tourism to meet industry requirements

- ● Eliminating 'red tape' and avoiding all administrative hurdles, including any conflict or overlapping of jurisdictions

- ● Ameliorating environmental quality

- ● Proactive management of change

Source: Adapted from Smeral (1998), as later reported by Wahab and Cooper (2005)

15.6 Yip's globalization driver framework

Yip (1992) argued that it is not simply the case that industries are 'global' or 'not global' but rather that they can be global in some respects and not in others.

Yip's globalization driver framework, shown in Figure 15.5, makes it possible to identify which aspects of an industry are global and which aspects differ locally. Analysis using this framework can play an important role in shaping the global strategy of a business. A global strategy, according to Yip, will be global in many respects but may also include features that are locally oriented.

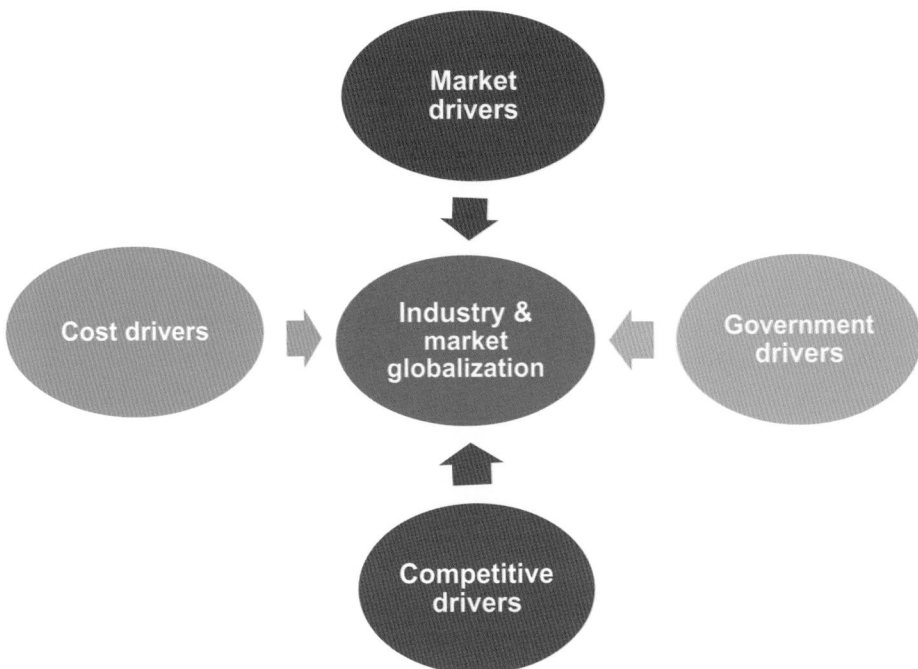

Figure 15.5 A framework describing drivers for globalization

Yip (1992) argued that to achieve the benefits of globalization, the manager of a worldwide business needs to recognize when industry conditions provide the opportunity to use global strategy drivers.

Yip identified four drivers (shown in Figure 15.5) that determine the nature and extent of globalization in an industry:

- *Market* drivers
- *Cost* drivers
- *Government* drivers
- *Competitive* drivers

The various aspects of each of these drivers are summarized in Table 15.2, and each of these drivers is considered in turn below.

15.6.1 Market globalization drivers

The degree of globalization of a market will depend on the extent to which there are common customer needs, global customers, global distribution channels, transferable marketing and lead countries. It is not simply a case of a market being 'global' or 'not global'. Managers must seek to establish which, if any, aspects of their market are global.

COMMON CUSTOMER NEEDS

Probably the single most important market globalization driver is the extent to which customers in different countries share the same need or want for a product. The extent of shared need will depend on cultural, economic, climatic, legal and other similarities and differences. There are numerous examples of markets where customer needs are becoming more similar. Examples include motor

Table 15.2 A summary of the globalization drivers

Market drivers	Cost drivers
• Common customer needs	Global scale economies
• Global customers	Steep experience curve effect
• Global distribution channels	Sourcing efficiencies
• Transferable marketing techniques	Differences in country costs (including exchange rates
• Presence in lead countries	High product development costs
	Fast-changing technology
Government drivers	**Competitive drivers**
• Favorable trade policies	High exports and imports
• Common marketing regulations	Competitors from different continents
• Government-owned competitors and customers	Interdependence between countries
• Compatible technical standards and common marketing regulations	Competitors globalized
• Host government concerns	

vehicles, soft drinks and fast food. Examples also extend to *THE*, where beach and ski resorts, cruise ships, global tours by bands, film and cinema and business travel might be cited.

> For example: *International business travel is highly fragmented, but a few large, internationally diversified companies have emerged (see the Short Case Illustration of BCD below) to service the needs of customers around the world. These suppliers include networks of international companies or franchisees such as Uniglobe Travel International, based in Vancouver, Canada, and UK-based Travel Solutions International (TSI) and GlobalStar. Some large travel management companies have also developed, such as American-based Carlson Wagonlit Travel and American Express, UK-based Hogg Robinson Group (HRG) and the Dutch-based company BCD. In addition, many tour operators, leisure-based travel agents and hotel companies operate subsidiaries to service corporate travel management requirements.*

Similarly, the various hospitality brands operated by international hotel groups such as Marriott Corporation, as well as McDonald's, Burger King and Pizza Hut in fast food or Coca-Cola and Pepsi in soft drinks, are illustrative of converging customer needs in certain markets. Levitt (1983) referred to this similarity of tastes and preference as increasing *market homogenization* – all markets demanding the same products, regardless of their domestic culture and traditional preferences.

15.2 SHORT CASE ILLUSTRATION

Market globalization drivers: BCD, international corporate travel management

CTM is a diverse field of activity that concerns the management of the travel arrangements for organizations in a strategic and cost-effective manner. Many organizations carry out this activity for themselves as an internal function, but many others contract the activity out to specialist suppliers. The market for supplying organizations is highly fragmented and varies considerably between countries, but a few large, internationally diversified suppliers have emerged as multinational corporations have spread their activities and require multicountry expertise.

Services carried out by such companies for their clients include:

- Planning and booking travel arrangements for companies at advantageous rates
- Analyzing travel market trends and providing consultancy and advice services
- Assessing the risks associated with travel to particular locations
- Documenting travel arrangements and reporting on expenditure
- Providing visa, passport and foreign currency services

The large CTM companies (or 'business travel agents') are often not well-known consumer brands but nevertheless constitute sizeable entities.

These companies include BCD, a privately owned company based in Utrecht, Netherlands, with regional centers in Atlanta, London and Singapore. The company, founded in 1975, operates in over 100 countries and had sales totaling US$25.7bn in 2017. The company operates a wide range of travel management products to meet the demands of internationally based corporate clients.

However, corporate travel is changing quickly, and the companies serving it (such as BCD) will have to be agile and adapt to survive and prosper. The demands of travelers, the promise of technology and the escalating sophistication of corporate clients will place demands on the providers of corporate travel solutions. Changes taking place include:

- Content disaggregation across multiple distribution platforms
- Evolving traveler expectations and services
- Enhanced virtual meeting systems
- Changing travel behavior

Source: www.bcdtravel.com

Questions

1. What would you consider to be the principal drivers of globalization in BCD's case?

2. What are the main activities carried out by CTM companies such as BCD, and why might the activities be viewed as strategically important for multinational companies?

GLOBAL CUSTOMERS AND CHANNELS

Global customers purchase products or services in a coordinated way from the best global sources. Yip identified two types of global customers:

1. *National global customers* – customers who seek the best suppliers in the world and then use the product or service in one country

> For example: *A theme park operator in a particular country might seek the best rides from many countries that are known for providing such specialist engineering skills, such as Germany, Switzerland, the USA and Japan.*

2. *Multinational global customers* – customers who similarly seek the best suppliers in the world but then use the product or service obtained in many countries

> For example: *Cruise lines source their ships from a number of companies in certain countries that are known for building cruise ships, such as Finland, France, Germany, Italy and Japan to ensure optimal quality standards delivered at a competitive price. They then use and market the product in many countries.*

Alongside global customers, there are sometimes global, or more often regional, distribution channels that serve the global customers. Global customers and channels will contribute toward the development of a global market.

15.3 TECHNOLOGY FOCUS

Globalization and personalization

Though the forces described by Yip's model of globalization can clearly be identified, there are nevertheless other pressures on organizations in *THE* (and other industries) working in the opposite direction: to communicate with customers individually; in other words, recognizing their individual differences and needs and not treating them as a homogeneous mass.

Technology is increasingly allowing companies to personalize their messages to customers but to do so in a cost-efficient way.

In 2018–19, CTM company BCD (see above) produced a series of three 'Inform' papers outlining the impact of technology on their business field. The third of these reports, *Communications, Emerging Technology and Travel Management* (BCD, 2019), explored how emerging technologies can be used to deliver effective, personalized messages to travelers and thereby engage them at exactly the right moment to encourage compliance. The report cited examples of the uses of technology such as:

- Using *machine learning* to communicate directly with travelers as individuals, basing messages on travel patterns, booking behavior and personal preferences

- Using a *blockchain*-based data storage system to keep traveler data safe, increasing traveler willingness to share personal information needed to craft personalized messaging

- Adopting *chatbot* technology to enable voice-controlled digital assistant travel bookings and automate routine travel management communication tasks, like answering policy questions

- Using *AR* and *VR* technologies to enhance interaction with travelers and, in some cases, replace travel

- Leveraging the IoT and location-based technology to keep travelers informed with timely and relevant messages throughout their journey, including warnings about flight cancellations and other disruptions

Source: BCD (2019)

TRANSFERABLE MARKETING

Transferable marketing describes the extent to which elements of the marketing mix like brand names and promotions can be used globally without local adaptations.

Clearly, when adaptation is not required, it is indicative of a global market. Brands like McDonald's, Coca-Cola and Nike are used globally, and increasingly travel brands such as Hilton, TUI and Lufthansa also have global recognition. Yet advertising for such brands can be both global and locally adapted according to the prevailing attitudes in local markets. If marketing is transferable, it will favor a global market.

LEAD COUNTRIES

When, as Porter (1990) found, certain countries lead in particular industries, it becomes critical for global competitors to participate in these lead countries to be exposed to the sources of innovation.

Lead countries are those that are ahead in product and/or process innovation in their industry. These lead countries help to produce global standards and hence global industries and markets.

For example: *The USA would clearly be seen as the lead country in terms of internet travel distribution systems, airline operations and new hotel and accommodation formats, whereas European companies have taken the lead in developing vertically and horizontally diversified leisure travel companies (such as TUI and Kuoni). A number of Asian airports such as Singapore, Hong Kong and Kuala Lumpur are consistently ranked among the world's best for the quality of the customer experience.*

15.6.2 Cost globalization drivers

The potential to reduce costs by global configuration of value-adding activities is an important impetus toward the globalization of certain industries. If there are substantial cost advantages to be obtained, an industry will tend to be global.

For example: *The international strategic alliances such as SkyTeam, oneworld and Star that have emerged in the airline industry have done so partly due to the need to add value for their customers by being able to offer global connectivity. However, their attraction to individual airlines also lies in their ability to save costs (such as business lounges, sales and marketing and procurement) through working cooperatively with other airlines.*

GLOBAL SCALE ECONOMIES

When an organization serves a global market, it is able to gain much greater economies of scale than if it serves only domestic or regional markets. Similarly, serving global markets has considerable potential for economies of scope. The differences between scale and scope economies are explained in the Key Concept below.

For example: *Internationally diversified THE companies such as Air France–KLM, Disney, Accor, Merlin Entertainments and TUI, which market their activities in many countries, gain large economies of scope in product development, marketing, procurement and financing.*

KEY CONCEPT

Economies of scale and scope

Economies of scale and economies of scope and are both widely used terms (for a discussion, see Ghoshal, 1987), encountered in a Key Concept in Chapter 8. Here we discuss the concepts further because it is important to understand the differences and be able to apply the terms correctly in various *THE* contexts.

- *Economies of scale* – describe the benefits that are gained when increasing volume results in lower unit costs

Although economies of scale can arise in all parts of the value chain, it is probably best understood by illustrating it using purchasing as an example. An individual purchasing one hotel room will pay more *per item* than a large company contracting to purchase hundreds of hotel rooms to provide for their customers for the season. Thus, the purchaser who is able to purchase in bulk (because of the size and structure of the buyer) enjoys scale economies over smaller organizations that buy in at lower volumes.

- *Economies of scope* – describe the benefits that can arise in one product or market area as a result of activity in another

Another way of putting it is that the cost of providing two distinct offers from the same organization is less than that for providing both separately. Thus, if a tour operator expands to market its activities in another country, the costs of the marketing activity can be shared with the activity in the countries in which it already operates through joint advertising, promotion and so on. Website development costs and brochure production costs can be shared between the various markets. Similarly, skilled and experienced staff can be transferred from one country to another to share the skills and expertise they have learned in a different market situation.

EXPERIENCE CURVE EFFECT

When there is a steep learning curve in operations and marketing, businesses serving global markets will tend to obtain the greatest benefits. In many service industries there are steep learning curves, thus yielding the greatest benefits to global businesses.

Experience and good practices from one country can be shared with other countries and regions, thereby increasing organizational learning and experience. Those organizations that are able to communicate the lessons from their experience – that is, learning around the organization quickly and effectively – are likely to be the most successful in global markets.

> For example: *For an international hotel group expanding internationally, it is crucial to get their market entry strategy right. However, experience from entering other country markets will help them make the correct decisions when they choose to enter subsequent markets.*

KEY CONCEPT

Learning curve

The idea of the learning curve has been used in many areas of life – not just in business. It describes the rate at which an individual or an organization learns to perform a particular task. The gradient of the beginning of the curve is referred to as its 'steepness' and is the most important part. The steeper this first part, the faster the learning. The general shape of a learning curve is described as *exponential* because the gradient usually decreases along its length as the time taken to perform the task decreases as those performing the task gain experience with it.

SOURCING EFFICIENCIES

If there are efficiency gains to be made by centralized sourcing carried out globally, this will drive an industry toward globalization. Businesses like those in sports apparel and clothing fashion benefit from global sourcing to obtain the lowest prices and highest quality standards.

> For example: *Cruise lines and airlines seeking crew and purchasing ships and aircraft will seek sourcing efficiencies by obtaining labor and equipment in the most cost-efficient ways. Many cruise lines select crew members from Asian countries where good quality staff members can be recruited at internationally competitive wage rates.*

FAVORABLE LOGISTICS

If transportation costs comprise a relatively high proportion of sales value, there will be every incentive to concentrate operations. If transport costs are relatively low, such as with consumer electronic goods, production can be located in several locations (thus favoring globalization of activities), which are chosen on the basis of other cost criteria such as land or labor costs.

DIFFERENCES IN COUNTRY COSTS

Operational costs (building, labor, etc.) vary from country to country, which can stimulate or impede globalization. Thus, countries with lower operational costs will be attractive to businesses in the process of globalization.

> For example: *Many Asian countries have attracted international hotel chains because of their favorable cost conditions and availability of high-quality labor at reasonable cost (as well as growing demand). Similarly, aircraft and ship maintenance and repair are often outsourced to countries with lower labor costs.*

FAST-CHANGING TECHNOLOGY AND HIGH PRODUCT DEVELOPMENT COSTS

Product life cycles are decreasing as the pace of technological change increases and consumers are becoming more discerning. At the same time, R&D costs are increasing in many industries. Such product development costs can only be recouped by high sales in global markets. Domestic markets simply do not yield the volumes of sales required to cover high R&D costs, particularly where the domestic market is small.

> For example: *Cruise lines and airlines face very rapidly changing technology and greater degrees of competition, together with high development and equipment purchase costs. These are facets they share with other industries such as pharmaceuticals and automobiles. As a consequence, they must operate in global markets in order to ensure they achieve the volumes of sales necessary to recoup these costs.*

15.6.3 Government globalization drivers

Many governments have taken individual and collective action to reduce barriers to global trade since World War II.

FAVORABLE TRADE POLICIES

The WTO (and its predecessor) has done much to reduce barriers to trade that have hindered globalization of many industries in the past. Although there are still significant barriers to trade in certain areas, the movement toward freedom of trade has been substantial, thus favoring globalization. The growth of customs unions and 'single markets' such as the EU and NAFTA have also made an important contribution in this regard.

> For example: *Since its inception, the airline sector has been subject to government regulation driven by the need for safety standards and the view that airlines represent important and prestigious national assets. This began to change in the late 1970s when airline deregulation occurred in the USA, followed by Europe in the 1990s and subsequently in many other parts of the world. Restrictions on the ownership of airlines by foreign owners remain as a constraint to full deregulation, however.*

COMPATIBLE TECHNICAL STANDARDS AND COMMON MARKETING REGULATIONS

Many of the differences in technical standards between countries that hindered globalization in the past have been reduced.

> **For example:** *Telecommunications standards, which have traditionally differed between countries, are increasingly being superseded by international standards. Similarly, standards are converging in the pharmaceutical, airline and computing industries, which makes it easier to produce globally accepted products.*

Airlines and shipping have long had common safety standards coordinated through UN agencies, as it is necessary to alleviate consumer safety concerns by developing common standards. Shipping, including cruising, is regulated by the IMO. IMO is the London, UK-based UN specialist agency with responsibility for the safety and security of shipping and the prevention of marine pollution by ships.

Similarly, the ICAO was created in 1944 as another specialist agency of the UN to promote the safe and orderly development of international civil aviation throughout the world. Based in Montreal, Canada, the agency sets standards and regulations necessary for aviation safety, security, efficiency and regularity, as well as for environmental protection in aviation.

There remain important differences in advertising regulations between countries; generally, however, these differences are being eroded (albeit slowly), which favors greater degrees of globalization.

GOVERNMENT-OWNED COMPETITORS AND CUSTOMERS

Government-owned competitors, which often enjoy state subsidies and other benefits, can act as a stimulus or a barrier to globalization. They frequently compete with other global competitors, thus being forced to become more efficient and global market oriented. On the other hand, government-owned competitors can make it very difficult for other competitors to compete in their home market (because they do not enjoy the same benefits).

There has, however, been a growing trend toward the privatization of many state-owned businesses in many countries worldwide, which has reduced this barrier to globalization. Thus, government-owned hotel, shipping and airline companies have been sold to the private sector so that governments can concentrate their scarce resources in other areas of activity.

> **For example:** *In recent years, many governments around the world have chosen to bring private capital and management techniques into the management of state assets such as hotels, airports and other transport infrastructure and airlines. The process of wholly or partly privatizing state assets has been facilitated by factors such as the decline in communism, the need for governments to raise money and reduce their debts and the recognition that such assets need specialist management skills.*
>
> *The European states of Croatia and Slovenia (among others) have privatized state-run hotels in recent years. Assaf and Cvelbar (2010) reported in relation to Slovenian hotels that privatization has led to an improved level of performance. Park et al. (2011) evaluated the possible effects of privatization on Incheon International Airport in Seoul, South Korea. Similarly, Miyoshi (2015) assessed the Japanese government's policy of reforming the ownership of government-owned airports to reduce its large financial burden by involving private entities.*

HOST GOVERNMENT CONCERNS

The attitudes and policies of host governments can either hinder or favor globalization. In certain circumstances, host governments may favor the entry of global businesses into domestic industries and markets and may provide financial or non-financial assistance to do so. Such measures will assist the process of globalization.

> **For example:** *In a study of foreign direct investment (FDI) in tourism and related sectors, Endo (2006) stated that many countries, including both developed (e.g., Australia, Canada,*

Switzerland) and developing (e.g., Egypt, India, Jamaica, Kenya) countries, are offering some sort of incentives to tourism-related activities to attract domestic and foreign investors.

The more governments that espouse such policies, the greater the globalization of an industry will be. Conversely, in other cases, host governments will seek to protect industries that they see as strategically important and will attempt to prevent entry of foreign businesses. Thus, legal restrictions placed on competition by governments act as a barrier to the globalization process.

For example: *Many countries such as the USA limit ownership of their airlines by foreign companies and restrict access to domestic airline routes for foreign-based competitors.*

15.6.4 Competitive globalization drivers

The greater the strength of the competitive drivers, the greater the tendency for an industry to globalize will be. Global competition in an industry will become more intense when:

- There is a high level of trade between countries
- Competitors in the industry are widely spread (often on different continents)
- The economies of the countries involved are interdependent
- Competitors in the industry are already globalized

HIGH EXPORTS AND IMPORTS

The higher the level of trade in products and services between countries, the greater the pressure for globalization of an industry will be.

COMPETITORS FROM DIFFERENT CONTINENTS

The more countries that are represented in an industry and the more widely spread they are, the greater the likelihood of globalization.

INTERDEPENDENCE OF COUNTRIES

If national economies are already relatively interdependent, this will act as a stimulus for increased globalization. Such interdependence may arise through, for example, multiple trading links in other industries, being a part of a single market or being in a shared political alliance.

COMPETITORS GLOBALIZED

If a competitor is already globalized and employing a global strategy, there will be pressure on other businesses in the industry to globalize as well. Globalization in the business travel sector is high because of the pressure on organizations to compete globally.

For example: *Travel agencies that specialize in providing travel arrangements for business customers, so-called CTM companies (such as BCD, illustrated previously), are often required to serve the needs of customers that are themselves global companies. Such companies often wish to deal with an organization that is able to service its travel needs on a global basis; that is, a company that offers potential economies of scope.*

15.6.5 Using the globalization driver framework

Yip's globalization driver framework provides a useful tool for analyzing the degree of globalization of an industry or market. Equally, it makes possible an understanding of which particular aspects of an industry or market are global and which aspects are localized.

Each of the drivers must be analyzed for the industry and market under consideration, and the results of the analysis will play an important role in assisting managers to form the global strategy of their organization. It is important that strategy be fit for purpose; that is, some aspects of strategy might be standardized across many countries, whereas others need to be modified for local conditions to be successfully implemented.

Yip (1992) argued that successful global strategy must be based on a comprehensive globalization analysis of the drivers encountered above. Managers of a global business must, he contended, evaluate the globalization drivers for their industry and market and must formulate their global strategy on the basis of this analysis.

> **For example:** *If they find that customer demand is largely homogeneous for their product, they can produce a largely standardized product for sale throughout the world. If, on the other hand they find that there are few cost advantages of global concentration of operations because of adverse economies of scale or scope, they may choose to disperse their operational activities around the world to be close to their customers in different parts of the world.*

The 'total global strategy' of an organization can be a mix of standardization and local adaptation as market and industry conditions dictate. Thus, the results of the analysis will help to determine:

- Which features of the strategy are globally standardized.
- Which features of the strategy are locally adapted.

Yip went on to identify three stages in developing a total global strategy.

- *Developing a core strategy* –building core competences and generic or hybrid strategy that can potentially give global competitive advantage
- *Internationalizing the core strategy* – introducing core competences and generic strategy to international markets and locating value-adding activities where competitive advantages, such as low-cost access to resources, are available. This will include choice of which markets the business will enter and the means by which it will enter them.
- *Globalizing the international strategy* – coordinating and integrating the core competences and strategy on a global basis, as well as deciding which elements of the strategy are to be standardized and which are to be locally adapted on the basis of the strength of the globalization drivers in the industry and market

15.4 SHORT CASE ILLUSTRATION

Internationalizing events: rugby sevens

Top-level sport is by nature international. If you want to be the best in any sport, it has to be proven through international competition. International sport is also highly competitive with regard to international attention, global television audiences, commercial sponsorship and global success.

Football, particularly the large European leagues (Spain's Primera División, Germany's Bundesliga, England's Premier League and Italy's Serie A) and the World Cup, held every 4 years, command global attention, as do the Olympic Games and American football. Other sports have to compete for such attention.

One of the ways many sports have competed is by 'internationalizing' sports events; that is, organizing sports events in countries around the world, thereby spreading interest and raising commercial revenue. Thus, tennis, golf, motor racing, snooker and badminton, for example, have successful and growing tours with events staged in succession in countries around the world. In some cases, such as the lucrative annual Formula 1 Motor Racing tour, cities compete with each other for the rights to stage one of the events. In 2008, Singapore staged the world's first F1 Grand Prix at night on its Marina Bay circuit.

Rugby union is a physical contact sport played with 15 players on each side that originated in late 19th-century England at Rugby School – hence the name. It has grown to become a worldwide sport with a loyal following, but success in this physically demanding sport has been concentrated in relatively few countries, with New Zealand having the preeminent record of achievement in the sport. The Rugby World Cup, organized by the sport's governing body (the International Rugby Board), held every 4 years since 1987 has spread interest in the game.

However, the game has complex rules and is usually played in winter, and it is difficult to win without players who are physically large, which serves to somewhat inhibit its global reach.

As with other sports (such as cricket and football), shorter, faster versions of the game have been developed to help spread its appeal. Thus, rugby sevens (which itself has a long history) has spread in recent years as the game has secured commercial sponsorship and television coverage. With a version of the game involving seven players, it has developed rapidly to become a global game with an annual worldwide series of events and Olympic recognition in Rio de Janeiro in 2016, with Fiji its first-ever Gold Medal winner in the inaugural tournament

The annual Hong Kong sevens competition (dating from 1976) attracts international tourists to Hong Kong from many countries and has played a significant role in raising the tourist profile of the Special Administrative Region. The sevens form of the game is played throughout the year, is less physically demanding while favoring athleticism, is far shorter in length and has simpler rules. As a result, it lends itself to tournament rather than one-off formats, can be followed more easily by casual spectators rather than rugby aficionados and represents an attractive package for television.

The profile of rugby sevens has grown considerably with the advent of the HSBC Sevens World Series, which is an annual series of international tournaments run by the International Rugby Board featuring national teams and sponsored by HSBC Bank. The series, organized for the first time in the 1999–2000 season, was formed to develop an elite-level competition series between rugby nations and develop the sevens game into a viable commercial product for the International Rugby Board. The series has developed into an annual competition held between October and April at nine venues around the world, including Australia, Dubai, South Africa, the USA, New Zealand, Japan, South Africa, Scotland and England. Since its inception, teams from some 36 countries have been involved, and both spectator numbers and television revenues have increased considerably.

Questions

1. How would you categorize the international growth of rugby sevens using the concepts of Yip and Porter covered in this chapter?

2. What are the difficulties and opportunities that might be encountered in internationalizing in this way?

15.7 Key strategic international decisions

Once a business has developed core competences and strategies that can potentially be exploited internationally and globally, decisions must be made as to where and how to employ them. Initial moves into overseas markets will involve (using Porter's terminology) *market development*, because such markets and segments can be regarded as new to the business. The initial market development may then be followed by product development and diversification (see Chapter 10).

When a business enters international and global markets, it is necessary to build new competences alongside those that have resulted in domestic competitive advantage. These new competences could well be in the areas of global sourcing and logistics and global management expertise.

The globalization of a business does not happen overnight. It may well involve entry to key countries with the largest markets first, followed by entry to less important countries later. In the initial stages of globalization, the key decisions are usually as follows:

- Which countries are to be entered first?
- In which countries are value-adding activities to be located?
- Which market development strategies are to be employed to gain entry to chosen overseas markets?

THINK POINTS

- Using relevant examples from *THE*:
- Explain each of Yip's globalization drivers.
- Explain how Porter developed the generic strategy framework to apply to global strategy.
- Explain the importance of configuration and coordination of value-adding activities to global strategy.

15.8 Market entry decisions

15.8.1 Decision criteria

The interest in market entry strategy derives from the internationalization and globalization frameworks and can be viewed as one of the most critical strategic decisions for an organization (Root, 1994). There has been extensive research into market entry strategies, and several models and theories have emerged. Canabal and White (2008) and Schellenberg et al. (2018) summarized and evaluated the literature in this field.

Much of the research related to market entry relates to manufacturing as opposed to services, and it can be argued (as elsewhere in this book) that there are crucial differences between the two. These differences in relation to foreign market entry were outlined by Brouthers and Brouthers (2003), Ekeledo and Sivakumar (2004), Blomstermo et al. (2006) and Sanchez-Peinado et al. (2007).

There is also a growing specific literature that relates to market entry decisions for *THE* organizations, though it is heavily skewed toward the hotel sector; see, for example, Quer et al. (2007), León-Darder et al. (2011), Choi and Parsa (2012), Villar et al. (2012), Andreu et al. (2017) and Kruesi et al. (2017).

The decision as to which countries and markets to enter first will be based on a number of important factors.

- *The potential size of the market* – Is the market for the product in the country likely to be significant?
- *Economic factors* – Are income levels adequate to ensure that significant numbers of people are likely to be able to afford the product?
- *Cultural and linguistic factors* – Is the culture of the country likely to favor acceptance of the product to be offered?
- *Political factors* – What are the factors that may limit entry to markets in the host country?
- *Technological factors* – Are levels of technology adequate to support provision of the product in the host market, and are technological standards compatible?

A business will choose to enter markets in those countries where the above conditions are most favorable.

The Short Case Illustration below outlines the balance of risk and opportunity encountered by TUI in entering the Russian and Commonwealth of Independent states (CIS) markets and how the company has chosen to deal with the circumstances that it faces. The case of TUI's entry into and subsequent retreat from the Russian market demonstrates some of the difficulties of international expansion.

15.5 SHORT CASE ILLUSTRATION

Market entry decisions: TUI enters and leaves Russia

Entering a new foreign market is one of the riskiest decisions a business can take and one that must be taken with great care, having analyzed not only the opportunities of the market itself but also the means of market entry.

The Russian market presents particular challenges, and companies such as furniture company Ikea have made costly mistakes in the past. Russia is a vast country, with a business culture that is still evolving in the post-communist period and weak legal protection for foreign investors and consumers who are generally inexperienced travelers. Russia has become increasingly isolated following its invasion of Ukraine in February 2022. Few Western companies are now willing to trade directly with Russia.

Nevertheless, Russia and the former Soviet states, generally referred to as Commonwealth of Independent States (CIS), represent enormous opportunities for foreign tour operators. The harsh winters, over 200 million consumers and few large existing competitors make Russia and CIS attractive markets for outbound travel.

TUI Travel plc is one of the world's leading leisure travel groups, serving some 27 million customers in many countries. Its core source markets, which include the UK and Ireland, Germany, France and Scandinavia, are mature and growing relatively slowly; hence the need to consider new growth opportunities. Its tour operating strategy is capable of being *stretched* in that it is similar (with some local adaptation) in all of its core source markets. It relies on its:

- *Content* – unique inclusive ('packaged') holidays and tailor-made holidays
- *Brands and distribution* – market-leading brands, trusted brands for safety and security and high levels of controlled distribution with a focus on online distribution

- *Technology* – flexible technological platforms to support growth
- *Growth and scale* – ability to leverage the advantages of scale and scope
- *People* – providing the business with knowledge and expertise and drive innovation

TUI identified the potential for travel growth in Russia and CIS in the early years of this century, but despite its power and size chose not to develop on its own. In 2009, a joint venture was formed with a Russian group controlled by Russian oligarch Alexei Mordashov (who also controls the large steel company Severstal). The Russian company had vital knowledge and experience of the Russian market to match the international travel expertise provided by TUI.

After forming the joint venture, TUI Russia acquired a number of Russian and Ukrainian tour operators and set up a network of travel agencies. Thus, TUI Russia and CIS's market entry strategy involved a combination of a joint venture and vertical and horizontal integration.

However, TUI has adopted a strategy of retrenchment, in that it has reduced its exposure to Russia (in common with many other Western and Asian companies), partly due to government sanctions being imposed. Mordashov invested in TUI and joined its supervisory board, but he was forced to resign in March 2022 as sanctions were introduced. TUI sold its stake in the joint venture at the end of March 2021 to KN-Holdings, a company owned by Mordashov's family.

The brand license agreement that allowed TUI Russia to continue using the TUI name in Russia, Ukraine, Belarus, Kazakhstan and Uzbekistan was cancelled in March 2022.

Sources: Jolly (2022); www.tuitravelplc.com

Questions

1. What other market entry methods might TUI have considered?

2. What are the main risks that TUI might encounter in entering a country like Russia, and what steps is the company taking to overcome them?

15.8.2 *Location of value-adding activities*

Managers must determine which countries they will locate key value-adding activities of their business in. They will seek to gain cost, skill and resource advantages. In other words, they will attempt to locate activities in countries where there are production advantages to be gained. Such advantages depend on:

- *Wage levels* – low wage levels will keep operational costs low
- *Skill levels* – suitably skilled labor must be available
- *Availability of resources* – suitable resources must be accessible
- *Infrastructure* – transport, communications and ICT must be favorable to the logistics of the business

The existence of these conditions within a country will, in turn, depend on:

- *Economic factors* – level of economic development, wage levels, exchange rate conditions
- *Social factors* – attitudes toward work, levels of education and training

- *Political factors* – legislation favoring investment etc.
- *Technological factors* – levels of technology and transport and communications infrastructure in the country

15.8.3 Market development methods

Once decisions have been made as to which countries' markets to enter and where value-adding activities are to be located, the task for management becomes the determination of which method of development to employ to enter another country.

Broadly speaking, a business can choose either *internal or external methods for development* of overseas markets (see Chapter 12). Internal methods are usually slower but tend to entail lower risk. External methods involve the business developing relationships with other businesses. Internal methods of development include direct exporting and establishing overseas offices and subsidiaries. External methods include joint ventures and alliances, mergers and acquisitions, franchising and licensing. The choice of method will depend on a number of factors:

- The size of the investment required or the amount of investment capital available
- Knowledge of the country to be entered and potential risk involved (e.g., of political instability)
- Revenue and cash flow forecasts and expectations
- Operating cost considerations
- Control considerations (some investment options will have implications for the parent company to control activity in the host country)

15.8.4 Internal development methods

Internal methods of development (as explained in Chapter 12) are based on the organization exploiting its own resources and competences and involve the organization carrying out some of its activities overseas. This may be exporting its expertise or setting up some form of operations abroad. The advantages of internal methods of development are that they maximize future revenue from sales abroad and they allow a high degree of control over overseas activities. On the other hand, they can involve significant risk if knowledge of the host country and its markets is limited, and they may require considerable direct investment.

DIRECT EXPORTING

Direct exporting is the transfer of services across national borders from the home operation. The service may simply be provided from the home country.

> For example: *A cruise line might advertise its products in a country in which they have no staff. Instead, customers are directed to a sales office in the cruise line's home country. As sales increase, a sales office may be set up in the overseas country.*

To avoid some of the pitfalls of direct exporting (such as lack of local knowledge and access to distribution channels), many businesses make use of local sales agents to distribute their products (sometimes known as a *piggyback* distribution arrangement). In this way, the company avoids direct investment in a foreign country in which it lacks expertise and relies on others with local knowledge to provide key services in a particular market.

Overseas operations

Organizations may choose to offer their products and services directly in foreign countries. There are a number of reasons for such direct investment. The investment allows the company to gain local knowledge, maintain control over the operations and tailor the products and marketing to local demands. Relationships can also be forged with local suppliers and government that might be helpful in developing the business.

Foreign subsidiary

Internal development may involve establishing a foreign subsidiary of the business such as when it is favorable for the parent company to have total control of its overseas operations, decision making and profits. Such a subsidiary may carry out the full range of activities of the parent business or it may be only an operational or marketing subsidiary.

15.8.5 External development methods

External methods of development (or entry 'modes', as they are often termed) are the 'vehicle' by which market entry is achieved. These entry modes involve the organization entering into relationships with businesses in a host country. External development methods can take the form of alliances or joint ventures, mergers or acquisitions or franchises (see Chapter 12 for a discussion of these topics).

Such methods (modes) have certain intrinsic advantages and disadvantages associated with them:

- Advantages – Providing local knowledge, potentially reducing risks and reducing investment costs (except in the case of mergers or acquisitions)
- Disadvantages – Providing reduced revenues and reduced control of activities as optimal income is traded off against the advantage of lower financial exposure (again except in the case of mergers and acquisitions)

International alliances and joint ventures

Alliances and joint ventures allow a business to draw on the skills, local knowledge, resources and competences of a locally based company. They reduce the risks of entry to overseas markets by providing local knowledge and help reduce investment costs.

International mergers and acquisitions

Mergers and acquisitions give a business access to the knowledge, resources and competences of a business based in the host country, thus reducing some of the risks of market entry.

International franchising and licensing

A franchise is an arrangement under which a franchiser supplies a franchisee with a tried-and-tested brand name, products and expertise in return for the payment of a proportion of profits or sales. The major advantage to the franchiser is that the risk, investment and operating costs of entering overseas markets are considerably reduced. At the same time, the franchisee can contribute their local knowledge while also benefiting from the lower risks associated with an established business idea.

> For example: *Much activity by THE organizations has taken place in foreign markets through franchisement. The expansion of Burger King, Holiday Inn and Choice hotels into overseas markets has come largely through franchise development.*

15.9 A conceptualization of market entry

This chapter has discussed a number of facets of market entry. The topic is clearly complex and multifaceted and has received considerable attention in the academic literature.

It is, however, useful to have a model or a conceptualization of the main facets of market entry to understand the decision-making process that needs to take place. One such conceptualization was provided by J. Johnson and Tellis (2008), who considered the drivers of success for market entry into China and India in particular, though the generic model could be applicable to other countries.

The conceptualization of J. Johnson and Tellis (2008) is shown in Figure 15.6. The authors suggested that there are two broad factors that drive firm performance in international market entry and a number of 'constructs' by which firm and country differentiation can be measured or estimated:

- *Firm differentiation* – This can be achieved through the strategy that is adopted and the way in which resources are accessed and deployed.

The key elements of the firm's strategy in this context relate to the mode (method) of entry that is chosen and the timing of the entry. The various modes of entry have been discussed previously but broadly include both external and internal methods. The timing of any strategic move is critical for its success and depends on environmental factors such as the stage in the economic cycle and the positioning of competitors. J. Johnson and Tellis (2008) reported that firm size is a measure of the resources a company has available.

- *Country differentiation* – The key variables with regard to country differentiation include the characteristics of the host country, the two most important of which are the risk associated with investing in a particular country and the openness of the country in terms of regulatory and other barriers to entry of foreign firms.

In addition to the constructs outlined (firm strategy, firm resources and country characteristics), firm and country differentiation can be viewed as shaping host home location. The two measures of this construct, which are discussed extensively in the academic literature, are economic and cultural distance (see, for example, the work of Hofstede [1980] on cultural distance, discussed in Chapter 4).

To measure or estimate the firm's performance in relation to the constructs outlined, the model uses historical data as reported in annual reports and other records.

Though the findings need to be treated cautiously, because they relate to two emerging markets only (albeit very significant markets), the survey was not limited to service companies and was based on historical data; nevertheless, the authors presented some interesting results. Using their model with historical data the authors drew several conclusions in relation to market entry in China and India:

- Success is greater for entry into China than for entry into India.
- Success is greater for smaller firms than for larger firms.
- Success is greater for entry into emerging markets with less risk and those that are economically close to the home market.
- Success is greater for firms that use a mode of entry with greater control.
- Joint ventures are the most popular mode of entry.

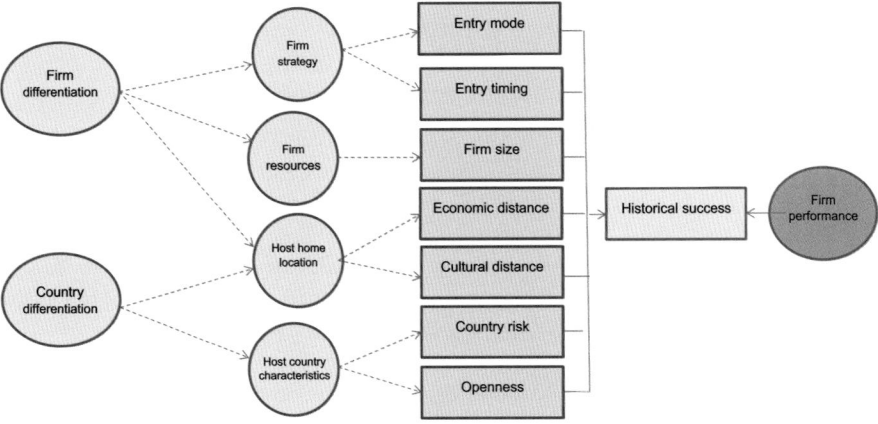

Figure 15.6 A conceptual framework: drivers of entry success

Source: Adapted from Johnson and Tellis (2008)

15.10 Globalization and market entry strategy – a focus on hospitality

Although we have considered globalization and market entry strategy separately, they are in reality closely related, because companies have to carefully consider how they will enter each market in which they plan to operate. Thus, here we use the hospitality sector (and international hotel groups in particular) to illustrate the connectedness of these two aspects.

The hospitality sector is at the forefront of globalization, and much of the internationalization and globalization literature focuses on this sector (see, for example, C. Johnson and Vanetti, 2005; Whitla et al., 2007; Y. Yu et al., 2014), and it is clear that the large branded hotel groups are spreading their interests around the world. International hotels serve to illustrate the opportunities and threats presented by globalization and the variety of market entry strategies that are being implemented in the various markets concerned. See, for example, Assaf et al. (2015), which considered the key locational factors in attracting international hotel groups; Niñerola et al. (2016), which related the experiences of Spain's Meliá Hotels in entering the Chinese market; and Berbel-Pineda et al. (2017), which assessed entry mode choice for hotel groups internationalizing.

The approach toward internationalization and globalization varies between hospitality companies, though increasingly companies are utilizing *asset-light* models that involve managing, leasing or franchising assets rather than owning them. By using such business models, companies are seeking to avoid the capital requirements of hotel development and the inherent property risks involved. Market entry strategies also vary considerably both between hotel groups and within each group. In most cases, the overall core elements of the strategy used remain in place, regardless of individual market characteristics, but then adaptation takes place for local market conditions.

The Short Case Illustration below outlines the globalization and market entry strategies that have been used by hotel companies, using IHG as an example. Though globalization will continue and the larger companies are actively increasing their property portfolios (though they do not necessarily own the properties concerned), it is clear that new competitors are emerging.

In addition, notwithstanding the continuing effects of globalization, the sector remains highly fragmented. Given the growth in demand and consumers seeking new product formats, there is still room for new and innovative formats in the market.

15.6 SHORT CASE ILLUSTRATION

Hospitality globalization and market entry strategy: IHG

In recent decades, the hospitality industry has been a significant force in globalization, as evidenced by the proliferation of multinational firms such as Accor, Best Western, Hilton, InterContinental and Marriott (Cunill, 2006). The internationalization of (primarily Western) brands has been motivated by a variety of factors, including sales expansion, geographic diversification, resource and labor acquisition and worldwide brand recognition (L. Yu, 1999). Most multinationals have deployed either a strategy of concentration or one of scale economies with a brand formula derived from the home country (Gross and Huang, 2011). The typical range of strategic choices for market entry modes includes strategic alliances, franchising, management contracts, joint ventures and acquisitions (Athiyaman and Go, 2003).

However, the large multinational groups are being challenged. As Gross and Huang (2011:261) pointed out, 'While established mega-chains have attracted the most attention, their corporate domination is being challenged by the growth of smaller domestic hotel chains in countries other than the traditional Western ones that may potentially emerge as hospitality exporters.'

Future multinational hotel chains may not come from Western sources; rather, domestic hotel groups (in countries such as China and India) are reaching a stage of development that potentially prepares them for international expansion. In the case of China, substantial stakes are held in Western developed chains such as Radisson and Hilton, and domestically developed brands such as Jin Jiang are quickly developing an international presence.

Nevertheless, many of the large Western chains and a few selected upscale Asian chains (such as Mandarin Oriental, Shangri-la and Nikko) are firmly established internationally in both emerging and developed markets, and they continue their growth strategies. They are not only targeting new countries in which to develop but also achieving greater geographic penetration in those countries in which they are already operating.

For example, IHG, one of the world's largest hotel groups, has built a strong global presence through a strategy that seeks to build preferred brands with scale positions in the most attractive markets globally.

IHG achieves this through concentrating growth in the largest markets so that IHG and owners can operate more efficiently and benefit from enhanced revenues and reduced costs. The key markets for the hotel brands that constitute IHG include large developed markets such as the USA, UK and Germany, as well as emerging markets like China and India.

IHG adapts its strategy and business model by market, choosing partnerships and joint ventures where appropriate.

IHG views the greatest opportunity for growth in any single country in China (where it is the largest international hotel company), in anticipation of increasing demand for hotels, driven by a large, emerging middle class and growing domestic and international travel. The company's strategy has been to:

- Enter the market early
- Develop a relationship with key local third-party owners
- Grow the company's presence rapidly

Outside the largest markets, IHG focuses on building presence in key gateway cities where its brands can generate revenue premiums from high business and leisure demand.

Thus, IHG has one of the largest pipelines (hotels being planned and developed) of any hotel group and continues to develop its global reach. In doing so, however, it maintains the principles underlying its strategy, but it carefully selects its targeted development markets and modifies its strategy according to the specific characteristics of that market.

Sources: Adapted from www.ihgplc.com/; Cunill (2006); L. Yu (1999); Athiyaman and Go (2003); Gross and Huang (2011)

Questions

1. What are the main elements of IHG's strategy and its adaptation for the Chinese market?

2. Consider the threats that IHG might face in its future development in China.

3. Consider the market entry conceptualization provided by J. Johnson and Tellis (2008) and apply it to IHG's entry to the Chinese hospitality market.

THINK POINTS

- Discuss the ways in which a business may develop a 'total global strategy'.

- Discuss the advantages and disadvantages of different market entry methods.

- Distinguish between the approaches adopted by IHG and TUI in the Short Case Illustrations in this chapter.

- Explain the main elements of J. Johnson and Tellis's (2008) conceptualization of market entry above and how it aids understanding of the process.

Small business focus

It might be thought that internationalization and globalization issues are not directly relevant to most SMEs operating in *THE* sectors because their size precludes them from competing except in the domestic market. Though many *THE* companies are often active internationally because of the inherent international nature of the products, many smaller *THE* companies sell their products only in domestic markets.

There are two reasons why internationalization and globalization should be of interest to *THE* managers in SMEs:

- International competitors may choose to compete in the domestic market, thereby challenging the market share of existing SMEs.
- New technology and other advances are increasingly enabling SMEs to internationalize rapidly.

SMEs in all industries (including *THE*) often face difficulties compared to larger competitors. The limited literature on the international activities of SMEs (Agndal and Elbe, 2007) emphasizes constraints to internationalization that inhibit international expansion. These constraints (summarized by Freeman et al., 2006) include:

- A lack of economies of scale
- A lack of financial and knowledge resources
- An aversion to risk
- An inability to manage uncertainty

However, though SMEs are extremely important in many parts of *THE*, with the accommodation, travel intermediaries and event management sectors remaining highly fragmented, large international groups are developing in each of these sectors and increasing their international market share. As a result, managers in smaller *THE* companies have to be aware of the strategic intentions of the larger internationally diversified companies, whether they intend to internationalize or not.

Multinational companies have the ability to switch substantial resources from one market to another quickly and decisively and can sustain short-term losses by cross-subsidizing the business venture from other markets in which they are active. Thus, they can quickly build market share, sometimes at the expense of smaller domestic companies already operating in the market. These SMEs have fewer resources and cannot afford to sustain losses by cross-subsidy from elsewhere.

Conceptualizations of the ongoing globalization of firms are dominated by stage models (Hjalager, 2007) that imply that firms normally proceed through a series of stages until they reach a global scale and that to trade globally, they will have reached a certain size and scale of operations.

However, a new stream of literature emerged in the early 1990s that takes a different view of globalization. It focuses on smaller entrepreneurial firms adopting a global focus from the outset and embarking on rapid and dedicated internationalization. The evolution of these so-called born global companies has been influenced by an inexorable trend toward globalization and the pervasive impact of new technologies (Knight and Cavusgil, 2004).

DEFINITION/QUOTATION

'Born global' companies

Born global companies can be defined as:

> Entrepreneurial start-ups that, from or near their founding, seek to derive a substantial proportion of their revenue from the sale of products in international markets.
>
> Knight and Cavusgil (2004:124)

The accelerated pace of entry into international markets is driven by a desire to gain *first-mover advantage* and to lock in new customers before competitors can. Bell et al. (2001) identified 'born again' global firms that have internationalized rapidly following a long period during which they concentrated on the domestic market. Studies of successfully internationalizing born global SMEs have found that such firms are characterized by an organizational culture that is proactive, risk-taking and innovative (Freeman et al., 2006). Bell et al. (2003) suggested an integrative model of SME internationalization that envisages different pathways by which the process can take place.

In inherently international industrial sectors such as *THE*, which are rarely directly regulated by government (except in the case of airlines), there is an opportunity for born global firms to develop (Hjalager 2007; Williams and Shaw, 2011). The approach adopted by the internet intermediary Skyscanner illustrated below provides an example of a born global approach.

15.7 TECHNOLOGY FOCUS

Born global companies: Skyscanner travel search engine

The emergence of new technologies, the coalescing needs of consumers and the influence of visionary entrepreneurs have allowed some SMEs to rapidly globalize in a way that was previously not possible for smaller firms.

Skyscanner is an example of such a born global company. Though comparatively recently formed, it has gone through a rapid internationalization process. Skyscanner's three founders, including CEO Gareth Williams, met at Manchester University and officially launched the company, based in Edinburgh, Scotland, in 2003.

Gareth became frustrated with the difficult and tedious process of searching multiple airline and travel agent websites to find the best fares and envisioned a solution: a single website that could collect, collate and compare prices for every commercial flight in the world. Skyscanner was born at a pub brainstorming session between the three friends, from a simple Excel spreadsheet.

Skyscanner's comprehensive proprietary flight search product has grown considerably since that time to become Europe's leading flight search engine, and offices have been opened in Singapore, Miami, Beijing and Glasgow. Skyscanner stresses its impartiality and that it is not an online travel agency; rather, it operates by showing customers all flight, hotel and car rental options available to them from its global partners and online travel resellers. Customers can then compare all options and select the best choice and price for their trip, going on to book with their chosen brand.

In this way, Skyscanner's partners control the distribution of prices, the rate they charge and also the booking and customer data. Because Skyscanner is not an online travel agent, one brand is not favored over another. Customers are simply directed to their purchases by market forces and product differentiation.

Skyscanner has demonstrated its appeal to consumers around the world through sister websites. The site is available in over 30 languages and used by 100 million people a month.

Thus, in less than 15 years, the travel-based technology company was able to grow from very small beginnings as an SME to a substantial global scale facilitated by the internet. It was bought by Trip.com Group (formerly Ctrip), China's largest travel firm, for $1.75bn in 2016.

Sources: www.skyscanner.com; www.trip.com

Questions

1. Explain what factors enabled Skyscanner to become a born global company.

2. What difficulties might Skyscanner have to overcome to ensure that its growth is maintained?

According to Knight and Cavusgil (2004), a number of recent trends have led to the emergence of born global firms. These include:

- The increasing role of niche markets and greater demand for specialized or customized products
- Advances in communications technology, email, the worldwide web and Skype, which means that small firms can manage international operations more efficiently and have greater access to information
- The inherent advantage of small firms in terms of quicker response time, flexibility and adaptability
- The internationalization of knowledge, tools, technology and facilitating institutions, which provides opportunities for technology transfer and access to funding
- Trends toward global networks, which facilitate the development of mutually beneficial relationships with international partners

Few born globals are actually 'born' global, but they internationalize soon after forming and often within three years of foundation. The 'born global' label has been adopted because it is an appealing phrase that conveys the importance of these firms and the new paradigm they represent in the world economy (Knight and Liesch, 2016). The early and rapid internationalization of born globals facilitated by the internet and mobile technologies can be viewed as an unprecedented form of international expansion (Sharma and Blomstermo, 2003).

The emergence of born global firms might represent a shift from a focus on the large, well-established multinational enterprises applying a logic of high monopolistic or oligopolistic profits, efficiency-seeking and power to a logic of young; resource-constrained firms emphasizing a logic of profit opportunity creation and resourceful innovation (Zander et al., 2015).

Nowhere in the commercial realm are the characteristics of born global entities, identified by Zander et al. (2015), more evident than in *THE*. Companies such as Airbnb, Skyscanner, Uber, Lyft and Trip.com, have demonstrated that SMEs are able to grow rapidly through:

- Early and rapid internationalization
- The adoption of highly innovative practices
- Holding out opportunities for investors to benefit from future profitability of their operations (rather than delivering immediate profits)

CHAPTER SUMMARY

The focus of global strategy is the attainment of global competitive advantage. Many industries and markets are becoming increasingly global, partly as a result of external factors but also as a result of the strategies of businesses themselves. Global strategy, like domestic strategy, is centered on the core competences of the business itself but it is equally dependent on an understanding of which aspects of the organization's industry and market are global and which require local adaptation.

Yip's (1992) globalization driver framework provides managers with an essential set of tools for beginning to understand the nature and extent of globalization in their particular industry and markets. Porter provided insight into the importance of global configuration and coordination of value-adding activities in achieving and sustaining competitive advantage, and Yip developed the concept of total global strategy to explain how a worldwide approach to strategy can be developed. Finally, the mode of entry by which organizations can develop global strategy by entering foreign markets has been explained.

The global business environment is particularly dynamic, and global strategy will have to be constantly adjusted and adapted as circumstances change if competitive advantage is to be sustained and developed. Some have questioned whether globalization has reached its peak and surmised that deglobalization will ensue. Certainly, the COVID-19 pandemic and the war in Ukraine have led to a temporary halt to the process.

The use of the frameworks developed in this chapter makes it possible for managers to constantly monitor and analyze their global environment and to develop global strategy accordingly.

Developing internationally is one of the riskiest decisions that mangers have to consider. In developing internationally, managers must carefully consider which markets they will enter and how this will be achieved. This chapter has considered the main modes of market entry strategy and provided examples of where these are applied in *THE*.

Internationalization and globalization are not just concerns for larger companies. SMEs have to understand internationalization processes to compete effectively. Furthermore, internet and mobile technologies have enabled some SMEs in *THE* to rapidly and successfully expand their international reach due to the phenomenon termed 'born global'.

REFERENCES AND WEBSITES

References

Agndal, H. and Elbe, J. (2007) 'The internationalization processes of small and medium-sized Swedish tourism firms', *Scandinavian Journal of Hospitality and Tourism*, 7(4): 301–327.

Al-Kaabi, H., Potter, A. and Naim, M. (2007) 'An outsourcing decision model for airlines' MRO activities', *Journal of Quality in Maintenance Engineering*, 13(3): 217–227.

Altinay, L. (2007) 'The internationalization of hospitality firms: Factors influencing a franchise decision-making process', *Journal of Services Marketing*, 21(6): 398–409.

Andreu, R., Claver, E. and Quer, D. (2017) 'Foreign market entry mode choice of hotel companies: determining factors', *International Journal of Hospitality Management*, 62: 111–119.

Assaf, A. G. and Cvelbar, L. K. (2010) 'The performance of the Slovenian hotel industry: Evaluation post-privatization', *International Journal of Tourism Research*, 12(5): 462–471.

Assaf, A. G., Josiassen, A. and Agbola, F. W. (2015) 'Attracting international hotels: Locational factors that matter most', *Tourism Management*, 47: 329–340.

Athiyaman, A. and Go, F. (2003) 'Strategic choices in the international hospitality industry', in B. Brotherton (Ed.), *The International Hospitality Industry*, Oxford, UK: Elsevier, 142–160.

Bartlett, C. A. and Ghoshal, S. (2002) *Managing across Borders: The Transnational Solution*, Cambridge, MA: Harvard Business Press.

BCD. (2019) *Communications, Emerging Technology and Travel Management*, Utrecht, Netherlands: BCD Travel, www.bcdtravel.com

Bell, J., McNaughton, R. and Young, S. (2001) ' "Born-again global" firms: An extension to the "born global" phenomenon', *Journal of International Management*, 7(3): 173–189.

Bell, J., McNaughton, R., Young, S. and Crick, D. (2003) 'Towards an integrative model of small firm internationalization', *Journal of International Entrepreneurship*, 1(4): 339–362.

Berbel-Pineda, J. M., Palacios-Florencio, B. and Ramírez-Hurtado, J. M. (2017) 'Determining factors in the internationalization of hotel industry: An analysis based on export performance', *Tourism Economics*, 23(4): 768–787.

Blomstermo, A., Sharma, D. D. and Sallis, J. (2006) 'Choice of foreign market entry mode in service firms', *International Marketing Review*, 23(2): 211–229.

Borodako, K., Berbeka, J. and Rudnicki, M. (2015) 'External and internal factors motivating outsourcing of business services by meeting-industry companies: A case study in Krakow, Poland', *Journal of Convention and Event Tourism*, 16(2): 93–115.

Brouthers, K. D. and Brouthers, L. E. (2003) 'Why service and manufacturing entry mode choices differ: The influence of transaction cost factors, risk and trust', *Journal of Management Studies*, 40(5): 1179–1204.

Canabal, A. and White, G. O., III. (2008) 'Entry mode research: Past and future', *International Business Review*, 17(3): 268–284.

Chen, J. J. and Dimou, I. (2005) 'Expansion strategy of international hotel firms', *Journal of Business Research*, 58(12): 1730–1740.

Choi, G. and Parsa, H. G. (2012) 'Role of intangible assets in foreign-market entry-mode decisions: A longitudinal study of American lodging firms', *International Journal of Hospitality and Tourism Administration*, 13(4): 281–312.

Cunill, O. M. (2006) 'The internationalization-globalization of hotel chains', in K. S. Chon and O. M. Cunhill (Eds), *The Growth Strategies of Hotel Chains: Best Business Practices by Leading Companies*, Binghamton, NY: Haworth Hospitality Press, 169–189.

Douglas, S. P. and Wind, Y. (1987) 'The myth of globalization', *Columbia Journal of World Business*, Winter: 19–29.

Dwyer, L. (2015) 'Globalization of tourism: Drivers and outcomes', *Tourism Recreation Research*, 40(3): 326–339.

Ekeledo, I. and Sivakumar, K. (2004) 'International market entry mode strategies of manufacturing firms and service firms: A resource-based perspective', *International Marketing Review*, 21(1): 68–101.

Endo, K. (2006) 'Foreign direct investment in tourism – Flows and volumes', *Tourism Management*, 27(4): 600–614.

Enright, M. J. and Newton, J. (2004) 'Tourism destination competitiveness: A quantitative approach', *Tourism Management*, 25(6): 777–788.

Espino-Rodríguez, T. F. and Padrón-Robaina, V. (2005) 'A resource-based view of outsourcing and its implications for organizational performance in the hotel sector', *Tourism Management*, 26(5): 707–721.

Etemad, H. and Motaghi, H. (2018) 'Internationalization pattern of creative-cultural events: Two cases from Canada', *International Business Review*, 27(5): 1033–1044.

Evans, N. G. (2012) 'Tourism: A strategic business perspective', in T. Jamal and M. Robinson (Eds), *The Sage Handbook of Tourism Studies*, Thousand Oaks, CA: Sage, 215–234.

Freeman, S., Edwards, R. and Schroder, B. (2006) 'How smaller born-global firms use networks and alliances to overcome constraints to rapid internationalization', *Journal of International Marketing*, 14(3): 33–63.

Fuster, B., Lillo-Bañuls, A. and Martínez-Mora, C. (2018) 'Offshoring of services as a competitive strategy in the tourism industry', *Tourism Economics*, 24(8): 963–979.

Ghoshal, S. (1987) 'Global strategy: An organizing framework', *Strategic Management Journal*, 8(5): 425–440.

Gil, R., Kim, M. and Zanarone, G. (2022) 'Relationships under stress: Relational outsourcing in the US airline industry after the 2008 financial crisis', *Management Science*, 68(2): 1256–1277.

Go, F. and Pine, R. (1995) *Globalization Strategy in the Hotel Industry*, London: Routledge.

Gonzalez, R., Llopis, J. and Gasco, J. (2011) 'What do we know about outsourcing in hotels?', *The Service Industries Journal*, 31(10): 1669–1682.

Gross, M. J. and Huang, S. S. (2011) 'Exploring the internationalization prospects of a Chinese domestic hotel firm', *International Journal of Contemporary Hospitality Management*, 23(2): 261–274.

Hamel, G. and Prahalad, C. K. (1985) 'Do you really have a global strategy', *Harvard Business Review*, 63(4): 139–148.

Hamel, G. and Prahalad, C. K. (1994) *Competing for the Future*, Watertown, MA: Harvard Business School Press.

Hanlon, J. P. (2007) *Global Airlines: Competition in a Transnational Industry*, Abingdon, UK: Routledge.

Hawkins, D. E. (2004) 'Sustainable tourism competitiveness clusters: Application to World Heritage Sites network development in Indonesia', *Asia Pacific Journal of Tourism Research*, 9(3): 293–307.

Hillebrand, E. E. (2010) 'Deglobalization scenarios: Who wins? Who loses?', *Global Economy Journal*, 10(2): 1850197.

Hjalager, A. M. (2007) 'Stages in the economic globalization of tourism', *Annals of Tourism Research*, 34(2): 437–457.

Hofstede, G. (1980) *Culture and Organizations: Software of the Mind*, London: McGraw-Hill.

Hong, W. C. (2009) 'Global competitiveness measurement for the tourism sector', *Current Issues in Tourism*, 12(2): 105–132.

Howells, J. (1999) 'Research and technology outsourcing', *Technology Analysis and Strategic Management*, 11(1): 17–29.

Hsu, C. C. and Liou, J. J. (2013) 'An outsourcing provider decision model for the airline industry', *Journal of Air Transport Management*, 28: 40–46.

Irwin, D. A. (2020) *The Pandemic Adds Momentum to the Deglobalization Trend*, Peterson Institute for International Economics, www.piie. com/blogs/realtime-economic-issues-watch/pandemic-adds-momentum-deglobalization-trend

Jackson, J. and Murphy, P. (2006) 'Clusters in regional tourism – An Australian case', *Annals of Tourism Research*, 33(4): 1018–1035.

Jensen, P. D. Ø. and Petersen, B. (2014) 'Value creation logics and internationalization of service firms', *International Marketing Review*, 31(6): 557–575. https://doi.org/10.1108/IMR-09-2013-0187

Johnson, C. and Vanetti, M. (2005) 'Locational strategies of international hotel chains', *Annals of Tourism Research*, 32: 1077–1099.

Johnson, J. and Tellis, G. J. (2008) 'Drivers of success for market entry into China and India', *Journal of Marketing*, 72: 1–13.

Jolly, J. (2022) 'TUI group terminates branding deal with TUI Russia', *The Guardian*, 10 March, www.theguardian.com

Knight, G. A. and Cavusgil, S. T. (2004) 'Innovation, organizational capabilities, and the born-global firm', *Journal of International Business Studies*, 35(2): 124–141.

Knight, G. A. and Liesch, P. W. (2016) 'Internationalization: From incremental to born global', *Journal of World Business*, 51(1): 93–102.

Kobrin, S. J. (1991) 'An empirical analysis of the determinants of global integration', *Strategic Management Journal*, 12(1), 17–31.

Kruesi, M., Kim, P. B. and Hemmington, N. (2017) 'Evaluating foreign market entry mode theories from a hotel industry perspective', *International Journal of Hospitality Management*, 62: 88–100.

Lamminmaki, D. (2005) 'Why do hotels outsource? An investigation using asset specificity', *International Journal of Contemporary Hospitality Management*, 17(6): 516–528.

León-Darder, F., Villar-García, C. and Pla-Barber, J. (2011) 'Entry mode choice in the internationalization of the hotel industry: A holistic approach', *The Service Industries Journal*, 31(1): 107–122.

Levitt, T. (1983) 'The globalization of markets', *Harvard Business Review*, May/June: 92–102.

Litteljohn, D., Roper, A. and Altinay, L. (2007) 'Territories still to find – The business of hotel internationalisation', *International Journal of Service Industry Management*, 18(2): 167–183. https://doi.org/10.1108/09564230710737817

Matheson, C. M., Foley, M. and McPherson, G. (2006) 'Globalisation and Singaporean festival', *International Journal of Event Management Research*, 2(1): 1–16.

Mathieson, A. and Wall, G. (1982) *Tourism: Economic, Physical and Social Impacts*, London: Longman.

McCartney, G. and Osti, L. (2007) 'From cultural events to sport events: A case study of cultural authenticity in the dragon boat races', *Journal of Sport Tourism*, 12(1): 25–40.

Miyoshi, C. (2015) 'Airport privatization in Japan: Unleashing air transport liberalisation?', *Journal of Airport Management*, 9(3): 210–222.

Mol, M. (2007) *Outsourcing: Design, Process and Performance*, London: Cambridge University Press.

Niewiadomski, P. (2020) 'COVID-19: From temporary de-globalisation to a re-discovery of tourism?', *Tourism Geographies*, 22(3): 651–656, doi:10.1080/14616688.2020.1757749

Niñerola, A. F., Campa-Planas, A., Hernández-Lara, A. B. and Sánchez-Rebull, M. V. (2016) 'The experience of Meliá Hotels International in China: A case of internationalization of a Spanish hotel group', *European Journal of Tourism Research*, 12: 191–196.

Park, J. W., Kim, K. W., Seo, H. J. and Shin, H. W. (2011) 'The privatization of Korea's Incheon International Airport', *Journal of Air Transport Management*, 17(4): 233–236.

Pla-Barber, J. and Ghauri, P. N. (2012) 'Internationalization of service industry firms: Understanding distinctive characteristics', *The Service Industries Journal*, 32(7): 1007–1010.

Porter, M. E. (1986a) 'Changing patterns of international competition', *California Management Review*, 28(2): 9–40.

Porter, M. E. (1986b) *Competition in Global Business*, Cambridge, MA: Harvard University Press.

Porter, M. E. (1990) *The Competitive Advantage of Nations*, New York: Free Press.

Porter, M. E., Bernard, M., Chaturvedi, R. S., Hill, A., Maddox, C. and Schrimpf, M. (2012) 'Tennessee music cluster: Microeconomics of competitiveness', Harvard Business School Presentation, May.

Postelnicu, C., Dinu, V. and Dabija, D. C. (2015) 'Economic deglobalization – From hypothesis to reality', *Ekonomie a Management (E&M)/Economics and Management*, 18(2): 4–14.

Promsivapallop, P., Jones, P. and Roper, A. (2015) 'Factors influencing hotel outsourcing decisions in Thailand: Modifications to the transaction cost economics approach', *Journal of Hospitality and Tourism Research*, 39(1): 32–56.

Quer, D., Claver, E. and Andreu, R. (2007) 'Foreign market entry mode in the hotel industry: The impact of country- and firm-specific factors', *International Business Review*, 16(3): 362–376.

Quinn, B. (2005) 'Changing festival places: Insights from Galway', *Social and Cultural Geography*, 6(2): 237–252.

Ramón-Rodríguez, A. B., Moreno-Izquierdo, L. and Perles-Ribes, J. F. (2011) 'Growth and internationalization strategies in the airline industry', *Journal of Air Transport Management*, 17(2): 110–115.

Ribes, J. F. P., Rodriguez, A. R. and Jiménez, M. S. (2011) 'Determinants of the competitive advantage of residential tourism destinations in Spain', *Tourism Economics*, 17(2): 373–403.

Richards, G. (2007) 'The festivalization of society or the socialization of festivals? The case of Catalunya', in G. Richards (Ed.), *Cultural Tourism: Global and Local Perspectives*, Binghampton, NY: Haworth Press, 257–276.

Rieple, A. and Helm, C. (2008) 'Outsourcing for competitive advantage: An examination of seven legacy airlines', *Journal of Air Transport Management*, 14: 280–285.

Root, F. R. (1994) *Entry Strategies for International Markets*, New York: Lexington Books.

Sanchez-Peinado, E., Pla-Barber, J. and Hébert, L. (2007) 'Strategic variables that influence entry mode choice in service firms', *Journal of International Marketing*, 15(1): 67–91.

Schellenberg, M., Harker, M. J. and Jafari, A. (2018) 'International market entry mode – A systematic literature review', *Journal of Strategic Marketing*, 26(7): 601–627.

Segal-Horn, S. (2004) 'The internationalization of service firms', in S. Segal-Horn (Ed.), *The Strategy Reader*, Oxford, UK: Blackwell.

Sharma, D. D. and Blomstermo, A. (2003) 'The internationalization process of born globals: A network view', *International Business Review*, 12(6): 739–753.

Smeral, E. (1998) 'The impact of globalization on small and medium enterprises: New challenges for tourism policies in European countries', *Tourism Management*, 19(4): 371–380.

Snowdon, B. and Stonehouse, G. (2006) 'Competitiveness in a globalised world: Michael Porter on the microeconomic foundations of the competitiveness of nations, regions, and firms', *Journal of International Business Studies*, 37(2): 163–175.

Sölvell, Ö. (2015) 'The competitive advantage of nations 25 years – Opening up new perspectives on competitiveness', *Competitiveness Review*, 25(5): 471–481.

Song, H., Li, G. and Cao, Z. (2018) 'Tourism and economic globalization: An emerging research agenda', *Journal of Travel Research*, 57(8): 999–1011. https://doi.org/10.1177/0047287517734943

Song, S. and Lee, S. (2020) 'Motivation of internationalization and a moderating role of environmental conditions in the hospitality industry', *Tourism Management*, 78: 104050. https://doi.org/10.1016/j.tourman.2019.104050

Stonehouse, G., Campbell, D., Hamill, J. and Purdie, T. (2007) *Global and Transnational Business: Strategy and Management*, 2nd ed., London: John Wiley and Sons.

Teo, P. (2002) 'Striking a balance for sustainable tourism: Implications of the discourse on globalisation', *Journal of Sustainable Tourism*, 10(6): 459–474.

Timothy, D. J. (Ed.). (2019) *Handbook of Globalisation and Tourism*, Cheltenham, UK: Edward Elgar.

Tribe, J. (1997) 'The indiscipline of tourism', *Annals of Tourism Research*, 24(3): 638–657.

Tsai, S. P. (2012) 'Place attachment and tourism marketing: Investigating international tourists in Singapore', *International Journal of Tourism Research*, 14(2): 139–152.

UNWTO. (2022) *From Crisis to Transformation*, Madrid: UNWTO, www.UNTWO.org

Villar, C., Pla-Barber, J. and León-Darder, F. (2012) 'Service characteristics as moderators of the entry mode choice: Empirical evidence in the hotel industry', *The Service Industries Journal*, 32(7): 1137–1148.

Wahab, S. and Cooper, C. (2005) 'Tourism, globalization and the competitive advantage of nations', in C. Cooper and S. Wahab (Eds), *Tourism in the Age of Globalization*, London: Routledge, 3–21.

Whitla, P., Walters, P. G. P. and Davies, H. (2007) 'Global strategies in the international hotel industry', *International Journal of Hospitality Management*, 26(4): 777–792.

Whittington, R., Regnér, P., Angwin, D., Johnson, G. and Scholes, K. (2020) *Exploring Strategy*, 12th ed., Harlow, UK: Pearson.

Williams, A. M. and Shaw, G. (2011) 'Internationalization and innovation in tourism', *Annals of Tourism Research*, 38(1): 27–51.

Yip, G. S. (1992) *Total Global Strategy – Managing for Worldwide Competitive Advantage*, Englewood Cliffs, NJ: Prentice Hall.

Yu, L. (1999) *The International Hospitality Business: Management and Operations*, Binghamton, NY: Haworth Hospitality Press.

Yu, Y., Byun, W. H. and Lee, T. J. (2014) 'Critical issues of globalisation in the international hotel industry', *Current Issues in Tourism*, 17(2): 114–118.

Zander, I., McDougall-Covin, P. and Rose, E. (2015) 'Born globals and international business: Evolution of a field of research', *Journal of International Business Studies*, 46(1): 27–35.

Websites

www.amadeus.com
www.asianaviation.com
www.bcdtravel.com
www.ihgplc.com
www.navitaire.com/
www.piie. com
www.qantas.com.au
www.skyscanner.com
www.theguardian.com
www.trip.com
www.tuitravelplc.com
www.UNTWO.org

Chapter **16**

Sustainability strategy for tourism, hospitality and event organizations

Introduction and chapter overview

Organizations and destinations have faced increasing pressures in recent years (exerted by stakeholder groups) to be more active in their approaches to the sustainability of the natural environment and to consider their social role in society (Aras and Crowther, 2008; Scherer and Voegtlin, 2020). Sustainability was introduced in Chapter 1 in relation to corporate governance, and analysis of the natural environment was considered in Chapter 7.

In this chapter, we build on these foundations to consider how the issues of sustainability can be considered by *THE* organizations and incorporated into a 'sustainability strategy' as part of the organization's overall strategy.

The chapter first discusses the meaning of sustainability and its application to businesses, before going on to consider the distinction between sustainable strategy and sustainable competitive advantage. Finally, the chapter considers which aspects should be considered by a sustainability strategy, with examples from *THE*.

LEARNING OBJECTIVES

After studying this chapter, you should be able to:

- Explain the meaning and origins of the term sustainability
- Understand how sustainability has been applied to business contexts

DOI: 10.4324/9781003318613-21

- Understand the differences between a sustainability strategy, CSR and TBL
- Clarify the distinction between sustainability strategy and sustainable competitive advantage
- Assess the key elements a sustainability strategy might include
- Critically evaluate examples of sustainability strategies from *THE*

16.1 Business sustainability: meaning

> **DEFINITION/QUOTATION**
>
> **'The house is on fire'**
>
> I want you to act as if the house is on fire, because it is.
>
> Environmental activist Greta Thunberg (2019)

Management scholars and practicing managers accept the veracity of Greta Thunberg's statement. In acknowledging that current resource use is unsustainable, Barnett et al. (2021:647), for example, stated that 'it is time to acknowledge that "the house is on fire", and that to sustain themselves and help to sustain all of us, firms must develop strategies to sustain their environments'.

But before we can proceed to forming a valid sustainability strategy for *THE* organizations, we must attempt to understand what we mean by 'sustainability' and, more specifically, the meaning of sustainability as applied to business; that is, *business sustainability*. Here we build on the discussion of sustainability in the context of evaluation of strategic options in Chapter 13.

The *Brundtland Report* (Brundtland Commission, 1987:1) described sustainable development as being that which 'meets the needs of the present without compromising the needs of future generations'.

Thus, sustainability aims to secure intergenerational equity, and its logic is clear in that most people want to live as well as their parents and be able to pass on similar opportunities to their offspring.

> **DEFINITION/QUOTATION**
>
> **Sustainable tourism**
>
> Building on the definition of sustainable development and applying it directly to tourism, the term 'sustainable tourism' is defined as:
>
> > Sustainable tourism that meets the needs of present vacationers and host districts while securing and enhancing opportunities for the future. It is visualized as leading to management of all resources in such a way that economic, social and aesthetic needs can be satisfied while maintaining cultural integrity, essential ecological processes, and biological diversity and life support systems.
> >
> > (UNWTO, 2018)

What we are particularly concerned with here is how the sustainability concept applies to businesses. The same logic applies (as above) in business in that most managers want their business to be at least as profitable as in the past and, ideally, for profits to grow. Based on this logic, business sustainability is defined below; from the definition, it can be seen that 'time' is central to the notion of sustainability.

DEFINITION/QUOTATION

Business sustainability

Business sustainability can be defined as:

> The ability of firms to respond to their short-term financial needs without compromising their (or others') ability to meet their future needs.
>
> Bansal and DesJardine (2014:71)

However, the definition provided by Bansal and DesJardine (2014) does not actually specify what aspects of business sustainability relates to or how it might be measured and evaluated. Hence, a number of authors have been more specific and specified that sustainability can be viewed as a 'business approach that creates long-term value by embracing opportunities and managing risks in three domains: economic, environmental and social' (Bonn and Fisher, 2011; see also Crane and Matten, 2007), which is consistent with the TBL approach that is widely adopted by organizations and is sometimes represented by the '3 Ps' of people, profit and planet.

Within this context, sustainability issues have gained greater prominence throughout *THE* organizations and the academic literature. To this end, many *THE* companies and international organizations (such as UNWTO, the World Bank and UNESCO) have developed policies and strategies to incorporate sustainable principles.

A vast literature relating to sustainability issues relating to *THE* has emerged and it is difficult to disagree with Higgins-Desbiolles' (2010) assertion that the application of sustainability principles to tourism is the predominant issue in current tourism discourse (see, for example, MacKenzie and Gannon, 2019; Streimikiene et al., 2021).

Sustainability has become the strategic imperative of the new millennium. Phrases such as 'sustainability', 'corporate social responsibility (CSR)', 'going green' and the 'triple bottom line' refer to organizations enhancing their long-term economic, social and environmental performance (Galpin et al., 2015).

Building on the concept of sustainability, and responding to the concerns of stakeholders, a corporate governance (discussed in Chapter 1) form emerged that takes into consideration not only the traditional economic 'bottom line' (profitability) but also less quantifiable indicators that measure social and environmental impact. This approach for measuring corporate performance is the so-called triple bottom line (TBL), a term that was popularized by John Elkington in the 1990s (Elkington, 1998).

Thus, the TBL represents a philosophical orientation whereby organizations not only develop and implement a traditional economically sustainable strategy but also explicitly include environmental and social sustainability strategies. Stoddard et al. (2012) discussed benefits of adopting this approach for tourism organizations seeking sustainable development.

However, CSR and TBL can be distinguished from sustainability. Sustainability requires trade-offs, especially across time. Firms must choose between investing less for smaller profits sooner and investing more for greater profits later (Laverty, 1996). CSR and TBL, on the other hand, do not necessarily require trade-offs. Most responsibility scholars argue that CSR represents the set of organizational activities that are good for society and the firm (McWilliams and Siegel, 2001; Bansal and DesJardine, 2014). 'Framed in this way, responsibility is nothing more than good business' (Bansal and DesJardine, 2014:71).

16.1.1 Sustainability and competitive advantage

Sustainability is not without controversy. Shareholders, who expect organizations to concentrate on maximizing their financial returns, frequently question company boards when the focus appears to have shifted to (natural) environmental concerns.

> **For example:** *In January 2022, the boss of UK-based consumer goods company Unilever was criticized by one of its leading investors: 'Unilever is laboring under the weight of a management which is obsessed with publicly displaying sustainability credentials at the expense of the fundamentals of the business' (Fletcher, 2022).*

However, counterbalancing some negative sentiment toward sustainability, as Galpin et al. (2015) stated, there is also an ever-expanding volume of literature underscoring the importance of sustainability to organizations and its positive impact on performance (see, for example, Willard, 2012; Bonini and Swartz, 2014; Winston, 2014; Laszlo and Zhexembayeva, 2017; Walsh and Dodds, 2017; McAteer, 2019).

KEY CONCEPT

Sustainability strategy: clarification of meaning

It is important to clarify the meaning of 'sustainability strategy' and distinguish it from other commonly used strategy terminology.

It is not an organization's 'plan to sustain its competitive advantage'. *Sustainable competitive advantage* is a common term used in strategy (and is discussed elsewhere in this book) that, like sustainable strategy, is focused on maintaining performance over time. Sustainable competitive advantage, though, is concerned with maintaining an advantage over rivals. By contrast, *sustainability strategy* looks beyond the organization in seeking to sustain the natural environments in which the organization operates.

However, importantly, sustainability strategy can in itself be a source of sustainable competitive advantage, but an organization's attempt at sustaining its competitive advantage may be to the detriment of the natural environment and hence to its sustainability strategy.

Sources: Barnett et al. (2015, 2021)

Environmental sustainability has often been reported as a means to providing a competitive advantage by encouraging efficiencies, attracting additional customers and generating positive brand images (Kumar and Christodoulopoulou, 2014; Walsh and Dodds, 2017).

> **For example:** *Walsh and Dodds (2017) considered the implementation of sustainability initiatives in North American hotels. Environmental sustainability strategies can employ a low-cost, differentiated or hybrid (a combination of the two) approach to creating a competitive advantage (Figure 16.1). The authors found that the hotels sampled used all three approaches but tended to rely on their need to create environmental sustainability legitimacy by placing an emphasis on differentiation through environmental sustainability branding.*

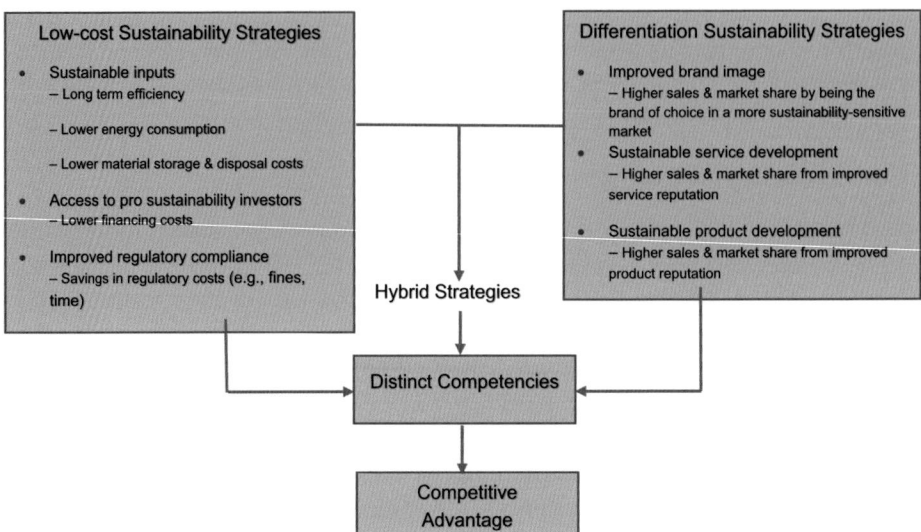

Figure 16.1 Deriving competitive advantage from sustainability strategies

Source: Adapted from Walsh and Dodds (2017)

16.2 Sustainability strategy: principal issues

It should be recognized that formulating and implementing a sustainability strategy for *THE* organizations is likely to be highly context specific. The necessary sustainability actions of an event organizer are likely to be very different to those of an airline, for example.

Many consultancy firms, intergovernmental organizations and industry organizations are encouraging governments, businesses and destinations to develop sustainability strategies, so it is unsurprising that they vary considerably. It is reassuring to consider that though most sustainable strategies are imperfect, at least the key issues are being considered so that organizations can move in the 'right' direction.

Underpinning the worldwide efforts is the 2030 Agenda for Sustainable Development (www.un.org/goals), adopted by all United Nations Member States in 2015, which provides a shared blueprint for peace and prosperity for people and the planet. At its heart are the 17 Sustainable Development Goals (SDGs), which are an urgent call for action by all countries in a global partnership. They recognize that ending poverty and other deprivations must go hand in hand with strategies that improve health and education, reduce inequality and spur economic growth – all while tackling climate change and working to preserve our oceans and forests.

A number of organizations are involved in encouraging organizations and destinations to adopt sustainable strategies for organizational development. These organizations include the UNWTO (www.untwo.org), WTTC (www.wttc.org), IISD (www.iisd.org) and GSTC (www.gstcouncil.org). Many organizations and companies are also involved with the GRI. The GRI (www.globalreporting.org) is an international independent standards organization (based in Amsterdam) that helps businesses, governments and other organizations understand and communicate their impacts on issues such as climate change, human rights and corruption. GRI also provides the world's most widely used sustainability reporting standards (the GRI Standards).

For example: *The GSTC has developed two sets of criteria over a number of years. These criteria serve as the global standards for sustainability in travel and tourism and are used as a basis for certification of organizations. The criteria (one set for tour operators and hotels and the other for destinations) are arranged in four pillars: sustainable management, socioeconomic impacts, cultural impacts and environmental impacts (including consumption of resources, reducing pollution and conserving biodiversity and landscapes).*

Sustainability strategies are written in many different styles, and some, it might be argued, are deliberately vague, include easily achieved goals or contain hyperbolic language. Nevertheless, many organizations now take sustainability issues seriously; not doing so has the potential to alienate many customers. Consequently, it makes commercial sense to formulate and implement a sustainability strategy and, where possible, integrate it within the overall organizational strategy.

The Norwegian ferry and cruise line Hurtigruten, operating in highly sensitive marine environments, has a longstanding commitment to sustainability issues.

16.1 SHORT CASE ILLUSTRATION

Sustainability strategy: Hurtigruten Group

Hurtigruten Group operates a Norwegian coastal ferry service linking towns along the jagged Norwegian coastline and a cruise line operating 'exploration' cruises to remote locations such as Greenland, Alaska and Antarctica. The shipping line, which is headquartered in Oslo, Norway, has been operating since the mid-19th century. The company's vision is to be 'the undisputed leader in sustainable adventure travel'. In its marketing, the company strongly features its sustainability focus and claims to be the world leader, in this respect, among cruise lines.

Transportation is the biggest single contributor to global GHG emissions (www.epa.gov/ghgemissions), with maritime transportation alone being responsible for 2.5% of the world's emissions. The company has publicly recognized that its ships have a negative impact on the environment with the emissions produced but has set a goal to be emission-free by 2050.

Working systematically toward emissions-free operations in 2050 is a dual process. The company cannot wait for technology to be in place, so the focus is on (1) a continuous process of improvement and (2) long-term development and collaboration that pushes for future solutions.

The company has been focused on lowering emissions for some time, with initiatives such as:

- Banning heavy fuel oil in all vessels (in 2009)
- Putting three new battery-hybrid ships into operation by 2021
- Upgrading all seven ships operating the coastal route (from 2021) to significantly reduce emissions. The upgrades, as well as the phasing in of sustainable biofuels, will reduce CO_2 emissions by around 25% and cut NO_x emissions by 80%.

- Becoming the first world cruise line to issue a green bond (in 2022). Green bonds are a way of raising funds for environmental and climate projects from external investors, giving investors a means to align sustainability and financial priorities.

- Setting a goal of 100% reuse and recycling of waste by 2030

Sources: www.hurtigruten.com; www.epa.gov/ghgemissions

Questions

1. Explain the commercial reasons for Hurtigruten emphasizing its sustainability strategy.

2. What are the main features of Hurtigruten's sustainability strategy?

It is difficult to be precise about what should be included in a sustainability strategy given the diversity of organizational contexts and the diversity of views, but in most cases the following might be considered:

- *Effective use of energy* – moving toward more sustainable sources such as vehicle electrification, utilizing solar and wind power and moving away from oil and gas
- *Sustainable use of natural resources* – protecting natural habitats, areas of scenic beauty and wilderness areas
- *Reducing emissions* – targeting positions of carbon neutrality. Clearly this is an issue of some difficulty for airlines, but tests are underway to use biofuels.
- *Reduction and disposal of waste* – reducing the amount of waste products produced and maximizing use of recycling
- *Having a positive influence on local cultures* – supporting small local authentic businesses

The tour operator Contiki has increasingly moved to emphasize the sustainability of its tours for younger travelers. The company claims to be carbon neutral and stresses the incorporation of authentic local experiences.

16.2 SHORT CASE ILLUSTRATION

Sustainability strategy: Contiki Tours

In 1962, New Zealander John Anderson was alone in Europe and short of money. He acquired a minibus, gathered a group of young people and spent 12 weeks exploring Europe. The success of the first trip led to further trips, and Contiki was born.

The company, which is now a subsidiary of the US-based private company The Travel Corporation (TTC), caters exclusively to the 18–35 age group, with tours operating in Europe, Australia, New Zealand, North America, South America, Africa, the Middle East and Asia.

Though the company had a reputation for partying, it has diversified and now stresses its sustainability credentials. In common with other TTC companies (such as Insight Vacations,

AAT Kings and Trafalgar Tours), Contiki has developed its sustainability strategy based on 11 stated goals. These include:

- Achieving carbon neutrality by 2030 or sooner. Contiki claims to have achieved this by 2022.
- Sourcing 50% of electricity from renewable sources by 2025
- Reducing food waste by 50% across all hotels and ships by 2025
- Increasing use of local and organic food products in the company's supply chain by 2025
- Reducing printed brochures by 50% by 2025
- Including at least one Make Travel Matter® Experience on 50% of TTC itineraries by 2025

Make Travel Matter® experiences are based on the positive social or environmental impact they have on their communities and those who experience them. The experiences are focused on 'people', 'planet', or 'wildlife'. For example, travelers to Laos dine at a restaurant run by The Tree Alliance (Training Restaurants for Employment & Entrepreneurship). In addition, around 200 at-risk young people are trained in each cohort to give them hands-on skills and experience they can use to thrive in the hospitality and tourism industry.

Sources: www.contiki.com; www.tree-alliance.com

Questions

1. What is meant by Make Travel Matter® experiences, and why does Contiki incorporate them into its itineraries?

2. Assess the main elements of Contiki's sustainability strategy.

Small business focus

The limited literature that does exist points to SMEs in *THE*, as in other industries, being viewed as relatively slow to adopt sustainability practices (Kornilaki et al., 2019). However, owner-managers often perceive the environment to be an important issue affecting their business (Coles et al., 2014). In comparison with larger firms, SME owners often lack time, financial resources, specialist staff and the expertise to formulate and implement sustainable strategies (Shields and Shelleman, 2015; Mohammed, 2022).

SMEs in the hospitality sector, for example, might experience less pressure than big chain hotels or franchises to adopt sustainability practice, because they are not under the same scrutiny as larger companies in the industry. Indeed, larger hotels are increasingly using sustainability as a marketing tool for their brands. The main motivation for independent hotels or restaurants to adopt sustainability practices appears to be the owner's beliefs and personal ethical values or cost reduction reasons (Abaeian et al., 2019; Musavengane, 2019).

The relatively slow adoption of sustainability strategies is somewhat surprising, because a number of studies have indicated that there is a positive correlation between environmental actions and financial performance, at least in the hospitality sector (Molina-Azorín, 2009; Singal, 2014).

> For example: *In reinforcing these findings, a study of smaller hotels in the Spanish Catalonia region (Bagur-Femenias et al., 2016) found that the implementation of*

environmental initiatives yielded internal improvements that enhanced efficiency and resulted in a better utilization of resources, with consequent cost savings.

CHAPTER SUMMARY

Industry leaders and academics have recognized that sustainability is a key factor in the long-term success of both firms and the communities in which they operate (Galpin et al., 2015). However, the terms sustainability and, by extension, sustainability strategy are difficult to define and are therefore open to interpretation.

This chapter has offered one such interpretation and has applied the term to business contexts, and *THE* in particular. A distinction is made between sustainable competitive advantage and sustainability strategy. The first of these terms is concerned with gaining an advantage over rivals. By contrast, sustainability strategy looks beyond the organization in seeking to sustain the natural environments in which the organization operates. In doing so, the sustainability strategy itself might become a source of competitive advantage.

Finally, the chapter moves to consider the principal component parts of a sustainable strategy. Though it is recognized that such a strategy is likely to be highly context specific, some of the major themes for such a strategy together with examples from *THE* have been considered in this chapter.

REFERENCES AND WEBSITES

References

Abaeian, V., Khong, K. W., Yeoh, K. K. and McCabe, S. (2019) 'Motivations of undertaking CSR initiatives by independent hotels: A holistic approach', *International Journal of Contemporary Hospitality Management*, 31(6): 2468–2487. https://doi.org/10.1108/IJCHM-03-2018-0193

Aras, G. and Crowther, D. (2008) 'Governance and sustainability: An investigation into the relationship between corporate governance and corporate sustainability', *Management Decision*, 46(3): 433–448.

Bagur-Femenias, L., Celma, D. and Patau, J. (2016) 'The adoption of environmental practices in small hotels, voluntary or mandatory? An empirical approach. *Sustainability*, 8(7): 695.

Bansal, P. and DesJardine, M. R. (2014) 'Business sustainability: It is about time', *Strategic Organization*, 12(1): 70–78.

Barnett, M. L., Darnall, N. and Husted, B. W. (2015) 'Sustainability strategy in constrained economic times', *Long Range Planning*, 48(2): 63–68.

Barnett, M. L., Henriques, I. and Husted, B. W. (2021) 'Sustainability strategy' in I. M. Duhaime, M. A Hitt and M. A. Lyles (Eds), *Strategic Management: State of the Field and Its Future*, New York: Oxford University Press, 647–662.

Bonini, S. and Swartz, S. (2014) 'Profits with purpose: How organizing for sustainability can benefit the bottom line', *McKinsey on Sustainability and Resource Productivity*, 2(1): 5–15.

Bonn, I. and Fisher, J. (2011) 'Sustainability: The missing ingredient in strategy', *Journal of Business Strategy*, 32(1): 5–14.

Brundtland Commission. (1987) *The World Commission on Environment: Our Common Future*, New York: United Nations.

Coles, T., Zschiegner, A. K. and Dinan, C. (2014) 'A cluster analysis of climate change mitigation behaviours among SMTEs', *Tourism Geographies*, 16(3): 382–399.

Crane, A. and Matten, D. (2007) *Business Ethics*, 2nd ed., New York: Oxford University Press.

Elkington, J. (1998) 'Partnerships from cannibals with forks: The triple bottom line of 21st-century business', *Environmental Quality Management*, 8(1): 37–51.

Fletcher, R. (2022) 'Unilever boss Alan Jope defends sustainability focus after shareholder attack', *The Times*, 23 May.

Galpin, T., Whittington, J. L. and Bell, G. (2015) 'Is your sustainability strategy sustainable? Creating a culture of sustainability', *Corporate Governance*, 15(1): 1–17.

Higgins-Desbiolles, F. (2010) 'The elusiveness of sustainability in tourism: The culture-ideology of consumerism and its implications', *Tourism and Hospitality Research*, 10(2): 116–129.

Kornilaki, M., Thomas, R. and Font, X. (2019) 'The sustainability behavior of small firms in tourism: The role of self-efficacy and contextual constraints', *Journal of Sustainable Tourism*, 27(1): 97–117.

Kumar, V. and Christodoulopoulou, A. (2014) 'Sustainability and branding: An integrated perspective', *Industrial Marketing Management*, 43(1): 6–15.

Laszlo, C. and Zhexembayeva, N. (2017) *Embedded Sustainability: The Next Big Competitive Advantage*, Abingdon, UK: Routledge.

Laverty, K. J. (1996) 'Economic "short-termism": The debate, the unresolved issues, and the implications for management practice and research', *Academy of Management Review*, 21(3): 825–860.

MacKenzie, N. and Gannon, M. J. (2019) 'Exploring the antecedents of sustainable tourism development', *International Journal of Contemporary Hospitality Management*, 31(6): 2411–2427.

McAteer, P. (2019) *Sustainability Is the New Advantage: Leadership, Change, and the Future of Business*, London: Anthem Press.

McWilliams, A. and Siegel, D. (2001) 'Corporate social responsibility: A theory of the firm perspective', *Academy of Management Review*, 26(1): 117–127.

Mohammed, A. H. A. (2022) 'SMEs' sustainable development challenges post-COVID-19: The tourism sector', *World Journal of Entrepreneurship, Management and Sustainable Development*, 18(3): 407–424.

Molina-Azorín, J. F., Claver-Cortés, E., López-Gamero, M. D. and Tarí, J. J. (2009) 'Green management and financial performance: a literature review', *Management Decision*, 47(7): 1080–1100. https://doi.org/10.1108/00251740910978313

Musavengane, R. (2019) 'Small hotels and responsible tourism practice: Hoteliers' perspectives', *Journal of Cleaner Production*, 220: 786–799.

Scherer, A. G. and Voegtlin, C. (2020) 'Corporate governance for responsible innovation: Approaches to corporate governance and their implications for sustainable development', *Academy of Management Perspectives*, 34(2): 182–208.

Shields, J. and Shelleman, J. M. (2015) 'Integrating sustainability into SME strategy', *Journal of Small Business Strategy*, 25(2): 59–78.

Singal, M. (2014) 'The link between firm financial performance and investment in sustainability initiatives', *Cornell Hospitality Quarterly*, 55(1): 19–30.

Stoddard, J. E., Pollard, C. E. and Evans, M. R. (2012) 'The triple bottom line: A framework for sustainable tourism development', *International Journal of Hospitality and Tourism Administration*, 13(3): 233–258.

Streimikiene, D., Svagzdiene, B., Jasinskas, E. and Simanavicius, A. (2021) 'Sustainable tourism development and competitiveness: The systematic literature review', *Sustainable Development*, 29(1): 259–271.

Thunberg, G. (2019) *Speech to World Economic Forum*, Davos, Switzerland, 24 January.

UNWTO. (2018) *UNWTO Tourism Highlights*, Madrid: UNWTO.

Walsh, P. R. and Dodds, R. (2017) 'Measuring the choice of environmental sustainability strategies in creating a competitive advantage', *Business Strategy and the Environment*, 26(5): 672–687.

Willard, B. (2012) *The New Sustainability Advantage: Seven Business Case Benefits of a Triple Bottom Line*, 2nd ed., Gabriola Island, BC, Canada: New Society Publishers.

Winston, A. (2014) *The Big Pivot: Radically Practical Strategies for a Hotter, Scarcer, and More Open World*, Boston: Harvard Business Review Press.

Websites

www.contiki.com
www.epa.gov/ghgemissions
www.globalreporting.org
www.gstcouncil.org
www.hurtigruten.com
www.iisd.org
www.tree-alliance.com
www.ttc.com
www.un.org/goals
www.untwo.org
www.wttc.org

17

Strategic management for tourism, hospitality and event organizations – strategy in practice

Introduction and chapter overview

This concluding chapter brings together a number of themes. Throughout the book, we have both considered theoretical concepts relating to strategic management and *THE* and stressed the linkages between the two. Practical applications and examples have also been provided. This chapter provides a practical summary of what factors might be considered in presenting a strategy and what the 'finished product' might look like.

The subject of this book is concerned with two quite young subjects, namely, the interrelated subjects of tourism, hospitality and events management and strategic management. It is also concerned with the application of one to the other; that is, applying strategic management concepts and frameworks to *THE*.

Tourism, hospitality and events are service sectors with particular characteristics that are highly distinctive, not only when compared with manufacturing but also when compared with many other services. In this chapter, we return to some of the themes introduced in Chapters 1 and 2. The distinctiveness of the subject area is discussed and the implications that are implied for the study and application of strategic management principles are considered.

> **LEARNING OBJECTIVES**

After studying this chapter, you should be able to:

- Understand the nature of the distinctive challenges that managers in *THE* face
- Explain the relevance of strategic management to managers operating in *THE*

DOI: 10.4324/9781003318613-22

- Understand the different approaches to strategy outlined in this book
- Understand how to present strategy in a clear, coherent and convincing way

17.1 The growth of *THE* and the managerial challenges presented

The antecedents of 'mass' international tourism and hospitality can be traced back to Thomas Cook in 1850s Britain (Withey, 1998; Zuelow, 2015). Events management is a highly diverse field, but performances, festivals and events of various descriptions have taken place throughout history. However, as highly structured sectors of many economies, *THE* can primarily be viewed as a creation of more recent times. The rise of these sectors, and the academic disciplines that have emerged to study them, has been traced by a number of authors, including Ottenbacher et al. (2009), Getz and Page (2016), Walker (2018) and Holloway and Humphreys (2022). Since the early 1950s, the growth of international tourism (and the associated sectors we are considering) 'has been phenomenal in its scale, and remarkably resilient to periodic economic and political adversity' (Evans, 2012:215).

However, because many more countries and new consumers are being drawn into the international tourism net, and despite periodic shocks (such as COVID-19 and the war in Ukraine), further growth is to be expected. Such growth will be uneven, both spatially and with regard to time, and is likely to take place against the backdrop of dramatic changes in the business environment, thereby creating both managerial and marketing opportunities and dilemmas for private sector leaders and public sector policymakers.

17.1.1 *Strategic management in* THE *contexts*

Given the dominance and drive of the private sector in the development of international tourism, hospitality and events management and the growth in the services that support these, a business management-oriented approach to *THE* studies has evolved over the past 30 years and has become the dominant frame for teaching *THE* in universities and colleges. The study of strategic management (or strategy) is a part of this development because it represents what is sometimes called a 'capstone' module on many courses. It is referred to in this way because strategic management:

- Takes a holistic approach integrating the study of different business subjects such as human resource management, finance and marketing
- Is usually studied toward the end of courses so that prior knowledge of relevant underpinning subjects can be integrated appropriately
- Takes a 'real- world' perspective in that, just as in business itself, there is rarely a 'right' or 'wrong' answer; it is concerned with the analysis of issues and the formulation and implementation of strategies to address the issues identified

Those working in *THE* contexts need to understand not only the actual business changes taking place but also the underlying characteristics of the industry. These underlying characteristics (discussed in Chapter 2 and throughout the book) raise a number of managerial issues that, if not necessarily unique, are certainly highly distinctive.

Managers working within *THE*, policymakers, regulators and others concerned with the industry's continuing development need to be knowledgeable about these characteristics and issues as well as recognize the potential managerial responses that are possible and the impact they might have. These managerial actions responding to identified challenges often fall within one of the recognized functional areas of business – marketing, human resource management, finance and operations – or, in bringing together the major issues in one place, they are considered as part of the emerging academic field we consider here of strategic management.

Throughout this book it has been argued that *THE* businesses are 'different' and, indeed, this provides the underlying rationale for the book itself. *THE* businesses are different in a number of ways from businesses that produce physical products, and they also have a different emphasis than other service industries.

These differences (discussed in Chapter 2) lead to important consequences, the implications of which managers of *THE* businesses must consider. The result lies in various distinctive managerial responses to the issues faced, which are discussed throughout the book.

17.1.2 Approaches to the study of strategic management

In all industries, including the component sectors of *THE*, some organizations prove to be more successful than others. The superior performers conceivably possess something special that competitors do not have access to that allows them to outperform their rivals. The sources of 'competitive advantage' lie in combining:

- The superior application of competences (skills)
- The deployment of superior resources (assets)
- Creating value for consumers.

Sustainability is achieved when the advantage resists erosion by competitive behavior (Porter, 1985).

Thus, to achieve the goal of competitive advantage, managers must have an understanding of how value is added in an organization. A number of approaches have been used in the emergence of a new managerial paradigm – 'strategic management'.

THINK POINTS

- Explain why *THE* managers need to understand the underlying characteristics of *THE*.
- Consider why *THE* organizations might benefit from taking a strategic approach.

The developing nature of strategy as a coherent academic study is reflected in debates revolving around what constitutes the most appropriate approach to strategic management; see, for example, Whittington (2001) and Jones (2004) for an overview of the various perspectives on strategy.

There is some disagreement among strategists on the best way of understanding the determinants of competitive advantage. Some writers advocate an approach to strategic management that is *planned* or *prescriptive* (sometimes called *deliberate*), whereas others argue that it is better to evolve strategy incrementally (the *emergent* approach to strategy; see the Key Concept in Chapter 1).

In this book we have primarily adopted a prescriptive approach while acknowledging that strategy in contemporary fast-moving environments must be flexible and thereby may include some elements that change and may be viewed as emergent.

Accordingly, it is suggested that strategy must be both inward and outward looking, planned and emergent, and a number of authors have taken an integrative and pragmatic approach to strategy (see, for example, Hitt and Tyler, 1991; Cravens et al., 1997; Lampel et al., 2013; Hill et al., 2014). By adopting this synthesis, a broader understanding of competitive advantage can be gained.

17.2 Strategy in practice

17.2.1 Factors determining how strategy is presented

We now turn our attention (briefly) to a consideration of strategy in practice.

How should the strategy be presented in *THE* contexts?

Of course, there is no absolute answer to this question, because the presentation of the strategy is a subjective matter, and styles vary enormously. The presentation of the strategy will vary according to a number of factors, including those shown in Table 17.1.

Table 17.1 Factors determining the way in which organizations present their strategies

Factor	Implication
Who is the strategy aimed at?	• Is it aimed mainly at the owners, or is it aimed at a range of stakeholders? • If it is aimed predominantly at shareholders and other investors, it will focus predominantly on financial information and financial prospects for the future.
Private or public companies	• Private companies normally do not disclose as much information as public companies, because they do not need to do so to attract investment and inform shareholders. • Many privately held companies are controlled by one person or a small team, and the strategy may be closely aligned with the vision and values of those particular individuals.
Size and complexity	• Some strategies are written for large and complex organizations in dynamic environments and therefore, to be meaningful, the strategy has to address a wide range of issues. • Conversely, other strategies may be written for smaller, less complex organizations, and thus the range of issues will be narrower.
Competitive pressures	• Sometimes the strategy (at least its published version) is deliberately vague or ambiguous. This reflects the competitive environment in which the organization is operating. • In some cases, the organization will not want to divulge too much information that could be useful to competitors.
Strategic approach	• This book has outlined different approaches or views of strategy. In particular, prescriptive vs emergent views have been highlighted. • Where the strategic approach is prescriptive, it implies that a detailed process has been undertaken and a strategic plan has been prepared. • Conversely, if an emergent view is taken, the view might be that the environment is too turbulent for a strategy to be written or that it should be minimalist in style.

17.2.2 Styles of strategy presentation

As a result of the factors outlined in Table 17.1, there are a wide range of styles adopted for the presentation of strategies. In fact, it is true to say that every strategy is unique.

Table 17.2 summarizes some of the ways in which the presentation of strategies differs.

Table 17.2 Differences in the presentation of an organization's strategy

Factor	Implication
Length	• Some strategies are long and complex. • Some strategies are short and simple. • In some cases, the strategy is mainly presented as a short summary with supporting reports and appendices that provide evidence and analysis.
Style	• Some strategies are very colorful, professionally produced documents, with many elaborate charts and illustrations. • Other strategies are drab and have few illustrations.
Language	• Some strategies use very simple language, whereas others are laden with jargon. • The 'language of strategy' is full of different words that are used to denote a similar aspect; for example, goals, targets, objectives, endpoints. Conversely, in some cases, the same words are used to denote differing aspects; for example, the words sustainable and sustainability are often used in ways that are open to interpretation and denote different aspects of strategy. • The situation is made more complicated by the fact that strategy is a field that has many gurus, academics and consultants involved, who make their own uses for words and sometimes create their own terminology.
Strategic terminology	• Closely linked to the previous point is the strategic terminology that is used. • In many cases, organizations will avoid using the strategic terminology we have used in this book (or any other strategic terminology that is commonly used). • Just as a doctor is likely to explain an illness to a patient in nontechnical language, the strategy is explained in nontechnical language to have meaning for all stakeholders involved. • Thus, the strategy may be presented as 'where we want to get to' rather than use the word 'vision'. Regardless of the language used, the intent is the same.
Detail	• Some strategies are highly detailed and clearly can be applied to all parts of the business. • Other strategies lack detail and apply only to the organization as a whole. • Some organizations do not have a strategy at all, either preferring to manage on a day-to-day basis or having a strategy that is not labeled as such and is embedded in other documents.
Measures of success	• Some strategies include measurable objectives, KPIs and an indication of CSFs that will allow for the strategy to be delivered – or not. • Other strategies include only vague qualitative statements that cannot be measured, and there is little indication of what might constitute success – or, to use the strategic terminology that is often used: What does success look like?

It is difficult to be precise about what constitutes good practice when it comes to presenting a strategy, or a *strategic plan* as it is usually termed, because, as outlined above, it is largely subjective and is determined by the context in which it is written. Kenny (2016) emphasized that going through the process of 'planning' is more important than the actual 'plan' itself and, in a later article, that it is important for the strategic plan to be truly 'strategic' in its focus (Kenny, 2018).

However, 'good' presentation of strategy is important in that it is a key part of informing both internal and external stakeholders of what the organization is trying to achieve.

> **For example:** *Investors will be reluctant to invest funds in an organization if they are unable to attain a clear picture of how the organization envisages its future progress and how likely it is to achieve its objectives as set out in its strategy. Similarly, employees and managers are more likely to be motivated and productive if they are clear about what the organization is striving to achieve.*

One way of considering and remembering the importance of presentation to producing a 'good' strategy is to think of the '8 Cs of presentation'

17.2.3 The 8 Cs of presentation

For a strategy to have impact, it should adhere to the principles of the 8 Cs of presentation, as shown in Table 17.3.

Following on from the 8 Cs of presentation are a number of guidelines, below in Table 17.4.

17.2.4 Strategy presentation: an example

An example of what a strategy might look like is shown in Table 17.5.

In this example, the strategy is summarized on a single page. One of the world's largest hotel groups, IHG, is used as an example.

Table 17.3 The 8 Cs of strategy presentation

Aspect of presentation	Description
1. Clear	It is written in a style that is easily comprehended and communicated.
2. Coherent	There is a logical flow throughout the document.
3. Consistent	Each aspect is consistent with all other aspects.
4. Concise	Excessive words and documentation are avoided.
5. Convincing	It is based clearly on analysis and presents arguments logically, with measurable targets.
6. Context specific	It takes into account the specific *THE* context for which it is written.
7. Creative	It is presented in an attractive and interesting way.
8. Comprehensive	It relates to all parts of the organization and deals with all key issues.

Source: Author's classification

Table 17.4 Suggested guidelines for the presentation of strategy

Aspect	Guidelines
Presentation	• The strategy should be clear, interesting and 'professional' in its presentational standards.
Length	• The strategy may be detailed, have supporting documents and have adaptations for all parts of the organization. Other strategies might be short but equally effective.
	• In either case, the outcome should be the result of a robust process.
	• However, the essence of the strategy should be capable of being captured on a single page for ease of communication and dissemination.
Language	• The strategy should be written in such a way that it is clear, concise and appropriate for the stakeholders being addressed.
Internal consistency	• All parts of the strategy should be consistent with each other, so that it is not ambiguous or contradictory and there is a logical flow to the document.
	• All parts of the organization should be aligned so that objectives (what is trying to be achieved) at every level and each part of the organization are consistent and complementary.
Measurement of success	• The strategy should include measurable and achievable objectives of some sort.
	• Unless there are measurable objectives, how does anyone know whether the strategy has been successful, and how will staff be motivated to achieve them?

In relation to Table 17.5, the following should be noted:

- *The left-hand column u*ses the sort of strategic terminology used in this text and others to describe the 'strategic hierarchy'. Most strategies involve *a* strategic hierarchy of some sort (though they vary in detail). It provides a logical journey through the strategic process

- *The middle column g*ives a description of what the strategic terms (used in the left-hand column) mean in short, easily understood sentences; for example, 'values' is described as 'what we want to be'.

- *The right-hand column* presents the IHG strategy, by way of an example taken from IHGs publicly available documentation.

The strategy, which is adapted from the company's 2021 annual report (IHG, 2021) and website, utilizes the same terminology and emphasis that the company uses in its document.

Note: As is commonly the case, the language used (in the IHG strategy) is different from the language in the left-hand column but is taken to mean the same thing. For example, what IHG describes as 'ambition' would appear to equate to its 'mission'.

Table 17.5 What a strategy document might look like – IHG

OUR STRATEGY		
MISSION	*Ambition* Why we exist?	• IHG is one of the world's leading hotel companies, with well-loved brands, a world-class loyalty program, and a purpose to provide 'True Hospitality for Good'.
VALUES	*Values* What we want to be?	• Build loved and trusted brands • Customer centric in all we do • Create digital advantage • Care for our people, communities and planet
VISION	*Cause* What we believe in? or Where we want to get to?	• Guided by a clear and proven asset-light strategy, focused on delivering industry-leading net-rooms growth over the medium term.
STRATEGY KEY THEMES	*Strategic Intent* What is our plan for the future?	• Use our scale and expertise to create the exceptional guest experiences and owner returns needed to grow our brands in the industry's most valuable markets and segments. Delivered through a culture that attracts the best people and has a positive impact on the world around us.

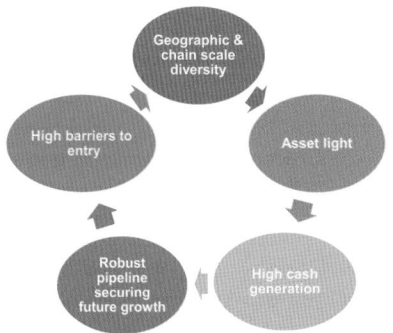

Strategic Model

Targeted Portfolio

- Targeting the most attractive markets & segments is critical to maximise growth.
- Prioritise resources & investments based on growth potential, strategic importance & ability to win.
- This is a key part of our ambition to accelerate growth trajectory, & build on strong global competitive position.
- Operate in the Mainstream, Upscale & Luxury segments – the highest opportunity segments based on guest needs.
- Focused on key geographic markets & key cities.

(continued)

Table 17.5 Continued

OUR STRATEGY		

STRATEGY IN ACTION	*Implementation*
	
	What we need to do?
		• ***Build loved and trusted brands –***
		  ➢ Transformed our portfolio, adding six new brands in the past four years alone.
		  ➢ Significantly strengthening luxury & lifestyle offer for guests and owners
		  ➢ Continued to invest significantly in the quality, design, service and technology that underpins existing well-established brands.
		  ➢ Supported by IHG Rewards, one of the industry's biggest loyalty program
		  ➢ A pipeline of almost 1,800 hotels
		
		• ***Customer centric in all we do***
		  ➢ Providing owners and teams with clear action plans, training and support for evolving brand standards and procedures to meet changing guest expectation.
		  ➢ Capturing demand through tailored marketing campaigns and promotions
		  ➢ To continue improving guest satisfaction scores and drive revenue for owners, updated guest room and public space design programmes are ongoing.
		  ➢ The IHG Rewards Program is critical to future growth. Members drive around half of all room nights globally. The loyalty offering was transformed in 2022.
		
		• ***Create digital advantage***
		  ➢ Hotels completed detailed room inventory assessments to prepare for attribute pricing powered by industry-leading Guest Reservation System (GRS).
		  ➢ Next generation IHG mobile app launched in 2022
		  ➢ AI voice-activated platforms are answering and routing customer calls to the most appropriate support area
		
		• ***Care for our people, communities and planet***
		  ➢ In 2021 '2030 Journey to Tomorrow' plan was launched
		  ➢ People – Achieve gender balance and a doubling of under-represented groups across leadership & cultivate a culture of inclusion for colleagues, owners and suppliers

OUR STRATEGY		
		➢ Communities – Drive economic and social change through skills training and innovation
		➢ Planet – Implement a 2030 1.5°C science-based target that delivers 46% absolute reduction in CO_2 from hotel portfolio
MEASURING SUCCESS	*Performance* How we know if we have been successful?	• Performance is measured with a set of carefully selected key performance indicators (KPIs), which monitor success in achieving the strategy & delivering high-quality growth

Sources: IHG 2021 Annual Report; www.ihg.com, accessed Dec. 2022.

CHAPTER SUMMARY

Strategic management is fundamentally concerned with understanding the nature of competitive advantage and the means by which it is acquired and sustained.

This chapter has argued (as elsewhere in this book) that the contexts presented in *THE* are different from those in other sectors. They are different from manufacturing in particular, but there are also defining characteristics that make *THE* different from other service-based sectors. Consequently, managers in *THE* must be aware of these distinctive factors and take them into account when designing appropriate strategies.

The chapter, in concluding the book, takes a practically oriented approach to strategy. In pulling all of the disparate threads together, what factors underpin the presentation of the strategy, and what should the 'finished product' look like? It is difficult to be definitive, because there is room for innovation and creativity, and judgments as to what constitutes successful presentation are subjective. However, guidelines are suggested that apply in most cases.

REFERENCES

References

Cravens, D. W., Greenley, G., Piercy, N. F. and Slater, S. (1997) 'Integrating contemporary strategic management perspectives', *Long Range Planning*, 30(4): 493–506.

Evans, N. G. (2012) 'Tourism: A strategic business perspective', in T. Jamal and M. Robinson (Eds), *The Sage Handbook of Tourism Studies*, Thousand Oaks, CA: Sage, 215–234.

Getz, D. (2002) 'Event studies and event management: On becoming an academic discipline', *Journal of Hospitality and Tourism Management*, 9(1): 12–23.

Getz, D. and Page, S. (2016) *Event Studies: Theory, Research and Policy for Planned Events*, 3rd ed., Abingdon, UK: Routledge.

Hill, C. W., Jones, G. R. and Schilling, M. A. (2017) *Strategic Management Theory: An Integrated Approach*, 12th ed., New York: Cengage Learning.

Hitt, M. A. and Tyler, B. B. (1991) 'Strategic decision models: Integrating different perspectives', *Strategic Management Journal*, 12(5): 327–351.

Holloway, J. C. and Humphreys, C. (2016) *The Business of Tourism*, 10th ed., Harlow, UK: Pearson.

IHG. (2021) *IHG 2021 Annual Report and Accounts*, www.IHG.com

Jones, G. (2004) 'Perspectives on strategy', in S. Segal-Horn (Ed.), *The Strategy Reader*, Oxford: Blackwell, 491–508.

Kenny, G. (2016) 'Strategic plans are less important than strategic planning', *Harvard Business Review*, June: 1–6.

Kenny, G. (2018) 'Your strategic plans probably aren't strategic, or even plans', *Harvard Business Review*, April: 6.

Lampel, J., Mintzberg, H., Quinn, J. B. and Ghoshal, S. (2013) *The Strategy Process: Concepts, Contexts and Cases*, 5th ed., Harlow, UK: Pearson.

Ottenbacher, M., Harrington, R. and Parsa, H. G. (2009) 'Defining the hospitality discipline: A discussion of pedagogical and research implications', *Journal of Hospitality and Tourism Research*, 33(3): 263–283.

Porter, M. E. (1985) *Competitive Advantage*, New York: The Free Press

Walker, J. R. (2018) *Exploring the Hospitality Industry*, 4th ed., Harlow, UK: Pearson.

Whittington, R. (2001) *What Is Strategy – And Does It Matter?*, 2nd ed., London: Cengage Learning.

Withey, L. (1998) *Grand Tours and Cook's Tours: A History of Leisure Travel, 1750 to 1915*, London: Aurum Press.

Zuelow, E. (2015) *A History of Modern Tourism*, London: Macmillan.

Part **6**

Case analysis for tourism, hospitality and events

Introduction

Case study analysis invariably forms a part of most courses in strategic management. Originally developed as a teaching tool in the major American business schools, particularly Harvard, case studies are now widely used by most universities in business-related courses.

Case studies are used to enable:

- An understanding of the complex nature of strategic decision making
- An understanding of the interrelated nature of decision making; that is, a decision taken in one part of a business will have an effect on other parts of the organization.
- An understanding of academic points illustrated in context rather than in an abstract way
- Learning to be more relevant and interesting and more easily comprehended

It has been argued throughout this book that managers in *THE* have to be aware of the distinctive characteristics of these sectors and the managerial implications that arise because of these characteristics. Cases that cover various facets of *THE* management provide an illustration of the specific strategic management challenges that managers face in these contexts.

Case studies are thus a valuable tool in several ways. Case studies:

- Provide experience of organizational problems and issues that it might not be possible or feasible to encounter directly
- Serve to illustrate the theory and concepts of strategic management applied to relevant examples from *THE*
- Allow active participation in strategic analysis, choice and implementation and the ability to present results persuasively
- Illustrate the linkages inherent in strategic management in that internal decisions have impacts on other parts of the organization and on external stakeholders
- Illustrate the holistic nature of strategic management in that decisions often require knowledge of other subject fields such as marketing, finance and human resource management

Although there is perhaps no substitute for management experience in the real world, case studies represent the next best thing!

What do case studies cover?

The case studies you are asked to analyze indicate the broad range of strategic decisions managers need to take in real-world *THE* organizations. The cases may vary in a number of ways, which may affect the type of analysis that is carried out and the way in which the results of the analysis are presented.

Cases are diverse and may relate to organizations:

- At both large and small scales
- That are either complex in their structure and management or are relatively simple to understand
- With exposure to particular types of risk
- That are successful or are experiencing difficulties
- That are known to you or are disguised to illustrate particular points

- That are totally fictitious and created for illustrative purposes or where the company name, names of managers, and so on are changed to disguise the real company under discussion
- Either in the present day or at a date in the past
- That work either collectively or independently

In all cases considered, however, it is important to realize that what you are normally being asked to do is:

> *Place yourself in the position of a manager of an organization or within an industry sector at a particular moment in time.*

The important point is not what *actually* happened to the organization but, given the available information, how you would have made sense of the information available to you at the time and what actions you would have recommended in these circumstances.

Reading and studying the case

In considering cases, you are expected to go beyond merely *describing* the circumstances of the case. The case method requires you to:

- Analyze the cases in detail
- Develop sound, reasoned judgments that will lead to recommendations being made

In so doing, it is important to recognize the key or strategic points of the case and to distinguish these points from less substantial or trivial points.

Many cases contain 'red herrings', which are designed to mislead and confuse. In this way, the 'real world' is replicated, because in real situations information:

- Comes from several directions in a disorderly way
- Reaches managers by different means
- Is often confusing or incomplete

A manager has to make sense of the information and discern the important or urgent from the less important or less urgent. So, in analyzing a case, it is important to ask:

> *What are the central issues?*

There will be instances when you feel that you do not have all of the information you need to make the best decision. The information presented in the case, however, is often incomplete by design and reflects the situation in the real world.

Managers often have to make decisions based on the information available to them at the time, and although they might wish they had further information, it is either unavailable or not available within the necessary time frame with the resources available. Thus, you are required to make the best possible use of the information that you have at your disposal.

You are also asked to make your analysis at the time of the case. Managers do not have the benefit of hindsight when managing their companies (much as they might want it) but have to manage with the information available to them at that time – so it is with case studies.

> For example: *A case considering a tour operator in 2019 would not have knowledge of, for instance, the COVID-19 pandemic that had major worldwide impacts in 2020 and 2021.*

One of the difficulties in analyzing cases is the lack of a 'right' answer. Though there may be some answers that are clearly 'wrong', it is less easy to prove that an answer is right.

> **For example:** *If you propose that a small events management company operating in its local market that has demonstrated growth of 10% per annum over the last 5 years should grow to become the largest event management company in the world over the next 3 years, it would almost certainly be unrealistic and therefore 'wrong', because it does not appear to be possible.*

However, there may be several strategic options available, and the strength of the answer depends on the strength of the arguments presented, which in turn depend upon the analysis carried out. The analysis of the case should be based on:

- The facts of the case
- Sound and logical reasoning
- The application of strategic principles, theories and concepts from the academic literature

Doing the analysis

A few tips on the analysis of cases are suggested in the table below:

Analysis aspect	Tips
Reading the case	• Read the case twice initially. First read the case quickly as if you were reading a newspaper to get a feel for the structure and layout of the case.
	• On the second reading of the case, make notes, underline important passages, mark sections for later analysis and identify the central issues. Once you have an adequate grasp of the case and the issues presented, you can begin an in-depth analysis.
Organize the case facts	• The facts of a case may be presented in a bewildering or misleading way.
	• It may be necessary for you to reorganize the information or label the data so that it makes more sense. **For example:** *Sometimes it might be necessary to reorder the material chronologically or to separate the organization into its constituent parts (SBUs).*
Avoid vacuous terms	• Terms that are hollow and lacking in context make the analysis unsound. **For example:** *'Good', 'bad', 'many', 'few' are vacuous, without precise meaning, because they can be interpreted differently by different individuals.*
	• Instead, use precise language.
Do not contact the company	• The case provides the information you need to analyze, and the information may have been changed for teaching purposes.
	• The case is designed to put you in the position of a company manager at a particular point in time.
	• What actually happened is not normally relevant, and companies should not be burdened by numerous enquiries unless you are specifically instructed to do so.

Analysis aspect	Tips
Appeal to authority	• Use of references, application of concepts, and use of empirical evidence to support your case are valid ways of justifying your arguments. • However, care must be taken. Just because an 'expert' supports a view does not necessarily make it correct, and different experts can present different views.
Applying concepts	• If you use a concept to organize the information or to support your views, make sure that it is applied appropriately. > For example: *Porter's five force model may be an appropriate way of analyzing the competitive environment, but make sure that it is applied to the facts of the case and not merely presented in its abstract form.* • A common mistake is to use every conceivable strategic concept or framework available. Be selective, because some concepts are more appropriate in the circumstances than others. • The concepts are only useful in that they aid understanding. • Which concepts are appropriate will depend on the facts of the case and the material presented to you.
Case linkages	• The case may be presented in a confusing manner, but look for opportunities to make links between different parts of the case and thereby demonstrate that you have understood the case and its complexities. > For example*: The case may state within the text that a new sales and marketing director was appointed. In another part of the case a table may indicate a falling sales trend and the financial statements may indicate a vastly increased advertising budget. By bringing together the three disparate pieces of information, appropriate conclusions can be drawn.* • Similarly, bringing together information from differing parts of the case and presenting it in a different form may be useful to aid understanding. For example, putting the figures into a graph or table might be useful.
Adding value to the information	• Look for opportunities when analyzing a case to add value through your analysis. In other words, it is of far more value to interpret the information rather than to merely repeat the information contained in the case in your answer. > For example: *A case on an airline might state that the aircraft fleet contains ten Boeing 737–800 and six Boeing 787 aircraft purchased at various stated dates between 2006 and 2019. Rather than repeat this information in your answer, it is much more useful to calculate the average age of the fleet. Is the fleet relatively young or relatively old?* • Similarly, a hotel operator may present sales figures for the last 10 years. A calculation showing the percentage growth (or decline) of sales from year to year would add value. Such a calculation would clearly show whether the rate of growth has increased or decreased. The information could also be presented as a graph.

CASE STUDY SUMMARY

Case	Strategy focus	Geographic focus	Sector focus
1. Competing or cooperating in the airline industry: strategic alliances or going it alone?	• History and development of international airlines • Alliances vs organic growth as strategic methods of growth • Competitive strategy • International regulation of airlines • Macro external analysis	Global	International airlines
2. Thomas Cook vs TUI: survival of the fittest	• Historic tourism development • Competitive strategy and strategic direction • Products and markets • Pandemic strategy • Comparative analysis • Financial analysis and performance • Change and leadership • Characteristics of *THE* products • Turnaround strategy	Europe and Global	Tour operators and tourism
3. Queensland Australia: tourism and events – strategic positioning and promotion	• Strategy for developing Queensland as an international tourism and events destination • Sustainability • Products and markets • Recovery strategy • Positioning and promoting destinations • Public–private partnerships	Asia-Pacific	Tourist destinations and events

4. IHG: competing on the world stage	• International growth strategies in the hotel industry • Methods of growth; e.g., organic, franchising and management contracts • Market segmentation and brand development • Financial analysis • Achieving competitive advantage • Corporate culture and governance • Internationalization	USA and Global	Hospitality
5. RX – strategic issues for a leading events management company	• Planning events • Understanding strategic risks • Pandemic strategy • Product and market strategy • Product innovation • Competitive strategy and strategic methods • Internationalization	Global	Events
6. Airbnb: back to the future – a 'disruptor' for global hospitality	• Strategic direction and competitive strategy • Strategic methods • Products and markets • Change and leadership • Corporate culture • Internationalization • The sharing economy • Disruptive innovation	Global	Hospitality

Part 6

CHAPTER/CASE CORRELATION

Chapter	Competing or cooperating in the airline industry: strategic alliances or going it alone?	Queensland Australia: tourism and events – strategic positioning and promotion	IHG: competing on the world stage	RX: strategic issues for a leading events management company	Thomas Cook vs TUI: survival of the fittest	Airbnb: back to the future – a 'disruptor' for global hospitality
1. Strategy and strategic objectives for tourism, hospitality and event organizations	✓	✓	✓	✓	✓	✓
2. Introduction to strategy for tourism, hospitality and events	✓	✓	✓	✓	✓	✓
3. Tourism, hospitality and event organizations – the operational context: sources of competitive advantage	✓	✓	✓	✓	✓	✓
4. Tourism, hospitality and event organizations – the human resources context			✓	✓		✓
5. Tourism, hospitality and event organizations – the financial context			✓	✓	✓	✓
6. Tourism, hospitality and event organizations – the products and markets context		✓	✓		✓	✓
7. The external environment for tourism, hospitality and event organizations – the macro context	✓	✓			✓	✓

8. The external environment for tourism, hospitality and event organizations – the competitive context	✓	✓	✓	✓	✓	✓
9. SWOT analysis for tourism, hospitality and event organizations	✓	✓	✓	✓	✓	✓
10. Competitive strategy for tourism, hospitality and event organizations	✓	✓	✓	✓	✓	✓
11. Strategic directions for tourism, hospitality and event organizations	✓	✓	✓	✓		✓
12. Strategic methods of development for tourism, hospitality and event organizations	✓	✓	✓	✓	✓	✓
13. Strategic evaluation and selection for tourism, hospitality and event organizations	✓	✓	✓	✓	✓	✓
14. Strategic implementation for tourism, hospitality and event organizations	✓	✓	✓	✓	✓	
15. International and global strategies for tourism, hospitality and event organizations	✓	✓	✓	✓	✓	✓
16. Sustainability strategy for tourism, hospitality and event organizations				✓		
17. Strategic management for tourism, hospitality and event organizations – strategy in practice		✓	✓	✓		

Case **1**

Competing or cooperating in the airline industry: strategic alliances or going it alone?

Introduction

The airline sector has a long history of working in partnership, exemplified by the IATA annual conferences and bilateral agreements (which split markets equally between pairs of national airlines). Under the auspices of IATA, on a global scale, a tradition of cooperation between airlines was built up, and on individual routes cooperation has commonly included revenue pooling agreements between the carriers operating a route.

Airlines also have a long history of cooperating on safety and planning issues. The ICAO is a specialized agency of the UN based in Montreal, Canada. It coordinates the principles and techniques of international air navigation and fosters the planning and development of international air transport to ensure safe and orderly growth.

In recent years, airlines have formed alliances for fear of being left behind, and the stage has now been reached where the international airline sector has coalesced into three large alliance groupings: the *Star Alliance*, *Oneworld Alliance* and *SkyTeam Alliance*. Each of the alliances includes one of the large American so-called legacy airlines.

It is not only the number of airline alliance agreements being made that is significant but the deepening relations between partners in these alliances. The alliances are no longer mere loose arrangements between a couple of carriers to share flight codes and cross-sell tickets. The alliances have developed in a way that is so wide-ranging that they have many of the characteristics of mergers, despite national rules often forbidding foreign ownership.

DOI: 10.4324/9781003318613-24

However, some notable gaps in the coverage of the major strategic alliances remain as some airlines have adopted a different competitive stance. In particular, the fast growing and cash-rich Middle East Airlines of Emirates and Etihad based in the developing hubs of Dubai and Abu Dhabi, respectively, have so far avoided joining the alliances and instead pursue their own individual strategies. By contrast, the other fast-growing Middle East airline – Qatar Airways – joined the Oneworld Alliance during 2014.

Emirates and Etihad have chosen different methods in striving for growth. These alternative methods involve individual partnership arrangements with other airlines, over which the respective the two United Arab Emirates airlines have some degree of control.

Emirates growth has been founded on a strategic geographical position (between the European, African and Asian markets with transpolar flights connecting to North America), a low cost base, generous frequent flyer benefits and state-of-the-art infrastructure at Dubai International Airport with no night flying restrictions, thereby increasing aircraft utilization rates. The low cost base is partly attributable to the operation of a fleet comprising all widebody aircraft (largely of Airbus A380s and Boeing 777s), which results in lower unit costs compared to other large airlines operating a mix of narrow and widebody fleets. It also allows the airline to use the aircraft's cargo capacity to increase its revenues. Competitors have frequently claimed they face unfair competition from the airline because it has received government support in various ways as a wholly owned subsidiary of the state.

A number of reasons have been forwarded for Emirates not joining one of the global airline alliances (although they had planned to join Star Alliance in 2000). The main reason cited is usually that freedom of action is compromised because of the common alliance goals imposed that mainly serve the interests of the alliance founders or smaller airlines. Other reasons are that the airline has grown its own network so widely that it does not need alliance partners to provide global coverage, and where such gaps occur codesharing agreements (such as with Qantas) suffice. Alliances can lead to customer dissatisfaction because in some cases passengers do not know with certainty which airline will provide the service.

Emirates' strategy has involved some individual cooperation agreements with airlines such as Qantas, Malaysia Airlines and 'low-cost' airlines such as Gol and WestJet (in South and North America, respectively) and Jetstar and Bangkok Airways in Asia-Pacific. An illustration of this approach was provided by Tim Clark, president of Emirates, when interviewed for the London-based *Financial Times* (Parker, 2013). He said, 'Emirates has no interest in joining one of the global alliances, because it does not want to be "beholden" to some of the most powerful carriers within these groupings. Etihad has taken a different route by taking several minority stakes in airlines including German carrier Air Berlin (which subsequently went bust) and financially troubled Italian carrier Alitalia.'

Low-cost carriers (such as AirAsia, easyJet and Southwest airlines) that have grown up around the world have also not joined the strategic alliances, and the alliances themselves have not welcomed the new competitors. However, the distinction between low-cost carriers and 'traditional' carriers has become increasingly blurred as low-cost carriers have sometimes added additional service features and traditional carriers have economized on some service aspects (such as in-flight food) to compete. Additionally, some members of the alliances have low-cost subsidiaries that sit outside the alliance structures. In the Star Alliance, for instance, Thai Airways has Thai Smiles, ANA has ANA Wings, Air Canada has Air Canada Express and South African has Mango.

The low-cost airlines have generally followed simple 'point-to-point' route networks as opposed to 'hub-and-spoke' networks based on large hub airports favored by the traditional carriers. Low-cost carriers by definition strive to minimize costs by cutting out added costs involved in aspects of operations such as passengers and baggage transferring airlines at hub airports, coordinating schedules with other airlines and ticketing and reservations coordination.

Motivations for alliance formation

Enormous changes have occurred in the world economy in recent years, including major developments in technology, education and world trade, and the pace of change has been quickening.

External drivers

INFORMATION REVOLUTION

In the 1960s and 1970s, information technologies played a role in international tourism, creating mass, standardized and rigidly packaged tourism but merely facilitating its development (Poon, 1993). The US Airline Deregulation Act of 1978 introduced airlines operating in the USA to a new world of competitive threats and opportunities. The key change, whereby price regulating power was removed from the Civil Aeronautics Board (CAB), enabled airlines to increase the variety of fares offered, and the increased frequency at which fares changed necessitated the extensive development of advanced computer reservations systems (CRSs).

The CRS systems allow airlines to monitor, manage and control their capacity through yield management and their clients through frequent flyer programs. CRS systems, originally in the USA and then in Europe and elsewhere, provided a marketing tool of considerable power, giving travel agents' preferences for booking flights to the first to appear on their screens. The spread in the coverage of CRS systems and their increasing sophistication, with functions other than reservations, has led to them being termed global distribution systems (GDSs).

In the past the airlines that owned the GDSs undoubtedly favored their own flights (or those of their codesharing partners), but to a significant extent such bias has now been eliminated at least in Europe and North America through codes of conduct. The power given to airlines by GDS systems has been replicated by the power given directly to consumers by the internet.

A vast amount of information is directly available to consumers to compare prices, and this growth has allowed airlines to communicate directly with consumers, cutting out the need for intermediaries. Internet search engines such as Expedia, Skyscanner, Opodo and Trip give enormous power to consumers because they are able to easily search available flight alternatives. Many airlines, particularly low-cost carriers, take the majority of their bookings through this distribution channel.

ECONOMIC RESTRUCTURING

Economic restructuring through the philosophy of 'economic disengagement' by governments in many parts of the world has, over the last few decades, had a major impact on airline industry structure. This philosophy, influenced by the widespread adoption of the 'theory of contestable markets' (which advocated the removal of restrictive market entry barriers) from the early 1980s (Baumol, 1982), manifested itself in the forms of deregulation and privatization.

The Chicago Convention of 1944 established the bilateral system of air service agreements between pairs of national governments that have since governed international air transport. The international market that developed was characterized by national airlines from each country serving routes and airlines charging the same fares and often sharing markets and revenues. Some bilateral agreements also stipulate conditions governing responsibility for matters such as ground handling. The terms of the bilateral agreements reflected the negotiating power and current aviation policies of the countries involved; thus, the resulting productivity was often low and costs were high (OECD, 1997).

Deregulation of domestic services occurred in the USA in 1978, followed by Canada, the United Kingdom, Australia and New Zealand in the 1980s and the completion of deregulation within the EU in April 1997. Parallel liberalization in international air services has taken place much more slowly. Notwithstanding the change that has occurred in some markets, even the liberalized structures are restrictive on market entry. Requirements for designated airlines to be owned by nationals of the states involved are common, and airport congestion and slot allocation practices often further impede effective market entry (Doganis, 2009). Evidence is, however, mounting that the removal of bilateral agreements and similar intervention barriers can reduce fares.

Another, and linked, aspect of *economic disengagement* is the worldwide movement toward the privatization of state-owned airlines. However, despite this gradual process, many international airlines remain publicly owned or have major government shareholdings. Controls on foreign ownership remain in most markets, but some foreign ownership of airlines or stakes in airline ownership now exist, and this will increase with planned privatizations.

The EU's third air transport package (implemented in April 1997), for instance, set no limit on the stake a Union national or a Union airline can hold in an airline registered in another EU state. With limited exceptions, however, non-EU investors cannot hold a majority stake in any EU airline. In the USA, foreign shareholdings of up to 49% of equity under certain circumstances and 25% of voting stock are possible, although the US government also imposes an ad hoc control test to determine whether the foreign shareholder would substantially influence decision making irrespective of equity held.

Liberalization, privatization, foreign ownership and transnational mergers will have a major impact on the future structure of the airline industry, but many regulatory and ownership barriers remain in force worldwide. As a result, alternative methods of strategic development, namely, internally generated growth and mergers and acquisitions, are often precluded as viable growth strategies for international airlines; consequently, the formation of strategic alliances has been, in many cases, the only available form of market entry.

GLOBAL COMPETITION

Organizational form has been dramatically influenced by the rise of globalization. Global competition is clearly well advanced in industries such as motor vehicles, pharmaceuticals, soft drinks and, more recently, financial services but is a more recent phenomenon in the airline business, having been restricted by regulation, government ownership and consumer preferences.

Airlines are seeking to maximize their 'global reach', in the belief that those that offer a global service (with a competitively credible presence in each of the major air travel markets) will be in the strongest competitive position. Within the overall framework of globalization there are certain key markets. The importance of what Ohmae (1989) termed the 'triad' markets of Japan, North America and Europe can, in a global airline context, be modified to broaden the Japanese leg of the triad to include the wider Asia-Pacific region (including the Middle East) and for the crucial markets to include not only the constituent markets of the triad but also the flows between them. Furthermore, indications are that the growth in international air travel will continue to outstrip the growth in economic activity as measured by gross domestic product, but it will not be uniform across the world, with some regions significantly outpacing others.

Internal drivers

RISK SHARING

Strategic alliances are seen as an attractive mechanism for hedging risk because neither partner bears the full risk and cost of the alliance activity. The need to spread the costs and risks of innovation has increased as capital requirements for development projects have risen. Developing new or existing routes, for instance, is far less risky if the partners operating the routes have firmly entrenched marketing strengths in the two markets at either end of the routes.

ECONOMIES OF SCALE, SCOPE AND LEARNING

A prime driver for alliance formation is for airlines to achieve cost economies, which can be categorized as economies of scale, scope and experience. Economies of scale exist where the average cost per unit of output declines as the level of output increases. Empirical evidence reveals little evidence of economies of scale, however, except for the smallest operators and specific areas such as marketing. Furthermore, evidence suggests that airlines' unit costs do not fall greatly as they expand their networks. Cost savings appear to stem largely from attracting more traffic to a given network rather than expanding it to cover more destinations.

The airline industry may lack substantial scale economies, but other economies related to the size and nature of operations exist (OECD, 1997) and help to explain the growing market concentration and the move toward alliances. Economies of scope occur when the cost of producing two (or more) products jointly is less than the cost of producing each one alone. Such economies can be achieved if alliance partners link up their existing networks so that they can provide connecting services for new markets and where marketing costs can be shared between alliance partners (Hanlon, 2007) that may have strong entrenched positions in certain markets.

A number of authors, such as Hamel (1991) and Inkpen (1998), have suggested that an important motivator to forming alliances is the benefit to be derived from economies of learning (such as experience). Incumbent suppliers have more information on the market being served and can tailor their services to specific customer needs, and alliances allow the information to be gained from existing suppliers, whereas new entrants would have to sink resources to acquire such information to win market share.

ACCESS TO ASSETS, RESOURCES AND COMPETENCES

Specific resource, skill or competence inadequacy or imbalance can be addressed by collaborating with partners which have a different set of such attributes and can therefore compensate for internal deficiencies. The regulatory framework of 'bilaterals' (see Appendix 2) and landing rights and congestion at certain airports means that airlines possessing licenses to operate on a route and slots at congested airports have important and marketable assets that are attractive to alliance partners. Alliances can thus offer relatively easy access to a route by allowing access to a partner's assets that may have been established over prolonged periods and that may have been protected by government intervention.

SHAPE COMPETITION

Strategic alliances can influence the companies that a firm competes with and the basis for competition because they can hinder the abilities of competing firms to retaliate by binding them as allies. Furthermore, current strategic positions may be successfully defended against forces that are too strong for one firm to withstand alone (Glaister and Buckley, 1996).

Strategic alliances may therefore be used as a defensive ploy to reduce competition, because an obvious benefit of strategic alliances is converting a competitor into a partner. Smaller, relatively weak airlines may view alliances as the only viable way to compete with larger, more sophisticated rivals. The purchase of a 40% share of Sri Lankan Airlines in 1998 by Emirates Airlines, for instance, can be viewed as part of a defensive alliance strategy aimed at retaining international competitiveness through allying with a commercially stronger rival.

Alternatively, alliance formation may form part of an offensive strategy, by linking with a rival, for example, to put pressure on the profits and market share of a common competitor. The long-standing operating alliance between British Airways and American on transatlantic routes, as part of the wider Oneworld Alliance, is an example of such an offensive positioning. As such, it has attracted criticism in that the two airlines have large market shares on these routes and dominant positions at their respective hubs (Heathrow in London and Dallas–Fort Worth).

Alliance structure and performance

Considerable time and effort may be expended in developing the structure and scope of an alliance. The unique nature and operating environment of the airline sector dictate that alliances must be structured around diverse requirements.

Evaluating the performance of alliances is complex given the multifaceted objectives of many alliances and the difficulties involved in ascribing financial measures. The situation is often further complicated by asymmetric performance: one firm achieves its objectives while others fail to do so. For instance, several studies have reported cases of alliances in which one partner had raced to learn the other's skills while the other partners had no such intentions. Despite these evident measurement obstacles, several authors (including, Evans, 2001; Min and Joo, 2016; Douglas and Tan, 2017; Yu et al. 2017) have attempted empirical studies of alliance performance primarily through examining the factors leading to the termination of alliance arrangements.

These studies, which have not focused directly on the airline industry, have cited various contributory factors in the termination of alliances, including partner asymmetry, the competitive overlap between partners, the presence of other concurrent ties and the characteristics of the alliance itself such as autonomy of operations and flexibility. Such an approach to the study of alliance performance is limited by two factors. Firstly, not all alliance terminations can be viewed as failures because in some cases they may have been intended as interim transitional arrangements. Secondly, not all ongoing alliances can necessarily be viewed as successful, because inertia or high exit costs may provide an explanation for their continuation.

Taking a more pragmatic approach to the evaluation of alliance success, Mockler (1999) suggested that four basic criteria should be fulfilled. Firstly, the alliance must add value to a participant. That is, it must be worth more to the company to enter into an alliance than to undertake a venture on its own. Secondly, the participant must be able to learn something from collaborating with partners. Thirdly, a participant must be able to protect its own competences even while interacting with the alliance over a continuing period of time and, fourthly, the firm must retain flexibility and not be overly reliant on any one partner.

Conclusion

Airlines have rushed to form alliances for fear of being left behind, and many have later changed their partners as they have become more sophisticated at identifying the potential 'strategic fit' between partners. The alliances have developed from individual relationships between pairs of airlines (which were subject to many changes and modifications) to a situation where there are now three major strategic alliances that have added member airlines over the years.

To some degree, alliance formation can be viewed as an inevitable result of the regulatory framework within which the international airline industry operates. Regulatory and legal restrictions often prevent the full ownership of airlines by foreign companies and, consequently, alliances have been perceived as the only viable market entry mechanism, at least in the short to medium term. However, some observers view strategic alliances as inherently unstable and transitory forms of organization, a 'second-best' solution that is disturbingly likely to break up under commercial pressure.

The role and characteristics of these strategic alliances have continued to evolve. In the late 1980s, strategic alliances were seen as a rather crude way to grow quickly by avoiding bilateral restrictions, and some airlines rushed to form alliances. The cyclical slump and heavy losses of the early 1990s turned attention to the efficiency improvements made possible by alliances and, consequently, airlines focused more clearly on the strategic logic of the particular partners that had been chosen. The importance of 'strategic fit' thus came to be stressed; that is, the proposed partners should have a compatible culture, management style and geographical coverage.

The commercial logic for airlines to form alliances was established as a range of external and internal drivers exerted pressure. This logic, if extended, has led to the larger, multi-airline, globally encompassing alliance structures that developed from the late 1990s and that are still evident in today's industry.

Less attention has been paid to the implications of airline alliances for consumers (both internationally and in local markets) and how alliance success can be determined (Wang, 2014). Consumers receive several benefits from those alliances that are successful in producing integrated products. Consumers are provided with an enhanced choice of destinations through the marketing of alliance partners' route networks. Schedule coordination between partners often produces shorter transfer times between connections, and coordination of flight timings can avoid bunching of flight schedules. Additionally, consumers benefit from one-stop check-in (even when taking a connecting flight provided by the partner airline), the pooling of frequent flyer programs, shared airport lounge facilities, shared ground handling arrangements and the improvement in technical standards brought about through the sharing of expertise.

However, a critical unknown remains: whether consumers are paying higher or lower fares because of the strategic alliances. If carriers collaborate on many of their activities, what incentive is there to compete on price? By their very nature alliances often limit supply and thereby would be expected to force up prices. Alliance arrangements often allow one carrier to fly aircraft in a market where two may have been doing so otherwise, possibly leading to higher fares. Thus, the fares outlook for consumers in airlines' rush to form alliances is far from clear.

A number of trends relating to strategic airline alliances are discernible:

- The number of airlines involved in alliances has continued to grow. Three key alliances have emerged, each including one of the major American airlines. The focus in the coming years will be on these alliances adding further airlines to fill gaps in their global coverage. In addition, second-level feeder airlines will be added to the existing alliances.

- Substantial new alliances may be difficult to form because most of the major international players are all now involved in alliances and new alliances would therefore lack the substantial marketing presence that appears to be necessary to ensure success.

- Airlines from more countries will increasingly become involved with the established alliances, though the alliances have sometimes been highly selective in terms of which airlines they allow to join. To date, airlines from Africa, South America and parts of Asia have largely been excluded from the major alliances.

- Though the case for alliances has robustly been made by the airlines, less attention has been focused on consumers. Increasingly, international regulators will be attempting to ensure that the supposed cost savings (that the airlines argue result from alliance activity) are passed on to consumers and that the dominant positions at hub airports are scaled down to allow more 'contestability' of markets.

- Competition between the alliance groupings as entities (as opposed to the individual airlines comprising them) is increasing. The alliances promote themselves as 'umbrella' brands, with the individual airlines being subbrands offering similar service standards, and an increasing level of integration between the constituent airlines will be evident.

References

Baumol, W. J. (1982) 'Contestable markets: An uprising in the theory of industry structure', *American Economic Review*, 72(1): 1–15.

Bilotkach, V. and K. Hüschelrath (2012) 'Airline alliances and antitrust policy: The role of efficiencies', *Journal of Air Transport Management*, 21: 76–84.

Doganis, R. (2009) *Flying Off Course: Airline Economics and Marketing*, 4th ed., London: Routledge.

Douglas, I. and Tan, D. (2017) 'Global airline alliances and profitability: A difference-in-difference analysis', *Transportation Research Part A: Policy and Practice*, 103: 432–443.

Evans, N. (2001) 'Collaborative strategy: An analysis of the changing world of international airline alliances', *Tourism Management*, 22(3): 229–243.

Glaister, K. W. and P. J. Buckley (1996) 'Strategic motives for international alliance formation', *Journal of Management Studies*, 33(3): 301–332.

Hamel, G. (1991) 'Competition for competence and inter-partner learning within international strategic alliances', *Strategic Management Journal*, 12: 83–104.

Hanlon, P. (2007) *Global Airlines: Competition in a Transnational Industry*, 3rd ed., Abingdon, UK: Routledge.

ICAO. (2013) National Restrictions on Air Carrier Ownership and Control, Working Paper, Montreal: International Civil Aviation Organization

Inkpen, A. (1998) 'Learning, knowledge acquisition, and strategic alliances', *European Management Journal*, 16(2): 223–229.

Min, H. and Joo, S. J. (2016) 'A comparative performance analysis of airline strategic alliances using data envelopment analysis', *Journal of Air Transport Management*, 52: 99–110.

Mockler, R. J. (1999) *Multinational Strategic Alliances*, London: John Wiley.

OECD. (1997) *The Future of International Air Transport Policy: Responding to Global Change*, Paris: OECD.

Ohmae, K. (1989) 'Managing in a borderless world', *Harvard Business Review*, May/June: 152–161.

Parker, A. (2013) 'Gulf carriers destabilize alliances', *The Financial Times*, 14 November.

Poon, A. (1993) *Tourism, Technology and Competitive Strategies*, Wallingford, UK: CAB International.

Wang, S. W. (2014) 'Do global airline alliances influence the passenger's purchase decision?' *Journal of Air Transport Management*, 37: 53–59.

Yu, M. M., Chen, L. H. and Chiang, H. (2017) 'The effects of alliances and size on airlines' dynamic operational performance', *Transportation Research Part A: Policy and Practice*, 106: 197–214.

Appendix 1 The major airline strategic alliance groupings

	Star Alliance	SkyTeam Alliance	Oneworld Alliance
Alliance founded	1997	2000	1999
Constituent airlines	26	19	13
Destinations	1,294	1,150	1,012

	Star Alliance	SkyTeam Alliance	Oneworld Alliance
Countries	195	175	170
Annual passengers (million)	762	630	490
Headquarters	Frankfurt, Germany	Amsterdam, Netherlands	Dallas, USA
Constituent airlines include	Aegean Airlines, Greece	Aerolíneas Argentinas, Argentina	American Airlines, USA
	Air Canada, Canada	Aeroméxico, Mexico	British Airways, UK,
	Air China, China	Air Europa, Spain	Cathay Pacific, Hong Kong
	Air India, India	Air France, France	Finnair, Finland
	Air New Zealand, New Zealand	China Airlines, Taiwan	Iberia Airlines, Spain
	All Nippon, Japan	China Eastern Airlines, China	Japan Airlines, Japan
	Asiana Airlines, South Korea	Czech Airlines, Czech Republic	Malaysia Airlines, Malaysia
	Austrian Airlines, Austria	Delta Air Lines, USA	Qantas, Australia
	Avianca, Colombia	Garuda Indonesia, Indonesia	Qatar Airways, Qatar
	Brussels Airlines, Belgium	ITA Airways, Italy	Royal Jordanian, Jordan
	Copa Airlines, Panama	Kenya Airways, Kenya	Sri Lankan Airlines, Sri Lanka
	Croatia Airlines, Croatia	KLM, Netherlands	S7 Airlines, Russia*
	Egypt Air, Egypt	Korean Air, South Korea	Oman Air, Oman**
	Ethiopian Airlines, Ethiopia	Middle East Airlines, Lebanon	
	EVA Air, Taiwan	Saudia, Saudi Arabia	
	LOT Airlines, Poland	TAROM, Romania	
	Lufthansa, Germany	Vietnam Airlines, Vietnam	
	Scandinavian Airlines, Denmark/Sweden/Norway	Virgin Atlantic, UK	
	Shenzhen Airlines, China	Xiamen Air, China	
	Singapore Airlines, Singapore	Aeroflot, Russia*	
	South African Airways, South Africa		
	Swiss International Air Lines, Switzerland		
	TAP, Portugal		
	Thai Airways, Thailand		
	Turkish Airlines, Turkey		
	United Airlines, USA		

*Currently suspended.
**Joining in 2024.

Appendix 2 Freedoms of the sky and bilateral agreements

Freedoms of the sky

In 1944, delegates from 52 nations met in Chicago to develop a multilateral treaty securing each nation's rights over its airspace. These 'freedoms of the sky' have been the fundamental building blocks of air transportation regulation and each subject to specific conditions, such as establishing the frequency of flights or airport usage.

There are five basic freedoms that are recognized by virtually all countries

- First freedom – The right to fly over another nation's territory without landing (overflight)

- Second freedom – The right to land in a foreign country for nontraffic reasons, such as maintenance or refueling, without picking up or setting down revenue traffic

- Third freedom – The right to carry traffic (people or cargo) from own State A to treaty partner State B

- Fourth freedom – The right to carry traffic (people or cargo) from treaty partner State B to own State A

- Fifth freedom – The right to carry traffic between two foreign countries with services starting or ending in own State A

Bilateral air service agreements

International air transport services are regulated by bilateral air services agreements (ASAs) between states. When negotiating ASAs, states generally wish to secure that the rights exchanged with their partners will benefit the air carriers of both parties but not air carriers of other states who are not parties to the agreement and thus not providing reciprocal rights.

The simplest way to reserve rights for each party's air carriers is for each party to restrict designation to air carriers that are majority owned and effectively controlled by that party. At the same time, restrictions are reflected in national laws of the parties. Indeed, an obvious reason for national restrictions has been the logic of ASAs with respect to securing the benefits as described above.

Source: ICAO (2013)

Appendix 3 Reasons for foreign ownership restrictions

A summary of the reasons for foreign ownership restrictions on airlines

- National air carriers dominantly government owned and controlled.

- National air carriers considered as key strategic assets.

- National security concerns about the foreign control of strategic assets.

- The intention to make aircraft readily available when needed for the purposes of national defense, emergency needs or providing air services for public interest.

- Market access rights, especially cabotage, reserved to national air carriers.

- Labor issues such as the concern that foreign investors may not maintain the same labor standards.

Source: ICAO (2013)

Case **2**

Thomas Cook vs TUI: survival of the fittest

Background

The growth in the number of tourist arrivals, particularly international arrivals, has been mirrored by the growth of a vast complex travel industry that supports the activity. Thomas Cook was one of the world's best-known brands in travel, and it has sometimes been referred to as the world's oldest travel company. Thomas Cook began his international travel company in 1841, with a successful one-day rail excursion he organized between the English cities of Leicester and Loughborough.

From these humble beginnings Thomas Cook began to develop first with domestic excursions and then, from the 1850s, the development of tours in Continental Europe. Thomas Cook Group plc developed into one of the world's leading leisure travel groups with sales of over £9.5bn and more than 11 million customers and 22,000 employees in the year ended 30 September 2018.

The 'package' concept

In Europe in particular, the world's largest international tourist destination, the leisure travel industry grew particularly from putting the various elements of travel and holidays together as part of a 'package'. Before this, tourists traveling abroad could purchase separate components of a holiday – accommodation, transportation, activities, ground handling, etc. – as individual items. During the 1960s, however, the foreign inclusive tour or package holiday became established in Western Europe (and later elsewhere) and brought with it a substantial expansion in the numbers of tourists venturing abroad.

DOI: 10.4324/9781003318613-25

A package can be defined (EU, 2015) as 'a pre-arranged combination, sold or offered for sale at an inclusive price, of not less than two of the following three elements: transport; accommodation; and other tourist services not ancillary to transport or accommodation and accounting for a significant part of the package'.

The role of tour operators has been the key element in the expansion, which has continued progressively since the 1950s. This role goes beyond that of the wholesaler, in that they not only purchase or reserve the separate components in bulk but, in combining these components into an 'inclusive tour', they also become producers, because a new product – the inclusive tour or package holiday – is created. A tour operator typically combines tour and travel components to create a holiday. The most common example of a tour operator's product would be a flight on a 'charter' airline plus a transfer from the airport to a hotel and the services of a local representative, all for one price.

The traditional appeal of the tour operator's product has been to offer a complete holiday package at the lowest price to a population often lacking the linguistic knowledge or the knowledge and confidence to organize independent travel. As a result, tour operation has become the dominant feature of the holiday market in most tourist-generating countries, though the companies involved vary in their structures. In North America, for instance, the activities are often carried out by vacation subsidiaries of the major scheduled airlines and hotel groups, whereas in Europe several large tour operating companies have come to dominate the industry.

Benefits of the package concept

Many predictions have been made that the package holiday product is set to decline and die. The growth of low-cost airlines, the ability of consumers to put their own packages together via the internet and the growth in number of more experienced travelers are all factors that have been cited as contributing to this demise. However, such predictions have generally proved unfounded because the companies concerned continue to allow consumers to benefit from the advantages of packaged products. These benefits include the convenience of purchasing all elements of a holiday in one purpose-designed 'bundle'; delivery of product quality assurance, reliability and protection; and perceived good monetary value.

Although the future of the package seems assured, changes in consumer preferences and changes in the environment in which tour operating products are provided are changing the characteristics of these packages and how they are delivered to customers.

Changes that have taken place in recent years include the growth of all-inclusive holidays (in which almost all holiday costs at the destination are prepaid), the growth of long-haul travel destinations and cruising and the emergence of significant outbound travel markets in the rapidly emerging economies of countries such as those of the BRIC group (Brazil, Russia, India and China).

The growth of UK outbound tour operations

Anyone who knows the climate of Northern Europe will be aware that summers are unpredictable and unseasonably cold and wet weather is common. Consequently, it is not surprising that warmer, more dependable climates within easy reach are sought when circumstances allow. When the necessary circumstances did indeed come together during the 1950s – rising incomes, paid holiday entitlements, aircraft technology and entrepreneurial vision – a new industrial sector was born. The 'air-inclusive tour' (AIT) industrial sector developed across Europe separately, taking different forms in various countries.

The reasons for this rapid growth of the UK outbound AIT market and that of the operators that service it are inextricably linked, but perhaps two major factors stand out. Firstly, many UK residents travel abroad for their holidays in search of reliable sunshine and warmth. The UK's island location has necessitated the development of well-organized packaged transportation to service this need. Secondly, UK residents accord holidays and travel a high priority in terms of their discretionary expenditure even in times of economic hardship. Again, a highly sophisticated holiday travel industry has developed to service this need.

Relatively low barriers to entry and continual striving among operators for increased market share have led to periodic price wars, which resulted in a highly volatile record of profitability since the industry's inception. The price wars, low margins and the vulnerability of the travel industry to external economic and political factors inevitably took their toll on operators, and a number of large operators failed.

Several large tour operators came to increasingly dominate the AIT market, as mass market operators were determined to increase their market share and to reap the anticipated rewards of market dominance. Since its inception, Thomson (now part of TUI plc), the market leader, had faced major challenges to its market leadership position but had hitherto always successfully defended its position.

A company's status as a plc necessitated the targeting of profitability rather than market share as the primary objective to satisfy their shareholders and, as a result, since 1991 competition has focused on matching supply much more closely to demand, thereby avoiding damaging price wars. The latter part of the 1990s saw a flurry of activity in the UK tour operating sector with Airtours, Thomson and First Choice consolidating their leading positions with the takeover of smaller groups, adding aircraft to their airline subsidiaries and acquiring further high street travel agents to boost their distribution outlets.

Clearly, given the scale and complexity of their operations and the vertically and horizontally integrated structure of their businesses, the largest operators in the UK came to dominate the sector. However, a marked polarization has occurred in the UK industry, dividing the industry into a relatively small number of 'mass' tour operators and a much larger number of 'independent' operators largely serving specialized niche markets.

One of the key features of independent tour operators is that they are not vertically integrated, in that they do not own their own travel agencies or other distribution channels, nor do they own their own airline, and thus they rely on the supply in the marketplace for individual components of the package. In the UK the term 'independent' tour operator also has a more precise meaning, in that it can refer to those companies that are members of the AITO. AITO, formed in 1976, has grown to represent about 120 members that collectively carry nearly a million customers per annum.

Tour operating risks

Increasingly, however, given the size and international complexity of the companies concerned, it became apparent in the in the late 1990s that a pan-European view of competition issues in the tour operating sector was necessary. Scale matters in a business where the better performers still only make thin profit margins of perhaps 4%. Consequently, if an operator can negotiate cost efficiencies of 1% to 2% cent through better buying of, say, hotel rooms and aircraft fuel, that has a very material impact on profitability. These are the sort of factors that have driven consolidation over the last 20 years or so.

Tour operating has always been viewed as an inherently risky business in which seasonal and cyclical effects are prominent and where the underlying product is relatively expensive and viewed as a luxury rather than a necessity. Most profits are generally made during a short summer period, and the sector experiences 'good' and 'bad' years as economic, climate and other external pressures exert their influences on consumers who can be fickle in their buying habits.

The principal risks usually perceived by external observers of the travel industry for a tour operating group are those of underutilized aircraft and excess hotel and other accommodation for which payment has already been made. The reality is that in many cases the major tour operators have considerable flexibility in contracting both of these services. Aviation contracts with third-party suppliers usually have a variety of cancellation options that can be exercised once booking patterns have been established. A great deal of the stock required for accommodation is not negotiated on an irrevocable basis, meaning that adjustments to capacity can be made, though such changes can prove costly.

Perhaps more critical to the business, and common to other businesses dealing with international conditions, are changes in exchange and interest rates and aviation fuel. Most companies develop policies of 'hedging' against all major risks on the financial and commodity markets prior to each holiday cycle. This usually involves the practice of negotiating a range of forward contracts and options. In this way, the costs of hedging these risks can be built into the overall selling prices that customers are asked to pay.

The holiday business is well known for generating substantial cash flows because customers traditionally pay in advance and holiday companies pay most of their suppliers in arrears. There is a degree of seasonality to this cash flow, with large cash surpluses commonly built up during the spring period (as sales are made), which are eroded as payments to suppliers are made during the summer period. Autumn and winter are the seasons of greatest risk because business costs are still incurred but relatively few customer payments are received. Thus, effective cash management of these balances and potential seasonal deficits has become a very important part of business management for many tour operators.

European expansion

Tour operators responded to the perceived risks in several ways in the two leading European markets (Germany and the UK). In the 1990s, the sector increasingly became vertically integrated, and horizontal expansion followed firstly at the national level and then internationally when domestic opportunities became more limited.

The new century, however, was characterized by the largest players in Germany and the UK purchasing smaller, weaker rivals but by consolidation among the largest players themselves, which eventually resulted in the emergence of two dominant groups: TUI and Thomas Cook. TUI Group, headquartered in the German city of Hannover, is quoted on the Frankfurt and London stock exchanges.

First Choice emerged in the mid-2000s reinvigorated, having modified its strategic positioning. First Choice's emphasis had been to shift away from high-volume, low-margin businesses toward a portfolio of individually branded, more specialist products with an emphasis on all-inclusive arrangements offering potentially higher returns. All-inclusive products that involve the provision of most destination services including food and beverages in the package price have proved increasingly popular. Such arrangements allow the tour operator to provide more rigorous quality standards through the control of a greater part of the supply chain and gain additional revenues from the services provided. Cost efficiency is maintained through the utilization of centralized systems and corporate buying power.

Like TUI, Thomas Cook has had a number of ownership changes. Thomas Cook passed through four different German owners before a 2007 merger with UK-based MyTravel plc returned it to the

London Stock Exchange. The mid-1990s were a period of rapid growth, with the acquisition of a number of well-known tour operator brands culminating in the company's merger with Carlson Leisure Group's UK travel interests, which included a large number of high street travel agents.

The summer of 2007 was pivotal in creating the two major European-based tour operating groups that came to dominate the industry sector. TUI in its present form was formed at that time as it merged with UK-based First Choice travel, as was the Thomas Cook Group. In June 2007, Thomas Cook AG and MyTravel Group plc (a major listed UK travel group, previously named Airtours) merged to form Thomas Cook Group plc. Thus, Thomas Cook acquired a brand with a poor record of profitability and took on considerable additional levels of debt.

Another merger followed in October 2011, when Thomas Cook amalgamated its UK high street travel and foreign exchange businesses with those of the Co-operative Group to create the UK's largest retail travel network of over 1,200 shops, at a time when the proportion of internet bookings in the UK was rising quickly and traditional 'high street' travel agencies were coming under severe financial pressures. In October 2013, Thomas Cook officially unveiled its new 'unified' brand to the world. The 'Sunny Heart' and 'Let's Go!' taglines.

European-based tour operators – challenges

The vertically integrated model whereby a single group became the full owner (or had equity in) airline operations, tour operations and travel retailing (and sometimes accommodation and cruise operations), is now firmly established. A few large integrated European-based groups emerged of which TUI and Thomas Cook were the largest, but other large European groups such as Kuoni and Globus based in Switzerland and France's Club Med also emerged. The industry does, however, retain a large number of smaller operators competing for customers in certain niches. Increasing polarization has occurred as companies have had to make the strategic choice to become complex vertically, horizontally or, in some cases, diagonally integrated organizations or to specialize as niche players targeted at discrete market segments.

One of the reasons often cited for ever greater concentration by a few large suppliers for an industry is that larger companies enjoy the advantages to be derived from economies of scale and scope. These economies clearly exist in tour operating, in terms of marketing, operational and purchasing economies, for instance, but savings have been hard to achieve in the recent adverse economic circumstances, particularly in Europe. The core Western European markets that the companies serve are increasingly 'mature', and there has been a trend away from standard 'summer sun' packages toward a more diverse range of package options. Tour operators are increasingly being forced to respond to a much more complex holiday market than has hitherto existed, through diversification, narrower market segmentation, responding to independently minded and increasingly experienced customers and embracing the all-inclusive market and cruising.

The larger European-based companies have also looked to spread their geographical coverage away from their focus on the mature markets of Western Europe. New markets have been sought with expansion into Eastern and Central Europe, Russia, India and China in particular. Large emerging middle classes with high propensities to spend on international travel make these markets attractive to travel company investors. However, each international marketplace is different, with its own complexities and varying stages of development. In such cases, companies have to carefully consider their mode of market entry and the business model to be adopted.

Companies have also had to consider the balance of their activities to avoid overstretching their resources and capabilities. Even for the larger, well-established companies, competitive and resource pressures and entry into new markets necessitate consideration of newer ways of working, including the increasing emphasis on collaborative strategy through the formation of strategic alliances and franchising, the separation of ownership of tourist assets from their management and outsourcing some activities previously handled 'in-house'.

Furthermore, tour operators have had to respond to two further challenges that place far more power in the hands of consumers.

Many new technology entrants to the travel industry and consumers were quick to recognize the power of the internet. It enables consumers to search for information online; to access reliable, accurate and up-to-date information; and to quickly compare comparative product offerings. Furthermore, the availability of such information enables consumers to make reservations in a fraction of the time necessary for some other methods and with a minimum of inconvenience. The internet is driven by both the increasing volume and diversity of tourism demand and by the power it gives consumers to buy personalized 'bundles' of tourism products. In some cases, this leads to the avoidance of traditional tourism packages, leading instead to consumers assembling their own packages (so-called dynamic packaging) from individual component parts on offer with prices fluctuating according to supply and demand at the time of booking.

Though such distribution does not totally undermine the advantages that tour operators enjoy or the need for specialist advice that can be offered by retail travel agents, it clearly has a significant impact. In particular, tour operators have had to adjust their own distribution activities, investing in enhanced interactive websites supported by call centers and reassessing the scale of their networks of retail shops. Additionally, the internet allows (at reasonable cost) suppliers an unprecedented opportunity to communicate globally with their target markets and to establish direct relationships with consumers. Some smaller companies have successfully developed a niche sector of the market, usually by targeting particular customer types or by focusing on specific destinations and often by using the internet as a cost-effective tool.

The rapid rise of low-cost airlines such as easyJet, Ryanair, Norwegian and Jet2 in Europe over the last 20 years has provided further challenges for managers at tour operating companies and, indeed, Jet2 has emerged as a major force in vertically integrated European tour operations. The airlines cut costs wherever possible and, by operating modern aircraft fleets, are able to ensure high rates of utilization for their planes. The low-cost carriers have also increasingly targeted routes to Mediterranean resort destinations that are served by the charter airlines. However, charter airlines such as those owned by the tour operating groups have provided stiff competition through careful exploitation of the inherent advantages of charter flights.

The low-cost airlines have to operate on a prearranged schedule regardless of sales level achieved. Managers of charter carriers (as in all airlines) watch load factors very carefully and are fully conscious of the load factor at which breakeven is achieved. Beyond the breakeven point (as in all travel operations), profitability quickly accumulates with each additional passenger. The charter carriers are usually able to achieve very high load factors by matching seats available to demand and, if necessary, changing the aircraft type, consolidating flights and even changing departures (or arrivals) to a different airport.

A broader challenge to tour operators is also provided by the low-cost carriers in that, as with the internet, they allow consumers to easily and at reasonable cost put their own packages together. A low-cost flight can easily be combined with accommodation, and ancillary services such as ground transportation can quickly be added. The multitude of search engines available can facilitate making these arrangements, and price comparisons are easy to make. Tour operators have had to respond to these challenges by offering more flexible products. Mass tourism is increasingly being replaced by mass customization in an industry that has to cater for ever more discerning and experienced consumers.

Thomas Cook Group in 2011

2011 was not a 'good' year for Thomas Cook; in fact, it was a year the company would wish to forget, for it was the year in which a respected and historic name in travel came perilously close to failure.

The travel group had been hit by tough trading brought on by the global economic downturn, high fuel costs and social unrest in popular destinations for the company such as Egypt, Tunisia and Greece. The cumulative effect forced the company to negotiate and renegotiate banking lifelines and make disposals to raise cash and reduce debt, which led to senior management changes.

The situation reached a crisis point in late November 2011, when the following statement was released by the company:

> Thomas Cook Group plc announces that as a result of deterioration of trading in some areas of the business in the current quarter, and of its cash and liquidity position since its year end, the Company is in discussions with its principal lending banks with regard to its facilities during the seasonal low period of cash in the business.

The group's long-serving chief executive resigned in the summer of 2011 as a result of the adverse reactions to profit warnings and the sliding share price. His departure had been widely anticipated, following discontent among shareholders as the group's debt burden rose to more than £900mn.

Although the company's position had deteriorated, with three profit warnings having been made during the year, the statement nevertheless was a bombshell, and shares subsequently lost 70% of their value later that week. Shares that had traded at 300 pence at their spring 2009 peak tumbled. The shares in Europe's second-biggest tour operator closed 75% down at just over 10 pence, giving it a market capitalization of just £89mn.

The newly installed interim chief executive said trading since the group's end of year in September had been worse than expected, piling further pressure on Thomas Cook's cash flow during the slow winter booking season.

He blamed the group's lack of bookings on a Eurozone crisis and a sluggish recovery in tourism to the Middle East and North Africa (Wembridge and Blitz, 2011). It was also acknowledged that costs had risen for holidays in Turkey, where the company was market leader, and that its fuel buying policy was only 80% hedged against fuel increases compared to rivals TUI TRAVEL's hedge at more than 90%. Weak performance in the UK had prompted the company to undergo a wide-ranging review of its British operations, a key component of the business, a step seen by some analysts as an admission that the business model was flawed.

Whereas rival TUI had weighted its offerings toward higher-margin 'differentiated' package holidays, Europe's second-biggest tour group was still heavily exposed to more basic trips, which people book later or reject completely in favor of planning their own flights and hotels (Wembridge and Jacobs, 2011). While Thomas Cook was suffering, its larger rival TUI, though not soaring, was certainly doing better. Customer numbers in its large British, German and French markets were either flat or only marginally ahead in 2010–11, full-year revenues increased by 9% and pretax profits were £144mn compared with a £73mn loss in the previous year.

TUI appeared to try to make the most of its rival's misfortunes. It ran adverts on its website in late 2011 containing lines such as, 'Unlike a certain holiday company we could mention, you don't need to worry about the way we run our business'. The adverts elicited complaints from Thomas Cook and were quickly removed.

The underlying problem faced by both Thomas Cook and TUI was that recession across its major European markets had taken its toll, and some important core destinations had become unattractive due to political instability. Thomas Cook's cash flow is seasonal because fewer holidays are booked and paid for in the winter, prompting speculation that the group could breach its obligations around Christmastime. However, an old adage in banking is that 'if you owe the bank a million pounds, you have a problem, but if it's a billion pounds the bank has a problem'. Consequently, whereas a smaller company might have been forced into failure as banks failed to agree to extended credit terms, Thomas Cook's lenders agreed that the group's net debt could now be up to 4.5 times earnings, before interest, tax, depreciation, amortization and restructuring costs at the end of December. That was an increase from 3.75 times EBITDA that was agreed in May 2010. This gave the company some leeway and it survived 2011, having had a close call.

Thomas Cook Group in 2013

Wind the clock forward 2 years and the position with the company is very different. In July 2012 a new CEO, Harriet Green, who had previously led an electronics distribution business, was appointed. Although the company had survived the previous winter, in an interview with the UK trade paper *Travel Weekly* she said (with understatement) that when she joined the company it was 'not very well' (Taylor, 2013). In the same interview she said that Thomas Cook business appeared to operate as a number of unconnected 'silos'. There had been many acquisitions, but there appeared to be little evidence of integration because it seemed that the synergies had stayed in the boardroom. For example, the online travel agent was a completely separate business competing with the company's own high street shops.

The new CEO worked from a modest office and was clearly not afraid to speak her mind. 'I don't really give a dam whether people like what I have say and I am not trying to win any popularity contests' (Saunders, 2014). While clearly having a strategic vision for the company, she was also not afraid to deal with operational detail and communicate freely. She had 3,000 followers on her Twitter account and dealt with all of her own emails, encouraging staff to contact her and providing answers within 24 hours. 'When people realized that, it sent the most symbolic ripple through the organization and it allowed me to say that we've got to do these things at pace' (Saunders, 2014).

By mid-2013, Thomas Cook's share price had recovered to about 145 pence, valuing the group at about £1.3bn. The company took advantage of the surge in the share price to make a £400mn rights issue of shares to help cut the holiday company's £1.5bn debt burden.

A series of asset sales (including its North American division) had been made and a cost-cutting regime had been implemented. In March 2013, 2,500 jobs were cut in its British business and around 200 high street travel agents were closed, though it retained a large presence in physical travel agent branches.

Thomas Cook in 2018

Though Harriet Green appeared to have made progress in a widely praised restructuring of the business and altering its culture, she abruptly left the company in November 2014.

Old problems came back to haunt Thomas Cook during the latter part of 2018. In June the share price had been close to 150 pence, but by December, following two profit warnings in 2 months, the share price tumbled, along with the valuation of Thomas Cook. An article in London's *Financial Times* pointed out that On the Beach, a listed online travel agent that only began trading in 2004 (and whose revenues were a fraction of Thomas Cook's), at that time had a larger market value than Thomas Cook, the company that gave rise to package holidays (Eley, 2018).

The firm blamed its profits drop on a prolonged UK summer heatwave hitting overseas bookings, but winter bookings were also down by 3%. Undoubtedly, weather was a factor, but most commentators felt that the problems at the company were deeper rooted. Simon Calder, travel editor of *The Independent*, recognized the value and heritage of the Thomas Cook brand but also pointed to other issues facing the company. He said, 'They have taken their eye off the ball and failed to spot trends, mainly the emergence of no-frills travel'.

Rival TUI, meanwhile, was thriving, relatively. TUI posted net profits of earnings before interest and tax of just over €1bn on turnover of €19.5bn in 2018). Thomas Cook had also been hit by the rise of the UK budget airline Jet2, which has now become the UKs second-largest tour operator: 'They have picked up a lot of the "bread and butter" holiday market that Thomas Cook used to have' (Calder, 2018). Though Thomas Cook had invested in new hotel concepts to generate new business and loyalty with repeat bookings, analysts maintain that it still lagged behind its larger UK/German rival. TUI had invested heavily in buying hotels and cruise ships and generating additional revenue from dynamic packaging, while slimming down its number of retail travel agent branches.

Some of the challenges facing Thomas Cook were common to all tour operators, but others seemed more specific to Thomas Cook itself. In addition to weather issues and stiff competition from asset-light online travel agents and low-cost airlines, other disruptive factors, included political unrest in important destination countries such as Turkey, persistently high levels of debt and costs incurred in restructuring the business (including the downward revaluation of some assets and costs incurred in closing retail branches). The high level of debt was particularly highlighted by the financial press because it restricted the company's ability to invest substantial sums in areas of the business where investment was required and could potentially lead to the company asking its shareholders to invest further funds.

During 2018, the introduction of a 'new operating model' for Thomas Cook led to implementation costs totaling £57mn (2017: £42mn). These costs primarily related to the ongoing transformation and efficiency programs in Continental Europe and the UK. These programs commenced in 2015 with a focus on generating synergies within the group by cooperating more closely across all source markets and harmonizing activities, rather than duplicating processes in each individual market across a number of teams. The transformation projects focused on aligning and integrating activities across the group in each business area, including finance, digital, marketing, product and yield management. The work represented an investment in the transformation of the group but resulted in a material level of incremental costs.

The trend toward increased personalization and tailoring of the traditional package holidays provided opportunities to appeal to more independently minded travelers. Thomas Cook had grown its range of holiday extras from private transfers to bookable sunbeds positions to take advantage of this trend but at a relatively slow pace. A small portfolio of own-brand hotels provided a point of differentiation, and the increased focus on design-led hotels and higher quality food offered customers further reasons to book with Thomas Cook, setting it apart from price-driven hotel aggregators and online travel agents.

Thomas Cook was a stand-out name in the travel business with a long and proud history. However, the total number of customers buying package holidays in its core European markets has barely changed in the last 20 years, yet new competitors have emerged (and continue to do so). At the same time, the company was operating a vertically integrated business model dating from the 1990s, and some question its continuing value.

At the time of Thomas Cook's demise, dynamic packaging was becoming of far greater importance in European tour operating. TUI was in the process of heavily investing in technology and adopting it across the group, whereas Thomas Cook had failed to fully take advantage of this opportunity.

Dynamic packaging refers to a trip or vacation with in-built flexibility and 'pick and mix' functions that customers can book online. It contrasts with the traditional travel industry business model in which the tour operator buys blocks of flights and overnight stays from wholesalers and sells them on to customers. This pre-internet model left the tour operator exposed to the cost of any unsold holidays and was a factor in the collapse of Thomas Cook.

Tour operators, including TUI, and their competitors in the form of online travel sites have made dynamic packages a core focus of their businesses. Customers making purchases on sites such as Expedia and Booking.com are sourcing flights, accommodation and car rental in real time. The term 'dynamic' applies to the package because it changes depending on the customer, who may want to add theater tickets, airport parking, activities, restaurant bookings or destination activities.

Crucially, dynamic also applies to prices. Dynamic pricing – that is, flexible pricing based on market demand – is particularly suited to perishable products such as hotel stays, airline seats and concert tickets.

As Simon Cooper, the founder of the online retailer On the Beach, was quoted as saying, in his view, 'you can either be a high-end, vertically integrated operator like TUI, or you can be a nimble, agile online operator like us. If you're somewhere in between, then what is it that makes you different?' (Eley, 2018).

Thomas Cook's demise 2019

Over the course of the decade, the company's failure to adapt to changing circumstances, including the growth of more flexible travel companies, online travel-related services, more confident consumers putting their own packages together, low-cost airlines and online accommodation platforms, took their toll. These factors had been exacerbated in the years immediately prior to collapse by an exceptionally warm Northern European summer in 2018 encouraging consumers to stay at home, and uncertainty caused by Brexit and the consequent fall in the value of sterling from 2016 onwards.

The leadership of Thomas Cook also appeared to question the merits of vertically integrated business model. In early 2019 it was reported that the company was considering selling its airline, with a possible asking price of asking price of £1bn, with a view to having additional funds to invest in developing hotel projects (Eley, 2018).

However, Thomas Cook's fate was sealed by the insurmountable debt burden. The company failed to clear a debt burden of £1.1bn that had almost destroyed it back in 2011. At the end, it had racked up debts of £1.7bn, meaning that it needed to sell 3 million holidays a year just to cover its interest payments (Hernandez, 2020).

Increasingly frantic negotiations took place in late summer and September to try to save the company, including calls for UK government support that fell on deaf ears. Thomas Cook's shares were listed on the London Stock Exchange. In the early hours of Monday, 23 September 2019, the UK company filed for compulsory liquidation. Following the failure of last-ditch rescue negotiations, the UK regulatory authority, the Civil Aviation Authority, announced that Thomas Cook had ceased trading with immediate effect. As with many previous European tour operator failures, liquidation occurred prior to the onset of winter, because creditors proved to be unwilling to support the company through the weaker seasonal trading conditions.

Following the failure, the Thomas Cook brand name was acquired by Chinese group Fosun International and now trades as an online-only travel brand, and Sunderland, UK-based Hays Travel paid £6mn to acquire 555 UK travel agency branches. TUI's share price surged by more than 10% on the day of the collapse, as the potential benefits from the demise of its competitor were recognized by shareholders. TUI, though, has faced challenging operating conditions of its own, having issued several profit warnings throughout 2019. With much smaller debts, the company was not expected to suffer the same fate as Thomas Cook. However, the subsequent effects of the COVID-19 pandemic from spring 2020 through 2021 meant that TUI had to rely on loan support offered by the German government to ensure its survival.

We speculate, but had Thomas Cook received the financial backing it sought in autumn 2019 to survive the oncoming winter, it would surely have been a casualty of the pandemic by the following spring.

REFERENCES AND WEBSITES

References

Calder, S. (2018) 'Thomas Cook: What's gone wrong at the holiday firm', BBC News, www.bbc.co.uk

Eley, S. (2018) 'Thomas Cook faces deeper challenges than hot summer and late bookings', interview with S. Cooper, *Financial Times*, 30 November.

EU. (2015) Directive (EU) 2015/2302 of the European Parliament and of the Council of 25 November 2015 on package travel and linked travel arrangements, amending Regulation (EC) No. 2006/2004 and Directive 2011/83/EU of the European Parliament and of the Council and repealing Council Directive 90/314/EEC.

Hernandez, V. (2020) 'The collapse of Thomas Cook: What happened and why', *International Banker*, 16 January, Internationalbanker.com/

Saunders, A. (2014) The MT interview: Harriet Green, *Management Today*, February.

Taylor, I. (2013) 'Big interview: Harriet Green on the transformation of Thomas Cook', *Travel Weekly*, 15 March.

Wembridge, M. and Blitz, R. (2011) 'Thomas cook plunges on debt concerns', *Financial Times*, 22 November.

Wembridge, M. and Jacobs, R. (2011) 'Thomas Cook chief stands down', *Financial Times*, 3 August.

Website

www.tuigroup.com

Appendix: Thomas Cook Group financial statements

	Income statement (£mn)							
	2018	2017	2016	2015	2014	2013	2012	2011
Revenue	9,584	9,006	7,810	7,834	8,588	9,315	9,195	9,809
Gross profit	1,933	1,990	1,820	1,772	1,866	2,020	2,031	2,098
Gross profit margin (%)	20.2	22.1	23.3	22.6	21.7	21.7	22.1	21.4
Profit/(loss) from operations	97	227	197	211	52	13	(170)	(267)
Interest	(150)	(184)	(163)	(169)	(168)	(177)	(168)	(135)
Profit/(loss) before taxation	(53)	43	34	50	(114)	(163)	(337)	(398)
Profit/(loss) for the financial year	(163)	9	1	(19)	(115)	(213)	(441)	(518)

	Statement of financial position (£mn)							
	2018	**2017**	**2016**	**2015**	**2014**	**2013**	**2012**	**2011**
Total assets	6,569	6,605	6,943	5,958	5,794	6,285	5,907	6,690
Current assets	2,113	2,231	2,645	2,035	1,829	1,933	1,524	1,646
Current liabilities	(4,222)	(4,339)	(4,633)	(3,702)	3,894)	(3,688)	(3,540)	(3,749)
Net pension deficit	(165)	(325)	(457)	(279)	(448)	(404)	(331)	(331)
Net assets	291	256	326	315	239	548	458	1,183
Net debt	(389)	(40)	(129)	(128)	(315)	(426)	(792)	(894)

3

Queensland Australia: tourism and events – strategic positioning and promotion

Background

Queensland is Australia's second largest and third most populous state, with a population of over 5 million and many natural attractions for tourists. These include the Great Barrier Reef; a long and spectacular coastline, areas of rainforest and the Outback. The state is vast, stretching over 1,500 miles (2,400 km) from north to south, and has diverse scenery including rainforest, desert, mountains and beaches.

Tourism is one of Queensland's key sectors, but the sector was (in common with many other destinations) decimated by the COVID-19 pandemic and is now in a phase of recovery. In 2020–21 tourism directly accounted for 121,000 (or 4.7%) jobs and indirectly accounted for 53,000 jobs, or a total of 6.7% of employment, in the state. Before COVID-19 (2018–19), tourism accounted for 9.1% of employment in the state.

Tourism and Events Queensland (TEQ) is the Queensland government's lead marketing, experience development and major events agency, representing the state's tourism and events industries. TEQ operates at national and international levels, looking at new and innovative ways to make the most out of emerging opportunities that benefit the Queensland tourism industry and economy.

For the year ended June 2021, overseas tourism exports were $362 million for Queensland. However, before COVID-19, tourism totaled $8.0 billion, which was the equivalent of 9.1% of tourism's goods exports and was the third largest export market behind coal and liquefied natural gas. In 2020–21, direct and indirect tourism GSP was $16.8bn, or 4.6% of total Queensland GSP. Tourism

DOI: 10.4324/9781003318613-26

contributes $8.3bn directly to the Queensland economy, accounting for 2.3% of Queensland's GSP. Tourism indirectly contributes an additional $8.5bn to the Queensland economy. Before COVID-19, tourism's total contribution accounted for 7.7% of Queensland's GSP.

TEQ works closely with the state's 13 membership-based RTOs, which together represent around 4,500 Queensland tourism operators, of which 9 out of 10 can be classified as 'small businesses'. The RTO network is widely regarded as one of the most influential in Australia and has played a major role in Queensland's tourism success.

TEQ provides strategic industry leadership and coordinates stakeholders in the planning, industry development, marketing and application of resources to grow tourism in each Queensland destination. Strategies and activities are developed in close consultation with the RTOs. TEQ operates from a head office located in Brisbane, with some staff based throughout Queensland and internationally, working closely with Tourism Australia (the national tourism body) to target established and emerging international markets. Queensland's experiences and destinations are promoted in 14 key source markets, managed by global hubs:

- Australia and New Zealand (Brisbane and Auckland)
- Americas, UK and Europe (London)
- Japan and Korea (Tokyo and Soeul)
- Mainland China, Hong Kong and Taiwan (Shanghai, Guangzou and Taipei)
- Southeast Asia (Singapore, Malaysia and Indonesia) and India (Singapore)

Queensland's tourism industry has developed greatly since 1929, when the Queensland Government Tourist Bureau was transferred to the Railway Department and the first attempt was made to correlate publicity with a travel booking organization. Tourism and Events Queensland began as the Queensland Tourist and Travel Corporation (QTTC). The QTTC was established by Act of Parliament in August 1979, taking over from the Department of Tourism.

As a statutory authority, under the jurisdiction of the then Minister for Maritime Services and Tourism, the corporation operated as a marketing and development organization, with the sales arm trading under the name Queensland Government Tourist Bureau.

QTTC pioneered the destination marketing approach in Australia, highlighting the many unique visitor experiences on offer in Queensland and working alongside a network of RTOs to support destination marketing and development.

In February 1999, the Where Else But Queensland marketing campaign was launched, positioning the state as the undisputed premier holiday destination in Australia. In keeping with the new Where Else branding, QTTC became Tourism Queensland, adopting the stylized Q (still being used) into all communications and making it synonymous with Queensland.

Early in 2006, a new brand was launched that flowed through to new websites being developed. The Queensland Holidays site (www.queensland.com/au) offers visitors a refreshing experience and aims to present Queensland as a vibrant, fun, warm, friendly, colorful and relaxing place to visit and provides booking options for users. The consumer site provides a comprehensive tool for retrieving up-to-date news, information, research, policies and plans and strategies relating to Queensland's 12 destinations, special interests and the international sector.

In November 2012 the Tourism and Events Queensland Bill 2012 was passed, successfully merging Tourism Queensland and Events Queensland into Tourism and Events Queensland.

Tourism and Events Queensland

Thus, in Queensland, the interaction and connectivity between tourism and events is explicitly recognized in the title and purposes of the statutory body established to promote and develop activity. Hospitality activities are not explicitly mentioned but are subsumed within the all-embracing umbrella of 'tourism'. Combining the resources and expertise of the former Tourism Queensland and Events Queensland formally into one entity enabled a continued focus on driving growth in Queensland's tourism and event industries in close partnership with government and industry.

Recognizing that tourism and events are intrinsically linked, the creation of Tourism and Events Queensland ensured the most coordinated and strategic approach to maximize domestic and international visitors.

TEQ operates in a highly competitive national and international environment in an industry where global economic conditions and other external shocks such as natural disasters and pandemics may influence visitor numbers and expenditure. Tourism and Events Queensland identifies new and innovative ways to maximize emerging opportunities for the benefit of industry and the Queensland economy as a whole. Events play an important role in the tourism industry by creating exposure, promoting community pride and driving visitation and expenditure to the host region.

TEQ's vision and operational focus is an efficient and collaborative tourism and events business system that engages and provides a sense of ownership for all stakeholders, working toward the goals of contributing significantly to the Queensland economy and growing the state's tourism and events market shares (relative to other states). To support the collaborative business system, Tourism and Events Queensland has developed a holistic business structure that supports the critical interrelationships between the Minister, Tourism and Events Queensland; the Department of Tourism, Major Events, Small Business Queensland destinations; other government partners; and industry.

The Queensland brand represents how Queensland is presented to the rest of the world. The Queensland tourism brand is evolving in line with consumer needs. Following a 2019 strategic review, Queensland adopted a 'purpose-led' brand position to 'travel for good', ensuring that TEQ realizes its consumer-led, experience-focused and destination-delivered marketing approach.

The evolution of the Queensland brand is a 15-year aspiration to inspire a new way of interacting with Queensland, positioning Queensland globally in the new era of transformational travel to embody the essence of Queensland tourism's purpose, to travel for good. It envisages a deeper, more meaningful and engaging travel destination where the experiences delivered will change travelers and the world for the better. Thus, travel for good is centered on regeneration – whether regenerating people by activating the mind and body and lifting their hearts or regenerating the world by positively contributing to humanity, communities and the environment.

Though the branding represents an umbrella brand to promote the whole of Queensland, the state has a unique position in Australia of having a number of strong destination brands, each having distinctive attributes, target markets and a sufficiently developed tourist industry to warrant a portfolio approach to their management as destinations. The approach reflects the diversity and scale of Queensland (and its tourism industry) and translates into different destination images, target markets and positional and promotional programs for each destination.

The state is divided into 13 tourism destination regions, each with a regional tourism plan aligned with the state strategies. Examples of the regions and the main elements of their positioning and brand themes are shown in the following table:

Destinations	Positioning	Brand themes
Tropical North Queensland	Feel the natural exhilaration of an Australian Tropical Adventure	• Great Barrier Reef • The world's oldest tropical rainforest • Tropical lifestyle and culture • Adventures • Aboriginal and Torres Strait Islander people
Brisbane	Feel the vitality of city life with a subtropical twist	• Vibrant • Relaxed • Urban outdoor lifestyle events • Culture • Nature at your doorstep bursting with color and life
Gold Coast	Welcoming, vibrant, diverse, fun and entertaining	• Surf • Taste • Escape • Play • Culture
Sunshine Coast	Feel the rejuvenating warmth of our beach culture	• Innovative food • Wonders of nature • Immersive encounters • Exhilarating events • Beachside culture
Whitsunday Islands	Feel the wonder of Australia's island paradise	• Diverse island paradise • Iconic landscapes in the heart of the Great Barrier Reef • Sailing, flying, snorkeling and diving • Airlie Beach and Mainland

The diverse tapestry of experiences that Queensland offers underpins the Queensland brand, and TEQ's marketing showcases the breadth and depth of experiences and events that are delivered within destinations. Research shows that Queensland's experiences are the primary driver of holiday planning and travel.

Queensland is home to not one but five World Heritage–listed wonders, including Gondwana Rainforest and the Great Barrier Reef. From world-class events and vast landscapes to the rainforests, beaches and the reef, these experiences refresh and transform visitors.

In the new era of travel, consumers are actively seeking these experiences in a way that will change them. Through TEQ's Experience Design program, developed and delivered in partnership with RTOs, TEQ is supporting the tourism and events industry to reimagine their experience offering in line with Queensland's travel for good brand purpose.

TEQ's long-term strategic focus has now been updated and outlined a strategic plan for tourism and events covering the period 2018–22. The strategy is underpinned by the TEQ Events Strategy 2025 and the TEQ Marketing Strategy 2025.

In light of COVID-19, TEQ is reviewing its global approach to tourism and events marketing for Queensland. TEQ has commenced development of a global marketing strategy that will propel Queensland forward as the world emerges post-COVID-19. The marketing strategy will be aligned to the Action Plan for Tourism Recovery and will generating a fresh approach to drive strategic, deliberate growth for the Queensland tourism and events industry. The Action Plan for Tourism Recovery was formulated by a government-appointed panel and envisages additional state funding for the industry to speed its recovery.

Appendix 1 About Tourism and Events Queensland

TEQ is a statutory body under the Tourism and Events Queensland Act 2012. It is the state's lead tourism marketing, destination and experience development and major events agency. Working across government and in partnership with RTOs and industry and commercial stakeholders, TEQ aims to grow Queensland's tourism and events industry and drive OVE.

Vision

Inspiring the world to experience the best address on Earth.

Purpose

Achieving economic and social benefits for Queensland by growing the tourism and events industry in partnership with industry and broader government. TEQ is a consumer-led, experience-focused, destination-delivered organization that connects people and places like never before through innovation and collaboration with the tourism and events industry.

Role and functions

The primary functions of TEQ are:

- To attract domestic and international travelers to travel to and within Queensland through
  - the promotion and marketing of Queensland; and
  - tourism experience and destination development
- To identify, attract, develop and promote major events for the state that
  - contribute to the Queensland economy;
  - attract visitors to Queensland;
  - enhance the profile of Queensland; and
  - foster community pride in Queensland
- To work collaboratively with the Department of Tourism, Innovation and Sport (DTIS) and other public-sector units and Queensland tourism industry stakeholders to identify opportunities to increase tourism and travel to and within Queensland
- To conduct research into, and analysis of, tourism in Queensland

Objectives

TEQ's objectives are to:

- Contribute to the Queensland economy

- Attract visitors to Queensland, generating OVE

- Enhance the profile of Queensland

- Foster community pride in Queensland

These objectives are being achieved through the implementation of TEQ's Strategic Plan and marketing and events strategies.

Strategic Plan 2021–25

TEQ's Strategic Plan 2021–25 sets out TEQ's strategic positioning and the way value is created for the state's tourism and events industry, particularly in growing OVE and market share for the state. The plan focuses on strengthening the visitor economy through innovation by building consumer demand, aviation capacity and the value of Queensland's events calendar to build market share.

Performance indicators

A range of performance indicators measure the extent to which TEQ is achieving its objectives. Service delivery measures are those that TEQ has a high degree of influence over, with industry outcome measures reflecting collective efforts across the tourism network.

Values

- *Lead together* – Guided by the Minister and TEQ Board, we are clear on our purpose, direction and priorities and our team is empowered to implement.

- *One team* – We work in partnership with our teammates and always act for the good of the whole.

- *Go beyond* – We are creative, innovative and solutions-driven. We strive for continuous improvement and make a difference where it really counts for Queensland.

- *Agile and responsive* – We embrace emerging trends and opportunities. To thrive in a competitive industry environment we are proactive, flexible and adaptable.

Landscape and operating environment

The tourism and events industry continues to operate in a highly competitive environment, impacted by social, economic, political, environmental and technological changes, which bring new challenges, threats and opportunities that can impact economic and social outcomes and the achievement of TEQ's objectives.

Current strategic risks include:

- Uncontrollable events such as climate change, natural disasters, global economic shocks, pandemics such as COVID-19 and geopolitical events impacting the visitor economy

- Variable social and economic conditions across source markets impacting visitation and recovery to pre-COVID-19 levels

- Supply challenges relating to tourism experience, product, workforce and aviation capacity that affect consumer perception and demand

- Changing consumer intention, sentiment and attitudes affecting consumer demand

- Cyber security challenges that threaten system and information security

Marketing strategy

To reach its full potential, Queensland's tourism industry must overcome a number of challenges, including intense competition from domestic and international destinations. TEQ marketing strategy aligns with the overall strategy and events strategy and aims to realize three objectives:

- Increase OVE from priority domestic and international source markets, supporting Queensland jobs

- Maintain and grow Queensland's share of Australian OVE

- Grow equity in the Queensland brand

To deliver the objectives, TEQ marketing is consumer led, experience focused and destination delivered:

- Consumer research has formed the basis for the marketing strategy.

- Marketing will be based on the 'Queensland Experience Framework', which focuses on those 'Hero Experiences' that are the heart and soul of Queensland.

- Hero Experiences will be brought to life by the 'Best of Queensland Experiences' – those tourism operators, events and iconic locations that showcase the best of what Queensland destinations have to offer.

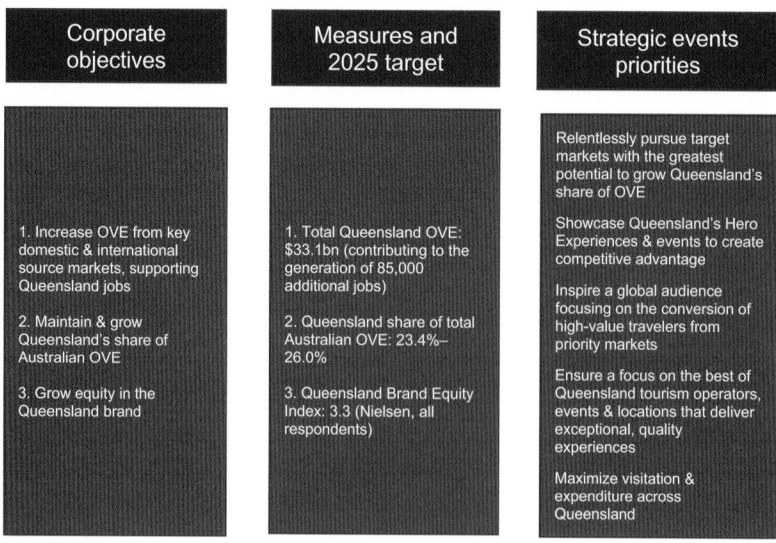

Figure 1 – Case 3

Research findings

- Experiences within Queensland are the primary driver of holiday planning and travel.

- Queensland owns a range of unique and aspirational experiences.

- Queensland remains one of the strongest brands in the travel category.

- Queensland is considered by holiday travelers to be the primary destination with regions within it considered more of an experience.

Domestic and international segmentation

To achieve the goals of gaining market share and increasing OVE in Queensland, TEQ targets domestic travelers who will generate a disproportionate share of OVE for Queensland. Those identified spend more than the average traveler on leisure trips (>A$2,000 per trip, or A$300 per night for shorter trips).

Three domestic high value traveler segments with different holiday preferences and behaviors have been identified, representing approximately 4 million Australians living interstate of Queensland and 1.1 million Queenslanders:

- Traveling with children

- 18–49 traveling without children

- 50+ traveling without children

Internationally, TEQ will align its target segments with the national tourism body, Tourism Australia (TA). TA has embarked on a journey to transition from predominantly demographically defined and based target audiences across markets to a global-based behavioral and attitudinal target audience.

Queensland's experience framework

Five key Experience Pillars and supporting Hero Experiences are identified that reflect the heart and soul of Queensland and represent where Queensland has a competitive advantage. The Framework will guide TEQ's marketing activities by focusing on Hero Experiences that have the best potential to drive visitation and expenditure.

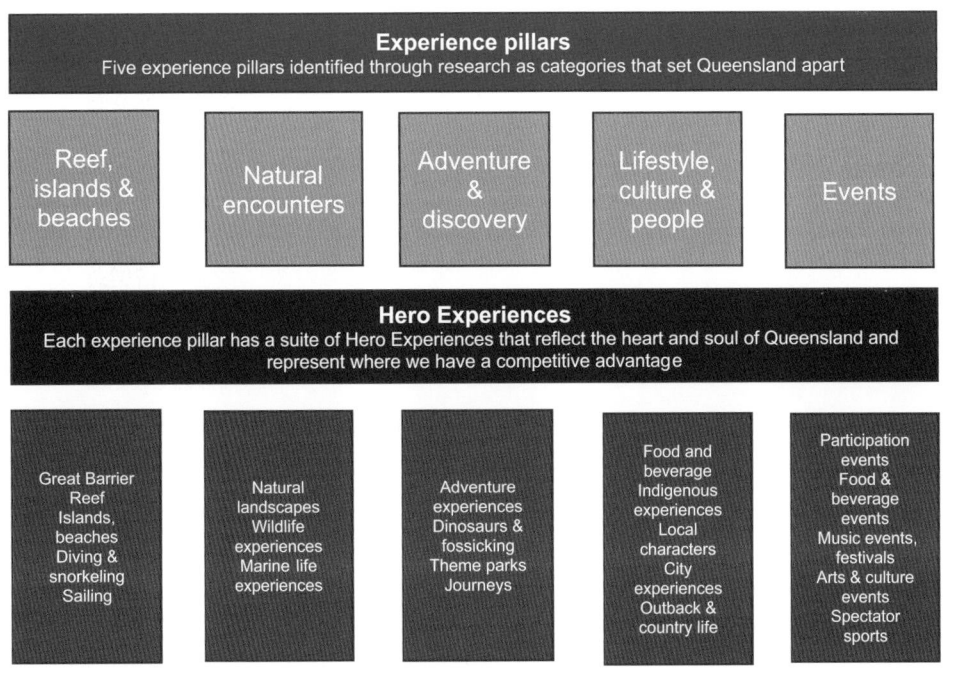

Figure 2 – Case 3

Queensland key source markets

Source market	Actual 2018 (A$bn)	Potential 2025 (A$bn)
Domestic	16,165.2	22,300.0
UK and Nordic	515.2	811.4
Europe	446.8	754.1
India	151.6	327.6
Greater China	1,603.9	3,564.1
Japan	397.5	793.2
South Korea	249.2	405.7
Southeast Asia	299.2	494.7
New Zealand	564.1	973.2
Americas	538.1	1,009.0

Events strategy

The opportunity

TEQ works collaboratively with government, industry and destination partners to identify, attract, develop and promote successful events in Queensland. The inclusion of events into an integrated TEQ approach to driving visitor growth and expenditure represents a major opportunity for the state – every dollar of event investment can also be seen as a dollar invested in experience and destination marketing. Events complement the leisure travel sector and are often the deciding factor to travel, especially outside peak holiday periods, while also encouraging greater visitor dispersal throughout regional Queensland.

The Events Strategy provides a framework to create a sustainable Queensland Events Calendar that ensures that government investment is prioritized, events are integrated into both experience and destination marketing initiatives, required economic and social outcomes are met and events continue to drive growth to achieve superior results against investment objectives.

Objectives

The objectives (set out previously) will be delivered by:

- Leveraging the competitive advantage of Tourism and Events Queensland
- Strategic partnerships with event and destination stakeholders
- Agreement and reliance on a set of event selection metrics that will inform optimal event investment

The Events Strategy is designed to be adaptive and to connect with industry, to inspire growth and to maintain currency through time with changing trends, funding and priorities. The Events Strategy is subject to existing capacity and capabilities, infrastructure and resources, including access, accommodation, transport, public infrastructure, venues and precincts.

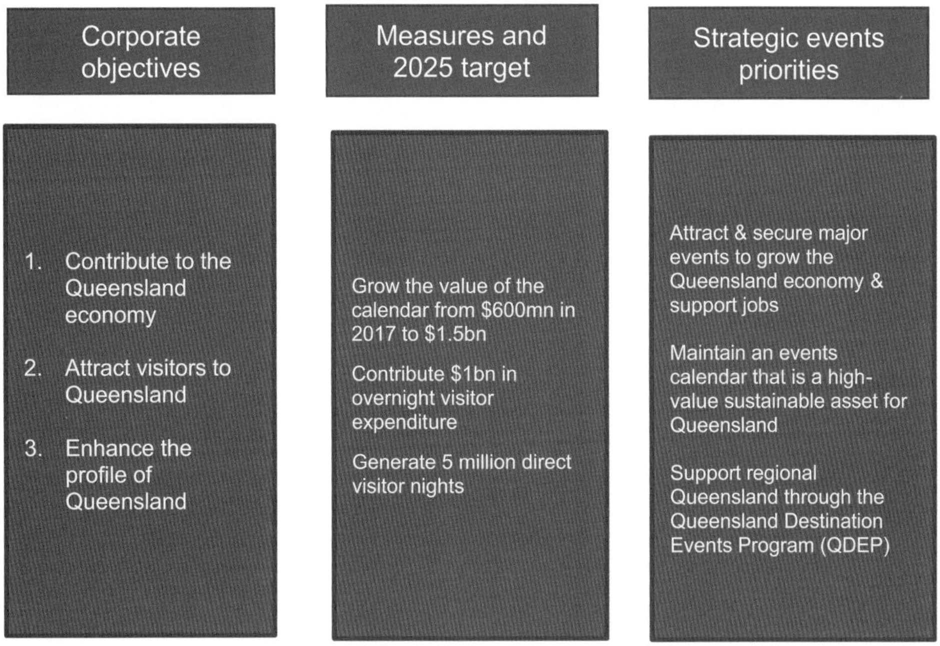

Corporate objectives	Measures and 2025 target	Strategic events priorities
1. Contribute to the Queensland economy 2. Attract visitors to Queensland 3. Enhance the profile of Queensland	Grow the value of the calendar from $600mn in 2017 to $1.5bn Contribute $1bn in overnight visitor expenditure Generate 5 million direct visitor nights	Attract & secure major events to grow the Queensland economy & support jobs Maintain an events calendar that is a high-value sustainable asset for Queensland Support regional Queensland through the Queensland Destination Events Program (QDEP)

Figure 3 – Case 3

Its Live! in Queensland

In addition to promoting the Queensland Events Calendar as a whole, the 'It's Live! In Queensland' platform can promote:

- Individual events or events within certain clusters or genres
- One or more events that might align with or strengthen a particular Queensland hero experience
- Events in individual destinations or those at certain times of the year

TEQ Event Investment Programs TEQ makes cash and value-in-kind investments in and/or supports events across three major program groups:

- *Major event investments* – Opportunistic events selected to provide variety and richness to the Events Calendar. Major events may be one-off or annually recurring.
- *Queensland destination events* – Currently the greatest in number and unique to its host destination, they create enormous value as destination marketing tools and form the platform or the foundation of the Events Calendar.
- *Business events* – A collective term referring to corporate and government meetings, incentive travel reward programs, association conventions and exhibitions. May be as small as 15 businesspeople, through to a large international scientific meeting attracting 10,000 delegates that could involve travel and accommodation for hundreds.

Appendix 2 Queensland tourism and events: megatrends

Megatrends that will shape the future of tourism and events in Queensland. There is evidence of some of the big shifts, or 'megatrends', that are likely to shape the industry over the coming decades, and we can use these to set the context for long-term planning. Research commissioned by the Queensland government identified seven megatrends:

Megatrend	Description
The Orient Express	The world economy will significantly change over the coming decades. Rapid income growth within emerging economies will create new markets and new sources of competition. There are major growth opportunities through attracting new tourists from the developing Asia region and ensuring that Queensland is a differentiated and aspirational destination for domestic and international travelers.
A natural advantage	Global biodiversity is decreasing. Natural habitats are disappearing at alarming rates, and remaining areas of pristine natural habitats are increasing in value. As the world's population grows and becomes more urbanized, tourists will be drawn to nature-based experiences. Queensland's natural assets will become an increasingly important drawcard for locals and visitors alike.
Great expectations	As incomes grow, people shift their discretionary expenditure toward experiences rather than products. Future tourists will seek experiences that are personalized, 'authentic' to the destination and its people, involve social interaction and create emotional connection.
Bolts from the blue	Sudden and unexpected events such as extreme weather and infectious disease outbreaks are more likely in a world with a changed climate, antimicrobial drug resistance and increased human mobility. When combined with the growing importance of safety perceptions, these events will have both positive and negative impacts on Queensland tourism expenditure, depending on where they occur in the world and the perceptions potential travelers have regarding their impacts.
Digital whispers	In the digital age, models of human communication and decision making are changing. Information flows much more rapidly and via more widely distributed channels than it did in even the recent past. The perceived credibility of information sources is also changing. The online world has created new risks and opportunities for the tourism sector.
On the move	People are becoming increasingly mobile. Though leisure remains a strong motivator for travel, people are traveling further and more frequently for many reasons, including trade, business, events, conferences, education and health care. Technological advances in the transport sector, particularly aviation, will enable the continued rise in mobility as people are able to move greater distances faster.
The lucky country	Queensland and Australia have weathered the financial turbulence of the last decade exceptionally well compared to many other countries. However, for some travelers, they are expensive destinations. Local tourism operators face higher costs than many overseas competitors.

Source: Hajkowicz et al. (2013)

Appendix 3 Tourism and Events Queensland: summary of recent performance

Visitor numbers

Over a third of all international visitors to Australia visit Queensland during their trip. International visitors tend to spend more on their visits than domestic visitors and often visit more than one state. During 2018 there were a range of impacts on international visitation to Australia that were felt in varying degrees by Queensland and the other states, which included the effect of domestic economic conditions in European markets and youth unemployment in many countries. Positive impacts on visitation included the growth of the Chinese market, and a range of world-class sporting and entertainment events also attracted a broad cross section of international visitors.

International visitation to Queensland grew by 4.6% to a record 2.8 million visitors in the year ending September 2018. These visitors spent a record $5.9bn in the state, up by 11.5% year on year. Queensland's top five source markets by expenditure were China, New Zealand, the UK, Japan and the USA.

Queensland closed its borders to:

- International tourism between March 2020 and January 2022 due to COVID-19 restrictions

- Domestic tourism (without a negative COVID test between August 2020 and January 2022)

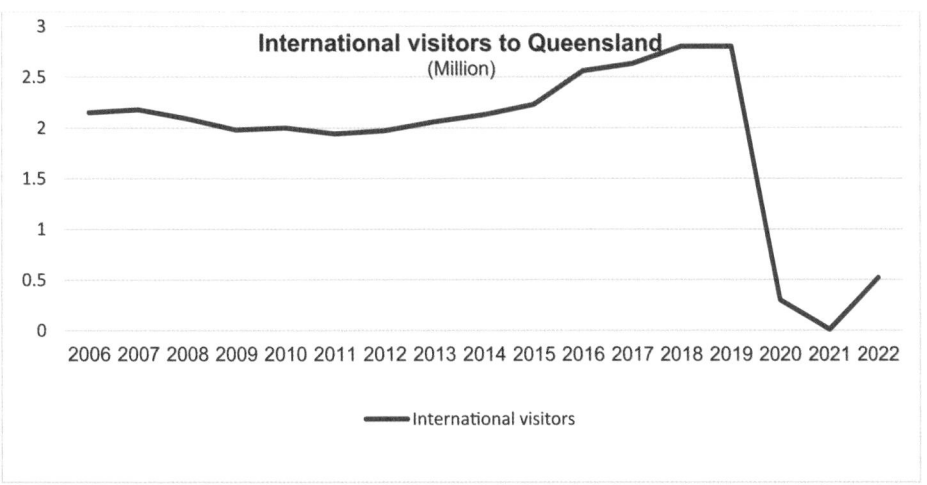

Figure 4 – Case 3

	Visitors (000)	Average stay (days)	Average spending (A$)
	Domestic visitors 2018		
Total Australia	102,735	3.6	684
Queensland	22,794	4.0	772

	Visitors (000)	Average stay (days)	Average spending (A$)
Domestic visitors 2018			
New South Wales	33,633	3.1	607
Victoria	25,366	2.9	575
Other states	24,130	4.0	704
Domestic visitors 2021			
Total Australia	87,359	3.8	702
Queensland	20,758	4.0	785
New South Wales	30,155	3.4	643
Victoria	16,611	3.2	533
Other states	22,037	4.2	762

REFERENCES AND WEBSITES

Reference

Hajkowicz, S., Cook, H. and Boughen, N. (2013) *The Future of Tourism in Queensland*, Brisbane: Commonwealth Scientific and Industrial Research Organisation (CSIRO); www.csiro.au

Websites

www.destq.com.au
www.queensland.com/au
www.tourism.australia.com
www.teq.queensland.com

Case 4

IHG – competing on the world stage

Background

InterContinental Hotel Group (IHG), marketed as IHG Hotels and Resorts, is a British multinational hospitality company headquartered in Windsor, UK. It is listed on the London Stock Exchange and the New York Stock Exchange and is also a constituent of the FTSE 100 Index of the UK's largest companies.

IHG is one of the largest hotel groups in the world by number of rooms, along with competitors such as US-based Marriott, Hilton and Wyndham; French-based Accor; and Chinese group Jin Jiang, which controls the Radisson Hotel Group, outside North America. It has about 6,000 hotels globally and over 900,000 rooms, many of which are in the USA. The vast majority of its hotels are franchises.

IHG has a series of statements representing their purpose, guiding values, ambition and strategic priorities.

Hospitality is an interesting industry sector in many respects. It is growing rapidly around the world and, though there are many individually owned properties or small chains, consolidation is taking place so that a small number of large internationally diversified groups have become established.

Many of the first groups to establish themselves internationally have been from the USA or Europe, but in more recent times chains from Asia and elsewhere have established substantial international operations. It is also a sector that represents the principal physical manifestation of business and leisure travel, because the buildings the hotels occupy are often prominent features of cities, resorts, roadside locations and scenic areas. A group such as IHG has a diversified portfolio of brands and is represented in over 100 countries across the world.

DOI: 10.4324/9781003318613-27

The industry has many of the characteristics often associated with service sectors such as the inseparability of production and consumption, the perishability of its product offerings and, at least in part, product intangibility. Managers operating in the business also have to deal with international currency risks. Revenues and expenditures will often be denominated in different currencies, and assets and debts may well be denominated in currencies other than the company's accounting currency.

Furthermore, the patterns of business activity often give rise to further need for managerial attention. Volatile levels of business and cash flow are common due to both cyclical patterns of the economy and seasonality. Hospitality generally follows, on a lagged basis, the overall economy. There is a history of increases and decreases in demand for hotel rooms, in occupancy levels and in rates realized by owners of hotels through economic cycles. Variability of results through some of the cycles in the past has been more severe due to changes in the supply of hotel rooms in given markets or in given categories of hotels. The industry suffered from a severe slowdown during the COVID-19 pandemic between 2020 and 2021, with many hotels having to completely close for part of the period.

Supply and demand

The $360bn worldwide hotel industry has compelling structural growth drivers, underpinned by factors including consumers' inherent desire to travel, population growth and an expanding middle class in emerging markets with increasing disposable incomes. Though the pandemic suppressed demand during 2020 and 2021, demand has returned rapidly in domestic markets as government restrictions were lifted and vaccination rates increased. This demand has predominantly been in markets not exposed to cross-border trips and across essential business travel, though discretionary corporate travel and group events have begun to return. Cost remains a significant barrier to building a scale position in the industry, whether due to the investment required to build and maintain hotels, to establish a strong loyalty program or to market brands in a competitive marketplace.

The combination of changes in economic conditions and in the supply of hotel rooms can result in significant volatility in results for owners, managers and franchisors (and franchisees) of hotel properties. The costs of running a hotel are typically more fixed than variable. Because of this, in an environment of declining revenues, the rate of decline in earnings will be higher than the rate of decline in revenues. Conversely, in an environment of increasing demand and room rates, the rate of increase in earnings is typically higher than the rate of increase in revenues.

For the industry as a whole, it is not yet clear what impact there will be on demand from structural changes brought about by the pandemic, such as technology replacing elements of business travel. However, this may be offset by a greater use of hotels to facilitate a global shift to increasingly flexible working arrangements. In addition, there is scope for 'bleisure' demand, where flexible working creates potential for leisure demand to be combined with business stays. It is likely that fluctuating COVID-19 restrictions will continue to create a volatile demand environment in the short term. However, it is anticipated that the attractive industry fundamentals will be fully restored in the longer term. For example, a key US forecast predicts that RevPAR will return to 2019 levels by the end of 2023.

The effects of seasonality are geographically specific. In a diversified portfolio of properties, its effects will vary from property to property and from country to country, driven by a number of factors such as climate, school holidays, cultural and religious festivals, sporting events and changing tastes and fashions. Beach resort hotels generally fill during summer months, for example, and city business hotels find that activity levels are lower.

How IHG competes

In the highly competitive hospitality industry in which hotel groups operate, trademarks, trade names and logos are very important in the successful sales and marketing of accommodation and vacation ownership properties and services. The major international chains work assiduously to establish their brands and their market positioning, and many subbrands have been formed to target perceived new segments and their needs. The companies concerned devote sizable revenues to promoting and positioning their brands effectively and in protecting their brands from intellectual property infringement.

But not everything is always as it appears in the hospitality industry. The branding can mean different things in different circumstances. The branding, or the 'sign above the door', can denote that the hotel building and the hotel operations are owned and managed by the owner of the brand. However, in many cases the position is far more complicated, with the ownership of the building, the management of the hotel and the provision of the brand and its values and attributes all being carried out by different companies.

Thus, there is frequently a three-way arrangement that separates the physical asset, its management and the brand holder. First, the hotel property may be owned by a commercial landlord or a real estate investment trust. Secondly, there are several large hotel management companies (and many smaller ones) that manage hotels under the 'umbrella' of several brands. These companies (which might also act as the property owner) include White Lodging, Highgate Holdings and Aimbridge Hospitality, as well as many other companies worldwide. In the business-to-business market in which they operate, these companies are well-known, sizeable and powerful companies in their own right with which the brand owners have to negotiate, but they are largely unrecognized by consumers.

IHG operates hotels in three different ways – as a franchisor, as a manager and on an owned and leased basis. The company focuses on the mainstream, upscale and luxury segments of the hotel industry and has a targeted portfolio of 18 brands. The key competitors against which IHG benchmarks itself, such as Marriott, Hilton, Accor and Wyndham, also have multiple brands with which to compete and, like IHG, have been progressively switching to an 'asset-light' model of operation.

Whether the company chooses to franchise or manage hotels on behalf of third-party hotel owners depends largely on market maturity, owner preference and, in some cases, the particular brand. In mature markets, such as the Americas and Europe, the franchise model is predominant, whereas a managed model is typically used in emerging markets such as 'Greater China'.

Owing to IHGs asset-light approach, the number of owned and managed leased hotels has dramatically reduced from over 180 hotels 20 years ago to just a handful today.

The franchise model (which is by far the largest operating model for IHG) allows franchisees to be in business for themselves but not by themselves. IHG franchisees can brand their hotel with one of IHG's well-known and popular brands and benefit from a powerful loyalty program and strong reservation system. A comprehensive set of tools such as revenue management and marketing programs is also provided by IHG to drive business and new demand.

IHG's franchise fee growth is driven by three levers – room growth, RevPAR and royalty fees. The franchise agreement is generally a standard contract, with some variation across the world. A sample contract would normally have a royalty fee of 5% to 6% of room revenue. However, this can vary by brand and country.

The managed model comes into force in situations where third-party owners want their hotel managed for them. In these cases, IHG manages the hotel but ownership of the physical building remains with a third-party owner. Typically, the senior management like the general manager and the financial controller are IHG employees who have oversight to build a successful team.

Management contracts can be bespoke but usually include two separate fees: base and incentive. The base fee is typically 1% to 3% of a hotel's total revenue, but the percentage varies by country and brand. The incentive fee is a share of profits, which is in place to align IHG's interests with those of the property owner and to reward IHG for running the hotel profitably.

Since 2003, IHG has completed the sale of almost 200 hotels as part of its move to an asset-light business model. In a few instances, the company still owns hotels to drive the growth of its brands and expand its presence in key markets.

As a result of this separation, brand changes are a regular feature of the industry. The changes are sometimes simply due to the expiration of the contract or the change of ownership of the building. The changes may also be due to the failure to agree after contract negotiations as all parties jostle for the most favorable terms. The franchise arrangements permit the branded hotel companies to roll out their brands more quickly with far less capital commitment but at the price of losing some degree of control over the brand. The franchisee takes most of the financial risk but is able to gain access to a respected branded product and the services provided by the brand owner.

There is intense competition in all areas of the hospitality industry. Competition exists for hotel guests, management agreements, franchise agreements and sales of vacation ownership properties. The number of branded lodging operators with a global reach and depth of product and offerings is, however, limited. Those companies that have a strong customer base, prominent brand recognition, strategic property locations and global development capabilities are likely to be most successful.

Hotel owners choose to work with IHG because they have faith in the company's brands and there is a track record in delivering strong returns. Reasons for continued success in attracting hotel owners to IHG brands are multifaceted and complex but include:

- The strength of brands – IHG has a portfolio of brands across industry segments, designed to drive owner returns
- A single loyalty program – IHG has a strong loyalty program, which is common to all of its portfolio of brands
- Digital advantage – IHG has invested in a cloud-based 'IHG Concerto' platform, including a guest reservation system, to better connect with guests and owners.
- Investment in hotel life cycle management and operations – Investment in technology, systems and processes has taken place to support performance, increase efficiencies and drive returns for IHG owners.
- Procurement – IHG uses its scale to reduce costs for owners, with procurement programs for hotel goods, services and construction.
- Sustainability tools and expertise – IHG has developed tools, training and programs to support hotels and provide better data and insights to enable them to reduce their energy, waste and water consumption.
- Global sales organization – IHG has developed a global sales structure to drive higher quality and achieve revenue at lower cost for hotels.

Guests are increasingly expressing a desire to travel more sustainably, and those companies embracing and responding to this shift in consumer sentiment are likely to be most successful. A recent study by the WTTC found that nearly 60% of travelers have chosen sustainable options within the past few years.

As environmental concerns continue to grow, guests are likely to be more selective in choosing companies that prioritize environmentally sustainable practices. With stakeholders increasingly expecting businesses to operate and grow responsibly, the onus is on travel companies to respond to shifting stakeholder values and expectations and drive positive change through their products and experiences. This ambition presents serious challenges to implement given the proliferation of the asset-light model across the industry and will require branded players to work with hotel owners of assets to drive positive change.

The advent of Airbnb has led to profound changes in the lodging market by creating a 'born global' competitor that utilizes technology efficiently in providing a new marketplace for rental rooms. By keeping hotel rates in check and making additional rooms available during peak periods when hotel rooms often sell out and rates increase, a serious competitor to hotel rooms has quickly emerged. Hotels have traditionally earned their largest margins when rooms are scarce and customers are forced to pay higher rates (Gerdeman, 2018).

Airbnb describes itself as 'a trusted community marketplace for people to list, discover, and book unique accommodations around the world – online or from a mobile phone' (www.Airbnb.com). The marketplace was founded in 2008 and has at least doubled in total transaction volume during every subsequent year. It has created a market for a previously rare transaction: the short-term rental of an apartment or room to strangers. In the past, these transactions were not commonly handled by single individuals because there were large costs to finding a match, securely exchanging money and ensuring safety. Though Airbnb is not the only company serving this market, it is the dominant platform (Farronato and Fradkin, 2018).

The global hotel industry appears to provide good continuing investment opportunities. Currently the industry consists of approximately 18 million rooms, of which about 54% are in branded properties, and the branded proportion is continuing to rise. Broadly, the growth of the industry has been in line with gross domestic product growth, and this trend is expected to continue with an average of about 2.6% per year but with large regional variations.

In the USA (the world's largest market), lodging demand, as measured by number of booked hotel rooms, has improved with the economic recovery in recent years; in contrast, over the last few years, US lodging industry capacity has grown at a rate well below its long-term average of 2.0%. This positive imbalance between demand and supply growth has contributed to a RevPAR growth in the USA over the last few years. The COVID-19 pandemic interrupted this pattern, at least temporarily, but projections indicate that this rate of growth will continue for the next few years.

The broader global macroeconomic climate also appears positive, which will continue to drive longer-term growth in the lodging sector, but periodic regional economic and political difficulties will make the growth spatially uneven. In particular, a growing middle class, which the OECD expects will grow from approximately 2 to 5 billion people by 2030, will exhibit the desire and have the resources to travel both within their home regions and elsewhere, which will support growth in global tourism. The UNWTO projects that global tourism will grow on average between 3% and 4% annually through to 2030.

Human resources

As a company working in hotels and offices in more than 100 countries in multiple time zones, employees represent multiple nationalities and many cultures, religions, races, sexualities, abilities, backgrounds and beliefs.

IHG aims to foster 'freedom to be yourself' among its employees, because giving space to a rich variety of backgrounds, experiences and perspectives sparks the innovation and ideas that IHG needs to succeed as a global business. Creating a diverse and inclusive culture is valued by guests and hotel owners and is embodied in the company's stated purpose to provide 'True Hospitality for Good'. Thus, it is viewed as being central to how the company views itself and is viewed by others – 'who we are' – to fostering teamwork – 'how we work together' – and, ultimately, to providing business success – 'how to grow our business'.

Its importance is reflected in 'caring for our people, communities and planet', one of ILG's four stated strategic priorities, and is supported by its 'Journey to Tomorrow' 2030 action plan. The plan has four themes relating to the business's culture: to drive gender balance and a doubling of under-represented groups across ILG's leadership; to cultivate an inclusive culture for ILG colleagues, owners and suppliers; to support all colleagues to prioritize their well-being and the well-being of others; and to drive respect for and advance human rights.

Financial performance

IHG's financial performance has been severely affected by the COVID-19 pandemic, but the company's strong balance sheet and geographic and brand diversity have enabled it to 'weather the storm' and emerge in a strong competitive position. A 5-year income statement and balance sheet for IHG is shown in Appendix 2.

Appendix 1 IHG: purpose, values, ambitions and strategic priorities

Our purpose: True Hospitality for Good

Simple but powerful, our purpose of 'True Hospitality for Good' inspires and informs everything we do – shaping our culture, bringing our brands to life and representing a commitment to make a difference to our guests, colleagues, owners and communities, and to protecting the world around us.

Acting with purpose in this way allows us to embrace opportunities to effect positive change so that True Hospitality for Good can be felt in different ways. It can be making connections that bring loved ones together, creating a feeling of belonging for our colleagues as they develop their careers at IHG, providing people in thousands of our communities with the skills to get ahead in the world of work through our IHG Academy or helping our hotels deliver sustainable solutions to preserve their beautiful surroundings.

www.IHGPlc.com

Our guiding values

- Do the right thing
- Show we care
- Aim higher
- Celebrate difference
- Work better together

    Our colleagues are supported by a set of values that are important to both IHG and our guests. As we work together as one team with our stakeholders, these collective values provide a shared sense of purpose that guide everything we do, from how we support and recognise our people to how we grow our business and work with our owners and communities.

www.IHGPlc.com

Our ambition

To deliver industry leading growth in our scale, enterprise platform and performance, doing so sustainably for all stakeholders, including our hotel owners, guests, and society as a whole.

Our strategic priorities

- Customers: Being customer centric in all we do
  - Strengthening the bond between IHG master brand and individual brands
  - Transformation IHG Rewards scheme delivering key improvements
  - Lowering costs and delivering efficiencies for owners
- Brands: Building loved and trusted brands
  - 18 hotel brands – One loyalty program
  - Luxury and lifestyle – 13% of rooms and 20% of pipeline
  - Premium – 4 brands tailored to target upscale market segments
  - Essentials – 3 brands – driving growth at scale
  - Suites – An expanding portfolio with notable growth potential
- Digital – Creating digital advantage
  - Innovating technology and distribution platforms
- Care: Caring for our people, communities and planet
  - Our people – Champion a diverse culture
  - Communities – Improving lives of 30 million people around the world
  - Carbon and energy – Reduce in line with climate science
  - Waste – Pioneer transformation to minimal waste hospitality industry
  - Water – Conserve water and help secure water access in areas of greatest risk

Source: ILG Investor Presentation, 21 February 2023, www.IHGPlc.com

Appendix 2 IHG: income statement and balance sheet

Income statement	31/12/2022	31/12/2021	31/12/2020	31/12/2019	31/12/2018
	$ (mn)	$ (mn)	$ (mn)	$ (mn)	$ (mn)
Revenue	3,892	2,907	2,394	4,627	4,337
Operating profit/(loss)	687	502	−139	633	583
Net interest	−96	−139	−140	−115	−96
Profit before tax	540	361	−280	545	482
Profit after tax	376	265	−260	386	350
Earnings per share					
Adjusted	282.30¢	147.00¢	31.30¢	303.30¢	293.20¢
Dividend per share	$1.38	$0.86	$0.00	$0.00	$3.52

Balance sheet:	31/12/2022	31/12/2021	31/12/2020	31/12/2019	31/12/2018
	$ (mn)	$ (mn)	$ (mn)	$ (mn)	$ (mn)
Assets					
Non-current assets					
Property, plant and equipment	437	411	504	799	786
Intangible assets	1,144	1,195	1,293	1,376	1,143
Investment properties	n/a	n/a	n/a	n/a	n/a
Investments	36	77	81	110	104
Other financial assets	163	173	168	284	267
Other non-current assets	758	794	750	690	419
	2,538	2,650	2,796	3,259	2,719
Current assets					
Inventories	4	4	5	6	5
Trade and other receivables	662	575	514	685	637
Cash at bank and in hand	976	1,450	1,675	195	704
Current asset investments	n/a	n/a	n/a	n/a	n/a
Other current assets	36	37	49	49	27
	1,678	2,066	2,243	916	1,373
Total assets	**4,216**	**4,716**	**5,039**	**4,194**	**4,092**

Income statement	31/12/2022	31/12/2021	31/12/2020	31/12/2019	31/12/2018
Liabilities					
Current liabilities					
Borrowings	81	327	903	152	159
Other current liabilities	1,463	1,297	964	1,213	1,248
	1,544	**1,624**	**1,867**	**1,365**	**1,407**
Non-current liabilities					
Borrowings	2,742	2,937	3,314	2,673	2,525
Provisions	121	134	139	140	141
Other non-current liabilities	1,417	1,495	1,568	1,481	1,150
	4,280	**4,566**	**5,021**	**4,272**	**3,816**
Total liabilities	**5,824**	**6,190**	**6,888**	**5,681**	**5,223**
Net assets	**−1,608**	**−1,474**	**−1,849**	**−1,465**	**−1,131**
Capital and reserves					
Share capital:	137	154	−1,857	−1,473	−1,139
Other reserves	−2,359	−2,539	n/a	n/a	n/a
Retained earnings	607	904	n/a	n/a	n/a
Minority interests/other equity	7	7	8	8	8
Total equity	**−1,608**	**−1,474**	**−1,849**	**−1,465**	**−1,131**

Appendix 3 IHG: scope of operations

IHG regional breakdown				
	Americas	Europe, Middle East, Asia-Pacific & Africa	Greater China	Global
Open hotels	4,356	1,169	639	6,164
Open rooms	515,496	229,664	166,467	911,627
Pipeline hotels	954	434	471	1,859
Pipeline rooms	100,319	83,410	97,739	281,648

HG Portfolio of Brands
IHG brands

Masterbrand and loyalty

IHG Hotels and Resorts	IHG One Rewards

Luxury and lifestyle

Six Senses	Regent	InterContinental	Vignette	Kimpton	Hotel Indigo
19 open	9 open	207 open	3 open	78 open	143 open
38 pipeline	10 pipeline	90 pipeline	7 pipeline	41 pipeline	119 pipeline

Premium

Voco	Hualuxe	Crowne Plaza	Even Hotels
45 open	21 open	403 open	22 open
39 pipeline	21 pipeline	111 pipeline	31 pipeline

Essentials

Holiday Inn Express	Holiday Inn	Avid
3,171 open	1,239 open	59 open
637 pipeline	238 pipeline	145 pipeline

Suites

Atwell Suites	Staybridge Suites	Holiday Inn Club Vacations	Candlewood Suites
2 open	314 open	28 open	368 open
30 pipeline	162 pipeline	1 pipeline	124 pipeline

Exclusive partners

Iberostar

33 open

15 pipeline

Total gross revenue in IHG's system (US$bn)		
	2022	2021
Candlewood Suites	0.7	0.7
Crowne Plaza	2.3	1.8
Even Hotels	0.1	0.0
Holiday Inn	4.0	2.8
Holiday Inn Express	6.5	4.2
Hotel Indigo	0.4	0.3
Hualuxe	0.1	0.1

Total gross revenue in IHG's system (US$bn)		
	2022	2021
InterContinental	2.7	2.0
Kimpton	0.7	0.4
Staybridge Suites	1.0	0.7
Other	0.9	0.5
Total	19.4	13.5

Part 6

Appendix 4 Selected hotel groups: portfolio of hotels

Hotel group	Owned and leased			Managed			Franchised			Total		
	2013	2017	2021	2013	2017	2021	2013	2017	2021	2013	2017	2021
IHG (UK)	10	8	9	658	907	939	3,954	4,433	5,216	4,622	5,348	6,164
Wyndham (USA)	2	2	0	45	116	179	7,290	8,304	8771	7,337	8,422	8,950
Accor (France)	1,324	1,081	117	986	1,172	2,343	770	2,030	2,838	3,080	4,283	5,298
Marriott (USA)	43	84	166	1,015	1,959	1,943	2,645	4,432	5,880	3,703	6,475	7,989
Starwood* (USA)	48	–	–	559	–	–	548	–	–	1,155	–	–
Hilton (USA)	156	73	54	530	656	745	3,394	4,555	6,038	4,080	5,284	6,837
Total	1,583	1,248	346	3,793	4,810	6,149	18,601	23,754	28,743	23,977	29,812	35,238

*Starwood was acquired by Marriott in September 2016.

Key brands:

- **Wyndham** – *Luxury/Upscale:* Wyndham, Wyndham, Wyndham Grand; *Midscale:* La Quinta, Ramada; *Economy:* Days Inn, Howard Johnson; *Suites:* Hawthorn.
- **Accor** – *Luxury/Upscale:* Raffles, Fairmont, Sofitel, Movenpick; *Midscale:* Mercure, Novotel; *Economy:* Ibis, Ibis Budget.
- **Marriott** – *Luxury/Upscale:* JW Marriott, Ritz Carlton, St Regis, W; *Midscale:* Marriott; Le Meridien, Renaissance, Westin, Sheraton; *Economy:* Courtyard, Moxy; **Suites:** Residence Inn, TownePlace.
- **Hilton** – *Luxury/Upscale:* Waldorf Astoria, Conrad, Hilton; *Midscale:* DoubleTree, Hilton Garden Inn; *Economy:* Hampton; *Suites:* Embassy, Homewood.

REFERENCES AND WEBSITES

References

Farronato, C. and Fradkin, A. (2018) *The Welfare Effects of Peer Entry in the Accommodation Market: The Case of Airbnb, No. w24361*, Cambridge, MA: National Bureau of Economic Research.

Gerdeman, D. (2018) 'The Airbnb effect: Cheaper rooms for travelers, less revenue for hotels', *Forbes Magazine*, 27 February.

Websites

www.accor.com
www.corporate.wyndhamhotels.com
www.hilton.com
www.IHGplc.com
www.marriott.com

Case **5**

RX – strategic issues for a leading events management company

Background

'Events management' is an all-encompassing term that covers a multitude of activities and subdivisions ranging from wedding planning to international festivals. The events that are organized differ in a number of ways.

The scale of events ranges from small local events to globally important events such as the Olympics and the World Cup. Events also differ in their target audiences in that some are clearly targeted to consumers (B2C), whereas others are targeted at other businesses (B2B). In most cases, though the event itself may have a very high profile, the organizations that organize the events are generally in the background and have a much lower public profile. Some events are organized in a regular cycle, such as every year, or, in the case of the Olympic Games or the World Cup, given their enormous scale, every 4 years. Other events are one-off events such as a concert by a particular artist at a particular venue.

There is a continuum of events in relation to their finances. Some are financed by local or national government and are viewed as a service that can be subsidized, whereas others are run as 'not-for-profit' ventures, often by PPPs, but do not receive a public subsidy. Other events are organized in a purely commercial way, with the company that manages the process expecting to do so in a way that is profitable for its shareholders.

Given the number and diversity of events and festivals being organized and managed and the sheer scale of the activities involved, it is not surprising that the industry that has grown up to provide these services remains highly fragmented. It is also the case that the overall events and festivals

DOI: 10.4324/9781003318613-28

sector is often broken down into various segments and that companies are often highly specialized in the type of events they manage, the customers they target and the specialist services they provide.

One such segment is the meetings, incentive travel, conventions and exhibitions segment, often referred to by the acronym MICE. The MICE set of events has been recognized as a significant events market segment over the past few decades. The segment is multifaceted in that it brings together hospitality services, including lodging, food and beverage, catering, convention service, convention facility supply, transportation, tourism, retail and entertainment and, consequently, often represents an economic driver of great importance for the local economy of a destination. Many destinations have developed large-scale facilities to cater for this segment. Convention centers, large-scale exhibition spaces and meeting resources have been developed in many cities around the world.

MICE activity is essentially urban in its focus because it requires ease of access, a nucleus of facilities and ancillary attractions and hospitality capacity. Some destinations, such as London, Dubai, Singapore, New York and Hong Kong, derive enormous revenues from attracting MICE tourism activity with delegates drawn by their status as major world cities. Others, such as Las Vegas and Macau, have built their MICE activity as an adjunct to gambling and utilizing the extensive hospitality resources developed in these cities. Other cities, such as Frankfurt and Geneva, as well-positioned trading cities, have ancient trade fairs that long predate the use of the MICE terminology. Resorts such as Davos in Switzerland, Australia's Gold Coast, the Indonesian island of Bali and Miami, Florida, have also targeted MICE activities because they represent highly attractive destinations for visitors, who provide a means of filling their large hospitality facilities during 'off-peak' and 'shoulder' seasons.

Companies have emerged to organize and manage much MICE activity. The industry is highly fragmented, with many local and regional companies operating, and many companies have particular specialisms such as meetings or exhibitions or a concentration on particular industry sectors such as health care or automotive. Notwithstanding the industry fragmentation that exists, there is very keen competition for organizing MICE events. Several large, diversified companies have emerged, and the major international hotel groups often commit large resources to developing these activities centered on their hotel properties and associated banqueting and convention spaces.

The scale of MICE activity is vast and growing quickly. One estimate valued the size of the industry at US$215bn in 2020 and forecasted growth to reach US$1,337bn by 2028 (AMR, 2022). The MICE industry is complex, consisting of participants, exhibitors, planners, sponsors, visitor and convention bureaus and venues. However, the COVID-19 outbreak severely restricted the global MICE industry during 2020 and 2021, mainly owing to the unprecedented lockdowns, restrictions of social gatherings and meetings, travel restrictions and social distancing measures to curb the spread of coronavirus. The majority of MICE events and destination venues were closed during the pandemic owing to the complete lockdown in many countries worldwide. The growing popularity of online MICE events, conducted on video conferencing platforms such as Zoom and Google Meet, had a profound impact on the industry, leading some to question the cost-effectiveness of face-to-face meetings.

This is a multifaceted business, in which convention and exhibition centers, specialized facilities, tourism, trading partners and distribution operate systematically in generating revenue. MICE activities are generally recognized as a high value-adding business opportunities worldwide, and many countries and cities are committed to strengthening and enhancing the infrastructure to accommodate internationally renowned events.

Exhibitions

Exhibitions are a large constituent part of MICE events, though many of them go relatively unnoticed by the general public because many are B2B events. The exhibitions vary considerably in their scale and focus, with many concentrating on very specialized industry sectors and subsectors. It is also sometimes difficult to disaggregate exhibitions from other MICE activity because many other activities such as meetings, conventions and conferences cluster around the exhibitions and delegates often benefit from incentive travel opportunities provided by their organizations.

A number of specialized companies have formed to organize and manage exhibitions around the world, and though there are many 'one-off' events, the companies and their partners have tried to create recognized exhibition brands in their chosen specialisms, the formats of which are repeated in subsequent years and 'cloned' and adapted to serve different geographical markets. Some of the companies that specialize in these events have long histories, whereas others are of much more recent origin. The trade fairs (*messe*) were established in large Continental European cities, particularly in Germany (such as Frankfurt, Munich and Hannover) in medieval times.

The global exhibitions have seen robust growth in recent years, after several years affected by the world economic downturn, expanding by about 5% per year prior to the COVID-19 pandemic. A particularly important constituent of this growth is likely to come from the emerging markets, and China has cemented itself in second place, with the rapid emergence of the Gulf Region also continuing to drive global growth. In addition to these countries, 'tier 2' emerging markets such as Indonesia and Malaysia are seeing heightened mergers and acquisitions and launch activity. The large international organizers are expanding into these countries as they continue to rebalance their portfolios to emerging markets. Substantial growth in mature markets is more difficult to achieve, but compelling offerings, including digital, can drive show value and provide additional revenue opportunities for organizers.

Apart from its solid growth prospects, the exhibitions sector remains highly attractive for many other reasons: events can be highly profitable; they have excellent cash flow characteristics, with stand space deposits often paid a year in advance; and there is a high degree of revenue integrity, with exhibitor renewal rates typically in the 65% to 85% range. Furthermore, the exhibitions market remains fragmented and still offers considerable opportunities for consolidation. The $950mn acquisition of a large American events management company illustrates the attractiveness of the exhibitions sector for investors. Nielsen Expositions, which had grown from a US publishing business (Miller Freeman). was acquired by Onex, a Canadian private equity investor. in 2013 and subsequently changed its name to Emerald Expositions. The subsequent acquisition of another US exhibition organizer (GLM) propelled Emerald to the position of the leading trade exposition organizer in the USA.

There are, however, significant differences between the world's most attractive exhibition markets and the requirements of the industry sectors on which the events focus. Thus, though organizers are trying to create branded concepts that can be replicated in various parts of the world, they nevertheless have to try to understand the local market dynamics and make relevant adaptations to their products accordingly. Local knowledge, expertise and contacts are hard to acquire, and though the industry is not heavily regulated, it is common for local partners to become involved. These partnerships may take the form of a joint venture but may also involve looser arrangements such as contractual agreements with local organizations such as venue owners; travel, hospitality and marketing companies; and trade associations. In doing so, event organizers are able to reduce risks by acquiring local expertise and knowledge, sharing marketing activities and having specialized support at the particular location.

Furthermore, an increasingly important part of the exhibition market is the digital interface that occurs between exhibitors, buyers and intermediaries prior to the event, during the event and after the event. These 'digital platforms' allow connections to be made, partnerships and alliances to be formed, a deeper understanding of products to be gained and price and product comparisons to be made. Generally, these digital platforms are an adjunct to the exhibition and related events, but in a small (but rapidly growing) number of cases, 'virtual exhibitions' have been held, thereby avoiding the costs and logistical effort of organizing a physical exhibition involving all parties meeting in one place at a specified time. This is likely to be a growing trend in the industry, though those with vested interests such as hotel operators, destination organizations, venue owners, travel companies and exhibition organizers are all involved in stressing the advantages of face-to-face meetings, which they claim are more effective in generating results.

Increasingly, event organizers are deploying extensive resources in developing and maintaining their digital platforms and making them part of their positioning relative to competitor offerings. Organizers who have developed digital platforms stress the quality, networking opportunities and business facilitation offered by their particular digital platforms and point to the inability of smaller organizers to provide similar coverage.

RELX Group

RELX Group (previously Reed Elsevier) is a major international business publisher and business services provider based in the UK and the Netherlands with offices and operations worldwide.

Reed Elsevier came into being in autumn 1992 as the result of a merger between Reed International, a British trade book and magazine publisher, and the Dutch science publisher Elsevier. In 2015 the company changed its name to RELX Group (pronounced Relex), with its shares listed in London (where it is a constituent of the FTSE 100 index of largest companies), New York and Amsterdam.

RX – origins and growth

RELX's exhibitions business is called RX, formerly Reed Exhibitions, and is one of the world's largest exhibition companies, running 400 events in 22 countries, though in a diverse, segmented industry, this claim is difficult to verify. Undeniably, it certainly is a very large event organizer and a market leader in its primary segment. RX is a global business, headquartered in London, and has further principal offices in Paris, Vienna, Moscow, Norwalk (Connecticut), Mexico City, São Paulo, Abu Dhabi, Beijing, Tokyo and Sydney. RX has 4,000 employees worldwide, and its portfolio of events serves 43 industry sectors.

The origins of Reed Exhibitions can be traced back to 1966 when a British publishing company, IPC, purchased a stake in the US company Cahners Publishing, which also had a portfolio of exhibitions that it organized. IPC was acquired by Reed International in 1970, and over the next 15 years, Reed and Cahners continued to grow their exhibition business in the USA, Asia and Europe through acquisitions and mergers, becoming Reed Exhibition Companies in 1986.

With the purchase of Miller Freeman Europe (a US publisher with a European exhibition business) in 2000, Reed Exhibitions became the world's largest exhibition organizer. In the decades since, there has been a strategic shift in emphasis toward the growth markets of China, Latin America and the Middle East, fueled by joint venture partnerships and the leveraging of market-leading Reed brands.

Reed's first major presence in China (Reed Huayin) was established in 2003, followed by Reed Sinopharm in 2005 and Reed Huabo in 2007. In 2007, Reed also acquired Alcantara Machado in Brazil, making it the number one organizer in Latin America.

RX is a global market leader in a fragmented industry, holding less than a 10% global market share. A powerful enlarged competitor emerged during 2018 as two other international exhibition organizers combined their activities as UBM was acquired by informa (which also includes the Taylor & Francis publishing business including the Routledge imprint), both of which are based in the UK. US-based Emerald and some of the larger German and Swiss *messe*, including Frankfurt, Düsseldorf, Cologne, Hannover, Munich and Basel, are also important competitors. Competition also comes from industry trade associations, convention center and exhibition hall owners and hospitality operators utilizing their function room spaces.

RX also has to compete in other ways. As a division of a large, diversified corporation, it has to compete with other parts of the business for investment and in the allocation of resources. It also has to consider the efficiency of its internal processes to ensure that it delivers in a value-for-money way, carrying out those tasks where it is important to have direct control but outsourcing and partnering where it is sensible and cost-effective to do so. The relevant balance will be different in each case and according to environmental circumstances and is likely to change over time as more experience is gained and learning is acquired by other parties. RX operates in many countries and in many sectors, but the company must continually monitor the relative performance of both sectors and countries to focus its activities appropriately.

RX – business model, competition and strategy

RX's stated strategic goal is to 'leverage industry expertise, large data sets and technology to enable customers to build their businesses by connecting face-to-face and digitally. This enables innovation and generates billions of dollars of revenues for the economic development of local markets and national economies around the world' (RELX, 2022).

The primary focus of Reed Exhibitions' activities is on B2B events, although it also runs a small number of consumer events and, consequently, the organization is not widely recognized by consumers. However, that is not to say that brands are unimportant, for it has acquired, developed and grown a number of strong market leading brands in its chosen B2B segments. The year 2022 represented a year of recovery for RX as it ran 254 face-to-face events in 22 countries (215 events in 2021), with the revenue performance of events relative to pre-COVID equivalents improving through the year, and a number of events trading above prepandemic levels. By the end of the year, RX was able to operate without disruption in almost all geographies.

RX also continues to focus on technology through growth in the number of digital products and their usage by customers. As face-to-face revenues recovered, digital products also grew strongly. The industry also has significant 'multiplier' effects in that it helps generate billions of dollars of business activity (for exhibitors), facilitates entry into new markets and boosts the local economies where the events are hosted.

The substantial majority of RX's revenues are from sales of exhibition space, with the balance being derived from other sources, which include conference fees, online and offline advertising, sponsorship fees and (for some events) admission charges. Exhibition space is sold directly or through local agents where applicable. RX often works in collaboration with trade associations, which use the events to promote access for members to domestic and export markets, and with governments, for whom events can provide important support to stimulate foreign investment and promote regional and national enterprise.

Increasingly, part of the business proposition is to offer visitors and exhibitors the opportunity to interact before and after the event through the use of online tools such as directories and matchmaking. In other parts of the RELX group, there has been transformational and rapid shift to electronic revenue generation. This has been far less pronounced in the Exhibitions division. Nevertheless, electronic revenues have more than doubled from their 2013 levels. It is likely that there will be some shift toward electronic revenue generation in future years, and its central role in supporting face-to-face activity will become more important. New and enhanced tools are likely to be developed.

Growth in the exhibitions market is influenced by both B2B marketing spend and business investment. Historically, these have been driven by levels of corporate profitability, which in turn has followed overall growth in gross domestic product. Emerging markets and higher growth sectors provide additional opportunities for RX. Because some events are held other than annually, growth in any one year is affected by the cycle of nonannual exhibitions.

Like most companies in its field, RX specializes in particular industry sectors where it can leverage its market knowledge, experience, marketing expertise, established networks and financial strength. RX organizes influential events in key markets focused on addressing the needs of the industry, where participants from around the world meet face to face to do business, to network and to learn. Its events encompass a wide range of sectors. They include construction, cosmetics, electronics, energy and alternative energy, engineering, entertainment, gifts and jewelry, health care, hospitality, interior design, logistics, manufacturing, media, pharmaceuticals, real estate, recreation, security and safety and transport and travel.

At an operational level, RX clearly has proven, geographically dispersed expertise in envisaging, designing, planning and delivering large-scale exhibition events. The strategic priorities of RX reflect broader concerns. A business such as Reed Exhibitions has to respond to investors' demands relating to growth and delivering attractive rates of return. In doing this, the company must be concerned with the 'one-off' nature of the underlying business and differential growth rates in various sectors and geographical localities.

Many events are one-off events that are successfully delivered and then the organizing company moves on to the next event. The company has to develop consistent returns, though. To counteract the one-off nature of this industry, the company has built up some strong B2B exhibition brands in certain sectors that have become well established and generally run annually or biannually.

Consequently, in considering its strategy, RX needs to focus on a number of aspects. These include how the company can build and develop successful exhibition propositions, responding to customer needs and market conditions, which methods of development should be utilized and which markets should be targeted. At the same time, the company has to be driven by deploying its resources effectively and in a highly competitive, fragmented and cost-sensitive sector, ensuring that cost-effective operational delivery can be achieved with appropriate quality assurance.

In delivering its strategic priorities, Reed Exhibitions tries to deliver a platform for industry communities to conduct business, to network and to learn through a range of market-leading events in growth sectors, especially in higher growth geographies, enabling exhibitors to target and reach new customers quickly and cost-effectively. The company believes that organic growth is an important part of its development because its product portfolio (existing and potential) is strong, is capable of further penetration in its existing markets and can be adapted to access new market opportunities.

Growth in this industry is difficult to achieve. The industry is highly susceptible to changes in the local economy and, in a fragmented industry with relatively low entry barriers, many companies are jostling for competitive advantage. Furthermore, as with most service sectors, there is a focus on the quality of the customer experience. However, there are human resource issues that managers have to address. Events are delivered by a workforce that is dispersed, under pressure to deliver results to tight schedules and includes many part-time employees, employees working for independent suppliers and, in some cases, volunteers. There is also a large supply chain of direct suppliers to the event such as lighting and sound suppliers, printers and caterers and indirect suppliers such hotels, restaurants and transportation.

For a company such as RX to compete effectively, it must leverage the advantages it derives from being large and well established and having a record of product innovation. Thus, a number of aspects regarding the way in which the company operates are likely to be crucial to future strategic growth prospects. These aspects might include continuing to generate greater customer value through the intelligent application of customer knowledge, developing a pipeline of new or 'cloned' events and building and maintaining the technology platforms to ensure the rapid deployment of innovation and best practice. In addition, RX is shaping its portfolio through a combination of strategic partnerships and acquisitions in high-growth sectors and geographies. At the same time, strategic withdrawal will be considered by the company in markets and industry sectors with lower long-term growth prospects.

RX makes selective acquisitions to enter or increase presence in attractive sectors with high growth potential. During 2022, for example, RX acquired Big Data London to access the high-growth market in data and analytics and secured the rights to produce the E3 show, strengthening its position in the attractive gaming and interactive entertainment market. Similarly, RX made selective launches to enter new attractive sectors (e.g., Femtech, Tokyo) or extend successful value propositions into new markets (such as INTERPHEX pharma and Biotech into Korea) or additional calendar slots for existing events.

RX continues to seek organic growth through launches that are tightly focused on industries and geographies that are well placed for long-term growth. The focus is on three main areas that position it for long-term success:

Digital initiatives: Digital tools and platforms have been widely deployed and enhanced to increase the value from face-to-face events.

Operational efficiency: A leaner and more flexible structure is in place that is better able to respond to changing circumstances and customer needs. This new structure, RX's global technology platforms and more specialist functions allow RX to accelerate revenue growth, while controlling costs and embedding sustainability throughout the organization. It also enables a faster and more agile deployment of digital products, new events and process innovation.

Portfolio optimization: Furthermore, through a combination of new launches, strategic partnerships and selective acquisitions in faster growing sectors and geographies, RX is seeking to optimize its portfolio of products.

RX – travel events

One sector in which Reed had developed particular expertise is the international travel industry, and the sector accounts for about 8% of the Exhibition division's revenues. Though the industry is clearly of massive proportions and has grown enormously (and will continue to do so), it is somewhat difficult to identify, define and communicate with. However, the expos that RX has developed enable diverse suppliers, buyers and those with an interest in the industry to be brought together in one place and at one time and for business negotiations and transactions to be carried out. The development of relevant and targeted electronic platforms supplements the face-to-face acuity with resources deployed in developing, maintaining and updating a series of dedicated websites, industry blogs, Twitter feeds and Facebook pages.

In the travel sector, RX has developed a number of leading brands, the formats of which it is increasingly 'cloning' and replicating, albeit in locally adapted ways for different geographical regions. The World Travel Market, for example is a well-established global event held annually in London since 1980 that has achieved strong brand recognition. The global brand strength has been utilized to produce regionally focused events in strong emerging regional markets. Similarly, EIBTM (the global meetings and events expo) and ILTM (International Luxury Travel Market) were acquired by RX in 1998 and 2005, respectively. EIBTM and ILTM are long-established leading global expos in their fields with annual events in Barcelona, Spain, and Cannes on the French Riviera. Subsequently, both events have been progressively cloned to encompass new geographies, though this has happened systematically so that Reed does not overstretch its resources, can learn from its experiences elsewhere and can ensure that existing successful events are not 'cannibalized'.

Though there has been much discussion and some development of electronic meetings, virtual exhibitions and other electronic communications, face-to-face expos remain highly relevant and popular in the global travel industry. Perhaps this is partly driven by the nature of the underlying product 'travel' and the propensity of industry professionals to gather together in one place, but the importance of such gatherings seems to be replicated in other sectors.

The travel events are often viewed by leading professionals as 'must attend' events, allowing exhibitors and visitors to achieve a number of objectives such as enhancing brand awareness, directly meeting relevant trade colleagues, education, media exposure, networking and competitor monitoring. In addition, crucially, the expos allow for commercial transactions to be initiated, discussed and, in some cases, concluded while at the event, allowing delegates to be able to demonstrate a return on investment for their involvement.

There is, however, an increasing focus on customer value, and in travel, as in other sectors, RX has to work hard on constant product evaluation and enhancements to its offerings. The ways in which a product might be enhanced include enhancing the face-to-face format, adding value through technology and extending community reach.

Innovation at large exhibitions includes clearly brokered relationships offering a customized experience and the arrangement of prescheduled meetings of exhibitors and buyers whereby both parties identify whom they want to meet. Formats have evolved further over the past few years with the development of so-called table-top summits for focused markets in which exhibitors purchase a table and receive a diary of prescheduled meetings with buyers. The benefits of table-top summits for exhibitors are that they are able to test new markets at lower cost (no stand build) and they have guaranteed time with buyers. For Reed Exhibitions' expansion, it represents a way of quickly becoming involved with new market opportunities.

Technology now permeates all RX Exhibitions (and those of many of its competitors), and it acts to enhance the face-to-face experience in that it provides a year-round community beyond the show-floor and provides content for users. Reed's position as a broker is thus strengthened, and it can charge for some of the content display. The technology can also extend to software that identifies preferences for meeting buyers and suppliers and creating customized schedules of meetings at mutually agreeable times. Smartphone apps and online tools allow customization for each visitor to build their own personalized schedules and to interact with exhibitors, event organizers and the media while receiving reminders and updates about activities within the event.

Increasingly, active steps are taken to extend the 'footprint' of events using social media, digital channels, TV and print media. At larger events, activities include roving social media reporters, dedicated onsite video teams for instant online content and conference sessions broadcast online. Such exposure increases brand awareness, beyond the exhibition, for the event itself but also for the products being promoted by exhibitors. At the same time, it spreads the perception of Reed Exhibitions that it is more than an exhibition organizer and that in an increasingly competitive industry (such as exhibitions), which on the face if it appears quite straightforward, innovation, technology and customer service are as important as in any other service-based sector.

REFERENCES AND WEBSITES

References

AMR. (2018) *Global Exhibition Market Report*, London: AMR International Strategy Consultants, www.amrinternational.com

AMR. (2022) *MICE Industry by Event Type (Meetings, Incentives, Conventions, and Exhibitions) – Global Opportunity Analysis and Industry Forecast, 2021–2028*, Portland, OR: Allied Market Research, www.amrinternational.com

RELX. (2022) Annual Report and Accounts, www.relx.com

UFI. (2018) *Global Exhibition Industry Statistics 2017*, Paris: UFI, The Global Association of the Exhibition Industry, www.ufi.org

Websites

www.amrinternational.com
www.alliedmarketresearch.com
www.informa.com
www.relx.com
www.ufi.org

Appendix 1 World exhibition space

Country	Exhibition space 2022 (in m²).	% of the World	Country	Exhibition space 2017 (in m²)	% of the World
China	10,216,681	25.2	USA	6,850,426	19.7
USA	6,936,197	17.1	China	5,753,724	16.6
Germany	3,181,205	7.8	Germany	3,228,020	9.3
Italy	2,361,690	5.8	Italy	2,293,748	6.6
France	1,978,787	4.9	France	2,245,311	6.5
Spain	1,638,795	4.0	Spain	1,526,319	4.4
Brazil	1,194,357	2.9	Canada	840,376	2.4
Russia	1,149,264	2.8	Brazil	788,011	2.3
Canada	760,914	1.9	Russia	768,276	2.3
Netherlands	720,101	1.8	Netherlands	709,701	2.2
Turkey	667,076	1.6	UK	648,121	2.0
UK	649,188	1.6	Turkey	602,030	1.9
Mexico	620,437	1.5	Switzerland	495,798	1.7
Belgium	460,621	1.1	Mexico	480,088	1.4
Switzerland	457,000	1.1	Poland	473,341	1.4
Japan	446,000	1.1	Japan	455,462	1.4

Appendix 2 RELX: market segments, revenues and profits

Market segments	RELX business focus	Segment position	Key brands
Scientific, technical and medical	Provide information and tools to help customers improve scientific and health care outcomes. Its products and services include electronic and print journals, textbooks, reference works and workflow solutions for researchers and practitioners.	Global No. 1	Elsevier
Risk solutions and business information	Provide data, analytics and insight that enable customers to evaluate and manage risks and develop market intelligence, supporting more confident decisions, improved economic outcomes and enhanced operational efficiency.	Global No. 1	LexisNexis, Risk Solutions, Reed Business Information
Legal	A world-leading provider of legal, regulatory and news and business information and analysis to legal, corporate, government and academic customers.	USA No. 2 Outside US No. 1 or No. 2	LexisNexis, Legal and Professional
Exhibitions	One of the world's leading events businesses, with 400 events in over 22 countries.	Global No. 2	RX

	RELX revenue by geographic market								
	Europe			North America			Rest of world		
	2013	2017	2022	2013	2017	2022	2013	2017	2022
Scientific, technical and medical	30%	25%	13%	38%	42%	80%	32%	33%	7%
Risk solutions and business information	59%	15%	21%	28%	80%	48%	13%	5%	31%
Legal	21%	20%	68%	68%	68%	20%	11%	12%	12%
Exhibitions	43%	39%	47%	16%	21%	19%	41%	40%	34%

	Revenue (£mn)			Operating profits (£mn)		
	2013	2017	2022	2013	2017	2022
Scientific, technical and medical	2,126	2,478	2,909	826	913	1,078
Risk solutions and business information	1,480	2,076	2,900	533	759	1,100
Legal	1,567	1,692	1,782	238	322	372
Exhibitions	862	1,109	953	213	285	162

Part 6

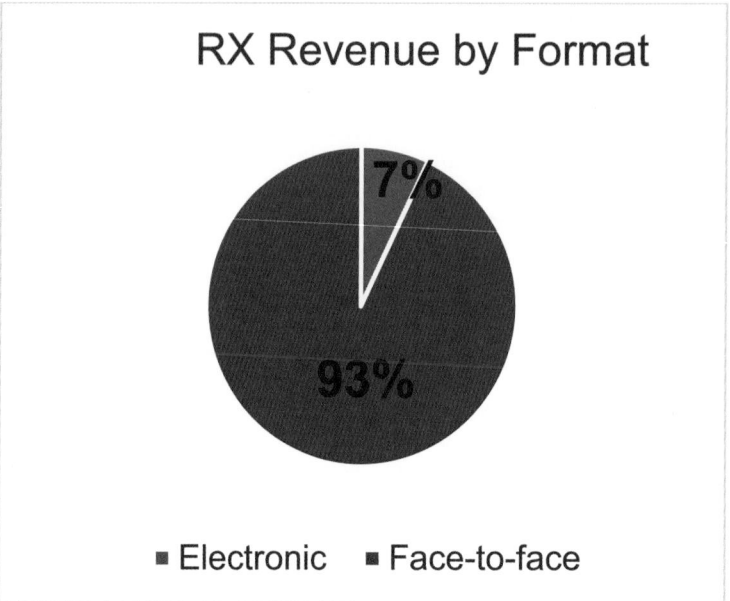

Figure 1 – Case 5

Figure 2 – Case 5

Appendix 3 RX: bringing together key travel industry professionals

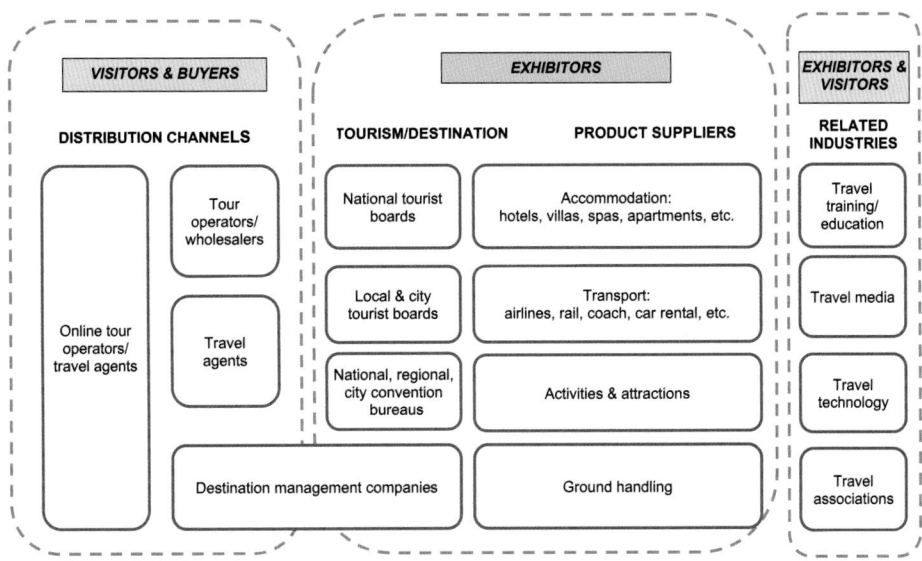

RX travel industry events			
Leisure travel	IBTM global events	Luxury travel	Sports travel
World travel market, London, November	EIBTM: Global Meetings and Events Expo, Barcelona, November	International luxury travel market, Cannes, France, November	International golf travel market, November
World travel market, Latin America, April/May	CIBTM: Incentives, Business Travel and Meetings Expo, China, August	International luxury travel market, Asia, April	International ski travel market, March
World travel market, Africa, April	AIBTM: Incentives, Business Travel and Meetings Expo, America, June	International luxury travel market, Americas, September	
Arabian travel market, Dubai, May	GIBTM: Incentives, Business Travel and Meetings Expo, Gulf, February/March	International luxury travel market, Africa, April	
IFTM, Paris, September	IBTM: Incentives, Business Travel and Meetings Expo, India, September	International luxury travel market, Japan, March	
	IBTM: Incentives, Business Travel and Meetings Expo, Africa, April	International luxury travel market, August	
	AIME: Asia-Pacific Incentives and Meetings Expo, Melbourne, Australia, February		

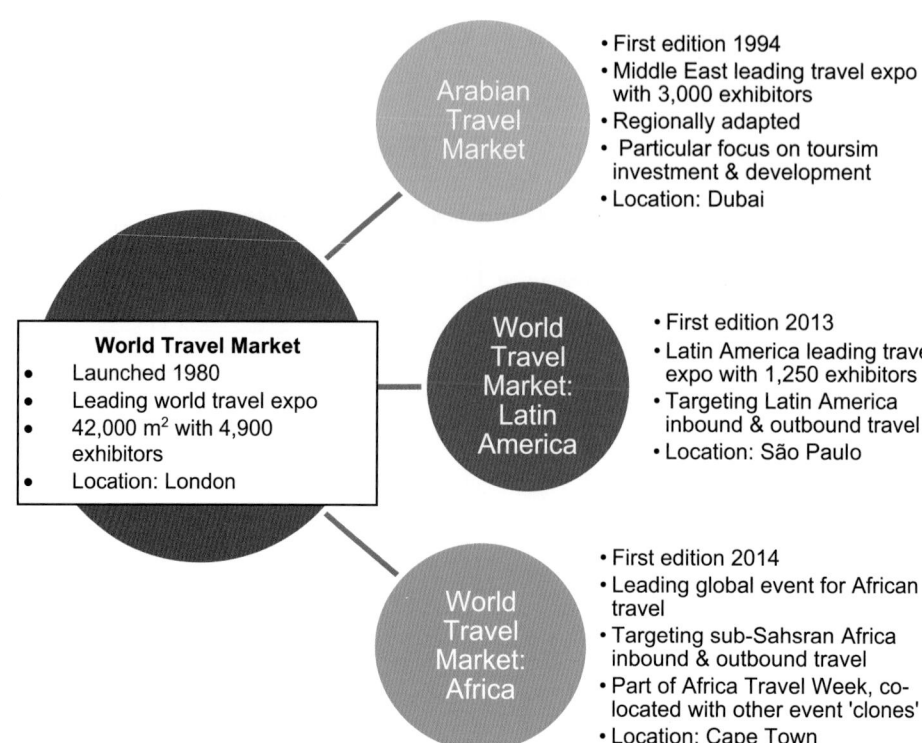

Arabian Travel Market
- First edition 1994
- Middle East leading travel expo with 3,000 exhibitors
- Regionally adapted
- Particular focus on toursim investment & development
- Location: Dubai

World Travel Market
- Launched 1980
- Leading world travel expo
- 42,000 m² with 4,900 exhibitors
- Location: London

World Travel Market: Latin America
- First edition 2013
- Latin America leading travel expo with 1,250 exhibitors
- Targeting Latin America inbound & outbound travel
- Location: São Paulo

World Travel Market: Africa
- First edition 2014
- Leading global event for African travel
- Targeting sub-Sahsran Africa inbound & outbound travel
- Part of Africa Travel Week, co-located with other event 'clones'
- Location: Cape Town

Case **6**

Airbnb: back to the future – a 'disruptor' for global hospitality

Introduction

Airbnb is creating the future by looking back to the past. This 'Back to the Future' vision of Airbnb is, as Gallagher (2017) pointed out in his popular book chronicling the meteoric rise of Airbnb, appropriate because Airbnb's basic idea is 'not new at all'. Brian Chesky (who with partner Joe Gebbia co-founded Airbnb) recalled 'that the only person who didn't tell him Airbnb was a horrible idea was his grandfather, who when he heard what his grandson was up to, just nodded and said, "Oh of course. That's how we used to travel"' Gallagher (2017:xvi). The point is that whether as tenants, boarders, visitors, pilgrims, etc., people stayed in some sort of home-share long before the birth of Airbnb, or the internet for that matter.

What was different, though, when Airbnb was launched is that it had an easy-to-use, accessible website that was firmly focused on urban properties, rather than the rural and resort, leisure focus of most existing sites. The two co-founders lacked corporate experience, management qualifications or technical expertise when Airbnb was initiated. They were both designers, having studied together at Rhode Island School of Design, which, though it gave them a poor understanding of the technical requirements of building a web-based company, nevertheless gave them a consumer's view of what a site should look like and how it should function. Astutely, the two co-founders quickly realized their own shortcomings and recruited a third, technically competent co-founder, Nathan Blecharczyk, after the first week (Gallagher, 2017). Blecharczyk was an engineer with a Harvard computer science degree who had previously shared an apartment with Joe Gebbia.

Unlike many other tech 'unicorns' (start-ups reaching $1bn turnover), the three co-founders are still very much in charge of the colossus they have assembled. The founders were early to recognize

DOI: 10.4324/9781003318613-29

the importance of a strong and supportive culture, and until 2013 they interviewed every job applicant. To this day anyone who is hired has to pass a 'core values' interview, where they are judged not
on their CV but on how they fit into the firm's culture, to ensure that people hired have a sense of
the company's mission ('A Different Breed of Unicorn', 2017).

Though of relatively recent birth, Airbnb has grown quickly to reach a market valuation of about
$70bn (in February 2023). By way of context, Marriott, the world's largest hotel operator (by most
measures), which traces its history back many decades, is valued in the range of $50–55bn. An
attention to costs, which is uncommon in tech start-ups, led by Chief Financial Officer Laurence
Tosi (who was recruited from private equity giant Blackstone in 2015), is beginning to show up in
results. Airbnb reportedly achieved profitability for the first time in the second half of 2016 and
subsequently traded profitably ('A Different Breed of Unicorn', 2017).

In the past, companies often took decades to establish themselves and create an international presence. Airbnb is different in this respect (as in others), a product of our times, which are characterized by tech companies owning and managing relatively few physical assets, which can rise at a
meteoric rate. Importantly, unlike most predecessors, given access to finance and the ability to use
internet and mobile technology creatively, these companies are able to quickly establish an international and global scale of operations.

From humble West Coast USA origins in 2007, Airbnb has, like Uber, and Amazon and Google
before them, grown exponentially to have a global footprint. In doing so, it has had significant
disruptive effects, not only on the traditional hospitality industry but also on urban property
markets, local communities and consumer behavior in hospitality. Its phenomenal success
has enabled homeowners to benefit from their most valuable asset and for travelers to find
authentic, well-located accommodation easily and to be able to compare the value of competing offerings. However, Airbnb's growth has not been without controversy; competitors are
gathering strength, and the ways in which continued growth for the company can be assured
are far from clear.

The Airbnb product

Airbnb is an online community marketplace facilitating short-term rentals ranging from shared
accommodations to entire homes (Zervas et al., 2017). Typically, the accommodation available
through the Airbnb website and app involves an entire home (house of apartment) or a room in a
residence where the host is also present. A particular feature of Airbnb's model is that its rental listings are usually not available on competitors' websites, because its hosts tend to be loyal. Whereas
Uber, in the 'ride-for-hire' sector, is locked in a fierce competition with rivals in many markets for
customers and drivers and has chosen to subsidize journeys to avoid losing market share, Airbnb
has no need to pay up to keep hosts and users.

From its inception, the Airbnb website (www.airbnb.com) has been quite straightforward and intuitive for users: a prospective guest searches based on destination, travel dates and party size; the
website returns a list of available spaces that can be refined by attributes like price, neighborhood
and amenities, and then individual listings can be selected for greater detail, including a description,
photographs and reviews from previous guests (Guttentag and Smith, 2017).

The story of Airbnb's birth has repeatedly been told and has become a tale of entrepreneurial folk-
lore. The two recent university graduates converted their home into an 'Air Bed & Breakfast' by
offering overnight stays on air mattresses during a San Francisco conference in 2007 (Guttentag,
2015), when other accommodation options were scarce. Since 2013, the company has operated
from five floors of a former battery factory in the fashionable SoMa (South of Market Street) area,

which was once San Francisco's industrial core. The building's two dozen conference rooms are exact replicas of some of Airbnb's property listings. Collectively Airbnb employees are referred to as the 'Air family' (or 'Airfam' for short), and many perks and special events are provided for staff, including 'Air Shares', at which employees can share particular skills, such as photography or tie-dyeing, with each other. The same elements are replicated at Airbnb offices around the world (Gallagher, 2017).

Web-driven initiatives in 'social travel' initially revolved around well-intentioned motives of offering people a place to stay and sharing experiences. Networked hospitality businesses, of which Airbnb is the market leader, turned the 'inviting strangers to your home' concept into a commercial phenomenon. Airbnb, which has now been joined by many other companies – some small and locally focused, others large and internationally diversified (such as Expedia subsidiaries Vrbo and Flipkey, Booking.com and Holiday Lettings) – created a commission-based web platform for room sharers and travelers).

Airbnb operates an accommodation marketplace that allows people to list their available living spaces to be leased or rented by users looking for short-term lodging. Airbnb also allows users to book experiences related to tourism and make reservations at restaurants, but these services form a negligible part of the company's revenues at present. Airbnb allows bookings at listings in cities and other locations worldwide, a scale that it was able to achieve over just a few years, because of its role as an intermediary (or broker) connecting people looking to rent out a living space and those looking for a place to stay.

Because Airbnb does not require investment in any real estate, unlike many hotel companies, its growth is purely dependent on the number of hosts and guests it can attract on its platform. The company makes money by charging the host as well as the guest a percentage of the booking cost as a service fee. Currently, the company charges its hosts a service fee of 3% to 5% of the booking amount, and the service fee for guests ranges between 5% and 15% of the booking amount. Airbnb's business model currently operates with minimal regulatory controls in most locations and, as a result, hosts and guests both have incentives to use signaling mechanisms to build trust and maximize the likelihood of a successful booking. Airbnb has built an online reputation system to reinforce this behavior, which enables and encourages each guest and host to leave a review upon completion of a stay. Guests use star ratings to rate features of their stay, such as cleanliness, location and communication, and both guests and hosts may provide other information about aspects of the stay, including personal comments.

The development of information technologies alongside the growth of Web 2.0 has enabled the development of online platforms that promote user-generated content, sharing and collaboration (Kaplan and Haenlein, 2010). However, though technological advances are clearly important in the growth of online platforms such as Airbnb, other factors are also important.

The rapid global growth of technology start-ups can be attributed to three factors: the problems they addressed were globally pervasive, they enabled customers to act entrepreneurially and they both provided innovative web-based services and adopted and deployed innovative web-based processes to allow them to innovate continuously and efficiently (Bailetti, 2012). Using this innovative web-based technology, Airbnb enables rental hosts to act in an entrepreneurial manner on a global basis. The rental hosts list their available accommodations on Airbnb and earn profits by renting them, usually at rates cheaper than comparable hotels, leading to savings for travelers (Varma et al., 2016). Many admirable technological advances have failed to take off in the past, but the availability of early and substantial financial backing in their Silicon Valley home through 'venture capital' financiers has changed the dynamics of initiatives (such as Uber and Airbnb), particularly by promoting more rapid expansion (Schor, 2016).

The sharing economy

Airbnb and other 'peer-to-peer' short-term rental companies represent part of the broader 'sharing economy' (also sometimes called 'collaborative consumption'; Guttentag and Smith, 2017). The sharing economy has been defined as 'consumers granting each other temporary access to underutilized physical assets ("idle capacity"), possibly for money' (Frenken and Schor, 2017). The sharing economy can be distinguished from other economic forms.

Sharing is about consumer-to-consumer platforms and not about renting or leasing a good from a company (business-to-consumer). The latter case would be an example of a product service economy, where a consumer gains access to a product while the service provider retains ownership. Sharing is also about consumers providing each other temporary access to a good and not about the transfer of ownership of the good. Thus, the sharing economy does not include the secondhand economy, in which goods are sold or given away between consumers (as occurs on online platforms such as eBay). Finally, sharing is about more efficient use of physical assets and not about private individuals delivering each other a service. Physical assets can be unused, but people cannot. Internet platforms that bring consumers together to provide each other with services represent the on-demand economy. An example of such a platform is Task Rabbit (which was acquired by Ikea), through which people can be hired to carry out work around the house and undertake errands (Frenken et al., 2015).

The operation and the long-term impacts of these sharing platforms are shaped by both their market orientation (for-profit vs nonprofit) and market structure (peer-to-peer vs business-to-peer). These dimensions shape the platforms' business models, logics of exchange and potential for disrupting conventional businesses (Schor, 2016). Though all sharing economy platforms effectively create 'markets in sharing' by facilitating exchanges, the imperative for a platform to generate a profit influences how sharing takes place and how much revenue devolves to management and owners. For-profit platforms push for revenue and asset maximization, whereas many sharing space initiatives, such as Time Banks and Makerspaces, are nonprofit organizations. They do not seek growth or revenue maximization but instead aim to serve needs, usually at a community scale (Schor, 2016).

Though the for-profit vs non-profit divide is the most important one, the divide between P2P (peer-to-peer) and B2P (business-to-peer) platforms is also significant. P2P entities earn money by commissions on exchanges, so revenue growth depends on increasing the number of trades. In contrast, B2P platforms often seek to maximize revenue per transaction, as traditional businesses often do. The differences between Zipcar (B2P) and Turo (P2P) illustrate the point. On the Turo site, owners earn income from renting out their own vehicles and setting rates and availability. Zipcar, on the other hand, functions like an ordinary short-term car rental company where cars can be rented for very short periods. With a P2P structure, as long as there is competition, the 'peers' (both providers and consumers) should be able to capture a higher fraction of value. If, however, there is little competition, the platform can extract excess profits (Schor, 2016).

In the sharing economy, consumers can be viewed as co-creators of value and have the potential to become entrepreneurs by dealing with their assets like solar energy and cars and, in the Airbnb context, renting out their houses and apartments (Oskam and Boswijk, 2016). Co-creation has been defined as 'the joint creation of value by the company and the customer; allowing the customer to co-construct the service experience to suit their context' (Prahalad and Ramaswamy, 2004: 8).

This represents a shift in thinking from the traditional 'firm-centric' view of value creation in which the firm controls the value chain for its products, which it then delivers to consumers, to a customer centric view in which the customer becomes part of the value creation process and customers start to manage their own value chains. In this way, the economy is developing into a networked economy instead of the traditional hierarchical structure.

To work in this co-created networked economy successfully, Prahalad and Ramaswamy (2004) argued that companies need to develop a range of capabilities to successfully work with customers to deliver technology-enabled co-created platforms (Mazur and Zaborek, 2014).

The four main building blocks or groups of competences that companies should develop to effectively engage in value co-creation with customers are dialogue, access, risk assessment and transparency, which taken together form the DART acronym and represent a model that has been widely followed. Dialogue represents interactivity between two equal problem solvers, eager to act together and learn. Access implies facilitating co-creation by offering the right tools for communication between customers and suppliers, and it also entails those marketing solutions that result in increased freedom of choice for customers. Risk assessment refers to the customer's right to be fully informed about the risks they face from accepting the value proposition. Transparency represents a retreat from the information asymmetry usually apparent between the customer and supplier and practicing openness of information.

Airbnb and hotels

Airbnb's relationship with the traditional hotel industry is complicated and has evolved over time. Hotel executives have glanced enviously over their shoulders at the high-tech start-up's eye-watering advances in valuation, but Airbnb itself has gone out of its way to stress that it is *not* a hotel and that it can benignly co-exist with them. In doing so, Airbnb is implying that its presence is responsible for expanding the entire demand for accommodation, as opposed to directly taking market share from hotels. Brian Chesky is reportedly fond of saying that 'for us to win hotels don't have to lose' (Gallagher, 2017:140). In supporting this contention, Airbnb maintains that its guests tend to stay longer, group sizes are larger and many properties are in areas that are poorly served by existing hotel chains.

For the most part, however, the hospitality industry was relatively slow in recognizing the potential threat that Airbnb might pose. However, a company selling millions of rooms in mainly urban locations to 'millennials' (who set trends for others and who will continue to consume for many decades) is bound to have a significant impact on existing providers in the marketplace. Increasingly, hotels have begun to catch on and respond to the new competition in various ways. The launch of a number of new subbrands in recent years by many of the major internationally diversified chains (such as Moxy and W by Marriott, Andaz by Hyatt, Tryp by Wyndham) can be viewed as a response to the new competition. The new brands are often urban focused and aimed at younger travelers, and their branding and images are distinct from the 'umbrella' brand.

The octogenarian chairman of Marriott International Hotels (speaking in 2015) recognized the potential impact of Airbnb when he was quoted as saying that 'it's a real disruptor for us' while noting that in Orlando, for instance, Airbnb had more rooms available than Marriott, with anyone owning a condominium property renting out their properties through the Airbnb site (Gallagher, 2017:42).

Disruptive innovation

Airbnb's innovative approach can be viewed through the lens of the disruptive innovation theory, which was proposed and popularized by Clayton Christensen in several seminal works (Bower and Christensen, 1995; Christensen, 1997). This theory outlines a process through which a disruptive product transforms a market, sometimes to the point of destroying previously dominant companies. Digital camera technology, for example, destroyed Kodak's dominant position in film products.

A disruptive product will, in general, initially underperform with regard to the prevailing product's key performance attributes but will offer a distinct set of benefits, typically focused around being cheaper, more convenient or simpler (Guttentag, 2015). Consequently, the disruptive product appeals to the low end of the market or creates a completely new market that is limited in size and profit margins. As such, it lacks appeal for the larger companies because they are content to focus on more profitable markets and continue with marginal product improvements through sustaining innovations. The disruptive product improves over time, which makes it appealing to more numerous customers. This shift toward the mainstream market may eventually attract attention from the leading companies, but the position of the disruptive product may be so entrenched by this time that the previously leading companies may struggle to compete (Guttentag, 2015).

Thus, disruptive innovation theory describes how companies may falter, not by falling behind the pace of advancement or ignoring their core consumers but rather by disregarding the upward encroachment of a disruptive product that lacks in traditionally favored attributes but offers alternative benefits (Schmidt and Druehl, 2008). Another facet of the disruption concerns the use of data. Airbnb (and the online travel intermediaries) generally compiles so-called big data more effectively than the hotel brands, allowing it to facilitate personalization.

The rise of online travel intermediaries (such as Expedia, Travelocity and Booking.com) illustrates the point. These websites cannot match the personalized service of a traditional physical travel agency, but they offer potential convenience and cost-savings (Guttentag, 2015). Previous concerns relating to aspects such as the security of booking travel reservations online have been assuaged, and over time these online travel agencies have captured an increasing share of the mainstream market (Law et al., 2004). Accordingly, online travel agencies have contributed to a significant decline in the number of traditional travel agencies, and those that remain have been forced to focus more specifically on complex and higher value purchases (Kracht and Wang, 2010).

The Airbnb effect

Hotel companies are now paying attention to 'the Airbnb effect'. Its true impact (and those of its imitators) is hard to gauge, because studies are few and the various factors involved are complex and difficult to unravel. Evidence from the studies that do exist and more anecdotal and journalistic evidence indicate that Airbnb is having a significant effect and that this impact goes beyond the hotel industry (as its closest rival) to encompass local communities and the urban property markets of tourist destinations. Furthermore, the wider impact has, in some cases, led to the intervention of policymakers, community groups and protestors.

One study that focused on Airbnb's entry into the Texas market (Zervas et al., 2017) showed that it had a quantifiable negative impact on local hotel revenues. The study also concluded that Airbnb represented a viable alternative for certain traditional types of overnight accommodation. However, the competitive threat posed by Airbnb to traditional hotels was not evenly spread across the quality spectrum of hotels. The study pinpointed lower-end hotels as those that are most vulnerable to increased competition from rentals enabled by firms like Airbnb.

Some European cities (such as Amsterdam, Berlin, London, Paris and Barcelona) are swamped by summer tourists, and though they welcome spending in the local economy, they can also produce a hostile reaction from local communities. Though Airbnb has not been the sole reason for the reaction of inhabitants, it has been seen as a reason for concern. As an article in *The Economist* put it: 'In several cities a theme has emerged. Airbnb out-of-towners warp districts and upset residents.

Grocery shops and libraries that cater for locals are replaced by identikit cafés and bike-rental outlets that serve tourists' ('Charlemagne: The Backlash against Airbnb', 2018). Whole areas of some of the leading tourist cities are colonized by Airbnb (with a reported 18% of all properties in Central Florence, for example, listed on the site), and residents are squeezed out as landlords favor high-value, short-term lets over long-term renters. In 2015, the new mayor of Barcelona promised to clamp down on the excesses of mass tourism, starting with Airbnb by fining it for letting out unregistered properties.

Challenges for Airbnb

In several cities, legislators have also tried to limit Airbnb's activities. Opposition to the firm is fierce in many big cities, especially those that have limited access to affordable housing, where residents blame Airbnb for taking apartments off the market. Several cities that could supply large profits, including Berlin, Barcelona and New York, have imposed rules that make offering short-term rentals difficult. New York, for example, which is Airbnb's third-largest market, has banned short-term rentals in apartment buildings for less than 30 days, unless a host is present. Berlin has passed a ban and requires a permit if someone wants to rent more than half of their apartment on a short-term basis. Airbnb has now opted for a new, more conciliatory approach, as Gallagher (2017), noted. In Amsterdam and London, it has agreed to police its listings to ensure that they comply with local laws on the number of days a year each unit can be rented. However, investors are concerned that more restrictive laws will dampen Airbnb's prospects.

The firm was conceived as a marketplace for renting spare rooms to tourists, but at issue is the way its business model has evolved. Entrepreneurs were quick to spot a lucrative opportunity, acquiring portfolios of empty properties and offering them as a direct, often cheaper, competitor to hotels while obtaining high short-term rents for their properties. According to data gathered by Tom Slee, author of a book on the sharing economy, 27% of Airbnb listings in New York are offered by people who own multiple properties, and the pattern is replicated in other key cities for Airbnb (Slee, 2017).

A 'customer-facing' business such as Airbnb (in common with other such businesses), faces the obvious risks to its future from catastrophic failure of some kind. Such failures might stem from a major data breach, a safety hazard at Airbnb's properties or a barrage of media criticism of its services. As the company has grown, controlling the risks has become more complex, and detractors and competitors are paying more attention to the company's activities. It is uncertain what the future might hold for managing business risks and dealing with actual and potential regulatory barriers and additional taxation, but one thing is abundantly clear: Airbnb will face additional competitive pressures in its core business.

Dozens of other companies (some predating Airbnb itself) have flooded the market with 'me-too' offerings, though none have captured the global reach currently enjoyed by Airbnb. Airbnb has sought growth by rapid organic expansion but also by targeted acquisitions, such as two that were completed before the pandemic in 2020: Hotel Tonight, a website for booking 'last-minute' hotel rooms, and Gaest, based in Aarhus, Denmark, which provides a platform for posting and booking venues for meetings and other events.

Knowledgeable and well-connected local competitors have sprung up (in China, Europe and North America) to serve many of the local markets in which Airbnb competes. Serious competition is also being provided by some of the travel industry's heavyweights. Three American-based companies are targeting Airbnb's short-term rental markets. TripAdvisor, itself a subsidiary of media giant Liberty, acquired HouseTrip (now renamed Holiday Lettings), and in fall 2015 Expedia acquired HomeAway for a hefty $3.9bn, a long-established site with over 1.2 million listings, and has subsequently acquired further rental companies in other markets such as CanadaStays (in 2019). However, perhaps the most fearsome potential competitor is Booking Holdings. The Connecticut-based company, owner of Booking.com (and a plethora of other sites), is valued at over $90bn and has been steadily building up a stock of non-hotel accommodation to offer as part of its inventory.

Hotels have also been taking the competitive threat of Airbnb seriously, and several, including Holiday Inn parent IHG, Wyndham (owner of many brands including Days Inn and Ramada) and Hyatt have acquired short-term rental companies. The most aggressive entry into the short rental P2P market, however, is the French hotel group Accor (which trades under a number of brands, including Sofitel, Novotel and Ibis). After two small forays into the market in Europe and America, the hotel group bought full control of Onefinestay in 2016 for $170mn. The Accor CEO was quoted as saying, 'It would be absolutely foolish to fight against any new concept like this, let alone fighting against the sharing economy' (Gallagher, 2017:154).

The COVID-19 pandemic had a profound impact on Airbnb, as with all travel and hospitality companies worldwide, though because its long-term prospects look favorable, the company was able to successfully float on the New York stock market during this period. Bookings dropped as much as 96% in some cities, though it rose in many rural areas. In March 2020 the company pledged $250mn in payouts to hosts to compensate them for guest cancellations due to the pandemic, and in April 2020, due in part to the decline in business from the pandemic, Airbnb raised $1bn in equity from private equity firms and $1bn in debt. During 2020, approximately 1,900 employees, or about 25% of its workforce in the Americas, Europe and Asia, were laid off. However, in December 2020 the company became a public company via an initial public offering, raising $3.5bn.

Airbnb – a challenging future?

The success of networked platforms such as Airbnb owes a great deal to a number of underlying drivers: technological advancements, sociocultural change and globalization (Oskam and Boswijk, 2016). Though the ways in which these drivers manifest themselves will be subject to change, they will remain as important themes into the future. These drivers will certainly continue to fuel the Airbnb phenomenon in the near future. What is less certain is how platforms such as Airbnb will be able to compete when faced with an uncertain landscape of competitors and increased regulatory pressures.

What does seem clear is that Airbnb's future development will not follow a 'one-size-fits-all' approach. How it competes in the different markets in which it operates will have to be flexible and varied in response to the differing challenges of local markets. Differential regulatory circumstances, community acceptance and different rates of tourism growth will require an adjustment in the business model to the individual circumstances. Some 62% of Airbnb's guests are 34 years old and younger, but as these guests and the company head toward greater maturity the challenge for the company will be how it is able to attract the next generation of travelers. However, further expansion of the brand is possible by rolling out the brand to different geographical areas. Co-founder and CEO Brian Chesky has identified Asia-Pacific as having huge growth potential, the Latin America market is expanding and Africa will become an important geographical area for the sector in the next 10 to 20 years.

To Oskam and Boswijk (2016), this differential positioning of the brand can be viewed on two dimensions: tourism demand and regulation, which give rise to four possible scenarios: 'status quo', 'experimentation', 'exclusivity' and 'commercialization'. The firm ultimately appears to aim to evolve from a platform for overnight stays into a comprehensive travel company, capturing an ever-greater share of tourists' spending. The company has made important strides in that direction, and business travelers are one target. Airbnb has made it easier for firms to place roving employees in hosts' rooms instead of in hotels, and it has set up partnerships with companies such as Hyundai and Domino's pizza chain to make it easier to find rooms that are suitable for their employees. Employees from 250,000 companies now regularly book travel on Airbnb ('A Different Breed of Unicorn', 2017), but many companies still view Airbnb's diverse offerings as lacking the consistency of delivery around the world that many companies demand.

The firm bought Canadian holiday rental site Luxury Retreats in February 2017 for around $300mn with the intent to appeal to wealthier travelers. The purchase brought a portfolio of expensive luxury urban and resort properties into Airbnb's orbit. However, the company faces important choices between the quantity and quality of its listings. Being the 'go-to' company for mass market travelers requires ever more inventory in mid-range properties, and in moving up-market it could alienate its existing core travelers.

Speculation about other potential revenue streams for Airbnb abounds. A move into airline bookings has been rumored, but this represents a notoriously low-margin business. Existing key platforms in the field (such as Expedia and sites operated by Booking Holdings) make most of their profits from hotel bookings rather than air tickets. The company has also moved tentatively into sales of ancillary services for tourists such as selling experiences at their destination, but there are many other possibilities in this highly diverse field of operations.

February 2019 saw Airbnb move into the meetings field for the first time with the acquisition of Gaest.com, a Danish platform for short-term meeting space rentals. It marks Airbnb's first big move into office spaces, where it competes with existing major brands in the field such as WeWork (which lets nomadic workforces rent out desk space and meeting rooms for short periods). On the face of it, meetings offer another appealing sector for a disruptor such as Airbnb because the sector is highly fragmented, with many small operators and poorly developed technology solutions. However, Airbnb would have to overcome significant hurdles if it were to have the same impact it has had in the short-term rental market.

Gaest, founded in Denmark in 2015, allows guests to book spaces for meetings and miscellaneous events. Like Airbnb, Gaest lets hosts list their own spaces for rent, based on the idea that meeting planners and mangers will pay a premium for interesting, new and innovative venues. Though diversification into meetings and events appears a logical step for Airbnb, buying a relatively small Danish platform in a notoriously fragmented field (event management) does not appear to be the key strategic move some had expected from Airbnb. Though the industry is ripe for an integrated approach and the introduction of an innovative disruptor, there is no indication, at least so far, that Airbnb will provide the impetus in this case.

Airbnb has risen very fast to establish its global platform, but potential investors, looking to the future rather than the past, query the sources of future growth as established hotel groups, numerous new start-ups and powerful existing travel brands encircle the company as regulatory pressures increase. Initially the website attracted cost-conscious millennials looking for more authentic travel experiences, but growth now depends on broadening its base.

In a 2023 interview, Brian Chesky stated, 'My general principle is I want the moat to get deeper every year and that means that every year, we need to give away more value than we're charging' (Schaal, 2023). The term 'moat', popularized by well-known business investor Warren Buffett, refers to a business's ability to maintain competitive advantages over its competitors to protect its long-term profits and market share. Just like a medieval castle, the moat serves to protect those inside the fortress and their riches from outsiders (www.Investopedia.com).

Airbnb offers its hosts a higher level of damage protection insurance than its key competitors with its 'AirCover' insurance and 24/7 support. It is likely that the company will also offer more free services to hosts and provide more value so that eventually it can start selling new or enhanced products to hosts as well. Undoubtedly, for both hosts and guests the Airbnb brand, which is extremely hard to replicate, is among its major advantages. The number of services available to guests, such as travel insurance, excursions and activities, is also likely to expand.

Airbnb has hitherto avoided having significant amounts of digital advertising on its pages and consequently earns negligible income from this source. Some might argue that this purity and clarity is part of its attraction, but it provides a point of contrast for Airbnb vs some of its key competitors such as Expedia and Booking.com. Such advertising is a significant portion of Booking.com's income, for example (and also for comparators such as Amazon, Etsy and Alibaba), and this income allows them to pay for higher ranking listings on search engines. However, Chesky urged some caution in this respect when he stated, 'I'd want it to be much more targeted and really abide by user experience principles and be very, very careful over turning that dial too quickly' (Schaal, 2023).

Airbnb's use of technology was groundbreaking when it first launched. Its ranking of accommodation using machine learning and various parameters such as location, accommodation type, price and size of party allows customers to quickly and accurately assess huge quantities of data using a simple user-friendly interface. But technology moves on, and competitors quickly copied both the look and the functionality of the Airbnb website and app. The application of artificial intelligence (AI) offers the possibility of another huge step forward, and if not grasped by Airbnb, it will surely be applied by others. AI searches allow users to obtain results based on their past behaviors, devices, locations and hundreds of other factors. Thus, search engines powered by AI increasingly know what users are likely to want.

Airbnb faces many competitors and challenges for future growth, and how the company will develop is uncertain. Its growth and culture (as a private company) have been closely linked with its founders, and staff at Airbnb are apt to refer to the 'Airbnb community' to describe its employees, hosts and customers. The company arranges an annual 3-day festival – Airbnb Open – for its employees and hosts (who attend at their own expense), at which speakers from inside and outside the organization make presentations and provide entertainment. Whether these ways of working will survive as the company grows ever larger and as a public company has external shareholders to satisfy remains to be seen.

REFERENCES AND WEBSITES

References

Bailetti, T. (2012) 'What technology startups must get right to globalize early and rapidly', *Technology Innovation Management Review*, 2(10): 5–16.

Bower, J. L. and Christensen, C. M. (1995) 'Disruptive technologies: Catching the wave', *Harvard Business Review*, Jan-Feb: 43–53.

Christensen, C. M. (1997) *The Innovator's Dilemma: When New Technologies Cause Great Firms to Fail*, Boston: Harvard Business School Press.

'Charlemagne: The Backlash against Airbnb: Protests Will Meet Holidaymakers' (2018) *The Economist*, 19 July, www.economist.com.

'A Different Breed of Unicorn' (2017) *The Economist*, 27 May, www.economist.com.

Frenken, K., Meelen, T., Arets, M. and Glind, P. V. (2015) 'Smarter regulation for the sharing economy', *The Guardian*, 20 May, www.theguardian.com.

Frenken, K. and Schor, J. (2017) 'Putting the sharing economy into perspective', *Environmental Innovation and Societal Transitions*, 23: 3–10.

Gallagher, L. (2017) *The Airbnb Story: How to Disrupt an Industry, Make Billions of Dollars and Plenty of Enemies*, London: Virgin Books.

Guttentag, D. (2015) 'Airbnb: Disruptive innovation and the rise of an informal tourism accommodation sector', *Current Issues in Tourism*, 18(12): 1192–1217.

Guttentag, D. A. and Smith, S. L. (2017) 'Assessing Airbnb as a disruptive innovation relative to hotels: Substitution and comparative performance expectations', *International Journal of Hospitality Management*, 64: 1–10.

Kaplan, A. M. and Haenlein, M. (2010) 'Users of the world, unite! The challenges and opportunities of social media', *Business Horizons*, 53(1): 59–68.

Kracht, J. and Wang, Y. (2010) 'Examining the tourism distribution channel: evolution and transformation', *International Journal of Contemporary Hospitality Management*, 22(5): 736–757.

Law, R., Leung, K. and Wong, R. (2004) 'The impact of the internet on travel agencies', *International Journal of Contemporary Hospitality Management*, 16(2): 100–107.

Mazur, J. and Zaborek, P. (2014) 'Validating DART model', *International Journal of Management and Economics*, 44(1): 106–125.

Oskam, J. and Boswijk, A. (2016) 'Airbnb: The future of networked hospitality businesses', *Journal of Tourism Futures*, 2(1): 22–42.

Prahalad, C. K. and Ramaswamy, V. (2004) *The Future of Competition: Co-Creating Unique Value with Customers*, Boston: Harvard Business Press.

Schaal, D. (2023) 'CEO Brian Chesky wants to deepen moat between Airbnb and competitors', 7 March, www.Skift.com/.

Schmidt, G. M. and Druehl, C. T. (2008) 'When is a disruptive innovation disruptive?' *Journal of Product Innovation Management*, 25(4): 347–360.

Schor, J. (2016) 'Debating the sharing economy', *Journal of Self-Governance and Management Economics*, 4(3): 7–22.

Slee, T. (2017) *What's Yours Is Mine: Against the Sharing Economy*, London: Scribe Publications.

Varma, A., Jukic, N., Pestek, A., Shultz, C. J. and Nestorov, S. (2016) 'Airbnb: Exciting innovation or passing fad?' *Tourism Management Perspectives*, 20: 228–237.

Whittington, R., Regnér, P., Angwin, D., Johnson, G. and Scholes, K. (2020) *Exploring Strategy*, 12th ed., Harlow, UK: Pearson.

Wyman, D., Mothorpe, C. and McLeod, B. (2022) 'Airbnb and VRBO: The impact of short-term tourist rentals on residential property pricing', *Current Issues in Tourism*, 25(20): 3279–3290.

Zervas, G., Proserpio, D. and Byers, J. W. (2017) 'The rise of the sharing economy: Estimating the impact of Airbnb on the hotel industry', *Journal of Marketing Research*, 54(5): 687–705.

Websites

www.airbnb.com
www.economist.com
www.ft.com
www.investopedia.com

Appendix 1 Platform market structure and orientation

		Platform market structure	
		Peer to peer	Business to peer
Platform orientation	Non-profit	Timebanks	Makerspace
	For profit	Turo	Zipcar

Figure 1 – Case 6

Source: Adapted from Schor (2016)

- *Makerspace* is a physical location where people gather to co-create, share resources and knowledge, work on projects, network, and build.
- *Timebanking* is a way of spending one hour of time helping someone out by, for example, mowing someone's lawn or doing their shopping. For every hour spent, you earn an hour in return. This can be spent on receiving an hour of someone else's time.
- *Turo* is an American-based peer-to-peer carsharing company.
- *Zipcar* provides vehicle reservations to its members, billable by the minute, hour or day; members may have to pay a monthly or annual membership fee in addition to car reservations charges.

Appendix 2 Airbnb: key metrics

Airbnb key metrics			
	2020	2021	2022
Nights and experiences booked	193.2mn	300.6mn	393.7mn
Gross booking value	$23.9bn	$46.9bn	$63.2bn
Revenue	$3.4bn	$6.0bn	$8.4bn
Net income (loss)	$(4.6)bn	$(352)mn	$1.9bn
EBITDA	$(251)mn	$1.6bn	$2.9bn

Appendix 3 Business model conceptualization

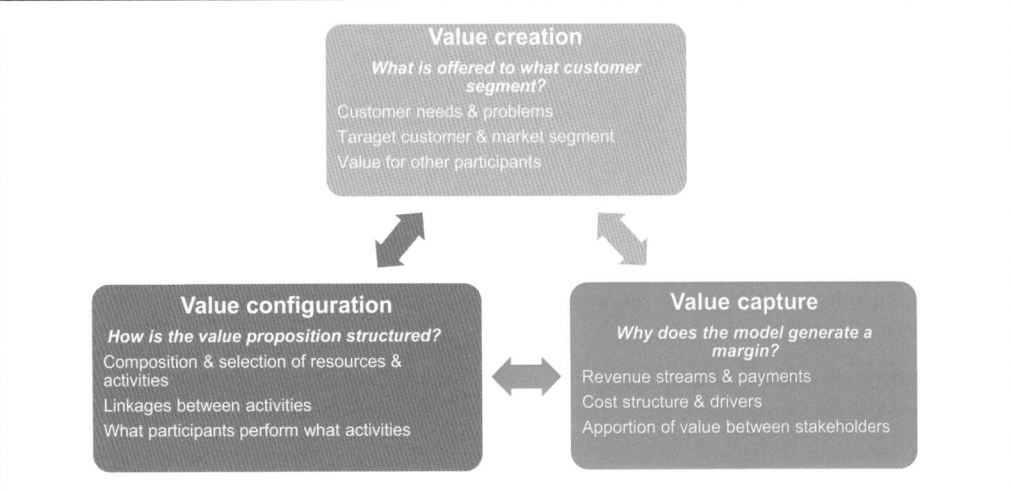

Figure 2 – Case 6

Business models describe business transactions and interrelationships between various parties internal to the organization and externally. To Whittington et al. (2020), business models are best explained as three interrelated components. The first component, *value creation*, represents a proposition that addresses a specific customer segment's needs and problems and those of other participants. Value *configuration* deals with how the resources and activities are configured to produce this value, and *value capture* seeks to explain revenue streams and cost structures that allow stakeholders to gain a share of the total value generated.

Appendix 4 Airbnb: scenarios for development

Oskam and Boswijk (2016) presented four possible scenarios of the environment faced by Airbnb in particular locations that will impact how the company develops. The possible development scenarios are based on the regulatory regime Airbnb faces and the relative growth of tourism demand.

- **Status quo:** Some locations are characterized by relatively stable tourism demand and a repressive regulatory environment toward Airbnb.

  For example: *Stuttgart is an example of a mid-sized European city with modest tourist activity and a hotel industry mainly catering to business travelers. Regulatory controls in resident areas have prevented Airbnb from becoming important in the city. Thus, 'business as usual' is maintained and the city's tourism will maintain its moderate growth trajectory.*

- **Experimentation:** Some locations are characterized by relatively stable tourism demand and no regulation or a welcoming attitude toward Airbnb.

  For example: *Portland, Oregon, reached an agreement with Airbnb to collect taxes and to impose basic safety regulations and closely cooperated with the rental company to promote the city internationally.*

- ***Exclusivity:*** Some locations are characterized by booming tourism demand and a relatively repressive regulatory attitude toward Airbnb.

  For example: *Barcelona's growing irritation with mass tourism culminated in a moratorium on hotel investments and a harsh crackdown on illegal short-term rentals in 2015. Frozen supply and growing demand allowed existing hotels to raise rates. Because new hotels could not be built, investors concentrated on upscaling two- and three-star hotels. The local authorities face the same challenge as previously: how to avoid tourism from displacing local residents from the city center. Barcelona City Council launched its Strategic Plan for Tourism 2020, which recognizes the city's dependence on tourism, but acknowledges that it must move away from constant promotion and increasing numbers and focus more on governance to ensure that tourism is sustainable.*

- ***Commercialization:*** Some locations are characterized by booming tourism demand and relatively light regulation or a welcoming attitude toward Airbnb.

  For example: *Amsterdam embraced P2P rentals during the financial crisis when it helped homeowners afford their mortgages. Airbnb was also seen as a means to increase visitor numbers and to spread tourist spend. The abundant availability of nontraditional accommodation also inspired numerous innovative hotel concepts and spin-offs for other creative businesses. But residential rental prices went up as landlords started to include an 'Airbnb premium' in popular tourist areas. This Airbnb premium has also been reported in other geographies such as South Carolina (Wyman et al., 2022). Tourism growth meant an investment opportunity for investors, who started building portfolios of popular Airbnb listings by purchasing properties.*

GLOSSARY

Acquisition The purchase of a controlling interest of one business's shares by another. The acquired business becomes a subsidiary of the acquirer but may be subsequently absorbed fully into the parent's structure.

Added value The difference between the full cost of a product and its financial value to the market. High added value is one of the objectives of strategy. It tends to be measured in terms of profit.

Annual report and accounts Audited annual communication between a limited company and its shareholders. In the UK, it has five compulsory statements by law (the chairman's statement, the auditor's statement, the profit and loss statement, the balance sheet and the cash flow statement).

Augmented benefits Benefits added to core (or basic) benefits that are intended to differentiate a product.

Backward vertical development The acquisition of one or more parts of the backward direction in the supply chain. This is typically done by acquisition of or merger with a supplier.

Barriers to entry Obstacles preventing entrant firms from being established in a particular market.

BCG matrix (Boston Consulting Group matrix) Framework used to rationalize and understand a business's product portfolio. It divides products according to their market share and the rate of market growth. Four categories are identified: stars (high market share in high growth market), cash cows (high market share in low growth market), question marks (low market share in high growth market) and dogs (low market share in low growth market).

Benchmarking A collection of techniques used to compare certain aspects of business practice and the transfer of good practice procedures from benchmark companies to 'followers'.

Breakeven point The point at which costs or expenses and revenue are equal; that is, there is no net loss or gain.

Business critical Those aspects of business that are viewed as crucial to the successful implementation of strategy.

Business ethics An area of research in which the nature of the relationship between business organizations and their role as moral agents is explored. It also describes research into the interface between business organizations and their social constituencies.

Capacity In *THE*, capacity refers to the number of people that can be accommodated in a hotel, aircraft, bus, resort, venue, etc. The important figure is how much of the capacity is actually used at any time. This can be measured in various ways but is usually expressed as the occupancy rate for accommodation and venues or the load factor for transportation.

Capital   The finance used to invest in a business with a view of making a return from it in future years. It is used to purchase the other resource inputs that enable an organization to carry out business activity.

Capital intensity   The amount of capital used in businesses relative to the other factors of production, particularly human resources.

Carrying capacity   The ability of a site, resort, region or country to absorb tourists without deteriorating. The notion of carrying capacity is central to the concept of sustainability.

Change agent   One of the models of change management wherein the change process is overseen and managed by a single individual (the change agent). Offers the advantages of specialist management of a change process and the personification of the need for change.

Clusters   In many industries, companies group together. Clusters are geographic concentrations of interconnected companies and institutions in a particular industrial field. They encompass an array of linked industries and other entities that are important to competition.

Collaboration   Businesses are said to collaborate when, instead of (or perhaps as well as) competing, they choose to work together in pursuit of both parties' strategic objectives.

Commercially sensitive   Confidential business information the disclosure of which may harm the business.

Competence building   Takes place when an organization builds new core competences, based on its resources and competences.

Competence leveraging   The ability of an organization to exploit its core competences in new markets or to modify and improve existing core competences.

Competences   The abilities that an organization possesses that enable it to compete and survive in an industry. Includes an element that is tangible (its physical resource base) and another that is intangible (know-how, networks, etc.).

Competitive advantage   The ability of an organization to outperform its competitors. It can be measured in terms of superior profitability, increase in market share or other similar performance measures.

Competitive positioning (school of thought)   The approach to business strategy that argues that an organization's success in strategy rests on how it positions itself in respect to its environment. This is in contrast to the resource-based approach.

Consortia/consortium   Various types of collaborative arrangements in which more than two organizations join together to undertake certain tasks (such as marketing and promotion) or for the duration of a certain project.

Contestable market   A contestable market is characterized by insignificant entry and exit barriers, so there are negligible entry and exit costs.

Core competences   Competences are core when they become the cause of the business's competitive advantage. Also called distinctive capabilities.

Corporate reports   *Same as annual report and accounts* (see above)

Cost–benefit analysis   One of the non-financial tools sometimes used in evaluating strategic options. It involves weighing up the benefits that will arise from a course of action against its costs.

Cost leadership (in generic strategy framework)   The approach to business that seeks to achieve higher than industry-average performance by keeping unit costs lower than those of competitors. It is characterized by an emphasis on the high-volume production of standard products.

Critical success factors (CSFs)   Those elements that are vital for a strategy to be successful.

Culture   The character or personality of an organization. A culture can be understood by examining its manifestations under the categories of the cultural web.

Delayering   Cutting costs through reducing the numbers of people employed, particularly at middle levels of the organization.

Deliberate strategy Strategy that is planned in advance and that follows a rational process through each stage from analysis through to implementation.

Demerger The disposal of a business (usually a subsidiary) by making it into a standalone business and selling it off, usually via a flotation.

Diagonal integration A process whereby firms use information technologies to logically combine services for best productivity.

Differentiation (in generic strategy framework) The approach to business that seeks to achieve higher than industry-average performance by being distinctive rather than cheap (more distinctive than competitors). It presupposes that markets will pay more for extra product features.

Disintermediation The removal of intermediaries in the supply chain, or 'cutting out the middleman', as it is often referred to. Customers can often deal directly with the supplier offering a service rather than through an intermediary such as a travel agent. This has been greatly facilitated through the growth of the Internet.

Distinctive capability See *core competence*.

Diversification Business growth that involves developing new products for new markets.

Dynamic capabilities The firm's ability to integrate, build and reconfigure internal and external competences/resources to address rapidly changing environments.

Earnings Profit after interest and tax. Attributable to the company's shareholders, who may elect to not withdraw the total earnings as dividends to leave some retained profit for future investment.

Economies of scale The benefits gained in unit costs (cost per item) of increases in size and, hence, the dilution of fixed costs.

Economies of scope The benefits gained in unit costs (cost per item) of increases in scope or number of services provided and, hence, the dilution of fixed costs.

Efficiency A comparison of a system's output to its inputs with a view to testing how well the input has been turned into output.

Emergent strategy Strategy that is not planned in advance and that arises from a consistent pattern of behavior.

Entry barriers The obstacles that a new entrant to an industry needs to negotiate to gain market entry. Examples include the cost of capital, the legal and regulatory obstacles, access to supply and distribution channels, the costs of competing (especially lack of scale economies), etc.

Environmental analysis Essentially the same as strategic analysis – an analysis of an organization's internal environment and its external macro environment and micro environment.

Experience effect Unit costs are reduced as companies learn from their experiences.

External analysis The analysis of the external environments in which an organization exists (micro and macro) with a view to identifying opportunities and threats.

External growth Growth of a business by merger or acquisition (in contrast to organic or internal growth).

Factors of production Inputs into an organizational process that make normal operation possible (otherwise called resources).

Fiscal policy Regulation of a national economy by the use of government revenues and expenditure.

Five forces analysis A conceptual framework for understanding an industry's or organization's position in respect to the forces in its micro environment. Can be used to explain the structure of the industry and the performance of competitors within it.

Focus strategy (in generic strategy framework) Competitive advantage gained through serving one (or few) market segments.

Foreign exchange risk Arises out of uncertainty about the future exchange rate between two currencies. The risk can be categorized as transaction, translation or economic (or political) exposure to risk.

Forward vertical development The acquisition of one or more parts of the forward direction in the supply chain. This is typically done by acquisition of or merger with a buyer.

Frame conditions Those conditions operating in the organization's commercial environment that frame (or influence) strategic decision making for a particular organization.

Franchising An arrangement for business growth where the idea or format is rented out (from a franchisor to a franchisee) rather than directly developed by the originator of the idea.

Generic strategy A distinctive posture that an organization adopts with regard to its strategy. It is suggested that superior performance arises from adopting a cost leadership or differentiation strategy with either a narrow or broad product and market scope.

Globalization The most extensive stage of business development in which an organization's interests are spread throughout the world and are configured to compete and respond to differing customer requirements in many different national and local cultures.

Heterogeneity of services Services, unlike mass-produced manufactured goods, are never identical. The human element and other factors in delivering services ensure that services will be heterogeneous; that is, varied.

Hierarchical congruence Objectives set at various levels must be aligned with each other in such a way that each level of organizational decision making contributes to the organization's overall strategic objectives.

Horizontal development Merger with or acquisition of a competitor or a business at the same stage of the supply chain. Increase in market share.

Hostile takeover An acquisition attempt that is not supported by the board of the target company.

Human resource One of four resource inputs that can be deployed to help create competitive advantage. Comprises the employees and any other people's skills that are used by the organization (such as consultancy skills that it has access to).

Human resource audit An investigation into the size, skills, structure and all other issues surrounding those currently employed by the organization.

Hybrid strategy An approach to generic strategy that adopts elements of both cost leadership and differentiation.

Implementation The part of the strategic process that involves carrying out the selected strategy. It involves making the requisite internal changes and reconfiguring the organization's resource base to make it possible.

Incremental change Organizational change that is carried out in many small steps rather than fewer large steps.

Industry A group of producers of close substitute products. The players in an industry compete against each other for resource inputs and in product markets.

Industry analysis Part of strategic analysis. The analysis of an industry, usually using the five forces framework, with a view to gaining a greater understanding of the micro environment.

Inseparability of services The production and consumption of service products are inseparable. The implication of this inseparability is that the consumers have direct experience of the production of the service in contrast to the production of a physical product.

Intangible resources Sometimes called intellectual resources – resource inputs that are not physical but that can be among the most important at causing competitive advantage. Examples include patents, legal permissions, licenses, registered logos, designs, brand names, etc.

Intangibility of services Services cannot normally be seen, touched, smelled, tasted, tried on for size or stored on a shelf prior to purchase. Their intangibility makes them harder to buy but easier to distribute.

Integration The collective name given to mergers and acquisitions. See also *diagonal integration*.

Intellectual resources See *intangible resources*.

Intermediaries   The individuals and companies that act as 'middlemen' by purchasing and packaging products and services and from their owners (the principals) and selling them on to customers. Travel agents and tour operators are examples of intermediaries.

Internal analysis   Part of strategic analysis (along with external analysis) wherein the internal parts are examined for strengths and weaknesses. The value chain framework is often used to assist the process.

Internal growth   Growth in the size of a business without the use of mergers and acquisition. It involves the reinvestment of previous years' retained profits in the same business venture.

Internationalization   Business growth involving development across national borders. Can be achieved by using market entry strategies such as exporting, direct investment, international joint ventures, alliances or franchising.

Job enrichment   Employees are given a greater deal of discretion or empowerment to make decisions

Job rotation   Employees rotate jobs between them so that teamwork is encouraged and knowledge and skills are gained.

Job sharing   Employees' jobs are shared between two or more employees, thereby sharing burdens and responsibilities.

Joint venture   A collaborative arrangement between two or more companies. JVs tend to be for limited time periods, usually for a project or similar. Can also take the form of multi-partner consortia.

Just-in-time   An operational philosophy that aims to carry out (usually) production without any waste. Sometimes called stockless production.

Key issues   The issues that 'fall out of' the SWOT analysis, which is, in turn, the summary of the strategic analysis. In practice, key issues are those issues that are the most pressing, the most important and the most critical.

Key performance indicators (KPIs)   Represent a measurement tool. They are measures that quantify management objectives and enable the measurement of strategic performance.

Leakages   Leakages in *THE* refers to the way in which revenue generated by *THE* activity is lost by the local, regional or national economy to the economies of other localities, regions or countries.

Licensing   The renting-out of a piece of intellectual property so that the licensee enjoys the benefits of the licensor's innovation upon the agreement of a royalty payment. Most commonly applied to recipes, formulations, brands (such as lager brands), etc. Not to be confused with franchising.

Limited liability   A type of liability that is limited to the amount that has been invested.

Macro environment   The outer 'layer' of environmental influence – that which can influence the micro environment. It comprises five categories of influence: sociodemographic, political, economic, natural and technological.

Management buyout   Occurs when a company is sold to its current management.

Management contracts   A popular form of joint development method whereby the ownership of the physical asset (such as a hotel or other accommodation) is separated from its management.

Market   The group of customers that a business or industry can sell its outputs to. Can also mean the specific part of a total market that an individual business sells to. In economics, market is taken to mean the 'place' or arena in which buyers and sellers come together.

Market segmentation   The practice of subdividing a total market up into smaller units, each of which shares a commonality of preference with regard to a buying motivation. Markets are segmented by applying segmentation bases – ways of dividing customers in a market from each other.

Market share   The proportion (usually expressed as a percentage) of the market for a product type held by a supplier to the market. Can be defined in terms of value of volume.

Mass tourism   Large-scale packaging of standardized leisure services at fixed prices for sale to a mass clientele

Mergers   A form of external growth involving the 'marriage' of two partners of (usually) approximately equal size. The identities of both former companies are merged into the new company.

Micro environment   The near or immediate business environment that contains factors that affect the business often and over which individual businesses may have some influence. Usually comprises competitors, suppliers and customers.

Mission statements   A formalized statement of the overall strategic purpose of an organization.

Moment of truth   See *service encounter*.

Near environment   See *micro environment*.

Objectives   The state of being to which an organization aims or purposes. It is the end to which strategy aims.

Oligopoly   A commercial environment in which a particular market is controlled by a small group of firms.

Operational objectives   To be distinguished from strategic objectives. The level of objective that tends to be short to medium term in timescale and that has the sole purpose of helping to achieve the higher-level strategic objective.

Opportunity cost   The cost of an alternative that must be forgone to pursue a certain action.

Organic growth   See *internal growth*.

Overtrading   Overtrading *often* occurs when companies expand their own operations too quickly and risk failure due to lack of financial resources.

Package holiday   A package holiday is a prearranged combination, sold or offered for sale at an inclusive price, including at least two of transport, accommodation and other tourist services ancillary to transport or accommodation.

Paradigm   The worldview or way of looking at the world held by an individual or organization. It is a very powerful determinant of the culture and behavior (and hence performance) of a business.

Perishability of services   Because production and consumption are simultaneous, services are instantly perishable if they have not been sold at the time of production.

Planned strategies   See *deliberate strategy*.

Portfolio   Can refer to the spread of interests in respect to products and markets. The principle behind any portfolio is to spread opportunity and risk with a view to making the organization less vulnerable to trauma in any one product or market segment and to enable it to be in the position to quickly exploit any opportunities.

Prescriptive strategy   See *deliberate strategy*.

Price elasticity of demand   The relationship between the price of a product and the quantity of the product sold. Price elastic products are those whose quantity sold is relatively price responsive. Price inelastic products are those where a change in price would be expected to bring about a proportionately lower change in quantity sold.

Product   The output of an organization intended for consumption by its markets. The result of the value adding process.

Product life cycle   The concept is based on the analogy with living things, in that all products would be expected to have a finite life, whether it is long or short, and that products move from introduction through growth toward maturity and eventually decline.

Profit   The surplus of sales against total costs. Tends to be measured either before or after tax.

Profit and loss account   One of the three compulsory financial statements in a company annual report. The profit and loss statement reports on the total sales, the costs incurred in creating those sales and hence (by subtraction), the profit made over a reporting period.

Profit Impact of Market Strategy (PIMS) study   On examining thousands of companies in many industries, this study found that one of the primary determinants of profitability is market share.

Public–private partnerships   Various forms of collaborative activity bringing public and private sector involvement together to develop assets and resources.

Quality   Usually defined as 'fitness for the purpose'. It is not to be defined in terms of luxury or premium.

Ratio analysis   A comparison (by quotient) of two items from the same set of accounts.

Related diversification   External growth by developing new products for new markets. Related diversification suggests that the new products or markets have something in common with existing products or markets such that the risk of diversification is lessened. Related diversification is in contrast to unrelated diversification.

Resource-based approach   A way of understanding the source of competitive advantage as arising from the way in which an organization obtains and deploys its resources to build and develop core competences.

Resource immobility   Many resources that are used cannot be moved in terms of either place or time.

Resource markets   The markets in which a business competes with other businesses for resource inputs. Examples include labor markets, real estate and property markets, finance markets (for capital), etc.

Resource substitution   The substitution of one resource category with those of another.

Resources   The key inputs into an organization that enable normal functioning to take place. There are four categories of resource: physical (e.g., stock, land, buildings, etc.), financial, human and intangible (or intellectual).

Retained profit   A balance sheet measure of the profit that is attributable to the shareholders once all other allocations are accounted for; that is, profit after interest, tax and extraordinary items.

Risk premium   The risk premium is the additional return an investor expects to receive from holding a risky investment instead of risk-free assets.

Satisficing   Behavior linked to the behavioral theory of the firm. In this view of the firm (which often applies to smaller companies), a critical level of profit is achieved by firms; thereafter, priority is attached to the attainment of other goals because the owners are satisfied with the levels of profit that have been achieved.

Selection of strategy   The second stage in the overall strategic process that takes the information gained in the strategic analysis and uses it to evaluate options and to decide upon the most appropriate option.

Service encounter   The time and place where the customer interacts with the organization.

SERVQUAL   A framework developed by to consider service quality.

Service profit chain   Assesses the sources of profitability and growth in labor-dominated service firms.

Stakeholder theory   The belief that the objectives of an organization are determined by the relative strengths of the various stakeholders.

Stakeholders   Any group or individual who can affect or be affected by the achievement of an organization's objectives.

STEEP analysis   The key stage in macro-environmental analysis. It involves auditing the macro environment for sociodemographic, political, economic, environmental and technological influences.

Stockholder position   The belief that business objectives should be determined predominantly for the financial benefit of the owners (shareholders). In practice, this position is taken to mean that the objectives of a business should be to maximize its profits.

Strategic alliance   A collaborative arrangement between (usually) two businesses where part or all of the two companies' value chains are shared for mutually beneficial strategic purpose.

Strategic analysis   The first part of the strategic purpose. Its purpose is to gather information about a business's internal and external environments so that sufficient information is available to make possible the informed evaluation of options.

Strategic congruence   The integration of multiple objectives either within an organization (at various levels) or between multiple groups so that they are aligned with each other.

Strategic groups   The subgroups within an industry that compete head on with each other for the same types of customers or for similar resource inputs. The members of a strategic group will normally consider an ongoing monitoring of each other's activities to be an essential part of their strategic analysis.

Strategic implementation   See *implementation*.

Strategic objectives   In contrast to operational objectives, strategic objectives are those pursued at the highest level of an organization. They concern the whole organization, are concerned with the overall product and market scope and tend to concern longer timescales than operational objectives.

Strategic options   Generated as part of the second stage of the strategic process (evaluation and selection). The options that are considered as possible courses of action for the future.

Strategic process   One way of looking at strategy is to conceptualize it as an iterative process. According to this view, the process has three distinct stages: strategic analysis, strategic evaluation and selection and then, finally, strategic implementation. In practice, all stages are carried out continually.

Strategic selection   See *selection*.

Strategy   There are a number of definitions of strategy, perhaps best understood in terms of Mintzberg's 5 Ps: plan, ploy, pattern, perspective and position. A strategy is usually taken to mean the process that is performed to close the gap between where an organization is now and where it aims to be in the future.

Strengths   Those internal features of an organization that can be considered to add to its ability to compete in its strategic group (or industry) and to increase its competitive advantage. Strengths are positive attributes that an organization owns.

Structure   The term used to describe the shape of an organization. In strategy, a consideration of structure usually refers to its height, width, complexity and the extent to which it is decentralized.

Stuck in the middle   A phrase used to describe the position of an organization that, in respect to the generic strategy framework, is neither purely cost leadership nor differentiation. It has been argued that to be stuck in the middle is to expose an organization to the probability or returning below-average profits because the organization experiences competition from those pursuing all other competitive strategies (narrow and broad, cost and differentiation). This view has been challenged.

Substitute products   Products that provide identical or comparable benefits to those of the organization's products.

Supply chain   Not to be confused with the value chain. Usually refers to the entire path that a product and its component parts take from the primary industry stage to when it is sold to the final consumer on the chain.

SWOT Analysis   Standing for strengths, weaknesses, opportunities and threats, it is the key technique for presenting the results of strategic analysis and provides a platform for going on to formulate the strategy for the future. Strengths and weaknesses should be based on the internal analysis of the organization, whereas the opportunities and threats should be based on an analysis of the organization's external environment.

Synergy   The effect that is observed after two or more parties (e.g., businesses in a merger) come together and the whole becomes greater than the sum of the parts. Sometimes expressed as $2 + 2 = 5$.

Targeting   When the possible range of segments has been identified and the characteristics of each of the segments has been analyzed, an organization then has to decide which market segments to target.

Tipping point   The critical point in a situation, process or system beyond which a significant effect or change takes place.

Tour operator   Tour operators purchase or reserve the separate components of a package holiday in bulk and combine these components into an 'inclusive tour' or package.

Tourist area life cycle (TALC)   Destinations go through a similar evolution to that of products, but visitor numbers are substituted for product sales. Destinations move from evolution through involvement, development and consolidation before reaching stagnation. Decline will follow unless actions are taken that result in rejuvenation.

Turnaround   A process dedicated to corporate renewal using analysis and strategy to turn troubled companies around and return them to solvency.

Unrelated diversification   External growth by developing new products for new markets. Unrelated diversification suggests that the new products or markets have little or nothing in common with existing products or markets such that the risk of diversification is increased but that portfolio benefits are maximized. Unrelated diversification is in contrast to related diversification.

Value adding   See *added value*.

Value chain analysis   A conceptualization of the internal activities of an organization. The framework divides the internal activities of an organization into two categories: those that directly add value (primary activities) and those that support the primary activities (support or secondary activities). The analysis of an organization's value chain is intended to show the strategic importance of any key linkages or any blockages – points where value is added less efficiently than it might be.

Vertical development   The acquisition of forward or backward competences such as through merger with, or acquisition of, a supplier (backward vertical development) or a customer (forward vertical development).

Waste   Anything that does not add value in an organizational process (such as machine inefficiencies, tooling up and tooling down, bad quality, stock, etc.).

Weaknesses   Those internal features of an organization that can be considered to detract from its ability to compete in its strategic group (or industry) and to reduce its competitive advantage. Weaknesses are negative attributes that an organization owns.

Weighted average cost of capital   The rate that a company is expected to pay on average to finance its assets weighted in accordance with proportion of finance provided.

Working capital   Working capital represents the difference between a company's current assets and current liabilities and is a measure of a company's liquidity and short-term financial health.

Subject index

Note: Page references in *italic* type refer to Figures; those in **bold** refer to Tables

3Rs (Reaction of shareholders, Returns, Risks) of acceptability 496–511
4Cs (complementary skills, cooperative cultures, compatible goals, commensurate levels of risk), partner selection for strategic alliances 452–453
4Ps (Product, Promotion, Price, Place) 247, *247*; SMEs 269; *see also* marketing mix
5Cs of credit (Character, Capacity, Capital, Collateral, Conditions) 217
5Ps of strategy (Mintzberg) 17–21
5Rs (Retirement, Retraining, Redeployment, Redundancy, Recruitment), human resource management 150
7 Days Inn 494
7-S model of performance (Peters and Waterman) 550–551, *551*
8Cs of strategic management presentation 631, **631**
9/11 terrorist attacks 53, 75–76, 415
2030 Agenda for Sustainable Development (UN) 620

Abu Dhabi, UAE 253, 647
acceptability (strategic evaluation) 486, **487**, *487*, 496–498; returns 496, 497–507; risk 496, 507–511, **509**
access 128
Accor Hotel Group 75–76, 111, 140–141, 190, *190*, 222, 314, 430, *471*, 606, 714
accounting rate of return 499, 501
accounts, presentation of 203–204; *see also* financial information; financial statements
ACORN (A Classification of Residential Neighborhoods) 237
adaptation, and change 545, *545*
advertising 241, 595
Aer Lingus 415
AerCap 180
Africa 68
age **234**, 310
AI (artificial intelligence) 127, 148–149, 285, 290, 716
Air Asia 28–29, 157, *182*, **183**
Air France/KLM 314, 431, 461
Air New Zealand 184–185, 200, *200*, 201, 292, 492, 510; financial analysis

194–195, *196*, *197*; refinancing *185*, 185–186
air pollution 297; *see also* GHG emissions
Air Travel Organisers' Licensing system, Civil Aviation Authority 324
Airbnb 128, 256, 329, 610, 685; case study 707–720
Airbus 258, 292
aircraft 292; emissions and air pollution 297, 505; leasing 96, 180, 313
Airline Deregulation Act of 1978, USA 300, 431, 648
airline industry 20–21, 92, 95, 97, 179, 211, 241, 253, 336, 461, 467, 492, 581, 595, 648, 649, 650; aircraft leasing 96, 180, 313; breakeven analysis 500, *501*; case study 646–655; codesharing agreements 445, 447, 452, 461, 466, 647, 648; collaborative process 448–449, *449*; cost leadership **378**, 378–379; deregulation 300, 431, 648, 649; economic factors **294**, 294–295; economic restructuring 648–649; foreign ownership restrictions 450, 489, 594,

596, 649, 655; frequent flyer programmes 56, 314, 382; jet fuel prices 509–510; low-cost 312, 328, 375, 378, **378**, 379, 431, 452, 513, 583, 647–648, 661; management contracts 465–466; outsourcing 120, 121–122, 577, 579; Porter's five forces model of industry analysis 327–328; seasonality *58*, 58–59; strategic alliances 184–185, 328, 445, 447–449, *449*, 450, 451–452, 489, 592, 646–655

airports 95, 105, 108, 253, 288, 330, 456, 579, 595, 647–648, 649, 650; environmental issues 295, 297, 298

airspace: national sovereignty and the five freedoms of the air 300, **300**, 655

AITO (Association of Independent Tour Operators) 78–79, 658

AITs (air-inclusive tours) 657

Alibaba 445–446

American Airlines 56, 291, 314, 382, 431, 489, 651

American Express 412, 575, 589

American Strategic Planning Institute 122

Amsterdam, Netherlands 720

ANA 179

Ansoff product-market matrix 484; diversification 400, *400*, 401, *408*, 408–414, *410*, *412*; market development 400, *400*, 401, 403–405; market penetration 400, *400*, 401, 402–403, *403*; product development 400, *400*, 401, 406–407

AR (augmented reality) systems 290–291, 591

arts, the, Ansoff product-market matrix 401–402

ASAs (air service agreements) 655

Ashfield Event Experiences 101, 102, 111

ASK (available seat kilometres) **294**

Asset: management 180, 313: ownership 180, 313

'asset stripping' 473

asset-light strategies 180, 339, 461, 470, 605, 606; IHG 462, 470, 683, 684, 685

assets: balance sheets 182; cash flow forecasting 213; disposal of non-core assets 473–474; strategic assets and distinctive capabilities 104–105

Assurance (RATER dimensions of service) 147

attendance rates 53, 54

attractions 61, *63*, **225**, 230, *261*, 297; joint developments 444, **444**

Australia 65, 68; *see also* Queensland, Australia

Australian: Council of National Trusts: stakeholders 38–39; Open tennis championships 138–139

authenticity 575

aviation 288, 300, 324; economic factors **294**, 294–295; infrastructure issues 287, 298; political factors 299–300, **300**; sustainability 197–198; technology advances 291–292

Avis 296, 460, 462

balance of payments 293

balance sheets *181*, 181–182, *182*, 198, 203

balance, strategic directions 419–420

Balearic Islands, Spain 65, 352, 353, 407

Baltimore Inner Harbor 457–458

Bangkok, Thailand 253

Bangladesh 352

Bank of England, Monetary Policy Committee 293

bankruptcy 415

banks 211

Barcelona, Spain 713, 720

barriers to entry 60, 253, 312–317, 380; SMEs 61, 77–78

BCD 589–590, 591, 596

BCG (Boston Consulting Group) matrix 122, 262–267, *263*, *264*, **266**, 399

benchmarking 99, 151–152, 197–198, 338

Bermuda Agreement, 1946 300

Best Western 129, 462–463, 467, 468, 606

Big Data 56, 127, 148, 231, 290, 712

blockchain 148, 285, 290, 291, 591

boards of directors **37**, 38, 40, 366, 496

Boeing 162, 179, 257–258, 292

bootstrap marketing 270

'born global' companies 608–610

Botswana 67, 68

brands 243, 382; brand loyalty 55–56, 313–314, 324, 336

breakeven analysis 499, 500–501, *501*

Brexit 299, 419

BRIC (Brazil, Russia, India and China) countries 73

British Airways 105, 309, 376, 431, 461, 489, 492, 651

Brundtland Report, 1987 295, 617

BSC (balanced scorecard) 123, 557–561, *560*, *561*, *562*, **563**, 563–564

BTG (Beijing Tourism Group) 494

Budget Travel 439

Burger King 460

Busan International Film Festival 456–457

business events 230, 577; *see also* MICE (meetings, incentive travel, conventions and exhibitions) industry

business objectives 26, **26**, 33

business travel 240–241, 252, 336, 589
business-to-business (B2B) marketing 238–239, 243, 694
business-to-peer (B2P) platforms 710
'buy, ally or DIY [do it yourself]' matrix 470–472, *471*
buyers' power 310, *311*, 317–318, 326, 327

CAA (Civil Aviation Authority) 324, 665
Calgary First Night Festival 543
California, US 329
Canada 343
CanadaStays 714
capabilities 99–100, 110;
capacity 53
capacity constraints 96; *see also* carrying capacity
capital 183, 190–191; cost of 191–193; loan capital 186–187, **187**, 192, 193; rights issue capital 184–186, *185*; share capital 183–184, 187, **187**, 192, 193
capital budgeting 528
capital intensity 179–181
car hire services 460–461, 467
carbon neutrality 296, 298, 621, 623; *see also* GHG emissions; sustainability
CARES evaluation criteria 486
Carlson group of companies 51, 454, 589
Carnival Corporation 180, 189, 190, *190*
carrying capacity 53, 70, 71, 96
case study analysis 638–645
cash flow 198, 485, 659; BCG matrix 263, 264, 265–266, **266**; seasonality of 57–58, 59
cash management 204, 209, 210, 211–212; cash flow forecasting 212–213, **213**, **214**, 215–216, 498
centralization 533, **533**, *533*, 565
CEOs 40, 198
change 544, *544*, 550; barriers to 539; change leadership

and management 519, 521, 523, 538–551, *539*, **541**, *544*, *545*, *548*, **549**, *551*; context of **541**, 541–546, *544*, *545*; inertia 544, *544*; Lewin's 3-step model *539*, 539–540; successful organizational change 547, *548*
change agents 549–551, *551*
charter airlines 661
chatbots 148, 149, 290, 591
Chicago Convention (Convention on International Civil Aviation), 1944 299, 300, 648
China 70, 120, 142–143, 316, 437, 445–446, 604; hotels 153–154, 475–476, 493–494, 606; human resources 139, 140, 153–154
Civil Aeronautics Board, USA 431, 648
climate change 67–69, 298; *see also* GHG emissions; sustainability
climatic factors 352–353
Club Med 407
clustering 170, 326, 328–331, 332–338, *333*, 346
co-creation of value 124, 127–128
collaboration 107, 307, 326, 334, 346, **370**, 427; airlines 448–449, *449*; SMEs 129–130, 475
collaborative consumption 128, 710
collaborative (cooperative) strategy 442
Colorado Convention Centre 455
combined market value 433
competences 87, 91, 99–100, *101*, 102–103, *103*, 113, 334; competence building 103, 104, 107; competence leveraging 103, 104, 394; competence-based strategy 389–392, **390**, *392*
competition 60, 94–95, 254

competitive advantage 35, 86, 89–90, 145, 296, 308–309, 366, 369, 388, 552, *552*; competences and capabilities 99–110, 389–392, **390**, *392*; competitive positioning 89, 90, 369, 439, 440; knowledge management 111–112;; Profit Impact of Market Strategy study 122, 123; relational approach 369, 439–440; resources 92–99, 388; service profit chain 122–124, *124*; service-dominant logic 124–128; SMEs 128–130; sources of 90–92; strategic marketing 220–221; sustainability 619, *620*; sustainable 91–92, 107–108, 109, 390–392, *392*, 619; value-adding activities 112–122; *see also* core competences
competitive environment analysis 3, 283–284, 307–308, 356; clustering 328–331; competitor profiling 339–341, **341–342**; CSFs (critical success factors) 342–344; industries 308–310; KPIs (key performance indicators) 343–344; markets 308–309; Porter's five forces model of industry analysis 310–328, *311*, *321*, *322*, **326**; resource-based approach 332–338, *333*; SMEs 344–346, *345*; strategic group analysis 308–309, 338–339
competitive positioning 89, 90, 369, 392, 439, 440
competitive strategy 366, *367*, 368–369, 372, 482, 483, 484; competence-based strategy 389–392, **390**, *392*; *THE* contexts 370, **370–372**; core competence, generic strategy and the value chain 392–394, **393**; Porter's generic strategies

369, *373*, 373–389, *374*, **378**, **385**, *389*, 580, 582–584, *583*, *584*; SMEs 394–396, *396*; strategy clock framework 388, *389*
competitors 323, 326, 334, 339, 595, 596; monitoring of 323; profiling of 339–341, **341–342**, 345, 346; rivalry between 310, *311*, 320–325, *321*, *322*, 328; SMEs 344–345
consortia 270; *see also* cooperation; strategic alliances
consumer behaviour 237
contestability, of markets 60, 315
Contiki Tours 233, 384, 622–623
contingency planning 76
continuous improvement 107
control 301–302, 354–355
conventions *see* MICE (meetings, incentive travel, conventions and exhibitions) industry
cooperation 326, 440; cooperative networks 443–444, **444**, 466–469, *467*
COP26 UN Climate Change Conference, Glasgow, Scotland, 2021 68
core activities, value-adding 119–122
core competences 91, 99–100, 100–103, 101, *101*, *103*, 106–107, 108, 113, 118, 186, 308, 310, 369, 394, 439, 552; competence-based strategy 389–392, **390**, *392*, 393, **393**
corporate governance 39–40, 366
corporate objectives 26, **26**, 33–35
cost leadership strategy 373, *373*, *374*, 374–380, **378**, **385**, 386, 387, 388, 393, **393**, 395, 484; global 582, **583**
cost of capital 191–192; WACC (weighted average cost of capital) 193

cost-benefit analysis 504–506
country differentiation 604, *605*
COVID-19 pandemic, impacts of 53, 73–75, 139, 148, 287, 294, 421, 580; Air New Zealand 184, 185, 194–195; Airbnb 714; Best Western 468; crisis response strategies 416, **417**, 417–418, **418**; Expedia Group 376; Las Vegas hotel occupancy rates 322, *322*; Lufthansa 545–546; TUI 474; Whitbread plc 341
creative clusters 329; *see also* clustering
'CRIME' (Communicable, Realistic, Internally Consistent, Measurable, Explicit) objectives 34
crisis management 75, 77
Croatia 595
cross-sectional analysis 194, 196–199, 203
crowdsourcing 259
CRSs (computer reservation systems) 648
cruising 317, 324, **371**, 380, 427, 513; sustainability 297, 621–622; *see also* shipping
CSF (critical success factors) 137, 152–155, 342–344; SMEs 344
CSR (corporate social responsibility) 35, 39, 296, 495, 618–619
CTM (corporate travel management) companies 589–590, 591, 596
'cultural dimensions theory' (Hofstede) 166–169, **168**
cultural distance 604
cultural web *160*, 160–163
customer loyalty 123, 314, 316, 382
customer satisfaction 123, 147
customer service 49–50, 52, 120; guest-employee encounter management 143–145, **144**, *145*; 'moments of truth' 144–145, *145*
'customer-centric' view 127, 128

customers 336, 590, 595; definition of markets by **225**, 225–226; and globalization 573, 588–590; power of 310, *311*, 317–318; switching costs 313–314, 316–317, 318; wants and needs 226, 334
Cyprus 385

DART (dialogue, access, risk assessment and transparency) 711
DCF (discounted cash flow) methods 499, 501–502
debt finance 186–187, 192, 193
decision making, levels of *21*, 21–23, **22**, 24–25, 483
declining markets 402, 485
deglobalization 580, 611
'degrees of turbulence' model, SMEs 302
deliberate (prescriptive) strategy 19, 486, 511, 628
Delta Airlines 431, 489
demand 53, 57, 96, 118, 221; demand conditions, Porter's diamond framework 585, *585*, 586
demergers 433, 472–473
demography 285, 287, demographic segmentation 336
Denver Performing Arts Complex 455
deregulation 300, **371**, 378, 431, 489, 576, 594, 648, 649
destination organizations 62, *63*, 444, **444**
destinations/destination marketing 230, 297, 313, 329, 343, **371**, 513, 695; 'eventful cities' 157–158; improving competitiveness of 586–587; positioning 244–245, **245–246**; Queensland, Australia 245, **245–246**, 668–680; strategy mapping 560–561, *562*, 563, **563**; TALC (tourism area life cycle) 254–255

diagonal diversification 411–412, *412*, diagonal integration 575
diamond framework, Porter *585*, 585–587
differentiation 241, 313, 324, 387, 604, *605*; global 582, **583**
differentiation strategy 373, *373*, 374, *374*, 380–384, **385**, 386, 387, 388, 392, 395, 484
digital platforms, exhibitions industry 696–697
direct marketing 241
direct substitutes 316, 317
Discover Halifax, Nova Scotia 563, **563**
disintermediation 256, **371**, 375, 648
disposals 472–474
disruptive innovation 256, 711–712
distinctive capabilities 99, 101, 104–106, 106–107, 308
distribution channels 315, 334, 382, 590, 602
diversification *408*, 408–409, 599; Ansoff product-market matrix 400, *400*, 401, *408*, 408–414, *410*, *412*
divestment strategies 415, 433, 472–473
dividends 183, 184
Doha, Qatar 253
Dubai 65, 253, 647
dynamic capabilities 108–110, *110*, 390–392, *392*

Earth Summit, Rio de Janeiro, 1992 295
ease of entry/exit **46**, 55, 60–61, 334, **555**
easyJet 497, 534, 540–541
economic factors (STEEP analysis) 3, 278, 280, 292–295
economic growth 293
economic impacts of tourism 65, *66*
economic objectives 34
economic policy 298
economies of scale 35, 120, 170, 225, 314–315, 331,

375, 592–593, 650; global 592–593; international services 574, **574–575**, 584
economies of scope 314–315, 331, 409, 592–593, 650; international services 574, **574–575**, 584
ecotourism 69, 73; *see also* sustainable tourism
Edinburgh Festival 380–381, 513
Edmonton, Canada 157–158
education level, psychographic segmentation variable **234**
Emerald Expositions 696
emergent strategy 19, 165, 486, 511–512
Emirates 253, 452, 647
Empathy (RATER dimensions of service) 147
employees 123, 150, 151; employee retention 140, 142, 159–160; *see also* human resources
employment conditions 139–143; *see also* human resources
energy efficiency 622
Enterprise Holdings 460461
entrepreneurs, experiential knowledge of 269
environmental impacts of tourism 65, *66*
environmental scanning 280
EPS (earnings per share) 202
Etihad 253, 452, 647
EU (European Union) 290, 594, 649; Brexit 299, 419; foreign ownership restrictions 450, 649; mergers and acquisitions regulation 438, 439
Europe 70, 325, 457, 594
Eurotunnel 309
evaluation criteria, strategic evaluation 486–487, **487**, *487*
'eventful cities' 157–158, **371**
events 8–9, 38, 56, 57, **225**, 285, 297, 343, 428, 456, 467, 577, 581; 'eventful cities' 157–158; human resources 138–139; internationalization

of 597–598; joint developments 444, **444**; positioning 244–245, **245–246**; Queensland, Australia 676–677; 'smart' 289–290;
events management 23, 61, *63*, 111, 120, 188, 211, 346, **371**, 409, 420, 455, 461, 488, 534; case study 694–706; markets and marketing 220, 223–224; screening 489–490; SMEs 41
executive directors, corporate governance 40
exhibitions 696–697, 702; *see also* MICE (meetings, incentive travel, conventions and exhibitions) industry
exit: exit barriers 324–325; exit costs 60–61; exit strategies **417**, **418**; *see also* ease of entry/exit
Expedia Group 375–376, 433
experience effect *263*, 263–264, 376–377, 593
exports 596, 602
external analysis 3, 5, 278–279; SMEs 301–302; *see also* competitive environment; competitive environment analysis; macro-environmental analysis; SWOT analysis
external feasibility 493–494, *494*
external linkages (value chain analysis) 119, **119**
external shocks **46**, 55, 73–77, 416, **556**; SMEs 420

factors of production 17, 523
far environment *see* macro-environmental analysis
FDI (foreign direct investment) 595–596
Feasibility: feasibility studies *261*; strategic evaluation 486, **487**, *487*, 491–494, 507
feedback 5, 512, 518, 521
festivals 157, 297, 343, 352, 461, 506, 513; film festivals

456–457; globalization 575, 581; strategic drift 542–543
film festivals 456–457
finance 176–177, 178–179; cash management 209–216; foreign exchange risk management 204–209; SMEs 216–217
financial analysis 179–181, 194–195, 357; balance sheets *181*, 181–182, *182*; capital intensity 179–181; cross-sectional analysis 194, 196–199, 203; financial management 177, 179; financial structure and profitability 181–182; longitudinal analysis 194, 195, *196*, *197*, 199203; ratio analysis 194, 199–203, *200*
financial planning 528
financial resources 17, 87, 92, 97, 98, 177–179; sources of 182–183, 188–191, **189**, *190*
financial statements 198, 203–204
firm differentiation 604, *605*
First Choice 472, 658, 659, 660
first-mover advantage 253, 513, 608
fiscal policy 292–293
five freedoms of the air 300, **300**, 655
'fixed-fee' management agreements 466
Fliggy 445, 446
Florida, US 329
focus strategy 373, *373*, *374*, 384–385, **385**, 395–396, **396**
foreign direct investment (FDI) 595–596
foreign exchange risk management 204–209
foreign ownership restrictions 450, 489, 594, 596, 649, 655
formal organizational structure 537
forward foreign exchange contracts 209
Fosun International 407

frame conditions 370, **370–372**, 396
France 129, 190, 258, 319, 321, 338, 403, 407, 590, 600; cross-channel travel 309, 316
franchising 313, 427, 443–444, **444**, 460–463, **463**; hotels 469, 470, **470**, 476, 683; international 602, 603, 604, 606; SMEs 475–476
free resources 93
'free riders' 513
frequent flyer programmes 56, 314, 382
Frontier Airlines 431, 433
FTK (freight tonne kilometres) **294**
functional specialization, and organizational structure 535
functions, definition of markets by **225**, 225–226

Gaest 713, 715
Gatwick Airport, London 318, 330, 492, 497
GDS (Global Distribution System) 291–292, **371**, 445, 581, 648
gearing 357; gearing ratio 192, 202–203
GE-McKinsey matrix *267*, 267–268
gender, psychographic segmentation variable **234**
General Electric Company 122; *see also* GE-McKinsey matrix
Generation Y 244
generic strategy framework (Porter) *see* Porter's generic strategy framework
geographic concentration, and organizational structure 535
Germany 314, 319, 321, 590, 600, 659, 696; Messe Frankfurt 428; Premier Inn 341–342; *see also* TUI Group
GHG emissions 67–68, 297; shipping 621–622; *see also* sustainability
GL Events 405

Glasgow Declaration on Climate Action in Tourism 68
global brands 591
Global Hotel Alliance 468
global industries 573, 574, 576, 581
global strategies 570–571; competitive advantage of nations or regions *585*, *585*, 585–587; globalization of markets and industries 573–580, **574–575**; internationalization and globalization 572–573; key strategic decisions 599; market entry strategy 571, 599–607, *605*; models of 580–584, *582*, *583*, *584*; multi-domesticity 581, *582*; Porter's global generic strategies 580, 582–584, *583*, *584*; SMEs 607–610; Yip's globalization driver framework 580, 584, *587*, 587–598, **588**; *see also* globalization
'global village' 573–574
globalization 404, 570, 571, 572–573, 590–591, 605–607; models of 580–584, *582*, *583*, *584*
globalization driver framework, Yip 580, 584, *587*, 587–598, **588**
GlobalStar 589
goods, tangible nature of 45
goods-dominant (G-D) logic 125, 126, **126**, 127
governments 121, 298, 595–596; mergers and acquisitions policy 437–439; Porter's diamond framework *585*, *585*, 586–587
GRI 620
Grootbos, South Africa 71–72
growth strategies, Ansoff product-market matrix *400*, 400–402
GSTC (Global Sustainable Tourism Council) 620, 621
guerrilla marketing 270

'hard services' 46
Hawaii, USA 352, 353
Heathrow Airport, London 58, *58*, 105, 297, 298, 318, 492, 651
'hedging' 659
Henn-na Hotel, Nagasaki, Japan 149
heritage tourism 290–291
Hertz 460
heterogeneity of service products 6, **46**, 47, 49–51, 138, 169, **554**; SMEs 78; *see also* IHIP (intangibility, heterogeneity, inseparability and perishability) characteristics of service products
hierarchy 24, 533; joint developments 442–443, *443*
high-cost of *THE* service products **46**, 55, 56–57, **555**
Hilton International 111, 149, 222, 314, 451, 606
HNA Group 413–414, 454
holding companies 535
Holiday Inn 377, 404, 415–416; franchising 460, 461–462
Home Inns, China 153–154, 494
HomeAway 713–714
Hong Kong 325, 528–529; Dragon Boat Festival 313–314, 575
horizon scanning 280
horizontal: diversification 411; integration 64, 411, 436
horizontal interorganizational relationships 444
hospitality 8, 56, 61, *63*, 74, 180, 220, 256, 285, 343; cooperative networks 466, *467*, 467–468; financial management 177–178; globalization and market entry strategy 605–607; human resources 137–138; joint developments 444, **444**
hotels 8, 56, 75, 92, 111, 118, 123, 139, 188, 208, 230, 313, 318, 320, 325, 331,

382, 420, 427, 434, 475, 500, 513, 595, 605, 682, 711; asset-light strategies 180, 339, 461, 462, 470, 683, 684, 685; competition 321, 322, *322*; consortia 129–130; franchising 460, 461–462, 469, 470, **470**, 476, 683; globalization 572, 581; management contracts 464, 469, 470, **470**; market concentration 222–223, **223**; NPV calculations **503**, 503–504, **504**; outsourcing 120, 577; owning or leasing 469, 470, **470**; position and perspective strategies 20–21; product positioning 243–244; referral networks 467, 469; resource audits 525–526, **527**; strategic alliances 453–454; strategic group analysis *345*, 345–346; sustainability 297, 619, *620*; *see also* hospitality
HouseTrip 713
HRG (Hogg Robinson Group) 589
human factors, heterogeneity of service products 49–50
human resources 17, 87, 92, 94, 97, 98, 136–139, 141–142, 528; audit of 149–155; composition of workforce 139–140; as CSF (critical success factor) 137, 152–155; employment and working conditions 139–143; guest-employee encounter management 143–145, **144**, *145*; IHG 685–686; organizational culture 155–169, **166**, **168**; organizational structure 536, *536*; service quality 145–149, *146*; SMEs 169–170; technology 148–149; 'virtuous circle' and business success *146*, 146–147
Hurtigruten Group 621–622
Hyatt hotels *471*, 714

Hybrid: competitive strategy 386–387; method of strategic development 441–442

IAG (International Airlines Group) 431, 489
IATA (International Air Transport Association) 298, 299, 646
Iberia 431, 461
ICAO (International Civil Aviation Organization) 299, 595, 646
ICT (information and communications technology) 289, **372**, 375, 648
IHG (Intercontinental Hotel Group) 222, 243, *471*, 714; asset-light strategy 462, 470, 683, 684, 685; case study 681–693; competition strategy 683–685; globalization and market entry strategy 606–607; human resources 685–686; strategic management presentation 631–632, **633–634**
IHIP (intangibility, heterogeneity, inseparability and perishability) characteristics of service products 6, **46**, 47
IISD (International Institute for Sustainable Development) 620
ILTM (International Luxury Travel Market) 701
IMO (International Maritime Organization) 595
impact analysis 506–507
impact of *THE* service products **46**, 55, 65–73, *66*, **556**; SMEs 78
incentive travel *see* MICE (meetings, incentive travel, conventions and exhibitions) industry
incremental change 544
India 70, 73, 604, Indian Ocean tsunami, 2004 68, 76

indirect substitutes 317

industries 106, 308–309, 337; other industries, resource-based approach to competitive environment analysis 332, 333, *333*, 337; related and supporting industries, Porter's diamond framework 585, *585*; resource-based approach to competitive environment analysis 332, 333, 334; structural change **371**

industry analysis 309–310; Porter's five forces model 310–328, *311, 321, 322*, **326**

inflation 293, 503

informal organizational structure 537

Inkaterra, Peru 335

innovation 104–105, 107, 383–384; disruptive innovation 256, 711–712; SMEs 513; strategies **417, 418**

innovativeness (entrepreneurial orientation) 421

inseparability of service products 6, 46, **46**, 47, 51–52, **553**; SMEs 78; *see also* IHIP (intangibility, heterogeneity, inseparability and perishability) of service products

insolvency 211

intangibility of service products 6, **46**, 47–49, 124, **553**; *see also* IHIP (intangibility, heterogeneity, inseparability and perishability) of service products

intangible (intellectual) resources 17, 92–93, 97, 98, 529

integration, mergers and acquisitions 433, 436, 437–439

interdependence of *THE* service products **46**, 55, 61–64, *63*, **65**, 73, **556**

intergeneration equity 495

intermediaries 144, **144**, 180, 256, 259, 269, 312, 410, 469, 609, 709, 712; technology 275–276

internal analysis 3, 5, 86–87, *88*; *see also* SWOT analysis

internal feasibility 491–492, **493**

internal linkages (value chain analysis) 119, **119**

internal (organic) growth 426, *426*, 427–430, **430**, 432, 441, 442, 469, 470, 475

International Certificate in Green Tourism, CU Green Choice Sustainable Tourism Standard 335

international strategies 4, 570–571, 599; competitive advantage of nations or regions *585*, 585–587; globalization of markets and industries 573–580, **574–575**; internationalization and globalization 572–573; market entry strategy 571, 599–607, *605*; models of 580–584, *582, 583, 584*; multi-domesticity 581, *582*; Porter's global generic strategies 580, 582–584, *583, 584*; SMEs 607–610; Yip's globalization driver framework 580, 584, *587*, 587–598, **588**; *see also* internationalization

internationalization **371**, 396, 404, 519, 570, 571, 573; events 597–598; models of 580–584, *582, 583, 584*

internet, the 292, **371**, 375, 382, 469, 661

investment appraisal 498–499; accounting rate of return 499, 501; breakeven analysis 499, 500–501, *501*; cost-benefit analysis 504–506; DCF (discounted cash flow) methods 499, 501–502; impact analysis 506–507; IRR (internal rate of return) 499, 502–503; NPV (net present value) 499, 502–503, **503**, 503–504, **504**; payback method 499–500

IoT (Internet of Things) 148, 290, 292, 591

IRR (internal rate of return) 499, 502–503

Italy 223, 321; MICE (meetings, incentive travel, conventions and exhibitions) industry clustering 330

Japan 70, 450

Jet Blue 123, 431, 433

jet fuel prices 509–510

Jet2 plc 59

Jin Jiang International Hotel Group 51, 154, 494

job enlargement/enrichment/ rotation/sharing 142; *see also* human resources

joint developments 426, *426*, 427, 440–444, *441, 443*, 469, 475, 476

joint ventures 443–444, **444**, 485, 602, 603, 606; SMEs 129–130

Kenes Group 489–491

knowledge management, and competitive advantage 111–112

Korea: Busan International Film Festival 456–457

Kotler's five levels of product features/benefits 248–249, 485

KPIs (key performance indicators) 343–344

Kruger National Park, South Africa 238

Kuala Lumpur, Malaysia 253

Las Vegas, USA 321–322, *322*

lead countries 591–592

leadership 4, 537–538, 546, 547; change leadership and management, strategic implementation 519, 521, 523, 538–551, *539*, **541**, *544, 545, 548*, **549**, *551*;

leadership styles 548–549, **549**; SMEs 565; *see also* management
learning curves 593
learning organization 111
leasing 61, 180, 191, 216, 313, 469, 470, **470**, 605, 710; *see also* asset-light strategies
Lego Group 377
leisure travellers 252, 336
Lewin's 3-step model of change *539*, 539–540
licensing, international 602, 603
lifestyle market segmentation 234–235
limited liability companies, share capital 183–184, 187, **187**
liquidation 415
Live Nation 205–206, 210, 508, **509**
load factors 53, 54, 199, 294, **294**, 500
loan capital 186–187, **187**, 192, 193, 427
longitudinal analysis 194, 195, *196*, *197*, 199, 203
low cost competition **371**, low-cost airlines 312, 328, 375, 378, **378**, 379, 431, 452, 513, 583, 647–648, 661
loyalty schemes 55–56, 446, 469; frequent flyer programmes 56, 314, 382
Lufthansa 309, 431, 461, 545–546
Luxury Retreats 715
Lyft 610

Macau, China, SWOT analysis 353, **353–354**
machine learning 591
Machu Picchu, Peru 335
macro segmentation, B2B (business-to-business) marketing 239
macro-environmental analysis 3, 278, 280–284, *283*; SMEs 301–302; STEEP analysis 278, 280, 282, *283*, 284–301
Madre de Dios, Peru 335

Make Travel Matter Experience 623
Makerspaces 710, 718
Maldives, the 68–69
management 546, 547; change leadership and management, strategic implementation 519, 521, 523, 538–551, *539*, **541**, *544*, *545*, *548*, **549**, *551*; management styles 156, 548–549, **549**, *see also* leadership
management consultants 550
management contracts 427, 443–444, **444**, 463–466, 469, 470, **470**, 606; IHG 683–684
managers, empowerment of 142–143
Manchester, UK 457–458
Mandarin Oriental hotels 382
mapping, of strategy 559–560, *561*, *562*
market concentration, hotels 222–223, **223**
market entry strategy 571, 599–607, *605*
market growth rate 221, 239; *see also* BCG (Boston Consulting Group) matrix
market homogenization 573–576, **574–575**, 589
market leadership, Inkaterra, Peru 335
market research 336
market segmentation 220, 227, 228–231, **230**, 334, 336; ACORN (A Classification of Residential Neighborhoods) 237; B2B (business-to-business) marketing 238–239; benefit 232, 237–238, 385; business travellers 240–241; criteria for 231–232; focus strategy 384–385; geo-demographic 232, 236–237, 241; geographic 232, 233, 384–385; global 582, **583**; international 574; lifestyle 234–235; Porter's generic strategy framework 374; psychographic 232,

233–236; sociodemographic 232–233, **234**; VALS (values, attitudes and lifestyles) 235
market share 35, 122, 224, 254, 334; hotels, China 493–494; *see also* BCG (Boston Consulting Group) matrix
market size 221, 239
market structures 320, 321, *321*; Porter's diamond framework 585, *585*, 586
market subgroups 335–336; *see also* market segmentation
marketing alliances 326
Marketing Manchester PPP 459
marketing mix 227, 247, *247*; SMEs 269
marketing regulations, compatibility of 594–595
marketing research 228
markets and marketing 106, 186, 219–220, 221, 308–309, 324, 485; B2B (business-to-business) marketing 238–239; definitions of 223–228; globalization of 573–580, **574–575**; joint developments 442–443, *443*; market attractiveness 221–223, **223**; SMEs 268–270; STP (segmenting, targeting and positioning) marketing 220, 227–228; strategic directions decisions 484–485; strategic marketing 220–221
Marriott hotels 56, 222, 383, 429, 434, 445–446, 460, *471*, 606, 711; product positioning 243–244; resource analysis 97–98; Courtyard brand, 97, **98**, 243–244, 429; Moxy brand, 243–244, 429, 484, 711
M&As *see* mergers and acquisitions
mass tourism 7, 69–71, 73
master franchises 462
mature markets 402, 485

McDonald's 403, 460, 462
McKinsey 550
measurability, target
  marketing 240
measurement issues, human
  resource audit 151
meetings: Airbnb 715; *see also*
  MICE (meetings, incentive
  travel, conventions and
  exhibitions) industry
megatrends 284, 285, 542;
  Queensland, Australia 678
Melbourne, Australia 158
mergers and acquisitions
  426, *426*, 427, 430–433,
  430–439, **435–436**,
  437, 441, 442, 469, 470;
  international 602, 603, 606;
  strategic methods 426,
  426, 427, 430–439,
  435–436, **437**, 441,
  442, 469, 470, 485
Merlin Entertainments Group
  377
Messe Frankfurt 428
me-too products 242, 252,
  253, 513
MICE (meetings, incentive
  travel, conventions and
  exhibitions) industry:
  clustering 330, 695
micro (near) environment 3,
  279, 283–284, 307; *see also*
  competitive environment
  analysis
microsegmentation 229, 239
Milan, Italy 330
Millennials 244, 711
Mintzberg's 5 Ps of strategy
  17–21
mission/mission statements
  26, 26–32
mobile-based marketing 241
'moments of truth'
  144–145, *145*
monetary policy 292–293
monopoly 320, 321, *321*;
  monopolistic competition
  320–321, *321*; monopolistic
  power, market segments 229
Mpumalanga,
  South Africa 238
multi-domesticity 581, *582*

multinational companies 572,
  573, 608, 610; multinational
  global customers 590
Mumbai, India, terror attacks,
  2008 73
Muslim contexts, service
  quality in 146
MyTravel Group plc 439,
  659, 660

NAFTA (North American Free
  Trade Agreement) 594
national responsiveness
  583, **583**
natural environment, attitudes
  towards 288, 295
nearshoring **372**, 578
networks 326, 346, 440;
  'networked' economy 127
'new tourism' 71
New Zealand 565
niche markets 222, 374,
  395–396, **396**, 475
Nielsen Expositions 696
no change strategy 414
noise pollution 297
non-core activities 120–122;
  non-core assets, disposal of
  473–474
non-executive directors 40
non-price competition 320
Northern Ireland 63
not-for-profit organizations
  34–35
NPV (net present value)
  499, 502–503, **503**,
  503–504, **504**

objectives 13, 16, 24, 34–35;
  'CRIME' (Communicable,
  Realistic, Internally
  Consistent, Measurable,
  Explicit) 34; hierarchy of
  26, **26**; objective-setting
  process 25–29, **37**, *37*;
  open and closed 25–26, **26**,
  33; stakeholder approach
  36–39, **37**; stockholder
  approach 35–36
occupancy rates 53, 54, 199,
  322, *322*
OECD 284, 285
offshoring **372**, 578

Okavango Delta, Botswana 67
oligopoly 320, 321, *321*
Olympic Games: Athens 352;
  London 49–50, 138; Tokyo
  506–507
Onefinestay 714
Oneworld Alliance 448, 452,
  592, 646, 651, 653–654
Onex 696
open skies agreements 300
operational-level decisions 483
opportunity cost 96, 505
organic (internal) growth 426,
  426, 427–430, **430**, 432,
  441, 442, 469, 470, 475
organic reduction 472
organizational culture 120,
  154, 165, 529, 534; cultural
  typologies 164–169,
  166, **168**; cultural web
  160, 160–163; Handy's
  culture types 164–165;
  Hofstede's cross-cultural
  differences 166–169, **168**;
  human resources 155–169,
  166, **168**; importance of
  156–160; Miles and Snow's
  culture types 165–166,
  166, 529–530; SMEs 565;
  strategic implementation 4,
  519, 521, 523, 529–530
organizational knowledge 107
organizational performance,
  7-S model (Peters and
  Waterman) 550–551, *551*
organizational structure 151;
  complexity of 533–535;
  divisionalization methods
  535–538, *536*; 'height' of
  531–532, *532*; 'hybrid'
  structures 535, *536*; matrix
  structures 534, 535–537,
  536; organizational
  culture 156, 534; strategic
  implementation 4, 519, 521,
  523, 530–538, *532*, **533**,
  533, *536*; 'width' of 533,
  533, *533*
organizations, resource-based
  approach to competitive
  environment analysis 333, *333*
outsourcing 120–122, 571,
  576–579, 584

overcapacity 325
overcapitalization 191
overtourism 70
overtrading 191, 414
ownership of *THE* service
    products **46**, 55–56, **554**;
    SMEs 78

P & O Ferries 309
P2P (peer-to-peer)
    platforms 710
packaged services 48–49, 237,
    656–657; intermediaries
    144, **144**
Pan Pacific Hotels 469
paradigms 161, 163
parallel processing 260
Paris agreement on climate
    change 298
partnerships 326, 430, 440;
    SMEs 270
pause/proceed with caution
    strategy 414
payback method, investment
    appraisal 499–500
penetration pricing 250, 251
perfect competition 320, 321, *321*
performance measurement 99
perishability of service
    products 6, **46**, 47,
    52–54, 73, 124, **553**; *see
    also* IHIP (intangibility,
    heterogeneity, inseparability
    and perishability) of service
    products
personalization, and
    globalization 590–591
PEST *see* STEEP (analysis
PESTEL *see* STEEP analysis
Philippines 65, 70–71,
    382–383
Phuket, Thailand 65
physical resources, planning
    528–529
physical (tangible) resources
    17, 92, 97, 98
piggyback distribution
    arrangements 602
PIMS (Profit Impact of Market
    Strategy) 122, 123, 264
pioneer companies 252
planning horizons, decision
    making 24–25

PLC (product life-cycle)
    250–254, **251**, *251*, 399,
    485, 594; critiques of 255;
    S-curve (technology life
    cycle analysis) 255–258,
    257; TALC (tourism area life
    cycle) 254–255
Plymouth, UK 457
Porter's diamond framework
    585, 585–587
Porter's five forces model of
    industry analysis 310–312,
    311; business rivalry 310,
    311, 320–325, *321*, *322*,
    328; limitations of 325–328;
    new entrants 310, *311*,
    312–316, 327; power of
    buyers/customers 310, *311*,
    317–318, 328; substitute
    products 310, *311*, 316–317,
    328; summary of 325, **326**;
    suppliers' power 310, *311*,
    318–320, 328
Porter's generic strategy
    framework 369, *373*,
    373–374, *374*, 392, 393,
    393; cost leadership strategy
    373, *373*, *374*, 374–380,
    378, **385**, 386, 387, 388,
    393, 395; critical evaluation
    of 385–388; differentiation
    strategy 373, *373*, 374,
    374, 380–384, **385**, 386,
    387, 388, 392, 395; focus
    strategy 373, *373*, *374*,
    384–385, **385**, 395–396,
    396; global strategies 580,
    582–584, *583*, *584*; and
    SMEs 395
position statements 355
positioning 220, 227;
    competitive positioning
    school of competitive
    advantage 89, 90, 369,
    439, 440
power: power distance 156,
    161, **168**;
PPPs (public-private
    partnerships) 95, 121, **371**,
    427, 441, 443–444, **444**,
    454–460, 505, 694
Premier Inn 331, 402–403, *403*
premium pricing 380

prescriptive (deliberate)
    strategy 19, 486, 511, 628
presentation styles, strategic
    management 630, **630**,
    631, **631–632**, 632–633,
    633–635
price 94, 241, 247, *247*,
    250, 316, 387; demand
    management 54, 96;
    penetration pricing 250, 251
price competition 320
price: elasticity of demand
    250, 252, 379–380, 383;
    inelasticity of demand 259;
    sensitivity 336; pricing
    power 35, 57
privatization 300, **371**, 595, 649
proactiveness (entrepreneurial
    orientation) 421
product markets, resource-based
    approach to competitive
    environment analysis 332,
    333, *333*, 334–336
product portfolio 262, 399;
    BCG (Boston Consulting
    Group) matrix 262–267,
    263, *264*, **266**; composite
    portfolio models *267*,
    267–268
product positioning 220, 227,
    241–245, *242*, **245–246**,
    247, *247*
productivity 293
products 87, 219–220,
    247, *247*, 366, 375, 377,
    380, 485; continuous
    improvement and
    competence building 107;
    definition and typology of
    248–249; Kotler's five levels
    of product features/benefits
    248–249, 485; new product
    development 258–261;
    product-based definitions
    of markets 224–225;
    SMEs 268–270; strategic
    directions decisions
    484–485; substitute
    products 252, 310, *311*,
    316–317, 318, 327
profit and loss (P&L)
    statements 181, 182, **183**,
    198, 203

profits 186, 203, 427; profit strategy 414
promotion 48, 96, 247, *247*, 257, *257*; differentiation 382–383; SMEs 269
protected markets 583, **583**
public sector organizations 91, 95, 372, 572
'pulsating' organization concept 138–139

Qantas 189, 190, *190*, 452, 579
Qatar Airways 253, 647
quality 241, 336; *see also* service quality
Queensland, Australia 245, **245–246**; case study 668–680

RACES evaluation criteria 486
Radisson Hotels 51, 453–454, 460, 606
RATER (Responsiveness, Assurance, Tangibles, Empathy, Reliability) dimensions of service 147
ratio analysis 194, 199–203, *200*
RBV (resource-based view) 90–91, 101, 108, 109, 389
R&D (research and development) 256–257, *257*, 594
'realized' strategy 486
reconstruction, and change 545, *545*
recruitment and selection 140, 142, 150, 151
Reed Exhibitions *see* RX Exhibitions
referral networks 467, 469
regional tourist organizations (RTOs), Queensland, Australia 669, 672
regulation 94, 298, 299–300, 315–316, 324
Relais et Chateaux 129, 467
relationship marketing 57
Reliability (RATER dimensions of service) 147
RELX Group 697
Reno-Taho territory, Nevada, USA 158

replacement effect 513
resource audits 525–526, **527**
resource markets 92, 309, 319, 524; resource-based approach to competitive environment analysis 332, 333, *333*, 336–337
resource substitution 148
resource-based approach to competitive environment analysis 332–338, *333*
resource/competence school of competitive advantage 89, 90–91
resources 92–99, 113, 186; bargaining power of suppliers 318–320; competences and core competences 100, *101*, 103, *103*, 439; development and control of 528–529; financial 17, 92, 97, 98, 524; intellectual (intangible) 17, 524; leveraging of 394, **395**; matching with strategy 525–526, **527**; physical (tangible) 17, 92, 97, 98, 524; resource analysis 87, 97–99; sourcing efficiencies 593; standardization of 377; strategic implementation 4, 519, 521, 523–529, **527**; strategy 16, 17; sustainability 622; SWOT analysis 352–353; *see also* human resources
responsible travel 69
Responsiveness (RATER dimensions of service) 147
restaurants 74, 180, 230, 248, 403, 460, 461, 574; Tree Alliance (Training Restaurants for Employment and Entrepreneurship) 623
retained profit 186
retrenchment 415–417, **417**, **418**, 419, 472–474
returns 34, 192, 497–498; accounting rate of return 499, 501; breakeven analysis 499, 500–501, *501*; cost-benefit analysis 504–506; DCF (discounted

cash flow) methods 499, 501–502; financial tools 498–504, *501*, **503**, **504**; impact analysis 506–507; investment appraisal 498–499; IRR (internal rate of return) 499, 501, 502–503; non-financial tools 504–507; NPV (net present value) 499, 501, 502–503, **503**, 503–504, **504**; payback method 499–500; strategic evaluation 496, 497–507
revenue: management systems 292; 'revenue sharing' management agreements 466
reverse segmentation, B2B (business-to-business) marketing 239
rights issue capital 184–186, *185*
risk 76, 507–508, **509**, 650; risk assessment, value co-creation 128; risk premium 503; risk taking (entrepreneurial orientation) 421scenario planning and sensitivity analysis 509–511; SMEs 421; strategic directions 419–420; strategic evaluation 496, 507–511, **509**
Ritz Hotel 338
Ritz-Carlton 143
Riu family holiday properties 474
robotics 148–149, 290
ROCE (return on capital employed) 34, 199, 200
Rome, Italy 330
Royal Caribbean cruise line 380
RPK (revenue passenger kilometres) **294**
RTOs (regional tourist organizations), Queensland, Australia 669, 672
rugby sevens 597–598
RX Exhibitions 432, 697–706
Ryanair 77, 328, 497, 540–541

Sabre 291, 581
safety 299, 595
Saga Holidays 225, 233, 412

Sales: agents, local 602; functions, SMEs 269
Salzburg Festival 352
satisficing 421
SBUs (strategic business units) 33, 311, 312, 366, 369, 372, 399; competitive strength, GE-McKinsey matrix *267*, 267–268; SMEs 395
Scandic Hotels 296
scanning stage, STEEP analysis 286
SCARE evaluation criteria 486
SCEPTICAL (Social, Cultural, Economic, Physical, Technical, International, Communications and Infrastructure, Administrative and Legal and Political factors) analysis 284
screening 489–491, **491**, 507
S-curve (technology life cycle analysis) 255–258, *257*
SDGs (Sustainable Development Goals) 620
seasonality 95, 191, 682; cash management 210, 211–212; of *THE* service products **46**, 55, 57–59, *58*, **555**
sell out strategies 415
Seoul, South Korea 158, 595
separable services 46
service delivery 25; guest-employee encounter management 143–145, **144**, *145*; 'moments of truth' 144–145, *145*
service orientation 130
service product characteristics 6, 45–54, **46**, **553**; *see also* *THE* (tourism, hospitality and events)-specific product characteristics
service profit chain 122–124, *124*, 557
service quality 146, 382; guest-employee encounter management 143–145, **144**, *145*; human resources 145–149, *146*
service value 123

service-dominant (S-D) logic 124–126, **126**, 127–128
services 45, 146, 366
services marketing mix 247, *247*; SMEs 269
SERVQUAL model of service quality 122, 147
SFA (suitability, feasibility, acceptability) framework 486
Shanghai, China 325
share capital 183–184, 187, **187**, 192, 193, 200, 427; EPS (earnings per share) 202
shareholders: disposals 473–474; dividends 183, 184; return on ordinary shareholders' funds 200; share capital 183–184, 187, **187**; sustainability strategy 618, 619
sharing economy, the 128, 710–711
shipping 313, 595, 621–622; *see also* cruising
Singapore 253
Singapore Airlines 253, 386–387
'single markets' 594
skills audit *see* human resource audit
Skyscanner 609, 610
SkyTeam Alliance 448, 452, 489, 592, 646, 653–654
SkyWest Inc. 465–466
Slovenia 595
Small Luxury Hotels of the World 129, 467
'smart' *THE* 289–290
SMEs 10, 77–79, 623; 4Ps (Product, Promotion, Price, Place) 269; barriers to entry 61, 77–78; collaborations and joint ventures 129–130, 475; competitive advantage 128–130; competitive environment analysis 344–346, *345*; competitive strategy 394–396, *396*; competitors 344–345; complexity 565; consortia 270; control 301–302; CSFs (critical success factors) 344; 'degrees of

turbulence' model 302; events management 41; external analysis 301–302; external shocks 420; finance 216–217; focus strategy 384; franchising 475–476; global strategies 607–610; heterogeneity characteristic of service products 78; hospitality 623; human resources 169–170; impact characteristic of *THE* service products 78; innovation 513; inseparability characteristic of service products 78; international strategies 607–610; joint ventures 129–130; leadership 565; lifestyle motives of business owners 475, 565; markets and marketing 268–270; organizational culture 565; partnerships 270; promotion 269; resource limitations 302; risk-averse strategies 421; sales functions 269; SBUs (strategic business units) 395; service product characteristics 78; services marketing mix 269; strategic alliances 270; strategic directions 420–421; strategic evaluation 512–513; strategic group analysis *345*, 345–356; strategic implementation 564–565; strategic management 40–41; strategic methods 475–476; supply chain issues 63; sustainability strategy 623–624; SWOT analysis 359–361, **360**; *THE* (tourism, hospitality and events)-specific product characteristics 78
social media marketing 270
soft: capabilities *471*, *472*; 'soft services' 47, 55, 124
Sorrel Hospitality 462–463
South Korea 330

Southwest Airlines 158–160, 309, 328, 377, 378, 379, 431, 497

Spain 34, 96, 169, 221, 252, 254, 314, 318, 319, 458, 586, 605, 701; hotels 302, 380, 605, 622–623, 623–624

Spirit Airlines 433

'spirit of service' 145

sporting events 230, 352; Dragon Boat Festival, Hong Kong 313–314, 575; rugby sevens 597–598

SRI International 235

Sri Lanka, Indian Ocean tsunami, 2004 76

stability (perseverance) strategies 414, 417, **417**, 419

staff turnover 140, 199

stakeholders 29, 38, 39–40; Australian Council of National Trusts 38–39; climate change and sustainable tourism 69; interest and power 36–37; internal and external **37**; mapping of 37, 37–38; objective-setting 36–39, **37**; strategic evaluation 496–497

Star Alliance 184–185, 448, 452, 489, 592, 646, 647, 653–654

Starwood Worldwide Inc 434

STEEP (sociodemographic, technological, economic, environmental and political) analysis 278, 280, 282, 283, 284–286, 301, 488; economic factors 3, 278, 280, 292–295; environmental factors 278, 280, 295–298; political, governmental, legal and regulatory factors 299–300, **300**; sociodemographic factors 3, 278, 280, 287–288; stages in 286; technological factors 289–292; what to analyse 286–287

STEP analysis 278, 280, 284; see also STEEP (sociodemographic, technological, economic, environmental and political) analysis

step change 544

stockholder approach to objective-setting 35–36

strategc alliances 326, 427, 440, 443, **444**, 444–446, 470, 485; airline industry 184–185, 328, 445, 447–449, 449, 450, 451–452, 489, 592, 646–655; difficulties in 450–452; international 602, 603, 606; motivations for 449–450; partner selection 452–454; THE sector 446–448; SMEs 270

strategic analysis 2, 3, 87, 88, 178, 522, 524, 524

strategic business units (SBUs) see SBUs (strategic business units)

strategic choice/selection 2, 4, 87, 88, 365, 366, 368, 483, 484, 505, 523, 524, 524

strategic congruence, mission statements 29

strategic decisions 483, 484

strategic development 178–179, 188, **189**, 192; 'hybrid' method of 441–442

strategic directions 366, 367, 368, 370, 394, 399–400, 482, 483; COVID-19 crisis response strategies 416, **417**, 417–418, **418**; growth strategies 399, 400, 400–414, 403, 408, 410, 412, 419, 484; product and market decisions 484–485; retrenchment strategies 399, 415–417, **417**, **418**, 419, 484; risk and balance 401, 419–420; risk-averse strategies 421; SMEs 420–421; stability (perseverance) strategies 399, 414, 417, **417**, **418**, 419, 484

strategic drift 542–543

strategic evaluation 366, 482–483; acceptability 486, **487**, 487, 496, 507; emergent strategies 511–512; evaluation criteria 486–487, **487**, 487; feasibility 486, **487**, 487, 491–494, 507; identifying options 483–486; process 487; returns 496, 497–507; risk 496, 507–511, **509**; screening 489–491, **491**, 507; SMEs 512–513; stakeholder reaction 496–497; suitability 486, **487**, 487, 488–491, 507; sustainability 486, **487**, 487, 495–496

strategic group analysis 308–309, 338–339; hotels 345, 345–346

strategic groups, competitive advantage 106

strategic implementation 2, 4–5, 87, 88, 518–519, 520–523; BSC (balanced scorecard) 521, 523, 557–561, 560, 561, 562, **563**, 563–564; change leadership and management 519, 521, 523, 538–551, 539, **541**, 544, 545, 548, **549**, 551; communication, coordination and measurement 519, 521, 523, 557–561, 560, 561, 562, **563**, 563–564; THE contexts 551–552, 552, **553–556**; organizational culture and structure 4, 519, 521, 523, 529–538, 532, **533**, 533, 536; resources 519, 521, 523–529, **527**; service product characteristics **553–554**; SMEs 564–565

strategic management 626–628; approaches to study of 628–629; cooperative networks 466–469, 467; definition 15; in practice 518–519; presentation factors 629,

629; presentation styles 630, **630**, 631, **631–632**, 632–633, **633–635**; relational approach 439–440
strategic marketing 220–221
strategic methods 366, *367*, 368, 370, 394, 425–427, *426*, 482, 483; 'buy, ally or DIY [do it yourself]' matrix 470–472, *471*; comparison between 469–472, **470**, *471*; cooperative networks 443–444, **444**; decisions 485–486; franchising 427, 443–444, **444**, 460–463, **463**, 469, 470, **470**, 475–476, 485; joint development 426, *426*, 427, 440–444, *441*, *443*, 469, 475, 476; joint ventures 443–444, **444**, 485; management contracts 427, 443–444, **444**, 463–466, 469, 470, **470**; mergers and acquisitions 426, *426*, 427, 430–439, **435–436**, **437**, 441, 442, 469, 470, 485; organic (internal) growth 426, *426*, 427–430, **430**, 432, 441, 442, 469, 470, 475, 485; PPPs (public-private partnerships) 427, 441, 443–444, **444**, 454–460; relational approach 425, 439–440; retrenchment 472–474; SMEs 475–476; strategic alliances 427, 432, 443, **444**, 444–454, *449*, 470, 476
strategic: objectives 179, 453; *see also* objectives; options 364–367, *365*, *367*, 483–486; process 87, *88*
strategic selection *see* strategic choice/selection
strategy 13–14, 44, 186; business level 365, *365*, 366–367, *367*; corporate level *365*, 365–366, 367; decision making levels 21–25; definitions 14–16; elements of

16–17; financial sources, strategic significance of 188–191, **189**, *190*; levels of *365*, 365–366; mapping of 559–560, *561*, *562*; Mintzberg's 5 Ps of 17–21; objectives 25–34; operational level 365, *365*, 366; practice of 16–21; *see also* competitive strategy
strategy clock framework 388, *389*
strategy formulation 370, **370–372**
strategy process 2, *2*, 4–5, 355; *see also* strategic analysis
structure (cultural web) 161, 163
stuck in the middle (Porter's generic strategy framework) 373, 386
substitute products: Porter's five forces model of industry analysis 310, *311*, 316–317, 318, 327; price elasticity of demand 252
'success factors' concept 342; *see also* CSF (critical success factor)
Sun Air 461
sunk cost effect 513
Sunvil 115, 118, 384–385
suppliers 222, 239, 318, 326; power of, Porter's five forces model of industry analysis 310, *311*, 318–320, 328
supply: 54, 57, 96, 118, 221; supply chains 62–65, 580, 593
sustainability 519, 685; corporate governance 40; globalization 575; stakeholders 39; strategic evaluation 486, **487**, *487*, 495–496; strategic implementation and management 4–5; supply chains 62–63
sustainability strategy 616–617; business sustainability 617–619, *620*; competitive advantage 619, *620*; principal issues 620–623; SMEs 623–624

sustainable competitive advantage 91–92, 107–108, 109, 390–392, *392*, 619
sustainable development 295, 620
sustainable tourism 38, 67–68, 93, 285, 297, 352, 617, 618; AITO (Association of Independent Tour Operators) guidelines 78–79; Grootbos, South Africa 71–72; Peru 335
Sweden 542–543
switching costs, between suppliers 319
SWOT analysis 3, 87, 278, 279, 351–352, 488; common errors 357; *THE* contexts 352–354, **353–354**; GE-McKinsey matrix 268; general principles 354–356; implementation **356**, 356–358, **358–359**; SMEs 359–361, **360**
symbols (cultural web) 161, 162
synergy 408, 434–435

tactical: alliances 445; objectives 24, 33
Taiwan 339
takeovers 430, 433; *see also* mergers and acquisitions
TALC (tourism area life cycle) 254–255
tangible (physical) resources 17, 92, 97, 98
Tangibles (RATER dimensions of service) 147
targeting/target marketing 220, 227, 228, 239–241
Task Rabbit 710
TBL (triple bottom line) 495–496, 618–619
technical standards, compatibility of 594–595
technology 156, 285; differentiation 380–381; disintermediation **371**; globalization 576, 591, 594; human resources 148–149, 170; intermediaries 275–276; S-curve (technology life cycle

analysis) 255–258, *257*; *see also* ICT (information and communications technology)

telecommunications standards 595

TEQ (Tourism and Events Queensland) 245, **245–246**, 668–680

Texas, USA 712

Thailand 70, 76

THE (tourism, hospitality and events) 9, 41, 61, *63*; joint development 443–444, **444**; operational level 6–7, 9–10; strategic alliances 446–448; strategy 6–10, 44; *see also* events; hospitality; tourism

THE (tourism, hospitality and events)-specific product characteristics **46**, 55–77, *58*, *63*, **65**, *66*, **555–556**; SMEs 78

theme parks 376–377, 506

third sector organizations 91

Thomas Cook 7, 64, 439, 656–667

Thompson 472, 658

time 96–97, 252

Time Banks 710, 718

time horizons 24–25, 33

time series analysis *see* longitudinal analysis

time value of money 498–499, 501

tipping points 500

top management, and organizational change 550

'total global strategy,' Yip's globalization driver framework 580, 597–598

total share volume 184

total supply chains (value chain analysis) 115

tour operators 62, *63*, 207, 209, 264, 325, 346, 486, 659; cash management 211, 212; economies of scale and scope 314–315; Europe 325, 438–439, 659–662; market segmentation 230, 237; merger control 438–439; package concept 48–49,

657–658; UK 78, 129, 204–205, 207, 212, 225, 233, 412, 657–658

tourism 7, 124, 125, 220, 233, 302, 343, 456, 513, 578; difference from travel 577–578; FDI (foreign direct investment) 595–596; globalization 572, 575, 581; human resources 137–138, 139; impacts of 65–73, *66*; loyalty schemes 55–56; market segmentation 71, 228; seasonality of demand 57–59, *58*; 'smart' 289–290; strategic drift 542; supply chain 63–65; SWOT analysis 359, **360**; value co-creation 124; *see also THE* (tourism, hospitality and events)

tourism consumers, awareness of impact of tourism 72–73

'Tourism for Tomorrow World Conservation Award,' WTTC 335

'tourism system' 144

'tourist carrying capacity' 71

tourist clusters 329

trade: fairs 428, 696; *see also* MICE (meetings, incentive travel, conventions and exhibitions) industry. policies, and globalization 594

Trailblazers Adventure Travel Pvt. Ltd. 235–236

Trailfinders plc 382

training and development 140–141, 151

transferable marketing 591

transformational change 544

transition economies 316

transnational companies 573

transparency 108, 128

transport 48, 61, *63*, 230, 594; breakeven analysis 500; clustering of transport hubs 330; joint developments 444, **444**; technology **372**, 576

travel agents 211, 382, 524

Travel Corporation, The (TTC) 622–623

Travel Counsellors 180–181

travel, difference from tourism 577–578

travel events: RX Exhibitions 700–701; *see also* MICE (meetings, incentive travel, conventions and exhibitions) industry

travel: intermediaries, franchising 461; organisers 62, *63*, 444, **444**

Travel Solutions International (TSI) 589

Travelodge 402

Treaty of Rome, 1957 438

Tree Alliance (Training Restaurants for Employment and Entrepreneurship) 623

trend analysis *see* longitudinal analysis

TripAdviser 376, 713

Trip.com Group 609, 610

TSI (Travel Solutions International) 589

TTC (The Travel Corporation) 622–623

TUI Group 64, **65**, 115, 308, 376, 439, 472, 474; case study 659, 660, 662, 664–665, 665–666

Turkey 53, 344

turnaround strategies 415–416

Turo 710, 718

Uber 610

UK 94, 97, 237, 293; arts 401; Brexit 299, 419; cross-channel travel 309, 316; destination marketing 458–460; outbound tour operations 657–658; PPPs (public-private partnerships) 457–458; regulation 324; tour operators 78, 129, 204–205, 207, 212, 225, 233, 412, 657–658

Ukraine war 580, 600, 611, 627

undercapacity 325

undercapitalization 191

unemployment levels 293
UNESCO 618
'unicorns' 707–708
Uniglobe Travel International 589
Unilever 619
uniqueness, and competence building 107
United Airlines 386, 431
UNWTO 618, 620
Upstream: diversification 409; linkages (value chain analysis) 115
urban development/renewal 454
US Airways 489
USA: airline industry 488–489; deregulation 300, 378, 431, 489, 594, 648, 649; foreign ownership restrictions 450, 489, 594, 596, 649, 655; mass tourism 70; PPPs (public-private partnerships) 457–458; tourist clustering 329–330
utility 225

VALS (values, attitudes and lifestyles) market segmentation 235
Value Alliance 448
value chains 113–115, *115*, **393**, 409; value chain analysis 87, 112, 114, 115, *118*, 118–119, **119**, 122, 375; value systems 115, *118*
value co-creation 124, 127–128, 711
value: measures of market share 224; value propositions 127; value, service profit chain 122

value-adding 112–113; competitive advantage 112–122; globalization 573, 583, **584**; mergers and acquisitions 435
value-for-money objectives, not-for-profit organizations 34
values **26**, 26–27, 29, 31–33
Vanilla Alliance 448
venture teams 260
vertical: backward diversification 409; forward diversification 409–411; integration 64, 411, 419, 436; interorganizational relationships 444
Vietnam 421
Virgin 452
'virtual exhibitions' 697
'virtuous circle,' of human resources and business success *146*, 146–147
vision **26**, 26–27, 28, 31–33
Visit Florida 31–32
volunteers 140, 142; London 2012 Olympic Games 49–50, 138
VR (virtual reality) systems 290–291, 591
VRIN (valuable, rare, inimitable and nonsubstitutable) resources 92, 108
VRIO (value, rarity, imitability and organizational capability) framework 108, *109*, 390, **390**

W Hotels 383–384

WACC (weighted average cost of capital) 193
wage levels 293
waste reduction and disposal 622
web-based marketing 241
WestJet 162–163
WeWork 715
'what if?' analysis 509
Whitbread plc 331, 340–341, **341–342**, 402
working capital 182, 191
working conditions 139–143; *see also* human resources
World Bank 618
World Hotels 130
WTO 576, 594
WTTC (World Travel and Tourism Council) 335, 620
Wyndham Hotels Group 222, 339, 470, *471*, 714

Yip's globalization driver framework 580, 584, *587*, 587–588, **588**; competitive drivers *587*, 588, **588**, 596; cost drivers *587*, 588, **588**, 592–594; government drivers *587*, 588, **588**, 594–596; market globalization drivers *587*, **588**, 588–592; use in practice 596–598
young people, employment in *THE* sector 139, 142
Your Hotels Worldwide 130
Yum! Brands Inc. 460

'zero defects' 144
Zipcar 710, 718

Name index

Note: Page references in *italic* type refer to Figures; those in **bold** refer to Tables.

Abdelkader, A. A. 146
Abou-Shouk, M. 129
Ackermann, F. 511
Adams, D. 498
Agyris, C. 112
Ahmed, P. K. 109, 391
Alamdari, F. 378, 379
Albers, S. 418, **418**
Albrecht, K. 145
Aldao, C. 71
Almeida-Santana, A. 55–56
Alon, I. 475
Altinay, L. 476
Andersen, V. 513
Anderson, J. 622
Andersson, T. D. 121, 352, 506, 542
Ansoff, I. *400*. 400–402, 484
Arasli, H. 56
Archer, B. H. 506
Argenti, J. 358
Armstrong, G. 227, 232
Arnold, G. 498
Asmelash, A. G. 496
Assaf, A. G. 595
Ateljevik, J. 565
Avcikurt, C. 344
Avery, G. C. 32
Ayoun, B. 199

Bain, J. 60
Balogun, J. 541, 544–545, *545*. 549

Banham, H.C. 302
Bansal, P. 618, 619
Bardolet, E. 352, 353
Barlow, M. 401
Barnett, M. L. 617, 619
Barney, J. B. 108, 389
Barney, Jay 330
Bartlett, C. A. 581
Bass, B. M. 547
Bass, R. 547
Baum, T. 57, 137, 144–145, *145*
Baumol, W. J. 60
Bec, A. 290
Becerra, M. 380
Beer, M. 550
Bell, J. 608
Bennett, M, M, 445
Bensoussan, B. E. 112, 114, 255, 509
Bernini, C. 330
Berry, L. L. 147
Biazzo, S. 564
Blanchard, K. 548
Blecharczyk, N. 707
Bleeke, J. 450
Blitz, G. 407
Bonn, I. 618
Bonoma, T. V. 239
Boswijk, A. 714, 719
Bosworth, G. 421
Bourguinon, P. 407
Bourne, L. 37

Bowdin, G. 9, 138
Bowman, C. 388
Brent Ritchie, C, R. 7
Breukel, A. 509
Brookes, M. 476
Brouthers, K. D. 452
Brown, R. 255
Bruch, H. 546
Buhalis, D. 127
Bull, A. 57, 93
Butler, R. W. 254–255

Cai, L. A. 56
Calder, S. 664
Camilleri, M. A. 239
Campbell, A. 30, 36
Campbell, N. 125
Capone, F. 329
Carlsen, J. 352, 543
Carlzon, J. 144
Cavusgil, S. T. 608, 610
Chadwick, R. 7
Chan, J. 468
Chandler, A. D. 15–16, 530
Chebat, J. 522
Chen, C. C. 56
Chen, J. J. 572
Chen, P. J. 142, 143
Chesky, B. 707, 711, 714, 715, 716
Cheung, C. 142–143
Child, J. 449–450
Choi, G. 92

Chon, K. 330
Chow, C. K. W. 437
Christensen, C. 256, 711
Clark, T. 451, 647
Collins-Kreiner, N. 71
Connell, J. 9, 57, 58
Cook, T. 7, 656
Cooper, C. 255, 586
Cooper, S. 665
Crotts, J. C. 169
Cyelbar, L. K. 595
Cyert, R. M. 421

Daniel, R. 342
De Wit, B. 440, 442
Deery, M. 139
DeFranco, A. L. 498
DeKay, F. 56
DeRoos, J. A. 464
DesJardine, M. R. 618, 619
Dess, G. G. 421
Dev, C. S. 441, 447
Dhir, S. and S. 409
Do, B. 421
Dobbs, M. E. 327
Dodds, R. 619, *620*
Doganis, R. 378
Dogru, T. 57
Dolnicar, S. 56, 228, 416–417
Domou, I. 572
Donaldson, T. 36
Doorne, S. 565
Douglas, S. P. 574
Drucker, P. F. 29
Dube, K. 68, 71
Duncan, J. 281, 282
Duterte, R. 71
Dwyer, L. 505, 542, 581
Dyer, J. H. 439, 440, 470

Eden, C. 511
Edwards, D. 542
Eid, R. 146
Elkington, J. 495
Endo, K. 595–596
Enz, C. A. 8
Ernst, D. 450
Evans, N. G. 7, 45, 47, 55.
    57–58, 64, 67, 73, 109, 113,
    123, 125, 137, 178, 204,
    206, 220, 252, 326, 391, 431,
    444, 446, *448*, 464, 522, 552,
    557–558, 563, 577. 627, 651

Fagan, S. 378, 379
Falshaw, J. R. 512
Farrell, H. 421
Farris, P. W. 122
Faulkner, D. 388, 442–443,
    443. 449–450
Ferrante, M. 57
Finlay, P. N. 107
Fisher, J. 618
Fitchett, J. M. 68
FitzPatrick, M. 92
Fleischer, C. S. 112, 114,
    255, 509
Fletcher, J. 7
Fletcher, R. 619
Freeman, R. E. 36
Frenken, K. 710
Friedman, M. 35–36
Fuller, M. B. 450
Fyall, A. 129, 467

Galan, J. I. 530
Gallagher, L. 707, 711, 714
Gallarza, M. G. 56
Galpin, T. 619
Garengo, P. 564
Garrod, B. 129, 467
Gartner, W. C. 56
Gebbia, J. 707
Gee, C. Y. 7
Getz, D. 9, 38, 121, 297, 343,
    542, 543
Ghoshal, S. 574, **574–575**.
    581
Gibson, L. D. 229
Gilmore, A. 63
Ginter, P. M. 281, 282
Giscard Estaing, H. 407
Gkoumas, A. 551
Glaister, K. W. 512
Glueck, F. 33
Go, F. M. 462, 509
Goeldner, C. R. 7
Goldblatt, J. 9
Gonzalez, R. 577
Gössling, S. 68
Graeff, C. L. 548
Graham, A. 297
Green, H. 663
Grönroos, C. 130, 147
Gross, M. J. 606
Grundy, T. 327
Gu, Z. 325

Gummesson, E. 47
Guttentag, D. 256

Haberberg, A. 484
Hahn, W. 522
Haji-Ioannou, S. 497
Hall, D. J. 530
Hallin, C. A. 111
Hamel, G. 29, 99–100, 101,
    102–103, 389, 576–577,
    581, 650
Han, M. X. 120
Handy, C. 155, 164–165, 529
Hanlon, C. 138, 139
Haque, S. 352
Harrington, R. J. 8
Harrison, A. 129
Harrison, J. S. 8, 103
Heeley, J. 457
Heldt, T. 543
Hembrow, I. 49
Heracleous, L. 386–387
Hersey, P. 548
Heskett, J. L. 122, 123, 124
Hickson, D. J. 167
Higgins-Desboilles, F. 618
Hill, C. W. 27
Hilton, C. 451
Hitt, M. A. 28
Hjalager, A. M. 256, 572
Hofstede, G. 166–169, **168**.
    529
Holbeche, L. 541
Hollensen, S. 228, 229
Holloway, C. 7
Hoogendoorn, G. 68
Horner, D. 498
Horton, B. A. 68
Howells, J. 579
Hsu, C. H. 56
Huang, S. S. 606
Hughes, K. 434
Humphreys, C. 7

Inkpen, A. 650

Jabeen, F. 148
Jacoby, S. 40
Jago, L. 138, 139
Jang, S. S. 325
Jauch, L. R. 33
Jiang, H. 288
Jogaratnam, G. 539

Johnson, G. 160, 470–472, *471*. 544
Johnson, J. 604, *605*
Jones, G. 628
Jones, P. 297, 523
Joussen, F. 474

Kantabrura, S. 32
Kanter, R. M. 444, 452
Kaplan, R. S. 123, 557–560, 564
Karadakis, K. 352
Kay, J. 99–100, 104–106, 308–309, 389, 435
Kayaman, R. 56
Kelleher, H. 159
Kenny, G. 631
Kenyon, A. 395
Kim, B. Y. 369, 440
Kim, S. S. 330
Kim, W. G. 199
Klein, S. 447
Knight, G. A. 608, 610
Knoke, D. 443
Knorr, A. 56
Konu, H. 236
Kotler, P. 220, 227, 232, 248–249, 484
Kotter, J. P. 546, 547, *548*
Krippendorf, J. 67
Kumar, S. 496
Kusluvan, S. 145–146

Lado, A. A. 145
Lam, T. 120
Lamminmaki, D. 120
Lattin, T. W. 498
Laws, E. 67
Le, D. 75
Lee, S. K. 325
Lee, W. 217
Lee, Y, J, A. 329
Legrand, W. 68
Leiper, N. 144
Lenz, R. T. 511
Lenzen, M. 67–68
Levitt, T. 573–574, 589
Lewin, K. *539*. 539–540
Lewis, D. 498
Li, X. R. 125
Liu, A. 139
Lockwood, R. D. 204
Long, P. E. 484
Lozano, J. 57

Lu, T. Y. 56
Lumpkin, G. T. 421
Lundberg, E. 506
Lundtorp, S. 57
Lusch, R. F. 125, **126**. 130
Lyles, M. A. 511
Lynch, R. 40, 282, 394, 409, 511

Madera, J.M. 137
Mair, J. 297
March, J. G. 421
Marnburg, E. 111
Maslow, A. 235
Mason, P. 67
Mathieson, A. 577
Mathur, S. S. 395
Mbaiwa, J. E. 67
McCamley, C. 63
McCartney, G. 575
McKercher, M. 55–56
McMahon-Beattie, U. 509
McSweeney, B. 167
Medcof, J. W. 452, 476
Mendelow, A. 36–37
Meyer, R. 440, 442
Miles, R. E. 165–166, **166**. 529–530
Mill, R. C. 147–148
Miller, S. 522
Mintzberg, H. 17–21, 387, 392, 484, 511, 531
Mitchell, A. 235
Miyoshi, C. 595
Mockler, R. J. 651
Moeller, S. 47
Mondal, M. 352
Moore, M. J. 122
Mordashov, A. 601
Moreno-Gil, S. 55–56
Morrison, A. J. 129, 302, 359, **360**
Moutinho, L. 255
Moyle, C. L. J. 68
Mules, T. 505, 506

Nduna, L. T. 238
Niewiadomski, P. 580
Nordvall, A. 543
Norton, D. P. 123, 557–560, 564
Norton, P. 57

O'Dwyer, M. 269
OECD 284, 285

Oh, H. 369, 440
Ohmae, K. 442, 649
O'Leary, M. 328, 540
Oreja-Rodriguez, J. R. 302
O'Shaughnessy, J. 125
O'Shaughnessy, N. 125
Oskam, J. 714, 719
Osti, L. 575
O'Sullivan, N. 436–437
Ottenbacher, M. C. 8
Oyewole, P. 288

Page, S. J. 7, 9, 259
Palatková, M. 551
Palmer, A. 269, 359
Palmer, R. 158
Parasuraman, A. 147
Parilla, J. C. 57
Park, J. W. 595
Parker, A. 431
Parsa, H. G. 92
Pearce, J. A. 415
Pearson, J. 92
Pechlaner, H. 440
Pehrsson, A. 60
Peiró-Signes, A. 329–330
Peluso, A. M. 287
Pemberton, J. D. 111, 112, 512
Peters, T. 550–551, *551*
Petrick, J. F. 125
Phi, G. 75
Pichierri, M. 287
Pine, R. 462
Plog, S. 233
Poetz, M. K. 259
Poon, A. 69–70, 112, *115*. 411
Porter, M. E. 89, 90, 112, 114, *115*. 286, 308, 310–329, 369, 373–388, 392, 395, 450, 484, 571, 580, 582–584, *583*. *584*. *585*. 585–587, 586, 591
Powers, E. L. 27, 28
Powers, T. L. 522
Prahalad, C. K. 29, 99–100, 101, 102–103, 127, 128, 389, 576–577, 581, 710–711
Prentice, R. 513
Preston, L. E. 36
Pugh, D. S. 167
Purkayastha, S. 409

Quinn, B. 575
Quinn, J. B. 544

Rahimi, R. 55–56
Raj, R. 9
Ram, Y. 71
Ramaswamy, V. 127, 128, 710–711
Rangan, U. S. 444–445
Rate, S. 284
Reisinger, Y. 169
Richards, G. 157, 158
Rieple, A. 484
Riesman, D. 235
Ro, H. 142, 143
Robbins, D. K. 415
Rockart, J. F. 342
Rosselló, J. 57
Roxas, F. M. Y. 38
Rubell, S. 383
Rumelt, R. P. 439
Rundshagen, V. 418, **418**
Ruzzier, M. K. 56

Saias, M. A. 530
Sainghi, R. 57
Sanchez-Bueno, M. J. 530
Sansó, A. 57
Schein, E. 155
Scholes, K. 498
Schor, J. 710
Schrager, I. 383
Schreier, M. 259
Scott, D. 68
Segal-Horn, S. 574, **574–575**. 575
Senge, P. M. 112
Shanley, M. 470
Shapiro, B. P. 239
Shauna, A. 68
Sheldon, P. J. 352, 353
Sheng, L. 323
Shibli, S. 401
Sidhu, J. 28
Sinarta, Y. 127
Singh, H. 439, 440
Škare, M. 416
Smeral, E. 586
Smith, A. 297
Smith, W. 227

Snow, C. C. 165–166, **166**. 529–530
Solomons, R. 243
Sorensen, A. 434
Stalk, G. 99–100, 389
Stoddard, J. E. 618
Stokes, D. 269
Stokes, R. 147
Stone, R. A. 30
Stonehouse, G. H. 111, 112, 512, 581
Stronza, A. L. 67
Sun, D. 154
Sundbo, J. 513
Swarbrooke, J. 259

Taylor, I. 474
Teece, D. 109, *110*. 391, 392
Teixeira, R. 302
Teixeira, R. 359, **360**
Tellis, G. J. 605, *605*
Teo, S. 457
Terwiesch, C. 259
Thunberg, G. 617
Timothy, D. J. 581
Tkaczynski, A. 147
Todd, L. 38
Todeva, E. 443
Topham, G. 540–541
Trigano, Gilbert 40
Tsai, H. 177–178, 325
Tse, E. C. Y. 539
Tsui, W. H. K. 437
Tuch, C. 436–437
Tum, J. 57

Ulrich, K. T. 259
UNWTO 71, 580, 617
Urbano, D. 169
Uslay, C. 122

Van Zyl, C. 238
Vargo, S. L. 125, 126, **126**. 130
Von Hippel, E. 259
Voyer, J. 544

Wahab, S. 586
Walker, D. H. 37
Wall, G. 139, 577
Walsh, P. R. 619, *620*

Wang, C. L. 109, 391
Waterman, R. 550–551, *551*
Waters, J. A. 484
WCED 295, 494
Weidenfeld, A. 409
Wenzel, M. 417
Wheelan, T. L. 414, 415
Whittington, R. 388, 408, 484, 496, 542, 628
Wild, J. 540–541
Williams, G. 609
Williams, L. S. 28
Williams, R. J. 421
Williamson, D. 167
Wilson, K. 415–416, 461–462
Wilson, M. C. 145
Wind, Y. 574
Wirtz, J. 386–387
Wood, R. 120
WTTC 139
Wu, E. 139
Wyatt, A. 39
Wynn, J. R. 157

Xiao, Q. 476
Xie, L. 56

Yan, J. 437
Yanes-Estévez, V. 302
Yao, T. 139
Yeoman, I. 509
Yin, X. 470
Yip, G. S. 571, 580, 584, *587*. 587–598, **588**
Yordanova, D. 169
Yoshino, M. M. Y. 444–445
Young, S. 30

Zaleznik, A. 546
Zander, I. 610
Zare, S. 416–417
Zehrer, A. 129
Zeithaml, V. A. 47, 122, 147
Zeng, Z. 148
Zhang, H. Q. 139, 154
Zhang, X. 63
Zhang, Y. 288
Zheng, T. 325
Zhuang, X. 67